PRINCIPLES OF
Accounting

PRINCIPLES OF
Accounting

Dempsey Dupree
Clarion University of Pennsylvania

Matthew Marder

ADDISON-WESLEY PUBLISHING COMPANY

Reading, Massachusetts
Menlo Park, California
London
Amsterdam
Don Mills, Ontario
Sydney

Sponsoring Editor: Frank Burns
Production Manager: Herb Nolan
Production Editors: Mary Crittendon
Jerrold Moore
Text Designer: Catherine Dorin
Illustrator: ARVAK, Inc.
Cover Designer: Vanessa Piñeiro
Copy Editor: Dorothy MacDonald
Art Coordinator: Robert Forget
Manufacturing Supervisor: Hugh Crawford
Cover Photograph: Marshall Henrichs

Library of Congress Cataloging in Publication Data

Dupree, Dempsey.
  Principles of accounting.

  1. Accounting.   I. Marder, Matthew.   II. Title.
HF5635.D94   1984   657   83-3714
ISBN 0-201-11333-3

Reprinted with corrections, May 1984

To William A. Paton,
eminent teacher and writer

Preface

Proficient and timely accounting becomes increasingly important as organizations, legal requirements, and technologies grow more complex. Investors, creditors, managers, government agencies, and the many other users of accounting results rightfully expect accounting to keep pace with their needs for data.

Constructing an accounting principles text for today and tomorrow presents a special challenge. Traditional topics must be covered within the context of constantly changing accounting standards, tax laws, regulatory requirements, expanding computer capabilities, and volatile economic conditions. Coverage must provide an understandable overview of accounting for nonaccounting majors, yet contain sufficient scope and detail for accounting majors to acquire a solid foundation for intermediate level courses in accounting.

In accepting the challenge we were convinced that we could construct a text that satisfies these requirements and, in so doing, present in a clear manner, in a logical progression, and in a fresh way the many facets of the intriguing field of accounting. *Principles of Accounting,* we believe, simultaneously presents sound methods and valid concepts, enhances effective learning and teaching, and provides flexibility of use of the material—all in a contemporary, readable style. We believe that both instructor and student will benefit from our method of presenting currently relevant and accurate textual matter.

LEARNING FEATURES

The book is divided into nine distinct parts, each having one or more chapters. Where appropriate, chapters are subdivided into two or more topical sections. In addition, two appendixes to both Chapter 3 and Chapter 16 are provided for those desiring more depth in the topics covered. Also, an appendix on international operations is included at the end of the book, as is an appendix illustrating corporate financial reports. The organization of material aids the instructor in selecting sections considered essential to a particular course, facilitates the assignment of questions, exercises, and problems, and makes the material more manageable for the student.

Performance Objectives

Undivided chapters begin with clearly stated performance objectives; subdivided chapters begin with a brief introduction to the chapter, and each section in the chapter begins with its own set of performance objectives. Objectives are repeated in the text margin at points where they are demonstrated. They represent a core of what we believe students completing the principles course should be able to do. Individual instructors may add or delete objectives if they wish.

A *Self-Quiz on Objectives* is included at the end of each section and undivided chapter. These quizzes consist of questions, exercises, and problems that require the student to demonstrate mastery of each objective. They test comprehension in greater depth than do true-false or multiple-choice questions. Students may immediately evaluate their competence by referring to the *Solutions to Self-Quizzes* (Appendix B). Thus they may discover whether additional work in an area is needed before they go on to subsequent assignments.

Emphasis on Important Information

Important terms appear in boldface italics when they are first used in the text. Each term and its definition (in italics) are further emphasized by color. Definitions are stated in clear nontechnical language to enhance comprehension at the principles level. Terms (in alphabetical order) and their definitions are repeated in a *Glossary* at the end of the section or undivided chapter in which they first appear.

Other information having particular importance is given visual impact by means of color illustrations. More than 130 functional illustrations help clarify, explain, and summarize concepts and procedures discussed in the accompanying text. Important rules, lists, analogies, and calculations are emphasized by color; facsimiles of accounting documents, journal pages, ledger accounts, work sheets, schedules, and statements appearing in the body of the text are also highlighted with color backgrounds.

Each chapter concludes with a brief *Chapter Summary* that emphasizes again some of the key matters covered in the chapter.

Assignment Materials

Provided at the end of sections and chapters are an exceptional range and abundance of assignment materials. Discussion questions, exercises, problems, comprehension problems, and alternate problems present the student with an interesting variety of assignment types and degrees of difficulty. For example, *Discussion Questions* stimulate student thought, either in class discussions or as out-of-class assignments. Many of the questions provide excellent opportunities for extending class discussions into interesting areas beyond text coverage. *Exercises* usually are confined to a single topic and require relatively short solutions, whereas *Problems* have a broader scope. Problems located at the end of subdivided chapters generally integrate the ideas presented in the different sections of the chapter. *Alternate Problems* (Appendix D) parallel certain of the section and chapter problems in order to provide greater assignment flexibility. Going beyond the basic text coverage, *Comprehension Problems* are conceptual in nature and require students to arrive at logical conclusions; from one to three of these problems are provided at the end of each chapter.

Accuracy and Correlation

We share with all accountants the concern for accuracy. Therefore great care, including the use of multiple proofreaders and reviewers, was exercised to ensure the accuracy and correlation of textual information, assignment matter, and supplementary materials.

TOPICAL FEATURES

Logical Order and Progression

Wherever possible, similar and reciprocal topics are treated together. For example, receivables and payables are covered simultaneously in recognition of their reciprocal nature. Accounting for branch operations and consolidated statements are presented as two sections of the same chapter because of the similarity between combining branch with home office data and consolidating statements of subsidiaries with those of parent corporations.

Because internal controls are paramount when accounting for cash, the chapter on Cash Controls (Chapter 9) is located in Part IV along with chapters on Payment Control Systems (Chapter 10) and Data Processing Systems and Controls (Chapter 11). Chapter 11 presents an internal control approach to the processing of data by whatever method: manual, mechanical, electronic, or a combination of them. It is brief, nontechnical, and cogent to the study of accounting principles.

In order to avoid undue complexity, some matters are deferred until students are better prepared to deal with them. Although forms of business organization are discussed briefly in Chapter 2, neither text illustrations nor problem materials involve partnerships or corporations until these legal entities are covered in depth in the text. Similarly, neither merchandising nor manufacturing is introduced before the points where they are specifically covered in depth.

Not only does the presentation of principles and techniques progress from the simple to the complex, but topics are also introduced in logical terms. For example, the adjusting entry (as opposed to the closing entry) approach for updating merchandise inventory is emphasized initially because of its conceptual clarity. Once students thoroughly grasp the relationship between the accounting records and the schedule of cost of goods sold, they generally have no trouble with procedural variations, such as combining the inventory adjustment with closing entries.

Conceptual Strengths

Accounting concepts are interwoven with methods throughout the text. Section 1.B sets the pace by introducing accounting concepts of entity, monetary unit, cost basis, realization, matching, and time periods—all in the context of reflecting transactions into the accounting equation. These concepts are reinforced, and others are introduced, as accounting techniques are developed in subsequent chapters.

Chapter 12 serves as a bridge between the more basic topics preceding it and the more complex ones that follow. Section 12.A reviews and pulls together the accounting concepts previously introduced, elaborates on them, and briefly traces the development of accounting principles. Section 12.B develops the contemporary topics of accounting for changes in purchasing power of money and changes in values of goods over time.

Not only are accounting concepts interwoven throughout, but concepts of economics, finance, management, marketing, and other disciplines are also introduced at appropriate points. For instance, both merchandising and manufacturing are examined in the context of the types of utility they deal in, and expenses and revenues are characterized as measures of the consumption and provision of economic resources. Financial Statement Analysis (Chapter 19) is developed in conjunction with the sometimes conflicting needs of owners, lenders, and managers.

Capital budgeting is treated in Chapter 25 (Alternative Choice Decisions) from the standpoint of selecting data relevant to making choices among competing and conflicting alternatives. Advantages and disadvantages of payback, net present value, and rate of return approaches are discussed, their results are compared, and the circumstances under which each leads to valid decisions are noted. A review of the chapter will show how this highly complex topic is clearly presented in conceptual terms.

Profiles

Career profiles of a number of practicing accountants indicate the variety of opportunities available in the accounting profession. The profiles are on the reverse side of the part title pages.

SEQUENCING

The text is intended for use in two-semester, three-quarter, or concentrated two-quarter sequences of the introductory accounting course. After Chapter 3, the order of use could be changed somewhat, and sections or chapters could be excluded according to the instructor's preference. Approximately one-half of the textual material is contained in the first five parts of the book. Consequently, the first semester of a two-semester sequence (or first quarter of a two-quarter sequence) may conveniently end with Chapter 12. However, those instructors who want to cover more material could include some or all of Part VI in the first term, while those who desire a slower pace initially could stop after Part IV. A three-quarter sequence might include Parts I through III in the first quarter, Parts IV through VII in the second, and Parts VIII and IX in the third.

SUPPLEMENTARY MATERIALS

For the Student

Working Papers: Volume I (Chapters 1–12) and Volume II (Chapters 13–26)

- Complete and convenient accounting forms provided for student use in solving text self-quizzes and all problems.
- Appropriate forms partially completed to reduce unnecessary labor.
- Solutions to problems and alternate problems fit on the same forms with a few exceptions (in which case additional forms are provided).

Study Guide (Richard Keith, Lynn Marples, and Charles Pineno, authors)

- Comprehensive guide to the textbook to assist the student while using the book and in preparing for examinations.
- Contains a description of chapter objectives, review of topics, terminology, and concepts that are presented in each chapter.
- Careful presentation of objective questions including many true-false, multiple-choice, and completion questions.
- Extensive exercises and short problems provided.
- Solutions provided for all of these assignments for each chapter—many with helpful explanations of the derivation of answers.

Manual Practice Sets I, II, and III (Jim Weglin, author)

- Three practice sets, each requiring about 8 to 12 hours completion time.
- Practice Set I—presents the complete accounting cycle for a proprietorship.
- Practice Set II—provides all the information needed to expose students to the full cycle for a corporation.
- Practice Set III—presents a manufacturing concern to allow reinforcement of the managerial coverage of the text.

Computer Practice Sets I, II, and III (George Miller and Jim Weglin, authors)

- Three sets utilizing information similar to that of the manual sets—provide the needed software and user documentation for effective utilization of a (micro)computer.
- Give a clear comparison of manual and electronic processing and provide exposure to automated data entry and report generation.
- First available for the Apple II® and IBM Personal Computer®.
- Computer expertise not a prerequisite.

Checklist of Key Figures

- Provides suggested key figures for problem solutions.
- Available in multiple quantities for student use at the instructor's option.

Software Tutor

- Independent software program—covers basic concepts of elementary financial accounting.
- Works as an overview and is useful as a primer for the first course or as a review.
- Provides innovative software design techniques such as branching, help commands, and menu selection.

For the Instructor

Solutions Manual: Volume I (Chapters 1–12) and Volume II (Chapters 13–26)

- Available in two convenient volumes.
- All components set in large bold type.
- Suggested answers for all discussion questions.

- Solutions to all exercises and problems in the text.
- Gradation of level and time for completion provided for each problem.
- Thoroughly proofed for textual correlation and accuracy.

Transparencies of Solutions

- Solutions to all problems on acetate for over-head projection.
- Set in large bold type.

Transparencies of Illustrations

- Two-color acetate.
- Aid in presentation of textual material.

Instructor's Resource Guide (Eric Carlsen, author)

- Manual for optional use by the instructor.
- Particularly helpful to inexperienced or part-time faculty.
- Contains outline of chapter topics and extensive instructional notes about text content and presentation.
- Direction in assignment of exercises and problems and guide to chapter problems by topic.

Test Bank (Richard Keith and Lynn Marples, authors)

- Data base of examination material.
- Available in hard copy form containing over 1,200 items.
- Good balance of objective tests (true-false, multiple choice, completion, matching) and more extensive exercises, including short problems.
- (Micro)computerized system called TESTGEN for selecting and editing test questions and printing exams (objective tests).

Achievement Tests (Richard Keith and Lynn Marples, authors)

- Separate and different test items providing an additional source of objective questions for test purposes.
- Cover two or three chapters as appropriate for convenient evaluation of student performance.

Solutions Manual for Practice Sets

- Contains solutions to manual and computerized practice sets.
- Documentation for computer use also included

Checklist of Key Figures

- Contains key figures of problem solutions as applicable.
- Available in quantity for optional distribution to students.

ACKNOWLEDGMENTS

The production of a new accounting principles text is a long and arduous process, and many individuals have contributed to this project during the years since its inception. It is impossible to identify and list all of the students, colleagues, staff members, editors, reviewers, and family members who in some way influenced this work. So, with apologies to all those deserving people omitted, appreciation is expressed to the following who were especially helpful.

- Editors Frank Burns, Mary Crittendon, and Jerrold Moore, for their encouragement, patience, guidance, and long hours of hard work; Herb Nolan, production manager for the parent text and Sherry Berg, production manager for the supplementary materials package—truly monumental tasks.

- Charles G. Carpenter, Miami University of Ohio, for reviewing, pruning, and helping to improve the early chapters.

- Our colleagues; Mary Lou Pae, in particular, who meticulously combed through the entire set of manuscripts for the text and the solutions manual; Roberta Jeannerat for top quality clerical assistance since the beginning of the project.

- Students who worked the exercises and problems and offered critical advice; in particular, Nancy Vernon, a graduate student; Mary Newland, a most dedicated student assistant; Steve Tamsula, a rare multitalented accounting student who materialized at a crucial moment to take on a host of chores with exceptional ability and efficiency—for which we shall be forever grateful.

- Our families, for the love, encouragement, and understanding without which we could not have found the fortitude to pursue this project to its conclusion, and for which there are no words sufficient to convey our gratitude.

- The many accounting instructors who reviewed portions of the work in various stages over the years, for their critical contributions that more often than not were incorporated into the manuscript. The following reviewers were particularly helpful.

Early Stages

Wayne Alderman, Auburn University
Herman Andress, Santa Fe Community College (Gainesville, Fla.)
Jay Paul Blazek, Milwaukee Area Technical College
Les Chadwick, University of Delaware
Kenneth Coffey, Johnson County Community College
E. A. Devine, Eastern Michigan University

Jamie T. Doran, CPA
Dwight M. Edmonds, Wilfried Laurier University, Ontario
John P. Farmer (retired), Orange Coast College
Ronald Gray, University of Alabama, Birmingham
Doug Hillman, Drake University
George Ihorn, El Paso Community College
Wayne Lyman, Allegheny Community College
Emily Miklis, Tri-County Community College, East Campus
Ronald D. Niemeyer, Central Missouri State University
Ida B. Pound, Alameda College
Robert R. Wennagal, College of the Mainland, Texas
Lee C. Wilson, Mesa Community College
Charles T. Zlatkovich (retired), University of Texas at Austin

Later Stages
James R. Barnhart, Ball State University
Nita J. Dodson, East Texas State University
Kenneth Ferris, Southern Methodist University
Roger Hehman, Raymond Walters College (University of
    Cincinnati)
Harold Holen, Montana State University
Kathleen McGahran, University of Michigan
Bill Magers, Tarrant County Community College
Vincent Pelletier, College of DuPage
George W. Wells, Jr., Tulsa Junior College
William Zahurak, Allegheny County Community College

- The following people who undertook the demanding task of proofing
  some or all of the final manuscript for both the text and solutions manual.

Samuel Chesler, Lowell University
Mark Dawson, Clarion University
Gregory Fox, Erie Community College
Lou Gilles, Coastal Carolina College
Robert Landry, Massasoit College
Melissa Martinson (retired), Portland Community College, Seattle
Mary Lou Pae, Clarion University
Ed Rinetti, Los Angeles City College

Clarion, Pa.   D.D.
November, 1983   M.M.

Contents

2
Accounting for Transactions   44

3
End-of-Period Work

PART II

Merchandising Operations

4

Merchandise Transactions   179

5

Special Journals and Subsidiary Ledgers

6
Cash Claims and Debts   287

7
Merchandise Inventories   330

8
Long-Term Assets and their Expiration 380

PART IV
Systems and Controls

9
Cash Controls 425

10
Payment Control Systems   458

11

Data Processing Systems and Controls

499

PART V

Accounting Concepts

12

Accounting Principles and Changing Prices

523

SECTION 12.A

Concepts Underlying Accounting Practice

524

PART VI

Multiple Ownership

13
Partnerships   579

14
Corporations: Capital Stock   604

15
Corporations: Earnings, Retained Earnings, and Statements 627

16
Long-Term Liabilities and Investments 652

SECTION 16.A
Long-Term Liabilities 653

PART VII

Using Financial Data

17
Consolidating Financial Data 711

18
Flows of Working Capital and Cash   757

19
Financial Statement Analysis

PART VIII
Manufacturing Operations

20
Manufacturing Accounting

21
Cost Accounting Systems 865

PART IX

Budgets and Decision Making

22
Budgetary Control 909

23
Cost and Revenue Behavior   946

24

Flexible Budgets and Standard Costs   984

25
Alternative Choice Decisions (Capital Budgeting)

26
Income Tax Considerations

PRINCIPLES OF
Accounting

PART I

FRAMEWORK OF ACCOUNTING

ACCOUNTANTS IN THE WORKPLACE

NAME: Eli Boyer

AFFILIATION: Laventhol & Horwath

POSITION: Audit Partner

SPECIALIZATION: Sports and Entertainment

With clients like Bob Hope, George Steinbrenner, and the San Diego Chargers, Eli Boyer has reached the top of his field. To reach this level, he emphasizes, "you've got to work hard and learn the field." And, he adds, there's no substitute for "knowing what a set of books is."

Upon graduating with a B.S. in accounting from UCLA, Boyer began his career with a small Los Angeles firm, "preparing trial balances and monthly statements." "It was the best experience I could ever have gotten," he says. One of the firm's clients—a law firm— specialized in the entertainment industry.

Others were added and when the firm merged with Laventhol & Horwath, it brought along a strong reputation in the sports and entertainment world.

The man who put drama and acting lessons into George Foreman's contract with ABC also established himself in the casino, hotel, and real estate businesses. "We do everything," says Boyer, "consulting, tax planning, contract negotiation, mergers, and acquisitions." Wealthy clients also depend on Boyer to keep them abreast of tax-shelter and investment opportunities.

Boyer advises young accountants to develop a "facility for figures." "One shouldn't reach for a calculator to do simple calculations," he says. He also stresses the importance of tax knowledge. Today taxes are "a critical part of almost any deal you're involved with," he explains.

NAME: Paul Nolan

AFFILIATION: FBI

POSITION: Supervisory Special Agent

SPECIALIZATION: Fraud, Corruption, Labor Racketeering

Few people think of accounting when they think of the FBI. But of the bureau's 8,000 agents, 1,100 are trained accountants. And when someone accused U.S. Secretary of Labor Raymond Donovan of taking a bribe, an accountant, Paul Nolan, began the investigation.

As a Supervisory Special Agent, Nolan monitors the performance of accountant agents throughout the country. He also supervises investigations arising out of the Ethics of Government Act, or "Watergate legislation," when a high-level government official is accused of a crime. If the investigation leads to the appointment of a special prosecutor, Nolan serves as liaison between the prosecutor and the Department of Justice.

"I am the prosecutor's representative in Washington," Nolan explains. "Whatever is needed—buildings, trucks, cars—I get it." At the same time, Nolan represents the DOJ to the special prosecutor.

With a B.A. in accounting and a master's in public administration, Nolan worked in public, corporate, and municipal accounting before joining the FBI. He likes the FBI best. "Most auditors spend their lives looking for unusual occurrences. Here we see them all the time."

Introduction to Accounting

Welcome to the study of accounting. A knowledge of accounting principles is essential for most businesspeople and quite useful to investors. In fact, many news reports on business events and economic conditions are difficult to understand for those with no knowledge of accounting. The principles of accounting course is a prerequisite for a number of other business courses, and it is the foundation course for students majoring in accounting.

Chapter 1 introduces you to accounting, which is often referred to as the language of business. The chapter is divided into two sections. Section A explores the nature of accounting by considering accounting definitions, types of accounting users, components of the main financial statements, and various specialized areas within the field of accounting. This section also briefly surveys the evolution of accounting over the course of time and discusses several agencies that influence the way in which accounting is practiced.

Section B introduces the accounting equation, on which almost all systems of accounting are based. The dual effects of transactions on the equation are illustrated in the context of six of the basic concepts of accounting. Also shown are balance sheet and income statement presentations of information gathered by reflecting transaction effects into the equation.

SECTION 1.A

The Nature of Accounting

OBJECTIVES

This section introduces you to the study of accounting. At the conclusion of your study, you should be able to

1. State in your own words the overall questions answered by these financial statements:
   a. An income statement.
   b. A balance sheet.
   c. A statement of changes in financial position.

2. Define these terms in your own words:
   a. Accounting.
   b. Asset.
   c. Liability.
   d. Owners' equity.
   e. Revenue.
   f. Expense.
   g. Net income.

3. Differentiate these expressions:
   a. Bookkeeper; accountant.
   b. Public accounting; private accounting; governmental accounting.
   c. General accounting; cost accounting; budgeting; auditing.
   d. Financial accounting; managerial accounting.

ACCOUNTING: A FINANCIAL LANGUAGE

Accounting is a language, a system that communicates information. It is often referred to as the language of business, although it is just as important in the operation of government agencies, churches, colleges, and other kinds of organizations.

You probably have some idea already of what the term *accounting* means. It is frequently used in everyday conversation to mean "answering for responsibility," and in a broad sense, accounting systems help individuals and groups do just that. Managers of business concerns account to owners, creditors, employee unions, government agencies, and other interested parties; managers of government units account to chief executives, boards, taxpayers, and others; charities to contributors; clubs to members; and so on.

Many accounting terms will be somewhat familiar to you; you have heard people speak of assets, liabilities, revenues, and expenses. In fact, accounting was developed by people, very much like you, who were seeking better ways to gather and report useful information about organizations.

Some type of orderly *system* is needed to account for an organization of any size and complexity. *An accounting system is used to collect, process, and report needed data* about a business, government unit, or other type of association. Information is usually collected, processed, and reported in *financial* terms, which simply means that *money* is the basis of measurement. In some cases, however, it may be more useful to state the information in terms of units produced or hours worked.

Accounting often goes beyond the preparation of reports to include the *analysis* of the information contained in a report and the *interpretation* of the report for particular people. Later you will study some of the techniques for analyzing reports that make them more useful for specific purposes. Some facts may be compared to others by means of ratios, or amounts may be combined in various ways to help answer particular questions. Also, accounting reports may be translated into everyday language for persons who do not understand accounting language.

Those who use accounting information are usually involved in making *decisions* of various kinds. In most cases decision makers are concerned with *future* outcomes. Therefore, accounting information about the past is often just a starting point for predicting future results. In recent years, accountants have become more involved in projecting possible future outcomes on a formal basis.

The term *accounting* is so broad that it is difficult to give a precise definition. Even so, you should be able to define it roughly in your own words. Several possible definitions appear in Illustration 1.1.

ILLUSTRATION 1.1

ACCOUNTING DEFINITIONS

1. *The act of collecting, processing, reporting, analyzing, interpreting, and projecting financial information.*

2. The system (or means) of providing quantified information about an organization to people who need such information.

3. ". . . a service activity. Its function is to provide quantitative information, primarily financial in nature, about economic entities that is intended to be useful in making economic decisions."[1]

4. ". . . the process of identifying, measuring, and communicating economic information to permit informed judgments and decisions by users of the information."[2]

OBJECTIVE 2a. Define accounting.

[1]*Statement of the Accounting Principles Board No. 4,* American Institute of Certified Public Accountants (New York, 1970) Par. 9.

[2]*A Statement of Basic Accounting Theory,* American Accounting Association (Evanston, Ill., 1966) p. 1.

ACCOUNTING USERS

The purpose of accounting is to provide useful information about an organization to people who need such information. A distinction should be made between accounting to those outside an organization (external users) and accounting to managers and others within an organization (internal users).

Financial Accounting

Practically all accounting reports are in financial (money) terms; yet the expression *financial accounting ordinarily means accounting to users outside of (external to) the organization being accounted for.* Financial accounting produces general-purpose reports for use by the great variety of people who are interested in the organization but who are not actively engaged in its day-to-day operation.

Among the users of financial accounting reports are investors in corporate securities, lenders (such as bankers and suppliers), government agencies, labor unions, and many other classes of external users.

Managerial Accounting

Managerial accounting provides managers (internal users) of the organization with information useful for decision making. Actually, much of the information for both managerial and financial accounting comes from the organization's general accounting system. However, reports prepared for management use are usually more specialized, and in more detail, than the general-purpose financial reports to external users. Also, management reports sometimes include additional information not normally supplied by the general accounting system. For instance, management reports might compare actual results with those that had been projected (budgeted) for the period, or with results of other companies. Or facts may be stated in something other than monetary units.

In brief, financial and managerial accounting may be summarized as follows:

OBJECTIVE 3d. Differentiate financial and managerial accounting.

Financial Accounting	*Managerial Accounting*
General-purpose reports for external users	Specialized reports for internal users

ACCOUNTING REPORTS

Accounting information is conveyed to users in a variety of reports and schedules. Generally, reports to internal (management) users are specially designed to meet their particular needs, which are usually known at the time the reports are prepared. Reports to external users tend to be more stan-

ILLUSTRATION 1.2

MINIM COMPANY Balance Sheet July 31, 19--			
ASSETS		**LIABILITIES**	
Cash	$ 435	Accounts payable	$1,185	
Accounts receivable	3,320	Wages payable	570	$1,755
Supplies inventory	860	**OWNER'S EQUITY**	
		Sue Minim, capital	2,860
		Total Liabilities and	
Total Assets	$4,615	Owner's Equity	$4,615

dardized and are often referred to as *financial statements*. Traditionally, two principal financial statements have been prepared for business concerns: a *balance sheet* and an *income statement*. Lately a third principal statement, the *statement of changes in financial position*, has been added, and a brief statement showing changes in ownership equity is often prepared.

Balance Sheet

*A **balance sheet** shows the financial position, or condition, of an organization at a particular point in time.* In fact, it is sometimes referred to as a *position statement*, or a *statement of condition*. A balance sheet is somewhat like a snapshot that attempts to show how well off the concern is, or where it stands at a particular instant.

It shows the *economic resources (properties, possessions) of an organization, referred to as **assets**,* and the claims that creditors and owners have against the assets. *Economic obligations of an organization (amounts owed to creditors) are called **liabilities**, and owners' claims are referred to as owners' equity, or capital.*[3]

A common arrangement of the balance sheet is to list assets on the left side and liabilities and owners' equity on the right. An example of a balance sheet for a small company owned by one individual is presented in Illustration 1.2.

The balance sheet in Illustration 1.2 shows the company's financial condition on July 31. At that time the company had assets of $4,615, of

---

[3]See *FASB Statement of Financial Accounting Concepts No. 3,* "Elements of Financial Statements of Business Enterprises," Financial Accounting Standards Board (Stamford, Conn., 1980) for more technically precise definitions of these and other terms used in this chapter. As pointed out later in this chapter, owners' equity may be characterized as the difference between the assets and liabilities of an organization.

ILLUSTRATION 1.3

OBJECTIVE 1b. State the
question answered by a
balance sheet.

OBJECTIVE 2b.
Define asset.

OBJECTIVE 2c.
Define liability.

OBJECTIVE 2d.
Define owners' equity.

Balance sheet (position statement, statement of condition). A financial statement that shows the position, or condition, of an organization at a point in time.
(Question answered by a balance sheet: Where does the organization stand at a point in time?)

Assets. Economic resources (properties) of an organization.

Liabilities. Economic obligations of (amounts owed by) an organization.

Owners' equity. Owners' claims on the assets of an organization.

which $1,755 was owed to others as liabilities and $2,860 remained for the owner. Note that the statement *heading* identifies the name of the concern, the title of the statement, and the date for which the position is shown. You will learn more about the balance sheet and its components later. For now, keep in mind the definitions in Illustration 1.3.

Income Statement

An *income statement shows the results of operating for a period of time. It is sometimes called an* **operating statement** *or* **statement of operations**. It shows how well an organization performed during the period covered.

An income statement shows the *revenues* generated, the *expenses* incurred, and the resulting *net income,* or *profit,* for a period of time.

Revenues	$XXXX
Less: Expenses	XXXX
Net income	$XXXX

The terms *revenue, expense,* and *income* should be somewhat familiar to you already. As used in accounting, revenue is a measure of *gross accomplishment,* and income is *net accomplishment* after allowing for the expenses, or sacrifices, undergone to generate the revenue. *Revenue is the inflow of assets in return for services performed or products delivered during a period; an* **expense** *is a* sacrifice, *or cost, incurred to generate revenue;* **net income** *is simply the amount by which the revenues for a period of time exceed the expenses incurred to generate them.*[4]

Revenues are usually considered earned when services are performed or goods are sold, regardless of when money is actually received. In other words, revenues are identified with the periods in which they are earned.

---

[4]See *FASB Statement of Concepts No. 3,* Paragraphs 63 and 65, for more technically precise definitions. For instance, *revenue* sometimes comes in the form of decreases in liabilities, and *expenses* may be either decreases in assets or increases in liabilities.

ILLUSTRATION 1.4

MINIM COMPANY Income Statement For the Month of July 19--		
Service revenue		$4,960
Expenses		
Wages	$1,970	
Rent	1,000	
Supplies used	750	3,720
Net Income		$1,240

For example, an auto repair business has earned revenue the day it repairs a customer's car, although the customer may not pay the charges right away. Similarly, a store earns revenue when a sale is made on credit. A right to receive money is recognized as an *account receivable*. An account receivable is an asset that will eventually be converted to cash.

Expenses are recognized in the period that is benefited, regardless of when payment is made in cash. For instance, wages earned by employees are considered an expense of the period in which employees work, even though they may not be paid in cash until the following period. Thus an obligation to pay money is recognized as a sacrifice (expense) when it arises; the obligation is viewed as a liability until it is paid with cash.

An example of an income statement for a small company is shown in Illustration 1.4. Some accountants arrange expenses on an income statement according to size, with the largest first, but this practice is not a uniformly accepted custom.

During July, Minim Company had total revenue of $4,960, total expenses of $3,720, and net income of $1,240. This statement shows how well the company performed during the month of July. Notice that the *heading* pins down the *period of time* covered by the statement.

In summary, keep in mind the definitions in Illustration 1.5 associated with an income statement.

ILLUSTRATION 1.5

> *Income statement (operating statement, statement of operations). An accounting report that pictures the results of operating for a period of time.* (Question answered by an income statement: How well did the organization do during a period of time?)
>
> *Revenue. The inflow of assets in return for services performed or products delivered during a period.*
>
> *Expense. A sacrifice, or cost, incurred to generate revenue.*
>
> *Net income. The amount by which the revenues for a period exceed the expenses incurred to generate them.*

OBJECTIVE 1a. State the question answered by an income statement.

OBJECTIVE 2e. Define revenue.

OBJECTIVE 2f. Define expense.

OBJECTIVE 2g. Define net income.

ILLUSTRATION 1.6

MINIM COMPANY		
Statement of Changes in Financial Position (Cash Basis)		
For the Month of July 19--		

FINANCIAL RESOURCES PROVIDED

Cash Provided by Operations		
Cash received for services performed	$4,520	
Cash applied to expenses	3,445	
Cash provided by operations	$1,075	
Financial Resources Provided by Other Sources		
Additional investment by owner	500	
Total financial resources provided		$1,575
FINANCIAL RESOURCES APPLIED		
Cash Withdrawn by Owner		1,525
Net Increase in Cash		$ 50

Statement of Changes in Financial Position

Today, a statement of changes in financial position is prepared as a third principal statement to accompany the balance sheet and income statement. *A statement of changes in financial position, sometimes called a funds statement, shows the sources and uses of financial resources during a period of time.*

The statement of changes in financial position may emphasize cash flows or working capital flows.[5] In either case, the statement will include the effects of all significant financing activities. Since you are probably more familiar with cash flows than with working capital flows,[6] the statement presented in Illustration 1.6 emphasizes cash flows.

Notice that the statement is not concerned with revenues or expenses of the month, but rather with the flows of resources in and out of the company. Keep in mind that we are purposely making our examples simple at this point, and that statement arrangements vary in practice. Statements of changes in financial position are covered in some depth in Chapter 18. For the moment, the following points are worth remembering.

OBJECTIVE 1c. State the questions answered by a statement of changes in financial position.

Statement of changes in financial position (funds statement). A financial statement that shows the sources and uses of financial resources during a period of time. (Questions answered by a statement of changes in financial position: Where did financial resources come from during the period? What were financial resources used for during the period?)

---

[5]*APB Opinion No. 19*, "Reporting Changes in Financial Position," American Institute of Certified Public Accountants (New York, 1971) Par. 12.

[6]Working capital, defined as current assets less current liabilities, is discussed in Chapter 18.

BOOKKEEPING VERSUS ACCOUNTING

Financial statements are the end products of an accounting system. A great deal of effort goes into gathering and processing data about a concern before the facts end up in an accounting report. Much of the work required is clerical in nature and can be performed by office workers, machines, and computers. The routine clerical tasks of collecting and processing financial information are often referred to as *bookkeeping*. Bookkeeping is a part of accounting, but accounting involves much more than bookkeeping.

Bookkeepers perform the routine, repetitive tasks of collecting and processing financial information. Accountants are responsible for designing the systems within which bookkeepers work; supervising the day-to-day work of bookkeepers; recording unusual and complex transactions; preparing, analyzing, and interpreting accounting reports; auditing the records; and performing a variety of other complex accounting activities.

OBJECTIVE 3a. Differentiate bookkeeper and accountant.

ACCOUNTING SPECIALTIES

There is no clear-cut way to categorize accounting specialties because of the variety of combinations of duties found in practice. However, Illustration 1.7 shows some of the more common accounting specialties.

Public Accounting

Public accountants work individually or in public accounting firms to provide accounting services to others for a fee. Public accountants who meet a state's educational and experience requirements and pass a uniform national examination may be licensed by the state as a CPA (Certified Public Accountant). The 2½-day CPA exam is prepared by the American Institute of Certified Public Accountants and is administered nationally twice a year. You can find out what the CPA requirements are for a particular state by writing to the state's board of accountancy.

OBJECTIVE 3b. Differentiate public, private, and governmental accounting.

ILLUSTRATION 1.7

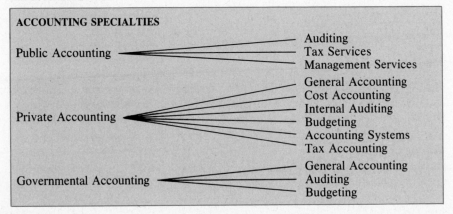

ACCOUNTING SPECIALTIES

Public Accounting
- Auditing
- Tax Services
- Management Services

Private Accounting
- General Accounting
- Cost Accounting
- Internal Auditing
- Budgeting
- Accounting Systems
- Tax Accounting

Governmental Accounting
- General Accounting
- Auditing
- Budgeting

OBJECTIVE 3c. Differentiate general and cost accounting, budgeting, and auditing.

CPAs provide auditing, tax, and management services to their clients. *Auditing is the process of examining a concern's financial statements and the underlying accounting records to determine whether the statements are presented fairly.* Investors, lenders, and others who use a concern's financial statements as a basis for deciding whether to buy or sell stock, lend money, or take some other action are interested in the CPA's *audit report.*

In the tax area, CPAs interpret tax rules and regulations, help clients develop plans for minimizing taxes, and aid in the preparation of federal and local tax returns. Management services include development of accounting and control systems, actuarial studies, product profitability analyses, and numerous other services to managers.

Private Accounting

OBJECTIVE 3b. Differentiate public, private, and governmental accounting.

*Accountants employed by organizations on a salaried basis are sometimes referred to as **private accountants**.* While the nature of their responsibilities depends on the size of the concern and the extent to which an accountant specializes, there are some common specialty areas.

OBJECTIVE 3c. Differentiate general and cost accounting, budgeting, and auditing.

*In **general accounting**, the accountant is responsible for the overall process of collecting, processing, and reporting financial information.*

*In **cost accounting**, the professional is responsible for the identification and control of costs, including the processing and reporting of cost information.*

Internal auditing is performed by an organization's own accountants to ensure that its record keeping is efficiently performed and relatively free of errors. Internal auditors also inform managers of instances where their directives are not being followed.

Budgeting is the process of projecting future financial outcomes for an organization, and subsequently comparing the projections to the actual results. Budgeting is a necessary part of a company's planning efforts.

Some accountants specialize in the design of accounting systems, others in helping organizations comply with the various tax laws.

Governmental Accounting

OBJECTIVE 3b. Differentiate public, private, and governmental accounting.

Like other organizations, *government units must collect and report financial information, a process sometimes referred to as **governmental accounting**.* Governmental accountants may specialize in budgeting, auditing, or a variety of other areas. The *Internal Revenue Service (IRS),* for example, employs accountants to make sure taxpayers comply with federal tax laws. Other governmental agencies are involved in a variety of accounting functions. The *General Accounting Office (GAO)* reports to Congress on whether federal agencies have expended funds in accordance with congressional legislation. The *Securities and Exchange Commission (SEC)* is responsible for ensuring that adequate information is available to investors.

EVOLUTION OF ACCOUNTING

Accounting, as it is practiced today, evolved gradually over the years, and we cannot pinpoint the time of the first accounting system. Accounting arose to satisfy people's needs for information, and its origins predate recorded history. Members of ancient tribes undoubtedly used some rudimentary means of accounting to tribal chiefs. An accounting system of some sort was also needed to keep track of trading activity between tribes.

As societies became more complex, accounting was needed for maintaining tax records, answering to wealthy landowners, and providing information about caravans, trading voyages, and other early business ventures.

Until fairly recent times, most businesses were small and easy to keep track of. The owner was usually involved in the daily operations of a business and had a pretty good idea of how well it was doing. Informal notations about important events were made in a diary, sometimes referred to as a *day book,* and as a rule that was sufficient to meet the owner's needs for information. However, with the industrial revolution, the increase in corporate business, and the advent of income taxation,[7] more sophisticated financial information was called for. As always, accounting concepts and practices were adapted to meet the needs of the times. It is an evolutionary process that is still going on.

ACCOUNTING AUTHORITIES

Changes in accounting practices occurred somewhat randomly during most of accounting's development. Only in this century have professional associations and government agencies begun to exert formal influences to bring about needed changes in accounting practice.

In the United States, the *American Institute of Certified Public Accountants (AICPA)* probably has had the most influence on accounting practices. It was largely the efforts of this institute that resulted in the formation of the independent *Financial Accounting Standards Board (FASB),* supported by CPAs and business people, which issues "Statements on Financial Accounting Standards." These official standards are generally adhered to in practice, and when auditing accounting records, CPAs attempt to ensure compliance with the standards.

An agency of the federal government, the *Securities and Exchange Commission (SEC),* also exerts a great deal of influence on accounting practice. The SEC attempts to ensure that investors are provided adequate and reliable information about corporations that issue new securities, as well as about those whose securities are traded through organized stock exchanges.

Another government agency, the *Internal Revenue Service (IRS),* has a considerable indirect influence on accounting practice. Although the IRS

---

[7]The first income tax law in the United States considered constitutional was effective March 1, 1913, four days after the Sixteenth Amendment was ratified.

has little interest in accounting reports other than tax returns, accounting systems must be designed to generate the information needed to comply with the tax laws.

A host of other government agencies and a number of associations of accountants have varying degrees of influence on how accounting is done. The *American Accounting Association,* made up largely of academic accountants, and the *National Association of Accountants,* most of whose members are private accountants, both sponsor formal research projects and issue occasional position papers on aspects of accounting practice. As you proceed in your business studies, you will come across references to a number of the other agencies and associations that influence accounting practice.

GLOSSARY FOR SECTION 1.A

Accountant   One who designs systems; supervises bookkeepers; prepares, analyzes, and interprets financial reports; audits accounting records; and/or performs other complex accounting activities.

Accounting   The act of collecting, processing, reporting, analyzing, interpreting, and projecting financial information. (See other definitions in Illustration 1.1.)

Accounting system   A method by which financial data are collected, processed, and reported.

Assets   Economic resources (properties) of an organization.

Auditing   The process of examining financial statements and the underlying accounting records to determine whether the statements are presented fairly.

Balance sheet (position statement, statement of condition)   A financial statement that shows the position, or condition, of an organization at a particular point in time.

Bookkeeper   One who performs routine record-keeping tasks in an accounting system.

Budgeting   The process of projecting future financial outcomes for an organization, and subsequently comparing the projections to actual results.

Cost accounting   The identification and control of costs, and the processing and reporting of cost information.

CPA   One who has passed the Uniform CPA Exam and has also attained the educational and experience background required for licensing by a state to practice as a *certified public accountant.*

Expense   A sacrifice, or cost, incurred to generate revenue.

Financial accounting   The act of gathering and reporting financial information to users outside of (external to) the organization being accounted for.

General accounting   The overall process of collecting, processing, and reporting financial information.

Governmental accounting   The act of processing and reporting financial information about governmental units.

Income statement (operating statement, statement of operations)   A financial statement that shows the results of operating for a period of time.

Internal auditing   Auditing that is performed by an organization's own accountants to ensure that record keeping is efficiently performed and relatively free of errors.

Liabilities   Economic obligations of (amounts owed by) an organization.

Managerial accounting   The act of providing useful information to managers (internal users) of the organization being accounted for.

Net income   The amount by which the revenues for a period exceed the expenses incurred to generate them.

Owners' equity (capital)   Owners' claims on the assets of an organization.

Private accountant   An accountant who is employed by a concern on a salary basis.

Public accountant   An accountant who works individually or in a public accounting firm to provide accounting services to others for a fee.

Revenue   The inflow of assets in return for services performed or products delivered during a period.

Statement of changes in financial position (funds statement)   A financial statement that shows the sources and uses of financial resources during a period of time.

SELF-QUIZ ON OBJECTIVES FOR SECTION 1.A
Solutions to Self-Quiz begin on page B-1.

1. **OBJECTIVE 1.** State in your own words the overall questions answered by these financial statements:
   a. An income statement.
   b. A balance sheet.
   c. A statement of changes in financial position.

2. **OBJECTIVE 2.** In your own words define the following:
   a. Accounting.
   b. Asset.
   c. Liability.
   d. Owners' equity.
   e. Revenue.
   f. Expense.
   g. Net income.

3. **OBJECTIVE 3.** Differentiate these expressions:
   a. Bookkeeper; accountant.
   b. Public accounting; private accounting; governmental accounting.
   c. General accounting; cost accounting; budgeting; auditing.
   d. Financial accounting; managerial accounting.

DISCUSSION QUESTIONS FOR SECTION 1.A

1. Why is accounting referred to as the language of business?

2. The expressions "account for" and "accounting" are common in everyday conversation. How are the everyday meanings of the expressions similar to (or different from) their more restricted meanings in accounting for organizations?

3. Why is it difficult to pinpoint clear-cut specialties within the practice of public accounting?

4. What is a CPA, and how do you become one?

5. How does a CPA's opinion increase the usefulness of an accounting report?

6. Why are most cost accountants employed by manufacturing concerns?

7. Why do organizations employ internal auditors?

8. Almost all budgeting specialists work for very large organizations. Why?

9. What is the purpose of the Securities and Exchange Commission?

10. How many types of users of accounting information can you list?

11. Why would a firm's suppliers be interested in its accounting reports?

12. How and why do you suppose accounting originated?

13. Ratification of the Sixteenth Amendment to the Constitution was quickly followed by an income tax law. What effects do you suppose this event had on the practice of accounting?

14. How has the rapid growth of government (in terms of people employed, services rendered, and controls imposed) affected the practice of accounting?

15. What is the Financial Accounting Standards Board (FASB), and what is its purpose?

SECTION 1.B

The Accounting Equation

OBJECTIVES

This portion of the chapter deals with the effects on the accounting equation of various kinds of transactions and events. At the conclusion of your study, you should be able to

1. Write the accounting equation.

2. Reflect into an accounting equation, by writing plus and minus amounts under account titles, events of the following kinds:
   a. An owner investment of cash.
   b. The payment of cash for another asset.
   c. The purchase of an asset on account.
   d. The purchase of an asset for a cash down payment and the remaining amount payable on account.
   e. Payment of cash on a liability.
   f. Withdrawal of cash by an owner.
   g. The receipt of revenue in cash.
   h. The recognition of revenue as a receivable.
   i. The payment of cash for an expense.
   j. An expense incurred on account.
   k. The expiration of an asset to expense.

3. Prepare in good form:
   a. A balance sheet that shows account totals within an accounting equation at a point in time.
   b. An income statement that shows the revenues and expenses that were reflected into an accounting equation during a period of time.

4. State in your own words each of the following accounting concepts:
   a. Entity.　　　　d. Realization.
   b. Monetary.　　　e. Matching.
   c. Cost.　　　　　f. Time period.

THE ENTITY CONCEPT

The purpose of accounting is to provide useful information about an organization to people who need such information. The activities of a new business concern are used here to introduce some of the basic concepts of accounting. George Metts has decided to start the Metts Delivery Service to deliver parcels throughout the city.

George—and others as well—needs information about the business, which is to be viewed as a separate *entity* for accounting purposes. Accounting reports are more clearly identified with the entity when the personal affairs of owners and other individuals are kept separate from the affairs of the entity.

The concept of an entity underlies much of what is done in accounting. It is mainly an assumption made to help identify the particular events to be accounted for. The assumption may be described as follows.

OBJECTIVE 4a. State the entity concept.

> *Entity concept. Each organization for which we account is an independent entity, separate from its owners, managers, customers, creditors, and all other persons and entities with which it deals.*

ASSETS

An entity usually consists of more than just a name. In most cases, various kinds of economic resources, or properties, are needed to carry on activities. *Resources* are things that are useful, productive, and valuable; as pointed out in the previous section, resources of an entity at a point in time are called *assets*.

To set his business venture into motion on March 2, George transfers $5,000 from his personal bank account to a new checking account in the name of the business, Metts Delivery Service. The cash is now to be viewed as an *asset* (property) possessed by the new entity, and is the first event to be recognized for accounting purposes.

Since there were no other assets before this, the event might be expressed as shown in Illustration 1.8.

OWNER'S EQUITY

At this point we can remember easily where the asset cash came from. As the entity acquires more and more assets, however, it will become increasingly difficult to pin down all the *sources* of the assets held. For this reason, the single event should be viewed as consisting of *two* elements.

> 1. The receipt of $5,000 cash
> 2. Supplied by the owner of the business

ILLUSTRATION 1.8

METTS DELIVERY SERVICE Assets	
Previously held	$ –0–
Cash received	+ 5,000
Total assets	$5,000

Remember, the business is to be viewed as an *independent* entity. In accounting for the entity, we will not be concerned with the owner's personal activities. Nevertheless, George still has a claim to the cash that is held by the business, because he owns the business entity.

Accounting always identifies the claims (or rights) against the assets held by the entity.

Resources	=	Sources
Assets	=	Claims against assets

*The expression of the equality of an entity's assets with the claims against them is referred to as the **accounting equation.*** You will come to see that all but the simplest of accounting systems are based on the accounting equation.

Another word for a claim against assets is *equity,* and an *owner's equity,* sometimes called *capital,* is the owner's claim against the assets of an entity. George's investment of $5,000 may be expressed in the entity's accounting equation as follows.

METTS DELIVERY SERVICE		
Assets	=	Owner's Equity
+ 5,000		+ 5,000

OBJECTIVE 2a. Reflect into an accounting equation an owner investment of cash.

TRANSACTIONS

At the outset George plans to run his business from his home, but he does need office supplies such as paper forms and envelopes. On March 2 he purchases these items from an office supply store and writes a $60 check on the new business bank account to pay for them.

The purchase of office supplies is a transaction that has changed the entity's position. *A **transaction** is simply an economic event that requires accounting recognition.* George's investment of money in his business was also a transaction.

The office supplies are assets (resources) held by the business. Part of the asset cash that was in the bank went to pay for the supplies. The decrease and increase in assets might be inserted into the accounting equation as shown in Illustration 1.9 on the next page.

Since one asset was exchanged for another, the overall picture has not changed. However, the *makeup* of the assets has changed.

The categories of assets (cash, office supplies) are referred to as *accounts.* As you will see later, accounts are also devices for keeping track

ILLUSTRATION 1.9

METTS DELIVERY SERVICE		
Assets	**=**	**Owner's Equity**
+ 5,000 ⎫ Cash		+5,000
− 60 ⎬		
+ 60 ⎭ Office Supplies		
5,000		

of increases and decreases in individual asset, liability, and owners' equity components. An account is therefore defined to encompass both meanings:

> **Account.** *A category, or class, of accounting information. A device for keeping track of increases and decreases in individual asset, liability, and owners' equity components.*

The arrangement of the equation in Illustration 1.10 shows the effects of the transaction in terms of individual accounts.

THE MONETARY CONCEPT

You may have noticed that the office supplies were reflected into the equation in dollars, rather than in numbers of envelopes or sheets of forms or whatever. Accounting recognizes transactions in monetary units, which involves another underlying assumption of accounting. The *monetary concept* might be stated as follows.

OBJECTIVE 4b. State the monetary concept.

> *Monetary concept. Transactions can be stated in terms of monetary units.*

The particular monetary unit used depends on the country in which the accounting takes place. In the United States, accounting is done in U.S. dollars; in England, the British pound is used; and so on.

ILLUSTRATION 1.10

METTS DELIVERY SERVICE				
Assets			**=**	**Owner's Equity**
Cash	+	Office Supplies	=	G. Metts, Capital
+ 5,000				+ 5,000
− 60	+	60		
4,940	+	60	=	5,000

OBJECTIVE 2b. Reflect into an accounting equation the payment of cash for another asset.

THE COST CONCEPT

The manner in which the purchase of office supplies was recognized involves another accounting concept. Once an asset is recorded at its cost basis, it is usually left at that figure until the asset, or a portion of it, is used or disposed of.[8] In accounting, a *cost is simply a sacrifice measured in monetary units,* and the cost concept may be stated as follows.

Cost concept. *Assets are recorded and maintained in accounting records at their cost bases.*

OBJECTIVE 4c. State the cost concept.

LIABILITIES

When George returns to the office supply store on March 3 to buy several additional items, the store manager offers to establish a charge account for the new business entity. Supplies costing $25 are charged (purchased on account). The promise of Metts Delivery Service to pay cash in the future is an *account payable* (to the office supply store, it is an *account receivable*). The account payable is a *liability* of the entity. Recall from the previous section that liabilities are economic obligations of an entity. They represent claims against an entity and are also sources of assets (resources), somewhat akin to owners' claims.

The purchase of supplies on account may be reflected into the equation as shown in Illustration 1.11.

A balance sheet is actually a formal presentation of the accounting equation at a point in time. Illustration 1.12 on the next page presents a balance sheet for Metts, showing the additional supplies and the liability to the store from which they came.

Now let's consider a slightly more complex transaction involving a liability. George would like to buy a panel truck for delivering parcels and

ILLUSTRATION 1.11

METTS DELIVERY SERVICE						
Assets			=	Liabilities	+	Owner's Equity
Cash	+	Office Supplies	=	Accounts Payable	+	G. Metts, Capital
+ 5,000					+	5,000
− 60	+	60				
4,940	+	60	=			5,000
	+	25		+ 25		
4,940	+	85	=	25	+	5,000

OBJECTIVE 2c. Reflect into an accounting equation the purchase of an asset on account.

[8] An exception to this generalization occurs when the value of an asset falls below its cost basis. This "lower of cost or market" approach will be discussed at a later point. As assets expire, their costs become expenses.

ILLUSTRATION 1.12

METTS DELIVERY SERVICE Balance Sheet March 3, 19--			
ASSETS		*LIABILITIES*	
Cash	$4,940	Accounts payable	$ 25
Office supplies	85		
		OWNER'S EQUITY	
	———	G. Metts, capital	5,000
		Total Liabilities and	
Total Assets	$5,025	Owner's Equity	$5,025

locates a used truck for $6,500. But we see from the balance sheet that the entity has only $4,940 of cash left. It would not be wise to use all the available cash to purchase a truck, because cash will probably be needed for other things.

George could invest more cash in the business if he has any that he could spare. Instead, he decides that the entity should borrow some of the money needed. On March 4 the truck dealer takes an initial cash payment of $2,500 and George's written promise to pay the remainder at $200 a month. A *written* promise to pay money in the future is called a *note payable* (to the truck dealer, it is a *note receivable*).[9]

The purchase of the truck is a **compound transaction** *in that it affects more than two accounts.* The purchase of the truck may be reflected into the equation as shown in Illustration 1.13.

OBJECTIVE 2d. Reflect into an accounting equation the purchase of an asset for a cash down payment and the remainder on account.

ILLUSTRATION 1.13

METTS DELIVERY SERVICE										
		Assets			=		Liabilities		+	Owner's Equity
		Office				Accounts		Note		G. Metts,
Cash	+	Supplies	+	Truck	=	Payable	+	Payable	+	Capital
+ 5,000									+	5,000
− 60	+	60								
4,940	+	60			=					5,000
	+	25				+ 25				
4,940	+	85			=	25			+	5,000
− 2,500			+	6,500			+	4,000		
2,440	+	85	+	6,500	=	25	+	4,000	+	5,000

---

[9]Note obligations are discussed in more detail in Chapter 6.

ILLUSTRATION 1.14

	METTS DELIVERY SERVICE **Balance Sheet** **March 4, 19—**		
ASSETS		*LIABILITIES*	
Cash	$2,440	Accounts payable	$ 25
Office supplies	85	Note payable	4,000
Truck	6,500		
		Total Liabilities	$4,025
		OWNER'S EQUITY	
	____	G. Metts, capital	5,000
		Total Liabilities and	
Total Assets	$9,025	Owner's Equity	$9,025

The balance sheet in Illustration 1.14 pictures the status of the accounting equation after the purchase of the truck.

On March 10 George makes the first $200 payment on the note. The effects of this transaction are:

1. A $200 decrease in cash
2. A $200 decrease in note payable

The payment on the note may be put into the equation as shown in Illustration 1.15.

OBJECTIVE 2e. Reflect into an accounting equation the payment of cash on a liability.

ILLUSTRATION 1.15

METTS DELIVERY SERVICE

		Assets			=	Liabilities			+	Owner's Equity
Cash	+	Office Supplies	+	Truck	=	Accounts Payable	+	Note Payable	+	G. Metts, Capital
+ 5,000									+	5,000
− 60	+	60								
4,940	+	60			=					5,000
	+	25				+ 25				
4,940	+	85			=	25			+	5,000
− 2,500			+	6,500	=		+	4,000		
2,440	+	85	+	6,500	=	25	+	4,000	+	5,000
− 200							−	200		
2,240	+	85	+	6,500	=	25	+	3,800	+	5,000

If you wish, you can prepare the balance sheet to reflect the equation as it now stands.

OWNER WITHDRAWALS

From time to time, George may need to withdraw money from his business for personal use. A $500 withdrawal on March 15 has the following effects.

> **1.** A $500 decrease in cash
> **2.** A $500 decrease in owner's equity

The withdrawal of cash reduces George's equity and may be reflected into the equation as shown in Illustration 1.16.

The balance sheet in Illustration 1.17 shows the accounts (categories) of the equation as they stand after all the foregoing transactions.

NATURE OF THE ACCOUNTING EQUATION

OBJECTIVE 2f. Reflect into an accounting equation the withdrawal of cash by the owner.

A clear understanding of the accounting equation is essential, because most accounting systems are based on it. The apparent simplicity of the equation tends to cloud its relative importance in the study of accounting. The equation is actually an *identity*, with the two sides representing different versions of the same thing. The left side of the equation, assets, consists of the resources (properties) held by the entity; the right side of the equation, equities, represents the claims against the resources.

ILLUSTRATION 1.16

METTS DELIVERY SERVICE

		Assets			=	Liabilities			+	Owner's Equity
Cash	+	Office Supplies	+	Truck	=	Accounts Payable	+	Note Payable	+	G. Metts, Capital
+ 5,000									+	5,000
− 60	+	60								
4,940	+	60			=					5,000
	+	25				+ 25				
4,940	+	85			=	25			+	5,000
− 2,500			+	6,500			+	4,000		
2,440	+	85	+	6,500	=	25	+	4,000	+	5,000
− 200							−	200		
2,240	+	85	+	6,500	=	25	+	3,800	+	5,000
− 500									−	500
1,740	+	85	+	6,500	=	25	+	3,800	+	4,500

ILLUSTRATION 1.17

METTS DELIVERY SERVICE			
Balance Sheet			
March 15, 19––			
ASSETS		*LIABILITIES*	
Cash	$1,740	Accounts payable	$ 25
Office supplies	85	Note payable	3,800
Truck	6,500		
		Total Liabilities	$3,825
		OWNER'S EQUITY	
	———	G. Metts, capital	4,500
		Total Liabilities and	
Total Assets	$8,325	Owner's Equity	$8,325

An element of an equation may be moved (transposed) from one side of the equals sign to the other by changing its sign. Thus the equation is mathematically correct in three different forms (Illustration 1.18).

This fact may be illustrated with the totals from the balance sheet of March 15 (Illustration 1.19).

Although all three variations of the equation are mathematically correct, the third is less useful as a model of the entity. The owner's claim is more of a *residual* than are liabilities, because creditors' claims take first priority. As mentioned previously, a balance sheet is a formal expression of the first arrangement of the accounting equation.

ILLUSTRATION 1.18

1. Assets = Liabilities   + Owner's Equity
2. Assets − Liabilities   = Owner's Equity
3. Assets − Owner's Equity = Liabilities

OBJECTIVE 1. **Write an accounting equation.**

ILLUSTRATION 1.19

1. Assets = Liabilities   + Owner's Equity
   $8,325 = $3,825   + $4,500

2. Assets − Liabilities   = Owner's Equity
   $8,325 − $3,825   = $4,500

3. Assets − Owner's Equity = Liabilities
   $8,325 − $4,500   = $3,825

ILLUSTRATION 1.20

METTS DELIVERY SERVICE								
	Assets			=	Liabilities		+	Owner's Equity
		Office			Accounts	Note		G. Metts,
Cash	+	Supplies	+ Truck	=	Payable	+ Payable	+	Capital
1,740	+	85	+ 6,500	=	25	+ 3,800	+	4,500
+ 1,200							+	1,200

OBJECTIVE 2g. Reflect into an accounting equation the receipt of revenue in cash.

REVENUE TRANSACTIONS

To illustrate the effects of revenues and expenses on the accounting equation, we will follow the operating activities of Metts Delivery Service. George Metts started his business on March 1, and by March 15 the entity had the financial position shown in the balance sheet in Illustration 1.17 on the preceding page.

Revenue in Cash

During the remainder of March, George delivers many parcels for his customers, who in turn pay the business $1,200 cash for the services rendered. The cash, which is deposited in the entity's bank account, also represents revenue earned. The event is viewed as consisting of *two* elements.

> **1.** The receipt of $1,200 cash
> **2.** Representing revenue earned (increase in owner's equity)

The receipt of cash revenue represents an increase in both assets and owner's equity and might be reflected into the equation as shown in Illustration 1.20.

Revenue on Account

Additional parcels are delivered during March for several customers who agreed to pay delivery fees of $500 during April. The amounts due from these customers are legal *accounts receivable* and should be recognized also as revenues that have been earned during March. The usual practice of showing revenues when the *legal claim* to cash arises is referred to as the *accrual basis* of reporting revenues.[10] To *accrue* simply means to grow, or come into existence.

---

[10]The recognition of revenue at the point that cash is received is called the *cash basis* of accounting. The *cash basis* is used by some small service concerns but is not generally acceptable for financial reporting purposes.

Realization Concept

The recognition of revenue as soon as it is *earned*, even though money will not be received until later, is referred to as the *realization concept*.

> *Realization concept. Revenue arises at the point of sale of property, or upon the rendering of a service.*

OBJECTIVE 4d. State the realization concept.

The two elements of the transaction involving revenue on account are as follows.

1. The recognition of $500 of accounts receivable
2. Representing revenue earned (increase in owner's equity)

The elements are expressed in the equation as shown in Illustration 1.21.

EXPENSE TRANSACTIONS

Matching Concept

Expenses are incurred for the purpose of generating revenues. In fact, accounting attempts to *match* expenses with the revenues they help to generate.

> *Matching concept. Revenues should be matched with the expenses that were responsible for their generation.*

OBJECTIVE 4e. State the matching concept.

An income statement is a formal expression of the matching concept in that the expenses shown thereon are presumed to have aided in the generation of the revenue for the period.

OBJECTIVE 2h. Reflect into an accounting equation the recognition of revenue as a receivable.

ILLUSTRATION 1.21

METTS DELIVERY SERVICE

	Assets				=	Liabilities			+	Owner's Equity
Cash	+	Office Supplies	+	Truck	+	Accounts Receivable	=	Accounts Payable	+	Note Payable	+	G. Metts, Capital
1,740	+	85	+	6,500			=	25	+	3,800	+	4,500
+ 1,200											+	1,200
					+	500					+	500

ILLUSTRATION 1.22

METTS DELIVERY SERVICE

		Assets			=	Liabilities			+	Owner's Equity
Cash	+	Office Supplies	+	Truck	+	Accounts Receivable	=	Accounts Payable	+	Note Payable	+	G. Metts, Capital

Cash	Office Supplies	Truck	Accounts Receivable	Accounts Payable	Note Payable	G. Metts, Capital	
1,740 +	85 +	6,500		= 25 +	3,800 +	4,500	
+1,200					+	1,200	} Delivery
			+ 500		+	500	} fees
− 400					−	400	Rent expense

<p>

OBJECTIVE 2i. Reflect into an accounting equation the payment of cash for an expense.

Cash Expense

Most organizations require a certain amount of office and storage space. Early in March, George rented a small garage-type building, and on March 16 he writes a check for $400 to pay that month's rent. As always, a transaction involves at least two effects on the accounting equation.

> 1. The payment of $400 cash
> 2. Representing rent expense (decrease in owner's equity)

Whereas revenues *increase* George's equity in the business, expenses *decrease* his equity (Illustration 1.22).

Expense on Account

George has arranged with a service station to buy gasoline on account for use in the truck. At the end of March, the station bills Metts Delivery Service for $180 worth of gasoline obtained during March. Let us assume that substantially all the gasoline was used in March. Here are the elements of this transaction.

> 1. The recognition of $180 of accounts payable
> 2. Representing gasoline expense (decrease in owner's equity)

These elements are reflected into the equation as shown in Illustration 1.23. Note that the gasoline consumption resulted in an expense, even though no cash was involved.

ILLUSTRATION 1.23

METTS DELIVERY SERVICE

					Assets	=	Liabilities			+	Owner's Equity	
Cash	+	Office Supplies	+	Truck	+	Accounts Receivable	=	Accounts Payable	+	Note Payable	+	G. Metts, Capital	
1,740	+	85	+	6,500			=	25	+	3,800	+	4,500	
+ 1,200											+	1,200 ⎱	Delivery
					+	500					+	500 ⎰	fees
− 400											−	400	Rent expense
						+ 180					**−**	**180**	Gas expense

Asset Expirations

OBJECTIVE 2j. Reflect into an accounting equation an expense incurred on account.

Recall that office supplies were purchased early in March at a total cost of $85. At that time, the supplies were classified as an asset—property belonging to Metts Delivery Service. The *cost* of the supplies represented the sacrifice incurred by the business to obtain them (in money paid, or due to be paid in the future).

Some of the supplies, $20 worth, were used during March. The cost of these supplies must be removed from the asset account and recognized as an expense (Illustration 1.24). The elements are as follows.

1. A $20 reduction of office supplies on hand
2. Representing supplies expense (decrease in owner's equity)

OBJECTIVE 2k. Reflect into an accounting equation the expiration of an asset to expense.

ILLUSTRATION 1.24

METTS DELIVERY SERVICE

					Assets	=	Liabilities			+	Owner's Equity	
Cash	+	Office Supplies	+	Truck	+	Accounts Receivable	=	Accounts Payable	+	Note Payable	+	G. Metts, Capital	
1,740	+	85	+	6,500			=	25	+	3,800	+	4,500	
+ 1,200											+	1,200 ⎱	Delivery
					+	500					+	500 ⎰	fees
− 400											−	400	Rent expense
						+ 180					−	180	Gas expense
		− 20									**−**	**20**	Supplies expense

The truck is another asset that has been helpful in earning revenue. Certainly some of its life has been used up in the process of earning revenues during March. Therefore, some of the cost of the truck should be *matched* with March revenues.

George estimates that the truck will be used in the business for two years, after which it can probably be sold for $1,700. Therefore, he proposes that for accounting purposes, the difference between the cost of $6,500 and the $1,700 residual value be spread evenly over the 24 months of use. Thus the truck is assumed to expire, or *depreciate,* at the rate of $200 per month.

$$\frac{\$6,500 - \$1,700}{24 \text{ months}} = \frac{\$4,800}{24 \text{ months}} = \$200 \text{ per month depreciation}$$

Depreciation is simply the conversion of a portion of the cost of a long-term productive asset to expense as the asset is worn out in the process of generating revenue. For the month of March, the truck depreciation elements are as follows.

1. The expiration of $200 of truck cost
2. To depreciation expense (decrease in owner's equity)

OBJECTIVE 2k. Reflect into an accounting equation the expiration of an asset to expense.

These elements are reflected into the equation as shown in Illustration 1.25.

ILLUSTRATION 1.25

METTS DELIVERY SERVICE

		Assets				=	Liabilities			+	Owner's Equity	
Cash	+	Office Supplies	+	Truck	+	Accounts Receivable =	Accounts Payable	+	Note Payable	+	G. Metts, Capital	
1,740	+	85	+	6,500		=	25	+	3,800	+	4,500	
+ 1,200										+	1,200 ⎱	Delivery
					+	500				+	500 ⎰	fees
− 400										−	400	Rent expense
							+ 180			−	180	Gas expense
	−	20								−	20	Supplies expense
	−	200								−	200	Depr. expense

Expense Versus Cost

Costs are sacrifices in the form of assets paid or liabilities assumed. Assets are accounted for in terms of their costs. *Expenses* are in effect *expired* (used up) costs, whereas assets are *unexpired* (deferred) costs. Thus expenses are costs, but not all costs are expenses. Expenses, on one hand, are the resources (costs) that have been used up (expired) in the generation of revenue. Assets, on the other hand, are the resources (costs) that are available (unexpired) for use in the future.

It is worth emphasizing at this point that an expense may occur without a simultaneous cash outlay, as illustrated by both the purchase of gasoline on account and the depreciation. Expenses result as costs expire, indicating that resources are being used up in the process of realizing revenues.

BALANCE SHEET

The net effects of the revenue and expense transactions on the *position* of Metts Delivery Service can be obtained by summing the equation (Illustration 1.26).

A balance sheet prepared on March 31 will show the position of the entity at that point in time (see Illustration 1.27 on the next page).

The asset accounts are usually listed in the balance sheet in the order of their nearness to cash. Accounts receivable will soon be collected in cash, so they are listed right after cash; the truck is the asset with the longest life, so it is listed last.

ILLUSTRATION 1.26

METTS DELIVERY SERVICE

		Assets			=	Liabilities		+	Owner's Equity	
Cash	+	Office Supplies	+ Truck +	Accounts Receivable	=	Accounts Payable	+ Note Payable	+	G. Metts, Capital	
1,740	+	85	+ 6,500		=	25	+ 3,800	+	4,500	
+ 1,200								+	1,200 }	Delivery
				+ 500				+	500 }	fees
− 400								−	400	Rent expense
						+ 180		−	180	Gas expense
	−	20						−	20	Supplies expense
			− 200					−	200	Depr. expense
2,540	+	65	+ 6,300	+ 500	=	205	+ 3,800	+	5,400	

ILLUSTRATION 1.27

**OBJECTIVE 3a. Prepare
a balance sheet.**

METTS DELIVERY SERVICE
Balance Sheet
March 31, 19— —

ASSETS		LIABILITIES	
Cash	$2,540	Accounts payable	$ 205
Accounts receivable	500	Note payable	3,800
Office supplies	65		
Truck (net of depreciation)	6,300	Total Liabilities	$4,005
		OWNER'S EQUITY	
		G. Metts, capital	5,400
		Total Liabilities and	
Total Assets	$9,405	Owner's Equity	$9,405

INCOME STATEMENT

George can see that his owner's equity has increased by $400 since he started
his business with an investment of $5,000. He recalls that he withdrew $500
during March for his personal use. Therefore, the business must have produced
$900 for him, as indicated by the following computation.

Capital balance March 31		$5,400
Original investment	$5,000	
Withdrawn in March	500	
Capital left after withdrawal		4,500
Increase in capital balance		$ 900

The $900 increase is the difference between revenues and expenses
during March—the *net income* earned by the business. The figures under
the Owner's Equity column of the equation show the effects of the revenue
and expenses (Illustration 1.28).

ILLUSTRATION 1.28

OWNER'S EQUITY	
G. Metts, Capital	
4,500	Balance March 15
+ 1,200 }	
+ 500 }	Delivery fees
− 400	Rent expense
− 180	Gas expense
− 20	Supplies expense
− 200	Depreciation expense
5,400	Balance March 31

ILLUSTRATION 1.29

METTS DELIVERY SERVICE Income Statement For the Period March 16 through March 31, 19--		
Delivery fees earned		$1,700
Expenses		
Rent	$400	
Truck depreciation	200	
Gasoline	180	
Office supplies used	20	800
Net Income		$ 900

OBJECTIVE 3b. Prepare an income statement.

An income statement can be prepared from the information contained within the equity section of the equation. This statement will show George how well his business performed during the portion of March when it was delivering parcels (see Illustration 1.29).

We should keep in mind that no allowance has been made for the time and effort that George himself put into the business. Thus the net income of a proprietorship represents both the owner's reward for this time and effort and the return on his investment of money in the business.

Had the expenses for the period been greater than revenue, the difference would have been labeled **net loss.**

Time Period Concept

The income statement in Illustration 1.29 is for the last half of March, because no revenues were being realized prior to March 16. However, most income statements picture operations for an entire month, a calendar quarter, or a year.

To be meaningful, operating results must be tied to specific time periods. *The period of time for which we account is referred to as the* **accounting period.** The time period concept may be stated as follows.

Time period concept. *The activities of an entity are capable of being identified with particular calendar accounting periods.*

OBJECTIVE 4f. State the time period concept.

The time period concept is interrelated with a number of other accounting concepts. Revenues are considered *realized* within specific time periods; expenses as expired *costs* are *matched* with the revenues within the context of a *time period*. For example, part of the cost of the truck was matched as depreciation against the revenues realized during the time period covered by the income statement that was previously shown.

An income statement prepared for a period of time helps to explain the changes in position that occurred between the beginning and end of the period. In other words, an income statement is a bridge between two balance sheets—one at the beginning and one at the end of a period.

GLOSSARY FOR SECTION 1.B

Account   A category, or class, of accounting information. A device for keeping track of increases and decreases in individual asset, liability, and owners' equity components.

Accounting equation   An expression of the equality of an entity's assets with the claims against them.

Accounting period   The period of time for which accounting is done.

Compound transaction   A transaction that affects more than two accounts.

Cost   A sacrifice measured in monetary units.

Cost concept   The accounting concept of recording and maintaining assets in the records at their cost bases.

Depreciation   The conversion of a portion of the cost of a long-term productive asset to expense as the asset is worn out in the process of generating revenue.

Entity concept   The accounting assumption that each organization for which we account is an independent entity, separate from its owners, managers, customers, creditors, and all other persons and entities with which it deals.

Matching concept   The idea that revenues should be matched with the expenses that were responsible for their generation.

Monetary concept   The accounting assumption that transactions can be stated in terms of monetary units.

Net loss   The amount by which expenses exceed revenues for a period of time.

Realization concept   The presumption that revenue arises at the point of sale of property, or upon the rendering of a service.

Time period concept   The presumption that the activities of an entity are capable of being identified with particular calendar accounting periods.

Transaction   An economic event that requires accounting recognition.

SELF-QUIZ ON OBJECTIVES FOR SECTION 1.B
Solutions to Self-Quiz begin on page B-2.

1.   OBJECTIVE 1.   Write the accounting equation.

2.   Reflect transactions (a) through (e) in an accounting equation like the one shown for the Flox Company.

	Assets			=	**Liabilities**	+	**Owner's Equity**
		Office			Note		
Cash	+	Supplies	+	Car	=	Payable	+	R. Flox, Capital

Transactions

a) **OBJECTIVE 2a.** Raymond Flox invested $3,000 cash in his new business, the Flox Company.

b) **OBJECTIVE 2b.** Office supplies were purchased for a $20 cash payment.

c) **OBJECTIVE 2d.** A new car was purchased for use in the business. Cash of $500 was paid, and a $5,000 note payable was signed for the remaining cost.

d) **OBJECTIVE 2f.** Raymond Flox withdrew $400 in cash from the company.

e) **OBJECTIVE 2e.** A cash payment of $200 was made on the note payable.

3. **OBJECTIVE 3a.** The account totals of the accounting equation for the Flox Company are shown below at September 30. Prepare a balance sheet in good form for the Flox Company.

		Assets			=	**Liabilities**	+	**Owner's Equity**
		Office				Note		
Cash	+	Supplies	+	Car	=	Payable	+	R. Flox, Capital
4,000	+	75	+	5,500	=	4,200	+	5,375

4. Reflect into the accounting equation given, by writing plus and minus amounts under account titles, the January transactions for the Ripe Company.

RIPE COMPANY

		Assets			=	**Liabilities**	+	**Owner's Equity**
		Accounts				Accounts		
Cash	+	Receivable	+	Gasoline	=	Payable	+	J. Ripe, Capital
1,000	+	500	+	280	=	330	+	1,450

Transactions

a) **OBJECTIVE 2i.** Paid January rent, $250.

b) **OBJECTIVE 2j.** Received by mail a $90 electric bill for the month of January. The bill will not be paid until February.

c) **OBJECTIVE 2k.** Used gasoline costing $50 from the company's gasoline storage tank.

d) **OBJECTIVE 2g.** Collected $400 cash for services rendered in January.

e) **OBJECTIVE 2h.** Billed a customer $600 for services rendered in January. The customer has promised to pay during February.

5. **OBJECTIVE 3b.** Prepare an income statement in good form to reflect the revenues and expenses in the accounting equation for the month of January, which follows.

ACORN TREE SERVICE

		Assets			=	Liabilities	+	Owner's Equity
Cash	+	Accounts Receivable	+	Truck	=	Accounts Payable	+	T. Acorn, Capital
500	+	1,100	+	8,000	=	3,000	+	6,600
+ 2,000							+	2,000 Service revenue
− 500							−	500 Wage expense
			−	150			−	150 Depr. expense
						+ 200	−	200 Gasoline expense
− 400							−	400 Rent expense
1,600	+	1,100	+	7,850	=	3,200	+	7,350

6. **OBJECTIVE 4.** State in your own words each of the following accounting concepts.

   a. Entity   **d.** Realization

   b. Monetary   **e.** Matching

   c. Cost   **f.** Time period

DISCUSSION QUESTIONS FOR SECTION 1.B

1. How does an exchange of one asset for another affect the accounting equation?

2. What is a cost, as the term is used in accounting?

3. Why is the accounting equation referred to as an identity?

4. Liability and owner's equity claims are sometimes said to *cut across* all the assets. Why?

5. How are the following pairs of accounting concepts interrelated, or interdependent?

   a. Realization; time period

   b. Cost; matching

   c. Realization; matching

6. How does an income statement help to explain the changes between two balance sheets?

7. How do assets differ from expenses?

8. How can an asset become an expense?

9. What is the importance of matching revenues and expenses?

10. What does the expression *accounting period* mean?

11. Why is it important that both revenues and expenses be identified with particular accounting periods?

EXERCISES FOR SECTION 1.B

1.B.1. Perry Company has assets totaling $88,600 and liabilities of $36,800 on December 31. Determine the owner's equity in the Perry Company on December 31.

1.B.2. Calculate the missing elements below.

	Assets	Liabilities	Owner's Equity
a.	120,000	70,000	?
b.	?	25,000	35,000
c.	62,000	30,400	?
d.	28,700	?	10,900

1.B.3. Calculate the missing amounts.

	Revenues	Expenses	Net Income
a.	250,000	198,000	?
b.	86,000	?	9,800
c.	?	150,000	28,000
d.	94,000	110,000	?

1.B.4. Indicate whether the following statements are true or false.

a. Revenues are recognized when they are earned, expenses when they are paid in cash.

b. When assets expire they become liabilities.

c. Net income is a measure of accomplishment.

d. An accounting period is never longer than one month.

e. The matching concept is that assets are matched against corresponding liabilities.

f. Revenues less expenses yield net income.

g. Revenues of a period should be matched with expenses of the same period.

h. The more revenues earned during a period, the higher will be the cash balance at the end of the period.

PROBLEMS FOR SECTION 1.B
Alternate Problems for this section begin on page D-1.

1.B.5. The following information is available for the Rigby Company, owned by C. Rigby, at December 31.

Cash	$ 800
Supplies	75
Calculator	420
Automobile	6,100
Note payable	3,600

Required

Prepare a balance sheet for the company at December 31.

1.B.6. Belwah Company's revenues and expenses for December are as follows.

Fees earned	$4,200
Wage expense	3,600
Rent expense	500
Supplies expense	200
Telephone and utilities expense	180
Entertainment expense	250

Required

Prepare an income statement for December.

1.B.7. Three transactions for Zap Company are shown here.

Transactions

a) U. Zap invested $7,000 cash in her new company on July 1.

b) Zap purchased land on July 5 for $10,000, paying $4,000 cash and signing a note for the remaining cost.

c) Tools were purchased on July 7 for $600 cash.

Required

Prepare a balance sheet for Zap Company after each of the transactions.

1.B.8. Selected data for the Alex Gander Company are provided for the month of April.

Cash	$2,800
Accounts receivable	1,750
Accounts payable	1,825
A. Gander, capital	1,280
Fees earned	3,300
Rent revenue	450
Wage expense	1,100
Utilities expense	125
Rent expense	900
Other expense	180

Required

Prepare an income statement for April.

1.B.9. Each of the following transactions has two or more effects on the financial position of Bundy Company, which started business on June 1.

Transactions

a) On June 1, O. Bundy invested $15,000 cash in her new business, the Bundy Company.

b) On June 2, Bundy paid cash for $150 worth of office supplies.

c) On June 2, Bundy purchased a typewriter for $500 cash.

d) On June 3, Bundy purchased a truck for $12,000. A $2,000 cash down payment was made, and a note was signed for the remaining amount.

Required

1) For each transaction state the amount of the effect, whether it is an increase or decrease, and whether an asset, liability, and/or owner's equity is changed.

2) Write the accounting equation, including the names of the assets, liabilities, and owner's equity accounts; and show under the equation the effects of the four transactions. Be sure to total the columns either after each transaction or at the bottom.

3) Prepare a balance sheet for Bundy Company after the fourth transaction.

1.B.10. Soho Company has been in business for some time. The following equation indicates Soho's position at the end of March, except that the capital balance for B. Soho is missing.

SOHO COMPANY

	Assets		=	Liabilities	+	Owner's Equity
Cash +	Office Supplies +	Accounts Receivable	=	Accounts Payable	+	B. Soho, Capital
3,000 +	50 +	800	=	500	+	?

Required

1) Determine B. Soho's capital balance at March 31, and write it in Soho's accounting equation.

2) Reflect into Soho's accounting equation, by writing plus and minus amounts under account titles, the following April transactions for the Soho Company.

Transactions

a) Paid wages of $1,500 to employees for work done in April.

b) Charged (purchased on account) gasoline costing $120 for use in the company truck during April.

c) Used $18 worth of office supplies out of the storeroom.

d) Received $25 water bill for April.

e) Received a $100 payment from a customer for services rendered and billed in March.

f) Received $2,500 from customers for services rendered in April.

g) Paid $30 water bill from March.

SUMMARY OF CHAPTER 1

Accounting developed over the years as a means of providing financial information about organizations to a variety of users. Reports prepared for managerial (internal) users tend to be somewhat specialized, whereas general purpose reports are prepared for financial (external) users. A number of organizations and government agencies influence how accounting is performed.

A balance sheet pictures the condition of an organization at a point in time in terms of its assets, liabilities, and owner's equity. An income statement indicates how well a concern has done for a period of time by showing the revenues earned, the expenses incurred, and the resulting net income for the period. A statement of changes in financial position shows where resources came from and how resources were used during a period.

Accountants specialize in a variety of ways within the general areas of public, private, and governmental accounting. Some work in general accounting, while others perform as auditors, provide tax or management services, or work in budgeting, cost accounting, systems, or other specialties.

Most accounting systems are based on the accounting equation, whereby the assets of an entity are shown to be equivalent to the creditor and owner claims against them. The major equation elements are further divided into account categories, which supply information for the financial statements.

Various accounting concepts underlie the way accounting is done in practice. Transactions of an *entity* are quantified in *monetary* units. Assets are recorded at their *cost* bases. Cost sacrifices that have no carryover value are classified as expenses. And expenses are *matched* with *realized* revenues in the context of *time periods*.

PROBLEMS FOR CHAPTER 1
Alternate Problems for this chapter begin on page D-2.

1.1. Waldo Grunen started his own advertising agency on March 2 of this year. Until the new firm is better established, Waldo expects to do all the work himself. During the first month of operations his business, Grunen Ad Agency, was involved in the following transactions.

Transactions

a) Waldo deposited $10,000 of personal funds in a bank account in the firm's name.

b) Purchased office equipment for $6,000 on account. The equipment is expected to last for five years, after which it will be worthless.

c) Purchased advertising supplies for $410 cash.

d) Billed clients $500 for services rendered.

e) Paid $600 office rent for March.

f) Paid $3,000 on the account incurred for purchase of office equipment.

g) Billed clients $2,200 for services performed.

h) Collected $500 on accounts receivable.

i) Waldo withdrew $1,000 of cash from the business for his personal use.

j) Received a $150 electric bill for March. Payment of the bill is due on April 20.

k) Work was performed in March for which clients will be billed $800 during April. Waldo was simply too busy during March to prepare and mail the bills.

l) A count of advertising supplies shows supplies costing $140 are still on hand at the end of March.

Required

1) Show the effects of the foregoing transactions, including any needed month-end adjustments, under an accounting equation like the following.

Assets				= **Liabilities** + **Owner's Equity**	
Cash +	Accounts Receivable +	Advertising Supplies +	Office Equipment =	Accounts Payable +	W. Grunen, Capital

2) Total the account categories and make sure that the equation is in balance.

3) Prepare an income statement for the month of March.

4) Prepare a balance sheet that shows the firm's position at month-end.

5) Explain in accounting concept terms why you handled transaction (k) as you did.

6) State why you did, or did not, include the owner's withdrawal— transaction (i)—in the income statement.

1.2. On June 1 of this year, Laura Brite resigned her position with a public accounting firm so that she could start her own company. The new concern, Laura Brite, CPA, experienced the following transactions during June.

Transactions

a) Laura withdrew $5,000 from her personal savings account and deposited the amount in a business checking account for Laura Brite, CPA.

b) Laura wrote a check for $800 to pay June rent for office space.

c) Purchased a desk-top printing calculator for $1,200 on account (for credit). The calculator is expected to last for five years, after which it will be worthless.

d) Wrote a $200 check for various office supplies.

e) Wrote a check for $2,400 for used office furniture. Laura plans to use the furniture for two years, after which she will junk it and purchase new furniture that will be more suitable.

f) Sent bills totaling $600 to clients for services rendered during June.

g) Wrote a check for $500 to apply against the obligation incurred for purchase of the calculator—transaction (c).

h) Laura wrote and cashed a $400 business check to obtain money for personal living expenses.

i) Collected and deposited $250 of cash received on account from a client.

j) Received a $60 phone bill for the office telephone. The charges are for the month of June, but will not be paid until some time during July.

k) At month-end, Laura established that office supplies costing $160 are still on hand, the remainder having been used during June.

Required

1) Reflect the foregoing transactions, including any end-of-month adjustments that are necessary, into an accounting equation like the following. Then total the account categories to make sure the equation is in balance after all transactions are shown.

Assets					**= Liabilities + Owner's Equity**	
	Accounts	Office			Accounts	Laura Brite,
Cash +	Receivable +	Supplies +	Calculator +	Furniture =	Payable +	Capital

2) Prepare an income statement for the month of June.

3) Prepare a balance sheet that shows the firm's position at month-end.

4) Which of the accounting concepts discussed in this chapter were involved in your month-end adjustments for office supplies and depreciation?

5) Comment on the implications of the net loss shown on the income statement for June. Do you think that such losses are unusual for new business concerns? Why?

COMPREHENSION PROBLEM FOR CHAPTER 1

1.3. A fire in the rented office space of Shuster's Refuse Company destroyed all files and records in early January 19X5, but no assets owned by the company were lost in the fire. Mel Shuster obtained from his bank's microfilm records copies of all checks and deposit slips for 19X4. From these records he established that $30,000 of cash receipts from customers had been deposited in 19X4, and that checks were written during 19X4 in the following total amounts.

Gasoline	$ 3,400
Truck repairs	540
Office rent	960
Withdrawal by Mel for personal use	24,000
Total Checks	$28,900

Shuster Refuse Company's cash on deposit with the bank on December 31, 19X4, was $3,200.

Mel was also able to determine that $1,250 collected and deposited during the first week of January 19X4 was for refuse hauled during 19X3, and that $1,800 was collected in January 19X5 for refuse hauled during 19X4. Customers pay each week for the previous week's services.

From the records of the service station that services the truck, Mel was able to determine that $220 was owed for gasoline on December 31, 19X3, and that $300 was owed on December 31, 19X4. There were no other business liabilities outstanding on those dates.

Mel's only business asset is a truck for which he paid $24,000 in early January 19X3. The truck is expected to last for two more years (a total life of four years), after which it will be virtually worthless.

Required

1) Prepare an income statement for Shuster Refuse Company for the year 19X4.

2) Prepare a balance sheet that shows the company's position at December 31, 19X4.

3) Mel would like to compare the company's position at the beginning of 19X4 with the position at year-end. Prepare a balance sheet for the company that shows its position at December 31, 19X3.

4) Explain how Mel's withdrawals during 19X4 could exceed his company's net income and still result in an increase in the cash balance.

2
Accounting for Transactions

Chapter 2 covers the techniques by which accounting systems gather and process financial data for use in accounting reports. The data-gathering process is illustrated as a manual system, but most electronic data processing systems are based on similar techniques. One needs to understand clearly the basic accounting model before proceeding on to other accounting topics.

Chapter 2 consists of two sections. Section A concentrates on the rules for summarizing data by reflecting transactions into accounts. Accounts are viewed initially as abbreviated T-forms that, when arranged as components of the accounting equation, represent a model of the concern in question. A variety of transactions involving assets, liabilities, revenues, and expenses are introduced into the equation accounts, and the summarized results are pictured as accounting statements. The three main legal forms of business ownership are briefly discussed at the end of the section.

Section B concentrates on the functions of accounting systems, by which accounting data are processed. Transactions are documented, recorded, and summarized in order to obtain the data for accounting reports. Although some electronic systems are capable of performing two or more of the functions simultaneously, it is helpful to think of them as a series of activities. Accepted procedures for recording and summarizing data are illustrated, as is the trial balance format for showing account balances. The kinds of errors that can occur in accounting systems are discussed briefly.

SECTION 2.A
Summarizing Data

OBJECTIVES

This section concentrates on the rules for reflecting accounting information into account categories. At the completion of the section, you should be able to

1. Define the terms *debit* and *credit*.
2. State what a T-account is and indicate which is the debit side.
3. Reflect transactions into T-accounts.
4. Name and differentiate the three most common legal forms of business organization.

ACCOUNTS

Accounting information is accumulated and summarized in categories called *accounts*. In a way, an account is like a container, or bin, for storing information. A particular accounting system may use any number of accounts (categories) to provide the needed information.

Chart of Accounts

Most entities have a *chart of accounts, which lists the accounts currently in use in the accounting system.* Accounts are usually numbered in some meaningful way and grouped under accounting equation headings. For example, in the chart of accounts for Metts Delivery Service (Illustration 2.1), the

ILLUSTRATION 2.1

METTS DELIVERY SERVICE	
Chart of Accounts	
100 Assets	*300 Owner's Equity*
111 Cash	311 G. Metts, Capital
112 Accounts Receivable	312 G. Metts, Withdrawals
113 Office Supplies	*400 Revenue*
121 Truck	411 Delivery Fees
0121 Accumulated Depreciation— Truck	*500 Expenses*
200 Liabilities	511 Rent Expense
	512 Gasoline Expense
211 Accounts Payable	513 Supplies Expense
212 Note Payable	514 Depreciation Expense

first digit of an account number indicates the accounting equation element under which the account falls. Accumulated Depreciation (0121), in the asset section, will be explained later. G. Metts, Withdrawals (312), in the owner's equity section, has been provided to keep track of George Metts's withdrawals of cash for personal use.

Revenue and expense accounts are actually subsections of the owner's equity section but usually appear in charts of accounts under separate headings.

Ledgers

Each account within an accounting system is maintained as a separate category of the *general ledger, which consists of the asset, liability, and owner's equity accounts that make up the accounting equation for a particular entity.*

Ledger categories (accounts) are designed to fit the needs for information. In manual (noncomputerized) systems, each account is maintained as a page in a ledger book. The accounts are designed with a combination of columns and lines for writing in words and numbers. One account arrangement is shown in Illustration 2.2. This particular arrangement is divided in the middle, with two identical sides.

ILLUSTRATION 2.2

ACCOUNT TITLE								ACCOUNT NO.
Date	Description	Ref.	Amount	Date	Description	Ref.	Amount	

Some modern accounting systems summarize information electronically (by computer). In these systems, the ledger accounts may be on magnetic tapes or disks or in computer memory banks of some kind. When information is needed, the computer can provide printouts or picture the data on a television type of tube.

T-Accounts

For now, we will use *abbreviated (shorthand) versions of ledger accounts, called **T-accounts** because they resemble the letter T.* Accountants frequently use T-accounts to picture in brief the effects that transactions have on the accounting system.

THE ENTITY MODEL

T-accounts may be portrayed under the accounting equation to represent an accounting model of an entity. For example, the Metts Delivery Service would be pictured as in Illustration 2.3.

ILLUSTRATION 2.3

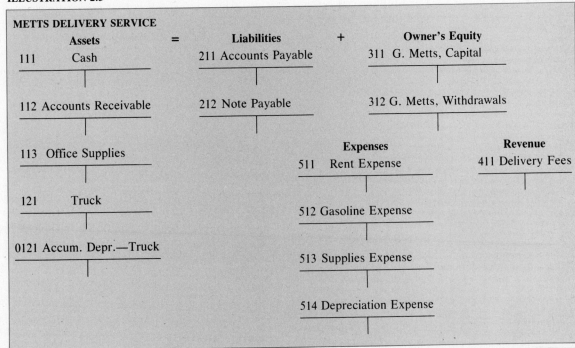

DEBIT AND CREDIT RULES

You can see from the following illustration that a T-account has two sides.

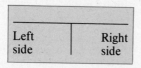

OBJECTIVE 1. Define debit and credit.

You have already come across a number of important terms that are part of the accounting language. The next two terms frequently cause confusion for accounting students. In accounting, we substitute the term *debit for left, and credit for right,* frequently abbreviated *Dr.* and *Cr.*[1] Try to avoid the common mistake of associating the terms *debit* and *credit* with the concepts of plus and minus. If you simply remember the definitions, you will avoid much confusion as you progress in accounting.

OBJECTIVE 2. Define a T-account and indicate the debit side.

Remember, a T-account is an abbreviated version of a ledger account, and the left side is called the debit side.

Another convention that must be memorized is that *increases* in asset accounts are shown on the debit (left) side of an account. Since there are only two sides, the credit (right) side must therefore reflect asset *decreases.*

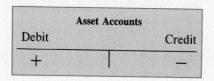

The accounting equation is an identity. The liability and owner's equity claims are simply claims against the total assets. One side of the equation is like a mirror image of the other side; they are merely two ways of looking at the same thing. From this, and from rules of algebra, we can logically conclude that whatever is true for one side of the equation is also true in the opposite for the other side. In other words, if assets increase on the debit side, then liabilities and owner's equity must increase on the credit

---

[1]*Dr.* and *Cr.* come from the expressions *debitor* and *creditor,* but these terms are no longer used in the way they once were.

side. Likewise, if assets are decreased by credits, then liabilities and owner's equity must be decreased by debits.

Assets	=	Liabilities	+	Owner's Equity
Dr. Cr.		Dr. Cr.		Dr. Cr.
+ | −		− | +		− | +

In summary, only two conventions have to be memorized.

1. Debit is left.
2. Debits increase assets.

The remaining debit and credit rules follow automatically.

DEBIT AND CREDIT RULES
Debit is left; therefore, credit is right.
Debits increase assets; therefore:
  Credits decrease assets.
  Debits decrease liabilities and owner's equity.
  Credits increase liabilities and owner's equity.

TRANSACTIONS

Recall how transactions affect the equation. George Metts's initial investment of $5,000 cash in his business was viewed as consisting of *two* elements.

1. The receipt of $5,000 cash
2. Supplied by the owner

This event is reflected in the equation by increasing both cash and owner's capital accounts. In terms of debits and credits, the equation is affected as follows.

Assets	=	Liabilities	+	Owner's Equity
111 Cash				311 G. Metts, Capital
5,000 |				| 5,000

Analyzing Transactions

The process of deciding how to reflect each event into the accounting model involves four mental steps, stated below in question form.

> 1. Which accounts are affected?
>
> 2. Are the accounts assets, liabilities, or owner's equity?
>
> 3. Are the accounts increased or decreased?
>
> 4. Should the affected accounts be debited or credited?

This process of analysis can be seen in Illustration 2.4. The investment of cash by George Metts was analyzed as shown in Illustration 2.5.

With experience, you will acquire the ability to analyze transactions almost automatically. For now, try analyzing the transactions in Illustration 2.6, before you trace their effects in the equation pictured in Illustration 2.7 on page 52.

Owner Withdrawals. The withdrawal of cash (f) represents a decrease in cash and owner's equity. The account G. Metts, Capital, could have been debited directly to show the decrease. However, George wants to keep a separate record of how much cash he withdraws. The two owner's equity

ILLUSTRATION 2.4

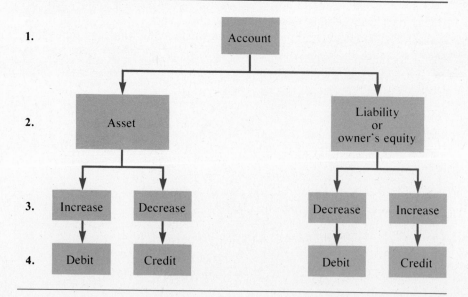

ILLUSTRATION 2.5

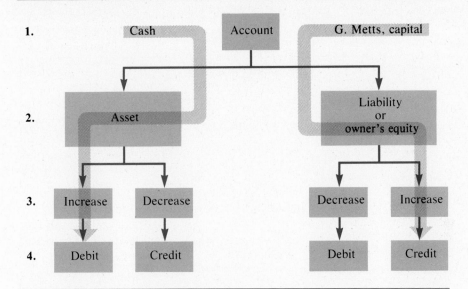

accounts should be viewed together, since the remaining owner's equity is the amount left after withdrawals. In other words, George's equity in the business at this point is $4,500, the amount shown in the Capital account less the amount shown in the Withdrawals account.

Operating Transactions

The effects of revenues and expenses could be introduced directly into an owner's capital account, but locating the information needed to prepare an income statement would then be difficult, especially in large, complex business firms.

ILLUSTRATION 2.6

> **TRANSACTIONS, MARCH 1 THROUGH MARCH 15**
> a) George invested $5,000 cash in the business.
> b) Office supplies were purchased for $60 cash.
> c) Office supplies were purchased for $25 on account.
> d) A truck was bought for $6,500. Cash of $2,500 was paid, and a note payable was signed for the remaining cost.
> e) A $200 cash payment was made on the note payable.
> f) George withdrew $500 cash from the business for personal use.

ILLUSTRATION 2.7

METTS DELIVERY SERVICE

Assets	=	Liabilities	+	Owner's Equity

111   Cash

a)	5,000	b)	60
		d)	2,500
		e)	200
		f)	500

211   Accounts Payable

		c)	25

311   G. Metts, Capital

		a)	5,000

112   Accounts Receivable

212   Note Payable

e)	200	d)	4,000

312   G. Metts, Withdrawals

f)	500

113   Office Supplies

b)	60
c)	25

121   Truck

d)	6,500

0121 Accum. Depr.—Truck

**OBJECTIVE 3.   Reflect
transactions into
T-accounts.**

Since many people want information about revenues and expenses, special accounts are provided to collect such data. Revenue and expense accounts are called *temporary equity (nominal) accounts because at the end of each accounting period their balances are transferred to a permanent (real) equity account. Permanent (real) accounts are the asset, liability, and owner's equity accounts that are not closed at the end of an accounting period.* Soon you will learn how to *close* temporary equity accounts.

Revenue accounts temporarily collect *increases* in owner's equity, so it is logical that these increases appear on the *credit* side of revenue accounts. Expenses, on the other hand, are *decreases* in owner's equity—so they are collected on the *debit* side of the expense accounts. Expense accounts accumulate decreases in owner's equity.

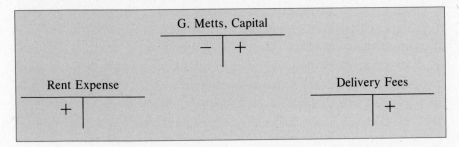

Actually, the owner's Withdrawals account is also a temporary equity account, but it should not be confused with expense accounts just because it also accumulates decreases in owner's equity. Unlike expenses, owner withdrawals do not assist in the production of revenue.

We can analyze revenue and expense transactions the same way we analyze other transactions. In Illustration 2.8, for example, cash revenue is analyzed.

The operating transactions for Metts Delivery Service during the last half of March are listed in Illustration 2.9 on the next page.

Note how each operating transaction was reflected in the equation pictured as Illustration 2.10 on the next page.

ILLUSTRATION 2.8

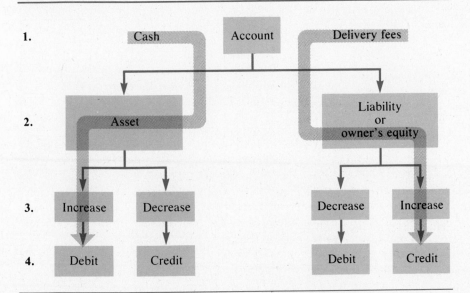

ILLUSTRATION 2.9

TRANSACTIONS, MARCH 16 THROUGH MARCH 31

g) Rent expense for March was paid in cash, $400.

h) Cash revenue of $1,200 was collected.

i) Revenue was earned but not yet collected, $500.

j) Gasoline was purchased on account, $180.

k) Office supplies were used, $20.

l) Truck depreciation recognized, $200.

**OBJECTIVE 3. Reflect
transactions into
T-accounts.**

ILLUSTRATION 2.10

METTS DELIVERY SERVICE

Assets	=	Liabilities	+	Owner's Equity

111   Cash

a)	5,000	b)	60
h)	1,200	d)	2,500
		e)	200
		f)	500
		g)	400

211 Accounts Payable

		c)	25
		j)	180

311 G. Metts, Capital

		a)	5,000

112 Accounts Receivable

i)	500	

212 Note Payable

e)	200	d)	4,000

312 G. Metts, Withdrawals

f)	500	

113 Office Supplies

b)	60	k)	20
c)	25		

Expenses

511   Rent Expense

g)	400	

Revenues

411 Delivery Fees

		h)	1,200
		i)	500

121   Truck

d)	6,500	

512 Gasoline Expense

j)	180	

0121 Accum. Depr.—Truck

		l)	200

513 Supplies Expense

k)	20	

514 Depreciation Expense

l)	200	

ACCUMULATED DEPRECIATION

As asset costs expire they are transferred to expense accounts. For example, the use of office supplies is shown as a credit to the Office Supplies account and a debit to Supplies Expense. In the case of depreciation, however, the credits are accumulated in a separate account called Accumulated Depreciation, a *contra (offset) account* that should be viewed along with the account showing the asset's original cost. A **contra account** *is one that accumulates decreases for another related account.*

   A contra account is used to accumulate depreciation so that the asset account can continue to show the full cost of the asset being depreciated. Depreciation is only an estimate of how much cost is expiring, and accumulated depreciation reflects the uncertainties involved in any estimating scheme. In our example, *the unexpired cost of the truck, called* **net book value,** is $6,300.

Truck	$6,500
Less: Accumulated Depreciation	200
Net Book Value of Truck	$6,300

ACCOUNT BALANCES

Where there is more than one amount in a T-account, an *account balance* may be determined by adding up each side and subtracting the smaller total from the larger. For example, the Cash account has a balance of $2,540, determined as follows.

111		Cash	
a)	5,000	b)	60
h)	1,200	d)	2,500
	6,200	e)	200
		f)	500
		g)	400
Balance 2,540			3,660

   When amounts appear on only one side of an account, the balance may be determined simply by adding the column of amounts.

STATEMENTS FROM T-ACCOUNTS

Income Statements

Once account balances are determined, an income statement and balance sheet may be prepared from them, provided that no errors have been made. An income statement shows the results of operations, as represented by the

ILLUSTRATION 2.11

METTS DELIVERY SERVICE Income Statement For the Period March 16 through March 31, 19– –		
Delivery fees		$1,700
Expenses		
Rent	$400	
Depreciation	200	
Gasoline	180	
Office supplies	20	800
Net Income		$ 900

revenue and expense account balances for Metts Delivery Service (Illustration 2.11).

Statements of Owner's Capital

Neither the owner's withdrawals nor the results of operations (net income) have yet been introduced into the permanent owner's capital account. A balance sheet would not be correct, and in fact would not *balance,* if the data collected in temporary equity accounts were ignored.

One approach is to prepare a brief statement called a *statement of owner's capital, which explains how the owner's equity account got from the balance at the beginning of a period to the balance at the end.*

The statement for Metts Delivery Service (Illustration 2.12) is for the entire month of March and starts with a zero beginning equity because the business did not previously exist.

Balance Sheets

A balance sheet prepared at March 31 (Illustration 2.13) will show the owner's equity at that date, as determined by the statement of owner's capital (Illustration 2.12).

ILLUSTRATION 2.12

METTS DELIVERY SERVICE Statement of Owner's Capital For the Month of March 19– –		
G. Metts, capital, March 1		$ –0–
Owner investment in March		5,000
Net income for March	$900	
Less: Owner's withdrawals	500	400
G. Metts, capital, March 31		$5,400

ILLUSTRATION 2.13

| METTS DELIVERY SERVICE |
| Balance Sheet |
| March 31, 19-- |

ASSETS			*LIABILITIES*	
Cash		$2,540	Accounts payable	$ 205
Accounts receivable		500	Note payable	3,800
Office supplies		65		
Truck	$6,500		Total Liabilities	$4,005
Less: Accumulated depreciation	200	6,300		
			OWNER'S EQUITY	
			G. Metts, capital	5,400
			Total Liabilities and	
Total Assets		$9,405	Owner's Equity	$9,405

Notice that the balance sheet shows the Accumulated Depreciation balance subtracted from the Truck balance to arrive at a net book value for the truck of $6,300. As the truck ages, the Accumulated Depreciation balance will grow, and the net book value of the truck will shrink.

Remember, a balance sheet shows the condition (position) of an entity at a *point* in time—in this example, at close of business on March 31. An income statement shows how well a business did for a *period* of time. A statement of owner's capital simply shows the changes in the owner's capital during a period of time.

FORMS OF BUSINESS ORGANIZATIONS

Metts Delivery Service has just one owner, George Metts. *A business with only one owner is called a **proprietorship**,* and the owner is referred to as the *proprietor*.

*A business concern jointly owned by two or more persons is called a **partnership**,* and the owners are called *partners*. We account for a partnership in much the same way as for a proprietorship, except that the equity claims of each of the partners are shown in a separate account. The business pictured in the balance sheet in Illustration 2.14 can be identified as a partnership, because owners' equity claims are shown for more than one owner. You will learn more about accounting for partnerships in Chapter 13.

A third form of business organization is the corporation. *A corporation is an association in which ownership is represented by shares of stock,* which can be bought and sold by *shareholders* without disturbing the entity itself. A corporation is created by the state government, which issues a legal document called a *charter*. Once created, the corporation has the power to contract and own property as though it were a person. For this reason, a corporation is frequently referred to as an artificial person.

ILLUSTRATION 2.14

ABC EXTERMINATING
Balance Sheet
September 30, 19--

ASSETS		LIABILITIES	
Cash	$ 2,000	Accounts payable	$ 3,300
Chemicals	300		
Equipment	8,000		

OWNERS' EQUITY	
J. Aaron, capital	$3,000
C. Martinez, capital	2,500
H. Clark, capital	1,500
Total Owners' Equity	7,000

Total Assets	$10,300	Total Liabilities and Owners' Equity	$10,300

A corporation may have any number of shareholders, whose ownership claims are combined in the equity section of a corporation's balance sheet and labeled *capital stock* or common stock. The business pictured in Illustration 2.14, for example, could have been organized as a corporation, in which case the owners' equity of $7,000 would have been listed simply as Capital Stock. All other parts of the balance sheet would have been the same. Several subsequent chapters of this text deal with accounting for corporations.

In summary, the three most common legal forms of business organization are:

OBJECTIVE 4. Name and differentiate the most common legal forms of business.

Proprietorship. A business owned by one individual.

Partnership. A business concern jointly owned by two or more individuals.

Corporation. An association in which ownership is represented by shares of stock.

GLOSSARY FOR SECTION 2.A

Chart of accounts   A list of accounts that are currently in use in an accounting system.

Contra account   An account that accumulates decreases for another, related account.

Corporation   An association in which ownership is represented by shares of stock.

Credit (Cr.)   An accounting term for the direction *right*, usually referring to an amount column to the right.

Debit (Dr.)   An accounting term for the direction *left*, usually referring to an amount column to the left.

General ledger   A collection of asset, liability, and owner's equity accounts that make up the accounting equation for a particular entity.

Net book value   The unexpired portion of the cost of an asset.

Partnership   A business concern jointly owned by two or more individuals.

Permanent (real) accounts   Asset, liability, and owner's equity accounts that are not closed at the end of an accounting period.

Proprietorship   A business owned by one individual.

Statement of owner's capital   A report that explains how the owner's equity account got from the beginning to the ending balance.

T-accounts   Abbreviated (shorthand) versions of ledger accounts that resemble the letter *T*.

Temporary equity (nominal) accounts   Accounts that collect data for one period only, after which they are closed and the data transferred to a permanent equity account. (Examples: revenues, expenses, owner's withdrawals.)

SELF-QUIZ ON OBJECTIVES FOR SECTION 2.A
Solutions to Self-Quiz begin on page B-3.

1.   **OBJECTIVE 1.**   Define the terms *debit* and *credit*.

2.   **OBJECTIVE 2.**   State what a T-account is and indicate which is the debit side.

3.   **OBJECTIVE 3.**   Reflect the following transactions into T-accounts.

   a. I. M. Worthy invests $20,000 cash in his business.

   b. A used truck costing $12,500 is purchased. A payment of $5,000 is made and a note signed for the balance.

   c. The company receives $500 in cash for delivering a piece of heavy equipment.

   d. Wages are paid to employees in the amount of $2,000.

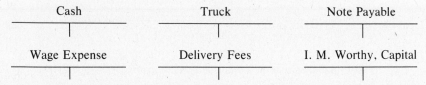

4.   **OBJECTIVE 4.**   Name and differentiate the three most common legal forms of business organization.

DISCUSSION QUESTIONS FOR SECTION 2.A

1. Why are debit and credit rules for increasing and decreasing accounts reversed on opposite sides of the accounting equation?

2. Why do expenses increase on the debit side, even though they are part of the equity section of the accounting equation?

3. What is a chart of accounts, and how is it useful to accountants and bookkeepers?

4. What are the four questions that must be answered to properly reflect an event into T-accounts?

5. Why are revenue and expense accounts referred to as temporary equity accounts?

6. The owner's withdrawals account is a temporary equity account used to accumulate decreases in owner's equity. Is the owner's withdrawals account an expense account? If not, how does it differ from an expense account?

7. What is a contra account, and how is it used?

EXERCISES FOR SECTION 2.A

2.A.1. Complete the following statements of debit and credit rules.

    a. Debit is left; therefore, credit is _____.

    b. Debits increase assets; therefore, credits _____ assets.

    c. _____ decrease liabilities and owner's equity.

    d. _____ increase liabilities and owner's equity.

2.A.2. Indicate whether each of the following statements is true or false.

    a. The purchase of an asset always increases a firm's total assets.

    b. Decreases in an owner's equity account appear on the left side of the T-account.

    c. A debit decreases liability and owner's equity accounts.

    d. The purchase of a truck for cash affects a liability account.

    e. A debit increases an asset account.

    f. Withdrawal of cash from the business by the owner for personal use results in a credit to the owner's capital account.

    g. An asset account is decreased by a credit.

2.A.3. The Taxi Company was established as a cab service. By analyzing the entries in the following T-accounts, describe the transaction that took place on each particular date. For example, what transaction took place on January 1?

Cash		Employee Uniforms		Land	
1/1 90,000	1/3 10,000	1/12 400		1/3 10,000	
1/17 20,000	1/4 15,000				
	1/10 40,000				
	1/16 2,000				
	1/21 30,000				

Taxi Cabs		Building		Accounts Payable	
1/10 40,000		1/4 30,000			1/12 400
1/21 40,000					
1/27 20,000					

Notes Payable		Mortgage Payable		M. Blain, Capital	
	1/17 20,000	1/16 2,000	1/4 15,000		1/1 90,000
	1/21 10,000				
	1/27 20,000				

2.A.4. For each of the transactions, answer the questions that follow.

Transactions

a) E. Grazio invested $50,000 cash in his business.

b) A building was purchased for $85,000. A cash payment of $25,000 was made and a note payable signed for the balance.

c) A $300 payment was made on an account payable.

d) An insurance expense of $800 was paid in cash.

e) E. Grazio made a cash withdrawal of $2,500 from the business.

Questions

1) Which accounts are affected?

2) Are the accounts assets, liabilities, or owner's equity?

3) Are the accounts increased or decreased?

4) Should the affected accounts be debited or credited?

PROBLEMS FOR SECTION 2.A
Alternate Problems for this section begin on page D-3.

2.A.5. The following transactions were experienced by TJ's Car Wash during October.

Transactions

a) T. J. Seth invested $5,000 to start a new car wash business.

b) The business borrowed $3,000 from a bank, and a note payable was signed.

c) Car wash equipment costing $8,000 was purchased for $4,000 cash and a note payable of $4,000.

d) Supplies costing $1,000 were purchased on account.

e) A $150 payment was made on notes payable.

f) Cash revenue of $1,800 was collected.

g) Revenue of $600 was earned but not yet collected.

h) Wages of $500 were paid in cash.

i) Rent expense of $600 was paid in cash.

j) Supplies costing $120 were used during October. *Note:* The supplies used were from supplies purchased in item (d).

k) Equipment depreciation of $133 was recognized.

l) T. J. withdrew $700 from the business for personal use.

Required

1) Reflect the October transactions into T-accounts.

2) Prepare an income statement for October.

3) Prepare a statement of owner's capital for October.

4) Prepare a balance sheet at month-end.

2.A.6. The following transactions were experienced by the Jones Company.

Transactions

a) The owner, Holly Jones, invested $18,500 in the business.

b) The company borrowed $10,000 from the bank.

c) Machinery costing $12,000 was purchased for cash.

d) A payment of $1,000 was made on the bank loan.

e) The owner withdrew $500 from the business for her personal use.

f) Office supplies were purchased on credit for $20.

Required

1) Record each of the transactions in T-accounts by debiting and crediting the accounts affected.

2) The accounting equation $A = L + OE$ will exist if your work in requirement (1) was correctly done. Show that the sum of the asset T-account balances is equal to the sum of the liability and owner's equity T-account balances.

2.A.7. The following T-accounts reflect the status of O'Connor Company at June 30.

Cash	
7,000	2,000
3,000	100
	1,000
	2,500
	1,200
	1,250
	400

Accounts Payable	
	200

J. O'Connor, Capital	
	7,000

Accounts Receivable	
6,000	

Note Payable	
400	4,000

J. O'Connor, Withdrawals	
1,000	

Office Supplies	
100	75
200	

Wage Expense	
2,500	

Service Revenue	
	3,000
	6,000

Equipment	
6,000	

Rent Expense	
1,200	

Accum. Depr.—Equipment	
	100

Supplies Expense	
75	

Insurance Expense	
1,250	

Depreciation Expense	
100	

Required

1) Prepare an income statement for the month of June.

2) Prepare a balance sheet at June 30.

2.A.8. Roadside Hot Dogs was established in April. The following transactions took place during that month.

Transactions

a) J. Marsh invested $10,000 cash to start the business.

b) Purchased a piece of land for $10,000 and a building for $20,000 by paying $6,000 cash and assuming a $24,000 mortgage.

c) Equipment costing $3,000 was purchased on account.

d) Office supplies of $60 were purchased for cash.

e) Paid $1,000 on accounts payable.

f) Borrowed $6,000 cash from the bank by signing a note.

g) Acquired some adjacent land for $4,000 cash in order to expand parking facilities.

h) Paid $500 for paper bags, wrappers, and cups.

i) J. Marsh transferred equipment valued at $1,000 to the entity. This equipment had been used previously in another business owned by Marsh.

Required

1) For each transaction, indicate which accounts will be debited and which will be credited, and by how much.

2) Set up T-accounts and show the effects of the transactions in the accounts.

3) Compute the balance in each T-account and prepare a list of account titles and balances.

4) Prepare a balance sheet for April 30.

2.A.9. The following T-accounts for the Dunlap Company show the balances on May 1, as well as the transactions that occurred during May.

Cash				Accounts Payable				A. Dunlap, Capital	
Bal.	2,000	b)	100	d)	1,000	Bal.	1,000	Bal.	2,700
a)	2,700	c)	200			e)	600		
i)	400	d)	1,000						
		f)	1,400						
		g)	800						

Accounts Receivable				Notes Payable				A. Dunlap, Withdrawals	
Bal.	500	i)	400	c)	200	Bal.	4,000	g)	800
h)	1,200								

Supplies				Wage Expense				Service Revenue	
Bal.	200	j)	200	f)	1,400			a)	2,700
b)	100							h)	1,200

Truck				Gasoline Expense		
Bal.	8,000			e)	600	

Accum. Depr.—Truck			Supplies Expense	
	Bal.	3,000	j)	200
	k)	300		

Depreciation Expense	
k)	300

Required

1) Prepare an income statement for May.

2) Prepare a statement of owner's capital for May.

3) Prepare a balance sheet at May 31.

SECTION 2.B

Functions of Accounting Systems

OBJECTIVES

This section deals with the functions by which information is processed in most accounting systems. When you have completed your study, you should be able to

1. List the four functions of accounting for transactions in the order in which they are normally performed.
2. Define in your own words the following devices and relate each to the accounting function it supports:
   a. Source documents.
   b. Journals.
   c. Ledgers.
   d. Accounting statements.
3. Prepare, in proper form, entries in a general journal to record transactions.
4. Post amounts from journal entries to ledger accounts, and tie entries and postings together with cross-reference numbers.

THE FRAMEWORK OF ACCOUNTING SYSTEMS

Each entity for which we account is in some ways different from every other entity. Likewise, the needs for accounting information differ for each unique entity being accounted for. Thus each accounting system must be designed to fit the specific needs of the particular entity. Even so, practically all systems share a common *framework*.

To provide useful information, every accounting system must identify bits of information, collect these bits, and process them to the point that they can be reported to people. In doing this, information is processed through certain phases, or *functions,* of the system.

Documenting

The various transactions experienced by an entity are usually noted on *business forms called **source documents**.* These documents, as the first step in the accounting system, can then act as triggers to get the events recorded into the system. Receipts, invoices, checks, and earning slips are just a few examples of the forms that help to document transactions.

The initial noting of events is not necessarily on paper documents. In some modern systems, it may be done electronically or mechanically. For example, long-distance telephone calls that you dial directly are noted elec-

OBJECTIVE 2a. Define source documents.

tronically for use later in making out bills and determining the revenue earned by the phone company.

Regardless of how it is done, transactions must somehow be noted for an accounting system to process the information for use in accounting reports. This is performed in a process called *documenting*.

> **Documenting.** *The accounting function of noting transactions by means of source documents.*

Recording

Information that has been documented must still be recorded in the accounting system for further processing. This is usually done in the order in which transactions occur—by date, in chronological order. This second function of accounting, known as *recording,* is often performed in a book called a journal. *A **journal** is sometimes referred to as a **place of original entry** because it is the place where transactions are first listed (entered) in a formal manner.*

OBJECTIVE 2b.
Define journals.

Of course, recording can be performed in ways other than by writing in a journal. In automated systems, information is recorded into punched cards or tapes, or on magnetic tapes or disks. Some documents, such as checks and deposit slips, may be encoded with printing that can be read by a special device, called a scanner, which automatically records the data into the computer "journal." Then, at some later time, the automated system can print out a written record of events as they have been registered in the internal journal.

Whatever the method, all accounting systems provide for recording transactions and events into one or more journals of some kind.

> **Recording.** *The accounting function of registering transactions and events in chronological order (by date).*

Summarizing

As you will recall, accounting information is classified into account categories, which is a way of *summarizing* the information so that it can be used in reports to people who need the information.

The data that are summarized in the third accounting function come from the journal (or journals). In some automated systems, the recording and summarizing functions are performed together. In other words, a computer may record directly into account categories, much as we did when we recorded transactions directly into T-accounts. The speed and flexibility of a computer then allows it to print out the recorded information in almost any form, including a listing of transactions in chronological order.

Remember, *a group of accounts is called a **ledger**.* One or more ledgers are used to accomplish the summarizing function of accounting. In automated systems, the ledger accounts may actually be maintained in the form of punched cards, or on magnetic tapes or disks.

OBJECTIVE 2c. Define ledgers.

> ***Summarizing.*** *The accounting function of classifying information into account categories.*

Reporting

The purpose of accounting is to provide useful information to people who need it. *Accounting data are frequently presented in formal **accounting statements**.* The fourth function of accounting, *reporting,* is the end product of the accounting system. The first three functions are performed mainly to attain the fourth (Illustration 2.15).

OBJECTIVE 2d. Define accounting statements.

> ***Reporting.*** *The accounting function of providing information to people who need it.*

Keep in mind that accounting also includes the analysis and interpretation of information that is reported, as well as the projection of future results in some cases. But the four functions of accounting are documenting, recording, summarizing, and reporting events that have *already* occurred.

ILLUSTRATION 2.15

OBJECTIVE 1. List the accounting functions in order.

OBJECTIVE 2. Relate source documents, journals, ledgers, and statements to the function each serves.

ACCOUNTING FUNCTIONS

1	2	3	4
Documenting	Recording	Summarizing	Reporting
Source documents	Journals	Ledgers	Statements

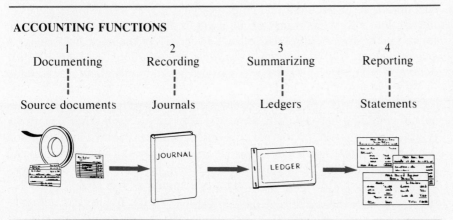

ILLUSTRATION 2.16

General Journal					*PAGE*
Date	Account Names and Explanations	A/C #	Debit	Credit	

JOURNAL ENTRIES

By now you probably have a general idea of how an accounting system processes information. At this point we will concentrate more specifically on the procedures for recording transactions in a journal.

Types of Journals

Transactions are usually recorded in one or more journals in chronological order. *The record of each transaction in a journal is called an **entry**, and the process of making the entry is referred to as **journalizing** or **entering**.*

An accounting system may employ any number of **special journals,** *each designed especially for recording transactions of a certain type.* For example, all transactions involving cash receipts might be recorded in a *cash receipts journal,* while all cash payments might be recorded in a *cash payments journal.* Special journals are also frequently used for purchases on account, sales on account, and employee payrolls, as well as other types of transactions.[2] Systems using special journals also employ a *general journal* for recording transactions that do not fit in any of the special journals. *A **general journal** is a journal that is suitable for recording any type of transaction.* For the time being, we will assume that all transactions are recorded in a general journal.

Journal entries are usually recorded in a standard format, which allows accountants and bookkeepers to more easily follow each other's work. A typical page in a general journal contains the columns shown in Illustration 2.16. The column heads may differ among companies. The column labeled A/C # is a reference column for ledger account numbers. The two columns at the right are for showing debit and credit amounts. You might notice that they form the letter *T*, with the debit column to the left of the credit column.

---

[2]Special journals are discussed in more depth in Chapter 5.

ILLUSTRATION 2.17

Assets		=	Liabilities		+	Owner's Equity	
Dr.	Cr.		Dr.	Cr.		Dr.	Cr.
+	−		−	+		−	+

		Expenses		Revenues	
		Dr.	Cr.	Dr.	Cr.
		+			+

Journalizing Transactions

Recall the debit and credit rules and the process for analyzing transactions, because they are essential to arriving at proper journal entries (see Illustrations 2.17 and 2.18).

Now consider the investment of $5,000 by George Metts in his new business, Metts Delivery Service. An analysis of this event would lead to the journal entry shown in Illustration 2.19 on the next page.

Note carefully the entry format. The A/C # column is usually left blank until the entry is reflected (posted) in the ledger accounts, a procedure that we will study later in this section. Debit account titles come first and are

ILLUSTRATION 2.18

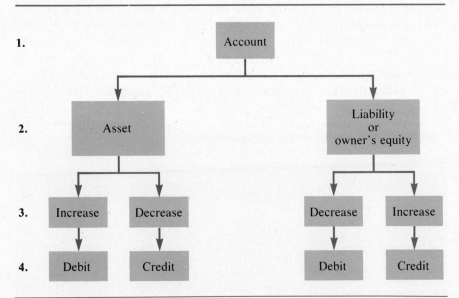

ILLUSTRATION 2.23

16	Rent Expense		400	
	Cash			400
	March rent paid; Check No. 5.			
31	Cash		1,200	
	Delivery Fees			1,200
	Revenue collected in cash; Deposit No. 2.			

ILLUSTRATION 2.24

OBJECTIVE 3. Prepare general journal entries.

	General Journal		PAGE 2	
Date	Account Names and Explanations	A/C #	Debit	Credit
19-- Mar. 31	Accounts Receivable		500	
	Delivery Fees			500
	Revenue earned but not yet collected.			
31	Gasoline Expense		180	
	Accounts Payable			180
	Gasoline purchased on account from Ace Service Station.			
31	Supplies Expense		20	
	Office Supplies			20
	Office supplies used during March.			
31	Depreciation Expense		200	
	Accumulated Depreciation—Truck			200
	Truck depreciation during March.			

reflected by journal entries on the remainder of journal page 1 and on journal page 2 (Illustrations 2.23 and 2.24).

LEDGERS

Journal entries picture transactions in terms of their debit and credit effects on accounts that are located in a *ledger*. *The act of transferring information from a journal to ledger accounts is called posting.* Posting distributes the effects of transactions into account categories to accomplish the third function of accounting, *summarizing* (Illustration 2.25).

The main ledger, containing the asset, liability, owner's equity, revenue, and expense accounts, is called the general ledger. Any number of subsidiary ledgers may also be used to supplement the main ledger with more detailed information. Subsidiary ledgers will be studied in Chapter 5.

ILLUSTRATION 2.25

ACCOUNTING FUNCTIONS

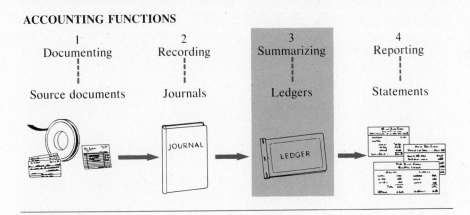

The ledger account form employed in this text is the one in Illustration 2.26, which provides separate columns for debit and credit balances. There are other formats in use, however, one of which provides for debit postings on the left half and credit postings on the right (like the T-accounts).

Let us look at several transactions for the Metts Delivery Service to see how the posting process works. To post George's investment of $5,000, we would open the general ledger to the first page, to the Cash account. As shown in Illustration 2.27 on the next page, the date and debit amount are written on the first line, and the journal page number is marked in the reference column of the account. The ledger account number is now written in the A/C # (reference) column of the journal. This last step serves two pur-

ILLUSTRATION 2.26

					ACCOUNT NO.	
					Balance	
Date	**Item**	**Ref.**	**Debit**	**Credit**	*Debit*	*Credit*

ILLUSTRATION 2.27

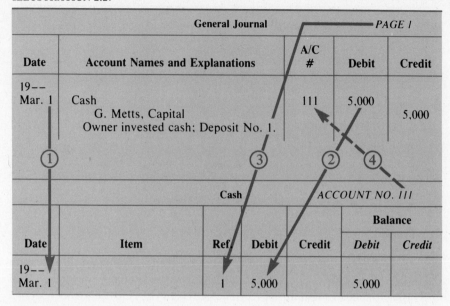

poses: it shows the page (account) in the ledger to which the posting was made, and it also serves as evidence that the amount has been posted. Amounts in the journal without account references still have not been posted.

Cross-referencing of journal entries and ledger postings permits verification (auditing) of data by working back through the system to the accounting documents. It also allows the effects of transactions to be traced from the accounting documents through the system to the accounting statements. The arrows show the steps that were followed in posting the cash account.

The account balance of $5,000 can be written in at the time of posting. However, some accountants and bookkeepers prefer to wait until the end of an accounting period and then calculate and write in only one account balance figure.

Next, we turn to the ledger account for G. Metts, Capital, and post the credit part of the entry shown in Illustration 2.28.

TRIAL BALANCE

The debit amounts of each journal entry should equal the credit amounts. If entries are recorded and posted properly, the ledger will reflect equal debits and credits, and the total credit account balances will then equal the

ILLUSTRATION 2.28

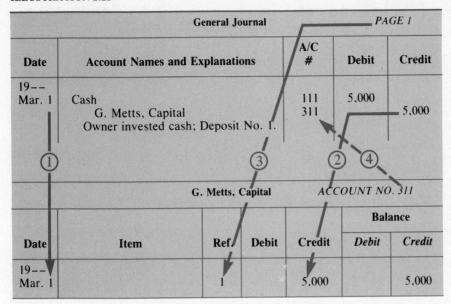

OBJECTIVE 4. Post from journal entries to ledger accounts, using cross-reference numbers.

total debit account balances. When debits are equal to credits, the accounting system is said to be *in balance*.

*A **trial balance** is an informal accounting schedule that lists the ledger account balances at a point in time and compares the total of debit balances with the total of credit balances.* One purpose of a trial balance is to ensure that the general ledger is in balance. The trial balance is not an accounting statement, although the information it contains can be used to prepare statements. Thus a trial balance serves two main purposes.

1. To check the equality of debits and credits
2. To provide information for use in preparing statements

A trial balance may have a heading similar to that of an accounting statement. Ledger accounts are listed in the order in which they appear in the ledger. Debit balances are shown in one column and credit balances in another, and the columns are totaled to ensure that they are equal. A trial balance prepared at March 31 for Metts Delivery Service appears in Illustration 2.29. Since the debit and credit column totals are equal, the system is in balance.

ILLUSTRATION 2.29

A/C #	Account	Debits	Credits
	METTS DELIVERY SERVICE **Trial Balance** **March 31, 19– –**		
111	Cash	1,040	
112	Accounts Receivable	1,500	
113	Office Supplies	165	
121	Truck	6,500	
0121	Accumulated Depreciation—Truck		200
211	Accounts Payable		1,205
212	Note Payable		800
311	G. Metts, Capital		5,000
312	G. Metts, Withdrawals	500	
411	Delivery Fees		4,700
511	Rent Expense	1,400	
512	Gasoline Expense	480	
513	Supplies Expense	120	
514	Depreciation Expense	200	
		11,905	11,905

ERRORS

Errors That Cause Imbalance

If the trial balance does not balance, one or more errors have caused an inequality of debits and credits. There are three common types of errors that disturb balance.

ERRORS THAT DISTURB BALANCE
1. Transposition of digits within an amount
2. Failure to post one side of a journal entry
3. Posting a credit as a debit, or vice versa

---

*A **transposition error** occurs when two digits of a number are reversed.* For example, 157 might be copied as 175. It is a noteworthy fact that errors resulting from transpositions are always divisible by 9. Also, the number of times that 9 goes into the error indicates the numerical *difference* between the digits transposed.

$$175 - 157 = 18$$
$$18 \div 9 = 2$$
$$7 - 5 = 2$$

Another common error occurs when one side of an entry is omitted in the posting process, resulting in the understatement of a ledger balance in the amount omitted. The imbalance will show up on a trial balance.

The third common mistake occurs when a figure is posted to the wrong side of a ledger account. When this happens, the imbalance will be twice the amount posted incorrectly.

Errors That Do Not Cause Imbalance

Certain errors do not upset the equality of debits and credits, and therefore do not cause an inequality on the trial balance. Thus a balanced trial balance does not ensure error-free records. There are three common types of errors that do not disturb the equality of debits and credits.

ERRORS THAT DO NOT DISTURB BALANCE
1. Double transposition
2. Reversing debits and credits
3. Omission of entries, or failure to post entire entries

NORMAL BALANCE

In Section 2.A you learned that some accounts are increased by debits and others are increased by credits. The accounting framework, based on the accounting equation, is devised so that increases to accounts normally exceed decreases. Thus the *normal balances* that one customarily expects to find in accounts are as follows.

NORMALLY SHOW DEBIT BALANCES	NORMALLY SHOW CREDIT BALANCES
Assets	Asset contras (e.g., Accum. Depr.)
Owner's Withdrawals	Liabilities
Expenses	Owner's Capital
	Revenues

An abnormal balance for an account suggests that either one or more errors have been made or unusual circumstances are present (such as a checking account overdrawn, throwing Cash into a credit balance).

STATEMENTS FROM A TRIAL BALANCE

Since a trial balance lists all accounts and their balances, statements can be prepared quite readily from it. Illustration 2.30 on the next page shows how the statements are simply rearrangements of trial balance data.

ILLUSTRATION 2.30

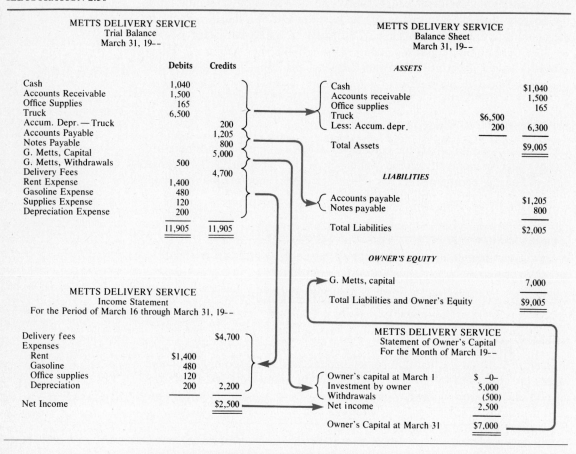

METTS DELIVERY SERVICE
Trial Balance
March 31, 19--

	Debits	Credits
Cash	1,040	
Accounts Receivable	1,500	
Office Supplies	165	
Truck	6,500	
Accum. Depr. — Truck		200
Accounts Payable		1,205
Notes Payable		800
G. Metts, Capital		5,000
G. Metts, Withdrawals	500	
Delivery Fees		4,700
Rent Expense	1,400	
Gasoline Expense	480	
Supplies Expense	120	
Depreciation Expense	200	
	11,905	11,905

METTS DELIVERY SERVICE
Income Statement
For the Period of March 16 through March 31, 19--

Delivery fees		$4,700
Expenses		
Rent	$1,400	
Gasoline	480	
Office supplies	120	
Depreciation	200	2,200
Net Income		$2,500

METTS DELIVERY SERVICE
Balance Sheet
March 31, 19--

ASSETS

Cash		$1,040
Accounts receivable		1,500
Office supplies		165
Truck	$6,500	
Less: Accum. depr.	200	6,300
Total Assets		$9,005

LIABILITIES

Accounts payable		$1,205
Notes payable		800
Total Liabilities		$2,005

OWNER'S EQUITY

G. Metts, capital		7,000
Total Liabilities and Owner's Equity		$9,005

METTS DELIVERY SERVICE
Statement of Owner's Capital
For the Month of March 19--

Owner's capital at March 1	$ –0–
Investment by owner	5,000
Withdrawals	(500)
Net income	2,500
Owner's Capital at March 31	$7,000

GLOSSARY FOR SECTION 2.B

Accounting statement   A formal presentation of accounting data.

Documenting   The accounting function of noting transactions by means of source documents.

Double-entry accounting   The requirement that debits of each entry be accompanied by an equal amount of credits.

Entry   A record of a transaction in a journal.

General journal   A journal suitable for recording any type of transaction.

General ledger   The main ledger for an entity, containing the asset, liability, owner's equity, revenue, and expense accounts.

Journal   A *place of original entry* for listing transactions in a formal manner (usually in chronological order).

Journalizing (entering)   The process of making entries in a journal.

Ledger   A group of accounts.

Normal balance The balance (debit or credit) that one customarily expects to find in an account.

Posting The act of transferring information from a journal to ledger accounts.

Recording The accounting function of registering transactions and events, usually in chronological order.

Reporting The accounting function of providing information to people who need it.

Source documents Business forms that serve as notations of transactions.

Special journal A journal specially designed for recording transactions of a certain type (for example, cash receipts).

Subsidiary ledger A ledger that provides detailed information as a supplement to the general ledger.

Summarizing The accounting function of classifying information into account categories.

Transposition error An error made by reversing two digits of a number.

Trial balance An informal listing of ledger accounts that compares the total of debit balances to the total of credit balances at a point in time.

SELF-QUIZ ON OBJECTIVES FOR SECTION 2.B
Solutions to Self-Quiz begin on page B-3.

1. **OBJECTIVE 1.** List the four functions of accounting for transactions in the order in which they are normally performed.

2. **OBJECTIVE 2.** Define in your own words the following devices and relate each to the accounting function it supports:

   a. Source documents.

   b. Journals.

   c. Ledgers.

   d. Statements.

3. **OBJECTIVE 3.** Prepare, in proper form, general journal entries for the following transactions for Pence Company. The chart of accounts shows the accounts currently in use.

   19--

   May 2 Pam Pence invested $1,800 cash to start a new business (Deposit No. 1).

   3 Purchased a sanding machine for $2,000, paying $500 cash (Check No. 101) and signing a note payable for the remaining cost.

   4 Purchased sanding supplies for $700 on credit (on account) from Gritty Company.

   15 Deposited in the bank $900 cash (Deposit No. 2), which was collected from customers for floor-sanding services performed in May.

   15 Pam withdrew $100 (Check No. 102) from the business for personal use.

25	Paid building rent for month of May, $300 (Check No. 103).
25	Paid $200 on accounts payable (Check No. 104).
31	Paid employee's wage for May, $600 (Check No. 105).
31	Billed customers for sanding work done in May, $1,300. Customers have agreed to pay their accounts in June.
31	Depreciation on sanding machine during May, $80.
31	An inspection of sanding supplies on hand shows that $150 worth of supplies have been used during May.

PENCE COMPANY
Chart of Accounts

100 Assets
111 Cash
112 Accounts Receivable
113 Sanding Supplies on Hand
151 Sanding Machine
0151 Accumulated
    Depreciation—Sanding
    Machine

200 Liabilities
211 Accounts Payable
212 Note Payable

300 Owner's Equity
311 Pam Pence, Capital
312 Pam Pence, Withdrawals

400 Revenues
411 Sanding Revenue

500 Expenses
511 Wage Expense
512 Sanding Supplies Expense
513 Rent Expense
514 Depreciation Expense

---

4. **OBJECTIVE 4.** Set up ledger accounts for Cash and for Pam Pence, Capital, and post the first entry you made in problem (3) to the accounts.

DISCUSSION QUESTIONS FOR SECTION 2.B

1. How do journal entries provide a useful link between source documents and ledger accounts?

2. Why is a journal referred to as the book of original entry?

3. What is meant by double-entry accounting?

4. What is a trial balance, and what are its two main purposes?

5. What is a transposition error? Under what conditions would you suspect that a transposition error had been made?

6. How do reference numbers help in tracing information through an accounting system?

EXERCISES FOR SECTION 2.B

2.B.1. S. Mertz, a self-employed plumber, made extensive plumbing repairs for the T&R Office Supply Store. Mertz accepted a filing cabinet, priced at $250, in payment for his services. Make the entry to record this transaction on May 21.

2.B.2. D. Beaty has just resigned her job and started a business by investing $10,000 cash, an old pickup truck that she owns, and a desk that had been given to her some years ago by her father. The estimated current value of the truck is $2,500, and the desk is worth about $200. Make the entry to record her investment on July 14.

2.B.3. A trial balance shows a total of $3,560 for the debit column and $3,380 for the credit column. Calculate the amount of the imbalance and, assuming that it is a result of a *single* error, list as many ways as you can that the error could have been made.

2.B.4. Indicate the amount by which each of the following errors will cause the trial balance totals to differ.

   a. A debit amount of $300 was posted in error as a credit.

   b. A debit figure of $2,980 was posted to the proper ledger account as $2,890.

   c. A debit to Wage Expense of $800 was posted erroneously to the Rent Expense account.

   d. A credit of $1,200 to Service Revenue was not posted at all because the bookkeeper overlooked it. The debit part of the entry was properly posted.

   e. A purchase of supplies for $200 on account was not entered in the journal, and therefore it was not reflected into the ledger accounts.

   f. The bookkeeper failed to post an entire entry for the owner's withdrawal of $400 cash.

   g. A machine purchased for $970 was entered incorrectly in the journal by debiting Machine for $790 and crediting Cash for $790.

   h. A $3,000 credit to Service Revenue was posted incorrectly as $300. The debit part of the entry was posted correctly.

PROBLEMS FOR SECTION 2.B
Alternate Problems for this section begin on page D-6.

2.B.5. Torgue Company was formed on August 1 and experienced the following transactions during August.

Transactions

Aug.	1	Sidney Torgue invested $10,000 cash in the business (Deposit No. 1).
	1	Tools were purchased for $800 on credit from Tally Company.
	2	A wrecker truck was purchased for a down payment of $2,000 (Check No. 1), and an $8,000 note was signed for the remaining cost.
	5	Torgue withdrew $200 (Check No. 2) for personal use.
	15	The $800 due to Tally Company was paid with Check No. 3.
	15	A payment of $300 (Check No. 4) was made on the note that was signed when the truck was purchased.
	31	Torgue invested an additional $2,000 cash into the business (Deposit No. 2).

Required

1) Journalize the transactions on journal page 1.

2) Set up ledger accounts and post the entries you made for requirement (1).

3) Prepare a trial balance at August 31.

4) Prepare a balance sheet at August 31.

2.B.6. Following are transactions for Dewey Company for the month of July.

Transactions

July 2   Collected $400 of accounts receivable that had been recorded in previous months (Deposit No. 210).

10   Collected $300 for services performed for customers in July (Deposit No. 211).

15   Paid July rent on building, $250 (Check No. 1225).

15   Paid balance due to Axon Service Station for gasoline purchased on credit during June, $180 (Check No. 1226).

19   Collected $520 for services performed for customers in July (Deposit No. 212).

25   Michael Dewey withdrew $600 for personal use (Check No. 1227).

31   Paid employee wages for July, $820 (Check No. 1228).

31   Received bill for $150 from Axon Service Station for gasoline purchased on credit during July.

31   Billed customers $950 for services performed in July (cash to be collected in August).

31   Monthly depreciation on the company truck was $140.

Required

1) Journalize the foregoing transactions on journal page 14. Choose titles that are brief and descriptive.

2) From the transactions journalized, prepare an income statement for July (without posting the entries to ledger accounts).

2.B.7. Following are April transactions and the chart of accounts for the Margaret Fong Company.

Transactions

Apr. 3   Paid $350 on accounts payable (Check No. 560).

5   Owner withdrew $500 for personal use (Check No. 561).

8   Collected $260 of accounts receivable (Deposit No. 140).

10   Collected $400 cash for services rendered in April (Deposit No. 141).

10   Purchased equipment for $4,000, paying $1,000 down (Check No. 562) and signing a note for the remaining cost.

18　Paid April rent on building, $600 (Check No. 563).

30　Paid April wages of $1,200 (Check No. 564).

30　Received bill for utilities used in April, $90.

30　Billed customers $2,600 for services rendered in April (to be collected in May).

30　Equipment depreciation for April was $210.

MARGARET FONG COMPANY
Chart of Accounts

100 Assets	*300 Owner's Equity*
111 Cash	311 M. Fong, Capital
112 Accounts Receivable	312 M. Fong, Withdrawals
121 Equipment	*400 Revenue*
0121 Accumulated Depreciation—Equipment	411 Service Revenue
200 Liabilities	*500 Expenses*
211 Accounts Payable	511 Rent Expense
212 Note Payable	512 Wage Expense
	513 Utilities Expense
	514 Depreciation Expense

Required

Journalize the transactions on journal page 5.

2.B.8. A chart of accounts and a number of journal entries for the Totsy Company follow. Kenneth Totsy started business on January 2.

TOTSY COMPANY
Chart of Accounts

10 Assets	*30 Owner's Equity*
11 Cash	31 K. Totsy, Capital
12 Accounts Receivable	32 K. Totsy, Withdrawals
13 Supplies on Hand	*40 Revenue*
16 Equipment	41 Service Revenue
016 Accumulated Depreciation—Equipment	*50 Expenses*
	51 Rent Expense
20 Liabilities	52 Wage Expense
21 Accounts Payable	53 Supplies Expense
26 Notes Payable	54 Depreciation Expense

	General Journal			*PAGE 1*
Date	**Account Names and Explanations**	**A/C #**	**Debit**	**Credit**
19-- Jan. 2	Cash		4,000	
	K. Totsy, Capital			4,000
	Owner invested cash; Deposit No. 1.			
3	Equipment		3,000	
	Cash			1,000
	Notes Payable			2,000
	Purchased equipment for cash and note; Check No. 101.			
3	Supplies on Hand		600	
	Accounts Payable			600
	Purchased supplies on account from George Co.			
10	Cash		700	
	Service Revenue			700
	Cash revenue received; Deposit No. 2.			
15	Rent Expense		200	
	Cash			200
	Paid January rent; Check No. 102.			
20	Cash		900	
	Service Revenue			900
	Cash revenue received; Deposit No. 3.			
25	K. Totsy, Withdrawals		300	
	Cash			300
	Owner withdrew cash for personal use; Check No. 103.			
31	Wage Expense		1,000	
	Cash			1,000
	Paid January wages; Check No. 104.			
31	Accounts Receivable		800	
	Service Revenue			800
	Billed customers for services performed in January.			
31	Supplies Expense		200	
	Supplies on Hand			200
	Supplies used in January.			
31	Depreciation Expense		100	
	Accum. Depr.—Equipment			100
	Depreciation for January.			

Required

1) Set up ledger accounts and post the entries. Use account forms that provide for a running balance, and be sure to cross-reference the entries and postings.

2) Prepare a trial balance for Totsy Company at January 31.

3) Prepare an income statement for January.

4) Prepare a statement of owner's capital for January.

5) Prepare a balance sheet at January 31.

2.B.9. Milton Zamost started Zamost Service Company on May 4. General journal entries, ledger accounts, and a trial balance prepared by Zamost are shown below and on the following pages.

	General Journal			PAGE 1
Date	**Account Names and Explanations**	**A/C #**	**Debit**	**Credit**
19––				
May 4	Cash	10	20,000	
	M. Zamost, Capital	31		20,000
	Owner's investment in business.			
8	Land	16	15,000	
	Notes Payable	21		10,000
	Cash	10		5,000
	Purchase of land.			
8	Building	17	20,000	
	Mortgage Payable	23		12,000
	Cash	10		8,000
	Purchased building on land in previous entry.			
15	Supplies	12	250	
	Accounts Payable	21		250
	Purchased supplies on account.			
16	Cash	10	15,000	
	M. Zamost, Capital	31		15,000
	Additional owner's investment.			
24	Office Equipment	15	2,800	
	Cash	10		2,800
	Purchased office equipment.			
26	Supplies	12	1,000	
	Cash	10		1,000
	Purchased supplies.			
28	Notes Payable	21	400	
	Cash	10		400
	Payment on note.			
28	Building	17	5,000	
	Cash	10		5,000
	Remodeling of building.			
30	M. Zamost, Withdrawals	32	750	
	Cash	10		750
	Owner's withdrawal.			

			Cash		ACCOUNT NO. 10	
					Balance	
Date	**Item**	**Ref.**	**Debit**	**Credit**	*Debit*	*Credit*
19-- May 4		1	20,000		20,000	
8		1		500	19,500	
8		1		8,000	11,500	
16		1	15,000		26,500	
24		1		2,800	23,700	
26		1		1,000	22,700	
28		1		400	21,300	
28		1		5,000	16,300	
30		1	750		17,050	

			Supplies		ACCOUNT NO. 12	
					Balance	
Date	**Item**	**Ref.**	**Debit**	**Credit**	*Debit*	*Credit*
19-- May 15		1	250		250	
26		1	1,000		1,250	

			Office Equipment		ACCOUNT NO. 15	
					Balance	
Date	**Item**	**Ref.**	**Debit**	**Credit**	*Debit*	*Credit*
19-- May 24		1	2,800		2,800	

			Land		ACCOUNT NO. 16	
					Balance	
Date	**Item**	**Ref.**	**Debit**	**Credit**	*Debit*	*Credit*
19-- May 8			15,000		15,000	

	Building			ACCOUNT NO. 17		
					Balance	
Date	**Item**	**Ref.**	**Debit**	**Credit**	*Debit*	*Credit*
19-- May 8		1	20,000		20,000	
28		1	5,000		25,000	

	Accounts Payable			ACCOUNT NO. 21		
					Balance	
Date	**Item**	**Ref.**	**Debit**	**Credit**	*Debit*	*Credit*
19-- May 15		1		520	520	

	Notes Payable			ACCOUNT NO. 21		
					Balance	
Date	**Item**	**Ref.**	**Debit**	**Credit**	*Debit*	*Credit*
19-- May 8		1		10,000		10,000
28		1	400			9,600

	Mortgage Payable			ACCOUNT NO. 23		
					Balance	
Date	**Item**	**Ref.**	**Debit**	**Credit**	*Debit*	*Credit*
19-- May 8		1		12,000		12,000

	M. Zamost, Capital			ACCOUNT NO. 31		
					Balance	
Date	**Item**	**Ref.**	**Debit**	**Credit**	*Debit*	*Credit*
19-- May 4		1		20,000		20,000
16		1		15,000		35,000

					Balance	
Date	Item	Ref.	Debit	Credit	Debit	Credit
19-- May 30		1		750		750

M. Zamost, Withdrawals   *ACCOUNT NO. 32*

ZAMOST SERVICE COMPANY
Trial Balance
May 31, 19--

	Debit	Credit
Cash	17,050	
Supplies	1,250	
Office Equipment	2,800	
Land	15,000	
Building	25,000	
Accounts Payable	520	
Notes Payable		9,600
Mortgage Payable		12,000
M. Zamost, Capital		35,000
M. Zamost, Withdrawals		750
	60,620	57,350

Required

1) Locate as many errors as you can find in the records. For each error that you locate, state how it occurred and the effect it had on the accounting system.

2) Prepare a corrected trial balance.

SUMMARY OF CHAPTER 2

The accounting model of an entity is based on the accounting equation, whereby the assets owned are equal to the creditor and owner claims against them. The major equation elements are further divided into account categories, and account changes are expressed as debits and credits. Assets are increased by debits, whereas credits increase liability and owner's equity accounts.

The revenues and expenses of each accounting period are collected in temporary equity accounts. Revenues represent equity increases and thus accumulate as credits; expenses, which decrease owner's equity, accumulate as debits. A record of owner's withdrawals is often maintained in a separate temporary account, which also accumulates a debit balance. A statement of owner's capital may be prepared to show the effects of net income (or net loss), which is the difference between revenues and expenses for a period, and the effects of withdrawals on the permanent capital account.

Accounting information is processed by means of four basic functions: documenting, recording, summarizing, and reporting. Accountants follow certain accepted procedures when working with documents, journals, and ledgers and when preparing statements that communicate accounting data.

A trial balance is prepared to test the equality of debits and credits and to provide information for use in preparing statements. An out-of-balance trial balance indicates that one or more errors have been made. However, an in-balance trial balance does not guarantee that the system is error free; some types of errors do not disturb the equality of debits and credits.

PROBLEMS FOR CHAPTER 2
Alternate Problems for this chapter begin on page D-10.

2.1. An opening trial balance for Dandy Company at May 1 follows, together with a list of transactions for May.

A/C #	Account	Debit	Credit
	DANDY COMPANY **Trial Balance** **May 1, 19– –**		
11	Cash	720	
12	Accounts Receivable	480	
13	Supplies	190	
16	Equipment	4,000	
016	Accumulated Depreciation—Equipment		2,800
21	Accounts Payable		90
31	J. Dandy, Capital		2,500
32	J. Dandy, Withdrawals	–0–	
41	Service Revenue		–0–
51	Rent Expense	–0–	
52	Wage Expense	–0–	
53	Supplies Expense	–0–	
54	Depreciation Expense	–0–	
		5,390	5,390

Transactions

May 5   Collected accounts receivable, $480 (Deposit No. 92).

     5   Purchased supplies on account, $50.

    10   Collected cash from customers for work done in May, $320 (Deposit No. 93).

    20   Paid May rent, $450 (Check No. 643).

    20   James Dandy withdrew $80 for personal use (Check No. 644).

    25   Paid on accounts payable, $90 (Check No. 645).

    31   Paid wages for month, $800 (Check No. 646).

    31   Billed customers $2,100 for work done in May.

    31   Supplies remaining on hand at month-end, $180.

    31   Depreciation on equipment during May, $150.

Required

1) Journalize the May transactions.

2) Set up T-accounts with balances as shown on the May 1 trial balance, and post the May journal entries to the T-accounts.

3) Prepare a trial balance at May 31.

4) Prepare an income statement for the month of May.

2.2. The Shop-for-You Company opening trial balance for November 1 follows. Also provided are the transactions for the month of November.

A/C #	Account	Debit	Credit
	SHOP-FOR-YOU COMPANY **Trial Balance** **November 1, 19--**		
11	Cash	260	
15	Car	5,000	
015	Accumulated Depreciation—Car		1,800
21	Note Payable		2,400
31	T. Treadmore, Capital		1,060
41	Shopping Fees		–0–
51	Advertising Expense	–0–	
52	Gasoline Expense	–0–	
53	Car Maintenance Expense	–0–	
54	Depreciation Expense	–0–	
		5,260	5,260

Transactions

Nov. 10   Deposited $300 in fees collected from customers (Deposit No. 206).

12   Paid $45 for newspaper advertising (Check No. 514).

15   Paid November installment on note, $200 (Check No. 515).

15   Paid $70 for car repairs (Check No. 516).

20   Deposited $450 in fees collected from customers (Deposit No. 207).

25   Paid $160 for radio advertising (Check No. 517).

29   Paid service station $110 for gasoline purchased during November (Check No. 518).

30   Deposited $550 in fees collected from customers (Deposit No. 208).

30   Automobile depreciation for November, $120.

Required

1) Journalize the November transactions on general journal page 11.

2) Set up ledger accounts on forms that allow for a running balance, showing the opening balances at November 1 for the first five accounts. Post the November entries to the ledger accounts, taking care to cross-reference the journal and ledger properly.

3) Prepare a trial balance at November 30.

4) Prepare an income statement and statement of owner's capital for November, and a balance sheet at November 30.

2.3. Maggie's Repair Service was started on February 1 by Maggie Charles. A chart of accounts and the February transactions are shown below.

MAGGIE'S REPAIR SERVICE
Chart of Accounts

100 Assets

111 Cash
112 Accounts Receivable
113 Supplies
121 Tools and Equipment
0121 Accumulated
     Depreciation—Tools
     and Equipment
131 Truck
0131 Accumulated
     Depreciation—Truck

200 Liabilities

211 Accounts Payable
212 Notes Payable

300 Owner's Equity

311 M. Charles, Capital
312 M. Charles, Withdrawals

400 Revenue

411 Service Revenue

500 Expenses

511 Wage Expense
512 Rent Expense
513 Gasoline Expense
514 Supplies Expense
515 Depreciation Expense

Transactions

Feb. 1   The owner, Maggie Charles, invested $6,000 in the business (Deposit No. 1).

3   The company borrowed $2,000 from the bank on a note payable (Deposit No. 2).

4   Tools and equipment costing $3,500 were purchased on account.

4   A truck was purchased for $8,000. A $3,000 cash down payment was made (Check No. 101), and a note was signed for the $5,000 balance.

5   Supplies were purchased for cash at a cost of $600 (Check No. 102).

6   Cash revenue of $300 was collected for making emergency repairs on a bulldozer (Deposit No. 3).

10   Billed a customer for $2,000 of revenue that was earned but not yet collected.

12   Bought gasoline (to be used during February) on account, $15.

12   Paid employee wages totaling $1,200 (Check Nos. 103–106).

15   Paid $3,500 owed for tools and equipment purchased on February 4 (Check No. 107).

15   Received $2,000 from the customer who was billed on February 10 (Deposit No. 4).

19   Paid employee wages totaling $800 (Check Nos. 108–110).

22   Received cash revenue of $1,800 for services rendered today (Deposit No. 5).

23   Bought gasoline (to be used during February) on account, $18.

26   Paid rent for February, $900 (Check No. 111).

26   Paid employee wages totaling $1,100 (Check Nos. 112–115).

29   Maggie withdrew $500 cash from business for her personal use (Check No. 116).

29   Recognized depreciation expense on truck for February in the amount of $200.

29   Recognized depreciation expense on tools and equipment for February in the amount of $50.

Required

1) Journalize the transactions for February, starting on page 1 of a general journal.

2) Set up appropriate ledger accounts on forms that provide for a running balance. Post the journal entries and be sure to cross-reference the entries and postings.

3) Prepare a trial balance at February 29.

4) Prepare an income statement and statement of owner's capital for the month of February, and a balance sheet at February 29.

COMPREHENSION PROBLEMS FOR CHAPTER 2

2.4. Muster Company was formed during March. Soon after, the company purchased land with a building on it, paying some cash down and signing a mortgage note for the remaining cost. The company also purchased equipment during March. The trial balance for Muster at March 31 follows.

MUSTER COMPANY Trial Balance March 31, 19––		
	Debit	**Credit**
Cash	3,500	
Equipment	6,000	
Building	40,000	
Land	8,000	
Mortgage Payable		36,000
K. Muster, Capital		23,000
K. Muster, Withdrawals	1,500	
	59,000	59,000

Required

1) Reflect into T-accounts the transactions that must have taken place during March.

2) Prepare journal entries for the transactions that must have taken place during March.

2.5. Milo Bargarino established a new law practice on May 1. During the month of June, the following transactions occurred.

Transactions

June 1   Milo withdrew $2,000 for his personal use.

2   Furniture costing $3,000 was purchased on account.

4   Paid $300 cash on accounts payable.

6   Supplies costing $200 were purchased on account.

12   Milo Bargarino, Attorney (the entity) borrowed $3,000 from a local bank on a note payable.

22   Law books costing $2,300 were purchased for cash.

At the end of June, the following trial balance was prepared. There were no revenues or expenses during May and June because Milo was occupied with getting the business organized during these months.

<table>
<tr><td colspan="3" align="center">**MILO BARGARINO, ATTORNEY**
Trial Balance
June 30, 19--</td></tr>
<tr><td></td><td>**Debit**</td><td>**Credit**</td></tr>
<tr><td>Cash</td><td>2,000</td><td></td></tr>
<tr><td>Supplies</td><td>600</td><td></td></tr>
<tr><td>Law Books</td><td>3,800</td><td></td></tr>
<tr><td>Furniture</td><td>3,000</td><td></td></tr>
<tr><td>Building</td><td>28,000</td><td></td></tr>
<tr><td>Land</td><td>4,000</td><td></td></tr>
<tr><td>Accounts Payable</td><td></td><td>4,100</td></tr>
<tr><td>Notes Payable</td><td></td><td>8,000</td></tr>
<tr><td>Mortgage Payable</td><td></td><td>22,000</td></tr>
<tr><td>Milo Bargarino, Capital</td><td></td><td>9,300</td></tr>
<tr><td>Milo Bargarino, Withdrawals</td><td>2,000</td><td></td></tr>
<tr><td></td><td>43,400</td><td>43,400</td></tr>
</table>

Milo would like to compare the June 30 balance sheet with the one for May 31, but he has misplaced the records for May.

Required

1) Use the information provided to prepare balance sheets for June 30 and May 31.

2) Prepare a schedule that lists the sources and uses of cash during June and that concludes with the net change in cash for the month.

2.6. During a storm on October 1, 19--, the offices of the Shock Installation Company were struck by lightning and burned to the ground. Fortunately, the ledger was in a fireproof safe, but all the other accounting records were destroyed. The ledger accounts follow.

					Balance	
Cash					**ACCOUNT NO. 111**	
Date	Item	Ref.	Debit	Credit	*Debit*	*Credit*
19--						
Aug. 30	Balance forward	X			3,800	
30		10	210		4,010	
Sept. 1		11		400	3,610	
5		11	250		3,860	
13		12	1,700		5,560	
15		12		1,500	4,060	
20		12		120	3,940	
30		12		750	3,190	
30		12		1,500	1,690	
30		12		500	1,190	

Accounts Receivable					**ACCOUNT NO. 112**	
					Balance	
Date	Item	Ref.	Debit	Credit	*Debit*	*Credit*
19--						
Sept. 1	Balance forward	X			400	
5		11		250	150	
5		11	2,000		2,150	
21		12	1,200		3,350	

Office Supplies					**ACCOUNT NO. 113**	
					Balance	
Date	Item	Ref.	Debit	Credit	*Debit*	*Credit*
19--						
Sept. 1	Balance forward	X			80	
1		11	80		160	
30		12		70	90	

Office Equipment and Furniture ACCOUNT NO. 121						
					Balance	
Date	Item	Ref.	Debit	Credit	Debit	Credit
19-- Sept. 1	Balance forward	X			2,400	

Accumulated Depreciation— Office Equipment and Furniture ACCOUNT NO. 0121						
					Balance	
Date	Item	Ref.	Debit	Credit	Debit	Credit
19-- Aug. 30 31 Sept. 30	Balance forward	X 11 12		50 50		250 300 350

Truck ACCOUNT NO. 131						
					Balance	
Date	Item	Ref.	Debit	Credit	Debit	Credit
19-- July 1		4	6,000		6,000	

Accumulated Depreciation—Truck ACCOUNT NO. 0131						
					Balance	
Date	Item	Ref.	Debit	Credit	Debit	Credit
19-- July 31 Aug. 31 Sept. 30		5 11 13		100 100 100		100 200 300

Installation Equipment				ACCOUNT NO. 141		
					Balance	
Date	Item	Ref.	Debit	Credit	Debit	Credit
19-- Sept. 1	Balance forward	X			1,800	

Accumulated Depreciation— Installation Equipment				ACCOUNT NO. 0141		
					Balance	
Date	Item	Ref.	Debit	Credit	Debit	Credit
19-- June 30		3		10		10
July 31		5		15		25
Aug. 31		11		30		55
Sept. 30		13		30		85

Accounts Payable				ACCOUNT NO. 211		
					Balance	
Date	Item	Ref.	Debit	Credit	Debit	Credit
19-- Sept. 1	Balance forward	X				1,105
1		11	400			705
1		11		80		785
17		12		16		801
27		12		20		821

J. Shock, Capital				ACCOUNT NO. 311		
					Balance	
Date	Item	Ref.	Debit	Credit	Debit	Credit
19-- Aug. 28	Balance forward	X				12,580
31		10		450		13,030

J. Shock, Withdrawals   *ACCOUNT NO. 312*

Date	Item	Ref.	Debit	Credit	Balance Debit	Balance Credit
19-- Sept. 30		12	500		500	

Installation Fees   *ACCOUNT NO. 411*

Date	Item	Ref.	Debit	Credit	Balance Debit	Balance Credit
19-- Sept. 5		11		2,000		2,000
13		12		1,700		3,700
21		12		1,200		4,900

Salary Expense   *ACCOUNT NO. 511*

Date	Item	Ref.	Debit	Credit	Balance Debit	Balance Credit
19-- Sept. 15		12	1,500		1,500	
30		12	1,500		3,000	

Rent Expense   *ACCOUNT NO. 512*

Date	Item	Ref.	Debit	Credit	Balance Debit	Balance Credit
19-- Sept. 30		12	750		750	

Insurance Expense   *ACCOUNT NO. 513*

Date	Item	Ref.	Debit	Credit	Balance Debit	Balance Credit
19-- Sept. 20		12	120		120	

	Depreciation Expense				ACCOUNT NO. 514	
					Balance	
Date	Item	Ref.	Debit	Credit	Debit	Credit
19-- Sept. 30		12	50		50	
30		13	100		150	
30		13	30		180	

	Gasoline Expense				ACCOUNT NO. 515	
					Balance	
Date	Item	Ref.	Debit	Credit	Debit	Credit
19-- Sept. 17		12	16		16	
27		12	20		36	

	Supplies Expense				ACCOUNT NO. 516	
					Balance	
Date	Item	Ref.	Debit	Credit	Debit	Credit
19-- Sept. 30		12	70		70	

Required

Reconstruct from the ledger accounts the journal entries that must have been made for September transactions. You may omit the explanations for the entries.

3
End-of-Period Work

The days and nights immediately following the end of an accounting period are indeed busy ones for bookkeepers and accountants. It is at this time that data contained in the accounting records must be updated and verified for use in accounting statements. Also, the records must be readied quickly for processing transactions for the next accounting period. Most entities are accounted for on an annual (12-month) basis, although months and calendar quarters may be viewed as subperiods of the year. In order to keep matters simple for learners, monthly accounting periods are often assumed for illustrations and accounting problems.

Chapter 3 contains three sections and two appendixes. Section A concentrates on the various kinds of adjusting entries that may be needed at the end of an accounting period. Much of the routine processing of data is done during the period by clerks and automated processes, but adjusting the accounting records is the accountant's responsibility.

Section B deals with use of a work sheet for organizing end-of-period work, and with the preparation of adjusting entries and financial statements directly from data contained in the work sheet.

Section C focuses on closing procedures used to ready the accounting records for the next accounting period. The purposes of closing entries are pointed out, and the closing process is illustrated. This section concludes with a list of steps that make up a complete accounting cycle.

Appendix I briefly covers the use of reversing entries at the beginning of an accounting period. Reversing entries are not absolutely necessary in an accounting cycle. Some accountants employ reversing entries, whereas others do not.

Appendix II explores prepaid expenses and unearned revenues beyond the discussion of deferrals provided in Section A. Adjustments for prepaid expenses and unearned revenues are illustrated, as are the related reversing entries that might be made at the start of a new accounting period.

SECTION 3.A

Adjusting Entries

OBJECTIVES

This section concentrates on adjusting entries needed to update and correct account balances. At the end of the section, you should be able to

1. State why adjusting entries are necessary.
2. Prepare journal entries to adjust for the following:
   a. Accrual of revenues and expenses.
   b. Deferral of revenues and expenses.
   c. Expiration of liabilities to revenues.
   d. Expiration of assets to expenses.

THE NEED FOR ADJUSTMENTS

The purpose of accounting is to provide useful information to people who need it. To be most useful, the information should be accurate and up to date. As you now know, financial information is presented by accountants in *statements,* which fall within the fourth function of accounting, *reporting* (Illustration 3.1).

ILLUSTRATION 3.1

ACCOUNTING FUNCTIONS

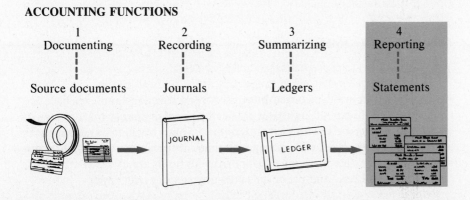

1	2	3	4
Documenting	Recording	Summarizing	Reporting
Source documents	Journals	Ledgers	Statements

ILLUSTRATION 3.2

31	Supplies Expense	20	
	Office Supplies		20
	Office supplies used during March.		
31	Depreciation Expense	200	
	Accumulated Depreciation—Truck		200
	Truck depreciation during March.		

Recall that the source documents provide information about transactions for use in making journal entries. Journal entries are then posted to a ledger, and ledger accounts provide data for statement preparation. Events that have not been documented will not have been recorded in the normal way, and the information in the ledger will not be complete.

OBJECTIVE 1. State why adjusting entries are necessary.

Accountants prepare adjusting entries to record events that have not been noted (documented) and recorded in the usual way. *Adjusting entries are special entries made at the end of an accounting period to update and correct information shown in the accounts.*

Special care is taken to ensure that revenues are reported in proper periods and that expenses are matched with reported revenues in accordance with the *matching concept.* Likewise, accountants are concerned that assets and liabilities be properly reported. In fact, the process of recognizing changes in expenses and revenues necessarily involves assets and liabilities. Recall, for example, that a debit to an expense account is followed by a credit to either an asset or a liability account. Usually, one side of an adjusting entry involves a revenue or expense (temporary) account while the other side involves an asset or liability (permanent) account.

Actually, we have already dealt with adjusting entries without labeling them as such. You may recall from the previous chapter the last two entries for Metts Delivery Service on March 31, which are shown again in Illustration 3.2. There were no source documents to act as signals to get these entries recorded. The accountant had to discover the need for adjusting entries—that some of the supplies had been used, and that the truck had depreciated since it was purchased.

TYPES OF ADJUSTMENTS

Accruals

At the end of a period, accrued but unrecorded revenues and expenses are recognized by means of adjusting entries. *Accrual is simply the process of growing, arising, or coming into existence.* Some revenues and expenses accrue constantly with the passage of time. Interest, for example, accumulates over the time that loaned (or borrowed) funds are used. Rent, wages, insurance premiums, and property taxes also accrue over time.

ILLUSTRATION 3.3

Date	Account Names and Explanations	A/C #	Debit	Credit
	ADJUSTING JOURNAL ENTRIES			
19-- Dec. 31	Accounts Receivable Repair Service Revenue To recognize revenue earned during the last week of December, but which will not be billed to customers until January.		780	780
31	Interest Receivable Interest Revenue To record interest earned during December on savings account balance at Mid-Town Bank.		60	60

OBJECTIVE 2a. Adjust for accrual of revenues.

In accounting, the term *accrual* is often interpreted broadly to include sales or service revenues earned but as yet unbilled, and purchased goods or services for which invoices have not yet arrived. Thus accrual adjustments involve increases in either receivables or payables.

Revenue Accruals.   To illustrate the accrual of revenues, let us consider the adjustments shown in Illustration 3.3. The first entry was needed to record December revenues for which bills were not prepared and mailed until January, because of normal delays in billing procedures. The second entry registers savings account interest that accrued during December.

Notice that revenue accruals involve the simultaneous recognition of receivables and revenues and take the following form.

Asset (Receivable) Account Debited Revenue Account Credited	XXX	XXX

Expense Accruals.   The adjusting entries in Illustration 3.4 on the next page show the accrual of expenses at the end of an accounting period. Study the entries carefully, particularly the explanations, to see why the expense accruals were needed.

Expense accruals take the following form.

Expense Account Debited Liability (Payable) Account Credited	XXX	XXX

ILLUSTRATION 3.4

OBJECTIVE 2a. Adjust for accrual of expenses.

Date	Account Names and Explanations	A/C #	Debit	Credit
19— Dec. 31	Wage Expense Wages Payable To recognize December wages to be paid in January.		520	520
31	Interest Expense Interest Payable To recognize accrued interest due on bank loan.		110	110
31	Repair Parts Used Accounts Payable To recognize repair parts purchased and used during December from Jones Parts Co. Jones sends a monthly statement on the first day of each month for all purchases made during the previous month.		75	75

Deferrals

Cash is occasionally received from customers before it is actually earned, and it is sometimes disbursed to prepay expenses. Rent, for example, is usually paid in advance, as are insurance premiums, magazine subscriptions, and certain other items. From a landlord's viewpoint, advance payment represents an obligation (liability) to the tenant; the tenant's prepayment of rent buys the right to use property in the future, which is an asset.

To simplify accounting procedures, cash receipts and payments are sometimes reflected immediately as revenues and expenses even though they represent deferred items. There is no harm in treating a month's rent as an expense when it is paid in advance on the first day of the month. After all, the entire amount will be an expense by month-end anyway. And in most cases, at least *some* of the insurance premiums, magazine subscriptions, or other prepayments belong to the period in which they are paid.

When an accountant discovers that a portion of what has been recorded as a revenue or expense should be assigned to a future period, an adjusting entry is made to defer the appropriate amount.

Deferred Revenue.   Revenues received before they are earned are liabilities, because they represent obligations to customers. When a magazine company collects money in advance for subscriptions, it has a *liability* to deliver magazine issues in the future; as magazines are delivered, portions of the liability are earned as revenue. The adjusting entries in Illustration 3.5 dem-

ILLUSTRATION 3.5

Date	Account Names and Explanations	A/C #	Debit	Credit
19-- Dec. 31	Rent Revenue Unearned Rent Revenue To defer January rent, which was received in December and recorded at that time as revenue.		800	800
31	Subscriptions Revenue Unearned Subscriptions Revenue To defer subscriptions revenue for magazines yet to be published.		1,600	1,600

OBJECTIVE 2b. Adjust for deferral of revenues.

onstrate the deferral of revenues that are as yet unearned at the end of a period.

Revenue deferral adjustments take the following form.

Revenue Account Debited Unearned Revenue (Liability) Account Credited	XXX	XXX

Accounting for unearned revenues is discussed in more detail in Appendix II of this chapter.

Deferred Expenses.   Adjustments that defer expenses to a future period are shown by the entries in Illustration 3.6.

ILLUSTRATION 3.6

Date	Account Names and Explanations	A/C #	Debit	Credit
19-- Dec. 31	Unexpired Insurance Insurance Expense To defer insurance premiums that apply to future months.		480	480
31	Prepaid Rent Rent Expense To defer rent prepaid for the first quarter of the coming year.		1,350	1,350
31	Office Supplies Supplies Expense To recognize unused office supplies at year-end.		140	140

OBJECTIVE 2b. Adjust for deferral of expenses.

Adjustments to defer expenses take the following form.

Prepaid Expense (Asset) Account Debited	XXX	
Expense Account Credited		XXX

Accounting for prepaid expenses is discussed in more detail in Appendix II of this chapter.

Expirations

In a sense, all assets are deferred charges (debits) and all liabilities are deferred credits. Assets and liabilities represent carryovers of costs and obligations into future accounting periods. As assets are used up or depreciated in the process of earning revenues, portions of their costs are written off (expired) to expenses; and liabilities in the form of deferred revenues are shifted to revenue accounts as the revenues are earned.

Liability Expirations to Revenue.   As we saw earlier, some revenues may be collected in advance, before they are earned, in which case they should be deferred as liabilities. The adjusting entries in Illustration 3.7 recognize the portions of previously deferred revenues that were earned during the month of January.

Liability expirations to revenue take the following form.

Unearned Revenue (Liability) Account Debited	XXX	
Revenue Account Credited		XXX

Asset Expirations to Expense.   As asset costs expire, they become expenses. Adjusting entries are commonly made to recognize depreciation of productive assets such as equipment, trucks, or buildings. Assume, for example, that a truck is purchased for $19,800, that it has an expected life of 48 months,

ILLUSTRATION 3.7

OBJECTIVE 2c. Adjust for expiration of liabilities to revenues.

Date	Account Names and Explanations	A/C #	Debit	Credit
19—— Jan. 31	Unearned Rent Revenue		800	
	Rent Revenue			800
	To recognize rent revenue for January.			
31	Unearned Subscriptions Revenue		730	
	Subscriptions Revenue			730
	To recognize revenue for magazines delivered during the month.			

ILLUSTRATION 3.8

Date	Account Names and Explanations	A/C #	Debit	Credit
19-- Jan. 31	Depreciation Expense—Truck Accumulated Depreciation—Truck To record truck depreciation for January.		400	400
31	Insurance Expense Unexpired Insurance To record insurance premiums for January.		20	20
31	Rent Expense Prepaid Rent To recognize rent expense for January.		450	450
31	Supplies Expense Office Supplies To record office supplies used during January.		30	30

OBJECTIVE 2d. Adjust for expiration of assets to expenses.

and that at the end of its life it is expected to be worth $600 as salvage. Also, the truck is expected to be equally useful (productive) during each month of its life. Depreciation per month can be determined as follows.

$$\frac{Cost - Salvage}{Months\ of\ life} = Depreciation\ per\ month$$

$$\frac{\$19,800 - \$600}{48} = \$400\ per\ month$$

Remember, depreciation of a long-lived productive asset is accumulated in an asset contra account called Accumulated Depreciation. The adjusting entry to record the truck depreciation is shown in Illustration 3.8, along with several other adjustments for asset expirations.

Asset expiration adjustments take the following form.

Expense Account Debited	XXX	
Asset (Contra Asset) Account Credited		XXX

IDENTIFYING THE NEED FOR ADJUSTMENTS

Adjusting entries are needed to recognize events for which no source documents have been prepared. So how does one know which accounts to adjust, and by how much?

Different accountants follow different approaches to uncover needed adjustments. One avenue is simply to review the adjustments that were made at the end of previous accounting periods. In some cases the same or similar adjustments are needed at the end of each accounting period.

Another approach is to scan the accounts in an unadjusted trial balance, looking for clues that suggest the need for adjustments. Certain receivables and payables involve interest, which must be accrued with the passage of time; depreciable assets must be depreciated each period; supplies can be checked to determine what is still on hand; and so on.

A more orderly approach is to examine or audit each account, starting at the beginning of the ledger, to determine if any adjustments are needed. Bank accounts are reconciled to bank statements to prove the cash account. Files of unpaid invoices, orders, and other documents are examined in an attempt to discover unrecorded payables or receivables. Receivables and payables are reviewed for any accrued interest receivable or payable. In fact, all available evidence is considered in an effort to locate any misstatements as each account is examined.

Your ability to identify the need for adjustments will improve as you become more skilled in accounting.

GLOSSARY FOR SECTION 3.A

Accrual   Growing, or arising, with the passage of time.

Adjusting entries   Special journal entries made at the end of an accounting period to update and correct information shown in the accounts.

SELF-QUIZ ON OBJECTIVES FOR SECTION 3.A
Solutions to Self-Quiz begin on page B-6.

1. OBJECTIVE 1.   State why adjusting entries are necessary.

2. OBJECTIVE 2.   Prepare adjusting journal entries, at October 31, for the following items.

   Adjustments Data

   a) Service revenues in the amount of $850 were earned during the last few days of October, but have not yet been billed to customers (and therefore have not yet been recorded).

   b) Interest of $40 accrued during October on a loan payable to the bank.

   c) Of the Service Revenue account credits during October, $500 represents advances from customers for services to be rendered during November.

   d) On October 1, $1,200 in rental charges was paid for building space during October, November, and December. The entire amount was debited to Rent Expense at the time of payment.

e) Of $700 credited to an Unearned Service Revenue account during September, $400 was earned during October.

f) A business automobile was purchased on October 1 for $8,200. It has an expected useful life to the business of 48 months, after which it can be sold for $1,000. (Record the depreciation expense for October.)

DISCUSSION QUESTIONS FOR SECTION 3.A

1. Why are adjusting entries needed?

2. How do accountants identify the accounts most likely to be in need of adjustment at the end of an accounting period?

3. What is an accrual? Give an example of an accrual that usually requires an adjusting entry at the end of an accounting period.

4. What does the expression *asset expiration* mean?

5. How is the realization concept related to the need for adjusting entries?

6. Why is depreciation usually recorded only as an adjusting entry at the end of each accounting period?

EXERCISES FOR SECTION 3.A

3.A.1. An adjustment will usually affect two of the following groups of accounts: assets, liabilities, expenses, and revenues. Set up a chart with headings as follows:

	Asset	Liability	Expense	Revenue
a)				
b)				
etc.				

For each of the following items, indicate the effect of the adjustment on assets, liabilities, expenses, or revenues by writing increase or decrease in the appropriate column.

Adjustments Data

a) Rent revenue collected in advance during the year was recorded in a revenue account. At the end of the year, a portion of the rent is still unearned.

b) An inventory of supplies shows some supplies on hand. All supplies, when purchased, were recorded as an expense.

c) Depreciation for the year has not been recorded.

d) All insurance premiums are recorded in a Prepaid Insurance account. An adjustment is needed to recognize insurance cost that has expired.

e) Interest earned on a note receivable has not been recorded.

f) Deposits paid by customers to apply on installation fees are recorded as unearned service revenue. An adjustment is needed to recognize the portion of advances that have now been earned.

g) Wages and salaries are owed to employees at the end of the accounting period.

h) An adjustment is needed to recognize interest that has accrued on a note payable.

3.A.2. On Tuesday, May 31, the Small Company had accrued wages of $200. On Friday, June 3, the Small Company paid employee wages of $500 for the week.

a. Make the adjusting entry on May 31 for accrued wages.

b. Make the entry on June 3 to record the payment of the week's wages.

3.A.3. On June 1, Josen Publishing Company received $600 from a law firm for a twelve-month subscription to *Court Decisions*. Josen follows the practice of recording subscriptions as liabilities at the time they are received. Make Josen's entries on June 1 and June 30 relative to the subscription.

3.A.4. Mocha Company paid insurance premiums of $600 on July 1 for fire insurance coverage for the last half of the year.

a. Assuming that the payment on July 1 was charged to Insurance Expense, make the needed adjusting entry on July 31.

b. Assuming that the payment on July 1 was charged to Unexpired Insurance, make the needed adjusting entry on July 31.

3.A.5. Farley Wrecking Service purchased a new tow truck for $11,000. The owner, Barbara Farley, estimated that the truck's useful life would be 36 months and that at the end of that time it would be worth $200 as salvage. She also assumed that the truck would be equally productive for each month of its life. Make an adjusting journal entry to record one month's depreciation at September 30.

PROBLEMS FOR SECTION 3.A
Alternate Problems for this section begin on page D-13.

3.A.6. Adjustments data are given below.

Adjustments Data

a) Service revenue of $85 was earned on the last day of June, but will not be billed to the customer until July 3.

b) Wages of $500, earned by employees during the last week in June, will not be paid until July 2.

c) The Supplies account shows a balance of $320. A check of supplies on hand shows that all but $105 of the supplies were used during June.

d) Depreciation on an automobile during June was $150.

Required

Prepare adjusting entries at June 30.

3.A.7. Jeb Smiley, a college student, started his own business on January 1. During the year he devised and kept his own accounting records. A friend who is studying accounting suggested that Jeb's records may require some year-end adjustments. Jeb and his friend accumulated the following adjustments information.

Adjustments Data

a) On January 1, Jeb borrowed $2,000 to help start his business. He promised to repay the loan, plus 10% per annum interest, 24 months from the day he borrowed the money.

b) During the year, Jeb paid $100 from his personal funds for supplies used in the business.

c) On July 1, Jeb purchased a used truck for $3,600 for use in his business. The truck is expected to have a useful life of 24 months, after which it is expected to be worthless.

d) During the year, a property tax liability of $250 accrued on business assets.

Required

Make any necessary adjusting entries, at December 31, for Jeb's business.

3.A.8. Able Company borrowed $10,000 cash from Baker Company on July 1 and agreed to repay the sum plus 12% per annum (1% per month) interest on August 31.

Required

1) Prepare for Able Company entries to record

   a) The loan proceeds on July 1.

   b) The adjustment to accrue interest on July 31.

   c) Payment of the loan plus interest on August 31.

2) Prepare for Baker Company entries to record

   a) The loan made to Able Company on July 1.

   b) The adjustment to accrue interest on July 31.

   c) Receipt of cash for loan repayment and interest on August 31.

3.A.9. On October 1, Conner Company paid Duncan Company $3,000 in rental charges for use of a building during October, November, and December.

Required

1) Assuming that Conner Company charged the rental payment to a temporary (expense) account, and that Duncan Company credited it to a temporary (revenue) account, show how the entries would appear in the journal of each company to record

   a) The initial payment of the rent.

   b) The needed adjustment on October 31.

2) Assuming that Conner Company charged the rental payment to a permanent (asset) account, and that Duncan Company credited it to a

permanent (liability) account, show how the entries would appear in the journal of each company to record

a) The initial payment of the rent.

b) The needed adjustment on October 31.

3.A.10. Following is an unadjusted trial balance for Rabanks Research Company for the year ended December 31. Adjusting entries are made only at year-end.

RABANKS RESEARCH COMPANY Trial Balance December 31, 19--		
	Debit	**Credit**
Cash	11,420	
Prepaid Rent	1,500	
Prepaid Computer Service	10,000	
Office Supplies	8,750	
Office Equipment	24,000	
Accounts Payable		6,540
Rabanks, Capital		25,000
Research Fees Earned		61,000
Office Salaries Expense	7,700	
Research Salaries Expense	21,500	
Telephone Expense	780	
Travel Expense	1,890	
Rent Expense	5,000	
	92,540	92,540

Additional Data

a) The prepaid rent represents three month's rent paid on November 1.

b) During the year, 95 hours of computer time were used at $100 per hour.

c) A physical count of office supplies on December 31 showed an inventory of $6,000.

d) All the office equipment was purchased a year ago and has a useful life of six years, after which it will be worthless.

e) Research services rendered to clients but not yet billed, $3,000.

f) Research salaries earned but not paid, $2,450.

Required

1) Make journal entries for all the necessary adjustments.

2) Construct an adjusted trial balance.

3) Prepare an income statement for the year and a balance sheet at December 31 from the adjusted trial balance.

SECTION 3.B

The Work Sheet

OBJECTIVES

This section deals with the preparation of an end-of-period work sheet and with the preparation of statements from the work sheet. At the conclusion of the section, you should be able to

1. Prepare a ten-column work sheet, given an unadjusted trial balance and adjustments data for a small service-type business.

2. From information contained in a work sheet, prepare an income statement, a statement of owner's capital, and a classified balance sheet in report form.

3. State the rules for classifying asset and liability accounts as current.

WORKING PAPERS

In addition to the formal source documents, journals, ledgers, and statements, many kinds of informal working papers are used in accounting. *A working paper is an informal but orderly arrangement of information that serves as an intermediate step in getting from one accounting function to another.*

Working papers are usually done in pencil and are seldom seen by anyone not working directly with the accounting system. They are organized scratch papers that serve as *tools* in the accounting process. The ability to devise and use working papers effectively is a skill that every good accountant has developed.

You have already been introduced to the trial balance, which is one type of working paper. A trial balance, you may remember, is an informal accounting schedule that verifies the equality of debit and credit balances in the ledger accounts.

Purpose of a Work Sheet

A trial balance prepared from the ledger before adjusting entries have been recorded and posted is called an **unadjusted trial balance.** The effects that adjustments have on an unadjusted trial balance are frequently worked out on a work sheet before any adjusting entries are actually made in the journal. *A work sheet is a form with a number of columns for organizing the work that must be performed at the end of an accounting period.* Thus a work sheet is simply an intermediate step between the summarizing and reporting functions of accounting (Illustration 3.9). Its purpose is to reflect the effects of adjustments into account balances and to arrange the adjusted balances in groups according to the statements in which the accounts appear.

ILLUSTRATION 3.9

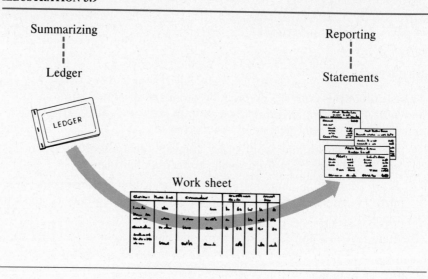

WORK SHEET PREPARATION

Work sheet formats vary according to the size and complexity of the entity and the preferences of individual accountants. We will use a ten-column arrangement to help organize data at July 31 for the firm of Beck Cleaning. Adjustments are required as shown in Illustration 3.10.

Look at the work sheet in Illustration 3.11 on page 116. Notice how the heading identifies the entity and period of time covered. The first two amount columns contain the firm's unadjusted trial balance at July 31. The next two columns reflect the effects of adjustments. Debit and credit amounts for each entry are keyed together in the adjustments columns with letters or numbers, so that the effects of each adjustment can be easily

ILLUSTRATION 3.10

BECK CLEANING Adjusting Entry Data July 31
a) Revenue earned but unbilled at July 31, $120.
b) Accrued wages at July 31, $30.
c) Supplies on hand at July 31, $70.
d) Truck depreciation for July, $100.

identified. Explanations for each adjustment may be noted at the bottom of the work sheet, or elsewhere, to be used when adjusting journal entries are prepared.

A work sheet may contain a set of columns with the heading Adjusted Trial Balance. The purpose of these columns is to show the adjusted account balances and to ensure that debits and credits are still in balance. The account balances for the adjusted trial balance are obtained by simply adding across the Unadjusted Trial Balance and Adjustments columns.

The revenue and expense amounts are carried from the Adjusted Trial Balance columns to a set of Income Statement columns, and the columns are totaled. The difference between the revenues and expenses is net income (or net loss). The net income is added to the debit column (or net loss to the credit column) to obtain a balanced set of columns, as shown in Illustration 3.11 on the next page, the work sheet for Beck Cleaning.

The balances of all accounts except revenues and expenses are carried to a set of Balance Sheet columns, and the columns are totaled. The totals should be out of balance by the amount of net income (or net loss), because the effects of revenues and expenses are not yet reflected in the Owner's Equity account. When net income is added to the credit column (or net loss to the debit column), the column totals should be equal, as they are on Beck's work sheet.

The net income (or net loss) required to balance the set of Balance Sheet and Income Statement columns should be identified, although the balancing figure appears on the credit side for one set of columns, on the debit side for the other.

USING THE WORK SHEET

Journalizing Adjustments

The adjustments columns in the work sheet provide the information needed to make the actual adjusting entries in the journal, as shown in Illustration 3.12 on the next page.

Preparing Statements

Keep in mind that the work sheet is only a tool. The columns on the work sheet are not statements, but rather a source of information from which the formal statements are prepared.

Income Statement. The income statement for Beck Cleaning shown in Illustration 3.13 on page 117, was prepared from the Income Statement columns of the Beck work sheet. Some accountants choose to list expenses according to size, with the largest first and the smallest last, regardless of their order on the work sheet.

ILLUSTRATION 3.11

OBJECTIVE 1. Prepare a
ten-column work sheet.

BECK CLEANING
Work Sheet
For the Month of July 19--

A/C #	Account	Unadjusted Trial Balance	
		Dr.	Cr.
11	Cash	520	
12	Accounts Receivable	340	
13	Cleaning Supplies	180	
15	Truck	5,000	
015	Accumulated Depreciation—Truck		1,300
21	Accounts Payable		60
22	Wages Payable		-0-
31	Sandra Beck, Capital		3,310
031	Sandra Beck, Withdrawals	750	
51	Cleaning Revenue		2,730
61	Wage Expense	410	
62	Rent Expense	200	
63	Supplies Expense	-0-	
64	Depreciation Expense	-0-	
		7,400	7,400
	Net Income		

ILLUSTRATION 3.12

Date	Account Names and Explanations	A/C #	Debit	Credit
	ADJUSTING JOURNAL ENTRIES			
19--	*a)*			
July 31	Accounts Receivable		120	
	Cleaning Revenue			120
	To recognize unbilled revenue at July 31.			
	b)			
31	Wage Expense		30	
	Wages Payable			30
	Accrued wages at July 31.			
	c)			
31	Supplies Expense		110	
	Cleaning Supplies			110
	To reflect as expense supplies used during July.			
	d)			
31	Depreciation Expense		100	
	Accumulated Depreciation—Truck			100
	To recognize truck depreciation for July.			

Adjustments		Adjusted Trial Balance		Income Statement		Balance Sheet	
Dr.	Cr.	Dr.	Cr.	Dr.	Cr.	Dr.	Cr.
		520				520	
a) 120		460				460	
	c) 110	70				70	
		5,000				5,000	
	d) 100		1,400				1,400
			60				60
	b) 30		30				30
			3,310				3,310
		750				750	
	a) 120		2,850		2,850		
b) 30		440		440			
		200		200			
c) 110		110		110			
d) 100		100		100			
360	360	7,650	7,650	850	2,850	6,800	4,800
				2,000			2,000
				2,850	2,850	6,800	6,800

Adjustment Explanations:
a) To recognize unbilled revenue at July 31.
b) Accrued wages at July 31.
c) To reflect as expense supplies used during July.
d) To recognize truck depreciation for July.

ILLUSTRATION 3.13

BECK CLEANING Income Statement For the Month of July 19--		
Cleaning revenue		$2,850
Expenses		
Wages	$440	
Rent	200	
Supplies	110	
Depreciation	100	850
Net Income		$2,000

OBJECTIVE 2. From information contained in a work sheet, prepare an income statement.

ILLUSTRATION 3.14

BECK CLEANING Statement of Owner's Capital For the Month of July 19– –	
Capital balance, July 1	$3,310
Net income for July	2,000
Total	$5,310
Less: July withdrawals	750
Capital balance, July 31	$4,560

Statement of Owner's Capital.   From the balances shown for Beck's capital and withdrawal accounts, and from the net income, the statement in Illustration 3.14 was prepared.

Balance Sheet.   The balance sheet in Illustration 3.15 shows the assets, liabilities, and capital accounts for Beck Cleaning as they stand at the *end* of July. Asset and liability account balances were taken directly from the Balance Sheet columns on the work sheet; the owner's capital balance at month-end was derived on the statement of owner's capital.

SUMMARY DIAGRAM

The work sheet facilitates end-of-period accounting tasks. Information for adjusting entries comes from the work sheet, as does the information for accounting statements, as pictured in Illustration 3.16.

ILLUSTRATION 3.15

BECK CLEANING Balance Sheet July 31, 19– –				
ASSETS			*LIABILITIES*	
Cash		$ 520	Accounts payable	$60
Accounts receivable		460	Wages payable	30
Cleaning supplies		70		
Truck	$5,000		Total Liabilities	$ 90
Less: Accumulated				
depreciation	1,400	3,600	*OWNER'S EQUITY*	
			Sandra Beck, capital	4,560
			Total Liabilities and	
Total Assets		$4,650	Owner's Equity	$4,650

ILLUSTRATION 3.16

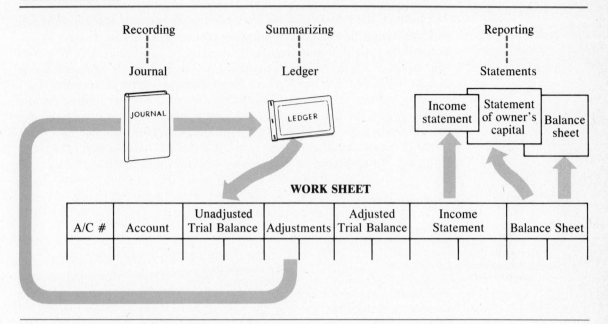

CLASSIFIED BALANCE SHEETS

You may recall that assets are normally listed on a balance sheet in the order of their relative nearness to cash. For example, the Accounts Receivable account usually follows the Cash account because accounts receivable are likely to turn into cash very soon. On the other hand, assets like Land and Buildings are normally listed toward the end, because they are expected to be around a long time.

A classified balance sheet is a balance sheet that divides its accounts into subgroups within the major sections of the statement. One approach is to divide asset accounts into two groups, current and noncurrent. *Current assets are cash and other assets that are relatively close to being cash.* In practice, an asset is classified as current if it can meet any of the following conditions within one year:

a. If it can reasonably be expected to turn into cash

b. If it can easily be converted to cash by the managers of the entity

c. If it can take the place of cash (as with prepaid expenses)

OBJECTIVE 3. State the rules for classifying asset and liability accounts as current.

When assets are divided into current and noncurrent categories, it is common practice to classify liabilities in a similar way. *Current liabilities are liabilities that can reasonably be expected to be paid within one year.* Naturally, liabilities that are not current are considered noncurrent.

Balance Sheet Form

The balance sheet form that we have been using presents assets on the left side and claims against assets (equities) on the right, similar to the way the accounting equation is arranged. *This balanced arrangement, with assets and equities side by side, is sometimes referred to as the **account form of balance sheet**,* because it resembles the traditional T-form of account.

An alternate arrangement, sometimes called the *report form of balance sheet, centers the asset section under the heading, with the equity claims shown below the assets.* The report form frequently fits on a standard sheet of paper better than the account form. A classified balance sheet for Demi Company at September 30 is shown in report form in Illustration 3.17.

ILLUSTRATION 3.17

OBJECTIVE 2. Prepare a classified balance sheet in report form.

DEMI COMPANY
Balance Sheet
September 30, 19– –

ASSETS			
Current			
Cash		$ 1,290	
Accounts receivable		1,090	
Supplies		540	
Prepaid insurance		220	
Total current assets			$ 3,140
Noncurrent			
Land		$ 3,000	
Building	$24,000		
Less: Accumulated depreciation	7,400	16,600	
Total noncurrent assets			19,600
Total Assets			$22,740
LIABILITIES			
Current			
Accounts payable	$ 220		
Wages payable	175		
Interest payable	25		
Total current liabilities		$ 420	
Noncurrent			
Note payable		5,000	
Total Liabilities			$ 5,420
OWNER'S EQUITY			
James Demi, capital			17,320
Total Liabilities and Owner's Equity			$22,740

GLOSSARY FOR SECTION 3.B

Account form of balance sheet   A balance sheet presented in a balanced arrangement, with assets and equities side by side.

Classified balance sheet   A balance sheet that divides its accounts into subgroups within the major sections of the statement.

Current assets   Cash and other assets that are relatively close to being cash.

Current liabilities   Liabilities that can reasonably be expected to be paid within one year.

Report form of balance sheet   A balance sheet that shows equity claims below the asset section of the statement.

Unadjusted trial balance   A trial balance prepared from the ledger before adjusting entries have been recorded and posted.

Working paper   An informal but orderly arrangement of information that serves as an intermediate step in getting from one accounting function to another.

Work sheet   A form with a number of columns for organizing the work that must be performed at the end of an accounting period.

SELF-QUIZ ON OBJECTIVES FOR SECTION 3.B
Solutions to Self-Quiz begin on page B-7.

1. **OBJECTIVE 1.** An unadjusted trial balance for Dibbs Company at April 30 follows. Also provided are adjustments at April 30. The firm uses a monthly accounting period. No additional capital was contributed by the owner during April. Prepare a ten-column work sheet for April.

A/C #	Account	Debit	Credit
\multicolumn{4}{c}{**DIBBS COMPANY** **Unadjusted Trial Balance** **For the Month of April 19– –**}			
111	Cash	450	
112	Accounts Receivable	520	
113	Supplies	190	
115	Land	5,000	
116	Building	25,000	
0116	Accumulated Depreciation—Building		4,500
211	Accounts Payable		110
212	Wages Payable		–0–
215	Mortgage Payable		10,000
311	B. Dibbs, Capital		15,850
312	B. Dibbs, Withdrawals	850	
411	Service Revenue		3,200
511	Wage Expense	1,400	
512	Supplies Expense	250	
513	Depreciation Expense	–0–	
		33,660	33,660

Adjustments Data

a) Revenue earned but unbilled (and unrecorded) at April 30, $230.

b) Accrued wages at April 30, $350.

c) Supplies on hand at April 30, $120.

d) Building depreciation for April, $200.

2. **OBJECTIVE 2.** Using the work sheet created in self-quiz item 1, prepare an income statement, a statement of owner's capital, and a classified balance sheet in report form.

3. **OBJECTIVE 3.** State the rules for classifying asset and liability accounts as current.

DISCUSSION QUESTIONS FOR SECTION 3.B

1. A work sheet shows the effects of end-of-period adjustments. Must these same adjustments also be recorded as journal entries? Why?

2. When and why is a work sheet prepared?

3. Why is the net income for a period added to the income statement's debit column and the balance sheet's credit column?

4. "A ten-column work sheet consists of five pairs of columns. If the column totals for each pair are *not* equal, then an error has been made. If the column totals for each pair *are* equal, then no errors have been made." Do you agree with this statement? Why?

5. The column totals for the balance sheet columns of the work sheet may differ from the amount of total assets and the total of liabilities and owner's equity shown on the balance sheet. Why is this true? (Assume that there are no errors on the balance sheet or work sheet.)

6. What is the difference between the way a net loss is treated on the work sheet and the way net income is treated?

7. How does the report form of a balance sheet differ from the account form?

EXERCISES FOR SECTION 3.B

3.B.1. Subtotals for the Income Statement and Balance Sheet columns of a work sheet follow. Complete the columns by balancing them in proper form, and label the balancing amount as either a net income or net loss.

	Income Statement		Balance Sheet	
	Dr.	*Cr.*	*Dr.*	*Cr.*
Totals	875,000	762,000	1,356,000	1,469,000

3.B.2. Shown here are four errors that were made during the preparation of a work sheet. For each error, determine the amount of imbalance it would cause, and indicate the set of work sheet columns in which the imbalance would first show up.

a. In copying the Cash account balance from the ledger to the Unadjusted Trial Balance, the $5,100 debit balance was written as $1,500.

b. In the work sheet Adjustments columns, a debit to Accounts Receivable and a credit to Service Revenue are both written incorrectly as $320 instead of $230, the correct amount.

c. In transferring amounts to the Adjusted Trial Balance columns, the $150 adjustment to Accumulated Depreciation is *subtracted* from the Accumulated Depreciation balance instead of being *added*.

d. The amount of Owner's Withdrawals is incorrectly copied in the balance sheet columns as a credit of $500, instead of as a debit.

PROBLEMS FOR SECTION 3.B
Alternate Problems for this section begin on page D-14.

3.B.3. G. Davis, attorney-at-law, has the following trial balance and adjustments data at the end of her first year of practice.

G. DAVIS, ATTORNEY-AT-LAW Unadjusted Trial Balance December 31, 19--		
	Debit	**Credit**
Cash	3,950	
Accounts Receivable	4,100	
Office Equipment	3,000	
Supplies	330	
Accounts Payable		600
G. Davis, Capital		3,000
Fees Earned		13,655
Salary Expense	4,000	
Utilities Expense	875	
Rent Expense	1,000	
	17,255	17,255

Adjustments Data

a) Office rent payable at the end of the year was $200.

b) Supplies inventory at December 31 was $240.

c) Depreciation expense on the office equipment was not recorded for the year; it has a five-year life and is being depreciated on a straight-line basis.

Required

Prepare a ten-column work sheet.

3.B.4. An unadjusted trial balance for Lunk Company at March 31 follows. Also provided are adjustments data at March 31. The firm uses a monthly accounting period. No additional capital was contributed by the owner during March.

A/C #	Account	Debit	Credit
	LUNK COMPANY		
	Unadjusted Trial Balance		
	March 31, 19——		
11	Cash	600	
12	Accounts Receivable	1,000	
13	Supplies	90	
15	Truck	6,800	
015	Accumulated Depreciation—Truck		340
21	Accounts Payable		800
22	Interest Payable		–0–
23	Note Payable		4,000
31	F. Lunk, Capital		2,550
32	F. Lunk, Withdrawals	500	
41	Fees Earned		2,000
51	Rent Expense	700	
52	Interest Expense	–0–	
53	Supplies Expense	–0–	
54	Depreciation Expense	–0–	
		9,690	9,690

Adjustments Data

a) Fees earned but unbilled and unrecorded at March 31, $150.

b) Accrued interest on note payable at March 31, $40.

c) Supplies on hand at March 31, $20.

d) Truck depreciation for March, $170.

Required

1) Prepare a ten-column work sheet for March.

2) Prepare an income statement and a statement of owner's capital for March, as well as a classified balance sheet in report form at March 31.

3) Prepare adjusting journal entries at March 31.

3.B.5. A partially completed ten-column work sheet for Martinez Auto Repair is shown on the next page. The data from which the adjustments were made are as follows. The work sheet contains a number of errors.

Adjustments Data

a) Wages accrued at December 31 were $450.

b) An inventory indicated that $2,550 worth of supplies were still on hand on December 31.

c) Rent expense of $300 for the month of December was not recorded.

MARTINEZ AUTO REPAIR
Work Sheet
For the Year Ended December 31, 19——

Account	Unadjusted Trial Balance Dr.	Unadjusted Trial Balance Cr.	Adjustments Dr.	Adjustments Cr.	Adjusted Trial Balance Dr.	Adjusted Trial Balance Cr.	Income Statement Dr.	Income Statement Cr.	Balance Sheet Dr.	Balance Sheet Cr.
Cash	3,475				3,475				3,475	
Accounts Receivable	3,025				3,025				3,025	
Prepaid Rent	5,200			c) 300	4,900				4,900	
Supplies	5,400			b) 2,850	2,550				2,550	
Land	10,100				10,100				10,100	
Building	17,500				17,500				17,500	
Accum. Depr.—Building		3,500		e) 875		4,375				4,375
Equipment	5,000				5,000				5,000	
Accum. Depr.—Equipment		2,000		f) 500		2,500				2,500
Accounts Payable		4,575		d) 100		4,675				4,675
P. Martinez, Capital		31,925				31,925				31,925
Service Fees		15,400				15,400		15,400		
Wages Expense	4,500		a) 450		4,950		4,950			
Rent Expense	3,200		c) 300		3,500		3,500			
	57,400	57,400								
Wages Payable				a) 450		450				450
Supplies Expense			b) 2,850		2,850		2,850			
Repair Expense			d) 100		100		100			
Depr. Expense—Building			e) 875		875		875			
Depr. Expense—Equipment			f) 500		500		500			

d) A bill of $100 for minor repairs to the building in December was not recorded.

e) Depreciation on the building for the year was $875.

f) Depreciation on the equipment for the year was $500.

Required

1) Total the work sheet columns.

2) List and describe the errors that were made.

3) Correct the work sheet by lining through all incorrect amounts and writing corrected figures above or beside them.

3.B.6. A work sheet for Marco Company is shown on the page opposite. The work sheet contains a number of errors. Adjustments information is shown correctly at the bottom of the work sheet.

Required

1) Locate and describe all errors on the work sheet.

2) Prepare a corrected work sheet.

3.B.7. A balance sheet at June 30 and the June income statement for Starbads repair are as follows. The owner made no withdrawal during June.

STARBADS REPAIR Balance Sheet June 30, 19--		
ASSETS		
Current		
Cash	$ 1,200	
Accounts receivable	21,000	
Prepaid insurance	1,400	
Supplies	1,100	
Total current assets		$24,700
Noncurrent		
Equipment	$20,000	
Less: Accumulated depreciation	2,500	17,500
Total Assets		$42,200
LIABILITIES		
Current		
Accounts payable	$7,000	
Notes payable	3,000	
Total current liabilities		$10,000
Noncurrent		
Notes payable		15,000
Total Liabilities		$25,000
OWNER'S EQUITY		
C. Brown, capital		17,200
Total Liabilities and Owner's Equity		$42,200

MARCO COMPANY
Work Sheet
For the Month of April 19--

A/C #	Account	Unadjusted Trial Balance Dr.	Unadjusted Trial Balance Cr.	Adjustments Dr.	Adjustments Cr.	Adjusted Trial Balance Dr.	Adjusted Trial Balance Cr.	Income Statement Dr.	Income Statement Cr.	Balance Sheet Dr.	Balance Sheet Cr.
11	Cash	500				500				500	
12	Accounts Receivable	2,000				2,000				2,000	
13	Supplies	900			a) 400	500				500	
14	Prepaid Insurance	800			b) 100	700				700	
16	Equipment	6,000				6,000				6,000	
016	Accum. Depr.—Equip.		800		c) 200		1,000				1,000
21	Accounts Payable		1,800				1,800				1,800
22	Notes Payable		1,500				1,500				1,500
23	Wages Payable		-0-		d) 150		150				150
24	Interest Payable		-0-		e) 20		20				20
31	E. Marco, Capital		4,000				4,000				4,000
41	E. Marco, Withdrawals	900				900				900	
51	Service Revenue		8,000				8,000		8,000		
61	Wage Expense	4,000		d) 150		4,150		4,150			
62	Rent Expense	1,000				1,000		1,000			
63	Supplies Expense	-0-		a) 400		400		400			
64	Interest Expense	-0-		e) 20		20		20			
65	Depreciation Expense	-0-		c) 200		200		200			
66	Insurance Expense	-0-		b) 100		100		100			
		16,100	16,100	870	870	16,470	16,470	5,870	8,000	10,600	8,470
	Net Income							2,130			2,130
								8,000	8,000	10,600	10,600

Adjustment Explanations:
a) Supplies used during April, $400.
b) Insurance expired during April, $100.
c) Equipment depreciation for April, $200.
d) Accrued wages at April 30, $150.
e) Accrued interest at April 30, $20.

STARBADS REPAIR
Income Statement
For the Month of June 19--

Fees earned		$20,000
Expenses		
Salaries	$12,000	
Rent	2,000	
Supplies	900	
Interest	100	
Depreciation	500	
Insurance	200	
Total expenses		15,700
Net Income		$ 4,300

Required

Reconstruct the Adjusted Trial Balance, Income Statement, and Balance Sheet columns as they must have appeared on the work sheet for June.

SECTION 3.C
Closing Procedures

OBJECTIVES

This section focuses on procedures for closing the temporary equity accounts and preparing the accounting records for the next accounting period. When you have completed this section, you should be able to

1. Identify the accounts that should be closed at the end of a period.
2. Prepare closing journal entries.
3. Post closing entries to ledger accounts.

ACCOUNTING PERIODS

Transactions and events are identified and reported within the context of time. An income statement reports on activities that occurred during a period of time, and a balance sheet pictures an entity's position at a point in time.

Fiscal Year

An accounting period may be of any desired length, but is usually a fiscal year, or a subdivision of a fiscal year. *A fiscal year is a twelve-month (annual) period that has been adopted for accounting purposes. A fiscal year may be a calendar year, or it may cut across two calendar years.* For example, a fiscal year may end on March 31, or June 30, or at the end of any other month.

Natural Business Year. A concern may adopt its natural business year as its fiscal year. *A natural business year is the twelve-month period ending when the entity is least busy.* Many merchandising firms use a fiscal year ending January 31, after the Christmas rush and January sales are over. Merchandise inventories and other end-of-period tasks can then be performed with the least disturbance to business activities.

Interim Reports. A fiscal year accounting period is chosen for most entities, although interim (partial year) accounting reports may also be prepared, depending on the needs for information. *An interim report is simply a report prepared for a portion of the year, such as a month or a quarter of a year.* Interim reports provide timely data for making decisions that cannot wait until annual statements are available.

Accounting Cycle. *The accounting practices involved in documenting, recording, summarizing, and reporting for a period are referred to as the* *accounting cycle because the process is repeated for each period.* Textbook examples of the accounting cycle usually assume monthly accounting periods to keep matters as simple as possible. But keep in mind that for most entities accounting involves a fiscal-year cycle, with interim reports being prepared as needed for portions of the year.

CLOSING ENTRIES

Purpose of Closing Entries

Recall that temporary equity (nominal) accounts are used to accumulate revenues, expenses, and owner's withdrawals for an accounting period. The temporary accounts supply information used to prepare the income statement and statement of changes in owner's capital, both of which picture activities for a *period* of time.

Temporary accounts must be cleared out, or closed, at the end of each accounting period. Otherwise the revenues, expenses, and withdrawals would continue to accumulate forever. Also, the data that have been collected in the temporary equity accounts must be reflected at some point into the permanent (real) equity account(s). For these reasons, closing entries are prepared at the end of each fiscal period.[1] *Closing entries are journal entries that transfer the effects of temporary equity account balances to the permanent owner's equity account (or owners' equity accounts).* Keep in mind that closing entries have two main purposes.

OBJECTIVE 1. Identify accounts that should be closed at the end of a period.

> **PURPOSES OF CLOSING ENTRIES**
> **1.** To bring temporary equity accounts to a zero balance
> **2.** To update the permanent owner's equity account

Preparing Closing Entries

In theory, closing entries are made at the very end of the last day of the accounting period. As a practical matter, however, they are usually prepared sometime later, after the rest of the end-of-period work has been completed. Nevertheless, closing entries appear in the journal as the last entries made on the last day of the accounting period.

Recall the work sheet for Beck Cleaning pictured in the previous section. The income statement columns show the balances of revenue and expense accounts as adjusted at July 31. We could close these accounts, one by one, to the owner's capital account. But a more efficient approach is to prepare

---

[1] Even when interim reports are prepared, closing entries are generally made only at the end of the fiscal year.

a compound journal entry that debits the revenue account, credits expense accounts, and credits the owner's capital account for the net income, as shown by the first closing entry in Illustration 3.18.

The second closing entry shown reduces (debits) the owner's capital for the amount withdrawn from the firm during July. Note that the closing entries come after the adjusting entries in the general journal.

ILLUSTRATION 3.18

	General Journal		PAGE 14	
Date	Account Names and Explanations	A/C #	Debit	Credit
	ADJUSTING JOURNAL ENTRIES			
19––	*a)*			
July 31	Accounts Receivable		120	
	Cleaning Revenue			120
	To recognize unbilled revenue at July 31.			
	b)			
31	Wage Expense		30	
	Wages Payable			30
	Accrued wages at July 31.			
	c)			
31	Supplies Expense		110	
	Cleaning Supplies			110
	To reflect as expense supplies used during July.			
	d)			
31	Depreciation Expense		100	
	Accumulated Depreciation—Truck			100
	To recognize truck depreciation for July.			
	CLOSING ENTRIES			
31	Cleaning Revenue		2,850	
	Wage Expense			440
	Rent Expense			200
	Supplies Expense			110
	Depreciation Expense			100
	Sandra Beck, Capital			2,000
	To close revenue and expense accounts, and to reflect net income into the owner's capital account.			
31	Sandra Beck, Capital		750	
	Sandra Beck, Withdrawals			750
	To close withdrawals to owner's capital account.			

OBJECTIVE 2. Prepare closing journal entries.

Posting the Closing Entries

Like all other journal entries, closing entries must be posted to the ledger. At that point, the temporary equity accounts are reduced to a zero balance. It is customary to note in the ledger account that a posting has come from a closing entry, as shown in the two accounts in Illustration 3.19.

When the two closing entries pictured earlier have been posted, the owner's capital and withdrawal accounts will appear as in Illustration 3.20.

The T-accounts in Illustration 3.21 show the effects of the closing entries made for Beck Cleaning.

Use of Income Summary Accounts

*Some accountants prefer to offset expenses against revenue in an intermediate account, called **Income Summary**, during the closing process. Other*

OBJECTIVE 3. Post closing entries to ledger accounts.

ILLUSTRATION 3.19

	Cleaning Revenue				ACCOUNT NO. 51	
					Balance	
Date	Item	Ref.	Debit	Credit	*Debit*	*Credit*
19––						
July 5		12		890		890
12		12		360		1,250
18		13		550		1,800
28		13		930		2,730
31	Adjusting	14		120		2,850
31	Closing	14	2,850			–0–

	Wage Expense				ACCOUNT NO. 61	
					Balance	
Date	Item	Ref.	Debit	Credit	*Debit*	*Credit*
19––						
July 15		12	205		205	
31		13	205		410	
31	Adjusting	14	30		440	
31	Closing	14		440	–0–	

ILLUSTRATION 3.20

					Balance	
Date	Item	Ref.	Debit	Credit	*Debit*	*Credit*
Sandra Beck, Capital				ACCOUNT NO. 31		
19−− July 1	Balance	X				3,310
31	Closing (Net Income)	14		2,000		5,310
31	Closing (Drawing)	14	750			4,560

					Balance	
Date	Item	Ref.	Debit	Credit	*Debit*	*Credit*
Sandra Beck, Withdrawals				ACCOUNT NO. 031		
19−− July 13		12	450		450	
24		13	300		750	
31	Closing	14		750	−0−	

ILLUSTRATION 3.21

EFFECTS OF CLOSING ENTRIES

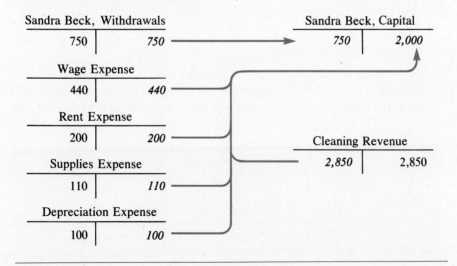

ILLUSTRATION 3.22

OBJECTIVE 2. Prepare closing journal entries.

		CLOSING ENTRIES		
	31	Cleaning Revenue	2,850	
		Income Summary		2,850
		To close revenue to income summary.		
	31	Income Summary	850	
		Wage Expense		440
		Rent Expense		200
		Supplies Expense		110
		Depreciation Expense		100
		To close expenses to income summary.		
	31	Income Summary	2,000	
		Sandra Beck, Capital		2,000
		To distribute net income to capital account.		
	31	Sandra Beck, Capital	750	
		Sandra Beck, Withdrawals		750
		To close withdrawals into capital account.		

*titles sometimes used for this account are **Income and Expense Summary** and **Profit and Loss Summary***. An Income Summary account is actually a temporary equity account that remains open only briefly during the process of making and posting closing entries. The closing entries in Illustration 3.22 show that an Income Summary account is being used for Beck Cleaning. These entries are equivalent to the closing entries presented earlier. The Income Summary account is closed by the entry that reflects the net income into the owner's capital account, as shown by Illustration 3.23.

POST-CLOSING TRIAL BALANCE

A trial balance prepared after closing entries have been posted is called a post-closing trial balance. The permanent accounts are the only ones with balances that carry over into the new accounting period. A post-closing trial

ILLUSTRATION 3.23

OBJECTIVE 3. Post closing entries to ledger accounts.

					Balance	
Date	Item	Ref.	Debit	Credit	*Debit*	*Credit*
19--						
July 31	Closing (Revenue)	14		2,850		2,850
31	Closing (Expenses)	14	850			2,000
31	Closing (Net Income)	14	2,000			-0-

Income Summary   *ACCOUNT NO. 40*

ILLUSTRATION 3.24

	BECK CLEANING Post-Closing Trial Balance July 31, 19--			
A/C #	**Account**	**Debit**	**Credit**
11	Cash	520	
12	Accounts Receivable	460	
13	Cleaning Supplies	70	
15	Truck	5,000	
015	Accumulated Depreciation—Truck		1,400
21	Accounts Payable		60
22	Wages Payable		30
31	Sandra Beck, Capital		4,560
		6,050	6,050

balance may list the temporary accounts with zero balances. If only the accounts with balances are shown, the post-closing trial balance for Beck Cleaning at July 31 will appear as in Illustration 3.24.

PREPARING FOR THE NEW PERIOD

Closing entries clear out the temporary equity accounts to get them ready for the new accounting period. Some accountants like to visibly separate the postings of different accounting periods so as to avoid confusion. One way of doing this is to draw a line across each ledger page (Illustration 3.25).

ILLUSTRATION 3.25

		Cash			ACCOUNT NO. 111	
					Balance	
Date	**Item**	**Ref.**	**Debit**	**Credit**	**Debit**	**Credit**
19-- Mar. 9	Balance Brought Forward	X			870	
11		27	100		970	
12		27		320	650	
15		27	460		1,110	
17		28	200		1,310	
18		28		510	800	
28		28		150	650	
19-- Apr. 3		29	80		730	

ILLUSTRATION 3.26

STEPS IN AN ACCOUNTING CYCLE

During the Period
1. Document transactions
2. Journalize transactions
3. Post journal entries to ledger accounts

End of Period
4. Prepare a work sheet that includes:
   a. An unadjusted trial balance
   b. The effects of needed adjustments
   c. An adjusted trial balance
   d. Income statement data
   e. Balance sheet data
5. Prepare an income statement
6. Prepare a statement of changes in owner's equity
7. Prepare a balance sheet
8. Journalize adjusting entries
9. Post adjusting entries
10. Journalize closing entries
11. Post closing entries
12. Prepare a post-closing trial balance
13. Ready accounts for the new period

Postings for the new accounting period can then be continued on the same page. Other accountants prefer to start the new period with new ledger pages.

SUMMARY OF STEPS IN AN ACCOUNTING CYCLE

As we approach the end of the section, let us review the accounting activities performed during a period. Illustration 3.26 shows one possible sequence of steps; it and Illustration 3.27 show how all the steps fit together within the accounting cycle.

GLOSSARY FOR SECTION 3.C

Accounting cycle   The accounting practices of documenting, recording, summarizing, and reporting that are repeated for each period.

Closing entries   Journal entries that transfer the effects of temporary equity account balances to the permanent owner's equity account.

Fiscal year   A twelve-month (annual) period that has been adopted for accounting purposes. A fiscal year may be a calendar year or it may cut across two calendar years.

ILLUSTRATION 3.27

ACCOUNTING CYCLE

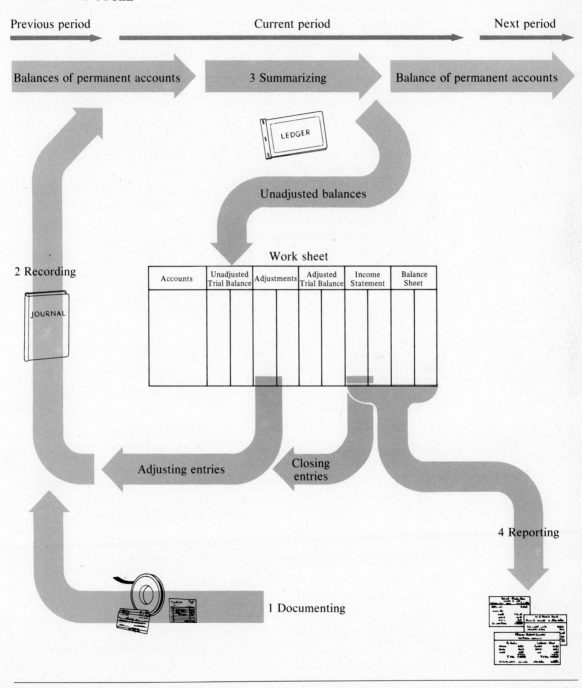

Income Summary (Income and Expense Summary, Profit and Loss Summary) An intermediate account used by some accountants for offsetting expenses against revenues during the closing process. The Income Summary balance (net income or net loss) is then closed to the permanent owner's equity account.

Interim report A report prepared for part of a year, such as a month or a quarter of a year.

Natural business year The twelve-month period ending when the entity is least busy.

Post-closing trial balance A trial balance prepared after closing entries have been posted.

SELF-QUIZ ON OBJECTIVES FOR SECTION 3.C
Solutions to Self-Quiz begin on page B-10.

1. **OBJECTIVES 1, 2, 3.** An adjusted trial balance for the Van Allen Company at October 31 is shown here followed by selected ledger accounts. Without using an Income Summary account, prepare closing entries for the Van Allen Company on journal page 28, and post the closing entries to ledger accounts like those shown.

VAN ALLEN COMPANY
Adjusted Trial Balance
October 31, 19– –

A/C #	Account	Debit	Credit
11	Cash	140	
12	Accounts Receivable	210	
21	Accounts Payable		70
31	H. Van Allen, Capital		230
32	H. Van Allen, Withdrawals	600	
41	Service Revenue		1,100
51	Rent Expense	300	
52	Supplies Expense	150	
		1,400	1,400

H. Van Allen, Capital   *ACCOUNT NO. 31*

Date	Item	Ref.	Debit	Credit	Balance Debit	Balance Credit
19– – Oct. 1	Balance	X				230

H. Van Allen, Withdrawals   ACCOUNT NO. 32

Date	Item	Ref.	Debit	Credit	Balance Debit	Balance Credit
19-- Oct. 15 31		27 27	50 550		50 600	

Service Revenue   ACCOUNT NO. 41

Date	Item	Ref.	Debit	Credit	Balance Debit	Balance Credit
19-- Oct. 10 25 31	 Adjusting	27 27 27		500 390 210		500 890 1,100

Rent Expense   ACCOUNT NO. 51

Date	Item	Ref.	Debit	Credit	Balance Debit	Balance Credit
19-- Oct. 15		27	300		300	

Supplies Expense   ACCOUNT NO. 52

Date	Item	Ref.	Debit	Credit	Balance Debit	Balance Credit
19-- Oct. 8 17		27 27	80 70		80 150	

DISCUSSION QUESTIONS FOR SECTION 3.C

1. Why are closing entries made?

2. At what point in the accounting cycle are closing entries made?

3. What is a fiscal year?

4. What is a natural business year?

5. How will a post-closing trial balance differ from an adjusted trial balance for a given firm?

6. Why are revenue, expense, and owner withdrawal accounts called temporary accounts?

7. What is an Income Summary account, and what purpose does it serve?

8. What is an interim report?

EXERCISES FOR SECTION 3.C

3.C.1. A list of account titles follows. Make a new list of those accounts that will need to be closed at the end of each accounting period.

Cash

Accounts Receivable

Fees Earned

Accumulated Depreciation—Truck

Depreciation Expense

Equipment

J. Smith, Capital

J. Smith, Withdrawals

Prepaid Rent

Insurance Expense

Rent Expense

Unexpired Insurance

3.C.2. Arrange the following procedures in the order in which they are usually performed during the accounting cycle.

a. Prepare work sheet

b. Post to ledger

c. Make closing entries

d. Prepare statements

e. Post adjusting and closing entries

f. Journalize transactions

g. Make adjusting entries

3.C.3. Following are selected account balances for Jervey Company at December 31. Prepare a single journal entry to close all the necessary accounts.

Cash	49,700
Accounts Payable	21,300
Building	48,000
Accumulated Depreciation—Building	12,000
Interest Revenue	720
Notes Receivable	12,000
Rent Expense	6,000
Salaries Expense	45,000
Service Revenue	70,280
N. Jervey, Capital	32,000
Depreciation Expense	6,000
Supplies Expense	2,400

3.C.4. An adjusted trial balance for the Bagwell Company at December 31 follows. Prepare closing journal entries, assuming that the company uses an intermediate account called Income Summary.

BAGWELL COMPANY Adjusted Trial Balance December 31, 19—		
	Debit	**Credit**
Cash	49,000	
Accounts Receivable	6,000	
Prepaid Insurance	800	
Land	14,000	
Building	60,000	
Accumulated Depreciation—Building		10,000
Equipment	18,000	
Accumulated Depreciation—Equipment		9,000
Notes Payable		30,000
D. Carper, Capital		81,660
Service Revenue		53,000
Insurance Expense	120	
Interest Expense	240	
Depreciation Expense—Building	5,000	
Depreciation Expense—Equipment	3,000	
Salaries Expense	27,500	
	183,660	183,660

PROBLEMS FOR SECTION 3.C
Alternate Problems for this section begin on page D-16.

3.C.5. The adjusted trial balance for Glick's Beauty Salon follows.

GLICK'S BEAUTY SALON Adjusted Trial Balance June 30, 19--		
	Debit	**Credit**
Cash	3,830	
Accounts Receivable	50	
Prepaid Rent	600	
Inventory of Supplies	220	
Salon Equipment	2,940	
Accumulated Depreciation—Salon Equipment		84
Accounts Payable		558
Notes Payable		2,000
Interest Payable		10
Harvey Glick, Capital		5,000
Harvey Glick, Withdrawals	600	
Fees Earned		1,600
Salaries Expense	780	
Rent Expense	120	
Office Supplies Expense	60	
Depreciation Expense	42	
Interest Expense	10	
	9,252	9,252

Required

Prepare closing entries, assuming that

1) An Income Summary account is used.

2) An Income Summary account is not used.

3.C.6. An adjusted trial balance for the Rocker Company at April 30 follows.

ROCKER COMPANY Adjusted Trial Balance April 30, 19--			
A/C #	**Account**	**Debit**	**Credit**
111	Cash	450	
112	Accounts Receivable	1,200	
211	Accounts Payable		750
311	J. Rocker, Capital		2,000
312	J. Rocker, Withdrawals	800	
411	Fees Earned		3,000
511	Rent Expense	1,100	
512	Laundry Expense	700	
513	Salary Expense	1,500	
		5,750	5,750

Required

1) Prepare closing entries at April 30.

2) Prepare a post-closing trial balance for the Rocker Company at April 30, assuming that the closing entries have been posted to ledger accounts.

3.C.7. The preclosing trial balance for Valley Cable-Vision at the end of September is as follows.

VALLEY CABLE-VISION Trial Balance September 30, 19---	Debit	Credit
Cash	2,050	
Accounts Receivable	450	
Interest Receivable	18	
Repair Parts	2,652	
Prepaid Insurance	90	
Equipment	3,000	
Accumulated Depreciation—Equipment		650
Accounts Payable		310
G. Stockdale, Capital		5,876
G. Stockdale, Withdrawals	938	
Cable Fees Earned		4,164
Repair Service Revenue		510
Interest Revenue		19
Interest Expense	8	
Salary Expense	1,450	
Building Rent Expense	180	
Truck Lease Expense	75	
Insurance Expense	87	
Utility Expense	62	
Depreciation Expense	50	
Repair Parts Used	419	
	11,529	11,529

Required

1) Prepare closing journal entries.

2) Prepare an income statement for the month of September.

3.C.8. The City Repair Service is engaged in providing electrical repair service. The adjusted trial balance for the firm at the end of July is as follows.

CITY REPAIR SERVICE Adjusted Trial Balance July 31, 19—		
	Debit	**Credit**
Cash	741	
Accounts Receivable	430	
Electrical Supplies	1,931	
Unexpired Insurance	183	
Tools	235	
Land	3,000	
Building	25,000	
Accumulated Depreciation—Building		7,000
Accounts Payable		520
Mortgage Payable		10,000
Jan Knight, Capital		14,860
Jan Knight, Withdrawals	430	
Service Revenue		2,110
Wages Expense	1,820	
Electrical Supplies Used	511	
Insurance Expense	69	
Interest Expense	15	
Depreciation Expense	50	
Utility Expense	75	
	34,490	34,490

Required

1) Prepare closing journal entries, using an Income Summary account.

2) Prepare a classified balance sheet as of July 31.

3.C.9. An adjusted trial balance for the Madre Company at December 31 is as shown here. Also provided are selected ledger accounts.

MADRE COMPANY Adjusted Trial Balance December 31, 19--			
A/C #	Account	Debit	Credit
111	Cash	500	
112	Accounts Receivable	1,300	
114	Equipment	1,500	
0114	Accumulated Depreciation—Equipment		420
211	Accounts Payable		200
311	M. Madre, Capital		2,000
312	M. Madre, Withdrawals	800	
411	Fees Earned		8,000
511	Rent Expense	1,200	
512	Wage Expense	5,000	
513	Supplies Expense	180	
514	Depreciation Expense	140	
		10,620	10,620

	M. Madre, Capital			ACCOUNT NO. 311		
					Balance	
Date	Item	Ref.	Debit	Credit	*Debit*	*Credit*
19-- Dec. 1	Balance	X				2,000

	M. Madre, Withdrawals			ACCOUNT NO. 312		
					Balance	
Date	Item	Ref.	Debit	Credit	*Debit*	*Credit*
19-- Dec. 14 30		82 83	400 400		400 800	

	Fees Earned			ACCOUNT NO. 411		
					Balance	
Date	Item	Ref.	Debit	Credit	*Debit*	*Credit*
19-- Dec. 30	Balance from preceding ledger page	X				8,000

	Rent Expense			ACCOUNT NO. 511		
					Balance	
Date	Item	Ref.	Debit	Credit	*Debit*	*Credit*
19-- Dec. 1		81	1,200		1,200	

					Balance	
Date	Item	Ref.	Debit	Credit	Debit	Credit
19-- Dec. 15 31		82 83	2,500 2,500		2,500 5,000	

Wage Expense   *ACCOUNT NO. 512*

					Balance	
Date	Item	Ref.	Debit	Credit	Debit	Credit
19-- Dec. 5 20		81 82	120 60		120 180	

Supplies Expense   *ACCOUNT NO. 513*

					Balance	
Date	Item	Ref.	Debit	Credit	Debit	Credit
19-- Dec. 31	Adjusting	83	140		140	

Depreciation Expense   *ACCOUNT NO. 514*

Required

1) Prepare closing entries for Madre Company on journal page 84.

2) Post the closing entries to ledger accounts like those shown. *(Note:* Open up an Income Summary account if you used that approach in closing.)

3) Prepare a post-closing trial balance at December 31, including only accounts with balances.

SUMMARY OF CHAPTER 3

Adjusting entries are prepared at the end of an accounting period to update and correct account balances prior to the preparation of accounting statements. Each adjusting entry normally involves one temporary account and one permanent account. A revenue accrual simultaneously increases an asset and a revenue, while an expense accrual increases an expense and a liability. Revenue deferral adjustments shift unearned revenues to liability accounts, and expense deferrals recognize prepaid expenses as assets. When previously deferred revenues are earned, the liabilities are shifted (expired) to revenue accounts; expired assets are shifted to expense accounts.

A work sheet is a useful tool for organizing end-of-period work. Needed adjustments are reflected on the work sheet, and adjusted account balances are distributed into sets of columns according to the statements in which they will appear. Adjusting journal entries may be prepared directly from the adjustments columns of a work sheet; information for statements comes from the appropriate work sheet columns.

Closing entries transfer the balances of temporary accounts to permanent equity accounts. The closing process updates permanent equity accounts and readies temporary accounts for the next accounting period.

PROBLEMS FOR CHAPTER 3
Alternate Problems for this chapter begin on page D-17.

3.1. A chart of accounts and other data for the Cycle Service Company are shown below.

CYCLE SERVICE **Chart of Accounts**	
Assets	*Owner's Equity*
111 Cash	311 B. Ross, Capital
112 Accounts Receivable	312 B. Ross, Withdrawals
113 Supplies	
115 Equipment	*Revenue*
0115 Accumulated Depreciation— Equipment	411 Service Revenue
Liabilities	*Expenses*
211 Accounts Payable	511 Rent Expense
212 Wages Payable	512 Supplies Expense
213 Interest Payable	513 Wage Expense
214 Notes Payable (long-term)	514 Interest Expense
	515 Depreciation Expense

	CYCLE SERVICE **Post-Closing Trial Balance** **June 30, 19- -**		
A/C #	**Account**	**Debit**	**Credit**
111	Cash	1,270	
112	Accounts Receivable	300	
113	Supplies	80	
115	Equipment	5,400	
0115	Accumulated Depreciation—Equipment		1,200
211	Accounts Payable		1,350
214	Notes Payable (long-term)		1,500
311	B. Ross, Capital		3,000
		7,050	7,050

Transactions

July 2   Received $600 cash for services rendered today (Deposit No. 985).

7   Purchased equipment costing $1,200. Paid $200 cash (Check No. 2492) and signed a note payable for balance.

13   Billed customers for services, $1,800.

20   Billed customers for services, $1,600.

21   Received $2,500 cash from customers billed last month (Deposit No. 986).

25   B. Ross withdrew $2,000 from the business for personal use (Check No. 2493).

26   Paid $120 to a supplier on accounts payable (Check No. 2494).

27   Paid employee wage, $1,200 cash (Check No. 2495).

30   Purchased supplies on account, $50.

30   Paid rent for July, $500 cash (Check No. 2496).

Adjustments Data

a) An examination of the supply room and supply requisitions indicates that supplies costing $100 were used during July.

b) Accrued interest for July on notes payable, $25.

c) Wages accrued but not paid for the month of July, $60.

d) Equipment depreciation for July, $200.

e) Revenue earned but not billed for July, $75.

Required

1) Open new ledger accounts with July 1 balances.

2) Prepare general journal entries in good form on journal page 30 for the July transactions.

3) Post July journal entries to the ledger.

4) Prepare a ten-column work sheet for the month of July.

5) Prepare an income statement and a statement of owner's capital for July, together with a classified balance sheet at July 31.

6) Prepare adjusting journal entries for July.

7) Prepare closing entries for July.

8) Post the adjusting and closing entries to the ledger and ready the ledger accounts for the new period.

3.2. A partially completed work sheet for the T.D.S. Company follows.

A/C #	Account	Unadjusted Trial Balance Dr.	Unadjusted Trial Balance Cr.	Adjustments Dr.	Adjustments Cr.	Adjusted Trial Balance Dr.	Adjusted Trial Balance Cr.
	T.D.S. COMPANY **Work Sheet** **For the Month of April 19--**						
11	Cash	1,000				1,000	
12	Accounts Receivable	6,800				6,800	
13	Supplies	2,100			c) 300	1,800	
14	Prepaid Insurance	2,400			a) 200	2,200	
15	Prepaid Rent	9,000			b) 750	8,250	
16	Equipment	16,400				16,400	
016	Accum. Depr.—Equipment		1,600		d) 150		1,750
21	Accounts Payable		7,700				7,700
22	Wages Payable		–0–		e) 450		450
23	Notes Payable (90 days)		10,000				10,000
24	Notes Payable (due in 7 years)		8,000				8,000
31	T. D. Sands, Capital		8,000				8,000
32	T. D. Sands, Withdrawals	1,000				1,000	
41	Service Revenue		13,000				13,000
51	Wage Expense	9,400		e) 450		9,850	
52	Insurance Expense	–0–		a) 200		200	
53	Rent Expense	–0–		b) 750		750	
54	Supplies Expense	–0–		c) 300		300	
55	Interest Expense	200				200	
56	Depreciation Expense	–0–		d) 150		150	
		48,300	48,300	1,850	1,850	48,900	48,900

Explanations
a) Insurance expired in April.
b) Prepaid rent expired in April.
c) Supplies used in April.
d) Equipment depreciation for April.
e) Accrued wages for April.

Required

1) Prepare a completed work sheet for T.D.S. Company.

2) Prepare an income statement and a statement of owner's capital for the month of April.

3) Prepare a classified balance sheet in report form at April 30.

4) Prepare adjusting and closing entries.

5) Prepare a post-closing trial balance.

3.3. Ledger accounts at December 31 are given for Moore Company, followed by adjustments information.

					Cash	ACCOUNT NO. 111

					Balance	
Date	Item	Ref.	Debit	Credit	*Debit*	*Credit*
19--						
Dec. 1	Balance	X			2,000	
2		42		1,300	700	
3		42	3,000		3,700	
7		42	4,000		7,700	
15		42		5,000	2,700	
16		42		400	2,300	
16		42		1,000	1,300	
19		42		100	1,200	
21		42	200		1,400	
30		42		300	1,100	

					Accounts Receivable	ACCOUNT NO. 112

					Balance	
Date	Item	Ref.	Debit	Credit	*Debit*	*Credit*
19--						
Dec. 1	Balance	X			3,500	
3		42		3,000	500	
21		42		200	300	
30		42	3,000		3,300	

					Supplies	ACCOUNT NO. 113

					Balance	
Date	Item	Ref.	Debit	Credit	*Debit*	*Credit*
19--						
Dec. 1	Balance	X			400	
19		42	100		500	
21		42	800		1,300	

Prepaid Insurance   *ACCOUNT NO. 114*

Date	Item	Ref.	Debit	Credit	Balance Debit	Balance Credit
19-- Dec. 1	Balance	X			50	

Land   *ACCOUNT NO. 117*

Date	Item	Ref.	Debit	Credit	Balance Debit	Balance Credit
19-- Dec. 1	Balance	X			10,000	

Building   *ACCOUNT NO. 118*

Date	Item	Ref.	Debit	Credit	Balance Debit	Balance Credit
19-- Dec. 1	Balance	X			50,000	

Accumulated Depreciation—Building   *ACCOUNT NO. 0118*

Date	Item	Ref.	Debit	Credit	Balance Debit	Balance Credit
19-- Dec. 1	Balance	X				1,100

Accounts Payable   *ACCOUNT NO. 211*

Date	Item	Ref.	Debit	Credit	Balance Debit	Balance Credit
19-- Dec. 1	Balance	X				400
16		42	400			-0-
21		42		800		800
30		42	300			500

Wages Payable *ACCOUNT NO. 212*

Date	Item	Ref.	Debit	Credit	Balance Debit	Balance Credit
19－－ Dec. 1	Balance	X				300
2		42	300			－0－

Interest Payable *ACCOUNT NO. 213*

Date	Item	Ref.	Debit	Credit	Balance Debit	Balance Credit

Mortgage Payable *ACCOUNT NO. 218*

Date	Item	Ref.	Debit	Credit	Balance Debit	Balance Credit
19－－ Dec. 1	Balance	X				30,000

Jo Moore, Capital *ACCOUNT NO. 311*

Date	Item	Ref.	Debit	Credit	Balance Debit	Balance Credit
19－－ Dec. 1	Balance	X				34,150

Jo Moore, Withdrawals *ACCOUNT NO. 312*

Date	Item	Ref.	Debit	Credit	Balance Debit	Balance Credit
19－－ Dec. 15		42	5,000		5,000	

			Service Revenue		ACCOUNT NO. 411	

					Balance	
Date	**Item**	**Ref.**	**Debit**	**Credit**	*Debit*	*Credit*
19-- Dec. 7		42		4,000		4,000
30		42		3,000		7,000

			Wage Expense		ACCOUNT NO. 511	

					Balance	
Date	**Item**	**Ref.**	**Debit**	**Credit**	*Debit*	*Credit*
19-- Dec. 2		42	1,000		1,000	
16		42	1,000		2,000	

			Supplies Expense		ACCOUNT NO. 512	

					Balance	
Date	**Item**	**Ref.**	**Debit**	**Credit**	*Debit*	*Credit*

			Insurance Expense		ACCOUNT NO. 513	

					Balance	
Date	**Item**	**Ref.**	**Debit**	**Credit**	*Debit*	*Credit*

			Depreciation Expense		ACCOUNT NO. 514	

					Balance	
Date	**Item**	**Ref.**	**Debit**	**Credit**	*Debit*	*Credit*

					Balance	
	Interest Expense				ACCOUNT NO. 515	
Date	Item	Ref.	Debit	Credit	Debit	Credit

Adjustments Data

a) Building depreciation for December, $100.

b) Accrued interest on mortgage payable at December 31, $250.

c) Supplies used during December, $500.

d) Accrued wages at December 31, $1,400.

e) Insurance expired during December, $50.

f) Earned but unbilled (and unrecorded) revenue at December 31, $200.

Required

1) Prepare a ten-column work sheet for Moore Company for December.

2) Prepare adjusting journal entries on journal page 43.

3) Prepare closing journal entries.

4) Post adjusting and closing entries to ledger accounts.

COMPREHENSION PROBLEMS FOR CHAPTER 3

3.4. A post-closing trial balance for Bucketshop Company is as follows. Carole Neely, Bucketshop's owner, intends to withdraw $10,000 cash during early July to use as a down payment on a vacation home.

	BUCKETSHOP COMPANY Post-Closing Trial Balance June 30, 19--		
A/C #	Account	Debit	Credit
111	Cash	14,000	
112	Accounts Receivable	25,000	
113	Supplies	6,000	
114	Land	30,000	
115	Building	32,000	
0115	Accumulated Depreciation—Building		5,000
211	Accounts Payable		9,000
212	Notes Payable (60 days)		6,000
213	Notes Payable (due in 5 years)		15,000
214	Mortgage Payable		20,000
311	C. Neely, Capital		52,000
		107,000	107,000

Required

1) Prepare a classified balance sheet in report form at June 30.

2) Comment on the advisability of Neely's intended withdrawal of cash. What additional information would be helpful in assessing the company's ability to withstand the $10,000 withdrawal?

3.5. Jim Shuster has come to you for assistance. He wants to know how well his business, the Shuster Company, did last year, and what the company's condition was at December 31. Jim remembers that he contributed cash to start the business during January of last year. He has analyzed his company's bank deposits and checks for last year to obtain the following information.

Deposits	
Owner's contribution to start the business	$ 40,000
Proceeds of bank loan	10,000
Collections from customers	200,000
Total deposits	$250,000

Checks	
Supplies	$ 25,000
Wages	140,000
Truck	20,000
Owner withdrawals	18,000
Gasoline, oil, and truck maintenance	6,000
Rent on building	13,000
Utilities	4,400
Insurance	3,960
Miscellaneous expenses	17,000
Total checks	$247,360

Jim is apprehensive about his business because he had to borrow $10,000 from the bank on November 1 of last year, and his business checkbook balance at December 31 was only $2,640. Through a series of inquiries, you have been able to extract from Jim the following facts.

   a. The bank loan bears interest of 12% per annum (1% per month), which is to be paid quarterly.

   b. Wages of $2,000 were owed at December 31.

   c. Supplies costing $5,000 were still on hand at year-end.

   d. The truck, purchased in early January of last year, is expected to last for three years, after which it can probably be sold as junk for $200.

   e. Several customers have paid a total of $4,700 in advance for services to be rendered in the following year.

   f. A three-year business insurance policy was taken out in early January. The full three-year premium of $3,960 was paid at that time.

	Deposits and Checks	
Account	Dr.	Cr.

g. Customers owe the company $22,000 for services rendered during the past year.

h. Jim is willing to pay you a fee of $250 for helping him. You can see no point in setting up a complete set of books for the previous year's activity, in view of the small fee involved.

Required

1) Summarize Shuster's deposits and checks data in the first two columns of a work sheet with columns headed as above. Write in needed account titles.

Adjustments		Adjusted Trial Balance		Income Statement		Balance Sheet	
Dr.	*Cr.*	*Dr.*	*Cr.*	*Dr.*	*Cr.*	*Dr.*	*Cr.*

2) Complete the work sheet by inserting adjustment data and distributing adjusted balances to the proper columns. Show column totals in acceptable form.

3) Prepare an income statement for the year and a balance sheet at December 31.

4) Comment generally on the performance of Jim's business and on its condition at December 31. Be sure to respond to his concern about having to borrow money.

APPENDIX **3.1**
Reversing Entries

Most of the routine tasks in accounting are performed by clerks, machines, and computers. Recurring transactions are recorded the same way each time they occur. For example, the payment of wages is recorded with a debit to Wage Expense and a credit to Cash, without regard to any accrued wages that may already appear in the accounts.

For this reason, some accountants, on the first day of the new accounting period, *reverse* any adjusting entries that involve transactions in the new period. *A reversing entry, then, is an entry made at the beginning of an accounting period to reverse the effects of an adjusting entry that was made at the end of the previous period.* Accrual and deferral adjustments are those most commonly reversed.

Consider the adjusting entries made for Beck Cleaning at July 31, as shown in Illustration 3.28.

The accounts affected by the adjustments appear as shown in Illustration 3.29, *after* both adjusting and closing entries have been posted.

The adjustment for cleaning revenue was necessary to pick up revenue that was earned but not yet billed (invoiced) to the customer at July 31. On August 2, when the invoice is prepared, the revenue might be recorded again if the bookkeeper is unaware of (or forgets about) the adjusting entry that

ILLUSTRATION 3.28

General Journal		A/C #	Debit	Credit
				PAGE 14
Date	**Account Names and Explanations**	**A/C #**	**Debit**	**Credit**
	ADJUSTING JOURNAL ENTRIES			
19--	*a)*			
July 31	Accounts Receivable	12	120	
	Cleaning Revenue	51		120
	To recognize unbilled revenue at July 31.			
	b)			
31	Wage Expense	61	30	
	Wages Payable	22		30
	Accrued wages at July 31.			

ILLUSTRATION 3.29

	Accounts Receivable			ACCOUNT NO. 12		
					Balance	
Date	Item	Ref.	Debit	Credit	Debit	Credit
19--						
July 10	Balance Brought Forward	X			340	
31	Adjusting	14	120		460	

	Wages Payable			ACCOUNT NO. 22		
					Balance	
Date	Item	Ref.	Debit	Credit	Debit	Credit
19--						
July 31	Adjusting	14		30		30

	Cleaning Revenue			ACCOUNT NO. 51		
					Balance	
Date	Item	Ref.	Debit	Credit	Debit	Credit
19--						
July 5		10		890		890
12		12		360		1,250
18		13		550		1,800
28		13		930		2,730
31	Adjusting	14		120		2,850
31	Closing	14	2,850			-0-

	Wage Expense			ACCOUNT NO. 61		
					Balance	
Date	Item	Ref.	Debit	Credit	Debit	Credit
19--						
July 15		12	205		205	
31		13	205		410	
31	Adjusting	14	30		440	
31	Closing	14		440	-0-	

was made. Similarly, all the wages paid on August 15 may be debited to the Wage Expense account, even though $30 of these wages were earned by employees during July.

In anticipation of these problems, the accountant for Beck Cleaning could make the reversing entries on August 1 that are shown as Illustration 3.30.

After these entries are posted, the Cleaning Revenue account will have a debit balance, and Wage Expense will show a credit balance, as we see in Illustration 3.31.

In effect, the Cleaning Revenue account temporarily shows the account receivable, and the Wage Expense account temporarily shows the amount owed to the employee. However, the debit balance in Cleaning Revenue will be offset when the invoice is recorded on August 2, as shown in Illustration 3.32 on page 162.

When the wage paid on August 15 is recorded and posted, the portion that was earned in July will be automatically canceled, as shown in Illustration 3.33 on page 162.

Reversing entries are not absolutely necessary, as long as the person who records the transactions is aware of (and can remember) the held-over effects of the prior period's adjustments. However, many accountants prefer making reversing entries to taking the chance that held-over effects of adjustments will be overlooked. Reversing entries just simplify the tasks of accounting for the new fiscal period.

ILLUSTRATION 3.30

	General Journal			PAGE 15
Date	**Account Names and Explanations**	**A/C #**	**Debit**	**Credit**
	REVERSING ENTRIES			

19--
Aug. 1
	Cleaning Revenue
	    Accounts Receivable
	    To reverse the adjustment for
	    unbilled revenue at July 31.
			120	120

1	Wages Payable
	    Wage Expense
	    To reverse the adjustment for
	    accrued wages at July 31.
			30	30

ILLUSTRATION 3.31

Accounts Receivable — ACCOUNT NO. 12

Date	Item	Ref.	Debit	Credit	Balance Debit	Balance Credit
19--						
July 10	Balance Brought Forward	X			340	
31	Adjusting	14	120		460	
Aug. 1	Reversing	15		120	340	

Wages Payable — ACCOUNT NO. 22

Date	Item	Ref.	Debit	Credit	Balance Debit	Balance Credit
19--						
July 31	Adjusting	14		30		30
Aug. 1	Reversing	15	30			-0-

Cleaning Revenue — ACCOUNT NO. 51

Date	Item	Ref.	Debit	Credit	Balance Debit	Balance Credit
19--						
July 5		10		890		890
12		12		360		1,250
18		13		550		1,800
28		13		930		2,730
31	Adjusting	14		120		2,850
31	Closing	14	2,850			-0-
Aug. 1	Reversing	15	120		120	

Wage Expense — ACCOUNT NO. 61

Date	Item	Ref.	Debit	Credit	Balance Debit	Balance Credit
19--						
July 15		12	205		205	
31		13	205		410	
31	Adjusting	14	30		440	
31	Closing	14		440	-0-	
Aug. 1	Reversing	15		30		30

ILLUSTRATION 3.32

2	Accounts Receivable	12	120	
	Cleaning Revenue	51		120
	Customer billed for services performed.			

			Cleaning Revenue		ACCOUNT NO. 51		
						Balance	
Date	**Item**	**Ref.**	**Debit**	**Credit**		*Debit*	*Credit*
19--							
July 5		10		890			890
12		12		360			1,250
18		13		550			1,800
28		13		930			2,730
31	Adjusting	14		120			2,850
31	Closing	14	2,850				–0–
Aug. 1	Reversing	15	120			120	
2		15		120			–0–

ILLUSTRATION 3.33

15	Wage Expense	61	205	
	Cash	11		205
	Employee wage paid; Check No. 972.			

			Wage Expense		ACCOUNT NO. 61		
						Balance	
Date	**Item**	**Ref.**	**Debit**	**Credit**		*Debit*	*Credit*
19--							
July 15		12	205			205	
31		13	205			410	
31	Adjusting	14	30			440	
31	Closing	14		440		–0–	
Aug. 1	Reversing	15		30			30
15		16	205			175	

GLOSSARY FOR APPENDIX 3.I

Reversing entry   An entry made at the beginning of an accounting period to reverse the effects of an adjusting entry that was made at the end of the previous period.

DISCUSSION QUESTIONS FOR APPENDIX 3.I

1. What is a reversing entry?
2. Why do some accountants choose to make reversing entries?

PROBLEM FOR APPENDIX 3.I

3.I.1. Adjusting journal entries and selected ledger accounts for the Reflections Company follow. To simplify procedures for the bookkeeper, the accountant for the Reflections Company makes reversing entries, where appropriate, on the first day of each new period.

	General Journal			PAGE 10
Date	**Account Names and Explanations**	**A/C #**	**Debit**	**Credit**
	ADJUSTING JOURNAL ENTRIES			
19--	*a)*			
May 31	Depreciation Expense	514	250	
	Accumulated Depreciation—Truck	0114		250
	Truck depreciation for May.			
	b)			
31	Accounts Receivable	112	1,200	
	Fees Earned	411		1,200
	To recognize unbilled revenue at May 31.			
	c)			
31	Wage Expense	511	300	
	Wages Payable	212		300
	Accrued wages at May 31.			
	d)			
31	Interest Expense	513	20	
	Interest Payable	213		20
	Accrued interest at May 31.			
	e)			
31	Supplies Expense	512	80	
	Supplies	113		80
	To adjust for supplies used during May.			

Accounts Receivable   ACCOUNT NO. 112

Date	Item	Ref.	Debit	Credit	Balance Debit	Balance Credit
19–– May 31	Balance	X			1,100	
31	Adjusting	10	1,200		2,300	

Supplies   ACCOUNT NO. 113

Date	Item	Ref.	Debit	Credit	Balance Debit	Balance Credit
19–– May 31	Balance	X			100	
31	Adjusting	10		80	20	

Accumulated Depreciation—Truck   ACCOUNT NO. 0114

Date	Item	Ref.	Debit	Credit	Balance Debit	Balance Credit
19–– May 31	Balance	X				3,000
31	Adjusting	10		250		3,250

Wages Payable   ACCOUNT NO. 212

Date	Item	Ref.	Debit	Credit	Balance Debit	Balance Credit
19–– May 31	Adjusting	10		300		300

Interest Payable   *ACCOUNT NO. 213*

Date	Item	Ref.	Debit	Credit	Balance *Debit*	Balance *Credit*
19--						
May 31	Adjusting	10		20		20

Fees Earned   *ACCOUNT NO. 411*

Date	Item	Ref.	Debit	Credit	Balance *Debit*	Balance *Credit*
19--						
May 31	Balance	X				4,000
31	Adjusting	10		1,200		5,200
31	Closing	10	5,200			–0–

Wage Expense   *ACCOUNT NO. 511*

Date	Item	Ref.	Debit	Credit	Balance *Debit*	Balance *Credit*
19--						
May 31	Balance	X			2,000	
31	Adjusting	10	300		2,300	
31	Closing	10		2,300	–0–	

Supplies Expense   *ACCOUNT NO. 512*

Date	Item	Ref.	Debit	Credit	Balance *Debit*	Balance *Credit*
19--						
May 31	Adjusting	10	80		80	
31	Closing	10		80	–0–	

	Interest Expense				ACCOUNT NO. 513	
					Balance	
Date	Item	Ref.	Debit	Credit	Debit	Credit
19-- May 31 31	Adjusting Closing	10 10	20	20	20 -0-	

	Depreciation Expense				ACCOUNT NO. 514	
					Balance	
Date	Item	Ref.	Debit	Credit	Debit	Credit
19-- May 31 31	Adjusting Closing	10 10	250	250	250 -0-	

Required

Make appropriate reversing entries at June 1 on journal page 11 and post the reversing entries to the appropriate accounts.

APPENDIX 3.II
Prepaid Expenses and Unearned Revenues

PREPAID EXPENSES

Nature of Prepaid Expenses

Under the *cost concept*, assets are recorded at their cost bases. If costs expire in the generation of revenues, they become expenses. If costs expire without generating revenues, they become losses. All assets are deferred costs until such time as they expire, or are otherwise used as payments for other assets, expenses, or liabilities, or as distributions to the owners of the business.

When services, supplies, and similar items that will soon become expenses are paid for in advance they are called **prepaid expenses**. The expression is somewhat confusing because prepaid expenses are not yet expenses— they are assets whose costs are being deferred until such time as they expire. Payments in advance for such items as rent, insurance, office supplies, and property taxes are generally classified as prepaid expenses.

Prepaid expenses are current assets because, had they not been paid in advance, they would have required cash payments within the next year or so. *Prepayments of expenses for periods far in the future are usually referred to as* **deferred charges**. Thus deferred charges are long-term prepayments, whereas prepaid expenses are short-term prepayments.

Adjustments for Prepaid Expenses

When prepaid expenses exist, they should be adjusted to their proper balances at the end of each accounting period. The way in which the adjustments are calculated and recorded depends to some degree on how the payments were recorded initially.

Clerks who process and record data are usually instructed to follow some consistent approach which does not require them to distinguish between expenses and prepayments. For example, all cash payments for rent, insurance, interest, and similar expense items may be debited directly to the respective expense accounts, leaving to accountants the job of shifting unexpired costs to prepaid expense accounts at the end of each accounting period. On the other hand, clerks may be instructed to debit asset accounts (Prepaid Rent, Prepaid Insurance, etc.) at the time that cash payments are made. In the latter case, accountants will determine at year-end the portions of costs that have expired during the period, and shift these expired costs to expense accounts.

First Recorded as Assets.   Consider the following asset accounts from Dale Company's unadjusted trial balance at December 31, 19X4.

Office Supplies	650
Prepaid Rent	6,000
Prepaid Insurance	2,400

The clerk responsible for recording Dale's transactions has been instructed to debit an appropriate asset account whenever cash is paid for supplies, rent, or insurance.

Further investigation by the accountant in charge uncovers the following facts.

a. Office supplies remaining on hand at December 31, 19X4, had cost the company $210.

b. Six months' store rent of $6,000 was paid in advance on November 1, 19X4.

c. Fire insurance premiums of $2,400 were paid on September 1, 19X4, to cover a period of one year from that date.

Adjusting journal entries that reduce each prepaid expense account to its proper balance are shown in Illustration 3.34.

ILLUSTRATION 3.34

	ADJUSTING ENTRIES		
19X4	*a)*		
Dec. 31	Office Supplies Expense	440	
	Office Supplies		440
	To reduce the supplies account to the balance on hand at year-end.		
	b)		
31	Rent Expense	2,000	
	Prepaid Rent		2,000
	To reflect into expense store rent for November–December 19X4.		
	c)		
31	Insurance Expense	800	
	Prepaid Insurance		800
	To recognize insurance expense for September–December 19X4.		

ILLUSTRATION 3.35

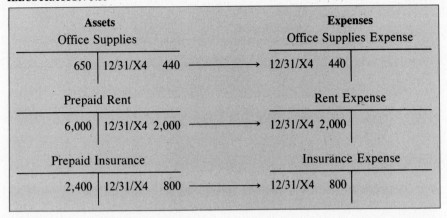

The adjusting entries shift expired costs from assets to expenses, as shown by the T-accounts in Illustration 3.35.

Each adjusting entry transferred *expired* cost to an expense account, and left *unexpired* cost in the asset account.

First Recorded as Expense.   Now, let us assume that Dale's clerk had been instructed to debit expense accounts (rather than asset accounts) whenever cash is paid for supplies, rent, and insurance. The unadjusted trial balance would then show expense account balances as follows.

Office Supplies Expense	650
Rent Expense	6,000
Insurance Expense	2,400

Using the same adjustments data as previously shown, adjusting journal entries must now transfer *unexpired* costs to asset accounts, as shown in Illustration 3.36 on the next page.

The effects of shifting costs from the expense accounts to asset accounts are shown by the T-accounts in Illustration 3.37 on the next page.

From the foregoing examples, you can see how the adjusting entries for prepayments will differ, depending on whether costs are recorded initially in asset accounts or in expense accounts.

Reversing Procedure.   When a company records prepayments by debiting asset accounts, the prepaid expenses are written down to their unexpired balances at the end of each period. If, on the other hand, prepayments were debited to expense accounts, adjusting entries shift the unexpired costs to prepaid expense accounts. Under both procedures, prepaid expenses are

ILLUSTRATION 3.36

	ADJUSTING ENTRIES		
19X4	*a)*		
Dec. 31	Office Supplies	210	
	Office Supplies Expense		210
	To recognize office supplies unused at year-end.		
	b)		
31	Prepaid Rent	4,000	
	Rent Expense		4,000
	To set up Prepaid Rent at year-end.		
	c)		
31	Prepaid Insurance	1,600	
	Insurance Expense		1,600
	To recognize unexpired insurance premiums at year-end.		

ILLUSTRATION 3.37

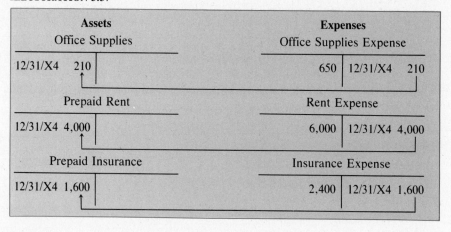

carried forward into the next period as assets, while expense accounts are reduced to zero balances by the closing entries.

When the prepayments were recorded initially as expenses, some accountants prefer to shift the prepaid expenses back to expense accounts on the first day of each new period. This is especially true when the prepayments are expected to expire during the new period anyway. The entries made to shift prepaid expense balances to expense accounts simply *reverse* the adjustments that were made at the end of the previous period, and are therefore referred to as *reversing entries*.[2]

---

[2]The overall concept of reversing entries is presented in Appendix I of this chapter.

ILLUSTRATION 3.38

	REVERSING ENTRIES		
19X5 Jan. 1	Office Supplies Expense	210	
	Office Supplies		210
	To reverse the December 31 adjustment for Office Supplies.		
1	Rent Expense	4,000	
	Prepaid Rent		4,000
	To reverse the December 31 adjustment for Prepaid Rent.		
1	Insurance Expense	1,600	
	Prepaid Insurance		1,600
	To reverse the December 31 adjustment for Prepaid Insurance.		

Entries that reverse the three adjustments pictured earlier in this section are shown in Illustration 3.38. Note that they are dated for the first day of the new accounting period.

When reversing entries are not made, the prepaid expense accounts will carry the beginning balances until the end of the new accounting period, at which time they must be adjusted, either upward or downward, to a balance which reflects the unexpired cost at that point in time.

UNEARNED REVENUES

Nature of Unearned Revenues

Under the *realization concept,* revenue is recognized at the point of sale of goods, or upon the performance of services. When payment is received for goods (or services) prior to the time that they are sold (or performed) the entity receiving payment is said to have unearned revenue. *Unearned revenue, sometimes called* **revenue received in advance,** *is an obligation to deliver in the near future goods or services for which payment has already been received.* This obligation is actually a *liability* in the amount of the payment received—if the goods or services are for any reason not delivered, the money will have to be returned to the party from whom it came.

Unearned revenues are in effect deferred revenues until such time as they are earned. *Collections in advance for revenues that are not expected to be earned within the near future are usually called* **deferred credits.** Thus unearned revenues are current liabilities, whereas deferred credits are long-term liabilities.

Insurance companies, magazine publishing firms, and rental property owners generally receive most of their revenues before they are earned.

Most other business concerns receive unearned revenues only infrequently. Merchandise firms, for example, may occasionally receive deposits from customers on goods that are being specially ordered for some reason.

Adjustment for Unearned Revenues

Like prepaid expenses, adjustments for unearned revenues depend to some extent on how entries were made initially.

First Recorded as a Liability. Consider, as an example, the other side of the store rent that was paid in advance by Dale Company. Farnum, Inc., entered into an agreement on November 1, 19X4, to rent a portion of its building to Dale for $12,000 a year, payable semi-annually in advance on May 1 and November 1 of each year. The $6,000 collection from Dale on November 1, 19X4, was credited by Farnum to a liability account, Unearned Rent Revenue. The adjusting entry required on December 31, 19X4, the end of Farnum's fiscal year, is as follows.

	ADJUSTING ENTRY		
19X4 Dec. 31	Unearned Rent Revenue	2,000	
	Rent Revenue		2,000
	To recognize rent earned during November and December 19X4.		

The entry shifts a portion of the liability account to revenue, as illustrated by the following T-accounts.

Liability Unearned Rent Revenue		Revenue Rent Revenue	
12/31/X4 2,000	6,000		12/31/X4 2,000

First Recorded as a Revenue. Now, assume that Farnum recorded the collection on November 1, 19X4, as Rent Revenue. The adjusting entry on December 31, 19X4, must now shift the portion *not yet earned* to a liability account, as follows.

	ADJUSTING ENTRY		
19X4 Dec. 31	Rent Revenue	4,000	
	Unearned Rent Revenue		4,000
	To recognize rent not yet earned at December 31, 19X4.		

The effect of the adjustment is illustrated by the following T-accounts.

Liability Unearned Rent Revenue		Revenue Rent Revenue	
	12/31/X4 4,000 ←	← 12/31/X4 4,000	6,000

Reversing Procedure.   The accountant for Farnum may prepare a reversing entry on January 1, 19X5, to reflect into the revenue account the rent that was unearned at the end of 19X4. You can see that the following entry is the reverse of the adjustment that was made on December 31, 19X4.

	REVERSING ENTRY		
19X5 Jan. 1	Unearned Rent Revenue	4,000	
	Rent Revenue		4,000
	To reverse the adjustment for unearned rent that was made on December 31, 19X4.		

GLOSSARY FOR APPENDIX 3.II

Deferred charges   Prepayments of expenses for periods far in the future.

Deferred credits   Collections in advance for revenues that are not expected to be earned within the near future.

Prepaid expenses   Payments in advance for services, supplies, and similar items that will soon become expenses.

Unearned revenue (revenue received in advance)   An obligation to deliver in the near future goods or services for which payment has already been received.

DISCUSSION QUESTIONS FOR APPENDIX 3.II

1. Why are prepaid expenses usually classified as current assets?

2. What do accountants call prepayments of expenses for periods far in the future?

3. Under what circumstances might an accountant reverse adjustments for prepaid expenses?

4. What are deferred credits?

5. Under what circumstances might an accountant reverse adjustments for unearned revenues?

6. What types of business tend to receive most of their revenues before they are earned?

7. What types of expenditure most often involve prepayments of expenses?

8. Why are unearned revenues usually classified as *current* liabilities?

EXERCISES FOR APPENDIX 3.II

3.II.1. On September 1, 19X4, Bud, Inc. paid $9,600 for a liability insurance policy covering a period of one year from the date of payment. The records are adjusted only at year-end. Make the adjusting entry on December 31, 19X4, the end of the fiscal year, assuming that the bookkeeper recorded the September 1 payment as:

   a. Prepaid Insurance

   b. Insurance Expense

3.II.2. Refer to part *b* of the previous exercise and assume that Bud, Inc. follows the practice of shifting prepaid expenses to expense accounts on the first day of each new period. Make the required reversing entry on January 1, 19X5.

3.II.3. On March 1, 19X4, Mobull Company received $3,600 in advance as payment for servicing Merkel Company's garbage trucks each month for the next year. Make the adjusting entry on December 31, 19X4, assuming that the bookkeeper recorded the March 1 collection as:

   a. Service Revenue

   b. Unearned Service Revenue

3.II.4. The Ozma Company borrowed $10,000 from the bank on December 1, 19X4. Ozma signed a 120-day note payable for $10,000. The bank deducted the agreed-upon interest of $300 in advance and gave Ozma $9,700 cash. The entry made on Ozma's books was:

19X4			
Dec. 1	Cash	9,700	
	Interest Expense	300	
	Notes Payable		10,000

Make the adjusting entry at December 31, 19X4, to recognize prepaid interest expense.

3.II.5. Refer to the previous exercise and make a reversing entry at January 1, 19X5, to reflect into the Interest Expense account the interest that was prepaid at the end of 19X4.

3.II.6. The New Clarion Magazine Company received $168,000 for advertising during 19X4, its first year of operation. Advertising was recorded by crediting the Advertising Revenue account. At December 31, 19X4, it is determined that advertising sold for $39,000 will appear in magazine issues to be published during 19X5. Make the required adjusting entry at December 31, 19X4.

PROBLEMS FOR APPENDIX 3.II

3.II.7. On October 1, 19X4, the LAF&C Commuter Railroad began selling three-month commuter passes to passengers for $120. During the last three months of 19X4 three-month passes were sold as follows:

October 1	$6,000
November 1	$7,200
December 1	$6,000

Assume that the bookkeeper records pass sales by crediting Unearned Ticket Revenue.

Required

1) Make an adjusting entry at December 31, 19X4.

2) Assume instead that the bookkeeper recorded sales of three-month passes by crediting Ticket Revenue and make an adjusting entry at December 31, 19X4.

3) If the bookkeeper followed the practice described in the preceding item, make a reversing entry at January 1, 19X5, to reflect into the Ticket Revenue account the revenue that was unearned at the end of 19X4.

3.II.8. On November 16, 19X4, WCU, Inc. accepted a $6,000, 180-day note in settlement of a delinquent account from ARG Company. By agreement, on November 16, ARG paid WCU $180 interest in advance.

Required

1) Make the entries for WCU to record receipt of the note and interest on November 16, assuming that a revenue account is credited for the interest.

2) Make an adjusting entry for WCU to recognize unearned interest at December 31, 19X4.

3) Make entries on ARG's books for the November 16 transactions, assuming that an expense account is debited for the interest.

4) Make an adjusting entry on ARG's books at December 31, 19X4, to recognize prepaid interest.

5) Assume that ARG follows the practice of shifting prepaid expenses to expense accounts on the first day of each new period and make the required reversing entry on January 1, 19X5.

PART II

MERCHANDISING OPERATIONS

ACCOUNTANTS IN THE WORKPLACE

NAME: Sybil C. Mobley, Ph.D.

AFFILIATION: Florida A&M University,
    School of Business and
    Industry

POSITION: Dean

SPECIALIZATION: Financial Accounting,
    Socioeconomic Accounting

In 1963, a young woman with a Ph.D. in accounting began teaching at Florida A&M University. Today, Dr. Sybil C. Mobley is Dean of the School of Business and Industry. From her academic base, where she is known for her contributions to accounting literature, Dr. Mobley has ranged far afield—in both the private and public sectors. She serves on the boards of directors (and audit committees) of Champion International, Anheuser Busch, and Sears Roebuck; she toured Africa twice

with the Agency for International Development, was a consultant to the IRS, is an educator consultant to the Controller General of the United States, and was just appointed to the Presidential Commission on Industrial Competitiveness.

Dr. Mobley stresses the importance of her decision to major in accounting, saying that "the background it provided has been crucial to my performance in every field I pursued." A university, she adds, is a "very stimulating environment; the insights and experiences it provides have helped to expand my career in many ways."

A graduate of Bishop College and the Wharton School, Dr. Mobley received her Ph.D. from the University of Illinois. She became head of her department at Florida A&M in 1971 and in 1974, founding dean of the newly created School of Business and Industry.

NAME: Margaret Anne Reins

AFFILIATION: Northwestern (Illinois)
    Memorial Hospital

POSITION: Assistant Director of Accounting

SPECIALIZATION: Electronic Data Processing

A biology major at Boston College, Margaret Anne Reins began her association with Northwestern Memorial Hospital as a researcher studying dialysis techniques. For three years, under a grant from the National Institutes of Health, she compared patient progress at area hospitals, analyzing the results with the help of a computer. Then, intrigued by the math, Reins enrolled in the Master of Science and Accountancy program at De Paul University. At the end of her Northwestern project, she went to work for the hospital as a beginning

accountant. Today Reins directly supervises 12 accountants and generally oversees all of Northwestern's accounting functions.

One of Reins's key responsibilities is the preparation of monthly financial statements, which involves use of the hospital's electronic data processing system and an intimate understanding of its capabilities. Each month, after running a general ledger computer program, Reins must carefully examine the results "to see what's missing," and make the necessary additions manually. The hospital has implemented a program—designed by an outside firm in conjunction with the hospital's own EDP people—to integrate accounts payable into the general ledger program. Already the computer can provide the staff with information, for example, that $500,000 will be needed to pay off debts next week.

4
Merchandise Transactions

Some firms regularly buy and sell goods without changing their form in any significant way. Accounting systems for merchandising companies normally provide for accumulating various kinds of data relative to buying and selling transactions.

Chapter 4 consists of three sections. Section A deals with accounting for purchases and sales of goods and adjusting for inventories on hand at the end of accounting periods. This section commences with a discussion of the different kinds of utility and the difference between manufacturing and merchandising. Entries for purchases and sales, including those for transportation charges, are illustrated. The approach for calculating the cost of goods sold is presented, as is a simple income statement for a merchandising concern.

Section B is concerned with accounting for returns, allowances, and discounts related to purchases and sales of merchandise. The presentation of returns, allowances, and discounts on a schedule of cost of goods sold is illustrated, along with an income statement. Also, an alternate approach for accounting for purchases and sales on a "net of discounts" basis is presented, along with a discussion of the merits of using this approach.

Section C deals with merchandise reporting and illustrates the end-of-period accounting work for a merchandising concern. Several income statement arrangements for a merchandising concern are shown, as are a statement of owner's capital and a balance sheet.

SECTION 4.A

Purchases and Sales

OBJECTIVES

This section deals with accounting for the purchases and sales of merchandise and with merchandise inventories. At the conclusion of this section, you should be able to

1. Define merchandising in your own words.
2. Differentiate retailing from wholesaling.
3. Make general journal entries to record the following:
   a. Purchases of merchandise.
   b. Transportation in.
   c. Sales of merchandise.
   d. Transportation out.
4. Prepare a schedule of cost of goods sold, given the amounts for beginning inventory, purchases, transportation in, and ending inventory.

UTILITY

Revenues are measures of overall accomplishments during a period of time; expenses are measures of the sacrifices made to earn revenues; *net income* represents net accomplishment for a period. Viewed another way, revenues are the *values* of the goods and services supplied to customers, and expenses are the *costs* of resources used. Costs represent the *values* of resources when they were purchased. Thus net income is in a sense the difference between the total value of the resources supplied to others (revenues) and the total value of the resources consumed (expenses).

   Market value is the price at which customers (buyers) are willing to buy and suppliers (sellers) are willing to sell a commodity or a service at a particular point in time. Market value is a measure of how *useful* an article or service is. *Another term for usefulness is* **utility.** If the total market value of economic goods and services supplied (revenues) is greater than the market value of goods and services used (expenses), then an entity must have created or added utility (usefulness) to the goods and services during the period. Net income, then, is a measure of the utility created by an entity during a period.

   If an entity's expenses exceed its revenues for a period, there is a *net loss,* which means that more utility has been used than has been supplied. If net losses continue long enough, an entity will go out of business, and the resources it has been using will then be available for use by more profitable entities. For example, former employees of a bankrupt concern will seek work elsewhere, and suppliers of the concern will attempt to sell their outputs to other businesses. In this way, our economic system channels available resources to profitable entities that are creating utility.

*The usefulness (value) of a service is sometimes called **service utility**. The usefulness added by transporting goods from one location to another, where they are in greater demand, is referred to as **place utility**. The usefulness added by storing goods until they are in greater demand is **time utility**. Usefulness added by making available to users small amounts of goods that are otherwise available only in large amounts is called **quantity utility**. And finally, usefulness created by combining resources to produce something that did not previously exist is referred to as **form utility**.*

*An entity that combines various resources to produce a commodity that did not previously exist is said to be engaged in **manufacturing**.* Manufacturing concerns concentrate primarily on the creation of form utility, although they may also be somewhat involved in creating other types of utility as well—particularly time and place utilities.

*An entity that buys goods (merchandise) and resells them without changing their basic form is said to be engaged in **merchandising**, or selling.* A merchandising concern usually concentrates on creating quantity, time, and place utilities.

OBJECTIVE 1.   Define merchandising.

Service businesses, of course, concentrate on the creation of service utility.

Illustration 4.1 summarizes the types of utility normally created by each of the three main classes of business entities.

MERCHANDISING CONCERNS

Merchandising concerns specialize in various ways. There are shoe stores, grocery stores, and others that sell at retail. *Retailing is the process of selling merchandise in relatively small quantities to consumers.* Retailers usually buy goods in fairly large quantities from *wholesalers*. Retail stores deal in quantity utility by making goods available in smaller quantities to their customers. *Wholesaling is the process of buying goods from manufacturers or other distributors and reselling them in relatively large quantities to retailers*

OBJECTIVE 2.   Differentiate retailing from wholesaling.

ILLUSTRATION 4.1

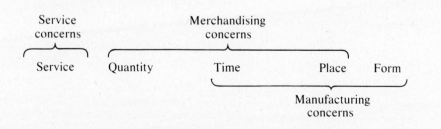

or other merchants. Wholesalers and retailers create time, place, and quantity utility by making merchandise available at the time and place, and in the quantities, desired by their customers.

MERCHANDISE INVENTORY

The amount of goods held for resale by a merchandising concern at any point in time is called **merchandise inventory.** The cost of merchandise on hand at the start of a period is known as *beginning inventory;* the goods on hand at the end of a period are *ending inventory.* The ending inventory for one accounting period is the beginning inventory for the following period. Cleaning supplies, office supplies, and other supplies held for *internal* use are not included in Merchandise Inventory accounts, but are shown instead in one or more Supplies on Hand accounts.

Some merchandisers buy and sell limited numbers of very expensive items. An automobile dealer, for instance, needs to know how many cars are on hand and the cost of each at all times. As a result, the dealership will continually (perpetually) keep track of its inventory, car by car. *A* **perpetual inventory system** *is one in which a running item-by-item record of the inventory is maintained.*

Many merchandisers deal in large numbers of relatively low-cost items, for which a perpetual inventory system may be impractical. Most small grocery stores, for example, do not keep continual track of the cost of all the items on their shelves.[1] Concerns of this type take a *physical inventory at the end of each period by counting the actual goods on hand. The costs of the various kinds of inventory are then summed to arrive at the total cost of inventory on hand. A* **periodic inventory system** *is one in which the inventory account is updated only at the end of each accounting period.* Physical inventories may also be taken to check the accuracy of perpetual inventory records.

Inventory systems are covered more fully in Chapter 7. Here our focus is on accounting for merchandise transactions when a periodic inventory system is used.

RECORDING PURCHASES AND SALES

Purchases

Under a periodic inventory system, merchandise purchases are accumulated in a temporary equity account called **Purchases.** If a purchase is paid for

---

[1] Some retail stores use optical scanners for registering merchandise sales. With such equipment perpetual inventory records might be maintained by continuously transmitting into computers the identities and quantities of goods being sold.

immediately, the entry will take the following form.

| June 2 | Purchases
    Cash
Purchased produce with Check No.
3672. | | 200 | 200 |

OBJECTIVE 3a. Record purchases of merchandise.

Most merchandising concerns purchase goods on credit, paying for them at some later date. A purchase on account is recorded as follows.

| June 3 | Purchases
    Accounts Payable
Canned goods purchased from Ace
Supply Co. on 30-day account. | | 1,000 | 1,000 |

The payment of the account will then be recorded as follows.

| July 2 | Accounts Payable
    Cash
Paid Ace Supply Co. for purchase of
June 3; Check No. 3750. | | 1,000 | 1,000 |

Note that the Purchases account is used *only* for accumulating the cost of merchandise bought for resale. Supplies, equipment, and other items bought for internal use are debited directly to appropriate accounts.

Transportation In

Goods are often hauled by a freight company for a fee. The fee may be paid by either the seller or the buyer, depending on the agreement they have made. *An agreement by which the seller pays the freight charges is referred to as f.o.b. destination, which stands for "free-on-board destination."* The expression might best be understood in relation to transportation by boat, where goods are loaded "on board" and transported to their destination at the seller's expense. *When goods are sold f.o.b. shipping point, the buyer pays the transportation charges.* An account called Transportation In (or Freight In) is debited to record payment of shipping charges on goods purchased f.o.b. shipping point, as follows.

| June 10 | Transportation In
    Cash
Paid freight charges on purchase;
Check No. 3681. | | 60 | 60 |

OBJECTIVE 3b. Record transportation in.

Transportation In is used only for accumulating the transportation costs associated with merchandise purchases. Freight charges paid on machinery and other purchases are generally combined with prices paid to arrive at the total costs of the items.

Sales

Goods may be sold either for cash or on credit. Cash sales, and possibly credit sales, may be keyed into a cash register, like those you see in most retail stores. At the end of each day a manager uses a special key to obtain from the machine the sales totals registered that day. These totals are then reconciled to the money in the cash register. Each day's cash receipts are usually deposited in a bank, leaving only a small "change fund" of cash in each register for starting the next business day.

The entry to record cash sales takes the following form.

OBJECTIVE 3c. Record sales of merchandise.

June 2	Cash	2,500	
	Sales		2,500
	Cash sales for June 2; Deposit No. 1475.		

Under a periodic inventory system, the *cost* of the merchandise sold is not accounted for until the end of an accounting period. Later in the section we will consider how to calculate the cost of goods sold.

Wholesaling concerns and some retailers sell mainly on credit. A credit sale is recorded as follows.

June 3	Accounts Receivable	960	
	Sales		960
	Sold goods to Stokes Co. on 30-day account.		

When cash is collected on account, the entry takes the usual form.

July 2	Cash	960	
	Accounts Receivable		960
	Collected from Stokes Co. for sale of June 3; Deposit No. 1490.		

One entity's sale is often another's purchase. If we are accounting for the seller of merchandise, a sale results in an increase in either cash or an account receivable. A purchase, on the other hand, involves either a payment of cash or the assumption of an account payable.

Transportation Out

When goods are sold f.o.b. destination, the seller must pay any freight charges for delivery of the merchandise. These charges are usually debited to an account titled Transportation Out (or Freight Out), as illustrated below.

June 8	Transportation Out		40	
	Cash			40
	Paid freight charges on items sold;			
	Check No. 3678.			

OBJECTIVE 3d. Record transportation out.

Transportation Out should not be confused with Transportation In, which is related to purchasing. Transportation Out is a selling expense.

COST OF GOODS SOLD

Under a periodic inventory system, the Merchandise Inventory account will show the cost of beginning inventory throughout an accounting period. At the end of an accounting period, a physical inventory is taken by counting the quantities of goods on hand and determining their costs. Unit costs are usually taken from purchase invoices, and the total cost of each type of inventory is determined by *extending*, or multiplying, the number of units by unit cost, as shown in Illustration 4.2.

Let's assume that the inventory depicted in Illustration 4.2 is for the Merkle Company, a merchandising firm that accounts for a calendar-year period. Merkle's inventory at the end of the previous year, 19X4, was $18,200, the balance still shown in the Merchandise Inventory account. The Purchases account indicates that goods costing $340,000 were purchased during 19X5, and Transportation In shows costs of $15,300 paid during the year. The

ILLUSTRATION 4.2

MERCHANDISE INVENTORY, DECEMBER 31, 19X5			
Description	**Units**	**Unit Cost**	**Total Cost**
Ball point pens, with eraser	200	.30	60.00
Staple pullers	50	1.00	50.00
Typewriter cleaning solvent	38	.50	19.00
Desk calendars	20	2.00	40.00
Total Inventory Cost			20,600.00

ILLUSTRATION 4.3

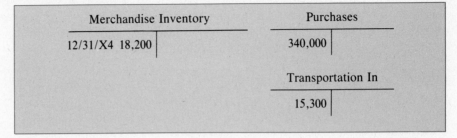

ILLUSTRATION 4.4

OBJECTIVE 4. Prepare a
schedule of cost of
goods sold.

MERKLE COMPANY Schedule of Cost of Goods Sold For the Year Ended December 31, 19X5		
Merchandise inventory at December 31, 19X4		$ 18,200
Purchases during 19X5	$340,000	
Transportation in	15,300	
Delivered cost of purchases		355,300
Cost of goods available for sale		$373,500
Merchandise inventory at December 31, 19X5		20,600
Cost of goods sold		$352,900

T-accounts in Illustration 4.3 portray the information needed to calculate the cost of goods sold.

The cost of the merchandise that was *available* for sale is the sum of the three accounts pictured in Illustration 4.3. The ending inventory of $20,600 was not sold, of course. The schedule in Illustration 4.4 shows the calculation for the cost of goods sold for 19X5.

Cost of goods sold represents the sum of the costs of all goods that were sold during the accounting period. These are expired costs, and thus are actually expenses for the year. The format of the schedule of cost of goods sold "backs into" the result, in a manner of speaking, by concluding that all available goods except those left on hand (ending inventory) must have been sold. The elements in the cost of goods sold calculation are summarized in Illustration 4.5.

The relationship between the various elements of Merkle's merchandise costs are pictured in Illustration 4.6.

The schedule of cost of goods sold may act as a supporting schedule for an income statement. The statement in Illustration 4.7 is supported by the cost of goods sold schedule shown in Illustration 4.4.

ILLUSTRATION 4.5

Beginning Inventory	• •	costs brought over from the previous period
Plus: Purchases	• •	costs incurred during the current period
Goods Available		
Less: Ending Inventory	• •	costs deferred to the following period
Cost of Goods Sold		

ILLUSTRATION 4.6

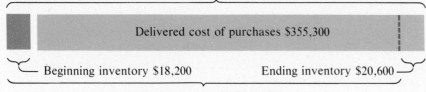

Goods available for sale $373,500

Delivered cost of purchases $355,300

Beginning inventory $18,200   Ending inventory $20,600

Cost of goods sold $352,900

ILLUSTRATION 4.7

MERKLE COMPANY Income Statement For the Year Ended December 31, 19X5		
Sales		$621,000
Expenses		
Cost of goods sold	$352,900	
Salaries	108,500	
Rent	42,000	
Utilities	8,600	
Insurance	1,800	
Depreciation	10,400	524,200
Net Income		$ 96,800

GLOSSARY FOR SECTION 4.A

Cost of goods sold   The sum of the costs of all goods sold during an accounting period; actually an *expense* of the period.

f.o.b. destination   An agreement providing that the seller of merchandise will pay freight charges. The abbreviation f.o.b. stands for "free-on-board."

f.o.b. shipping point   An agreement providing that the buyer of goods will pay freight charges.

Form utility   Usefulness created by combining resources to produce something that did not previously exist.

Manufacturing   The process of combining various resources to produce a commodity that did not previously exist.

Market value   The price at which customers (buyers) are willing to buy and suppliers (sellers) are willing to sell a commodity or a service at a particular point in time.

Merchandise inventory   The amount of goods held for resale by a merchandising concern at any point in time.

Merchandising   The process of buying and reselling goods without changing their basic form.

Periodic inventory system   A system in which the inventory account is updated only at the end of each accounting period.

Perpetual inventory system   A system for maintaining an accurate item-by-item record of the inventory on hand at all times.

Physical inventory   The amount of inventory as determined by counting the actual goods on hand, extending to get costs, and summing to arrive at the total cost of all goods on hand.

Place utility   Usefulness added by transporting goods from one location to another.

Purchases   A temporary equity account for recording purchases of merchandise for resale.

Quantity utility   Usefulness added by making large amounts of goods available to users in smaller amounts.

Retailing   The process of selling merchandise in relatively small quantities to consumers.

Service utility   Usefulness of a service rendered.

Time utility   Usefulness added by storing goods until they are in greater demand.

Utility   The overall usefulness, or value, of something.

Wholesaling   The process of buying goods from manufacturers or other large distributors and reselling them to retailers or other merchants.

SELF-QUIZ ON OBJECTIVES FOR SECTION 4.A
Solutions to Self-Quiz begin on page B-11.

1. **OBJECTIVE 1.** Define merchandising in your own words.

2. **OBJECTIVE 2.** Differentiate retailing from wholesaling.

3. **OBJECTIVE 3.** Journalize the following transactions for a merchandising concern that uses a periodic inventory system.

Transactions

19—

Mar. 1   Purchased merchandise on account, at a cost of $8,000, from Doby Supply Company. Goods were shipped f.o.b. shipping point.

2   Purchased merchandise for $400 cash (Check No. 5062).

4   Paid freight bill of $60 with Check No. 5063. Charges were for transporting goods purchased from Doby Supply on March 1.

5   Sold merchandise for $500 cash (Deposit No. 1055).

7   Sold merchandise for $4,000 on account to Jay Mooney. Goods were shipped f.o.b. destination.

8   Paid freight bill of $40 with Check No. 5064. Charges were for transporting goods sold to Jay Mooney on March 7.

9   Paid $8,000 to Doby Supply Company for purchase of March 1 (Check No. 5065).

14   Collected $4,000 from Jay Mooney for sale of March 7 (Deposit No. 1056).

4. **OBJECTIVE 4.** From the following data prepare a schedule of cost of goods sold for Inland Sales Company for the year ended December 31, 19X5.

Merchandise inventory, December 31, 19X4	$ 40,000
Merchandise inventory, December 31, 19X5	30,000
Purchases during 19X5	500,000
Sales during 19X5	800,000
Transportation in during 19X5	10,000
Transportation out during 19X5	5,000

DISCUSSION QUESTIONS FOR SECTION 4.A

1. How is a merchandising concern's ability to earn net income related to the utility it provides its customers?

2. What is the difference between the utility created by manufacturing concerns and the utility created by merchandising concerns?

3. What is the difference between a perpetual inventory system and a periodic inventory system?

4. How does the cost of goods available for sale during a period differ from the cost of goods sold for the same period?

5. What does the expression market value mean?

6. What is the difference between f.o.b. destination and f.o.b. shipping point? What does f.o.b. stand for?

7. Why is the ending merchandise inventory of one accounting period the same as the beginning merchandise inventory of the next period?

8. The manager of Dobb Merchandising Company does not think it is necessary to take physical inventories. In fact, he has the company bookkeeper report as cost of goods sold the current period's purchases plus freight in for the period. What is wrong with ignoring beginning and ending inventories in the calculation of cost of goods sold?

EXERCISES FOR SECTION 4.A

4.A.1. Use the information that follows to calculate the cost of goods available for sale by the Johnson Company for the fiscal year ended November 30, 19X5.

Merchandise inventory, December 1, 19X4	$ 40,000
Merchandise inventory, November 30, 19X5	32,000
Cost of goods sold for year ended November 30, 19X5	456,000

4.A.2. Use the following information to calculate the cost of goods available for sale during the month of April.

Merchandise inventory, April 1	$ 8,000
Merchandise inventory, April 30	19,000
Purchases during April	112,000
Sales during April	201,000
Transportation in for April	4,000
Transportation out for April	2,000

4.A.3. Use the information provided in exercise 4.A.2. to calculate the cost of goods sold for April.

4.A.4. Compute the cost of goods sold for each firm for which information is given below.

	Firm A	Firm B	Firm C
Beginning inventory	$ 48,000	$ 38,000	$ −0−
Ending inventory	38,000	48,000	38,000
Purchases	176,000	176,000	176,000

4.A.5. Joan Adelman, a college student, started a business selling student artwork. She purchases works of art from student artists and resells them to other students, faculty members, and townspeople. She began in February by purchasing a number of art items for $150. During February Joan had sales of $250. On February 28 Joan had several items on hand for which she had paid $50. In March she paid $200 for art items and had sales of $300. At the end of March Joan had art left in stock that she had purchased for $80.

    a. Determine Joan's cost of goods sold for February.

    b. Determine Joan's cost of goods sold for March.

PROBLEMS FOR SECTION 4.A
Alternate Problems for this section begin on page D-24.

4.A.6. The following transactions are for a merchandising concern that uses a periodic inventory system.

Transactions

May	1	Purchased merchandise for $1,000 cash, f.o.b. destination (Check No. 1188).
	8	Purchased merchandise on account at a cost of $2,000; terms f.o.b. shipping point.
	13	Paid freight for merchandise purchased on May 8, $40 cash (Check No. 1189).
	14	Sold merchandise for $800 cash (Deposit No. 650).
	20	Sold merchandise on account for $5,000; goods shipped f.o.b. destination.
	23	Paid freight bill of $50 for goods shipped May 20 (Check No. 1190).

Required

Journalize the transactions.

4.A.7. The data that follow are for the Weltzing Company.

Merchandise inventory, June 1	$ 21,000
Merchandise inventory, June 30	30,000
Purchases during June	220,000
Sales during June	410,000
Freight in during June	3,800
Freight out during June	5,600

Required

Prepare a schedule of cost of goods sold for Weltzing Company for the month of June.

4.A.8. The Smithfield Store purchases merchandise for resale from Giant Wholesalers. Transactions for September are as follows.

Transactions

Sept. 3   Smithfield purchased merchandise on account from Giant Wholesalers at a cost of $300; f.o.b. shipping point.

8   Smithfield paid $15 freight charges on September 3 purchase.

12   Smithfield purchased merchandise on account from Giant Wholesalers at a cost of $5,000, f.o.b. destination. Freight charges of $50 were paid by Giant on this date.

Required

1) Journalize the transactions for Smithfield Store.

2) Journalize the appropriate transactions as they would appear in Giant's records.

4.A.9. Information follows for Rewrite Stores.

Freight in for August	$ 1,100
Purchases for August	108,000
Increase in merchandise inventory during August	12,000

Required

1) Calculate the cost of goods sold for August.

2) Assume that the *increase* in inventory had been a *decrease*. Calculate the cost of goods sold.

SECTION 4.B

Returns, Allowances, and Discounts

OBJECTIVES

This section is concerned with accounting for returns, allowances, and discounts related to purchases and sales of merchandise. When you have completed this section, you should be able to

1. Make general journal entries to record the following:
   a. Purchases returns and allowances and sales returns and allowances.
   b. Purchases discounts and sales discounts.
2. Prepare a schedule of cost of goods sold when purchases discounts and purchases returns and allowances are involved.
3. Make general journal entries to record the following on a net-of-discounts basis:
   a. Purchases on account.
   b. Sales on account.
   c. Payment of payables within the discount period.
   d. Collection of receivables within the discount period.
   e. Purchases discounts lost.
   f. Sales discounts forfeited.

RETURNS AND ALLOWANCES

Merchandise may be returned by purchasers for a variety of reasons. In some cases the wrong goods are mistakenly shipped by the seller. On other occasions the merchandise is damaged or defective.

A seller will sometimes agree to reduce the price of damaged or defective merchandise (grant an ''allowance'') to induce the purchaser to keep the goods. Or an allowance may be granted because of a mistake in billing, or because of some misunderstanding between the parties about the terms of the sale.

Let's assume that a portion of bought goods, $100 worth, is defective, and these defective items are returned by the Buying Company to the Selling Company. A special form called a debit memorandum may be used to notify the Selling Company that the account payable to Selling Company is being debited (reduced) on the books of the Buying Company. *A debit memorandum is a document that explains to a creditor the reasons for a reduction in the buyer's Accounts Payable.* The form prepared by the Buying Company appears in Illustration 4.8.

The Selling Company may also issue a credit memorandum to the Buying Company. *A credit memorandum is a document that notifies a customer that*

ILLUSTRATION 4.8

DEBIT MEMORANDUM

Buying Company
Dubois, Pennsylvania

Date   May 25, 19--

To: Selling Company
Detroit, Michigan

We debit your account as follows:

Loopers received in damaged condition
and returned today   10 @ $10 $100

J. L. Dobbs
Purchasing Agent

---

a reduction in the seller's Accounts Receivable is being allowed. Illustration 4.9 shows the relationship between debit and credit memorandums.

Returns of merchandise and allowances on merchandise could conceivably be recorded as direct reductions in Sales and Purchases accounts. However, the volumes of defective goods purchased or sold are matters that concern managers, owners, and others. For this reason, most accounting

ILLUSTRATION 4.9

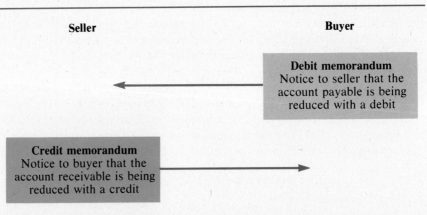

Seller	Buyer

Debit memorandum
Notice to seller that the account payable is being reduced with a debit

Credit memorandum
Notice to buyer that the account receivable is being reduced with a credit

---

ILLUSTRATION 4.10

Selling Company			Buying Company		
Accounts Receivable	1,000		Purchases	1,000	
Sales		1,000	Accounts Payable		1,000
Sales Ret. and Allow.	100		Accounts Payable	100	
Accounts Receivable		100	Purchases Ret. and Allow.		100

OBJECTIVE 1a. Record purchases returns and allowances and sales returns and allowances.

systems provide special accounts for accumulating returns and allowances related to sales and purchases.

Entries to record a sale of merchandise and a subsequent return of part of the goods might appear as is on the seller's and buyer's books shown in Illustration 4.10.

Sales Returns and Allowances is a contra account to Sales, whereas Purchases Returns and Allowances is a contra account to Purchases. You may recall that a contra account is an account for accumulating reductions in some other account.

DISCOUNTS

Trade Discounts

A merchandising company may sell goods to two or more classes of customers. A wholesaling business, for example, may sell to retailers, to institutions such as schools and hospitals, and even directly to consumers. To avoid publishing different price lists, the wholesaler might have just one list of prices for consumers, with trade discounts allowed to other classes of customers. Retailers, for example, might be granted a trade discount of 30% off the *list prices* of all merchandise. *A **trade discount** is a percentage reduction from list prices for a certain class of customers.*

In practice, both sellers and buyers record transactions at the *discounted* prices (net of trade discounts). In other words, there is no attempt to account for either the list prices or the amount of trade discounts. When goods that list for $1,000 are sold at a trade discount of 30%, the transaction is simply recorded as a $700 sale. Likewise, the buyer records a purchase in the amount of $700.

Cash Discounts

Many companies encourage their customers to pay promptly by providing a cash discount. *A **cash discount** is a reduction in the amount due when an account is paid within a stated period of time.*

ILLUSTRATION 4.11

TERMS OF 2/10, n/30

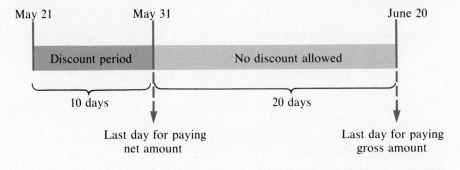

*The part of a sales agreement covering the manner in which an account is to be paid is often referred to as the **credit terms**.* Credit terms allowing for a cash discount may be stated in various ways, but they usually include both the discount period and the maximum time for paying the account. Terms of "2/10, n/30" translate into "2%, 10 days; net, 30 days." Use of the word "net" is somewhat misleading, because what is really meant is that a 2% discount will be allowed if the account is paid within 10 days of the invoice date, but that the *gross* amount of the invoice must be paid after the 10 days. The maximum period of time allowed for payment is 30 days from the billing date.

Suppose, for example, that the $1,000 sale was billed (invoiced) by Selling Company on May 21 and that the credit terms were 2/10, n/30. The terms may be pictured as in Illustration 4.11. Thus Buying Company may settle the account during the first 10 days by paying $980 cash (the discount is 2% of $1,000, or $20). But if payment is not made within 10 days, then $1,000 cash must be paid by the thirtieth day.

ILLUSTRATION 4.12

Amount of purchase on May 21	$1,000
Less: Merchandise returned on May 25	100
Balance of account due	$ 900
Less: Discount of 2% for payment by May 31	18
Net payment due by May 31	$ 882

ILLUSTRATION 4.13

Selling Company				Buying Company		
May 31	Cash	882		May 31	Accounts Payable	900	
	Sales Discounts	18			Purchases Discounts		18
	Accounts Receivable		900		Cash		882
	Collected for sale of				Paid for purchase of		
	May 21, less return of				May 21, less return		
	May 25.				of May 25.		

OBJECTIVE 1b. Record
purchases discounts and
sales discounts.

Credit terms may provide for a variety of discounts, discount periods, and maximum periods. For example, credit terms may call for payment by a certain day of the month following the billing. Terms of n/10 EOM mean that the amount billed is due 10 days after the end of the month (EOM), which simply means by the tenth day of the following month.

*The Selling Company will refer to cash discounts on sales as **sales discounts**; cash discounts on purchases are called **purchases discounts**.* Let's use our earlier example to see how cash discounts are recorded. Remember, on May 25, $100 worth of goods purchased by Buying Company were returned to Selling Company. Naturally, *the cash discount cannot be taken on goods that were returned*. Thus Selling Company can settle the remaining $900 account by paying $882 on or before May 31, which is 10 days from the date of the invoice. The calculation is shown in Illustration 4.12.

Entries on the books of the two companies are as shown in Illustration 4.13.

What if Buying Company did not make payment within the discount period? If full payment were made on June 20, the entries in Illustration 4.14 would appear on the books of the two companies.

ILLUSTRATION 4.14

Selling Company				Buying Company		
June 20	Cash	900		June 20	Accounts Payable	900	
	Accounts Receivable		900		Cash		900
	Collected for May 21				Paid for May 21		
	sale, less return of				purchase, less		
	May 25.				return of May 25.		

ILLUSTRATION 4.15

Merchandise Inventory	Purchases
Jan. 1 60,000	580,000

	Purchases Returns and Allowances
	6,000

	Purchases Discounts
	10,000

Transportation In	
40,000	

COST OF GOODS SOLD

Now let's see how the calculation of cost of goods sold is affected by purchases returns and allowances and by purchases discounts. The accounts that accumulate these items are contra accounts to Purchases. The T-accounts in Illustration 4.15 show the beginning inventory and the accounts related to merchandise purchased by Weils Company for the year.

ILLUSTRATION 4.16

OBJECTIVE 2. Prepare a schedule of cost of goods sold.

WEILS COMPANY
Schedule of Cost of Goods Sold
For the Year Ended December 31, 19 --

Merchandise inventory at January 1			$ 60,000
Purchases		$580,000	
Less: Purchases returns and allowances	$ 6,000		
Purchases discounts	10,000	16,000	
Net purchases		$564,000	
Plus: Transportation in		40,000	
Delivered cost of net purchases			604,000
Cost of goods available for sale			$664,000
Merchandise inventory at December 31			55,000
Cost of goods sold			$609,000

ILLUSTRATION 4.17

WEILS COMPANY Income Statement For the Year Ended December 31, 19--		
Sales		$1,040,000
Less: Sales returns and allowances	$12,000	
Sales discounts	18,000	30,000
Net sales		$1,010,000
Expenses		
Cost of goods sold	$609,000	
Wages	150,000	
Rent	80,000	
Depreciation	7,000	
Utilities	11,000	857,000
Net Income		$ 153,000

A physical inventory taken at year-end shows that merchandise costing $55,000 remained unsold. The schedule in Illustration 4.16 presents the cost of goods sold calculation for the year.

The cost of goods sold is one of the *expenses* shown on an income statement. The income statement for Weils Company (Illustration 4.17) shows how sales returns and allowances and sales discounts are offset against sales before expenses are subtracted to arrive at net income.

RECORDING NET OF CASH DISCOUNTS

Most business managers take advantage of all cash discounts allowed because *lost discounts* usually represent a very high cost for the relatively short period that payment can be delayed. Consider, for example, a $1,000 purchase with credit terms of 2/10, n/30. The discount allowed for paying by the tenth day is 2% of $1,000, or $20. The true cost of the merchandise is $980. Delaying payment for an additional 20 days will result in the *loss* of the $20 discount, as shown in Illustration 4.18 on the next page.

The cost of deferring payment of $980 for 20 days is $20. A lost discount is not logically a part of merchandise cost, but rather a *financing cost* similar to interest. In fact, we can approximate the annual interest rate that would be equivalent to the discount rate that is lost when payment is delayed beyond the discount period.

For most short-term interest calculations, the year is assumed to have 360 days. The 20-day period that is allowed beyond the discount period is

ILLUSTRATION 4.18

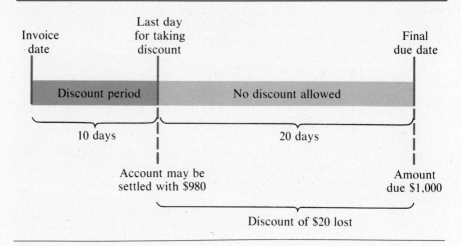

one-eighteenth of a year. By multiplying the 2% discount rate times 18, we see that the equivalent interest cost is about 36% per year.[2]

$$2\% \left(\frac{360 \text{ days}}{20 \text{ days}} \right) = 2\%(18) = 36\%$$

Some accountants believe that an accounting system should identify the purchases discounts that were *lost* during an accounting period, rather than identify discounts that were taken. Discounts lost would then be treated as an expense. Taking purchases discounts is simply good business, while losing discounts regularly can be extremely costly.

One way to account for lost purchases discounts is simply to record purchases (and accounts payable) initially at their net cost. Then, if the

---

[2]Actually, the equivalent interest cost is higher than 36%, because the rate is applied to the gross invoice amount, whereas only 98% of that amount is in fact being "borrowed." The "true" interest cost is slightly more than 36.7%, as determined by the following calculation.

$$I = PRT,$$

and

$$R = \frac{I}{PT},$$

where I = interest in dollars, P = amount borrowed, R = interest rate, and T = period of loan in years. Therefore,

$$R = \frac{\$20}{\$980(20/360)} = \frac{\$20}{\$980(1/18)} = \frac{\$20}{\$54.44} = \text{about } 36.7\%.$$

account is paid within the discount period, no discount will be registered in the books. If the account is not paid within the discount period, however, purchases discounts lost will have to be recognized.

Sales may also be recorded on a net basis so as to highlight sales discounts forfeited by customers, rather than sales discounts taken. Sales Discounts Forfeited is viewed as revenue earned from lending money to customers and is thus kept separate from sales revenue. The entries recording the earlier transactions on a net basis appear in Illustration 4.19. Compare these entries to the earlier ones made on a gross basis and see the difference in emphasis.

Most companies today continue to record purchases and sales on a gross basis, which is the traditional method. Nevertheless, the net approach would appear to be superior in that it highlights discounts lost (an expense) and also records purchases (or sales) at the "true" *cash* prices of the merchandise—in other words, at the prices they would sell for on a cash basis.

OBJECTIVE 3. Record, on a net-of-discount basis, purchases and sales on account, payment of payables and collection of receivables within the discount period, purchases discounts lost, and sales discounts forfeited.

ILLUSTRATION 4.19

	Selling Company				Buying Company		
May 21	Accounts Receivable	980		May 21	Purchases	980	
	Sales		980		Accounts Payable		980
	Billed Buying Co. for $1,000 on terms of 2/10, n/30				Goods purchased for $1,000 on terms of 2/10, n/30		
25	Sales Ret. and Allow.	98		25	Accounts Payable	98	
	Accounts Receivable		98		Pur. Ret. and Allow.		98
	Defective goods returned by Buying Co.				Returned defective goods to Selling Company		
31	Cash	882		31	Accounts Payable	882	
	Accounts Receivable		882		Cash		882
	Collected for sale of May 21, less return of May 25.				Paid for purchase of May 21, less return of May 25.		

If payment were not made by May 31, the third entry above would be replaced by:

	Selling Company				Buying Company		
June 20	Cash	900		June 20	Accounts Payable	882	
	Accounts Receivable		882		Purchases Discounts Lost	18	
	Sales Disc. Forfeited		18		Cash		900
	Collected for sale of May 21, less return of May 25.				Paid for purchase of May 21, less return of May 25.		

Moreover, the Accounts Payable (or Accounts Receivable) account is not overstated by the discounts that are to be taken, as happens when the gross approach is used.

In accordance with predominant practice, the gross approach is assumed in this text except where otherwise indicated.

GLOSSARY FOR SECTION 4.B

Cash discount   A reduction in the amount due when an account is paid within a stated period of time.

Credit memorandum   A document that notifies a customer that a reduction in the seller's Accounts Receivable is being allowed.

Credit terms   The part of a sales agreement covering the manner in which an account is to be paid.

Debit memorandum   A document that explains to a creditor the reasons for a reduction in the buyer's Accounts Payable.

Purchases discounts   Cash discounts from the viewpoint of a buying company.

Sales discounts   Cash discounts from the viewpoint of a selling company.

Trade discount   A percentage reduction from list prices for a certain class of customers.

SELF-QUIZ ON OBJECTIVES FOR SECTION 4.B
Solutions to Self-Quiz begin on page B-13.

1. **OBJECTIVE 1.** Prepare journal entries for each of the following events. Record the purchase and sale at "gross" amounts.

   Transactions

   Apr. 4   Purchased $3,000 worth of merchandise from Duke Company on credit terms of 2/10, n/30.

   6   Sold $600 worth of merchandise to Ray Company on credit terms of 1/10, n/60.

   7   Sent a debit memorandum to Duke Company stating that items costing $500 were missing from the purchase of April 4. Duke Company agreed by phone to the $500 allowance.

   9   Mailed a credit memorandum to Ray Company granting them a $100 adjustment for goods that they returned. The goods were from the April 6 sale.

   13   Mailed a check to Duke Company to cover the amount owed on the purchase of April 4.

   16   Received a check from Ray Company for the amount due on the sale of April 6.

2. **OBJECTIVE 2.** The following account balances were taken from a trial balance at December 31 for Alley Company.

	Debit	Credit
Merchandise inventory, January 1	30,000	
Sales		700,000
Purchases	400,000	
Purchases discounts		5,000
Purchases returns and allowances		2,000
Transportation in	10,000	
Transportation out	18,000	
Depreciation expense	50,000	

A physical inventory taken at December 31 shows that merchandise costing $45,000 is left on hand at year-end.

Required

Prepare a schedule of cost of goods sold for Alley Company for the year.

3. **OBJECTIVE 3.** On March 5 Ace Company purchased $5,000 worth of merchandise from Bee Company on credit terms of 2/10, n/30.

   a. Make journal entries on a net-of-discounts basis for Bee Company to record

   (1) The sale on March 5.

   (2) Proceeds from the sale, assuming that a check for the net amount was received on March 15.

   (3) Proceeds from the sale, assuming that a check for the gross amount was received on March 30.

   b. Make journal entries on a net-of-discounts basis for Ace Company to record

   (1) The purchase on March 5.

   (2) Payment, assuming that a check was written on March 14.

   (3) Payment, assuming that a check was written on March 29.

DISCUSSION QUESTIONS FOR SECTION 4.B

1. What is a debit memorandum and how is it used?

2. What is a credit memorandum and how is it used?

3. Why are Sales Returns and Allowances and Purchases Returns and Allowances called contra accounts?

4. What is the difference between a trade discount and a cash discount?

5. What do credit terms of 2/10, n/60 mean?

6. Why is it usually considered good business to pay within the discount period, and preferably toward the end of the discount period?

7. What are the advantages of recording purchases and sales on a net-of-discounts basis?

8. When sales and purchases are recorded on a gross basis, the contra accounts Sales Discounts and Purchases Discounts are used to accumulate discounts taken. On a net-of-discounts approach, the accounts Sales Discounts Forfeited and Purchases Discounts Lost are used to accumulate discounts not taken. What is the nature of the accounts Sales Discounts Forfeited and Purchases Discounts Lost?

EXERCISES FOR SECTION 4.B

4.B.1. Make journal entries on a gross basis for the following events as they would appear in both Y Company's journal and Z Company's journal.

Transactions

Mar. 1   Y Company purchased $5,000 worth of merchandise from Z Company on credit terms of 2/10, n/30.

5   Y Company was granted an allowance of $1,000 because the goods purchased on March 1 were defective.

8   Y Company paid Z Company for the March 1 purchase.

4.B.2. For each of the credit terms below, calculate the approximate interest rate that lost discounts represent.

a. 2/10, n/30

b. 2/10, n/60

c. 2/30, n/60

d. 1/10, n/30

4.B.3. Make journal entries for the following events as they would appear in both B Company's journal and S Company's journal on a net-of-discounts basis.

Transactions

May 1   B Company purchased $1,000 worth of merchandise from S Company on credit terms of 2/10, n/30.

2   B Company returned damaged merchandise to S Company for a $200 allowance.

16   B Company paid S Company for the May 1 purchase.

4.B.4. On June 5, Nosko Company purchased merchandise with list prices totaling $2,000, subject to a trade discount of 20% and credit terms of 2/10, n/30. Nosko paid for the merchandise on June 12. Make journal entries for Nosko to record the purchase and the payment, assuming use of

    a. The gross basis.

    b. The net basis.

4.B.5. Use the information below to calculate the missing inventory figure.

Merchandise inventory, June 1	$?
Merchandise inventory, June 30	12,000
Purchases during June	64,000
Purchases discounts	1,200
Transportation in	1,100
Cost of goods available for sale	78,500

PROBLEMS FOR SECTION 4.B
Alternate Problems for this section begin on page D-25.

4.B.6. Purchases and sales transactions of the Tops and Bottoms Boutique are listed below.

Transactions

May	1	Purchased merchandise on account, $3,000; terms 2/10, n/30.
	7	Paid for merchandise purchased on May 1.
	10	Purchased merchandise on account, $5,000; terms 1/10, n/30.
	11	Returned part of merchandise purchased on May 10, $200.
	14	Sold merchandise on account, $2,000; terms 2/10, n/30.
	25	Paid amount owed on May 10 purchase.
	27	Received payment for goods sold May 14.
	28	Sold merchandise on account, $4,000; terms 2/10, n/30.
	31	Received payment for goods sold May 28.

Required

Make journal entries to record the transactions, assuming that

    1) Purchases and sales are recorded at gross (before cash discounts).

    2) Purchases and sales are recorded net of cash discounts.

4.B.7. The following transactions were experienced by Glib Company, which records purchases and sales on a gross basis.

Transactions

June 2   Purchased merchandise on account for $3,000; terms 2/10, n/30.

    3   Sold merchandise for cash, $125.

    5   Customer returned merchandise sold on June 3 for a cash refund.

   14   Paid for merchandise purchased on June 2.

   14   Purchased merchandise on account for $8,000; terms 2/10, n/30.

   15   Returned part of the June 14 purchase to the vendor for credit. The returned merchandise had been invoiced at a gross cost of $2,000.

   21   Paid for merchandise purchased on June 14, less returns and discounts.

   24   Sold merchandise on credit for $300; terms 1/10, n/30.

   30   Customer paid account for June 24 sale.

Required

Record the transactions in Glib's journal.

4.B.8. January transactions for XL Marketing are as follows.

Transactions

Jan. 2   Sold $500 worth of merchandise to Arl Company on credit terms of 2/10, n/30.

    4   Purchased $1,000 worth of merchandise from Ralph Company on credit terms of 1/10, n/30.

    5   Received a debit memorandum from Arl Company stating that goods costing $100 were received in damaged condition. Arl is granted a $100 credit on account due for the sale of January 2.

    6   Sent a debit memorandum to Ralph Company for a $50 shortage of goods purchased on January 4.

   11   Received a check from the Arl Company for the amount due on the January 2 sale.

   12   Mailed a check to Ralph Company for the balance due on the January 4 purchase.

Required

1) Prepare journal entries for each transaction, assuming purchases and sales are recorded on a gross basis.

2) Prepare journal entries for each transaction on a net-of-discounts basis.

3) Assume that the January 12 transaction took place on January 20 instead. Make a journal entry to record the January 20 transaction on

   a) A gross basis.

   b) A net-of-discounts basis.

4.B.9. Information for the year just ended is shown here for the Smithfield Soap Company.

Merchandise inventory, January 1	$ 57,800
Merchandise inventory, December 31	57,800
Purchases	860,450
Purchases returns and allowances	8,900
Purchases discounts lost	1,100
Transportation in	12,600
Transportation out	2,000
Sales discounts forfeited	5,650
Sales returns and allowances	14,000

Required

Prepare a schedule of cost of goods sold for the company.

4.B.10. Information for the Crossland Marketing Company for the month of November is as follows.

Merchandise inventory, November 1	$ 87,000
Merchandise inventory, November 30	55,000
Purchases during November	290,000
Purchases discounts for November	2,150
Purchases returns and allowances for November	800
Transportation in during November	4,000
Transportation out during November	6,400
Sales discounts for November	3,000
Sales returns and allowances for November	100
Sales for November	578,000
Wage expense	80,000
Rent expense	6,000
Depreciation expense	12,000
Consultant expense	34,000

Required

1) Prepare a schedule of cost of goods sold for the month.

2) Prepare an income statement for the month.

4.B.11. The following information relates to the Clothing Paraphernalia Company for the year just ended.

Purchases	$400,800
Purchases discounts	3,000
Transportation in	5,000
Decrease in merchandise inventory during the year	48,000

Required

1) Calculate the cost of goods sold during the year.

2) Assume instead that the inventory increased by $48,000 during the year. Calculate the cost of goods sold for the year.

3) Assume instead that the ending inventory was the same as the beginning inventory. Calculate the cost of goods sold for the year.

SECTION 4.C

Merchandise Reporting

OBJECTIVES

This section is concerned with end-of-period accounting work for a merchandising entity, including preparation of financial statements. When you have completed this section, you should be able to

1. Prepare the following items for a merchandising concern:
   a. A ten-column work sheet.
   b. Adjusting journal entries.
   c. Closing journal entries.
   d. A multiple-step income statement.
   e. A classified balance sheet.
2. Define gross profit (gross margin).

WORK SHEETS FOR MERCHANDISING CONCERNS

Work sheets for merchandising concerns look much like those for service firms. The major differences come from the adjustments needed to arrive at the cost of goods sold for the period. Procedures for adjusting for cost of goods sold vary in practice, but they all arrive at the same result.[3]

A work sheet for the Wixon Merchandising Company is presented in Illustration 4.20. Let's concentrate for the moment on adjustments (d) through (i), which pertain to cost of goods sold. Adjustment (d) in effect transfers the *beginning* inventory to the Cost of Goods Sold account, leaving the Merchandise Inventory account with a zero balance at this point. Next, adjustment (e) transfers Purchases to Cost of Goods Sold. But we must remember that both Purchases Discounts and Purchases Returns and Allowances are contra accounts to Purchases, so adjustments (f) and (g) transfer these balances to the credit side of Cost of Goods Sold. Also Transportation In is related to Purchases, so this account balance is transferred by adjust-

---

[3]Many accountants avoid the use of a Cost of Goods Sold account by combining the inventory adjustment with the closing entries. With this approach, the components of Cost of Goods Sold show up in the income statement columns of the work sheet.

Although the approach just described is an efficient one, this text, for conceptual reasons, emphasizes the steps in determining Cost of Goods Sold by means of a series of adjusting entries. The adjusting entry approach seems to help students gain an understanding of the concepts involved, as opposed to memorizing a set of procedural steps for getting the job done. With a clear understanding of the concepts, one can usually deal with procedural variations that are encountered in practice.

Problem 4.C.6 at the end of this section and Alternate Problem 4.C.6 in Appendix D require the use of the closing entry approach for adjusting the Merchandise Inventory account. Once you thoroughly understand the ways in which data from the accounts relate to the Cost of Goods Sold calculation, you should not only be able to adapt to alternative approaches, but you should understand why they arrive at the same result.

ILLUSTRATION 4.20

OBJECTIVE 1a. Prepare a ten-column work sheet for a merchandising concern.

WIXON MERCHANDISING COMPANY
Work Sheet
For Year 19--

A/C #	Account	Unadjusted Trial Balance Dr.	Cr.
101	Cash	22,000	
102	Accounts Receivable	100,000	
103	Merchandise Inventory	70,000	
151	Furniture and Fixtures	40,000	
0151	Accumulated Depreciation—Furn. and Fix.		18,000
152	Land	10,000	
153	Building	80,000	
0153	Accumulated Depreciation—Building		26,000
201	Accounts Payable		60,000
251	Note Payable (due in 5 years)		30,000
351	J. Wixon, Capital		123,000
352	J. Wixon, Withdrawals	4,000	
401	Sales		950,000
402	Sales Discounts	13,000	
403	Sales Returns and Allowances	17,000	
405	Rent Revenue		5,000
502	Purchases	640,000	
503	Purchases Discounts		10,000
504	Purchases Returns and Allowances		6,000
505	Transportation In	25,000	
601	Salaries Expense	182,000	
602	Advertising Expense	14,000	
603	Utilities Expense	11,000	
		1,228,000	1,228,000
202	Salaries Payable		
604	Depreciation Expense		
605	Interest Expense		
203	Interest Payable		
500	Cost of Goods Sold		
	Net Income		

Adjustments		Adjusted Trial Balance		Income Statement		Balance Sheet	
Dr.	Cr.	Dr.	Cr.	Dr.	Cr.	Dr.	Cr.
		22,000				22,000	
		100,000				100,000	
i) 75,000	d) 70,000	75,000				75,000	
		40,000				40,000	
	b) 4,000		22,000				22,000
		10,000				10,000	
		80,000				80,000	
	b) 2,000		28,000				28,000
			60,000				60,000
			30,000				30,000
			123,000				123,000
		4,000				4,000	
			950,000		950,000		
		13,000		13,000			
		17,000		17,000			
			5,000		5,000		
	e) 640,000	–0–	–0–				
f) 10,000			–0–				
g) 6,000			–0–				
a) 1,200	h) 25,000	–0–					
		183,200		183,200			
		14,000		14,000			
		11,000		11,000			
	a) 1,200		1,200				1,200
b) 6,000		6,000		6,000			
c) 1,800		1,800		1,800			
	c) 1,800		1,800				1,800
d) 70,000	f) 10,000	} 644,000		644,000			
e) 640,000	g) 6,000						
h) 25,000	i) 75,000						
835,000	835,000	1,221,000	1,221,000	890,000	955,000	331,000	266,000
				65,000			65,000
				955,000	955,000	331,000	331,000

Adjustment Explanations:
a) Accrued wages at December 31.
b) Depreciation for the year.
c) Accrued interest payable at year-end.
d) Beginning inventory to Cost of Goods Sold.
e) Purchases to Cost of Goods Sold.
f) Purchases Discounts to Cost of Goods Sold.
g) Purchases Returns and Allowances to Cost of Goods Sold.
h) Transportation In to Cost of Goods Sold.
i) Set up ending inventory.

ILLUSTRATION 4.21

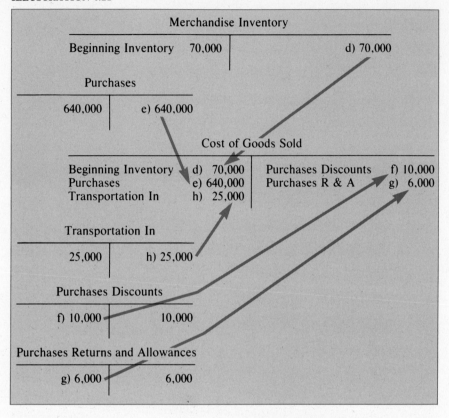

ment (h). The effects of adjustments (d) through (h) are shown by the
T-accounts in Illustration 4.21.

Note that the T-account for Cost of Goods Sold contains all the necessary information for calculating cost of goods available for sale, as shown
in Illustration 4.22.

ILLUSTRATION 4.22

Beginning inventory			$ 70,000
Purchases		$640,000	
Less: Purchases discounts	$10,000		
Purchases returns and allowances	6,000	16,000	
Net purchases		$624,000	
Plus: Transportation in		25,000	
Delivered cost of net purchases			649,000
Cost of goods available for sale			$719,000

ILLUSTRATION 4.23

Merchandise Inventory		
Beginning Inventory 70,000		d) 70,000
Ending Inventory i) 75,000		

Cost of Goods Sold			
Beginning Inventory	d) 70,000	Purchases Discounts	f) 10,000
Purchases	e) 640,000	Purchases R & A	g) 6,000
Transportation In	h) 25,000	Ending Inventory	i) 75,000

Finally, adjustment (i) removes the ending inventory from Cost of Goods Sold and places it in the Merchandise Inventory account, as illustrated in Illustration 4.23, since this represents merchandise that remained unsold at year-end.

At this point, the Cost of Goods Sold account should net out to the proper balance, because it contains all the ingredients for calculating cost of goods sold. The schedule in Illustration 4.24 simply rearranges the data shown in the account.

The remainder of the work sheet for Wixon Merchandising Company is much the same as work sheets for service businesses. The Income Statement columns in the work sheet show Sales for the year as a credit, and Sales Discounts and Sales Returns and Allowances as debit amounts. Cost of Goods Sold appears as one figure in the debit column.

ILLUSTRATION 4.24

WIXON MERCHANDISING COMPANY **Schedule of Cost of Goods Sold** **For the Year Ended December 31, 19--**		
Merchandise inventory at January 1		$ 70,000
Purchases		$640,000
Less: Purchases discounts	$10,000	
Purchases returns and allowances	6,000	16,000
Net purchases		$624,000
Plus: Transportation in		25,000
Delivered cost of net purchases		649,000
Cost of goods available for sale		$719,000
Merchandise inventory at December 31		75,000
Cost of goods sold		$644,000

ADJUSTING JOURNAL ENTRIES

The adjusting journal entries for Wixon Merchandising Company are shown in Illustration 4.25. The first three entries (a, b, and c) are omitted because they are similar to those you worked with for service firms. Adjustments (d) through (i) follow the approach used in the work sheet to arrive at Cost of Goods Sold and to set up the correct ending balance in the Merchandise Inventory account. You should keep in mind that different accountants prefer different approaches, but they all arrive at the same result.

ILLUSTRATION 4.25

OBJECTIVE 1b. Prepare adjusting journal entries for a merchandising concern.

Date	Account Names and Explanations	A/C #	Debit	Credit
	ADJUSTING ENTRIES			
19––	*d)*			
Dec. 31	Cost of Goods Sold		70,000	
	Merchandise Inventory			70,000
	To transfer beginning inventory to Cost of Goods Sold.			
	e)			
31	Cost of Goods Sold		640,000	
	Purchases			640,000
	To transfer Purchases to Cost of Goods Sold.			
	f)			
31	Purchases Discounts		10,000	
	Cost of Goods Sold			10,000
	To transfer Purchases Discounts to Cost of Goods Sold.			
	g)			
31	Purchases Returns and Allowances		6,000	
	Cost of Goods Sold			6,000
	To transfer Purchases Returns and Allowances to Cost of Goods Sold.			
	h)			
31	Cost of Goods Sold		25,000	
	Transportation In			25,000
	To transfer Transportation In to Cost of Goods Sold.			
	i)			
31	Merchandise Inventory		75,000	
	Cost of Goods Sold			75,000
	To set up ending inventory.			

ILLUSTRATION 4.26

Date	Account Names and Explanations	A/C #	Debit	Credit
	CLOSING ENTRIES			
19--				
Dec. 31	Sales		950,000	
	Rent Revenue		5,000	
	Sales Discounts			13,000
	Sales Returns and Allowances			17,000
	Salaries Expense			183,200
	Advertising Expense			14,000
	Utilities Expense			11,000
	Depreciation Expense			6,000
	Interest Expense			1,800
	Cost of Goods Sold			644,000
	J. Wixon, Capital			65,000
	To close revenue and expense accounts to owner's equity.			
31	J. Wixon, Capital		4,000	
	J. Wixon, Withdrawals			4,000
	To close withdrawals to owner's equity.			

OBJECTIVE 1c. Prepare closing journal entries for a merchandising concern.

CLOSING ENTRIES

The purpose of closing entries is to clear out temporary equity accounts and update permanent equity accounts. The first closing entry in Illustration 4.26 debits all balances shown in the Income Statement credit column of the work sheet and credits all balances shown in the debit column. The difference, net income, is added into the owner's equity account. The second entry closes the withdrawals account to owner's equity.

INCOME STATEMENTS

Recall that an income statement shows the amount of revenues *realized* during a period and the related costs being *matched* with the revenues. Sales revenues are recognized at the time that legal title to merchandise is passed from the seller to the buyer—in other words, at the point of sale. In a retail store, title usually changes hands when the buyer takes possession of the merchandise after paying for it or signing for it (in the case of credit).

When goods are being shipped from the seller to the buyer, f.o.b. terms usually determine when title changes hands. The legal rule is that the hauling company acts as the agent of whoever pays the freight bill. When goods are sold f.o.b. shipping point, title to goods passes to the buyer as soon as the transportation firm takes possession. On the other hand, when goods are sold f.o.b. destination, title does not pass to the buyer until the goods are delivered to the buyer.

Expenses that appear on an income statement are costs that have expired. Expired costs are those that have no holdover value for the future. The cost of goods sold for a period is actually an expense, since the goods have left the entity. In exchange for the merchandise sold, revenues have been generated in the form of cash or accounts receivable. Thus cost of goods sold is probably more directly matchable against revenue than any other expense an entity incurs.

The format of an income statement varies with the needs of users, preferences of accountants, and other circumstances. Some income statements show a great deal of detail; others are highly condensed, showing data only in summarized categories. Income statements may be arranged in either a single-step or multiple-step format.

Single-Step Income Statements

A *single-step income statement groups revenues together and expenses together and then deducts expenses from revenues in one step to arrive at net income.* You have already prepared income statements in single-step format for service firms. A single-step income statement for a merchandising concern lists Cost of Goods Sold along with the other expenses for the period covered by the statement. A single-step income statement for Wixon Merchandising Company is presented in condensed form in Illustration 4.27.

Multiple-Step Income Statements

A *multiple-step income statement derives gross profit, operating income, and net income in successive steps.* It may be presented in condensed form, in

ILLUSTRATION 4.27

WIXON MERCHANDISING COMPANY Income Statement For the Year Ended December 31, 19--		
Revenues		
Net sales	$920,000	
Rent revenue	5,000	$925,000
Expenses		
Cost of goods sold	$644,000	
Salaries	183,200	
Advertising	14,000	
Utilities	11,000	
Depreciation	6,000	
Interest	1,800	860,000
Net Income		$ 65,000

ILLUSTRATION 4.28

WIXON MERCHANDISING COMPANY
Income Statement
For the Year Ended December 31, 19--

Sales			$950,000
Less: Sales discounts		$13,000	
Sales returns and allowances		17,000	30,000
Net sales			$920,000
Cost of goods sold			
Merchandise inventory, Jan. 1			$ 70,000
Purchases		$640,000	
Less: Purchases discounts	$10,000		
Purchases returns and allowances	6,000	16,000	
Net purchases		$624,000	
Plus: Transportation in		25,000	
Delivered cost of net purchases			649,000
Cost of goods available for sale			$719,000
Merchandise inventory, Dec. 31			75,000
Cost of goods sold			644,000
Gross Profit			$276,000
Operating expenses			
Salaries		$183,200	
Advertising		14,000	
Utilities		11,000	
Depreciation		6,000	
Total operating expenses			214,200
Net Operating Income			$ 61,800
Other revenue			
Rent		$ 5,000	
Other expense			
Interest		1,800	3,200
Net Income			$ 65,000

OBJECTIVE 1d. Prepare a
multi-step income state-
ment for a merchandising
concern.

considerable detail, or somewhere in between. A multiple-step income statement for Wixon Merchandising Company, which includes a cost of goods sold calculation, is presented in Illustration 4.28.

You can see how cluttered a statement appears when a great deal of detail is shown. The size of the income statement could have been greatly reduced simply by showing the cost of goods sold on one line, with a supporting schedule available to anyone who might be interested in the details. In fact, the multiple-step format can be even further condensed, as Illustration 4.29 on the next page shows.

Presented briefly following the illustration are the items that appear in a condensed multiple-step income statement.

ILLUSTRATION 4.29

WIXON MERCHANDISING COMPANY Income Statement For the Year Ended December 31, 19--		
Net sales		$920,000
Cost of goods sold		644,000
Gross Profit		$276,000
Operating expenses		214,200
Net Operating Income		$ 61,800
Other revenues and expenses		
Rent revenue	$5,000	
Interest expense	1,800	3,200
Net Income		$ 65,000

Net Sales. Sales Discounts and Sales Returns and Allowances are contra accounts to Sales. Therefore, they are subtracted from gross sales to arrive at net sales.

Gross Profit. Merchandisers naturally try to sell goods for more than cost. *Gross profit, sometimes referred to as gross margin, is what remains after cost of goods sold is deducted from net sales.* This is the margin that is available to cover the other expenses for a period and to yield net income, if there is any.

OBJECTIVE 2. Define gross profit (gross margin).

A percentage of gross profit can be determined by dividing gross profit by net sales.

$$\frac{\text{Gross profit}}{\text{Net sales}} = \frac{\$276,000}{\$920,000} = 30\%$$

This tells us that, on the average, 30¢ of each sales dollar is left over after allowing for merchandise costs (70¢ of each sales dollar). A gross profit percentage for one period may be compared to percentages of other periods, or of other concerns, to help evaluate an entity's performance. Gross profit percentages are also helpful in estimating inventories in budgeting, as well as in other business situations.

Operating Expenses. Merchandising concerns incur operating expenses in addition to cost of goods sold. *Operating expenses are the expenses responsible for the generation of revenues from the sales of goods.*

Net Operating Income. Operating expenses are deducted from gross profit to arrive at net operating income. *Net operating income is what is left after both cost of goods sold and operating expenses for a period have been*

ILLUSTRATION 4.30

WIXON MERCHANDISING COMPANY Statement of Owner's Capital For the Year Ended December 31, 19--		
J. Wixon, capital, January 1		$123,000
Net income	$65,000	
Withdrawals	4,000	61,000
J. Wixon, capital, December 31		$184,000

deducted from net sales. For a merchandising firm, it is what has been earned from the normal operations of buying and selling merchandise. Net operating income does not include the effects of nonsales revenues or the effects of expenses or losses not associated with buying and selling activities.

Other Revenues and Expenses. Nonsales revenues and nonoperating expenses are reported toward the bottom of a multiple-step income statement as other revenues and expenses. Included in other revenues are revenue from rentals, interest income, gains on sales of assets other than merchandise, and other miscellaneous revenue items. Under other expenses are interest expense (the cost of using borrowed funds), losses on sales of assets other than merchandise, and other nonoperating expenses and losses.[4]

Net Income. As defined in Chapter 1, net income is the difference between revenues earned for a period of time and the expenses incurred to generate them. A multiple-step income statement identifies different *levels* of income, with the final result labeled as *net* income. Revenues other than sales cannot be included at the top of the statement because they would distort the amount of reported gross profit, which is in effect a gross income earned on sales. Nonoperating expenses cannot be considered until after net operating income is determined.

STATEMENTS OF OWNER'S CAPITAL

A statement of owner's capital is no different for a merchandising concern than for service entities. It simply shows the beginning capital balance, the effects of net income and withdrawals for the year, and the ending capital balance (Illustration 4.30).

---

[4]*Accounting Principles Board Opinions Nos. 9, 15, and 30* and *Financial Accounting Standards Board Statements Nos. 4 and 16* deal with aspects of how unusual and extraordinary gains and losses should be reported in financial statements. In general, where extraordinary items have a material effect, they should be reported separately at the bottom of an income statement. Such items are added to (or deducted from) net income before extraordinary items to arrive at the final net income for the period. *APB Opinion No. 15* also specifies how earnings per share of stock should be reported on the face of an income statement for a corporation.

BALANCE SHEETS

Balance sheets for merchandising concerns are similar to those for service firms. The ending Merchandise Inventory represents a deferred cost and is shown as one of the current assets owned by the entity. A classified balance sheet for Wixon Merchandising Company at December 31 is shown in Illustration 4.31. This statement shows the position of the company at a point in time, December 31. Assets are reported at their cost bases. The costs of depreciable assets are reduced by the amounts of accumulated depreciation to arrive at their net book values.

ILLUSTRATION 4.31

OBJECTIVE 1e. Prepare a classified balance sheet for a merchandising concern.

WIXON MERCHANDISING COMPANY Balance Sheet December 31, 19--			
ASSETS			
Current			
Cash		$ 22,000	
Accounts receivable		100,000	
Merchandise inventory		75,000	$197,000
Noncurrent			
Furniture and fixtures	$40,000		
Less: Accumulated depreciation	22,000	$ 18,000	
Land		10,000	
Building	$80,000		
Less: Accumulated depreciation	28,000	52,000	80,000
Total Assets			$277,000
LIABILITIES			
Current			
Accounts payable		$ 60,000	
Salaries payable		1,200	
Interest payable		1,800	$ 63,000
Noncurrent			
Note payable			30,000
Total Liabilities			$ 93,000
OWNER'S EQUITY			
J. Wixon, capital			184,000
Total Liabilities and Owner's Equity			$277,000

GLOSSARY FOR SECTION 4.C

Gross profit (gross margin)   What remains after cost of goods sold is deducted from net sales.

Multiple-step income statement   An income statement that derives gross profit, operating income, and net income in successive steps.

Net operating income   What is left after both cost of goods sold and operating expenses for a period have been deducted from net sales.

Operating expenses   The expenses that are responsible for the generation of revenues from the sale of goods.

Single-step income statement   An income statement that groups revenues together and expenses together and deducts expenses from revenues in one step to arrive at net income.

SELF-QUIZ ON OBJECTIVES FOR SECTION 4.C
Solutions to Self-Quiz begin on page B-15.

1. **OBJECTIVE 1.** An unadjusted trial balance for the Duxal Company follows, along with adjustments information.

DUXAL COMPANY Unadjusted Trial Balance September 30, 19X5	Debit	Credit
Cash	8,000	
Accounts Receivable	25,000	
Merchandise Inventory	15,000	
Land	11,000	
Building	60,000	
Accumulated Depreciation—Building		22,000
Accounts Payable		12,000
Note Payable (long-term)		20,000
Francine Duxal, Capital		29,000
Francine Duxal, Withdrawals	5,000	
Sales		215,000
Sales Discounts	2,000	
Sales Returns and Allowances	3,000	
Rent Revenue		5,000
Purchases	130,000	
Purchases Discounts		1,000
Purchases Returns and Allowances		2,000
Transportation In	5,000	
Salaries Expense	35,000	
Advertising Expense	3,000	
Utilities Expense	4,000	
	306,000	306,000

Adjustments Data

a) Building depreciation, $2,000.

b) Merchandise inventory, 10/1/X4, $15,000.

c) Merchandise inventory, 9/30/X5, $7,000.

Required

1) Prepare the work sheet.

2) Prepare a multiple-step income statement for the year ended September 30, 19X5.

3) Prepare a classified balance sheet at September 30, 19X5.

4) Prepare adjusting and closing journal entries.

2. **OBJECTIVE 2.** Define the expression gross profit.

DISCUSSION QUESTIONS FOR SECTION 4.C

1. What is a single-step income statement?

2. What are the advantages and disadvantages of multiple-step income statements, as compared to single-step statements?

3. How are each of the following accounting concepts involved in accounting for merchandise transactions?

    a. Cost

    b. Realization

    c. Matching

    d. Time period

4. What is net operating income?

5. Why are sales discounts and sales returns and allowances subtracted from sales on an income statement?

6. Business firms occasionally experience unusual gains or losses during an accounting period. How should a large loss of assets due to fire be reported on the income statement?

EXERCISES FOR SECTION 4.C

4.C.1. Selected data for the Kingsville Company follow. Prepare adjusting entries on December 31 to set up the Cost of Goods Sold account and correct the Inventory account.

Merchandise inventory, January 1	$ 28,000
Purchases	279,000
Purchases returns and allowances	2,300
Purchases discounts	4,100
Freight in	4,800
Sales	580,000
Sales discounts	8,000
Merchandise inventory, December 31	41,000

4.C.2. With the data provided in the previous exercise calculate Kingsville's percentage of gross profit for the year.

4.C.3. A partial income statement follows. The inventory at selling price was $1,300,000 at year-end. Estimate the cost of the ending inventory, assuming that the firm has followed a consistent markup policy.

CLANCY'S DEPARTMENT STORE **Income Statement** **For the Year Ended December 31, 19--**	
Sales	$9,000,000
Cost of goods sold	5,400,000
Gross profit	$3,600,000

PROBLEMS FOR SECTION 4.C
Alternate Problems for this section begin on page D-26.

4.C.4. A partially completed work sheet for Lemeg Stores is presented below. The merchandise inventory at December 31 is $48,000.

		Unadjusted Trial Balance		Adjustments	
A/C #	Account	Dr.	Cr.	Dr.	Cr.
111	Cash	18,000			
112	Accounts Receivable	156,000			
113	Merchandise Inventory	41,000			
121	Furniture and Equipment	30,000			
0121	Accumulated Depreciation—Furn. and Equip.		11,000		b) 3,000
131	Land	15,000			
141	Building	100,000			
0141	Accumulated Depreciation—Building		12,500		b) 2,500
211	Accounts Payable		18,000		
221	Mortgage Payable (10 years)		49,000		
311	W. Lemeg, Capital		116,500		
312	W. Lemeg, Withdrawals	5,000			
411	Sales		995,000		
412	Sales Returns and Allowances	12,000			
413	Rent Revenue		6,000		
511	Purchases	580,000			
512	Purchases Discounts		8,000		
513	Purchases Returns and Allowances		5,000		
514	Transportation In	14,000			
612	Salaries Expense	210,000		a) 4,800	
613	Advertising Expense	21,000			
614	Utilities Expense	16,000			
615	Interest Expense	3,000			
		1,221,000	1,221,000		
212	Salaries Payable				a) 4,800
616	Depreciation Expense			b) 5,500	
611	Cost of Goods Sold				

LEMEG STORES
Work Sheet
For the Year Ended December 31, 19--

Adjustment Explanations:
a) Accrued salaries at year-end.
b) Depreciation for the year.

Required

1) Prepare a completed work sheet for Lemeg Stores.

2) Prepare a multiple-step income statement for Lemeg Stores for the year and a classified balance sheet at December 31.

4.C.5. An unadjusted trial balance for Goldberg Company follows. Adjustments information for the fiscal year ended June 30, 19X5 is also provided.

A/C #	Account	Debit	Credit
	GOLDBERG COMPANY		
	Unadjusted Trial Balance		
	June 30, 19X5		
111	Cash	5,000	
112	Prepaid Insurance	1,200	
113	Accounts Receivable	26,000	
115	Merchandise Inventory (6/30/X4)	42,000	
116	Supplies	1,400	
118	Store Equipment	18,000	
0118	Accumulated Depreciation—Store Equipment		1,200
211	Accounts Payable		6,400
212	Notes Payable (due in 4 years)		24,000
311	M. Goldberg, Capital		37,950
312	M. Goldberg, Withdrawals	15,000	
411	Sales		220,000
412	Sales Returns and Allowances	2,800	
413	Sales Discounts	1,050	
420	Rental Income		2,400
512	Purchases	127,000	
513	Purchases Returns and Allowances		3,400
514	Purchases Discounts		800
515	Transportation In	1,100	
516	General Salaries Expense	20,900	
517	Advertising Expense	1,500	
518	Sales Salaries Expense	26,000	
519	Supplies Expense	–0–	
520	Depreciation Expense	–0–	
521	Rent Expense	7,200	
522	Insurance Expense	–0–	
511	Cost of Goods Sold	–0–	
		296,150	296,150

Adjustments Data

a) Insurance expired during fiscal year, $600.

b) Supplies on hand at June 30, 19X5, $600.

c) Store equipment depreciation for fiscal year, $1,800.

d) Merchandise inventory at June 30, 19X5, $13,000.

Required

1) Prepare a ten-column work sheet for Goldberg for the year ended June 30, 19X5.

2) Prepare a multiple-step income statement for the year ended June 30, 19X5.

3) Prepare a classified balance sheet at June 30, 19X5.

4) Prepare adjusting and closing entries at June 30.

5) Prepare a condensed single-step income statement for the year ended June 30, 19X5, supported by a separate schedule of cost of goods sold.

4.C.6. Accountants use a variety of approaches for accomplishing end-of-period work. One work sheet approach carries all temporary accounts related to purchases directly into the income statement columns of the work sheet. The income statement columns also show the beginning merchandise inventory balance in the debit column and the ending merchandise inventory balance in the credit column.

Required

1) Use the unadjusted trial balance and adjustments data provided in problem 4.C.5 to prepare a work sheet for Goldberg Company that follows the approach just described.

2) Prepare closing entries for Goldberg Company that are consistent with the work sheet approach used for the preceding requirement. (*Hint:* The inventory account will be updated and accounts related to purchases closed, as part of the closing entries. One compound closing entry may be made for all items in the income statement columns.)

4.C.7. Selected account balances are shown below for Travis Discount Stores.

TRAVIS DISCOUNT STORES Selected Account Balances December 31, 19--		
	Debit	**Credit**
Sales		11,000,000
Sales Returns and Allowances	98,000	
Sales Discounts	380,000	
Rental Revenue		100,000
Merchandise Inventory, January 1	1,400,000	
Purchases	6,700,000	
Purchases Returns and Allowances		300,000
Purchases Discounts		410,000
Transportation In	200,000	
Salaries and Wages Expense	1,000,000	
Rent Expense	900,000	
Depreciation Expense	650,000	
Other Expense	500,000	

NOTE: Merchandise inventory, at cost, on December 31 was $950,000.

Required

1) Prepare a single-step income statement for the year.

2) Prepare a multiple-step income statement for the year.

4.C.8. A trial balance for O'Connor Stores follows, along with some additional data.

O'CONNOR STORES Trial Balance December 31, 19--		
	Debit	
Cash	10,000	
Accounts Receivable	85,000	
Merchandise Inventory, January 1	180,000	
Store Fixtures	60,000	
Accumulated Depreciation		8,000
Accounts Payable		88,000
Bank Loan Payable		35,000
M. O'Connor, Capital		105,000
M. O'Connor, Withdrawals	20,000	
Sales		420,000
Purchases	185,000	
Wage Expense	80,000	
Rent Expense	24,000	
Other Expense	12,000	
	656,000	656,000

Additional Data

a) The company uses the periodic inventory method.

b) Merchandise inventory, December 31, was $125,000.

c) Depreciation expense for the year is $6,000.

Required

1) Prepare a ten-column work sheet.

2) Prepare a multiple-step income statement and a balance sheet.

3) Make the adjusting and closing entries.

4.C.9. An operating statement for Telesales Company follows.

TELESALES COMPANY Operating Statement For the Year Ended June 30, 19--		
Sales		$2,000,000
Cost of goods sold		
Beginning inventory	$ 350,000	
Purchases	1,350,000	
Goods available for sale	$1,700,000	
Less: Ending inventory	400,000	1,300,000
Gross Profit		$ 700,000
Operating expenses		
Salaries and wages	$340,000	
Rent	20,000	
Depreciation	8,000	
Insurance	5,000	
Other	30,000	403,000
Net Income		$ 297,000

Required

1) What is the gross profit percentage?

2) What is the cost of goods sold percentage?

3) What was the average markup *on cost*?

4) What is the importance of the gross profit percentage to a merchandiser?

5) Make adjusting entries to set up the Cost of Goods Sold account and update the Inventory account.

SUMMARY OF CHAPTER 4

Merchandising concerns purchase goods and resell them without altering their form in any significant way. Purchases and sales of merchandise are often on credit, and terms frequently provide cash discounts for payment within a specified period of time. Purchases and sales may be accounted for either on a gross basis, which keeps track of discounts taken, or on a net basis, which highlights discounts forfeited. Accounting systems for merchandising concerns also account for returns and allowances related to goods purchased and sold.

End-of-period work sheets for merchandising entities are a bit more complex than those for service concerns, mainly because they must allocate the cost of goods available for sale between cost of goods sold and cost of ending inventory.

Merchandise income statements may be prepared in either a single-step or multiple-step format. Under the multiple-step approach, the cost of goods sold is matched directly with sales to derive a gross profit for the period. Cost of goods sold is the difference between the cost of goods available for sale and ending inventory; cost of goods available for sale is the sum of the beginning inventory and the net delivered cost of goods purchased during the period.

PROBLEMS FOR CHAPTER 4
Alternate Problems for this chapter begin on page D-29.

4.1. Halfsales Company sells merchandise at wholesale prices to retail stores. A post-closing trial balance at February 28, a list of transactions for March, and adjustments information follow.

A/C #	Account	Debit	Credit
	HALFSALES COMPANY **Post-Closing Trial Balance** **February 28, 19– –**		
111	Cash	20,000	
112	Accounts Receivable	85,000	
113	Merchandise Inventory	60,000	
116	Furnishings	48,000	
0116	Accumulated Depreciation—Furnishings		18,000
211	Accounts Payable		35,000
212	Wages Payable		–0–
213	Notes Payable (due in 2 years)		30,000
311	Paul Half, Capital		130,000
312	Paul Half, Withdrawals	–0–	
411	Sales		–0–
412	Sales Discounts	–0–	
413	Sales Returns and Allowances	–0–	
510	Cost of Goods Sold	–0–	
511	Purchases	–0–	
512	Purchases Discounts		–0–
513	Purchases Returns and Allowances		–0–
514	Transportation In	–0–	
611	Wage Expense	–0–	
612	Depreciation Expense	–0–	
613	Rent Expense	–0–	
		213,000	213,000

Transactions

Mar.	1	Purchased merchandise on account, $30,000; terms 2/10, n/30.
	5	Returned defective merchandise costing $500 from purchase of March 1.
	8	Sold merchandise on account, $100,000; terms 2/10, n/30.
	10	Customer returned goods sold on March 8, $1,000.
	16	Received payment for March 8 sale.
	18	Purchased merchandise on account, $40,000; terms 2/10, n/30.
	18	Paid transportation charges on March 18 purchase, $300.
	24	Paid for March 18 purchase.
	26	Paid for March 1 purchase.
	27	Paid March rent, $3,000.
	27	Paid wages through March 27, $12,000.
	30	Received payments on accounts receivable, $25,000. These accounts were not subject to any discounts.

30   Sold merchandise on account, $60,000; terms 2/10, n/30.

31   The proprietor, Paul Half, withdrew $500 for personal use.

Adjustments Data

a) Wages accrued but not paid at March 31, $1,100.

b) Depreciation on furnishings for March, $500.

c) Merchandise inventory at March 31, $18,000.

Required

1) Make journal entries to record the March transactions (begin on journal page 115).

2) Open appropriate ledger accounts with beginning balances, and post the March transactions.

3) Prepare a work sheet for March.

4) Prepare a multiple-step income statement for March.

5) Prepare a classified balance sheet at March 31.

6) Prepare and post adjusting and closing entries at March 31.

4.2. The following information is presented for Moneysaver Sales Company: post-closing trial balance at December 31, a list of transactions for January, and adjustments information at January 31.

	MONEYSAVER SALES COMPANY Post-Closing Trial Balance December 31, 19--		
A/C #	**Account**	**Debit**	**Credit**
11	Cash	13,000	
12	Accounts Receivable	90,000	
13	Merchandise Inventory	20,000	
15	Furniture and Fixtures	64,000	
015	Accumulated Depreciation—Furniture and Fixtures		12,000
21	Accounts Payable		55,000
22	Salaries Payable		–0–
23	Interest Payable		200
24	Loan Payable (due in 3 years)		20,000
31	N. Ravis, Capital		99,800
32	N. Ravis, Withdrawals	–0–	
41	Sales		–0–
42	Sales Discounts	–0–	
43	Sales Returns and Allowances	–0–	
51	Cost of Goods Sold	–0–	
52	Purchases	–0–	
53	Purchases Discounts		–0–
54	Purchases Returns and Allowances		–0–
55	Freight In	–0–	
61	Salary Expense	–0–	
62	Rent Expense	–0–	
63	Depreciation Expense	–0–	
64	Interest Expense	–0–	
		187,000	187,000

Transactions

Jan. 3   Purchased merchandise on account, $10,000; terms 2/10, n/30.

5   Returned damaged merchandise costing $1,000 from purchase of January 3.

10   Paid for January 3 purchase.

13   Sold merchandise on account, $40,000; terms 1/10, n/30.

17   Customer returned goods sold on January 13, $800.

18   Purchased merchandise on account, $30,000; terms 2/10, n/30.

20   Paid freight charges on January 18 purchase, $900.

22   Sold merchandise for cash, $10,000.

25   Customer paid for merchandise sold January 13.

26   Sold merchandise on account, $25,000; terms 1/10, n/30.

27   Paid salaries through January 27, $15,000.

29   Received payment for January 26 sale.

30   Paid $20,000 on accounts payable. These accounts were not subject to any discounts.

30   Paid January rent, $2,800.

30   Paid for January 18 purchase.

31   Cash withdrawn by owner, $1,000.

Adjustments Data

a) Additional interest accrued during January on loan payable, $100.

b) Depreciation for January, $600.

c) Salaries accrued but not paid at January 31, $1,500.

d) Merchandise inventory at January 31, $28,000.

Required

1) Make journal entries to record the January transactions (begin on journal page 69).

2) Open appropriate ledger accounts with beginning balances, and post the January transactions.

3) Prepare a work sheet for January.

4) Prepare a multiple-step income statement for January.

5) Prepare a classified balance sheet at January 31.

6) Prepare and post adjusting and closing entries at January 31.

COMPREHENSION PROBLEMS FOR CHAPTER 4

4.3. On New Year's Day, 19X5, the Flambe Bazaar, a gourmet cooking supply store, burned to the ground. Fortunately, the accounting records had been stored in a fireproof cabinet and the concern carried fire insurance on all its assets. Unfortunately, the year-end physical inventory (for 19X4) had not been taken.

The inventory destroyed must be approximated so that an insurance claim may be filed. An income statement for 19X3 is provided here. Also shown is an income statement for 19X4 with missing data represented by question marks. Pricing policies were the same in 19X4 as they were in 19X3, so that the rate of gross profit should be approximately the same.

THE FLAMBE BAZAAR
Income Statement
For the Year Ended December 31, 19X3

Net sales		$100,000
Cost of goods sold		
Merchandise inventory, 1/1/X3	$20,000	
Net purchases	70,000	
Cost of goods available	$90,000	
Merchandise inventory, 12/31/X3	25,000	
Cost of goods sold		65,000
Gross Profit		$ 35,000
Expenses		20,000
Net Income		$ 15,000

THE FLAMBE BAZAAR
Income Statement
For the Year Ended December 31, 19X4

Net sales		$120,000
Cost of goods sold		
Merchandise inventory, 1/1/X4	$ 25,000	
Net purchases	90,000	
Cost of goods available	$115,000	
Merchandise inventory, 12/31/X4	?	
Cost of goods sold		?
Gross Profit		$?
Expenses		25,000
Net Income		$?

Required

1) Calculate the approximate cost of the inventory that was destroyed by fire.

2) What effects did the fire have on the accounting statements for 19X4? Would you, as an accountant, feel any obligation to inform the users of 19X4 financial statements of the fire and its effects? Why?

3) What effects might the fire have on the 19X5 financial statements?

4.4. At mid-year, the owner of Buymore Store wants to know how much additional merchandise will have to be purchased for the last half of 19X5 if the company is to achieve its sales goal of $500,000 while maintaining the same *rate* of gross profit as 19X4. The income statement for 19X4 and some year-to-date data for 19X5 are provided here. Buymore follows a practice of holding its inventory as level as possible.

BUYMORE STORE Income Statement For the Year Ended December 31, 19X4		
Net sales		$400,000
Cost of goods sold		
Merchandise inventory, 1/1/X4	$ 30,000	
Net purchases	280,000	
Goods available for sale	$310,000	
Merchandise inventory, 12/31/X4	30,000	
Cost of goods sold		280,000
Gross Profit		$120,000
Expenses		80,000
Net Income		$ 40,000

BUYMORE STORE Year-to-Date Data Six Months Ended June 30, 19X5	
Sales	$300,000
Purchases	210,000
Expenses	42,000

Required

1) Calculate the approximate cost of purchases for the remainder of 19X5 if sales goals are to be attained without disturbing the inventory level.

2) Suppose that suppliers increase their prices by 10% during the latter part of 19X5. What action must be taken by Buymore managers if they wish to maintain the same gross profit percentage as in the past?

3) Speculate on the possible reaction of customers to the action you came up with for requirement (2), and on the likely consequences of those reactions for Buymore Store.

4.5. Following are unadjusted and post-closing trial balances for Martin Company.

	Unadjusted		Post-Closing	
MARTIN COMPANY Trial Balances December 31, 19--				
	Debit	*Credit*	*Debit*	*Credit*
Cash	10,000		10,000	
Accounts Receivable	80,000		80,000	
Merchandise Inventory	100,000		120,000	
Unexpired Insurance	2,000		1,500	
Building	400,000		400,000	
Accumulated Depreciation—Building		280,000		300,000
Accounts Payable		75,000		75,000
Unearned Rent Revenue		-0-		1,000
T. Martin, Capital		153,600		235,500
T. Martin, Withdrawals	65,000		-0-	
Sales		800,000		-0-
Rent Revenue		13,000		-0-
Purchases	480,000		-0-	
Purchases Discounts		5,000		-0-
Transportation In	8,000		-0-	
Wage Expense	160,000		-0-	
Insurance Expense	1,600		-0-	
Depreciation Expense	-0-		-0-	
Miscellaneous Expense	20,000		-0-	
	1,326,600	1,326,600	611,500	611,500

Required

1) Prepare adjusting journal entries for Martin Company that are consistent with the foregoing data.

2) Prepare the closing journal entries at December 31 for Martin Company.

CHAPTER 5

Special Journals and Subsidiary Ledgers

Thus far only the general journal has been used for recording all types of transactions. This chapter deals with the use of special journals for recording large numbers of similar transactions and also with the use of detailed subsidiary ledgers controlled by general ledger accounts.

Section A of this chapter outlines the purposes of subsidiary ledgers and special journals before examining the use of special journals for recording sales on account, sales returns and allowances, and cash receipts. Also covered are the techniques for posting from the special journals both to subsidiary customer accounts and to general ledger accounts, and the process by which the subsidiary ledger is reconciled with the Accounts Receivable account in the general ledger.

Section B introduces special journals for recording purchases on account, purchases returns and allowances, and cash payments. Postings from special journals to subsidiary creditor accounts and general ledger accounts are illustrated, as is the reconciliation of subsidiary payables to the Accounts Payable account in the general ledger. Section B closes with a brief discussion of the wide variety of formats and types of subsidiary ledger records actually used.

Throughout this chapter—and for that matter, throughout the remainder of this text—sales and purchases are assumed to be recorded initially at their gross amounts (before cash discounts) unless otherwise indicated. As was pointed out in Chapter 4, recording at net amounts is in some ways superior to recording at gross invoice amounts. However, the predominant approach in practice is to record sales and purchases at gross amounts and to recognize discounts taken whenever payments are made.

SECTION 5.A

Sales and Cash Receipts Journals and the Receivables Ledger

OBJECTIVES

This section concentrates on accounting for sales and cash receipts by means of special journals and on the use of a subsidiary ledger for customers' accounts. At the conclusion of this section, you should be able to

1. State in your own words the purposes of
   a. Subsidiary ledgers.
   b. Special journals.
2. Record transactions in special sales journals and cash receipts journals.
3. Balance and rule sales and cash receipts journals.
4. Post from sales journals and cash receipts journals to
   a. Accounts receivable ledger accounts.
   b. General ledger accounts.
5. Prepare a schedule of customer account balances and make sure the receivables ledger reconciles with the control account.

SUBSIDIARY INFORMATION

An account is a category of information. An accounting system may be designed with a large number of categories or with just a few broad categories, depending on the needs and preferences of the people involved. For example, one company may choose to maintain a separate account for each type of cash that it has (Cash on Hand, Cash in Bank A, Cash in Bank B, and so on), while another firm may include all its cash in one account (Cash on Hand and in Bank).

A firm with just one Cash account must still keep track of the amount of cash on deposit with each bank. One approach is to keep a running record of the balance in a particular bank on check stubs. The check stubs thus provide *subsidiary information* in support of the Cash account. *Subsidiary information is a subcategory of information contained in some larger category.*

It is often impractical to have a separate ledger account for every identifiable category of information. For instance, a large manufacturing corporation may use a great many machines in its production processes. Usually, the costs of all the various machines are grouped in one Machinery account. *Subsidiary* information about each of the machines is then maintained separately.

Subsidiary Ledgers

Subsidiary information is sometimes organized quite formally in a subsidiary ledger. *A **subsidiary ledger** is a group of accounts that represent subdivisions of a general ledger account. The **general ledger** is the main ledger, or controlling ledger, that is maintained for an entity. A general ledger account for which a subsidiary ledger is maintained is referred to as a **control account**.*

Ledgers, subsidiary or general, may be maintained on pages in a book, on punched cards, or on magnetic disks, tapes, or drums. You will learn more about automated information systems later in this text.

Purposes of Subsidiary Ledgers.   Subsidiary ledgers provide detailed information that supplements and supports control accounts in a general ledger. Through the use of subsidiary ledgers, information can be broken down into many detailed accounts while the general ledger is kept to a manageable size.

Subsidiary ledgers are also helpful in dividing up the work that must be done in accounting for large entities. A different employee can be responsible for each subsidiary ledger, and a number of persons can post and maintain accounts at the same time.

Here, then, are the main purposes of subsidiary ledgers.

OBJECTIVE 1a.   State the purposes of subsidiary ledgers.

> 1. To help keep the general ledger to a manageable size
> 2. To help divide work and responsibility among employees so that transactions can be processed efficiently

Accounts Receivable Ledgers

Subsidiary ledgers can be maintained for any general ledger account for which detailed information is needed. In this unit we will concentrate only on the accounts receivable subsidiary ledger.

Business concerns and other entities must keep close track of, and maintain control over, their receivables. Most entities maintain a formal subsidiary ledger for accounts receivable, which is controlled by an Accounts Receivable control account in the general ledger.

The relationship between the control account and the subsidiary ledger can be illustrated by T-accounts as shown in Illustration 5.1.

You can see that the sum of the balances in the subsidiary ledger accounts equals the balance in the general ledger control account. The process by which postings are made to the accounts receivable subsidiary ledger will be illustrated later in this section.

ILLUSTRATION 5.1

GENERAL LEDGER

Accounts Receivable

644.25

ACCOUNTS RECEIVABLE SUBSIDIARY LEDGER

Carl Darwin   Harry Pitts

332.75   180.40

Gerri Jones   Marge Ritz

76.10   55.00

SPECIAL JOURNALS

The only journal we have used so far is the general journal with two amount columns. It is called a *general journal because it can handle all kinds of transactions.* But recording entries in a general journal and posting amounts one by one to ledger accounts is cumbersome when there are a great many transactions to be processed. Therefore, specially designed journals may be used to help process transactions more efficiently. *A special journal is one that has been designed to handle transactions of a particular type.*

Through careful design of special journals, the process of recording transactions can be speeded up. Any number of special journal columns can be provided for collecting changes in accounts frequently debited or credited. An entry may fit on just one journal line, and explanations may be omitted where they are obvious. In this way, both space and time can be saved, and the journalizing effort can be substantially reduced. Where a number of special journals are in use, several people may journalize at the same time. In fact, clerks may specialize in recording certain types of transactions.

The posting process can also be made more efficient. Rather than posting each amount separately, all of the debits (or credits) to a particular account for a period may be totaled and posted as one figure. This saves posting time and keeps ledger accounts uncluttered.

In summary, here are the main purposes of special journals.

1. To help divide journalizing work into segments
2. To improve efficiency by reducing journalizing effort, reducing posting effort, and permitting specialization

OBJECTIVE 1b. State the purposes of special journals.

There are many varieties and designs of special journals. In this section we concentrate on the special journals used for recording sales and cash receipts.

Sales Journals

The main source of revenue for merchandising concerns is the sale of goods to customers. Sales terms vary with different types of merchandisers. Wholesaling concerns usually sell large quantities of merchandise on a credit basis. On the other hand, some retailers deal almost entirely in cash sales, while others sell both on credit and for cash.

Because sales transactions occur so frequently and are so similar, they fit well in journals designed especially for them. Sales transactions fall into two categories—credit sales and cash sales. To keep track of all cash receipts in one place, cash sales are usually recorded in a cash receipts journal, which is discussed later. Credit sales represent a simultaneous increase in Accounts Receivable and Sales revenue. Credit sales are usually recorded in a *sales journal designed especially for recording sales on account.*

When sales taxes are not involved, the debit and credit amounts for each sales transaction are identical, and a sales journal with a single amount column, like the one in Illustration 5.2, may be used. At the end of the month, the amount column may be totaled and then posted to both the Accounts Receivable control account and the Sales account in the general ledger.

Sales Taxes. Many merchandising concerns are required by state and/or local law to collect sales taxes from customers and to remit them to governmental units. *A sales tax is a tax imposed by a government on certain kinds of sales made within the boundaries of the governmental unit (state, county, or city).* Some sales are subject to sales tax while others are not.

ILLUSTRATION 5.2

OBJECTIVE 2. Record transactions in special sales journals.

SALES JOURNAL FOR THE MONTH OF January 19--				PAGE S51
Date	Customer	Invoice Number	Ref.	Amount
Jan. 7	Terse Merchandising Company	5744		500

ILLUSTRATION 5.3

				Accounts Receivable	Sales Tax Payable	Sales
SALES JOURNAL FOR THE MONTH OF March 19--						*PAGE S5*
Date	**Customer**	**Invoice Number**	**Ref.**	*Debit*	*Credit*	*Credit*
Mar. 2	Marge Ritz	301		74.20	4.20	70.00
2	Ralph Royal	302		47.70	2.70	45.00
5	Carl Darwin	303		88.51	5.01	83.50
6	Ruth Motts	304		42.29	2.39	39.90
8	Macho Fong	305		63.60	3.60	60.00
11	Marrie Topps	306		37.52	2.12	35.40
15	Gerri Jones	307		57.24	3.24	54.00
17	Harry Pitts	308		19.08	1.08	18.00
17	Mark Fritz	309		28.62	1.62	27.00
20	Carl Darwin	310		34.45	1.95	32.50
23	Marge Ritz	311		127.20	7.20	120.00
24	Allen Dinger	312		66.57	3.77	62.80
28	Susan Dozer	313		79.82	4.52	75.30
30	Fawn Knight	314		26.24	1.49	24.75
31				793.04	44.89	748.15

OBJECTIVE 3. Balance and rule sales journals.

For example, a state law may exempt medicines and drugs. In this case, a drugstore will collect sales taxes on sales of cosmetics and other items, but not on sales of medicines. The sales journal shown in Illustration 5.3 was designed to accommodate sales taxes.

Sales Journal Entries.   The sales recorded in the sales journal in Illustration 5.3 were all subject to a 6% sales tax. As you can see, the amounts in the Accounts Receivable column include the sales taxes that must be collected from customers. Naturally, the sum of the two credit columns must be equal to the debit column for the journal to be in balance.

The customers' names are needed for purposes of posting to individual customer accounts, as illustrated later in this unit. If credit terms are allowed to customers, they may be shown either in the Customer column or in a special column provided for that purpose. It is not necessary to note the credit terms when all customers are allowed the same terms.

*The process of totaling the columns of a special journal and ensuring that debits and credits are in balance is referred to as **balancing the journal**.*

ILLUSTRATION 5.4

SALES JOURNAL FOR THE MONTH OF <u>March 19--</u>　　　　　　　　　　　　　　*PAGE <u>S5</u>*

Date	Customer	Invoice Number	Ref.	Accounts Receivable *Debit*	Sales Tax Payable *Credit*	Sales *Credit*
Mar. 2	Marge Ritz	301	√	74.20	4.20	70.00

NAME   <u>Marge Ritz</u>
ADDRESS   <u>627 Maple Street, Hibbs, PA 15443</u>

Date	Item	Ref.	Debit	Credit	Balance
19-- Mar. 1 2	Balance	X S5	74.20		55.00 129.20

OBJECTIVE 4a. Post from sales journals to accounts receivable ledger accounts.

At the end of each posting period, the columns are double-ruled, as our example illustrates.

Posting from a Sales Journal to Subsidiary Accounts

Amounts in the Accounts Receivable column must be posted individually to customer accounts in the subsidiary ledger. A check mark is noted in the Reference column as each subsidiary posting is made. The process of posting to a subsidiary account is shown in Illustration 5.4.

Posting from a Sales Journal to General Ledger Accounts

Column totals for a sales journal are posted to the general ledger accounts named in the column headings. Illustration 5.5 shows the posting process. Notice that the general ledger account numbers are put in parentheses at the bottom of the amount columns of the journal.

OBJECTIVE 4b. Post
from sales journals to
general ledger accounts.

ILLUSTRATION 5.5

SALES JOURNAL FOR THE MONTH OF <u>March 19--</u>   PAGE <u>S5</u>

Date	Customer	Invoice Number	Ref.	Accounts Receivable Debit	Sales Tax Payable Credit	Sales Credit
Mar. 2	Marge Ritz	301		74.20	4.20	70.00
30	Fawn Knight	314		26.24	1.49	24.75
31				793.04	44.89	748.15
				(112)	(213)	(411)

Accounts Receivable   ACCOUNT NO. 112

Date	Item	Ref.	Debit	Credit	Balance Debit	Balance Credit
19-- Mar. 1	Balance	X			644.25	
31		S5	793.04		1437.29	

Sales Tax Payable   ACCOUNT NO. 213

Date	Item	Ref.	Debit	Credit	Balance Debit	Balance Credit
19-- Mar. 1	Balance	X				185.50
15		CP6	185.50			-0-
31		S5		44.89		44.89

Sales   ACCOUNT NO. 411

Date	Item	Ref.	Debit	Credit	Balance Debit	Balance Credit
19-- Mar. 31		S5		748.15		748.15

ILLUSTRATION 5.6

SALES RETURNS AND ALLOWANCES JOURNAL FOR <u>March 19--</u> *PAGE SP3*					
			Sales Ret. & Allow.	Sales Tax Payable	Accounts Receivable
Date	**Customer**	**Ref.**	*Debit*	*Debit*	*Credit*
Mar. 7	Carl Darwin	✓	40.00	2.40	42.40

Sales Returns and Allowances Journal

When sales returns and allowances are few, they are usually recorded in the general journal. When sales returns and allowances occur frequently, a special journal like the one in Illustration 5.6 may be used to record them. The entry shown reflects the return of merchandise that was sold for $40, plus a $2.40 sales tax, for a credit to the customer's account. The check mark in the reference column shows that the posting has been made to the customer's account in the subsidiary ledger.

Cash Receipts Journal

For control purposes, *all* cash received should be recorded in a *cash receipts journal, designed especially for recording transactions involving the receipt*

ILLUSTRATION 5.7

OBJECTIVE 2. Record transactions in special cash receipts journals.

CASH RECEIPTS JOURNAL FOR THE MONTH OF <u>March --</u>				
			General	
Date	**Account and Explanation**	**Ref.**	*Debit*	*Credit*
Mar. 29	Brought Forward		50.00	2,000.00
30	Allen Dinger	✓		
30	Cash Sales			
30	Bank Credit Card Sales			
31	J. Darby, Capital	311		1,000.00
31	Mark Fritz	✓		
31	Cash Sales			
31	Bank Credit Card Sales			
31			50.00	3,000.00
			(✓)	(✓)

of cash. This rule helps separate the duties of recording and handling cash and pinpoints the responsibility for properly recording cash. Also, recording all cash receipts in one place makes it easier to compare the bank deposits during a period with the cash receipts shown in the accounting records for that period.

You may recall that cash comes into an entity for a variety of reasons. A merchandising concern may get cash from cash sales, collections on account, borrowings, owner investments, and other sources. As with other special journals, a cash receipts journal is designed with special columns for accounts that are frequently debited or credited. A set of general columns can handle items that occur only infrequently. The cash receipts journal pictured in Illustration 5.7 was designed for a merchandising firm that sells both for cash and on credit, accepts bank credit cards, grants credit to charge customers, and collects sales taxes for payment later to a governmental unit.

Collections on Account. The first entry on March 30 reflects the collection of a charge sale that was recorded on March 24 in the sales journal shown earlier. To illustrate how sales discounts are recorded, we are assuming that this retail firm allows customers a 2% discount for payment within ten days of the invoice date.

Cash Sales. The second entry on March 30 records the cash sales made on that date. The sales taxes collected are recorded as a liability, since they must be paid to a governmental unit at some future date. It is assumed that this company records cash sales at net amounts, without formally recognizing in the accounts any discounts allowed customers for paying immediately. Of course, under some circumstances, cash customers are in a different class

					PAGE CR7
Accounts Receivable	Sales	Sales Tax Payable	Credit Card Expense	Sales Discount	Cash
Credit	*Credit*	*Credit*	*Debit*	*Debit*	*Debit*
790.30	18,534.50	1,112.07	307.54	15.05	22,064.28
66.57				1.33	65.24
	1,002.45	60.15			1,062.60
	418.30	25.10	26.60		416.80
					1,000.00
28.62					28.62
	585.67	35.14			620.81
	345.17	20.71	21.95		343.93
885.49	20,886.09	1,253.17	356.09	16.38	25,602.28
(112)	(411)	(213)	(612)	(412)	(101)

OBJECTIVE 3. **Balance and rule cash receipts journals.**

from credit customers. For instance, an auto parts store may sell only on a cash basis to retail customers, but sell parts on credit (and perhaps for lower prices) to operators of auto repair shops.

Posting from the Cash Receipts Journal

OBJECTIVE 4. Post from cash receipts journals to accounts receivable and general ledger accounts.

Amounts in the Accounts Receivable column must be posted individually to customer accounts in the subsidiary ledger, just as was done for the sales journal earlier. Check marks are noted in the Reference column as postings are made to the subsidiary accounts.

Amounts in the General columns are posted individually to general ledger accounts, and ledger account numbers are noted in the Reference column. For example, the March 31 credit of $1,000 to the owner's capital account was posted individually and referenced to Account No. 311.

Special column totals are posted to the general ledger accounts named in the column headings. The journal page (CR7 in the example) is referenced in the ledger accounts, and account numbers are noted below the column totals in the journal, just as was done for the sales journal. Of course, the general column totals are not posted anywhere, as indicated by the checkmarks under these amounts.

Bank Credit Card Sales.   The third entry on March 30 reflects sales that were made to customers who used their bank credit cards. *A bank credit card is an identification card issued by a financial institution that authorizes sellers to provide goods and services to the cardholder on credit and collect immediately from the institution, which in turn collects from the cardholder.* Credit card receipt forms are prepared in multiple copies that usually bear an impression of the data on the card. The selling concern deposits copies of the credit card receipts in its bank account (much the same as checks) less a discount charge borne by the seller. Thus bank credit card sales are recorded as cash sales. For the March 30 entry, the credit card discount was 6% of the total charges, including sales taxes, and the amount has been debited to a Credit Card Expense account.

A bank credit card should not be confused with a *company credit card, which is an identification card issued by a particular company for use only in buying goods and services on account from that company.*

Investment by Owner.   The first entry on March 31 reflects an additional contribution of capital to the business. Remember, *all* cash that flows into the entity should be recorded in the cash receipts journal.

Balancing the Cash Receipts Journal

The column totals were balanced on page CR6 of the cash receipts journal before being carried forward to page CR7. The journal is balanced at month-

ILLUSTRATION 5.8

					Balance	
		Accounts Receivable			ACCOUNT NO. 112	
Date	Item	Ref.	Debit	Credit	*Debit*	*Credit*
19-- Mar. 1	Balance	X			644.25	
31		S5	793.04		1,437.29	
31		SR3		76.80	1,360.49	
31		CR7		885.49	475.00	

OBJECTIVE 5. **Prepare a schedule of customer account balances and reconcile with the control account.**

RUNT COMPANY
Schedule of Accounts Receivable
March 31, 19--

Carl Darwin	$241.74
Susan Dozer	79.82
Fawn Knight	26.24
Marge Ritz	127.20
Total	$475.00

end by making sure that debit column totals are equivalent to credit column totals, and the monthly totals are double-ruled below the totals as shown.

RECONCILING THE RECEIVABLES LEDGER

A list of customers' accounts and balances, called a *schedule of accounts receivable*, may be prepared at any point in time. Normally, however, a schedule is prepared at the end of each month, at which time the subsidiary ledger is *reconciled* to its control account in the general ledger. *Reconciled means "brought into agreement."* If the totals for the schedule of accounts receivable does not equal the Accounts Receivable account balance, then the error(s) must be located and corrected. The customers' account balances at March 31 in the example in Illustration 5.8 reconcile with the Accounts Receivable balance.

GLOSSARY FOR SECTION 5.A

Balancing a journal   The process of totaling the columns of a special journal and ensuring that the debits and credits are in balance.

Bank credit card   An identification card issued by a financial institution that authorizes sellers to provide goods and services to the cardholder on credit and collect immediately from the institution, which in turn collects from the cardholder.

Cash receipts journal   A journal designed especially for recording transactions involving the receipt of cash.

Company credit card   An identification card issued by a particular company for use only in buying goods and services on account from that company.

Control account   A general ledger account for which a subsidiary ledger is maintained.

General journal   A journal with two amount columns that can handle all kinds of transactions.

General ledger   The main ledger, or controlling ledger, that is maintained for an entity.

Reconcile   To bring into agreement.

Sales journal   A journal designed especially for recording sales on account.

Sales tax   A tax imposed by a government on certain kinds of sales made within the boundaries of the governmental unit.

Special journal   A journal designed to handle transactions of a particular type.

Subsidiary information   A subcategory of information contained in some larger category.

Subsidiary ledger   A group of accounts that represent subdivisions of a general ledger account.

SELF-QUIZ ON OBJECTIVES FOR SECTION 5.A
Solutions to Self-Quiz begin on page B-20.

1. **OBJECTIVE 1.** State in your own words the purposes of subsidiary ledgers and special journals.

2. Provided below and on the following pages are the last three transactions of Nelly Company for September, page 25 of the cash receipts journal and page 16 of the sales journal. Also provided are two general ledger accounts and two accounts from the subsidiary accounts receivable ledger.

Transactions

Sept. 30   Sold merchandise on account to Alan Wahoo for $200 plus 5% sales tax (Invoice No. 1435).

30   Received $150 on account from Archie Ball.

30   Cash sales for September 30 were $6,531.60. Sales taxes of $326.58 were collected from customers and placed in the cash register along with the proceeds from cash sales made on that date.

CASH RECEIPTS JOURNAL FOR THE MONTH OF <u>September 19--</u>   *PAGE CR25*

Date	Accounts & Explanation	Ref.	General Debit	General Credit	Accounts Receivable Credit	Sales Credit	Sales Tax Payable Credit	Cash Debit
Sept. 30	Brought Forward		85.00	1,000.00	16,750.40	45,218.60	2,260.90	65,144.90

SALES JOURNAL FOR THE MONTH OF <u>September 19--</u>   *PAGE S16*

Date	Customer	Invoice Number	Ref.	Accounts Receivable Debit	Sales Tax Payable Credit	Sales Credit
Sept. 30	Brought Forward			18,411.96	876.76	17,535.20

GENERAL LEDGER ACCOUNTS

	Accounts Receivable				*ACCOUNT NO. 114*	Balance	
Date	Item	Ref.	Debit	Credit		Debit	Credit
19-- Sept. 1	Balance	X				8,460.75	

	Sales				*ACCOUNT NO. 411*	Balance	
Date	Item	Ref.	Debit	Credit		Debit	Credit

ACCOUNTS RECEIVABLE LEDGER ACCOUNTS

NAME   Archie Ball

ADDRESS   1436 Tee Street, Tarrytown, NY 10591

Date	Item	Ref.	Debit	Credit	Balance
19-- Sept. 20		S15	150.00		150.00

NAME   Alan Wahoo

ADDRESS   3285 Bee Street, Tarrytown, NY 10591

Date	Item	Ref.	Debit	Credit	Balance
19-- Sept. 1 10	Balance	X CR24		 240.00	240.00 –0–

Required

1) **OBJECTIVE 2.** Record the three transactions in the special journals.

2) **OBJECTIVE 4a.** Post to the accounts receivable subsidiary accounts.

3) **OBJECTIVE 3.** Total the journal columns, and balance and rule the journals.

4) **OBJECTIVE 4b.** Post from the journals to the general ledger accounts provided.

3. **OBJECTIVE 5.** Consider your work for problem 2 and the following T-accounts for Nelly's *remaining* customers whose accounts have balances at September 30. Prepare a schedule of subsidiary account balances, and make sure that the subsidiary ledger reconciles to the control account.

Sheldon Artoo	**Farley Craig**
972.50	1,615.14
Ann Craft	**Jane Franz**
499.00	1,284.12
Ralph Hartle	**Mary Rooney**
3,740.25	1,530.50
Mark Stafford	
330.80	

DISCUSSION QUESTIONS FOR SECTION 5.A

1. What are control accounts and subsidiary ledgers, and how are they related?

2. How can the use of subsidiary ledgers be considered efficient when subsidiary postings duplicate postings to the general ledger?

3. Why should the sum of the individual account balances in a subsidiary ledger be equal to the balance in its control account?

4. Are sales to customers who use bank credit cards recorded by the selling company as cash sales or as credit sales? Why?

5. What kinds of transactions are recorded in a sales journal?

6. What kinds of transactions are recorded in a cash receipts journal?

7. How does the use of a cash receipts journal aid in attaining internal control over cash?

EXERCISES FOR SECTION 5.A

5.A.1. Listed here are selected transactions for the Nulf Corporation.

Transactions

Oct. 2   Received $250 on account from A. Sumers.

2   Cash sales for today were $700. Sales taxes of $42 were collected from customers in addition to the sales proceeds.

3   Borrowed $5,000 from the bank. Signed a note payable due 90 days from today with interest at 12%.

Required

Set up a cash receipts journal, with columns as shown here, and record the foregoing transactions.

Date	Accounts & Explanation	Ref.	General Debit	General Credit	Accounts Receivable Credit	Sales Credit	Sales Tax Payable Credit	Cash Debit

5.A.2. Following are selected transactions for the Flax Company.

Transactions

Jan. 3   Sold merchandise on account to H. Dinger for $500 plus 6% sales tax (Invoice No. 1286).

    4   Sold merchandise on account to B. Gett for $600 plus 6% sales tax (Invoice No. 1287).

    4   Sold merchandise on account to K. Carnal for $100 plus 6% sales tax (Invoice No. 1288).

Required

Set up a sales journal, with columns as shown here, and record the foregoing transactions.

Date	Customer	Invoice Number	Ref.	Accounts Receivable Debit	Sales Tax Payable Credit	Sales Credit

5.A.3. Shown opposite is the last page of the January sales journal for Usmac Company. Also shown are T-accounts representing two general ledger accounts and three customer accounts. Post from the sales journal to the T-accounts, and note the posting references in the sales journal in acceptable form.

WB
26a

SALES JOURNAL FOR THE MONTH OF <u>January 19--</u>			PAGE <u>S3</u>	
Date	**Customer**	**Invoice Number**	**Ref.**	**Amount**
Jan. 29	Brought Forward			87,100
30	Dan Arno	J102	✓	500
30	Mary Bard	J103	✓	450
31	Jeff Carr	J104	✓	80
31				88,130

	Accounts Receivable			103
Jan. 1 Bal.	120,000	Jan. 31	CR3	104,000
	Sales			601
	Dan Arno			
Jan. 1 Bal.	250	Jan. 5	CR1	250
	Mary Bard			
	Jeff Carr			
Jan. 25 S2	40			

PROBLEMS FOR SECTION 5.A
Alternate Problems for this section begin on page D-33.

5.A.4. Serle Appliance Company commenced business on June 20. Following are transactions relating to sales and cash receipts during June.

Transactions

19--

June 20   Mark Serle deposited $40,000 in a checking account for his company.

23   Sold an appliance on account to S. Morris for $400 plus 5% sales tax.

24   Sold an appliance on account to M. Able for $740 plus 5% sales tax.

26   Sold appliances for $1,260 cash, of which $60 represents sales tax.

27   Sold an appliance on account to T. Zallys for $620 plus 5% sales tax.

27   Collected $100 from S. Morris to apply on his account.

29   Sold an appliance on account to B. Calley for $360 plus 5% sales tax.

29   Sold an appliance on account to R. Nellis for $500 plus 5% sales tax.

29   Collected $777 on account from M. Able.

30   Sold an appliance on account to N. Dolby for $380 plus 5% sales tax.

30   Sold appliances for $945 cash, of which $45 represents sales tax.

Required

1) Record the June transactions in sales and cash receipts journals with column headings as indicated below.

SALES JOURNAL FOR THE MONTH OF _____					*PAGE* _____	
				Accounts Receivable	Sales Tax Payable	Sales
Date	Customer	Invoice Number	Ref.	*Debit*	*Credit*	*Credit*

CASH RECEIPTS JOURNAL FOR THE MONTH OF _____							*PAGE* _____
			General		Accounts Receivable	Sales	Sales Tax Payable	Cash
Date	Accounts & Explanation	Ref.	*Debit*	*Credit*	*Credit*	*Credit*	*Credit*	*Debit*

2) Balance and rule the journals.

3) Set up subsidiary ledger accounts for customers, and post appropriate amounts from the journals to the accounts.

4) Set up general ledger accounts for Cash (111), Accounts Receivable (112), Sales Tax Payable (213), Mark Serle, Capital (311), and Sales (411). Make all necessary postings from the journals to the general ledger accounts.

5) Reconcile the customers' ledger to its control account by preparing a schedule of accounts receivable whose total equals the control account balance.

5.A.5. Shown below are page CR13 of the cash receipts journal and page S8 of the sales journal for Nox Company. The beginning balances on March 1 for four general ledger accounts are as follows.

Account #	Account	Balance Debit	Balance Credit
111	Cash	4,200	
112	Accounts Receivable	3,500	
212	Sales Tax Payable		1,230
411	Sales		–0–

Required

1) Set up cash receipts and sales journals like those shown, and balance and rule the journals.

2) Set up four general ledger accounts to reflect the balances indicated, and post from the journals to the four accounts, taking care to properly cross-reference the postings.

CASH RECEIPTS JOURNAL FOR THE MONTH OF March 19--   *PAGE CR13*

Date	Accounts & Explanation	Ref.	General Debit	General Credit	Accounts Receivable Credit	Sales Credit	Sales Tax Payable Credit	Cash Debit
Mar. 31	Brought Forward		400	3,800	8,750	12,100	363	24,613
31	R. Beckwith	✓			800			800

SALES JOURNAL FOR THE MONTH OF March 19--   *PAGE S8*

Date	Customer	Invoice Number	Ref.	Accounts Receivable Debit	Sales Tax Payable Credit	Sales Credit
Mar. 28	Brought Forward			8,652	252	8,400
30	M. Fortz	111	✓	206	6	200
31	J. Fonze	112	✓	412	12	400

5.A.6. Provided below are the last three transactions for May, the May 1 balances for two general ledger accounts and two subsidiary accounts receivable accounts, page CR22 of the cash receipts journal, and page S12 of the sales journal.

Transactions

May 31   Sold merchandise on account to Hugh Howards for $150 plus 4% sales tax (Invoice No. 508).

31   Received $250 on account from Zelda Meeks.

31   Cash sales for today were $3,000. Sales taxes of $120 were collected from customers in addition to the sales proceeds.

Selected Account Balances, May 1

Accounts Receivable (Account No. 112)	$4,100
Sales (Account No. 411)	–0–
Hugh Howards	104
Zelda Meeks	520

Required

1) Set up journal pages like those illustrated and record the three transactions.

2) Set up accounts receivable ledger accounts for Howards and Meeks, and reflect any postings required by the transactions.

3) Total the journal columns, and balance and rule the journals.

4) Set up general ledger accounts for Accounts Receivable and Sales, and post from the journals to those accounts.

CASH RECEIPTS JOURNAL FOR THE MONTH OF May 19--   *PAGE CR22*

Date	Accounts & Explanation	Ref.	General Debit	General Credit	Accounts Receivable Credit	Sales Credit	Sales Tax Payable Credit	Cash Debit
May 30	Brought Forward		300	2,600	4,700	3,650	146	10,796

SALES JOURNAL FOR THE MONTH OF May 19--   *PAGE S12*

Date	Customer	Invoice Number	Ref.	Accounts Receivable Debit	Sales Tax Payable Credit	Sales Credit
May 29	Brought Forward			8,424	324	8,100

SECTION 5.B

Purchases and Cash Payments Journals and the Payables Ledger

OBJECTIVES

This section deals with accounting for purchases and cash payments by means of special journals and with the use of a subsidiary ledger for creditor accounts. When you complete your study, you should be able to

1. Record transactions in
   a. Purchases journals.
   b. Cash payments journals.
2. Balance and rule a cash payments journal.
3. Post from purchases journals and cash payments journals to
   a. Accounts payable ledger accounts.
   b. General ledger accounts.
4. Explain how each of the following helps to provide internal control over cash:
   a. Use of a cash payments journal.
   b. Separating the duties of handling and recording cash.

ACCOUNTS PAYABLE LEDGERS

As stated in the preceding section, a subsidiary ledger may be maintained whenever detailed information in support of a control account is needed. You have seen how a receivables ledger is helpful in keeping track of amounts owed by customers. An accounts payable subsidiary ledger serves a similar purpose in keeping track of amounts owed to creditors.

One entity's receivable is another's payable, so it is not surprising that accounting for payables is somewhat similar to accounting for receivables. The sum of the creditor accounts must equal the Accounts Payable balance, as illustrated by the T-accounts in Illustration 5.9 on the next page.

PURCHASES JOURNALS

The Nature of the Purchases Journal

Most merchandising concerns make frequent purchases of merchandise, which are recorded in a special journal. *A **purchases journal** is specially designed for recording purchases on account.* Purchases for cash are recorded in a **cash payments journal**, *designed specifically for recording cash disbursements.*

ILLUSTRATION 5.9

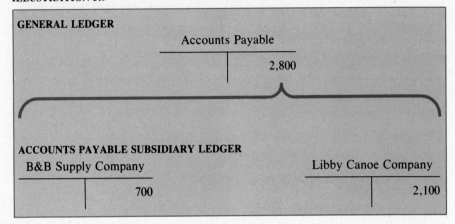

Although a purchases journal may be designed to handle nonmerchandise purchases, most concerns use it only for recording purchases of merchandise for resale. A purchase on account is recorded by debiting Purchases and crediting Accounts Payable for the amount of the purchase. Since the debit and credit amounts are identical, a purchases journal may contain only one amount column. At the end of a month, the total of the month's credit purchases can be posted to both the Purchases and Accounts Payable control accounts, as is demonstrated later. One possible arrangement for a purchases journal appears in Illustration 5.10.

Purchases Journal Entries

In recording a purchase, the creditor's name is needed for posting to the subsidiary account in the accounts payable ledger. The invoice date and credit terms are also needed to ensure that payment is made within the discount period. The purchases journal in Illustration 5.10 also provides a

OBJECTIVE 1a. Record transactions in a purchases journal.

ILLUSTRATION 5.10

PURCHASES JOURNAL FOR THE MONTH OF January 19--						PAGE *P1*
Date	Creditor	P.O. No.	Invoice Date	Terms	Ref.	Amount
Jan. 8	Tallyhoe Suppliers	2562	1/7--	2/10, n/30		500

ILLUSTRATION 5.11

PURCHASES JOURNAL FOR THE MONTH OF <u>January 19--</u>						*PAGE P1*
Date	Creditor	P.O. No.	Invoice Date	Terms	Ref.	Amount
Jan. 8	Tallyhoe Suppliers	2562	1/7/--	2/10, n/30	√	500

NAME <u>Tallyhoe Suppliers</u>					
ADDRESS <u>728 Market Street, Toledo, Ohio 43602</u>					
Date	Item	Ref.	Debit	Credit	Balance
Jan. 8		P1		500	500

OBJECTIVE 3a. Post from the purchases journal to accounts payable ledger accounts.

column for showing the number of the purchase order on which the merchandise was ordered.

Posting to the Accounts Payable Subsidiary Ledger

Entries are posted to subsidiary accounts in the accounts payable ledger at the time they are made, or soon after, to keep creditors' accounts as current as possible. The purchases journal page is referenced in the creditor's account, and a check mark is made in the journal to show that the amount has been posted. When a number of special journals are used, a reference number must also indicate the particular journal from which the posting came. One approach is to indicate purchase journal pages as P1, P2, and so on. Illustration 5.11 shows the process by which the Tallyhoe purchase is posted to the subsidiary account. The check mark is noted in the journal at the time the amount is posted.

Posting to General Ledger Accounts

At month-end the purchases journal is totaled, and the total amount is posted both as a debit to the Purchases account and as a credit to the Accounts Payable control account in the general ledger. The general ledger account numbers are written below the total amounts, as shown in Illustration 5.12 on the next page.

OBJECTIVE 3b. Post from
the purchases journal to
general ledger accounts.

ILLUSTRATION 5.12

PURCHASES JOURNAL FOR THE MONTH OF January 19--   *PAGE P1*

Date	Creditor	P.O. No.	Invoice Date	Terms	Ref.	Amount
Jan. 8	Tallyhoe Suppliers	2562	1/7/--	2/10, n/30	✓	500
10	M&R Corporation	2564	1/9/--	n/30	✓	680
10	Arnold Company	2565	1/8/--	2/10, n/30	✓	300
14	Marvi, Inc.	2563	1/10/--	2/10, n/30	✓	800
15	Lee Merchandising Company	2568	1/14/--	1/10, n/30	✓	200
17	M&R Corporation	2566	1/15/--	n/30	✓	550
17	Tippy Supply Company	2570	1/16/--	n/30	✓	160
20	Tallyhoe Suppliers	2572	1/19/--	2/10, n/30	✓	50
24	Lee Merchandising Company	2567	1/23/--	1/10, n/30	✓	630
25	M&R Corporation	2569	1/23/--	n/30	✓	360
31	Tippy Supply Company	2574	1/30/--	n/30	✓	490
31	Purchases Dr., Accounts Payable Cr.					4,720
						(511) (211)

ACCOUNTS PAYABLE   *ACCOUNT NO. 211*

Date	Item	Ref.	Debit	Credit	Balance Debit	Balance Credit
19-- Jan. 1	Balance	X				2,800
31		PR1	50			2,750
31		P1		4,720		7,470

PURCHASES   *ACCOUNT NO. 511*

Date	Item	Ref.	Debit	Credit	Balance Debit	Balance Credit
19-- Jan. 31		P1	4,720		4,720	

ILLUSTRATION 5.13

PURCHASES RETURNS AND ALLOWANCES JOURNAL FOR January 19--		*PAGE PR1*	
Date	Creditor	Ref.	Amount
Jan. 8	Tallyhoe Suppliers	√	50

PURCHASES RETURNS AND ALLOWANCES

Large firms that frequently return purchases and request allowances may use a special journal for recording purchases returns and allowances. From the special journal in Illustration 5.13, we see that merchandise has been returned that was purchased earlier at a cost of $50.

CASH PAYMENTS JOURNALS

The Nature of the Cash Payments Journal

For control purposes, *all cash payments should be recorded in a special cash payments journal* when such a journal is being used. *A cash payments journal is sometimes called a* **cash disbursements journal** *or, when cash payments are all represented by checks, a* **check register.** Cash is a difficult asset to safeguard, and special care must be taken to prevent its theft or misuse. Funneling all cash payments through one journal makes it easier to keep a close watch on where cash goes and to pinpoint responsibility for recording cash payments.

OBJECTIVE 4a. Explain how the use of a cash payments journal helps to provide internal control over cash.

Ideally, the person responsible for recording cash transactions should not have access to the actual cash that comes and goes. The likelihood of cash being stolen by an employee is reduced by *separating the duties* of handling cash and recording cash transactions. It is true that an employee who handles cash will still have an opportunity to misuse it; but without access to the books, the theft cannot be concealed for long.

OBJECTIVE 4b. Explain how separating the duties of handling and recording cash helps to provide internal control over cash.

Cash Payments Journal Format

As with all special journals, a cash payments journal should be designed to fit the needs of the particular entity in which it is used. Special columns may be provided for any accounts that are frequently debited or credited as part of cash payments entries. The cash payments journal in Illustration 5.14 on the next page has a set of general columns to handle debits and credits that do not fit in the four special columns provided.

ILLUSTRATION 5.14

CASH PAYMENTS JOURNAL FOR THE MONTH OF January 19--									PAGE CP1
				General		Freight In	Accounts Payable	Purchases Discounts	Cash
Date	Accounts and Explanation	Ck. No.	Ref.	Debit	Credit	Debit	Debit	Credit	Credit
Jan. 3 {	Truck		151	8,000					
	Notes Payable—1st Nat. Bank	4755	251		5,000				3,000
4	Farway Truck Lines	4756	—			75			75
6	B&B Supply Co.	4757	√				700	14	686
9	Rent Expense	4758	614	1,500					1,500
9	Advertising Expense	4759	613	160					160
10	Lippy Canoe Co.	4760	√				2,100		2,100
14	Cross Freight Lines	4761	—			110			110
15	Wage Expense	4762	612	1,800					1,800
16	Tallyhoe Suppliers	4763	√				450	9	441
16	Arnold Company	4764	√				300	6	294
19	Marvi, Inc.	4765	√				800	16	784
19	Farway Truck Lines	4766	—			60			60
22	Lee Merchandising	4767	√				200	2	198
25	Utilities Expense	4768	615	410					410
27	Tallyhoe Suppliers	4769	√				50	1	49
31	Wage Expense	4770	612	1,700					1,700
31				13,570	5,000	245	4,600	48	13,367
				(√)	(√)	(514)	(211)	(512)	(111)

OBJECTIVE 1b. Record transactions in a cash payments journal.

OBJECTIVE 2. Balance and rule a cash payments journal.

Cash Payments Journal Entries

As shown in Illustration 5.14, the first entry, on January 3, is unusual in that it requires the use of three journal lines and involves a credit to Notes Payable for the purchase of a truck.

A special column has been provided for recording Freight In, which, for this company, is recorded at the time cash is paid out to transportation firms. The second entry, on January 4, reflects the payment of cash for freight charges on merchandise purchased.

It is general practice to record purchases at gross invoice prices and to recognize discounts taken at the time accounts are paid. For this reason, a special Purchases Discounts column is usually provided in the cash payments journal. You can see from the entry on January 6 how the credit to Purchases Discounts balances the line. Notice how the cash payments journal was balanced and ruled at the bottom of Illustration 5.14.

Posting to Subsidiary and General Ledger Accounts

Amounts in the Accounts Payable column of the cash payments journal are posted individually to suppliers' accounts in the subsidiary ledger. The check marks in the Reference column indicate that the subsidiary accounts have been posted. The amounts in the General columns are posted individually to the general ledger accounts. The account numbers in the Reference column of the journal show that these accounts have been posted (Illustration 5.14). The journal page is also referenced to the postings in the accounts (Illustration 5.15).

OBJECTIVE 3a. Post from the cash payments journal to accounts payable ledger accounts.

As with other special journals, only the totals of columns dedicated to specific accounts are posted to the general ledger. The account numbers in

OBJECTIVE 3b. Post from the cash payments journal to general ledger accounts.

ILLUSTRATION 5.15

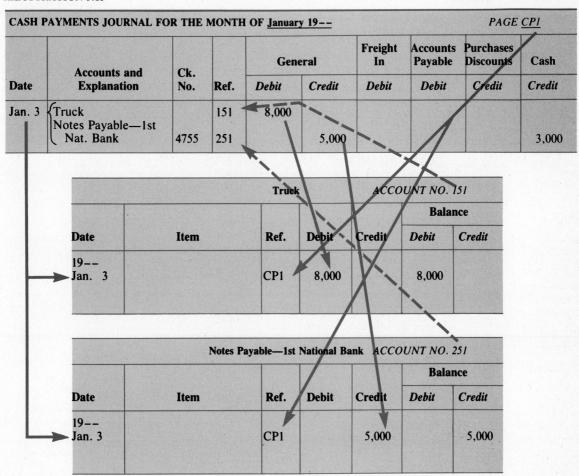

parentheses at the bottom of the columns indicate that the totals were posted to those accounts (Illustration 5.14). The check marks at the bottom of the General columns indicate that those totals are not posted anywhere. As pointed out earlier, the amounts in the General columns are posted individually to the respective accounts involved.

RECONCILING THE PAYABLES LEDGER

An accounts payable subsidiary ledger is reconciled to its control account in a manner similar to that for receivables. A schedule of accounts may be prepared and the total compared to the balance of the Accounts Payable account in the general ledger. Any errors must be located and corrected so that the control account and the subsidiary ledger are in agreement. The creditors' accounts in Illustration 5.16 reconcile to the control account.

OTHER SPECIAL JOURNALS

Special journals of all kinds may be designed to fit the particular needs of an entity. Some smaller concerns use a *combined cash journal in which both cash receipts and cash payments are recorded.* In very small concerns, a *combination journal is sometimes designed to handle all types of transactions.*

ILLUSTRATION 5.16

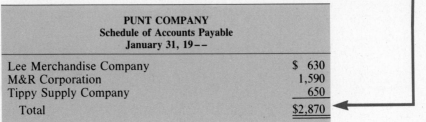

Date	Item	Ref.	Debit	Credit	Balance Debit	Balance Credit
				Accounts Payable		ACCOUNT NO. 211
19--						
Jan. 1	Balance	X				2,800
31		PR1	50			2,750
31		P1		4,720		7,470
31		CP1	4,600			2,870

PUNT COMPANY
Schedule of Accounts Payable
January 31, 19--

Lee Merchandise Company	$ 630
M&R Corporation	1,590
Tippy Supply Company	650
Total	$2,870

A combination journal is a specially designed journal that offers some of the advantages of special journals, such as efficiency in journalizing and posting, but does not facilitate the division of duties and responsibilities among employees.

It is not possible to cover every type of special journal available. But a basic understanding of the nature of special journals will allow you to work with whatever you may encounter.

OTHER SUBSIDIARY RECORDS

Subsidiary payables ledgers are sometimes maintained in the form of unpaid invoices. Copies of unpaid invoices can be filed in a folder by vendor name; then, when they are paid they can be moved to a file of paid invoices. The total of all the unpaid invoices in the folders should equal the Accounts Payable account balance if the records have been maintained correctly.

Of course, the same method can be used for accounts receivable by maintaining files of sales invoices that customers have not paid; the total of all these invoices should equal the balance in the Accounts Receivable control account.

Subsidiary records, other than for receivables and payables, are maintained for many purposes, depending on the individual needs of the particular entity. For example, a company with an automobile fleet might maintain a subsidiary ledger for automobiles. Subsidiary ledgers may be kept to show subcategories of investments, partners' capital balances, sales by categories, manufacturing expenses, or any general ledger account for which detailed information is needed.

GLOSSARY FOR SECTION 5.B

Cash payments journal (cash disbursements journal)   A journal designed specifically for recording cash disbursements.

Check register   A name sometimes used for the cash payments journal when all payments of cash are represented by checks.

Combination journal   A journal specially designed for an entity, but which will handle all types of transactions.

Combined cash journal   A journal specially designed for recording both cash receipts and cash payments.

Purchases journal   A journal specially designed for recording purchases on account.

SELF-QUIZ ON OBJECTIVES FOR SECTION 5.B
Solutions to Self-Quiz begin on page B-22.

1. Provided below and on the page opposite are a company's last two transactions for January, page 2 of the purchases journal, and page 2 of the cash payments journal. Also provided are two general ledger accounts and two accounts from the subsidiary accounts payable ledger.

   Transactions

   Jan. 31 Received merchandise purchased from the Art Supply Company at a cost of $500 (Purchase Order No. 1362). Invoice date January 29; credit terms 2/10, n/30.

   31 Paid Jazzy Corporation invoice dated January 23. The invoice amount is $600, subject to a 2% discount if paid within ten days. Payment was made with Check No. 2832.

PURCHASES JOURNAL FOR THE MONTH OF January 19--						PAGE P2
Date	Creditor	P.O. No.	Invoice Date	Terms	Ref.	Amount
Jan. 30	Brought Forward Varco, Inc.	1361	1/28/--	n/30	√	20,765 620

CASH PAYMENTS JOURNAL FOR THE MONTH OF January 19--									PAGE CP2
		Ck. No.	Ref.	General		Accounts Payable	Purchases Discounts	Cash	
Date	Accounts and Explanation			Debit	Credit	Debit	Credit	Credit	
Jan. 31	Brought Forward Wage Expense	2831	612	6,542 2,400	2,000	18,600	204	22,938 2,400	

GENERAL LEDGER ACCOUNTS

		Accounts Payable		ACCOUNT NO. 211		
					Balance	
Date	Item	Ref.	Debit	Credit	Debit	Credit
19-- Jan. 1	Balance	X				10,400

					Balance	
Date	Item	Ref.	Debit	Credit	*Debit*	*Credit*

Purchases   *ACCOUNT NO. 511*

ACCOUNTS PAYABLE LEDGER ACCOUNTS

NAME   Art Supply Company
ADDRESS   210 First Street, Clarion, PA 16214

Date	Item	Ref.	Debit	Credit	Balance

NAME   Jazzy Corporation
ADDRESS   2114 Fifth Ave., Knox, PA 16232

Date	Item	Ref.	Debit	Credit	Balance
19-- Jan. 23		P1		600	600

Required

1) **OBJECTIVE 1a,b.** Record the two transactions in the special journals.

2) **OBJECTIVE 3a.** Post to the accounts payable subsidiary accounts.

3) **OBJECTIVE 2.** Total the journal columns, and balance and rule the cash payments journal.

4) **OBJECTIVE 3b.** Post the total of the purchases journal column to the general ledger accounts.

5) **OBJECTIVE 3b.** Post the total of the accounts payable column from the cash payments journal to the general ledger accounts.

2. Explain how each of the following helps to provide internal control over cash:

    a. **OBJECTIVE 4a.** Use of a cash payments journal

    b. **OBJECTIVE 4b.** Separating the duties of handling and recording cash

DISCUSSION QUESTIONS FOR SECTION 5.B

1. What kinds of transactions are recorded in a purchases journal?

2. If a company uses a purchases journal, a cash payments journal, and a general journal, where will a transaction involving the purchase of merchandise for cash be recorded?

3. What kinds of transactions are recorded in a cash payments journal?

4. How should an entity decide if a special journal would be useful in its accounting system?

5. Is each of the following statements true or false?

    a. When a cash payments journal is used, only column totals need to be posted.

    b. A purchases journal is used to record purchases of merchandise both for cash and on account.

    c. When a purchases journal has only one amount column, the credit part of the entry must be recorded in the *general* journal.

    d. Special journals should be designed to meet the needs of the particular entity in which they will be used.

    e. The use of special journals increases the amount of posting work.

EXERCISES FOR SECTION 5.B

5.B.1. Record the selected transactions for the Bentool Corporation in a cash payments journal with column headings as shown here.

CASH PAYMENTS JOURNAL FOR THE MONTH OF_____									PAGE ____
Date	Accounts and Explanation	Ck. No.	Ref.	General		Freight In	Accounts Payable	Purchases Discounts	Cash
				Debit	*Credit*	*Debit*	*Debit*	*Credit*	*Credit*

Transactions

19--

July 2   Purchased equipment for cash, $1,200 (Check No. 448).

     5   Paid freight charges to Super Freight Lines on merchandise delivered today, $48 (Check No. 449).

    8   Paid Krackoff Company for merchandise purchased on account on June 30 (Check No. 450). Invoice cost, $1,000; terms 2/10, n/30.

  15   Paid salary to Inez Johnson, $750 (Check No. 451).

5.B.2. Record the selected transactions for the Rockart Company in a purchases journal with headings as shown here.

Transactions

19--

Apr. 8   Received merchandise from the Keper Corporation at a cost of $800 (Purchase Order No. 616). Invoice dated April 5; terms 1/10, n/30.

  12   Received merchandise from the Flimax Company at a cost of $1,000 (Purchase Order No. 598). Invoice dated April 10; terms n/10.

  21   Received merchandise from Hardy, Inc., at a cost of $11,000 (Purchase Order No. 621). Invoice dated April 16; terms 2/10, n/30.

PURCHASES JOURNAL FOR THE MONTH OF_____					*PAGE* ____	
Date	**Creditor**	**P.O. No.**	**Invoice Date**	**Terms**	**Ref.**	**Amount**

5.B.3. Following is the last page of the January purchases journal for Usmac Company. Also shown, on the next page, are T-accounts representing two general ledger accounts and two creditor accounts. Post from the purchases journal to the T-accounts, and note the posting references in the purchases journal in acceptable form.

PURCHASES JOURNAL FOR THE MONTH OF January 19--					*PAGE P3*	
Date	**Creditor**	**P.O. No.**	**Invoice Date**	**Terms**	**Ref.**	**Amount**
Jan. 29	Brought Forward					68,500
30	Danny's Doodad's, Inc.					1,200
31	Jeanie's Clothiers					2,700
31						72,400

		Accounts Payable		201
Jan. 31	CP3	85,000	Jan. 1 Bal.	90,000

	Purchases		701

		Danny's Doodad's, Inc.		
Jan. 15	CP2	4,000	Jan. 5 P1	4,000

	Jeanie's Clothiers	

PROBLEMS FOR SECTION 5.B
Alternate Problems for this section begin on page D-36.

5.B.4. Bolo Parts Company commenced business on May 15. Following are transactions relating to purchases and cash payments during May.

Transactions

May 16   Purchased parts from DM Company for $5,000 on account; terms 2/10, n/30.

16   Purchased parts from JR Company for $2,000 on account; terms 1/10, n/30.

17   Purchased parts from BMX, Inc., for $8,000 on account; terms n/60.

18   Purchased parts from Nilo Company for $800 cash (Check No. 0001).

24   Paid DM Company account incurred on May 16 (Check No. 0002).

24   Paid JR Company account incurred on May 16 (Check No. 0003).

27   Paid employee wages of $700 (Check No. 0004).

28   Purchased parts from JR Company for $3,000; terms 1/10, n/30.

28   M. Bolo, the owner, withdrew $1,000 cash from the business for his personal use (Check No. 0005).

29   Purchased parts from RD Company for $1,800; terms 2/10, n/30.

30   Paid building rent for May, $1,600 (Check No. 0006).

31   Purchased parts from DM Company for $3,600; terms 2/10, n/30.

Required

1) Record the May transactions in purchases and cash payments journals with column headings as shown.

CASH PAYMENTS JOURNAL FOR THE MONTH OF_____								PAGE ____
Date	Accounts and Explanation	Ck. No.	Ref.	**General**		**Accounts Payable**	**Purchases Discounts**	**Cash**
				Debit	*Credit*	*Debit*	*Credit*	*Credit*

PURCHASES JOURNAL FOR THE MONTH OF_____			PAGE ____	
Date	Creditor	Terms	Ref.	Amount

2) Balance and rule the journals.

3) Set up subsidiary ledger accounts for creditors, and post appropriate amounts from the journals to the accounts.

4) Set up general ledger accounts for Cash (111), Accounts Payable (201), M. Bolo, Withdrawals (302), Purchases (501), Purchases Discounts (502), Wages (604), and Building Rent (608). (*Note:* Assume that the owner invested $80,000 in the business, and include that amount in the Cash account on May 15, with a reference to the cash receipts journal page CR1.) Make all necessary postings.

5) Reconcile the creditor ledger to its control account by preparing a schedule of accounts payable whose total equals the control account balance.

5.B.5. Provided below and on the following page are the last three transactions for the month of May, page 18 of the purchases journal, and page 21 of the cash payments journal. Two general ledger accounts and two accounts from the subsidiary accounts payable ledger are also provided on pages 272 and 273.

Transactions

May 31   Paid Hotsy Company invoice dated May 15 (Check No. 3007). The invoice amount is $800, and credit terms are 2/10, n/30.

31   Paid DNA Corporation invoice dated May 22 (Check No. 3008). The invoice amount is $900, and credit terms are 2/10, n/30.

31   Received merchandise from the Hotsy Company at a cost of $600 (Purchase Order No. PO868). Invoice dated May 29; terms 2/10, n/30.

PURCHASES JOURNAL FOR THE MONTH OF May 19--   PAGE *P18*

Date	Creditor	P.O. No.	Invoice Date	Terms	Ref.	Amount
May 31	Brought Forward Barfeo, Inc.	PO867	5/26	1/10, n/30	√	40,500 300

CASH PAYMENTS JOURNAL FOR THE MONTH OF May 19--   PAGE *CP21*

Date	Accounts and Explanation	Ck. No.	Ref.	General Debit	General Credit	Freight In Debit	Accounts Payable Debit	Purchases Discounts Credit	Cash Credit
May 29	Brought Forward Office Supplies	3006	115	7,500 80	3,700	480	31,000	640	34,640 80

GENERAL LEDGER ACCOUNTS

		Accounts Payable			ACCOUNT NO. 211	
Date	Item	Ref.	Debit	Credit	Balance Debit	Balance Credit
19-- May 1	Balance	X				12,400

		Purchases			ACCOUNT NO. 511	
Date	Item	Ref.	Debit	Credit	Balance Debit	Balance Credit

ACCOUNTS PAYABLE LEDGER ACCOUNTS

NAME   DNA Corporation
ADDRESS   111 Fifth Ave., Summerville, PA 15864

Date	Item	Ref.	Debit	Credit	Balance
19-- May 22		P17		900	900

NAME   Hotsy Company
ADDRESS   68407 Telegraph Rd., Thornwood, NY 10590

Date	Item	Ref.	Debit	Credit	Balance
19-- May 15		P16		800	800

Required

1) Set up journals like those shown and record the three transactions.

2) Total the journal columns, and balance and rule the journals.

3) Post from the journals to ledger accounts like those shown, taking care to reference the postings properly.

5.B.6. The last page of a cash payments journal for February is shown here.

CASH PAYMENTS JOURNAL FOR THE MONTH OF <u>February 19--</u>									*PAGE CP28*
				General		Freight In	Accounts Payable	Purchases Discounts	Cash
Date	Accounts and Explanation	Ck. No.	Ref.	*Debit*	*Credit*	*Debit*	*Debit*	*Credit*	*Credit*
Feb. 27 27 28	Brought Forward Meeter Company Equipment Harkwell, Inc.	0133 0134 0135		10,000 4,000	8,040	80	12,000 980 1,200	70 20	13,970 980 1,200

Required

1) Set up a journal like the one shown, and balance and rule the journal. If the journal is not in balance, locate and correct the error(s) by lining through incorrect amounts and writing in the correct amounts. Check stubs show that Check No. 0133 was written for $980; No. 0134 for $4,000; and No. 0135 for $1,200.

2) Set up ledger accounts with balances as indicated, and post from the journal to the accounts.

GENERAL LEDGER ACCOUNTS		
A/C #	Account	Balance 2/1--
111	Cash	$28,000
116	Equipment	40,000
211	Accounts Payable	24,000
513	Purchases Discounts	–0–
514	Freight In	–0–

ACCOUNTS PAYABLE LEDGER ACCOUNTS			
Date	Ref.	Credit	Balance
Harkwell, Inc.			
Feb. 10	P9	$1,200	$1,200
15	P9	860	2,060
Meeter Company			
Feb. 20	P9	$1,000	$1,000

5.B.7. Following is page 8 of the purchases journal for Bagelox Company. Also provided are the balances at March 1 for two general ledger accounts and four accounts from the accounts payable subsidiary ledger.

PURCHASES JOURNAL FOR THE MONTH OF March 19--						PAGE P8
Date	Creditor	P.O. No.	Invoice Date	Terms	Ref.	Amount
Mar. 3	Great Company	611	2/28	n/30		1,500
8	Zebox, Inc.	590	3/6	1/10, n/30		2,000
11	Great Company	613	3/10	n/30		800
12	Aaron Supply	620	3/10	n/30		400
18	Hearfelt, Inc.	610	3/15	2/10, n/30		3,000
25	Zebox, Inc.	621	3/22	1/10, n/30		1,500
25	Great Company	622	3/23	n/30		2,100
30	Great Company	612	3/28	n/30		600
31	Aaron Supply	614	3/30	n/10		1,400
						13,300

GENERAL LEDGER ACCOUNTS		
A/C #	Account	Balance March 1
211	Accounts Payable	$12,500
512	Purchases	–0–

SUBSIDIARY LEDGER ACCOUNTS	
Creditor	Balance March 1
Aaron Supply	$ 900
Great Company	1,300
Hearfelt, Inc.	–0–
Zebox, Inc.	–0–

Required

Set up ledger accounts with balances as shown, and post from the journal to the accounts.

SUMMARY OF CHAPTER 5

The time and effort required for the recording and posting processes may be reduced through the use of specially designed journals. Many entries will fit on one journal line, and only the totals of special columns have to be posted.

An entity that employs a number of clerks in the recording process may use several special journals to help divide the work. Internal control can also be strengthened by having a different person responsible for processing each class of transactions.

A cash receipts journal is used only for recording transactions involving receipts of cash, and only cash payment transactions are recorded in a cash payments journal. Sales on account are recorded in a sales journal, and purchases on credit are recorded in a purchases journal. Transactions that do not fit in any of the special journals are recorded in a general journal.

Subsidiary ledgers provide detailed information in support of control accounts in a general ledger. Subsidiary ledgers help divide work and responsibility and help keep general ledgers to a manageable size.

An accounts receivable subsidiary ledger keeps track of amounts due from a concern's customers; an accounts payable ledger shows how much is due to each creditor. Other subsidiary ledgers may be maintained for any general ledger account for which detailed information is needed.

PROBLEMS FOR CHAPTER 5
Alternate Problems for this chapter begin on page D-40.

5.1. Provided below and on the following page are a company's last six transactions for the month of June, page 18 of the purchases journal, page 24 of the sales journal, page 20 of the cash payments journal, and page 31 of the cash receipts journal. Beginning balances for four general ledger accounts and the June activity so far for four subsidiary accounts are also provided on page 278.

Transactions

June 28   Paid HYZ Company invoice dated June 16 (Check No. 2111). The invoice amount is $1,200, and credit terms are 2/10, n/30.

28   Received $300 on account from George Garbarino.

29   Sold merchandise on account to J. Habla for $600 plus 6% sales tax (Invoice No. 1286).

30   Paid Alky Corporation invoice dated June 25 (Check No. 2112). The invoice amount is $800, and credit terms are 2/10, n/30.

30   Received merchandise from Alky Corporation at a cost of $1,500 (Purchase Order No. PO22). Invoice dated June 28; terms 2/10, n/30.

30   Cash sales for today were $2,300. Sales taxes of $138 were collected from customers and placed in the cash register along with the proceeds from the cash sales.

PURCHASES JOURNAL FOR THE MONTH OF June 19--   *PAGE P18*

Date	Creditor	P.O. No.	Invoice Date	Terms	Ref.	Amount
June 27	Brought Forward Frame Company	PO28	6/25	1/10, n/30	√	38,200 500

SALES JOURNAL FOR THE MONTH OF June 19--   *PAGE S24*

Date	Customer	Invoice Number	Ref.	Accounts Receivable Debit	Sales Tax Payable Credit	Sales Credit
June 28	Brought Forward Hintzen, Inc.	1285	√	42,930 848	2,430 48	40,500 800

CASH PAYMENTS JOURNAL FOR THE MONTH OF June 19--   *PAGE CP20*

Date	Accounts and Explanation	Ck. No.	Ref.	General Debit	General Credit	Freight In Debit	Accounts Payable Debit	Purchases Discounts Credit	Cash Credit
	Brought Forward			6,800	2,600	390	32,600	550	36,640

CASH RECEIPTS JOURNAL FOR THE MONTH OF June 19--   *PAGE CR31*

Date	Accounts and Explanation	Ref.	General Debit	General Credit	Accounts Receivable Credit	Sales Credit	Sales Tax Payable Credit	Cash Debit
	Brought Forward		5,060	3,900	11,900	16,000	840	27,580

GENERAL LEDGER ACCOUNTS			
		June 1 Balance	
A/C #	Title	Debit	Credit
111	Cash	$15,450	
112	Accounts Receivable	8,600	
211	Accounts Payable		$ 5,960
411	Sales		400,000

SUBSIDIARY LEDGER ACCOUNTS				
			Balance	
Date	Name	Ref.	Debit	Credit
Receivables				
June 14	George Garbarino	S23	$300	
—	J. Habla		–0–	
Payables				
June 25	Alky Corporation	P17		$ 800
June 16	HYZ Company	P17		1,200

Required

1) Set up journal pages with brought forward and entry amounts like those illustrated, and record the six transactions.

2) Total, balance, and rule the journals.

3) Set up the four general ledger accounts and four subsidiary accounts, and post to them from the journals.

5.2. Case Company accounts on a monthly accounting cycle. Provided below and on the following pages are the last six transactions for April, the last pages of the four special journals used by Case, a post-closing trial balance at March 31, lists of receivable and payable account balances as of April 26, general ledger accounts to which postings were made during April, and adjustments information for April.

Transactions

Apr. 27   Sold merchandise on account to B. Quano for $400 plus 6% sales tax (Invoice No. 2186).

  28   Paid Alex Company invoice dated April 20 (Check No. 412). The invoice amount is $2,000, and credit terms are 1/10, n/30.

28   Received merchandise from Ace Wholesale Company at a cost of $3,000 (Purchase Order No. PO71). Invoice dated April 26; terms 2/10, n/30.

29   Cash sales for today were $1,800. Sales taxes of $108 were collected from customers and placed in the cash register along with the proceeds from cash sales.

30   Received $424 on account from B. Quano.

30   Paid wages for the period April 16 through April 30, $4,500 (Check No. 413).

PURCHASES JOURNAL FOR THE MONTH OF April 19––   *PAGE P20*

Date	Creditor	P.O. No.	Invoice Date	Terms	Ref.	Amount
	Brought Forward					23,800

SALES JOURNAL FOR THE MONTH OF April 19––   *PAGE S22*

Date	Customer	Invoice Number	Ref.	Accounts Receivable *Debit*	Sales Tax Payable *Credit*	Sales *Credit*
	Brought Forward			47,700	2,700	45,000

CASH PAYMENTS JOURNAL FOR THE MONTH OF April 19––   *PAGE CP12*

Date	Accounts and Explanation	Ck. No.	Ref.	General *Debit*	General *Credit*	Freight In *Debit*	Accounts Payable *Debit*	Purchases Discounts *Credit*	Cash *Credit*
	Brought Forward			9,500	1,400	700	21,100	450	29,450

CASH RECEIPTS JOURNAL FOR THE MONTH OF April 19––   *PAGE CR16*

Date	Accounts and Explanation	Ref.	General *Debit*	General *Credit*	Accounts Receivable *Credit*	Sales *Credit*	Sales Tax Payable *Credit*	Cash *Debit*
	Brought Forward		–0–	–0–	21,600	8,200	492	30,292

A/C #	Account	Debit	Credit
	CASE COMPANY **Post-Closing Trial Balance** **March 31, 19--**		
111	Cash	6,100	
112	Accounts Receivable	26,350	
113	Merchandise Inventory	42,000	
116	Equipment	11,000	
0116	Accumulated Depreciation—Equipment		4,000
211	Accounts Payable		27,000
212	Sales Tax Payable		200
215	Bank Loan Payable (due in 3 years)		10,000
216	Interest Payable		250
311	S. Case, Capital		44,000
312	S. Case, Withdrawals	–0–	
411	Sales		–0–
511	Purchases	–0–	
512	Freight In	–0–	
513	Purchases Discounts		–0–
611	Cost of Goods Sold	–0–	
612	Wage Expense	–0–	
613	Rent Expense	–0–	
614	Advertising Expense	–0–	
615	Utilities Expense	–0–	
616	Depreciation Expense	–0–	
617	Interest Expense	–0–	
		85,450	85,450

CASE COMPANY **Schedule of Accounts Receivable** **April 26, 19--**		**CASE COMPANY** **Schedule of Accounts Payable** **April 26, 19--**	
P. Baker	$10,700	Ace Wholesale	$ –0–
R. Cone	972	Alex Company	2,000
N. Early	18,650	Paul Company	14,040
A. Grady	1,100	Raul Company	11,200
M. Jarvy	13,800	Sauls Company	1,610
B. Miles	5,220	Vale Company	850
B. Quano	–0–	Total	$29,700
T. Tully	2,008		
Total	$52,450		

GENERAL LEDGER ACCOUNTS

						Equipment — ACCOUNT NO. 116

Equipment — ACCOUNT NO. 116

Date	Item	Ref.	Debit	Credit	Balance Debit	Balance Credit
19-- Apr. 1	Balance	X			11,000	
1		CP9	1,000		12,000	

Bank Loan Payable — ACCOUNT NO. 215

Date	Item	Ref.	Debit	Credit	Balance Debit	Balance Credit
19-- Apr. 1	Balance	X				10,000
1		CP9		1,400		11,400

Wage Expense — ACCOUNT NO. 612

Date	Item	Ref.	Debit	Credit	Balance Debit	Balance Credit
19-- Apr. 15		CP10	4,600		4,600	

Rent Expense — ACCOUNT NO. 613

Date	Item	Ref.	Debit	Credit	Balance Debit	Balance Credit
19-- Apr. 26		CP11	2,900		2,900	

Advertising Expense — ACCOUNT NO. 614

Date	Item	Ref.	Debit	Credit	Balance Debit	Balance Credit
19-- Apr. 19		CP10	550		550	

| | | | | | Balance | |
Date	Item	Ref.	Debit	Credit	Debit	Credit
19-- Apr. 25		CP11	450		450	

Utilities Expense *ACCOUNT NO. 615*

Adjustments Data

a) Depreciation expense (equipment) for April, $100.

b) Interest expense accrued but not paid during April, $114.

c) Merchandise inventory at April 30, $31,500.

Required

1) Set up journal pages like those illustrated and record the six transactions.

2) Total the journal columns, and balance and rule the journals.

3) Set up general ledger accounts for the accounts included on the post-closing trial balance of March 31. Include appropriate balances, as shown on the trial balance, and the additional postings shown in the ledger accounts illustrated.

4) Set up an accounts receivable ledger account for B. Quano and accounts payable ledger accounts for Ace Wholesale and Alex Company. Reflect a $2,000 purchase of April 20, referenced as P19, in the Alex Company account.

5) Post from the journals to the general and subsidiary ledger accounts.

6) Prepare a work sheet for the month of April.

7) Prepare schedules of the subsidiary receivable and payable account balances at April 30, and reconcile to the general ledger control accounts.

8) Prepare an income statement for April.

9) Prepare a balance sheet at April 30.

10) Prepare adjusting and closing entries for April on general journal page 8.

11) Post adjusting and closing entries to the ledger accounts.

5.3. Selected general and subsidiary ledger accounts for Daco Company are listed below with their balances at December 1. Also provided is a list of December transactions that involve cash receipts and cash payments.

GENERAL LEDGER ACCOUNTS			
A/C #	Title	Debit	Credit
111	Cash	$ 8,000	
112	Accounts Receivable	12,500	
212	Notes Payable		$6,000

ACCOUNTS RECEIVABLE LEDGER ACCOUNTS		
A/C #	**Account Name**	**Amount**
AR4	G. B. Three	$600
AR12	B. Trout	900

Transactions

19--

Dec. 2   Purchased equipment for cash, $1,400 (Check No. 1107).

     5   Received $600 on account from G. B. Three.

     7   Borrowed $10,000 from the bank by signing a note payable due 90 days from today with interest at 12%.

     8   Paid salary to J. Jenks, $1,200 (Check No. 1108).

   11   Paid Snap & Crackle for merchandise purchased on account on December 3 (Check No. 1109). Invoice cost, $1,500; terms 2/10, n/30.

   13   Cash sales for today were $900. Sales taxes of $45 were collected from customers in addition to the sales proceeds.

   15   Paid freight charges to DGB Trucking on merchandise delivered today, $109 (Check No. 1110).

   16   Purchased merchandise for cash, $210 (Check No. 1111).

   20   Received $400 on account from B. Trout.

   22   Cash sales for today were $840. Sales taxes of $42 were collected from customers in addition to the sales proceeds.

   23   Paid Sundown Suppliers for merchandise purchased on December 5 (Check No. 1112). Invoice cost, $1,200; terms 1/10, n/30.

Required

1) Set up a cash payments journal (page 18) and a cash receipts journal (page 20), and record the transactions given for December. (*Note:* Review the transactions to determine the special columns you want to include in the journals.)

2) Balance and rule the journals.

3) Set up the three general ledger accounts and two customer accounts to reflect the December 1 balances provided, and post to the accounts from the journals.

COMPREHENSION PROBLEM FOR CHAPTER 5

5.4. John Parks, D.M.D., is starting his own dental practice. He expects to employ one dental assistant and another employee who will act as a receptionist, bookkeeper, file clerk, and typist. John anticipates that about half his patients will pay in cash and the other half will ask to be billed on account. The two employees will be paid on a monthly basis. There will be frequent charges from dental laboratories for such things as false teeth and inlays, and some of these charges will have to be paid in cash. In addition to the lab charges and wages, John expects that there will be periodic charges for office rent, utilities, and supplies.

John will have to purchase some expensive equipment initially, the cost of which will be spread over the expected useful life of the equipment. To help purchase the equipment, a local bank has agreed to lend John a substantial sum of money, which is to be repaid in monthly installments plus interest.

John expects to withdraw money for his personal use once each month.

John has come to you for help in setting up an accounting system for his practice. Once the system is established, the bookkeeper will make routine entries, but you will be responsible for posting, making adjustments, and preparing statements on a monthly basis.

Required

1) Set up a chart of accounts, showing account numbers and titles.

2) Design a combination journal in which the bookkeeper will be able to record all entries, but which provides special columns for accounts frequently debited or credited.

3) What subsidiary ledgers will be needed for the practice?

4) Briefly outline appropriate posting procedures you would use at the end of each month. Should the subsidiary ledgers be posted more frequently than once each month? Why?

5) What procedures would you suggest to help safeguard the firm's cash from employee thefts?

PART III

ASSETS AND LIABILITIES

ACCOUNTANTS IN THE WORKPLACE

NAME: Ronnie Patterson

AFFILIATION: City of Atlanta

POSITION: Director, Bureau of Accounting
          and Budget Administration

SPECIALIZATION: Municipal Accounting

Ask Ronnie Patterson what he does for the accounting office of the City of Atlanta, and he'll tell you succinctly: "I do what has to be done." Accounting for a city with a population of 425,000 means keeping all systems functioning smoothly. Atlanta has 46 separate funds (within a centralized accounting system), which merge into a general accounting ledger, and the flow of money is immense.

While an undergraduate at Georgia State University, Patterson was employed by Eastern Air Lines. He then went to work for the City of Atlanta and found that job more to his liking. His career progressed through the bureau's data processing, employee benefits, and revenue collection systems. It took him only nine years to become director of the bureau (while picking up B.A. and MBA degrees).

Patterson's office once helped prepare the budget but today mainly administers it. He is accountable to city officials, the general public, and the Municipal Financial Officers' Association code of municipal accounting.

Patterson advises young accountants to learn all they can about management. They should also be well aware, he says, of a current trend to address the dual needs of cash and accrual accounting.

NAME: Virginia B. Robinson

AFFILIATION: General Accounting Office

POSITION: Associate Director, Financial
          Systems Group

SPECIALIZATION: Governmental Accounting

The General Accounting Office, with which Virginia B. Robinson holds a supervisory position is charged with reporting to Congress and agency heads on the integrity of accounting systems used by federal executive branch and District of Columbia agencies. Her office works with agencies to implement proper accounting standards and performs reviews to ensure that they are being followed.

Agencies are required by law to obtain approval of their accounting systems from the GAO. But sometimes, says Robinson, "There will be problems with an agency and Congress will say, 'why don't you pay some attention to this one.'" Alternatively, an agency may ask for guidance or for relief from some rule. For example, explains Robinson, the GAO used to require agencies to capitalize assets that cost $300 or more. Agencies complained that inflation made this standard unrealistic; as a result, the GAO raised it to $1,000.

A graduate of Howard University, Robinson originally "wanted to be an FBI investigator, but in those days that wasn't open to women." She took a job with the Department of Commerce as a cost accountant. Moving to the Navy, back to Commerce, and then to the Department of Energy, Robinson assumed her present position with the GAO in 1981.

Accounting, she says, is a good field for women. They possess "a patience for detail, a willingness to see things through to the end" that, in accounting, goes a long way.

CHAPTER 6
Cash Claims and Debts

Receivables and payables usually represent delays in the transfer of cash from one party to another. Naturally, one entity's receivable is another's payable. Just as naturally, accounting for a receivable is the "mirror image" of accounting for the related payable on the debtor's books.

Chapter 6 consists of two sections. Much of Section A is devoted to problems related to interest-bearing receivables and payables, including the discounting of notes in order to obtain cash. The section begins with a discussion of the nature of receivables and payables and ends with brief remarks on other accruals, contingent liabilities, and classification of receivables and payables.

Section B deals with estimating and accounting for uncollectible receivables. Various approaches for recognizing uncollectible accounts are examined. The section also briefly covers the estimation of sales discounts and sales returns and allowances, and it illustrates possible balance sheet presentations of the various receivables accounts.

SECTION 6.A

Receivables and Payables

OBJECTIVES

This section concentrates on accounting for short-term receivables and payables and the interest charges that relate to them. At the conclusion of the section, you should be able to

1. Calculate:
   a. Interest accrued for a period of time.
   b. Proceeds from discounting a note receivable.

2. Make journal entries to record:
   a. Assumption and payment of a note payable.
   b. Acceptance and collection of a note receivable.
   c. Discounting of a note receivable.
   d. Dishonor of a note receivable.

3. Define in your own words:
   a. Contingent liability.
   b. Discount period.
   c. Discount rate.
   d. Dishonored note.
   e. Maturity value.
   f. Proceeds from discounting.

THE NATURE OF RECEIVABLES AND PAYABLES

An *asset* is a resource, a thing of value, held by an entity. *A receivable is an asset, since it is a right to receive an asset or service in the future.* A receivable most often represents a delay in the receipt of cash. Something is usually given up for a receivable. There is a sacrifice of goods, services, or cash in return for the right to receive something in the future.

One party's receivable is always another party's payable. *A payable is a promise to provide an asset or service in the future* and is therefore a liability of the party that owes the money. *A person who owes a payable is often referred to as a debtor,* while the *one to whom a debt is owed is known as a creditor.* The relationship between the parties might be diagramed as shown in Illustration 6.1.

Our economy depends heavily on the use of *debt*, which is in effect a substitute for money. A consumer may buy goods on account from a retailer who owes a wholesaler who is in debt to the manufacturer that owes its suppliers, and so on. Each entity buys inventories and other resources on account, converts them to receivables through sales, and eventually collects

ILLUSTRATION 6.1

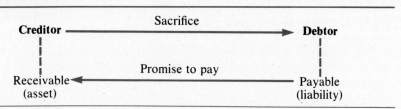

cash that is used, at least in part, to pay creditors. Although Illustration 6.2 is oversimplified in that it ignores profits, owners' withdrawals, and other matters, it nevertheless gives some idea of the way the receipts and payments of cash are delayed by debt.

Debt is often referred to as *credit,* which should not be confused with the credit rules for reflecting transactions into accounts. The lender (creditor) actually *debits* a receivable account to show an increase. However, the borrower (debtor) *credits* a payable account for the liability assumed. A loan of $1,000 cash would be reflected in the journals of the lender and borrower as follows.

LENDER			BORROWER		
Loan Receivable	1,000		Cash	1,000	
Cash		1,000	Loan Payable		1,000

You can see how the borrower's entry mirrors the lender's entry.

TRADE RECEIVABLES AND PAYABLES

Receivables arising as a result of sales of merchandise or services in the ordinary course of business are sometimes referred to as **trade receivables,** whereas *amounts owed for the purchase of goods for resale are known as* **trade payables.** Most entities keep trade receivables and payables separated (in separate accounts) from other types of receivables and payables.

ILLUSTRATION 6.2

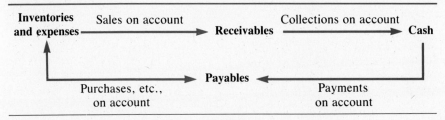

Accounts Receivable and Payable

All receivables are based on legal agreements (contracts) between two or more parties. These agreements may be either oral or written. *Trade receivables based on oral or informally written orders are known as **accounts receivable**, and amounts owed for the purchase of goods for resale are called **accounts payable**. A claim to cash that is supported by a formal written promise to pay, signed by the debtor, is referred to as a **note receivable**. From the debtor's viewpoint the obligation is a **note payable**.*

Remember, one party's receivable is another's payable. A buyer may order goods or services from a supplier by phone or in writing. But no entry is required until goods are sold or services performed, in accordance with the *realization concept* introduced in Chapter 2. The point at which goods are considered sold may depend on the f.o.b. terms. At any rate, a sale (and purchase) of goods on credit for $2,000 is reflected in the seller's and buyer's journals as follows.

SELLER			BUYER		
Accounts Receivable	2,000		Purchases	2,000	
Sales		2,000	Accounts Payable		2,000

When the buyer pays the account, both the receivable and the payable are canceled. The end result is that the sale brings in cash, and the purchase requires the payment of cash, as suggested by the entries in Illustration 6.3.

Notes Receivable and Payable

*When a written agreement to pay cash is signed by the debtor, it is called a **promissory note**. The debtor who signs a note is called the **maker**, and a creditor named in the note is known as the **payee**.*

ILLUSTRATION 6.3

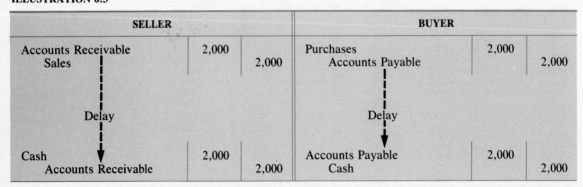

SELLER			BUYER		
Accounts Receivable	2,000		Purchases	2,000	
Sales		2,000	Accounts Payable		2,000
Delay			Delay		
Cash	2,000		Accounts Payable	2,000	
Accounts Receivable		2,000	Cash		2,000

ILLUSTRATION 6.4

PROMISSORY NOTE

$8,000.00   June 6   , 19 --

Ninety   days after date   we   promise to pay to the order

of   Creditor Corporation

Eight Thousand and no/100   dollars

Debtor Corporation

Jean Baker, Treasurer

Negotiable Notes. *Notes and other credit documents that meet certain requirements stated in the Uniform Commercial Code are referred to as **negotiable instruments**. A **negotiable promissory note** is "one that is signed by the maker and contains an unconditional promise to pay a sum certain in money, on demand or at a definite time, to the order of the payee or to the bearer (holder) of the note."*[1] The note in Illustration 6.4 meets all the requirements for negotiability.

The payee's right to receive money may be passed on (negotiated) to another party by *endorsement* or, if the note is made payable "to bearer," simply by *delivery*. *An **endorsement** is accomplished when the noteholder signs the back of the note. A party receiving a note by endorsement is referred to as an **endorsee**.* An endorsee may in turn endorse the note to another endorsee, and so on.

Unless the endorsement is *qualified* by writing the words "without recourse" above the endorser's signature, each endorser assumes a contingent liability to pay the noteholder if the maker does not pay. *A **contingent liability** is a possible obligation that will arise only at the occurrence of some uncertain event.* If, for example, the maker of the note fails to pay (defaults) at the due date, the noteholder can call upon any regular (unqualified) endorser to pay the amount due. Of course, an endorser who pays a dishonored note has a legal right to recover the amount paid from the defaulting maker of the note.

OBJECTIVE 3a. Define contingent liability.

The relationships between the parties to a negotiable note are shown in Illustration 6.5 on the next page.

---

[1]Uniform Commercial Code, Article 3, Section 3–104.

ILLUSTRATION 6.5

PARTIES TO A NEGOTIABLE NOTE

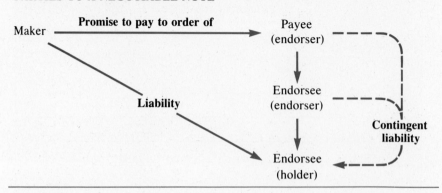

Recording Notes.   Business concerns sometimes borrow cash from financial institutions by giving them notes payable at future dates. Equipment and other long-term assets are sometimes purchased by signing notes payable in installments. More commonly, notes arise in connection with merchandise sales or purchases.

Accounting for a note resulting from a sale is much the same as accounting for accounts receivable. The selling firm debits a Notes Receivable account, and the buying firm credits a Notes Payable account. When the note is paid, the receivable and payable accounts are canceled, as Illustration 6.6 shows.

A note often results when a debtor is unable to pay an account at its due date. The creditor may agree to accept a note because it is excellent evidence in the event that future legal action is necessary to collect what is due, and also because the note may be negotiated (endorsed) to a bank to obtain cash, should the need arise.

ILLUSTRATION 6.6

	CREDITOR (SELLER)			DEBTOR (BUYER)		
June 6	Notes Receivable	8,000		Purchases	8,000	
	Sales		8,000	Notes Payable		8,000
	Delay			Delay		
Sept. 4	Cash	8,000		Notes Payable	8,000	
	Notes Receivable		8,000	Cash		8,000

ILLUSTRATION 6.7

	CREDITOR (SELLER)			DEBTOR (BUYER)		

June 6	Notes Receivable
	    Accounts Receivable
		8,000	8,000	Accounts Payable
				    Notes Payable
					8,000	8,000

Sept. 4	Cash
	    Notes Receivable
		8,000	8,000	Notes Payable
				    Cash
					8,000	8,000

If the note previously illustrated had resulted from the conversion of an account to a note, the conversion and subsequent collection of cash at the note's due date would be accounted for on the books of the parties as shown in Illustration 6.7.

OBJECTIVE 2a. Record assumption and payment of a note payable.

OBJECTIVE 2b. Record acceptance and collection of a note receivable.

ACCRUED INTEREST

Some expenses and revenues *accrue* with the passage of time. As expenses accrue, so do the liabilities to pay for them; the accrual of revenues involves the accrual and recognition of receivables. Interest, rent, property taxes, insurance, and wages are all examples of items that accrue with the passage of time. For the moment let's concentrate on *interest,* which is in effect a rental charge for the use of money.

Interest Rates

Interest is usually stated in terms of an *annual rate.* A rate of 12% per annum means that a borrower must pay (and a lender receive) 12¢ *per year* for each dollar (or $12 for each $100) that is borrowed. Naturally, if the money is used for less than a year, the interest charge should be reduced proportionately. Thus a 12% interest rate amounts to 6% per half-year, and so on, as Illustration 6.8 demonstrates.

ILLUSTRATION 6.8

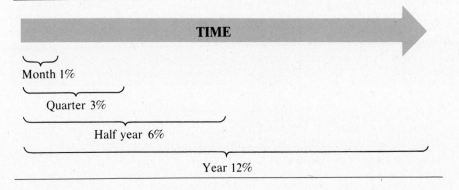

TIME

Month 1%

Quarter 3%

Half year 6%

Year 12%

The Interest Formula

To calculate interest for a period of time, *the amount borrowed, often referred to as the principal,* is multiplied by the interest rate, which is in turn multiplied by the time period.

INTEREST FORMULA

Interest = Principal × Rate × Time

$$I \quad = \quad P \quad \times \quad R \quad \times \quad T$$

When a loan is for less than a year, time is stated as a fraction of the year. For convenience (ease of calculation), the commercial world usually assumes that a year consists of 360 days. However, calculation of interest due to, or from, governmental units is usually based on a 365-day year.

The following calculation computes the interest on $1,000 for 60 days at 12% per annum.

$$P \times R \times T = I$$
$$\$1,000 \times 0.12 \times \frac{60}{360} = \$20$$

Interest on Notes

Notes and other credit instruments frequently provide for an interest charge on the principal amount borrowed. For example, let's assume that Creditor Company has accepted an $8,000, 90-day note as settlement for an overdue account receivable from Debtor Company. The note is dated June 6 and bears 9% per annum interest. In other words, the note is the same as the one pictured earlier in the section except that a line has been added that reads, *"with interest at 9%."* Recall that the entries recording the note were as follows.

		CREDITOR COMPANY			DEBTOR COMPANY		
June 6	Notes Receivable		8,000		Accounts Payable	8,000	
	Accounts Receivable			8,000	Notes Payable		8,000

The due date of the note can be determined by counting 90 days from June 6 on a calendar. The usual rule is to exclude the date of the instrument and include the due date in the term of the note. A similar way to arrive at the due date is as follows.

Days remaining in June (30 − 6)	24
Days in July	31
Days in August	31
Total days through August 31	86
Due Date September	4
Term of note	90

This approach simply plugs in the due date that will total to the term of the note.

The important features of the note held by Creditor Company are as follows.

Date of note	June 6
Term of note	90 days
Due date	September 4
Principal amount	$8,000
Interest rate	9%

The interest on the note may be calculated in the following way.

$$P \quad \times \quad R \quad \times \quad T \quad = \quad I$$
$$\$8,000 \times 0.09 \times \frac{90}{360} = \$180$$

OBJECTIVE 1a. Calculate interest accrued for a period of time.

The entries made by the companies upon payment of the note are as follows.

		CREDITOR COMPANY			DEBTOR COMPANY		
Sept. 4	Cash		8,180		Notes Payable	8,000	
	Notes Receivable			8,000	Interest Expense	180	
	Interest Revenue			180	Cash		8,180

Adjusting Entries for Interest

Interest accrues with the passage of time and is normally recorded at the time it is received (or paid). When the accounting period ends *during* the term of a note, an adjusting entry is necessary to recognize the accrued revenue (or expense) up to the end of the period.

Suppose, for example, that both Creditor Company and Debtor Company account for fiscal years ending on June 30. Each company must recognize the interest accrued between June 6, the date of the note, and June 30—a period of 24 days. The amount of accrued interest is determined in the following way.

$$\$8,000 \times 0.09 \times \frac{24}{360} = \$48$$

The adjusting entries would be as follows.

	CREDITOR COMPANY			DEBTOR COMPANY		
June 30	Interest Receivable	48		Interest Expense	48	
	Interest Revenue		48	Interest Payable		48

Since part of the interest was accrued on June 30, the entries to record payment of the note on September 4 would look like this.

	CREDITOR COMPANY			DEBTOR COMPANY		
Sept. 4	Cash	8,180		Notes Payable	8,000	
	Notes Receivable		8,000	Interest Payable	48	
	Interest Receivable		48	Interest Expense	132	
	Interest Revenue		132	Cash		8,180

Discounting Notes

If a noteholder needs cash, a negotiable note may be endorsed to a financial institution in return for money. The financial institution can then look forward to collecting the maturity value of the note from the maker on the due

OBJECTIVE 3e. Define maturity value.

date of the note. *The maturity value of any credit instrument is the principal amount plus any interest due when the instrument falls due (matures).*

A financial institution will not advance to an endorser the full maturity value of a note, since it will demand some return on the money it is giving up to get the note. *The financial institution's charge for taking a note by endorsement is referred to as the amount of discount.* The amount of discount

OBJECTIVE 3b. Define discount period.

OBJECTIVE 3c. Define discount rate.

OBJECTIVE 3f. Define proceeds from discounting.

depends on *the length of time from the date of discounting until the due date (maturity date) of the note, called the discount period, and the percentage per annum at which the maturity value of a note is discounted, called the discount rate. The amount of cash received by the endorser of a note, called the proceeds from discounting, is the maturity value of the note less the amount of discount charged.*

To illustrate the discounting process, let us assume that Creditor Company discounts Debtor Company's note at the bank on June 24 at a 12% discount rate. Recall that the interest for 90 days at 9% interest comes to $180, and the maturity value is $8,180.

The discount period, during which the bank must wait for payment, is 72 days, determined as follows.

Days remaining in June (30 − 24)		6
Days in July		31
Days in August		31
Due date	September	4
Discount period in days		72

The discount formula is similar to the interest formula.

DISCOUNT FORMULA

Maturity value × Discount rate × Discount period = Amount of discount

$$M \quad \times \quad R_d \quad \times \quad T_d \quad = \quad D$$

And the amount of bank discount in our example is therefore:

$$M \times R_d \times T_d = D$$
$$\$8{,}180 \times 0.12 \times \frac{72}{360} = \$196.32$$

Thus Creditor Company will get cash proceeds from the bank as follows.

Maturity value − Amount of discount = Proceeds from discounting

$$\$8{,}180.00 \quad - \quad \$196.32 \quad = \quad \$7{,}983.68$$

OBJECTIVE 1b. Calculate the proceeds from discounting a note receivable.

No entry is needed on Debtor Company's books, since the note is still payable to someone. After being notified of the endorsement, Debtor Company will simply pay the bank on the due date, instead of paying Creditor Company. Upon discounting the note, the difference between the principal amount of the note and the proceeds from discounting is reflected as interest expense by Creditor Company.

OBJECTIVE 2c. Record discounting of a note receivable.

CREDITOR COMPANY			
June 24	Cash	7,983.68	
	Interest Expense	16.32	
	Notes Receivable		8,000.00

Had cash proceeds been *more* than the principal amount of the note, then Interest Revenue would have been credited. This can happen when the bank discount rate is less than the note interest rate and the note is discounted late in the term of the note.

Illustration 6.9 portrays all elements of the discounting example.

ILLUSTRATION 6.9

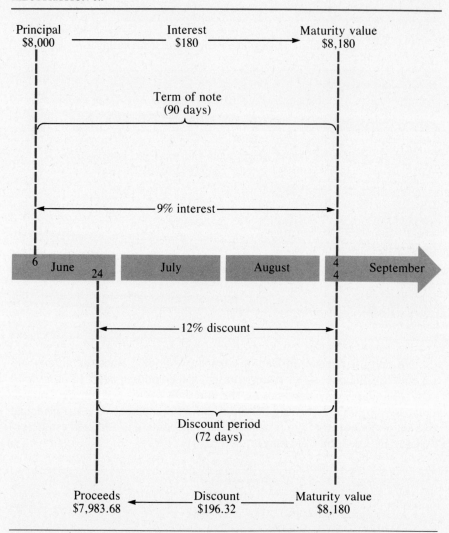

An Alternate Approach

Some accountants argue that where a *contingent liability* exists, the note should not be removed from the endorser's accounts until the maker has paid the note (and therefore canceled the contingent liability). When a note is discounted, these accountants prefer to credit a *contra* account, Notes Receivable—Discounted, for the principal amount of the note. Following this approach, the entry on June 24, recording the receipt of cash by Creditor Company, would have been as shown here.

June	24	Cash	7,983.68	
		Interest Expense	16.32	
		Notes Receivable—Discounted		8,000.00

The asset section of the ledger would then reflect the following picture during the remaining term of the note.

Notes Receivable		Notes Receivable—Discounted	
8,000			8,000

You can see that the Notes Receivable—Discounted account simply offsets Notes Receivable that have been discounted. If a balance sheet were prepared at this point in time, the canceling out would appear as follows.

Notes Receivable	$8,000	
Less: Notes Receivable—Discounted	8,000	$–0–

If the note is paid to the bank at maturity, the entry on each company's books, assuming that Debtor Company has not previously accrued any interest payable, is as follows.

		CREDITOR COMPANY			**DEBTOR COMPANY**		
Sept. 4		Notes Rec.—Discounted	8,000		Notes Payable	8,000	
		Notes Receivable		8,000	Interest Expense	180	
					Cash		8,180

Creditor Company cancels the contra account against Notes Receivable to indicate that there is no longer any contingent liability.

Dishonored Note

OBJECTIVE 3d. Define dishonored note.

A *dishonored note* is a note that the maker failed to pay on its due date. Since a dishonored note is no longer negotiable, the noteholder normally transfers the amount of the note, plus accrued interest, to Accounts Receivable. If, for example, Creditor Company had failed to pay Debtor Company on the note's due date (assuming, of course, that the note had not been discounted), Creditor Company would have made the following entry.

OBJECTIVE 2d. Record dishonor of a note receivable.

CREDITOR COMPANY			
Sept. 4	Accounts Receivable	8,180	
	Notes Receivable		8,000
	Interest Revenue		180

As pointed out earlier, a noteholder may call upon any regular endorser to pay a dishonored note. If, for example, the dishonored note had been discounted at the bank, Creditor Company would most likely have to pay the maturity value of the note to the bank. The entries to reflect such a payment, and to recognize the right to recover the amount from the maker, assuming that Creditor Company had used a contra account to show its contingent liability, would be as follows.

CREDITOR COMPANY			
Sept. 4	Accounts Receivable	8,180	
	Cash		8,180
4	Notes Receivable—Discounted	8,000	
	Notes Receivable		8,000

Interest Versus Discount

In essence, interest and discount charges represent the same thing—rent for the use of money. However, the effects of interest and discount *rates* are different because interest is based on the *amount borrowed,* while discount is based on the *maturity amount* of an obligation.

To illustrate this difference, let us consider two ways of borrowing from a bank by signing a $1,000, one-year note. If the bank charges *interest* of 12% per annum, the borrower will get $1,000 cash and pay back $1,120 (maturity value) at the end of one year.

Note face (principal)	$1,000
Interest (12%, 1 year)	120
Amount due	$1,120

Now, suppose instead that the bank *discounts* the note at 12%. In this case the borrower will receive only $880 in cash, determined as follows.

Note face	$1,000
Less: Discount (12%, 1 year)	120
Proceeds	$ 880

At the end of one year, the borrower will have to pay back only $1,000, the face amount of the note, which is also the maturity value. Yet the borrower had the use of only $880 during the year, for which $120 was paid. By relating the charge to the money available, we can see that the effective *interest* rate is slightly higher than 13.6%.

$$\frac{\$120}{\$880} = \text{about } 13.6\%$$

We can generalize that a discount rate is equivalent to a higher interest rate. Since discount is deducted in advance, the actual amount available to the borrower is the maturity value *less* the discount. The approximate effective interest rate can be derived for any discount rate by dividing the discount rate by 100% less the discount rate.

$$\frac{\text{Discount rate}}{100\% - \text{Discount rate}} = \text{Interest rate}$$

To demonstrate this formula, let us convert a 12% discount rate to its equivalent effective interest rate.

$$\frac{0.12}{1.00 - 0.12} = \frac{0.12}{0.88} = \text{about } 13.6\%$$

OTHER ACCRUALS

Wages, fees, and other payments for human services are usually based on a measure of the time involved. For example, people may be paid for their services by the hour, week, month, or year. Similarly, property rental charges are normally based on the time period during which the property is used. Insurance premiums are also based on time periods.

You have already seen how accrued interest revenue and expense are recorded. One party's accrued revenue is another's accrued expense. The same is true for other kinds of accruals. For example, the recognition of fees accrued at the end of a period increases the creditor's assets and the debtor's liabilities.

CREDITOR			DEBTOR		
Fees Receivable	XXX		Fees Expense	XXX	
Fees Earned		XXX	Fees Payable		XXX

CONTINGENT LIABILITIES

You have seen how an endorser can become contingently liable for a promissory note. Contingent (uncertain) liabilities may also result from lawsuits, product warranties, premium and coupon marketing schemes, and so on. If the possible future event is likely to occur, and if the resulting liability can be reasonably estimated, a contingent liability should be recorded and properly shown in the financial statements.[2] An adjusting entry to recognize the obligation to honor future product warranty claims related to sales of the period would take the following form.

Dec. 31	Product Warranty Expense	XXX	
	Estimated Warranty Liability		XXX
	To recognize estimated future warranty claims related to sales made this year.		

If a contingent liability is highly unlikely to materialize, or if a reasonable estimate is impossible, the contingency will be disclosed to users of financial statements in some manner. One disclosure approach was illustrated earlier in this section, where an offsetting contra account, Notes Receivable—Discounted, is maintained until the due date of a discounted

---

[2]FASB Statement of Financial Accounting Standards No. 5, "Accounting for Contingencies" (Stamford, Conn.: Financial Accounting Standards Board, 1975), par. 8.

note. The contra account then appears as a subtraction from the Notes Receivable balance (which includes discounted notes) on the balance sheet. Another approach is to explain the contingency in a footnote to the financial statements. The accounting doctrine of disclosure is discussed in more detail in Section 12.A of this text.

CLASSIFICATION OF RECEIVABLES AND PAYABLES

Receivables and payables may be classified in various ways, according to the purposes to be served. On most balance sheets, a distinction is made between current and noncurrent assets and liabilities. Short-term receivables—that is, receivables that are collectible within one year—are usually classified as *current;* receivables not collectible within one year are classified as *noncurrent.* Similarly, short-term payables—due within one year—are normally classified as current; longer-term payables as noncurrent.

In this section we have focused on accounting for short-term receivables and payables, which are classified as current assets and liabilities. We must keep in mind, however, that some long-term receivables and payables come due in installments, in which case the amounts that are due within one year should be classified as current.

GLOSSARY FOR SECTION 6.A

Accounts payable   Trade payables based on oral or informally written orders.

Accounts receivable   Trade receivables based on oral or informally written orders.

Amount of discount   A financial institution's charge for taking a note by endorsement.

Contingent liability   A possible obligation that will arise only at the occurrence of some uncertain event.

Creditor   One to whom a debt is owed.

Debtor   One who owes a payable.

Discount period   The period of time between the discount date and the due date of a note.

Discount rate   The percentage per annum at which the maturity value of a note is discounted.

Dishonored note   A note that the maker failed to pay on its due date.

Endorsee   A party who receives a note by endorsement.

Endorsement   A noteholder's signature on the back of a note.

Maker   A debtor who has signed a promissory note.

Maturity value   The principal amount of a credit instrument plus any interest that will be due when the instrument falls due.

Negotiable instruments   Notes and other credit documents that meet certain requirements stated in the *Uniform Commercial Code*.

Negotiable promissory note   A note that is signed by the maker and that contains an unconditional promise to pay a sum certain in money, on demand or at a definite time, to the order of the payee or the bearer of the note.

Note payable   An obligation to pay cash that is supported by a written promise signed by the debtor.

Note receivable   A claim to cash that is supported by a written promise signed by the debtor.

Payable   A promise to provide an asset or service in the future.

Payee   A creditor named in a promissory note as having a right to receive cash from the maker.

Principal   An amount of money borrowed by one party from another.

Proceeds from discounting   The cash received as a result of discounting a note.

Promissory note   A written promise, signed by the debtor, to pay cash.

Property taxes   Taxes based on the amount of assets (properties) owned.

Receivable   A right to receive an asset or service in the future.

Trade payables   Amounts owed for the purchase of goods for resale.

Trade receivables   Receivables arising from the sale of merchandise or services.

SELF-QUIZ ON OBJECTIVES FOR SECTION 6.A
Solutions to Self-Quiz begin on page B-23.

1. **OBJECTIVE 1a, 2a, 2b.** On December 1, 19X4, Darling Company received a 60-day, $4,000 note dated December 1, 19X4, from Blake Company in settlement of an overdue account receivable. The note provides for interest at a 9% per annum rate. Make general journal entries to record the note, the accrual of interest at December 31, 19X4, and the payment of the note on its due date on the books of

   a. Darling Company.

   b. Blake Company.

2. **OBJECTIVE 1b, 2c, 2d.** On June 10, Swift Company received a 90-day, $6,000 note dated June 10 from Dundi Company in settlement of an overdue account receivable. The note bears 12% per annum interest. On July 10, Swift Company discounted the note at the bank at a 9% per annum discount rate, receiving cash for the amount of proceeds. The note was dishonored on its due date, and Swift Company paid the bank the amount of the maturity

value. Record in Swift Company's general journal the acceptance of the note, the proceeds from discounting the note, and the effect of the note's dishonor on its due date.

3. OBJECTIVE 3. Define each expression in your own words:

    a. Contingent liability.

    b. Discount period.

    c. Discount rate.

    d. Dishonored note.

    e. Maturity value.

    f. Proceeds from discounting.

DISCUSSION QUESTIONS FOR SECTION 6.A

1. What is a promissory note?

2. What features must a promissory note possess to be negotiable?

3. How does endorsement of a note affect the payee's right to receive money?

4. Why might a creditor agree to accept a note from a debtor who cannot pay an account at its due date?

5. What are some expenses that tend to accrue with the passage of time?

6. What is the difference between a discount rate and an interest rate?

7. What kind of account is Notes Receivable—Discounted, and how is it used?

EXERCISES FOR SECTION 6.A

6.A.1. For each of the following notes, calculate the amount of interest that will be due at maturity.

	Principal	Interest Rate	Term
a.	$1,000	10%	60 days
b.	$1,100	10%	90 days
c.	$1,000	9%	60 days
d.	$1,000	12%	60 days
e.	$1,000	12%	120 days
f.	$6,979	10%	60 days
g.	$5,000	8%	90 days

6.A.2. Calculate the missing items for the following notes.

	Date Written	Principal	Interest Rate	Days to Maturity	Maturity Date	Maturity Value
a.	July 20	$1,000	12%	60	Sept. 18	_____
b.	Mar. 15	$1,000	9%	___	June 13	_____
c.	Sept. 2	$1,000	12%	___	_____	$1,030
d.	Aug. 13	$1,000	12%	60	_____	_____
e.	Jan. 15	_____	9%	___	Mar. 16	$2,030
f.	_____	$1,000	12%	___	June 30	$1,010
g.	_____	$9,000	___	120	Nov. 30	$9,270

6.A.3. Calculate the proceeds from discounting the following notes receivable.

	Date Written	Principal	Interest Rate	Maturity Date	Date Discounted	Discount Rate
a.	June 30	$10,000	12%	Aug. 29	July 30	12%
b.	June 30	$10,000	12%	Aug. 29	July 30	15%
c.	June 30	$10,000	12%	Aug. 29	Aug. 14	15%

6.A.4. The Fozzie Company accepted a 12%, 60-day, $10,000 note dated July 31 from Greef Corporation in settlement of an overdue account receivable. On August 15 Fozzie Company discounted the note at the bank at a 15% per annum discount rate. Calculate the proceeds to Fozzie Company, and make the general journal entry on August 15 to record discounting of the note.

6.A.5. On June 20 IDM Corporation accepted a 120-day, 18% note (dated June 20) for $9,000 from Skoshi Suppliers in settlement of an overdue account receivable. On August 19 IDM discounted the note at the bank at a 12% per annum discount rate. The note was dishonored on its due date, and IDM paid the bank the amount of the maturity value. Record in IDM's general journal the acceptance of the note, the proceeds from discounting, and the effect of the note's dishonor on its due date.

6.A.6. Calculate the equivalent effective interest rate for a 12% discount rate.

PROBLEMS FOR SECTION 6.A
Alternate Problems for this section begin on page D-44.

6.A.7. On July 10 Bimimi Company accepted a 90-day, 12% note (dated July 10) for $10,000 from CYA Company in settlement of an overdue account receivable. On August 9 Bimimi discounted the note at the bank at a 9% per annum discount rate. The note was paid by CYA on its due date, and Bimimi received notice from the bank of the payment.

Required

1) Make general journal entries to reflect the foregoing events for

   a) Bimimi Company.

   b) CYA Company.

2) Assume instead that the interest rate had been 6% and the discount rate 12%. Make the necessary entries for

   a) Bimimi Company.

   b) CYA Company.

6.A.8. Smorg Company experienced the following events during the year.

a. City real estate taxes of $8,000 for the period July 1, last year, through June 30, this year, were paid on May 25, this year. The city announced that the same taxing rate was expected for the following tax period.

b. On October 2 an $8,000, 15%, 120-day note was received from Antco Corporation. The note was dated October 2.

c. Borrowed $20,000 from the bank on September 2 by signing a 9% per annum note due in 180 days.

Required

Make any adjusting journal entries needed on Smorg's books at December 31. Smorg accounts on a calendar-year basis and records adjusting entries only at year-end.

6.A.9. On November 1, 19X4, Marco Company accepted a $5,000, 90-day, 12% note (dated November 1, 19X4) from J&K Stores in settlement of an overdue account receivable.

Required

1) Make general journal entries for Marco to record the note, the accrual of interest at December 31, 19X4, and the collection of the note on its due date.

2) Make the general journal entries for J&K Stores to record issuance of the note, the accrual of interest at December 31, and payment at the note's due date.

6.A.10. On September 2, 19X4, Horatio Alge, a student at Acme University, borrowed $2,000 from the Acme University Alumni Association. Horatio signed a note promising to repay the $2,000 on December 31, 19X5, plus interest at 6% per annum.

Required

1) Make the adjusting entry at December 31, 19X4, to accrue interest receivable on the Alumni Association's books.

2) Make the entry at December 31, 19X5, to record the collection of Alge's note and interest.

6.A.11. Bark Company sells to customers on credit terms of n/30. Some customers are slow to pay, causing Bark to experience frequent cash shortages. In an attempt to speed up cash inflow, Bark decides to seek 60-day, 9% notes from customers whose accounts become overdue. If necessary, Bark may then discount the notes with a local bank. Selected transactions experienced by Bark Company are provided below.

Transactions

July 1   Sold merchandise on account to Able Company, $3,000.

3   Required Baker Company to sign a 60-day, 9% note to cover an overdue account receivable for $4,000.

5   Discounted Baker Company's note with the bank at a 12% discount rate.

12   Received $2,030 from Charlie Company in settlement of a $2,000 note plus interest.

20   Notification received from the bank that Delta Company defaulted on a $4,000 discounted note with a maturity value of $4,060.

22   Collected from Delta the $4,060 due on the dishonored note.

31   Required Able Company to sign a 60-day, 9% note for the balance due from the July 1 sale.

Required

Make general journal entries to record the foregoing transactions.

SECTION 6.B

Uncollectible Receivables

OBJECTIVES

This section examines the various aspects of accounting for uncollectible receivables. At the conclusion of your study, you should be able to

1. Write off uncollectible receivables by
   a. The direct write-off approach.
   b. The allowance approach.
2. Record the collection of receivables that were previously written off as uncollectible by
   a. The direct write-off approach.
   b. The allowance approach.
3. Determine the needed adjustment for and prepare an adjusting entry under the
   a. Percentage of revenue method.
   b. Percentage of receivables balance method.
   c. Aging schedule method.
4. State in your own words why the use of an aging schedule is superior to other approaches for estimating uncollectibles.

CREDIT RISK

Every entity that has receivables bears some credit risk. *Credit risk is the likelihood that some receivables will never be collected.* Some debtors are unable to pay their debts because of financial hardships; others may simply be unwilling to pay what they owe.

Credit risk can be avoided by refusing to accept receivables—by dealing only on a cash basis, as do some retail stores. However, many business concerns must grant credit because their competitors do. And others grant credit in the belief that their revenues will be greater than the related costs, which will in turn result in a larger net income.

Some accountants contend that uncollectible receivables are *expenses*, voluntarily assumed by entities that accept receivables. Expenses, you may recall, are costs that expire in the process of generating revenues. Other accountants argue that uncollectible accounts are not expenses, but rather asset losses. *A loss is a cost expiration (asset sacrifice) that is involuntarily borne and does not help to produce any revenue.*

You may decide for yourself whether bad accounts are expenses or losses. In either case, the effects of uncollectible accounts have to be recognized sooner or later, and when they are, revenues of some period will be reduced.

DIRECT WRITE-OFF APPROACH

Uncollectible Accounts

The simplest way to account for an uncollectible receivable is to recognize it as an expense (or loss) during the period in which it is proved to be bad. The following entry writes off J. Dirsmith's account on November 5, when it was judged uncollectible. The credit part of the entry is posted both to the Accounts Receivable control account and to Dirsmith's account in the subsidiary ledger.

OBJECTIVE 1a. Write off uncollectible receivables by the direct write-off approach.

Nov. 5	Uncollectible Accounts Expense	500	
	Accounts Receivable—J. Dirsmith		500
	To write off an uncollectible account.		

This approach is sometimes referred to as the *direct write-off of an account, since the expense is recognized in the accounting period when the account is written off.* No attempt is made to identify the amount with the period in which the revenue was recognized, which violates the *matching concept.* Also, the Accounts Receivable amount on a balance sheet will be overstated by any uncollectible accounts to be written off in future periods.

Recovery of Written-Off Accounts

Sometimes an account that has been written off is later discovered to be collectible after all. Perhaps there has been an improvement in the debtor's financial status, or perhaps just a change of mind.

The usual approach for recording recoveries of accounts that were written off is first to reinstate the receivable account, to show that it was good after all, and then to record its collection. For example, if J. Dirsmith were to unexpectedly pay his account in December, the previously recognized expense would be canceled as the receivable is reinstated, as illustrated here, assuming use of the direct write-off approach.

OBJECTIVE 2a. Record the collection of receivables that were previously written off as uncollectible by the direct write-off approach.

Dec. 20	Accounts Receivable—J. Dirsmith	500	
	Uncollectible Accounts Expense		500
	To reinstate an account previously written off.		
20	Cash	500	
	Accounts Receivable—J. Dirsmith		500
	Collection of an account.		

ALLOWANCE FOR DOUBTFUL ACCOUNTS

Matching Write-Offs with Revenues

Under the *matching concept* of accounting, we attempt to match costs with the revenues they help to generate. Whether bad accounts are viewed as expenses or losses, they should be identified with the revenues that were recorded at the time the receivables arose. If uncollectibles are viewed as expenses, they should be matched with the sales or service revenues of the accounting period in which the receivables were recorded. If they are viewed as losses, then the receivables were not really valid revenues at the time they were recorded. In other words, although not proved until later, receivables were not collectible at the time they were recorded.

The direct write-off approach will result in matching write-offs with revenues only when accounts are written off in the accounting period when the revenues were recorded. When an account is not identified as bad until a later period, the direct write-off approach will show the Uncollectible Accounts Expense (or Loss) in a period *different* from the one in which the revenue was recorded.

Allowance Approach

In accordance with the matching concept, current accounting practice requires that uncollectibles related to the current period's revenues be *estimated* so as to approximate the Uncollectible Accounts Expense of the period.[3] The usual approach is to establish an Allowance for Doubtful Accounts as a contra account to Accounts Receivable. Other familiar titles for the contra account are Allowance for Bad Debts, Allowance for Uncollectibles, Reserve for Bad Debts, and simply Estimated Uncollectibles. Whatever the title, *the process of estimating uncollectibles is usually referred to as the* **allowance approach for recognizing uncollectibles**.

Let us assume, for example, that a new entity has Accounts Receivable of $80,000 at the end of its first year of operations. A careful review of the credit risks suggests that perhaps $4,000 of the receivables may never be collected. An adjusting entry to set up the allowance account could be made as follows.

	ADJUSTING ENTRY		
19X4			
Dec. 31	Uncollectible Accounts Expense	4,000	
	Allowance for Doubtful Accounts		4,000
	To adjust for estimated uncollectibles.		

---

[3]*FASB Statement No. 5*, par. 22.

An asset contra account represents a reduction in the asset account to which it is related. *The amount remaining after the contra account is offset against the asset account is called the **asset net book value**.* For the example just given, the net book value of Accounts Receivable is $76,000 as depicted by the T-accounts that follow.

Accounts Receivable		Allowance for Doubtful Accounts	
12/31/X4 80,000			12/31/X4 4,000

Note the similarity between Allowance for Doubtful Accounts and Accumulated Depreciation. They are both contra accounts based on approximations, although one is a reduction of a current asset while the other is a reduction of a noncurrent asset.

There is another reason why a contra account is used for estimated uncollectibles. Accounts Receivable is a *control* account in the general ledger, and the balances in the customers' subsidiary accounts must total to the balance of the control account. If part of the control account balance is written off, then something must also be reduced in the subsidiary ledger. But we do not yet know *which* individual accounts receivable will end up uncollectible. If we did, there would be no need for the allowance approach; we would simply use the direct write-off approach and anticipate all bad debts.

Write-Offs to an Allowance Account

When an allowance approach is used, uncollectible accounts are always written off against the allowance. For example, if A. Rogers' account is determined to be uncollectible on January 13, 19X5, then the entry to write off the account is as follows.

OBJECTIVE 1b. Write off uncollectible receivables by the allowance approach.

19X5			
Jan. 13	Allowance for Doubtful Accounts	300	
	Accounts Receivable—A. Rogers		300
	To write off an uncollectible account.		

The accounts would now look like this.

Accounts Receivable				Allowance for Doubtful Accounts			
12/31/X4	80,000	1/13/X5	300	1/13/X5	300	12/31/X4	4,000

Notice the changes in the accounts.

	Before Jan. 13	Jan. 13	After Jan. 13
Accounts Receivable	$80,000	− $300	$79,700
Less: Allowance for			
Doubtful Accounts	4,000	− 300	3,700
Net book value	$76,000		$76,000

You can see that the write-off entry did not change the net book value of Accounts Receivable; it merely changed both accounts by the same amount. Note, however, that the net book value was reduced by the *adjusting* entry of December 31.

Recovery of Written-Off Accounts

As pointed out earlier, an account that has been written off as uncollectible will occasionally be collected at some later date. When this occurs, the customer's account is put back on the books before it is shown to be collected. Under the allowance approach, recoveries are credited back to the allowance account (rather than to the expense account, as is done under the direct write-off approach). For example, if A. Rogers pays his account, the following entries are made.

19X5			
May 10	Accounts Receivable—A. Rogers	300	
	Allowance for Doubtful Accounts		300
	To reinstate an account previously written off.		
10	Cash	300	
	Accounts Receivable—A. Rogers		300
	Collection of account.		

OBJECTIVE 2b. Record the collection of receivables that were previously written off as uncollectible by the allowance approach.

ESTIMATING METHODS

Percentage of Revenue

The basis for any forecast is experience. The amount of bad debts in the past may be correlated with revenues to establish a company's bad debts experience rate. By allowing for expected differences a current experience rate can be approximated.

A new company has no past on which to base its forecast. The company's managers may have had experience with other companies, however, and may have information on the rates of losses experienced by similar concerns in the industry.

Cash sales, of course, can never be the source of bad debts. Therefore, the estimate of uncollectibles should be based on credit sales—not total revenues.

Suppose that in the past approximately 1% of sales on account have proved to be uncollectible. If credit sales are $600,000 during the current year, the company will make the following entry to recognize the estimated uncollectibles ($600,000 × 1%).

OBJECTIVE 3a. Prepare an adjusting entry under the percentage of revenue method.

	ADJUSTING ENTRY		
Year 1 Dec. 31	Uncollectible Accounts Expense	6,000	
	Allowance for Doubtful Accounts		6,000
	To adjust for estimated uncollectibles.		

Any balance already in the allowance account is ignored under the percentage of revenue method. The expense is being estimated on the basis of credit sales. The allowance results from approximating this year's uncollectibles.

The problem with this method is that eventually the balance in the allowance account may become unreasonable (when compared with Accounts Receivable). No estimate can be expected to predict future events perfectly; even small amounts of overestimates or underestimates may pile up over time to result in an allowance that is either too high or too low when compared with the amount of receivables. Of course, the percentage can be adjusted upward or downward when the allowance balance gets out of line.

Percentage of Receivables Balance

Another method of estimating uncollectible accounts bases the adjustment on the amount of receivables at the end of a period, rather than on the amount of revenue during the period.

When the amount of estimated uncollectibles is based on ending receivables, Uncollectible Accounts Expense is the *resulting* figure, determined in the following manner.

	Rate × Ending Accounts Receivable
	Plus: Debit balance in Allowance for Doubtful Accounts
or	Less: Credit balance in Allowance for Doubtful Accounts
	Uncollectible Accounts Expense

Suppose, for example, that a company follows the practice of maintaining an allowance balance equal to 10% of ending Accounts Receivable, and that the accounts show the following balances before the adjustment for estimated uncollectibles is made.

Accounts Receivable	Allowance for Doubtful Accounts
40,000	500

The adjustment would be made as follows.

	10% × $40,000	$4,000	
	Plus: Debit balance	500	
	Expense provision	$4,500	
	ADJUSTING ENTRY		
Dec. 31	Uncollectible Accounts Expense	4,500	
	Allowance for Doubtful Accounts		4,500

OBJECTIVE 3b. Prepare an adjusting entry under the percentage of receivables balance method.

When the preceding adjustment is posted, the contra account will show a balance equal to 10% of ending receivables.

Accounts Receivable	Allowance for Doubtful Accounts
40,000	500 12/31 4,500
	Balance
	4,000

Had the allowance account shown a *credit* balance of $500 before the adjusting entry was made, only $3,500 would have been needed to bring it to the required balance.

OBJECTIVE 3b. Prepare an adjusting entry under the percentage of receivables balance method.

10% × $40,000	$4,000	
Less: Credit balance	500	
Expense provision	$3,500	
ADJUSTING ENTRY		
Dec. 31 Uncollectible Accounts Expense	3,500	
Allowance for Doubtful Accounts		3,500

Aging Schedule

The collectibility of Accounts Receivable may vary considerably from year to year. During economic recessions, customers may have difficulty in meeting their credit obligations; more companies go broke during hard times than during good times.

One measure of the quality of receivables is their age. The longer a receivable remains unpaid, the greater the likelihood that it will eventually be written off as uncollectible. The amounts of receivables that fall within various age categories can be determined with the aid of an aging schedule.

OBJECTIVE 3c. Determine the needed adjustment under the aging schedule method.

A receivables aging schedule groups amounts due from customers according to the length of time the receivables have remained on the books. The schedule in Illustration 6.10 is one approach toward estimating uncollectibles.

ILLUSTRATION 6.10

DREYFUSS COMPANY Receivables Aging Schedule December 31, 19––					
Customer	**Balance**	**1–30 Days**	**31–61 Days**	**61–120 Days**	**Over 120 Days**
T. Arch	450	450			
R. Chang	280	280			
E. Jones	635		635		
J. Traub	500				500
C. Warez	790			790	
Total	40,000	31,000	2,800	2,900	3,300
Estimated Loss Rate		× 2%	× 10%	× 20%	× 80%
Estimated Uncollectibles	4,120	620	280	580	2,640

As you can see, the estimated loss rate increases with the age of the receivables. The percentage used for each age category will vary according to each entity's experience. The adjustment for uncollectibles, assuming a $500 credit balance in the allowance account, would be made as follows.

Estimated Uncollectibles	$4,120	
Less: Credit balance	500	
Expense required	$3,620	
ADJUSTING ENTRY		
Dec. 31	Uncollectible Accounts Expense	3,620	
	Allowance for Doubtful Accounts		3,620

OBJECTIVE 3c. Prepare an adjusting entry under the aging schedule method.

The aging schedule is considered superior to the other approaches because it takes into consideration the *quality* of the receivables, as measured by their ages, at the time that the adjustment is being made.

Practically all sizable concerns with many receivables have computerized their accounting systems. Receivables aging can be performed readily by computers as long as sales dates are carried in the receivables data bank.

OBJECTIVE 4. State why use of an aging schedule is superior to other approaches for estimating uncollectibles.

Summary of Approaches

The various approaches for recognizing uncollectible accounts may be summarized as shown in Illustration 6.11.

It should be pointed out that the direct write-off approach is acceptable only when uncollectibles are inconsequential in amount. The best estimates of uncollectibles consider the relative ages of the ending receivables.

OTHER RECEIVABLES ALLOWANCES

Receivables may be overstated for reasons other than bad accounts. Any significant amounts that are not expected to be collected from customers should be estimated and recognized with end-of-period adjusting entries.

ILLUSTRATION 6.11

APPROACHES FOR RECOGNIZING UNCOLLECTIBLE ACCOUNTS

1. Direct write-off approach (bad accounts recognized at the time they are proved uncollectible)

2. Estimating approaches (attempt to match uncollectible accounts with appropriate revenues)

   a. Estimate uncollectible revenues (applies a rate to credit revenues)

   b. Estimate uncollectibles in ending receivables (emphasizes the proper statement of assets)

      1) By using one rate for all receivables, *or*

      2) By considering the age of receivables

Estimated Sales Discounts

Where credit terms are granted, there will usually be some receivables that are still within the discount period. If, for example, terms of 2/10, n/30 are granted to all customers, any account less than ten days old may bring in only 98% of the recorded receivable. Suppose that Dreyfuss Company has $20,000 in Accounts Receivable at December 31 that is subject to a 2% discount. And suppose experience indicates that 90% of the company's customers take the discounts that are permitted. The following adjustment recognizes the ending receivables that are not expected to be collected because of sales discounts.

Dec. 31	Sales Discounts	360	
	Allowance for Sales Discounts		360
	2% (90% × $20,000)		

Estimated Returns and Allowances

When anticipated returns and allowances are significant in amount, they too should be recognized by means of an end-of-period adjustment. Suppose Dreyfuss Company estimates that in the future, customers will return (or request allowances for) about $1,000 worth of the goods sold in the year just ended. The adjusting entry to reflect this estimate would take the following form.

	ADJUSTING ENTRY		
Dec. 31	Sales Returns and Allowances	1,000	
	Allowance for Sales Returns and Allowances		1,000

STATEMENT PRESENTATIONS OF RECEIVABLES

Accounts Receivable should be viewed along with all contra accounts that represent potential reductions in the cash to be realized in the future. Assume, for example, that receivables and allowances for Dreyfuss Company at December 31 are as depicted by the following T-accounts.

Accounts Receivable		Allowance for Doubtful Accounts	
40,000			4,120

Allowance for Sales Discounts		Allowance for Sales Returns & Allowances	
	360		1,000

ILLUSTRATION 6.12

DREYFUSS COMPANY
Balance Sheet
December 31, 19– –

ASSETS

Current

Cash			$ 10,600
Accounts receivable		$40,000	
Less allowances for: Doubtful accounts	$4,120		
Sales discounts	360		
Sales returns and allowances	1,000	5,480	34,520
Inventories			95,000
Total current assets			$140,120

A balance sheet should then show Accounts Receivable net of the allowances, or the allowances may be shown on the balance sheet as reductions in Accounts Receivable, as in Illustration 6.12.

Notes receivable, interest receivable, and other receivables may also turn out to be uncollectible. Where such losses are likely, they should be estimated and recognized by means of adjusting entries. In fact, all such estimates might be included in one allowance account and presented on a balance sheet, as in Illustration 6.13.

ILLUSTRATION 6.13

CORRY COMPANY
Balance Sheet
December 31, 19– –

ASSETS

Current

Cash			$ 8,300
Receivables			
Accounts receivable		$80,000	
Notes receivable	$30,000		
Less: Notes receivable discounted	12,000	18,000	
Interest receivable		200	
Total		$98,200	
Less: Allowances for doubtful accounts		6,400	91,800
Inventories			210,000
Total current assets			$310,100

GLOSSARY FOR SECTION 6.B

Allowance approach for recognizing uncollectibles An approach for estimating uncollectibles in an attempt to match Uncollectible Accounts Expense with the revenues that were recognized when the receivables were recorded.

Asset net book value The amount remaining after a contra account is offset against the asset account to which it relates.

Credit risk The likelihood that some receivables will never be collected.

Direct write-off of an account An approach for recognizing Uncollectible Accounts Expense in the accounting period when the accounts are written off.

Loss A cost expiration (asset sacrifice) that is involuntarily borne and does not help to produce any revenue.

Receivables aging schedule A schedule that groups amounts due from customers according to the length of time the receivables have remained on the books.

SELF-QUIZ ON OBJECTIVES FOR SECTION 6.B
Solutions to Self-Quiz begin on page B-25.

1. Tallyhoe Company uses the direct write-off approach for recognizing uncollectibles. On July 5 an $800 account receivable from J. Dobbs was judged to be uncollectible.

   a. OBJECTIVE 1a. Make the journal entry to write off the account.

   b. OBJECTIVE 2a. On November 10 Tallyhoe received a check for $800 from J. Dobbs, who explained that she had just inherited a large sum of money. Make the entries to record the recovery of Ms. Dobbs's account.

2. Nile Company uses the allowance approach for estimating uncollectibles. On March 12 a $700 account receivable from R. Troup was judged to be uncollectible.

   a. OBJECTIVE 1b. Make the journal entry to write off the account.

   b. OBJECTIVE 2b. On September 14 a check for $700 was received from R. Troup, in full payment of the account that had been written off on March 12. Make the journal entries to reflect the recovery of the account.

3. Marve Company uses the allowance approach for recognizing uncollectibles. At December 31 an unadjusted trial balance shows the following balances for selected accounts.

	Debit	Credit
Accounts Receivable	90,000	
Allowance for Doubtful Accounts		200
Sales		600,000
Uncollectible Accounts Expense	–0–	

a. **OBJECTIVE 3a.** Experience indicates that 1% of credit sales turn out to be uncollectible. All sales were made on account. Make the adjusting entry for estimated uncollectibles using the percentage of revenue method.

b. **OBJECTIVE 3b.** Ignore the preceding part and assume instead that experience indicates that 5% of ending Accounts Receivable turn out to be uncollectible. Make the adjusting entry for estimated uncollectibles at December 31 using the percentage of receivables balance method.

4. **OBJECTIVE 3c.** Joci Company estimates uncollectibles with the aid of an aging schedule. At December 31 Allowance for Doubtful Accounts shows a *debit* balance of $600. A summary of the aging results and the estimated rate of uncollectibles for each age group are given below.

	Total	0–30 Days	31–90 Days	Over 90 Days
Accounts Receivable	$87,500	$62,400	$21,100	$4,000
Estimated Uncollectible		1%	5%	25%

Make the adjusting entry for estimated uncollectibles at December 31.

5. **OBJECTIVE 4.** State in your own words why the use of an aging schedule is superior to other approaches for estimating uncollectibles.

DISCUSSION QUESTIONS FOR SECTION 6.B

1. A company can avoid uncollectible accounts by selling on a cash basis only. Why do so many concerns grant credit to their customers?

2. In your opinion, should uncollectible receivables be labeled expenses or losses? Why?

3. How does a direct write-off approach to uncollectibles often fail to meet the objectives of the matching concept of accounting?

4. What is the allowance approach for recognizing uncollectibles?

5. Why are uncollectibles estimated?

6. Why is the amount of estimated uncollectibles maintained in a contra account (Allowance for Doubtful Accounts) instead of being deducted directly from the asset account (Accounts Receivable)?

7. Under the percentage of revenue method, how does a balance already in Allowance for Doubtful Accounts affect the adjustment?

8. Under the percentage of receivables balance method, how does a balance already in Allowance for Doubtful Accounts affect the adjustment?

9. What is an asset net book value?

EXERCISES FOR SECTION 6.B

6.B.1. On May 21 a $1,200 account receivable from A. L. Windall was determined to be uncollectible.

 a. Using the direct write-off approach, make the journal entry to write the account off.

 b. On January 15 of the following year a check for $1,200 was unexpectedly received from A. L. Windall. Make journal entries to record the recovery of Windall's account.

6.B.2. Experience indicates that 1.5% of the F. K. M. Company's credit sales turn out to be uncollectible. Credit sales for the year were $800,000. At December 31 Allowance for Doubtful Accounts shows a credit balance of $500. Make an adjusting entry at December 31 to recognize Uncollectible Accounts Expense by the percentage of revenue method.

6.B.3. The balance of Accounts Receivable at December 31 is $120,000. Allowance for Doubtful Accounts shows a credit balance of $500. Experience indicates that 4% of ending Accounts Receivable turn out to be uncollectible. Make the entry at December 31 to adjust the allowance account by the percentage of receivables balance method.

6.B.4. Seth Company uses the allowance approach for estimating uncollectibles. On April 15 a $2,400 account from Barry Company was determined to be uncollectible.

 a. Make the journal entry to write the account off.

 b. On July 20 a $2,400 check is received from Barry Company in full payment of the account that had been written off. Make the journal entries to record the recovery of the account.

6.B.5. The College Bookstore gives students a 2% discount for paying their accounts within 30 days. The bookstore manager uses an allowance system for matching sales discounts with revenue. On December 31 Allowance for Sales Discounts has a credit balance of $30. There are $10,000 worth of accounts receivable on which the 2% discount may be taken. Experience has shown that 60% of the students take the discount. Make an entry on December 31 to adjust Allowance for Sales Discounts.

PROBLEMS FOR SECTION 6.B
Alternate Problems for this section begin on page D-45.

6.B.6. Joshua Company uses an aging schedule to estimate uncollectibles. Here are the results of an aging schedule at December 31.

	0–30 Days	31–90 Days	Over 90 Days
Accounts Receivable	$54,000	$15,000	$6,000
Estimated Loss Rate	2%	6%	20%

Required

1) Assume that Allowance for Doubtful Accounts shows a credit balance of $350 at December 31. Make an entry to adjust the allowance account at December 31.

2) Assume that Allowance for Doubtful Accounts shows a debit balance of $350. Make an entry to adjust the allowance account at December 31.

6.B.7. Altru Company offers its credit customers terms of 2/10, n/30. At December 31 Accounts Receivable includes $40,000 of customer accounts still subject to the 2% discount. In the past, 85% of the customers have taken advantage of sales discounts.

Required

1) Make an adjusting entry at December 31 to allow for the ending receivables that will probably not be collected because of sales discounts.

2) Assume that a $1,000 receivable included in the December 31 balance is collected on January 4, net of the 2% discount. Make the required journal entry.

6.B.8. On December 31, 19X4, Sanchez Company estimated that during 19X5 customers will return (or request allowance for) about $500 worth of goods sold in 19X4.

Required

1) Make an adjusting entry at December 31, 19X4, to record this estimate.

2) Assume that a customer returns merchandise and receives a cash refund of $75 on January 15, 19X5. The sale had been made on December 30, 19X4. Make the required journal entry.

6.B.9. Current asset accounts for Exaam Company are shown in the following partial adjusted trial balance.

EXAAM COMPANY Partial Adjusted Trial Balance December 31, 19--		
	Debit	**Credit**
Cash	14,600	
Accounts Receivable	38,000	
Allowance for Doubtful Accounts		2,100
Allowance for Sales Discounts		250
Allowance for Sales Returns and Allowances		800
Inventories	111,000	

Required

Prepare a partial balance sheet for Exaam Company at December 31 to show how the accounts in the adjusted trial balance should be presented.

6.B.10. Burns Company records show the following customer accounts at June 30.

Account Receivable	Amount	Date
Abate Co.	$ 1,500	May 20
Axe Co.	2,000	June 15
Bates, Inc.	6,000	May 11
Bend	500	June 15
Emex	7,500	June 2
Falex Corp.	600	Jan. 15
Flakey, Inc.	1,000	Feb. 28
Gross	1,200	June 20
Linton, Inc.	5,500	June 7
Seth Products	20,000	May 2
Winnie Pop, Ltd.	7,500	June 10
Zap, Inc.	800	Apr. 11

Required

Prepare an aging schedule for Burns Company as of June 30. Use these column headings: 0–30 Days, 31–60 Days; 61–90 Days; and Over 90 Days.

6.B.11. Farling Stores uses an aging schedule to help estimate uncollectibles. The results of an aging schedule and other selected information follow.

FARLING STORES Aged Accounts Receivable December 31, 19––			
	0–30 Days	**31–60 Days**	**61–90 Days**	**Over 90 Days**
Accounts Receivable	$200,000	$110,000	$40,000	$10,000
Estimated Loss Rate	1%	2%	10%	40%

Accounts Receivable		Allowance for Doubtful Accounts	
360,000			2,100

Required

1) Calculate the amount of uncollectible accounts by the aging schedule approach.

2) Calculate the amount of the adjustment needed to bring Allowance for Doubtful Accounts to the required balance.

3) Make the adjusting entry on December 31.

SUMMARY OF CHAPTER 6

Receivables and payables represent delays in the receipt and payment of cash. Accounts receivable and payable are based on informal agreements, whereas notes receivable and payable are based on formal written promises. One party's receivable is always another party's payable; the entry to record a payable on the debtor's books mirrors the entry to record the receivable on the creditor's books.

Some receivables and payables provide for the payment of interest, which is in effect a rental charge for the use of money. Interest charges are usually stated as annual rates. An adjusting entry to recognize accrued interest is required when the accounting period ends during the term of an interest-bearing receivable or payable.

A noteholder may convert a negotiable note into cash by discounting it with a financial institution. The amount of cash proceeds from discounting a note depends on the discount rate charged and the discount period. A discount rate is equivalent to a higher interest rate because the discount amount is deducted in advance to arrive at the proceeds from discounting. When a note is negotiated (transferred) with an unqualified endorsement, the endorser assumes a contingent liability to pay the note if the maker dishonors it.

Various kinds of receivables and payables may arise from transactions that do not involve sales or purchases of merchandise. Wages, fees, rental charges, and insurance premiums result in receivables for some and payables for others.

Uncollectible receivables are viewed by some accountants as asset losses, by others as necessary expenses of doing business on credit. Some concerns recognize uncollectibles only when they are proved to be bad, under the direct write-off approach. A better matching of expenses (or losses) with revenues is attained with the allowance approach for recognizing uncollectibles. Under the allowance approach, uncollectibles are estimated and recorded as an adjusting entry at the end of each accounting period. Estimated uncollectibles are shown in Allowance for Doubtful Accounts, a contra asset account that is offset against receivables.

An estimate of uncollectibles may be based either on the amount of revenues for a period or on the amount of receivables held at the end of a period. An estimate based on a receivables aging schedule takes into consideration the relative quality of the receivables, as measured by the length of time the receivables have remained on the books.

End-of-period adjustments should also recognize any other significant amounts of receivables that are not expected to be collected from customers. Estimates of sales discounts that are likely to be taken and anticipated returns and allowances should be shown in contra asset allowance accounts as offsets against receivables.

PROBLEMS FOR CHAPTER 6
Alternate Problems for this chapter begin on page D-46.

6.1. Following are selected events experienced by Barco Company.

19X3

Dec.   31   Barco estimates uncollectibles at 1% of sales. Sales for 19X3 were $700,000. Allowance for Doubtful Accounts showed a credit balance of $400 before the year-end adjustments.

19X4

Mar.   3   A $900 account receivable from the Hummer Company was judged uncollectible.

July   15   A 90-day, 9% note (dated July 15) for $6,000 was accepted from EKL, Inc., in settlement of an overdue account receivable.

July   30   The EKL note was discounted at the bank at a 6% per annum discount rate.

Aug.   4   Hummer Company paid the $900 balance due that was written off as uncollectible on March 3.

Oct.   14   Barco was notified by the bank that EKL defaulted on its note due October 13. Barco paid the bank the maturity amount.

Oct.   30   EKL paid the maturity amount of the note defaulted on October 13 plus interest at 9% per annum calculated from the due date of the note.

Nov.   19   A 60-day, 12% note (dated November 19) for $8,000 was accepted from Jodi Company in settlement of an overdue account receivable.

Dec.   15   Various customer accounts totaling $7,600 were written off as uncollectible.

Dec.   31   Adjusting entries were made for uncollectible accounts expense and to accrue interest on the Jodi Company note. Sales for 19X4 were $850,000.

19X5

Jan.   18   Cash was received in settlement of the Jodi Company note, plus interest.

Required

Record in Barco's general journal all entries required by the foregoing events.

6.2. A partial work sheet for R. H. Mays Company follows, along with adjustments data.

A/C #	Account	Unadjusted Trial Balance	
		Dr.	*Cr.*

R. H. MAYS COMPANY
Work Sheet
For the Year Ended December 31, 19X4

A/C #	Account	Dr.	Cr.
111	Cash	3,000	
112	Prepaid Insurance	1,800	
113	Accounts Receivable	12,000	
0113	Allowance for Doubtful Accounts	30	
114	Note Receivable	2,000	
116	Merchandise Inventory	22,000	
121	Furniture and Equipment	20,000	
0121	Accumulated Depreciation—Furn. and Equip.		1,800
211	Accounts Payable		10,800
215	Bank Loan Payable		8,000
311	R. H. Mays, Capital		32,260
312	R. H. Mays, Withdrawals	–0–	
411	Sales		170,000
412	Sales Returns and Allowances	6,000	
511	Purchases	111,930	
512	Purchase Returns and Allowances		200
513	Freight In	500	
612	Salary Expense	31,000	
613	Advertising Expense	5,000	
614	Utilities Expense	1,800	
615	Rent Expense	6,000	
		223,060	223,060
616	Insurance Expense		
617	Depreciation Expense		
618	Interest Expense		
212	Interest Payable		
619	Uncollectible Accounts Expense		
115	Interest Receivable		
413	Interest Revenue		
611	Cost of Goods Sold		

Adjustments Data

a) On January 1, 19X4, a two-year insurance premium of $1,800 was paid.

b) Depreciation on furniture and equipment is $3,000 per year.

c) The bank loan was dated December 1, 19X4. It requires interest at 9% per annum to be paid quarterly and falls due on December 1, 19X6.

d) Experience indicates that 3% of ending accounts receivable turn out to be uncollectible.

e) The note receivable is dated November 1, 19X4, and bears 8% interest payable when the note matures on January 30, 19X5.

f) The merchandise inventory at December 31, 19X4, is $13,000.

Required

1) Use the information provided to complete a ten-column work sheet for R. H. Mays Company.

2) Prepare an income statement for 19X4.

3) Prepare a balance sheet at December 31, 19X4.

6.3. Following are a list of accounts receivable for the Bono Company at December 31 and a summary of loss experience.

ACCOUNTS RECEIVABLE		
Transaction Date	Name	Amount Due
July 20	J. Alpha	$ 2,000
Nov. 15	Barton Co.	4,000
Dec. 1	T. Crew	8,000
Jan. 30	L. Dampkin	500
Oct. 27	V. Echo	950
Dec. 16	M. Frank	1,100
Nov. 30	Juliet Co.	1,300
Dec. 28	R. King	6,000
Nov. 12	Packer Co.	12,000
Nov. 30	Stinger Co.	2,100
Sep. 15	TDX Co.	3,200
Nov. 10	Zeta Co.	4,000

LOSS EXPERIENCE	
Account Age	% Uncollectible
1–30 days	1
31–60 days	2
61–120 days	5
Over 120 days	20

Required

1) Prepare a receivables aging schedule at December 31. Group accounts as follows: 1–30 days, 31–60 days, 61–120 days, and over 120 days.

2) Assume that Allowance for Doubtful Accounts shows a debit balance of $400. Make the adjusting entry for estimated uncollectibles at December 31.

3) Assume instead that Allowance for Doubtful Accounts shows a credit balance of $500 before the adjustment. Make the adjusting entry at December 31.

COMPREHENSION PROBLEMS FOR CHAPTER 6

6.4. The Randy Company, which was started four years ago, has been using the direct write-off approach for recognizing bad debts. An accountant suggests that revenues and expenses would be better matched by using an allowance approach. The accountant has gathered the following data.

	RANDY COMPANY Selected Data		
	19X4	**19X3**	**19X2**
Sales	$240,000	$180,000	$150,000
Actual Bad Debts	2,300	1,850	1,490

Required

1) Determine the approximate percentage of sales that has tended to go bad in the past.

2) Assume that sales in 19X5 were $260,000 and that $2,500 worth of bad accounts were written off in 19X5. Of the 19X5 write-offs, $1,300 were 19X4 accounts and $1,200 were 19X5 sales. Make an entry to put Randy Company on the allowance approach, basing the estimate on the percentage determined in the preceding part.

3) Comment on the matching problems created by converting to the allowance approach in 19X5. Suggest possible solutions to these problems.

6.5. Before adjusting entries were made, Miller Company's Allowance for Doubtful Accounts showed a debit balance at December 31, 19X3, of $2,000; and at December 31, 19X4, the account showed a credit balance of $5,000. A junior accountant said it was obvious that accountants had underestimated uncollectibles at December 31, 19X2, and overestimated uncollectibles in December 31, 19X3. A senior accountant said it was more obvious that the junior's accounting background was defective, because he failed to recognize other possible reasons for the end-of-year balances.

Required

1) Explain in writing to the junior accountant how the account could show a *debit* balance at year-end even though the previous year's adjustment was right on target.

2) Explain how the account could show a *credit* balance when the previous year's adjustment was on target.

7
Merchandise Inventories

Almost all entities hold inventories of some kind. You have already dealt with adjustments for supplies owned by concerns that perform services. Merchandise inventories were first introduced in Chapter 4. Chapter 7 concentrates on special kinds of problems associated with accounting for merchandise inventories. Some of the concepts that you learn here will also be applicable to accounting for manufacturing inventories, which is the focus of much of Chapters 20 and 21.

Chapter 7 is presented in three sections. Section A concentrates primarily on the three most common assumptions about the flow of inventory costs. The relative effects of the three methods on income statements and balance sheets are discussed, and tax consequences are also touched upon briefly. The section closes with a discussion of the concept of inventory replacement cost.

Section B introduces inventory accounting systems that continuously keep track of goods on hand, and it compares the techniques and results of perpetual systems to those of periodic inventory systems. This section also discusses the conservative practice of reporting inventories at the lower of either the original cost or the replacement cost.

Section C focuses on techniques for estimating inventory costs when it is either impractical or impossible to match invoice costs with actual counts of items on hand.

SECTION 7.A

Inventory Costing Methods

OBJECTIVES

In this section you will study the effects of alternative assumptions about how inventory costs flow through an entity. When you have completed your study, you should be able to

1. State why it is usually necessary, and certainly desirable, to adopt an assumption about cost flow for inventory costing purposes.

2. Determine cost of ending inventory and cost of goods sold using the
   a. First-in, first-out (FIFO) method.
   b. Last-in, first-out (LIFO) method.
   c. Weighted average method.

3. Summarize the relative effects of each of the most commonly used cost-flow assumptions on income statement and balance sheet data during periods of rising costs of purchases.

TYPES OF INVENTORIES

Inventories are quantities of goods or materials on hand. *Merchandise* inventories are goods that are held for resale by merchandising concerns. Inventories of office supplies, cleaning supplies, and similar items that are consumed within an entity are usually viewed as prepaid expenses. This is because as they are used up, they become operating expenses rather than part of cost of goods sold. Manufacturing concerns have several different kinds of inventories, which are discussed later in connection with accounting for manufacturing activities.

In this section our concern is primarily with accounting for costs of merchandise inventories.

MATCHING MERCHANDISE COSTS

Recall from Chapter 4 the general format of the cost of goods sold calculation.

Beginning Inventory
Plus: Purchases
Goods Available for Sale
Less: Ending Inventory
Cost of Goods Sold

In effect, the cost of goods available for sale is allocated between ending inventory and cost of goods sold. The more the cost that is allocated to ending inventory, the less that goes into cost of goods sold, and vice versa. Ending inventory costs are carried forward as assets into the next accounting period; costs of goods sold are matched with (that is, subtracted from) revenues of the current period.

You can see that a proper determination of ending inventory cost is important, since both the income statement (through cost of goods sold) and the balance sheet (through merchandise inventory) are affected. If, for example, too much cost is allocated to ending inventory, cost of goods sold will be understated. And when cost of goods sold is understated, net income will be overstated.

We must also keep in mind that the ending inventory of one period is the beginning inventory of the following period. Any misstatement of the ending inventory of one period will therefore distort the cost of goods available for sale for the next period. An overstatement of ending inventory cost has the effect of shifting some of the cost, properly allocable to one year, into the next. Suppose, for example, that the ending inventory of 19X4 was overstated by $1,000. This would result in an understatement of cost of goods sold for 19X4 and an overstatement for 19X5, as illustrated here.

19X4		19X5	
Beginning inventory		Beginning inventory	$1,000 over
Plus: Purchases		Plus: Purchases	
Goods available for sale		Goods available for sale	$1,000 over
Less: Ending inventory	$1,000 over	Less: Ending inventory	
Cost of goods sold	$1,000 under	Cost of goods sold	$1,000 over

If, on the other hand, ending inventory is understated, the cost of goods sold for that year will be overstated, and in the following period, cost of goods sold will be understated.

Because the income statement and balance sheet are interrelated, inventory misstatements affect both. An overstatement of ending inventory results not only in overstated total assets, but also in overstated net income for the period (because of understated cost of goods sold). On the other hand, an understatement of ending inventory not only understates assets but also understates net income for the period.

COSTING INVENTORIES

*The process of assigning costs to inventory items is referred to as **inventory costing, inventory pricing, or inventory valuation.*** As pointed out in Chapter 4, unit costs from a purchase invoice may be multiplied by physical inventory counts to arrive at total costs for inventory items.

When purchase prices have changed over time, the particular costs to be assigned to inventory items must somehow be determined. It is this problem that causes the most difficulty in inventory costing. A number of approaches to assigning inventory costs are acceptable, as long as the method selected is consistently followed. The most commonly used costing methods are discussed in this unit.

IDENTIFIABLE COSTING METHOD

One might argue that the best way to keep track of inventory costs is to somehow *identify the actual cost of each inventory item by using an **identifiable costing method.*** This method may be practical when the inventory consists of a limited number of expensive items. Even with a large number of items, the cost of each item might be marked, or tagged, on each unit of inventory.

But identifying the actual purchase prices with inventory units may not really be the best approach. A business may have on hand a number of identical inventory items that were acquired at different times and at different costs. Simply by choosing which particular unit to sell first, a concern's managers can manipulate the amount of reported profit (and inventory cost remaining).

Consider, for example, the case where two units are on hand on the last day of the year. Although identical in appearance and usefulness, one unit purchased early in the year cost $600 and the other one purchased late in the year cost $700. One of the units is being sold to a customer for $850. If the unit that cost $600 is chosen to be sold, $250 of gross profit will be shown, and the $700 unit will remain in inventory. If, on the other hand, the $700 unit is sold, gross profit of only $150 will be shown, and the $600 unit will remain in inventory. It is apparent that the identifiable costing method provides an opportunity for manipulation of a concern's reported profits.

COST-FLOW ASSUMPTIONS

Need for Assumptions

Ideally, reported accounting results should not be subject to distortion or manipulation by a company's managers. One problem with the identifiable costing method is that it is not systematic. The adoption of an assumption about how costs move through the entity compels everyone to live with the outcome, provided the assumption is applied consistently over time.

Another difficulty with the identifiable costing method is that of associating specific costs with particular units of inventory. The greater the number of items in inventory there are, and the more costs vary over time, the less practical is the identifiable method.

Thus some assumption about inventory cost flow is needed for the following reasons.

> 1. To help prevent manipulation of accounting results.
> 2. To avoid the problem of identifying specific costs with particular units of inventory.

A cost-flow assumption need not duplicate the manner in which goods physically flow through an entity; it is simply a presumption about the costs that are to be matched with a period's revenues, without regard for the order in which units of merchandise are sold. If purchase prices were stable, all cost-flow assumptions would yield the same results. However, costs have tended to change over time, with most concerns experiencing steadily rising costs because of inflation.

A particular cost-flow assumption may be used in conjunction with either periodic or perpetual inventory systems. Recall that a periodic inventory system records purchases of merchandise in a Purchases account, adjusting the Merchandise Inventory account only at the end of each accounting period when cost of goods sold is determined. Examples in this section involve the use of a periodic inventory system. Perpetual inventory systems are discussed in the next section.[1]

First-In, First-Out (FIFO) Method

As the words imply, *the first-in, first-out (FIFO) cost-flow assumption is that the first costs incurred are assignable to the first goods sold. Conversely, the last costs incurred are assigned to the items left in inventory.*

Consider the problem of assigning cost to an ending inventory of 100 jackets, given the following information.

COST OF JACKETS AVAILABLE FOR SALE			
Jan. 1	Beginning inventory	80 units at $15	$1,200
May 10	Purchased	150 units at 20	3,000
Sept. 18	Purchased	60 units at 25	1,500
Available for sale		290 units	$5,700

Since the first costs in are assumed to be the first out, the ending inventory is made up of the most recent costs (the last costs incurred).

---

[1]See Section 4.A for definitions of periodic and perpetual inventory systems.

JACKET INVENTORY COSTED UNDER FIFO		
Purchased on Sept. 18	60 units at $25	$1,500
From purchase of May 10	40 units at 20	800
Inventory at Dec. 31	100 units	$2,300

OBJECTIVE 2a. Determine cost of ending inventory and cost of goods sold using the first-in, first-out (FIFO) method.

The cost of jacket units sold may be determined by subtracting the ending inventory from the cost of units available for sale.

COST OF JACKETS SOLD UNDER FIFO		
Available for sale	290 units	$5,700
Inventory at Dec. 31	100 units	2,300
Sold	190 units	$3,400

The allocation of costs between cost of goods sold and ending inventory, using the FIFO method, is shown in Illustration 7.1.

Notice that when costs are rising, the FIFO method matches the lower (earlier) costs with revenues, and the higher (later) costs are deferred as ending inventory.

Last-In, First-Out (LIFO) Method

*The **last-in, first-out (LIFO)** cost-flow assumption is that the latest costs incurred are assignable to the first goods sold, while the earliest costs are assigned to items in inventory.* Consider the previous example once again, this time using the LIFO method, as shown on the next page.

ILLUSTRATION 7.1

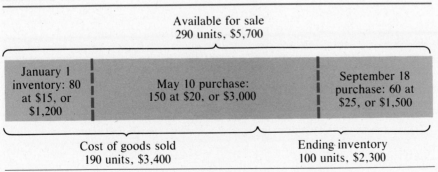

Available for sale
290 units, $5,700

January 1 inventory: 80 at $15, or $1,200

May 10 purchase: 150 at $20, or $3,000

September 18 purchase: 60 at $25, or $1,500

Cost of goods sold 190 units, $3,400

Ending inventory 100 units, $2,300

COST OF JACKETS AVAILABLE FOR SALE

Jan. 1	Beginning inventory	80 units at $15	$1,200
May 10	Purchased	150 units at 20	3,000
Sept. 18	Purchased	60 units at 25	1,500
	Available for sale	290 units	$5,700

The ending inventory of 100 units is now assumed to be made up of the *earliest* costs.

OBJECTIVE 2b. Determine cost of ending inventory and cost of goods sold using the last-in, first-out (LIFO) method.

JACKET INVENTORY COSTED UNDER LIFO

Inventory on Jan. 1	80 units at $15	$1,200
From purchase of May 10	20 units at 20	400
Inventory at Dec. 31	100 units	$1,600

And the cost of units sold is calculated as follows.

COST OF JACKETS SOLD UNDER LIFO

Available for sale	290 units	$5,700
Inventory at Dec. 31	100 units	1,600
Sold	190	$4,100

Illustration 7.2 shows how the costs are allocated using the LIFO method. During periods of rising costs, the LIFO method matches the higher (later) costs with revenues and carries the lower (earlier) costs forward as ending inventory.

ILLUSTRATION 7.2

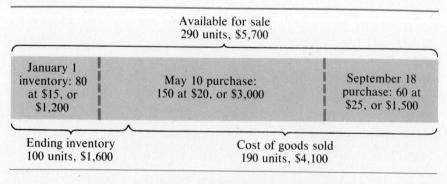

Weighted Average Method

*The **weighted average** cost-flow assumption is that each unit available for sale bears an equal share of the total cost of goods available for sale.* The unit cost for costing inventory is determined by dividing the cost of goods available for sale by the number of units available for sale. We can apply this method to our earlier example.

$$\frac{\text{Cost of jackets available}}{\text{Units available}} = \frac{\$5,700}{290} = \$19.6552$$

Inventory is then costed at the weighted average unit cost.

JACKET INVENTORY COSTED UNDER WEIGHTED AVERAGE		
Inventory at Dec. 31	100 units at $19.6552	$1,965.52

OBJECTIVE 2c. **Determine cost of ending inventory and cost of goods sold using the weighted average method.**

And cost of goods sold using the weighted average is as follows.

COST OF JACKETS SOLD UNDER WEIGHTED AVERAGE		
Available for sale	290 units	$5,700.00
Inventory at Dec. 31	100 units	1,965.52
Sold	190 units	$3,734.48

Note that the cost of goods sold could have been calculated directly by multiplying 190 units times the average cost of $19.6552.

You can see that the results from using the weighted average method fall somewhere in between those obtained from the FIFO and LIFO methods.

Comparing the Results

The three cost-flow assumptions yielded quite different results for the jacket inventory and cost of goods sold.

	FIFO	Weighted Average	LIFO
Available for sale	$5,700.00	$5,700.00	$5,700.00
Inventory at Dec. 31	2,300.00	1,965.52	1,600.00
Cost of jackets sold	$3,400.00	$3,734.48	$4,100.00

The more cost assigned as cost of goods sold, the less gross profit there will be, and the less net income will be reported. In our example, the FIFO method resulted in the most income, the LIFO method the least. Had costs been declining over time, the opposite would have been true.

Most merchandising concerns have many kinds of inventory items. Although the change in cost may vary for different items—and some purchase prices may actually decrease—we can generalize about the likely results during inflation. As purchase prices increase, so will cost of goods sold. However, more or less of the increases in costs can be deferred as inventories, depending on the costing method used. Illustration 7.3 summarizes the relative effects of the three cost-flow methods when costs are continually *rising*.

Note that we have *not* said a particular method overstates or understates income or ending inventory cost. Such conclusions require judgments about the wrongness of a method. Although there is disagreement as to which method is the best, all the methods discussed so far are acceptable in practice. However, because different results emerge from different methods, we must be cautious about comparing the data reported by different firms. If the firms being compared do not employ the same inventory costing method, no comparison of accounting data affected by inventory costing can be completely valid.

Tax Considerations

Income Taxes.   Federal, state, and local income taxes are based on the amount of taxable income, as defined in the laws that levy the taxes. These laws usually allow cost of goods sold as a deductible expense in arriving at taxable income. The higher the cost of goods sold, the lower will be taxable

ILLUSTRATION 7.3

OBJECTIVE 3.   Summarize the relative effects of the common cost-flow assumptions during periods of rising costs of purchases.

PERIODS OF RISING COSTS			
	FIFO	**Weighted Average**	**LIFO**
INCOME STATEMENT			
Cost of Goods Sold	Lowest	In between	Highest
Gross Profit	Highest	In between	Lowest
Net Income	Highest	In between	Lowest
BALANCE SHEET			
Ending Inventory	Highest	In between	Lowest
Current Assets	Highest	In between	Lowest
Total Assets	Highest	In between	Lowest

income and, as a result, the lower the income tax that must be paid. Taxpayers, including corporate managers, usually try to hold taxes to the minimum permitted by law.

Methods used for determining taxable income do not necessarily have to be the same as those for determining the net income reported on an income statement. However, federal tax laws provide that when the *last-in, first-out* inventory method is used for determining taxable income, it *must also be used* for financial reporting purposes.[2]

As we have seen, the LIFO cost method results in a lower net income (and taxable income) than do the other methods when the costs of purchases are increasing. The fact that the LIFO method has become more popular as inflation and tax rates have risen should come as no surprise.

Floor Taxes. Some state and local taxing jurisdictions impose a floor tax on inventories on hand at year-end. *Floor taxes (inventory taxes) are property taxes based on the cost of inventories owned at a point in time.*

Business concerns may attempt to minimize floor taxes in two ways: (1) by reducing the quantity of inventory items on hand before the physical inventory is taken and (2) by assigning the lowest permissible cost to inventories on hand. As we have seen, during times of rising costs, LIFO assigns a lower cost to ending inventory than do the other methods.

REPLACEMENT COSTS

In a sense, the matching of costs with revenues represents a recovery of costs from the revenue stream. Net income is the accountant's measure of what remains after all costs have been recovered, or allowed for.

In order to continue in business, a company must *replace* the inventory it sells. If purchase prices are continually rising, the cost of a unit sold will likely be less than the cost to replace that unit in inventory. In other words, the replacement cost will exceed cost recovery. *Replacement cost at a point in time is the price that would have to be paid to replace an asset.*

A statement issued by the Financial Accounting Standards Board requires the largest of corporations (and encourages other business concerns) to disclose in a supplement to the financial statements the replacement cost amounts of inventory and certain other assets.[3] This requirement and other aspects of accounting for changing prices are discussed in more detail in Section 12.B.

Net income is usually viewed as representing resources available for either distribution to owners or reinvestment in the business as owner's

---

[2]Internal Revenue Code, Sec. 472(c).

[3]*FASB Statement No. 33,* "Financial Reporting and Changing Prices" (Stamford, Conn.: Financial Accounting Standards Board, 1979), par. 30.

equity. However, when a portion of the reported net income must be used to supplement cost recovery in order to replace inventories, then not all the net income is available for distribution to owners or to finance growth.

The problem can be illustrated with the simple example of Jim's Peanut Wagon. Jim sells roasted peanuts from his wagon for 50¢ a bag. Each morning he buys 100 bags of roasted peanuts at 30¢ a bag, and he sells all of them during the day. His daily income statement is as follows.

Sales, 100 bags at 50¢	$50
Cost of goods sold, 100 bags at 30¢	30
Net Income	$20

Each day Jim puts aside $30 of the $50 he takes in for the next day's peanut purchase. The net income of $20 he uses for his daily living expenses.

One morning Jim's supplier informs him that starting with the next day's purchase, Jim must pay 40¢ a bag for peanuts. At the end of that day Jim has the usual $50 in hand, and has supposedly made $20 of net income. However, he must set aside $40 for the next day's purchase of 100 bags of peanuts, leaving only $10 available for his living expenses.

If Jim had raised his selling price to 60¢ a bag on the *day before* his purchase prices went up, he would have shown a net income of $30. However, $10 of his reported net income must still go into the replacement of his inventory, because the cost recovery was not enough to cover the new purchase price.

The implications of our illustration are applicable to General Motors as much as they are to Jim's Peanut Wagon. Net income will represent available resources only *if* replacement costs are used as a measure of cost of goods sold. Such a costing method might be called the ***next-in, first-out (NIFO)*** *costing method, because the inventory replacement costs are assigned to the goods sold.* Replacement costing, or NIFO, is not currently an accepted method for financial reporting, although some large firms provide some information of this type. We examine the problem in more detail in Chapter 12.

Recall our comparison of results obtained from the three most commonly used cost-flow assumptions. Of the three, LIFO comes closest to matching current (replacement) costs with revenues. As pointed out, LIFO assigns the most recent costs to cost of goods sold. However, LIFO assigns the oldest costs to ending inventories, which tends to widen the gap between reported ending inventory cost and the cost of replacing the inventory. In other words, LIFO sacrifices balance sheet relevance to attain more relevant data for the income statement.

GLOSSARY FOR SECTION 7.A

First-in, first-out (FIFO)   A costing method based on the assumption that the earliest costs incurred go into cost of goods sold and that the latest costs incurred go with inventories on hand.

Floor taxes (inventory taxes)   Property taxes that are based on the cost of inventories owned at a point in time.

Identifiable costing method   A method for costing inventories which identifies for each item the actual price paid for it.

Inventories   Quantities of goods or materials on hand.

Inventory costing (inventory pricing, inventory valuation)   The process of assigning costs to inventory items.

Last-in, first-out (LIFO)   A costing method based on the assumption that the latest costs incurred go into cost of goods sold and that the earliest costs incurred go with inventories on hand.

Next-in, first-out (NIFO)   A costing method that assigns to cost of goods sold the cost of replacing the inventory items sold.

Replacement cost   The price that would have to be paid to replace an asset at a point in time.

Weighted average   A costing method based on the assumption that each unit available for sale bears an equal share of the total cost of goods available for sale.

SELF-QUIZ ON OBJECTIVES FOR SECTION 7.A
Solutions to Self-Quiz begin on page B-27.

1. **OBJECTIVE 1.** State why it is desirable to make a cost-flow assumption for inventory costing purposes.

2. **OBJECTIVE 2.** Data from the records of Ninmitz Company show that the following units of fans were available for sale.

Jan. 1	Beginning inventory	70 units at $18	$1,260
Mar. 6	Purchased	200 units at 19	3,800
June 20	Purchased	50 units at 20	1,000
Aug. 11	Purchased	120 units at 21	2,520
Available for sale		440 units	$8,580

There are 130 fans on hand at December 31, the end of the fiscal year. Determine the cost of ending inventory and cost of goods sold using

a. The first-in, first-out (FIFO) method.

b. The last-in, first-out (LIFO) method.

c. The weighted average method.

3. **OBJECTIVE 3.** Summarize the relative effects that use of FIFO, LIFO, and weighted average costing methods have on income statement and balance sheet data during periods of rising costs of purchases.

DISCUSSION QUESTIONS FOR SECTION 7.A

1. If purchase prices were stable over time, what would be the relative results obtained from the various cost-flow assumptions? Explain.

2. How does the identifiable costing method permit manipulation of accounting results?

3. A taxpayer must obtain the consent of the Internal Revenue Service before changing the method of accounting for inventories, at least for purposes of filing tax returns. What reasons can you suggest for such a requirement?

4. Net income is the accountant's measure of what remains after applicable costs have been recovered from revenues. In theory, net income should be available for distribution to owners or for financing growth. How are the foregoing statements affected by changing costs?

5. What are floor taxes?

6. Retail firms that use the identifiable costing method sometimes tag each item with its cost, coded in some way to prevent customers from knowing the cost. Why do you suppose a business might not want its customers to know its purchase costs?

7. Of the most commonly used inventory costing methods, which comes closest to matching replacement costs with revenues? Explain.

EXERCISES FOR SECTION 7.A

7.A.1. Determine the missing words in the following sentences.

If the cost of ending inventory is understated, cost of goods sold for that accounting period will be (a) _____, and in the next period, cost of goods sold will be (b) _____. If the cost of ending inventory is overstated, net income for that period will be (c) _____, and in the next period, net income will be (d) _____.

7.A.2. Identify the acceptable costing method that approximates the result described in each of the following statements.

    a. Reports inventory at the most current cost.

    b. Matches current costs with revenues.

    c. Reports inventory at average cost.

    d. Reports inventory at the oldest (earliest) cost.

7.A.3. Inventory and purchasing data for one type of merchandise sold by Duke Company are as follows. The company uses a periodic inventory system.

Jan.	1	Beginning inventory	100 units at $50	$ 5,000
May	7	Purchased	400 units at 45	18,000
Sept.	16	Purchased	600 units at 42	25,200
Dec.	8	Purchased	150 units at 40	6,000
Dec.	31	Ending inventory	200 units	

a. Identify the inventory costing method that would result in the least taxable income for the year.

b. Assume an income tax rate of 40%. Calculate the taxes that can be avoided or deferred by using the method you chose in the preceding part (as compared to the method resulting in the highest taxable income).

PROBLEMS FOR SECTION 7.A
Alternate Problems for this section begin on page D-48.

7.A.4. Inventory and purchasing data for one kind of inventory held by Milo Company are shown here. Milo employs a periodic inventory system.

Jan.	1	Beginning inventory	80 units at $15	$1,200
Feb.	28	Purchased	300 units at 16	4,800
May	16	Purchased	400 units at 18	7,200
Oct.	20	Purchased	50 units at 19	950
Dec.	1	Purchased	100 units at 20	2,000
Dec.	31	Ending inventory	170 units	

Required

Determine the cost of ending inventory and cost of goods sold using

1) The LIFO method.

2) The FIFO method.

3) The weighted average method.

7.A.5. Inventory and purchasing data for one type of inventory held by Lump Company follow. Lump uses a periodic inventory system.

Jan.	1	Beginning inventory	100 units at $30
Apr.	1	Purchased	100 units at 32
July	1	Purchased	100 units at 34
Oct.	1	Purchased	100 units at 36
Dec.	31	Ending inventory	100 units

Required

1) Determine the cost of ending inventory and cost of goods sold using

   a) The FIFO method.

   b) The LIFO method.

   c) The weighted average method.

2) Assume instead that Lump's purchases on April 1, July 1, and October 1 were all at unit costs of $30. Determine the cost of ending inventory and the cost of goods sold using

   a) The FIFO method.

   b) The LIFO method.

   c) The weighted average method.

7.A.6. The following data relate to the mineral water inventory of Margo Company, which uses a periodic inventory system.

Jan. 1	Beginning inventory	80,000 liters at 40¢	$ 32,000
13	Purchased	200,000 liters at 42¢	84,000
15	Purchased	300,000 liters at 41¢	123,000
30	Purchased	100,000 liters at ?	?
31	Ending inventory	120,000 liters ?	?
Cost of goods sold			$233,200

Required

Assuming use of the LIFO method:

1) Determine the cost of the ending inventory.

2) Determine the unit cost and total cost of the January 30 purchase.

SECTION 7.B

Inventory Systems

OBJECTIVES

In this section we concentrate on perpetual inventory systems and on the lower of cost or market concept. When you have finished your study, you should be able to

1. State why it is necessary to take physical inventories even though perpetual inventory records are maintained.

2. State in your own words the principal reasons for using perpetual inventory systems.

3. Determine the cost of goods sold and the cost of ending inventory assuming use of a perpetual inventory system and the
   a. First-in, first-out (FIFO) method.
   b. Last-in, first-out (LIFO) method.
   c. Moving average method.

4. State why the last-in, first-out (LIFO) method will usually produce different results for the periodic and perpetual systems.

5. State what is meant by the term *market* in the expression *lower of cost or market*.

6. Determine the cost of ending inventory using the lower of cost or market approach.

PERIODIC INVENTORY SYSTEMS

Chapters 4 and 5 have already illustrated certain aspects of accounting for merchandise transactions within a periodic inventory system, and a periodic system was assumed for the discussion of cost-flow assumptions in the previous section. When a periodic system is used, a Purchases account is charged with the cost of goods purchased. For example, a purchase of merchandise costing $5,000 is recorded as follows.

AT TIME OF PURCHASE		
Purchases	5,000	
Accounts Payable		5,000
Merchandise purchased.		

No entry is made to recognize cost of goods sold when a sale is made. A sale of merchandise for $500 is simply recorded in the following way.

AT TIME OF SALE		
Accounts Receivable	500	
Sales		500
Merchandise sold.		

At the end of an accounting period, the Merchandise Inventory account is brought up-to-date and Cost of Goods Sold is recognized. In summary form, and ignoring purchases returns, purchases discounts, and transportation, an end-of-period adjustment for Cost of Goods Sold may take the following format.[4]

END-OF-PERIOD ADJUSTMENT		
Cost of Goods Sold	78,000	
Merchandise Inventory (Ending)	12,000	
· Purchases		80,000
Merchandise Inventory (Beginning)		10,000
To set up Cost of Goods Sold and the actual inventory on hand at the end of the period.		

PERPETUAL INVENTORY SYSTEMS

Recording Purchases and Sales

When a perpetual inventory system is used, continuing records are maintained for various items in inventory. The Merchandise Inventory account in the general ledger serves as a control account for subsidiary inventory records. When goods are purchased, the Merchandise Inventory account is charged with the cost, as follows.

AT TIME OF PURCHASE		
Merchandise Inventory	5,000	
Accounts Payable		5,000
Merchandise purchased.		

The units purchased and their costs are reflected into the subsidiary inventory records, so that they will show the quantities and costs of goods actually on hand. Subsidiary inventory records are usually posted directly from receiving slips or purchase invoices. *An invoice is a billing form on which a seller shows details about goods or services that have been sold, including the charges for them; a receiving report, sometimes called a re-*

---

[4]Refer back to Chapter 4 for a more detailed example of end-of-period adjustments for a merchandising concern.

ILLUSTRATION 7.4

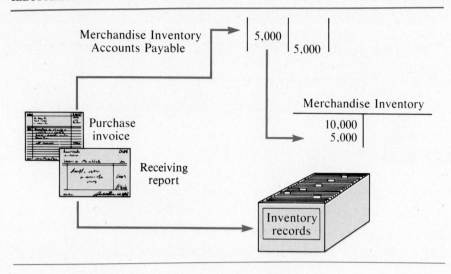

ceiving slip, is a form on which a buyer's own employees list the quantity, description, and condition of goods that are received. The recording and posting process is shown in Illustration 7.4.

When a sale occurs, an entry must be made to record the sale and reduce the inventory balance by the cost of the goods sold (Illustration 7.5).

Subsidiary inventory records must also reflect the decrease in inventory units and their costs. These subsidiary postings are usually made directly from shipping tickets or copies of sales invoices. *A shipping ticket is a form on which the seller's employees list the quantity and description of goods being shipped to a customer.* The recording and posting process is depicted in Illustration 7.6 on the next page.

Of course, many purchases and sales occur during an accounting period. A merchandising firm of any size would probably use specialized journals, similar to those illustrated in Chapter 5, for recording purchases and sales

ILLUSTRATION 7.5

AT TIME OF SALE		
Accounts Receivable	200	
Sales		200
Merchandise sold.		
Cost of Goods Sold	120	
Merchandise Inventory		120
To recognize the cost of merchandise sold.		

ILLUSTRATION 7.6

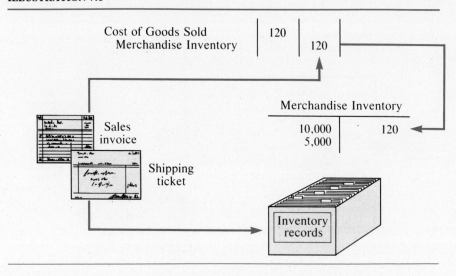

of merchandise. The journalizing and posting processes may be computerized for purposes of speed and efficiency.

Reconciling the Inventory Balance

Although subsidiary inventory records may be reconciled to the inventory control account at any time during an accounting period, they should *always* be reconciled at the *end* of each period. The cost balances on the individual inventory records are simply totaled to ensure that they are in agreement with the control account balance. Naturally, any disagreement must be investigated, and any errors that are discovered should be corrected.

Adjusting Inventory Records

As already pointed out, the Merchandise Inventory account and subsidiary inventory records in a perpetual system should reflect the actual inventories on hand. However, the physical inventories on hand may differ from the accounting records for at least two reasons. First, clerical mistakes are occasionally made when purchases and sales are recorded and posted. And second, inventory units may disappear as a result of shoplifting, employee theft, or spoilage.

OBJECTIVE 1. State why physical inventories are necessary even though perpetual inventory records are maintained.

Therefore, inventories must be physically counted, and the counts for various items compared to subsidiary inventory records in an attempt to discover any differences between what the records show and the actual quantities on hand. Where differences show up, the subsidiary inventory records are corrected, and an entry is made to decrease or increase the Merchandise Inventory control account for the total of the cost adjustments.

If, for example, merchandise shortages costing $850 are discovered, the following entry might be made.

END-OF-PERIOD ADJUSTMENT		
Inventory Shortage Expense	850	
Merchandise Inventory		850
To adjust the inventory account to the actual on hand at the end of the period.		

Comparison of Entries Under Periodic and Perpetual Systems

You can see from Illustration 7.7 how entries differ under the periodic and perpetual inventory systems.

Reasons for Perpetual Systems

Perpetual inventory systems are most often used by concerns that keep a limited amount of high-cost items on hand. These concerns must exercise

ILLUSTRATION 7.7

PERIODIC SYSTEM			PERPETUAL SYSTEM		
AT TIME OF PURCHASE					
Purchases	5,000		Merchandise Inventory	5,000	
Accounts Payable		5,000	Accounts Payable		5,000
Merchandise purchased.			Merchandise purchased.		
AT TIME OF SALE					
Accounts Receivable	200		Accounts Receivable	200	
Sales		200	Sales		200
Merchandise sold.			Merchandise sold.		
			Cost of Goods Sold	120	
			Merchandise Inventory		120
			To recognize the cost of merchandise sold.		
END-OF-PERIOD ADJUSTMENT					
Cost of Goods Sold	78,000		Inventory Shortage Expense*	850	
Merchandise Inventory (End)	12,000		Merchandise Inventory		850
Purchases		80,000	To adjust the inventory account to the actual on hand at the end of the period.		
Merchandise Inventory (Beg.)		10,000			
To set up Cost of Goods Sold and the inventory on hand at the end of the period.					

*No entry is necessary when physical inventory is in agreement with perpetual records.

constant control over their inventories to discourage thefts of these valuable items. An automobile dealership, for example, cannot afford to be careless with its inventory of cars.

Perpetual inventory records also help identify the types and numbers of inventory units available for sale to customers. By referring to subsidiary records, the seller can tell a potential customer immediately whether a particular item is in stock.

Subsidiary inventory records can also ensure that sufficient levels of inventories are maintained. Purchase orders may be issued automatically by clerks or computers when inventory stocks drop below established reorder points.

In summary, here are the principal reasons for using perpetual inventory systems.

OBJECTIVE 2.　State the principal reasons for using perpetual inventory systems.

REASONS FOR PERPETUAL INVENTORY SYSTEMS
1. To help discourage thefts of inventory
2. To help identify the types and numbers of inventory units available for sale
3. To help ensure that sufficient levels of inventory are maintained.

Types of Inventory Records

There are many ways of keeping track of inventory items. Where items are few in number, purchase invoices may be used to keep track of units on hand. An automobile dealership, for example, can identify each car by its serial number. When a car is sold, it may be marked off the purchase invoice. Invoice costs for unsold cars can be readily totaled to determine if subsidiary data are equal to the Merchandise Inventory control account in the general ledger.

When inventories include numbers of identical units for each category, more formal subsidiary records may be needed. A tire dealer, for example, may have on hand twenty tires of one type, eighteen tires of another type, and so on. Each distinct type of item is then viewed as a subsidiary account, or category.

Subsidiary inventory accounts do not have to be kept in a ledger book. Card files are sometimes used, with each card representing a type of item. Or, when the inventory system is computerized, details may be in the form of punched cards, or they may be encoded on magnetic tapes or disks.

The subsidiary inventory record in Illustration 7.8 shows the kinds of information usually kept for each inventory category.

ILLUSTRATION 7.8

Perpetual System, FIFO Method									
Item: *R2K Jackets*						Location: *Storeroom*			
	Received			**Sold**			**Balance**		
Date	Units	Unit Cost	Amount	Units	Unit Cost	Amount	Units	Unit Cost	Amount
19--									
Jan. 1							80	15.00	1,200.00
Mar. 5				60	15.00	900.00	20	15.00	300.00
May 10	150	20.00	3,000.00				20	15.00	
							150	20.00	3,300.00
July 21				20	15.00				
				110	20.00	2,500.00	40	20.00	800.00
Sept. 18	60	25.00	1,500.00				40	20.00	
							60	25.00	2,300.00

First-In, First-Out (FIFO) Method

A careful examination of Illustration 7.8 shows that the first-in, first-out (FIFO) cost-flow method was used in costing the goods sold. Note, for example, that the 130 units sold on July 21 were assumed to be made up as follows.

COST OF JACKET UNITS SOLD ON JULY 21 UNDER FIFO		
Remaining units from beginning inventory	20 units at $15	$ 300
From purchase of May 10	110 units at 20	2,200
Total sold	130 units	$2,500

The inventory remaining after the September 18 purchase consists of 40 units at $20 and 60 units at $25, for a total cost of jacket inventory on hand of $2,300. This is the same result obtained in the previous section using

OBJECTIVE 3a. Determine the cost of goods sold and the cost of ending inventory assuming use of a perpetual inventory system and the FIFO method.

a periodic inventory system and the FIFO costing method. The principal difference is that the periodic system subtracts ending inventory cost to arrive at cost of units sold, whereas the perpetual system subtracts cost of units sold to arrive at ending inventory cost. We can therefore generalize that the FIFO method produces identical results for both perpetual and periodic systems, assuming, of course, we are dealing with the same facts.

Last-In, First-Out (LIFO) Method

Now let us look at the perpetual inventory record when the last-in, first-out (LIFO) method is used (Illustration 7.9). The sale on March 5 was costed the same under LIFO as it was under FIFO, since all the units available for sale on that date had the same cost. However, the July 21 sale under LIFO was assumed to be entirely from the May 10 purchase. And the inventory as of September 18 was viewed as consisting of three layers.

OBJECTIVE 3b. Determine the cost of goods sold and the cost of ending inventory assuming use of a perpetual inventory system and the LIFO method.

Not only is the result under LIFO perpetual different from that under FIFO, but it is also different from that shown for LIFO periodic in the previous unit. The different results for LIFO perpetual and LIFO periodic stem from the simplifying assumption for the periodic system that all pur-

ILLUSTRATION 7.9

Perpetual System, LIFO Method

Item: R & K Jackets   Location: Storeroom

Date	Received Units	Received Unit Cost	Received Amount	Sold Units	Sold Unit Cost	Sold Amount	Balance Units	Balance Unit Cost	Balance Amount
19--									
Jan. 1							80	15.00	1,200.00
Mar. 5				60	15.00	900.00	20	15.00	300.00
May 10	150	20.00	3,000.00				20	15.00	
							150	20.00	3,300.00
July 21				130	20.00	2,600.00	20	15.00	
							20	20.00	700.00
Sept. 18	60	25.00	1,500.00				20	15.00	
							20	20.00	
							60	25.00	2,200.00

chases are made before any sales occur during the period. Under the perpetual system, on the other hand, a sale at a particular point during the period can be made only from stocks on hand at that date. Therefore, except by coincidence, LIFO periodic results will differ from LIFO perpetual results.

OBJECTIVE 4. State why the LIFO method will usually produce different results for the periodic and perpetual systems.

Moving Average Method

Average costing with a perpetual system requires that a new average unit cost be calculated each time goods are purchased. *This approach is called the* **moving average costing method,** and *the* **moving average unit cost** *is calculated by dividing the cost of units available at a point in time by the number of units in stock at that time.* A perpetual inventory record employing the moving average method is shown in Illustration 7.10. When moving averages are calculated, unit costs will probably be rounded to the nearest cent to simplify record keeping. As a result, the units on hand times the rounded unit cost may not precisely equal the balance amount shown. This is not serious, for a new average unit cost figure is computed each time goods are received.

OBJECTIVE 3c. Determine the cost of goods sold and the cost of ending inventory assuming use of a perpetual inventory system and moving average method.

ILLUSTRATION 7.10

	Perpetual System, Moving Average Method								
Item: *Ra K Jackets*						Location: *Storeroom*			
	Received			Sold			Balance		
Date	Units	Unit Cost	Amount	Units	Unit Cost	Amount	Units	Unit Cost	Amount
19--									
Jan. 1							80	15.00	1,200.00
Mar. 5				60	15.00	900.00	20	15.00	300.00
May 10	150	20.00	3,000.00				170	19.41	3,300.00
July 21				130	19.41	2,523.30	40	19.41	776.70
Sept. 18	60	25.00	1,500.00				100	22.77	2,276.70

The moving average approach should not be confused with the weighted average (periodic) method discussed in the previous section. The weighted average method spreads the cost of units available for sale *during a period* evenly over the units available during the period, whereas the moving average method spreads the cost of units available at a *point in time* over the units on hand at that time.

Comparison of Results

Notice how the results depend on the costing method and inventory system used. The following table compares the results obtained under a periodic system to those obtained under a perpetual system.

	FIFO		Weighted Average	Moving Average	LIFO	
	Periodic	*Perpetual*			*Periodic*	*Perpetual*
Available for sale	$5,700.00	$5,700.00	$5,700.00	$5,700.00	$5,700.00	$5,700.00
Inventory at year-end	2,300.00	2,300.00	1,965.52	2,276.70	1,600.00	2,200.00
Cost of jackets sold	$3,400.00	$3,400.00	$3,734.48	$3,423.30	$4,100.00	$3,500.00

COMPONENTS OF INVENTORY COSTS

In principal, at least, all costs that can be associated with inventory items should be included in inventory costs.[5] Thus transportation charges, customs (import) duties, storage and insurance charges, and even the expenses incurred in running a purchasing department should, in theory, be allocated to inventory items. On the other hand, Purchases Discounts taken should be excluded from inventory costs.

In most cases, however, it is impractical if not impossible to allocate *all* costs related to inventories to individual inventory items. Most concerns show purchasing department expenses and similar outlays as general and administrative expenses. Transportation in and similar costs directly associated with goods purchased are usually added to cost of goods purchased to arrive at the cost of goods available for sale. Still, it is common practice to ignore transportation and similar costs when costing the ending inventory. Where transportation and similar costs are significant, a portion of these costs may be allocated to Ending Inventory.

---

[5]*ARB No. 43*, "Restatement and Revision of Accounting Research Bulletins" (New York: American Institute of Certified Public Accountants, June 1953), Chap. 4, Inventory Pricing, par. 5.

ILLUSTRATION 7.11

Inventory Item	Quantity	Per Unit Invoice Cost	Per Unit Replacement Cost	Lower of Cost or Market
USE OF LOWER OF COST OR MARKET RULE				
A	4	$ 50	$ 40	$ 160
B	10	180	185	1,800
C	5	200	200	1,000
D	3	730	710	2,130
E	20	60	62	1,200
Total				$6,290

OBJECTIVE 6. Determine the cost of ending inventory using the lower of cost or market approach.

THE LOWER OF COST OR MARKET RULE

Ordinarily, assets are stated at their cost bases, in accordance with the *cost concept* of accounting. However, when an asset is worth less than its cost basis, most accountants insist that the lower, more conservative, "value" should be used for reporting purposes. *Conservatism, a traditional doctrine (tenet) of accounting, has to do with reporting cautious, less than optimistic pictures to users of accounting results.*[6] Users may then be assured that although the real situation may be somewhat better than the accounting reports show, it is not likely to be any worse. In the words of the Accounting Principles Board: "Historically, managers, investors, and accountants have generally preferred that possible errors in measurement be in the direction of understatement rather than overstatement of net income and net assets."[7]

Conservatism is accomplished in inventory costing by means of the *lower of cost or market rule*. This expression is somewhat confusing in that the word "market," in this instance, refers to the market in which *purchases* are made, rather than to the *sales* market. Thus lower of cost or market really means lower of cost or replacement cost. *The lower of cost or market rule requires that inventory items be shown at replacement costs whenever these costs are less than the invoiced costs of the goods.*

OBJECTIVE 5. Give the meaning of *market* in *lower of cost or market*.

Illustration 7.11 shows the application of the lower of cost or market rule to individual inventory items.

---

[6]*FASB Statement of Financial Concepts No. 2,* "Qualitative Characteristics of Accounting Information," defines conservatism as "a prudent reaction to uncertainty to try to ensure that uncertainty and risks inherent in business situations are adequately considered" (Stamford, Conn.: Financial Accounting Standards Board, May 1980), par. 171.

[7]*Statement of the Accounting Principles Board No. 4,* "Basic Concepts and Accounting Principles Underlying Financial Statements of Business Enterprises" (New York: American Institute of Certified Public Accountants, October 1970), par. 171.

In practice, sales prices are taken into consideration to ensure that the replacement cost figures used are not too far removed (over or under) from what is likely to be realized from the sale of the items.[8] The lower of cost or market rule is especially applicable to goods that are damaged or outdated. Since goods are not normally purchased in those conditions, the amounts realizable from their sale are more likely to be used for inventory purposes than replacement costs. These additional sales value tests are rather complex and are not critical to the understanding of the basic concepts presented here.

The lower of cost or market rule may be used in conjunction with any of the cost-flow methods and with either a periodic or a perpetual inventory system. The costs of inventory items are first established by means of the costing method being used. Then the lower of cost or market test is applied to make sure that the inventory is stated conservatively.

Inventory reductions under the lower of cost or market rule will result in a larger part of cost of goods available for sale being allocated to Cost of Goods Sold. This will in turn lead to a lower gross profit and net income than would result from a pure cost approach. The ending inventory will also appear among the assets on the balance sheet at a lower (more conservative) figure.

ITEMS INCLUDED IN INVENTORY

A great deal of care must be exercised when inventory items are being counted, so that nothing is missed and no item is counted more than once. All items owned by the entity at the date of the inventory should be included, even though some of them may not be physically present at the time of the count.

Goods in Transit

Goods that are in transit from suppliers to customers should be included in inventory to the extent that they are owned by the entity being accounted for. In general, legal title transfers from a seller to a buyer when the buyer takes possession of the goods. When goods are shipped *f.o.b. destination,* legal title remains with the seller until the goods are delivered to the buyer.[9] The carrier is assumed to be the seller's agent, and the buyer takes possession of the goods only when they are delivered by the carrier.

---

[8] *Accounting Research Bulletin No. 43,* (New York: American Institute of Certified Public Accountants, June 1953), Chap. 4, Inventory Pricing, par. 8.

[9] See Chapter 4 for definitions of f.o.b. destination and f.o.b. shipping point.

When goods are shipped *f.o.b. shipping point,* the carrier is the agent of the buyer and takes possession of the goods in the buyer's name. In this case, legal title changes hands as soon as the goods are picked up by the carrier (at shipping point).

We can thus conclude that a firm may own goods in transit as a result of (1) purchases from suppliers on terms of f.o.b. shipping point and (2) sales to customers on terms of f.o.b. destination. On the other hand, goods purchased f.o.b. destination and goods sold f.o.b. shipping point should not be included in inventory unless they are physically present on the inventory date.

Goods on Consignment

Consigned goods are merchandise items that have been entrusted by the owner (consignor) to an agent (consignee), who is to sell the goods for the owner. Consigned goods should be included in the owner's (consignor's) inventory until such time as the goods have been sold by the consignee. Conversely, an entity in possession of consigned goods (as consignee) must be careful to exclude such goods from inventory.

GLOSSARY FOR SECTION 7.B

Conservatism   A traditional doctrine (tenet) of accounting that has to do with reporting cautious, less than optimistic pictures to users of accounting results.

Consigned goods   Merchandise items that have been entrusted by the owner (consignor) to an agent (consignee), who is to sell the goods for the owner.

Invoice   A billing form on which a seller shows details about goods or services that have been sold, including the charges for them.

Lower of cost or market rule   An approach for stating inventory items at replacement costs when these costs are less than the invoiced costs of the goods.

Moving average costing method   An inventory costing method that determines a new average unit cost each time goods are purchased.

Moving average unit cost   The unit cost determined by dividing the cost of units available at a point in time by the number of units in stock at that time.

Receiving report (receiving slip)   A form on which a buyer's own employees list the quantity, description, and condition of goods that are received.

Shipping ticket   A form on which the seller's employees list the quantity and description of goods being shipped to a customer.

SECTION 7.C

Estimating Inventory Costs

OBJECTIVES

This section deals with circumstances under which it is necessary or desirable to approximate the cost of inventory at a point in time. When you have finished your study, you should be able to

1. State how markup is related to gross profit.
2. Name three situations for which it may be necessary or desirable to estimate the amount of inventory at a point in time.
3. Estimate the cost of inventory at a point in time by means of the gross profit method.
4. Reduce ending inventory taken at selling prices to approximate cost, using the retail inventory method.
5. Calculate an estimated inventory loss using
   a. The gross profit method.
   b. The retail inventory method.

MARKUP

A grasp of the relationship between markup rates and gross profit is helpful in understanding inventory estimation techniques. *Markup is the difference between the cost of an inventory item and its selling price.* The total of all the markups on goods sold during a period is the gross profit for that period. *Gross profit* is what remains of sales after allowing for the cost of goods sold. Therefore, markups become gross profit as units of inventory are sold.

OBJECTIVE 1. State how markup is related to gross profit.

   A markup rate is the percentage relationship between a markup and some other amount, such as the selling price or cost. Markup rates are most often based on selling prices, but sometimes they are based on unit costs. Some people refer to a rate of markup on cost as *markon*, but there is no consistent use of that term. To avoid confusion, it is always best to state just what a markup rate is based on—*rate of markup on selling price*, for instance, or *rate of markup on cost*.

   Let us consider a simple example: an item of merchandise purchased for $4 that is *marked up* to sell for $5. The $1 markup can be stated as a percentage of selling price or of cost, as illustrated here.

$$\text{Rate of markup on selling price} = \frac{\text{Markup}}{\text{Selling price}} = \frac{\$1}{\$5} = 20\%$$

$$\text{Rate of markup on cost} = \frac{\text{Markup}}{\text{Cost}} = \frac{\$1}{\$4} = 25\%$$

You can see that the rate depends on just what base figure we assume to be 100%. A markup rate of 20% on selling price is the same as a markup rate of 25% on cost.

Gross profit is the *result* of the markup on items sold during a period. If, for example, all merchandise were priced to realize a markup rate of 20% on selling price, we would then expect to achieve a gross profit rate of 20% on sales. Of course, in most instances, different types of inventory are marked up at different rates. A department store may price clothing to include a markup rate of 20% on sales, while toys may be priced to yield a markup rate of 40% on sales. A gross profit rate, then, is actually a weighted average of all the different markup rates for items sold.

When only the unit cost and desired rate of markup on selling price are known, the selling price can be determined by two methods. Suppose, for example, that we wish to price an item costing $8 so as to achieve a markup of 20% on selling price. One approach is illustrated here.

$$\text{Selling price} = \frac{\text{Cost}}{100\% - \text{Rate of markup on selling price}} = \frac{\$8}{100\% - 20\%}$$

$$= \frac{\$8}{0.80} = \$10$$

Note that we did *not* increase the cost by 20% to get the selling price. If we had, the result would have been only $9.60, which does not yield a markup rate of 20% on selling price. However, we could have converted the markup rate on selling price to an *equivalent* rate based on cost. This alternate method is illustrated here.

$$\text{Rate of markup on cost} = \frac{\text{Rate of markup on selling price}}{100\% - \text{Rate of markup on selling price}}$$

$$= \frac{20\%}{100\% - 20\%} = \frac{20\%}{80\%} = 25\%$$

Now the selling price can be computed by increasing cost by the rate of markup on cost.

$$\text{Selling price} = \text{Cost} \times (100\% + \text{Rate of markup on cost})$$

$$= \$8 \times (100\% + 25\%) = \$8 \times 125\% = \$10$$

ESTIMATING INVENTORY BY THE GROSS PROFIT METHOD

Interim Statements

A concern may need to estimate the inventory on hand at a point in time for various reasons, such as for the preparation of *interim statements* and reports. Most entities report to owners, creditors, government agencies, and others on an annual basis. However, information is needed at more frequent intervals by the managers of the entity. And owners, creditors, and others may want, and demand, to know how well a concern is doing at various times during the accounting year. For these purposes, interim statements are prepared. *An interim statement is a statement prepared for a portion of an accounting year.*

Concerns that keep track of inventories by means of a *perpetual inventory system* can readily determine the total inventory at a point in time. But entities that employ a *periodic inventory system* must take a *physical inventory* to establish what is on hand. And it simply may be impractical to count and cost all inventory items each time interim statements are needed. For this reason, the total cost of inventories on hand may be estimated by means of the gross profit method. *The gross profit method of estimating inventory approximates total inventory cost by deducting the estimated cost of goods sold from the cost of goods available for sale,* as shown by the accounting records.

An estimate of the cost of goods sold can be made by removing the approximate gross profit from net sales. An approximation of the gross profit rate is usually made by adjusting the previous year's gross profit rate for any known changes in pricing (markup) policy. In the absence of any known changes in policy, the previous year's rate is used.

The calculation in Illustration 7.12 shows the process by which inventory may be estimated at a point in time, assuming an estimated gross profit rate of 25%.

ILLUSTRATION 7.12

OBJECTIVE 3. Estimate the cost of inventory at a point in time by the gross profit method.

INVENTORY ESTIMATED BY THE GROSS PROFIT METHOD		
Beginning inventory		$130,000
Purchases during period		500,000
Available for sale		$630,000
Sales during period	$720,000	
Less: Estimated gross profit (25% × $720,000)	180,000	
Estimated cost of goods sold		540,000
Estimated inventory at this point in time		$ 90,000

ILLUSTRATION 7.13

INVENTORY LOSS ESTIMATED BY THE GROSS PROFIT METHOD		
Beginning inventory		$130,000
Purchases during period		500,000
Available for sale		$630,000
Sales during period	$720,000	
Less: Estimated gross profit (25% × $720,000)	180,000	
Estimated cost of goods sold		540,000
Estimated inventory at this point in time		$ 90,000
Less: Inventory remaining (at cost)		60,000
Estimated inventory loss (at cost)		$ 30,000

OBJECTIVE 5a. Calculate an estimated inventory loss using the gross profit method.

Audit Technique

Auditors may employ the gross profit method of estimating inventory to test the reasonableness of a physical inventory. Mistakes made when counting, costing, and extending types of inventory can seriously distort the inventory figure. By estimating inventory by means of the gross profit approach, an auditor can determine whether the inventory figure is in line with what one might reasonably expect to find on hand. If there are serious doubts about the accuracy of the physical inventory, the auditor may require that it be retaken.

Inventory Losses

An entity may sometimes suffer a loss of inventory items because of fire, flood, theft, or other casualty. When this happens, the cost of items lost must be determined, or at least estimated, in order to include the effects in the accounting statements. If the entity carries insurance against such losses, the amount of any loss must be established in order to submit a claim to the insurance company.

Inventories that have disappeared, or that are damaged beyond recognition, cannot be counted. Under a periodic inventory system, an inventory loss is usually estimated by the gross profit method. By deducting the inventory that remains from the estimated inventory, the loss can be estimated (see Illustration 7.13).

In summary, there are three common situations for which inventories are estimated.

1. For interim statements
2. To check the reasonableness of a physical inventory figure
3. To establish the approximate amount of an inventory loss

OBJECTIVE 2. Name three situations that may call for estimating the amount of inventory at a point in time.

ESTIMATING INVENTORY BY THE RETAIL INVENTORY METHOD

Retail stores often display a considerable amount of inventory with selling prices clearly marked on the inventory items. Normally, costs are not marked on the merchandise items because retailers do not want their customers to know the amount of markup. A physical inventory is taken periodically (usually at year-end) by listing counts and retail prices for the various inventory items. The total retail value for each type of item is calculated, and these amounts in turn are added together to arrive at the total inventory at retail (Illustration 7.14).

Determining the invoiced costs of retail merchandise is difficult when there are large quantities of items on hand.

Some retail stores keep track of purchases at both cost and retail values. In other words, the selling prices of purchases are accumulated in some manner at the same time that costs are recorded in the Purchases account. With this additional information, a percentage relationship can be established between goods available at retail and goods available at cost, and that percentage can then be used to reduce retail inventory to an approximate cost basis. This approach is referred to as the retail inventory method. In summary, *the **retail inventory method** is an approach for reducing inventory at selling prices to approximate cost by multiplying the retail inventory by the percentage that goods available at cost is of goods available at retail.*

The retail inventory method is shown in Illustration 7.15.

Inventory Shortage

Retail stores frequently lose inventories through customer and employee thefts, as well as through spoilage. In addition, employees may sometimes pocket cash from sales that they do not properly register. An approximation

ILLUSTRATION 7.14

RETAIL INVENTORY LISTING			
Description	**Units**	**Price**	**Total**
Del Marrow Tomatoes, #2 Can	25	$0.30	$ 7.50
Tarte Tomato Paste	14	0.40	5.60
Liddy Small Lima Beans	52	0.65	33.80
White Cloud Flour, 5 lb.	33	1.50	49.50
Total inventory at retail			$70,000.00

ILLUSTRATION 7.15

INVENTORY COST APPROXIMATED BY THE RETAIL INVENTORY METHOD				
	Cost		Retail	
Beginning inventory	$ 60,000		$ 80,000	
Purchases	260,000		320,000	
Goods available	$320,000	÷	$400,000	= 80%
Inventory at retail prices			$ 70,000	× 80% =⌐
Inventory at approximate cost	$ 56,000	◄-----------------------------┘		

OBJECTIVE 4. Reduce ending inventory taken at selling prices to approximate cost, using the retail inventory method.

of the inventory shortage for a period can be determined with the retail inventory method (Illustration 7.16).

This approach may also be used to estimate losses suffered as a result of fires, floods, or robberies, provided that the retail value of purchases has been accumulated in the records.

Interim Statements

The retail inventory method may also be used to estimate inventories for use in interim statements. The procedure is shown in Illustration 7.17 on the next page.

ILLUSTRATION 7.16

INVENTORY SHORTAGE APPROXIMATED BY THE RETAIL INVENTORY METHOD				
	Cost		Retail	
Beginning inventory	$ 60,000		$ 80,000	
Purchases	260,000		320,000	
Goods available	$320,000	÷	$400,000	= 80%
Sales			325,000	× 80% =⌐
Approximate cost of goods sold	260,000	◄-- --------------┘		
Estimated inventory	$ 60,000		$ 75,000	
Inventory at retail prices			70,000	× 80% =⌐
Inventory at approximate cost	56,000	◄-- --------------┘		
Estimated inventory shortage	$ 4,000		$ 5,000	

OBJECTIVE 5b. Calculate an estimated inventory loss using the retail inventory method.

ILLUSTRATION 7.17

INVENTORY ESTIMATED BY THE RETAIL INVENTORY METHOD					
	Cost		**Retail**		
Beginning inventory	$ 60,000		$ 80,000		
Purchases during period	120,000		160,000		
Available for sale	$180,000	÷	$240,000	=	75%
Sales during period			170,000	×	75% =
Approximate cost of goods sold	127,500	◄ — — — — — — — — — — — — —			
Estimated inventory at this point in time	$ 52,500		$ 70,000		

GLOSSARY FOR SECTION 7.C

Gross profit method of estimating inventory   An approach for approximating total inventory cost by deducting the estimated cost of goods sold from the cost of goods available for sale.

Interim statement   A statement prepared for a portion of an accounting year.

Markup   The difference between the cost of an inventory item and its selling price.

Markup rate   The percentage relationship between markup and some other amount, such as selling price or cost.

Retail inventory method   An approach for reducing inventory at selling prices to approximate cost by multiplying the retail inventory by the percentage that goods available at cost is of goods available at retail.

SELF-QUIZ ON OBJECTIVES FOR SECTION 7.C
Solutions to Self-Quiz begin on page B-29.

1. **OBJECTIVE 1.**   State how markup is related to gross profit.

2. **OBJECTIVE 2.**   Name three situations for which it may be desirable to estimate the amount of inventory at a point in time.

3. The books of a retail concern show the following data.

Sales, January 1 through March 31	$300,000
Purchases, January 1 through March 31	200,000
Inventory at January 1	50,000

The gross profit rate has always held steady at about 40% of sales.

   a. OBJECTIVE 3. Estimate the cost of inventory on hand at March 31.

   b. OBJECTIVE 5a. A physical inventory at March 31 established an actual inventory at cost of $40,000. Determine the estimated cost of the inventory shortage.

4. Records of a retail concern show the following data.

Inventory at January 1	
At selling prices	$100,000
At cost	72,000
Purchases during the year	
At selling prices	$800,000
At cost	558,000

The December 31 inventory, taken at selling prices, was $150,000.

   a. OBJECTIVE 4. Reduce the December 31 inventory at retail to approximate cost, using the retail inventory method.

   b. OBJECTIVE 5b. If sales for the year were $700,000, determine the estimated cost of the inventory shortage.

DISCUSSION QUESTIONS FOR SECTION 7.C

1. What is the difference between a markup and a markup rate?

2. What is an interim statement? Why do some firms prepare interim statements?

3. What is a retail inventory method?

4. A retail merchant tells you that all merchandise in his store is priced at a 40% markup. Is this information sufficient to approximate the percentage of gross profit on sales? Why?

5. A business firm may arrange for a line of credit with a bank, which enables the firm to borrow up to a previously agreed upon limit without any additional credit investigation or approvals when funds are needed. Why might a bank (creditor) want to see the firm's interim statements at periodic intervals as part of a line of credit arrangement?

EXERCISES FOR SECTION 7.C

7.C.1. An item of merchandise purchased for $10 is marked up to sell for $15. State the markup as

   a. A percentage of cost.

   b. A percentage of selling price.

7.C.2. Compute the missing amounts (a) through (g) in the following exhibit.

Cost	Selling Price	Rate of Markup on Selling Price	Rate of Markup on Cost
$ 4	$ 5	_(a)_	_(b)_
_(c)_	$10	30%	_(d)_
$12	_(e)_	_(f)_	25%
—	—	60%	_(g)_

7.C.3. If a rate of markup on cost is 30%, determine the equivalent rate of markup on selling price.

7.C.4. The accounting records of Pier 6 Stores show the following data.

Sales, January 1 through June 30	$800,000
Purchases, January 1 through June 30	400,000
Inventory at January 1	100,000

The gross profit rate has held steady at about 45% of sales for the last few years. Estimate the cost of inventory on hand at June 30.

PROBLEMS FOR SECTION 7.C
Alternate Problems for this section begin on page D-51.

7.C.5. On May 15, Francois's Furs was robbed of a large part of its inventory of fur garments. Selected data are shown here.

	Cost	Retail
Beginning inventory, January 1	$ 64,000	$ 96,000
Purchases through May 14	300,000	424,000
Sales through May 14		400,000
Inventory remaining after robbery		30,000

Required
Estimate the cost of the stolen inventory.

7.C.6. The following data are available from the records of G. B. Three Department Stores.

Inventory at Jan. 1	
At selling prices	$ 50,000
At cost	30,000
Purchases, Jan. 1 through Dec. 31	
At selling prices	$600,000
At cost	379,500

The December 31 inventory at selling prices was $80,000.

Required

Reduce the December 31 inventory to approximate cost, using the retail inventory method.

7.C.7. Farnum Company inventory at December 31, 19X4, taken on a retail basis, is $620,000. Other data relative to the company follow.

	Cost	Retail
Sales for 19X4		$3,700,000
Purchases during 19X4	$2,468,000	4,000,000
Inventory at December 31, 19X3	260,000	400,000

Required

1) Reduce the retail inventory at December 31, 19X4, to cost, using retail inventory procedure.

2) The owner of the company suspects that shoplifting has been widespread during the year. Estimate the cost of the inventory that was stolen or that otherwise disappeared during 19X4.

7.C.8. An insurance adjuster comes to you for advice. One of the stores insured by his company was completely destroyed by fire on New Year's Day, 19X5, when the store was closed. The year-end inventory for 19X4 had not been taken at the time of the fire. Fortunately, the accounting records were stored in a fireproof vault and were not destroyed by the fire. The adjuster wants you to estimate the cost of the ending inventory so that the insurance company can settle the claim. Income statements for 19X3 and 19X4 are as follows.

STIFLE STORES
Income Statement
For the Year Ended December 31, 19X3

Sales		$100,000
Cost of goods sold		
Inventory, January 1	$25,000	
Net purchases	70,000	
Goods available for sale	$95,000	
Inventory, December 31	20,000	
Cost of goods sold		75,000
Gross Profit		$ 25,000
Expenses		15,000
Net Income		$ 10,000

STIFLE STORES
Income Statement
For the Year Ended December 31, 19X4

Sales		$140,000
Cost of goods sold		
Inventory, January 1	$ 20,000	
Net purchases	100,000	
Goods available for sale	$120,000	
Inventory, December 31	?	
Cost of goods sold		?
Gross Profit		$?

Required

Estimate the cost of the inventory destroyed by fire.

7.C.9. Vinny Sales Company was organized in February 19X4, and accounts on a fiscal year ending January 31. The company is seeking a bank loan during May 19X5, and the bank requires an interim statement for the three-month period ending April 30, 19X5.

On February 1, 19X5, the owner, Joan Vinny, changed her pricing policy to obtain an additional 4 percentage points of gross profit. This increase was effected immediately by changing prices of inventory on hand to reflect the higher markup. Vinny does not accumulate the retail value of purchased goods as they are received.

Provided on the page opposite are an income statement for the year ended January 31, 19X5, and a partial trial balance at April 30, 19X5.

VINNY SALES COMPANY
Income Statement
For the Year Ended January 31, 19X5

Sales	$860,000	
Less: Returns and allowances	20,000	$840,000
Cost of goods sold		
Inventory, Feb. 1, 19X4	$ –0–	
Purchases	$790,000	
Less: Returns and allowances	18,000	772,000
Available for sale	$772,000	
Inventory, Jan. 31, 19X5	100,000	672,000
Gross Profit		$168,000
Administrative and selling expenses		114,000
Net Income		$ 54,000

VINNY SALES COMPANY
Partial Trial Balance
April 30, 19X5

	Debit	Credit
Sales		283,000
Sales Returns and Allowances	8,000	
Purchases	238,000	
Purchases Returns and Allowances		6,000
Administrative and Selling Expenses	31,000	

Required

Prepare for Vinny an interim income statement for the three months ended April 30, 19X5.

SUMMARY OF CHAPTER 7

Although some concerns identify specific costs with inventory items, most entities adopt an assumption about how costs flow through the entity. The most common assumptions are first-in, first-out; last-in, first-out; and average costing. Except for the FIFO assumption, costing results may be different for periodic and perpetual inventory systems. A periodic system assumes that all purchases are made before any sales occur, whereas a perpetual system assigns costs only from goods available for sale.

The lower of cost or market rule can be applied in conjunction with any of the cost-flow assumptions or inventory systems. This rule is a conservative practice that costs inventory items at the lower of invoiced costs or replacement costs.

Inventory cost may be estimated for the purpose of preparing interim statements or establishing inventory losses, or as an audit technique to test the reasonableness of a physical inventory count. The usual estimating approach is to remove approximate gross profit from net sales to arrive at estimated cost of goods sold. Estimated ending inventory is then the difference between the cost of goods available for sale and the estimated cost of goods sold.

Most retail stores price their physical inventory counts at selling prices, which must then be reduced to approximate cost for statement purposes. When a store keeps track of the selling prices of goods purchased, the retail inventory method of costing inventory can be used. This method reduces inventory at selling prices to approximate cost by multiplying the retail inventory by the percentage that goods available at cost is of goods available at retail.

PROBLEMS FOR CHAPTER 7
Alternate Problems for this chapter begin on page D-52.

7.1. Agra Feed Stores have experienced sharply increasing purchase costs for an animal feed nutrient during the last six months of the year. Inventory and sales data for the nutrient follow.

		Pounds	Unit Cost	Unit Sales Price
July	Beginning inventory	4,000	$0.63	
	Purchases	3,000	0.67	
	Sales	6,000		$0.80
Aug.	Purchases	10,000	0.67	
	Sales	6,000		0.85
Sept.	Purchases	5,000	0.70	
	Sales	6,000		0.85
Oct.	Purchases	5,000	0.75	
	Sales	4,000		0.95
Nov.	Purchases	8,000	0.76	
	Sales	10,000		0.95
Dec.	Purchases	7,000	0.80	
	Sales	5,000		1.00

Agra Feed Stores uses a periodic inventory system.

Required

1) Identify the inventory method that will result in the most reported net income for the six-month period.

2) Identify the inventory method that will show the least net income.

3) How much more (or less) gross profit will result from using the first-in, first-out method than from using the last-in, first-out method?

4) The use of FIFO will result in the same inventory figure under either a periodic or a perpetual system, whereas LIFO inventory will differ with the two systems. Explain why these differences will occur.

7.2. Marilu Company sells only one product. Inventories are costed on a last-in, first-out basis, using a periodic inventory system. An unadjusted trial balance and adjustments information follow.

A/C #	Account	Debit	Credit
	MARILU COMPANY		
	Unadjusted Trial Balance		
	December 31, 19X4		
111	Cash	8,000	
112	Prepaid Insurance	–0–	
113	Prepaid Advertising	–0–	
115	Accounts Receivable	88,000	
0115	Allowance for Doubtful Accounts	200	
116	Merchandise Inventory	121,000	
118	Equipment	40,000	
0118	Accumulated Depreciation—Equipment		13,600
211	Accounts Payable		11,000
212	Bank Loan Payable		16,000
213	Interest Payable		–0–
311	M. Stockdale, Capital		57,100
312	M. Stockdale, Withdrawals	5,000	
411	Sales		805,000
412	Sales Returns and Allowances	4,800	
511	Purchases	471,500	
512	Purchases Discounts		1,800
513	Purchases Returns and Allowances		400
514	Freight In	5,400	
610	Cost of Goods Sold	–0–	
611	Salary Expense	110,000	
612	Rent Expense	16,000	
613	Insurance Expense	12,100	
614	Advertising Expense	16,100	
615	Utilities Expense	6,800	
616	Depreciation Expense	–0–	
617	Interest Expense	–0–	
618	Uncollectible Accounts Expense	–0–	
		904,900	904,900

Adjustments Data

a) Equipment depreciation for the year, $4,800.

b) A two-year fire insurance premium was paid on September 1, 19X4. Insurance Expense was debited for the entire amount, $2,400.

c) On September 1 the company paid $3,600 in advance for ads that were to appear in six monthly issues of a magazine, starting with October 19X4. The entire amount was debited to Advertising Expense.

d) The bank loan payable was incurred on October 2, 19X4, when a note bearing interest at 10% per annum was signed. Interest is to be paid on January 30, 19X5, the due date of the note.

e) It is expected that 1% of Accounts Receivable will prove to be uncollectible.

f) Inventory activity

Jan. 1	Beginning inventory	1,210 units @ $100
Feb. 4	Purchased	1,000 units @ 110
Mar. 8	Sold	1,800 units
May 3	Purchased	2,100 units @ 115
July 18	Sold	1,900 units
Sept. 1	Sold	300 units
Nov. 13	Purchased	1,000 units @ 120
Dec. 28	Sold	400 units

Required

Prepare a ten-column work sheet for the year 19X4.

7.3. Janeway Company has provided the following information to the accounting firm that does its annual audit.

Inventory, January 1, 19X4	$ 150,000
Purchases during 19X4	2,300,000
Inventory, December 31, 19X4	347,000
Sales during 19X4	3,010,000
Average gross profit rate during previous four years	30%

Required

1) Describe an approach for testing the reasonableness of the ending inventory figure.

2) Use the approach you just described to test the ending inventory figure, and indicate whether you would consider the inventory within reason.

7.4. Reported data for C.S. Stores are as shown.

	Cost	Retail
Beginning inventory	$ 55,000	$ 96,000
Purchases	830,000	1,396,000
Sales		1,280,000
Ending inventory	95,000	
Historic gross profit rate	40%	

Required

Test the reasonableness of the reported cost of ending inventory by two estimating methods, and indicate whether you consider the reported figure to be reasonable.

COMPREHENSION PROBLEMS FOR CHAPTER 7

7.5. The following information has been discovered by Emanon Company auditors in the process of auditing accounting records for the year ending December 31, 19X4.

    a) On June 1, 19X4, Emanon paid $12,000 to Person Magazine for a series of 12 ads that are to appear in 12 monthly issues of the magazine beginning with June 19X4. The payment on June 1 was recorded as Prepaid Advertising.

    b) Merchandise purchased on account for $25,000 on December 15, 19X4, was recorded by mistake as a $15,000 purchase. Entries have already been made on December 31 to set up cost of goods sold and update the ending inventory figure.

    c) On July 1, 19X4, the company paid a one-year insurance premium and debited Insurance Expense for the $10,800 paid.

    d) Inventory in Storage Room C, which cost $22,000, was counted twice when the physical inventory was taken. The double count has been reflected into the records by the entry to update the Merchandise Inventory account.

Required

1) Make adjusting journal entries for the foregoing information.

2) What is the net effect of items b and d on Emanon's ending inventory balance?

3) Determine the effect that each of the adjustments you made for the first part will have on net income, as well as the aggregate effect on net income of all four adjustments.

7.6. Jane Torres is considering the purchase of Mays Company. Jane is studying the following income statement data provided by Mays.

	19X4	19X3	19X2
Sales	$405,000	$375,000	$355,000
Cost of goods sold	220,000	205,000	195,000
Gross Profit	$185,000	$170,000	$160,000
Operating expenses	130,000	125,000	120,000
Net Income	$ 55,000	$ 45,000	$ 40,000

Jane's financial adviser, a CPA, has been able to determine that, intentionally or otherwise, the ending inventories of Mays have been misstated in the past as follows.

    December 31, 19X2: Understated by $10,000

    December 31, 19X3: Understated by $5,000

    December 31, 19X4: Overstated by $20,000

Required

1) Recalculate cost of goods sold, gross profit, and net income for each year by reflecting the inventory corrections.

2) How are the corrections likely to affect Jane's willingness to purchase Mays? Explain your answer fully.

8
Long-term Assets and their Expiration

Insofar as accounting records are concerned, assets are costs deferred to future periods. You have already learned that an asset's cost should be matched with the revenues it helps to generate during its useful life. Chapter 8 concentrates on some of the concepts and techniques used in accounting for long-lived assets.

This chapter consists of two sections. Section A deals with accounting for the acquisition and disposition of long-term assets as well as with accounting for improvements and renovations of existing assets. Techniques for accounting for natural resources and intangible assets are also introduced; and the concepts of depreciation, depletion, and amortization are differentiated.

Section B focuses on systematic approaches for recognizing expirations of long-term asset costs. The depreciation methods most frequently used are discussed and illustrated, and their results are compared. Also covered are accepted approaches for recognizing depletion of natural resources and amortization of intangible assets.

SECTION 8.A

Long-term Assets

OBJECTIVES

In this section we concentrate on accounting for plant assets, natural re-sources, and intangible assets. Long-term investments, another long-term asset category, are covered in Chapter 16. At the conclusion of this sec-tion, you should be able to

1. Record acquisitions of long-term assets.

2. Record dispositions of long-term assets.

3. Record trade-ins of old plant assets for new plant assets.

4. Record improvements and renovations of plant assets.

5. Differentiate between
   a. Long-term and current assets.
   b. Tangible and intangible assets.
   c. Depreciation, depletion, and amortization.

LONG-TERM VERSUS CURRENT ASSETS

Current assets are short-term in that they are expected to leave the entity or be used up within one year. All assets that are not current may be referred to as long-term (or long-lived) assets. *Long-term assets, then, are assets that are expected to remain within an entity for more than one year.*

OBJECTIVE 5a.
Differentiate between long-term and current assets.

PLANT ASSETS

Long-term assets are grouped under various headings in balance sheet pre-sentations. *The term **plant assets** is frequently used for tangible productive assets that are used over a number of years in the operation of an entity. Tangible assets are properties that have physical substance—in other words, assets that can be seen and touched. **Intangible assets**, on the other hand, are property rights that have value but no physical substance.* Patents, copyrights, and other intangible assets are discussed later in the section.

OBJECTIVE 5b.
Differentiate between tangible and intangible assets.

Furniture, equipment, machinery, buildings, and the land on which they are located are usually included under *plant assets* or an alternate label, *property, plant, and equipment.* A presentation of plant assets within a balance sheet might appear as follows.

	Cost	Accumulated Depreciation	Book Value
PLANT ASSETS			
Land	$100,000		$100,000
Buildings	400,000	$130,000	270,000
Furniture and fixtures	120,000	40,000	80,000
Machinery and equipment	160,000	90,000	70,000
Total plant assets	$780,000	$260,000	$520,000

Acquisitions

Plant assets are recorded at their cost bases, in accordance with the *cost concept*. All necessary expenditures of getting a plant asset delivered and ready for use should be included in its cost basis. Thus costs of transportation, sales taxes, installation, and so forth are added to the invoice cost of an asset. Any purchases discounts or other reductions in cost should be excluded from the cost basis of an asset.

Consider the following transactions relative to the purchase of a machine.

19X3

Mar. 27   Purchased an extruding machine for a list price of $50,000, less 2% discount for paying cash, plus sales taxes at 6% of net cost.

Mar. 29   Paid freight charges on the extruding machine, $800.

Apr. 1   Paid for installation of the extruding machine, $1,860.

Journal entries to record the acquisition of the machine might appear as shown in Illustration 8.1.

Land cost should include real estate commissions, surveying charges, title fees, and other costs associated with acquiring full ownership rights.

ILLUSTRATION 8.1

OBJECTIVE 1. Record acquisitions of long-term assets.

19X3			
Mar. 27	Machinery and Equipment	51,940	
	Cash		51,940
	Purchased extruding machine at list price of $50,000, less 2% discount, plus 6% sales tax.		
29	Machinery and Equipment	800	
	Cash		800
	Freight charges on extruding machine.		
Apr. 1	Machinery and Equipment	1,860	
	Cash		1,860
	Cost of installing extruding machine.		

Sometimes, land with old buildings on it is purchased with the intention of having the buildings removed. Under these conditions, the cost of the buildings themselves, along with the cost of demolishing and removing them, is added to the land cost. The cost of leveling and grading land to make it more useful or attractive is also added to the cost basis of the land.

Plant Asset Records

The Machinery and Equipment account debited in the earlier entries is a general ledger control account. An entity that owns numerous pieces of machinery and equipment is likely to keep a subsidiary record for each piece of machinery. Similarly, subsidiary records will be maintained for items of Furniture and Fixtures, Buildings, Land, and other categories of plant assets. These *subsidiary records that provide details about plant assets are sometimes referred to collectively as a plant ledger.* A subsidiary plant ledger record is pictured in Illustration 8.2.

Note that the card provides space for showing accumulated depreciation and net book value of the asset. As pointed out in Chapter 2, the *net book value* of an asset is the unexpired portion of an asset's cost.

ILLUSTRATION 8.2

SUBSIDIARY PLANT LEDGER RECORD

Item *Extruding Machine*   General Ledger Account *Machinery & Equipment*

Serial Number *EM-81-5480032*   Location *Department 4*

Estimated Life *5 years*   Estimated Salvage *$600*   Depreciation per Year *$10,800*

Date	Explanation	Cost			Accumulated Depreciation			Book Value
		Debit	Credit	Balance	Debit	Credit	Balance	
19X3								
Mar. 27	Net cost plus sales tax	51,940		51,940				51,940
29	Freight	800		52,740				52,740
Apr. 1	Installation	1,860		54,600				54,600

Depreciation

Plant asset costs are matched with revenues over the useful lives of the assets, in accordance with the matching concept. As a plant asset expires over time, portions of its cost are shifted to a Depreciation Expense account. You may recall that *depreciation* is the process of converting portions of the cost of a long-term productive asset to expense as the asset is worn out in the process of generating revenues. A contra account, Accumulated Depreciation, is used to show the total depreciation that has been accumulated for each category of plant assets.

A number of methods are acceptable for allocating plant asset cost as depreciation. Some of these are discussed later. For the moment, let us assume that the cost of an asset is spread evenly over the periods that are served.

To determine the depreciation for the period, both the life of the asset and its salvage value must be estimated. *Salvage value is the market value of a plant asset at the time it is sold or traded in on another asset.* The machine represented by the subsidiary record card in Illustration 8.2 is expected to last five years. At the end of five years, it is expected to have a salvage value of $600. The annual depreciation cost is determined as follows.

$$\frac{\text{Cost} - \text{Salvage value}}{\text{Expected life}} = \frac{\$54,600 - \$600}{5 \text{ Years}} = \$10,800$$

Since the asset was used for only nine months during 19X3, only three-fourths of a year's depreciation should be charged to that calendar year. Accountants normally record depreciation on all plant assets with one adjusting entry. If we were to assume that the extruding machine was the only depreciable asset owned, the entry for 19X3 would be as follows.

19X3			
Dec. 31	Depreciation Expense	8,100	
	Accum. Depr.—Machinery and Equipment		8,100
	Depreciation on extruding machine put into		
	service on April 1, 19X3.		
	(9/12 × $10,800 = $8,100)		

When the depreciation for 19X3 is reflected on the subsidiary record card, there will be a net book value of $46,500, as shown in Illustration 8.3.

ILLUSTRATION 8.3

SUBSIDIARY PLANT LEDGER RECORD

Item _Extruding Machine_   General Ledger Account _Machinery & Equipment_

Serial Number _EM-81-5480032_   Location _Department 4_

Estimated Life _5 years_   Estimated Salvage _$600_   Depreciation per Year _$10,800_

Date	Explanation	Cost			Accumulated Depreciation			Book Value
		Debit	Credit	Balance	Debit	Credit	Balance	
19X3								
Mar. 27	Net cost plus sales tax	51,940		51,940				51,940
29	Freight	800		52,740				52,740
Apr. 1	Installation	1,860		54,600				54,600
Dec. 31	Depreciation for 19X3					8,100	8,100	46,500

Since land is not normally worn out over time, it is not depreciated. For this reason, a lump-sum purchase price paid for a building and land must be allocated between the depreciable building and the nondepreciable land.

Dispositions

As a rule, depreciable assets do not cease to be useful precisely at the end of their estimated lives. Some assets are disposed of before the end of their predicted lives; other assets are used long after they were expected to expire. The cost and accumulated depreciation accounts are left on the books for fully depreciated assets until they are sold or junked.

Presumably, an entity will sell an asset whenever its sales value is greater than its usefulness value to the entity. When the proceeds from the sale of a plant asset exceed the asset's book value, a *gain* is recognized; when proceeds are less than book value, a *loss* is recorded.

Consider the extruding machine purchased in 19X3. On June 30, 19X7, the machine is sold for $10,000. Although depreciation has previously been recorded only at the end of each calendar year, it will be necessary to recognize depreciation for 19X7, up to the date of the sale. The entries to

ILLUSTRATION 8.4

OBJECTIVE 2. Record dispositions of long-term assets.

19X7 June 30	Depreciation Expense	5,400	
	Accum. Depr.—Machinery and Equipment		5,400
	Depreciation on extruding machine for the period Jan. 1 through June 30.		
	(6/12 × $10,800 = $5,400)		
30	Cash	10,000	
	Accum. Depr.—Machinery and Equipment	45,900	
	Machinery and Equipment		54,600
	Gain on Sale of Plant Assets		1,300
	Extruding machine sold.		
	($10,000 − $8,700 book value = $1,300 gain)		

record depreciation and disposition of the machine at June 30 are shown in Illustration 8.4.

Both the cost and the accumulated depreciation related to the machine have been written off, as shown by the subsidiary record card in Illustration 8.5.

ILLUSTRATION 8.5

SUBSIDIARY PLANT LEDGER RECORD

Item *Extruding Machine*   General Ledger Account *Machinery & Equipment*

Serial Number *EM-81-5480032*   Location *Department 4*

Estimated Life *5 years*   Estimated Salvage *$600*   Depreciation per Year *$10,800*

Date	Explanation	Cost Debit	Cost Credit	Cost Balance	Accumulated Depreciation Debit	Accumulated Depreciation Credit	Accumulated Depreciation Balance	Book Value
19X3								
Mar. 27	Net cost plus sales tax	51,940		51,940				51,940
29	Freight	800		52,740				52,740
Apr. 1	Installation	1,860		54,600				54,600
Dec. 31	Depreciation for 19X3					8,100	8,100	46,500
19X4 Dec. 31	Depreciation for 19X4					10,800	18,900	35,700
19X5 Dec. 31	Depreciation for 19X5					10,800	29,700	24,900
19X6 Dec. 31	Depreciation for 19X6					10,800	40,500	14,100
19X7 June 30	Depreciation for 19X7					5,400	45,900	8,700
30	Machine sold for $10,000		54,600	—0—	45,900		—0—	—0—

ILLUSTRATION 8.6

19X7			
June 30	Depreciation Expense	5,400	
	Accum. Depr.—Machinery and Equipment		5,400
	Depreciation on extruding machine for the period Jan. 1 through June 30. (6/12 × $10,800 = $5,400)		
30	Cash	5,000	
	Accum. Depr.—Machinery and Equipment	45,900	
	Loss on Sale of Plant Assets	3,700	
	Machinery and Equipment		54,600
	Extruding machine sold. ($5,000 − $8,700 book value = $3,700 loss)		

OBJECTIVE 2. Record dispositions of long-term assets.

Now let us assume instead that the machine was sold for $5,000 on June 30, 19X7. The resulting loss would be recorded as shown by the second entry in Illustration 8.6.

Actually, so-called gains or losses from the sale of depreciable assets represent the amounts by which the assets were overdepreciated or underdepreciated during the periods in which they were used. Sale proceeds that are more or less than book value of an asset indicate that the asset's service life to the entity, or its salvage value, or both, could not be precisely predicted at the time the asset was acquired. The recognition of a gain or loss upon disposition of a depreciable asset is an expediency; correcting depreciation expenses and net incomes of prior years is simply not practical.

Trade-Ins

Depreciable assets are not always junked or sold outright. An entity may *trade in* a used asset toward the purchase of a replacement, in which case the trade-in value allowed by the supplier becomes part of the cost of the newly acquired asset. If the trade-in value is less than the old asset's book value, a loss is recorded. However, under current practice, no gain is recognized when trade-in value exceeds an asset's book value except where cash is *received* as part of the trade-in agreement.[1] Instead the cost of the newly acquired asset is recorded at the total of the old asset's book value plus any additional consideration given (in cash or payables).

Consider again the extruding machine example, only now assume that it was traded in for a new machine on June 30, 19X7. A trade-in allowance

---

[1]*Opinion of the Accounting Principles Board No. 29,* "Accounting for Nonmonetary Transactions" (New York: American Institute of Certified Public Accountants, 1973). *APB No. 29* calls for the recognition of gain *in proportion to* the cash received (as compared to total value received).

ILLUSTRATION 8.7

19X7			
June 30	Depreciation Expense	5,400	
	Accum. Depr.—Machinery and Equipment		5,400
	Depreciation on extruding machine for the		
	period Jan. 1 through June 30.		
	(6/12 × $10,800 = $5,400)		
30	Accum. Depr.—Machinery and Equipment (old)	45,900	
	Machinery and Equipment (new)	58,700	
	Machinery and Equipment (old)		54,600
	Cash		50,000
	Extruding machine traded in on new machine.		

OBJECTIVE 3. Record trade-ins of old plant assets for new.

of $10,000 is made toward the $60,000 cost of the new machine. The second entry in Illustration 8.7 records both the disposition of the old machine and the acquisition of the new one.

The cost recorded for the new machine is the $50,000 cash plus the $8,700 book value of the old machine at the date the trade-in occurred. This treatment has the effect of reducing the future depreciation that will be recorded on the new machine by the amount of the overdepreciation (as indicated by the implied gain of $1,300) that was recorded in the past.

Now assume that only $5,000 is allowed for the old machine when it is traded in on the $60,000 new machine. The loss of the old machine is recognized in the second entry in Illustration 8.8.

ILLUSTRATION 8.8

19X7			
June 30	Depreciation Expense	5,400	
	Accum. Depr.—Machinery and Equipment		5,400
	Depreciation on extruding machine for the		
	period Jan. 1 through June 30.		
	(6/12 × $10,800 = $5,400)		
30	Accum. Depr.—Machinery and Equipment (old)	45,900	
	Machinery and Equipment (new)	60,000	
	Loss on Sale of Plant Assets	3,700	
	Machinery and Equipment (old)		54,600
	Cash		55,000
	Extruding machine traded in on new		
	machine.		
	($5,000 trade-in allowance − $8,700 book		
	value = $3,700 loss)		

OBJECTIVE 3. Record trade-ins of old plant assets for new.

Federal Income Tax Treatment.   Federal tax law provides that for income tax purposes, neither gains nor losses are to be recognized when assets are traded in on assets of like kind.[2] Accounting practice is therefore in partial agreement with the tax law in avoiding the recognition of gains on property traded in on similar property. In the case of trade-in losses, however, accounting practice differs from the treatment required by the tax law. This is just one of many situations where tax reporting differs from financial reporting.

Capital and Revenue Expenditures

Accountants sometimes refer to costs incurred for long-term assets as capital expenditures. *A capital expenditure is a deferred cost that is expected to help generate revenue over a number of future periods.* Thus the costs of plant assets are capital expenditures.

Costs that are assumed to benefit only the period in which they are incurred are referred to as revenue expenditures. These costs are shown as expenses on the income statement for the period; in other words, they are matched with current revenues. Ordinary maintenance and repair of plant assets are recorded as expenses of the period in which they are incurred (revenue expenditures).

Expenditures for low-cost assets that are expected to last a long time are often treated as revenue expenditures as a matter of convenience. A letter opener, for example, usually lasts for many years. Yet its cost is so low that it is hardly worth keeping track of, and depreciating, as a plant asset. Most entities establish a minimum amount—say, $50 or $100—below which all expenditures for assets are written off immediately as revenue expenditures.

Improvements

Care must be taken to distinguish between ordinary maintenance costs (revenue expenditures) and costs that make plant assets more useful in the future (capital improvements). *An improvement, sometimes referred to as a betterment, is a change in an existing asset that makes it more useful to its owner.* Land may be improved by landscaping, drainage, paving, and various other means. And frequently buildings are improved by the installation of partitions, better lighting, insulation, or suspended ceilings.

The cost of improving a depreciable asset must be spread over the *remaining life* of the improved asset. For example, insulation installed in an old building will be useful only as long as the building is safe for use. For this reason, improvements are frequently charged to a separate asset account, as illustrated by the following entry.

---

[2]*Internal Revenue Code,* Sec. 1031(a). Gains, however, must be recognized *to the extent of* cash or other unlike property *received* by the taxpayer.

OBJECTIVE 4. Record improvements of plant assets.

19X4 July 5	Building Improvements—19X4 Cash Cost of insulation installed to reduce future heating costs.	30,000	30,000

Renovations

Costs are sometimes incurred to renovate (overhaul) an old asset. *A reno-vation is a change in the condition of an asset that extends its useful life.* Renovation, in effect, puts back into an asset some of the usefulness that expired in prior years. Therefore, renovation cost should be debited to the Accumulated Depreciation account, and the revised book value should then be spread over the estimated remaining life of the revitalized asset.

Consider, for example, a building that is 30 years old and had an anticipated life of 40 years when it was new. The accounts related to the building now show the following balances.

Building		Accumulated Depreciation—Building	
400,000			300,000

At this point, the building is renovated at a cost of $200,000, which is expected to extend its useful life by 10 years (20 years of life remaining). The renovation is recorded as follows.

OBJECTIVE 4. Record renovations of plant assets.

Accumulated Depreciation—Building Cash Cost of building renovation.	200,000	200,000

The book value of the building is now $300,000, as indicated by the T-accounts that follow.

Building		Accumulated Depreciation—Building	
400,000		200,000	300,000

After renovation, building depreciation will be $15,000 per year, calculated as follows.

Original cost of building	$400,000
Less: Accumulated depreciation	100,000
Book value after renovation	$300,000
	÷
Remaining life	20 years
Depreciation per year	$ 15,000

Replacement Costs

The cost of replacing worn-out plant assets with new assets of comparable productivity has been steadily increasing for many years. Depreciation expenses, based on original cost of plant assets owned, do not provide sufficient recovery from a concern's revenue stream to provide for replacing plant assets. As a result, entities frequently have to finance the increased cost of new plant assets by using assets accumulated through profits or borrowings.

Of course, accumulated depreciation accounts do not represent stores of funds for use in replacing plant assets; they are simply accumulated reductions in the plant asset accounts, which is to say that they are *negative* assets. Nevertheless, depreciation expenses do recover costs, in a sense, from revenue streams. And, provided that the cost recoveries from revenues are not used for other purposes, portions of the assets brought in by revenues can be used to replace old, worn-out plant assets.

Some people have argued that plant assets on balance sheets should be shown at their replacement costs, and that depreciation should also be calculated to recover sufficient costs to provide for replacing assets. *Replacement cost, as used here, is the amount of money that would have to be spent at a point in time to replace one asset with another asset of equal usefulness.* For example, the replacement cost of a used machine would be the price that would have to be paid to obtain another machine of the same age and condition.

In many instances, the price of a specific item will have increased more than prices have generally; in other cases, the price may have decreased. For example, prices of computers and hand-held calculators have decreased in recent years. The point is that prices of specific items may increase dramatically, decrease dramatically, or stay the same in relation to the general level of prices.

Another way the impact of changing prices can be measured is through the use of an index to adjust the cost of assets acquired for the effects of inflation generally. (The Consumer Price Index could be used, for example.) There is a big difference of opinion among accountants and other informed users of financial information as to which approach is more relevant. Section 12.B deals with a requirement by the Financial Accounting Standards Board that large publicly held companies disclose selected information about changing prices.[3]

NATURAL RESOURCES

Natural resources are products of nature (nature's resources) that are valuable as raw materials in their natural state. Natural resources are located on land (for example, timber) or under land (oil, gas, minerals), until such time as they are extracted for use.

The right to a natural resource is sometimes purchased separately from the land of which it is a part. For example, the purchase of *mineral rights* would be recorded as an asset.

Dec. 5	Ore Deposits	200,000	
	Cash		200,000
	Ore rights purchased.		

As natural resources are removed from the land, a portion of the resource cost is allocated to the units extracted. *The allocation of natural resource cost to units that have been removed from land is called* **depletion.** Like depreciation, depletion is usually accumulated in a contra asset account.

Dec. 31	Ore Depletion Cost	40,000	
	Accumulated Depletion—Ore Deposits		40,000
	To adjust for cost of ore mined.		

If all ore extracted during a period is sold, the ore depletion cost winds up in cost of goods sold. If some of the extracted ore remains as ending inventory, the depletion cost must be allocated between the ore that was sold and that which remains on hand. The allocation process is similar to the allocation of the cost of merchandise available for sale between cost of goods sold and ending inventory.

Intangible Assets

As pointed out earlier, intangible assets are valuable property rights that have no physical substance. Actually, accounts and notes receivable, prepaid expenses, and even cash are intangible in form. However, for accounting purposes, the expression *intangibles* is usually viewed as consisting of noncurrent (long-term) intangible assets such as patents, copyrights, franchises, trademarks, goodwill, and leaseholds.

---

[3]*FASB Statement No. 33,* "Financial Reporting and Changing Prices" (Stamford, Conn.: Financial Accounting Standards Board, 1979).

The cost of an intangible asset should be spread over its useful life. *The allocation of the cost of an intangible asset to accounting periods is called* ***amortization.*** (The process of spreading premiums and discounts on debt instruments such as bonds over the debt periods is also referred to as *amortization.* Amortization related to long-term liabilities and investments is covered in Chapter 16.)

Note the difference in the terms used to describe the expiration of different types of long-term assets.

Depreciation. *The process of converting portions of the cost of a long-term productive asset to expense as the asset is worn out in the process of generating revenues.*

Depletion. *The allocation of natural resource cost to units that have been removed from land.*

Amortization. *The allocation of the cost of an intangible asset to accounting periods.*

OBJECTIVE 5c. Differentiate between depreciation, depletion, and amortization.

Patents

*A **patent** is a right of ownership to an invention that is protected by a government for a limited number of years.* In the United States, an exclusive ownership right to a new invention may be granted to the inventor for a period of 17 years. After 17 years, any company may produce, use, and market the device that was previously restricted by the patent.

A patent right may be sold, or the right to use the patent may be licensed to other parties by the owner. Patent cost is apportioned (amortized) over the remaining *useful* life of the patent, which may sometimes be less than its *legal* life.

Copyrights

Copyrights *are exclusive rights to the benefits from artistic works* such as music compositions, books, or artworks. In the United States a copyright is granted for the life of the author plus 50 years.[4] The cost of a copyright should be amortized over its expected useful life, which is oftentimes much shorter than the maximum legal life of the right.

Organization Costs

Organization costs are the start-up costs of forming a new business enterprise. These costs may be negligible for proprietorships and partnerships; they are

---

[4]Copyrights issued before January 1978 have a life of 28 years, with the possibility of renewal for another 28 years.

apt to be sizable for new corporations. Legal fees, incorporation fees, and other costs associated with the initial creation of an entity are included in organization costs.

In theory, organization costs should be spread over the expected life of an entity. As you may recall, the life of an entity is usually assumed by accountants to be indefinite (infinite). Any amount of organization cost spread over an infinite number of periods would yield an infinitely small amount of amortization per period. However, the Accounting Principles Board has stated that the amortization period for intangible assets should not exceed 40 years.[5]

Federal tax law allows new businesses to amortize organization costs, for tax purposes, over 5 years or more.[6] As might be expected, most new business entities choose to write off organization costs over 5 years, the minimum period allowed by the tax law.

Research and Development Costs

Large concerns, especially those engaged in manufacturing, spend a great deal of money on the research and development of new products. A pronouncement by the Financial Accounting Standards Board in 1974 requires concerns to expense most research and development costs in the periods in which they are incurred.[7] Consequently, research and development costs are usually not treated as intangible assets.

Goodwill

The term *goodwill* is difficult to define and is the source of much confusion among people who use accounting statements. *Goodwill is that intangible something that represents a company's ability to earn an extraordinary rate of net income.* In other words, a company that is able to earn an *above-average* rate of return on its identifiable assets possesses an additional asset, goodwill, representing its excess earning power.

Assets are reported in accounting statements at their cost bases. If an asset is worth more than it cost, the value above cost is usually ignored. If an asset exists that was not contributed (invested) by owners and was not purchased at a cost, it will not normally show up on the company's books. Therefore, goodwill will not normally appear on accounting statements unless it has been purchased from another entity.

---

[5] *Opinions of the Accounting Principles Board No. 17,* "Intangible Assets" (New York: American Institute of Certified Public Accountants, 1970), par. 29.

[6] *Internal Revenue Code,* Sec. 248.

[7] *Statement of Financial Accounting Standards Board No. 2,* "Accounting for Research and Development Costs" (Stamford, Conn.: Financial Accounting Standards Board, 1974), par. 12.

Actually, goodwill consists of elements that may be difficult to pin down, but are not mysterious. Unusually high earning power, relative to the identifiable assets, is due to such attributes as reputation, location, brand names, and the like. These attributes, in turn, are built on past delivery of quality merchandise and service, liberal refund policies, top-notch employees, effective advertising, and similar factors. Upon reflection, most of the attributes of goodwill *cost* something during past periods, but the costs were written off as expenses during the periods in which they were incurred. Accountants simply have no way of knowing just how much of a cost like advertising will benefit the generation of revenues in the future. Consequently, the conservative practice of expensing such costs leaves goodwill with no cost basis unless it is purchased from someone else.

Goodwill is sometimes acquired by purchasing a going concern—an entire operating entity or subentity. The difference between the price paid for the entity and the appraised (apparent) value of the identifiable assets acquired is then labeled goodwill, as illustrated here.

Cost of entire acquisition	$260,000
Value of identifiable assets	220,000
Cost of goodwill	$ 40,000

Such an acquisition would be recorded by recognizing the identifiable assets at their appraised value and by assigning the remaining cost to goodwill.

May 15	Land	20,000	
	Building	90,000	
	Furniture and Fixtures	30,000	
	Inventory	80,000	
	Goodwill	40,000	
	Cash		260,000
	Jones store purchased.		

The cost of goodwill should be amortized over its useful life, which is usually rather difficult to determine. An opinion of the Accounting Principles Board requires that the amortization period for intangibles, including goodwill, must not exceed 40 years.[8] (Federal tax law does not permit amortization of goodwill for purposes of determining taxable income.)

Leased Assets

Plant assets are frequently rented (leased) from others under a lease contract. *A lease is a written rental agreement. The owner of the property is referred*

---

[8] *Opinions of the Accounting Principles Board No. 17,* par. 29.

to as the **lessor,** while *the party using the rented property is known as the* **lessee.** *The right to use the rented property is sometimes referred to as a* **leasehold.**

In the past, leased property did not appear on the lessee's balance sheet except as prepaid rent and the cost of leasehold improvements. *Leasehold improvements are expenditures made by a lessee to make the leased property more useful in the lessee's business.* The cost of leasehold improvements should be spread (amortized) over their useful lives, which cannot exceed the legal life of the lease.

A statement by the Financial Accounting Standards Board in 1980 defines various types of lease arrangements and prescribes methods by which both lessors and lessees are to account for them.[9] The pronouncement is long and involved, owing to the complexities of the problems dealt with. Under certain circumstances, leases that are essentially financing arrangements for the purchase of assets must be accounted for as though the leased assets were actually purchased by the lessee from the lessor. Under these circumstances, the present value of future lease obligations is shown as both an asset and a liability on the lessee's books. The problems of accounting for long-term leases are dealt with at the intermediate and advanced levels of accounting study.

GLOSSARY FOR SECTION 8.A

Amortization   The allocation of the cost of an intangible asset to accounting periods.

Capital expenditure   A deferred cost that is expected to help generate revenue over a number of future periods.

Copyright   An exclusive right to the benefits from an artistic work.

Depletion   The allocation of natural resource cost to units that have been removed from land.

Depreciation   The process of converting portions of the cost of a long-term asset to expense as the asset is worn out in the process of generating revenues.

Goodwill   That intangible something that represents a company's ability to earn an above-average rate of return on its identifiable assets.

Improvement (betterment)   A change in an existing asset that makes it more useful to its owner.

Intangible assets   Property rights that have value but no physical substance.

Lease   A written rental agreement.

Leasehold   The right to use rental property.

---

[9]*Statement of Financial Accounting Standards Board No. 13,* "Accounting for Leases" (Stamford, Conn.: Financial Accounting Standards Board, revised May 1980).

Leasehold improvements   Expenditures by a lessee to make leased property more useful in the lessee's business.

Lessee   The party using rental property.

Lessor   The owner of rental property.

Long-term assets   Assets that are expected to remain within an entity for more than one year.

Natural resources   Products of nature (nature's resources) that are valuable as raw materials in their natural state.

Organization costs   The start-up costs of forming a new business enterprise.

Patent   A right of ownership to an invention that is protected by a government for a limited number of years.

Plant assets   Tangible productive assets that are used over a number of years in the operation of an entity.

Plant ledger   A set of subsidiary records that provides details about plant assets.

Renovation   A change in the condition of an asset that extends its useful life.

Replacement cost   The amount of money that would have to be paid at a point in time to replace one asset with another asset of equal usefulness.

Revenue expenditure   A cost that is assumed to benefit only the period in which it is incurred.

Salvage value   The market value of a plant asset at the time it is sold or traded in on another asset.

Tangible assets   Properties that have physical substance.

SELF-QUIZ ON OBJECTIVES FOR SECTION 8.A
Solutions to Self-Quiz begin on page B-31.

1. **OBJECTIVES 1, 2, 3, 4.** Make journal entries to record the following events.

    Jan. 4   Purchased a new shaving machine for $20,000, less 5% discount for paying cash, plus sales taxes of 6% on net cost. Costs of machines are charged to a general ledger control account titled Machinery.

    5   Paid freight charges on the machine purchased on January 4, $300.

    6   Paid cash to a contractor for installing the machine purchased on January 4, $700.

    8   Sold an old grinding machine for $800 cash. The machine had originally cost $8,000 and had accumulated depreciation to date of $7,000.

    10   Traded in an old truck for a new truck that had a list price of $16,000. The truck dealer allowed $4,000 for the old truck, and the remaining cost, $12,000, was paid in cash. The old truck had cost $10,000 and had accumulated depreciation of $8,000 at the time it was traded. All autos and trucks are controlled by a general ledger account titled Automotive Equipment.

11   An electronic smoke detector and burglar alarm system was installed in the building at a cash cost of $60,000. The building is now 20 years old and has an estimated remaining life of 20 years.

15   An old polishing machine, fully depreciated on the books, was overhauled at a cash cost of $4,000. As a result of the overhaul, the machine is expected to last for another 2 years. The machine had cost $12,000 when it was purchased 10 years ago.

2. **OBJECTIVE 5.** Differentiate between the following expressions:

   a. Long-term and current assets.

   b. Tangible and intangible assets.

   c. Depreciation, depletion, and amortization.

DISCUSSION QUESTIONS FOR SECTION 8.A

1. What are plant assets?

2. What is the difference between capital expenditures and revenue expenditures?

3. Under what circumstances might a firm sell or trade an asset that is not fully depreciated and is in good working order?

4. How does accounting for ordinary maintenance costs differ from accounting for the costs of asset improvements?

5. What is the difference between ordinary maintenance costs and renovation costs?

6. What account is usually debited to record the cost of renovating a depreciable asset, and why?

7. Why do some people argue that depreciation should be based on the *replacement* cost of an asset?

8. Why would a manager dispose of an asset when a *loss* on its disposition is anticipated? Does the accounting recognition of a loss on disposition of an asset mean that the decision to get rid of the asset was a bad one?

9. How does accounting for a trade-in differ from accounting for an outright sale of an old asset and the purchase of a replacement? Speculate on how such a difference in treatment might be justified.

10. In what ways does the tax treatment of trade-ins differ from accepted accounting practice? What problems may be expected to result from these differences?

11. What is goodwill, and under what circumstances will goodwill be recorded as an asset?

EXERCISES FOR SECTION 8.A

8.A.1. On May 15 the Dart Company purchased a new duplicating machine for $10,000 less a 2% discount for paying cash. Purchases of office machines are charged to a general ledger account titled Office Equipment. On the same date, freight charges of $185 were paid with cash. A special 220-volt electrical outlet was installed for the machine by an electrical contractor at a cost of $240, which was paid by check on May 15. Make general journal entries to record the transactions just described.

8.A.2. Use the information that follows, taken from a trial balance, to prepare the plant assets section of a balance sheet.

	Debit	Credit
Land	175,000	
Buildings	700,000	
Accumulated Depreciation—Buildings		190,000
Furniture and Equipment	160,000	
Accumulated Depreciation—Furniture and Equipment		80,000

8.A.3. Calculate the new amount of straight-line annual depreciation for a machine that originally cost $8,000 and had accumulated depreciation of $7,000 when it was overhauled for $3,000. The machine is expected to last for 3 more years, after which it will have a salvage value of $400.

8.A.4. On April 15 the SHM Company purchased as a going concern an operating retail store known as Sara's Sewing Shop. The appraised values of the assets purchased were as follows.

Land	$ 80,000
Building	360,000
Furniture	40,000
Equipment	50,000
Inventory	90,000

SHM paid $750,000 for the acquisition. Make the journal entry on SHM's books to record the purchase of Sara's Sewing Shop.

PROBLEMS FOR SECTION 8.A
Alternate Problems for this section begin on page D-55.

8.A.5. On July 1 the JCM Company purchased a stamping machine, serial number SM–1156, for $11,300. The machine was installed in Building A. Costs of machines are charged to a general ledger control account titled Machinery and Equipment. Freight on the machine was $600, which was paid July 3. The estimated useful life of the machine is 5 years, after which it is expected to have a salvage value of $1,400.

Required

Set up a subsidiary plant ledger record card similar to the one in this section, showing the preceding information on the card. Include half a year's straight-line depreciation recorded on December 31.

8.A.6. Following are selected events for June.

June 8   Traded an old truck for a new truck that had a list price of $20,000. The truck dealer allowed $6,000 for the old truck, and the remaining cost, $14,000, was paid in cash. The old truck had cost $12,000 and had accumulated depreciation of $9,000 at the time it was traded.

15   Sold an old lathe for $2,000 cash. The machine had originally cost $12,000 and had accumulated depreciation to date of $10,800. Factory machinery and equipment are controlled by a general ledger account titled Machinery.

18   An old grinding machine that had originally cost $8,000 and had accumulated depreciation of $7,000 and a remaining life of one year was overhauled at a cash cost of $2,000. As a result of the overhaul, the machine is expected to last for 2 additional years (a total of 3 years of life remaining).

25   An air-conditioning system was installed in a 15-year-old building that has a remaining life of 20 years. The air-conditioning system cost $200,000, which was paid in cash.

Required

Make journal entries to record the preceding events.

8.A.7. On April 15, 19X3, the Fortz Company purchased a custom-made piece of equipment at a cost of $96,000. Terms of the sale were 2/30, n/60. Freight charges of $2,400 and installation costs of $1,800 were paid on April 15, 19X3. The machine was paid for on May 1, 19X3. It is the company's policy to use straight-line depreciation and to record depreciation on long-lived assets as if they were acquired on the first day of the month of purchase. The equipment is expected to have a useful life of 10 years and a salvage value of $8,000. On January 2, 19X7, the company paid $21,615 cash for a major overhaul of the equipment. As a result of the overhaul, the machine has an expected useful life of 8 years from the date of the overhaul, with an expected salvage value of $8,000.

Required

Make journal entries to record the transactions just described, including depreciation for the years ended December 31, 19X3 through 19X7.

8.A.8. The following assets were sold by Quincy Company on January 5.

Asset	Cost	Accumulated Depreciation	Cash Proceeds from Sale
Bus	$80,000	$48,000	$29,000
Equipment	50,000	43,000	10,000
Machinery	8,000	7,600	400

Required

Make journal entries to record the sale of each of the assets.

8.A.9. Following are selected events for the Evergreen Company.

19X2

Jan.   2   Purchased office furniture on account, $10,000. Estimated life, 5 years; salvage value, $1,000.

       5   Paid installation and delivery charges on the office furniture, $200.

      10   Paid the January 2 account less 2% cash discount.

Dec. 31   Adjusting entry to record straight-line depreciation on office furniture purchased in January.

19X3

Dec. 31   Adjusting entry for depreciation on furniture purchased January 19X2.

19X4

Dec. 31   Record depreciation on furniture.

19X5

July   1   Sold the office furniture for cash, $4,000.

Required

1) Make journal entries to record the preceding events.

2) Assume that the furniture sold on July 1, 19X5, yielded cash proceeds of $3,000. Make the entry to record the sale.

SECTION 8.B

Cost Expirations

OBJECTIVES

In this section we concentrate on methods for allocating the cost of long-term assets to accounting periods. At the conclusion of this section, you should be able to

1. Calculate and record depreciation of a plant asset for a period, using
   a. The straight-line time and use methods.
   b. The double-declining-balance method.
   c. The sum-of-years'-digits method.
2. Compare straight-line (time), double-declining-balance, and sum-of-years'-digits depreciation methods in terms of their relative effects on income statements and balance sheets.
3. Calculate and record depletion of a natural resource for a period.
4. Calculate and record amortization of an intangible asset for a period.

DEPRECIATION

Purpose of Depreciation

A variety of depreciation methods are used to allocate the cost of depreciable assets to accounting periods. Any depreciation method should be systematic (based on a system) to prevent arbitrary manipulation of accounting results. Once a method is selected, it should be *consistently* followed—at least for the particular asset for which it was chosen.

Under the *matching concept,* expenses are matched with the revenues they helped to produce. Thus it would seem that the purpose of a depreciation method should be *to spread the cost of an asset, less any expected salvage value, over its productive life in proportion to the expected contribution of the asset toward the production of revenues.* If, for example, an asset's usefulness declines as it grows older, each period the depreciation expense should decrease accordingly. If, on the other hand, an asset is expected to be equally useful during its life, its cost should be spread evenly over the periods in which it is being used.

Recall that the *book value* of an asset is its original cost less the depreciation accumulated to date. Under current practice, we are not concerned with having the book value of an asset approximate either its replacement cost or its market value during its life. However, at the end of an asset's anticipated useful life, the estimated salvage value will be equal to cost less accumulated depreciation. Thus it is only at the end of an asset's useful life that we are concerned with equating book value with market value.

Causes of Depreciation

The rate at which an asset expires (depreciates) depends on a number of factors. Some assets deteriorate primarily with the passage of time. Other assets wear out as they are used. Buildings, for example, seem to depreciate over time, regardless of the extent to which they are used. Machinery and equipment, on the other hand, tend to wear out more with use than with time.

As a company grows, some of its assets may become inadequate. A computer that served the needs of a medium-size company may be traded for one with more capacity when the company expands. Compressors, generators, pumps, and other kinds of factory equipment may become inadequate as production increases. Predictable future inadequacy should be considered when the expected life of an asset is determined.

Improvements in technical processes that increase productivity may make assets obsolete (unsuitable for use) before they are physically worn out. Although difficult to predict, the possibility of future obsolescence should be considered when the expected lives of new assets are being determined.

Straight-Line Methods

The simplest way to recognize depreciation is to *spread the depreciable cost of an asset (cost less estimated salvage) evenly over the asset's useful life by means of a* **straight-line depreciation method**. Straight-line methods are based on the following formula.

$$\frac{\text{Cost} - \text{Salvage}}{\text{Units of life}} = \text{Depreciation per unit of life}$$

The base (useful life) over which depreciable cost is spread may be stated either in terms of *time* or in terms of *units of service* that the asset is expected to provide.

Based on Time.   In practice, asset lives are most frequently stated in terms of time. Under this method, depreciation is spread evenly over the months or years that an asset is expected to last. The following example is used to illustrate the method.

STAMPING MACHINE

Purchase price	$15,500
Date purchased	July 10, 19X4
Estimated life	5 years
Estimated salvage value	$500

The company would probably assume, for simplicity, that the machine was purchased on July 1. (A machine purchased between July 15 and July 31 would be viewed as having been bought on August 1.) Under the straight-line time method, annual depreciation for this machine would be as follows.

OBJECTIVE 1a. Calculate and record depreciation of a plant asset for a period, using the straight-line time method.

$$\frac{\text{Cost} - \text{Salvage}}{\text{Life in time periods}} = \text{Depreciation per time period}$$

$$\frac{\$15,500 - \$500}{5 \text{ years}} = \$3,000 \text{ per year}$$

The following adjusting entry records depreciation for the last half of 19X4.

19X4 Dec. 31	Depreciation Expense	1,500	
	Accum. Depr.—Stamping Machine		1,500
	($3,000 × 6/12 = $1,500)		

For each full year of use after 19X4, a depreciation expense of $3,000 would be recognized.

Based on Use. Depreciation is supposed to represent the cost of an asset's productivity that has been used up during a period. It would make sense, then, to base the depreciation charge on the extent to which an asset has been used for productive purposes during a period of time. For assets that wear out more from use than from age, the use method of depreciation, sometimes called the *units of service method,* seems to be most practical.

Suppose the life of the stamping machine were stated in terms of the number of parts it stamps out, rather than in terms of time, and that it is expected to stamp 100,000 parts during its life. Depreciation cost per part is figured as follows.

OBJECTIVE 1a. Calculate and record depreciation of a plant asset for a period, using the straight-line use method.

$$\frac{\text{Cost} - \text{Salvage}}{\text{Life in service units}} = \text{Depreciation per service unit}$$

$$\frac{\$15,500 - \$500}{100,000 \text{ parts}} = 15\text{¢ per part}$$

Unless production is maintained at a stable level, this method will result in uneven amounts of depreciation per period. If 12,000 parts were stamped during the last half of 19X4, the depreciation adjustment would be as follows.

19X4			
Dec. 31	Depreciation Expense	1,800	
	Accum. Depr.—Stamping Machine		1,800
	(12,000 × $0.15 = $1,800)		

Decreasing-Charge Methods

Many companies use *decreasing-charge methods* for recognizing depreciation. *A **decreasing-charge depreciation method** recognizes a large amount of depreciation expense in an asset's first year of life, and progressively smaller amounts of depreciation as the asset ages.* Because large portions of an asset's cost are expired during the early years of its life, a *decreasing-charge method is often referred to as **accelerated depreciation**.*

Companies became interested in decreasing-charge depreciation when these methods became acceptable for federal income tax purposes in 1954. By accelerating depreciation, companies were able to reduce taxable income for the early years of an asset's life, and thereby defer payments of federal income taxes until later years.

When the accelerated methods were considered for general accounting purposes, they were found to have a certain amount of merit. Many assets tend to be somewhat more useful (productive) when they are new than when they begin to wear out. As an asset ages, it tends to require more maintenance; and an asset cannot be used for productive purposes while it is being repaired.

If rising maintenance costs are added to the results of straight-line depreciation, the *total* cost of operating a productive asset will tend to increase over time. Thus increasing total operating costs may actually be shown when asset productivity is declining. Use of a decreasing-charge method for depreciation can sometimes show a more reasonable relationship between total costs and productivity.

Declining-Balance Method.   There are a number of methods by which depreciation can be calculated as a decreasing charge. The method most frequently used, the *declining-balance method of depreciation, applies a constant percentage to the asset's book value at the beginning of each year of the asset's life.* The declining-balance formula follows.

Constant %(Cost − Accumulated depreciation) = Depreciation for year

The result of this calculation is then spread evenly over the year to obtain depreciation expense for subannual accounting periods.

Salvage value is not normally considered when figuring depreciation under the declining-balance method. Some book value will always remain, however, since the method continually reduces book value by a constant percentage. Still, it is only coincidental if book value approximates salvage value at the time of the asset's disposition.[10]

The constant rate most often used is twice the straight-line rate, which is determined as follows.

$$2\left(\frac{100\%}{\text{Estimated life in years}}\right)$$

*When the rate used is twice the straight-line rate, the declining-balance method is called the **double-declining-balance method of depreciation**.*

Using the double-declining-balance method, depreciation on the stamping machine referred to previously would be as follows for its first full year of life.

OBJECTIVE 1b. Calculate and record depreciation of a plant asset for a period, using the double-declining-balance method.

$$2\left(\frac{100\%}{5 \text{ years}}\right)(\$15,500) = 40\% \times \$15,500 = \$6,200$$

Since the machine was used for only one-half of 19X4, the following depreciation adjustment would be made at year-end.

19X4 Dec. 31	Depreciation Expense	3,100	
	Accum. Depr.—Stamping Machine		3,100
	($6,200 × 6/12 = $3,100)		

Depreciation for 19X5 will consist of one-half of the first year's depreciation and one-half of the second year's depreciation as depicted in Illustration 8.9. Depreciation for the second full year of the machine's life is calculated as shown.

$$40\%(\$15,500 - \$6,200) = \$3,720$$

Thus depreciation for 19X5 will be as follows.

January 1 through June 30 (½ × $6,200)	$3,100
July 1 through December 31 (½ × $3,720)	1,860
19X5 depreciation expense	$4,960

---

[10]In practice, an asset is not depreciated below its estimated salvage value, and accountants will change to a straight-line approach at the point where the remaining depreciable cost spread over the asset's remaining estimated life will amount to more depreciation per year than would be obtained by continuing on the declining-balance method.

ILLUSTRATION 8.9

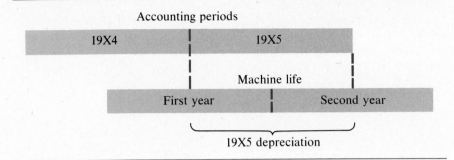

Note, however, that the same result is obtained by simply taking 40% of the book value at January 1, 19X5.

$$40\%(\$15,500 - \$3,100) = \$4,960$$

Therefore, we do not have to apportion for fractions of machine years, except in the first and last years of the machine's life.

Sum-of-Years'-Digits Method.   Another way to obtain decreasing-charge depreciation results is to *apply a decreasing fraction to the constant depreciable cost of an asset. The decreasing fraction is usually determined by placing the number of remaining years of life over a denominator that is the sum of the digits in the asset's life. The formula for this method, known as the **sum-of-years'-digits depreciation method**,* is as follows.

$$\frac{\text{Remaining years of life}}{\text{Sum of digits in total years of life}} (\text{Cost} - \text{Salvage}) = \text{Depreciation for year}$$

The numerator is the number of years of life remaining at the *beginning* of the asset year; it declines by one each year. For the stamping machine, depreciation for its first year of life, rounded to the nearest whole dollar, is figured in the following way.

$$\frac{5}{5 + 4 + 3 + 2 + 1} (\$15,500 - \$500) = \frac{5}{15} (\$15,000) = \$5,000$$

OBJECTIVE 1c. Calculate and record depreciation of a plant asset for a period using the sum-of-years'-digits method.

The denominator can be calculated by a short-cut technique that is useful when the life of an asset is quite long. Simply multiply the number of years of life (*n*) by one-half the life plus one year.

$$n\left(\frac{n+1}{2}\right) = \text{Sum of digits in } n$$

To illustrate the formula, we can use the relatively short life of the stamping machine.

$$n\left(\frac{n+1}{2}\right) = 5\left(\frac{5+1}{2}\right) = 5(3) = 15$$

To record a half-year's depreciation under the sum-of-years'-digits method, the following entry would be made.

19X4 Dec. 31	Depreciation Expense	2,500	
	Accum. Depr.—Stamping Machine		2,500
	($5,000 × 6/12 = $2,500)		

Depreciation for the second year of the machine's life is calculated as follows.

$$(4/15)(\$15,500 - \$500) = (4/15)(\$15,000) = \$4,000$$

Depreciation for 19X5 involves two different years of the asset's life.

January 1 through June 30 (½ × $5,000)	$2,500
July 1 through December 31 (½ × $4,000)	2,000
19X5 depreciation expense	$4,500

To avoid the problem of apportioning cost from different asset years, firms that calculate depreciation by the sum-of-years'-digits method often assume that assets are acquired and disposed of only on the first day of a year. Under this assumption, known as the *half-year convention,* assets bought or sold during the first half of a year are identified with the first day of the year, while assets bought or sold during the last half of a year are identified with the first day of the following year.

Comparing the Methods

Illustration 8.10 compares depreciation charges calculated by each of the three depreciation methods over the 5-year life of the stamping machine.

ILLUSTRATION 8.10

Stamping Machine	Cost:	$15,500
	Estimated Life:	5 years
	Estimated Salvage:	$500

| Machine Life Year | Depreciation Charge | | |
	Straight-Line	Double-Declining-Balance	Sum-of-Years'-Digits
1	$ 3,000	$ 6,200	$ 5,000
2	3,000	3,720	4,000
3	3,000	2,232	3,000
4	3,000	1,424*	2,000
5	3,000	1,424	1,000
Total Depreciation	$15,000	$15,000	$15,000

*Continuation of the declining-balance method in year 4 would result in only $1,339 of depreciation for that year. But $2,848 more depreciation is needed to bring the total depreciation over the 5 years to $15,000, in accordance with the practice described in footnote 10. That is, the firm switched to the straight-line method in year 4, depreciating the remaining $2,848 over years 4 and 5.

The double-declining-balance method shows the largest depreciation charge for the first year of an asset's life and therefore the smallest book value for the asset during the early years of its life. Reported net income during the first year of an asset's life will be smallest under the double-declining-balance method and largest under the straight-line method.

Accelerated Cost Recovery System (ACRS)

For property acquired after 1980, the *Internal Revenue Code* (Section 168) prescribes a uniform accelerated depreciation approach for tax return purposes. *The accelerated cost recovery system (ACRS) applies a percentage selected from a table to the cost of a depreciable asset to obtain the cost recovery permitted for tax purposes.* For example cars, light trucks, and certain kinds of machinery and equipment are designated "3-year property." This type of property bought from 1981 through 1984 is depreciated 25% in the tax year when it is acquired, 38% in the following year, and 37% in the last year, regardless of the anticipated life or salvage value. Under ACRS, a full year's recovery is taken for property acquired during the year, no matter how late in the year the property was purchased. Depreciable property is classified by definition as either 3-, 5-, 10-, or 15-year property. The tables provide for greater deductions in the early years of an asset's life (and smaller ones in later years) for property bought after 1984.

One must keep in mind that ACRS is prescribed by law for purposes of filing federal income tax returns; to date, no official pronouncement has recommended the system for general accounting purposes.

DEPLETION

The cost of a natural resource is usually spread evenly over the units that are expected to be extracted. The approach is similar to the straight-line method of depreciation based on use rather than time. The most difficult problem is estimating the number of units of the resource, especially when the resource is underground (as with mineral ores, oil, and natural gas).

To illustrate this approach, let us assume that land containing ore is purchased outright during 19X4 for $200,000, and that the land is expected to be worth $60,000 after an estimated 35,000 tons of ore are removed. The formula for determining the cost per ton of ore is as follows.

$$\frac{\text{Land cost} - \text{Residual value}}{\text{Estimated units}} = \frac{\$200,000 - \$60,000}{35,000 \text{ tons}} = \$4 \text{ per ton}$$

If 10,000 tons of ore were mined during the first year, depletion of $40,000 would be recorded.

19X4 Dec. 31	Ore Depletion	40,000	
	Accumulated Depletion—Ore Deposits		40,000
	(10,000 tons × $4 = $40,000)		

Should the estimate of ore reserves change as mining operations progress, the cost per unit will be adjusted. If, for example, it appears by the end of the second year that there will be 5,000 fewer tons of ore than was originally estimated, the depletion cost per ton will be increased to $5 per ton, as indicated by the following calculation.

OBJECTIVE 3. Calculate and record depletion of a natural resource for a period.

$$\frac{\text{Land cost} - \text{Residual value} - \text{Cost already recovered}}{\text{Estimated units at beginning of second year}}$$
$$= \frac{\$200,000 - \$60,000 - \$40,000}{20,000 \text{ tons}} = \frac{\$100,000}{20,000 \text{ tons}} = \$5 \text{ per ton}$$

Assuming that 10,000 tons of ore were mined during the second year, the entry to record depletion would appear as follows.

19X5 Dec. 31	Ore Depletion	50,000	
	Accumulated Depletion—Ore Deposits		50,000
	(10,000 tons × $5 = $50,000)		

The remaining cost assignable to the natural resource is simply spread over the estimated remaining units at a point in time.

AMORTIZATION

Intangible assets are usually spread over the periods of time during which they are estimated to be useful in much the same manner as for straight-line depreciation on a time basis. However, unlike depreciation and depletion, expirations of an intangible asset are usually credited directly to the asset account, rather than to a contra account. Assume, for example, that a patent with an expected remaining life of 5 years was purchased on January 1 for $50,000. The entry to record amortization for each full year of the patent's useful life would take the following form.

Dec. 31	Patent Amortization Expense	10,000	
	Patent		10,000
	($50,000 ÷ 5 years = $10,000)		

OBJECTIVE 4. Calculate and record amortization of an intangible asset for a period.

GLOSSARY FOR SECTION 8.B

Accelerated cost recovery system (ACRS)   A depreciation method prescribed by the *Internal Revenue Code,* which applies percentages selected from tables to the costs of depreciable assets to obtain cost recoveries for tax purposes.

Declining-balance method of depreciation   A decreasing-charge depreciation method that calculates depreciation for each year by applying a constant percentage to an asset's book value at the beginning of the year.

Decreasing-charge depreciation method (accelerated depreciation)   A depreciation approach that recognizes a large amount of depreciation expense in an asset's first year of life, and progressively smaller amounts of depreciation as the asset ages.

Double-declining-balance method of depreciation   A declining-balance depreciation method that uses a rate that is twice the straight-line rate.

Straight-line depreciation method   A depreciation method that spreads the depreciable cost of an asset evenly over the asset's life.

Sum-of-years'-digits depreciation method   A decreasing-charge depreciation method that applies a decreasing fraction to the constant depreciable cost of an asset. The decreasing fraction is the number of remaining years of life over a denominator that is the sum of the digits in the asset's life.

SELF-QUIZ ON OBJECTIVES FOR SECTION 8.B
Solutions to Self-Quiz begin on page B-32.

1. **OBJECTIVE 1.** Darwin Company purchased a truck on July 3, 19X4, at a cost of $36,800. The truck has an expected useful life of 8 years and an estimated salvage value of $800. Darwin Company calculates depreciation to the nearest

whole month. Make the adjusting journal entry at December 31, 19X4, assuming use of

   a. The straight-line time method.

   b. The straight-line use method (the truck is expected to be useful for 100,000 miles; was driven 10,000 miles during the last half of 19X4).

   c. The double-declining-balance method.

   d. The sum-of-years'-digits method.

2. **OBJECTIVE 2.** Blake Company purchased a costly piece of equipment. The choice of depreciation method will affect the amounts of reported income and assets during the first and subsequent years of the asset's life. Complete the following chart by placing a 1 in the appropriate space to indicate the largest reported figure, a 2 to indicate the middle figure, and a 3 to indicate the smallest figure for the first year of the asset's life.

Method	Size of Reported Net Income	Size of Reported Total Assets
Straight-line		
Double-declining-balance		
Sum-of-years'-digits		

3. **OBJECTIVE 3.** Enco, Inc., purchased land containing ore deposits for $250,000 during 19X4. It is estimated that the land will be worth $50,000 after 100,000 tons of ore are removed. During 19X4, 15,000 tons of ore were mined. Make the entry on December 31, 19X4, to record ore depletion for the year.

4. **OBJECTIVE 4.** Marco Publishing Company purchased a copyright on January 2, 19X4, for $60,000. The copyright is expected to be useful for a total of 5 years. Make the entry on December 31, 19X4, to record copyright amortization for the year.

DISCUSSION QUESTIONS FOR SECTION 8.B

1. Why do accountants usually prefer depreciation methods that are *systematic*?

2. What is the purpose of depreciation?

3. What do the terms *obsolescence* and *inadequacy* mean, and what do they have to do with depreciation?

4. Under what circumstances would you recommend the straight-line use (units of service) method of depreciation?

5. How can decreasing-charge methods be defended under the matching concept?

6. Both declining-balance and sum-of-years'-digits are decreasing-charge depreciation methods. What are the basic differences between the two methods?

7. How is the rate determined in the double-declining-balance depreciation method?

8. The cost of a natural resource is usually spread evenly over the units that are expected to be extracted. This approach to depletion is similar to the straight-line method of depreciation based on use. What theoretical argument might be offered in defense of an accelerated method of depletion?

EXERCISES FOR SECTION 8.B

8.B.1. Calculate the first year's depreciation for the machine described here, using

   a. The straight-line time method.

   b. The double-declining-balance method.

   c. The sum-of-years'-digits method.

LATHE	
Purchase price on January 4	$8,000
Estimated useful life	8 years
Estimated salvage value	$800

8.B.2. The Joshua Company purchased a new injection molding machine on April 1, 19X4, at a cost of $15,000. It has been estimated that the machine will last about 7 years and produce about 700,000 molds. The salvage value is estimated at $1,000.

   a. Calculate straight-line depreciation for 19X4 based on time.

   b. Calculate straight-line depreciation for 19X4 based on production of 90,000 molds.

8.B.3. During the current year the SVM Coal Company purchased 100 acres of land under which lay an estimated 400,000 tons of coal. The land was purchased for $1,250,000 and is expected to have a residual value of $250,000 after the coal has been removed. Calculate the amount of depletion for the current year, assuming that 150,000 tons of coal were removed.

8.B.4. Make journal entries to record the following events.

   Aug. 2   Purchased ore reserves estimated at 100,000 tons for cash, $75,000.

         31   Removed 10,000 tons of ore during August from reserves purchased on August 2.

8.B.5. The Rational Paper Company purchased land containing marketable timber for $360,000 during 19X4. It is estimated that the land will be worth $40,000 after

8,000,000 board feet of timber are removed. During 19X4, 1,400,000 board feet of timber were cut. Make the entry at December 31, 19X4, to record timber depletion for the year.

8.B.6. Shwartz Scientific purchased a patent on July 2, 19X4, for $420,000. The patent is expected to be useful for a total of 7 years. Make the entry on December 31, 19X4, to record patent amortization for the year.

8.B.7. Chick's Drilling Company is considering the purchase of a new rig. Compare the differences in reported annual income for the first year of a drilling rig's life for the double-declining-balance, sum-of-years'-digits, and straight-line methods, assuming the following facts about the rig.

Cost	$860,000
Life	8 years
Salvage	$140,000

PROBLEMS FOR SECTION 8.B
Alternate Problems for this section begin on page D-56.

8.B.8. Benton Adjusters purchased three new cars for their insurance adjusters on September 1, 19X4, at a total cost of $39,200. The cars have an expected life of 3 years and an estimated salvage value of $2,600.

Required

Make the adjusting journal entry at December 31, 19X4, assuming use of

1) The straight-line time method.

2) The straight-line use method (the cars are expected to be driven a total of 300,000 miles; they were driven 45,000 miles through December 31).

3) The double-declining-balance method.

4) The sum-of-years'-digits method.

8.B.9. The DGB Construction Company purchased a large bulldozer on January 4, 19X3, at a cost of $260,000. Freight charges of $3,000 for delivery of the bulldozer were also paid on January 4. The estimated useful life is 5 years, after which the expected salvage value is $33,000.

Required

Prepare a chart like the one following, showing the depreciation that would be recorded at the end of each year, and the total for each method.

Date	Depreciation			
	Straight-Line	*Sum-of-Years'-Digits*	*Double-Declining-Balance*	*150% Declining-Balance*
12/31/X3				
12/31/X4				
12/31/X5				
12/31/X6				
12/31/X7				
Total				

8.B.10. On May 15, 19X3, Colt Coal Company purchased 500 acres of land for a cash cost of $1,600,000. Core-drilling samples indicated that the land contained approximately 2,000,000 tons of coal reserves. It is estimated that after all the coal is removed, the land will have a residual value of $200,000. During 19X3, 300,000 tons of coal were removed. During 19X4, 350,000 tons were removed. On June 15, 19X5, the land was sold for $1,100,000 cash. From January 1, 19X5, through June 15, 19X5, 250,000 tons of coal were removed.

Required

Make journal entries to record

1) The purchase of the land.

2) Depletion for 19X3, 19X4, and 19X5.

3) The sale of the land.

8.B.11. Data for four assets are as follows.

Asset	Cost	Estimated Salvage Value	Estimated Life	Amount of Use During Year
a. Truck	$ 10,000	$ 400	4 years	3 months
b. Truck	10,000	400	100,000 miles	3,000 miles
c. Patent	84,000	–0–	14 years	2 months
d. Timberland	100,000	10,000	900,000 board feet	100,000 board feet

Required

Make a separate adjusting entry at December 31 to record the cost expiration associated with each of these assets, assuming that cost is spread evenly over asset lives.

8.B.12. The Duper Company purchases a truck on June 28, 19X4, at a cost of $24,000. The truck has an estimated life of 6 years and an estimated salvage value of $3,000. The company employs the sum-of-years'-digits depreciation method.

Required

1) Record depreciation for the years ended December 31, 19X4 and 19X5.

2) Record depreciation for 19X4 and 19X5 assuming that the company follows the practice of figuring depreciation from the first of the year closest to the purchase date.

8.B.13. The trial balance for the Plank Company at the end of its first year of operation follows.

PLANK COMPANY Trial Balance December 31, 19--		
	Debit	**Credit**
Cash	40,000	
Accounts Receivable	85,000	
Equipment	200,000	
Accounts Payable		28,000
Notes Payable		80,000
C. Plank, Capital		140,000
C. Plank, Withdrawals	12,000	
Service Revenue		344,000
Salary Expense	200,000	
Rent Expense	40,000	
Interest Expense	5,000	
Other Expense	10,000	
	592,000	592,000

The only adjustment required is to recognize depreciation on the equipment, all of which was purchased on January 8. The equipment has an estimated life of 8 years and an expected salvage value of $20,000.

Required

1) Calculate the amount of net income that would result from using

   a) Straight-line depreciation based on time.

   b) Sum-of-years'-digits depreciation.

   c) Double-declining-balance depreciation.

2) Calculate the total assets that would result from using each of the three depreciation methods.

SUMMARY OF CHAPTER 8

Plant assets are long-term tangible assets that are used over a number of periods in the operation of an entity. Natural resources are products of nature that are valuable in their natural state. Intangible assets are valuable long-term property rights that have no physical substance.

Long-term assets are recorded at their cost bases. Except for assets, like land, that do not expire, long-term asset costs are spread over the periods that benefit from their use. The expiration of plant assets is called depreciation; natural resource cost assigned to extracted units is referred to as depletion; the expiration of intangibles is known as amortization.

When plant assets are sold for more or less than their book values, gains or losses are recorded. In the case of depreciable assets, these gains or losses actually represent overdepreciations or underdepreciations in prior periods.

The cost of improving a plant asset is often debited to a separate asset account and spread over the remaining life of the improved asset. The cost of renovating a plant asset is debited to the accumulated depreciation account, and the new book value is then spread over the extended life of the renovated asset.

Depreciation of plant assets may be calculated by a variety of methods. The most common are straight-line or decreasing-charge. Straight-line methods are usually based on time or use. The declining-balance and sum-of-years'-digits methods both show decreasing amounts of depreciation as assets grow older.

Depletion of natural resources is almost always determined by spreading the cost of the resources evenly over the estimated units that are available for extraction. The cost of an intangible asset is usually spread evenly over the estimated useful life of the asset.

PROBLEMS FOR CHAPTER 8
Alternate Problems for this chapter begin on page D-57.

8.1. Savama Company purchased a spotwelding machine on July 1, 19X3, at a cash cost of $42,300. On the same date, installation charges of $2,800 were paid. The machine has an expected useful life of 10 years and an estimated salvage value of $3,800.

Required

1) Make journal entries to record the acquisition of the machine.

2) Make adjusting journal entries to record depreciation at December 31, 19X3, and December 31, 19X4, assuming use of

    a) The straight-line time method.

    b) The double-declining-balance method.

    c) The sum-of-years'-digits method.

8.2. On January 2, 19X3, Herd Company traded in an old truck for a new truck that had a list price of $36,000. The truck dealer allowed $5,000 for the old truck, and the remaining cost of $31,000 was paid in cash. The old truck had cost $16,000 and had accumulated depreciation of $12,000. Herd Company uses the double-declining-balance method of depreciation. The new truck is expected to last 5 years and have a salvage value of $3,800.

Required

1) Make the journal entry at January 2, 19X3, to record the acquisition of the new truck.

2) Make the adjusting entry at December 31, 19X3, to record the year's depreciation on the new truck.

3) Make the adjusting entry to record depreciation on the truck for 19X4.

4) On January 2, 19X5, the truck was sold for $15,000 cash. Record the sale of the truck.

5) Make the entry on January 2, 19X5, to record the sale of the truck for $15,000, assuming that straight-line time depreciation had been used (instead of the double-declining-balance method).

8.3. An unadjusted trial balance for the Marde Company is as shown here, followed by adjustments information.

MARDE COMPANY Unadjusted Trial Balance December 31, 19X4		
	Debit	**Credit**
Cash	12,000	
Accounts Receivable	35,000	
Land	25,000	
Machinery	19,600	
Accumulated Depreciation—Machinery		6,000
Automotive Equipment	24,000	
Accumulated Depreciation—Automotive Equipment		12,000
Building	140,000	
Accumulated Depreciation—Building		16,296
Accounts Payable		15,000
Notes Payable (due 6/30/X5)		12,000
Mortgage Payable		82,000
L. Marde, Capital		63,304
Fees		265,000
Salary Expense	170,000	
Utilities Expense	6,000	
Supplies Expense	14,000	
Interest Expense	6,200	
Gasoline Expense	7,800	
Other Expense	12,000	
	471,600	471,600

Adjustments Data

a) All machinery was purchased during January, 19X3. Estimated life is 5 years, with a salvage value of $1,600. The sum-of-years'-digits depreciation method is used.

b) All automotive equipment was purchased during January, 19X1. Estimated life is 5 years, with a salvage value of $4,000. The straight-line time depreciation method is used.

c) The building was occupied during January 19X2. Estimated life is 25 years, with a scrap value of $18,000. The depreciation method used is 150% declining-balance (150% of the straight-line rate). (*Suggestion:* For convenience, calculate depreciation to the nearest whole dollar.)

Required

1) Prepare a ten-column work sheet.

2) Prepare an income statement for the year ended December 31, 19X4.

3) Prepare a balance sheet at December 31, 19X4.

8.4. On January 3, 19X4, the J&S Company purchased a computer, serial number MC–0098, for $120,000. A cash payment of $40,000 was made, and a note was signed for the balance. The computer was installed in the company headquarters at 10 Smith Street on January 4, 19X4. An installation fee of $1,800 was paid in cash on that date. The cost of the computer is to be charged to a general ledger control account titled Office Equipment. The estimated useful life of the computer is 10 years, after which it is expected to have a salvage value of $10,000. The company rounds depreciation calculations to the nearest whole dollar.

Required

1) Make general journal entries to record the events just described.

2) Fill in information for the computer on a subsidiary plant ledger record card like the one illustrated in the chapter.

3) Make an adjusting journal entry at December 31, 19X4, to record depreciation on the computer. The company uses the sum-of-years'-digits depreciation method.

4) Indicate the first year's depreciation on the subsidiary record card.

8.5. On January 2, 19X3, the Gragg Company traded in an old truck tractor for a new tractor that had a list price of $80,000. The truck dealer allowed $20,000 for the old tractor, and the remaining cost, $60,000, was paid in cash. The old tractor had cost $38,000 and had accumulated depreciation of $24,000 when it was traded. The company uses double-declining-balance depreciation. It is estimated that the new tractor will have a useful life of 10 years and a salvage value of $6,000. On July 1, 19X4, Gragg sold the tractor for $55,000. The company accounts on a calendar year basis.

Required

Make journal entries to record

1) The trade-in on January 2, 19X3.

2) The depreciation for 19X3.

3) The depreciation for 19X4.

4) The sale on July 1, 19X4.

COMPREHENSION PROBLEMS FOR CHAPTER 8

8.6. On July 5, 19X3, Deasey Company purchased from AGI, Inc., a stamping machine at a price of $80,000, subject to terms of 2/15, n/60. Transportation charges of $1,200 were paid when the machine arrived on July 8. On July 12, a local contractor was paid $3,900 for installing the machine. AGI, Inc., was paid in full on July 15. Company employees began learning how to operate the new machine on July 8, and during that week materials costing $500 were ruined while the machine was being adjusted and the operators were growing accustomed to the machine. Operator time costing $800 was used in the process of learning to operate the machine. No usable product was turned out by the machine during the learning period. The machine is expected to serve the company 8 years, after which it is expected to have a salvage value of $2,000. The anticipated units of output and maintenance cost of each of the years of machine life are as follows. The output is expected to be spread evenly over each machine year of life.

Machine Year	Expected Units of Output	Anticipated Maintenance Cost
1	200,000	$1,000
2	190,000	2,000
3	180,000	3,000
4	170,000	4,000
5	160,000	5,000
6	150,000	6,000
7	140,000	7,000
8	130,000	8,000

Required

1) Ignore accepted accounting practice and determine what you believe to be the true cost of the machine.

2) Using the machine cost you derived for part (1), prepare adjusting journal entries at December 31, 19X3, and December 31, 19X4, to record depreciation under each of the following methods. (Show your work, and record amounts to the nearest whole dollar.)

   a) Straight-line time

   b) Units of output, assuming 100,000 units of output in 19X3 and 195,000 units in 19X4

   c) Sum-of-years'-digits

   d) Double-declining-balance

3) Choose the method (or devise one of your own) that in your opinion will best match the costs of production with revenues; defend your answer.

8.7. Cyrus Grunenwald is considering the purchase of a business currently owned by Nancy McCoy. Nancy's business, the McCoy Craft Shop, has done exceptionally well for a number of years, and she has decided to sell out and retire to the Caribbean. The Craft Shop has reported in the neighborhood of $200,000 annual net income in recent years. The condensed balance sheet at the close of the previous year follows.

McCOY CRAFT SHOP Balance Sheet December 31, 19--			
ASSETS		*LIABILITIES*	
Cash	$ 2,000	Accounts payable	$ 51,000
Receivables	10,000	Notes payable	67,000
Inventories	460,000	Total Liabilities	$118,000
Equipment	230,000		
Accumulated depreciation—Equipment	(184,000)	*OWNER'S EQUITY*	
		N. McCoy, capital	400,000
		Total Liabilities and	
Total Assets	$518,000	Owner's Equity	$518,000

Nancy contends that the business is worth $1 million, and that at that price it will return 20% per annum to Cyrus ($1,000,000 × 20% = $200,000 net income). The cash and other assets are to go with the business, and the liabilities are to be assumed by the new owner.

An investigation by Cyrus turns up the following facts.

a) Inventories with a cost basis of $50,000 are virtually worthless because of changes in the interests of hobbyists. The *replacement* costs of the remaining inventories total to $520,000.

b) The current value of the equipment is approximately $186,000. The equipment has an average expected remaining life of 5 years, with no salvage value anticipated. Depreciation expense has been running at $17,200 per year in recent years.

c) The owner of the building in which the shop is located has decided to raise the annual rent by $20,000.

d) The business is a proprietorship, and therefore there has been no allowance made for the value of Nancy's services. Nancy is a very capable craft specialist, and to hire a person of her ability would cost at least $30,000 per year.

Required

1) What value for goodwill would a purchase price of $1 million imply?

2) Considering the facts provided, what is the maximum price that Cyrus could pay Nancy for the shop if he demands a 20% return on his investment?

3) If Cyrus were to pay the price calculated for part (2), how much would he be paying for goodwill?

4) What risks should Cyrus be warned about?

PART IV

SYSTEMS AND CONTROLS

ACCOUNTANTS IN THE WORKPLACE

NAME: Daniel S. Mahoney

AFFILIATION: John Hancock Insurance
Company

POSITION: Administrative Auditor

SPECIALIZATION: Internal Auditing

As an internal auditor, Daniel S. Mahoney draws on many talents to help keep John Hancock Insurance Company shipshape. His varied roles include: scheduling audits; seeing to the training, progress, and performance of John Hancock's operational staff; conducting research into audit theory; and sometimes tackling a special auditing project of his own.

Mahoney, a graduate of Stonehill College in Massachusetts, worked for several finance and insurance companies before joining John Hancock in 1967 as an auditor. Given his effective performance in the department, he received two promotions—first to senior auditor and then, in 1980, to administrative auditor, his present position.

Mindful of the need for training and development to further career goals, in 1975 he became a Certified Internal Auditor (CIA). Roughly analagous to the CPA, the CIA designation recognizes a certain level of achievement. It is earned by demonstrated competence in the field and by successful completion of an examination.

A typical audit at John Hancock involves four separate stages. First, an auditor must make a study of "existing controls or lack thereof." This is essentially a systems analysis, during which he establishes the exact procedure the subject of his audit follows. For example, in death claims the auditor initially would establish exactly how they are processed from beginning to end at John Hancock.

Second, based on an analysis of the system, the auditor develops his "audit program." The key is to determine those areas where the greatest potential exposure exists and determine the relative strengths and weaknesses of the internal controls.

Third, the audit is actually performed. In the death-claims example, the auditor may have decided to look at a certain percentage of all such claims processed during one quarter. Each of the cases selected would then be examined carefully to establish exactly what had transpired. Typically, the auditor will have singled out 15 to 20 verification steps of the process to check. Examination of the actual cases will show whether all were properly carried out.

Finally, the auditor presents his recommendations in a written report to the second vice-president, auditing, who, after careful review, sends them on to the senior officer in charge of the area in which the audit was performed.

While ability and dedication remain an auditor's most important assets, Mahoney points to the growing importance of specialization. Like many of its competitors, John Hancock has expanded considerably from its life insurance base. "Today we're really a diversified financial services company," explains Mahoney. "A knowledge of stock brokerage, for example, would prove a valuable asset to an internal auditor, and a working knowledge of electronic data processing is a must."

CHAPTER 9
Cash
Controls

Because cash is such a desirable asset, care should be exercised to protect it from both internal misuse and external theft. This chapter covers some of the techniques used to maintain control over an entity's cash.

Chapter 9 is presented in two sections. After discussing the nature of cash, Section A concentrates on eight procedures that are helpful in controlling cash. One of the control procedures, the imprest fund, is discussed in some detail, whereas another, the bank reconciliation, is the main focus of Section B.

Section B concentrates on the bank reconciliation, a cash control device that can become rather involved. The section starts with a discussion of checking accounts, and it contrasts the depositor's and bank's viewpoints. Some reasons for differences between the bank's records and those of the depositor are considered, and the procedures for reconciling a bank statement to the depositor's books are then presented. Adjusting entries needed to correct the depositor's records are illustrated, and the importance of the bank reconciliation as a control procedure is summarized.

SECTION 9.A

Internal Control Over Cash

OBJECTIVES

This section concentrates on the nature of cash and cash control procedures. At the conclusion of this section, you should be able to

1. List the types of items that are classified as cash.
2. State why control over cash is important.
3. Make journal entries to record the establishment and replenishment of a petty cash fund.
4. List at least five procedures for attaining control over cash.

THE NATURE OF CASH

What Is Cash?

OBJECTIVE 1. List the types of items that are classified as cash.

Most people think of *cash as coin and paper money. For accounting purposes, however, cash also includes checking account balances and the checks, money orders, traveler's checks, and credit card sales slips that are awaiting deposit in bank checking accounts.*

Accounting does not usually distinguish between types of cash, although an entity may choose to have separate ledger accounts for change funds, petty cash funds, cash in various banks, cash at branch offices, and cash at other locations. In this section, separate accounts are used for Cash in Bank, Oil Field Advance, and Petty Cash.

Needs for Cash

Entities need some cash on hand for making change and for making small day-to-day disbursements for incidental expenses such as cleaning supplies, postage and delivery charges, and similar items. Also, most entities keep a cash balance in a checking account to take care of those times when cash disbursements exceed receipts or emergencies arise.

Although some cash is necessary in the operation of an entity, large amounts of idle cash are unproductive assets. Money must be invested in some way for revenues to be earned. Excess cash can be temporarily invested in marketable securities. *Marketable securities are temporary investments in government notes and bonds and other securities that are relatively stable in value and readily salable.* Marketable securities are sometimes referred to as near-cash assets.

CASH CONTROL PROCEDURES

Cash must be carefully controlled because it is such a desirable asset. With cash, people can acquire most of the things they want. Paper money can be pocketed with ease and spent without proof of ownership. In fact, unless serial numbers have been listed, the identity of stolen money is difficult to prove. For these and other reasons, cash is the asset most subject to theft.

OBJECTIVE 2.   State why control over cash is important.

Entities lose more cash through employee theft than through outside theft. The problem is much greater than most people think because most discovered thefts are not even reported by employers, and many thefts by employees are never discovered at all.

Strong internal controls over cash are important. *Internal control refers to the methods by which an entity's operations are controlled and its assets safeguarded. The ways in which accounting helps to attain internal control are often referred to as **internal check**.* There are a number of internal control procedures that help safeguard cash.

Separation of Duties

The most basic of internal control procedures is the *division of duties* among employees in a manner that permits them to serve as checks on one another. A proper separation of duties reduces the likelihood of wrongdoing by employees and increases the probability that wrongful acts that do occur will be discovered.

Employees who handle cash should not be involved in the accounting process, and vice versa. Whenever possible, accounting duties should be distributed among employees so that each person's work is in some way verified by one or more other persons. This technique may not entirely prevent thefts and frauds, but it makes it practically impossible to conceal them without collusion (cooperation) among employees.

Prompt Records of Cash Receipts

Cash should be documented as soon as it is received. When cash is received directly from a customer, the normal procedure is to register it promptly by machine, written receipt, or both.

Cash Registers.   The kind of cash register you see in most retail stores is an excellent cash control device, provided it is properly used. Sales are imprinted on a paper receipt for the customer, as well as registered internally within the machine. Usually, the amounts being registered are displayed so that the customer can see them, and a bell or tone sounds when the cash drawer is opened. These devices discourage employees from registering incorrect amounts and help prevent thefts of incoming cash. Some modern electronic cash registers are wired directly to computers, so that sales are automatically recorded as they are registered.

At the end of each day, the cash register provides a total of the day's collections, which can be read by a manager who has a special key to the register. The cash present in each register drawer may then be reconciled in the following manner.

CASH REGISTER NO. 1	
Beginning change fund	$ 100
Plus: Cash register total	3,600
Cash that should be on hand	$3,700
Less: Cash counted	3,695
Cash shortage	$ 5

Small amounts of shortages or overages of cash are common when many sales are being made. These are recorded in a Cash Short and Over account, as illustrated here.

May 16	Cash	3,595	
	Cash Short and Over	5	
	Sales		3,600
	Cash sales for the day.		

The usual amount of cash change fund is left in the register drawer for starting the next day's activities.

If cash shortages exceed overages for an entire accounting period, the debit balance in the account is viewed as an expense; when overages exceed shortages, the credit balance is treated as a revenue.

Prenumbered Receipts.   All forms used to document transactions should bear printed numbers in consecutive order, so that missing forms will be apparent to anyone who checks the duplicate copies on file. This device prevents employees from disposing of copies of forms to hide wrongdoing.

Handwritten receipts should be made on multiple-copy, prenumbered forms, with the original copies given to customers as proof of payment. One or more carbon copies are then available for determining the total collections made, which are reconciled to the cash on hand in the same manner as in the cash register illustration.

Check Listings.   Checks and other cash items received by mail should be immediately listed in triplicate by the clerk who opens the mail. One copy of the listing is retained by the clerk, one copy is given to the employee who makes the bank deposit, and the third copy goes to the accounting department for recording the collections. Should bank deposits disagree with the accounting records, the differences will show up when a *bank reconciliation* is made. Bank reconciliations are discussed in the next section.

Daily Deposits of Cash

A basic rule of cash control is that *each day's cash receipts should be deposited intact*. If the bank closes before the day's receipts are ready for deposit, the company may have to keep the receipts overnight in a safe and deposit them the following morning. Or the deposit might be dropped in a special night-deposit chute at the bank.

Most banks are better equipped than most companies to protect cash. They have guards, heavy vaults, and a variety of other safeguards. When a theft does occur at a bank, the banking company bears the loss. A business can therefore shift the risks of loss by putting its cash into a bank.

When we say that each day's receipts should be deposited in total (intact), we mean that receipts of different days should not be mixed together. Also, a company should not make payments out of the cash it receives. If this rule is followed, the bank statement will show as a separate deposit the total cash received for each day. The cash receipts records of the business can then be easily compared with the bank's record of the firm's deposits.

The importance of daily intact deposits in controlling cash cannot be overemphasized. If you ever get the job of auditing the cash transactions for a business, you will then appreciate the neatness of daily cash deposits. If the business you are auditing makes payments out of daily cash receipts, you will discover how much that complicates your audit.

Payments by Check

Another rule of cash control is that *cash payments should be made by check*. When disbursements are made by check, the check itself serves as a written basic data device. The canceled check is returned by the bank after it has been paid. The party named on the check must endorse it before it can be cashed or deposited. The endorsement serves as proof that the cash payment was received by the proper party.

Only responsible officials of an entity should be allowed to sign checks. These officials will require proper documentation that payments are being made for good reasons, and to the right parties.

An arrangement is sometimes made with the bank whereby *two signatures* are required on checks, especially where the dollar amounts are large. This procedure can help prevent unauthorized checks, provided that both officials carefully examine each check they sign.

Voucher Systems

Liability controls, which are discussed in the next chapter, are closely related to cash controls because practically all liabilities are eventually settled with cash. An excellent way to help attain control over cash is through a *voucher system*, which requires a properly approved voucher form as authorization for each check that is written. A full-fledged voucher system views all cash payments as settlements of liabilities, although, admittedly, obligations for cash purchases are canceled immediately by payments of cash. Voucher systems are covered in Section 10.A.

Imprest Funds

*An **imprest fund** is an advance of cash, usually to an employee for use in carrying on the entity's activities.* Invoices and other documents are then accepted as proof that the funds were properly disbursed.

Revolving Accounts. *An imprest fund that is regularly reimbursed upon the submission of documents proving expenditures is sometimes called a revolving account.* Revolving accounts are often used to control the expenses of distant branch operations, particularly when the operation is temporary. Thus the manager of an oil exploration team might be provided with $10,000 for meeting expenses while exploring for oil in a certain area. The account might be established with the following entry, assuming that cash on deposit with the bank is shown in an account titled Cash in Bank.

June 5	Oil Field Advance	10,000	
	Cash in Bank		10,000
	Advance to oil exploration team manager.		

When the team manager wants more funds, he or she simply submits the invoices and other basic data forms as proof that the money has been spent properly. A check is written for the amount of the expenditures already made from the advance. The reimbursement is then recorded by recognizing the expenses and reducing the bank account balance.

June 30	Travel Expense	1,150	
	Exploration Tools	4,600	
	Machinery Repair	2,300	
	Legal Charges	450	
	Cash in Bank		8,500
	Oil field advance reimbursed.		

Note that the revolving account balance of $10,000 remained undisturbed by the expenditures and reimbursement for them.

Petty Cash Funds. *A small imprest fund (revolving account) for making small (petty) payments in money is called **petty cash**.* A journal entry for establishing a $50 petty cash fund would look like this.

Jan. 3	Petty Cash	50	
	Cash in Bank		50
	To establish petty cash fund.		

OBJECTIVE 3. Record the establishment of a petty cash fund.

To start the fund a check is written to Petty Cash for the amount of the fund. The check is then cashed at the bank by the employee who is to administer the fund. Petty cash money is normally kept in a small box in the petty cash clerk's desk.

*Small disbursements of money from a petty cash fund are evidenced by a form called a **petty cash voucher**,* like the one in Illustration 9.1. The petty cash clerk will insist that a voucher be properly filled in for each payment of money from the fund. The money and the vouchers in the petty cash box should always total to the amount of the fund.

No journal entries are made at the time petty cash is paid out. An entry is made when a check is written to replenish the petty cash fund. In effect, the petty cash clerk trades the vouchers for a check, which is cashed for money. The entry to replenish petty cash takes the following form.

Jan. 31	Freight In	13	
	Postage Expense	21	
	Office Expense	8	
	Cash in Bank		42
	To reimburse the petty cash fund.		

OBJECTIVE 3. Record the replenishment of a petty cash fund.

ILLUSTRATION 9.1

PETTY CASH VOUCHER

No. 002

Amount _$6.00_　　　　　Date _January 4, 19--_

Paid to _Central Express_

For _Parcel delivery_

Charge to _Freight In_

Approved by _D. D._

Received by _Mosey Knight_

The petty cash fund should be replenished at the end of each accounting period, regardless of how much cash is left in the fund. It is only through replenishment that the expenses represented by petty cash vouchers are recognized on the books. If petty cash vouchers are not exchanged for cash at the end of the period, expenses will be understated—and the balance sheet will show slightly more cash than the company actually has.

The Petty Cash account remains at a constant balance in the ledger unless the size of the fund is increased or decreased. An increase in petty cash from $50 to $75 is recorded as follows.

Feb. 15	Petty Cash	25	
	Cash in Bank		25
	To increase the petty cash fund to $75.		

When there is no longer any need for the petty cash fund, it is closed out, and any remaining cash is returned to the regular bank account. An entry would be made to abolish the petty cash fund and recognize the last disbursements, as follows.

May 31	Cash in Bank	60	
	Postage Expense	12	
	Office Expense	3	
	Petty Cash		75
	To close the petty cash fund.		

Bank Reconciliations

An important cash control procedure, reconciliation of bank accounts, is covered at length in the next section.

Small Concerns

A small company with few employees may not be able to use certain cash control procedures. For example, an office that is run by one all-purpose clerk does not permit much in the way of division of duties. This problem can be largely overcome by the close attention of the owner, manager, or other person with the overall responsibility for the entity.

An owner of a small proprietorship can keep a close watch on the business operation. He or she knows how much cash usually comes and goes and will probably make deposits and sign checks personally. It is only when a concern is large, complex, and spread out that the more involved cash controls become imperative.

The following list summarizes the major control procedures discussed in this section.

CASH CONTROL PROCEDURES
1. Separation (division) of duties
2. Prompt documentation of cash receipts by means of cash registers, prenumbered receipt forms, and check listings
3. Daily intact deposits of cash
4. Payments by check
5. Use of a voucher system
6. Use of imprest funds
7. Bank reconciliations
8. Close attention to the business operation by an owner or manager of a small concern.

OBJECTIVE 4. List the procedures for attaining control over cash.

Control Constraints

Perhaps it is worth noting that although controls over cash are desirable, there is a limit to what concerns can afford. In general, internal controls should be adopted as long as the benefits exceed the costs. Since potential benefits and costs are often difficult to pin down, decisions may have to be based on subjective judgments about the net benefits to be derived from particular internal control procedures.

Electronic Data Processing

The trend for many years has been toward increasing automation of accounting. Electronic computers process data rapidly and are capable of turning out a great deal of information arrayed and summarized in a variety of ways.

Computers offer both advantages and disadvantages in attaining internal control. Whereas data can be processed accurately and consistently with computers, separation of duties becomes more difficult to attain. Elements of internal control are discussed in some detail in Chapter 11, along with the potential benefits and disadvantages of electronic data processing.

GLOSSARY FOR SECTION 9.A

Cash Coin and paper money, checking account balances, and checks and other items that banks will accept as deposits in checking accounts.

Imprest fund An advance of cash, usually to an employee for use in carrying on the entity's activities.

Internal check The ways in which accounting helps to attain internal control.

Internal control   The methods by which an entity's operations are controlled and its assets safeguarded.

Marketable securities   Temporary investments in government notes and bonds and other securities that are relatively stable in value and readily salable.

Petty cash   A small imprest fund (revolving account) for making small (petty) payments of money.

Petty cash voucher   A form for evidencing small disbursements of money from a petty cash fund.

Revolving account   An imprest fund that is regularly reimbursed upon the submission of documents proving expenditures.

SELF-QUIZ ON OBJECTIVES FOR SECTION 9.A
Solutions to Self-Quiz begin on page B-33.

1. **OBJECTIVE 1.** List the types of items that accountants classify as cash.

2. **OBJECTIVE 2.** State why control over cash is important.

3. **OBJECTIVE 3.** Make general journal entries to record the following events.

   Jan. 3   Established a $100 petty cash fund.

   31   Replenished the petty cash fund for January disbursements as follows.

Postage expense	$23
Office expense	36
Travel expense	21
Total	$80

4. **OBJECTIVE 4.** List at least five procedures for attaining control over cash.

DISCUSSION QUESTIONS FOR SECTION 9.A

1. Under what circumstance are investments classified as marketable securities?

2. Accountants usually advise that each day's cash receipts be deposited intact and that cash payments be made by check. How do these practices aid in the attainment of internal control over cash?

3. What can be done in small concerns to compensate for the inability to separate the duties of handling and recording cash?

4. Under what circumstances would additional internal control procedures become undesirable?

5. How does the separation of duties among employees help to attain cash control?

6. What does the term revolving account mean as it is used in this section?

7. Why is it important to replenish a petty cash fund at the end of each accounting period, regardless of how much cash is left in the fund?

EXERCISES FOR SECTION 9.A

9.A.1. The manager of the shoe department in Charles Brothers Department Store prepared the following reconciliation for the department's cash register at the close of business on May 6.

SHOE DEPARTMENT CASH REGISTER May 6, 19––	
Beginning change fund	$ 200
Plus: Cash register total	4,150
Cash that should be on hand	$4,350
Less: Cash counted	4,356
Cash overage	$ 6

Make a journal entry to record the sales for May 6, including the cash overage.

9.A.2. Make general journal entries to record the following events.

June 1   Established a $150 petty cash fund.

     30   Replenished the petty cash fund for June disbursements as follows.

Travel expense	$49
Postage expense	18
Entertainment expense	27
Total	$94

9.A.3. On May 1 the Jantz Company established a petty cash fund of $100. On September 30 a decision was made to increase the fund to a total of $130. Make the general journal entry (or entries) to increase the size of the fund and to record replenishment of the fund for September's expenditures, as follows.

Postage expense	$22
Travel expense	75
Total	$97

9.A.4. Make an entry to abolish a $150 petty cash fund on April 1. The fund was fully replenished on March 31.

9.A.5. A cash shortage was discovered when the petty cash clerk totaled the cash and vouchers in the petty cash box. The amounts of the shortage and expenditures follow. Make a general journal entry on May 31 to replenish the petty cash fund.

Office expense	$14
Travel expense	32
Cash shortage	3
Total	$49

9.A.6. Data for one of the cash registers in Harry's Grocery are as follows at close of business on April 1.

REGISTER NO. 3	
Change fund	$ 100
Cash register total (sales)	1,273
Cash counted	1,368

Make a general journal entry to record the sales for Register No. 3, including any cash overage or shortage.

PROBLEMS FOR SECTION 9.A
Alternate Problems for this section begin on page D-59.

9.A.7. Events relating to petty cash are as follows.

May	1	Established a $50 petty cash fund.
	3	Paid delivery charges (freight in) to Mailer's Truckers, $18.
	13	Reimbursed employee for travel expenses, $15.
	16	Paid postage expense, $1.75.
	17	Paid for office supplies, $10.
	20	Replenished petty cash for expenditures through this date.
	29	Increased petty cash fund to $100.
June	3	Abolished petty cash fund.

Required

1) Assume that the May 13 expenditure was to reimburse Montag Nants and that payment was approved by his supervisor, Sally Boltz. Prepare a petty cash voucher similar to the one illustrated in the section.

2) Make general journal entries to record the aforementioned events.

9.A.8. The following events relating to petty cash are provided for the H&H Company.

Feb.	3	Established a $100 petty cash fund.
	7	Paid postage expense, $13.
	10	Paid travel expense, $74.

14   Paid freight in, $8.

16   The fund was replenished. When vouchers were summarized, it was discovered that the fund was short $1.

Required

Make appropriate journal entries to record the foregoing events.

9.A.9. Events relating to petty cash for Molegart Company follow.

July 8   Established a $50 petty cash fund.

12   Paid delivery charges (freight in) to ABC Freight Company, $5.

15   Purchased postage stamps (postage expense), $10.

19   Paid delivery charges (freight in), $8.

24   Received a collect telegram, $6.

25   Purchased office supplies, $12.

26   Replenished petty cash fund for expenditures made through this date.

28   Increased petty cash fund to $100 balance.

Required

1) Prepare a petty cash voucher for the July 12 expenditure. Use fictitious names and initials where necessary.

2) Make the journal entries needed to record the events just listed.

9.A.10. The Galen Company has a $50 petty cash fund. Events relating to petty cash follow.

Aug. 2   Made a travel advance to an employee, $25.

5   Paid delivery charges (freight in), $3.

6   Reimbursed employee for telephone calls for company business, $5.

9   Purchased postage stamps, $10.

10   Replenished petty cash fund.

12   Increased petty cash fund to $125.

Required

Make any general journal entries needed to record the foregoing events.

SECTION 9.B

Bank Reconciliations

OBJECTIVES

This section deals with bank reconciliations. At the conclusion of this section, you should be able to

1. State two overall reasons for differences between cash account and bank statement balances.
2. List the four general steps for preparing a bank reconciliation.
3. Prepare a two-part bank reconciliation.
4. Make adjusting journal entries to correct a cash account balance.

CHECKING ACCOUNTS

Although most people are familiar with checks, many do not know the technical terms associated with their use. *A **checking account** is an arrangement (agreement) with a bank that permits a depositor to write checks on funds (moneys) that have been deposited with the bank. A **check** is a bill of exchange that calls upon a bank to make payment to a third party. A **bill of exchange** is an order by one party directing a second party to pay a third party.*

*The party who writes and signs a bill of exchange is known as the **drawer**; the party directed by a bill of exchange to pay money is called the **drawee**; the party named in a bill of exchange to receive payment is the **payee**.* In the case of a check, the depositor with money in the bank is the drawer and the bank is the drawee.

A payee named in a check may *endorse* (negotiate) the check to another party, an *endorsee*, by signing on the back of the check. The endorsee may in turn endorse the check to yet another endorsee, and so on. An endorsee has the right to collect the amount of the check from the drawee bank. The relationship between the parties to a check is shown in Illustration 9.2.

ILLUSTRATION 9.2

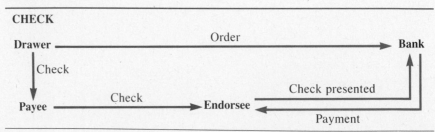

CHECK

From a bank's viewpoint, depositors' accounts are liabilities in that they represent amounts owed to depositors. Thus a bank *credits* a depositor's account when deposits are made and *debits* the account when checks are paid. The bank's entries mirror those made by the depositor, as illustrated here. However, keep in mind that all banks today employ highly computerized systems that journalize and post transactions automatically.

DEPOSITOR			BANK		
Cash in Bank	5,000		Cash	5,000	
Accounts Receivable		5,000	Demand Deposits		5,000
Collections deposited.			Deposit received.		
Accounts Payable	2,000		Demand Deposits	2,000	
Cash in Bank		2,000	Cash		2,000
Check issued.			Check cleared.		

At certain intervals, usually monthly, a bank sends each depositor a *bank statement, which is a record of the beginning balance, any increases and decreases that have occurred since the previous statement, and the ending balance of the depositor's account with the bank.* The bank statement in Illustration 9.3 on the next page shows one way the information may be arranged. In practice, of course, bank statements for business firms show many more debit and credit items than the statement illustrated.

REASONS FOR DIFFERENCES

The final balance shown on a bank statement is usually different from that shown in the depositor's Cash in Bank account. This difference is due to *time lags, errors,* or both.

OBJECTIVE 1. State two reasons for differences between cash account and bank statement balances.

Time Lags

A bank registers deposits, checks, and other items on the date when they arrive at the bank, which may be different from the date when they are recorded in the depositor's accounting records.

Deposits in Transit.   Recall that an important control procedure is the deposit of each day's cash receipts intact, without mixing them with receipts of other days and without making any disbursements directly from them. However, the bank may not be open when a day's receipts are ready for deposit, in which case the deposit will have to be made on the next banking day. Monday's receipts will be deposited on Tuesday, and so on. If the bank is not open on weekends, then Friday's receipts will be deposited on Monday, as will Saturday's and Sunday's receipts (as separate deposits), if applicable.

ILLUSTRATION 9.3

| CLARION NATIONAL BANK | | | | | | | | STATEMENT OF ACCOUNT |

WOODS SUPPLY COMPANY
1550 Wood Street
Clarion, PA 16214

21–5937–0
ACCOUNT NUMBER

7/31/––
DATE OF STATEMENT

Balance From Previous Statement	Debits		Credits		Statement Balance
	Number	*Amount*	*Number*	*Amount*	
$10,574.86	27	12,277.43	12	10,556.16	8,853.59

Checks—Debits						Deposits—Credits		
No.	Amount	Date	No.	Amount	Date	Amount	Date	Balance
*1025	75.00	7/1	1042	8.33	7/14	1,322.18	7/1	11,722.04
*1027	100.00	7/1	1043	798.00	7/17	835.76	7/2	11,967.30
*1030	32.00	7/6	1044	83.18	7/20	503.12	7/6	10,747.42
1031	1,691.00	7/6	1045	216.55	7/20	2,210.90	7/7	12,197.20
1032	590.50	7/2	1046	6.21	7/20	496.00	7/9	11,455.62
1033	5.62	7/7	1047	15.50	7/17	223.75	7/10	11,108.77
1034	75.50	7/7	1048	1,283.40	7/25	1,005.60	7/14	9,495.04
1035	135.00	7/10	RT	76.75	7/25	514.32	7/17	9,195.86
1036	38.14	7/9	1049	17.86	7/26	331.80	7/20	9,221.72
1037	1,199.44	7/9	*1051	14.00	7/26	700.00	7/21	9,921.72
1038	680.00	7/7	1052	2,010.00	7/31		7/25	8,561.57
1039	21.00	7/10	1053	68.25	7/31	1,620.47CM	7/26	10,150.18
1040	414.60	7/10	SC	10.60	7/31	792.26	7/31	8,853.59
1041	2,611.00	7/14						

SC—Service Charge   DM—Debit Memo   CM—Credit Memo
RT—Returned Check   OD—Overdraft   *—Previous Check(s) Missing

A concern will usually record cash as being received on the day it is collected. A day's collections may be stored in the company safe until they are deposited, or they may be dropped into a night-deposit chute at the bank. If cash is received only as customer checks, a deposit may even be mailed to the bank. *Deposits that have been recorded by an entity, but have not been received and recorded by the bank, are called **deposits in transit** or outstanding deposits.* Deposits in transit represent cash that the depositor has, but that has not yet been reflected into the bank statement balance.

Outstanding Checks. A check seldom gets to a bank on the day it is written, even when the drawer and payee have accounts with the same bank. Many checks are sent through the mail, and several days may go by before a check is deposited or cashed by the payee or endorsee. If the payee or endorsee deals with a different bank from the one on which the check is drawn, the check must first pass through that bank's clearing system before it can arrive at the drawee bank. *Checks that have been written and recorded by a depositor (drawer), but have not been presented to the drawee bank, are called outstanding checks or checks in transit.* Checks in transit represent cash decreases that have not yet been deducted from the bank statement balance.

Bank Debit and Credit Memos. Banks occasionally decrease or increase a depositor's account before the depositor is informed of the action. If, for example, a customer's check that has been deposited as cash is returned because of insufficient funds in the customer's bank account, the amount of the bad check will be automatically deducted from the depositor's account. The bank will then send a *debit memo* to notify the depositor of the reduction in the depositor's account. *A bank debit memo is simply a bank form for notifying a depositor of a reduction in the depositor's bank account.* Debit memos are also sent for deductions due to bank service charges and for other account reductions made by the bank.

A bank credit memo is a bank form for notifying a depositor of an increase in the depositor's bank account. Banks occasionally act as collection agencies for depositors by collecting notes and other credit instruments for them. When a collection is received by a bank on behalf of a depositor, the funds are credited directly to the depositor's bank account and a credit memo is sent to notify the depositor of the increase.

A depositor does not receive a debit or credit memo from the bank until some time after the change has been made by the bank. During this time lag, the depositor's Cash in Bank account will not be in agreement with the bank's records.

Errors

Errors made by either the depositor or the bank will naturally bring about disagreements between the two sets of records. Most bank errors are discovered, and corrected, by the bank on the day they were made. Banks balance out their cash records at the end of each banking day. Occasionally, however, banks clear stolen checks with forged signatures, and sometimes they mistakenly process checks for which stop-payment orders have been issued by depositors. *A stop-payment order is a depositor's request to a bank that an outstanding check not be cleared (paid).* Unless the depositor is at fault, the bank bears the loss when a check drawn illegally on a depositor's account is cashed.

Recording errors by depositors are much more common, where checks or deposits are recorded at erroneous amounts. The most common type of recording error transposes the digits in an amount (transposition error). If both the debit and credit figures reflect the same error, the books will remain in balance, in which case the error may not be discovered until the Cash in Bank account is reconciled to the bank statement balance.

RECONCILIATION PROCEDURES

Reconciliation Format

To reconcile means to bring into agreement. A Cash in Bank account may be reconciled to a bank statement, or the bank statement balance may be reconciled to the balance in the Cash in Bank account. However, it is best to *reconcile both the Cash in Bank account and the bank statement balance to the correct amount of disposable cash at the reconciliation date with a schedule called **two-part bank reconciliation**.* Arrangements vary in practice, but the items that must be considered in a two-part bank reconciliation are as follows.

TWO-PART BANK RECONCILIATION FORMAT	
Bank Statement	**Books**
Statement balance	Account balance
+ Deposits in transit	+ Unrecorded receipts
− Outstanding checks	− Unrecorded payments
± Bank errors	− Returned checks
	± Book errors
<u>Correct disposable cash</u>	<u>Correct disposable cash</u>

Naturally, the correct disposable cash amount must be the same for both sides of the reconciliation.

Reconciliation Steps

Although the order in which they are performed may vary, the steps necessary in preparing a bank reconciliation are shown on the page opposite.

Illustration

A bank reconciliation for Woods Supply Company is shown in Illustration 9.4 on page 444. The bank statement balance at July 31 is from the statement

BANK RECONCILIATION STEPS

OBJECTIVE 2. List the four general steps for preparing a bank reconciliation.

1. Compare deposits shown on the bank statement with deposits that have been recorded in the accounting records. Any recent deposits that have not yet been reflected in the bank statement should be marked as deposits in transit. Also, note any errors that might have been made in recording deposits.

2. Arrange, in numerical order, the canceled checks returned with the bank statement, and

   a. Compare any canceled checks that were written in the preceding period with the outstanding checks listed for the last bank reconciliation prepared. Note any checks that are still outstanding at the current reconciliation date.

   b. Compare canceled checks written in the period just ended with the checks recorded in the accounting records, noting the outstanding checks. Also, note any errors that might have been made in recording checks.

   c. Prepare a list of checks outstanding at the reconciliation date.

3. Identify any increases or decreases on the bank statement that have not already been recorded in the books. Increases and decreases for other than routine deposits and checks will usually be keyed with special symbols on the bank statement.

4. Reconcile both the bank statement balance and the Cash in Bank account balance to the current disposable cash at the reconciliation date.

in Illustration 9.3. The account balance of $7,857.69 comes from the Cash in Bank account in the general ledger for Woods Supply Company.

The bank statement side of the reconciliation shows a deposit in transit on July 31. This represents July collections that did not get deposited until August.

The right side of the reconciliation shows an unrecorded receipt from a note and related interest. This collection by the bank on behalf of Woods Supply is marked CM in the deposits column of the bank statement shown in Illustration 9.3. The debits section of the bank statement shows an amount marked RT for returned check. This was a customer check that was deposited but then returned because the drawer had insufficient funds on deposit. The debit item marked SC was for service charges levied by the bank. None of these items had been recorded in the books of Woods Supply Company.

In the process of comparing canceled checks with company records, it was discovered that a check for $1,283.40 in payment of Accounts Payable had been erroneously recorded as $1,238.40. This resulted in a transposition error of $45. Also, among the canceled checks is one for $100 that the bank had improperly cleared after a stop-payment request had been made. This

ILLUSTRATION 9.4

WOODS SUPPLY COMPANY Bank Reconciliation July 31, 19--					
BANK STATEMENT			**BOOKS**		
Statement balance		$8,853.59	Account balance		$7,857.69
Add: Deposit in transit	$625.15		Add: Unrecorded receipt		
Error (stop-pmt. Ck.			Note	$1,600.00	
cleared by bank)	100.00	725.15	Interest	20.47	1,620.47
		$9,578.74			$9,478.16
Less: Outstanding checks			Less: Returned check	$76.75	
No. 1021	$ 6.14		Service charge	10.60	
1050	72.80		Error (Ck. No. 1048)	45.00	132.35
1054	120.00				
1055	33.99	232.93			
Disposable cash		$9,345.81	Disposable cash		$9,345.81

OBJECTIVE 3. Prepare a two-part bank reconciliation.

bank error appears on the bank reconcilation as an addition to the bank statement balance.

Cash Adjustments

As the bank reconciliation shows, the Cash in Bank account balance at July 31 does not reflect the correct disposable cash that is available. Adjusting entries are required for all items on the books side of a two-part bank reconciliation. The adjusting entries might be made as shown in Illustration 9.5.

ILLUSTRATION 9.5

OBJECTIVE 4. Make adjusting journal entries to correct a cash account balance.

19--			
July 31	Cash in Bank	1,620.47	
	Notes Receivable		1,600.00
	Interest Revenue		20.47
	Customer's note collected by bank.		
31	Accounts Receivable	76.75	
	Cash in Bank		76.75
	Customer returned check reclassified to Accounts Receivable.		
31	Bank Service Charges	10.60	
	Cash in Bank		10.60
	Bank service charges for July.		
31	Accounts Payable	45.00	
	Cash in Bank		45.00
	To correct for error in recording Check No. 1049.		

ILLUSTRATION 9.6

19-- July 31	Cash in Bank	1,488.12	
	Accounts Receivable	76.75	
	Bank Service Charges	10.60	
	Accounts Payable	45.00	
	Notes Receivable		1,600.00
	Interest Revenue		20.47
	To adjust cash per bank reconciliation of July 31.		

As an alternative, all the previous adjusting entries might have been combined into one entry (Illustration 9.6).

Internal Control

As pointed out in the previous section, a bank reconciliation is an important internal control device. Most intentional and unintentional cash misstatements are uncovered as bank statement increases and decreases are compared with those shown in the entity's records. Keeping deposits of all cash receipts intact and using checks for all cash payments help ensure that the bank's records will serve as a check on those of the entity. The separation of duties element of internal control is best served when a bank reconciliation is prepared by someone independent of both the cash-handling and the cash-recording processes.

GLOSSARY FOR SECTION 9.B

Bank credit memo A bank form for notifying a depositor of an increase in the depositor's bank account.

Bank debit memo A bank form for notifying a depositor of a reduction in the depositor's bank account.

Bank statement A record of a depositor's account that is sent by a bank, showing the beginning balance, any increases and decreases that have occurred since the previous statement, and the ending balance.

Bill of exchange An order by one party directing a second party to pay a third party.

Check A bill of exchange that calls upon a bank to make payment to a third party.

Checking account An arrangement (agreement) with a bank that permits a depositor to write checks on funds (moneys) that have been deposited with the bank.

Deposits in transit (outstanding deposits)   Deposits that have been recorded by an entity, but have not been reflected into the bank statement balance.

Drawee   The party directed by a bill of exchange to pay money.

Drawer   The party who writes and signs a bill of exchange.

Outstanding checks (checks in transit)   Checks that have been written and recorded by the depositor (drawer), but have not been presented to the drawee bank.

Payee   The party named in a bill of exchange to receive payment.

Stop-payment order   A depositor's request to a bank that an outstanding check not be cleared (paid).

Two-part bank reconciliation   A schedule that reconciles both the Cash in Bank account and the bank statement balance to the correct disposable cash at the reconciliation date.

SELF-QUIZ ON OBJECTIVES FOR SECTION 9.B
Solutions to Self-Quiz begin on page B-34.

1. **OBJECTIVE 1.** State two overall reasons for differences between cash account and bank statement balances.

2. **OBJECTIVE 2.** List the four general steps for preparing a bank reconciliation.

3. The following information is provided for Dunkle Company.

   a. Bank statement balance at May 31, $3,785.40.

   b. Cash in Bank account balance at May 31, $1,523.13.

   c. Deposits in transit at May 31, $631.

   d. Outstanding checks at May 31, $2,911.27.

   e. A customer's check marked "insufficient funds" was included with the bank statement, along with a debit memo for $32, the amount of the check.

   f. A bank service charge of $13 appears on the bank statement but has not been recorded by the company.

   g. Check No. 4126 for $758 in payment on Accounts Payable was erroneously recorded by the company as $785.

   Required

   1) **OBJECTIVE 3.** Prepare a two-part bank reconciliation for Dunkle Company.

   2) **OBJECTIVE 4.** Make an entry, or entries, to adjust the Cash in Bank account balance at May 31.

DISCUSSION QUESTIONS FOR SECTION 9.B

1. What is meant by the expression *two-part bank reconciliation*, and why is the two-part format preferred by accountants?

2. What is a bill of exchange, and which type is most commonly used?

3. Why does a bank *credit* a depositor's account for deposits made?

4. How does a bank reconciliation help control cash?

5. How is cash control affected when the person who maintains the accounting records and the checkbook also reconciles the bank account?

6. When a bank reduces a depositor's account for a service charge, a returned check, or a similar item, it sends the depositor a *debit memo*. Why is the notice called a debit memo when the depositor's cash account must be *credited* for such items?

7. On July 31, the balance shown by a company's Cash in Bank account agrees with the balance shown on its bank statement. Is it necessary to prepare a bank reconciliation under these circumstances? Why?

8. Why is there usually a time lag between the issuance of a check and the reflection of the check on the bank's records?

9. "All adjusting entries involving Cash in Bank should stem from a bank reconcilation." Do you agree with this statement? Why?

10. Why are there usually more outstanding checks than there are deposits in transit at the time a reconciliation is prepared?

EXERCISES FOR SECTION 9.B

9.B.1. Determine if each statement is *true* or *false*.

a. The only time there is a difference between the Cash in Bank account balance and the bank statement balance is when an error has been made.

b. A credit memo is issued by a bank to notify a depositor of a decrease in the depositor's account.

c. Outstanding deposits are added to the Cash in Bank account balance when preparing a two-part bank reconciliation.

d. Outstanding checks are deducted from the bank statement balance when preparing a two-part bank reconciliation.

e. In a two-part bank reconciliation, the bank statement balance is reconciled to the Cash in Bank account balance in the ledger.

9.B.2. For each of the following items, indicate the needed adjustment to correct the Cash in Bank account balance by writing the word "increase" or "decrease," followed by the amount by which the cash balance should be increased or decreased. If no adjustment is necessary, write the words "no entry."

a. A $450 deposit was recorded in the books as $540.

b. A $600 deposit made for the last day of the month is not shown on the bank statement.

c. A $4.50 service charge appears on the bank statement but has not been recorded on the books.

d. A customer's check for $85 that had been deposited as cash was returned by the bank marked "insufficient funds."

e. Check No. 2037 in the amount of $460 was not among the canceled checks returned with the bank statement.

9.B.3. Make adjusting entries on December 31 to correct for the following.

   a. The Sara Vee Company recorded a $340 payment on account as $430 in its cash disbursements journal. The error was discovered when the canceled checks were compared with the company records.

   b. A check for $200 received and deposited by Sara Vee in settlement of an account was returned marked "insufficient funds."

   c. A bank service charge of $12 appears on the bank statement but has not been recorded by the company.

9.B.4. Information from the Fortz Company bank reconciliation at June 30 is as follows. Make adjusting journal entries to correct the company's Cash in Bank account balance. (Some items may not require an adjusting entry.)

   a. Deposits in transit at June 30 total $2,800.

   b. There was an unrecorded bank service charge of $15.

   c. Outstanding checks total $3,700.

   d. A $96 cash sale was erroneously recorded as $69.

   e. A $49 payment to a supplier on account was recorded in error as $94.

9.B.5. Use the information that follows to calculate the correct balance in the Cash in Bank account.

   a. Cash in Bank July 31, unadjusted, $11,840.

   b. Deposits in transit, $1,200.

   c. Outstanding checks, $850.

   d. Unrecorded bank service charge, $11.

   e. Check No. 1185 recorded as $89 instead of $98.

   f. Note collected by bank on behalf of company, $5,000; not yet recorded in the books.

PROBLEMS FOR SECTION 9.B
Alternate Problems for this section begin on page D-60.

9.B.6. The following information is provided for the Josh Redram Company.

   a. The bank statement balance at June 30 was $5,755.61.

   b. The Cash in Bank account balance at June 30 was $5,755.61.

   c. Deposits in transit at June 30 totaled $1,673.50.

   d. A comparison of the paid checks returned with the bank statement and the check register showed three checks outstanding at June 30 totaling $2,142.

   e. A customer's payment on account of $2,643.42 was recorded in the cash receipts journal as $2,634.42.

   f. A customer's check marked "insufficient funds" was included with the bank statement, along with a debit memo for $189, the amount of the check.

   g. Check No. 2131 for $274.50 was not recorded by the company. It had been written and sent as a payment of an account payable.

h. The bank statement included a service charge of $14 that was not recorded by the company.

Required

1) Prepare a two-part bank reconciliation at June 30 for Josh Redram Company.

2) Make an entry (or entries) to adjust the Cash in Bank account balance at June 30.

9.B.7. The following data are provided for the BJM Company.

a. The November 30 balance in the company's Cash in Bank account is $7,800.

b. The November 30 bank statement shows a balance of $9,661.

c. Deposits in transit at November 30, $980.

d. Outstanding checks at November 30, $500.

e. A $720 payment on account was recorded in the cash payments journal during November as $270.

f. On November 29, the bank collected a $2,800 non-interest-bearing note from a customer and credited the proceeds to the company's account.

g. There was an unrecorded bank service charge of $9 for November.

Required

1) Prepare a two-part bank reconciliation at November 30.

2) Make an entry (or entries) to adjust the Cash in Bank account to the correct balance at November 30.

9.B.8. The Hardy Company received a bank statement showing a balance of $7,650 at September 30. The company's Cash in Bank account indicated a balance of $8,468 on the same day. The following information has been gathered.

a. Outstanding deposits at September 30, $450.

b. Outstanding checks at September 30, $1,200.

c. The bank erroneously deducted from Hardy's account a $120 check written by the Bardy Company.

d. A deposit of $1,600 was erroneously recorded by the bank as $160.

e. There was an unrecorded bank service charge of $8.

Required

1) Prepare a two-part bank reconciliation at September 30.

2) Make an entry (or entries) to adjust the Cash in Bank account to the correct balance at September 30.

3) State what action Hardy Company should take as a result of the errors made by the bank.

9.B.9. The bank statement received by Fernandez Company for the month of May shows an ending balance of $2,328.61. The bank statement also shows service charges of $24 and a returned customer check (for insufficient funds) in the amount of $1,085, neither of which has been recorded by Fernandez. Toward the end of May the bank collected for Fernandez a $600 note receivable plus $20 interest. Provided here are data pertaining to the bank statement and Fernandez Company's records. The T-account for Cash in Bank shows postings from the cash receipts and cash payments journal for May.

FERNANDEZ COMPANY
Bank Reconciliation
April 30, 19--

BANK STATEMENT			*BOOKS*		
Statement balance		$2,198.42	Account balance		$2,182.00
Add: Deposit in transit		566.13			
		$2,764.55			
Less: Outstanding checks			Less: Recording error	$100.00	
No. 485	$ 54.35		Returned check	562.17	
488	762.19		Service charge	28.00	690.17
498	385.96				
499	70.22	1,272.72			
Disposable cash		$1,491.83	Disposable cash		$1,491.83

Cash in Bank			
Balance, May 1	1,491.83	CP 12	4,682.43
CR 14	5,701.23		

Canceled Checks Returned with the May Bank Statement		Checks Recorded During May	
No. 485	$ 54.35	No. 501	$ 219.85
488	762.19	502	444.73
498	385.96	503	500.00
501	219.85	504	92.11
502	444.73	505	78.00
503	50.00	506	100.00
504	92.11	507	36.99
505	78.00	508	1,515.20
507	36.99	509	925.15
508	1,515.20	510	377.22
509	925.15	511	10.60
511	10.60	512	96.33
513	62.85	513	62.85
		514	223.40
		Total	$4,682.43

Deposits Shown on the May Bank Statement	Deposits of May Receipts	
$ 566.13	No. 54	$1,950.80
1,950.80	55	2,185.00
2,185.00	56	555.24
620.00 CM	57	1,010.19
555.24	Total	$5,701.23

Required

1) Prepare a two-part bank reconciliation at May 31. Assume that any differences between bank statement amounts and book amounts are due to recording errors.

2) Make an entry (or entries) to adjust the Cash in Bank account at May 31. Assume that any returned checks were received initially in payment of Accounts Receivable, and that any recording errors relate to Accounts Payable.

SUMMARY OF CHAPTER 9

For accounting purposes, cash consists of coins and paper money, checking account balances, and checks and other items that banks will accept as deposits in checking accounts. Because it is such a desirable asset, cash must be carefully controlled with such internal control procedures as separation of duties, prompt records of cash receipts, daily cash deposits, payments by check, bank reconciliations, and imprest funds. A petty cash fund is an imprest fund used for making small disbursements. Expenses are recorded when a check is issued to replenish the petty cash fund.

Banks issue checking account statements periodically to depositors. Because of time lags and errors, a bank statement balance rarely agrees with the depositor's Cash in Bank account balance. Both the bank statement balance and the Cash in Bank account balance should be reconciled to correct disposable cash at the reconciliation date. Deposits shown on the bank statement and canceled checks are compared with the accounting records to establish the outstanding deposits and outstanding checks as of the reconciliation date. Unrecorded receipts and charges, returned checks, and any errors discovered are also considered in arriving at the correct disposable cash. Entries to adjust cash must be made for all items on the "books" side of a two-part bank reconciliation.

PROBLEMS FOR CHAPTER 9
Alternate Problems for this chapter begin on page D-62.

9.1. During their freshman year in college, Fritz and Francine were married. They opened a joint checking account in a bank near their college. Because of a number of distractions, they did not keep careful records in their checkbook. On June 2, a bank official called to inform the newlyweds that their account was overdrawn. Fritz and Francine gathered the following information together from their own records and from a previously unopened envelope containing their bank statement for the month of May.

   a. The checkbook record showed a balance of $41.19 on May 31.

   b. Francine had recorded Check No. 21 as $57 instead of $75.

   c. Fritz had failed to record Check No. 27 in the amount of $18.60.

   d. Francine had failed to record Check No. 28 for $20.50.

   e. Fritz recorded a deposit of $25, which Francine had also recorded.

   f. The following checks were outstanding:

No. 26	$15.40
29	30.00
30	1.84

   g. There was a $3 bank service charge for overdrawing the account in May.

   h. The May 31 bank statement showed a balance of $3.33.

Required

Find Fritz and Francine's correct amount of disposable cash at May 31 by preparing a two-part bank reconciliation.

9.2. Selected information follows for the BK Company.

   a. Bank statement balance at December 31, $8,776.

   b. Cash in Bank account balance at December 31, $13,442.

   c. Check No. 1190 for $88 had been cashed by the bank and was returned with the statement. BK Company had issued a stop-payment order to the bank three days before the check was cashed.

   d. Check No. 1203 for $100 was written on December 31 to replenish the petty cash fund. It was not included with the canceled checks.

   e. A bank service charge of $6 appeared on the bank statement.

   f. Cash receipts for December 31 of $4,672 were not deposited in the bank until January 2.

Required

1) Prepare a two-part bank reconciliation at December 31.

2) Make an entry (or entries) to adjust the Cash in Bank account at December 31.

3) State what should be done about Check No. 1190.

4) Give a possible explanation for the fact that Check No. 1203 did not clear, even though it was written to Petty Cash and did not have to be mailed anywhere.

9.3. Selected information is shown here for the Cacti Company.

   a. Bank statement balance at June 30, $21,630.

   b. Cash in Bank account balance at June 30, $18,443.

   c. The bank statement included a late payment charge of $120 that was erroneously deducted by the bank from Cacti's account.

   d. The deposit for June 15 of $8,654 was erroneously recorded in Cacti's books as $6,854.

   e. There were a number of outstanding checks totaling $1,187.

   f. A customer's check for $210 was returned with the notation "insufficient funds."

   g. Deposits in transit at June 30 totaled $530.

   h. A credit amount for $1,060 was listed on the statement for a note collected by the bank on the company's behalf.

Required

1) Prepare a two-part bank reconciliation at June 30.

2) The bookkeeper who prepared the reconciliation complained about the large number of outstanding checks for small amounts. Many of these checks were written for delivery charges, miscellaneous purchases of supplies, and postage. Suggest ways that the company might improve its cash control and reduce the number of checks written for small amounts each month.

9.4. Following are a bank reconciliation, list of deposit slips, bank statement, and portion of the check register (cash payments journal) for Naomi Company. Naomi's checks are encoded in such a manner as to permit the bank's computer system to list check numbers on the bank statement. No entry has yet been made for a collection by the bank of a $4,000 note receivable plus interest of $110.80. Neither has there been any recognition in the company's records of a customer's check for $158 that was returned for insufficient funds or the March service charges of $35. A stop-payment order for Check No. 1907 was properly communicated to the bank on March 26, because the merchandise for which that check was issued was found to be defective. The balance of the Cash in Bank account at March 31 is $133.38. Any differences between the amounts on the bank statement and amounts in the company's records are due to Naomi's recording errors. Returned customer checks are charged back to Accounts Receivable. Except where otherwise apparent, company checks were written in payment of Accounts Payable.

NAOMI SALES COMPANY
Bank Reconciliation
February 28, 19--

BANK STATEMENT			*BOOKS*	
Statement balance		$6,784.93	Account balance	$5,520.26
Add: Deposit in transit		2,789.43	Add: Recording error	18.00
		$9,574.36		$5,538.26
Less: Outstanding checks			Less: Service charge	42.00
No. 1885	$1,364.50			
1887	2,275.60			
1889	10.18			
1890	400.00			
1893	27.82	4,078.10		
Disposable cash		$5,496.26	Disposable cash	$5,496.26

DEPOSIT SLIPS FOR MARCH COLLECTIONS		
Date on Deposit Slip	Deposit Slip No.	Amount
Mar. 4	85	$1,995.20
6	86	3,681.00
10	87	750.00
11	88	1,111.90
18	89	3,085.72
24	90	2,500.00
27	91	855.23
29	92	1,619.67
31	93	1,292.19

LAKEVIEW BANK

NAOMI SALES COMPANY
9219 Sixth Avenue
Quincy, OH 43343

36–942–1
Account Number

3/31/– –
Date of Statement

Balance From Previous Statement	Debits		Credits		Statement Balance
	Number	*Amount*	*Number*	*Amount*	
$6,784.93	22	26,031.30	10	22,498.95	3,252.58

	Checks—Debits				
Date	**Ck. No.**	**Amount**	**Deposits—Credits**	**Date**	**Balance**
3/8	*1885	1,364.50	2,789.43	3/1	9,174.36
3/2	*1887	2,275.60		3/2	6,898.76
3/4	*1889	10.18		3/4	6,888.58
3/1	1890	400.00	1,995.20	3/5	8,883.78
3/18	*1893	27.82	3,681.00	3/8	5,483.28
3/8	1894	5,717.00	750.00	3/11	5,303.28
3/11	1895	930.00			
3/12	1896	87.24	1,111.90	3/12	4,327.94
3/14	1897	261.73		3/14	4,066.21
3/25	1898	14.17		3/18	3,293.39
3/12	1899	2,000.00	3,085.72	3/19	6,379.11
3/18	*1901	745.00		3/22	5,374.21
3/24	1902	811.19		3/24	4,563.02
3/22	1903	1,004.90	2,500.00	3/25	7,048.85
3/26	1904	3,960.15		3/26	2,568.50
3/27	1905	92.18	4,110.80CM	3/27	6,587.12
3/26	1906	520.20	855.23	3/29	5,292.11
3/29	1907	716.98	1,619.67	3/30	6,753.78
3/29	1908	1,433.26		3/31	3,252.58
3/30		158.00RT			
3/31	*1912	3,466.20			
3/31		35.00SC			

SC—Service Charge   DM—Debit Memo   CM—Credit Memo
RT—Returned Check   OD—Overdraft   *—Previous Check(s) Missing

CASH PAYMENTS JOURNAL FOR THE MONTH OF March 19--			
Date	**Accounts and Explanation**	**Ck. No.**	**Cash Credit**
Mar. 1	Macaw Supply Co.	1894	5,717.00
2	Farway Electric Co.	1895	930.00
2	Lee Trucking	1896	87.24
4	Darby and Darby	1897	216.73
5	James Joice	1898	14.17
8	Wong Supplies	1899	2,000.00
8	Jean Artoo	1900	25.50
12	Macaw Supply Co.	1901	745.00
14	Anchor Co.	1902	811.19
18	L & T Co.	1903	1,004.90
18	Wage Expense	1904	3,960.15
22	Roughway Freight Lines	1905	92.18
22	Wong Supplies *payment*	1906	520.20
25	~~Shiptown Products Co.~~ *stopped*	~~1907~~	~~716.98~~
26	Macaw Supply Co.	1908	1,433.26
29	James Joice	1909	85.80
29	Jean Artoo	1910	72.98
29	Anchor Co.	1911	614.85
31	Wage Expense	1912	3,466.20
31	Darby and Darby	1913	390.10
31	Lang Co.	1914	66.34
			22,253.79

Required

1) Prepare a two-part bank reconciliation at March 31.

2) Make an entry (or entries) to adjust Cash in Bank at March 31.

3) What needs to be done in regards to the stop-payment order that the bank failed to honor?

COMPREHENSION PROBLEMS FOR CHAPTER 9

9.5. Flash Developers sent Brian Slye, one of their brightest acquisitions specialists, out to buy land along a planned interstate highway. The firm hoped to be able to acquire land at the sites of future interchanges and resell the land later for a good profit. Brian was given authority to write checks on a $100,000 imprest (revolving) fund bank account that was to be used for buying land and related costs. After about four months in the field, Slye disappeared. A long investigation turned up the following information.

a. Only $110.50 was left in the company's imprest fund account.

b. The imprest fund had been replenished four times for $31,000, $68,000, $92,000, and $79,000, respectively.

c. An audit of the documents submitted by Slye to support replenishment of the fund revealed that many of the documents had been falsified. For example, rather than paying the full amount for properties, as shown on the documents, Slye had made only small down payments to landowners. In some cases, copies of supporting documents for a payment had been submitted several times. Other documents were totally false.

d. A careful audit of the documents showed that up to the last replenishment, there was $23,543.50 worth of valid expenditures.

e. Since the last replenishment, Slye had made $2,400.60 worth of valid expenditures. The balance of the expenditures since the last replenishment all went into Slye's pocket.

f. The last check was written to purchase an airline ticket to the Orient.

Required

1) Determine the amount of money apparently embezzled by Slye.

2) Suggest some controls that might have been used to limit the amount of the loss.

9.6. George Trusting started an industrial supply business called Trusting Tool and Supply Company. George spent much of his time on the road, making sales to customers. After a two-week road trip, George learned from other company employees that the company cashier/bookkeeper/office manager had been missing for several days. As the day progressed, George began receiving strange phone calls. The first was from the bank, reporting that the company's bank account was overdrawn by $10,000. Then, several suppliers called to inquire about payments that the bookkeeper had promised to make. It became obvious that George's bookkeeper had run off with the company's cash. George called several customers showing large Accounts Receivable balances in an effort to raise cash, but all insisted that they had recently paid their accounts in full. An investigation and audit yielded the following information.

a. The cashier/bookkeeper/office manager had been pocketing some of the cash received over the counter for the last four months and had hidden the thefts by recording false merchandise returns.

b. The bookkeeper cashed some checks received from customers as payments on account and pocketed the money without making any record of the customers' payments.

c. Falsified vouchers were put through the petty cash fund maintained by the bookkeeper. The cash was pocketed.

d. The bookkeeper wrote checks to himself and recorded them as payments to creditors.

e. Some of the bookkeeper's personal expenditures, including the purchase of a car, were paid for with company funds.

Required

Suggest specific control devices that could have been used to help prevent each of the foregoing embezzlement schemes.

CHAPTER # 10
Payment Control Systems

The previous chapter dealt with establishing and maintaining controls over cash. Because liabilities usually represent cash payment delays, errors or intentional misstatements of payables can eventually result in misuses of cash. Therefore, controls over payables are viewed as particular kinds of cash controls.

Chapter 10 is presented in two sections. Section A focuses on the control of liabilities other than payroll obligations, which is the topic of Section B. Section A first addresses the need for liability controls, the goals of a liability control system, and common basic data documents used in the purchasing process. The rest of the section is devoted to voucher systems, which are used by some concerns in order to attain tight control over cash payments. Recall that use of a voucher system was one of the eight cash control procedures mentioned in Section A of Chapter 9.

Section B covers payroll systems used to account for employee earnings. The need for internal control over payrolls and the goals of payroll systems are considered. The discussion then turns to the manner by which wages earned, payroll deductions, and net pay due are determined. The various methods used in most payroll systems are identified, and entries are shown for recording payroll obligations and payments.

SECTION 10.A

Liability Controls

OBJECTIVES

This section concentrates on systems for attaining control over liabilities and cash payments. At the conclusion of this section, you should be able to

1. State why control over liabilities is important.
2. List three goals of a control system for liabilities.
3. Complete a voucher form.
4. Record vouchers in a voucher register.
5. Record payments of vouchers.
6. List six basic steps for processing vouchers.

NEED FOR CONTROL OVER LIABILITIES

The need for maintaining control over assets has already been emphasized. Cash, as you may recall, is an asset that is especially difficult to control.

At first glance, one might think that liabilities should present few control problems. Surely, no one would wish to steal a firm's liabilities. However, the establishment of an invalid liability is sometimes the first step in a scheme to obtain cash from an entity illegally. Most liabilities are paid with cash at some future time. For this reason, the recording of liabilities must be carefully controlled.

OBJECTIVE 1. State why control over liabilities is important.

Even valid (legal) liabilities can sometimes present problems. Most business failures result at least in part from mismanagement of liabilities. Managers should guard against overcommitting a concern's ability to pay cash in the future, and only responsible managers should be allowed to commit the entity to liabilities. It is their responsibility to make sure that the entity benefits from the assumption of each liability and that the liability can with reasonable certainty be paid when it falls due.

Goals of Liability Control

A good control system for liabilities will help ensure that each liability assumed is valid, that it is stated at the correct amount, and that it is paid at the proper time. An obligation is valid when it has been authorized by a responsible manager and when the entity has received the goods, services, or other considerations for which the liability was incurred.

Care must be taken that liabilities are properly stated in amount. Purchase invoices should be checked for mathematical accuracy and compared to purchase orders and other documents to make certain that terms and unit prices are as agreed upon.

Finally, liabilities should be paid when they are due, but *no earlier* than is necessary. In general, liabilities subject to cash discounts should be paid within the discount periods. Losing a 2% discount on terms of 2/10, n/30 is equivalent to paying an interest rate of more than 36% per annum.[1] However, paying liabilities before they need to be paid means giving up the use of money that could otherwise be working for the entity.

In summary, here are the main goals of a control system for liabilities.

OBJECTIVE 2. List three goals of a control system for liabilities.

1. To ensure that obligations are valid
   a. Properly authorized
   b. Goods, services, and other considerations have been received
2. To ensure that amounts are correctly stated
   a. Terms are as agreed upon
   b. Amounts are mathematically correct
3. To ensure that obligations are paid at the proper time
   a. Cash discounts are taken
   b. Obligations are paid no earlier than necessary

DOCUMENTING LIABILITIES AND PAYMENTS

Some of the forms used to document liabilities and payments have already been introduced in earlier sections. Large entities may use many kinds of documents; very small concerns may require only a few.

Some forms originate within the entity being accounted for, some come to the concern from other entities. In general, forms coming from outside an entity are viewed as stronger evidence than forms originating within the entity. Dishonest employees may find it somewhat easier to construct invalid documents with the entity's own forms than with forms used by suppliers and other entities.

Some of the more commonly used forms are discussed in the paragraphs that follow.

Purchase Requisition

Most merchandising concerns make frequent purchases of goods for resale. These purchases are evidenced by a variety of forms. A large firm usually has a purchasing department to take care of all purchasing for the company. Special forms called *purchase requisitions may be used within the company*

---

[1]See Section 4.B for a discussion on the interest equivalents of discounts lost.

to let the purchasing department know what kinds of goods need to be purchased.

Purchase Order

A good manager tries to get the highest quality of resources at the lowest possible cost. A company may have to contact several potential suppliers to determine which one will furnish the needed resource at the lowest cost. Sometimes a supplier is invited to make a *bid, which is an offer to furnish goods or services at specified prices and terms.* A bid may be made by letter, or it may be made on a special bid form used by the supplier.

Presumably, each supplier submitting a bid will quote the lowest possible prices in an effort to win the right to furnish the resources. An entity may then choose the supplier whose bid is most attractive.

All orders should be written on *purchase order forms designed especially for ordering goods from suppliers.* If an order is made by phone, it should be confirmed by a written order. A purchase order should state the description, quality, quantity, and price of the goods or services ordered, and it should be signed by the manager who authorized the order.

The original of the purchase order is sent to the company selected to supply the needed resources. At least one copy of the order is retained by the purchasing company as evidence of the kind, quantity, and price of resources ordered.

A carbon copy of each purchase order may be sent to the receiving department as advance notice that a shipment will be coming. Sometimes the quantity is omitted from the copy sent to the receiving department. The reason for this is that advance knowledge of the number of units expected may condition receiving clerks to assume that the number was actually received. An independent count of actual units received is desired.

Receiving Report

When goods are received, *a written record of their quantity, description, and condition should be made on a **receiving report** (receiving ticket, receiving slip) form.* A receiving report provides proof of what was received and helps establish the validity of the obligation to pay for the goods. A copy of the receiving report is routed to the accounting department as evidence that the goods have been received.

Bill of Lading

Sometimes the goods are delivered by the suppliers themselves. More often, however, a transportation company is hired to haul goods from a seller to a buyer. In this event, there is usually *a special contract between the carrier and the seller called a **bill of lading**, which contains a description of the* *items being transported, the name of the shipper, and the name of the company expecting the delivery.* The receiving company usually gets a copy of the bill of lading, which is useful as external evidence that goods were actually shipped to it.

Purchase Invoice

A supplier usually mails an invoice at the time the goods are shipped, or soon after. *An **invoice** is a billing form that gives details about goods or services that have been sold, including the charges for them.* A selling company refers to its own billing forms as sales invoices, whereas a buying company refers to billings received from suppliers as purchase invoices. *A **sales invoice**, then, is a bill that is sent to a customer; a **purchase invoice** is a bill received from a supplier.* These terms are simply different ways of viewing the same basic data document.

Other Controls

Most liabilities are paid by check, usually accompanied by *a written explanation of what the payment is for, called a **check advice** or **remittance advice**.* Canceled checks returned with bank statements serve as evidence that payees have actually received payment.

Forms used by an entity are usually *prenumbered* sequentially so that all forms can be accounted for. This tends to reduce errors and discourage improper action by employees. Forms ruined accidentally should be marked "void" and filed, to show that all numbers are accounted for.

VOUCHER SYSTEMS

Voucher Forms

*A document containing written evidence in support of a transaction is called a **voucher**. But accountants often use the term in a more restricted sense to refer to a form especially designed to give information about a liability.* Some companies center their liability controls around the use of these special voucher forms.

It has already been pointed out that most liabilities are eventually paid with cash. Some companies go a step further and assume that *all* cash payments reduce liabilities. Even a cash purchase is viewed first as the creation of a liability and then as immediate payment of that liability with cash. *If a properly approved voucher is required to support every cash disbursement, the company is said to employ a **voucher system**.*

Voucher forms are designed in many different ways to fit the needs of particular firms. Some forms provide room on both back and front for noting a great deal of data. The voucher form in Illustration 10.1 is a simple one that documents a purchase of merchandise from a supplier.

ILLUSTRATION 10.1

GARY STORES, INC.	VOUCHER	No. X2-465

Pay To _Perry Supply Company_
1672 Hill Street
Perryville, Ohio 44864

Voucher Date _April 3, 19--_
Invoice Date _April 1, 19--_
Due Date _April 10, 19--_

Invoice No. _2673_
P.O. No. _316_

Gross Amount _$1,250.00_
Discount _25.00_
Net _1,225.00_

Verifications

Quantities _C.D_
Prices _C.D_
Terms _C.D_
Extensions and Footings _M.M._
Account Distribution _M.M._
Approved _W. Dale_

Account Distribution

Account	*Amount*
Purchases	_$1,250.00_

Vouchers Payable (Cr.) $ _1250.00_

Paid: _4/10/--_   Check No. _2285_   Amount _$1,225.00_

OBJECTIVE 3. Complete a voucher form.

As you can see, information about the purchase invoice is noted on the voucher. Also on the voucher are the initials of the persons who verified the quantities, prices, terms, arithmetic, and account distribution, as well as the signature of the official who approved the voucher for payment when it comes due. The due date noted is the end of the discount period. If no discount were allowed, the due date would be the end of the period allowed by the supplier for paying the invoice.

The account distribution is used for recording the voucher in a journal. The voucher pictured should be recorded as a debit to Purchases and a credit to Vouchers Payable—which is the liability control account in a voucher system.

The date, number, and amount of the check were noted at the bottom of the voucher form at the time of payment. The voucher in Illustration 10.1 is a paid voucher. Until the blanks at the bottom have been filled in, a voucher is still open (unpaid).

Forms Flow

Copies of purchase orders, receiving reports, and other forms related to the liability are usually attached to the voucher form. After the liabilities have been journalized, vouchers and related forms are usually filed in a suspense (date) file according to due date. Each day, the vouchers representing liabilities due that day are pulled for payment. Payment data are entered on the vouchers, the payments are journalized, and the voucher packets, including copies of the check advices, are then filed in a permanent file, usually alphabetically by suppliers' names. The manner in which the forms flow through the entity is shown in the flowchart in Illustration 10.2.

Recording Vouchers

*In a voucher system, a special journal called a **voucher register** is usually used for recording all vouchers.* A purchases journal is not needed, since purchases, along with all other transactions that require cash payments, are represented by vouchers. The voucher in Illustration 10.1 was journalized as shown on the first line of the voucher register pictured in Illustration 10.3 on page 466. Each voucher is recorded by crediting Vouchers Payable and debiting the appropriate account(s). As payments are made, the check dates and numbers are noted in the voucher register. Lines without check notations represent vouchers that are as yet unpaid.

Note that vouchers are prepared and recorded for all obligations to pay cash, even when the cash payments are made immediately. For example, the purchase of an office machine for cash was recorded as a voucher payable on April 6, although a check was written on the same date to pay for the machine.

Posting the Voucher Register

The voucher register is a special journal, and postings from it are made in a manner similar to postings from other special journals. The totals of special columns are posted to the accounts involved, and amounts in the other debits column are posted individually to the proper accounts. Voucher No. X2–467 required two debits in the other debits column. Account numbers are referenced at the bottom of the special columns and in the reference column for amounts posted individually. The check mark at the bottom of the other debits column indicates that the total of that column is not posted anywhere.

Recording Payments

Payments of vouchers are recorded in a *check register*.[2] Each check is recorded as a debit to Vouchers Payable and a credit to Cash. The check register in Illustration 10.4 on page 466 provides a special column for Purchases Discounts.

---

[2]As pointed out in Section 5.B, a cash payments journal is called a check register when all cash disbursements are represented by checks.

ILLUSTRATION 10.2

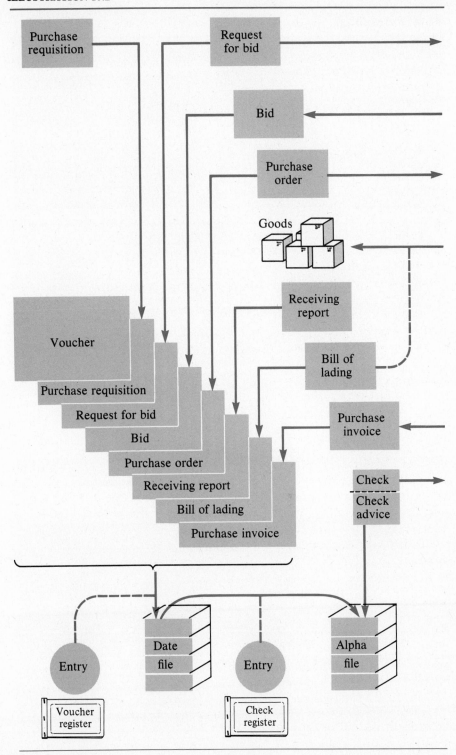

ILLUSTRATION 10.3

OBJECTIVE 4. Record vouchers in a voucher register.

			Paid	
Voucher No.	Date	Payee	Date	Ck. No.
X2–465	19–– Apr. 3	Perry Supply Co.	19–– Apr. 10	2285
X2–466	4	Torry Trucking	5	2280
X2–467	4	Sligo National Bank	4	2279
X2–468	6	Machine Supply Co.	6	2281
X2–484	28	J.C. Benny Co.		
X2–485	30	Valley Power Co.		
X2–486	30	Payroll	30	2305

VOUCHER REGISTER

OBJECTIVE 5. Record payments of vouchers.

ILLUSTRATION 10.4

CHECK REGISTER *PAGE 7*

Check No.	Date	Payee	Voucher No.	Vouchers Payable Dr.	Purchases Discounts Cr.	Cash Cr.
2277	19–– Apr. 2	D. M. Co., Inc.	X2–460	1,000	20	980
2278	2	Jervey Co.	X2–458	740		740
2279	4	Sligo National Bank	X2–467	4,060		4,060
2280	5	Torry Trucking	X2–466	146		146
2303	29	Merkle Supply Co.	X2–479	2,200	44	2,156
2304	29	Western Telephone Co.	X2–470	93		93
2305	29	Payroll	X2–486	3,520		3,520
	30			44,926	560	44,366
				(31)	(62)	(11)

							PAGE 8
Vouchers Payable	Purchases	Freight In	Supplies	Salaries	Other Debits		
Cr.	Dr.	Dr.	Dr.	Dr.	Account	Ref.	Amount
1,250 146 4,060 2,100	1,250	146			⎰Notes Payable ⎱Interest Expense Office Machines	32 76 23	4,000 60 2,100
900 740 3,520	900			3,520	Utilities Expense	75	740
46,782	30,272	470	620	7,090			8,330
(31)	(61)	(64)	(11)	(72)			(√)

The Unpaid Vouchers File

As mentioned earlier, unpaid vouchers are usually filed according to their due dates. The unpaid vouchers file is in effect a subsidiary ledger for the Vouchers Payable control account in the general ledger. Therefore, no Accounts Payable subsidiary ledger is needed. The unpaid vouchers are usually reconciled to the control account at the end of each month when the total of the unpaid vouchers is shown to be equal to the Vouchers Payable account balance, as depicted in Illustration 10.5.

Illustration 10.6 summarizes the six steps in processing vouchers. Both illustrations are on the next page.

GLOSSARY FOR SECTION 10.A

Bid An offer to supply goods or services at certain prices and terms.

Bill of lading A contract with the carrier of goods, which contains a description of the items being transported, the name of the shipper, and the name of the company expecting the delivery.

Check advice (remittance advice) A written explanation of what a check is for.

Invoice A billing form that gives details about goods or services that have been sold, including the charges for them.

Purchase invoice A bill that is received by a buyer from a supplier.

ILLUSTRATION 10.5

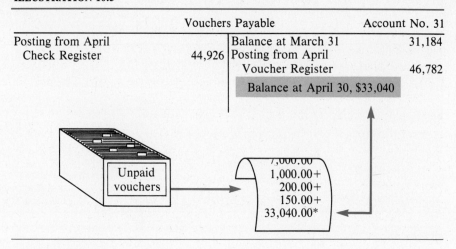

	Vouchers Payable		Account No. 31
Posting from April Check Register	44,926	Balance at March 31	31,184
		Posting from April Voucher Register	46,782
		Balance at April 30, $33,040	

Unpaid vouchers

7,000.00
1,000.00+
200.00+
150.00+
33,040.00*

ILLUSTRATION 10.6

OBJECTIVE 6. List six basic steps for processing vouchers.

VOUCHER PROCESSING STEPS

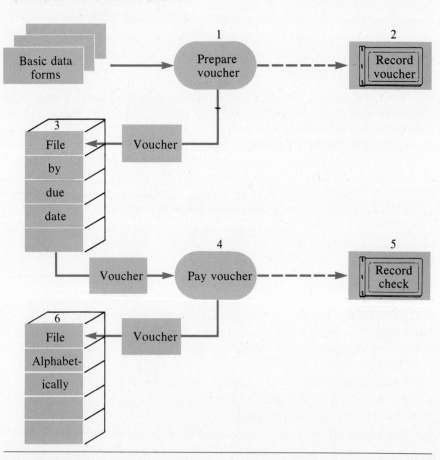

Basic data forms

1 Prepare voucher

2 Record voucher

3 File by due date

Voucher

4 Pay voucher

5 Record check

6 File Alphabetically

Voucher

Voucher

Purchase order   A form used to order goods from a supplier.

Purchase requisition   A special form used within an entity to let a purchasing department know what kinds of goods need to be purchased.

Receiving report (receiving ticket, receiving slip)   A form for listing the quantity, description, and condition of goods received.

Sales invoice   A bill that is sent by a seller to a customer.

Voucher   A document containing written evidence in support of a transaction. The term is often used in a more restricted sense to refer to a form especially designed to give information about a liability.

Voucher register   A special journal for recording vouchers.

Voucher system   A control system that requires a properly approved voucher for every cash disbursement.

SELF-QUIZ ON OBJECTIVES FOR SECTION 10.A
Solutions to Self-Quiz begin on page B-36.

1. **OBJECTIVE 1.** State why control over liabilities is important.

2. **OBJECTIVE 2.** List three goals of a control system for liabilities.

3. A purchase invoice form is shown here. The invoice received on July 2 is for merchandise bought by Buckley Company for resale to customers. Quantity, price, and terms were verified by Earl Foss. Extensions and footings were checked by Bill Doran, who also made the account distribution. Fred Males, the controller, approved the voucher for payment. Payment was made on July 10 with Check No. 1466.

INVOICE			NO. 2175

TABBY SUPPLY COMPANY
825 South Byers Street
Knox, PA 16232

July 1, 19--

Sold to:

Buckley Company
240 Forest Ave.
Clarion, PA 16214

Buyer's Purchase Order
No. *585*

Quantity	Item	Unit Price	Amount
80 sets	*Drill bits*	*10.00*	*800.00*

Terms: *2/10, n/30*

    a. OBJECTIVE 3. Complete Voucher No. X2-792, on a form similar to the one illustrated in this section.

    b. OBJECTIVE 4. Record the voucher in a voucher register.

    c. OBJECTIVE 5. Record the payment in a check register, and make the proper notations of payment on the voucher form and in the voucher register.

4. OBJECTIVE 6. List six basic steps for processing a voucher.

DISCUSSION QUESTIONS FOR SECTION 10.A

1. What are the two tests that should be met before a manager allows the entity to assume a liability?

2. Why is it usually a bad practice to pay liabilities before they come due?

3. How can well-managed entities ensure that quality resources are obtained at the lowest possible prices?

4. Why are the order quantities sometimes omitted from purchase order copies that are sent to the receiving department?

5. How does the use of prenumbered printed forms help to discourage employee theft and other wrongdoing?

6. What is a voucher system?

7. Why is a purchases journal not needed when a voucher system is used?

8. Why are unpaid vouchers filed by due date, and paid vouchers filed alphabetically by suppliers' names?

EXERCISES FOR SECTION 10.A

10.A.1. The Beta Company uses a voucher system. Several transactions for Beta are as follows.

Mar. 3   Voucher No. X2–466 is prepared as a result of merchandise purchased from 2N Manufacturing Company for $5,000.

      10   Check No. 2411 is issued in payment of Voucher No. X2–466.

      12   Voucher No. X2–470 is prepared as a result of equipment purchased from H&H Tool Company for $12,000.

      12   Check No. 2416 is issued in payment of Voucher No. X2–470.

Record each of the transactions in general journal form, and indicate after each entry the name of the journal that a company using a voucher system would normally use to record the transaction.

10.A.2. Explain how purchase orders, receiving reports, purchase invoices, vouchers, and canceled checks all help to provide evidence that the assumption and payment of liabilities were properly handled.

10.A.3. List at least three documents that help prove that purchase transactions were properly authorized. Briefly describe each document and its functions.

PROBLEMS FOR SECTION 10.A
Alternate Problems for this section begin on page D-63.

10.A.4. Information from a number of invoices received by the Timis Company is summarized as follows.

Invoice					Account		
Date	*No.*	**P.O. No.**	**Payable To**	**Amount**	*Name*	*No.*	**Terms**
19--							
Aug. 3	1213	P–107	B-Imports	$1,800	Purchases	51	2/10, n/30
3	4067	P–103	Bobbie Jeans, Inc.	560	Purchases	51	n/30
5			A. C. Crual, CPA	1,250	Acc't. Exp.	65	n/30
6	A218	P–121	B&G Suppliers	69	Supplies	14	2/10, n/30
11	1516	P–106	Art Manufacturing	2,700	Purchases	51	n/30
13	486	P–109	General Equipment	600	Equipment	18	2/10, n/30
20	2121	P–115	B-Imports	2,100	Purchases	51	2/10, n/30
20	1211		Electric Edison Co.	620	Util. Exp.	64	n/30
21	616	P–104	Redram, Inc.	1,400	Purchases	51	n/30

Timis uses a voucher system. Quantities, prices, and terms shown on a voucher are verified by D. Duper. Extensions and footings and account distributions are verified by M. Mauler. Vouchers are approved for payment by B. Jeannerat.

Required

1) Prepare Voucher No. 2152, dated August 5, for the first invoice just listed.

2) Record the invoices in a voucher register starting with Voucher No. 2152. Assume that each voucher was prepared two days after the invoice date.

3) Balance and rule the register and note appropriate account reference numbers as they would appear after postings to ledger accounts have been completed. (Vouchers Payable is Account No. 21.)

10.A.5. Three situations for the Schlep Company are as follows.

June 8 Received an invoice, dated June 5, from Doodles Wholesale for merchandise purchases. The amount of the invoice was $2,400, terms 2/10, n/30. The invoice was paid on June 13 with Check No. 1823.

10 Check No. 1822 for $120 was made payable to Petty Cash to replenish petty cash and to increase the amount of the fund by $50. Expenditures from petty cash consisted of $40 for travel expense, $10 for postage expense, and $20 for freight in.

13   Merchandise was received on a C.O.D. shipment. Check No. 1824 was drawn to D&G Company for $1,554. The merchandise cost $1,530 and the freight charge, including the C.O.D. charge, was $24.

Required

1) Prepare a voucher form to reflect the information provided for each situation. (Number vouchers serially starting with No. 101.)

2) Record the three vouchers in a voucher register.

3) Record payments of the vouchers in a check register, and note the payments properly in the voucher register.

10.A.6. Beer's Department Store received the following invoice from Job Wholesale. James Clark verified the invoice on the date received, September 16. A. C. Crual approved the voucher. The merchandise was ordered on Purchase Order No. X4–575.

INVOICE   **NO. 400013**

JOB WHOLESALE
113 Watergate Road
Brooklyn, NY

Sold to: *September 15, 19--*

Beer's Department Store
New York, NY

Quantity	Item	Unit Price	Amount
480	Slacks	11.00	5,280

Terms: *2/10, n/30*

Required

Prepare Voucher No. 6648, dated September 17, for the preceding invoice.

10.A.7. A list of vouchers follows.

Date Recorded	Voucher No.	Payable To	Account	Amount
19--				
May 5	X5–198	Buzz Telephone	Telephone Expense	$ 45.75
5	X5–199	NOD Corporation	Purchases	2,800.00
8	X5–200	Petty Cash	Petty Cash	150.00
10	X5–201	G. B. Garbarino	Legal Fees	4,800.00

Required

Record the vouchers in a voucher register similar to the one illustrated in this section.

10.A.8. A list of vouchers follows.

Date Paid	Voucher No.	Payable To	Account	Amount
19--				
May 8	X5–200	Petty Cash	Petty Cash	$ 150.00
14	X5–199	NOD Corporation	Purchases	2,800.00
31	X5–198	Buzz Telephone	Telephone Expense	45.75
June 3	X5–201	G. B. Garbarino	Legal Fees	4,800.00

Required

Record payment of the vouchers in a check register similar to the one illustrated in this section. Start with Check No. 3186 and assume that a 2% cash discount is taken on all merchandise purchases.

SECTION 10.B

Payroll Systems

OBJECTIVES

This section concentrates on accounting for the accrual and payment of employee salaries and wages and on accounting for related payroll deductions and taxes. At the conclusion of this section, you should be able to

1. State three overall goals of payroll systems.
2. Calculate gross wages, deductions, and net pay for individual employees, given hours worked, wage rates, and deductions data.
3. Make entries to record the following, given payroll register totals and related data:
   a. Wages earned and related liabilities for a payroll period.
   b. The employer's payroll tax expenses and related liabilities for a payroll period.

NEED FOR INTERNAL CONTROL OVER WAGES AND SALARIES

Various kinds of resources are used in the process of generating revenues. *Human services, often called **labor**, make up an important share of the resources used by most entities. Labor costs are called wages or salaries. **Wages** usually refer to the earnings of lower-level employees who work for an hourly or weekly rate of pay. **Salaries** usually refer to the compensation of employees who work at administrative or managerial levels for a monthly or annual rate of pay.*

Before they are paid to employees, *salaries and wages are usually accumulated (accrued) for a number of days or weeks, called the **pay period**. A listing of the wages or salaries due to employees for a pay period is called a **payroll**. The procedures used to account for wages and salaries are referred to as the **payroll system**.* An entity's payroll system is part of its overall accounting system.

In Chapter 9 we discussed the need for controls over cash payments. Because wages and salaries are paid with cash, and because of the sheer size of most payrolls, internal control over wages and salaries is very important.

Goals of Payroll Systems

One goal of a payroll system is to allow accruals of salaries and wages only for services actually rendered to the entity. Responsibility for this goal is sometimes divided among several departments within an entity. A personnel department, for example, may be responsible for authorizing the employment of workers at given rates of pay. A timekeeping department may be charged with keeping track of the time employees work. And a payroll department may be responsible for computing amounts due and for ensuring that payments are made only to those persons authorized to receive them.

Gathering and processing payroll data take considerable time. Yet employees expect to be paid on scheduled pay dates. Therefore, another goal of a payroll system is to process data quickly enough to permit prompt payment of the salaries and wages that are due.

Employers must comply with a variety of requirements by federal, state, and local governments. Some of these requirements have to do with taxes that must be withheld from employee earnings. Others subject employers to taxes that are measured by the amount of wages and salaries paid to employees. Still other requirements are concerned with fair treatment of employees by their employers. Payroll records must be kept in sufficient detail to provide information for use in complying with the various government regulations.

In summary, here are the three overall goals of a payroll system.

1. To allow accruals of salaries and wages only for services actually rendered to the entity.
2. To process data quickly enough to permit prompt payment of salaries and wages that are due.
3. To comply with government regulations.

OBJECTIVE 1. State three overall goals of payroll systems.

These goals help attain internal control over payroll obligations and the resulting cash payments. Whenever possible, sound internal control procedures should be built into payroll systems. For example, payroll accounting duties should be separated so that employees act as checks on each other; prenumbered forms should be used; payments of wages and salaries should always be made by check; and bank accounts from which payrolls are disbursed should be promptly and carefully reconciled.

CALCULATING WAGES

Gross Pay

An employee's *gross pay for a pay period is the total amount earned by the employee during the period, before any payroll deductions are made.* The amount of gross pay earned by an employee is determined by the employee's pay rate and the units of service rendered during the pay period. Salaries stated as monthly or annual rates of pay are frequently paid over a number of shorter pay periods. Wages (as opposed to salaries) are usually stated as hourly or weekly rates.

Although most often stated in terms of time units, wage rates are sometimes stated on a *piecework rate of pay, an earnings rate based on units of work performed.* For example, factory workers' wages may be based on the number of parts (pieces) they process during a pay period. Salespeople are sometimes paid *commissions, usually stated in percentage terms, based on the sales they make.* For example, a salesperson may be paid at the rate of 5% of total sales made during a pay period.

Occasionally, employees are paid both wages (or salaries) and commissions or piecework rates to encourage them to be productive. High-level managers are sometimes paid a bonus stated in terms of a percentage of the net income earned by the entity. *A **bonus** is extra compensation for helping to generate a good net income for the entity.* Even lower-level employees sometimes share in company earnings through *profit-sharing plans, which provide yearly bonuses to employees based on the level of company profits for the year.*

Time Cards.   As we have said, wages are often earned at hourly rates. To ensure that wages are accrued only for services actually rendered, the hours worked by employees must be carefully tallied. In a small concern, the owner or manager may informally note the hours worked by each employee each day. Larger concerns use time cards to keep track of hours worked.

*A **time card** is a special form for noting the hours worked by an employee each day.* Most large companies have *time clocks, which are designed to stamp the time on an employee's time card as the employee enters or leaves the place of work.* A time card designed for use with a time clock is pictured in Illustration 10.7. Time cards and time clocks are excellent internal control devices.

Overtime Rates.   Many firms pay their employees an *overtime premium for working more than a standard number of hours, for working on weekends, or for working on holidays.* In fact, a federal law, the Fair Labor Standards Act, requires most employers engaged in interstate commerce to pay a premium of one-half the regular hourly rate for hours worked in excess of 40 hours each week. The act also sets a minimum hourly wage. Salaried employees are exempt from certain provisions of the law, and a few occupations are also exempt from its provisions. Of course, employers are free to pay more than the minimum prescribed by the act, and many pay double or triple time for work on Sundays and holidays.

Calculating Gross Pay.   Consider the example of an employee, Karen Mortimer, who worked 42 hours the first week and 47 hours the second week of a biweekly pay period. Karen is paid at the rate of $8 per hour, with 50% overtime pay for any hours over 40 each week. Karen's gross pay may be figured by either of the approaches shown in Illustration 10.8 on page 478.

ILLUSTRATION 10.7

DEPT. NO. 4

EMPLOYEE NO. 23

NAME John W. Doe

WEEK ENDING Dec. 8,19--

ABSENCE (days)				
1. Sick 2. Holiday 3. Vacation 4. Personal*	SATURDAY	4	OUT	DEC 1 7 .5
			IN	DEC 1 11 .5
			OUT	
			IN	
ABSENCE (days) 1. Sick 2. Holiday 3. Vacation 4. Personal*	SUNDAY		OUT	
			IN	
			OUT	
			IN	
ABSENCE (days) 1. Sick 2. Holiday 3. Vacation 4. Personal*	MONDAY	8	OUT	
			IN	DEC 3 4 .5
			OUT	DEC 4 12 .5
			IN	
ABSENCE (days) 1. Sick 2. Holiday 3. Vacation 4. Personal*	TUESDAY	8	OUT	
			IN	DEC 4 4 .5
			OUT	DEC 5 12 .5
			IN	
ABSENCE (days) 1. Sick 2. Holiday 3. Vacation 4. Personal*	WEDNESDAY	8	OUT	
			IN	DEC 5 4 .5
			OUT	DEC 6 12 .5
			IN	
ABSENCE (days) 1. Sick 2. Holiday 3. Vacation 4. Personal*	THURSDAY	8	OUT	
			IN	DEC 6 4 .5
			OUT	DEC 7 12 .5
			IN	
ABSENCE (days) 1. Sick 2. Holiday 3. Vacation 4. Personal*	FRIDAY	8	OUT	
			IN	DEC 7 4 .5
			OUT	DEC 8 12 .5
			IN	

*Jury duty, Death. etc.

TOTAL HRS. [ ][ ].[ ]   Signature *John W. Doe*

SUPERVISOR RECAP

Regular	Overtime	Sick
4 0 . 0 HRS.	4 . 0 HRS.	[ ][ ].[ ] HRS.

Personal Absence Payable	Personal Absence Non-Payable	Vacation Payable
[ ][ ].[ ] HRS.	[ ][ ].[ ] HRS.	[ ][ ].[ ] HRS.

F-421   Signature *Marg Roe*

ILLUSTRATION 10.8

OBJECTIVE 2. Calculate gross wages, given hours worked and wage rates.

GROSS PAY CALCULATIONS	
Approach 1. One-half Time Premium for Overtime	
Regular pay	
89 hours at $8	$712
Overtime premium	
9 hours at $4	36
Gross pay	$748
Approach 2. Time and One-half for Overtime	
Regular pay	
80 hours at $8	$640
Overtime pay	
9 hours at $12	108
Gross pay	$748

The first approach specifically identifies the cost of overtime premiums. Overtime premium cost is frequently classified as an overhead (indirect) item for cost accounting purposes. Cost accounting concepts and procedures are introduced in Chapters 20 and 21.

Deductions

Amounts must be withheld from employee wages and salaries to comply with federal, state, and local tax laws. In addition, amounts may be withheld, at the request of employees, for union dues, insurance premiums, savings programs, and other purposes. *Withholdings from gross pay of employees are called payroll deductions.*

Income Taxes.   Employers are required by federal law to withhold income taxes from salaries and wages earned by most employees and to pay over the withheld amounts to the federal government at periodic intervals.[3] Employees then apply the withheld (prepaid) taxes against the actual taxes due when they file their individual tax returns at year-end. State and local taxing jurisdictions may also require the withholding of income taxes from employee earnings.

The amount of income taxes withheld from an employee's earnings depends on the amount of earnings and the number of allowances for dependents (exemptions) that the employee has claimed.[4] To establish the number of allowances claimed, each employee must furnish the employer with an Employee's Withholding Allowance Certificate (Form W–4), as shown in Illustration 10.9.

---

[3]*Internal Revenue Code,* Sec. 3401–3404.

[4]The term *dependent* is defined in technical terms in Section 152 of the *Internal Revenue Code.*

ILLUSTRATION 10.9

Form **W-4** (Rev. January 1983)	Department of the Treasury—Internal Revenue Service **Employee's Withholding Allowance Certificate**	OMB No. 1545–0010 Expires 8–31–85

1 Type or print your full name
Karen Marie Mortimer

2 Your social security number
177 34 8117

Home address (number and street or rural route)
620 Toby Road

City or town, State, and ZIP code
Parker, PA 16049

3 Marital Status
☐ Single ☒ Married
☐ Married, but withhold at higher Single rate
Note: If married, but legally separated, or spouse is a nonresident alien, check the Single box.

4 Total number of allowances you are claiming (from line F of the worksheet on page 2) 1

5 Additional amount, if any, you want deducted from each pay . . . . $

6 I claim exemption from withholding because (see instructions and check boxes below that apply):

  a ☐ Last year I did not owe any Federal income tax and had a right to a full refund of **ALL** income tax withheld, **AND**

  b ☐ This year I do not expect to owe any Federal income tax and expect to have a right to a full refund of **ALL** income tax withheld. If both a and b apply, enter the year effective and "EXEMPT" here . . ▶ | Year

  c If you entered "EXEMPT" on line 6b, are you a full-time student? . . . . ☐ Yes ☐ No

Under the penalties of perjury, I certify that I am entitled to the number of withholding allowances claimed on this certificate, or if claiming exemption from withholding, that I am entitled to claim the exempt status.

Employee's signature ▶ Karen Marie Mortimer   Date ▶ January 10 , 19 — —

7 Employer's name and address (Employer: Complete 7, 8, and 9 only if sending to IRS)
Farnsworth Sales Co., 1288 River Blvd., Parker, PA 16049

8 Office code

9 Employer identification number
99000888

The amount of income taxes to be withheld from each employee may be determined either by referring to a wage bracket withholding table or by using an approved percentage withholding formula.[5] The percentage method is generally used by entities that process payrolls by computer. A portion of a wage bracket withholding table for married persons paid on a biweekly basis is shown in Illustration 10.10 on the next page. Withholding tables are changed whenever tax rates are increased or decreased.

FICA Tax.   Most employers are required by the Federal Insurance Contributions Act (FICA) to withhold a percentage of each employee's gross earnings for FICA tax. The employer then contributes an equal amount of FICA tax and pays the total FICA tax to the federal government along with the federal income taxes withheld. Proceeds of *FICA taxes are used by the federal government to provide social security benefits to persons who are retired or disabled or who are surviving dependents of deceased workers.*

FICA tax is levied on employee earnings up to a maximum amount each year. Both the maximum earnings and the rate of tax have been increased from time to time by Congress. For simplicity, we will assume an FICA tax rate of 7% on the first $30,000 of each employee's annual earnings. Earnings in excess of the maximum (by our assumption, over $30,000) are not subject to FICA tax.

Other Deductions.   A variety of other deductions may be taken from employee earnings. Most common are deductions for union dues, savings programs, employee insurance, and charitable contributions.

---

[5]Percentage withholding formulas and wage bracket tables are included in Section 3402 of the *Internal Revenue Code.*

ILLUSTRATION 10.10

BIWEEKLY Payroll Period — Employee MARRIED — Effective July 1, 1982

And the wages are-		And the number of withholding allowances claimed is—										
At least	But less than	0	1	2	3	4	5	6	7	8	9	10 or more
		The amount of income tax to be withheld shall be—										
$700	$720	$100.70	$93.40	$86.00	$78.70	$71.40	$64.10	$56.80	$50.10	$43.90	$37.80	$31.60
720	740	105.30	97.20	89.80	82.50	75.20	67.90	60.60	53.30	47.10	41.00	34.80
740	760	110.10	101.00	93.60	86.30	79.00	71.70	64.40	57.10	50.30	44.20	38.00
760	780	114.90	105.70	97.40	90.10	82.80	75.50	68.20	60.90	53.60	47.40	41.20
780	800	119.70	110.50	101.30	93.90	86.60	79.30	72.00	64.70	57.40	50.60	44.40
800	820	124.50	115.30	106.10	97.70	90.40	83.10	75.80	68.50	61.20	53.90	47.60
820	840	129.30	120.10	110.90	101.60	94.20	86.90	79.60	72.30	65.00	57.70	50.80
840	860	134.10	124.90	115.70	106.40	98.00	90.70	83.40	76.10	68.80	61.50	54.20
860	880	138.90	129.70	120.50	111.20	102.00	94.50	87.20	79.90	72.60	65.30	58.00
880	900	143.70	134.50	125.30	116.00	106.80	98.30	91.00	83.70	76.40	69.10	61.80
900	920	148.60	139.30	130.10	120.80	111.60	102.40	94.80	87.50	80.20	72.90	65.60
920	940	154.00	144.10	134.90	125.60	116.40	107.20	98.60	91.30	84.00	76.70	69.40
940	960	159.40	149.00	139.70	130.40	121.20	112.00	102.70	95.10	87.80	80.50	73.20
960	980	164.80	154.40	144.50	135.20	126.00	116.80	107.50	98.90	91.60	84.30	77.00
980	1,000	170.20	159.80	149.40	140.00	130.80	121.60	112.30	103.10	95.40	88.10	80.80
1,000	1,020	175.60	165.20	154.80	144.80	135.60	126.40	117.10	107.90	99.20	91.90	84.60
1,020	1,040	181.00	170.60	160.20	149.80	140.40	131.20	121.90	112.70	103.50	95.70	88.40
1,040	1,060	186.40	176.00	165.60	155.20	145.20	136.00	126.70	117.50	108.30	99.50	92.20
1,060	1,080	191.80	181.40	171.00	160.60	150.20	140.80	131.50	122.30	113.10	103.80	96.00
1,080	1,100	197.20	186.80	176.40	166.00	155.60	145.60	136.30	127.10	117.90	108.60	99.80
1,100	1,120	202.60	192.20	181.80	171.40	161.00	150.70	141.10	131.90	122.70	113.40	104.20
1,120	1,140	208.90	197.60	187.20	176.80	166.40	156.10	145.90	136.70	127.50	118.20	109.00
1,140	1,160	215.30	203.00	192.60	182.20	171.80	161.50	151.10	141.50	132.30	123.00	113.80
1,160	1,180	221.70	209.40	198.00	187.60	177.20	166.90	156.50	146.30	137.10	127.80	118.60
1,180	1,200	228.10	215.80	203.50	193.00	182.60	172.30	161.90	151.50	141.90	132.60	123.40
1,200	1,220	234.50	222.20	209.90	198.40	188.00	177.70	167.30	156.90	146.70	137.40	128.20
1,220	1,240	240.90	228.60	216.30	204.00	193.40	183.10	172.70	162.30	151.90	142.20	133.00
1,240	1,260	247.30	235.00	222.70	210.40	198.80	188.50	178.10	167.70	157.30	147.00	137.80
1,260	1,280	253.70	241.40	229.10	216.80	204.50	193.90	183.50	173.10	162.70	152.30	142.60
1,280	1,300	260.10	247.80	235.50	223.20	210.90	199.30	188.90	178.50	168.10	157.70	147.40

At least	But less than	0	1	2	3	4	5	6	7	8	9	10 or more
1,300	1,320	266.50	254.20	241.90	229.60	217.30	205.00	194.30	183.90	173.50	163.10	152.70
1,320	1,340	273.60	260.60	248.30	236.00	223.70	211.40	199.70	189.30	178.90	168.50	158.10
1,340	1,360	281.00	267.00	254.70	242.40	230.10	217.80	205.50	194.70	184.30	173.90	163.50
1,360	1,380	288.40	274.20	261.10	248.80	236.50	224.20	211.90	200.10	189.70	179.30	168.90
1,380	1,400	295.80	281.60	267.50	255.20	242.90	230.60	218.30	206.00	195.10	184.70	174.30
1,400	1,420	303.20	289.00	274.80	261.60	249.30	237.00	224.70	212.40	200.50	190.10	179.70
1,420	1,440	310.60	296.40	282.20	268.00	255.70	243.40	231.10	218.80	206.40	195.50	185.10
1,440	1,460	318.00	303.80	289.60	275.30	262.10	249.80	237.50	225.20	212.80	200.90	190.50
1,460	1,480	325.40	311.20	297.00	282.70	268.50	256.20	243.90	231.60	219.20	206.90	195.90
1,480	1,500	332.80	318.60	304.40	290.10	275.90	262.60	250.30	238.00	225.60	213.30	201.30
1,500	1,520	340.20	326.00	311.80	297.50	283.30	269.00	256.70	244.40	232.00	219.70	207.40
1,520	1,540	347.60	333.40	319.20	304.90	290.70	276.50	263.10	250.80	238.40	226.10	213.80
1,540	1,560	355.00	340.80	326.60	312.30	298.10	283.90	269.70	257.20	244.80	232.50	220.20
1,560	1,580	362.40	348.20	334.00	319.70	305.50	291.30	277.10	263.60	251.20	238.90	226.60
1,580	1,600	369.80	355.60	341.40	327.10	312.90	298.70	284.50	270.20	257.60	245.30	233.00
1,600	1,620	377.20	363.00	348.80	334.50	320.30	306.10	291.90	277.60	264.00	251.70	239.40
1,620	1,640	384.60	370.40	356.20	341.90	327.70	313.50	299.30	285.00	270.80	258.10	245.80
1,640	1,660	392.00	377.80	363.60	349.30	335.10	320.90	306.70	292.40	278.20	264.50	252.20
1,660	1,680	399.40	385.20	371.00	356.70	342.50	328.30	314.10	299.80	285.60	271.40	258.60
1,680	1,700	406.80	392.60	378.40	364.10	349.90	335.70	321.50	307.20	293.00	278.80	265.00
1,700	1,720	414.20	400.00	385.80	371.50	357.30	343.10	328.90	314.60	300.40	286.20	271.90
		37 percent of the excess over $1,720 plus—										
$1,720 and over		417.90	403.70	389.50	375.20	361.00	346.80	332.60	318.30	304.10	289.90	275.60

BIWEEKLY — Married — Wages $700 to 1,720 and over

Net Pay

*Whatever is left of an employee's gross pay after all deductions are made is called **net pay**.* An employee's net pay for a period is paid by check or in cash on the scheduled payroll date.

Consider the example used earlier. Karen Mortimer earned a gross pay of $748 during a biweekly pay period, and her Form W–4 showed that she claims one exemption allowance. The withholding table in Illustration 10.10 indicates that federal income tax of $101.00 should be withheld from $748 earned during a biweekly pay period by a married taxpayer claiming one exemption.

If we assume an FICA tax rate of 7% and an authorized withholding of union dues of $12 for each biweekly pay period, Karen's net pay can be figured as follows.

NET PAY CALCULATION		
Gross pay		$748.00
Less deductions		
Federal income tax	$101.00	
FICA tax (7% × $748)	52.36	
Union dues	12.00	165.36
Net pay		$582.64

OBJECTIVE 2. Calculate deductions and net pay for individual employees.

CALCULATING THE PAYROLL

Most concerns employ more than one employee. The calculations to arrive at gross and net pay for employees are normally combined on a payroll register. *A **payroll register** is a record form that shows detailed payroll information for each employee for the pay period and shows the summarized totals* for all employees included on the register. Separate registers may be used for salaried and hourly employees. A payroll register is designed to fill the needs of a particular entity. The register in Illustration 10.11 on the next page shows one possible arrangement.

RECORDING THE PAYROLL

The payroll register can be viewed as a special journal, with the gross wages total posted directly to the Wage Expense account and the deductions and net pay totals to liability accounts. However, some entities view the payroll register as supporting data for an entry that is made in the general journal. The entry to record the payroll liability for the payroll register in Illustration 10.11 is shown on page 482 below the illustration.

ILLUSTRATION 10.11

PAYROLL REGISTER

			Earnings		
Name	**Hours**	**Regular Rate**	***Regular***	***Overtime Premium***	***Gross***
Merle Ash	80	6.00	480.00		480.00
Karen Mortimer	89	8.00	712.00	36.00	748.00
Jack Cross	75	7.40	555.00		555.00
Mazue Fittle	80	6.80	544.00		544.00
Maxine Long	81	9.00	729.00	4.50	733.50
Mark Poke	91	10.00	910.00	55.00	965.00
Corry Wright	80	9.25	740.00		740.00
			4,670.00	95.50	4,765.50

OBJECTIVE 3a. Record wages earned and related liabilities for a payroll period.

19--			
May 23	Wage Expense	4,765.50	
	Federal Income Taxes Payable		598.20
	FICA Taxes Payable		333.59
	Union Dues Payable		87.00
	Wages Payable		3,746.71
	To record wages for pay period ended May 23.		

PAYING EMPLOYEES

The usual manner of paying employees is to write checks to them for their net pay amounts. A small concern may use regular checks for paying employees. Each payroll check is then recorded by crediting the Cash in Bank account and debiting Wages Payable for the amount of net pay. If a check register (cash disbursements journal) is used, the checks are recorded in that special journal.

Large concerns are more likely to write payroll checks on a special bank account used only for disbursing payrolls. One regular check, made payable to "Payroll," may be written to transfer cash from the regular bank account to the payroll bank account. The cash transfer can be viewed, for accounting purposes, as equivalent to the payment of the payroll and recorded as follows.

FOR BIWEEKLY PERIOD ENDED MAY 23, 19--				
Deductions				**Net Pay**
Federal Income Tax	*FICA Tax*	*Union Dues*	*Total*	
58.90	33.60	12.00	104.50	375.50
101.00	52.36	12.00	165.36	582.64
55.30	38.85	12.00	106.15	448.85
63.40	38.08	12.00	113.48	430.52
86.20	51.35	12.00	149.55	583.95
124.30	67.55	15.00	206.85	758.15
109.10	51.80	12.00	172.90	567.10
598.20	333.59	87.00	1,018.79	3,746.71

19-- May 23	Wages Payable Cash in Bank To record transfer of funds to payroll account.	3,746.71	
			3,746.71

Special payroll checks are then written immediately to disburse all the cash in the payroll bank account. This procedure helps limit the number of checks clearing through the regular checking account. The payroll bank account is fairly easy to reconcile, since the outstanding checks must reduce the bank statement balance to zero. Some payroll registers are designed with a column for noting the payroll check numbers.

EMPLOYEE'S INDIVIDUAL EARNINGS RECORD

An *employee's individual earnings record is used to accumulate for each employee the earnings, deductions, and other payroll data for a calendar year.* Information for a pay period is shown on one line of the record, and totals are shown for each calendar quarter and for the year, as shown by the partial record pictured in Illustration 10.12 on the next page. Information for the individual earnings record is usually taken from the payroll register.

ILLUSTRATION 10.12

EMPLOYEE'S INDIVIDUAL EARNINGS RECORD

Name _Mortimer, Karen M._
Address _620 Toby Road_
Parker, PA 16049
Phone _343-5266_
Classification _Driver_
Pay Rate _$8.00 per hour_

Period Ending	Earnings			
	Regular	Premium	Gross	Cumulative
Jan. 3	640.00		640.00	640.00
First Quarter	4480.00		4480.00	4480.00
Apr. 11	640.00		640.00	5120.00
25	720.00	40.00	760.00	5880.00
May 9	640.00		640.00	6520.00
23	712.00	36.00	748.00	7268.00
June 6	704.00	32.00	736.00	8004.00
20	640.00		640.00	8644.00
Second Quarter	4056.00	108.00	4164.00	8644.00
Year	17040.00	400.00	17440.00	17440.00

EMPLOYER OBLIGATIONS

Payroll Tax Expenses

An employer must contribute an FICA tax equal to the amount withheld from an employee. This employment tax on the employer is in effect an additional payroll expense and is charged to a Payroll Tax Expense account.

Most entities are also required by the Federal Unemployment Tax Act to pay *unemployment taxes on employee wages and salaries, the proceeds of which are used to pay unemployment compensation and to administer the unemployment programs of the various states.*

Unemployment taxes are computed as a percentage of wages earned by employees, up to a maximum amount of earnings by each employee during a calendar year. Both the rate and the earnings maximum are subject to change by Congress; at the present time, the tax is 3.5% of the first $7,000 of wages earned by each employee during a year.

YEAR _19--_

Social Security No. _177-34-8117_
Birthdate _4-1-44_
Employment Date _7-15-78_
Termination Date _____
Tax Status: [x] Married ☐ Single
No. Allowances _____

Deductions				Net Pay
Federal Income Tax	FICA Tax	Union Dues	Total	
82.00	44.80	12.00	138.80	501.20
590.60	313.60	84.00	988.20	3491.80
82.00	44.80	12.00	138.80	501.20
105.70	53.20	12.00	170.90	589.10
82.00	44.80	12.00	138.80	501.20
101.00	52.36	12.00	165.36	582.64
97.20	51.52	12.00	160.72	575.28
82.00	44.80	12.00	138.80	501.20
549.90	291.48	72.00	913.38	3250.62
2304.20	1220.80	312.00	3837.00	13603.00

The Unemployment Tax Act requires that 2.7% of taxable wages be paid to the state in which the wages are earned; the remaining 0.8% of taxable wages is paid to the federal government.

States may tax at a rate higher than 2.7% if they wish, and they may set the maximum at more the $7,000. A state may also levy an unemployment tax on employees, in which case the unemployment tax is withheld from wages along with FICA and income taxes.

States may reduce the unemployment tax rate for employers that have had little or no unemployment history. Employers that pay a state unemployment tax at a lower "experience" rate still pay 0.8% of the taxable wages to the federal government.

Employee individual earnings records are helpful in determining the point at which employee earnings have exceeded the maximum amount taxable for either FICA or unemployment tax purposes. Once the payroll tax expenses are determined for a pay period, they are recorded in the following manner.

OBJECTIVE 3b. Record the employer's payroll tax expenses and related liabilities for a payroll period.

19-- May 23	Payroll Tax Expense	500.38	
	FICA Taxes Payable		333.59
	State Unemployment Taxes Payable		128.67
	Federal Unemployment Taxes Payable		38.12
	Payroll tax expense for the pay period ended May 23.		

Tax Deposits

Payroll taxes due the federal government are deposited at specified times with a member bank of the Federal Reserve System. If federal income and FICA tax liabilities come to less than $3,000 per pay period, but more than $500 per month, they are deposited monthly. The employer submits a Federal Tax Deposit card (Form 501) along with each deposit; a portion of Form 501 is detached, stamped by the bank, and retained by the employer as proof of payment.

When payroll taxes are deposited or paid directly to taxing authorities, tax liabilities are decreased by an entry similar to the following.

19-- June 10	Federal Income Taxes Payable	1,429.80	
	FICA Taxes Payable	1,334.36	
	Cash		2,764.16
	Deposited federal payroll taxes for May.		

Payroll Tax Returns

FICA and federal income taxes withheld from employees are reported quarterly on Form 941 (Employer's Quarterly Federal Tax Return). As shown in Illustration 10.13, the income taxes withheld are added to the FICA taxes for the quarter. The FICA tax is reported at the combined rate at which the employees and the employer are taxed. Since Farnsworth has already deposited all the taxes, nothing is due when the return is filed.

Form 941 must be filed for each quarter by the end of the first month of the next quarter. If all taxes due have already been deposited, however, the return due date is extended to the tenth day of the second month of the following quarter.

Each state requires that wages earned within the state be reported on a quarterly unemployment tax return. The state unemployment tax is paid with the return, or it is deposited according to the requirements of the particular state.

An Employer's Annual Federal Unemployment Tax Return (Form 940) must be filed with the Internal Revenue Service. The return is due by January

ILLUSTRATION 10.13

Form **941**

Department of the Treasury
Internal Revenue Service

Employer's Quarterly Federal Tax Return

▶ For Paperwork Reduction Act Notice, see page 2.

T	
FF	
FD	
FP	
I	
T	

Your name, address, employer identification number, and calendar quarter of return. (If not correct, please change.)

▶

Name (as distinguished from trade name)
Marcos T. Farnsworth
Trade name, if any
Farnsworth Sales Co.
Address and ZIP code
1288 River Blvd., Parker, PA 16049

Date quarter ended
June 30 19--
Employer identification number
99 000888

If address is different from prior return, check here ▶ ☐

Record of Federal Tax Liability
(Complete if line 13 is $500 or more)

If you made eighth-monthly deposits using the 95% rule, check here . . . . ▶ ☐

If you are a first-time 3-banking-day depositor, check here . . . . ▶ ☐

See the instructions under rule 4 on page 4 for details.

If you are not liable for returns in the future, write "FINAL" . . . . ▶ _____

Date final wages paid . . . . ▶ _____

Date wages paid	Tax liability
Day	
First month of quarter	
1st through 3rd . . . A	
4th through 7th . . B	
8th through 11th . . C	
12th through 15th . . D	
16th through 19th . . E	
20th through 22nd . . F	
23rd through 25th . . G	
26th through last . . H	
I Total . . . . . ▶	2,631.94
Second month of quarter	
1st through 3rd . . . I	
4th through 7th . . . J	
8th through 11th . . K	
12th through 15th . . L	
16th through 19th . . M	
20th through 22nd . . N	
23rd through 25th . . O	
26th through last . . P	
II Total . . . . . ▶	2,764.16
Third month of quarter	
1st through 3rd . . . Q	
4th through 7th . . . R	
8th through 11th . . . S	
12th through 15th . . T	
16th through 19th . . U	
20th through 22nd . . V	
23rd through 25th . . W	
26th through last . . . X	
III Total . . . . . ▶	2,591.45
IV Total for quarter (add lines I, II, and III)	7,987.55

1 Number of employees (except household) employed in the pay period that includes March 12th (complete first quarter only) . . . . . . ▶ **7**

2 Total wages and tips subject to withholding, plus other employee compensation . . . . . ▶ **27,480 00**

3 Total income tax withheld from wages, tips, pensions, annuities, sick pay, gambling, etc. . . ▶ **4,140 35**

4 Adjustment of withheld income tax for preceding quarters of calendar year . . . . ▶

5 Adjusted total of income tax withheld . . . ▶ **4,140 35**

6 Taxable FICA wages paid:
$____27,480 00____ × 14.0% (.140) equals tax **3,847 20**

7 a Taxable tips reported:
$_____ × 7.0% (.070) equals tax . . . . ▶

b Tips deemed to be wages (see instructions):
$_____ × 7.0% (.070) equals tax . . . . ▶

8 Total FICA taxes (add lines 6, 7a, and 7b) . . . **3,847 20**

9 Adjustment of FICA taxes (see instructions) . ▶

10 Adjusted total of FICA taxes **3,847 20**

11 Total taxes (add lines 5 and 10) . . . . . ▶ **7,987 55**

12 Advance earned income credit (EIC) payments, if any . . . . ▶

13 Net taxes (subtract line 12 from line 11). This must equal line IV . . . . ▶ **7,987 55**

14 Total deposits for quarter, including any overpayment applied from a prior quarter, from your records . ▶ **7,987 55**

15 Undeposited taxes due (subtract line 14 from line 13). Enter here and pay to Internal Revenue Service . ▶ **-0-**

16 If line 14 is more than line 13, enter overpayment here ▶ $ _____ and check if to be: ☐ Applied to next return, or ☐ Refunded.

Under penalties of perjury, I declare that I have examined this return, including accompanying schedules and statements, and to the best of my knowledge and belief it is true, correct, and complete.

Signature ▶ *Marcos T. Farnsworth*   Title ▶ Owner   Date ▶ July 15, 19--

Please file this form with your Internal Revenue Service Center (see instructions on "Where to File").   Form **941**

ILLUSTRATION 10.14

1 Control number	22222	OMB No. 1545-0008		

2 Employer's name, address, and ZIP code	3 Employer's identification number	4 Employer's State number
Farnsworth Sales Co. 1288 River Blvd. Parker, PA 16049	99 000888	111 2222

5 Stat. employee ☐	Deceased ☐	Pension plan ☐	Legal rep. ☐	942 emp. ☐	Sub-total ☐	Correction ☐	Void ☐

6	7 Advance EIC payment

8 Employee's social security number	9 Federal income tax withheld	10 Wages, tips, other compensation	11 FICA tax withheld
177-34-8117	$2,304.20	$17,440.00	$1,220.80

12 Employee's name, address, and ZIP code	13 FICA wages	14 FICA tips
Karen M. Mortimer 620 Toby Road Parker, PA 16049	$17,440.00	

16 Employer's use

17 State income tax	18 State wages, tips, etc.	19 Name of State
$383.68		PA

20 Local income tax	21 Local wages, tips, etc.	22 Name of locality
$174.40		Parker

Form **W-2 Wage and Tax Statement 1982**   Copy D For employer   Department of the Treasury Internal Revenue Service

31 of the following year; if all tax due has previously been deposited, the return is not due until February 10. Unpaid federal unemployment tax in excess of $100 must be paid by the end of the month following each quarter. If the total tax for the year is less than $100, it can be paid when the return is filed at the end of the year.

Wage and Tax Statement Forms

At the end of each calendar year, every employee must receive multiple copies of a Wage and Tax Statement (Form W-2) like the one in Illustration 10.14. The employee submits copies of this form along with federal, state, and local tax returns. The form will also show the amount of wages subject to state and local taxation, and the taxes withheld for these taxing jurisdictions.

GLOSSARY FOR SECTION 10.B

Bonus   Extra compensation for helping to generate a good net income for the entity.

Commissions   Earnings based on the amount of sales made.

Employee's individual earnings record   A form used to accumulate for each employee the earnings, deductions, and other payroll data for a calendar year.

FICA taxes   Payroll taxes imposed by the Federal Insurance Contributions Act for the purpose of providing social security benefits to persons who are retired or disabled or who are surviving dependents of deceased workers.

Gross pay   The total amount earned by an employee during a pay period, before any payroll deductions are made.

Labor   Human services used as resources in the process of generating revenues.

Net pay   Whatever is left of an employee's gross pay after all deductions are made.

Overtime premium   Additional employee compensation per hour for working beyond a standard number of hours or for working on weekends or on holidays.

Pay period   The number of days or weeks during which employee earnings are accumulated before they are paid.

Payroll   A listing of wages or salaries due to employees for a pay period.

Payroll deductions   Withholdings from gross pay of employees.

Payroll register   A record form that shows detailed payroll information for each employee for a pay period and shows the summarized totals.

Payroll system   The procedures used to account for wages and salaries.

Piecework rate of pay   An earnings rate based on units of work performed.

Profit-sharing plans   Agreements whereby employees share in company earnings by means of yearly bonuses based on the level of company profits.

Salaries   Compensation of employees working at administrative or managerial levels for a monthly or annual rate of pay.

Time card   A form for noting the hours worked by an employee each day.

Time clock   A specially designed clock that stamps the time on an employee's time card as the employee enters or leaves the place of work.

Unemployment taxes   Taxes imposed by the Unemployment Tax Act for the purpose of providing compensation to unemployed workers and administering the unemployment programs of the various states.

Wages   Earnings of lower-level employees who work for an hourly or weekly rate of pay.

SELF-QUIZ ON OBJECTIVES FOR SECTION 10.B
Solutions to Self-Quiz begin on page B-38.

1. **OBJECTIVE 1.** State three overall goals of payroll systems.

2. **OBJECTIVE 2.** Payroll data for an employee of Farnsworth Enterprises are as follows.

   Employee: Sam Tuthill

   Wage Rate: $7 per hour

   Overtime Premium: One-half pay for all hours in excess of 40 hours per week

   FICA Tax Rate: 7%

   Hours Worked: January 19–24, 40 hours; January 26–31, 46 hours

   a. Calculate Sam's gross wages for the biweekly period ended January 31.

   b. Calculate Sam's net pay for the biweekly period ended January 31, assuming that, in addition to FICA tax, federal income tax of $90 and state income tax of $12.46 are withheld.

3. **OBJECTIVE 3.** In addition to FICA taxes, Farnsworth Enterprises is subject to a state unemployment tax rate of 2.7% and a federal unemployment tax rate of 0.8% on the first $7,000 of wages earned by each employee. The payroll register for the biweekly pay period ended January 31 shows the following totals.

Gross pay	$12,640.00
FICA tax withheld	884.80
Federal income tax withheld	1,910.00
State income tax withheld	252.80
Net pay	9,592.40

a. Make the journal entry to record the payroll, assuming actual payment of wages is made at a later date.

b. Make the journal entry to record the employer's payroll tax expense for the pay period, assuming that no employee has earned $7,000 by the end of the pay period.

DISCUSSION QUESTIONS FOR SECTION 10.B

1. Why are controls over wages and salaries so important?

2. What determines the amount of federal income taxes to be withheld from an employee's earnings?

3. What is FICA tax, and who pays it?

4. What is the difference between gross pay and net pay?

5. What are the advantages of writing payroll checks on a special bank account used only for disbursing payrolls?

6. Who pays unemployment taxes, and for what purpose are the taxes collected?

EXERCISES FOR SECTION 10.B

10.B.1. Joe Shultz earns $9 per hour and is paid an overtime premium of one-half pay for all hours in excess of 40 hours per week. Calculate Joe's gross pay for each of the following pay periods.

a. Week ended June 9, 37½ hours

b. Week ended June 16, 45 hours

10.B.2. For the biweekly pay period ended June 23, Ed Moore earned gross wages of $730. His wages are subject to federal income tax withholding, an FICA tax rate of 7%, and a city tax rate of 0.3%. Ed claims three withholding allowance exemptions for federal income tax purposes. Determine Ed's net pay for the pay period. (*Note:* Use the withholding tax table provided in Illustration 10.10 to find the federal income tax to be withheld.)

10.B.3. The following data come from the payroll register of the Seth Company for the two-week pay period ended December 4.

Gross wages	$8,650.00
Deductions	
Federal income tax	1,220.60
FICA tax	605.50
U.S. savings bonds	360.00

Make a general journal entry to record the payroll liability.

10.B.4. For the monthly pay period ended March 31, Blithe Company's employees earned gross salaries totaling $9,840. The entire amount was subject to employer payroll taxes as follows.

FICA taxes at 7%

State unemployment taxes at 2.7%

Federal unemployment taxes at 0.8%

Make an entry to recognize the employer's payroll tax expense for March.

10.B.5. Federal payroll tax liabilities at the end of July for Josh Corporation were as follows.

Federal income taxes payable	$3,180.46
FICA taxes payable	429.32

On August 10 the payroll taxes are deposited with the Frogtown National Bank. Make a general journal entry to record payment (deposit) by the corporation.

10.B.6. Year-to-date earnings for the three employees of the Jacker Cracks Company at August 31 and earnings for the month of September are shown here.

	Earnings Through August 31	Earnings for September
J. Bond	$30,000.00	$3,750.00
S. Holmes	28,000.00	3,500.00
S. Spade	4,800.00	1,800.00

FICA taxes are levied at a rate of 7% on the first $30,000 of each employee's earnings. State unemployment taxes are levied at 2.7%, and federal unemployment taxes at 0.8%, on the first $7,000 of each employee's earnings. Make the entry to record the employer's payroll tax expense for September.

PROBLEMS FOR SECTION 10.B
Alternate Problems for this section begin on page D-65.

10.B.7. The Benco Company incurred wage expenses of $15,400 for the pay period ended April 11. FICA taxes were withheld from all earnings at a 7% rate.

Additionally, $2,310 was withheld for federal income taxes, and $154 was withheld for union dues.

Required

1) Make a general journal entry to record the payroll, assuming actual payment of wages is made at another time.

2) Make a general journal entry to record the employer's payroll tax expense for the pay period. Assume a state unemployment tax rate of 2.7% and a federal unemployment tax rate of 0.8% on the total amount of wages.

3) Prepare a single general journal entry to take the place of both the foregoing entries.

10.B.8. A payroll register for Peckwith Enterprises is provided here. Peckwith pays its employees biweekly, five days after the payroll period ends.

PAYROLL REGISTER		*FOR BIWEEKLY PERIOD ENDED AUGUST 15, 19--*				
		Deductions				
Name	**Gross Pay**	**Fed. Inc. Tax**	**FICA Tax**	**Union Dues**	**Total**	**Net Pay**
R. Flutz	800.00	140.50	56.00	15.00	175.50	624.50
C. Hakura	480.00	41.20	33.60	15.00	89.80	390.20
U. Nicorn	480.00	46.80	33.60	15.00	95.40	384.60
X. Piper	700.00	89.00	49.00	15.00	153.00	547.00
A. Sudden	1,200.00	237.80	84.00	–0–	321.80	878.20
Total	3,660.00	519.30	256.20	60.00	835.50	2,824.50

Required

1) Make an entry in general journal form to record the payroll on August 15.

2) Record the employer's FICA tax expense for the August 15 payroll.

3) Make an entry on August 20 to record the transfer of cash to a payroll bank account for payment to employees.

4) Assume that the taxes related to the August 15 payroll are deposited with a bank on August 20. Make the appropriate journal entry.

10.B.9. Joan Cromwell works for the Aras Company as a lathe operator for $9 an hour. She receives an overtime premium of one-half her regular rate for hours worked in excess of 40 each week. For the biweekly pay period ended January 12, she worked 41 hours and 49 hours, respectively. She is married and claims two exemptions. Ms. Cromwell's wages are subject to deductions for FICA tax at 7%, federal income tax, and union dues of $10 each biweekly period.

Required

Using the foregoing data and the federal withholding tax table provided in Illustration 10.10, fill in the first line of an employee's individual earnings record for Ms. Cromwell.

SUMMARY OF CHAPTER 10

Control over liabilities is important because they require the use of assets in the future. A good system of liability control will ensure that liabilities are valid, correctly stated, and paid only when due. A variety of different forms aid in documenting the incurrence and payment of liabilities.

In a voucher system, every cash payment is supported by a specially designed voucher form, which gives details about the liability. Vouchers are recorded in a special journal called a voucher register. Unpaid vouchers, along with copies of related forms, are usually filed according to due date. The unpaid vouchers file is in effect a subsidiary vouchers payable ledger. As vouchers are paid they are transferred to an alphabetical file, where they are filed according to suppliers' names.

A payroll system is part of an entity's overall accounting system. A payroll system should be designed to ensure that salaries and wages are paid only for services rendered, to process data quickly so that salaries and wages can be paid on time, and to comply with all government regulations.

An employee's gross pay is determined by the amount of services rendered and the rate of pay. Employees may be paid overtime premiums for working beyond the standard number of hours per week, for working on weekends, or for working on holidays. Time cards are often used for keeping track of the hours worked by employees.

An employee's gross pay is reduced by withholdings for taxes, union dues, and other payroll deductions to arrive at the net pay that is usually paid by check. Gross pay and deductions for employees are summarized for each pay period on a payroll register, which serves as the basis for the journal entry to record the payroll. Payroll data for each employee are also accumulated on an individual earnings record. At the end of the calendar year, each employee is given a Wage and Tax Statement form, which shows gross earnings for the year and the income taxes and FICA taxes withheld.

Employers must contribute an FICA tax in an amount equal to withholdings from employees. Federal income taxes withheld and FICA taxes withheld and contributed are deposited with a member bank of the Federal Reserve System. For each calendar quarter, an employer files an Employer's Quarterly Federal Tax Return to report on federal income taxes and FICA taxes withheld and contributed.

Most employers are required to pay unemployment taxes, based on wages and salaries, to state and federal governments. Unemployment taxes and the employer's share of FICA taxes are usually charged to a Payroll Tax Expense account.

weather bureaus keep statistics on rainfall and temperature, health departments keep track of contagious diseases, police departments keep track of types and numbers of crimes, accountants keep track of financial transactions, and so on.

A set of procedures for locating and processing data constitutes a data processing system. You are already familiar with some of the procedures used in *accounting,* which is a system for processing *financial* data.

DATA PROCESSING FUNCTIONS

Data processing can be viewed in terms of stages, or functions, performed. First, the data must be selected and *collected* in their basic, or raw, form. The next stage (function) is that of *converting* the data to a format suitable for use in a particular processing system. The data are then *rearranged* to arrive at results, which are then *communicated* to the persons needing the information. The four data processing functions can therefore be listed as follows.

OBJECTIVE 1. List the four data processing functions.

1. Collecting
2. Converting
3. Rearranging
4. Communicating

Now compare the data processing functions with the accounting functions you have studied.

Data Processing	Accounting
1. Collecting	1. Documenting
2. Converting	2. Recording
3. Rearranging	3. Summarizing
4. Communicating	4. Reporting

The similarities are not surprising when we remember that accounting is a data processing system. The last function, reporting (communicating), is the all-important one. The first three functions are important only insofar as they aid in accomplishing the fourth. The objective of any data processing system (including accounting) should be to communicate useful information to those who desire it.

SYSTEMS DESIGN

A data processing system should be designed to fit the entity involved and to meet its informational needs. The first step in the design of a new data processing system is usually to analyze the needs for data, keeping in mind that the information provided should be at least as valuable as the cost of providing it. Also, adequate controls must be designed into the system to ensure that the information provided is reliable.

Flowcharts

Once the informational needs are determined, it is usually helpful to establish the steps by which data will flow through the system. A *flowchart may be prepared to graphically portray the processing steps by means of symbols.* Over time, some of these symbols have taken on certain meanings. A few of the more common flowcharting symbols appear in Illustration 11.1.

OBJECTIVE 5a. Define flowchart.

Words may be written inside the symbols to show just what happens at each step. As a simple example, a flowchart for determining the gross weekly wages for employees is shown in Illustration 11.2 on the next page. We will leave the more involved flowcharting techniques for courses in data processing.

Attaining Internal Control

To be most useful, information provided by any processing system must be reliable. The reliability of the information depends on the accuracy and consistency with which information is processed. Accuracy pertains to avoiding (or minimizing) errors; consistency pertains to treating like events the same way. For example, making an arithmetic mistake or failing to record a transaction is an inaccuracy; classifying the cost of postage stamps as Office Expense one time and Postage Expense another time is an inconsistency.

ILLUSTRATION 11.1

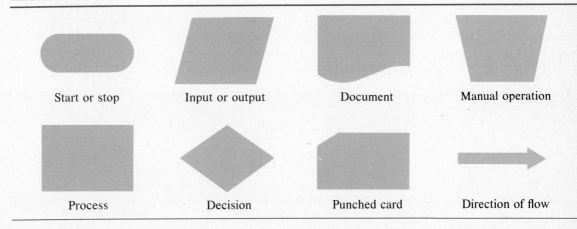

Start or stop Input or output Document Manual operation

Process Decision Punched card Direction of flow

ILLUSTRATION 11.2

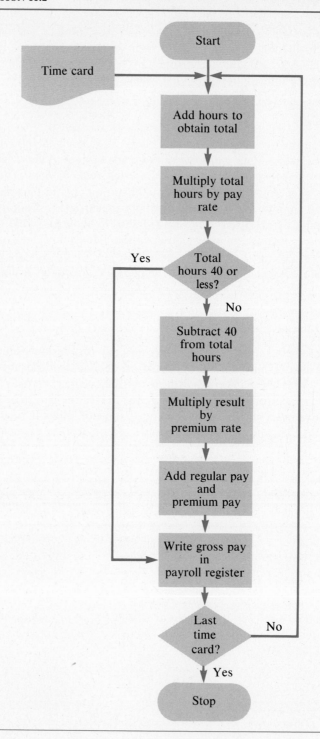

You may recall that the methods by which an entity's operations are controlled and its assets safeguarded are referred to as *internal controls,* and the ways in which accounting helps achieve internal control are often called *internal checks.*[1] Internal control is an important element of any data processing system because it contributes to the reliability of the information that is available from the system.

Collecting Data

One element, or goal, of internal control is the attainment of accuracy and consistency in collecting source data. A carefully designed system for collecting basic data can aid in attaining accuracy and consistency. Written procedures, flowcharts, and prenumbered multicopy forms are just a few of the features that might be included in such a system. Thus the first element of internal control parallels the first accounting (and data processing) function.

Processing Data

Another element of internal control is the attainment of accuracy and consistency while data are being processed. This element relates to the accounting functions of recording and summarizing transactions, and to the data processing counterparts of converting and rearranging data within the system. A well-designed data processing system provides for automatic checks and balances to aid in attaining accuracy and consistency.

Checking Data

Control can be improved by checking, or auditing, the information being collected and processed. *Auditing* is the process of examining records in an attempt to determine their reliability. It is preferable, of course, that the auditor be someone other than the person who did the work being checked. It is rather difficult to be critical (and objective) about one's own work.

Although people usually associate auditing with the end of an accounting period, most entities employ procedures that test and verify data at various points during the period. For example, a company would probably want to reconcile subsidiary ledgers with control accounts at frequent intervals. Such reconciliations are actually auditing techniques. And someone, perhaps a supervisor, may be assigned the task of checking to make sure that there are no missing numbers in the files of receipts, invoices, and other prenumbered forms. Many other auditing tasks can be performed during the period to ensure reliability of the information being processed.

---

[1]The expressions *internal control* and *internal check* were introduced in Chapter 9.

Auditing End Results

Information can be further verified at the end of a period. When errors, distortions, or omissions are discovered, adjustments are made to correct the information for reporting purposes.

Auditing techniques are too numerous and involved to be covered here. They include all kinds of reviews, analyses, and verifications of the information being reported. Some accounts may be verified by tracing information back to basic documents; balances in subsidiary accounts receivable or payable may be confirmed by mail by customers or creditors. These and other tests are aimed at determining the reliability of information that is to be communicated in accounting reports.

Division of Duties

Most people find it difficult to evaluate their own work objectively. One of the best internal control devices is therefore to have employees check each other's work. A different person can often find errors or omissions more readily than the one who did the work originally. An individual doing a self-check may repeat the same mistakes that were made the first time around.

When work and responsibilities have been carefully divided, employees can serve as checks on each other. This practice is referred to as *division of duties*. It helps in discouraging dishonesty among employees, in uncovering thefts and other wrongdoing when they do occur, and in discovering unintentional mistakes as well.

The division of duties helps to achieve all the other elements of internal control. Illustration 11.3 shows the relationship of each of the elements of

ILLUSTRATION 11.3

Function	Elements of internal control
1. Documenting (collecting)	1. Accuracy and consistency in collecting data
2. Recording (converting)	2. Accuracy and consistency in processing data
3. Summarizing (rearranging)	3. Review and testing at intermediate points
4. Reporting (communicating)	4. Review, analysis, and verification of end results

Division of duties

internal control to the data processing functions. As suggested by the illustration, division of duties is basic to the achievement of all the other elements.

IMPLEMENTATION

After a system has been designed, it must be implemented. Employees are trained, necessary equipment is acquired, and the various forms to be used are drawn up. If the new system will be replacing one that has been in use, it may be desirable to operate both the old and new system during a trial period. The process of running a new system for a while on a test basis helps to locate any flaws, or bugs, in the system so that they may be corrected. Thus a manual accounting system may be continued while a new computerized accounting system is being debugged.

DATA PROCESSING METHODS

Data may be processed in a variety of ways, but the techniques and procedures usually involve one or more of the following kinds of methods.

1. Manual methods
2. Mechanical methods
3. Electronic methods

OBJECTIVE 2. List the three kinds of methods for processing data.

Manual Methods

You already know something about manual, or handwritten, data processing. You do this when you work on accounting problems. Most people also handwrite their checks, bank reconciliations, tax returns, and other items involved in *personal* accounting.

Handwritten systems are still used in accounting for some small business concerns, although many small concerns use the services of data processing centers, and some have their own small, inexpensive computers for use in accounting. But even where electronic or mechanical processing systems are being used, some portions of the processing work may still be performed manually.

Mechanical Methods

Machines can be very helpful in processing data. Adding machines, cash registers, bookkeeping machines, and punched-card equipment have been in use for many years. In recent years, electronic calculators and cash registers have been widely adopted, although they perform much the same work that the earlier mechanical models did.

Bookkeeping machines are combined typewriters and calculators that are capable of producing specialized journals simultaneously with ledger postings. In other words, the recording and summarizing functions are accomplished together.

Punched-card equipment has been around for years. *A keypunch machine is used to encode data onto standardized cards by punching combinations of holes that represent numbers, letters, and other symbols.* The card may then be "read" by various machines that perform special tasks. *A card sorter automatically separates a deck of punched cards into categories. A card collator arranges two separate decks of punched cards into some desired order. A tabulating machine converts data on punched cards into printed output.* Other pieces of machinery perform various special tasks with punched cards. Card-punch equipment is frequently used in conjunction with computerized information systems.

Electronic Methods

OBJECTIVE 5b. Define computer.

Computers are devices that perform calculations and process data electronically. Electronic data processing (EDP) refers to the processing of information by means of electrical circuits—in other words, with computers. Computer technology has undergone dramatic changes in the last forty years. Advancements in the use of integrated circuits imbedded in minute electronic chips have led to the development of smaller and smaller computers that are able to process more and more data at a reasonable cost.

WHAT ARE COMPUTERS?

Computers were defined earlier as devices that perform calculations and process data electronically. A computer system requires *devices called input units for putting data into the computer.* Also needed are *output units for getting data out of the computer.* The computer itself acts as a *central processing unit (CPU), which consists of a storage unit, a control unit, and an arithmetic and logic unit.*

OBJECTIVE 5c. Define central processing unit.

OBJECTIVE 5d. Define computer program.

The storage unit of a computer, sometimes referred to as the memory, stores the program to be followed and portions of the data as they are being processed. A computer program is a set of instructions telling a computer how to process data for a particular purpose. A program is processed by the computer's control unit. Addition, subtraction, multiplication, and division, as well as comparisons of data, are performed by the arithmetic and logic unit of the CPU. The components of an electronic data processing (EDP) system are shown in Illustration 11.4.

INPUT MEDIA

Computer programs and the data to be processed must be fed into the computer in the form of a special machine language. Various types of input

ILLUSTRATION 11.4

EDP SYSTEM

CPU

| Storage unit (memory) |
| Control unit |
| Arithmetic and logic unit |

Input units → Control unit → Output units

devices have been designed to translate data from their existing forms into a language that the CPU recognizes. The particular input device used will depend on the form in which the data are expressed.

Keyboard Input

Data may be conveyed directly to the CPU by means of a special typewriter that converts typed words and figures into machine language that is transmitted to the CPU as a series of electrical signals. Keyboard input is only as fast as the typing skills of the operator, which is very slow compared with the other methods of input.

Keyboard input is most commonly used in connection with typewriter terminals that are located some distance from the CPU. *A terminal is a physical point at which data may either enter or leave a computer.* Terminals may be connected to the CPU by phone lines, which permit them to be located almost anywhere. Messages to the CPU are typed on a terminal, and the CPU may automatically respond with typewritten output messages.

OBJECTIVE 5e. Define terminal.

Punched Cards or Tapes

Information may be put directly into a CPU from punched cards by means of a special card-reading machine. Card input is much faster than keyboard input. However, cards must be punched before they can be used as inputs. If punching is done by hand on a keypunch machine, their initial preparation is still a slow process.

In some systems, punched cards are produced automatically as a by-product of other tasks. For example, cards may be punched automatically by a special machine attached to the typewriter used for preparing customer invoices. Some punched cards that are used as inputs were previously produced as computer outputs. In fact, checks, invoices, and other forms of basic data are sometimes computer-printed directly on punched cards. Perhaps you have seen these forms with holes in them, usually carrying a plea for people not to bend, fold, or mutilate them.

Punched tapes work on the same principle as punched cards. Information is encoded as holes in continuous paper tape, which can then be used for putting data into the CPU.

Magnetic Tapes or Disks

A tremendous amount of information may be stored on a reel of *magnetic tape, which is thin plastic tape on which information may be encoded in the form of magnetic bits, or spots.* The principle is similar to that of punched tape, except that coding is done with tiny magnetic impressions on the tape, rather than with holes. Data from magnetic tapes may be read into the CPU at extremely high speeds.

*Magnetic disks are round plastic sheets on which information may be encoded in the form of magnetic bits or spots. A number of disks may be grouped together in a container called a **disk pack**.* When placed in a disk-reading machine, information may be taken at random from points on the disks and communicated to the CPU.

Character Readers

Several kinds of modern machines are able to read data directly from basic data documents by recognizing special characters (symbols) encoded on them. Characters may be encoded in *special magnetic ink that can be sensed by a machine called a **magnetic ink character reader**,* through which the documents are passed. The character reader can then transmit data directly to the CPU for further processing.

*An **optical character reader** (**optical scanner**) is a machine capable of recognizing printed symbols and converting them for use in a data processing system.* You may have noticed peculiar-looking numbers, on checks and other documents, that are uniform enough to be automatically read by optical scanners.

Special Data Processing Languages

Various input devices are able to convert data into the special symbols recognized by computers. However, the computer must also be supplied with a set of instructions, the *program,* telling it how to process the data for the particular needs of users. Although computers can perform amazing feats, they are not yet able to deal with the almost infinite variations of our regular written languages.

Instructions for computers must be stated in one of the formal languages that either the computer or the input device has been designed to recognize. There are a number of special computer languages, and various modifications of each are required for use with the ever growing numbers of types, brands, and models of computers available. The special languages are usually known by acronyms. For example, *a computer language often used for accounting purposes is* **COBOL,** *which stands for COmmon Business Oriented Language.* **FORTRAN,** *which stands for FORmula TRANslation, is a computer language commonly used in the areas of mathematics and science.* **BASIC,** *which stands for Beginners All-purpose Symbolic Instructional Code, is frequently used in connection with inputs by means of typewriter terminals.* The intricacies of these and other computer languages will be left to data processing courses.

OUTPUT MEDIA

Data may be transmitted out of a CPU in a variety of formats. Information that is to be used directly by people is oftentimes typed or printed by special machines connected to the CPU by wires. In some cases, information may be visually shown on a *cathode-ray tube, which is a television device tied to the CPU by wires.* Typewriter and cathode-ray tube outputs are frequently used in connection with terminals located some distance away from the CPU.

Data outputs may also be in the form of magnetic tapes and disks or punched cards and tapes. Optical or magnetic characters may be printed as part of computer outputs. In these cases, the computer outputs usually serve at later times as computer inputs.

Illustration 11.5 on the next page summarizes the types of input and output media that we have discussed.

ADVANTAGES AND DISADVANTAGES OF ELECTRONIC DATA PROCESSING

Advantages

Electronic data processing systems can help in attaining internal control. By their very nature, computers are faster, more accurate, and more consistent than people. Computers are not capable of being dishonest. Therefore, when processing chores are shifted from clerks to computers, we can expect to have greater accuracy and consistency and fewer incidents of wrongdoing. Computers can also help in reviewing, testing, and analyzing data. In fact, a computer can practically audit itself. A variety of checks and balances can be incorporated right into the computer programs for processing data.

OBJECTIVE 3. State the advantages of EDP methods in the attainment of internal control.

ILLUSTRATION 11.5

EDP SYSTEM

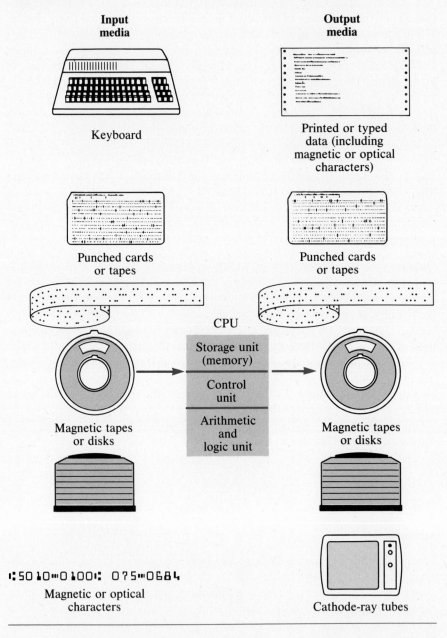

Input media

Keyboard

Punched cards or tapes

Magnetic tapes or disks

Magnetic or optical characters

CPU

Storage unit (memory)

Control unit

Arithmetic and logic unit

Output media

Printed or typed data (including magnetic or optical characters)

Punched cards or tapes

Magnetic tapes or disks

Cathode-ray tubes

Potential Disadvantages

From the standpoint of internal control, there are some potential disadvantages of electronic data processing. For one thing, information may be in a format that is unfamiliar to the person who is trying to audit the records. Information on punched cards and magnetic tapes cannot be easily "read" by people. Some information is even within the innards of a computer at certain points in time. However, the lack of access to information can be overcome by having the computer print out desired data in readable form. Thus a person who is familiar with a particular system can gain access to the data.

OBJECTIVE 3. State the disadvantages of EDP methods in the attainment of internal control.

As the number of employees is reduced, division of duties often becomes impractical. A sharp but dishonest computer operator may be able to distort outputs with minimum risk of discovery. However, a number of precautions can be taken to prevent wrongdoing.

The small number of employees required for a computerized system may be carefully selected, thus decreasing the likelihood of having dishonest employees. Also, the computer operators can be kept away from most of the company's liquid assets. Where several computer operators are employed, the jobs can be rotated so that the operators, in effect, check on each other.

Computer programming can be separated from the job of operating the computer. Furthermore, auditors can employ checks of various kinds in an attempt to uncover any mistakes or wrongdoing. Large corporations generally have separate programming departments, and they usually have their own internal auditors to check on computer operations. In this way, a division of duties is achieved even when data processing has been concentrated under the control of only a few persons.

Once dependence on a computer has been established, a computer breakdown may cause serious problems for an entity. The possibility of a computer malfunction is a necessary hazard of gaining the advantages of electronic data processing. In some cases, firms purchase insurance against potential large losses stemming from computer malfunctions and employee dishonesty.

COMPUTER APPLICATIONS

Use of the computer in the processing of data is practically unlimited. Of course, we should always keep in mind that the data produced by any system should be at least as valuable as the cost of obtaining it. Computers may be used for processing data within selected parts of an accounting system, for the entire accounting system, or for an integrated data processing system that may go far beyond the traditional boundaries of accounting. Discussions of a few of the more common applications of EDP follow.

Perpetual Inventories

Subsidiary records on perpetual inventories require numerous postings as various inventory items are purchased and sold. Errors are bound to occur as people perform clerical work. On the other hand, computers and related equipment are extremely accurate, once basic data have been put into the automated systems.

Computer systems are ideally suited for maintaining perpetual inventory records. A great deal of information may be processed rapidly, and data may be stored in coded form until needed. Magnetic tapes and disks allow large amounts of data to be stored in very small areas. Magnetic disks offer the further advantage of instant access to any of the data once the disks containing perpetual inventory information are placed into the computer system. Units on hand, sizes, locations of inventory, and other useful information may be available by means of cathode-ray or typewriter terminals located at points convenient to employees needing the information.

Computers may even be programmed to automatically prepare purchase orders whenever inventory stocks drop below established levels. Lists of items on hand at various locations can be printed out for comparison with actual physical inventory counts. Adjustments to the records may then be made to keep the perpetual records in line with the actual stocks on hand.

Payrolls

A great deal of clerical work is needed for keeping track of hours worked by employees; for computing gross pay, deductions, and net pay; for preparing payroll checks; for reconciling payroll bank accounts; for maintaining individual earnings records; for preparing payroll tax returns; and for a host of other payroll activities. A major portion of the clerical activity can be automatically, accurately, and speedily performed by computers.

Employee names, social security numbers, rates of pay, and other data that remain relatively constant may be stored on magnetic tapes or disks or on punched cards or tapes. Simply putting into the system the time worked by each employee during a pay period may be sufficient to permit most of the other work to be done automatically by the computer. Payroll checks may be printed on punched cards or coded with machine-readable ink, so that canceled checks can be processed automatically to reconcile the payroll bank account. Payroll tax returns, earnings statements, and other forms can be prepared automatically from the payroll data that has been accumulated.

Billings and Receivables

When sales and collections data are put into the computer, customer subsidiary records may be maintained in much the same manner as perpetual inventories. Information on balances due, delinquent accounts, aging schedules, and other matters can be readily taken from the system. Customer billings can be prepared as computer printouts. And analyses of sales by type, sales territory, and the like may be done simply by providing the computer with the proper program.

Integrated Data Processing

*Various data processing systems may be united into one **integrated data processing system*** to minimize duplications of effort and make the maximum information available for all purposes. When the entire accounting system is computerized, the system is, in a sense, an integration of subsystems for inventories, receivables, payrolls, and so on. Similarly, accounting systems for divisions and branches of an entity may be integrated.

  We tend to think that accounting systems are concerned only with financial data. However, information about product units, hours worked, and quantities of raw materials on hand may be more useful for certain purposes than monetary amounts. Because of the tremendous capacities of EDP systems, many kinds of data may be put in, stored, and reported out of fully integrated data processing systems.

OBJECTIVE 5f. Define integrated data processing system.

SUMMARY OF CHAPTER 11

Many kinds of data are constantly being collected, converted, rearranged, and communicated to interested persons. Accounting is a system for processing financial data. Sometimes a number of data processing systems are united into one overall integrated system.

Data processing systems should be carefully designed to serve specific purposes and to provide for internal checks so that the results will be accurate and reliable. Flowcharts are frequently used to graphically portray processing steps by means of symbols.

Data may be processed manually, mechanically, or electronically. EDP systems are very accurate and consistent, but usually provide limited opportunity for dividing duties among people.

Data may enter or leave the central processing unit of a computer system by means of a variety of media devices. Information may be put into the CPU by keyboard, or data may be automatically read from punched cards or optical characters or by other means. In some cases, data inputs come from earlier computer outputs on magnetic tapes, disks, or punched media. Data outputs that will be used directly by people are generally typed, printed, or visually displayed on cathode-ray tubes.

GLOSSARY FOR CHAPTER 11

Arithmetic and logic unit   The part of a computer that performs addition, subtraction, multiplication, and division and that makes comparisons of data.

BASIC   The acronym for Beginners All-purpose Symbolic Instructional Code, a computer language frequently used in connection with inputs by means of typewriter terminals.

Bookkeeping machines   Combined typewriters and calculators that are capable of producing specialized journals simultaneously with ledger postings.

Card collator   A machine that merges two separate decks of punched cards into some desired order.

Card sorter   A machine that automatically separates a deck of punched cards into categories.

Cathode-ray tube   A television device tied to a CPU by wires.

Central processing unit (CPU)   The main part of a computer consisting of a storage unit, a control unit, and an arithmetic and logic unit.

COBOL   The acronym for COmmon Business Oriented Language, a computer language often used for accounting purposes.

Computer program   A set of instructions telling a computer how to process data for a particular purpose.

Computer   A device that performs calculations and processes data electronically.

Control unit   The part of a computer that processes programs.

Data   The plural form of the word *datum*.

Data processing   Collecting, converting, rearranging, and communicating information.

Data processing system   A set of procedures for locating and processing data.

Datum   A fact, or an item of information.

Disk pack   A number of magnetic disks grouped together in a container.

Electronic data processing (EDP).   The processing of information by means of electrical circuits.

Flowchart   A graphical portrayal of processing steps by means of symbols.

FORTRAN   The acronym for FORmula TRANslation, a computer language commonly used for mathematics and science.

Input unit   A device for putting data into a computer.

Integrated data processing system   A system in which various data processing systems are united into one overall system.

Keypunch machine   A machine used to encode data onto standardized cards by punching combinations of holes that represent numbers, letters, and other symbols.

Magnetic disk   A round plastic sheet on which information may be encoded in the form of magnetic bits, or spots.

Magnetic ink character reader   A machine that can sense (read) characters encoded in special magnetic ink.

Magnetic tape   Thin plastic tape on which information may be encoded in the form of magnetic bits, or spots.

Optical character reader (optical scanner).   A machine capable of recognizing printed symbols and converting them for use in a data processing system.

Output unit   A device for getting data out of a computer.

Storage unit (memory)   The part of a computer that stores the programs to be followed and portions of the data as they are being processed.

Tabulating machine   A machine that converts data on punched cards into printed output.

Terminal   A physical point at which data may either enter or leave a computer.

SELF-QUIZ ON OBJECTIVES FOR CHAPTER 11
Solutions to Self-Quiz begin on page B-39.

1. OBJECTIVE 1.   List the four data processing functions.

2. OBJECTIVE 2.   List the three methods of processing data.

3. OBJECTIVE 3.   State in your own words at least two advantages and two disadvantages of EDP methods in the attainment of internal control.

4. **OBJECTIVE 4.** List at least three types of EDP input media and three types of EDP output media.

5. **OBJECTIVE 5.** Define these expressions in your own words:
   a. Flowchart.
   b. Computer.
   c. Central processing unit.
   d. Computer program.
   e. Terminal.
   f. Integrated data processing system.

DISCUSSION QUESTIONS FOR CHAPTER 11

1. What does the expression data processing mean?

2. What is the first, and probably the most important, step in designing a new data processing system?

3. Why is internal control such an important element of data processing systems?

4. Why is a computer potentially better able to audit its own work than a person is able to audit his or her own work?

5. How do computerized data processing systems sometimes hinder the achievement of division of duties?

6. It may not be economically feasible for very small business entities to use computers for all or part of their accounting work. What factors are more likely to be present in larger firms to make the use of EDP practical and cost effective?

EXERCISES FOR CHAPTER 11

11.1. Draw a simple diagram showing the main components of a computer system and the flow of data through the system.

11.2. Locate and read one or more articles in the popular press or in business periodicals dealing with the trend toward a cashless or checkless society. Try to relate what you read to the material in this chapter.

11.3. Talk to an official of a bank that offers always-open or twenty-four-hour banking services. Find out how the system works. What controls or safeguards are built into the system? Where is the computer located that serves the system?

PROBLEMS FOR CHAPTER 11
Alternate Problems for this chapter begin on page D-70.

11.4. Account numbers, rather than account names, are usually used for coding transactions data for computer input. Account numbers may be assigned so as to indicate the categories into which accounts fall. The accounts for the Braintree Company, in alphabetical order, are as follows.

Braintree Accounts

Accounts Payable
Accounts Receivable
Accumulated Depreciation—Equipment
Advertising Expense
Bank Loan Payable (due in five years)
Cash
Cost of Goods Sold
Depreciation Expense
Equipment
Freight In
Interest Expense
Interest Payable
Merchandise Inventory
Purchases
Purchases Discounts
Rent Expense
Sales
Sales Tax Payable
T. Braintree, Capital
T. Braintree, Withdrawals
Utilities Expense
Wage Expense

Required

Prepare a chart of accounts for Braintree using three-digit account (coding) numbers. The first digit should identify the account classification as asset, liability, owner's equity, revenue, or expense. For assets and liabilities, the second digit should disclose whether the account is current or noncurrent. For example, Cash might be numbered 111, with the first 1 signifying that it is an asset, the second 1 that it is current, and the third 1 that it is the first account in the current asset category.

11.5. Numbers are generally more efficient than words as symbols for communication. In fact, transactions data are often coded into numbers for input to computer processing. For example, a date might be stated as a six-digit number, followed by a three-digit account number, followed by the number 1 for a debit or 2 for a credit, followed by an eight-digit space for dollars and cents. A credit to the Cash account (111) on May 13, 1985, for $2,500.67 might be coded as follows.

| | | Dr.
or | |
| Date | Acct. no. | cr. | Amount |

1	2	3	4	5	6	7	8	9	10	11	12	13	14	15	16	17	18
0	5	1	3	8	5	1	1	1	2	0	0	2	5	0	0	6	7

Five transactions for the Braintree Company are shown here, along with a partial list of accounts.

Transactions

1985

Apr. 27	Sold merchandise on account for $400 plus 6% sales tax.
28	Paid account payable in the amount of $2,000 less purchases discount of 1%.
29	Cash sales for today were $1,800. Sales taxes of $108 were collected from customers and placed in the cash register along with the proceeds from cash sales.
30	Received $424 as payment on a customer's account.
30	Paid wages of $4,500.

PARTIAL LIST OF ACCOUNTS	
111	Cash
112	Accounts Receivable
211	Accounts Payable
212	Sales Tax Payable
411	Sales
513	Purchases Discounts
522	Wage Expense

Required

Code the transactions in an eighteen-digit format like the one illustrated in this problem. Write zeros in any of the 18 spaces not otherwise used.

11.6. There are eight wooden blocks stacked one on top of the other. Each block is painted either red, white, or blue. The blocks have to be moved *one at a time* from the stack and sorted into bins A, B, or C. A is for red blocks, B for white blocks, and C for blue blocks.

Required

1) Write a set of numbered instructions (a program) so that a not-too-bright worker can sort the blocks into the proper bins. Each numbered step in the instructions should contain only one command.

2) Diagram the program you have just written. Use square boxes for commands and diamond-shaped boxes for decision or question steps.

COMPREHENSION PROBLEMS FOR CHAPTER 11

11.7. On August 1, Brownlee Dairy switched from a manual accounting system to a computerized one. The salesperson who sold the computer assured Brownlee that there would be no implementation problems because only computer programs and subsystems proven by use in other dairy companies would be used.

Company bookkeepers were at first uncomfortable with the new system, but by month-end they were acting like seasoned computer technicians. However, on

September 5 it was discovered that the Cash account would not reconcile to the bank statement. Also, retail store managers began calling to complain that Brownlee's billings for August were incorrect. Collections on Accounts Receivable dropped to practically nothing.

In a state of panic, and considerably embarrassed, Brownlee's salespeople began visiting retail customers in an attempt to obtain from them the correct balances of their accounts with Brownlee. In the meantime, the cash activities were manually reconstructed from the bank statement data.

Upon inquiry of the computer company, it was discovered that the particular computer model purchased by Brownlee was different from the one used in the dairy company for which the programs were developed. Several modifications should have been made to adapt the programs to the computer model purchased by Brownlee. Also, company bookkeepers had made numerous mistakes in the process of feeding data into the computer system.

Required

Suggest some commonsense measures that could have prevented Brownlee's catastrophe.

11.8. Fuddle Company has grown from a small retail store to a chain of large department stores. Two years ago, company managers decided that it was time to computerize the accounting system, and turned the project over to a newly hired computer director. The speed with which the director converted the system surprised everyone.

Under the new system, all source documents were funneled to the director's office for coding on specially designed forms in preparation for computer input. The director also prepared special control programs which, he assured everyone, would make errors virtually impossible. Payroll checks and payments on account were computer-printed on presigned check forms. Furthermore, the computer automatically prepared monthly bank reconciliations.

Recently, without warning, the computer director disappeared. Almost as suddenly, it was discovered that merchandise inventories had fallen below acceptable levels and, in fact, many items were completely out of stock. Although the accounting records showed cash in the bank of $340,000, bank records indicated only an $8,400 balance. This was discovered when most of the computerized paychecks bounced.

A hurried audit of the firm's records revealed the following additional information.

a. Numerous "ghost" employees had been added to the payroll during the last six months. The endorsements on many of the paychecks appear to have been made in the handwriting of one individual.

b. There were no source documents for some entries that had been coded for computer input.

c. Payments were made to fictitious suppliers for goods that were never received.

Required

Consider the events just described and suggest controls that would have helped prevent the apparent thefts.

PART V

ACCOUNTING CONCEPTS

ACCOUNTANTS IN THE WORKPLACE

NAME: J. M. Andrews
AFFILIATION: Army Audit Agency
POSITION: Supervisory Auditor
SPECIALIZATION: Defense Auditing

"If it's olive drab, we look at it," says J. M. Andrews of the Army Audit Agency. "But if not, we may look at it anyway." That covers everything from tanks to training to tieclips—whether in Texas, Timbucktoo, or two hundred miles off the coast of Australia. Unquestionably, accounting for the Army poses some interesting challenges—and has prompted some unique solutions.

The Army performs three distinct types of audit: a "mandatory" audit for such "commercial" activities as commissaries and officers' clubs; a "single-location" audit to examine a specific installation; and a "multi-location" audit to track such things as clothing, weaponry, and computers. All three involve the "audit by objective" concept. Before beginning to collect information, the auditors decide on the objectives they hope to attain. In other words, says Andrews, "You don't start until you know where you're going."

The point of the audit is to present concrete suggestions. In fact, says Andrews, "85% of our work is in management consulting."

A graduate of the University of Texas at Arlington, Andrews spent five and a half years with Montgomery Ward before going with Uncle Sam. Of his present position, he says, "Above all I like the latitude and challenge of being a front-line supervisor."

NAME: Marco E. Gonzalez
AFFILIATION: Internal Revenue Service
POSITION: Examination Group Manager
SPECIALIZATION: Tax Shelters

"Tax shelters are getting more and more sophisticated every year," says Marco E. Gonzalez of the IRS. But, he adds, "so are we." Gonzalez works in one of the thorniest areas of all tax law, partnerships, and supervises a group of some 15 accountants.

First, he must determine who's involved in a tax shelter. If there is a separate partnership tax return, the computer can pull the personal returns of all the partners. If not, Gonzalez has to identify the participants in other ways, perhaps by locating the original promoter.

Second, he must check the accuracy of returns. Investigating coal mines—for which investors may report start-up costs as tax-deductible business expenses—Gonzalez has found that some mines did not even exist, along with a host of other irregularities. The benefits of other tax shelters are based on the depreciation of an asset. In these cases, Gonzalez asks the IRS's Department of Engineering Evaluation to establish a value and depreciation schedule for the asset in question.

A graduate of Rutgers University, Gonzalez spent five and a half years with the Equitable Life Assurance Society before joining the IRS. Gonzalez sees computers as the greatest force for change in the field. "Just like everywhere else, they're having a tremendous impact," he says.

Accounting Principles and Changing Prices

As has been mentioned before, accounting is often referred to as the language of business. Like other languages, rules for the practice of accounting evolved gradually over a long period of time. Only in relatively recent years have there been authoritative agencies to deal with nonuniform practices and other recognized problems with accounting reporting. This chapter examines critically some of the notions that influence the practice of accounting.

Chapter 12 is presented in two sections. Section A examines the various concepts that underlie current accounting practice and some of the shortcomings that result from these practices. The six basic accounting concepts introduced in Section B of Chapter 1 are reviewed and tied together, and a seventh concept is added to the list. Also examined are a number of doctrines that seem to influence the way in which accountants behave. The standard auditor's report is introduced, and sources of authoritative accounting pronouncements are covered briefly.

Section B deals with the effects of changing price levels on the validity of accounting results. The nature of the price-level problem in accounting is outlined, and some of the resulting distortions and inequities are discussed. Two alternate solutions to the price-level problem are presented, and a summary is given of the reporting requirements of an important accounting pronouncement concerned with changing prices.

SECTION 12.A

Concepts Underlying Accounting Practice

OBJECTIVES

This section deals with the various concepts that underlie accounting practice and with some of the shortcomings of accounting that have resulted from accepted practices. At the conclusion of this section, you should be able to

1. State in your own words the overall goal of accounting.
2. State in your own words the seven traditional concepts of accounting.
3. Define in your own words each of the following doctrines of accounting:
   a. Conservatism.
   b. Objectivity.
   c. Materiality.
   d. Consistency.
   e. Disclosure.
4. State what an auditors' report is.

GOAL OF ACCOUNTING

Accounting information is conveyed by means of reports. To be most useful, the information contained in accounting reports should be as timely, reliable, and relevant as possible. An accounting system, however, is expensive to install and operate. An entity's managers must determine how much useful accounting information the entity can afford to provide. Of course, accounting reports are expected to provide at least the minimum information required by applicable authoritative accounting pronouncements.

    The cost of accounting can be justified only in terms of the value of its products. Extra effort (and money) should be devoted toward improving the reliability and relevance of accounting data as long as the value of an improvement exceeds its cost.[1] The overall goal of accounting should be *to communicate the most useful information feasible with the means (resources) available.*[2]

OBJECTIVE 1. State the overall goal of accounting.

---

[1] *FASB Statement of Financial Accounting Concepts No. 2,* "Qualitative Characteristics of Accounting Information (Stamford, Conn.: Financial Accounting Standards Board, 1980), outlines in Figure 1 the qualitative considerations pertaining to accounting outputs, of which reliability and relevance are referred to as "primary decision-specific qualities," and the cost/benefit quantitative consideration is referred to as a "pervasive constraint" on the qualitative characteristics.

[2] The FASB has stated that the goal of *financial* reporting (as contrasted with managerial reporting) should be to ". . . provide information that is useful to present and potential

ACCOUNTING CONVENTIONS

Accounting is a language, of sorts, in that it is a means for communicating information. As with other languages, certain practices are simply accepted by convention. *A convention is a practice that has gained general acceptance over time.* Spelling and punctuation rules are conventions of written language that have gained rather uniform acceptance over time.

The notions of debit and credit are examples of accounting convention. Accounting could be just as effective if the definitions of those two words were reversed, but convention arbitrarily dictates that debit is left and credit is right. The accounting equation, journal entry and account formats, and report arrangements are all examples of accounting convention.

It is usually best to follow the accepted conventions, unless there is enough to be gained from change to justify any confusion that may result. Arbitrary departures from accepted practice tend to confuse and irritate people without serving any useful purpose.

TRADITIONAL ACCOUNTING CONCEPTS

A close examination of the way accounting is performed reveals a number of basic concepts that serve as an underlying framework for accounting. Six of the seven basic accounting concepts discussed in the following paragraphs were introduced in Section 1.B. They are presented here again so that you can better see their interrelationships and how they have influenced the accounting practices you have been learning.

You should realize that the various accounting concepts are known by a variety of labels, such as assumptions, principles, and postulates. At this point, we are not primarily concerned with terminology. As you progress, you will become aware of some of the finer distinctions that are currently being made in regard to terms.[3]

Entity Concept

We account for the effects of economic transactions and events on entities. An accounting entity may be an identifiable organization, part of an organization, or a group of organizations for which economic data are desired. Most business entities take the legal forms of corporations, partnerships, or proprietorships. However, governmental units, charities, churches, schools, fraternities, and even informal social groups may be viewed as distinct accounting entities.

---

investors and creditors and other users in making rational investment, credit, and similar decisions." *FASB Statement of Financial Accounting Concepts No. 1,* "Objectives of Financial Reporting by Business Enterprises" (Stamford, Conn.: Financial Accounting Standards Board, 1978), par. 34.

[3]See, for example, the *Statements of Financial Accounting Concepts* that have been issued by the Financial Accounting Standards Board.

As first pointed out in Section 1.B, the entity concept is basically an assumption that is made to help identify the particular events that are to be accounted for. You may recall that the concept (assumption) was stated as follows.

OBJECTIVE 2. State the traditional concepts of accounting.

> *Entity concept. Each organization for which we account is an independent entity, separate from its owners, managers, customers, creditors, and all other persons and entities with which it deals.*

The entity concept is evident in the way we account for investments, withdrawals, and other dealings of equity holders. When a proprietor puts money into a proprietorship venture, the investment is recorded as a distinct business event. Of course, the proprietor owns the entity and therefore still controls the money. In accounting for the proprietorship, however, the event is viewed from within the assumed entity; we do not account for the proprietor's personal transactions and events. If the proprietor withdraws money from the business, a shrinkage in entity assets is recorded. What the proprietor does with the funds is of no concern to the accountant for the entity.

Monetary Concept

Information about an entity is conveyed through accounting reports, usually in quantified form. It is not surprising that accountants have chosen to use the monetary unit as their quantitative measure. The monetary concept was introduced in Section 1.B, where it was stated as follows.

OBJECTIVE 2. State the traditional concepts of accounting.

> *Monetary concept. Transactions and events can be stated in terms of monetary units.*

As you know, different countries have different monetary units. This causes problems for companies that operate in international markets. Information that has been quantified in a foreign currency must be converted to domestic monetary units by means of a currency exchange rate at some particular point in time.[4]

The choice of the monetary unit as a measuring standard has never been seriously questioned. However, the changing *value* of the monetary unit over time has caused problems.

We think of the value of goods and services in terms of numbers of monetary units. However, the monetary units themselves have value in terms of the amounts of goods and services they will buy. When the prices of

---

[4]*FASB Statement No. 52*, "Foreign Currency Translation" (Stamford, Conn.: Financial Accounting Standards Board, 1981), deals with conversion of foreign amounts to domestic currency units.

goods and services in general rise, we have *inflation, which means that each unit of money buys less. If prices of goods and services drop, deflation occurs, and each unit of money buys more.*

For accounting purposes, we have in the past tended to ignore the changing value of money, our measuring stick. In other words, we have *assumed* that monetary units remained stable, and comparable between years, when in fact they have not. The assumption that the monetary unit is stable is definitely one of expediency. The relative value of the monetary unit is constantly changing, depending on the supply of money, the supply of goods, and people's expectations about the future.

There have been increasing demands over time for recognition in accounting of the effects of changing price levels, and progress is being made in this regard. Section 12.B introduces some approaches for dealing with the price-level problem in accounting.

Cost Concept

The cost concept was also introduced in Section 1.B, where it was stated as follows.

> *Cost concept. Assets are recorded and maintained in the accounting records at their cost bases.*

OBJECTIVE 2. State the traditional concepts of accounting.

An entity is viewed as consisting of its assets, measured in terms of monetary units. Assets may be thought of as economic rights—the right to use present property, the claims to future property, the right to service in the future. The balance sheet attempts to portray the condition of an entity at some point in time. Assets form the real basis for the balance sheet; liabilities and owners' equity are simply claims against the assets.

An entity acquires assets as a result of transactions. The monetary units sacrificed to attain assets may be in the form of current payments of cash or other assets. Or sacrifices may be in the form of promises to pay cash in the future—the incurrence of liabilities. In any case, a sacrifice is measured and recorded as *cost* at the time it is incurred. In general, accounting keeps track of assets on a *cost basis* until such time as the economic rights expire as expenses or losses, or they are distributed to owners.

The cost basis concept is neither inherently true nor inherently false, since it simply directs how something is to be done. This concept is one of convenience for the accountant. Original costs are known when transactions are being recorded. Maintaining assets at their cost bases obviates the need to keep reappraising the value of assets. When an asset is converted (expired) to expense, cost is still the most readily available figure.

The cost basis assumption has come under attack in recent times. The most frequent complaint is that past cost is *irrelevant* to the present needs of those who use accounting information. Cost represents a value in some marketplace at a certain time in the past. Perhaps a current value, or current cost, would be more relevant, provided that such a figure could be determined. Section 12.B deals in part with reporting data in value terms.

Time Period Concept

In ancient times, business activities were often performed as ventures. An ocean voyage or an overland caravan would be viewed as the entity to be accounted for. An investment of assets financed the venture, expenses and revenues resulted, and an accounting was made at the end of the venture. The endeavor might take months to complete, or it might take years. In any case, there was a start and a finish to the venture that did not necessarily coincide with any particular calendar period. The time period for accounting for a venture was from its start to its finish.

The lives of most present-day entities for which we account are indefinite. Timely data about entities are needed during their existence. Managers need information in order to manage an entity effectively. Investors, creditors, government bureaus, and others demand current financial information. To satisfy these demands, accountants must adopt accounting periods for which to account.

Calendar periods are chosen as accounting periods because people are accustomed to thinking in those terms. Weeks, months, and years pass, marking points of reference. The time period concept was stated in Section 1.B as follows.

OBJECTIVE 2. State the traditional concepts of accounting.

> *Time period concept. The activities of an entity are capable of being identified with particular calendar accounting periods.*

The adoption of a fiscal year, or a natural business year, is only a slight modification of the calendar basis. The calendar is still the point of reference, but the business year may be assumed to end at a more convenient time than December 31. Sometimes an accounting year is chosen that ends with the cycle of activity of the entity. Thus the fiscal year for a ski lodge may end with the skiing season.

The choice of calendar periods as accounting periods is natural enough, but the division of the life of a business into such periods is not so natural. In fact, the chopping up of entities' lives into calendar time periods gives rise to more accounting problems than anything else that accountants do. The problems associated with apportioning revenues and expenses between calendar periods and with stating assets and liabilities at points in time stem directly from the time period concept. As you will see, the remaining three concepts are closely related to the division of the life of an entity into accounting periods.

Realization Concept

People need timely information about the entities in which they have an interest. They want to know how a business stood at a fairly recent *point in time* and how well it performed during a recent *period of time*. The determination of an entity's position requires that the assets, and the claims against them, be identified at a certain point in time.

The determination of the amount of assets at a point in time requires that transactions be identified with periods of time. For instance, the amount of receivables depends on whether certain *revenues* have been earned, and vice versa. Some assumption about when revenue arises is necessary to assign revenues, and the resulting assets, to their proper periods. The realization concept was stated in Section 1.B as follows.

> *Realization concept. Revenue arises at the point of sale of property or upon the rendering of a service.*

OBJECTIVE 2. State the traditional concepts of accounting.

Once again we have an assumption that serves the practical needs of accounting for an entity. Few people would argue that revenues actually leap into the picture as legal sales occur or as conditions of service contracts are completed. Revenue is a measure of *accomplishment* and arises as a result of the expenditure of effort and money. Accountants generally do not recognize revenue, however, until new assets (usually cash or receivables) have been received by the entity. Potential revenue associated with transactions that are incomplete, insofar as accounting practice is concerned, is usually ignored.

Matching Concept

Revenues are measures of an entity's accomplishment. They are identified with the time periods in which they are earned, and they are quantified in terms of monetary units. When the appropriate expenses are offset against the revenues of a period, the amount remaining is net income, or profit. The overall goal of most business entities is to maximize profit over time.

Costs are sacrifices—such as the expenditure of assets or the incurrence of liabilities. *Deferred* costs are assets; *expired* costs are either expenses or losses. An expense is a sacrifice undergone in the process of producing revenues. Expenses may result from current expenditures, assumptions of liabilities, or expirations of all or part of the cost of assets. Expenses are usually borne voluntarily in the hope of producing revenues. When expenses exceed revenues, the result is called a net loss (negative net income). Sometimes the involuntary sacrifice of assets through some casualty, such as fire or theft, is also described as a loss.

The expenses on an income statement are assumed to be the costs (sacrifices) of producing the period's revenues. The process of relating expenses and revenues is called *matching*. The matching concept was stated in Section 1.B as follows.

OBJECTIVE 2. State the traditional concepts of accounting.

> *Matching concept. Revenues should be matched with the expenses that were responsible for their generation.*

The matching concept is the root of many of the accountant's problems. The particular expenses that helped to generate a certain revenue are not always determinable. The accountant's solution has been to rely on subassumptions in attempting to match revenues and expenses. For example, many *costs are first related to an accounting period and then assumed to be responsible for the revenues identified with that period. These types of sacrifices are often referred to as period costs.* Advertising and other selling and administrative costs are usually treated as period costs even though they may help to produce revenues in future periods. A cost that cannot reasonably be associated with particular future benefits is treated as an expense.

Going Concern Concept

An entity's assets are accounted for on a cost basis. As assets expire, part of their costs become expenses (or losses) to be matched against revenues. Some assets are so permanent that they can be expected to help produce revenues as long as the entity exists, or even longer. Examples of such assets are trademarks, franchises, letterheads, and organization cost.[5]

The balance sheet is a picture of the concern at a point in time, subject to the entity, cost basis, realization, and other concepts. If an entity were closed out, some assets would probably sell for more than their net book values, some for less. The differences between the cost and value of assets may not be as great as they first appear, if we assume that the concern will continue indefinitely.

By viewing how accounting is done, we can conclude that an assumption has been made that entities will continue as *going concerns*. This going concern concept might be stated as follows.

OBJECTIVE 2. State the traditional concepts of accounting.

> *Going concern concept. The life of an entity is considered unlimited unless (or until) there is concrete evidence that it will end at some approximately determinable future time.*

---

[5]However, as was pointed out in Chapter 8, organization cost and other intangible assets with indefinite lives may still be amortized over a limited number of accounting periods. Such treatment reflects the conservative attitude of accountants in regard to intangible assets.

ACCOUNTING CONCEPTS AND ACCOUNTING REPORTS

Accounting results are communicated in various reports. The basic concepts discussed here underlie the information that is reported to users of accounting information. Report users should keep in mind the effects that the concepts have on the reported data. A balance sheet, for example, represents the position, or condition, of an entity at a point in time. Many users of accounting reports think that the worth, or value, of the entity is at least being approximated by a balance sheet. However, assets have been traditionally reported at their costs, and only by chance would the costs coincide with the current market values of the entity's assets.

Even the reported costs of assets may not represent real sacrifices in terms of current monetary units. Costs were recorded in monetary units sacrificed at the specific times that assets were purchased. To the extent that inflation (or deflation) of monetary units has occurred, the costs will not reflect the sacrifices in *current dollar terms*. Also, the dollars paid for assets at various times in the past will not be comparable—that is, unlike quantitative units are combined in the balance sheet. In other words, the costs of the various assets are not stated in common, or like, dollars. Section 12.B deals with approaches for disclosing the effects of inflation or deflation.

A balance sheet also reflects the realization and matching concepts. Recall that revenues bring assets into the entity. When recognition of revenue is deferred, asset recognition is also deferred.

If expenses are overstated or understated, assets or liabilities will be misstated. Remember, either an asset or a liability is credited when an expense is debited.[6]

The important thing is that you recognize that a balance sheet is an accountant's picture of the condition of an entity at a point in time—subject to the cost basis, realization, monetary unit, and other accounting concepts.

An income statement pictures the results of operating for a period of time. It is also a kind of bridge from one balance sheet to the next. Imperfections in an income statement may result from defects in previous balance sheets or may cause distortions in subsequent statements, or both.

The various accounting concepts are interrelated. Entity revenues for a period are reported according to the realization concept. Expenses are matched against revenues, but in terms of costs (sacrifices) as measured in the monetary units of preceding time periods. The amount of asset cost that has expired to expense depends on the going concern concept.

People who use accounting reports should be aware of the effects of the various accounting concepts. They should recognize what reports do *not* represent, as well as what they do represent.

---

[6]Of course, accountants choose in some instances to accumulate asset credits in contra accounts, as with accumulated depreciation and estimated uncollectibles.

ACCOUNTING DOCTRINES

There are some similarities in how accountants think and act that seem to stem from certain doctrines, or tenets. *A doctrine is a belief that is accepted by a class of people, pretty much on faith.* Doctrines are generally taught or handed down by one generation to the next, as with religious doctrines, political doctrines, and so on.

Several of the more obvious doctrines observed by most accountants are discussed in the following paragraphs. Here again, you will find that some people prefer different labels; what we call doctrines others may call concepts, conventions, or principles.

Conservatism

OBJECTIVE 3a. Define conservatism.

Conservatism, as it applies to the practice of accounting, is the tendency of accountants to be cautious, or moderate, when making judgments and estimates. Accountants have leaned toward pessimism in the belief that understatements of assets and net income are less damaging than overstatements. The doctrine might be simply stated as "when in doubt, lean toward understatement." Or, in the words of the Accounting Principles Board:

> Historically, managers, investors, and accountants have generally preferred that possible errors in measurement be in the direction of understatement rather than overstatement of net income and net assets.[7]

The FASB has indicated a need to moderate the practice of conservatism from one of "deliberate, consistent understatement of net assets and profits"[8] to one of ensuring "that risks inherent in business situations are adequately considered."[9] In place of outright understatements, the board says, "The aim must be to put the users of financial information in the best possible position to form their own opinion of the probable outcome of the events reported."[10]

Some of the concepts discussed earlier appear to be based at least in part on the doctrine of conservatism. For example, under the *cost concept* assets are left at cost when values are higher. However, if asset values are lower than cost, accountants tend to write the assets down under the *lower of cost or market* approach.[11]

---

[7]*APB Statement No. 4,* "Basic Concepts and Accounting Principles Underlying Financial Statements of Business Enterprises" (New York: American Institute of Certified Public Accountants, 1970), par. 171.

[8]*FASB Statement of Concepts No. 2,* par. 93.

[9]*Ibid.,* par. 95.

[10]*Ibid.,* par. 97.

[11]The lower of cost or market approach, as applied to inventories, is discussed in Chapter 7.

Objectivity

In an accounting context, *objectivity refers to freedom from bias and prejudice.* To the extent possible, accounting entries are based on objective evidence as provided by basic data documents. When subjective judgments must be made, as with depreciation and other adjustments, care is taken to assure that the judgments are objectively made. Thus accountants strive for objective (unbiased) subjectivity in judgmental matters.

OBJECTIVE 3b. Define objectivity.

The doctrine of conservatism is closely allied with that of objectivity. The reluctance to depart from an *objectively* measured cost basis is a conservative practice. The realization concept specifies that revenues, and resulting net incomes, are not recognized until *objective* evidence of actual sales prices is available.

The FASB has recommended that in the future the expression *verifiability* be used in place of objectivity,[12] and has defined *verifiability as "the ability through consensus among measurers to ensure that information represents what it purports to represent. . . .*[13] The FASB also proposed that *neutrality* be adopted as a qualitative characteristic of accounting. *Neutrality is the "absence in reported information of bias intended to attain a predetermined result or to induce a particular mode of behavior."*[14] Thus the traditional doctrine of objectivity may henceforth be subdivided into the characteristics of verifiability and neutrality.

Materiality

Materiality is the relative importance of the result of an accounting action. Absolute accuracy in accounting is neither practical nor necessary for purposes of reporting reliable information. Where the effect of a transaction is very small (immaterial), the simplest and least expensive approach will be chosen to account for it. For example, a letter opener costing $1 may have a practical useful life of 100 years or more. To record the letter opener as a depreciable asset would be proper, but impractical, so it will be recorded as an expense of the year in which it is purchased. Similar treatment may be accorded to purchases of all long-term assets costing less than some specified amount, such as $50 or $100.

OBJECTIVE 3c. Define materiality.

The materiality of an amount will depend on its relative size and effect on reported data. A considerable sum may be immaterial in a giant corporation reporting many millions of net income, whereas the same figure might be quite important to a smaller concern. Also, accountants must keep in mind that the aggregate of many small amounts may be quite material. The

---

[12]*FASB Statement of Concepts No. 2*, par. 158.

[13]*Ibid.*, Glossary of Terms.

[14]*Ibid.*

real test of materiality is whether the manner of accounting for an item will affect the decisions that are made by the users of accounting data.

Consistency

OBJECTIVE 3d. Define consistency.

In order for accounting data for an entity to be comparable over time, accounting practices must remain somewhat consistent from period to period. *Consistency is the act of continuing to treat like items the same way over time.* Consistent treatment of transactions and adjustments helps to make accounting results more meaningful for each period as well as more comparable over time. If, for example, expenditures for postage are classified as Office Expense one time and as Miscellaneous Expense another time, the amounts of these reported expenses will be difficult to interpret. And you can imagine the confusion that would result from continually switching from one inventory costing method to another.

The consistency doctrine should not prevent changes from a less desirable accounting practice to one that is more meaningful in the accountant's view. However, when a change in method has a material effect on accounting results, both the change and the effect of the change should be disclosed to the users of accounting data.[15]

Disclosure

OBJECTIVE 3e. Define disclosure.

The doctrine of *disclosure refers to the attempt by accountants to communicate all material facts that are considered to be important to users of accounting data.* Information supplementary to reported amounts in statements and schedules may be disclosed in parenthetical remarks, footnotes, or other written comments accompanying the formal reports.

A parenthetical remark is a disclosure of information within the body of an accounting statement or schedule, often set apart by parentheses. Parenthetical remarks frequently follow an account title or other category of data. For example, inventories may be reported in a balance sheet in the following manner.

Merchandise inventory (at cost, using a last-in, first-out approach)	125,460

An accounting statement footnote is a separate explanation that is tied to an item within an accounting statement by a numerical, alphabetical, or

---

[15]Some guidelines on how to report the effects of accounting changes are provided in *APB Opinion No. 20,* "Accounting Changes" (New York: American Institute of Certified Public Accountants, 1971).

ILLUSTRATION 12.1

Note 3. Buildings are depreciated on a straight-line basis. Machinery and equipment are depreciated on a double-declining-balance basis. The cost and accumulated depreciation of plant asset categories are as follows.

Asset Category	Cost	Accumulated Depreciation	Net Book Value
Land	$ 120,000	$ –0–	$120,000
Buildings	500,000	350,000	150,000
Machinery	594,000	260,000	334,000
Equipment	280,000	120,000	160,000
Totals	$1,494,000	$730,000	$764,000

other symbol. For example, all items of plant and equipment may be grouped together in a balance sheet presentation as follows.

Plant and equipment (see note 3)	764,000

A footnote that accompanies the balance sheet may provide details about plant and equipment, perhaps as shown in Illustration 12.1.

Any information that may help to make accounting data more useful to users may be disclosed by supplementary notes to the accounting statements. The accounting methods and policies employed, changes in methods and the effects of such changes, contingent liabilities, and major events that occur subsequent to the time that the statements are dated are all disclosed by accountants when the effects are considered important to the users of accounting data.

Contingent liabilities are possible obligations that will arise only at the occurrence of some uncertain future event. Contingent liabilities in connection with customer notes that have been discounted with lending institutions are discussed in Chapter 6. Other types of contingent liabilities that may require disclosure are pending lawsuits, long-term contracts for purchases of materials or services, and all other unpredictable but potentially important events.[16]

Accounting reports present information for particular periods and points in time. *Occurrences after the statement dates, but before the statements are distributed to users, are called subsequent events.* Significant subsequent

---

[16]Some guidelines for "Accounting for Contingencies" are provided in *Statement of Financial Accounting Standards No. 5* (Stamford, Conn.: Financial Accounting Standards Board, 1975).

ILLUSTRATION 12.2

AUDITORS' REPORT

To the Shareholders and Board of Directors, Baker Corporation:

We have examined the balance sheet of Baker Corporation as of December 31, 19--, and the related statements of income, retained earnings, and changes in financial position for the year then ended. Our examination was made in accordance with generally accepted auditing standards, and accordingly included such tests of the accounting records and such other auditing procedures as we considered necessary in the circumstances.

In our opinion, the accompanying financial statements present fairly the financial position of Baker Corporation as of December 31, 19--, and the results of its operations and changes in its financial position for the year then ended, in conformity with generally accepted accounting principles applied on a basis consistent with that of the preceding year.

New York, New York
March 15, 19--   Smith, Rhodes & Co.

events that would be of interest to statement users should be disclosed in some manner. An example of a significant subsequent event would be the loss of a major company asset in a fire, flood, theft, or similar casualty that occurred after the close of the accounting year.

AUDITORS' REPORT

OBJECTIVE 4. State what an auditors' report is.

An accounting statement that has been audited by certified public accountants is accompanied by a report of the auditors. *An **auditors' report** is a statement of the scope of the work done by the auditors and an expression of the auditors' opinion about the fairness of the accounting statements.* When the auditors have been able to apply all the necessary audit tests, and when they believe the statements are fairly presented, their report will be concisely stated, like the example in Illustration 12.2.

The first paragraph of the auditors' report is called the *scope* paragraph, because it deals with the extent of the examination performed. Generally accepted auditing standards have been prescribed by the American Institute of Certified Public Accountants.[17] Failure to attain the prescribed auditing standards is disclosed by the auditors in the scope paragraph of their report.

The second paragraph of the auditors' report is called the *opinion* paragraph, because it states the auditors' opinion as to the fairness of the accounting statements.

[17]*AICPA Professional Standards, Volume 1* (New York: Commerce Clearing House, loose-leaf reporter), sec. AU100–AU500.

ACCOUNTING PRINCIPLES

It would appear that the expression *accounting principles, as it is used in an auditors' report, encompasses all the concepts, conventions, doctrines, and methods of accounting commonly found in use.* A number of alternative practices appear to be generally accepted for many areas of accounting. Consider, for example, the variety of acceptable inventory costing methods and the diversity of depreciation methods in use.

As long as the doctrine of consistency is observed, we can expect the accounting results for an entity to be somewhat comparable over time. However, we must be very cautious about comparing accounting results for different entities because of the variety of accounting practices adhered to. The comparability of accounting data for different firms is improved as accounting practices become more uniform.

Only in fairly recent times have there been any formal pronouncements on accounting principles. The present-day *Financial Accounting Standards Board (FASB)* was preceded by two earlier rule-making bodies.

Committee on Accounting Procedure

The Committee on Accounting Procedure (CAP) was the first formal group established by the American Institute of Certified Public Accountants (AICPA) to make pronouncements on accounting principles. Between the years 1939 and 1959, fifty-one *Accounting Research Bulletins* were issued by the committee as guidelines for acceptable accounting practice.

Accounting Principles Board

An Accounting Principles Board (APB) was formed by the AICPA to replace the Committee on Accounting Procedure. Between 1959 and 1973, thirty-one *APB Opinions* and four *APB Statements* were issued by the board. In addition, fifteen *Accounting Research Studies* on various topics were commissioned and published by the board.

The first study commissioned was an attempt to arrive at a number of basic *postulates* of accounting,[18] and the third was an attempt to state *principles* of accounting that could be derived from the postulates set out in the first study.[19] The conclusions of these two studies were never adopted by the APB, nor did they receive widespread acceptance by practicing accountants. In 1965, another *Accounting Research Study (No. 7)* attempted

---

[18]Maurice Moonitz, "The Basic Postulates of Accounting," *Accounting Research Study No. 1* (New York: American Institute of Certified Public Accountants, 1961).

[19]Robert T. Sprouse and Maurice Moonitz, "A Tentative Set of Broad Accounting Principles for Business Enterprises," *Accounting Research Study No. 3* (New York: American Institute of Certified Public Accountants, 1962).

to list all the generally accepted accounting principles then in use.[20] Whereas *Study No. 3* was an attempt to arrive at what the accounting principles should be, *Study No. 7* was an attempt to set down just what principles were actually being practiced at that time.

Financial Accounting Standards Board

The Financial Accounting Standards Board (FASB) was formed in 1973 to replace the APB. The FASB operates independently of the AICPA, and some board members are drawn from areas other than public accounting practice. The FASB issues official pronouncements called *Statements of Financial Accounting Standards*. The board also issues numbered *FASB Interpretations* dealing with certain aspects of the official pronouncements of the FASB and its predecessor organizations. Staff members serving the FASB are authorized to issue *FASB Technical Bulletins* to resolve particular reporting problems on a timely basis.

The FASB has undertaken an ongoing study of the conceptual framework for financial accounting and reporting. As the study progresses, *Statements of Financial Accounting Concepts* are issued. Early concepts statements dealt with reporting objectives,[21] qualitative characteristics of accounting information,[22] financial statement elements,[23] and reporting by nonbusiness organizations.[24]

It is likely that the FASB will continue to be the primary source of generally accepted accounting principles for some time to come.

Other Authoritative Bodies

Influence by other authoritative bodies on existing accounting practices should not be overlooked. As pointed out in Section 1.A, the *Securities and Exchange Commission* influences the way in which accounting is practiced, as do the *Internal Revenue Service,* the *American Accounting Association,* and a number of other agencies and associations.

---

[20]Paul Grady, ''Inventory of Generally Accepted Accounting Principles for Business Enterprises,'' *Accounting Research Study No. 7* (New York: American Institute of Certified Public Accountants, 1965).

[21]*FASB Statement of Concepts No. 1,* ''Objectives of Financial Reporting by Business Enterprises'' (1978); and *FASB Statement of Concepts No. 4,* ''Objectives of Financial Reporting by Nonbusiness Organizations'' (Stamford, Conn.: Financial Accounting Standards Board, 1980).

[22]*FASB Statement of Concepts No. 2,* ''Qualitative Characteristics of Accounting Information.''

[23]*FASB Statement of Concepts No. 3,* ''Elements of Financial Statements of Business Enterprises'' (Stamford, Conn.: Financial Accounting Standards Board, 1980).

[24]*FASB Statement of Concepts No. 4,* ''Objectives of Financial Reporting by Nonbusiness Organizations.''

GLOSSARY FOR SECTION 12.A

Accounting principles   All the concepts, conventions, doctrines, and methods of accounting that are commonly found in use.

Accounting statement footnote   A separate explanation that is tied to an item within an accounting statement by a numerical, alphabetical, or other symbol.

Auditors' report   A statement of the scope of the work done by the auditors and an expression of the auditors' opinion about the fairness of the accounting statements.

Conservatism   The tendency of accountants to be cautious, or moderate, when making judgments and estimates.

Consistency   The act of continuing to treat like items the same way over time.

Convention   A practice that has gained general acceptance over time.

Deflation   A general drop in the prices of goods and services, the result being that each unit of money will buy more than it would previously.

Disclosure   The attempt by accountants to communicate all material facts that are considered to be important to users of accounting data.

Doctrine   A belief that is accepted by a class of people, pretty much on faith.

Going concern concept   A traditional accounting assumption that the life of an entity is considered to be unlimited unless (or until) there is concrete evidence that it will end at some approximately determinable future time.

Inflation   A general rise in the prices of goods and services, the result being that each unit of money will buy less than it would previously.

Materiality   The relative importance of the result of an accounting action.

Neutrality   The absence in reported information of bias intended to attain a predetermined result or to induce a particular mode of behavior.

Objectivity   Freedom from bias and prejudice.

Parenthetical remark   A disclosure of information, often set apart by parentheses, within the body of an accounting statement or schedule.

Period costs   Costs (sacrifices) that are first related to an accounting period, and then assumed to be responsible for the revenues that were generated during that period.

Subsequent events   Occurrences after the statement dates, but before the statements are distributed to users.

Verifiability   The ability through consensus among measurers to ensure that information represents what it purports to represent.

SELF-QUIZ ON OBJECTIVES FOR SECTION 12.A
Solutions to Self-Quiz begin on page B-39.

Solutions to Self-Quiz begin on page B-39.

1. **OBJECTIVE 1.**   State in your own words the overall goal of accounting.

2. **OBJECTIVE 2.**   State in your own words each of the seven traditional concepts of accounting.

3. **OBJECTIVE 3.** Define in your own words each of the following doctrines of accounting.

   a. Conservatism

   b. Objectivity

   c. Materiality

   d. Consistency

   e. Disclosure

4. **OBJECTIVE 4.** State what an auditors' report is.

DISCUSSION QUESTIONS FOR SECTION 12.A

1. What is a convention, as this expression is used in Section 12.A? Give some examples of accounting conventions.

2. How is the entity concept evident from the way we account for owners' equity?

3. How does continued inflation affect the monetary concept?

4. What is the basis for the complaint by some people that cost figures are irrelevant to present needs?

5. Why is the time period concept necessary?

6. What are period costs, as the expression is used in Section 12.A?

7. What is a parenthetical remark within the context of an accounting statement?

8. What is an accounting statement footnote?

9. What are subsequent events?

10. How does the Financial Accounting Standards Board differ organizationally from its predecessor organizations, the Accounting Principles Board and the Committee on Accounting Procedure?

EXERCISES FOR SECTION 12.A

12.A.1. Computer Software Company shows a $50,000 balance in an account titled Brokerage Expense. Investigation reveals that the $50,000 was actually a bribe paid to an official of a foreign government in order to obtain a contract for computer services. Bribes are apparently commonplace in dealings with the government in question, and the contract would not have been obtained without the payment. If you were the accountant who discovered the bribe, what action would you take, and why?

12.A.2. In December 19X4 Burle Company paid an advertising concern in cash for three separate advertising campaigns. One $30,000 contract calls for advertising Christmas merchandise during the month of December. Another contract, involving $5,000, is for advertising during late December for a sale to be held during the first week of January. The third contract, costing $10,000, is for advertising during January of an inventory reduction sale to be held the last week of January. Monthly income statements are prepared for Burle Company. How much of the advertising cost should appear in the December income statement? State your reasons for including or excluding the cost of each of the campaigns.

12.A.3. Maze Company was notified on January 20 that it was being sued for $20,000 by a party who became seriously ill from eating soup canned by Maze. Further investigation revealed that some of the cans of soup processed between December 10 and December 15 of the previous year contained salmonella. Maze immediately recalled all the suspected soup and undertook an information campaign to warn consumers in the area where the defective soup was marketed. The information campaign is costing $50,000, and it is anticipated that $120,000 will be refunded to purchasers for return of cans of soup from the defective batch. Statements are just being prepared for the previous fiscal year ending December 31. Discuss the accountant's responsibility relative to the various aspects of the soup catastrophe.

12.A.4. Land on which Bob's Auto Service is located was acquired many years ago at a cost of $5,000. Owing largely to the fact that the land is located near an interchange for a newly constructed expressway, an interested party recently offered $300,000 for the land, declaring that if the offer were accepted the existing building would be demolished to make way for a new structure. Bob Treadway, proprietor of Bob's Auto Service, refused the offer because business has been very good since the new expressway was opened. At what figure should the land be shown on the entity's balance sheet? Defend your answer, and state which accounting concepts are applicable to the matter. Which figure is most relevant to Bob for decision making purposes, and why?

PROBLEMS FOR SECTION 12.A
Alternate Problems for this section begin on page D-72.

12.A.5. Jack Farnsworth operates the Farnsworth Funeral Home. Jack lives with his family on the second floor of the funeral home, which represents approximately one-half the building space. Jack's bookkeeper has prepared the following income statement for 19X4.

FARNSWORTH FUNERAL HOME
Income Statement
For the Year Ended December 31, 19X4

Revenues		
Service revenue	$125,000	
Sales	60,000	
Interest	2,000	$187,000
Expenses		
Cost of goods sold	$32,000	
Salaries	46,000	
Depreciation	34,700	
Utilities	4,200	
Maintenance	2,300	
Gasoline	2,100	
Other	3,000	124,300
Net Income		$ 62,700

A balance sheet prepared for December 31, 19X4, showed total business assets of $700,000 and owner's equity of $450,000.

An audit of the accounting records turned up the following facts.

a. The entire funeral home building is included as a business asset at a net book value on December 31 of $300,000. Building depreciation for the entire building in the amount of $18,000 was included in depreciation expense for 19X4. About two-thirds of the $4,200 of utilities were applicable to the residence portion of the building.

b. A speedboat was included among business assets at a net book value at December 31 of $6,000. Boat depreciation in the amount of $3,000 was charged to depreciation expense during 19X4. Jack maintains that the boat was acquired to recover drowning victims from a nearby lake. When questioned, Jack admits that no victims have been recovered since the boat was acquired 18 months ago, but he states that various family members have "spent much time searching on the lake."

c. About one-fifth of the maintenance expense was attributable to the personal part of the building.

d. The interest revenue reported in the income statement was earned on government securities owned by Mrs. Farnsworth. The securities, which were purchased for $30,000, are not included among business assets, but the interest proceeds were deposited in the business bank account.

Required

1) State the accounting concept that has been most violated in accounting for the funeral home, and defend your answer.

2) Under three column headings like those that follow, show the effects of correcting for each situation just described and determine the corrected net income, total assets, and owner's equity figures.

| | **19X4** | **December 31, 19X4** | |
	Net Income	*Assets*	*Owner's Equity*
As Reported	$62,700	$700,000	$450,000

12.A.6. Ace Company insured the life of one of its key employees for $300,000. The cash surrender value of the insurance policy is carried in an account titled *Cash Surrender Value of Life Insurance*. On June 5, 19X4, the insured employee died. On that date, the cash surrender value of the policy was carried at $120,000.

Required

1) Suggest reasons why a company may wish to insure the life of a key employee.

2) Prepare an entry on June 5 to record the death of the employee. Assume that the receivable will be collected from the insurance company at a later date. Devise descriptive titles for the accounts affected by the entry.

3) State whether you think the entry you made conveys the real economic consequences of the employee's death, and give reasons why you answered as you did.

12.A.7. A Veje Manufacturing Company income statement for calendar year 19X4 shows sales of $800,000 and cost of goods sold of $560,000. During December 19X4 Veje completed production of a special order of private brand merchandise which will be shipped to José Company in January. José has agreed to pay $100,000 for the specially ordered goods for which Veje's total production costs were $80,000. Veje accounts in accordance with generally accepted accounting principles.

Required

1) State whether the revenues and costs related to the special José order are likely to be included in the figures reported in Veje's 19X4 income statement, and give reasons for your response in accounting concept terms.

2) What will appear in Veje's December 31, 19X4, balance sheet relative to the José merchandise?

3) Disregarding generally accepted accounting principles, during what calendar year was the revenue actually earned by Veje? Why?

4) Speculate on reasons why Veje managers may have intentionally delayed shipment of the goods to José until 19X5.

SECTION 12.B

Accounting for Changing Prices

OBJECTIVES

This section deals with the effects that changing price levels have on the validity of accounting results. At the conclusion of this section, you should be able to

1. State in your own words the price-level problem as it relates to accounting.
2. State whether conventional accounting practices will tend to overstate or understate each of the following during periods of continued inflation:
   a. Assets.
   b. Net incomes.
   c. Rates of return.
   d. Sales growth trends.
3. Convert dollars of one point in time to equivalent dollars of another point in time, when given the necessary index numbers.
4. Approximate the purchasing power gain or loss that resulted from holding monetary assets and owing monetary liabilities for a period of time, when given the necessary index numbers.
5. Differentiate in your own words the following expressions as they relate to reporting financial data:
   a. Nominal dollar.
   b. Constant dollar.
   c. Current cost.
6. State in your own words the five general types of financial data that *FASB Statement No. 33* requires large corporations to disclose as supplements to their conventional financial statements.

MONETARY INFLATION

Since monetary inflation is a much discussed topic, you are probably aware of some of the problems that result from it. In simple terms, *monetary inflation refers to the overall increase in the price of goods and services that results when the supply of money rises at a faster rate than the supply of goods and services. A **price level** refers to the relative prices of goods and services at one point in time, as compared to some other point in time.* As monetary inflation continues, the price level rises and the purchasing power of money declines. *Purchasing power is the relative amount of goods and services that a given monetary unit will buy.*

Most of the world's people have lived with monetary inflation for years. In the United States, except for a couple of years, inflation at varying levels has been a fact of life since the Great Depression of the 1930s.

The extent of monetary inflation over time can be viewed in the form of price indexes. *A price index is a ratio of the price level at one point in time to the price level at some base period of time.* A price index may be calculated for a particular class of goods or services by dividing the cost of a representative sample of such items at one point in time by the cost of a similar sample at some base point in time.

A number of price indexes are calculated by agencies of the federal government. *A Consumer Price Index is a general index of price levels for goods and services commonly purchased by people for their own use. A Producer Price Index is an index of price levels of resources used by producers.* There are also indexes for construction costs, farm goods, and so on. The most general index in the United States is the *Gross National Product Implicit Price Deflator (GNP Deflator) which is an overall index of the general price level.* The GNP deflator index is available on a quarterly basis whereas the consumer and producer price indexes are available on a monthly basis.

The graph in Illustration 12.3 on the next page shows the movement of consumer, producer, and GNP deflator indexes for the years 1970 through 1982, with prices for 1967 representing 100 for each index.

PRICE-LEVEL PROBLEM IN ACCOUNTING

Let us now recall the monetary unit, cost, and matching concepts of accounting, as they were stated in the previous section. Transactions are quantified in terms of monetary units. Costs are measured in monetary units, as are expired costs (expenses) that are matched against revenues. Note that none of the concepts make any reference to the fluctuating value (purchasing power) of the monetary units being used. Thus *accounting has traditionally reported financial data in terms of the actual numbers of monetary units recorded at the various times when transactions occurred, without any adjustments to make the units equivalent—an approach variously referred to as **nominal dollar, unit-of-money** or **mixed dollar reporting.***

OBJECTIVE 5a. Define nominal dollar reporting.

Although the monetary unit is a measuring device, it does not remain constant, as do the measuring standards for distance, weight, and time. It is as though the measuring stick used for accounting has been shrinking as inflation has occurred. Dollars at different points in time are simply not equivalent measuring units.

Whereas no one would think of combining meters and yards, or Canadian dollars and U.S. dollars, without first converting to a common measure,

ILLUSTRATION 12.3   Price level

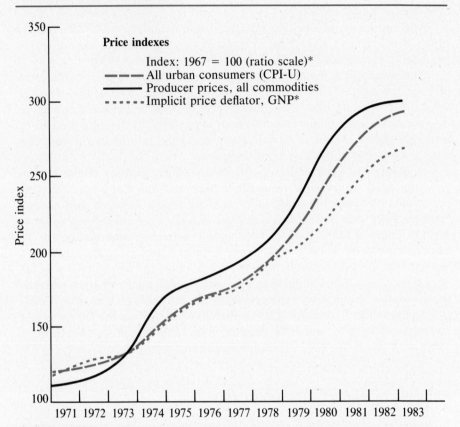

*GNP Deflator Index numbers are reported by the Department of Commerce with 1972 prices representing 100. The reported index numbers have been converted for use in this graph to index numbers for which 1967 prices represent 100.

SOURCES: Department of Labor, Bureau of Labor Statistics for Consumer and Producer Prices; and Department of Commerce, Bureau of Economic Analysis for Implicit Price Deflators.

most people seem content to combine dollars of one time period with those of other time periods without any attempt at conversion to uniform dollars. In fact, meters and yards are likely to be more nearly equivalent than are dollars of different time periods.

The price-level problem in accounting is essentially that *the quantification unit used in accounting (the monetary unit) is continually changing in value.* The problem can be outlined in somewhat more detail by the following series of observations.

PRICE-LEVEL PROBLEM IN ACCOUNTING

1. Accounting data are communicated by means of statements and reports.
2. Accounting data are reported (quantified) in terms of monetary units.
3. Accounting statements and reports commonly include monetary units of different time periods.
4. The value of monetary units is constantly changing over time.
5. Accounting has traditionally ignored the changing value of monetary units over time.
6. Unlike measuring units are combined in conventional accounting statements and reports.
7. Therefore, accounting communication is distorted.

OBJECTIVE 1. State the price-level problem as it relates to accounting.

Thus accounting communication is distorted when unlike measures are combined in accounting statements and reports. The magnitude of the distortion depends on a number of factors, however, as we shall now see.

Balance Sheet Distortions

Assets are reported in a balance sheet in terms of their costs. These costs stem from the various points in time at which the assets were acquired by the entity. Because of the effects of inflation, past dollars were more valuable than present dollars; old dollars are *equivalent to* a greater number of current dollars. The problem is further compounded by the fact that the dates at which various costs were incurred are not normally disclosed in a balance sheet. The further back in time that assets were purchased, the more will the real cost sacrifice be understated in terms of current dollars. Thus we can conclude as follows.

During times of continued inflation, the reported total cost of an entity's assets will tend to be understated in current dollar terms.

OBJECTIVE 2a. State whether conventional accounting practices tend to overstate or understate assets during inflation.

We should recognize, however, that *monetary assets* represent claims to current dollars, even though their costs may be stated in past dollars. *Monetary assets consist of money and claims to money.* Cash on hand and in banks and most receivables are monetary assets. As inflation occurs, anyone holding cash and receivables suffers monetary losses as these assets lose purchasing power. The cash simply will not buy as much as it would have in the past, and creditors will repay receivables with less valuable dollars than those they originally owed.

On the other hand, most liabilities are also in monetary terms. As inflation occurs, debtors realize monetary gains on their liabilities because the liabilities may be paid with cheaper dollars that have less purchasing power than those originally owed. Thus monetary gains on liabilities may cancel out some or all of the losses on monetary assets. In other words, the monetary gain on each dollar of liabilities will exactly offset the loss on a dollar of monetary assets as long as both were outstanding throughout a period of time. An entity is said to be hedged (protected) against monetary losses to the extent that its liabilities offset its monetary assets.

Income Statement Distortions

Revenues are usually stated in dollars that are relatively current. This year's sales are stated in this year's dollars. However, some of the expenses on an income statement are expirations of costs that were incurred in past years. This means that unlike dollars are being matched to arrive at net income for a period.

Depreciation expense and other expirations of long-term assets are most apt to be seriously understated in current dollar terms. The old valuable dollars of cost are being matched against current revenue dollars that are less valuable in comparison. An *understatement* of expenses will naturally result in an *overstatement* of net income. We therefore come to the following conclusion.

OBJECTIVE 2b. State whether conventional accounting practices tend to overstate or understate net incomes during inflation.

> During times of continued inflation, an entity's reported net income will tend to be overstated in current dollar terms.

Any net monetary losses on monetary accounts will further reduce an entity's real income for a period, whereas net monetary gains have a positive effect on real income.

Rate of Return Distortions

*A **rate of return** is a percentage obtained by dividing an income by the amount of investment required to obtain the income.* An income earned by an entity for a period may be related to the entity's total assets as follows.[25]

$$\frac{\text{Net income}}{\text{Total assets}} = \text{Rate of return on assets}$$

We have previously concluded that during times of continued inflation, total assets are likely to be understated, and net income is likely to be

---

[25]Rates of return are discussed in more detail in Chapter 19.

overstated, in current dollar terms. The effect of both an overstated numerator (net income) and an understated denominator (total assets) will be to greatly overstate the rate of return. To illustrate, suppose an entity reported the following rate of return.

$$\frac{\text{Reported net income}}{\text{Reported total assets}} = \text{Reported rate of return}$$

$$\frac{\$50,000}{\$500,000} = 10\%$$

Now let us suppose that the adjusted net income stated in *current dollars* is only one-half of that reported.

$$\frac{\text{Adjusted net income}}{\text{Reported total assets}} = \text{``Adjusted'' rate of return}$$

$$\frac{\$25,000}{\$500,000} = 5\%$$

Also, let us assume that total asset cost in *current dollars* is double that reported.

$$\frac{\text{Adjusted net income}}{\text{Adjusted total assets}} = \text{``Real'' rate of return}$$

$$\frac{\$\ \ \ 25,000}{\$1,000,000} = 2.5\%$$

We can therefore conclude as follows.

During times of continued inflation, an entity's reported rate of return on assets will tend to be greatly overstated in current dollar terms.

OBJECTIVE 2c. State whether conventional accounting practices tend to overstate or understate rates of return during inflation.

Trend Distortions

Data from current statements are frequently related to data from preceding periods to gauge an entity's progress, or lack of it, over time. For example, gross sales may be compared with sales of preceding periods to determine the revenue growth trend; net incomes may be compared to show the growth in profitability; rates of return may be compared to establish the relative effectiveness with which the firm's resources are being used. Thus data may be compared in gross, net, or rate terms.

Any comparison of time-series data in monetary units is affected by price-level changes. The longer the period of time over which comparisons are made, the more likely that the figures being compared are in materially different measuring units.

During times of inflation, it takes more current dollars to be equivalent to a given number of past dollars. Suppose, for example, that the price level has doubled over a period of years during which sales doubled. It takes twice as many sales dollars in the later period to be equivalent to the sales level of the earlier period. However, if they aren't otherwise informed, accounting statement users are left with the impression that sales volume has doubled between the two points in time. Thus we can arrive at the following conclusion.

OBJECTIVE 2d. State whether conventional accounting practices tend to overstate or understate sales growth trends during inflation.

> During times of continued inflation, an entity's reported revenue growth will tend to be overstated in current dollar terms.

Inequities

The various effects of the price-level problem already discussed are bad enough. More serious, however, are the inequities that occur between different types of businesses. Some companies, by their very nature, suffer the effects of inflation more than others.

Conventional accounting data have tended to be distorted more over long periods of time than over short periods. Assets that were purchased many years ago are most apt to be substantially understated in current dollar terms—at least under continuing inflation. Depreciation of older assets will be materially understated (in terms of current dollars), which results in an overstatement of net income. Net income overstatement leads to greater tax payments, and pressures for larger dividend payments, than are warranted.

If all companies were in approximately the same position, the problem would still be worth worrying about. However, certain types of companies have considerably more long-lived assets, and depreciation expense, than do others. As a rule, personal service businesses (lawyers, accountants, plumbers) need relatively little in the way of long-term assets. Merchandising businesses (retailers, wholesalers) need somewhat more long-term facilities than do personal service businesses. Generally speaking, however, it is the manufacturing business that requires large amounts of long-term (heavy fixed) resources in order to operate effectively. Consider, for example, the amount of investment in plant and equipment necessary for the production of steel, or for the generation and distribution of electricity.

Utilities, transportation companies, and companies engaged in heavy manufacturing are hardest hit by the effects of inflation.[26] It is probably no coincidence that these kinds of companies are beginning to falter after so many years of continuous inflation. Many of the assets they report were acquired long ago, for dollar sacrifices that are equivalent to a great many more current dollars than their accounting reports indicate.

Depreciation expenses shown in the operating statements of manufacturing companies and utilities are likely to be greatly understated in terms of equivalent sacrifices in current dollars. The overstated net incomes reported result in greater amounts of taxes and dividends than should be paid from the companies' real incomes. In some instances, concerns are paying more in taxes and dividends than they are actually generating in current dollars. No one should be surprised, then, when these companies are forced to borrow ever increasing amounts to replace wornout plant facilities in order to continue in operation.

The problems are aggravated for utilities by the actions of rate regulation authorities. Rate regulation commissions control what utilities may charge for their services so as to limit each company's profit to a fair return on the assets it uses. When the company's assets are severely understated, and when reported net income is substantially overstated, you can anticipate the reaction from rate regulation authorities who are supposed to act in the best interests of those who use the company's services.

CONSTANT DOLLAR ACCOUNTING

One way to deal with the price-level problem in accounting is to convert unlike monetary units into equivalent (constant) units of some time period. *Constant dollar reporting,* sometimes referred to as **uniform dollar** or **common dollar** reporting, has been defined as "a method of reporting financial statement elements in dollars each of which has the same (i.e., constant) general purchasing power."[27] Statements might conceivably be presented in terms of constant dollars of any time period. However, dollars reported in accounting statements are in all likelihood viewed by statement readers as though they were *current* dollars, because these are the dollars most familiar to them at the time they are using the accounting data. For this reason, the most sensible choice for a common measuring unit would seem to be the dollars of the most recent reporting period.

OBJECTIVE 5b. Define constant dollar reporting.

---

[26]However, some utilities and other companies have been able to counter some of the negative effects of inflation with monetary gains on high levels of long-term debt.

[27]*FASB Statement of Financial Accounting Standards No. 33,* "Financial Reporting and Changing Prices" (Stamford, Conn.: Financial Accounting Standards Board, 1979), par. 22.

Converting Monetary Units

The process of converting an amount of dollars at one point in time to equivalent dollars at a later point is relatively simple, provided we know price index numbers for the two points. The formula for conversion may be stated as follows.

$$\frac{\text{Index of later point}}{\text{Index of earlier point}} \times \text{Earlier dollars} = \text{Equivalent later dollars}$$

For example, let us assume that a price index at a time during 1972 was 125, and the index at a time during 1980 stood at 250. Since the later index is twice the earlier one, any given amount of earlier dollars will be equivalent to twice as many later dollars, as follows.

OBJECTIVE 3. Convert dollars of one point in time to equivalent dollars of another point in time.

$$\frac{250}{125} \times \$60,000 = \$120,000$$

If, on the other hand, one wishes to restate dollars of a later time to equivalent dollars of an earlier time, the formula would appear as follows.

$$\frac{\text{Index of earlier point}}{\text{Index of later point}} \times \text{Later dollars} = \text{Equivalent earlier dollars}$$

Assume, for instance, that $80,000 of cost incurred during 1980 when the index was 250 is being restated to 1967 dollars when the index was 100. The result would appear as follows.

$$\frac{100}{250} \times \$80,000 = \$32,000$$

A Simple Illustration of Conversion

Here is an oversimplified example to illustrate the process of converting to constant end-of-year dollars. In this way, you may more easily grasp the techniques without getting lost in a variety of details. Keep in mind, however, that only the largest of corporations are presently *required* to report anything in constant dollar terms.

First, assume that considerable inflation occurred evenly during a single year, as the following price-level index numbers show.

	Index
January 1, 19X0	120
Average during 19X0	160
December 31, 19X0	200

Let us assume that Future Company began business at the start of 19X0. Sales and expenses were evenly spread over the year, receivables and payables grew evenly over the year, and other assets and liabilities remained constant throughout the year, except that the net book value of Buildings and Equipment declined evenly as depreciation occurred. A comparative balance sheet and an income statement for the year stated in nominal (mixed) dollars are shown in Illustrations 12.4 and 12.5 (next page).

ILLUSTRATION 12.4

FUTURE COMPANY Comparative Balance Sheet	12/31/X0	1/1/X0
ASSETS		
Cash	$ 10,000	$ 10,000
Accounts receivable	80,000	–0–
Inventory (LIFO basis)	40,000	40,000
Buildings and equipment (net of depreciation)	70,000	100,000
Land	50,000	50,000
Total Assets	$250,000	$200,000
LIABILITIES		
Accounts payable	$ 10,000	$ –0–
Note payable	20,000	20,000
Total Liabilities	$ 30,000	$ 20,000
OWNER'S EQUITY		
J. Morley, capital		
Invested, 1/1/X0	$180,000	$180,000
Net income, 19X0	40,000	–0–
Total Owner's Equity	$220,000	$180,000
Total Liabilities and Owner's Equity	$250,000	$200,000

ILLUSTRATION 12.5

FUTURE COMPANY Income Statement For the Year Ended December 31, 19X0		
Sales		$300,000
Cost of goods sold		170,000
Gross Profit		$130,000
Operating expenses		
Depreciation	$30,000	
Other	60,000	90,000
Net Income		$ 40,000

The company suffered a purchasing power loss on net monetary items during the year, as approximated in Illustration 12.6.

The income statement can be converted to end-of-year dollars as shown in Illustration 12.7. Of course, simplifying assumptions have been made that

ILLUSTRATION 12.6

MONETARY ACCOUNTS		
	Nominal Dollars	
	12/31/X0	*1/1/X0*
Cash	$ 10,000	$ 10,000
Accounts receivable	80,000	–0–
Accounts payable	(10,000)	–0–
Note payable	(20,000)	(20,000)
Net monetary assets	$ 60,000	$(10,000)

OBJECTIVE 4. Approximate the purchasing power gain or loss from holding monetary assets and owing monetary liabilities for a period.

APPROXIMATION OF MONETARY LOSS			
	Nominal Dollars	Conversion Factor	Constant 12/31/X0 Dollars
Net monetary assets at 1/1/X0	$(10,000)	200/120	$(16,667)
Increase in net monetary assets during year	70,000*	200/160	87,500
			$ 70,833
Net monetary assets at 12/31/X0	$ 60,000	200/200	60,000
Purchasing power loss on net monetary items			$ 10,833

*Assumed to be in average 19X0 dollars. In actuality, the inflows and outflows of cash and other monetary accounts may not occur evenly during the year, nor will the price level change evenly. The approach illustrated above is similar to that shown in *FASB Statement No. 33,* par. 232, except that in *FASB 33* the constant dollars are stated in terms of average purchasing power for the year.

ILLUSTRATION 12.7

FUTURE COMPANY Income Statement For the Year Ended December 31, 19X0			
	Nominal Dollars	**Adjustment Factor**	**Constant 12/31/X0 Dollars**
Sales	$300,000	200/160	$375,000
Cost of goods sold	170,000	200/160	212,500
Gross Profit	$130,000		162,500
Operating expenses			
Depreciation expense	$ 30,000	200/120	$ 50,000
Other expense	60,000	200/160	75,000
	$ 90,000		$125,000
Operating Income	$ 40,000		$ 37,500
Net monetary loss	—		10,833
Net Income	$ 40,000		$ 26,667

revenues, expenses, and the index all rose evenly during the year. Therefore, revenues and expenses are converted by use of the average index except for Depreciation Expense, which stems from the asset that was acquired at the first of the year. The net monetary loss comes directly from the schedule previously shown.

A balance sheet stated in both nominal and constant dollars appears in Illustration 12.8 on the next page. The monetary assets and liabilities are not converted at year-end because they are correctly stated from a legal standpoint. The monetary loss is reflected into the owner's equity. In fact, the net income drop of $13,333 is the combined effect of the $2,500 decrease in operating income and the net monetary loss of $10,833.

The process of converting the statements of large, complex entities to constant dollars is considerably more complex than our simple illustration would indicate. However, the concepts are essentially the same, and the conversion techniques have been known for years. These techniques were clearly set forth in both *Accounting Research Study No. 6*[28] and *APB Statement No. 3*.[29] Preparation of constant dollar statements requires some additional effort and expense, but these sacrifices are small when compared with the costs already incurred to derive the nominal dollar data that are reported in accounting statements.

---

[28]*Accounting Research Study No. 6,* "Reporting the Financial Effects of Price-Level Changes" (New York: American Institute of Certified Public Accountants, 1963).

[29]*Statement of the Accounting Principles Board No. 3,* "Financial Statements Restated for General Price-Level Changes" (New York: American Institute of Certified Public Accountants, 1969).

ILLUSTRATION 12.8

FUTURE COMPANY
Balance Sheet
December 31, 19X0

	Nominal Dollars	Adjustment Factor	Constant 12/31/X0 Dollars
ASSETS			
Cash	$ 10,000		$ 10,000
Accounts receivable	80,000		80,000
Inventory (LIFO basis)	40,000	200/120	66,667
Buildings and equipment (net)	70,000	200/120	116,667
Land	50,000	200/120	83,333
Total Assets	$250,000		$356,667
LIABILITIES			
Accounts payable	$ 10,000		$ 10,000
Note payable	20,000		20,000
Total Liabilities	$ 30,000		$ 30,000
OWNER'S EQUITY			
J. Morley, capital			
Invested, 1/1/X0	$180,000	200/120	$300,000
Net income, 19X0	40,000		26,667
Total Owner's Equity	$220,000		$326,667
Total Liabilities and Owner's Equity	$250,000		$356,667

We should keep in mind that constant dollar reporting is still based on the *cost concept,* as well as on the other traditional concepts of accounting. It only abandons the implied assumption that monetary units remain uniform as time passes. Historical costs are simply reported in terms of equivalent dollars.

VALUE-BASED ACCOUNTING

Arguments can be made as well for use of value-based data for statement purposes. Most assets must be replaced as they are used or expire if an entity is to continue in existence. When assets are purchased, current prices must be paid. Cost expirations do not provide sufficient recovery for replacing assets at ever higher costs. In other words, depreciation and other cost expirations may not represent the true costs of using assets that have to be replaced eventually.

Also, gains may be *realized* on some assets that become more valuable over time even though they are not generally *recognized* by conventional accounting until the assets are sold. Suppose, for example, that you own securities worth much more than you paid for them. Do you not *feel* wealthier as a result of their appreciation in value? And, if some of the appreciation subsequently disappears as a result of market declines, haven't you suffered a loss? In other words, a person's wealth—and an entity's—fluctuates up and down as the values of assets change over time.

Relevance of Values

Under the *cost basis* concept, assets have traditionally been accounted for in terms of their *costs*—the sacrifices undergone to obtain them. Cost sacrifices are usually in the form of cash or other assets given up, or liabilities assumed, at the time that assets are acquired. A cost, then, did represent the *value* of an asset in the purchase market when the asset was acquired.

As time passes and costs change, the historical costs of assets become outdated. Recorded costs continue to represent the sacrifices that were made to obtain assets, but only by chance will they be the same as the current values of the assets.

Try, for a moment, to pin down your own financial position. What difference does it make what you paid for a painting, a car, or even a house several years ago? Isn't it the current *value* of your assets that determines how well off you are?

And consider these questions. Would we insure a building against fire loss in the amount of its depreciated cost or its current value? Should real estate taxes be based on costs or on values? When property is pledged as security for a loan, which is more relevant—historical cost or current value?

It is apparent that asset values are useful for a number of purposes. In fact, continuing to own an asset implies that the owner desires the asset more than the money that could be obtained from selling it. Each asset owned by an entity should be worth at least as much to the entity as the price for which it could be sold—otherwise it should be sold. By continuing to hold assets, owners in effect reinvest in the assets what they forgo by not selling them for their current values.

Value-Based Versus Constant Dollar Accounting

Value-based accounting should not be confused with constant dollar accounting. Constant dollar accounting does not abandon any of the traditional concepts of accounting, although it does take note of the changing values of monetary units. *Value-based reporting, however, substitutes for the cost concept the requirement that assets be reported at their current values.* Reporting current values requires that value increments be recognized before the point of sale (*realization concept*), although some accountants distinguish between unrealized gains and those realized through sales. Conservative accounting practices, incidentally, have long recognized *losses* in value under the *lower of cost or market* rule.

Whereas constant dollar accounting recognizes the changing values of *money,* value-based accounting recognizes the changing value of *assets* in terms of their worth in money. The value of money is measured by the quantity of goods and services that it will buy; an asset's value is stated in terms of its worth in money.

The differences between conventional *nominal dollar, constant dollar,* and *value-based* reporting may be illustrated by an example. Suppose that an entity owns two parcels of land, essentially identical, but purchased at different points in time. Parcel A was bought in 19X1 for $120,000, when a general price index was 120; parcel B was purchased for $150,000 in 19X2, when the index was 125. In 19X8, when the price index was 200, each parcel of land had a current market value of $300,000. The following table summarizes the different amounts at which the land parcels might have been reported on a 19X8 balance sheet. You can see that only value-based reporting will show the two assets as being equivalent.

	Historical Cost	Conversion Factor	Cost in Uniform 19X8 Dollars	Market Value in 19X8
Parcel A	$120,000	200/120	$200,000	$300,000
Parcel B	$150,000	200/125	$240,000	$300,000

A balance sheet presented in current value terms should automatically be stated in uniform end-of-period dollars. And the owner's equity will necessarily reflect the net effects of price-level changes, as well as the gains and losses from changing asset values. Whether a value-based income statement shows the detailed effects of price-level changes will depend on the format used by the accountant preparing it.

VALUE CONCEPTS

The term *value* is somewhat vague, and it is often accompanied by a modifier, as in *current* value or *market* value. Three kinds of value that might be used for value-based accounting are defined as follows.

OBJECTIVE 5c. Define current cost.

> **TYPES OF VALUE**
>
> *Current cost (replacement cost, entrance value). The cost of replacing an asset at a point in time.*
> *Net realizable value (exit value). The expected selling price of an asset less the estimated costs of getting it ready for sale and selling it.*
> *Value in use (economic value). The net present value of all expected future cash flows, inward and outward, associated with the use of an asset.*[30]

---

[30]Discounting techniques are covered in Appendix I of Chapter 16.

REPORTING REQUIREMENTS

The price-level problem has been considered by every influential accounting organization. In 1979 the Financial Accounting Standards Board (FASB) issued *FASB Statement No. 33* on "Financial Reporting and Changing Prices."[31] That statement encourages the disclosure of price-level adjusted data in addition to the conventional financial statements and requires the largest of business corporations to provide a minimum amount of adjusted data as supplements to the conventional statements. The requirements apply to corporations meeting either of the following tests.[32]

SIZE TESTS OF *FASB STATEMENT NO. 33*

1. Corporations with inventories and property, plant, and equipment (before deducting depreciation, depletion, and amortization) amounting in aggregate to more than $125 million; or

2. Corporations with total assets amounting to more than $1 billion (after deducting accumulated depreciation)

The supplemental information required to be disclosed by *Statement No. 33* is as follows.[33]

FASB STATEMENT NO. 33 DISCLOSURE REQUIREMENTS

1. Income from continuing operations for the current fiscal year on both a constant dollar basis and a current cost basis

2. The purchasing power gain or loss on net monetary items for the current fiscal year

3. The current cost amounts of inventory and property, plant, and equipment at the end of the current fiscal year

4. Increases or decreases for the current fiscal year in the current cost amounts of inventory and property, plant, and equipment, net of the effects of monetary inflation

5. A five-year summary of selected financial data, adjusted for price-level changes, about revenues, income, assets, monetary gains and losses, dividends per common share, and market prices of common shares

---

OBJECTIVE 6. State the types of financial data that FASB *Statement 33* requires large corporations to disclose.

Statement No. 33 specifies that the Consumer Price Index for all Urban Consumers (CPI-U) published by the Bureau of Labor Statistics of the U.S. Department of Labor is to be used to compute information on a constant dollar basis.[34] Where complete (comprehensive) financial statements in con-

---

[31]*FASB Statement No. 33,* "Financial Reporting and Changing Prices" (Stamford, Conn.: Financial Accounting Standards Board, 1979).

[32]*Ibid.,* par. 23. Inventories and property, plant, and equipment are intended to include land and other natural resources and leaseholds, but exclude goodwill and other intangible assets.

[33]*Ibid.,* pars. 29–35.

[34]*Ibid.,* par. 39. The index is published in the *Monthly Labor Review.*

stant dollars are prepared, amounts may be stated either in end-of-year constant dollars or in average-for-the-year constant dollars.[35]

When comprehensive financial statements in constant dollars are not prepared, supplementary disclosures in constant dollars are stated in terms of average-for-the-year dollars. If an entity prefers to do so, the five-year summary of selected financial data may be stated in dollars of the CPI-U base period (the period for which the CPI-U is 100).[36]

Whenever recoverable amounts are less than constant dollars or current costs, the recoverable amounts are to be used for disclosure purposes. *A recoverable amount is the net present value of expected cash from the use or sale of an asset.*[37] *Thus **recoverable amount** may be either value in use or net realizable value, depending on the accountant's judgment.*

Disclosure Formats

FASB Statement No. 33 provides, in its Appendix A, illustrations of possible disclosure formats. Illustration 12.9 shows how one corporation, Quaker State Oil Refining Corporation, chose to present the required data in its 1982 Annual Report. The Quaker State data are presented in average-for-the-year 1982 dollars. Note that, except for revenues, dividends, and share prices, adjusted data for years prior to the 1979 pronouncement need not be disclosed.

For another example of how an actual corporation has complied with the reporting requirements, see Schedule A, "Comparison of Selected Data Adjusted for Effects of Changing Prices," and Schedule B, "Schedule of Income Adjusted for Changing Prices," of the General Motors Corporation financial statements presented in Appendix C near the back of this book. The five-year comparison data for General Motors are presented in constant 1967 dollars (1967 is the base year for which the CPI-U is 100) while the data in Schedule B are presented in average 1982 dollars.

In closing, the status of financial reporting at the time of this writing is as follows.

PRESENT STATUS OF FINANCIAL REPORTING

1. Conventional statements must be prepared in nominal dollars, without regard to either specific or general changes in prices.

2. It is recommended that all business concerns disclose selected financial data adjusted for price changes, and large corporations are required to disclose this information as supplements to the conventional statements.

3. Concerns may, if they wish, present comprehensive financial statements in constant dollars and/or current costs as supplements to the conventional statements.

---

[35]*Ibid.*, par. 40.

[36]*Ibid.*, pars. 43, 65.

[37]*Ibid.*, par. 62.

ILLUSTRATION 12.9

Statement of Income Adjusted for Changing Prices

(Thousands of Dollars)

For the year ended December 31, 1982	As Reported in the Primary Statements	Adjusted for General Inflation	Adjusted for Changes in Specific Prices
Sales, operating and other revenues	$936,972	$936,972	$936,972
Cost of sales and operating costs	717,642	720,245	717,795
Selling, general and administrative	104,908	104,908	104,908
Depreciation and depletion	34,644	56,467	60,769
Interest	9,410	9,410	9,410
Provision for income taxes	31,800	31,800	31,800
	898,404	922,830	924,682
Net income	$ 38,568	$ 14,142	$ 12,290
Gain from decline in purchasing power of net amounts owed			$ 5,465
Increase in specific prices (current cost) of inventories and property, plant and equipment*			$ 6,740
Effect of increase in general price level			27,650
Excess of increase in general price level over increase in specific prices			$ 20,910

*At December 31, 1982, the current cost of inventory was $149,464,000 and the current cost of property, plant and equipment, net of accumulated depreciation and depletion, was $568,800,000.

Five Year Comparison of Selected Supplementary Financial Data Adjusted for Effects of Changing Prices

(in thousands except per share data) (in average 1982 dollars)	1982	1981	1980	1979	1978
Sales, operating and other revenues	$936,972	$986,221	$981,430	$926,131	$768,448
Historical cost information adjusted for general inflation:					
Income from continuing operations	$ 14,142	$ 3,150	$ 6,498	$ 25,796	—
Income from continuing operations per share	$ .65	$ .15	$ .30	$ 1.19	—
Net assets at year end	$456,510	$452,190	$454,945	$449,258	—
Current cost information:					
Income from continuing operations	$ 12,290	$ (6,162)	$ 3,072	$ 21,916	—
Income from continuing operations per share	$ .57	$ (.28)	$ .14	$ 1.01	—
Excess of increase in specific prices over increase in general price level	$ (20,910)	$ (2,988)	$ 8,488	$ 16,250	—
Net assets at year end	$583,992	$609,759	$627,875	$618,391	—
Gain from decline in purchasing power of net amounts owed	$ 5,465	$ 13,387	$ 19,260	$ 21,673	—
Cash dividends declared per share	$ .80	$ .85	$ .93	$ 1.00	$ 1.04
Market price per common share at year end	$ 15.45	$ 12.45	$ 22.66	$ 19.66	$ 14.96
Average consumer price index	289.1	272.4	246.8	217.4	195.4

SOURCE: Quaker State Oil Refining Corporation, *1982 Annual Report*, Oil City, Pa., pp. 23–24.

GLOSSARY FOR SECTION 12.B

Constant (uniform, common) dollar reporting   A method of reporting financial statement elements in dollars each of which has the same (i.e., constant) general purchasing power.

Consumer Price Index   A general index of price levels for goods and services commonly purchased by people for their own use.

Current cost (replacement cost, entrance value)   The cost of replacing an asset at a point in time.

Gross National Product Implicit Price Deflator (GNP Deflator)   An overall index of the general price level.

Monetary assets   Money and claims to money.

Monetary inflation   The overall increase in the price of goods and services that results when the supply of money rises at a faster rate than the supply of goods and services.

Net realizable value (exit value)   The expected selling price of an asset less the estimated costs of getting it ready for sale and selling it.

Nominal dollar (unit-of-money, mixed dollar) reporting   Conventional reporting of financial data in terms of actual numbers of monetary units recorded at the various times that transactions occurred, without any adjustments to make the units equivalent.

Price index   A ratio of the price level at one point in time to the price level at some base period of time.

Price level   The relative prices of goods and services at one point in time, as compared to some other point in time.

Producer Price Index   An index of price levels of resources used by producers.

Purchasing power   The relative amount of goods and services that a given monetary unit will buy.

Rate of return   A percentage obtained by dividing an income by the amount of investment required to obtain the income.

Recoverable amount   The net present value of expected cash from the use or sale of an asset (either value in use or net realizable value, depending on the accountant's judgment).

Value-based reporting   An approach to accounting that substitutes for the cost concept the requirement that assets be reported at their current values.

Value in use (economic value)   The net present value of all expected future cash flows, inward and outward, associated with the use of an asset.

SELF-QUIZ ON OBJECTIVES FOR SECTION 12.B
Solutions to Self-Quiz begin on page B-40.

1. **OBJECTIVE 1.** State in your own words the price-level problem as it relates to accounting.

2. **OBJECTIVE 2.** Indicate the likelihood that conventional accounting during inflationary periods will result in an overstatement or understatement for each of the following:

   a. Assets.

   b. Net incomes.

   c. Rates of return.

   d. Sales growth trends.

3. Selected balance sheet data for Welbe Company are provided here.

	12/31/X9	12/31/X8
Cash	$ 8,000	$ 6,000
Accounts receivable	60,000	40,000
Land	80,000	80,000
Accounts payable (credit balance)	(50,000)	(60,000)

   Price index numbers were as follows.

December 31, 19X8	110
Average for 19X9	132
December 31, 19X9	154

   a. **OBJECTIVE 3.** Assuming that the land was purchased on December 31, 19X8, calculate its cost stated in dollars of December 31, 19X9.

   b. **OBJECTIVE 4.** Assuming that changes in Cash, Accounts Receivable, and Accounts Payable balances were in average 19X9 dollars, approximate the purchasing power gain or loss on net monetary items during 19X9, stated in December 31, 19X9 dollars.

4. **OBJECTIVE 5.** Differentiate in your own words the following expressions as they relate to reporting financial data:

   a. Nominal dollar.

   b. Constant dollar.

   c. Current cost.

5. **OBJECTIVE 6.** State in your own words the five general types of financial data that *FASB Statement No. 33* requires large corporations to disclose as supplements to their conventional financial statements.

DISCUSSION QUESTIONS FOR SECTION 12.B

1. How can the managers of a concern prevent or minimize purchasing power losses owing to inflation?

2. What are some everyday reasons why the current values of an individual's personal assets may be more relevant than the original costs of the assets?

3. How does value-based accounting differ from price-level accounting?

4. To what extent are replacement cost concepts presently used in accounting in the United States?

5. When might the current value of a business asset be considered more relevant than its cost basis?

6. What is the difference between the expressions current cost, net realizable value, and value in use?

7. What are the differences between nominal dollar, constant dollar, and current cost presentations of:

   a. A balance sheet?

   b. An income statement?

EXERCISES FOR SECTION 12.B

12.B.1. Inflato Corporation built a warehouse at a cost of $1,400,000 when a price index was 120. Restate the cost of the building to equivalent dollars at a later time when the index is 168, and determine the percentage increase in the price level between the two points in time.

12.B.2. If the price index is 140 at a time that $28,000 was paid for a certain quantity of assets, what must the price index have been when the calculated equivalent dollar cost was $43,400?

12.B.3. Assume that a general price index rose from 120 in 1971 to 360 in 1991. Suppose that in 1971 a wealthy relative had put $100,000 in trust for you with the stipulation that any interest earned was to be used for homeless cats until you were paid the $100,000 principal in 1991. Calculate the monetary gain or loss that occurred on the $100,000 principal amount during the 20-year period.

12.B.4. Jalax Company reported total assets of $600,000 at December 31, and net income of $120,000 for the year then ended. It has been determined that total assets stated in constant end-of-year dollars would be 50% greater than the nominal dollars reported, and that the market value of total assets is double the reported amount. An income statement prepared in constant end-of-year dollars shows a net loss of $90,000. A value-based income statement, which includes real gains in value of assets held during the year, shows a net income of $72,000. Calculate the rate of return on total assets for the year assuming use of:

   a. Nominal dollar reporting.

   b. Constant dollar reporting.

   c. Value-based reporting.

Required

1) Comment on the inclusion of each of the three mentioned items as expenses for the year. Consider in your discussion both the accounting principles involved and the logical realities.

2) One of Vickey's owners was heard to remark: "The reported loss is mislabeled. It is instead a cost of profits to be earned in later years." Comment on the validity or invalidity of the owner's remarks.

12.8. Vinney Farms incurred $20,000 of costs in the current year for measures taken to fight a Botwala fruit fly infestation of its farms. Also during the current year, fruit with a normal sales value of $300,000 was destroyed to prevent the spread of the fruit fly to other areas. As a result of the extraordinary measures taken by growers and the state government, the Botwala fly was eradicated and is not expected to return to the area.

Required

1) State how you would account for the $20,000 costs incurred in fighting the fruit fly infestation, and give the reasoning behind your answer.

2) Should the $300,000 worth of fruit that was destroyed be reported in the financial statement for the year? If your answer is yes, explain where and how the reporting would appear in the statements. State the reasons for your answers.

PART VI

MULTIPLE OWNERSHIP

ACCOUNTANTS IN THE WORKPLACE

NAME: Katherine L. Miller

AFFILIATION: 3M Company

POSITION: International Financial
Accounting Coordinator

SPECIALIZATION: International

When in Rome, people do as the Romans do, and in foreign countries subsidiaries of American companies must obey foreign laws and comply with local accounting standards. When financial results are reported to the parent company in the United States, though, earnings and other data must be stated in accordance with generally accepted accounting principles in this country. At 3M Company, that's where Katherine L. Miller comes in. As International Financial Accounting Coordinator, Miller is responsible for the conformity of financial reports for 3M operations in fifty-two countries worldwide to U.S. standards.

"Our subsidiaries are usually staffed by local people," Miller explains. They, of course, must keep books for local purposes. To help them keep U.S. style records, as well, the company has prepared a four-volume manual explaining U.S. standards and 3M procedures. In addition, 3M staff from St. Paul visit the subsidiaries and the company brings foreign managers here for periodic training sessions.

As a rule, subsidiaries wire their results to the United States in terms of local currencies.

"We have a computer program that translates those figures into dollars," Miller explains. Sometimes, though, further adjustments are necessary. For example, Miller cites the cases of Brazil and Argentina.

In both countries, high rates of inflation make it necessary to periodically revalue fixed assets. Otherwise, depreciation charges would be unnaturally low. In the United States, however, this practice is not permitted. So 3M must "back those numbers out" before entering them on the St. Paul ledger.

A high school dropout, Miller took an equivalency test and entered Northern Michigan University, where she earned a degree in accounting. After working for two years with Peat, Marwick, Mitchell & Co., she moved to 3M. Miller quickly learned what she needed to know, though she had had no previous international experience, and steadily worked her way up to her present position.

A significant fringe benefit of her job has been the opportunity to meet "interesting people from throughout the world." That, in turn, has interested her in perhaps working in a foreign subsidiary in the future.

In addition to her work at 3M, Miller teaches Principles of Financial Accounting at the University of Minnesota.

Among trends in the accounting world, Miller cites a growing preference for cash flow information as particularly significant. Generally speaking, "there's more and more cash consciousness," she observes.

Partnerships

OBJECTIVES

Chapter 13 deals with accounting for those aspects of partnerships that differ from other legal forms of business entities. At the conclusion of this chapter, you should be able to

1. Journalize the formation of a partnership.

2. Make closing entries to distribute partnership net income or loss to partners' equity accounts in accordance with a partnership agreement.

3. Record the admission of a new partner who purchases a partnership interest by paying cash directly to old partners, assuming that
   a. The amount paid is ignored.
   b. Partnership assets are adjusted.

4. Record the admission of a new partner who purchases a partnership interest by contributing assets to the partnership, assuming that
   a. The bonus approach is used.
   b. Partnership assets are adjusted.

5. Prepare a partnership liquidation schedule that shows the allocation of gains or losses and the distribution of cash.

6. Record the liquidation of a partnership.

7. Prepare a cash distribution schedule for a liquidating partnership that shows how available cash should be distributed as it becomes available.

THE NATURE OF A PARTNERSHIP

A **partnership** is defined in the Uniform Partnership Act as "an association of two or more persons to carry on as co-owners a business for profit."[1] The **Uniform Partnership Act,** enacted by most states within the United States, is a set of laws governing the formation, operation, and dissolution of partnerships.

Although many partnerships are formed by only a loose verbal agreement a written agreement covering areas of potential conflict is advisable. A formal written contract among partners is called a **partnership agreement** or **articles of partnership.**

Conflict between partners is often due to an overlap of authority and responsibility. Unless the partnership agreement provides otherwise, the relationship between the partners is one of **mutual agency,** which means that each partner may legally commit the firm (and therefore its partners) to contracts in any area within the apparent scope of the firm's business. This can easily lead to confusion, with partners duplicating each other's efforts.

It is usually advisable that the partnership agreement provide for one **managing partner,** who is assigned the overall responsibility of administering the firm. Particular partners may be assigned responsibilities for sales management, purchasing, production, and other functional areas within the firm.

A partnership may own assets and incur debts in the name of the firm. However, partners are personally liable for debts that the partnership cannot pay—a feature often referred to as **unlimited liability.** From the viewpoint of partners, unlimited liability is a disadvantage of the partnership form of business organization.

Technically, at least, a partnership is terminated by the death, bankruptcy, incapacity, or withdrawal of any of its partners. The life expectancy of a partnership is therefore quite limited. As a practical matter, however, a new partnership can take the place of an old one without any interruption in business affairs and without any outward appearance of change.

PARTNERS' INITIAL INVESTMENTS

Except for the owners' equity accounts, accounting for partnerships is much the same as accounting for other business forms. Naturally, each partner's equity share must be individually accounted for. Where there are only a few partners, each partner's equity is shown in a separate permanent equity account. For firms with many partners, subsidiary accounts may be kept for the partners' shares of the business.

Let us assume that on January 2 Tripp and Pierce form the T&P Company with a contribution by Tripp of $200,000 in cash, and with Pierce contributing assets with agreed-upon fair values as indicated in the second entry of Illustration 13.1.

---

[1]Uniform Partnership Act, Sec. 6.

ILLUSTRATION 13.1

19--			
Jan. 2	Cash	200,000	
	Tripp, Capital		200,000
	Investment by Tripp in T&P Company.		
2	Land	30,000	
	Building	60,000	
	Truck	10,000	
	Pierce, Capital		100,000
	Investment by Pierce in T&P Company.		

OBJECTIVE 1. Journalize the formation of a partnership.

Partners' capital accounts do not have to show equal balances, and frequently partners agree to own unequal shares of a partnership.

DIVISION OF EARNINGS AND LOSSES

Partnership net income is derived in the same way as proprietorship net income: expenses are subtracted from revenues for the accounting period. Once derived, however, partnership net income is divided among the partners' equity accounts when the temporary equity accounts are closed at the end of a period. Unless the partners have agreed otherwise, they share equally in partnership profits and losses. However, it is usually best for partners to formally agree on an equitable income distribution. The responsibilities to be assumed, skills contributed, and capital invested by each partner are just some of the factors that should be considered.

Partners may agree to divide net incomes and losses any way they wish. For instance, net incomes and losses might be split 60:40, with one partner getting 60% and another 40%. A three-partner agreement might provide for division of incomes and losses on a 50:30:20 basis. Or the partners may agree that profits and losses be divided in proportion to their relative capital balances. Under certain circumstances, partners may agree to share net losses in a different ratio from net incomes.

Partners' Salaries

The differences in skill and effort contributed by each partner can be given consideration through partners' salaries. *Partners' salaries are allowances to individual partners for services rendered* and are deducted from partnership net income to arrive at a residual income to be divided among the partners.

Although partners' salaries are sometimes shown along with partnership expenses on an income statement, they are not actually expenses; they are merely a part of the agreed-upon formula for dividing the firm's net income. Partners' salaries are not subject to social security taxes, and the firm does not withhold income taxes from them. However, partners pay social security tax personally on earnings from self-employment, which includes their shares of partnership profits.

Partnership salaries are reported on the personal income tax returns of the partners, along with their other shares of partnership profits or losses. A partnership is required to file an information return (Form 1065) with the Internal Revenue Service, but the partnership pays no income taxes in its own name.

Interest on Partners' Capital

To encourage partners to contribute capital to the business, the partnership agreement may provide for an interest return on the partners' equity balances. The interest might be figured on capital balances at the beginning or end of a period or on average capital balances during the period. As with partners' salaries, interest on capital balances is simply a part of the overall plan for dividing net incomes and losses among partners. Partners' salary and interest allowances are *not* expenses of the partnership.

Partnership Income Statement

Except possibly for the firm name, partnership income statements look no different from those for proprietorships. In Illustration 13.2, a condensed statement for T&P Company shows an earned net income of $60,000 for the year, before any allowance for partners' salaries or interest on capital balances.

Income Distribution Schedule

Let us assume that Tripp and Pierce have agreed that Pierce will receive $1,000 per month salary allowance, which she will withdraw in cash each month, and that each partner will be allowed 10% interest on his or her

ILLUSTRATION 13.2

T&P COMPANY Income Statement For the Year Ended December 31, 19--		
Service revenue		$270,000
Expenses		
Employee wages	$150,000	
Depreciation	20,000	
Other	40,000	210,000
Net Income		$ 60,000

ILLUSTRATION 13.3

INCOME DISTRIBUTION SCHEDULE			
	Tripp	Pierce	Total
Partner's salary	$ –0–	$12,000	$12,000
Partners' interest	20,000	10,000	30,000
Remaining income	9,000	9,000	18,000
Net income	$29,000	$31,000	$60,000

capital balance at the beginning of the year. Residual profits or losses are to be divided equally between the partners. The schedule in Illustration 13.3 shows how the partnership net income for a year is distributed.

Partners' interest was figured at 10% of $200,000 of initial capital for Tripp and $100,000 of initial capital for Pierce.

Closing Entries

Closing entries for partnerships are very similar to those for proprietorships. Assuming that revenues and expenses for T&P have been closed into an Income Summary account, the final closing entries would appear as shown in Illustration 13.4.

Distributing Negative Amounts

Let us assume for a moment that T&P had earned only $36,000 of net income during its first year. The excess of salary and interest allowances would then be distributed as shown in Illustration 13.5 on the next page.

Had the income statement shown a net loss, a similar distribution would be made, with the net loss viewed simply as a *negative* net income. However, the partners' capital accounts would be *decreased* by the closing entries.

ILLUSTRATION 13.4

Dec. 31	Income Summary	60,000	
	Tripp, Capital		29,000
	Pierce, Capital		31,000
	To close net income to partners' capital accounts.		
31	Pierce, Capital	12,000	
	Pierce, Withdrawals		12,000
	To close partner's salary withdrawals to her capital account.		

OBJECTIVE 2. Distribute partnership net income or loss to partners' equity accounts.

ILLUSTRATION 13.5

INCOME DISTRIBUTION SCHEDULE			
	Tripp	**Pierce**	**Total**
Partner's salary	$ –0–	$12,000	$12,000
Partners' interest	20,000	10,000	30,000
Excess salary and interest	(3,000)	(3,000)	(6,000)
Net income	$17,000	$19,000	$36,000

THE STATEMENT OF PARTNERS' CAPITAL

A statement is usually prepared for a partnership that explains the changes in the partners' capital accounts for the year. Under the first assumption of $60,000 net income earned, the statement of partners' capital for T&P Company might appear as in Illustration 13.6.

THE BALANCE SHEET

A balance sheet for a partnership shows each partner's share of the owners' equity. Otherwise, partnership balance sheets look like those for proprietorships. A condensed balance sheet for T&P Company is shown in Illustration 13.7.

ADMISSION OF NEW PARTNERS

Purchase from Old Partners

When a partner sells a partnership interest to another person, most accountants simply transfer the old partner's capital balance to a capital account in

ILLUSTRATION 13.6

T&P COMPANY Statement of Partners' Capital For the Year Ended December 31, 19– –			
	Tripp	**Pierce**	**Total**
Initial capital balances	$200,000	$100,000	$300,000
Net income distribution	29,000	31,000	60,000
	$229,000	$131,000	$360,000
Less: withdrawals	–0–	12,000	12,000
Year-end capital balances	$229,000	$119,000	$348,000

ILLUSTRATION 13.7

T&P COMPANY
Balance Sheet
December 31, 19--

ASSETS		*LIABILITIES*		
Cash	$ 10,000	Accounts payable	$ 20,000	
Accounts receivable (net)	50,000	Notes payable	10,000	$ 30,000
Property, plant, and equipment (net)	318,000			
		PARTNERS' EQUITY		
		Tripp, capital	$229,000	
		Pierce, capital	119,000	348,000
		Total Liabilities and		
Total Assets	$378,000	Partners' Equity		$378,000

the new partner's name. Suppose that Beels sells his interest in the A&B Company to Catz for $150,000. Immediately before the sale, the old partners had the following capital balances.

Ames, Capital		Beels, Capital	
	150,000		150,000

The transfer of Beels's capital to Catz could be made in the partnership journal as follows.

Beels, Capital	150,000	
Catz, Capital		150,000
To transfer Beels's capital to Catz.		

Payment Amount Ignored.   The amount paid for a partnership interest may be more or less than the amount shown in the old partner's capital account. Also, a proportionate interest might be purchased from more than one old partner. Suppose, for example, that Catz had purchased a one-third interest in the A&B Company by paying Ames and Beels $60,000 each. The firm's accountant would most likely make the following entry to record Catz's entry into the partnership.

OBJECTIVE 3a. Record
the admission of a new
partner who pays cash
directly to old partners,
assuming that the amount
paid is ignored.

Ames, Capital	50,000	
Beels, Capital	50,000	
Catz, Capital		100,000
To record Catz's purchase of a one-third interest directly from Ames and Beels. $300,000 ÷ 3 = $100,000		

The three equity accounts would now stand as follows.

Ames, Capital		Beels, Capital		Catz, Capital
50,000	150,000	50,000	150,000	100,000

The foregoing entry ignores the amounts paid to the individual partners, and it credits the new partner with his proportionate share of the total equity as shown on the books. A firm's accountant may not know the details of private transactions between buying and selling partners. Even when the amount paid is known, some people argue that it should be ignored because the firm's assets and liabilities remain unchanged. Another view of the same transaction is discussed in the following paragraphs.

Assets Adjusted. If the accountant knows that Catz has paid $120,000 for equity that is shown on the books at $100,000, he should be at least mildly uneasy. Either Catz is a nitwit or the records do not reflect the full value of the partners' equity (and therefore the firm's assets). The latter conclusion would not be too shocking, since the accounting records usually show assets at their *cost* rather than their current *value*. Still, accountants do recognize the increased value of assets when they are sold—when there is objective evidence that someone is willing to pay more than their cost basis.

It might be argued that Catz's willingness to pay $120,000 to the old partners for a one-third interest is adequate evidence that he, at least, thinks the partnership equity must be worth three times that much, or $360,000. It then follows that the firm's assets should be increased by $60,000 at the time of Catz's entrance into the firm. If the firm's identifiable assets do not appear to be undervalued, perhaps the firm has *goodwill,* an intangible asset representing a firm's ability to earn an unusually high rate of net income.[2] With this approach, the entries in Illustration 13.8 might be made to reflect Catz's entrance into the firm.

---

[2] Goodwill is discussed in Chapter 8.

ILLUSTRATION 13.8

Goodwill (or other asset accounts)	60,000	
Ames, Capital		30,000
Beels, Capital		30,000
To recognize goodwill as suggested by the amount Catz is willing to pay for a one-third interest.		
Ames, Capital	60,000	
Beels, Capital	60,000	
Catz, Capital		120,000
To record Catz's purchase of a one-third interest directly from Ames and Beels. $360,000 \div 3 = \$120,000$		

OBJECTIVE 3b. Record the admission of a new partner who pays cash directly to old partners, assuming that partnership assets are adjusted.

Catz's equity account now reflects the full amount he paid for his interest.

Ames, Capital		Beels, Capital		Catz, Capital
60,000	150,000	60,000	150,000	120,000
	30,000		30,000	

If Catz had paid less for his share of the partnership than the book value of the equity he acquired, a downward adjustment of assets would be in order.

Of the two approaches for recording the purchase of a partnership interest directly from old partners, practicing accountants usually prefer to stick with the cost basis of assets, ignoring the actual amount paid by the new partner.

Contribution to the Partnership

Instead of buying an interest in a partnership directly from old partners, a new partner may contribute assets to the firm in exchange for an interest. Let us assume that Catz pays cash of $165,000 into the firm for a one-third share of the partnership.

Bonus Approach. If the new partner's investment of $165,000 is added to the $300,000 of old equity and the result is split three ways, each partner will have an equity balance of $155,000. The entry in Illustration 13.9 on the next page reflects into the new partner's capital account one-third of the total partnership equity.

This entry suggests that Catz has been generous to Ames and Beels by contributing $5,000 to each of them. *This manner of recording the admission*

ILLUSTRATION 13.9

OBJECTIVE 4a. Record
the admission of a new
partner who contributes
assets to the partnership,
assuming that the bonus
approach is used.

Cash	165,000	
Ames, Capital		5,000
Beels, Capital		5,000
Catz, Capital		155,000
To record Catz's payment for a one-third interest in the partnership.		
($300,000 + $165,000) ÷ 3 = $155,000		

*of a new partner, whereby the old partners' equity accounts are credited
for portions of the new partner's investment, is called the **bonus approach**.*
The bonus approach implies that the new partner pays a premium to the old
partners for the privilege of becoming a partner in the firm.

Assets Adjusted. It is unlikely that a new partner pays more than he or she
thinks the purchased interest is worth. Instead, the new partner probably
believes that the firm's equity (and its assets) are understated at the time
the interest is purchased. If Catz's one-third interest is really worth the
amount he pays, $165,000, then the original partners' shares must also be
worth $165,000 each. The first entry in Illustration 13.10 adjusts the firm's
assets to their implied value, and the second entry gives Catz full credit for
the amount he pays into the firm.

The partners' equity accounts now show balances consistent with the
amount Catz has paid for his interest in the firm.

Ames, Capital		Beels, Capital		Catz, Capital	
	150,000		150,000		165,000
	15,000		15,000		

ILLUSTRATION 13.10

OBJECTIVE 4b. Record
the admission of a new
partner who contributes
assets to the partnership,
assuming that partnership
assets are adjusted.

Goodwill (or other assets)	30,000	
Ames, Capital		15,000
Beels, Capital		15,000
To recognize goodwill as suggested by the amount Catz is willing to pay for a one-third interest.		
Cash	165,000	
Catz, Capital		165,000
To record Catz's admission to a one-third partnership interest.		

ILLUSTRATION 13.11

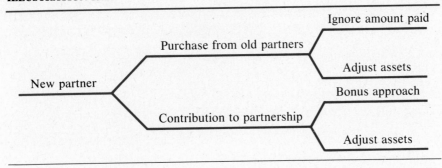

The diagram in Illustration 13.11 summarizes the approaches to recording a new partner's entry into a partnership. Keep in mind that most accountants prefer to avoid any adjustments of the asset accounts.

Perhaps it has occurred to you that a new partner might purchase an interest in a partnership for *less* than the partnership's assets seem to warrant. In that case, the accountant must choose one or more of the following three approaches to recording the new partner's investment.

1. Writing down overstated partnership assets to their fair values
2. Shifting portions of the old partners' equity balances to the new partner, as a bonus to the new partner
3. Recording as a new asset any goodwill brought to the firm by the new partner

PARTNERSHIP LIQUIDATIONS

The average life span of a partnership is much shorter than that of other forms of business. A partnership may terminate because of a disagreement between partners, the death of a partner, business failure, or other reasons. *The process of distributing the assets of a partnership among creditors and partners is known as **partnership liquidation**.*

Creditors' Claims

If a partnership is unable to pay a creditor, the creditor may seek payment from the personal assets of any of the partners because of the partners' *unlimited liability*. It is true, however, that partners' personal creditors have first claim on their personal assets, while partnership creditors have first claim on assets of the partnership.

If a partner pays partnership debts from personal funds, that partner is entitled to reimbursement from the other partners for their share of the obligation. This legal entitlement may be small consolation, however, if the

ILLUSTRATION 13.12

ABC COMPANY Condensed Balance Sheet November 30, 19––			
Cash	$ 50,000	Liabilities	$450,000
Other assets	600,000	A, capital	90,000
		B, capital	70,000
		C, capital	40,000
Total	$650,000	Total	$650,000

other partners have insufficient personal assets from which to meet their obligations.

In a partnership liquidation, care must be taken to distribute the firm's available cash to those who have the best legal claims to it. Creditors' claims should be satisified first, after which partners may receive cash according to their relative equity balances.

Gain on Liquidation

Any gains on liquidation of partnership assets are shared by partners in proportion to their profit-sharing ratios. As an example, consider the ABC Company, which has three partners who share profits and losses equally. A condensed balance sheet at November 30 appears as in Illustration 13.12.

Now, suppose the other assets are sold on November 30 for $630,000 cash. The liquidation schedule in Illustration 13.13 shows how the available cash should be distributed.

OBJECTIVE 5. Prepare a partnership liquidation schedule that shows the allocation of gains or losses and the distribution of cash.

Notice that final distributions of cash to partners are determined by their capital account balances, *not* their profit- and loss-sharing ratios. The balances of partners' capital accounts, after recognition of all liquidation gains and losses, are their respective claims to the cash that remains to be distributed.

ILLUSTRATION 13.13

ABC COMPANY Liquidation Schedule November 30, 19––						
					Equity	
	Cash	Other Assets	Liabilities	A	B	C
Balance before liquidation	$ 50,000	$600,000	$450,000	$ 90,000	$70,000	$40,000
Other assets sold	+ 630,000	− 600,000		+ 10,000	+ 10,000	+ 10,000
	$680,000	$ –0–	$450,000	$100,000	$80,000	$50,000
Cash distributed	− 680,000		− 450,000	− 100,000	− 80,000	− 50,000
	$ –0–	$ –0–	$ –0–	$ –0–	$ –0–	$ –0–

ILLUSTRATION 13.14

Nov. 30	Cash	630,000	
	Other Assets		600,000
	Gain on Sale of Assets		30,000
	Noncash assets sold.		
30	Gain on Sale of Assets	30,000	
	A, Capital		10,000
	B, Capital		10,000
	C, Capital		10,000
	Gain allocated to partners.		
30	Liabilities	450,000	
	Cash		450,000
	Liabilities paid.		
30	A, Capital	100,000	
	B, Capital	80,000	
	C, Capital	50,000	
	Cash		230,000
	Cash distributed to partners to close accounts.		

OBJECTIVE 6. Record the liquidation of a partnership.

In summary form, the journal entries to record the liquidation of ABC Company are as shown in Illustration 13.14.

Loss on Liquidation

No Capital Deficiencies. Partners will share any losses incurred during liquidation in proportion to their loss-sharing ratios. Suppose that ABC Company had sold its other assets for only $540,000. The liquidation schedule would then appear as in Illustration 13.15. And the journal entries to liquidate the partnership would be as shown in Illustration 13.16 on the next page.

OBJECTIVE 5. Prepare a partnership liquidation schedule that shows the allocation of gains or losses and the distribution of cash.

ILLUSTRATION 13.15

				Equity		
	Cash	Other Assets	Liabilities	A	B	C
ABC COMPANY **Liquidation Schedule** **November 30, 19--**						
Balance before liquidation	$ 50,000	$600,000	$450,000	$90,000	$70,000	$40,000
Other assets sold	+ 540,000	− 600,000		− 20,000	− 20,000	− 20,000
	$590,000	$ −0−	$450,000	$70,000	$50,000	$20,000
Cash distributed	− 590,000		− 450,000	− 70,000	− 50,000	− 20,000
	$ −0−	$ −0−	$ −0−	$ −0−	$ −0−	$ −0−

ILLUSTRATION 13.16

OBJECTIVE 6. Record
the liquidation of a
partnership.

Nov. 30	Cash	540,000	
	Loss on Sale of Assets	60,000	
	Other Assets		600,000
	Noncash assets sold.		
30	A, Capital	20,000	
	B, Capital	20,000	
	C, Capital	20,000	
	Loss on Sale of Assets		60,000
	Loss allocated to partners.		
30	Liabilities	450,000	
	Cash		450,000
	Liabilities paid.		
30	A, Capital	70,000	
	B, Capital	50,000	
	C, Capital	20,000	
	Cash		140,000
	Cash distributed to partners to close		
	accounts.		

Capital Deficiency. If losses are so great as to throw a partner's equity account to a negative balance (deficiency), the partner is obligated to pay that amount of cash into the firm—provided, of course, that the partner is able to do so. If ABC Company had sold its other assets for only $420,000, the liquidation schedule would appear as in Illustration 13.17.

Insolvent Partner. Now let us suppose that the facts are as we just described them except that C is personally *insolvent, which means he has insufficient assets from which to pay his debts.*

ILLUSTRATION 13.17

| | | | | Equity | | |
	Cash	Other Assets	Liabilities	A	B	C
Balance before liquidation	$ 50,000	$600,000	$450,000	$90,000	$70,000	$ 40,000
Other assets sold	+ 420,000	− 600,000		− 60,000	− 60,000	− 60,000
	$470,000	$ −0−	$450,000	$30,000	$10,000	$(20,000)
C pays in cash	+ 20,000					+ 20,000
	$490,000					$ −0−
Cash distributed	− 490,000		− 450,000	− 30,000	− 10,000	
	$ −0−	$ −0−	$ −0−	$ −0−	$ −0−	$ −0−

ABC COMPANY
Liquidation Schedule
November 30, 19−−

ILLUSTRATION 13.18

				Equity		
	Cash	Other Assets	Liabilities	A	B	C
Balance before liquidation	$ 50,000	$600,000	$450,000	$90,000	$70,000	$ 40,000
Other assets sold	+ 420,000	− 600,000		− 60,000	− 60,000	− 60,000
	$470,000	$ −0−	$450,000	$30,000	$10,000	$(20,000)
C's balance allocated				− 10,000	− 10,000	+ 20,000
				$20,000	$ −0−	$ −0−
Cash distributed	− 470,000		− 450,000	− 20,000		
	$ −0−	$ −0−	$ −0−	$ −0−	$ −0−	$ −0−

ABC COMPANY
Liquidation Schedule
November 30, 19−−

account must then be absorbed by the remaining partners in accordance with their relative loss-sharing ratios, as shown in the liquidation schedule in Illustration 13.18.

Cash Distribution Schedule

Noncash assets of a partnership may be sold off gradually over a period of time. To help ensure that available cash is distributed only to those parties with the best claims to it, a cash distribution schedule may be prepared. This schedule is derived by determining the relative size of the partners' equity balances, taking into consideration their loss-sharing ratios. For the ABC Company, where partners share losses equally, the relative abilities of the partners to absorb losses, as measured by their capital balances, can be determined as in Illustration 13.19.

ILLUSTRATION 13.19

ABC COMPANY
Relative Ability of Parties to Absorb Losses
At November 30, 19−−

	Total	A	B	C
Capital balances	$200,000	$90,000	$70,000	$40,000
Loss that would eliminate C's equity	− 120,000	− 40,000	− 40,000	− 40,000
Remainder	$ 80,000	$50,000	$30,000	$ −0−
Loss that would eliminate B's equity, assuming that C were insolvent	− 60,000	− 30,000	− 30,000	
Remainder	$ 20,000	$20,000	$ −0−	

ILLUSTRATION 13.20

OBJECTIVE 7. Prepare a
cash distribution schedule
for a liquidating
partnership showing how
available cash should be
distributed.

	ABC COMPANY Cash Distribution Schedule From November 30, 19– – Forward			
Cash Available	**Liabilities**	**A**	**B**	**C**
First $450,000	All			
Next $20,000		All		
Next $60,000		½	½	
Remaining cash		⅓	⅓	⅓

From the foregoing computation, we can prepare a schedule for the distribution of cash as it becomes available. This schedule, shown in Illustration 13.20, will honor the relative legal positions of the various parties, no matter what the gains or losses from liquidation turn out to be.

SUMMARY OF CHAPTER 13

Compared with other forms of business organizations, partnerships have a relatively short life expectancy. Conflicts between partners can be minimized by having a written partnership agreement specifying the responsibilities assigned to each partner.

Except for the owners' equity accounts, accounting for partnerships is much the same as accounting for other forms of business. Net incomes and net losses are allocated to the partners' capital accounts in accordance with the partnership agreement. Partners frequently agree to salary allowances to partners for services rendered, as well as to an interest allowance on partners' capital balances. Salary and interest allowances are not genuine expenses, but rather part of the overall plan for dividing profits among the partners.

A statement of partners' capital is usually prepared to explain the changes in the partners' capital accounts during an accounting period. Partnership income statements and balance sheets look much like those for other forms of business, except for the equity section of the balance sheets.

New partners may enter a partnership either by purchasing an interest directly from the old partners or by contributing assets to the partnership entity. Some accountants argue that partnership assets and equity accounts should be adjusted to reflect the firm's value implied by the amount paid by a new partner. However, most accountants prefer to leave the partnership's assets at their cost bases and to equalize the partners' equity accounts by means of bonus adjustments.

When a partnership is liquidated, care must be taken to ensure that cash is properly distributed among the creditors and partners in accordance with their legal rights. A liquidation schedule may be prepared to show how liquidation gains or losses are distributed and how the available cash is to be disbursed. A cash distribution schedule ensures that cash will be distributed to the proper parties as it becomes available during the process of liquidating a partnership.

GLOSSARY FOR CHAPTER 13

Bonus approach   A manner of recording the admission of a new partner, whereby the old partners' equity accounts are credited for portions of the new partner's investment.

Insolvent   Having insufficient assets from which to pay one's debts.

Managing partner   A partner who is assigned the overall responsibility of administering the partnership.

Mutual agency   The overlapping rights of partners, in the absence of a contrary agreement, to represent the firm as agents in any areas within the apparent scope of the firm's business.

Partnership   An association of two or more persons to carry on as co-owners a business for profit.

Partnership agreement (articles of partnership)   A formal written agreement among partners in a partnership.

Partnership liquidation   The process of distributing the assets of a partnership among creditors and partners.

Partners' salaries   Allowances to individual partners for services rendered to the partnership.

Uniform Partnership Act   A set of laws, enacted by most states, governing the formation, operation, and dissolution of partnerships.

Unlimited liability   The responsibility of a partner to stand personally liable for partnership debts.

SELF-QUIZ ON OBJECTIVES FOR CHAPTER 13
Solutions to Self-Quiz begin on page B-42.

1. Traude and Weil agreed to form the Traude-Weil Company on January 2, 19X4, with initial cash investments of $80,000 from Traude and $20,000 from Weil. The partners are to be allowed 8% interest on their capital balances at the beginning of each year, and Weil is to draw a cash salary allowance of $900 each month. Residual profits and losses are to be shared equally by the partners. Revenues and expenses for 19X4 have been closed to an Income Summary account, which shows a net income balance of $24,000 before any salary and expense allowances to the partners.

   a. **OBJECTIVE 1.** Journalize the formation of the partnership.

   b. **OBJECTIVE 2.** Make the entries to close the Income Summary and Weil, Withdrawals accounts at year-end.

2. Reede and Farley are equal partners with capital balances of $90,000 each. Record at July 1 Lyon's purchase of a one-third interest in the Reede & Farley Company, assuming the following:

   a. **OBJECTIVE 3.** Lyon pays cash of $35,000 directly to each of the old partners and

   1) The amount of the payment is ignored.

   2) Goodwill is recognized at the time that Lyon is admitted to the partnership.

   b. **OBJECTIVE 4.** Lyon pays cash of $96,000 into the partnership and

   1) The bonus approach is used.

   2) Goodwill is recognized at the time that Lyon is admitted to the partnership.

3. The LMN Company has been doing poorly, and the partners have agreed to liquidate the partnership. A condensed balance sheet at May 31 is shown here. The partners share profits and losses equally, and all partners are personally wealthy.

LMN COMPANY Condensed Balance Sheet May 31, 19--			
Cash	$ 6,000	Liabilities	$160,000
Other assets	294,000	L, capital	60,000
		M, capital	50,000
		N, capital	30,000
Total	$300,000	Total	$300,000

a. OBJECTIVE 7. Prepare a cash distribution schedule to show how cash should be distributed as it becomes available.

b. Assuming that noncash assets are sold for $249,000 cash on May 31 prepare

   1) OBJECTIVE 5. A partnership liquidation schedule.

   2) OBJECTIVE 6. Formal entries to record the liquidation of the partnership, assuming all cash is distributed on May 31.

DISCUSSION QUESTIONS FOR CHAPTER 13

1. A partnership may be formed by means of a loose verbal agreement. Why is it advisable for partners to have a written partnership agreement?

2. What are the possible consequences of the unlimited liability to which partners are exposed?

3. What are some events that can result in the termination of a partnership?

4. Unless otherwise agreed, how do partners share in profits and losses?

5. How is partnership income reported for purposes of federal income taxation?

6. A new partner, entering a partnership, may agree to pay an amount that implies that partnership assets and equity accounts are understated on the books. In such cases, how do most accountants choose to reflect the new partner's entry into the firm?

7. What does partnership liquidation mean?

8. Do partnership creditors have claims on the personal assets of partners that are equivalent to those of the partners' personal creditors? Explain.

9. Under what circumstances may one partner become a creditor to the other partners during a partnership liquidation?

EXERCISES FOR CHAPTER 13

13.1. On January 1 Foster and Daily form a partnership called the Foster and Daily Company. Foster contributes $150,000 cash to the company and Daily contributes equipment valued at $30,000 and wild animals valued at $20,000. Journalize the formation of the company.

13.2. Foster and Daily agree that they are each to be allowed 10% interest on their capital balances at the beginning of the year and that the residual net income or loss is to be shared equally. At the beginning of the year, the capital balances are $150,000 and $50,000, respectively. Revenue and expenses for the year have been closed to an Income Summary account, which shows a net income balance of $36,000.

    a. Make entries to close the Income Summary account on December 31.

    b. Prepare a statement of partners' capital for the year ended December 31.

13.3. At December 31, 19X4, the capital balances for Blake and Moss in the Blake & Moss Company were $60,000 and $120,000, respectively. With Moss's approval, Blake sells his share of the partnership to Carpenter for $75,000 on January 2, 19X5.

    a. Assuming that the difference between total cost and implied value of the firm's assets is to be ignored, make the entry to reflect the admission of the new partner.

    b. Assuming that implied goodwill is to be recognized, make the entries to reflect the admission of the new partner.

13.4. Fenton and Folker are law partners. At April 1 the balances in their capital accounts are $60,000 each. They agree to take Fipps in as a one-third partner if she pays $78,000 into the firm. Record the transaction:

    a. Using the bonus approach.

    b. Adjusting assets for implied goodwill.

    c. Using the bonus approach, but assuming that Fipps paid only $51,000 for a one-third interest.

13.5. Benton, Barton, and Bowls agreed to form a partnership on January 2 with initial cash investments of $120,000, $60,000, and $20,000, respectively. Each year, partners are to be allowed 10% interest on their capital balances at the beginning of the year, and Bowls is to draw a cash salary allowance of $1,000 per month. Residual profits and losses, after partners' interest and salary, are to be shared equally by the partners. Revenues and expenses for the first year have been closed to an Income Summary account, which shows a net income balance of $41,000 before any salary and interest allowances to the partners.

    a. Journalize on January 2 the formation of the partnership.

    b. Make the entries on December 31 to close the Income Summary and Bowls, Withdrawals accounts.

PROBLEMS FOR CHAPTER 13
Alternate Problems for this chapter begin on page D-78.

13.6. Axel and Rod are equal partners with capital balances of $54,000 each at September 1.

Required

Record Gump's purchase of a one-third interest in the Axelrod Company on September 1, assuming the following:

1) Gump pays cash of $30,000 directly to each of the old partners, and

   a) The amount of the payment is ignored by the accountant.

   b) Goodwill is recognized at the time Gump is admitted.

2) Gump pays cash of $20,000 directly to each of the old partners, and the amount of the payment is ignored.

13.7. Jenks, Barker, and Love are partners with capital balances of $60,000 each on October 15.

Required

Record Smith's purchase of a one-fourth interest in the Jenks, Barker, and Love Company on October 15 assuming the following:

1) Smith pays cash of $52,000 into the partnership, and

   a) An appropriate bonus is credited to the new partner.

   b) Goodwill of $8,000 is brought to the firm in the form of the new partner's business contacts and previous experience.

   c) The price paid by the new partner reflects the fact that one of the firm's assets, Trademarks, is overstated by $24,000.

2) Smith pays cash of $72,000 into the partnership, and

   a) The bonus approach is used in making the entry.

   b) Goodwill is recognized at the time that Smith is admitted.

13.8. The partners who own the Quirk Company have agreed to liquidate the partnership. A condensed balance sheet at August 31 is shown here. The partners share profits and losses equally, and all partners are personally wealthy.

QUIRK COMPANY Condensed Balance Sheet August 31, 19--			
Cash	$ 20,000	Liabilities	$160,000
Other assets	380,000	Abel, capital	120,000
		Baker, capital	80,000
		Charlie, capital	40,000
Total	$400,000	Total	$400,000

Required

1) Assuming that noncash assets are sold for $311,000 cash on August 31,

   a) Prepare a partnership liquidation schedule.

   b) Prepare formal entries to record the liquidation of the partnership, assuming that all cash is distributed on August 31.

2) Assuming that noncash assets are sold for $230,000 cash on August 31,

   a) Prepare a partnership liquidation schedule.

   b) Prepare formal entries to record the liquidation of the partnership, assuming that all cash is distributed on August 31.

13.9. The Colt Resources Company is owned by four partners whose capital account balances at May 31 are as follows.

Alex, Capital	$100,000
Gordo, Capital	80,000
Flip, Capital	300,000
Uze, Capital	120,000

The partners share profits and losses equally.

Required

Prepare a cash distribution schedule that shows how cash should be distributed as it becomes available, assuming that the company has liabilities of $425,000.

13.10. The following selected events pertain to the JCW partnership.

19X4

Jan. 2   James and Carter contributed $25,000 cash each and Williams contributed equipment valued at $25,000 to form the JCW Company.

Mar. 31   Parker contributed $37,000 to the partnership and was admitted as a one-fourth partner (use the bonus approach).

Dec. 31   The credit balance of $45,000 in the Income Summary account was closed to the partners' capital accounts. Because Parker was a partner for only part of the year, she gets only three-quarters of a normal share. (The credit balance in the Income Summary account resulted from closing the revenue and expense accounts for the year.)

19X5

Jan. 2   James decided to start his own company and forced liquidation of the partnership. Cash showed a balance of $40,000 before noncash assets carried on the books at $214,000 were sold for $150,000 cash. Liabilities totaled $97,000. Liquidation losses were borne equally by the partners.

Required

Make general journal entries to record the foregoing events.

13.11. Boggs and Slover are partners in the B&S Company. For the year ended December 31, 19X4, the partnership earned a net income of $60,000, which appears as a credit balance in the Income Summary account. On January 1, 19X4, Boggs's capital balance was $90,000 while Slover's balance was $30,000.

Required

Make closing journal entries to allocate the net income to the partners' capital accounts, assuming the following:

1) Profits and losses are shared equally.

2) Profits and losses are shared 60% by Boggs, 40% by Slover.

3) Profits and losses are shared in proportion to the partners' capital balances at the beginning of the year.

4) Profits and losses are shared equally, except that partners first receive 8% interest on their beginning capital balances.

5) Slover receives a $20,000 salary allowance, with residual income shared in proportion to partners' beginning capital balances.

13.12. A balance sheet for the NOP Company is shown here. Nichol, Oliver, and Paris share partnership profits and losses in the ratio of 6:3:1.

NOP COMPANY **Balance Sheet** **December 31, 19 – –**		
ASSETS		
Cash		$ 40,000
Equipment	$ 60,000	
Less: Accumulated depreciation	12,000	48,000
Building	300,000	
Less: Accumulated depreciation	120,000	180,000
Land		50,000
Total Assets		$318,000
LIABILITIES		
Accounts payable	$ 38,000	
Notes payable	100,000	
Total Liabilities		$138,000
PARTNERS' EQUITY		
Nichol, capital	$108,000	
Oliver, capital	54,000	
Paris, capital	18,000	
Total Partners' Equity		180,000
Total Liabilities and Partners' Equity		$318,000

Required

Make journal entries to record the liquidation of the partnership on December 31, with each of the following assumptions.

1) Noncash assets are sold for the following amounts of cash.

Land	$ 80,000
Building	220,000
Equipment	40,000

2) Noncash assets are sold for the following amounts of cash.

Land	$50,000
Building	50,000
Equipment	18,000

13.13. D&P Refrigeration Service was started on October 1 with partners agreeing to share profits and losses equally. Transactions for October are as follows.

Transactions

Oct. 1   D. Dunkin and F. Pollin each deposited $7,500 in a bank account in the name of D&P Refrigeration Service.

3   Purchased supplies for $200 cash. All supplies are expected to be used in October.

4   Received $1,000 cash for services rendered.

9   Billed customers for services rendered on account, $1,200.

15   Paid October rent, $800.

15   Paid employee wages, $600.

19   Collected $1,200 of accounts receivable.

20   Purchased land for $9,000 cash as a future building site.

30   Purchased office equipment for $6,000 by paying $1,000 cash and signing a note for the balance.

30   D. Dunkin and F. Pollin each withdrew $500 for their personal use.

31   Billed customers for services rendered, $2,000.

31   Paid employee wages, $600.

31   Paid utilities bills for October totaling $150.

Required

1) Make general journal entries for the October transactions, starting with journal page 1.

2) Open up ledger accounts and post the October entries. Number each account and cross-reference postings.

3) Prepare an income statement for October and a balance sheet at October 31.

4) Make closing entries and post to ledger accounts.

COMPREHENSION PROBLEM FOR CHAPTER 13

13.14. Kelly, Rose, and Smith own the KRS Company. Smith, without the knowledge of his partners, made several investments in the name of the partnership that now have little or no value. Kelly and Rose are personally wealthy, while Smith only has net personal assets (after meeting the claims of personal creditors) of $10,000. The partnership agreement provides that Kelly, Rose, and Smith share profits and losses in the ratio 40:40:20. A condensed balance sheet at September 30 is shown here.

KRS COMPANY Condensed Balance Sheet September 30, 19--			
Cash	$ 12,000	Liabilities	$252,000
Other assets	420,000	Kelly, capital	72,000
		Rose, capital	72,000
		Smith, capital	36,000
Total	$432,000	Total	$432,000

Required

1) Assuming that noncash assets are sold for $100,000 cash on September 30, prepare a partnership liquidation schedule.

2) Prepare journal entries to record the liquidation of the partnership, assuming all cash is distributed on September 30.

3) What recourse, if any, do Kelly and Rose have against Smith?

4) What could Kelly and Rose have done in the past to protect themselves against the losses they suffered?

5) Smith was heard to remark, "Kelly and Rose have nothing to complain about because they can recover their losses by offsetting them against profits from other sources." Comment on the validity, or lack thereof, of Smith's remark.

14

Corporations: Capital Stock

OBJECTIVES

This chapter deals with the nature of corporations and capital stock transactions. At the conclusion of this chapter, you should be able to

1. State in your own words at least five attributes that distinguish corporations from other forms of business organizations.
2. Record subscriptions receivable and their subsequent collection.
3. Record the issuance of capital stock.
4. Record the acquisition and reissuance of treasury stock.
5. State what a stock split is.
6. Differentiate between the expressions *par value, book value,* and *market value* as these terms relate to shares of stock.

WHAT IS A CORPORATION?

A corporation is conceived initially by one or more persons (promoters, incorporators) with an idea for a new business. *A corporation is an artificial, but independent, legal entity that has the right to contract and own property as though it were a person, and in which ownership is represented by shares of stock. A corporation is officially created by a state government through the issuance of a document called a* **certificate of incorporation,** *which is a grant of authority for the corporation to exist.* [1] The operation of a corporation

---

[1] Some corporations have been created by actions of the federal government. For instance, national banks and quasi-government corporations such as the Tennessee Valley Authority are federally chartered.

is governed by the corporation laws of the various states and by the provisions of its certificate of incorporation.

Equity Potential

It was no accident that the Industrial Revolution was marked by a greater use of the corporate form of business. A corporation allows numerous investors to pool their wealth (capital) in order to gain the economic benefits of large-scale operations.

*Ownership rights in a corporation are represented by **capital stock shares** that can be legally transferred to others. Owners of corporate stock are called **shareholders** or **stockholders**.*

A corporation's equity capital can continue to grow as long as people are willing to invest in its stock. In addition, a corporation can reinvest (retain) annual earnings that are not paid out as dividends to shareholders.

The ability of a corporation to accumulate equity capital is potentially much greater than that of a proprietorship or partnership. The equity of a proprietorship or partnership is limited to the wealth of its owners. Although a partnership may legally have any number of partners, the close identity of all partners with the entity tends to make a large partnership somewhat awkward and difficult to manage.

We should mention, however, that some corporations have only one or a very few shareholders. In fact, the outward appearance of many corporations is no different from that of proprietorships or partnerships. Nevertheless, the *potential* for a corporate form of business to accumulate capital is tremendous, as evidenced by the giant international corporations.

Transferability of Ownership

One of the characteristics of a corporation is transferability of ownership. This means that shareholders are free to sell all or any portion of their shares any time they wish—provided, of course, there are buyers. Unlike proprietorships and partnerships, sales of ownership rights do not interrupt the legal lives of corporations.

Limited Liability

Perhaps the most important single attribute of the corporate form is that shareholders are not personally liable for the corporation's debts unless they personally guarantee payment. In other words, the potential financial losses of shareholders are limited to their investments in the shares they own.

Consider, on the other hand, the legal position of proprietors and partners. They are personally liable for business debts. If the business should fail, a proprietor or partner could end up losing his or her home, car, and other personal assets.

The limited liability feature of a corporation stems from the fact that contracts are made in the corporation's name with the understanding that creditors can collect only from the corporation. As a result, creditors should be cautious in dealing with corporations. Lenders sometimes overcome the limited liability feature by requiring the shareholders in small corporations to personally endorse (guarantee) corporate obligations.

Unlimited Life

The potential life of a corporation is unlimited, or infinite, because a corporation is legally an independent entity, not tied to the lives of people. A proprietorship ends with the owner's death, and the death of one partner legally terminates a partnership. Since a corporation is an artificial entity, its life does not necessarily end when human lives do.

Management

Corporate managers are salaried employees of the corporation and are not required to own any shares of the business they manage. The limited liability, free transferability of ownership, and other corporate features encourage a greater separation of ownership and management than is found in proprietorships and partnerships. Large corporations, in particular, tend to rely on hired managers to run their daily operations and plan for future developments.

Shareholders do exercise some measure of control over the corporation in which they own shares. At annual shareholder meetings, a *board of directors* is elected. The board of directors establishes operating policies and employs the principal officers who manage the corporate operations. Depending on the size and complexity of the corporation, middle-level and lower-level managers may be employed by the officers to help run the corporation. Illustration 14.1 shows the relationship between the shareholders, directors, and officers of a corporation.

ILLUSTRATION 14.1

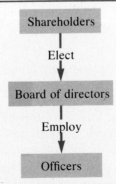

Government Control

Corporations are subject to more government control than are proprietorships and partnerships. To begin with, a corporation is more difficult to create than other types of business. Forms must be filled out, and fees must be paid for the privilege of having a new corporate entity created by the state. Thereafter, annual reports to the state may be required, minutes of stockholders' and directors' meetings must be written and properly filed, and names and addresses of stockholders must be kept accurate and up to date.

When a corporation publicly issues securities (equity shares or debt instruments) above a specified amount, or when any new securities are sold interstate or through the U.S. Postal Service, the corporation must file a *registration statement* with the Securities and Exchange Commission (SEC). The purpose of this is to ensure that potential investors have adequate information for making investment decisions. When a corporation's stock is traded on an organized securities exchange, the corporation is required to file annual reports with the SEC, and these must contain accounting statements audited by certified public accountants. Corporations may be subject to additional regulations by the securities exchanges on which their shares are traded.

Corporations may have to comply with numerous other federal, state, and local reporting requirements, depending on the particular circumstances. Banking, insurance, and utility corporations, as well as many other types, are regulated by special government agencies.

Taxation

As an independent legal entity, a corporation is required to pay income taxes on taxable earnings. On the other hand, proprietorships and partnerships do not pay income taxes; net incomes of these concerns are reported by the individual owners on their personal tax returns.

Contrary to popular belief, the corporate form of organization does not always offer tax advantages. In fact, operating as a corporation can be a rather severe tax disadvantage. The circumstances under which incorporation can be advantageous for tax purposes are discussed in the next chapter.

Some of the more important distinguishing attributes of corporations, as compared with proprietorships and partnerships, are summarized here.

1. Greater potential for accumulating equity capital
2. Easy transferability of ownership
3. Limited liability of owners for business debts
4. Potential for unlimited life
5. Tendency for separation of management from ownership
6. Greater control by governments
7. Obligation of the entity to pay income taxes

OBJECTIVE 1. State the attributes that distinguish corporations from other forms of business organizations.

WHAT IS STOCK?

Stock Certificates

As previously pointed out, corporate ownership rights are represented by shares of stock. Investors pay cash or other assets into a corporation in exchange for shares. The corporation issues *a formal document called a stock certificate to each investor to evidence the number of shares acquired.* If an investor acquires additional shares of stock at a later time, another certificate is issued to cover them. A specimen stock certificate is shown in Illustration 14.2. A stock certificate shows the owner's name, the number of shares held, and the date on which they were purchased.

A shareholder may transfer ownership of shares by endorsing the back of a stock certificate. A new stock certificate is then issued by the corporation or its transfer agent in the name of the new owner. If only some of the shares represented by a stock certificate are sold, then a new certificate must also be issued to evidence the smaller number of shares retained by the seller.

An entry to record the issuance of stock takes the following form.

Cash (or other assets)	XXX	
Capital Stock		XXX

ILLUSTRATION 14.2

SOURCE: Reproduced with permission of AT&T

When different classes of stock (common, preferred, etc.) are present, the entry must indicate which class of stock is being issued.

Common Stock

A certificate of incorporation may authorize the issuance of several classes of capital stock. The most common type is called, aptly enough, common stock. *Common stock represents the most basic ownership equity of a corporation.* Owners of common shares have a right to vote at shareholder meetings and share in the profits that are left after all prior claims are met. For this reason, the equity of owners of common stock is sometimes referred to as *residual* equity.

Although different classes of common stock sometimes exist (Class A Common, Class B Common, and so on), most corporations issue only one class of common stock.

In addition to their voting and profit-sharing rights, in most states owners of common stock have the *preemptive right to maintain their proportionate ownership interest in the corporation.* This means that a shareholder who owns 10% of the outstanding common stock has the right to acquire 10% of any new common stock that is issued. If a shareholder does not care to exercise this preemptive right, the shares may be issued to other persons. Shareholders may vote at shareholder meetings to waive their preemptive rights.

If the corporation goes out of business, owners of common shares have the right to share in any assets that are left over after satisfying all parties with prior claims. This right is of little consequence when a corporation is in financial difficulty, since few bankrupt companies have assets enough to satisfy even their creditors.

Preferred Stock

Shares of stock that provide preference claims to profits and to corporation assets in the event of liquidation are called **preferred stock**. Whereas all business corporations must have common shareholders, relatively few corporations issue preferred stock. The issuance of preferred stock is recorded in the following manner.

Cash (or other assets)	XXX	
Preferred Stock		XXX

Although preferred stock may differ from one corporation to the next, preferred shares have historically provided for a fixed dividend return but no voting power. The fixed return may be stated as a certain number of dollars per year (for example, $8 preferred) or as a percentage of par value

OBJECTIVE 6.
Differentiate between
par value, book value,
and market value.

per share (for example, 8%, $100 par preferred). Some modern preferred issues provide for floating dividend rates that change along with prevailing interest rates. *Par value is a stated face amount per share.* Do not confuse par value with market value (sales value) or book value. *The book value per share of stock is simply the amount of equity shown in the accounts for a class of stock divided by the number of shares of stock outstanding.*

Most preferred shares outstanding today are cumulative, nonparticipating, and callable. *Cumulative preferred stock provides that if preferred dividends are not declared for any year, these dividends accumulate, and all accumulated preferred dividends must be paid before any dividends may be paid on common shares. Accumulated, but undeclared, preferred dividends, referred to as **dividends in arrears**,* are not recognized by accountants as liabilities of the corporation. However, they should be disclosed by means of a footnote to, or parenthetical remark in, the balance sheet.

Participating preferred stock permits preferred shareholders to share in profits of the corporation beyond a minimum fixed dividend rate. As we have said, most preferred stock is *non*participating.

*Callable preferred stock allows the shares to be redeemed (called in) by the corporation, usually at some stipulated premium amount per share known as the call premium. A **call premium** is an extra amount above the par value of a security that must be paid upon forced redemption by the corporation.* For example, preferred shares with $100 par value may provide that the corporation can redeem the stock at $110 per share—that is, a call premium of $10 per share. However, in the event of liquidation of the corporation, preferred shareholders could expect to receive at most only the par value of their shares.

Since both dividends and asset claims are tied to par value, the market value of a preferred share will not normally fluctuate far away from par, unless the share is convertible into common shares at the shareholder's option. *A convertible preferred stock share can be exchanged for a specified number of common stock shares at the request of the preferred shareholder.* The market value of a convertible preferred share will most likely fluctuate along with the value of the number of common shares into which it is convertible, with the par value of the preferred share acting as an approximate minimum price.

FORMATION OF A CORPORATION

Organization Costs

A corporation is usually formed through the efforts of *a group of individuals known as **incorporators**, who undertake the legal and other work necessary to bring the corporation into existence.* The legal, accounting, and charter fees, as well as the other costs incurred in forming a corporation, are called *organization costs*.[2] These costs are considered an intangible corporate asset, and theoretically, they should be matched against all future revenues that the entity generates. As pointed out in Chapter 8, intangible assets are amortized in practice over periods of time not exceeding 40 years.[3] Most accountants choose to amortize organization costs over the first 5 years of a firm's life, probably because the Internal Revenue Code sets 60 months as the minimum amortization period for tax purposes.

Stock Subscriptions

Incorporators may get potential stockholders to sign *stock subscriptions, which are agreements to take certain numbers of shares at a specified issue price.* Stock subscriptions are in effect offers to purchase shares; the subscriptions become contracts when they are accepted by the corporation. When a new corporation comes into existence through issue of its certificate of incorporation, subscriptions are accepted and recorded in the accounts.

Assume, for example, that investors have agreed to purchase 20,000 shares of common stock at their par value of $10 per share. Until such time as the shares are issued, the equity will be shown in a Common Stock Subscribed account as follows.

Jan. 15	Subscriptions Receivable—Common	200,000	
	Common Stock Subscribed		200,000
	20,000 shares, $10 par, common subscribed at par.		

OBJECTIVE 2. Record subscriptions receivable and their subsequent collection.

Common Stock Subscribed is viewed as an equity claim against the corporation. In fact, it is balanced by the asset Subscriptions Receivable, and the accounts can be portrayed in an accounting equation as follows.

Assets	=	Liabilities	+	Shareholders' Equity
Subscriptions Receivable—Common				Common Stock Subscribed
200,000				200,000

As cash or other assets are received in payment, the receivable is reduced.

---

[2]Organization costs were defined in Chapter 8 as the start-up costs of forming a new business enterprise.

[3]APB, "Intangible Assets," *Opinion of the Accounting Principles Board No. 17* (New York: American Institute of Certified Public Accountants, 1970), par. 29.

OBJECTIVE 2.   Record
subscriptions receivable
and their subsequent
collection.

Jan. 25	Cash	50,000	
	Subscriptions Receivable—Common		50,000
	Collected from subscribers.		

When shares have been fully paid for, they are issued by the corporation to the subscribers. The entry to reflect the issuance of the subscribed stock would appear as follows.

OBJECTIVE 3.   Record
the issuance of capital
stock.

Feb. 10	Common Stock Subscribed	200,000	
	Common Stock		200,000
	20,000 shares issued to subscribers.		

If a subscriber pays part but not all of the subscription due, the result will depend on the state law and on the attitude of the board of directors. The partial payment may be (1) returned to the defaulting subscriber, (2) considered forfeited and kept by the corporation, or (3) applied toward the purchase of a smaller number of shares.

Now let us assume that subscribers had agreed to pay $15 per share for the 20,000 shares of $10 par stock. Accountants traditionally have differentiated between the par value of equity shares and payments by shareholders in excess of par. The following entry reflects only the par value of the shares into the Common Stock Subscribed account.

OBJECTIVE 2.   Record
subscriptions receivable
and their subsequent
collection.

Jan. 15	Subscriptions Receivable—Common	300,000	
	Common Stock Subscribed		200,000
	Capital in Excess of Par		100,000
	20,000 shares, $10 par, common subscribed at		
	$15 per share.		

As shares are fully paid, the Capital Stock Subscribed account is reduced, and the Common Stock account increased, for the par value of shares that are issued. The amount in the Capital in Excess of Par account is left undisturbed on the books as permanent shareholders' equity.

Par value per share has been viewed traditionally as the legal minimum of capital that is committed to the corporate entity. Actually, par value may be arbitrarily set at any amount and has little practical significance today. It is not unusual for shares of $1 par to be issued for many times the par amount (say, $20 per share). And after years of successful operation, par value becomes even more distant from any reasonable value of the shares.

No-Par Stock

Some states now permit corporations to issue *no-par stock—that is, stock without any designated legal face value.* When no-par common stock is issued, whatever is received for it can be recorded in the Common Stock account.

Even with no-par stock, incorporators, directors, and others seem to feel the need for some stated amount per share. *Frequently, no-par shares will be designated an arbitrary stated value per share.* As with par value, the stated value of shares is usually identified separately in the accounts. For example, an issue of 20,000 shares of $1 stated value stock at $15 per share would likely be recorded as follows.

Cash	300,000	
Common Stock		20,000
Capital in Excess of Stated Value		280,000
20,000 shares, $1 stated value, issued at $15 per share.		

OBJECTIVE 3. Record the issuance of capital stock.

OTHER STOCK TRANSACTIONS

Stock Issued in Exchange for Property

Corporations sometimes issue shares of stock in exchange for property, in which case the property is recorded on the books at fair market value.[4] For example, if 10,000 shares of $10 par common stock are issued for land and building worth $50,000 and $80,000, respectively, the entry might appear as follows.

Land	50,000	
Building	80,000	
Common Stock		100,000
Capital in Excess of Par		30,000
To record the fair value of property received for 10,000 shares of $10 par common stock.		

OBJECTIVE 3. Record the issuance of capital stock.

New Issues of Stock

As corporations grow, they may need new infusions of equity capital beyond that which they accumulate through retention of earnings. Subsequent issues

---

[4] For federal tax purposes a corporation adopts, for property acquired from a controlling shareholder, that shareholder's cost basis (Code Sec. 362[a]). Also, there may be special basis problems associated with business combinations, a topic covered in advanced accounting classes.

of new securities may be accomplished with stock subscriptions or with direct issues of stock for cash. In either case, corporations will attempt to issue the new shares for approximately what the old shares are selling for in the stock markets. The difference between the *market value* of the new shares and their par or stated value is then recorded in a Capital in Excess of Par (or Stated Value) account.

The preemptive rights of shareholders must be honored when new shares are issued. That is, shareholders must be given the right to maintain their proportionate ownership interests in the corporation. This is usually accomplished by providing each present shareholder with stock rights, which they may either exercise or sell to others. *A **stock right** is the privilege that is associated with each outstanding share of stock to acquire a proportionate amount of new shares issued.* For example, if 100,000 shares of common stock are already outstanding when 50,000 new shares are being issued, each shareholder is given a right to purchase one-half new share for each old share held. In other words, present shareholders can buy one new share with two stock rights. Problems associated with accounting for stock rights are left to more advanced courses in accounting.

Redemption of Stock

A corporation may redeem (retire) some of the outstanding shares by purchasing them from shareholders and canceling the stock certificates. The reason for doing this may be that excess cash is available and not needed for other purposes. Reducing the number of outstanding shares means that future earnings of the corporation will be spread over fewer shares, resulting in a larger return for the remaining shareholders.

When shares are retired, the amounts that were originally put into equity accounts are removed, and any excess amount that was paid for the shares is debited to the Retained Earnings account. Suppose, for example, that 500 shares of $10 par common stock, issued originally for $15 per share, are acquired by the corporation for $18 a share and canceled. The entry would be recorded as follows.

Common Stock	5,000	
Capital in Excess of Par	2,500	
Retained Earnings	1,500	
Cash		9,000
Redeemed 500 shares of common at $18 per share.		

Retained earnings are the accumulated profits (net incomes) of a corporation that have not been declared as dividends. Retained earnings activities are discussed at greater length in the next chapter.

If shares are bought back for less than the original issue price, the difference may be left in the Capital in Excess of Par account. If the previously mentioned shares are bought back for $13 per share, the entry would appear as follows.

Common Stock	5,000	
Capital in Excess of Par	1,500	
Cash		6,500
Redeemed 500 shares of common at $13 per share.		

Treasury Stock

Sometimes a corporation will acquire shares of its own stock and hold them as treasury stock. *Treasury stock is reacquired but uncanceled stock that may be reissued by the corporation without concern for the preemptive rights of the shareholders.* Legally, the preemptive right of shareholders applies only to *new issues* of shares.

Treasury shares may be acquired at bargain prices and reissued when share prices are high. Such trading in one's own stock helps to stabilize share prices over time, and long-time shareholders benefit from trading "gains." However, a corporation is not viewed as profiting from treasury stock transactions, because treasury shares are not assets of the corporation.

Treasury shares are sometimes acquired and reissued to officers or other employees of the corporation as part of their compensation—and as an incentive to help make the corporation a highly profitable one.

The cost of treasury stock is debited to an account by that name, as illustrated by the following entry.[5]

Treasury Stock	4,000	
Cash		4,000
200 shares of treasury stock acquired at $20 per share.		

OBJECTIVE 4. Record the acquisition of treasury stock.

Since the shares were not canceled, the equity accounts were not reduced directly. However, the Treasury Stock account does represent a reduction in common equity and is thus a contra equity account. *Do not* be misled into thinking that treasury stock is an asset of the corporation. A corporation cannot own portions of itself.

The balance in the Treasury Stock account is generally viewed as a restriction against retained earnings available for dividends. This restriction is therefore disclosed in some way in balance sheet presentations. The equity section pictured in Illustration 14.3 discloses the restriction as a parenthetical remark.

---

[5]Some accountants prefer to carry Treasury Stock on the books at the par or stated value of the shares. Alternative approaches to accounting for treasury shares are left to more advanced courses in accounting.

ILLUSTRATION 14.3

SHAREHOLDERS' EQUITY		
Common stock, $10 par, 20,000 shares issued, of which 500 shares are held as treasury stock	$200,000	
Capital in excess of par	100,000	
Retained earnings ($4,000, the cost of treasury stock, is unavailable for dividends)	40,000	
	$340,000	
Less: Treasury stock, 200 shares at cost	4,000	
Total Shareholders' Equity		336,000

Reissue of Treasury Stock. No gains or losses are recognized by corporations from buying and selling their own shares. If treasury shares are reissued for more than their cost, the excess is credited to a Capital from Reissue of Treasury Shares account, as illustrated here.

OBJECTIVE 4. Record the reissuance of treasury stock.

Cash	4,200	
Treasury Stock		4,000
Capital from Reissue of Treasury Shares		200
200 shares of treasury stock, $20 cost, reissued for $21 per share.		

In the rare instance where treasury shares are reissued for less than their cost, the difference is debited to Retained Earnings, unless there is a sufficient balance in Capital from Reissue of Treasury Shares as a result of prior treasury stock transactions. The following entry illustrates the reissue of treasury shares for less than their cost.

OBJECTIVE 4. Record the reissuance of treasury stock.

Cash	3,800	
Retained Earnings	200	
Treasury Stock		4,000
200 shares of treasury stock, $20 cost, reissued for $19 per share.		

Stock Splits

There are those who believe that high share prices discourage people with limited means from buying a corporation's stock. To reduce the market value per share, corporations sometimes *split* their shares. *A stock split is the replacement of old shares of stock with a greater number of new shares at a fixed multiple rate.* When two new shares are issued for each old share

OBJECTIVE 5. State what a stock split is.

called in, the result is referred to as a 2 for 1 split, and the market value per share should go down to approximately one-half of what it was before the split. However, if enough investors perceive a split as evidence of unusual success, the price per share may decline by less than would otherwise be expected.

Although the par value per share is usually split in the same proportion, no formal journal entries are required to record stock splits. The ledger account balances are not changed by splits, and each shareholder has the same equity claim as before. If desired, a memorandum entry may be made in the journal, or directly in the Capital Stock account. *A memorandum entry is a written explanation of some event, without any accompanying debits and credits to accounts.*

SHAREHOLDERS' EQUITY PRESENTATIONS

Presentations of shareholders' equity accounts in various corporate balance sheets are by no means uniform. Most corporations, however, do disclose the numbers of shares authorized, their par or stated values, and the number of shares issued along with the dollar amounts for each equity category. Illustration 14.4 presents one way of arranging the shareholders' equity section of a balance sheet.

BOOK VALUE PER SHARE

The Common Stock Subscribed amount in the foregoing presentation will be transferred to the regular Common Stock account when the subscribed shares are issued. The subscribed shares might reasonably be included with the outstanding shares in the calculation of book value per share of common stock. *Book value per share* has previously been defined as the equity shown

ILLUSTRATION 14.4

SHAREHOLDERS' EQUITY		
Preferred stock, $100 par, 8%, cumulative,		
10,000 shares authorized, 5,000 shares issued	$ 500,000	
Common stock, $10 par, 100,000 shares		
authorized, 20,000 shares issued	200,000	
Common stock subscribed, 4,000 shares	40,000	
Capital in excess of par	180,000	
Retained earnings ($24,000, the cost of treasury		
stock, unavailable for dividends)	310,000	
	$1,230,000	
Less: Treasury stock, at cost, 600 shares	24,000	
Total Shareholders' Equity		1,206,000

in the accounts for a class of stock divided by the number of shares of stock outstanding. Of the common shares issued, 600 are held as treasury stock. Thus the shares of equity to be used as a divisor for the book value calculation would be derived as follows.

Common shares issued	20,000
Less: Treasury shares	600
	19,400
Plus: Subscribed shares	4,000
Total common shares	23,400

The book value calculation would then be made as follows.

$$\frac{\text{Total equity} - \text{Preferred equity*}}{\text{Total common shares}} = \text{Book value per share}$$

$$\frac{\$1,206,000 - \$500,000}{23,400} = \$30.17 \text{ per share}$$

*Including any preferred dividends in arrears.

OBJECTIVE 6.
Differentiate between par value, book value, and market value.

Keep in mind the differences between the book value, market value, and par value of corporate shares. *Market value per share is simply the selling price of stock at a given point in time.* Market prices are affected by many factors, among which are expected future earnings, industry and economic conditions, and the prevailing mood in the stock markets.

SUMMARY OF CHAPTER 14

Corporations are independent legal entities created by states through the issuance of certificates of incorporation. Limited shareholder liability, easy transferability of shares, and unlimited life are some of the distinguishing characteristics of the corporate form of organization.

Corporate ownership rights are represented by shares of stock. All business corporations issue common stock shares, and some also issue preferred stock, which provides special preferences to income and/or corporate assets. Common stockholders elect directors who are responsible for determining operating policies and employing officers to run the corporation.

Subscriptions to stock are recorded as receivables. As subscriptions are fully collected, the par value of shares issued is shifted from a Stock Subscribed account to a Capital Stock account. Common shareholders have a preemptive right to acquire a sufficient number of any subsequently issued new shares to maintain their proportionate interest in the corporation.

A corporation may reacquire shares of its stock by buying them from shareholders. The reacquired shares may be either canceled or held as treasury stock for possible reissuance. Treasury Stock is viewed as a contra equity account.

GLOSSARY FOR CHAPTER 14

Book value per share   The amount of equity shown in the accounts for a class of stock divided by the number of shares of stock outstanding.

Callable preferred stock   Preferred shares that permit redemption by the corporation, usually at a call premium.

Call premium   An extra amount above the par value of a security that must be paid upon forced redemption by the corporation.

Capital stock share   An ownership right in a corporation, represented by a formal certificate that can be legally transferred to someone else.

Certificate of incorporation   A government document granting authority for the creation of a corporation.

Common stock   Shares that represent the most basic ownership equity of a corporation. (All business corporations have common shareholders, and many corporations have no other classes of stock outstanding.)

Convertible preferred stock   Preferred shares that can be exchanged for a specified number of common stock shares at the request of the preferred shareholder.

Corporation   An artificial, but independent, legal entity that has the right to contract and own property as though it were a person, and in which ownership is represented by shares of stock.

Cumulative preferred stock   Preferred shares for which undeclared preferred dividends must be accumulated and paid before any dividends may be paid on common shares.

Dividends in arrears   Accumulated, but undeclared, preferred dividends.

Incorporators   A group of individuals who undertake the legal and other work necessary to bring a corporation into existence.

Market value per share   The selling price of stock at a given point in time.

Memorandum entry   A written explanation of some event, without any accompanying debits and credits to accounts.

No-par stock   Shares of stock with no designated legal face value.

Participating preferred stock   Preferred shares that permit their owners to share in profits of the corporation beyond a minimum fixed dividend rate.

Par value   A stated face amount per share of stock.

Preemptive right   The legal right of common shareholders to maintain their proportionate ownership interest in a corporation.

Preferred stock   Shares of stock that provide preference claims to profits and corporation assets.

Retained earnings   The accumulated profits (net incomes) of a corporation that have not been declared as dividends.

Shareholders (stockholders)   Owners of corporate stock.

Stated value   An arbitrary per share amount designated to no-par stock.

Stock certificate   A formal document issued to an investor to evidence the number of shares of stock acquired.

Stock right   The privilege that is associated with each outstanding share of stock to acquire a proportionate amount of new shares issued.

Stock split   The replacement of old shares of stock with a greater number of new shares at a fixed multiple rate.

Stock subscriptions   Agreements to take certain numbers of corporate shares at a specified issue price.

Treasury stock   Reacquired but uncanceled stock that may be reissued by the corporation without concern for the preemptive rights of the shareholders.

SELF-QUIZ ON OBJECTIVES FOR CHAPTER 14
Solutions to Self-Quiz begin on page B-45.

1. **OBJECTIVE 1.** State in your own words at least five attributes that distinguish corporations from other forms of business organization.

2. **OBJECTIVES 2, 3, 4.** Make the necessary journal entries to record the following events for Spruce Corporation.

    Jan.   4   Spruce Corporation incorporated with authorization to issue 200,000 shares of $5 par common stock. Incorporators had previously obtained subscriptions for 20,000 shares of common stock at $20 per share.

           15   Collected $200,000 of the subscriptions receivable.

Feb. 8 Collected remaining subscriptions receivable, and issued the subscribed shares.

June 10 Reacquired 400 shares of common stock at $24 per share. Shares are to be held in the treasury for possible reissue in the future.

Aug. 14 Reissued at $30 per share the treasury stock acquired on June 10.

3. **OBJECTIVE 5.** State what a stock split is.

4. **OBJECTIVE 6.** Differentiate between the expressions *par value, book value,* and *market value* as these terms relate to shares of stock.

DISCUSSION QUESTIONS FOR CHAPTER 14

1. How may creditors overcome the limited liability associated with corporations so as to make corporate shareholders personally responsible for corporate debts?

2. Corporations are usually characterized by a greater separation of ownership from management than is found in proprietorships and partnerships. How do shareholders keep control over the corporations in which they own stock?

3. What are some examples of government controls that are imposed on corporations?

4. What is a preemptive right as it applies to common shareholders under the laws of most states?

5. Is treasury stock an asset? Explain.

6. How would you explain the fact that practically all large, well-known business concerns are corporations, while most proprietorships and partnerships are relatively small by comparison?

7. On the average, corporations have longer lives than unincorporated concerns. Why?

8. What is the difference between common stock and preferred stock?

9. Why do corporations acquire treasury stock?

EXERCISES FOR CHAPTER 14

14.1. On July 1, the three original incorporators of the Dank Corporation paid, from personal funds, $15,000 for various legal and other work involved in organizing the new corporation. Assuming that the corporation was formed the same day, make an entry to record these costs on the corporate books.

14.2. Investors signed a written agreement on September 1 to purchase at a future date 50,000 shares of common stock of the Bangor Corporation at par value of $20 per share.

  a. Make an entry on Bangor's books to reflect the equity resulting from the agreement on September 1.

b. Make an appropriate entry at September 30 to show the collection from each subscriber of half the amount due for subscribed shares.

14.3. Make an entry at April 1 to reflect the issuance of 200,000 shares of $10 par common stock that had previously been subscribed.

14.4. Subscribers agreed on January 31 to pay at a future date $16 per share for 50,000 shares of $10 par common stock. Record the subscriptions in the corporation's journal.

14.5. Record the issuance on May 15 of 100,000 shares of $1 stated value common stock for $20 cash per share.

14.6. From the following data, prepare a balance sheet for the AKA Corporation at June 15.

	Debit	Credit
Cash	$ 43,000	
Subscriptions receivable—common	300,000	
Organization costs	27,000	
Due to incorporators		$ 20,000
Common stock subscribed		300,000
Common stock		50,000
	$370,000	$370,000

14.7. Make entries to record the acquisition on October 16 of 1,000 shares of treasury stock at a cost of $15,000, and the reissue of the shares on December 8 for $15,700.

14.8. Use the information presented here to calculate the book value per common share.

Common shares issued	100,000
Treasury shares, common	5,000
Subscribed common shares	15,000
Total stockholders' equity	$4,003,000
Preferred shareholders' equity	$1,500,500

PROBLEMS FOR CHAPTER 14
Alternate Problems for this chapter begin on page D-79.

14.9. Selected events pertaining to Alex Corporation are as follows.

Mar. 15   Incorporators of Alex Corporation paid $32,000 in legal and other organization costs.

15   The charter obtained for Alex Corporation authorized the issuance of 1,000,000 shares of $1 par common stock and

100,000 shares of $100 par, 7% cumulative preferred stock. Incorporators had previously obtained subscriptions for 50,000 shares of common stock at $20 per share.

30   Collected $400,000 of the subscriptions receivable.

Apr. 15   Issued 10,000 shares of preferred stock for $100 cash per share.

20   Collected remaining subscriptions receivable and issued common stock.

July 21   Reacquired as treasury stock 1,000 shares of common stock at $18 per share.

Sept. 16   Reissued at $17 per share the treasury stock acquired on July 21.

18   Paid amount due incorporators for organization costs.

Required

Prepare general journal entries for Alex Corporation to record the foregoing events.

14.10. An adjusted trial balance for Simutech Corporation is shown here.

SIMUTECH CORPORATION Adjusted Trial Balance June 30, 19– –		
	Debits	**Credits**
Cash	48,000	
Marketable securities	170,000	
Subscriptions receivable—common	20,000	
Accounts receivable	320,000	
Buildings and equipment	500,000	
Accumulated depreciation—buildings and equipment		56,000
Accounts payable		111,000
Notes payable		150,000
Preferred stock		200,000
Common stock		400,000
Common stock subscribed		20,000
Capital in excess of par		64,000
Capital from reissue of treasury stock		12,000
Treasury stock	110,000	
Retained earnings		61,000
Sales		820,000
Salaries expense	240,000	
Rent expense	88,000	
Other expenses	398,000	
	1,894,000	1,894,000

Required

Prepare a balance sheet at June 30.

14.11. The shareholders' equity section of a balance sheet for the Markoo Corporation is shown here.

SHAREHOLDERS' EQUITY		
Preferred stock, $100 par, 9%, 20,000 shares authorized, 10,000 shares issued	$1,000,000	
Common stock, $10 par, 100,000 shares authorized, 30,000 shares issued	300,000	
Common stock subscribed, 5,000 shares	50,000	
Capital in excess of par	955,000	
Retained earnings (the cost of treasury stock, $34,000, unavailable for dividends)	480,000	
	$2,785,000	
Less: Treasury stock at cost, 1,000 shares	34,000	
Total Shareholders' Equity		2,751,000

Required

1) Calculate the book value per common share.

2) Calculate the new book value per common share after an additional 10,000 shares of common stock are issued at $55 per share.

14.12. At June 15, the records of the Flyer Corporation provided the following information.

$100 par value common shares issued	100,000
Common shares subscribed	18,000
Treasury stock shares	6,000
Preferred shares issued	10,000
Total shareholders' equity	$31,860,000
Preferred shareholders' equity	$1,200,000
Market value per common share	$420

Required

1) Calculate the book value per common share at June 15.

2) Assume that the common stock is split 4 for 1 on June 16. Calculate the par value, book value, and probable market value per share immediately after the stock split.

3) Can you think of any practical reason for splitting the stock?

14.13. Selected events pertaining to Evermore, Incorporated, are described here.

Apr. 15   Reacquired as treasury stock 5,000 shares of common stock at $20 per share.

    30   Board of directors authorized a new issue of Class B Common Stock, 100,000 shares, no par value. Subscriptions were immediately obtained for 50,000 shares of the new stock at $22 per share.

May 15	Collected all subscriptions for the new Class B stock.	
June 18	Reissued at $24 per share the treasury stock acquired April 15.	
Sept. 1	All 10,000 shares of $100 par preferred stock issued 10 years ago are called at $110 per share. The stock was originally issued at par. The shares are canceled (retired).	
30	The board of directors declared a 2 for 1 stock split on Class B Common Stock.	
Dec. 1	20,000 shares of Class B Common are issued for cash at $13 per share.	

Required

Prepare general journal entries for Evermore, Incorporated, to record the foregoing events.

COMPREHENSION PROBLEM FOR CHAPTER 14

14.14. The Garcia Systems Company is a small but growing computer software and systems design company. Juan Garcia, who owns the firm, would like to make the company one of the leaders in the field. On January 2, 19X5, the Garcia Corporation is formed, and the assets and liabilities of the proprietorship are taken over by the new corporation. The values of the assets at January 2 are difficult to assess, but it appears that they are worth approximately what is shown in the accounts. A balance sheet for the Garcia Systems Company at December 31, 19X4, is shown here.

GARCIA SYSTEMS COMPANY
Balance Sheet
December 31, 19X4

ASSETS		
Cash		$140,000
Accounts receivable		118,000
Supplies		15,000
Equipment and furnishings	$88,000	
Less: Accumulated depreciation	21,000	67,000
Total Assets		$340,000
LIABILITIES		
Accounts payable	$44,000	
Notes payable	58,000	
Total Liabilities		$102,000
OWNER'S EQUITY		
Juan Garcia, capital		238,000
Total Liabilities and Owner's Equity		$340,000

Required

1) Prepare the following for the *proprietorship* books:

   a) A compound journal entry to record the receipt of 23,800 shares of $10 par corporate shares in exchange for the firm's net assets

   b) The entry to distribute the corporate shares to Juan and close the proprietor's capital account

2) Prepare for the *corporate* books an opening compound journal entry to record the issuance of shares in exchange for the net assets of the proprietorship.

3) Explain why you did, or did not, bring the accumulated depreciation onto the corporate books.

4) Suppose it was determined that equipment and furnishings were worth $75,000 on January 2. Explain why you would, or would not, recognize the difference between book value and market value of the assets in your entries.

5) Explain how the corporate form may be helpful to Juan in making the business one of the leaders in the field.

6) Juan fears that he may lose control of the corporation as a result of going public with the issuance of shares. Explain why Juan is, or is not, justified in his fears, and advise him on ways that he might minimize the possibility of such an occurrence.

CHAPTER **15**

Corporations: Earnings, Retained Earnings, and Statements

OBJECTIVES

This chapter deals with accounting for, and reporting, corporate earnings, their retention by the corporation, and the declaration and payment of dividends. Also covered are some aspects of corporate income taxation. At the conclusion of this chapter, you should be able to

1. Calculate earnings per share and state where they are usually shown in accounting statements.

2. Define and state the significance of each of the following expressions as they relate to corporate dividends:
   a. Date of declaration.
   b. Date of record.
   c. Date of payment.

3. Make journal entries to record
   a. The declaration and subsequent payment of cash dividends.
   b. The declaration and subsequent issuance of stock dividends.

4. Differentiate between cash dividends and stock dividends.

5. State in your own words the four circumstances that must be present for the corporate form of business to be advantageous for tax purposes.

CORPORATE INCOME

Corporate income statements look much like income statements for proprietorships and partnerships. One major difference is that corporate income tax is shown as an expense of the corporation. Since owners report their shares of proprietorship and partnership incomes on their personal tax returns, income taxes do not appear in income statements of unincorporated entities. Illustration 15.1 highlights some distinguishing features of a corporate income statement.

Another difference, not so readily apparent, is that salaries earned by shareholders employed by the corporation are genuine expenses of the entity. Proprietors do not earn salaries and, as pointed out in Chapter 13, salary allowances to partners are nothing more than a way of dividing partnership income.

Dividends are *not* shown in the corporation's income statement because they are neither expenses nor losses of the entity. *Dividends are distributions of assets to shareholders of a corporation,* and are roughly equivalent to withdrawals by proprietors and partners. Dividends for a period are shown in a statement of retained earnings.

Extraordinary Items

Investors, lenders, and others try to assess a corporation's future profitability by looking at past earnings data. A corporation's normal income, uncolored by extraordinary items, is thought to be the best starting point for predicting future profitability. For this reason, it is accepted practice to differentiate normal operating results from extraordinary items in an income statement.[1]

ILLUSTRATION 15.1

VELMA CORPORATION Income Statement For the Year Ended December 31, 19--	
Sales	$900,000
Cost of goods sold	500,000
Gross Profit	$400,000
Operating expenses	270,000
Net Income before Tax	$130,000
Income Taxes	30,000
Net Income	$100,000
Earnings per share of common stock	$2.00

[1]*Opinions of the Accounting Principles Board No. 9,* "Reporting the Results of Operations" (New York: American Institute of Certified Public Accountants, 1966), pars. 17–20.

ILLUSTRATION 15.2

TNT CORPORATION Income Statement For the Year Ended June 30, 19--	
Sales	$4,000,000
Net Income from Continuing Operations before Tax	$ 650,000
Income taxes	270,000
Net Income from Continuing Operations	$ 380,000
Explosion loss, net of $140,000 tax savings	210,000
Net Income	$ 170,000

Extraordinary items are events that are both unusual and nonrecurring in nature. The effects of fires, tornadoes, and other casualties are examples of extraordinary items, as are one-time effects of changes in accounting methods.

When extraordinary events occur, their effects are reported, net of the related tax effects, below the normal earnings for the period, as portrayed in Illustration 15.2. TNT's income tax due for the year nets out to $130,000, which is the difference between the $270,000 that would have been due on the income from continuing operations and the $140,000 tax savings (recovery) as a result of the extraordinary loss that occurred. The idea is to report as income from continuing operations the amount of after-tax income that would have resulted if the extraordinary loss had not occurred.

Earnings per Share

Net income is an accounting measure of net accomplishment for a period. Shareholders view corporate net income as an increase in their equity, and they like to know how much of the net income goes with the shares of stock they own. It is for this reason that the amount of earnings per common share is shown on the face of a corporation's income statement.[2] Earnings per share figures are most commonly shown immediately below the final net income for the year.

When only common stock is outstanding, earnings per share are calculated by dividing net income after taxes by the weighted average number of common shares outstanding during the year. The weighted average approach used here is similar to the one illustrated in Section 7.A for determining unit inventory costs, except that here shares are weighted according to the portion of the year they were outstanding. For example, 10,000 shares

OBJECTIVE 1. Calculate earnings per share and state where they are usually shown in accounting statements.

[2]*Opinions of the Accounting Principles Board No. 15,* "Earnings Per Share" (New York: American Institute of Certified Public Accountants, 1969), pars. 12–13.

ILLUSTRATION 15.3

TNT CORPORATION Income Statement For the Year Ended June 30, 19--	
Sales	$4,000,000
Earnings (loss) per share of common stock	
Continuing operations before extraordinary items	$ 3.80
Explosion damage, net of tax savings	(2.10)
Net income	$ 1.70

issued at midyear are counted as 5,000, 10,000 shares issued at the beginning of the fourth quarter are counted as 2,500, and so on.

Where preferred stock is present, the return to preferred shareholders (preferred dividends) must be subtracted from net income to arrive at the net income belonging to common shareholders. The following computation is for a corporation with $300,000 of net income after taxes, preferred dividends of $40,000, and 100,000 shares of common stock outstanding throughout the year.

$$\frac{\text{Net income after taxes} - \text{Preferred dividends}}{\text{Average common shares outstanding}} = \text{Earnings per share}$$

$$\frac{\$300,000 - \$40,000}{100,000 \text{ shares}} = \$2.60$$

For years during which extraordinary items occur, per share amounts are usually shown for normal operations, for extraordinary items, and for final net income. Illustration 15.3 presents earnings per share for the statement that was shown in Illustration 15.2, assuming 100,000 shares of common stock outstanding during the year, with no preferred stock in the picture.

Determining earnings per share figures can become quite complex for years during which new shares were issued, as well as for corporations with convertible securities and/or stock options outstanding. Where applicable, past and potential dilutions of earnings per share must be considered, but such complications are left to intermediate and advanced accounting courses.

RETAINED EARNINGS

The Nature of Retained Earnings

Retained earnings were defined in Chapter 14 as the accumulated profits of a corporation that have not been paid out as dividends. Closing entries for

ILLUSTRATION 15.4

Dec. 31	Sales	900,000	
	Cost of Goods Sold		500,000
	Salaries and Wages Expense		200,000
	Depreciation Expense		50,000
	Other Expenses		20,000
	Income Tax Expense		30,000
	Retained Earnings		100,000
	To close temporary equity accounts and reflect net income into retained earnings.		

a corporation update the Retained Earnings account for the net income or net loss for the period as Illustration 15.4 shows.

From a legal viewpoint, retained earnings are available for the payment of dividends. However, the balance in a Retained Earnings account is nothing more than a portion of the shareholders' equity. And shareholders' equity represents the shareholders' claims against corporate assets. The amount of cash dividends that can be paid is limited to the amount of cash available for such payments. A cash dividend simultaneously reduces corporate assets and shareholders' equity, as illustrated by the following entry.

Retained Earnings	XXX	
Cash		XXX
Cash dividend declared and paid.		

The balance in a corporation's Retained Earnings account represents the total earnings of the corporation since it began less all dividends declared during the corporation's life. Retained earnings are sometimes more appropriately called *reinvested* earnings. The assets into which earnings have been reinvested may be in the form of buildings, machinery, and other long-term items that are not practically available for distribution to shareholders. In most corporations, the major portion of retained earnings has been rather permanently reinvested back into the entity.

For corporations that have been in operation a great many years, retained earnings may represent the major portion of shareholders' equity. For example, the consolidated balance sheet for General Motors Corporation at December 31, 1982, presented in the Appendix at the end of the book, shows $15.6 billion of net income retained for use in the business out of total stockholders' equity of $18.3 billion.[3] In other words, more than 85% of the reported shareholders' equity came from reinvested earnings. That same balance sheet reported only $279.6 million in cash. If General Motors had

---

[3]General Motors Annual Report, 1982, consolidated balance sheet, p. 18.

ILLUSTRATION 15.5

VELMA CORPORATION Statement of Retained Earnings For the Year Ended December 31, 19--		
Retained earnings, January 1		$800,000
Net income	$100,000	
Dividends declared	60,000	40,000
Retained earnings, December 31		$840,000

paid *all* its cash as dividends on the balance sheet date, less than 2% of the reported retained earnings would have been paid out as cash dividends.

Legal status notwithstanding, the Retained Earnings balance should not be viewed as any indication of a corporation's ability to pay cash dividends. Rather, it represents the corporation's growth through reinvestment of its own earnings.

Retained Earnings Statement

A statement of retained earnings shows the starting balance, the net income or loss for the period, any dividends declared, and the ending balance. Illustration 15.5 presents one possible arrangement.

The retained earnings statement is sometimes added to the bottom of an income statement. One format for a combined statement of income and retained earnings is shown in Illustration 15.6.

ILLUSTRATION 15.6

VELMA CORPORATION Statement of Income and Retained Earnings For the Year Ended December 31, 19--	
Sales	$900,000
Cost of goods sold	500,000
Gross Profit	$400,000
Operating expenses	270,000
Net Income before Tax	$130,000
Income taxes	30,000
Net Income	$100,000
Dividends declared during the year	60,000
Net Income Retained in the Business	$ 40,000
Retained earnings, January 1	800,000
Retained earnings, December 31	$840,000
Earnings per share of common stock	$ 2.00

Retained Earnings Restrictions

Portions of retained earnings may be restricted for various purposes. A *retained earnings restriction is a designation that a portion of the Retained Earnings balance is not available for dividends, even if funds are on hand from which to pay them.* For example, you may recall from the previous chapter that a Treasury Stock balance is generally viewed as a restriction against retained earnings.

Sometimes debt agreements with creditors will restrict a certain amount of retained earnings from being paid out as dividends. In other words, the corporate assets represented by that portion of retained earnings must remain in the corporation. The purpose of such restrictions is to assure creditors that an adequate equity base will be maintained for their protection.

Corporate directors occasionally place their own restrictions on retained earnings to prepare for certain possible (contingent) events. Contingencies of concern to the directors may be pending lawsuits against the corporation or uninsured potential losses from fires or other catastrophes.[4]

Retained earnings restrictions may be disclosed by parenthetical remarks or in footnotes to financial statements. In some cases, however, a journal entry is made to formally *appropriate* a portion of the Retained Earnings balance. *A retained earnings appropriation is the transfer by journal entry of a portion of a Retained Earnings balance to a special appropriation account* as a way of showing some restrictions against retained earnings. An entry to appropriate retained earnings for possible contingent losses follows.

Retained Earnings	200,000	
Retained Earnings Appropriated for Contingencies		200,000
To earmark retained earnings in the amount of possible losses from catastrophe.		

You should understand that an appropriation of retained earnings in no way absorbs a loss when it occurs. The loss from fire of an uninsured building must be borne whether or not there has been an appropriation of retained earnings for possible fire losses. Before the fire, the corporation owned a building; after the fire, the building is gone. Replacement of a burned building requires the use of cash and/or additional debt. Credit balances in equity accounts are not resources, but only claims to resources. A fire loss reduces both assets and shareholders' equity.

In fact, losses are not permitted to be debited directly to retained earnings appropriation accounts.[5] Losses must be closed to the Retained Earnings

---

[4]A contingent liability was defined in Chapter 6 as a possible obligation that will arise only at the occurrence of some unpredictable event.

[5]*Financial Accounting Standards Board Statement No. 5,* "Accounting for Contingencies" (Stamford, Conn.: Financial Accounting Standards Board, 1975), par. 15.

account during the closing process, along with the other temporary equity accounts. When the reason for having a retained earnings appropriation no longer exists, the balance of the appropriation account is returned to the Retained Earnings account.

CASH DIVIDENDS

In almost all cases, assets distributed to shareholders as dividends are in the form of cash. It is the responsibility of the corporate directors to determine whether any dividends will be paid, how much will be paid, and when they will be paid. Dividend declarations commonly involve three important dates.

> 1. Date of declaration
> 2. Date of record
> 3. Date of payment

Date of Declaration

OBJECTIVE 2a. Define and state the significance of date of declaration.

The date on which corporate directors declare a dividend is known as the date of declaration. Once the dividends are declared, they become a legal liability of the corporation. In effect, a portion of shareholders' equity is shifted to the liability category, as illustrated by the following entry made on the date of declaration of a cash dividend.

OBJECTIVE 3a. Record the declaration of cash dividends.

19X4			
Dec. 20	Retained Earnings	50,000	
	Common Dividends Payable		50,000
	Dividend of 50¢ per share payable January 17		
	to shareholders of record on January 3.		

Date of Record

OBJECTIVE 2b. Define and state the significance of date of record.

The date of record is the date specified by corporate directors for determining the shareholders who will receive a dividend. Dividend checks are mailed out on the date of payment to the shareholders listed in corporate records as owning shares on the date of record. It is customary to allow two to four weeks between the date of declaration and the date of record.

Date of Payment

OBJECTIVE 2c. Define and state the significance of date of payment.

The date specified by corporate directors for paying a dividend is known as the date of payment. The payment date is normally two to four weeks after

ILLUSTRATION 15.7

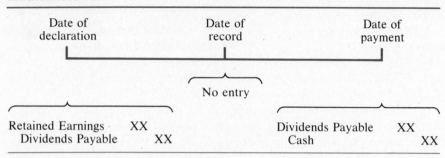

Date of declaration	Date of record	Date of payment
	No entry	
Retained Earnings XX Dividends Payable XX		Dividends Payable XX Cash XX

the date of record. The following entry reflects the payment of cash dividends on the date of payment.

19X5
Jan. 17
	Common Dividends Payable
	    Cash
	    To record payment of the dividend declared
	    on December 20.
		50,000	50,000

OBJECTIVE 3a. **Record the payment of cash dividends.**

Illustration 15.7 shows the relationship between the dividend dates and entries on the corporate records.

STOCK DIVIDENDS

The Nature of Stock Dividends

In lieu of, or in addition to, paying cash dividends, the directors of some corporations declare stock dividends. *A stock dividend is a proportional distribution of additional shares of stock to a corporation's shareholders.*

OBJECTIVE 4. **Differentiate between cash dividends and stock dividends.**

Stock dividends are a source of considerable confusion among shareholders, business persons, accountants, and others. In fact, they are *not truly dividends,* since no assets are distributed as a result of stock dividend declarations. Neither total corporate assets nor total shareholders' equity are affected by stock dividends.

Reasons for Stock Dividends

Various reasons have been given for declaring stock dividends. Some people contend that they help to conserve corporate cash by avoiding the payment of cash dividends. This implies that shareholders somehow equate the receipt of additional shares of stock with the receipt of cash dividends. Stock dividends conserve corporate cash because they are equivalent to no dividends at all.

Others argue that stock dividends avoid income taxation. It is true that no taxable income results when shareholders receive stock dividends. However, the same result is achieved by the absence of *any* dividends for the year. Stock dividends are not taxed because tax law recognizes that the corporation has given up no resources to the shareholders.

Another reason sometimes given for the declaration of stock dividends is that they help to hold down the market price of the shares and therefore aid in the buying and selling of shares in the stock market. It is true that stock dividends dilute equity per share and therefore tend to keep share prices lower then they otherwise would be. However, the same effect can be obtained by splitting the shares at periodic intervals.

Recording Stock Dividends

Stock dividends show up in the accounts as a shift of some of the Retained Earnings to other equity accounts. The prevailing practice is to transfer an amount equivalent to the market value of the shares to be distributed in the stock dividend.[6]

The entries in Illustration 15.8 reflect the declaration and distribution of a 10% stock dividend.

Stock Dividends Versus Stock Splits

As pointed out in the preceding chapter, stock splits do not require journal entries, since they do not disturb any of the equity accounts. Although stock dividends have the same logical effect as small stock splits, the stock market does not perceive them as being the same, at least not in the short run. Per-share prices of stocks do not tend to decline immediately to reflect the dilutions that result from stock dividends.

Accountants have attempted to distinguish between small stock dividends, involving the issuance of new shares amounting to less than 20% of the shares already outstanding, and those greater than 20%. Stock dividends in excess of 20% of outstanding shares may be viewed as essentially equivalent to stock splits. For these large distributions of additional shares, no transfer of retained earnings need be made unless required by state law. Where retained earnings are transferred (capitalized), only an amount equal to the *par* value of the new shares (as opposed to the *market* value) is shifted to capital stock accounts.[7]

---

[6]*Accounting Research Bulletin No. 43, Chapter 7B* (New York: American Institute of Certified Public Accountants, 1961), par. 10.

[7]Ibid., pars. 10–16.

ILLUSTRATION 15.8

Mar. 16	Retained Earnings	220,000	
	Common Stock Dividend Distributable		100,000
	Capital in Excess of Par		120,000
	10% stock dividend declared on 100,000		
	shares of common stock outstanding, par $10,		
	market value $22 per share, to be distributed		
	on April 5 to shareholders of record on March		
	26.		
Apr. 5	Common Stock Dividends Distributable	100,000	
	Common Stock		100,000
	Stock dividends declared on March 16 distrib-		
	uted to shareholders.		

OBJECTIVE 3b. Record the declaration and subsequent issuance of stock dividends.

CORPORATION BALANCE SHEET

Except for the owners' equity section, a corporation balance sheet looks pretty much like a balance sheet for a proprietorship or partnership. As suggested earlier, a number of accounts are used in accounting for shareholders' equity. The total par or stated value of outstanding shares is kept separate from the capital in excess of par or stated value. Earnings not paid out as dividends are accumulated in a Retained Earnings account. Illustration 15.9 on the next page highlights the distinguishing features of a balance sheet for a corporation with a simple capital structure.

When preferred stock is outstanding, more accounts are needed to account for the equity of preferred shareholders. The presentation of shareholders' equity may be further complicated by stock subscribed, treasury stock, retained earnings appropriations, and other matters, as shown in Illustration 15.10 on page 639.

CORPORATE INCOME TAXES

As independent legal entities, corporations are subject to income taxation unless they are exempted by the tax laws.[8] *An income tax is a tax based on the amount of income earned during a period.* Income taxes may be levied by federal, state, or local governments.

Taxable income is the difference between taxable revenues and allowable deductions, as provided by the law by which the tax is levied. Taxable income is frequently a different figure from the one reported as net income (before income taxes) on an income statement.

---

[8]Certain charitable, educational, and religious corporations are exempt from federal income tax under provisions of the Internal Revenue Code. The code also provides that elections may be filed for certain small-business corporations to have the tax on their income paid directly by the shareholders, similar to the way partnership incomes are treated.

ILLUSTRATION 15.9

VELMA CORPORATION		
Balance Sheet		
December 31, 19--		

ASSETS		
Current		
Cash	$ 70,000	
Accounts receivable (net)	240,000	
Inventories	290,000	$ 600,000
Noncurrent		
Land	$160,000	
Buildings and equipment (net)	810,000	
Other assets	130,000	1,100,000
Total Assets		$1,700,000

LIABILITIES		
Current		
Accounts payable	$180,000	
Noncurrent		
Mortgage payable	320,000	
Total Liabilities		$ 500,000

SHAREHOLDERS' EQUITY		
Common stock, $10 par, 20,000 shares issued		
and outstanding	$200,000	
Capital in excess of par	160,000	
Retained earnings	840,000	
Total Shareholders' Equity		1,200,000
Total Liabilities and Shareholders' Equity		$1,700,000

Tax rates are changed from time to time by the government unit that levies the tax. In 1983 the federal income tax rates as they applied to corporations were as follows.

Taxable Income		Tax Rate
First	$25,000	15%
Next	$25,000	18%
Next	$25,000	30%
Next	$25,000	40%
Over	$100,000	46%

ILLUSTRATION 15.10

FIDDLER CORPORATION
Partial Balance Sheet
December 31, 19--

SHAREHOLDERS' EQUITY

Contributed Capital

Preferred stock, $100 par, 10,000 shares issued and outstanding	$1,000,000	
Common stock, $10 par, 300,000 shares issued of which 5,000 shares are held in treasury stock	3,000,000	
Common stock subscribed, 8,000 shares	80,000	
Capital in excess of par—preferred	50,000	
Capital in excess of par—common	1,400,000	
Total contributed capital		$ 5,530,000
Retained Earnings		
Appropriated for contingencies	$ 600,000	
Unappropriated (restricted in the amount of $110,000, the cost of treasury stock)	4,200,000	4,800,000
Total contributed and retained		$10,330,000
Less: Treasury stock, 5,000 shares at cost		110,000
Total Shareholders' Equity		$10,220,000

Based on the 1983 tax rates, here is the calculation of federal income tax for a corporation with taxable income of $160,000.

Tax Rate	Taxable Income Increment	Tax
15%	$ 25,000	$ 3,750
18%	25,000	4,500
30%	25,000	7,500
40%	25,000	10,000
46%	60,000	27,600
	Total $160,000	$53,350

The entries to record the tax and the subsequent payment are as follows.

19X3 Dec. 31	Federal Income Tax	53,350	
	Federal Income Tax Payable		53,350
	To provide for federal income tax due on 19X3 income		
19X4 Mar. 15	Federal Income Tax Payable	53,350	
	Cash		53,350
	Payment of 19X3 federal income taxes.		

Marginal Tax Rate

According to the tax rates shown earlier, any corporation with taxable earnings in excess of $100,000 is subject to a marginal federal income tax rate of 46%. *A marginal income tax rate is the rate at which a given amount of additional taxable income would be taxed.* The marginal rate is increased, of course, by any rate imposed by the state in which the income is earned. Suppose, for example, that a corporation regularly has taxable earnings in excess of $100,000 each year. If the corporation were subject to a flat (proportional) state tax of 10%, any *additional* earnings would appear to be taxed at a combined *marginal* rate of 56%. However, since the 10% state tax reduces taxable income for federal tax purposes, the effective combined marginal rate would only be 51.4%, determined as follows.[9]

$$\text{Combined marginal rate} = 0.46(1 - 0.10) + 0.10 = 0.514$$

Double Taxation

A common misconception is that the corporate form of business offers an automatic tax advantage. Actually, operating as a corporation can be very costly from a tax standpoint. In the first place, the marginal rates at which corporations are taxed are generally quite high; corporations pay close to half their taxable earnings in excess of $100,000 as federal income tax. The tax burden is further increased by the various state and local income taxes.

What remains of earnings after income taxes is supposedly available for reinvestment within the corporation or for distribution to shareholders as dividends.[10] However, dividends received by shareholders are also subject

---

[9]If the federal income tax is also deductible for state income tax purposes, the combined marginal rate becomes approximately 49.06%.

[10]But keep in mind the price-level problems discussed in Section 12.B. Net incomes, and therefore taxable incomes, tend to be overstated. When all is said and done, only liquid assets not needed by the corporation are available for paying dividends.

to *personal* income taxes.[11] Since dividends paid by a corporation are not deductible on the corporate tax return, the same earnings are taxed twice: once as corporate income and again as personal income.

At this writing, the income tax rates imposed on individuals by the Internal Revenue Code range from a low of 11% to a high of 50%. The maximum rate applies to taxable income above $81,800 for unmarried individuals (above $162,400 for married individuals filing joint returns).

To illustrate the effects of double taxation, let us assume that a corporation has net taxable income of $200,000, and that it intends to pay as dividends what is left of the top $100,000 of income after taxes on that increment. Assume also that the corporation's shareholders are taxed at an average marginal tax rate of 50%. From the following calculation, we see that from the top $100,000 of corporate income, only $27,000 is left after corporate and individual taxes.

Element of corporate income	$100,000
Less corporate taxes at 46%	46,000
Left for payment of dividends	$ 54,000
Less shareholder taxes at 50%	27,000
Left for shareholders to spend	$ 27,000

A marginal corporate rate of 46% means that a corporation must earn $1.85 before taxes for each $1 of dividends it pays ($1 ÷ 0.54 = $1.85185). The combined effective rate at which the $100,000 of corporate income has been taxed is 73%, determined as follows.[12]

$$\frac{\text{Total tax}}{\text{Income}} = \frac{\$46,000 + \$27,000}{\$100,000} = \frac{\$73,000}{\$100,000} = 0.73$$

You can see that what was left of the $100,000 after corporate taxes, $54,000, dwindled to $27,000 when it was taken out of the corporation as dividends. The shareholders would have been wealthier had the money been left in the corporation, since shareholders own the corporation anyway. If earnings are reinvested after taxes, the corporation should presumably earn more income in the future, and the value of the shares should increase due to the greater wealth and increased earning power of the corporation.

Should any of the shareholders wish to realize cash from their shares, they may sell some of the shares in the marketplace. Proceeds from the sale

---

[11]The first $100 of dividends received each year by individuals ($200 on a joint return) is excluded from taxable income. (See Internal Revenue Code, Sec. 116(a).

[12]Actually, the effects are even more severe than illustrated here because of the additional burdens of state and local taxation. An approach for figuring the combined marginal rate of federal and state income taxes was shown earlier.

of shares are taxed much less heavily than dividends, since only the gains are taxed—and then only at capital gain rates.[13]

Double taxation is always a tax disadvantage. But double taxation can be avoided by allowing the corporation to keep what is left after taxes for reinvestment within the entity. To do this the business must be an expanding one, with attractive investment alternatives available.

For a corporation to be a tax advantage, the tax brackets of its shareholders must be higher than the rate at which the corporation is taxed. Also, shareholders must be able and willing to leave their earnings in the corporation. Otherwise, operation of the business as a partnership is less costly from a tax standpoint. Partnership income is taxed in the partner's personal tax returns at their personal tax rates. And when partners withdraw money from a partnership, their withdrawals are not taxed again, as are dividends from a corporation.

A corporation cannot be advantageous for tax purposes unless it is profitable. A corporate net loss is locked inside the corporate shell, since there is no such thing as negative dividends. In other words, shareholders cannot offset their shares of corporate losses against taxable income from other sources.[14] Corporations may be able to offset losses of one year against profits of prior or later years by means of loss carrybacks and carryforwards.[15]

For the corporate form of business to be a tax advantage, *all* of the following conditions must be met.

OBJECTIVE 5. State the circumstances that must be present for the corporate form of business to be advantageous for tax purposes.

CONDITIONS THAT MUST BE MET FOR THE CORPORATE FORM TO BE A TAX ADVANTAGE

1. The corporation must be profitable. Corporate losses are locked into the entity and can only be realized by shareholders through sale of their shares of stock at a loss.

2. The corporation must be able to retain and reinvest a substantial part of its earnings after taxes in profitable ways. Through corporate growth, the market value of shares should increase over time. If a shareholder realizes this increase in value by selling shares, the capital gain may receive favorable tax treatment.

3. Shareholders must already be subject to higher personal tax brackets than the rate at which the corporation income is being taxed. Otherwise, the tax they would pay as partners would be less than the corporate income tax.

4. Shareholders must be willing to leave a substantial portion of the corporation's net income in the business. If most of the net income left after corporate taxes is distributed as dividends, it will be taxed twice—once as corporate income and again as personal income to the shareholders.

---

[13]The concept of capital gains and the manner in which they are taxed are covered in Chapter 26. Suffice it to say here that capital gains from the sale of securities are accorded favorable tax treatment. Under some circumstances, 60% of the capital gain is tax free.

[14]An exception to this statement occurs with Subchapter S corporations (discussed later),

If any one of the foregoing conditions is not met, the corporate device cannot be a tax advantage. Even so, other advantages of incorporation (limited liability, for instance) may be sufficient to more than offset negative taxation effects.

Subchapter S Corporations

Subchapter S of the Internal Revenue Code permits shareholders of *certain corporations to elect to have the corporate entities treated, for federal tax purposes, as though they were partnerships. A corporation for which such a tax election has been made is known as a Subchapter S corporation, or small-business corporation.*[16] These corporations file yearly a special form similar to the one used by partnerships. No federal income tax is paid by the Subchapter S corporation (except, under certain circumstances, for capital gains tax); instead, the shareholders report their shares of the corporate income in their personal tax returns as though the entity were a partnership. Thus the effects of double taxation can be avoided when a corporation can be treated as a Subchapter S corporation.

Actually, the size of the corporation has little to do with its ability to qualify under the small-business provision of the code. The three most important requirements are as follows.

SUBCHAPTER S CORPORATION REQUIREMENTS

1. The corporation may not have more than 35 shareholders.
2. All shareholders must be either individual (noncorporate) citizens or residents of the United States or domestic estates.
3. The corporation may not issue more than one class of stock.

---

which are treated as partnerships for tax purposes. Also, corporate losses may be realized indirectly as *capital losses* at the time that capital stock is disposed of by the shareholder.

[15]Internal Revenue Code, Sec. 172, provides for net operating loss carrybacks and carryforwards under prescribed circumstances and with definite limitations.

[16]Internal Revenue Code, Subtitle A, Chapter 1, Subchapter S.

SUMMARY OF CHAPTER 15

Except for the presence of income taxes, corporate income statements look much the same as those for proprietorships and partnerships. The after-tax effects of extraordinary events should be reported separately from the income or loss from continuing operations. Current practice requires that earnings per share figures be shown on the face of corporate income statements. Earnings per share calculations become quite complex for corporations with potential equity dilutions, changing numbers of shares outstanding, and/or extraordinary items present during the year.

Retained earnings of a corporation are accumulated earnings that have not been declared as dividends. The major portion of the retained earnings of most corporations has been reinvested in noncash assets that are not readily available for payment of dividends. Portions of retained earnings may be restricted for various reasons to ensure that an adequate equity base will be maintained within the corporation.

Cash dividends represent the distribution to shareholders of a portion of their equity claims to corporate assets. Stock dividends, on the other hand, only dilute equity per share by having a greater number of shares represent the same total shareholders' equity. Payments of cash dividends subject corporate earnings to double taxation, resulting in very high combined effective rates of tax. Stock dividends do not result in any taxable income to shareholders.

Contrary to popular belief, the corporate form of business is often a serious tax disadvantage because of the effects of double taxation. To be a tax advantage, a corporation must be profitable and expanding, and the shareholders must be in high personal tax brackets and have little or no need for cash dividends. Double taxation may be avoided when a corporation qualifies for Subchapter S tax treatment.

GLOSSARY FOR CHAPTER 15

Date of declaration   The date on which corporate directors declare a dividend.

Date of payment   The date specified by corporate directors for paying a dividend.

Date of record   The date specified by corporate directors for determining the shareholders who will receive a dividend.

Dividends   Distributions of assets to the shareholders of a corporation.

Extraordinary items   Events that are both unusual and nonrecurring in nature.

Income tax   A tax based on the amount of income earned during a period of time.

Marginal income tax rate   The rate at which a given amount of additional taxable income would be taxed.

Retained earnings appropriation   The transfer by journal entry of a portion of a Retained Earnings balance to a special appropriation account.

Retained earnings restriction   A designation that a portion of the Retained Earnings balance is not available for dividends, even if funds are available from which to pay them.

Stock dividend   A proportional distribution of additional shares of stock to a corporation's shareholders.

Subchapter S corporation (small-business corporation)   A qualifying corporation for which a tax election has been made to have it treated like a partnership.

Taxable income   The difference between taxable revenues and allowable deductions, as provided by the law by which the tax is levied.

SELF-QUIZ ON OBJECTIVES FOR CHAPTER 15
Solutions to Self-Quiz begin on page B-46.

1. **OBJECTIVE 1.** Nick Corporation had net income after taxes of $600,000 for 19X4. Preferred dividends of $100,000 were declared and paid during 19X4. There were 200,000 shares of common stock outstanding throughout 19X4.

   a. Calculate earnings per share for 19X4.

   b. Where would the earnings per share most likely be shown in the accounting statements?

2. **OBJECTIVE 2.** Define and state the significance of each of the following expressions as they relate to corporate dividends:

   a. Date of declaration.

   b. Date of record.

   c. Date of payment.

3. **OBJECTIVE 3.** Make the journal entries needed to record the following events.

   Events

   Jan.   20   Directors of Jay Corporation declared common dividends of $1 per share of common stock to be paid in cash on March 1 to stockholders of record on February 8. There are 100,000 shares of Jay Corporation common stock outstanding.

   Feb.   8   Date of record for cash dividends.

   Mar.   1   Common dividends paid in cash.

   July   15   Directors of Jay Corporation declared a 2% stock dividend to be issued on August 20 to shareholders of record on August 1. There are 100,000 shares of common stock outstanding on July 15. On July 15, Jay common shares are selling for $18, and they have a par value of $5 and a book value of $12.

   Aug.   1   Date of record for stock dividend.

   Aug.   20   Stock dividend shares issued to common shareholders.

4. **OBJECTIVE 4.** Differentiate between cash dividends and stock dividends.

5. **OBJECTIVE 5.** State in your own words the four conditions that must be met for the corporate form of business to be advantageous for tax purposes.

DISCUSSION QUESTIONS FOR CHAPTER 15

1. Under what circumstances are corporate earnings subject to double taxation?

2. In what ways do financial statements for business corporations differ from those for unincorporated businesses?

3. What is a Subchapter S corporation as specified by the Internal Revenue Code? What are the three most important requirements that must be met by a business to be classified as a Subchapter S corporation?

4. A shareholder was overheard to remark that the amount of cash dividends that a corporation can pay is limited only by the balance in the Retained Earnings account. Do you agree or disagree, and why?

5. What is the major source of equity for mature corporations?

6. Why might the payment of cash dividends be objectionable, assuming that the goal of shareholders is to maximize their wealth?

7. What are the similarities and differences between stock dividends and stock splits?

8. What is a retained earnings restriction?

9. Why do creditors sometimes insist on a retained earnings restriction as a condition to granting credit?

EXERCISES FOR CHAPTER 15

15.1. Platz Corporation is subject to a marginal federal income tax rate of 46% and a flat 12% state corporate income tax. State taxes are deductible for federal tax purposes, but state law does not permit the deduction of federal taxes. Calculate the combined (federal and state) effective marginal tax rate for Platz.

15.2. A shareholder who is subject to a marginal tax bracket of 50% has received cash dividends of $20,000 from the SHM Corporation. The corporation earned $1 million and pays income tax at the rate of 46% on all income over $100,000.

   a. Determine the combined effective rate at which the cash dividend to the stockholder was taxed.

   b. Under the circumstances described, how much must the corporation earn to pay a dividend sufficient to leave the shareholder $1 after corporate and personal income taxes are paid?

15.3. Make all necessary entries to reflect a 10% stock dividend on 500,000 outstanding shares of $1 par common stock with a market value of $20 per share. The stock dividend was declared on June 15, to be distributed on July 13 to shareholders of record on June 30.

15.4. Make all necessary entries to reflect a $100,000 cash dividend declared on September 30, to be paid on October 30 to common shareholders of record on October 15.

15.5. For which of the following dates would a formal journal entry be made?

   a. Date on which a cash dividend is declared by board of directors.

   b. Date on which stockholders who are listed in corporate records become eligible to receive dividends.

   c. Date on which dividends are paid.

   d. Date on which stock split is declared by board of directors.

   e. Date on which a 10% stock dividend is declared by board of directors.

15.6. The following information pertains to SVM Corporation. Calculate earnings per share for 19X4.

Net income for 19X4	$5,000,000
Cash dividends on preferred stock during 19X4	$400,000
Common shares outstanding at January 1, 19X4	220,000
New common shares issued on July 1, 19X4	90,000

PROBLEMS FOR CHAPTER 15
Alternate Problems for this chapter begin on page D-81.

15.7. Following are selected events for ACB Corporation.

Events

Mar. 1   Directors of ACB Corporation declared common dividends of 48¢ per share to be paid in cash on April 15 to stockholders of record on March 21. There are 1,200,000 shares of common stock outstanding.

   11   Directors earmarked $250,000 of Retained Earnings for possible loss from a product liability lawsuit.

   21   Date of record for cash dividend.

Apr. 15   Common dividends paid in cash.

Sept. 1   Directors declared a 5% stock dividend to be issued on October 15 to stockholders of record on September 20. There are 1,200,000 shares outstanding, market value $22 per share, par value $10 per share.

   20   Date of record for stock dividend.

Oct. 15   Stock dividend shares issued to common shareholders.

   20   The product liability lawsuit prompting the directors' action on March 1 was settled out of court with a cash payment by ACB of $78,000 to the plaintiff.

Required

Make all journal entries needed to reflect the foregoing events.

15.8. Alka Corporation had net income after taxes for 19X4 of $18,000,000. Preferred dividends of $250,000 were paid during 19X4. There were 1,500,000 shares of common stock outstanding at January 1, 19X4, and 40,000 shares of common stock were issued on July 1, 19X4.

Required

1) Calculate earnings per share for 19X4.

2) State where earnings per share figures are normally shown in the accounting statements.

15.9. Selected data are given here for the Eman Corporation.

SELECTED DATA For the Fiscal Year Ended June 30, 19X5	
Sales	$120,000,000
Cost of goods sold	72,000,000
Selling, administrative, and general expenses	12,000,000
Interest expense	8,000,000
Federal income taxes	13,000,000
Cash dividends paid on common stock	6,000,000
Cash dividends paid on preferred stock	1,000,000
Retained earnings at July 1, 19X4	114,860,000
Retained earnings at June 30, 19X5	122,860,000
Average number of common shares outstanding: 1,150,000	

Required

Prepare a combined statement of income and retained earnings for Eman for the year ended June 30, 19X5. Be sure to include earnings per share in your statement.

15.10. The balance in the Retained Earnings account of the Zorb Corporation at January 1, 19X4, is $8,962,413. Selected transactions are as follows.

Transactions

19X4

Jan. 15   Common dividends of $896,000 declared November 30, 19X3, are paid.

Mar. 30   Directors declared a 4% stock dividend to be distributed on May 15 to stockholders of record on April 20. There are 2,500,000 shares of $10 par value stock outstanding, market value $15 per share.

Apr. 20   Date of record for stock dividend.

May 15   Stock dividend shares issued to common stockholders.

      24   Acquired 110,000 shares of treasury stock at a cost of $14 per share.

June 30   Directors declared common dividends of 38¢ per share to be paid in cash on August 15 to stockholders of record on July 20. There are 2,600,000 shares of issued stock, including 110,000 shares of treasury stock.

July 20   Date of record for cash dividend.

Aug. 15   Cash dividend paid.

Required

1) Make journal entries needed to reflect the events just listed.

2) Open a Retained Earnings ledger account at January 1, 19X4, and post entries made in part (1). Disregard cross-referencing numbers.

15.11. The Baggs Corporation has net taxable income of $6,400,000. Assume that corporate income is taxed at a uniform rate of 50% and that the average holder of Baggs Corporation stock is subject to federal, state, and local income taxes of 52%.

Required

1) How much must the corporation earn before taxes to be able to provide its stockholders with $1 million of disposable income after all corporate and personal income taxes (on the dividends) are paid?

2) What percentage of net corporate income after taxes must be paid out in order to provide the $1 million of disposable income to shareholders?

15.12. Following are selected events for the Dolff Corporation.

Events

June   1   Directors of Dolff Corporation declared preferred dividends of $5 per share to be paid on July 15 to preferred stockholders of record on June 30. There are 100,000 shares of preferred stock outstanding.

       1   Directors declared a 2 for 1 common stock split to become effective July 1. The $10 par value common stock is selling at $96 per share. There are 1,000,000 shares outstanding.

      15   Directors decided to appropriate $150,000 of Retained Earnings as a Reserve for Contingencies because of a patent infringement claim against Dolff in that amount.

      30   Date of record for preferred dividend.

July   1   Effective date of stock split.

      15   Preferred dividends paid in cash.

Aug.   1 $100,000 is paid to settle the patent infringement claim for which Retained Earnings were appropriated on June 15.

Required

Make the journal entries needed to reflect the foregoing events.

15.13. Data concerning liabilities and shareholders' equity for Gordo Corporation are as follows.

GORDO CORPORATION Selected Data June 30, 19--	
Accounts payable	$ 180,000
Salaries payable	41,000
Dividends payable—Common	240,000
Current maturities of mortgage payable	1,100,000
Mortgage payable (long-term)	10,000,000
Preferred stock, $100 par value, 10,000 shares issued and outstanding	1,000,000
Common stock, $1 par value, authorized 1,000,000 shares, issued 684,000 shares	684,000
Capital in excess of par	14,790,000
Retained earnings	28,640,138
Cost of common stock in treasury, 18,470 shares	383,495

Required

Prepare the liabilities and shareholders' equity sections of the balance sheet for Gordo Corporation at June 30.

15.14. Assume that corporate tax rates are as follows.

First	$25,000	15%
Next	$25,000	18%
Next	$25,000	30%
Next	$25,000	40%
Over	$100,000	46%

Required

1) Calculate the amount of tax due on each of the following taxable incomes:

   a) $20,000.

   b) $40,000.

   c) $80,000.

   d) $120,000.

2) Indicate the marginal and average tax rates for (a), (b), (c), and (d).

COMPREHENSION PROBLEM FOR CHAPTER 15

15.15. Myron Corporation shares had been selling on a stock exchange for $44 per share for several months when a 10% stock dividend was declared on February 18 to be distributed on March 15 to shareholders of record on March 1.

Required

1) Assuming that all shareholders are fully informed and act rationally, by how much, and in what direction, should the per-share market price have changed on or about the following dates?

a) February 18

b) March 1

c) March 15

2) Give the reasons for the changes you indicated in part (1).

3) Speculate on the probable changes in the per-share market price of the shares on each of the dates, given the way many shareholders perceive stock dividends.

4) Suppose Myron Corporation had split its shares on an 11 for 10 basis (each shareholder receives 11 new shares for each 10 old shares held). Discuss any differences in

a) The accounting treatment of the split as compared to the stock dividend.

b) The likely market reaction to the split as compared to the stock dividend.

16
Long-Term Liabilities and Investments

For every debtor, there exists a creditor; for every payable, there is a corresponding receivable held by another entity. As Section A of Chapter 6 illustrated, accounting for a receivable is in effect the "mirror image" of accounting for the corresponding payable. Such a relationship between two sets of accounts is sometimes referred to as symmetry of accounting. These remarks apply both to current and to long-term debt arrangements.

Chapter 16 is presented in two sections. Much of Section A is devoted to various aspects of accounting for bonds payable, including the issuance and retirement of bonds, the accrual of bond interest, and the amortization of bond premium and bond discount. Also included in this section are a discussion of the nature of long-term liabilities and brief remarks on liabilities for leases and pensions.

Section B deals with both short-term and long-term investments. The section commences with a discussion about the nature of investments and then goes on to treat short-term investments. Several types of long-term investments are covered, including sinking funds and ownership of corporate bonds and stocks. Some special problems in accounting for stock investments are introduced, and a balance sheet is presented to illustrate how investments are reported to statement users.

SECTION 16.A

Long-Term Liabilities

OBJECTIVES

This section deals with accounting for long-term liabilities. At the conclusion of your study, you should be able to

1. State the valuation basis for a long-term liability.
2. State the circumstances under which bonds will sell
   a. At a discount.
   b. At a premium.
3. Make journal entries to record the issuance of bonds.
4. Use the effective interest method to make journal entries to
   a. Adjust for accrued bond interest, including the discount or premium effects, at the end of an accounting period.
   b. Record the payment of bond interest on the due dates.
5. Make journal entries to retire bonds
   a. At maturity dates.
   b. By purchase or recall.

THE NATURE OF LONG-TERM LIABILITIES

Recall that a balance sheet pictures the condition of an entity at a point in time, in terms of the resources (assets) owned and the claims against those resources. The claims, consisting of liabilities and owners' equity, can also be viewed as the *sources* of the resources.

It is generally agreed that long-term needs for funds should not be financed with current liabilities, which will have to be paid before long with current assets. Thus current liabilities should help finance current assets, while long-term liabilities and ownership equity should supply an entity's remaining need for funds.

Current liabilities were discussed in Section 6.A. *Long-term liabilities are debt obligations that do not have to be paid within the next year, or within the operating cycle if it is longer than one year.* Illustration 16.1 shows the relationship between an entity's resources and the sources of those resources.

The relative amounts of current liabilities, long-term liabilities, and owners' equity vary by entity and over time. In general, debt is riskier than owners' equity because of the legal obligations to pay interest and repay the debt at specific times. On the other hand, borrowed funds may be invested so as to make more than the interest charges, leaving the extra earnings for the entity's owners. These considerations are explored in depth in finance

ILLUSTRATION 16.1

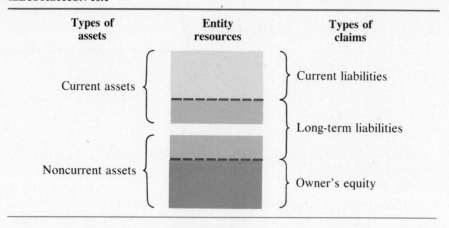

Types of assets	Entity resources	Types of claims
Current assets		Current liabilities
		Long-term liabilities
Noncurrent assets		Owner's equity

courses. Some approaches for measuring the effectiveness with which debt is employed are covered in Chapter 19.

Long-term liabilities are usually represented by formal, written debt instruments. Most debt instruments provide for fixed interest charges and definite maturity dates when the obligations must be paid. In some cases the principal (face) amount of the debt is paid off in installments. *An installment loan is repaid in periodic payments over the life of the loan.*

Debt obligations may be secured or unsecured. *A secured loan is guaranteed by granting the creditor a claim (lien) on specific property.* If the loan is not repaid as agreed, the property assigned as security may be taken (repossessed) and sold, with the sale proceeds used to apply against the loan amount. *When real estate is pledged as security for a loan, the agreement is known as a mortgage.*

Liabilities are claims against assets and are valued (in a negative sense) in terms of the assets they command. Amounts of cash or other assets due in the distant future must be discounted in order to arrive at their *present values*. Thus the valuation basis for a long-term liability is the net present value of the resources required to satisfy the obligation. Naturally, long-term receivables are valued in the same manner, because one party's liability is another's receivable. Present value concepts are covered in Appendix I of this chapter.

OBJECTIVE 1. State the valuation basis for a long-term liability.

BONDS PAYABLE

The Nature of Bonds

A bond is a formal negotiable note, usually specifying a long interval (5 to 50 years) between issuance and maturity. A bond certificate is a binding agreement (bond) to pay money in the future. Most bonds are issued in large denominations by business corporations or governments and provide for periodic interest payments over the bond life. Bond certificates, like stocks, are usually printed on paper bordered with ornamental designs and seals intended to discourage counterfeiting. A bond certificate states the obligations of the issuer and the rights of the bondholder, as shown in Illustration 16.2.

Bonds may be sold or purchased in the same securities markets as stocks. Bonds are sometimes referred to as senior securities, because bondholders' claims against a corporation are legally superior to those of stockholders.

Bond prices are usually stated as a percentage of face amount, but with decimal points and percent signs omitted. Bonds selling at 96 are priced at $96 per $100 of face amount; a $1,000 bond can be bought for $960. On the other hand, a $1,000 bond priced at 104 sells for $1,040. Security prices usually quote fractions of a dollar as fractions, rather than as decimals. Thus a $1,000 bond priced at 98⅛ will sell for $98.125 per $100 of face amount, which means that $981.25 must be paid for the bond.

Bond Indenture

The statement of terms on the bond certificate is usually *backed up by a more detailed contract known as the **bond indenture***. This agreement is en-

ILLUSTRATION 16.2

SOURCE: General Motors Acceptance Corporation

trusted to a *trustee,* who looks after the bondholders' rights during the life of the bond.

A bond indenture may contain any number of special provisions, depending on the concessions needed to attract lenders. For instance, management's freedom may be restricted in a variety of ways. The purpose of such restrictions is to protect the position of bondholders relative to other parties with interests in the corporation. A maximum permitted ratio of debt to equity may be specified to ensure that an adequate buffer of owners' equity is maintained to absorb possible future losses. Similar restrictions may be placed on the corporation's current ratio, on the payment of dividends, or on other aspects of the corporation's operations.

*Bonds may be secured by a real estate mortgage, in which case they are called **mortgage bonds**.* Or they may be secured by a lien on nonreal property such as machinery, equipment, or even stocks and bonds of other corporations that are owned by the borrowing corporation.

The bond indenture may permit the issuing corporation to call in (retire) the bonds prior to their maturity. If so, a *call premium* is usually specified as a penalty on the corporation for retiring the bonds early, similar to the call premium on preferred stock discussed in Chapter 14. The call feature enables corporations to take advantage of downward changes in interest rates by paying off outstanding bonds and issuing new bonds that pay less interest.

A bond indenture normally provides for a single maturity date for all bonds. This means that a corporation must be prepared at maturity to either pay out a large sum of cash or refinance the bonds with an issue of new bonds. To minimize the risk to bondholders, the indenture may provide for redemption of bonds gradually over the life of the bond issue. *Bonds may be issued in groups that fall due at various times; or the selection of bonds by chance (lot) may determine which ones will be redeemed at each redemption point. Bonds issued under these circumstances are called **serial bonds**.*

Sometimes the bond indenture requires that the issuing corporation *set aside money gradually to build up a **sinking fund** to be used to redeem the bonds at their maturity.* The purpose of a sinking fund provision is to ensure that there will be funds available for redemption when the bonds fall due. Sinking fund monies are usually invested in securities so as to earn a return until the funds are needed at the maturity of the bonds.

Benefits from Issuing Bonds

Although borrowing money is risky, it allows owners to profit from the use of money supplied by others. *The act of earning more on borrowed funds than they cost in interest is called **trading on the equity** or **using financial leverage**.* The use of owners' equity as a buffer (lever) for borrowing is discussed in Chapter 19.

When a large infusion of new money is needed in a corporation, managers must decide which source of funds would be most desirable. Since ready markets already exist for stocks and bonds, the choice frequently is between these two types of securities.

Bond interest is a deductible expense for tax purposes, while cash dividends on stocks are considered distributions of earnings to the stockholders. For a corporation in a 46% marginal tax bracket, each $1 of interest deduction reduces taxable income by $1, and consequently reduces taxes by 46¢. Therefore, the *after-tax* cost of the interest is only 54¢ per $1 of interest paid, or 54% of the stated interest rate. The after-tax cost of a 12% interest rate is only 6.48% for a corporation in a 46% marginal tax bracket, as demonstrated here.

Interest rate(1 − Tax bracket) = After tax rate of interest

$$0.12(1 - 0.46) = 0.12(0.54) = 0.0648$$

To understand how issuing bonds can benefit shareholders, consider a corporation currently earning $400,000 net income per year before income taxes. The corporation has no interest-bearing debt at present. There are 100,000 shares of common stock outstanding, which are selling at $20 per share. Directors believe that with $1,000,000 of new money the corporation can earn an *additional* $200,000 before interest and taxes. The choice comes down to either issuing 50,000 new common shares at $20 each or issuing 1,000 bonds bearing 12% interest for $1,000 per bond. The schedule in Illustration 16.3 shows the expected outcomes from each alternative, assuming for simplicity that a 46% tax rate applies to all income. You can see that the earnings per share are higher when the additional funds are obtained from issuing bonds.

ILLUSTRATION 16.3

	Issue Bonds	Issue Stock
Earnings before interest and taxes	$600,000	$600,000
Less bond interest	120,000	–0–
Net income before tax	$480,000	$600,000
Tax at 46%	220,800	276,000
Net income after tax	$259,200	$324,000
Earnings per share		
100,000 shares	$2.59	
150,000 shares		$2.16

Bond Interest

Borrowers prefer low rates of interest; lenders seek high returns on their money. The market (going) rate of interest for a particular type of loan is determined in the money market by the relationship between the amount of funds sought by borrowers (demand) and the amount available from lenders (supply). *The market rate of interest, then, is the rate that lenders are willing to accept for the use of their money at a particular point in time.*

In general, the level of *risk* involved directly affects the rate of interest—the higher the risk of loss, the higher the interest rate demanded by lenders. *The market rate of interest charged at any point in time for loans of minimum risk is called the prime rate of interest.* The difference between the prime rate and a particular rate borne by a high-risk loan is essentially the enticement needed to get lenders to assume the higher risk.

Interest rates may also vary according to the time duration of a loan. When interest rates are high, lenders prefer to lend on a long-term basis; when rates are low, lenders prefer to tie their money up for shorter periods, in the hope that they can transfer their money to high-interest loans in the near future. Therefore, long-term debt should bear a higher interest rate than short-term debt during periods when future interest rates are expected to rise. The opposite should be true during periods when future interest rates are expected to fall.

Since bond certificates must be printed prior to the time that they are issued, a corporation's officers and directors attempt to predict the interest rate the money market will require for the corporation's bonds, and *a stated rate of interest is printed along with other terms on the certificates. The bond contract requires the corporation to pay the stated rate of interest on the face value (principal amount) of the bonds.*

Market conditions may change between the time bonds are printed and the time they are issued. Also, the persons who decided on the stated interest rate may not have guessed correctly the exact rate that will satisfy lenders. Since the bond terms are already determined, these factors can only be reflected in the *price* of the bonds at the time of issue. If the stated rate of interest is less than lenders require, the bonds will sell at a discount. *Bond discount is the amount by which the face (principal) amount of a bond exceeds the issue price.* The lower the stated rate of interest, relative to the going market rate, the less lenders will pay for the bonds and therefore the greater the bond discount.

An attractive bond interest rate, relative to the going market rate, will cause lenders to compete for the bonds, thereby causing the bonds to sell at premium prices. *Bond premium is the amount by which the issue price of a bond exceeds the face amount.* Bond premiums and discounts are the means by which the bond markets convert the stated rates of interest to the market rates of interest that lenders are willing to accept. As market rates of interest change, bond prices change in the *opposite* direction. Increases

OBJECTIVE 2a. State the circumstances under which bonds will sell at a discount.

OBJECTIVE 2b. State the circumstances under which bonds will sell at a premium.

in interest rates cause the values of existing bonds to fall; decreased interest rates make bonds worth more.

Bonds Issued at Face Amount

The entry to record the issuance of bonds at their face value is rather straight-forward. The following entry reflects the issue of 1,000 bonds for their face value of $1,000 each

19X4 Nov. 1	Cash	1,000,000	
	Bonds Payable		1,000,000
	Issued 1,000, 12%, ten-year bonds at $1,000 each.		

OBJECTIVE 3. Record the issuance of bonds.

If the corporation accounts on a calendar-year basis, an adjusting entry will be needed on December 31 to accrue two months of interest expense.

19X4 Dec. 31	Bond Interest Expense	20,000	
	Bond Interest Payable		20,000
	Bond interest at 12% for two months.		
	$(0.12 \times \$1,000,000 \times \frac{2}{12} = \$20,000)$		

Bond interest is usually paid either semiannually or quarterly. Assuming semiannual payment of interest, the following entry reflects the cash payment for interest on May 1, 19X5.

19X5 May 1	Bond Interest Expense	40,000	
	Bond Interest Payable	20,000	
	Cash		60,000
	Semiannual interest payment.		
	$(0.12 \times \$1,000,000 \times \frac{6}{12} = \$60,000)$		

Bonds Issued between Interest Dates

Sometimes the issue of bonds is delayed beyond the date stated on the bond certificates. This presents a problem because the bond agreement calls for a full interest payment on the first interest date; however, bondholders will not have earned interest for the full period. The problem is usually resolved by having the bondholders pay for the accrued interest up to the time that

ILLUSTRATION 16.4

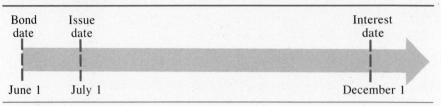

Bond date	Issue date		Interest date
June 1	July 1		December 1

the bonds are issued; this part of their payment is then returned to them as part of the first interest payment they receive.

Consider a situation where 12%, ten-year bonds, dated June 1, 19X4, are issued at $100,000 face value plus accrued interest on July 1. Important dates in this example are shown in Illustration 16.4.

The accrued interest for the 30 days between bond date and issue date is $1,000. This would probably be credited to Bond Interest Expense to offset that much of the full interest payment that will be paid on December 1.

OBJECTIVE 3. Record the issuance of bonds.

19X4 July 1	Cash	101,000	
	Bonds Payable		100,000
	Bond Interest Expense		1,000
	Issued 12%, ten-year bonds dated June 1, 19X4.		
	$(0.12 \times \$100,000 \times \frac{1}{12} = \$1,000)$		

When the semiannual interest payment is made on December 1, it is recorded just as though the bonds had been outstanding for a full six months.

19X4 Dec. 1	Bond Interest Expense	6,000	
	Cash		6,000
	Paid semiannual interest on bonds.		
	$(0.12 \times \$100,000 \times \frac{6}{12} = \$6,000)$		

At this point the Bond Interest Expense account will show the correct interest cost for five months, as illustrated by the following T-account.

Bond Interest Expense			
Dec. 1	6,000	July 1	1,000

Bonds Issued at a Discount

When bonds carry a stated interest rate that is less than the going market rate, lenders will take the bonds only at a discount. For example, a $1,000, 10%, ten-year bond paying interest semiannually will bring only about $885.30 if the going interest rate is 12%.[1] The market price of $885.30 is the present value of the future stream of interest payments ($50 each six months) plus the present value of the principal amount ($1,000) to be received at maturity.[2] The discount of $114.70 per bond is what it takes to make the bonds earn 12% interest for the bond buyer.

Most accountants prefer to show as Bonds Payable the full face amount that must be paid at maturity. Yet when bonds are issued at a discount, the corporation does not realize that much cash from the issue. In other words, the amount borrowed initially is less than the amount that must be paid back at maturity. The problem is usually resolved by recording the amount of discount in a contra liability account. If 1,000 bonds are issued at $885.30 each, the entry on the books of the corporation appears as follows.

19X4			
Nov. 1	Cash	885,300	
	Discount on Bonds Payable	114,700	
	Bonds Payable		1,000,000
	Issued 1,000, 10%, ten-year bonds at $885.30.		

OBJECTIVE 3. Record the issuance of bonds.

The Discount on Bonds Payable account should be viewed along with the Bonds Payable account, as depicted by the following T-accounts.

Bonds Payable	Discount on Bonds Payable
1,000,000	114,700

---

[1]Actually, the bonds would likely be quoted on a securities market at 88½, which would make the price $885 per bond. Securities prices are normally quoted with fractions stated in eighths of a dollar, including fourths or halves as lowest common denominators. Thus ⅜ would be quoted as ¼, ⅜ as ½, and ⅝ as ¾.

[2]Present value concepts are covered in Appendix I of this chapter. The calculation of the present value of the bond is as follows:

Interest per 6-month period, 5% × $1,000	$50	
Present value annuity factor, 6%, 20 periods	× 11.469921	
Present value of interest payments		$573.496
Principal amount	$1,000	
Present value factor, 6%, 20 periods	× 0.311805	
Present value of principal		311.805
Present value of bond contract		$885.301

The *net liability* immediately after issue is equivalent to the amount borrowed. At this point, the face of the bonds less the discount is shown as a long-term liability on the corporation's balance sheet, in a form similar to the following.

Bonds payable	$1,000,000	
Less: Discount on bonds payable	114,700	$885,300

Straight-Line Amortization of Bond Discount.   The full face amount of the bonds must be repaid at maturity; the discount amount should be gradually amortized over the life of the bonds by writing off the balance in the contra account. One way to accomplish this is to spread (amortize) the discount evenly (on a straight-line basis) over the number of bond interest periods. For ten-year bonds paying interest semiannually, the discount is spread over 20 semiannual periods.

$$\frac{\$114,700}{20 \text{ periods}} = \$5,735 \text{ discount amortization each interest period}$$

The entry for each semiannual period recognizes $5,735 more in interest expense than is paid out in cash.

Bond Interest Expense	55,735	
Discount on Bonds Payable		5,735
Cash		50,000
To record semiannual bond interest charges (straight-line method).		
(0.10 × $1,000,000 × 6/12 = $50,000)		

The amortization of the discount actually *increases* the net bond liability by $5,735 each six months, so that at the end of ten years there will be no balance in the contra liability account. In effect, a portion of the interest cost each period is added to the carrying value of the bond liability. It is for this reason that the reduction of the Discount on Bonds Payable account is sometimes called discount accumulation rather than discount amortization.

We must not forget to accrue interest at the end of each accounting period. For a corporation accounting on a calendar-year basis, the following entry would be needed on December 31 to recognize interest and discount amortization for November and December. For convenience, amounts are rounded to the nearest whole dollar.

| 19X4
Dec. 31 | Bond Interest Expense
 Discount on Bonds Payable
 Bond Interest Payable
Bond interest charges for two months
(straight-line method).
(0.10 × $1,000,000 × $\frac{2}{12}$ = $16,667)
($5,735 × $\frac{2}{6}$ = $1,912) | 18,579 | 1,912
16,667 |

Now, when the interest is paid on May 1, 19X5, the following entry will be made.

| 19X5
May 1 | Bond Interest Expense
Bond Interest Payable
 Discount on Bonds Payable
 Cash
Paid semiannual interest on bonds (straight-
line method).
($5,735 × $\frac{4}{6}$ = $3,823) | 37,156
16,667 | 3,823
50,000 |

Although the straight-line method for amortizing bond discount is simple, it yields somewhat misleading results. As the net bond liability increases from $885,300 to $1,000,000 over the ten-year bond period, we might expect the semiannual interest charges to go up accordingly. For this reason, the straight-line method is acceptable only when the results are not materially different from the effective interest approach described next.[3]

Effective Interest Amortization of Bond Discount. The 10% bonds described earlier had to be issued at a discount because the market (effective) rate of interest was 12% at the time they were issued. Instead of yielding 5% return per semiannual period, the issue price allows 6% yield to bondholders every six months.

The net bond obligation during the first six months of the bond issue stood at $885,300. At a 6% rate, the effective interest cost of using $885,300 for the six-month period would be $53,118. The discount amortization is then the difference between that figure and the cash interest that must be paid out ($53,118 − $50,000 = $3,118). Illustration 16.5 on the next page shows the manner in which the bond obligation increases as the discount is amortized by means of the effective interest approach. Note that the effective interest amount for each period is the result of multiplying the effective

---

[3]*Opinions of the Accounting Principles Board No. 21,* "Interest on Receivables and Payables" (New York: American Institute of Certified Public Accountants, 1971), par. 15.

ILLUSTRATION 16.5

EFFECTIVE INTEREST TABLE FOR BONDS ISSUED AT A DISCOUNT					
6-Month Period	Interest Paid (5% × $1,000,000)	Effective Interest (6% × Net Liability)	Discount Amortization	Bond Discount Balance	Net Bond Liability
				$114,700	$ 885,300
1	$50,000	$53,118	$3,118	111,582	888,418
2	50,000	53,305	3,305	108,277	891,723
3	50,000	53,503	3,503	104,774	895,226
4	50,000	53,714	3,714	101,060	898,940
5	50,000	53,936	3,936	97,124	902,876
6	50,000	54,173	4,173	92,951	907,049
7	50,000	54,423	4,423	88,528	911,472
8	50,000	54,688	4,688	83,840	916,160
9	50,000	54,970	4,970	78,870	921,130
10	50,000	55,268	5,268	73,602	926,398
11	50,000	55,584	5,584	68,018	931,982
12	50,000	55,919	5,919	62,099	937,901
13	50,000	56,274	6,274	55,825	944,175
14	50,000	56,651	6,651	49,174	950,826
15	50,000	57,050	7,050	42,124	957,876
16	50,000	57,473	7,473	34,651	965,349
17	50,000	57,921	7,921	26,730	973,270
18	50,000	58,396	8,396	18,334	981,666
19	50,000	58,900	8,900	9,434	990,566
20	50,000	59,434	9,434	–0–	1,000,000

NOTE: $1,000,000 face, 10%, ten-year, semiannual interest bonds issued to yield 12% return to bondholders.

(yield) interest rate times the net bond liability during the period. The effective interest rate, sometimes referred to as the yield rate, is the market rate of interest in effect at the time the bonds were issued.

Data used in preparing journal entries may be taken from the table in Illustration 16.5. For instance, we know that the interest expense for the first six-month period is $53,118, while the discount amortization is $3,118. For the adjusting entry at December 31, 19X4, we can take one-third of the interest and discount amounts for the first six-month period (two months are one-third of six months).

OBJECTIVE 4a. Use the effective interest method to adjust for accrued bond interest, including the discount or premium effects.

19X4			
Dec. 31	Bond Interest Expense	17,706	
	Discount on Bonds Payable		1,039
	Bond Interest Payable		16,667
	Bond interest charges for two months (effective interest method).		

ILLUSTRATION 16.6

19X5 May 1	Bond Interest Expense
	Bond Interest Payable
	    Discount on Bonds Payable
	    Cash
	    Paid semiannual interest on bonds (effective
	    interest method).
		35,412
		16,667
			2,079
			50,000

OBJECTIVE 4b. Use the effective interest method to record the payment of bond interest on the due dates.

19X5 Nov. 1	Bond Interest Expense
	    Discount on Bonds Payable
	    Cash
	    Paid semiannual interest on bonds (effective
	    interest method).
		53,305	3,305
			50,000

Although interest charges increase for each six-month period during the life of the bonds, prorations *within* interest periods are made on a straight-line basis. The entries to record the first two interest payments are shown in Illustration 16.6.

The information for the second entry in Illustration 16.6 came directly from the second-period row of Illustration 16.5.

Bonds Issued at a Premium

Bonds that pay interest at a rate greater than the market (effective) rate will be bid upward by bond investors to a price that will yield the market rate of interest. For example, a $1,000,000 bond issue of ten-year, 10% bonds that pay interest semiannually should bring in $1,135,903 of cash if the going annual rate of interest is 8%.[4]

The entry to record the bond issue would reflect the bond premium in a separate liability account.[5]

---

[4]The present value of the bond issue described is calculated as follows:

Interest per 6-month period, 5% × $1,000,000	$50,000	
Present value annuity factor, 4%, 20 periods	× 13.590326	
Present value of interest payments		$ 679,516
Principal amount	$1,000,000	
Present value factor, 4%, 20 periods	× 0.456387	
Present value of principal		456,387
Present value of bond contract		$1,135,903

[5]On securities markets, it is likely that these bonds would be priced at 113⅜, which would amount to $1,136.25 per bond.

OBJECTIVE 3.   Record the issuance of bonds.

19X4			
Nov. 1	Cash	1,135,903	
	Premium on Bonds Payable		135,903
	Bonds Payable		1,000,000
	Issued 1,000, 10%, ten-year bonds at $1,135.903 each.		

Straight-Line Amortization of Bond Premium.   Only $1,000,000 will be due at the maturity date of the bonds, so the premium amount must be written off (amortized) over the ten-year life of the bonds. If the premium is spread evenly by the straight-line method, $6,795.15 will be written off for each half-year. In effect, the bondholders are getting back in their interest checks each period part of the extra amount they paid initially for the bonds. Ignoring accruals needed at the end of each accounting year, and rounding to the nearest dollar, the entry at the end of each interest period would appear as follows.

Bond Interest Expense	43,205	
Premium on Bonds Payable	6,795	
Cash		50,000
Paid semiannual interest on bonds (straight-line method).		

Effective Interest Amortization of Bond Premium.   As the premium amount is written down (amortized), the gross bond liability is reduced. It should then follow that the effective interest cost should decline along with the bond liability. As with amortization of bond discounts, the amortization of bond premiums is normally carried out by the effective interest method.

Illustration 16.7 shows the effective interest and premium amortization for each six-month period of the life of the bonds described earlier.

The entry to accrue interest for the two months ending December 31, 19X4, will reflect one-third of the effective interest and premium amortization from the first row of the table.

OBJECTIVE 4a.   Use the effective interest method to adjust for accrued bond interest, including the discount or premium effects.

19X4			
Dec. 31	Bond Interest Expense	15,145	
	Premium on Bonds Payable	1,522	
	Bond Interest Payable		16,667
	Bond interest charges for two months (effective interest method).		

The entries to record the first two interest payments are shown in Illustration 16.8.

ILLUSTRATION 16.7

	EFFECTIVE INTEREST TABLE FOR BONDS ISSUED AT A PREMIUM				
6-Month Period	Interest Paid (5% × $1,000,000)	Effective Interest (4% × Gross Liability)	Premium Amortization	Premium Balance	Gross Bond Liability
				$135,903	$1,135,903
1	$50,000	$45,436	$4,564	131,339	1,131,339
2	50,000	45,254	4,746	126,593	1,126,593
3	50,000	45,064	4,936	121,657	1,121,657
4	50,000	44,866	5,134	116,523	1,116,523
5	50,000	44,661	5,339	111,184	1,111,184
6	50,000	44,447	5,553	105,631	1,105,631
7	50,000	44,225	5,775	99,856	1,099,856
8	50,000	43,994	6,006	93,850	1,093,850
9	50,000	43,754	6,246	87,604	1,087,604
10	50,000	43,504	6,496	81,108	1,081,108
11	50,000	43,244	6,756	74,352	1,074,352
12	50,000	42,974	7,026	67,326	1,067,326
13	50,000	42,693	7,307	60,019	1,060,019
14	50,000	42,401	7,599	52,420	1,052,420
15	50,000	42,097	7,903	44,517	1,044,517
16	50,000	41,781	8,219	36,298	1,036,298
17	50,000	41,452	8,548	27,750	1,027,750
18	50,000	41,110	8,890	18,860	1,018,860
19	50,000	40,754	9,246	9,614	1,009,614
20	50,000	40,386*	9,614	–0–	1,000,000

NOTE: $1,000,000 face, 10%, ten-year, semiannual interest bonds issued to yield 8% return to bondholders.

*Adjusted to compensate for the accumulated effects of rounding.

ILLUSTRATION 16.8

19X5 May 1	Bond Interest Expense	30,291	
	Premium on Bonds Payable	3,042	
	Bond Interest Payable	16,667	
	Cash		50,000
	Paid semiannual interest on bonds (effective interest method).		

OBJECTIVE 4b. Use the effective interest method to record the payment of bond interest on the due dates.

19X5 Nov. 1	Bond Interest Expense	45,254	
	Premium on Bonds Payable	4,746	
	Cash		50,000
	Paid semiannual interest on bonds (effective interest method).		

Bond Retirements

Since bond premiums and discounts are written off as adjustments over the life of the bonds, only the face amount of bond liability remains in the accounts at the time bonds mature. The entry to record the redemption of bonds at maturity is rather straightforward.

OBJECTIVE 5a. Retire bonds at maturity dates.

19Y4 Nov. 1	Bonds Payable	1,000,000	
	Cash		1,000,000
	To record the redemption of bonds.		

Redemption by Purchase.   A corporation with sufficient cash available may purchase some of its own bonds in the securities markets to effect a partial redemption of the bond liability. If bonds are acquired for less than the liability accounts reflect, a gain is recognized. For example, the entry to record the purchase at 96 of ten bonds that were issued initially for $1,000 each would appear as follows.

OBJECTIVE 5b. Retire bonds by purchase or recall.

19X6 Nov. 1	Bonds Payable	10,000	
	Cash		9,600
	Gain on Bond Retirement		400
	Redeemed ten bonds at 96.		

The gain represents an increase in shareholders' equity because more liabilities than assets are removed from the corporation's accounting equation, as illustrated here.

Assets	=	Liabilities	+	Shareholders' Equity
− $9,600		− $10,000		+ $400

If on the other hand, bonds are redeemed for more than the liability accounts show, a *loss* is recognized on the books.

OBJECTIVE 5b. Retire bonds by purchase or recall.

19X6 Nov. 1	Bonds Payable	10,000	
	Loss on Bond Retirement	400	
	Cash		10,400
	Redeemed ten bonds at 104.		

And the loss is a decrease in shareholders' equity.

Assets	=	Liabilities	+	Shareholders' Equity
− $10,400		− $10,000		− $400

Redemption by Call.   As pointed out earlier, a bond indenture may permit the corporation to call in the bonds by paying a call premium. If the call option is exercised, the entry will reflect a loss when the cash paid out exceeds the liability paid off. Consider the case where $1,000,000 face amount of ten-year bonds were issued initially for $885,300. Midway through the life of the bonds the liability should stand as follows.

Bonds Payable		Discount on Bonds Payable	
	1,000,000	114,700	41,098

If, at this point, the foregoing bonds were called at 102, the redemption entry would appear as follows.

19X9			
Nov. 1	Bonds Payable	1,000,000	
	Loss on Bond Redemption	93,602	
	Discount on Bonds Payable		73,602
	Cash		1,020,000
	Bonds called at 102.		

OBJECTIVE 5b. Retire bonds by purchase or recall.

The loss of $93,602 is the difference between the cash paid of $1,020,000 and the net bond liability of $926,398 (see line 10 of Illustration 16.5) at the end of 10 semiannual periods after the issue date.

You might wonder why a corporation's officers and directors would permit it to incur a loss voluntarily. The answer is that they probably would not, *if* the loss were a real one. When a book loss results from a bond redemption, the officers are probably trying to improve the long-run profitability of the corporation. Bonds may be called at a premium because the rate of interest being paid is substantially above the current market rate of interest. In attempting to improve future profitability, corporations sometimes redeem bonds at a book loss and replace them with new bonds at a lower interest rate.

LEASE LIABILITIES

Leased assets are discussed briefly in Chapter 8. As suggested there, accounting for leased assets is often complex and is best covered in intermediate and advanced accounting courses.[6]

Where leased properties are shown among the lessee's assets, corresponding lease liabilities appear among the liability accounts. In most cases, lease liabilities are long term and are generally reduced as cash payments are made and as the lessee's rights to use the leased properties expire.

PENSION LIABILITIES

Another area of considerable complexity is accounting for pension plans. *A pension plan is an employer's agreement to provide employees with an income during their retirement years.* Most pension plans currently in effect are *funded,* which means that money is paid periodically to an insurance company or other agency during an employee's working years; when the employee retires, the insuring agency provides the employee with retirement income.

The great majority of pension plans currently in effect were strongly influenced by the Internal Revenue Code, which sets the conditions under which pension costs may be deducted for tax purposes.[7] In 1974 the U.S. Congress passed a complicated law that requires extensive reporting by employers to ensure that employees' retirement funds are protected.[8] At this writing, accounting for pension costs by employers is still governed by a 1966 pronouncement by the Accounting Principles Board,[9] although the Financial Accounting Standards Board has for some time been considering the need for changes.

At this level it is sufficient for you to know that accrual of pension liabilities by employers is generally required for each year that employees are covered by a pension plan. The entry would take the following form.

Pension Plan Expense	XXX	
Accrued Pension Plan Liability		XXX
To record pension liability for the year.		

---

[6]*FASB Statement No. 13 as Amended and Interpreted Through May 1980* (incorporating Statements 13, 17, 22, 23, 26, 27, 28, and 29 and Interpretations 19, 21, 23, 24, 26, and 27) (Stamford, Conn.: Financial Accounting Standards Board, 1980) is a long and involved pronouncement on accounting for leases.

[7]Internal Revenue Code, Sec. 401–407.

[8]The Employees' Retirement Income Security Act of 1974, commonly referred to as ERISA.

[9]*Opinions of the Accounting Principles Board No. 8,* "Accounting for the Cost of Pension Plans" (New York: American Institute of Certified Public Accountants, 1966).

Cash payments to the pension funding agency would reduce the liability, as indicated by the following entry.

Accrued Pension Plan Liability	XXX	
Cash		XXX
Paid pension plan requirement for the year.		

Further study in this area must be left to more advanced accounting courses.

GLOSSARY FOR SECTION 16.A

Bond   A formal negotiable note, usually specifying a long interval (5 to 50 years) between issuance and maturity.

Bond discount   The amount by which the face amount of a bond exceeds the issue price.

Bond indenture   A detailed contract that backs up the bond terms stated on the bond certificates.

Bond premium   The amount by which the issue price of a bond exceeds the face amount.

Installment loan   A loan that is repaid in periodic payments over the life of the loan.

Long-term liabilities   Debt obligations that do not have to be paid within the next year, or within the operating cycle if it is longer than one year.

Market rate of interest   The interest rate that lenders are willing to accept for the use of their money at a particular point in time.

Mortgage   An agreement whereby real estate is pledged as security for a loan.

Mortgage bonds   Bonds that are secured by a real estate mortgage.

Pension plan   An employer's agreement to provide employees with an income during their retirement years.

Prime rate of interest   The market rate of interest charged at any point in time for loans of minimum risk.

Secured loan   A loan that is guaranteed by granting the creditor a claim (lien) on specific property.

Serial bonds   Bonds that are issued in groups that fall due at various times, or by agreement that provides for selection of bonds by chance (lot) to determine which will be redeemed at each redemption point.

Sinking fund   A pool of assets, usually in the form of securities, gradually built up from cash contributions made by a corporation for purposes of redeeming bonds at their maturity.

Stated rate of interest The contracted interest rate that must be paid on the principal amount of a loan.

Trading on the equity (using financial leverage) The act of earning more on borrowed funds than they cost in interest.

SELF-QUIZ ON OBJECTIVES FOR SECTION 16.A
Solutions to Self-Quiz begin on page B-48.

1. **OBJECTIVE 1.** State the valuation basis for a long-term liability.

2. **OBJECTIVE 2.** Under what circumstances will bonds sell at a discount? At a premium?

3. On December 1, 19X3, bonds with a face value of $100,000 were issued at 107, a price that yields an 8% per annum effective interest rate. The bonds pay $4,500 in interest on June 1 and December 1 of each year of their 10-year life (9% per annum). Using the effective interest method, make the following journal entries:

   a. **OBJECTIVE 3.** Record the bond issuance on December 1, 19X3.

   b. **OBJECTIVE 4a.** Recognize accrued interest on the bonds at December 31, 19X3, the end of the accounting year.

   c. **OBJECTIVE 4b.** Record payment of bond interest on June 1, 19X4.

   d. **OBJECTIVE 4b.** Record payment of bond interest on December 1, 19X4.

   e. **OBJECTIVE 5a.** Record the retirement of the bonds on December 1, 19Y3, assuming that the entry to record the final interest payment has already been made.

4. **OBJECTIVE 5b.** Lute Corporation bonds are called at 104 on August 1 when the accounts show Bonds Payable of $1,000,000 and Premium on Bonds Payable of $15,000. Make the entry in Lute's journal to record the redemption of the bonds.

DISCUSSION QUESTIONS FOR SECTION 16.A

1. Why are bonds sometimes referred to as senior securities?

2. What is a call premium as the term relates to corporate bonds?

3. How are risk levels reflected in bond interest rates?

4. What is a *market rate of interest,* and how is it determined?

5. What purpose is served by the account Discount on Bonds Payable?

6. Why might a corporation be willing to incur a loss by retiring its bonds at a call premium?

7. A bond indenture is a contract between a borrower (the issuing corporation) and lenders (the bondholders). In addition to specifying the maturity date and interest rate, a bond indenture may impose special restrictions on the borrower. What are some typical restrictions that may be placed on the issuing corporation by a bond indenture?

8. Bonds that are traded in organized securities markets may fluctuate in price after their initial issue by the corporation. What kinds of circumstances might cause a particular bond to fluctuate in price from time to time on the bond market?

EXERCISES FOR SECTION 16.A

16.A.1. State the selling price in dollars and cents of a $5,000 bond quoted at

   a. 98

   b. 106

   c. 100

   d. 96⅜

   e. 103¾

16.A.2. Calculate the amount of bond discount that would be amortized on a straight-line basis for each of 40 semiannual periods for $1,000,000 face amount of bonds issued at a price of 96⅜.

16.A.3. Calculate the amount of bond premium that would be amortized on a straight-line basis for each of 30 semiannual periods for $10,000,000 face amount of bonds issued at a price of 104½.

16.A.4. The Wenkle Corporation issued $1,000,000 face value bonds on October 31, 19X4, at 93½, a price that yields a 9% per annum effective interest rate. The bonds pay $40,000 in interest on April 30 and October 31 of each year of their 10-year life (8% per annum). Use the effective interest method to calculate the accrued interest expense at December 31, 19X4, and the bond discount to be amortized on that date.

16.A.5. The Pam Corporation issued bonds with a face value of $1,000,000 on June 30, 19X4, at 108⅝, a price that yields about 8% per annum effective interest. The bonds pay $45,000 in interest on June 30 and December 31 of each year of their 15-year life (9% per annum). Use the effective interest method to

   a. Calculate the interest expense to be recorded at December 31, 19X4.

   b. Calculate the amount of bond premium that should be amortized at December 31, 19X4.

PROBLEMS FOR SECTION 16.A
Alternate Problems for this section begin on page D-83.

16.A.6. On October 31, 19X4, the Megan Corporation issued bonds with a face value of $10,000,000. The bonds pay $450,000 in interest on April 30 and October 31 of each year of their 10-year life (9% per annum).

Required

   1) Assume that the bonds were issued at 93¾, a price that yields about 10% per annum effective interest rate. Using the effective interest method, make journal entries to

   a) Record the bond issuance on October 31, 19X4

SECTION 16.B

Investments

OBJECTIVES

This section deals with accounting for investments. At the conclusion of your study, you should be able to

1. Differentiate between current marketable securities and long-term investments.
2. Record the following entries in the issuing corporation's journal:
   a. The contribution of cash to a bond sinking fund.
   b. Earnings of the sinking fund.
   c. The retirement of bonds with sinking fund cash and the termination of the sinking fund.
3. Record the following in an investor's journal:
   a. Purchases of securities.
   b. Revenues from investments.
   c. Sales of investment assets.
4. Differentiate between the cost method and the equity method of accounting for investments in common stock.

THE NATURE OF INVESTMENTS

Idle cash is a most unproductive asset. In order to earn a return, cash must be invested into other asset forms. *When assets are acquired that are not directly related to the principal activities of the entity, they are usually referred to as investments.* Investments allow an entity to earn a return on funds that are not needed immediately in the entity's operations.

SHORT-TERM INVESTMENTS

Investments may be held for either short or long periods of time. *Where it is management's intention to hold investment assets for a relatively short period, the assets are referred to as temporary investments or short-term investments.*

Although idle funds may be invested in practically any kind of asset, they are most often invested in securities issued by corporations and governments. *Investments in stocks, bonds, treasury bills, and similar securities are called current marketable securities when (1) the securities are readily salable (marketable) and (2) the investing entity's managers view the securities as a ready source of cash. Investments that do not qualify as marketable securities are classified as long-term investments.*

OBJECTIVE 1.
Differentiate between current marketable securities and long-term investments.

Marketable securities are usually listed on the balance sheet just below the asset cash. In fact, for balance sheet purposes some entities show Cash and Current Marketable Securities as a single asset category. Marketable debt securities (bonds, notes, and so forth) are generally carried in the accounts at their costs. *FASB Statement No. 12* provides that marketable equity securities are to be reported at the *lower* of their total cost or total market value.[10] *Equity securities are investments in ownership shares (common or preferred) of other corporations.*

The amount by which the total cost of current marketable equity securities exceeds their total value at a point in time is reported as a *net unrealized loss on marketable equity securities* in the income statement for the period.[11] Let us assume, for example, that marketable equity securities owned by a corporation had cost $300,000, but are now worth only $270,000. The following entry establishes a contra asset allowance for the decline in market value.

Unrealized Loss on Cur. Marketable Equity Securities	30,000	
Allow. for Mkt. Decl. of Cur. Marketable Equity Sec.		30,000
To reflect the decline in market value of		
securities.		

The securities would be reported in the balance sheet at their cost of $300,000, with the allowance of $30,000 shown as a deduction, to arrive at the net book value of the securities.

Subsequent increases in market prices may be recognized in the accounts, but not to exceed the amount of the contra allowance. For example, should the market value of the securities increase to $280,000 in the next period, the following entry would be made.

Allow. for Mkt. Decl. of Cur. Marketable Equity Sec.	10,000	
Unrealized Gain on Cur. Marketable Equity Sec.		10,000
To reflect the partial recovery of previous		
declines in market value of securities.		

At this point, the remaining allowance of $20,000 would be deducted from the cost of the marketable securities, as shown on the balance sheet pictured in Illustration 16.13 on page 686.

---

[10]*Statement of Financial Accounting Standards No. 12,* "Accounting for Certain Marketable Securities" (Stamford, Conn.: Financial Accounting Standards Board, 1975), par. 8.

[11]Ibid., par. 9.

LONG-TERM INVESTMENTS

Entities commit funds to long-term investments for a variety of reasons. As pointed out in the previous section, a bond indenture may require that funds be set aside periodically in a *sinking fund* to ensure that money will be available to redeem the bonds at their maturity date. Bond sinking fund money is usually invested in securities so that it may earn a return for the corporation. In other instances of long-term investments, land may be purchased and held for some planned future use, or funds may be set aside and invested in securities to provide for future expansion of plant facilities.

Most large corporations hold substantial investments in *subsidiary corporations* for purposes of controlling their operations. Securities of related subsidiary corporations are always classified as long-term investments.

Bond Sinking Funds

Contributions to a bond sinking fund are usually deposited with a *sinking fund trustee* named in the bond indenture. *A sinking fund trustee may be an individual but is usually a bank or other financial institution charged with managing the fund.* At the time that cash is deposited with the trustee, an entry is made on the corporation's books.

OBJECTIVE 2a. Record the contribution of cash to a bond sinking fund.

Bond Sinking Fund	10,000	
Cash		10,000
Quarterly contribution to sinking fund.		

The sinking fund trustee will invest the money so it can earn a return for the corporation. When earnings on sinking fund investments are reported by the trustee, they are registered in the corporation's journal.

OBJECTIVE 2b. Record earnings of the sinking fund.

Bond Sinking Fund	1,200	
Sinking Fund Revenue		1,200
Sinking fund earnings as reported by trustee.		

In fact, some of the very bonds secured by the sinking fund may be purchased in the securities markets by the sinking fund trustee. If the bonds are turned over to the corporation for cancellation, an entry will be required to show the reduction of bond liability.

Bonds Payable	8,000	
Bond Sinking Fund		8,000
Eight $1,000 bonds acquired by bond trustee and canceled.		

When bonds mature there may be more or less money in the sinking fund than is required for retiring the bonds. If the fund is short, the corporation will be required to contribute additional cash to make up the shortage. If some cash is left over, it is paid over to the corporation, as reflected by the following entry.

Bonds Payable	860,000	
Cash	4,500	
Bond Sinking Fund		864,500
Bonds retired and sinking fund closed out.		

OBJECTIVE 2c. Record the retirement of bonds with sinking fund cash and the termination of the sinking fund.

Keep in mind that the foregoing entries are made on the books of the corporation. We are not concerned here with the bond trustee's accounting procedures.

Bond Investments

Corporation and government bonds may be held by an entity as either marketable securities or long-term investments. Bonds may be acquired directly from the issuer or in the securities markets. If bonds are purchased between interest dates, the purchaser will have to pay for the interest that has accrued since the last interest date. For example, if $10,000 face amount of 8% bonds are purchased for face value midway between semiannual interest dates, an entry is made as follows.

Apr. 15	Investment in Bonds	10,000	
	Bond Interest Receivable	200	
	Cash		10,200
	Purchased ten $1,000 bonds at 100 plus accrued interest.		

OBJECTIVE 3a. Record purchases of securities.

The entry to record receipt of bond interest on the next interest date would then appear as follows.

July 15	Cash	400	
	Bond Interest Receivable		200
	Bond Interest Revenue		200
	Semiannual interest received.		

OBJECTIVE 3b. Record revenues from investments.

In Section 16.A you learned how to account for bond discounts and premiums from the issuer's viewpoint. Now let's take the viewpoint of the investor. Since the same essential concepts are involved, this procedure should present few difficulties.

When bonds are obtained directly from the issuer, the investor's discount or premium per bond is the same as that of the issuing corporation. However, when bonds are purchased in the securities markets, the discount or premium is often different from that being accounted for on the issuer's books. Remember, the amount of discount or premium is determined by the difference between the stated bond interest rate and the market (effective) rate *at the time that bonds are acquired.*

Bonds Acquired at a Discount.   Let us assume that an investor buys bonds at a discount, as indicated by the following entry.

**OBJECTIVE 3a.   Record
purchases of securities.**

19X4			
Oct. 1	Investment in Tripp Bonds	9,600	
	Cash		9,600
	Purchased ten $1,000, 7% bonds of Tripp Corporation at 96, a price that yields approximately 8% effective interest per annum.		

Note that the cost of the bonds is recorded as an asset, *without* stating the amount of discount as a contra account. In this respect, accounting for bond investments differs from accounting for bond liabilities.

An investor may choose not to amortize discounts or premiums on bonds held as current marketable securities, since it is unlikely that the bonds will be held until they mature. However, bonds held as long-term investments should gradually be increased in the case of discounts, or decreased in the case of premiums, to arrive at their face value by their maturity date. As with bond liabilities, the accepted approach for adjusting bond investments for discount or premium expirations is the effective interest method.[12]

Now let us suppose that the ten bonds of Tripp Corporation were purchased as a long-term investment, that they pay interest semiannually, and that they mature on October 1, 19X9, five years from the date they were purchased. The entries to record the year-end interest adjustment and the receipt of cash interest are as shown in Illustration 16.9.

Notice that effective interest for the first six-month period ending April 1, 19X5, was obtained by multiplying the effective interest rate (4% per half-year) times the original cost of the bonds ($9,600), to get $384. The difference between the effective interest ($384) and the stated interest ($350) is the discount amortization ($34) for the six-month period. The adjusting entry at December 31, 19X4, recognizes half the revenue and discount in 19X4. The other half is recognized on April 1, 19X5, when the cash is received.

The entry on October 1, 19X5, will recognize effective interest for a full six months.

---

[12]*Opinions of the Accounting Principles Board No. 21,* "Interest on Receivables and Payables" (New York: American Institute of Certified Public Accountants, 1971), par. 15.

ILLUSTRATION 16.9

19X4 Dec. 31	Bond Interest Receivable	175	
	Investment in Tripp Bonds	17	
	Bond Interest Revenue		192
	To accrue interest for three months on Tripp bonds.		
	(½)(0.04 × $9,600) = $192		

OBJECTIVE 3b. Record revenues from investments.

19X5 Apr. 1	Cash	350	
	Investment in Tripp Bonds	17	
	Bond Interest Receivable		175
	Bond Interest Revenue		192
	To record receipt of interest on Tripp bonds and adjustment for discount.		

19X5 Oct. 1	Cash	350	
	Investment in Tripp Bonds	35	
	Bond Interest Revenue		385
	To record receipt of interest on Tripp bonds and adjustment for discount.		
	(0.04)($9,600 + $34) = $385		

Note that effective interest for the period was calculated by multiplying the effective interest rate per half-year (4%) times the *adjusted* cost of the bonds ($9,600 + $34). For this and other examples, amounts have been rounded to the nearest whole dollar.

Bonds Acquired at a Premium. Procedures for amortizing premiums on bond investments must gradually *decrease* original cost to maturity value. To illustrate the process, let us assume that $10,000 face amount of 7% Foster Corporation bonds are purchased on March 1, 19X4, at a price to yield approximately 6%. The bonds mature five years from date of purchase and pay interest semiannually on March 1 and September 1. The entries needed during 19X4 are shown in Illustration 16.10 on the next page.

Stock Investments

In some respects, accounting for stocks is less complicated than accounting for bond investments. Stock purchases are simply recorded at cost, with no concern for premiums or discounts. Also, since dividends do not accrue like

ILLUSTRATION 16.10

19X4 Mar. 1	Investment in Foster Bonds	10,425	
	Cash		10,425
	Purchased ten $1,000, 7% bonds of Foster Corporation at 104¼, a price to yield approximately 6% effective interest per annum.		

19X4 Sept. 1	Cash	350	
	Investment in Foster Bonds		37
	Bond Interest Revenue		313
	To record receipt of interest on Foster bonds and adjustment for premium.		
	(0.03 × $10,425 = $313)		

19X4 Dec. 31	Bond Interest Receivable	233	
	Investment in Foster Bonds		25
	Bond Interest Revenue		208
	To accrue interest for four months on Foster bonds.		
	(⁴⁄₆)(0.03 × $10,388) = $208		

interest, purchases of stocks between dividend dates do not involve any recognition of accrued income.

Brokerage charges on purchased securities are added to the cost of the investment. *Brokerage charges are fees charged by a brokerage firm for assistance in buying or selling property.* Brokerage charges involved in *selling* securities are usually deducted from the sales proceeds, and the net proceeds are recorded by the seller without formally recognizing the brokerage charges. Entries for the purchase and sale of securities are shown in Illustration 16.11.

Had the debit for net cash received in the November 20 entry been less than the cost basis of the shares sold, a loss would have been recognized. Note that stock prices are quoted in dollars and fractions of dollars per share, as they appear in the stock market pages of many daily newspapers. Shares bought at 10⅛ cost $10.125 per share; shares sold at 12½ bring $12.50 per share.

There are two acceptable approaches by which investor corporations may account for cash dividends, depending on the circumstances. When enough shares are owned to significantly influence the management of the

ILLUSTRATION 16.11

May 14	Investment in McGoo Stock	20,450	
	Cash		20,450
	Purchased 2,000 shares of McGoo common at 10⅛, plus broker's fee of $200.		

OBJECTIVE 3a. Record purchases of securities.

Nov. 20	Cash	24,750	
	Investment in McGoo Stock		20,450
	Gain on Sale of Securities		4,300
	Sold 2,000 shares McGoo common at 12½, less broker's fee of $250.		

OBJECTIVE 3c. Record sales of investment assets.

investee corporation, the investment may be accounted for by the equity method. Otherwise the shares are accounted for on a cost basis.

Cost Method versus Equity Method. An investor corporation seldom owns enough shares of another corporation to exercise any significant influence over its management. When the investor's influence is negligible, the investment is accounted for under the cost method. *The cost method of accounting for investments in stocks recognizes as revenue cash dividends but ignores the reported earnings of the investee corporation.* The following entries illustrate the recognition of dividend revenue, and the subsequent receipt of cash, under the cost method.

July 10	Dividends Receivable	5,000	
	Dividends Revenue		5,000
	To record dividends declared at 50¢ per share on Marte common stock.		

OBJECTIVE 3b. Record revenues from investments.

Aug. 5	Cash	5,000	
	Dividends Receivable		5,000
	Received cash dividends on Marte common stock.		

When an investing corporation owns sufficient voting shares to exercise significant influence over the related corporation, the securities may be accounted for by the equity method. As a general rule, ownership of 20% or more of a corporation's voting shares is presumed sufficient for exercising significant influence.[13] *Under the equity method of accounting for investments*

[13]*Opinions of the Accounting Principles Board No. 18,* "The Equity Method of Accounting for Investments in Common Stock" (New York: American Institute of Certified Public Accountants, 1971), par. 17.

OBJECTIVE 4.
Differentiate between the
cost and equity methods
of accounting for
investments.

in stocks, the investor recognizes a proportionate share of the related corporation's net income, and a cash dividend is recorded as a reduction in the investment. The following entries illustrate the recognition of income and the receipt of cash dividends under the equity method.

June 30	Investment in Marte Corporation Shares	10,000	
	Investment Income		10,000
	To recognize 20% of Marte Corporation net income.		

Aug. 5	Cash	5,000	
	Investment in Marte Corporation Shares		5,000
	Marte dividends received in cash.		

OBJECTIVE 3b.   **Record**
revenues from
investments.

The entries in Illustration 16.12 contrast the two methods of accounting for investments in shares of other corporations. Notice that under the equity

ILLUSTRATION 16.12

INVESTOR'S ENTRIES				
Cost Method		**Equity Method**		
WHEN SHARES ACQUIRED				
Investment in Marte Corp. Shares	80,000		Investment in Marte Corp. Shares	80,000	
Cash		80,000	Cash		80,000
Purchased 5,000 shares at 16.			Purchased 20% of Marte Corporation at 16.		
WHEN INCOME REPORTED BY INVESTEE				
No Entry			Invest. in Marte Corp. Shares	10,000	
			Investment Income		10,000
			To recognize 20% of Marte Corporation net income.		
WHEN DIVIDENDS DECLARED				
Dividends Receivable	5,000		No Entry		
Dividend Revenue		5,000			
To record dividends declared on Marte Corporation shares.					
WHEN CASH RECEIVED				
Cash	5,000		Cash	5,000	
Dividends Receivable		5,000	Invest. in Marte Corp. Shares		5,000
Marte dividends rec'd in cash.			Marte dividends rec'd in cash.		

method the investment account is increased by the investor's share of the earnings and reduced by cash dividends received.

Lower of Cost or Market. Recall that current marketable equity securities are reported at the lower of their total cost or market. Noncurrent equity securities are reported in a similar manner except that net unrealized losses are not shown on the income statement as a deduction in arriving at net income. Instead, such losses are charged directly to a contra shareholders' equity account.[14] For instance, if the total market value of noncurrent equity securities falls below their total cost by $70,000 during the current period, an adjusting entry similar to the following is required.

Accum. Unrealized Losses on Noncurrent Equity Sec.	70,000	
Allow. for Mkt. Decl. of Noncurrent Equity Sec.		70,000
To reflect the decline in market value of securities.		

The debit portion of the foregoing entry is a negative equity account, and appears on a balance sheet as a subtraction from shareholders' equity. The credit portion is a contra asset account that reduces long-term investments. Illustration 16.13 on the next page offers one approach for showing these contra balances on the balance sheet. Subsequent recoveries of value are recognized by reversing portions of the contra account balances up to the point where the noncurrent equity securities are again stated at cost.

Stock Dividends and Stock Splits. No revenue is recognized upon either the declaration or the receipt of additional shares as a result of stock dividends. Both stock dividends and stock splits result in a reduction of the cost per share of stock owned.[15] For example, the receipt of a 10% stock dividend on 1,000 shares that had cost $11 per share reduces the cost per share to $10, as shown by the following calculation.

$$\frac{\text{Cost of 1,000 shares}}{\text{1,000 shares} + \text{100 shares}} = \frac{\$11,000}{\text{1,100 shares}} = \$10 \text{ per share}$$

By the same measure, a 2-for-1 stock split will reduce the cost per share to half the original cost.

---

[14]*FASB Statement No. 12,* par. 11. However, par. 21 of this pronouncement provides that "other than temporary" value declines below cost are to be reported as realized losses.

[15]Stock dividends and stock splits are discussed in Chapters 14 and 15.

ILLUSTRATION 16.13

FARLEY CORPORATION
Balance Sheet
December 31, 19– –

ASSETS

Current

Cash		$100,000	
Marketable securities, at cost	$300,000		
Less: Allowance for market decline of current marketable equity securities	20,000	280,000	
Accounts receivable	$480,000		
Less: Allowance for doubtful accounts	40,000	440,000	
Inventories, at lower of cost or market		560,000	
Total current assets			$1,380,000

Noncurrent

Land		$110,000	
Buildings and equipment	$900,000		
Less: Accumulated depreciation	300,000	600,000	
Long-term investments, at cost	$400,000		
Less: Allowance for market decline of noncurrent equity securities	70,000	330,000	
Total noncurrent assets			1,040,000
Total Assets			$2,420,000

LIABILITIES

Current

Accounts and notes payable		$360,000	

Noncurrent

Bonds payable, 10%, due in ten years	$500,000		
Premium on bonds payable	10,000	510,000	
Total Liabilities			$ 870,000

SHAREHOLDERS' EQUITY

Common stock, par $10, 70,000 shares outstanding		$700,000	
Capital in excess of par		260,000	
Retained earnings	$660,000		
Less: Accumulated unrealized losses on noncurrent equity securities	70,000	590,000	
Total Shareholders' Equity			1,550,000
Total Liabilities and Shareholders' Equity			$2,420,000

Investments in Other Assets

Investments in assets other than securities are shown as long-term investments when the assets are not currently being used in regular business operations. These assets are presented in balance sheets at their cost bases.

GLOSSARY FOR SECTION 16.B

Brokerage charges   Fees charged by a brokerage firm for assistance in buying or selling property.

Cost method of accounting for investments in stocks   A method for accounting for investments in shares whereby the investor recognizes as revenue cash dividends but ignores the reported earnings of the investee corporation.

Current marketable securities   Investments in stocks, bonds, treasury bills, and similar securities that are readily salable and are viewed as a ready source of cash.

Equity method of accounting for investments in stocks   A method for accounting for investments in shares of a related corporation whereby the investor recognizes a proportionate share of net income that is reported by the related corporation, and receipt of a cash dividend is recorded as a realization of part of the investment.

Equity securities   Investments in ownership shares of other corporations.

Investments   Assets not directly related to the principal activities of an entity, usually held for the purpose of earning a return on funds not needed immediately in the entity's operations.

Long-term investments   Investments that do not qualify as marketable securities.

Sinking fund trustee   A financial institution or individual charged with managing a sinking fund.

Temporary investments (short-term investments)   Investment assets that managers intend to hold for only short periods of time.

SELF-QUIZ ON OBJECTIVES FOR SECTION 16.B
Solutions to Self-Quiz begin on page B-49.

1. **OBJECTIVE 1.** Differentiate between current marketable securities and long-term investments.

2. **OBJECTIVE 2.** Record the following transactions in the journal of Cloe Corporation.

   Transactions

   19X4

   Dec. 28   Paid quarterly contribution of $30,000 cash to the trustee of the corporation's bond sinking fund.

31   The bond sinking fund trustee reported that the fund earnings for 19X4 were $10,000.

19X9

Jan.   10   A check for $1,200 was received from the trustee, who reported that corporation bonds in the face amount of $2,000,000 were retired on this maturity date, January 10, and the sinking fund has been closed out.

3. **OBJECTIVE 3.** Record the following events in the journal of Danko Corporation.

Events

Feb.   10   Purchased 4,000 shares of Merkle common stock at 8¼, plus broker's commission of $600. These shares represent a small fraction of total Merkle shares outstanding.

Apr.   30   Purchased 20 bonds of Doel Corporation at 100 plus three months' accrued interest. The bonds have a face amount of $1,000 each, bear 8% per annum interest, and pay interest semiannually on February 1 and August 1.

May   6   Received 200 shares of Merkle common stock as a 5% stock dividend on the shares acquired on February 10.

June   14   Sold 1,000 shares of Merkle common stock at 9½ less brokerage commission of $150.

Aug.   1   Received semiannual interest on Doel Corporation bonds.

Nov.   12   Received notice from Merkle Corporation that a 50¢ per share common dividend was declared on November 12 to be paid on December 10 to shareholders of record on November 20.

Dec.   10   Received cash dividend on Merkle stock that had been declared on November 12.

4. **OBJECTIVE 4.** Differentiate between the cost method and the equity method of accounting for investments in common stock.

DISCUSSION QUESTIONS FOR SECTION 16.B

1. What is a bond *sinking fund,* and what is its purpose?

2. Why do corporations invest in securities of other corporations?

3. Why must the purchaser pay the seller for accrued interest on bonds bought between interest dates?

4. How are bond premiums and discounts shown in the records of the investing entity?

5. An investor may choose not to amortize premiums or discounts on bonds held as marketable securities. Why?

EXERCISES FOR SECTION 16.B

16.B.1. On July 1, Darwin Corporation deposited $50,000 in cash with a sinking fund trustee, in accordance with provisions of the indenture contract associated with bonds payable. On December 31 the bond trustee reported that sinking fund investments had earned $6,000 during the year. Make any needed entries to record these events in Darwin's general journal.

16.B.2. On November 1 Hart Corporation purchased as a long-term investment 25 $1,000 bonds at 95 plus accrued interest. The bonds bear interest at 9% per annum and pay interest semiannually on October 1 and April 1. Assume that the going market (effective) rate of interest is 10% and that Hart uses the effective interest method for accumulating bond discounts. Make entries in Hart's journal to record the purchase of the bonds on November 1 and to adjust for accrued interest on December 31.

16.B.3. Norton Corporation 8% bonds with a face value of $40,000 were bought by Jarvis Corporation some years back for a price to yield 7½%. The bonds, which pay interest on January 1 and July 1, show a book value of $40,400 at December 31, 19X4. Interest has not been accrued since the last interest check was received. Make the adjusting journal entry at December 31, 19X4, to accrue interest on the Norton bonds by the effective interest approach.

16.B.4. Vista Corporation owns 60% of the voting stock of East Corporation and accounts for its investment by the equity method. On January 20, 19X5, East Corporation reported that $800,000 of net income had been earned for the year ended December 31, 19X4. On February 18, 19X5, Vista received a $200,000 check from East Corporation in payment of common stock dividends. Make general journal entries for Vista Corporation, which reports on a calendar-year basis, to record the foregoing events.

PROBLEMS FOR SECTION 16.B
Alternate Problems for this section begin on page D-84.

16.B.5. Following are selected transactions for the Lamb Corporation.

Transactions

Jan. 15   Purchased 2,000 shares of Harden common stock at 24⅞ plus broker's commission of $800. These shares represent less than 1% of total Harden's shares outstanding.

Feb. 8   Received 80 shares of Harden common as a 4% stock dividend on the shares acquired January 15.

     28   Purchased 30 bonds of BJ Corporation at 100 plus four months' accrued interest plus broker's commission of $500. The bonds have a face amount of $1,000 each, bear 9% per annum interest, and pay interest semiannually on April 30 and October 31.

Apr. 30   Received semiannual interest on BJ Corporation bonds.

May 28   Sold 1,000 shares of Harden common at 27¼ less brokerage commission of $400.

Oct. 31   Received semiannual interest on BJ Corporation bonds.

     31   Harden Corporation declared a $1 per share common dividend to be paid on December 1 to shareholders of record on November 15.

Dec. 1   Received cash dividend on Harden stock that had been declared on October 31.

Required

Record the transactions in the journal of Lamb Corporation.

16.B.6. Selected transactions of Nebo Corporation are shown here.

Transactions

19X3

Oct. 1   Purchased as a long-term investment 20 $1,000, 9% bonds of GB III Corporation at 93¾, a price that yields 10% per annum effective interest. The bonds pay interest semiannually on April 1 and October 1.

Nov. 1   Purchased as a long-term investment 20 $1,000, 10% bonds of Marko Corporation at 105⅝, a price that yields 9% per annum effective interest. The bonds pay interest semiannually on May 1 and November 1.

Dec. 31   Adjusted for accrued interest on GB III and Marko bonds.

19X4

Apr. 1   Received interest check from GB III Corporation.

May 1   Received interest check from Marko Corporation.

Oct. 1   Received interest check from GB III Corporation.

Nov. 1   Received interest check from Marko Corporation.

Required

Make general journal entries to reflect the foregoing events on Nebo's books, using the effective interest method for recognizing interest earned. Round all computations to the nearest cent.

16.B.7. Following are selected transactions for the Krako Corporation.

Transactions

19X4

June 1   Krako called (retired) bonds at 105 when the accounts showed Bonds Payable of $15,000,000 and Discount on Bonds Payable of $75,000.

July 1   Issued new bonds, $10,000,000 face value, at 100.

Sept. 30   Paid quarterly contribution of $148,000 cash to the trustee of the corporation's bond sinking fund.

Dec. 31   Paid quarterly contribution of $148,000 to bond sinking fund.

31   The bond sinking fund trustee reported that the fund earnings for 19X4 were $3,710.

19X5

Jan.   2   The sinking fund trustee reported that $100,000 face amount of Krako bonds were purchased in the securities market at face value. The bonds were turned over to the corporation for cancellation.

19Z4

June 30   A check for $11,000 was received from the sinking fund trustee, who reported that corporation bonds in the face amount of $9,900,000 were retired on this the maturity date and the sinking fund was closed out.

Required

Record the foregoing transactions in the journal of Krako Corporation.

16.B.8. Following are selected transactions for the NTL Corporation.

Transactions

19X3

Jan.   2   Purchased 60% (a controlling interest) of the outstanding common shares of the Zeno Corporation for $460,000 cash.

Sept. 30   Received $20,000 cash dividend on Zeno Corporation shares.

Dec. 31   Zeno Corporation reported net income of $95,000 for the year ended this date.

19X4

Sept. 20   Received $15,000 cash dividend on Zeno Corporation shares.

Dec. 31   Zeno Corporation reported a net loss of $40,000 for the year ended this date.

Required

Record the foregoing transactions for the NTL Corporation.

16.B.9. A post-closing trial balance for Kramer Corporation is as shown here.

	Debit	Credit
KRAMER CORPORATION **Post-Closing Trial Balance** **December 31, 19 – –**		
Cash	49,000	
Marketable securities, at cost	784,000	
Allowance for market decline of current marketable equity securities		30,000
Accounts receivable	240,000	
Allowance for doubtful accounts		24,000
Inventories	369,000	
Land	75,000	
Buildings and equipment	650,000	
Accumulated depreciation		290,000
Long-term investments, at cost	360,000	
Allowance for market decline of noncurrent equity securities		48,000
Accounts payable		400,000
Bonds payable		800,000
Discount on bonds payable	36,000	
Common stock, par $20		400,000
Capital in excess of par		100,000
Retained earnings		519,000
Accumulated unrealized losses on noncurrent equity securities	48,000	
	2,611,000	2,611,000

Required

Prepare a classified balance sheet for Kramer Corporation.

SUMMARY OF CHAPTER 16

Funds supplied by long-term liabilities are usually used for financing non-current assets. Most long-term liabilities are represented by formal debt instruments that provide for fixed interest charges and definite maturity dates.

Bonds are formal negotiable notes that are issued as long-term debts by corporations and governments. When the stated rate of interest is less than the going market rate, bonds sell at a discount; when the stated rate is more than the market rate, bonds sell at a premium. Bond discounts and bond premiums should be amortized over the life of the bonds to which they relate. Under current practice, the effective interest approach is used for amortizing bond premiums and discounts, except when results from the straight-line method are not materially different.

Idle cash may be invested on either a long-term or a short-term basis in order to earn a return on the money. The most common way to invest idle cash is to buy bonds, stocks, treasury notes, or other securities. Securities that are readily salable and are intended by managers to serve as a substitute for cash are called current marketable securities.

A bond sinking fund is viewed as a long-term investment of the corporation that issued the related bonds. Bond sinking fund money is ordinarily invested in securities of corporations or governments. Revenue earned by a bond sinking fund is recognized by the corporation when it is reported by the fund trustee.

Bond discounts or premiums should be amortized for bonds held as long-term investments. The equity method is used in accounting for stocks when a sufficient amount is owned to exercise significant influence over the management of the corporation that issued the shares.

PROBLEMS FOR CHAPTER 16
Alternate Problems for this chapter begin on page D-85.

16.1. The following selected events were experienced by Corry Corporation.

Events

19X4

Sept. 14   Issued for cash 60,000 shares of $10 par common stock at $15 per share.

Oct.   5   Purchased 1,000 shares of Bland Corporation $5 par common stock for $20 per share. All the remaining 50,000 shares of Bland stock are owned by members of the Bland family.

Nov.   1   Issued 20-year bonds with a face value of $500,000 at 110, a price that yields effective interest of 8% per annum compounded semiannually. The bonds provide for paying 9% per annum interest on May 1 and November 1 each year.

Dec.   1   Purchased 20 $1,000 bonds of Masi Corporation at 96. The bonds provide for 7% per annum interest payable on May 31 and November 30 of each year. The bonds, to be held for an indefinite period of time, bear effective interest of 8% per annum.

19X5

Jan.   20   Cash dividends of $1 per share on 60,000 shares were declared and paid by Corry Corporation.

Feb.   2   Received a check for $500 in payment of dividends of 50¢ per share on Bland Corporation common stock.

May   1   Paid semiannual interest on bonds.

June   1   Received check for semiannual interest on Masi Corporation bonds purchased on December 1, 19X4.

Required

1) Prepare for Corry Corporation, in general journal form, entries for the events listed, including any needed adjusting entries at December 31, 19X4, the end of Corry Corporation's accounting year.

2) Explain why year-end adjusting entries are made for accrued interest payable and receivable but no entries are made to recognize accrued dividends.

16.2. The Sharmeg Corporation issued $1,000,000 face amount bonds on September 1, 19X4, at 106½, a price that yields about 9% per annum effective interest rate. The bonds pay $50,000 of interest on March 1 and September 1 of each year of their 10-year life (10% per annum).

Required

1) Use the effective interest method to complete the following table for the first three years of bond life.

Six-Month Period	Interest Payment	Effective Interest	Premium Amortization	Premium Balance	Gross Bond Liability
At issue				$65,000	$1,065,000
1	$50,000				
2					
3					
4					
5					
6					

2) Make journal entries to record the bond issue; accrued interest at December 31, 19X4; interest payments on March 1, 19X5, and September 1, 19X5; and accrued interest at December 31, 19X5.

3) On their issue date, DDC Corporation acquired as a long-term investment one-tenth of the Sharmeg bonds. Make general journal entries on DDC books to record the acquisition of the bonds; accrued interest on

December 31, 19X4; receipt of interest on March 1, 19X5, and September 1, 19X5; and accrued interest at December 31, 19X5. DDC employs the effective interest method for amortizing premiums on long-term investments.

COMPREHENSION PROBLEMS FOR CHAPTER 16

16.3. Mazoo Corporation managers are thinking of borrowing enough money on a 10-year, 10% real estate mortgage note secured by a factory building to call in $2,000,000 face amount, 12% bonds that are callable at 105. The bonds, which pay interest annually and mature in 10 years, are currently carried at $1,980,000 net after deducting the discount balance. Interest has just been paid, and the discount has been adjusted up to date.

Required

1) Determine for the managers the advisability of replacing the bonds with the mortgage note. (*Hint:* Use present value factors from Appendix II.)

2) Assuming that the bonds are to be called, prepare the entries to record the mortgage note and recall the bonds. Mazoo is to borrow just enough money to pay off the bonds.

3) If you recognize a gain or loss on the redemption of the bonds, explain what that element of your entry truly represents.

16.4. Jaxrax Corporation needs $4,000,000 for expansion of the company, from which it is estimated that additional annual net income of $800,000, before related interest and income taxes, can be derived. The company will pay taxes on additional earnings at a 46% marginal rate. The funds may be obtained by issuing bonds at a 10% effective interest rate or by issuing new common shares at $20 per share. Earnings per common share were $2.05 last year and are expected to remain about the same if the expansion does not occur. Jaxrax shareholders held a total of 400,000 shares of common stock throughout the previous year.

Required

1) Determine the after-tax rate of interest that would result from issuing bonds.

2) Do you think the corporation should expand? If so, should the expansion be financed with the issuance of bonds or new shares? Explain fully and show your work.

APPENDIX 16.I
Present Value Concepts

THE NATURE OF INTEREST

Money, like other kinds of property, can be rented. *The rental charge for the use of money is called interest.* A lender earns *interest revenue* for the use of money; from a borrower's viewpoint, the cost of renting money is an *interest expense.*

Except as a medium of exchange and a store of value, money is of little use. Most people want what money will buy more than they want money itself. To encourage people to lend their money, additional money—or interest—is paid to lenders. Interest, then, is the reward a lender receives for deferring the right to spend money until some future time.

An interest charge is usually stated as an annual (per annum) percentage, known as the interest rate. Assume, for example, that you lend someone $1,000 for a period of five years, with 6% interest to be paid by the borrower at the end of each year. You should then receive $60 at the end of each of the first four years, and $1,060 at the end of the five-year period, as shown in Illustration 16.14.

Thus over the course of five years you will receive a total of $1,300 in return for the $1,000 initial loan. The $1,300 figure is relatively meaningless, however, because it is a total of dollars at five different points in time; it is a total of *unlike* dollar units, which have not been adjusted for *time value.*

ILLUSTRATION 16.14

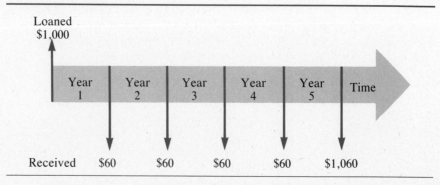

ILLUSTRATION 16.15

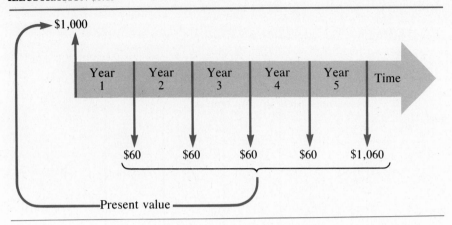

Money is said to have a time value that varies according to how near or how far it is from the present. The right to receive money in the future is worth less and less, in present value terms, the further in the future it is. Actually, provided that the 6% return is considered reasonable, the dollars to be received in the future are *equivalent to* the initial $1,000. Or we might say that the present value of the total of all the future cash amounts is $1,000, as suggested in Illustration 16.15.

FUTURE VALUE OF AN AMOUNT AT COMPOUND INTEREST

In place of taking interest periodically, you might agree to let the interest accumulate as part of the total loan. In other words, you agree to also lend the interest as it is earned and to take one lump sum at the end of the loan period. *When interest accumulations also earn interest, the process is called compounding of interest.* The loan balance will now accumulate as shown in Illustration 16.16 on the next page.

You can see from the illustration that the balance at the end of each year is 1.06, or 106% of what it was at the beginning of the year. The same end result can be obtained with the following series of multiplications.

$$\$1,000(1.06)(1.06)(1.06)(1.06)(1.06) = \$1,338.23$$

This can also be written in the following way.

$$\$1,000(1.06)^5 = \$1,338.23$$

ILLUSTRATION 16.16

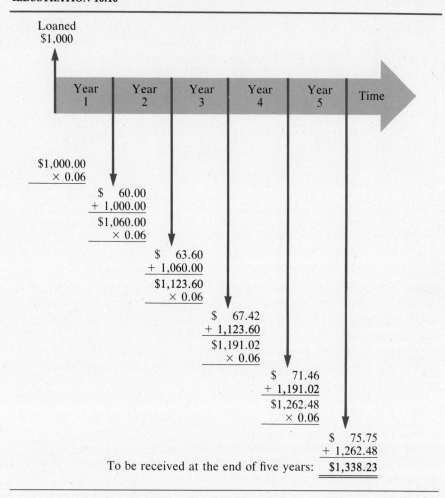

Loaned
$1,000

| Year 1 | Year 2 | Year 3 | Year 4 | Year 5 | Time |

$1,000.00
× 0.06

$ 60.00
+ 1,000.00
$1,060.00
× 0.06

$ 63.60
+ 1,060.00
$1,123.60
× 0.06

$ 67.42
+ 1,123.60
$1,191.02
× 0.06

$ 71.46
+ 1,191.02
$1,262.48
× 0.06

$ 75.75
+ 1,262.48

To be received at the end of five years: $1,338.23

From the foregoing example we can generalize that a *future value* can be determined by compounding any present amount p at interest rate i for n years.

$$p(1 + i)^n = \text{Future value}$$

PRESENT VALUE OF AN AMOUNT

Present value is the reverse of future value. *Determining the present values of future amounts is called* **discounting**. Whereas the accumulation (com-

ILLUSTRATION 16.17

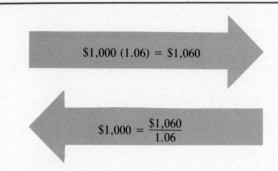

$1,000 (1.06) = $1,060

$1,000 = \dfrac{\$1,060}{1.06}

pounding) process involves multiplication, the discounting process involves division, as Illustration 16.17 shows.

When p is the present value amount and a is the future value (accumulated) amount, the relationship between them can be expressed as follows.

$$p(1 + i)^n = a$$
$$p = \frac{a}{(1 + i)^n}$$
$$p = (a)\frac{1}{(1 + i)^n}$$

A present value table can be constructed by calculating *factors* for various values of i and n. A ***present value factor*** *represents the present value of $1 at a given interest rate and for a given number of time periods.* The factors that follow have been rounded to three decimal places.

PRESENT VALUE FACTORS

Years		6% Factor
1	$\dfrac{1}{(1.06)^1}$	0.943
2	$\dfrac{1}{(1.06)^2}$	0.890
3	$\dfrac{1}{(1.06)^3}$	0.840
4	$\dfrac{1}{(1.06)^4}$	0.792
5	$\dfrac{1}{(1.06)^5}$	0.747

ILLUSTRATION 16.18

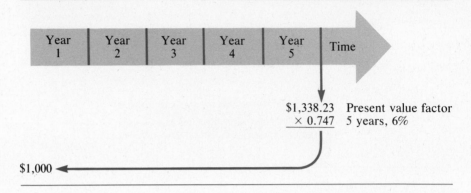

The factors in Illustration 16.21 in Appendix 16.II were derived in a similar manner. Keep in mind that future values and present values are *equivalents* for given rates of interest and time periods. For instance, the $1,338.23 to which $1,000 will accumulate in five years can be *discounted* back to $1,000 by multiplying the future amount by the appropriate present value factor as shown in Illustration 16.18.

If, on the other hand, the interest was received annually, the present value of all cash received is still $1,000 as Illustration 16.19 demonstrates.

Note that the present value factors used in Illustration 16.19 could have been obtained directly from Illustration 16.21 in Appendix 16.II. You will find them in the 6% column as factors for the first five periods. Keep in mind that the factors represent present values of $1 at various points of time in the future. In other words, at 6% interest, $1 one year from now is worth 94.3¢ now; $1 five years from now is worth only 74.7¢ now.

Compounding at More Frequent Intervals

Although interest is usually stated as a per annum rate, circumstances may necessitate compounding the interest at more frequent intervals. Interest may be compounded semiannually, quarterly, monthly, or even daily. If 8% interest is compounded semiannually, then 4% interest is added each six months; 8% interest compounded quarterly is simply 2% interest per quarter; and so on.

Present value tables may be used for compounding periods of other than one year, since they are set up for *periods* of time. For example, the present value factor for 16% interest compounded quarterly for five years may be located in the 4% column across from 20 periods. The per annum interest rate is simply divided by the number of times the interest is compounded

ILLUSTRATION 16.19

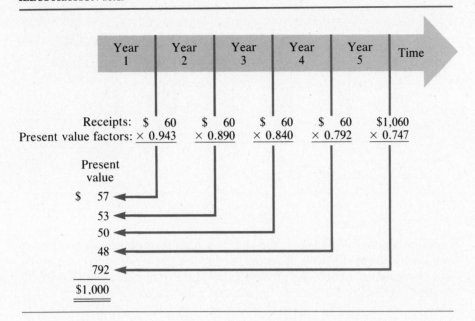

each year, and the years are multiplied by the same number. The present value of $1,000 five years in the future, assuming 16% interest compounded quarterly, may be calculated for 4% interest and 20 periods as follows. Of course, it is easier to obtain the present value factor (0.456) directly from Illustration 16.21 and simply multiply the factor by the $1,000 future amount in order to get the present value equivalent amount of $456.

$$p = (a)\frac{1}{(1 + i)^n}$$

$$p = (\$1,000)\frac{1}{(1 + 0.04)^{20}}$$

$$p = (\$1,000)(0.456)$$

$$p = \$456$$

PRESENT VALUE OF AN ANNUITY

*An **annuity** is a series of equal payments at the end of fixed intervals of time.* For instance, the equal annual payment of interest in the example we have been using can be viewed as an annuity, as shown in Illustration 16.20 on the next page. We may view this case as either a five-year annuity of $60 plus a

ILLUSTRATION 16.20

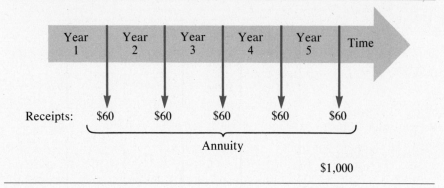

one-time amount of $1,000 at the end or a four-year annuity of $60 plus a one-time amount of $1,060. If we choose to view the series of payments as a five-year annuity of $60, the present value of the annuity can be derived by multiplying $60 by the *sum* of the present value factors.

$60(0.943) + $60(0.890) + $60(0.840) + $60(0.792) + $60(0.747)

$$= \$60(0.943 + 0.890 + 0.840 + 0.792 + 0.747)$$
$$= \$60(4.212)$$
$$\text{Annuity factor}$$
$$= \$253$$

The sum of the present value factors is the *present value of annuity factor* for five periods, 6% interest. In other words, $1 at the end of each of the five periods has a present value of $4.212 when the interest rate is 6% per period. *A **present value of annuity factor**, then, is the present value of $1 per period for a prescribed number of periods at a given rate of interest per period.*

The present value of all the amounts in our example may now be calculated in either of the following ways.

Present value of a five-year annuity	$60(4.212)	=	$ 253
Present value of lump sum	$1,000(0.747)	=	747
Total present value			$1,000
or			
Present value of a four-year annuity	$60(3.465)	=	$ 208
Present value of lump sum	$1,060(0.747)	=	792
Total present value			$1,000

Selected present value annuity factors are given in Illustration 16.22. When annuity intervals are less than one year, the years are multiplied by the number of payments per year, and the per annum interest rate is divided by the number of payments per year. The appropriate factor is then located in the column for the interest rate per annuity period, across from the number of annuity periods.

Now consider how the present value tables may be used to calculate the current value of bonds or other long-term debt securities that pay periodic interest. The current value of a $1,000, 8% bond that pays interest semiannually would be calculated as follows if the bond matures in five years and the going market (effective) rate of interest is 12%.

PRESENT VALUE OF INTEREST ANNUITY		
Semiannual interest at 4%	$ 40	
Annuity factor, 6%, 10 periods	× 7.360	
Present value of interest		$294
PRESENT VALUE OF LUMP SUM		
Bond principal	$ 1,000	
Present value factor, 6%, 10 periods	× 0.558	
Present value of principal		558
Present Value of Bond		$852

Since the bonds pay interest twice each year, the interest rates are halved and the years are doubled. Naturally, since the bond pays interest at less than the going market rate, it will sell for less than its face amount. On the other hand, when the market rate is less than the stated bond rate, a bond will sell at a premium.

GLOSSARY FOR APPENDIX 16.I

Annuity   A series of equal payments at the end of fixed intervals of time.

Compounding of interest   The process of accumulating interest amounts so that they also earn future interest.

Discounting   The process of determining present values of future amounts.

Interest   The rental charge for the use of money.

Interest rate   An interest charge, usually stated as an annual (per annum) percentage.

Present value factor   The present value of $1 at a given interest rate and for a given number of time periods.

Present value of annuity factor   The present value of $1 per period for a prescribed number of periods at a given rate of interest per period.

DISCUSSION QUESTIONS FOR APPENDIX 16.I

1. If someone offered you a choice of $100 today or $102 one year from today, which would you choose? Explain your answer.

2. How can the Present Value of One Dollar table presented in Appendix 16.II be converted to a compound interest table (the amount to which $1 will grow when invested for a specified period at a specified rate)?

3. How can the Present Value of Ordinary Annuity of One Dollar table provided in Appendix 16.II be derived from the Present Value of One Dollar table?

4. If money can be invested at a 7% rate, what is the future value of $100 invested today for two years?

5. If money can be invested at a 7% rate, what is the present value of $107 received one year from now?

6. Why is it invalid to compare or combine amounts of cash at different points in time without adjustment?

7. What is the definition of each of the following expressions?
   a. Compounding of interest
   b. Discounting
   c. Present value factor
   d. Annuity
   e. Present value of annuity factor

EXERCISES FOR APPENDIX 16.I

1. Use the present value tables in Appendix 16.II to calculate the present value of
   a. $10,000, ten years from now, at 16% per annum interest compounded quarterly
   b. $1,000 at the end of each six months for 12 years at 12% per annum interest compounded semiannually
   c. 20 $1,000, 10% bonds, which pay interest annually, when the market (effective) rate of interest is 8% and the bonds mature in 20 years.

2. On April 1, Marshall Doaks is considering the purchase of ten $1,000 face amount bonds that pay interest at 6% on March 31 of each year. The bonds mature on March 31, eight years hence. On April 1, the market rate of interest for bonds of this type stands at 10%. Calculate what Marshall should expect to pay for the bonds. (*Suggestion:* Refer to the material in Appendix 16.II.)

3. On July 1, 19X4, Nob Corporation is issuing $2,000,000 face amount 12% bonds that will mature in ten years. The bonds bear interest semiannually on January 1 and July 1. If the market rate of interest is 8% on July 1, 19X4,

determine the amount the bond issue should bring in. (*Suggestion:* Refer to the material in Appendix 16.II.)

4. Use the present value tables in Appendix 16.II to calculate the present value of

   a. $8,000, eight years from now, at 12% per annum interest.

   b. $1,000 at the end of each year for eight years at 12% per annum interest.

   c. $1,000 at the end of each year for eight years at 24% per annum interest.

APPENDIX 16.II
Present Value Tables

ILLUSTRATION 16.21

PRESENT VALUE OF ONE DOLLAR

Periods	4%	6%	8%	10%	12%	14%	16%	18%	20%	22%	24%	26%	28%	30%	40%
1	0.962	0.943	0.926	0.909	0.893	0.877	0.862	0.847	0.833	0.820	0.806	0.794	0.781	0.769	0.714
2	0.925	0.890	0.857	0.826	0.797	0.769	0.743	0.718	0.694	0.672	0.650	0.630	0.610	0.592	0.510
3	0.889	0.840	0.794	0.751	0.712	0.675	0.641	0.609	0.579	0.551	0.524	0.500	0.477	0.455	0.364
4	0.855	0.792	0.735	0.683	0.636	0.592	0.552	0.516	0.482	0.451	0.423	0.397	0.373	0.350	0.260
5	0.822	0.747	0.681	0.621	0.567	0.519	0.476	0.437	0.402	0.370	0.341	0.315	0.291	0.269	0.186
6	0.790	0.705	0.630	0.564	0.507	0.456	0.410	0.370	0.335	0.303	0.275	0.250	0.227	0.207	0.133
7	0.760	0.665	0.583	0.513	0.452	0.400	0.354	0.314	0.279	0.249	0.222	0.198	0.178	0.159	0.095
8	0.731	0.627	0.540	0.467	0.404	0.351	0.305	0.266	0.233	0.204	0.179	0.157	0.139	0.123	0.068
9	0.703	0.592	0.500	0.424	0.361	0.308	0.263	0.225	0.194	0.167	0.144	0.125	0.108	0.094	0.048
10	0.676	0.558	0.463	0.386	0.322	0.270	0.227	0.191	0.162	0.137	0.116	0.099	0.085	0.073	0.035
11	0.650	0.527	0.429	0.350	0.287	0.237	0.195	0.162	0.135	0.112	0.094	0.079	0.066	0.056	0.025
12	0.625	0.497	0.397	0.319	0.257	0.208	0.168	0.137	0.112	0.092	0.076	0.062	0.052	0.043	0.018
13	0.601	0.469	0.368	0.290	0.229	0.182	0.145	0.116	0.093	0.075	0.061	0.050	0.040	0.033	0.013
14	0.577	0.442	0.340	0.263	0.205	0.160	0.125	0.099	0.078	0.062	0.049	0.039	0.032	0.025	0.009
15	0.555	0.417	0.315	0.239	0.183	0.140	0.108	0.084	0.065	0.051	0.040	0.031	0.025	0.020	0.006
16	0.534	0.394	0.292	0.218	0.163	0.123	0.093	0.071	0.054	0.042	0.032	0.025	0.019	0.015	0.005
17	0.513	0.371	0.270	0.198	0.146	0.108	0.080	0.060	0.045	0.034	0.026	0.020	0.015	0.012	0.003
18	0.494	0.350	0.250	0.180	0.130	0.095	0.069	0.051	0.038	0.028	0.021	0.016	0.012	0.009	0.002
19	0.475	0.331	0.232	0.164	0.116	0.083	0.060	0.043	0.031	0.023	0.017	0.012	0.009	0.007	0.002
20	0.456	0.312	0.215	0.149	0.104	0.073	0.051	0.037	0.026	0.019	0.014	0.010	0.007	0.005	0.001
21	0.439	0.294	0.199	0.135	0.093	0.064	0.044	0.031	0.022	0.015	0.011	0.008	0.006	0.004	0.001
22	0.422	0.278	0.184	0.123	0.083	0.056	0.038	0.026	0.018	0.013	0.009	0.006	0.004	0.003	0.001
23	0.406	0.262	0.170	0.112	0.074	0.049	0.033	0.022	0.015	0.010	0.007	0.005	0.003	0.002	
24	0.390	0.247	0.158	0.102	0.066	0.043	0.028	0.019	0.013	0.008	0.006	0.004	0.003	0.002	
25	0.375	0.233	0.146	0.092	0.059	0.038	0.024	0.016	0.010	0.007	0.005	0.003	0.002	0.001	
26	0.361	0.220	0.135	0.084	0.053	0.033	0.021	0.014	0.009	0.006	0.004	0.002	0.002	0.001	
27	0.347	0.207	0.125	0.076	0.047	0.029	0.018	0.011	0.007	0.005	0.003	0.002	0.001	0.001	
28	0.333	0.196	0.116	0.069	0.042	0.026	0.016	0.010	0.006	0.004	0.002	0.002	0.001	0.001	
29	0.321	0.185	0.107	0.063	0.037	0.022	0.014	0.008	0.005	0.003	0.002	0.001	0.001	0.001	
30	0.308	0.174	0.099	0.057	0.033	0.020	0.012	0.007	0.004	0.003	0.002	0.001	0.001	0.001	
40	0.208	0.097	0.046	0.022	0.011	0.005	0.003	0.001	0.001						

ILLUSTRATION 16.22

PRESENT VALUE OF ORDINARY ANNUITY OF ONE DOLLAR

Periods	4%	6%	8%	10%	12%	14%	16%	18%	20%	22%	24%	25%	26%	28%	30%	40%
1	0.962	0.943	0.926	0.909	0.893	0.877	0.862	0.847	0.833	0.820	0.806	0.800	0.794	0.781	0.769	0.714
2	1.886	1.833	1.783	1.736	1.690	1.647	1.605	1.566	1.528	1.492	1.457	1.440	1.424	1.392	1.361	1.224
3	2.775	2.673	2.577	2.487	2.402	2.322	2.246	2.174	2.106	2.042	1.981	1.952	1.923	1.868	1.816	1.589
4	3.630	3.465	3.312	3.170	3.037	2.914	2.798	2.690	2.589	2.494	2.404	2.362	2.320	2.241	2.166	1.849
5	4.452	4.212	3.993	3.791	3.605	3.433	3.274	3.127	2.991	2.864	2.745	2.689	2.635	2.532	2.436	2.035
6	5.242	4.917	4.623	4.355	4.111	3.889	3.685	3.498	3.326	3.167	3.020	2.951	2.885	2.759	2.643	2.168
7	6.002	5.582	5.206	4.868	4.564	4.288	4.039	3.812	3.605	3.416	3.242	3.161	3.083	2.937	2.802	2.263
8	6.733	6.210	5.747	5.335	4.968	4.639	4.344	4.078	3.837	3.619	3.421	3.329	3.241	3.076	2.925	2.331
9	7.435	6.802	6.247	5.759	5.328	4.946	4.607	4.303	4.031	3.786	3.566	3.463	3.366	3.184	3.019	2.379
10	8.111	7.360	6.710	6.145	5.650	5.216	4.833	4.494	4.192	3.923	3.682	3.571	3.465	3.269	3.092	2.414
11	8.760	7.887	7.139	6.495	5.988	5.453	5.029	4.656	4.327	4.035	3.776	3.656	3.544	3.335	3.147	2.438
12	9.385	8.384	7.536	6.814	6.194	5.660	5.197	4.793	4.439	4.127	3.851	3.725	3.606	3.387	3.190	2.456
13	9.986	8.853	7.904	7.103	6.424	5.842	5.342	4.910	4.533	4.203	3.912	3.780	3.656	3.427	3.223	2.468
14	10.563	9.295	8.244	7.367	6.628	6.002	5.468	5.008	4.611	4.265	3.962	3.824	3.695	3.459	3.249	2.477
15	11.118	9.712	8.559	7.606	6.811	6.142	5.575	5.092	4.675	4.315	4.001	3.859	3.726	3.483	3.268	2.484
16	11.652	10.106	8.851	7.824	6.974	6.265	5.669	5.162	4.730	4.357	4.033	3.887	3.751	3.503	3.283	2.489
17	12.166	10.477	9.122	8.022	7.120	6.373	5.749	5.222	4.775	4.391	4.059	3.910	3.771	3.518	3.295	2.492
18	12.659	10.828	9.372	8.201	7.250	6.467	5.818	5.273	4.812	4.419	4.080	3.928	3.786	3.529	3.304	2.494
19	13.134	11.158	9.604	8.365	7.366	6.550	5.877	5.316	4.844	4.442	4.097	3.942	3.799	3.539	3.311	2.496
20	13.590	11.470	9.818	8.514	7.469	6.623	5.929	5.353	4.870	4.460	4.110	3.954	3.808	3.546	3.316	2.497
21	14.029	11.764	10.017	8.649	7.562	6.687	5.973	5.384	4.891	4.476	4.121	3.963	3.816	3.551	3.320	2.498
22	14.451	12.042	10.201	8.772	7.645	6.743	6.011	5.410	4.909	4.488	4.130	3.970	3.822	3.556	3.323	2.498
23	14.857	12.303	10.371	8.883	7.718	6.792	6.044	5.432	4.925	4.499	4.137	3.976	3.827	3.559	3.325	2.499
24	15.247	12.550	10.529	8.985	7.784	6.835	6.073	5.451	4.937	4.507	4.143	3.981	3.831	3.562	3.327	2.499
25	15.622	12.783	10.675	9.077	7.843	6.873	6.097	5.467	4.948	4.514	4.147	3.985	3.834	3.564	3.329	2.499
26	15.983	13.003	10.810	9.161	7.896	6.906	6.118	5.480	4.956	4.520	4.151	3.988	3.837	3.566	3.330	2.500
27	16.330	13.211	10.935	9.237	7.943	6.935	6.136	5.492	4.964	4.524	4.154	3.990	3.839	3.567	3.331	2.500
28	16.663	13.406	11.051	9.307	7.984	6.961	6.152	5.502	4.970	4.528	4.157	3.992	3.840	3.568	3.331	2.500
29	16.984	13.591	11.158	9.370	8.022	6.983	6.166	5.510	4.975	4.531	4.159	3.994	3.841	3.569	3.332	2.500
30	17.292	13.765	11.258	9.427	8.055	7.003	6.177	5.517	4.979	4.534	4.160	3.995	3.842	3.569	3.332	2.500
40	19.793	15.046	11.925	9.779	8.244	7.105	6.234	5.548	4.997	4.544	4.166	3.999	3.846	3.571	3.333	2.500

PART VII

USING
FINANCIAL DATA

ACCOUNTANTS IN THE WORKPLACE

NAME: Frank S. Schneider

AFFILIATION: Schneider & Shuster

POSITION: Managing Partner

SPECIALIZATION: SEC Filings, Oil & Gas, Real Estate, Construction

"Our firm probably doesn't look any different from the local office of a large national company," says Frank Schneider of Schneider & Shuster, CPAs. As a former partner in the national accounting firm of Touche Ross & Co., he has "seen both sides" of public practice. He particularly enjoys his present role, "knowing that we control our own destiny."

While still in the MBA program at the University of Denver, Schneider worked in a small accounting firm. After graduation he stayed with the firm and became a partner. In 1971, the firm merged with Touche Ross & Co. For several years, Schneider was Partner-in-Charge of their Miami office.

In 1976, he left the company to return to Denver and start his own practice. Coincidentally, back in Denver a previous associate was having similar thoughts. The result was formation of Schneider & Shuster.

The firm has matured and grown to a total of 40 people, with seven partners. Denver is a center for new stock offerings and the firm specializes in helping small companies go public. It also provides a broad range of other services, including tax planning and management advisory services for public and private clients.

NAME: Chrysta R. Stine

AFFILIATION: York (Pennsylvania) Hospital

POSITION: Assistant Controller, Costs and Budgets

SPECIALIZATION: Cost Accounting, Budgets

Accounting learned in the classroom is a sound basis for solving problems accountants face in the workplace, according to Chrysta R. Stine. "In the classroom," she says, "I learned to account for the cost of widgets. Now I'm using what I learned to account for the cost of nursery days!"

After graduating from Indiana University of Pennsylvania, she went to work for Peat, Marwick, Mitchell & Co. in their Harrisburg office. Stine feels that her exposure to business, industrial, utility, and public clients "was invaluable, because it taught me that accounting takes many forms and that opportunities for specialization are virtually endless." She chose the health field after two years at PMM & Co., moved to a medical center, and then a year later to York Hospital.

At York she had the opportunity, as the hospital's first internal auditor, to develop "the mission, policies, and procedures of the internal audit function—a very effective way to gain experience in dealing with top management and the board of directors."

Her current responsibilities lie in three areas: cost reimbursement (Medicare, Medicaid, and Blue Cross), budgeting (preparation and status reporting), and financial analysis (for capital expenditures and new services). Stine is now working on a project that is "particularly interesting and challenging: preparing for the changes in Medicare reimbursement that were recently passed by Congress"—while pursuing an MBA degree.

Consolidating
Financial Data

As you will probably recall, accountants usually view each organization for which they account as an independent entity. Nevertheless, there are circumstances under which it is desirable to merge accounting data from two or more distinct (balanced) accounting systems. In fact, an organization may be viewed for one purpose as an independent entity and for another purpose as a subpart of a larger entity. This chapter deals with approaches to merging accounting statements of two or more related entities in order to obtain combined statements for a redefined aggregate entity.

Chapter 17 is in two sections. Section A concentrates first on accounting for branch operations as identifiable entities and then on techniques for combining branch and home office statements.

Section B deals with accounting for related corporations. Some time is taken initially to define important terms and to consider reasons for having separate but closely related legal entities. The section then covers some accounting consequences of transactions between related corporations as well as techniques for merging statements of related corporations in order to obtain consolidated statements for the corporate "family."

SECTION 17.A

Accounting for Branch Operations

OBJECTIVES

This section deals with accounting for operations at branch locations and with combining branch and home office statements. At the conclusion of your study, you should be able to

1. Record intracompany transfers of assets in both home office and branch books.
2. Make closing entries in the branch journal, including adjustment of inventory to the ending balance.
3. Prepare an income statement and a balance sheet for a branch.
4. Prepare an income statement and a balance sheet for a home office.
5. Prepare a work sheet for combining home office and branch income statements.
6. Prepare a work sheet for combining home office and branch balance sheets.

REASONS FOR BRANCH OPERATIONS

Managers and others need accounting information about departments, divisions, and other subdivisions of entities that are large and complex. Such information is useful both in evaluating past operations and in planning for the future. Departmental and divisional reporting is discussed in Section 22.B, which deals with responsibility accounting. At this point we are concerned primarily with accounting for branch operations located at some distance from a home office. For purposes of our discussion, *a home office is the controlling facility of an entity that conducts operations at more than one location. A branch, or branch operation, is an identifiable subentity that is located at some distance from the home office of an entity.*

CENTRALIZED VERSUS DECENTRALIZED RECORDS

Branch operations may be accounted for at the home office by means of *a centralized accounting system, which processes all accounting data at one location. Under a centralized system, branches send the various basic data forms to the home office to be recorded.* A centralized accounting system may then provide information about branch operations in much the same way as for departments and divisions located at one site.

Entities with decentralized accounting systems maintain branch accounting records at each branch location. *A decentralized accounting system is one where all the accounting functions are performed within each of the identifiable subunits of an entity.* Basic data are collected, recorded in journals, and summarized in ledgers, and statements are prepared to report branch accounting data.

There are advantages and disadvantages associated with both systems of accounting for branches. A centralized system may be more economical. Computers and other devices may be employed to process large amounts of data efficiently, and qualified accountants and well-trained, specialized clerks may be hired to work with the large volumes of information being processed. Clearly, it would be less expensive to maintain this kind of equipment and staff in one location, rather than in several branch locations.

On the other hand, information being processed at a central location may not be readily available to people working at branch locations. For example, a branch manager may be unable to respond immediately to customer inquiries about their account balances, orders, or other matters.

Most of the disadvantages of either system may be overcome through special procedures—provided, of course, that the solution to the problem is not too costly. For example, branch personnel may be given access to centralized data by means of computer terminals tied into the home office computer by telephone lines.

RECORDING INTRACOMPANY TRANSACTIONS

Our focus is primarily on decentralized systems of accounting for branches, since these systems involve some unique accounting problems. Also, to keep our illustrations simple, our discussion is limited to accounting for a small entity with only one branch operation. Keep in mind, however, that decentralized accounting systems are most useful for large, complex entities with many branches located over wide geographical areas.

Let us assume that P. Page, who owns a retail store, has just opened a small second store that is to be known as the Tottown Branch. Branch operations will be carried on in a rented, fully furnished store building. When $1,000 of cash is transferred to a new bank account in the branch name, entries are made in the home office and branch journals as shown in Illustration 17.1.

ILLUSTRATION 17.1

	HOME OFFICE		
May 1	Tottown Branch	1,000	
	Cash		1,000
	Cash transferred to Tottown branch.		

	TOTTOWN BRANCH		
May 1	Cash	1,000	
	Home Office		1,000
	Cash received from home office.		

OBJECTIVE 1. Record intracompany transfers of assets in both home office and branch books.

The Tottown Branch account on the home office books and the Home Office account on the branch books are referred to as *reciprocal accounts,* *because they are supposed to show equal balances, but on opposite sides of the accounts.* Some differences may occur temporarily because of time lags in communication or because of mistakes made by one office or the other. Reciprocal accounts should be reconciled at periodic intervals, the way bank accounts are, so as to locate any differences that result from errors.

When the journal entries are posted, the reciprocal accounts show balances as depicted by the following T-accounts.

Home Office	Branch Office
Tottown Branch	Home Office
1,000	1,000

The Tottown Branch account in the home office ledger is viewed as an asset—an investment in the branch operation. The Home Office account in the branch ledger is in essence the owner's equity account.

It is common for home offices to supply branches with some or all of the goods they sell. The usual practice is to keep track of the cost of the goods transferred in special accounts, as the entries in Illustration 17.2 demonstrate.

The account Shipments to Tottown Branch carries a credit balance and is viewed as a contra account to Purchases. Shipments from Home Office is a purchases account on the branch books. Branches may buy goods from other suppliers as well, but we are avoiding such complications to keep our example simple.

ILLUSTRATION 17.2

OBJECTIVE 1. Record intracompany transfers of assets in both home office and branch books.

		HOME OFFICE		
May 2	Tottown Branch		5,000	
	Shipments to Tottown Branch			5,000
	Merchandise shipped to Tottown branch.			

		TOTTOWN BRANCH		
May 3	Shipments from Home Office		5,000	
	Home Office			5,000
	Merchandise received from home office.			

ILLUSTRATION 17.3

	HOME OFFICE		
May 15	Cash	10,000	
	Tottown Branch		10,000
	Cash received from branch.		

OBJECTIVE 1. Record intracompany transfers of assets in both home office and branch books.

	TOTTOWN BRANCH		
May 15	Home Office	10,000	
	Cash		10,000
	Cash paid over to home office.		

During an accounting period, there may be any number of entries involving shipments from the home office, as well as additional transfers of cash from the home office to the branch. As sales are made and receivables collected, excess cash may be accumulated at the branch. Unneeded cash at the branch will likely be paid over to the home office and recorded as shown in Illustration 17.3.

END OF PERIOD WORK FOR BRANCH

Branch Trial Balance

Sales and expenses are recorded in the branch books just as for any other operation. At the end of May, a trial balance is prepared from the ledger accounts for the Tottown branch, as shown in Illustration 17.4.

ILLUSTRATION 17.4

PAGE COMPANY—TOTTOWN BRANCH Trial Balance May 31, 19--		
	Debit	Credit
Cash	25,500	
Home Office		21,000
Sales		90,000
Shipments from Home Office	60,000	
Rent Expense	3,000	
Wages Expense	20,000	
Utilities Expense	2,000	
Miscellaneous Expense	500	
	111,000	111,000

ILLUSTRATION 17.5

OBJECTIVE 3. Prepare an income statement for a branch.

PAGE COMPANY—TOTTOWN BRANCH		
Income Statement		
For the Month of May 19—		
Sales		$90,000
Cost of goods sold		
Inventory, May 1	$ –0–	
Shipments from home office	60,000	
Available for sale	$60,000	
Inventory, May 31	5,000	55,000
Gross Profit		$35,000
Operating expenses		
Rent	$ 3,000	
Wages	20,000	
Utilities	2,000	
Miscellaneous	500	25,500
Net Income		$ 9,500

Branch Income Statement

For our example, we will assume a monthly accounting period and a physical count at May 31 showing that Tottown branch has inventory on hand costing $5,000. An income statement for the branch for the month of May might appear as in Illustration 17.5.

Branch Closing Entries

The inventory adjustment may be handled as an adjusting entry or combined with the closing entry. Under the first approach, the adjusting entry in Illustration 17.6 would be made to distribute Shipments from Home Office between ending inventory and Cost of Goods Sold. Had there been a beginning inventory, the entry would have credited that amount to the Merchandise Inventory account.

The closing entry can then be made to close the temporary accounts and to reflect the net income in the Home Office account (Illustration 17.6).

The alternative approach is to combine the two entries (Illustration 17.6) into one closing entry (Illustration 17.7).

Branch Balance Sheet

The Home Office account, which previously showed a balance of $21,000, has been increased by the branch's net income of $9,500 to a total balance of $30,500, as reflected in the balance sheet in Illustration 17.8.

ILLUSTRATION 17.6

	ADJUSTING ENTRY		
May 31	Merchandise Inventory	5,000	
	Cost of Goods Sold	55,000	
	Shipments from Home Office		60,000
	To set up ending inventory and recognize cost of goods sold.		
	CLOSING ENTRY		
31	Sales	90,000	
	Cost of Goods Sold		55,000
	Rent Expense		3,000
	Wages Expense		20,000
	Utilities Expense		2,000
	Miscellaneous Expense		500
	Home Office		9,500
	To close temporary accounts.		

ILLUSTRATION 17.7

May 31	Sales	90,000	
	Merchandise Inventory	5,000	
	Shipments from Home Office		60,000
	Rent Expense		3,000
	Wages Expense		20,000
	Utilities Expense		2,000
	Miscellaneous Expense		500
	Home Office		9,500
	To set up ending inventory and close temporary accounts.		

OBJECTIVE 2. Make closing entries in the branch journal, including adjustment of inventory to the ending balance.

ILLUSTRATION 17.8

PAGE COMPANY—TOTTOWN BRANCH	
Balance Sheet	
May 31, 19--	
ASSETS	
Cash	$25,500
Merchandise inventory	5,000
Total Assets	$30,500
EQUITY	
Home office	$30,500

OBJECTIVE 3. Prepare a balance sheet for a branch.

HOME OFFICE STATEMENTS

Upon receiving notice of the amount of branch net income, the home office makes the following entry on its own books to show the increased investment in the branch.

May 31	Tottown Branch	9,500	
	Tottown Branch Net Income		9,500
	To recognize branch net income.		

The home office statements in Illustration 17.9 and 17.10 show how the reciprocal account balances and branch net income are presented in these statements.

COMBINING STATEMENTS

Owners, managers, creditors, and others may want to see statements that show combined (consolidated) figures for the entire company. Home office and branch statements may be merged together, but care must be taken to avoid duplications of amounts.

ILLUSTRATION 17.9

OBJECTIVE 4. Prepare an income statement for a home office.

PAGE COMPANY—HOME OFFICE Income Statement For the Month Ended May 31, 19--			
Sales			$200,000
Cost of goods sold			
Inventory, May 1		$ 40,000	
Purchases	$190,000		
Less: Shipments to branch	60,000	130,000	
Available for sale		$170,000	
Inventory, May 31		37,000	133,000
Gross Profit			$ 67,000
Operating expenses			
Wages		$ 42,000	
Utilities		3,000	
Depreciation		5,000	
Maintenance		1,000	
Miscellaneous		800	51,800
Net Income—Home Office			$ 15,200
Net Income—Tottown Branch			9,500
Total Net Income			$ 24,700

ILLUSTRATION 17.10

PAGE COMPANY—HOME OFFICE		
Balance Sheet		
May 31, 19--		
ASSETS		
Cash		$ 8,400
Merchandise inventory		37,000
Tottown branch		30,500
Land		40,000
Furniture and fixtures	$ 60,000	
Less: Accumulated depreciation	32,000	28,000
Building	$120,000	
Less: Accumulated depreciation	40,000	80,000
Total Assets		$223,900
LIABILITIES		
Accounts payable		$ 26,000
Mortgage payable		50,000
Total Liabilities		$ 76,000
OWNER'S EQUITY		
P. Page, capital		147,900
Total Liabilities and Owner's Equity		$223,900

OBJECTIVE 4. **Prepare a balance sheet for a home office.**

Combining Income Statements

When income statements for the home office and branch are combined, balances in the reciprocal accounts Shipments to Tottown Branch and Shipments from Home Office are canceled against each other. These eliminations simply remove from the picture the effects of internal transfers of goods from one entity segment to another. A work sheet such as the one in Illustration 17.11 is helpful in arriving at combined amounts. A combined income statement may then be prepared from the work sheet data as shown in Illustration 17.12. These two illustrations are on the next page.

Combining Balance Sheets

As the work sheet in Illustration 17.13 shows, the balances in the reciprocal accounts Tottown Branch and Home Office are canceled against each other to arrive at combined balance sheet figures. These eliminations remove from the picture the asset account Tottown Branch because it duplicates assets held by the branch, and the corresponding equity account on the books of the branch. It is now a simple matter to prepare a combined balance sheet like the one in Illustration 17.14. Both illustrations are on page 721.

ILLUSTRATION 17.11

PAGE COMPANY
Work Sheet for Combining Income Statements
For the Month Ended May 31, 19– –

	Home Office	Tottown Branch	Eliminations		Combined Income St.
			Debit	*Credit*	
Sales	200,000	90,000			290,000
Cost of goods sold					
Inventory, May 1	40,000				40,000
Purchases	190,000				190,000
Shipments from home office		60,000		60,000	
Shipments to branch	(60,000)		60,000		
Inventory, May 31	(37,000)	(5,000)			(42,000)
Cost of goods sold	133,000	55,000			188,000
Gross Profit	67,000	35,000			102,000
Operating expenses					
Wages	42,000	20,000			62,000
Rent		3,000			3,000
Utilities	3,000	2,000			5,000
Depreciation	5,000				5,000
Maintenance	1,000				1,000
Miscellaneous	800	500			1,300
Total operating expenses	51,800	25,500			77,300
Net Income	15,200	9,500	60,000	60,000	24,700

OBJECTIVE 5. Prepare a work sheet for combining home office and branch income statements.

ILLUSTRATION 17.12

PAGE COMPANY
Income Statement
For the Month Ended May 31, 19– –

Sales		$290,000
Cost of goods sold		
Inventory, May 1	$ 40,000	
Purchases	190,000	
Available for sale	$230,000	
Inventory, May 31	42,000	188,000
Gross Profit		$102,000
Operating expenses		
Wages	$ 62,000	
Rent	3,000	
Utilities	5,000	
Depreciation	5,000	
Maintenance	1,000	
Miscellaneous	1,300	77,300
Net Income		$ 24,700

ILLUSTRATION 17.13

PAGE COMPANY
Work Sheet for Combining Balance Sheets
May 31, 19――

| | Home Office | Branch | Eliminations | | Combined Bal. Sheet |
			Debit	*Credit*	
Cash	8,400	25,500			33,900
Merchandise inventory	37,000	5,000			42,000
Tottown branch	30,500			30,500	–0–
Land	40,000				40,000
Furniture and fixtures	60,000				60,000
Accumulated depr.—furn. and fix.	(32,000)				(32,000)
Building	120,000				120,000
Accumulated depr.—building	(40,000)				(40,000)
Total Assets	223,900	30,500			223,900
Accounts payable	26,000				26,000
Mortgage payable	50,000				50,000
Home office		30,500	30,500		–0–
P. Page, capital	147,900				147,900
Total Liabilities and Owner's Equity	223,900	30,500	30,500	30,500	223,900

OBJECTIVE 6. Prepare a work sheet for combining home office and branch balance sheets.

ILLUSTRATION 17.14

PAGE COMPANY
Balance Sheet
May 31, 19――

ASSETS

Cash		$ 33,900
Merchandise inventory		42,000
Land		40,000
Furniture and fixtures	$ 60,000	
Less: Accumulated depreciation	32,000	28,000
Building	$120,000	
Less: Accumulated depreciation	40,000	80,000
Total Assets		$223,900

LIABILITIES

Accounts payable	$ 26,000
Mortgage payable	50,000
Total Liabilities	$ 76,000

OWNER'S EQUITY

P. Page, capital	147,900
Total Liabilities and Owner's Equity	$223,900

INTRACOMPANY MARKUPS

*Shipments to branches may be transferred at more than the inventory cost the home office. The excess over cost is referred to as an **intracompany markup** or **intracompany inventory profit.*** For now, it is sufficient that you know that such practices exist. The procedures for accounting for intracompany markups are covered in advanced courses in accounting.

GLOSSARY FOR SECTION 17.A

Branch (branch operation)   An identifiable subentity located at some distance from the home office of an entity.

Centralized accounting system   An accounting system in which all basic data documents for an entity are sent to one location for processing.

Decentralized accounting system   An accounting system where all the accounting functions are performed within each of the identifiable subunits of an entity.

Home office   The controlling facility of an entity that conducts operations at more than one location.

Intracompany markup (intracompany inventory profit)   The difference between the home office's cost of shipments to a branch and the amount that the branch is charged for the goods.

Reciprocal accounts   Two accounts that are supposed to show equal balances, but on opposite sides of the accounts.

SELF-QUIZ ON OBJECTIVES FOR SECTION 17.A
Solutions to Self-Quiz begin on page B-51.

1. **OBJECTIVE 1.** Make general journal entries on both home office and branch books for the following events.

   Events

   Jan. 5   The Parker Company established the Eastside Branch by transferring $4,000 cash to a bank account in the branch name.

   7   Merchandise costing $12,000 transferred from the home office to Eastside Branch.

   20   Eastside Branch transferred $6,000 in cash to the home office.

2. Trial balance figures at December 31 are provided here for the Parker Company—Home Office and Eastside Branch. The company accounts on a calendar-year accounting period. Adjustments have already been made for everything except inventories and cost of goods sold. Also provided are ending inventory figures.

   a. OBJECTIVE 4. Prepare an income statement for the home office.

   b. OBJECTIVE 5. Prepare a work sheet for combining home office and branch income statements.

c. **OBJECTIVE 2.** Prepare a closing entry (or entries) at December 31 for the Eastside branch books. Either include the inventory adjustment as part of the closing entry or prepare an adjusting entry to set up the ending inventory before making the closing entry.

d. **OBJECTIVE 6.** Prepare a work sheet for combining home office and branch balance sheets.

Note to student: Although the self-quiz does not specifically require the preparation of an income statement and balance sheet for Eastside branch, or the preparation of a balance sheet for the home office, you should be able to prepare these statements from the data available. You are encouraged to prepare the statements to ensure that you can meet Objectives 3 and 4. The statements would take much the same form as those illustrated in the section.

<table>
<tr><th colspan="5">PARKER COMPANY
Trial Balance
December 31, 19--</th></tr>
<tr><th></th><th colspan="2">Home Office</th><th colspan="2">Eastside Branch</th></tr>
<tr><th></th><th>Debit</th><th>Credit</th><th>Debit</th><th>Credit</th></tr>
<tr><td>Cash</td><td>5,000</td><td></td><td>4,000</td><td></td></tr>
<tr><td>Accounts Receivable</td><td>40,000</td><td></td><td>20,000</td><td></td></tr>
<tr><td>Merchandise Inventory, Jan. 1</td><td>80,000</td><td></td><td>-0-</td><td></td></tr>
<tr><td>Eastside Branch</td><td>16,000</td><td></td><td></td><td></td></tr>
<tr><td>Furniture and Fixtures</td><td>60,000</td><td></td><td></td><td></td></tr>
<tr><td>Accumulated Depreciation</td><td></td><td>25,000</td><td></td><td></td></tr>
<tr><td>Accounts Payable</td><td></td><td>50,000</td><td></td><td>8,000</td></tr>
<tr><td>Notes Payable</td><td></td><td>12,000</td><td></td><td></td></tr>
<tr><td>Home Office</td><td></td><td></td><td></td><td>16,000</td></tr>
<tr><td>J. Parker, Capital</td><td></td><td>43,000</td><td></td><td></td></tr>
<tr><td>Sales</td><td></td><td>600,000</td><td></td><td>270,000</td></tr>
<tr><td>Purchases</td><td>510,000</td><td></td><td></td><td></td></tr>
<tr><td>Shipments to Eastside Branch</td><td></td><td>180,000</td><td></td><td></td></tr>
<tr><td>Shipments from Home Office</td><td></td><td></td><td>180,000</td><td></td></tr>
<tr><td>Rent Expense</td><td>60,000</td><td></td><td>24,000</td><td></td></tr>
<tr><td>Wages Expense</td><td>120,000</td><td></td><td>58,000</td><td></td></tr>
<tr><td>Depreciation Expense</td><td>5,000</td><td></td><td></td><td></td></tr>
<tr><td>Utilities Expense</td><td>11,000</td><td></td><td>7,000</td><td></td></tr>
<tr><td>Miscellaneous Expense</td><td>3,000</td><td></td><td>1,000</td><td></td></tr>
<tr><td></td><td>910,000</td><td>910,000</td><td>294,000</td><td>294,000</td></tr>
</table>

Inventory, December 31	
Home Office	$75,000
Eastside Branch	15,000

DISCUSSION QUESTIONS FOR SECTION 17.A

1. What are some advantages and disadvantages of a centralized system of accounting for branch operations?

2. Is a Home Office account an asset, liability, or owners' equity account? Explain.

3. Is a Branch Office account an asset, liability, or owners' equity account? Explain.

4. Why are Branch Office and Home Office accounts referred to as reciprocal accounts?

5. What kind of an account is Shipments to Branch, and would you expect to find it on the home office or branch office books?

6. What is the name of the account that is reciprocal to Shipments to Branch?

EXERCISES FOR SECTION 17.A

17.A.1. Assume that branch office accounting is decentralized. Make journal entries on both the home office and branch books to record the following events.

Events

May	15	Herbie Stores opens a Brookville Branch by transferring $25,000 cash to a bank account in the branch name.
	29	Merchandise costing $98,000 is transferred from the home office to the Brookville Branch.
June	8	The branch transfers $8,000 excess cash back to the home office.

17.A.2. Make an entry on branch office books to record a $5,000 cash sale by the branch. Is an entry required on the home office books? Why?

17.A.3. Adjustments information follows for the Frogtown Branch.

Beginning Merchandise Inventory	$ 6,000
Shipments from Home Office	108,000
Ending Merchandise Inventory	13,000

There were no outside purchases made by the branch. Make an adjusting entry on the branch office books to set up ending inventory and recognize cost of goods sold.

17.A.4. Closing information is provided below for Branch 8.

Beginning Merchandise Inventory	$ 18,000
Shipments from Home Office	106,000
Rent Expense	21,000
Wage Expense	38,000
Other Expenses	12,000
Ending Merchandise Inventory	14,000

Sales for the period were $184,000. There were no outside purchases. Make a closing entry to set up ending inventory and close temporary accounts.

17.A.5. Refer to exercise 17.A.4. Assuming that sales were only $174,000, make the closing entry.

17.A.6. The Yonkers branch of Redram Industries reported net income of $78,000 for the year ended December 31. Make an entry on the home office books at December 31 to recognize the branch earnings.

PROBLEMS FOR SECTION 17.A
Alternate Problems for this section begin on page D-87.

17.A.7. The following events pertain to Lexen Company and its branch operation.

Events

Jan. 3   The Lexen Company established Branch 1 by transferring $10,000 cash to a bank account in the branch name.

4   Merchandise costing $18,000 transferred from the home office to Branch 1.

15   Excess merchandise costing $6,000 returned by Branch 1 to the home office.

28   Branch 1 transferred $7,000 cash to the home office.

Required

Prepare journal entries for both home office and branch books to reflect the foregoing events.

LYDECKER STORES
Work Sheet for Combining Balance Sheets
June 30, 19X4

	Home Office	Brookville Branch	Eliminations		Combined Bal. Sheet
			Debit	*Credit*	
Cash	48,000	12,000			
Accounts receivable	80,000	18,000			
Merchandise inventory, 6/30/X4	64,000	31,000			
Brookville branch	60,000				
Furniture and fixtures	160,000	16,000			
Accumulated depreciation	(30,000)	(2,000)			
Total Assets	382,000	75,000			
Accounts payable	50,000	15,000			
Notes payable	98,000				
D. Lydecker, capital	234,000				
Home office		60,000			
Total Liabilities and Owner's Equity	382,000	75,000			

LYDECKER STORES
Work Sheet for Combining Income Statements
For the Year Ended June 30, 19X4

	Home Office	Brookville Branch	Eliminations		Combined Income St.
			Debit	*Credit*	
Sales	600,000	100,000			
Cost of goods sold					
Inventory, 7/1/X3	58,000	15,000			
Purchases	400,000	20,000			
Shipments to branch	(80,000)				
Shipments from home office		80,000			
Available for sale	378,000	115,000			
Inventory, 6/30/X4	(64,000)	(31,000)			
Cost of goods sold	314,000	84,000			
Gross Profit	286,000	16,000			
Operating expenses					
Wages	40,000	10,000			
Rent	22,000	4,000			
Depreciation	10,000	1,000			
Utilities	11,000	3,000			
Miscellaneous	14,000	6,000			
Total operating expenses	97,000	24,000			
Net Income (Loss)	189,000	(8,000)			

Required

1) Set up and complete work sheets similar to those illustrated.

2) Prepare a combined income statement for the fiscal year and a combined balance sheet at June 30, 19X4.

SECTION 17.B

Consolidating Statements of Corporations

OBJECTIVES

This section deals with consolidating statements of parent and subsidiary corporations. At the conclusion of your study, you should be able to

1. Define in your own words each of the following expressions:
   a. Controlling interest.
   b. Subsidiary corporation.
   c. Parent company.
   d. Consolidated statement.
   e. Minority interest.
2. State in your own words three significant reasons for the formation or acquisition of subsidiary corporations by parent corporations.
3. Prepare a work sheet for consolidating simple income statements of a parent company and a subsidiary corporation.
4. Prepare a work sheet for consolidating simple balance sheets for a parent company and a subsidiary.
5. Differentiate between a purchase of a subsidiary and a pooling of interests.

AFFILIATED CORPORATIONS

Significant Influence

Practically all large, well-known corporations exercise control over smaller corporations. As pointed out in Section 16.B, corporations may own shares of stock in other corporations. *Where one corporation owns a sufficient number of voting shares of another corporation to exercise significant influence over its operations, the two entities are referred to as* **affiliated** *corporations.* In general, the ownership of 20% or more of the voting stock of a corporation is presumed sufficient for exercising significant influence over that corporation.[1] You may recall from Section 16.B that where such influence (or potential influence) is present, the shares may be accounted for on the investor's books by the *equity method.*

---

[1]*Opinions of the Accounting Principles Board No. 18,* "The Equity Method of Accounting for Investments in Common Stock" (New York: American Institute of Certified Public Accountants, 1971), par. 17.

Controlling Interest

OBJECTIVE 1a. Define controlling interest.

Ownership of more than half the voting shares of a corporation constitutes a controlling interest. With a controlling interest, a shareholder may elect the majority of the members of the board of directors, which ensures control over the corporation's operations.

OBJECTIVE 1b. Define subsidiary corporation.

OBJECTIVE 1c. Define parent company.

A corporation controlled by one individual or a group of related individuals is known as a closely held corporation. If a corporation is controlled by another corporation, it is called a subsidiary corporation, and the controlling corporation is known as the parent company. Subsidiary and closely held corporations are sometimes referred to as controlled corporations. When all the outstanding voting shares of a subsidiary corporation are owned by the parent company, the subsidiary corporation is referred to as a wholly owned subsidiary.

Economic versus Legal Entities. *A parent corporation and its subsidiaries may be thought of as a family of corporations. Although the corporations are separate legal units, they actually operate as one economic entity.* Corporate members of the economic entity are not free to act independently, because each must consider the welfare of the other members of the corporate family.

The financial statements of subsidiary corporations in which a parent corporation owns more than 50% controlling interest may be *consolidated* with those of the parent to show overall pictures for the economic entity.[2]

OBJECTIVE 1d. Define consolidated statement.

A consolidated statement is a financial statement that shows combined amounts for a family of corporations. In other words, a consolidated statement reports on a parent corporation and its subsidiaries as though they were a single entity. The assumption is that consolidated statements are more meaningful, at least to some users, than separate statements.

Minority Interest

OBJECTIVE 1e. Define minority interest.

When a controlling interest represents less than 100% of the voting shares, *the equity that is not part of the controlling interest is known as the minority interest in the controlled corporation. Owners of voting shares outside of the controlling interest are called minority shareholders.*

Minority shareholders have very little influence on the operation of a controlled corporation. However, if minority shareholders believe that the corporation is not being operated so as to benefit all shareholders in the long

---

[2]*Accounting Research Bulletin No. 51,* "Consolidated Financial Statements" (New York: American Institute of Certified Public Accountants, 1959), par. 2. *ARB 51* (pars. 2–4) points out circumstances under which it would not be advisable to consolidate statements of a controlled corporation with those of the parent.

run, they may seek relief in the courts. And the majority shareholders are of course not allowed to do anything illegal or in conflict with the corporate charter.

REASONS FOR HOLDING SUBSIDIARIES

There are many reasons for the formation or acquisition of subsidiary corporations. Under certain circumstances, subsidiary corporations may help to minimize income taxes. However, the area of corporate tax planning is a bit complex for an introductory course in accounting. (Conditions under which the corporate form of business may serve as a tax advantage are outlined in Chapter 15.)

Subsidiary corporations may be a convenient mechanism for decentralizing control, encouraging intercompany competition, and achieving many other administrative advantages. Three of the most significant reasons for holding subsidiary corporations are discussed in the paragraphs that follow.

Meeting Legal Requirements

Large corporations often conduct business in many states and countries, and they must take care to comply with the local laws, including a confusing variety of regulatory and taxation requirements. In some cases, a locally formed corporation is treated more favorably than a "foreign" one, especially when some of the shares are owned by local citizens. For this and other reasons, a subsidiary corporation may be formed to do business in a particular locality.

A corporation that operates in a number of countries is sometimes referred to as a **multinational corporation***.* Quite frequently, what appears to be one multinational corporation is actually a parent company that controls a number of subsidiary corporations operating in the various foreign countries.

Corporations involved in highly regulated areas, such as insurance, banking, and utility companies, may not be permitted to carry on other diverse activities at the same time. In other words, the regulated corporations must be kept relatively pure so that the regulatory agencies can more easily keep track of their activities. Therefore, if a large, complex corporation wishes to do business in one of the highly regulated areas, a separate corporate entity must be formed for that purpose. The parent corporation can then control the subsidiary's activities, provided that regulatory requirements are met.

Limiting Potential Losses

Recall that the corporate form of organization offers the advantage of limited liability in that shareholders' losses are limited to their investments in the corporation. Shareholders, unlike proprietors and partners, are not *personally* liable for their entity's debts—provided, of course, that they have not been involved in any fraud or other wrongdoing.[3]

The limited liability advantage of corporations may be enhanced through the use of subsidiary corporations. When all activities are carried on within one corporate shell, the entire corporation must absorb losses generated by any of its subdivisions. If, however, an identifiable high-risk division is separately incorporated, potential losses are limited to the parent corporation's investment in the subsidiary. The remaining assets of the parent corporation, and of any other subsidiary corporations, are protected from losses incurred by a subsidiary corporation. One unsuccessful subsidiary may go bankrupt without causing undue harm to the other more prosperous members of a corporate family.

Expanding Control Over Assets

As already pointed out, minority shareholders have little to say about how a corporation is operated. A majority shareholder or a controlling group of shareholders can exercise effective control over *all* of a corporation's assets.

The amount of assets that are controlled can be greatly expanded by use of subsidiary corporations. For example, assume that a majority shareholder owns 51% of the shares of P Corporation, which in turn owns 51% of S Corporation. The majority shareholder may then control S Corporation through P Corporation. Illustration 17.15 depicts the manner by which indirect ownership in only 26% of S Corporation gives effective control over all its assets.

The amount of corporate assets controlled may be further multiplied through *tier investments, whereby subsidiary corporations own stock in other subsidiary corporations.* As Illustration 17.16 indicates, an indirect investment of just over 13% will permit a majority investor in P Corporation to control the operation of T Corporation. The minority investors in Corporations P, S, and T are all rather powerless in that they have little to say about how the corporations are run.

In summary, here are the three significant reasons for the formation or acquisition of subsidiary corporations:

OBJECTIVE 2. State three significant reasons for the formation or acquisition of subsidiary corporations.

1. To meet legal requirements
2. To limit potential losses
3. To expand control over assets

---

[3]Shareholders of closely held or subsidiary corporations are sometimes persuaded by a lender to endorse or otherwise guarantee a corporate debt, in which case the shareholders can be called upon to pay the obligation.

ILLUSTRATION 17.15

CONTROL THROUGH INDIRECT OWNERSHIP

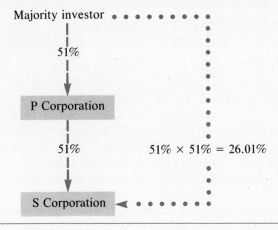

Majority investor

51%

P Corporation

51%   51% × 51% = 26.01%

S Corporation

ILLUSTRATION 17.16

CONTROL THROUGH INDIRECT OWNERSHIP

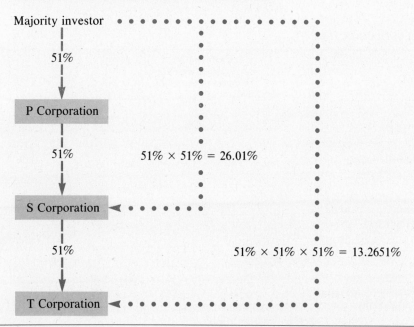

Majority investor

51%

P Corporation

51%   51% × 51% = 26.01%

S Corporation

51%   51% × 51% × 51% = 13.2651%

T Corporation

WHOLLY OWNED SUBSIDIARIES

Let us now concentrate on the techniques for consolidating financial statements. Examples are kept simple in order to get across the concepts without becoming enmeshed in details.

Subsidiary Acquisition

Consider the case of P Company, whose condensed balance sheet at December 31, 19X3, appears as in Illustration 17.17.

No business was conducted on New Year's Day. On Monday morning, January 2, 19X4, S Company was formed as a wholly owned subsidiary with a transfer of $50,000 of cash to a bank account in the name of the new company. P Company received 5,000 shares of $10 par stock in S Company. The entries on the books of the two companies are as shown in Illustration 17.18.

At this point S Company has one asset, Cash, which is duplicated by the asset account Investment in S Company on P Company's books. Likewise, S Company's equity is duplicated in the equity accounts of P Company. Illustration 17.19 shows how the subsidiary's assets and equity accounts are duplicated within the accounting equation of the parent corporation. The tall bar diagram on the left represents the assets of P Company and the corresponding claims against the assets. The short bar on the right represents

ILLUSTRATION 17.17

P COMPANY Balance Sheet December 31, 19X3		
ASSETS		
Cash		$100,000
Accounts receivable		80,000
Other assets		220,000
Total Assets		$400,000
LIABILITIES		
Accounts payable	$ 60,000	
Notes payable	140,000	
Total Liabilities		$200,000
SHAREHOLDERS' EQUITY		
Common stock	$130,000	
Retained earnings	70,000	
Total Shareholders' Equity		200,000
Total Liabilities and Shareholders' Equity		$400,000

ILLUSTRATION 17.18

	P COMPANY		
Jan. 2	Investment in S Company	50,000	
	Cash		˙50,000
	S Company formed as subsidiary. Received		
	5,000 shares of $10 par stock in S Company.		

	S COMPANY		
Jan. 2	Cash	50,000	
	Common Stock		50,000
	5,000 shares of $10 par common issued to		
	P Company at par value.		

S Company's asset of $50,000 cash and P Company's equity claim of an equal amount.

We must keep in mind that P Company's Investment in S Company account balance duplicates S Company's asset Cash. S Company's equity is also duplicated by P Company's equity, since P Company's shareholders

ILLUSTRATION 17.19

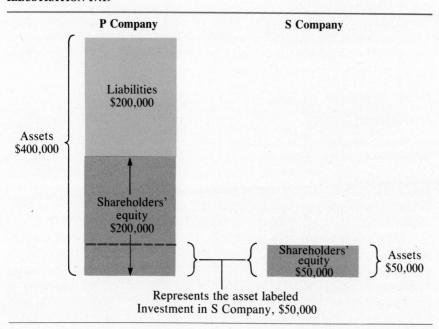

Represents the asset labeled
Investment in S Company, $50,000

ILLUSTRATION 17.20

P AND S COMPANIES
Work Sheet for Consolidating Balance Sheets
January 4, 19X4

	P Company	S Company	Eliminations Debit	Eliminations Credit	Consol. Bal. Sheet
Cash	50,000	50,000			100,000
Accounts receivable	80,000				80,000
Investment in S Company	50,000			50,000	
Other assets	220,000				220,000
Total Assets	400,000	50,000		50,000	400,000
Accounts payable	60,000				60,000
Notes payable	140,000				140,000
Common stock—P Company	130,000				130,000
Retained earnings—P Company	70,000				70,000
Common stock—S Company		50,000	50,000		
Total Liabilities and Shareholders' Equity	400,000	50,000	50,000		400,000

OBJECTIVE 4. Prepare a work sheet for consolidating simple balance sheets for a parent company and a subsidiary.

indirectly own S Company. The work sheet in Illustration 17.20 shows how the duplications are eliminated to arrive at a consolidated balance sheet immediately after the formation of the subsidiary. By comparing the right-hand column of the work sheet with the balance sheet for P Company (Illustration 17.17), you can see that the consolidated accounts are identical to the position of P Company before the subsidiary was formed.

Intercompany Sales

Corporate members of an economic entity are expected to help each other. Whenever possible, goods and services are purchased from family members rather than from outsiders, to keep suppliers' profits within the economic entity. Here is a simple example to illustrate intercompany sales between affiliated companies and to demonstrate the work sheet technique to eliminate double counting of intercompany sales and purchases.

Let us assume that P Company purchases goods on account from an outside supplier for $12,000 and sells them to S Company for $20,000. S Company then sells the goods to outside customers for $35,000. The entries in Illustration 17.21 reflect the effects of the transactions on the books of the parent and subsidiary corporations.

ILLUSTRATION 17.21

P COMPANY		
Purchases	12,000	
Accounts Payable		12,000
Accounts Receivable—S Company	20,000	
Sales		20,000

S COMPANY		
Purchases	20,000	
Accounts Payable—P Company		20,000
Accounts Receivable	35,000	
Sales		35,000

cost of sales

From the standpoint of the *economic* entity, only the original purchase by P and the sale by S are relevant. The intercompany sale cancels out against purchases, and the intercompany debt also cancels out, leaving the result shown in Illustration 17.22.

To further simplify matters, let us assume that S Company purchases no other goods during January 19X4. A work sheet to consolidate income statements is provided in Illustration 17.23 on the next page. As you can see, the intercompany sales are simply canceled out against intercompany purchases.

ILLUSTRATION 17.22

P COMPANY		
Purchases	12,000	
Accounts Payable		12,000
~~Accounts Receivable—S Company~~	~~20,000~~	
~~Sales~~		~~20,000~~

S COMPANY		
~~Purchases~~	~~20,000~~	
~~Accounts Payable—P Company~~		~~20,000~~
Accounts Receivable	35,000	
Sales		35,000

ILLUSTRATION 17.23

	P Company	S Company	Eliminations		Consol. Income St.
P AND S COMPANIES **Work Sheet for Consolidating Income Statements** **For the Month of January 19X4**			Debit	Credit	
Sales	100,000	35,000	20,000		115,000
Cost of goods sold	60,000	20,000		20,000	60,000
Gross Profit	40,000	15,000			55,000
Operating expenses	30,000	10,000			40,000
Net Income	10,000	5,000	20,000	20,000	15,000

OBJECTIVE 3. Prepare a work sheet for consolidating simple income statements of a parent company and a subsidiary corporation.

Recognition by Parent Company of Subsidiary Income

Under the *equity method* of accounting for investments, P Company makes an adjusting entry to recognize the net income reported by S Company.[4] Since S Company is totally owned by P Company, all the reported net income is recognized, as illustrated by the following entry.

	P COMPANY		
19X4 Jan. 31	Investment in S Company	5,000	
	S Company Net Income		5,000
	To recognize income reported by S Company.		

In most cases a parent company adjusts for its share of subsidiary net income only at the end of the subsidiary's fiscal year. We are assuming a monthly accounting period in order to keep things as simple as possible.

Intercompany Debt

When affiliated corporations are viewed as an economic entity, intercompany receivables and payables become irrelevant. They simply represent obligations between members of the corporate family. The work sheet in Illustration 17.24 demonstrates the elimination of both intercompany debt and intercompany investment. The subsidiary's accounts payable and shareholders' equity are both duplicated in the parent's equity accounts and in the assets they represent. Illustration 17.25 shows the nature of the duplications.

---

[4]The equity method of accounting for long-term investments is discussed in Section 16.B.

ILLUSTRATION 17.24

| | | | Eliminations | | Consol. |
	P Company	S Company	*Debit*	*Credit*	Bal. Sheet
P AND S COMPANIES Work Sheet for Consolidating Balance Sheets January 31, 19X4					
Cash	70,000	15,000			85,000
Accounts receivable	90,000	35,000		a) 20,000	105,000
Investment in S Company	55,000			b) 55,000	
Other assets	210,000	25,000			235,000
Total Assets	425,000	75,000		75,000	425,000
Accounts payable	70,000	20,000	a) 20,000		70,000
Notes payable	140,000				140,000
Common stock—P Company	130,000				130,000
Retained earnings—P Company	85,000				85,000
Common stock—S Company		50,000	b) 50,000		
Retained earnings—S Company		5,000	b) 5,000		
Total Liabilities and Shareholders' Equity	425,000	75,000	75,000		425,000

a) Elimination of intercompany debt.
b) Elimination of intercompany investment.

OBJECTIVE 4. Prepare a work sheet for consolidating simple balance sheets for a parent company and a subsidiary.

ILLUSTRATION 17.25

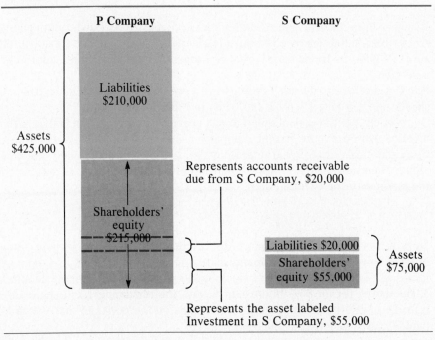

739

ILLUSTRATION 17.26

P AND S COMPANIES
Work Sheet for Consolidating Balance Sheets
February 1, 19X4

	P Company	S Company	Eliminations Debit	Eliminations Credit	Consol. Bal. Sheet
Cash	70,000	15,000			85,000
Accounts receivable	90,000	35,000		a) 20,000	105,000
Investment in S Company	55,000			b) 55,000	
Other assets	210,000	55,000			265,000
Total Assets	425,000	105,000		75,000	455,000
Accounts payable	70,000	20,000	a) 20,000		70,000
Notes payable	140,000	30,000			170,000
Common stock—P Company	130,000				130,000
Retained earnings—P Company	85,000				85,000
Common stock—S Company		50,000	b) 50,000		
Retained earnings—S Company		5,000	b) 5,000		
Total Liabilities and Shareholders' Equity	425,000	105,000	75,000		455,000

a) Elimination of intercompany debt.
b) Elimination of intercompany investment.

OBJECTIVE 4. Prepare a work sheet for consolidating simple balance sheets for a parent company and a subsidiary.

External Debt

Whereas intercompany debts within an economic entity cancel out against receivables, liabilities owed to outsiders expand the size of the consolidated entity. Suppose, for example, that S Company purchases some additional assets on February 1 by signing a note for $30,000. Assuming that no other transactions occur during February, a work sheet to consolidate balance sheets on February 1 would appear as in Illustration 17.26.

Notice that the consolidated assets are now greater by $30,000 than the amount owned by the parent company. Also, the liabilities owed by the economic entity are $30,000 larger than those of the parent company standing alone. Illustration 17.27 shows how the consolidated picture is greater by the amount of the external debt.

MINORITY OWNERSHIP INTEREST

Now let us go back and change the original illustration to include some minority ownership of S Company shares. On January 3, 19X4, S Company issues 6,250 shares of common stock at $10 per share. P Company acquires 5,000 shares for an 80% interest in S, and the remaining 1,250 shares are issued to minority shareholders. The entries on the books of the two companies now appear as in Illustration 17.28.

ILLUSTRATION 17.27

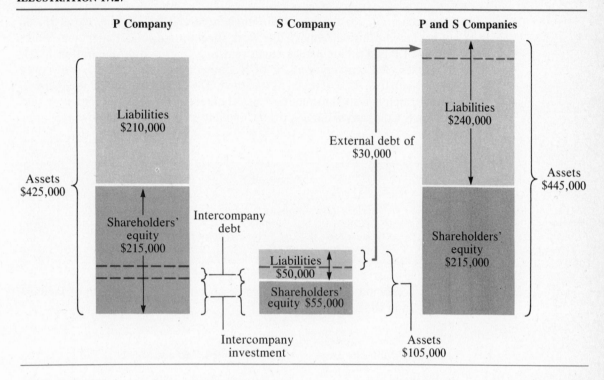

ILLUSTRATION 17.28

	P COMPANY		
19X4 Jan. 3	Investment in S Company 　　Cash Acquired 80% interest in S Company by pur- chasing 5,000 shares at $10 per share.	50,000	50,000

	S COMPANY		
19X4 Jan. 3	Cash 　　Common Stock 6,250 shares of $10 common issued at par.	62,500	62,500

Effects of Minority Interest on Consolidated Income Statements

If all other circumstances remain unchanged and S Company earns $5,000 of net income during January, the work sheet for consolidating income statements of P and S Companies might remain as pictured in Illustration 17.23. However, P Company's share of S Company's net income is now only $4,000—that is, 80% of the $5,000 earned. The remaining 20% of the income, $1,000, belongs to the minority shareholders. The adjusting entry to recognize S Company's income on P Company's records would now appear as follows.

	P COMPANY		
19X4 Jan. 31	Investment in S Company	4,000	
	S Company Net Income		4,000
	To recognize 80% of income reported by S Company.		

A combined (consolidated) income statement for the month of January is shown in Illustration 17.29.

Effects of Minority Interest on Consolidated Balance Sheets

A work sheet for consolidating balance sheets of the two companies must reflect the minority interest that is present. The work sheet at February 1, which also includes the external debt, will now appear as in Illustration 17.30. Note that the Cash and Common Stock accounts of S Company are greater by the amount of the initial investment by minority shareholders, $12,500; the Investment in S Company and Retained Earnings accounts of

ILLUSTRATION 17.29

P AND S COMPANIES Consolidated Income Statement For the Month of January 19X4	
Sales	$115,000
Cost of goods sold	60,000
Gross Profit	$ 55,000
Operating expenses	40,000
Net income including minority interest	$ 15,000
Minority interest in net income	1,000
Consolidated Net Income	$ 14,000

ILLUSTRATION 17.30

P AND S COMPANIES
Work Sheet for Consolidating Balance Sheets
February 1, 19X4

Accounts	P Company	S Company	Eliminations Debit	Eliminations Credit	Consol. Bal. Sheet
Cash	70,000	27,500			97,500
Accounts receivable	90,000	35,000		a) 20,000	105,000
Investment in S Company	54,000			b) 54,000	
Other assets	210,000	55,000			265,000
Total Assets	424,000	117,500		74,000	467,500
Accounts payable	70,000	20,000	a) 20,000		70,000
Notes payable	140,000	30,000			170,000
Common stock—P Company	130,000				130,000
Retained earnings—P Company	84,000				84,000
Common stock—S Company		62,500	b) 62,500		
Retained earnings—S Company		5,000	b) 5,000		
Minority interest				b) 13,500	13,500
Total Liabilities and Shareholders' Equity	424,000	117,500	87,500	13,500	467,500

a) Elimination of intercompany debt.
b) Elimination of intercompany investment and recognition of minority interest (20% × $67,500 = $13,500).

OBJECTIVE 4. Prepare a work sheet for consolidating simple balance sheets for a parent company and a subsidiary.

P Company are $1,000 less than they were in the previous work sheet example, owing to the minority interest share in net income of that amount.

Illustration 17.31 shows how the consolidated position of the two companies is greater than that of the parent company by the amount of external debt and minority interest. A consolidated balance sheet for the two companies at February 1 is shown in Illustration 17.32 on page 745. Note that the equity claims of minority shareholders are shown apart from the controlling interest.

PURCHASE VERSUS POOLING OF INTERESTS

So far, our examples have dealt with new subsidiaries formed by parent corporations. But existing corporations are sometimes acquired by parent companies as subsidiaries. When controlling interest in a corporation is obtained by buying shares from the corporation's shareholders, the acquisition is treated as a purchase. The acquisition of a controlling interest by exchanging shares of the parent for shares of the subsidiary—in accordance with the provisions of *APB Opinion No. 16*—is treated as a pooling of

ILLUSTRATION 17.31

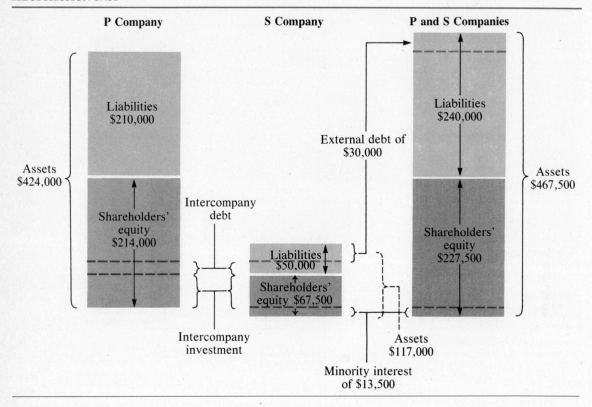

OBJECTIVE 5.
Differentiate between the
purchase of a subsidiary
and the pooling of
interests.

interests. Basically, a *purchase of a subsidiary* is viewed *"as the acquisition of one company by another,"* whereas a *pooling of interests* is seen *"as the uniting of the ownership interests of two or more companies by exchanges of equity securities."*[5]

Actually, *APB Opinion No. 16* applies to all types of business combinations, including those in which two or more corporations merge legally into one corporate entity. A number of tests for differentiating between purchases and poolings are set forth in that *Opinion.* For our purposes, suffice it to say that a pooling occurs when the majority of the common shares of one corporation are acquired over a short period of time in exchange for common shares of the acquiring company.

---

[5]*Opinions of the Accounting Principles Board No. 16,* "Business Combinations" (New York: American Institute of Certified Public Accountants, 1970), pars. 11 and 12.

ILLUSTRATION 17.32

P AND S COMPANIES **Consolidated Balance Sheet** **February 1, 19X4**		
ASSETS		
Cash		$ 97,500
Accounts receivable		105,000
Other assets		265,000
Total Assets		$467,500
LIABILITIES		
Accounts payable	$ 70,000	
Notes payable	170,000	
Total Liabilities		$240,000
SHAREHOLDERS' EQUITY		
Minority interest		$ 13,500
Controlling interest		
Common stock	$130,000	
Retained earnings	84,000	214,000
Total Shareholders' Equity		$227,500
Total Liabilities and Shareholders' Equity		$467,500

Under the purchase method of consolidating subsidiary statements with those of a parent, the subsidiary's retained earnings accumulated prior to acquisition are eliminated, and the subsidiary's assets at time of acquisition are consolidated at their fair values at that time, less any depreciation that occurred since the acquisition date. The pooling method, on the other hand, combines the subsidiary's retained earnings with those of the parent and combines the subsidiary assets at their book values as shown in the subsidiary's accounting records.

The finer distinctions between purchase and pooling methods and the circumstances under which they apply become rather involved. These matters, as well as the more complex aspects of consolidating financial statements, are studied in advanced accounting courses.

GLOSSARY FOR SECTION 17.B

Affiliated corporations Two (or more) corporations interrelated by means of the exercise of significant influence by one corporation over the other(s) through ownership of a sufficient number (20% or more) of its (their) voting shares.

Closely held corporation   A corporation controlled by one individual or a group of related individuals.

Consolidated statement   A financial statement that shows combined amounts for a family of corporations.

Controlled corporations   Corporations controlled either as subsidiaries of other corporations or as closely held corporations of individuals.

Controlling interest   Ownership of more than half the voting shares of a corporation.

Economic entity   A family of corporations consisting of a parent corporation and one or more subsidiary corporations.

Minority interest   The portion of a corporation's equity that is not part of the controlling interest of a controlled corporation.

Minority shareholders   Owners of voting shares outside of the controlling interest of a controlled corporation.

Multinational corporation   A corporation that operates in a number of countries.

Parent company   A corporation that owns a controlling interest in one or more other corporations.

Pooling of interest   The uniting of ownership interests of two or more companies by exchange of equity securities.

Purchase of a subsidiary   The acquisition of one corporation by another, usually by purchasing a controlling interest in the acquired company from that company's shareholders.

Subsidiary corporation   A corporation that is controlled by another corporation, which owns the majority of the first corporation's voting stock.

Tier investments   Subsidiary corporations' ownership of stock in other subsidiary corporations.

Wholly owned subsidiary   A subsidiary corporation whose outstanding voting shares are all owned by the parent company.

SELF-QUIZ ON OBJECTIVES FOR SECTION 17.B
Solutions to Self-Quiz begin on page B-54.

1. OBJECTIVE 1. Define the following expressions:
   a. Controlling interest
   b. Subsidiary corporation
   c. Parent company
   d. Consolidated statement
   e. Minority interest

2. OBJECTIVE 2. State three significant reasons for the formation or acquisition of subsidiary corporations by parent corporations.

3. OBJECTIVES 3, 4. Par Company owns 90% of the outstanding shares of Sub Company. Sub Company buys merchandise only from Par Company and had

no beginning or ending inventories. All of Sub Company's Accounts Payable are owed to Par Company, but the Note Payable is owed to a bank. Set up work sheets like the ones shown, and complete them to arrive at consolidated data for the economic entity.

PAR AND SUB COMPANIES Work Sheet for Consolidating Income Statements For Year Ended December 31, 19--					
	Par Company	Sub Company	Eliminations		Consol. Income St.
			Debit	Credit	
Sales	500,000	100,000			
Cost of goods sold	300,000	60,000			
Gross Profit	200,000	40,000			
Operating expenses	120,000	25,000			
Net Income	80,000	15,000*			

*Minority interest in net income (10% × $15,000 = $1,500).

PAR AND SUB COMPANIES Work Sheet For Consolidating Balance Sheets December 31, 19--					
	Par Company	Sub Company	Eliminations		Consol. Bal. Sheet
			Debit	Credit	
Cash	20,000	5,000			
Accounts receivable	80,000	18,000			
Investment in Sub Company	54,000				
Other assets	200,000	102,000			
Total Assets	354,000	125,000			
Accounts payable	104,000	25,000			
Note payable		40,000			
Common stock—Par Company	50,000				
Retained earnings—Par Co.	200,000				
Common stock—Sub Company		30,000			
Retained earnings—Sub Co.		30,000			
Minority interest					
Total Liabilities and Shareholders' Equity	354,000	125,000			

4. **OBJECTIVE 5.** Differentiate between a purchase of a subsidiary and a pooling of interests.

DISCUSSION QUESTIONS FOR SECTION 17.B

1. What are affiliated corporations?

2. Is it possible for a wholly owned corporation to be also an affiliated corporation? Explain.

3. What is an economic entity as that expression is used in this section?

4. What are tier investments, and of what advantage are they in obtaining control over corporations?

5. Why is intercompany debt eliminated in the process of consolidating financial statements?

6. Why is the account representing the parent's investment in the subsidiary eliminated in the process of consolidating financial statements?

EXERCISES FOR SECTION 17.B

17.B.1. On February 1 the Are Company was formed as a wholly owned subsidiary of the Ess Company with a transfer of $100,000 cash to a bank account in the name of the new company. Ess Company received 10,000 shares of $10 par common stock in Are Company. Make entries to record these events on both Are Company and Ess Company books.

17.B.2. Are Company, a wholly owned subsidiary of Ess Company, purchased $50,000 worth of merchandise from Ess on account on March 1. Make entries on the books of both companies to record this transaction.

17.B.3. Newton Corporation has just received notice that Ocho Corporation has earned $120,000 of net income for the year just ended. Prepare for Newton's journal any entries needed to recognize Ocho's earnings, assuming that

    a. Ocho is a wholly owned subsidiary of Newton.

    b. Newton owns 75% of Ocho's common stock.

    c. Newton owns 10% of Ocho's common stock.

17.B.4. On June 1 the Quix Corporation was formed through the issue of 12,000 shares of $10 par common stock at $20 per share. USX Corporation acquired 10,200 shares for an 85% interest in Quix, and the remaining 1,800 shares were issued to minority shareholders. Make entries to record these events on both Quix Corporation and USX Corporation books.

17.B.5. Riox Corporation owns 80% of the voting shares of Stoh Corporation; Stoh owns 60% of Tuff's shares; Tuff owns 52% of Ulrich's shares. Determine the percentage of indirect investment that Riox has in Ulrich, and explain how Riox directors can exercise effective control over Ulrich's operations.

PROBLEMS FOR SECTION 17.B
Alternate Problems for this section begin on page D-89.

17.B.6. A balance sheet for the WQPD Corporation is shown here.

WQPD CORPORATION Balance Sheet February 28, 19--		
ASSETS		
Cash		$ 98,000
Accounts receivable		170,000
Furniture and fixtures	$760,000	
Less: Accumulated depreciation	192,000	568,000
Total Assets		$836,000
LIABILITIES		
Accounts payable	$240,000	
Notes payable	110,000	
Total Liabilities		$350,000
SHAREHOLDERS' EQUITY		
Common stock	$250,000	
Retained earnings	236,000	
Total Shareholders' Equity		486,000
Total Liabilities and Shareholders' Equity		$836,000

On March 1 WQPD Corporation formed a wholly owned subsidiary by transferring $50,000 cash to a bank account in the name of the PVOK Corporation, for which WQPD received 5,000 shares of $10 par PVOK stock. There were no other transactions on March 1.

Required

1) Make journal entries for WQPD and PVOK Corporations to record the March 1 event.

2) Prepare a work sheet for consolidating balance sheets for the two corporations at March 1.

3) Prepare a consolidated balance sheet at March 1.

17.B.7. Zekkon Corporation owns 80% of the outstanding shares of Oxor Incorporated. All the goods sold by Oxor were purchased during the year from Zekkon, and all of Oxor's accounts payable are owed to Zekkon. Oxor's notes payable are owed to banks. Partial consolidating work sheets are shown here.

	ZEKKON AND OXOR CORPORATIONS Work Sheet for Consolidating Balance Sheets December 31, 19--				
	Zekkon Corp.	**Oxor Inc.**	**Eliminations**		**Consol. Bal. Sheet**
			Debit	*Credit*	
Cash	50,000	8,000			
Accounts receivable	160,000	20,000			
Investment in Oxor, Inc.	76,000				
Other assets	300,000	97,000			
Total Assets	586,000	125,000			
Accounts payable	130,000	21,000			
Notes payable	60,000	9,000			
Common stock—Zekkon	150,000				
Retained earnings—Zekkon	246,000				
Common stock—Oxor		50,000			
Retained earnings—Oxor		45,000			
Minority interest					
Total Liabilities and Shareholders' Equity	586,000	125,000			

	ZEKKON AND OXOR CORPORATIONS Work Sheet for Consolidating Income Statements For Year Ended December 31, 19--				
	Zekkon Corp.	**Oxor Inc.**	**Eliminations**		**Consol. Income St.**
			Debit	*Credit*	
Sales	900,000	180,000			
Cost of goods sold	558,000	108,000			
Gross Profit	342,000	72,000			
Operating expenses	225,000	43,000			
Net Income	117,000	29,000			

Required

Set up and complete work sheets like those shown.

17.B.8. XL Corporation is a wholly owned subsidiary of JAL Corporation. JAL purchases merchandise items from a number of manufacturers and wholesales them to XL for sale in XL's chain of retail stores. All of JAL's sales are made to XL. Income statements for the two corporations are as follows.

JAL CORPORATION Income Statement For the Year Ended December 31, 19– –	
Sales	$898,000
Cost of goods sold	506,000
Gross Profit	$392,000
Operating expenses	287,000
Net Income	$105,000

XL CORPORATION Income Statement For the Year Ended December 31, 19– –	
Sales	$4,690,000
Cost of goods sold	1,840,000
Gross Profit	$2,850,000
Operating expenses	1,908,000
Net Income	$ 942,000

Required

1) Prepare a work sheet for consolidating income statements.

2) Prepare a consolidated income statement for JAL and XL Corporations.

17.B.9. Helter Corporation owns 90% of the outstanding shares of Jewel Corporation. Jewel's Accounts Payable includes $36,000 owed to Helter Corporation. Helter's Notes Payable include $100,000 owed to its subsidiary. A partial work sheet for consolidating balance sheets is shown here.

HELTER AND JEWEL CORPORATIONS Work Sheet for Consolidating Balance Sheets December 31, 19– –			Eliminations		Consol. Bal. Sheet
	Helter Corp.	Jewel Corp.	*Debit*	*Credit*	
Cash	58,000	20,000			
Accounts receivable	220,000	190,000			
Investment in Jewel Corp.	333,000				
Notes receivable		100,000			
Other assets	450,000	250,000			
Total Assets	1,061,000	560,000			
Accounts payable	280,000	190,000			
Notes payable	210,000				
Common stock—Helter Corp.	350,000				
Retained earnings—Helter Corp.	221,000				
Common stock—Jewel Corp.		200,000			
Retained earnings—Jewel Corp.		170,000			
Minority interest					
Total Liabilities and Shareholders' Equity	1,061,000	560,000			

Required

1) Set up and complete a work sheet similar to the one illustrated.

2) Prepare a consolidated balance sheet at December 31.

SUMMARY OF CHAPTER 17

Entities sometimes carry on branch operations at locations distant from the home office. If branch operations are accounted for by means of a decentralized accounting system, it is necessary to combine (merge) branch and home office statements to obtain statements for the entire entity. In the process of combining statements, care must be taken to avoid duplication of amounts. Credit balances in Shipments to Branch accounts are offset against debit balances in Shipments from Home Office accounts in work sheets for combining income statements. In work sheets for combining balance sheets, debit balances in Branch accounts on home office books are offset against credit balances in Home Office accounts on the books of branches.

Parent corporations form or acquire subsidiary corporations for a variety of reasons. The statements of parent and subsidiary corporations may be consolidated to obtain statements for the economic entity consisting of the family of corporations. Intercompany investments and debt are eliminated to arrive at a consolidated balance sheet, and the effects of intercompany sales are eliminated to arrive at a consolidated income statement. Outside debt and minority investments increase the overall size of an economic entity, and therefore are not eliminated in the consolidating process.

PROBLEMS FOR CHAPTER 17
Alternate Problems for this chapter begin on page D-91.

17.1. Summarized transactions for the first month's operations of Midwest Branch of Harko, Inc., are as follows.

Transactions

Mar.	1	Received $30,000 from home office.
	3	Received merchandise costing $190,000 from home office.
	7	Sales on account, $98,000.
	10	Purchased merchandise on account, $28,000.
	16	Cash sales, $8,000; sales on account, $92,000.
	28	Sales on account, $123,000.
	29	Collected $76,000 on account.
	30	Paid rent for March, $3,000.
	30	Paid salaries for March, $41,000.
	30	Paid $18,000 on accounts payable.
	31	Transferred $7,000 cash to home office.

Merchandise inventory at March 31 was $11,000.

Required

1) Record the transactions in the branch general journal.

2) Prepare an income statement for the branch.

3) Prepare a closing entry (or entries) at March 31 for the branch. If you do not set up ending inventory as part of the closing entry, prepare a separate adjusting entry to do so.

4) Make an entry on the home office books to recognize branch net income.

17.2. Gino Corporation owns 70% of the common stock of Renn Corporation. Renn operates a branch store for which separate accounting records are maintained. Trial balances at year-end for Gino, Renn, and Renn's branch store are presented here. Renn's Purchases balance represents merchandise purchased from Gino, whereas the Purchases account for Renn Branch represents goods purchased from unrelated suppliers. Renn's Accounts Payable are all due to Gino, while the Accounts Payable of Renn Branch are due to unrelated firms. Ignore any problems associated with possible intercompany markups in inventories.

	Trial Balances December 31, 19--					
	Gino		**Renn**		**Renn Branch**	
	Debit	*Credit*	*Debit*	*Credit*	*Debit*	*Credit*
Cash	50,000		20,000		10,000	
Accounts Receivable	200,000		85,000		64,000	
Merchandise Inventory, Jan. 1	160,000		90,000		70,000	
Investment in Renn Corporation	280,000					
Renn Branch			145,000			
Other Assets	620,000		232,000		58,000	
Accounts Payable		86,000		52,000		24,000
Renn Home Office						145,000
Common Stock		700,000		300,000		
Retained Earnings		384,000		100,000		
Sales		900,000		500,000		350,000
Purchases	400,000		350,000		80,000	
Shipments to Renn Branch				140,000		
Shipments from Renn Home Office					140,000	
Rent Expense	120,000		20,000		12,000	
Wage Expense	150,000		110,000		60,000	
Other Expense	90,000		40,000		25,000	
	2,070,000	2,070,000	1,092,000	1,092,000	519,000	519,000
Inventory, December 31	150,000		85,000		68,000	

Required

1) Prepare a work sheet for combining the income statements of Renn and its branch store.

2) Prepare one or more entries for Renn Branch to update the Merchandise Inventory balance and close the branch's temporary equity accounts at December 31.

3) Prepare entries for Renn to recognize the branch net income for the year, update Renn's Merchandise Inventory balance, and close Renn's temporary equity accounts at December 31.

4) Prepare a work sheet for combining the balance sheets of Renn and its branch store. Keep in mind that the balances of some permanent accounts have been changed by the entries made for requirements (2) and (3).

5) Prepare a work sheet for consolidating the income statement of Gino with the combined income statement of Renn that resulted from requirement (1).

6) Prepare entries for Gino to recognize its share of Renn's net income, update Gino's Merchandise Inventory balance and close Gino's temporary equity accounts at December 31.

7) Prepare a work sheet for consolidating the balance sheet of Gino with the combined balance sheet of Renn that resulted from requirement (4). Keep in mind that the balances of some of Gino's permanent accounts have been changed by the entries made for requirement (6).

8) Assume for purposes of this requirement that Renn's beginning and ending inventories (but not branch inventories) were all purchased from Gino, and that Gino consistently realizes a gross profit rate of 20% on sales. What further changes would need to be made in the consolidated statements you have prepared, and why?

17.3. Able Corporation has for some years operated a branch in another city. The post-closing trial balances at the end of the fiscal year are shown for the corporation and its Baker Branch. There are no intracompany receivables or payables at June 30.

ABLE CORPORATION Trial Balance June 30, 19X4		
Cash	90,000	
Accounts Receivable	500,000	
Merchandise Inventory	740,000	
Baker Branch	350,000	
Other Assets	430,000	
Accounts Payable		940,000
Common Stock		400,000
Capital in Excess of Par		200,000
Retained Earnings		570,000
	2,110,000	2,110,000

ABLE CORPORATION—BAKER BRANCH Trial Balance June 30, 19X4		
Cash	5,000	
Accounts Receivable	80,000	
Merchandise Inventory	210,000	
Other Assets	175,000	
Accounts Payable		120,000
Home Office		350,000
	470,000	470,000

On July 1, 19X4, before conducting any business for the new year, Able's branch operation was incorporated as Baker Corporation. The branch assets and liabilities were taken over by the new corporation at their book values, and 20,000 shares of $10 par common stock in Baker Corporation were issued to Able Corporation.

Required

1) Prepare a work sheet for combining the Able Corporation and Baker Branch balance sheets at June 30, 19X4.

2) Make general journal entries to record the effects of terminating Baker Branch and creating Baker Corporation:

   a) In Able Corporation's journal.

   b) In Baker Branch's journal.

   c) In Baker Corporation's journal.

3) Prepare a work sheet for consolidating the balance sheets of Able Corporation and Baker Corporation immediately after Baker's formation on July 1.

4) In what ways are the work sheets prepared for requirements (1) and (3) different? Explain why both procedures reach the same results.

COMPREHENSION PROBLEMS FOR CHAPTER 17

17.4. Verban, Inc., is a closely held corporation in which all shares are owned by members of the Verban family. The corporation consists primarily of a large auto parts store located in a fair-size city.

Verban is a profitable but stable corporation, with no prospects for further growth at its present location. Several family members are employed by the corporation, and no member of the family has income from sources other than the corporation.

The Verban family has arranged to open a smaller auto parts outlet in a nearby suburb. There is some disagreement among family members concerning the business form that would be most suitable for the suburban store. You have been asked to advise the family.

Required

Outline for the Verban family some of the relative advantages and disadvantages of operating the suburban store as a family partnership, as a branch of Verban, Inc., or as a subsidiary corporation with Verban, Inc., as the parent company.

17.5. Managers of TEX Corporation have made arrangements to acquire 90% of the outstanding common shares of NIX Corporation. These shares are now owned by members of a family that controls NIX Corporation. The family members are willing to accept either $12 cash per share or one share of TEX common stock (currently selling for $24 per share) in exchange for each two shares of NIX stock. TEX Corporation could obtain the cash to buy NIX shares with an issue of 10% 30-year bonds. TEX Corporation and NIX Corporation each has 100,000 shares of common stock outstanding.

TEX Corporation earned $400,000 after taxes during the previous year, and NIX earned $240,000 after taxes for the same period. Both corporations are taxed at a marginal rate of 46%. It is believed that past earnings are representative of future earnings potential of the corporations.

Required

1) Advise TEX Corporation about the relative effect of purchasing NIX shares with cash as compared to exchanging TEX shares for them.

2) There are some indications that the remaining 10% of NIX shares could be obtained under the same terms. Should TEX managers attempt to acquire the remaining shares of NIX? Why?

CHAPTER **18**

Flows of Working Capital and Cash

An income statement shows revenues and expenses for a period, and a balance sheet pictures an entity's resources and obligations at a point in time. However, neither statement deals specifically with how changes in resources came about. This chapter presents two alternate approaches to preparing statements that show changes in financial resources.

Section A of Chapter 18 focuses on the net current asset (working capital) approach to presenting changes in financial resources. The nature of working capital is considered before going on to the determination of working capital changes. Techniques for preparing a statement of changes in financial position on a working capital basis are covered, and the steps in preparing the statement are summarized.

Section B is concerned with the cash flow approach to preparing statements of changes in financial position. The section commences with a discussion about how cash tends to circulate through most entities. Approaches to identifying cash flows from accrual basis accounting data are presented, and the steps in preparing cash flow statements are summarized.

SECTION 18.A

Statements of Changes in Financial Position

OBJECTIVES

This section deals with working capital flows and with the preparation of statements of changes in financial position. At the conclusion of your study, you should be able to

1. Define the expression *working capital.*
2. Prepare a comparative schedule of working capital, given balance sheets for the beginning and end of a period.
3. State the overall purpose of a statement of changes in financial position prepared on a working capital basis.
4. List the steps in the preparation of a statement of changes in financial position on a working capital basis.
5. Prepare a statement of changes in financial position on a working capital basis, given an income statement for a period, balance sheets for the beginning and end of the period, and other needed data.

THE NATURE OF WORKING CAPITAL

Assets are usually listed in balance sheets in the order of their relative *liquidity, or nearness to cash.* In fact, a classified balance sheet presents all current assets together as a subgroup of assets. Current assets, you may recall, include cash and other assets that are relatively close to cash.

Liabilities are usually listed in balance sheets in the order in which they are expected to be paid. Current liabilities are those that can reasonably be expected to be paid within one year, or one operating cycle if that is longer than one year.

Business managers, owners, and others are interested in current assets and current liabilities because of their effect on the liquidity of a concern.

OBJECTIVE 1. Define working capital. *The amount by which an entity's current assets exceed its current liabilities at a point in time is referred to as* **working capital** *or* **net current assets.**

Current assets − Current liabilities = Working capital

Working capital is sometimes referred to as *funds,* but the two expressions are not necessarily synonymous. Funds may mean different things to different people. Most individuals probably equate funds with cash. To some people the expression means *cash plus marketable securities and accounts receivable, sometimes referred to as* **quick assets** because they are just one step away from cash. It is probably a good idea to define the word *funds* according to the context in which it is used.

A word of caution may be in order about what working capital really represents. Many people mistakenly believe that working capital is readily available for paying dividends or for use in purchasing long-term assets. However, a certain amount of working capital must circulate continuously within the entity if the entity is to remain stable. As receivables are collected in cash, other receivables take their place. Much, if not all, of the cash collected will have to be used for expenses and for paying liabilities as they come due. Certain levels of receivables, inventories, and other current assets represent rather *permanent* investments for a business—more permanent, in many ways, than long-term depreciable assets such as machinery and equipment. Of course, a certain level of current liabilities is also rather permanent in that new payables arise as others are paid off.

Perhaps it would make more sense in some circumstances to identify the current assets that are not part of the normal requirements. For example, merchandise purchased specifically for sale during a Christmas season may be in excess of the normal inventory carried by a retail store. Garden supplies and winter sports equipment are other examples of seasonal buildups of inventory. Receivables may reach higher than normal levels as a result of seasonal sales on credit. Any current assets not crucial to operations, such as marketable securities, could be thought of as excess, or available, current assets.

In a similar manner, payables resulting from seasonal activity may not be replaced as they are paid. Accounts payable for seasonal merchandise, wages payable for seasonal help, and short-term bank loans are examples of noncirculating current liabilities.

The working capital that will be available for disbursement outside the cycle of operations could be determined in the following manner.

> Excess current assets − Excess current liabilities = Available working capital

COMPARATIVE SCHEDULE OF WORKING CAPITAL

As pointed out earlier, an entity's working capital is defined as its current assets less the current liabilities it owes. From the comparative balance sheets of Drissy Corporation presented in Illustration 18.1, we can determine that the working capital at December 31, 19X4, was $176,500.

> **Current assets − Current liabilities = Working capital**
> $265,300   − $88,800   = $176,500

ILLUSTRATION 18.1

	DRISSY CORPORATION Comparative Balance Sheet December 31, 19X4 and 19X3		
	19X4	19X3	Increase (Decrease)
ASSETS			
Current			
Cash	$ 14,500	$ 12,400	$ 2,100
Accounts receivable	97,800	73,600	24,200
Merchandise inventory	150,000	160,000	(10,000)
Prepaid rent	3,000	2,000	1,000
Total current assets	$265,300	$248,000	$ 17,300
Noncurrent			
Equipment	$480,000	$330,000	$150,000
Accumulated depreciation	(186,000)	(131,000)	(55,000)
Total noncurrent assets	$294,000	$199,000	$ 95,000
Total Assets	$559,300	$447,000	$112,300
LIABILITIES			
Current			
Accounts payable	$ 87,000	$ 74,000	$ 13,000
Wages payable	1,800	2,300	(500)
Total current liabilities	$ 88,800	$ 76,300	$ 12,500
Noncurrent			
Notes payable	140,000	100,000	40,000
Total Liabilities	$228,800	$176,300	$ 52,500
SHAREHOLDERS' EQUITY			
Common stock	$ 55,000	$ 50,000	$ 5,000
Capital in excess of par	75,000	30,000	45,000
Retained earnings	200,500	190,700	9,800
Total Shareholders' Equity	$330,500	$270,700	$ 59,800
Total Liabilities and Shareholders' Equity	$559,300	$447,000	$112,300

NOTE: Cash dividends were paid during 19X4 in the amount of $40,000.

Note that we have determined what the working capital was at a *point in time,* December 31, 19X4. Perhaps it would also be useful to know the working capital at the beginning of 19X4 and how much it changed during the year. The comparative schedule of working capital in Illustration 18.2 simply offsets the current liability sections of the comparative balance sheets against the current asset sections, thereby disclosing the detailed changes in working capital between two points in time.

ILLUSTRATION 18.2

DRISSY CORPORATION Comparative Schedule of Working Capital December 31, 19X4 and 19X3			
	19X4	**19X3**	**Increase (Decrease)**
Current Assets			
Cash	$ 14,500	$ 12,400	$ 2,100
Accounts receivable	97,800	73,600	24,200
Merchandise inventory	150,000	160,000	(10,000)
Prepaid rent	3,000	2,000	1,000
Total current assets	$265,300	$248,000	$17,300
Current Liabilities			
Accounts payable	$ 87,000	$ 74,000	$13,000
Wages payable	1,800	2,300	(500)
Total current liabilities	$ 88,800	$ 76,300	$12,500
Working capital	$176,500	$171,700	$ 4,800

OBJECTIVE 2. Prepare a comparative schedule of working capital.

From the schedule we can see that working capital increased by $4,800 during 19X4 and that the change represents an increase of $17,300 in current assets, offset by an increase of $12,500 in current liabilities. Still, the working capital presentation is a static one. We have calculated the increase in working capital, but we have not explained how the increase came about.

We must be careful at this point to avoid falling into a common trap. There is a tendency to say that working capital changed *because* individual current accounts went up or down. But working capital is *made up* of the current accounts, and thus these accounts cannot be considered sources or uses of working capital. To say that working capital went up because Accounts Receivable increased would be like saying that cash increased because cash increased. Working capital changes can best be explained by examining the changes in *noncurrent* accounts. Later in this section you will see how the increase or decrease in each of the noncurrent accounts is analyzed in the process of preparing the statement of changes in financial position.

STATEMENTS OF CHANGES IN FINANCIAL POSITION

Purpose of Statements of Changes in Financial Position

A statement of changes in financial position shows the sources and uses of financial resources during a period. APB Opinion No. 19, issued in 1971, prescribed that a statement of changes in financial position be prepared and

OBJECTIVE 3. State the purpose of a statement of changes in financial position prepared on a working capital basis.

presented as one of the basic financial statements.[1] *Opinion 19* permits the statement to be prepared on either a working capital flow or a cash flow basis.[2] However, in the past most accountants have preferred the working capital approach. This section concentrates on working capital flows; Section 18.B deals with cash flows.

A number of questions can be answered more readily from information contained in statements of changes in financial position than from income statements and balance sheets. Here are just some of the questions that may be answered by a statement of changes in financial position prepared on a working capital basis.

1. Where did the working capital come from to finance
   a. The payment of dividends?
   b. The purchase of noncurrent assets?
   c. The payment of long-term debt?
2. Why weren't dividends larger?
3. Where did the working capital go that was derived from
   a. Net income?
   b. Sale of noncurrent assets?
   c. Long-term borrowing or new investment in the entity?
4. Why did working capital increase (or decrease) during the period?

Format of Statement of Changes in Financial Position

The usual format of a statement of changes in financial position shows sources of working capital first, followed by uses of working capital, as outlined in Illustration 18.3.

The Accounting Principles Board stated in *Opinion 19* that statements should be "all inclusive" in disclosing changes in financial position, prescribing that "each reporting entity should disclose all important aspects of its financing and investing activities regardless of whether cash or other elements of working capital are directly involved."[3] As a result, property purchased with long-term debt or equity securities, property exchanged for other property, debt refinancing, and similar transactions are treated as though they involved both inflows and outflows of working capital. In this manner, the results of all financing and investment activities are disclosed to financial statement users.

---

[1]*Opinions of the Accounting Principles Board No. 19,* "Reporting Changes in Financial Position" (New York: American Institute of Certified Public Accountants, 1971), pars. 7 and 8.

[2]*Ibid.,* par. 12.

[3]*Ibid.,* par. 8.

ILLUSTRATION 18.3

NAME OF COMPANY **Statement of Changes in Financial Position** **Period Covered**
SOURCES OF WORKING CAPITAL Operations Disposal of long-term assets Long-term borrowing New investment by owners
Total sources
USES OF WORKING CAPITAL Purchase of long-term assets Payment of long-term debt Payment to owners
Total uses
Change in working capital

Working Capital from Operations

Revenues normally bring in working capital, since both Cash and Accounts Receivable are current (working capital) accounts. Also, most expenses are paid with cash or they increase current liabilities, both of which decrease working capital. Except for the effects of write-offs of long-term assets and deferred revenues, net income from operations does represent working capital generated from operations.

The simplest way to arrive at working capital from operations is by the following calculation.

Net income from operations Add back: Any expenses that did not consume working capital Subtract out: Any revenues that did not provide working capital
Working capital from operations

The most common expense that has no effect on working capital is depreciation. You will recall that *depreciation* is the process of converting portions of the cost of long-term productive assets to expenses. Depreciation Expense is recorded with an adjusting entry, at which time no working capital leaves the entity. Amortization of intangible assets and depletion of natural resources are other instances where portions of long-term assets are expired as expenses, requiring no use of working capital. Also, the portion of interest

ILLUSTRATION 18.4

DRISSY CORPORATION Income Statement For the Year Ended December 31, 19X4		
Sales		$950,000
Expenses		
Cost of goods sold	$530,000	
Wages	255,200	
Rent	36,000	
Depreciation	55,000	
Miscellaneous	24,000	900,200
Net Income		$ 49,800

expense attributable to the accumulation of bond discount uses no working capital; on the other hand, the amortization of bond premium does represent a use of working capital because that much more cash was paid than was recorded as interest expense. By the same logic, interest revenues on long-term investments may result in greater or smaller working capital flows when discounts or premiums are involved.[4]

Revenues that do not bring in working capital are unusual. Long-term magazine subscriptions and lease contracts may result in unearned revenues that are spread over a number of years. The act of converting part of a deferred revenue balance (which is a long-term liability) to earned revenue does not produce any working capital. Working capital comes in when cash is received in advance, and it is at that time that the source of working capital is reported in a statement of changes in financial position.

Consider Illustration 18.4, an income statement for Drissy Corporation. Since the income statement shows no indications of deferred revenues or other complications, working capital from operations may be determined very simply as follows.

Net Income	$ 49,800
Add back: Depreciation expense	55,000
Working capital from operations	$104,800

The complicating effects of taxes and extraordinary items are ignored here. Where extraordinary incomes or losses appear, their effects on working capital should be shown separately in the statement of changes in financial

---

[4]Refer to Chapter 16 for the effects of premiums and discounts on interest expense and interest revenue.

position, and working capital from operations should be exclusive of extraordinary items.[5]

Other Sources and Uses of Working Capital

The comparative schedule of working capital prepared earlier (Illustration 18.2) showed that working capital increased by only $4,800, although we have just determined that operations alone generated $104,800 worth of working capital during 19X4. Other sources and uses of working capital are revealed when the changes in balance sheet accounts are analyzed.

Since the changes in current account balances are used to determine the amount of working capital change, these same items cannot also be used to explain how the change came about. In other words, the current items are, collectively, working capital; as was pointed out earlier, saying that working capital increased because cash or some other current asset increased is like saying that cash increased because cash increased. We will examine the changes in noncurrent accounts to discover sources and uses of working capital.

From the Drissy Corporation comparative balance sheet (Illustration 18.1) we can see that the Equipment account balance increased by $150,000 during 19X4, which suggests that new equipment was purchased in that amount. It is possible, of course, that some equipment might also have been sold during 19X4, but the income statement (Illustration 18.4) reveals no gains or losses from such sales. Therefore, we are fairly safe in assuming that there were no sales of equipment during the year and that $150,000 was paid out for purchases of equipment.

The increase in Notes Payable suggests that $40,000 was borrowed during 19X4. Some or all of that amount might have directly financed some of the equipment that was purchased, but we have no evidence to that effect. At any rate, the *assumption* that working capital was borrowed and then subsequently used is consistent with the all-inclusive approach for viewing working capital flows.

The increase of $9,800 in Retained Earnings is consistent with the information we have about net income and dividends paid (disclosed by the note at the bottom of the balance sheet) as illustrated by the following calculation. Note that the declaration of dividends represents an outflow of working capital.

Retained earnings, 12/31/X3		$190,700
Net income, 19X4	$49,800	
Less: Dividends paid	40,000	9,800
Retained earnings, 12/31/X4		$200,500

---

[5]*Ibid.*, par. 10.

Common Stock increased by $5,000, and Capital in Excess of Par by $45,000, which suggests that new shares were issued for $50,000 during the year. We must be careful here, since the capital accounts might possibly have increased as a result of a stock dividend. However, Retained Earnings is decreased when a stock dividend is recorded, and we have already reconciled the change in Retained Earnings without uncovering any evidence of a stock dividend.

ILLUSTRATION 18.5

OBJECTIVE 5. Prepare a statement of changes in financial position on a working capital basis.

DRISSY CORPORATION
Statement of Changes in Financial Position (Working Capital Basis)
For the Year Ended December 31, 19X4

Financial Resources Provided

Operations			
Operating income for 19X4	$49,800		
Add back: Depreciation	55,000		
Working capital provided by operations		$104,800	
Borrowed on long-term notes payable		40,000	
Proceeds of common stock issue		50,000	
Total financial resources provided			$194,800

Financial Resources Applied

Purchased equipment		$150,000	
Paid cash dividends		40,000	
Total financial resources applied			190,000
Net Increase in Working Capital			$ 4,800

COMPARATIVE SCHEDULE OF WORKING CAPITAL

	End of Year	Beginning of Year	Increase (Decrease)
Current Assets			
Cash	$ 14,500	$ 12,400	$ 2,100
Accounts receivable	97,800	73,600	24,200
Merchandise inventory	150,000	160,000	(10,000)
Prepaid rent	3,000	2,000	1,000
Total current assets	$265,300	$248,000	$17,300
Current Liabilities			
Accounts payable	$ 87,000	$ 74,000	$13,000
Wages payable	1,800	2,300	(500)
Total current liabilities	$ 88,800	$ 76,300	$12,500
Working capital	$176,500	$171,700	$ 4,800

Preparing a Statement of Changes in Financial Position

Let us now use the information we have derived for Drissy Corporation to prepare a statement of changes in financial position. The change in working capital should always be calculated as a check on the accuracy of the bottom line of the statement. Many accountants include a schedule of changes in working capital accounts as part of the statement, as does the presentation in Illustration 18.5.

Listed here are the steps for preparing a statement of changes in financial position on a working capital basis.

STEPS IN PREPARING A STATEMENT OF CHANGES IN FINANCIAL POSITION ON A WORKING CAPITAL BASIS

1. Obtain or prepare balance sheets for the beginning and end of the period, and determine the amounts of increases and decreases in balance sheet items between the two dates.

2. Prepare a comparative schedule of working capital for the beginning and end of the period, noting the amount and direction of change in working capital.

3. Obtain or prepare an income statement for the period.

4. Determine the working capital provided by operations.

5. Analyze the changes in all noncurrent balance sheet items, noting each source or use of working capital as it is discovered.

6. Prepare the statement of changes in financial position, *making sure that the final amount of change in working capital is in agreement with that derived in the comparative schedule of working capital.*

OBJECTIVE 4. List the steps in the preparation of a statement of changes in financial position on a working capital basis.

GLOSSARY FOR SECTION 18.A

Liquidity Nearness to cash.

Quick assets Cash plus marketable securities and accounts receivable.

Statement of changes in financial position A report that shows the sources and uses of financial resources during a period of time.

Working capital (net current assets) The amount by which an entity's current assets exceed its current liabilities at a point in time.

SELF-QUIZ ON OBJECTIVES FOR SECTION 18.A
Solutions to Self-Quiz begin on page B-55.

1. **OBJECTIVE 1.** Define the expression *working capital.*

2. **OBJECTIVE 3.** State the overall purpose of a statement of changes in financial position prepared on a working capital basis.

3. **OBJECTIVE 4.** List the steps in the preparation of a statement of changes in financial position on a working capital basis.

4. **OBJECTIVES 2, 5.** From the data provided for Trapid Corporation, prepare a statement of changes in financial position on a working capital basis accompanied by a separate comparative schedule of working capital.

TRAPID CORPORATION Comparative Balance Sheet December 31, 19X4 and 19X3			
	19X4	**19X3**	**Increase (Decrease)**
ASSETS			
Current			
Cash	$ 18,000	$ 30,000	$(12,000)
Accounts receivable	110,000	120,000	(10,000)
Merchandise inventory	220,000	200,000	20,000
Prepaid rent	3,000	6,000	(3,000)
Total current assets	$351,000	$356,000	$ (5,000)
Noncurrent			
Fixtures and equipment	$390,000	$350,000	$ 40,000
Accumulated depreciation	(150,000)	(114,000)	(36,000)
Total noncurrent assets	$240,000	$236,000	$ 4,000
Total Assets	$591,000	$592,000	$ (1,000)
LIABILITIES			
Current			
Accounts payable	$ 60,000	$ 85,000	$(25,000)
Wages payable	10,000	8,000	2,000
Total current liabilities	$ 70,000	$ 93,000	$(23,000)
Noncurrent			
Notes payable	100,000	150,000	(50,000)
Total Liabilities	$170,000	$243,000	$(73,000)
SHAREHOLDERS' EQUITY			
Common stock	$ 80,000	$ 70,000	$ 10,000
Capital in excess of par	180,000	137,000	43,000
Retained earnings	161,000	142,000	19,000
Total Shareholders' Equity	$421,000	$349,000	$ 72,000
Total Liabilities and Shareholders' Equity	$591,000	$592,000	$ (1,000)

NOTE: Cash dividends of $155,000 were paid during 19X4.

TRAPID CORPORATION Income Statement For the Year Ended December 31, 19X4		
Sales		$1,200,000
Expenses		
Cost of goods sold	$700,000	
Wages	230,000	
Rent	48,000	
Depreciation	36,000	
Miscellaneous	12,000	1,026,000
Net Income		$ 174,000

DISCUSSION QUESTIONS FOR SECTION 18.A

1. Consider the statement, "Depreciation is a source of working capital." Do you agree? Why?

2. At year-end, an entity owes $49,318 on an 8% mortgage that calls for level payments of $1,000 at the end of each month for five years. Would it be proper to classify 12 monthly payments, or $12,000, as a current liability? Why?

3. A current asset may be roughly defined as an asset that can be converted to cash within one year. Does this mean that a corporation's current assets at year-end will be available for paying cash dividends during the coming year? Explain.

4. Why would it be unsatisfactory to say that an increase in working capital was caused by an increase in Accounts Receivable?

5. *APB Opinion No. 19* specifies an "all inclusive" approach for preparing a statement of changes in financial position. How does an "all inclusive" approach differ from one that simply presents the sources and uses of working capital?

EXERCISES FOR SECTION 18.A

18.A.1. Use the trial balance provided on the next page to calculate the amount of working capital present at December 31.

JARVIS CORPORATION
Post-Closing Trial Balance
December 31, 19– –

Cash	48,000	
Marketable securities	50,000	
Accounts receivable	180,000	
Allowance for doubtful accounts		30,000
Inventories	200,000	
Land	70,000	
Plant and equipment	500,000	
Accumulated depreciation		190,000
Accounts payable		130,000
Wages payable		81,000
Bonds payable (due in 10 years)		300,000
Common stock		140,000
Retained earnings		177,000
	$1,048,000	$1,048,000

18.A.2. Use the following data to calculate the change in working capital during 19X4.

	12/31/X4	12/31/X3
Current assets	$401,000	$386,000
Current liabilities	205,000	183,000

18.A.3. Use the income statement here to calculate working capital provided by operations.

NIFTY CORPORATION
Income Statement
For the Year Ended June 30, 19– –

Sales		$3,000,000
Expenses		
Cost of goods sold	$1,800,000	
Wages	400,000	
Depreciation	300,000	
Utilities	60,000	
Miscellaneous	40,000	
Income taxes	120,000	2,720,000
Net Income		$ 280,000

18.A.4. For each of the following events, indicate the immediate effect on working capital (*increased, decreased,* or *no change*):

    a. Purchased merchandise for cash.

    b. Purchased equipment for cash.

    c. Purchased equipment on 30-day credit.

    d. Paid an account payable.

    e. Borrowed money on a long-term note.

    f. Rendered services on credit.

    g. Recorded depreciation.

18.A.5. On January 15, 19X4, Bigley Company sold a piece of land it owned for $20,000 cash. On the same day, a new truck was purchased for $35,000 with a $5,000 cash down payment and a note promising to pay the balance in three equal installments on December 15, 19X4, 19X5, and 19X6. Determine the net effect on working capital in 19X4 of the foregoing transactions.

PROBLEMS FOR SECTION 18.A
Alternate Problems for this section begin on page D-94.

18.A.6. An income statement and comparative balance sheet for Belco, Incorporated, are provided below and on the following page.

BELCO, INC. Income Statement For the Year Ended December 31, 19X5		
Sales		$4,800,000
Cost of goods sold		2,976,000
Gross Profit		$1,824,000
Operating expenses		
Wages	$1,350,000	
Rent	98,000	
Depreciation	46,000	
Miscellaneous	54,000	
Total expenses		1,548,000
Net Income		$ 276,000

	19X5	19X4
BELCO, INC. **Comparative Balance Sheet** **December 31, 19X5 and 19X4**		
ASSETS		
Current		
Cash	$ 40,000	$ 31,000
Accounts receivable	180,000	128,000
Merchandise inventory	310,000	350,000
Prepaid rent	8,000	6,000
Total current assets	$538,000	$515,000
Noncurrent		
Furniture and equipment	$520,000	$390,000
Accumulated depreciation	(147,000)	(101,000)
Total noncurrent assets	$373,000	$289,000
Total Assets	$911,000	$804,000
LIABILITIES		
Current		
Accounts payable	$230,000	$245,000
Wages payable	36,000	33,000
Total current liabilities	$266,000	$278,000
Noncurrent		
Notes payable	250,000	230,000
Total Liabilities	$516,000	$508,000
SHAREHOLDERS' EQUITY		
Common stock	$120,000	$100,000
Capital in excess of par	51,000	40,000
Retained earnings	224,000*	156,000
Total Shareholders' Equity	$395,000	$296,000
Total Liabilities and Shareholders' Equity	$911,000	$804,000

*Cash dividends of $208,000 were paid during 19X5.

Required

1) Prepare a comparative schedule of working capital.

2) Prepare a statement of changes in financial position for 19X5 on a working capital basis.

18.A.7. Statements for Femme Health Clubs, Inc., are provided here.

FEMME HEALTH CLUBS, INC. Income Statement For the Year Ended June 30, 19X5		
Fees		$1,430,000
Expenses		
Salaries and wages	$840,000	
Depreciation	127,000	
Rent	120,000	
Advertising	38,000	1,125,000
Net Income		$ 305,000

FEMME HEALTH CLUBS, INC. Comparative Balance Sheet June 30, 19X5 and 19X4			
	19X5	**19X4**	**Increase (Decrease)**
ASSETS			
Cash	$110,000	$ 97,000	$ 13,000
Accounts receivable	165,000	108,000	57,000
Furniture and equipment	850,000	700,000	150,000
Accumulated depreciation	(207,000)	(80,000)	(127,000)
Total Assets	$918,000	$825,000	$ 93,000
LIABILITIES			
Accounts payable	$107,000	$ 60,000	$ 47,000
Salaries payable	62,000	40,000	22,000
Long-term notes payable	100,000	190,000	(90,000)
Total Liabilities	$269,000	$290,000	$(21,000)
SHAREHOLDERS' EQUITY			
Common stock	$400,000	$350,000	$ 50,000
Retained earnings	249,000*	185,000	64,000
Total Shareholders' Equity	$649,000	$535,000	$114,000
Total Liabilities and Shareholders' Equity	$918,000	$825,000	$ 93,000

*Dividends paid during 19X5, $241,000.

Required

Use the foregoing data to prepare a statement of changes in financial position on a working capital basis for the year ended June 30, 19X5.

18.A.8. An income statement and comparative balance sheet for Tee Corporation are as follows.

TEE CORPORATION Income Statement For the Year Ended December 31, 19X5		
Service revenue		$100,000
Expenses		
Salaries	$60,000	
Rent	17,000	
Gasoline	4,000	
Insurance	5,000	
Repairs	2,000	
Depreciation	4,500	92,500
Net Income		$ 7,500

TEE CORPORATION Comparative Balance Sheet December 31, 19X5 and 19X4	19X5	19X4
ASSETS		
Cash	$ 8,000	$ 5,000
Accounts receivable	10,000	4,000
Equipment	40,000	40,000
Accumulated depreciation—equipment	(4,000)	(1,000)
Trucks	9,000	9,000
Accumulated depreciation—trucks	(2,000)	(500)
Total Assets	$61,000	$56,500
LIABILITIES		
Salaries payable	$ 4,000	$ 5,000
Rent payable	6,000	8,000
Notes payable (noncurrent)	30,000	27,500
Total Liabilities	$40,000	$40,500
SHAREHOLDERS' EQUITY		
Common stock	$15,000	$15,000
Retained earnings	6,000*	1,000
Total Shareholders' Equity	$21,000	$16,000
Total Liabilities and Shareholders' Equity	$61,000	$56,500

*Dividends of $2,500 paid during 19X5.

Required

1) Calculate the change in working capital during 19X5.

2) Calculate working capital provided by 19X5 operations.

3) Prepare a statement of changes in financial position for 19X5 on a working capital basis.

SECTION 18.B

Cash Flow

OBJECTIVES

This section is concerned with cash flows and with the preparation of cash flow statements. At the conclusion of your study, you should be able to

1. Differentiate between accrual basis and cash basis accounting.
2. Define the expression *cash flow statement*.
3. List the steps in the preparation of a cash flow statement.
4. Prepare a cash flow statement accompanied by a schedule of cash from operations, given an income statement for a period, balance sheets for the beginning and end of the period, and other needed data.

CASH CYCLE

The nature of *cash* and the importance of maintaining careful control over cash are discussed in Chapter 9. A reasonable amount of cash is necessary for the smooth operation of an entity, but idle cash earns no return. To be productive, cash must be invested or paid out as expenses.

*The process by which cash is used in business operations to produce more cash is called the **cash cycle**.* Although somewhat oversimplified, Illustration 18.6 depicts the cash cycle.

Cash is applied to expenses that help generate cash from revenues. Of course, business managers hope to have a larger amount of cash returned than has been paid out. The extra cash on hand can then be paid to owners or used for expanding the business.

ILLUSTRATION 18.6

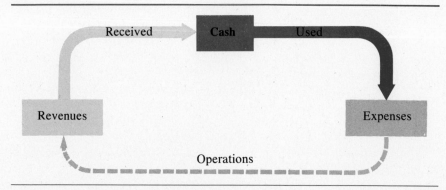

ILLUSTRATION 18.7

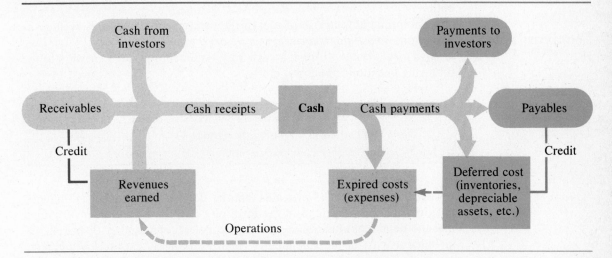

Most entities operate, at least in part, on credit. They do not pay cash for all expenses immediately, nor do they collect all revenues in cash as soon as these are earned. On occasion, new assets are acquired for cash or on credit. Also, the entity may receive new cash from investors or pay out some of its cash to owners. Thus the cash cycle might be more appropriately pictured as in Illustration 18.7. Receivables and payables represent delays in the flow of cash. Most assets other than receivables and cash are deferred costs that eventually end up as expenses of some accounting period.

The accounting concepts you have learned in this course underlie the *accrual basis of accounting, by which an entity attempts to recognize revenues as soon as they have been earned and to match expenses with the revenues they helped to generate.* Some entities, usually small service concerns, use a *cash basis of accounting, which recognizes revenues and expenses at the time that cash is received or paid out.* In these concerns, owners are usually associated closely with their business entities and are able to keep track of business affairs with a minimum of formal accounting data.

Use of a cash basis system does not mean that an entity's receivables and payables are completely ignored. Informal records of receivables, payables, and deferred costs may be maintained external to the cash basis accounting system. For example, the amount of accounts payable at any time might be determined by summing unpaid invoices kept in a desk drawer.

OBJECTIVE 1.
Differentiate between accrual basis and cash basis accounting.

CASH FLOW STATEMENTS

Accrual basis accounting provides more useful information than does a cash basis system. However, because of the importance of cash and the necessity for close control over it, a statement showing the inflows and outflows of cash for an accounting period is very helpful in managing and evaluating an entity.

The principal purpose of a cash flow statement also serves well as its definition. *A cash flow statement is a report that shows the sources and uses of cash for a period of time.* A cash flow statement provides answers to the following questions about the entity.

> **1.** Where did cash come from during the period?
> **2.** What was cash used for during the period?
> **3.** What was the change in cash position during the period?

APB Opinion No. 19 provides that the statement of changes in financial position may be presented in the form of a cash flow statement, provided that the details of changes in working capital accounts other than cash are included as part of the statement.[6] This condition can be met by including a comparative schedule of working capital below the cash flow presentation.

The major source of cash for most business concerns is revenue—either directly as cash revenue or indirectly as collections of accounts receivable. Of course, normal business operations involve both inflows and outflows of cash. However, most cash flow statements offset cash outflows for expenses against cash inflows from revenues to arrive at net cash from operations. In other words, the income statement for a period is converted to a cash basis, and net cash from operations is viewed as just one source of cash. The other common sources of cash are the sale of assets other than merchandise, borrowing, and additional investments by owners.

The most common uses of cash are for the purchase of assets, debt payments, and payments to owners. Illustration 18.8 shows the usual sources and uses of cash in a cash flow statement.

Cash from Operations

Cash from operations may be derived by converting an accrual basis income statement to a cash basis. To do this we generally need comparative balance sheets for the beginning and end of a period, as well as an income statement for the period. We will use data from the Drissy Corporation statements, presented as Illustrations 18.1 and 18.4 in the preceding section, to illustrate the process of conversion. To keep our example simple, we will ignore income taxes and avoid such things as dealings in marketable securities and sales of productive assets.

---

[6]*Ibid.*, par. 12.

ILLUSTRATION 18.8

NAME OF COMPANY
Cash Flow Statement
Period Covered

SOURCES OF CASH

Operations
Disposal of assets
Borrowing
Investment by owners

Total sources

USES OF CASH

Purchase of assets
Debt payments
Payment to owners

Total uses

Change in cash

Cash from Sales.   Beginning Accounts Receivable represent prior-period sales that were not collected until the current period, while ending Accounts Receivable are sales that have not yet been collected. Therefore, cash inflow during 19X4 can be derived by the following calculation.

Sales during 19X4	$950,000
Beginning accounts receivable	73,600
Ending accounts receivable	(97,800)
Cash from sales	$925,800

As an alternative to adding beginning receivables and subtracting ending receivables, Sales may be reduced by an increase in receivables or increased by a decrease in receivables to arrive at the cash inflow from sales. For our example, the cash derived during 19X4 can be calculated as follows.

Sales during 19X4	$950,000
Less: Increase in accounts receivable	24,200
Cash from sales	$925,800

ILLUSTRATION 18.9

Cost of goods sold
Less: Beginning inventory
Plus: Ending inventory
Plus: Beginning accounts payable
Less: Ending accounts payable

Cash paid for merchandise

or

Cost of goods sold
Plus: Increase in inventory (or Less: Decrease in inventory)
Plus: Decrease in accounts payable (or Less: Increase in accounts payable)

Cash paid for merchandise

Cash Paid Out for Merchandise.　Changes in both Merchandise Inventory and Accounts Payable must be considered in the process of converting Cost of Goods Sold to cash paid for merchandise. Inventories are deferred costs, while Accounts Payable are deferments of cash payments for merchandise purchases. The amount of cash paid for merchandise can be derived in either of the ways shown in Illustration 18.9.

Using the second approach in Illustration 18.9, cash paid by Drissy Corporation for merchandise during 19X4 is calculated as follows.

Cost of goods sold	$530,000
Decrease in merchandise inventory	(10,000)
Increase in accounts payable	(13,000)
Cash paid for merchandise	$507,000

Wages Expense, the next item on the income statement, can be converted to cash paid for wages by adding beginning Wages Payable and subtracting ending Wages Payable. Or Wages Expense may be increased by the decrease in Wages Payable, as follows.

Wages expense	$255,200
Plus: Decrease in wages payable	500
Cash paid for wages	$255,700

You may have noticed that Wages Payable affect cash paid for wages in the same way that Accounts Payable affect cash paid for merchandise. Now we shall see that Prepaid Rent affects cash paid for rent in much the same way that Inventories affect cash for merchandise.

Rent expense	$36,000
Plus: Increase in prepaid rent	1,000
Cash for rent	$37,000

Depreciation Expense, the next item on the income statement, can be ignored as having no cash effect. Depreciation Expense is nothing more than an expiration of cost reflected in the accounts by means of an adjusting journal entry. Any purchases of depreciable assets during the year will appear separately on the cash flow statement as a use of cash.

The last expense listed on the income statement, Miscellaneous Expense, must already be stated in terms of cash paid out, since no other accrued liabilities or prepayments are listed on the balance sheet. The schedule in Illustration 18.10 shows the cash flow derived from operations.

Other Sources and Uses of Cash

The comparative balance sheet for Drissy Corporation shows that cash increased by $2,100 during 19X4. So far, we have found that net cash derived from operations during 19X4 was $102,100. The changes in all balance sheet items must be analyzed for their cash effects to pin down the various sources and uses of cash. Changes in Accounts Receivable, Merchandise Inventory, Prepaid Rent, Accumulated Depreciation, and Accounts Payable were considered in deriving net cash from operations. Now the remaining changes must be considered one by one.

OBJECTIVE 4. Prepare a schedule of cash from operations.

ILLUSTRATION 18.10

DRISSY CORPORATION Schedule of Cash from Operations For the Year Ended December 31, 19X4			
Cash from sales			
Sales		$950,000	
Less: Increase in accounts receivable		24,200	$925,800
Cash paid for expenses			
Cost of goods sold		$530,000	
Less: Decrease in merchandise inventory	$10,000		
Increase in accounts payable	13,000	23,000	$507,000
Wages expense		$255,200	
Plus: Decrease in wages payable		500	255,700
Rent expense		$ 36,000	
Plus: Increase in prepaid rent		1,000	37,000
Miscellaneous expense			24,000	823,700
Net cash from operations			$102,100

As it turns out, the nonoperating sources and uses of cash are identical to those in Drissy's statement of changes in financial position shown in the previous section. This is often the case, because working capital flows related to noncurrent accounts usually involve exchanges of cash. The purchase of Equipment for $150,000 required, in all likelihood, a payment of cash in 19X4. Of course, it is possible that up to $40,000 of that amount was financed with the increase in Notes Payable, but no harm is done by *assuming* that cash was borrowed and subsequently paid out. In fact, as pointed out in the previous section, the all-inclusive approach prescribed by APB *Opinion 19* requires the disclosure of changes in resources, regardless of whether cash is involved. Proceeds of the capital stock issue were most likely in cash form, and, of course, cash dividend payments require the use of cash.

Preparing a Cash Flow Statement

With the information we have derived, we can prepare the cash flow statement shown in Illustration 18.11. Note the similarity between the cash flow statement and the statement of changes in financial position shown in Illustration 18.5. The bottom line of the cash flow statement must agree with the change in the cash account balance during the year. Here is one place where we know the final figure even before we begin to prepare the statement.

The cash flow statement presented in Illustration 18.11 should probably be accompanied by the schedule of cash from operations (Illustration 18.10). An alternative arrangement would be to show the details of the schedule as part of the cash flow statement, analogous to the way the calculation of cost of goods sold is sometimes shown within the body of an income statement.

The steps for preparing a cash flow statement are shown at the top of the page opposite.

ILLUSTRATION 18.11

OBJECTIVE 4. Prepare a cash flow statement.

DRISSY CORPORATION Cash Flow Statement For the Year Ended December 31, 19X4		
SOURCES OF CASH		
Net cash from operations	$102,100	
Borrowed on notes payable	40,000	
Proceeds of capital stock issue	50,000	
Total Sources		$192,100
USES OF CASH		
Purchased equipment	$150,000	
Paid cash dividends	40,000	
Total Uses		190,000
Net Increase in Cash		$ 2,100

STEPS IN PREPARING A CASH FLOW STATEMENT

1. Obtain or prepare balance sheets for the beginning and end of the period, and determine the amounts of increases or decreases in balance sheet items between the two dates.

2. Note the amount and direction of change for the Cash account. The cash flow statement for the period must agree with this amount.

3. Obtain or prepare an income statement for the period.

4. Prepare a schedule of cash from operations.

5. Analyze the changes in all balance sheet items not already considered during the process of preparing the schedule of cash from operations. Note each source or use of cash as it is discovered.

6. Prepare the cash flow statement, making sure that the final net cash change agrees with the cash change determined in step 2.

OBJECTIVE 3. List the steps in preparing a cash flow statement.

ILLUSTRATION 18.12

DRISSY CORPORATION
Statement of Changes in Financial Position (Cash Basis)
For the Year Ended December 31, 19X4

Financial Resources Provided

Net cash from operations (see accompanying schedule)	$102,100	
Borrowed on notes payable	40,000	
Proceeds of capital stock issue	50,000	
Total financial resources provided		$192,100

Financial Resources Applied

Purchased equipment	$150,000	
Paid cash dividends	40,000	
Total financial resources applied		190,000
Net Increase in Cash		$ 2,100

COMPARATIVE SCHEDULE OF WORKING CAPITAL

	End of Year	Beginning of Year	Increase (Decrease)
Current Assets			
Cash	$ 14,500	$ 12,400	$ 2,100
Accounts receivable	97,800	73,600	24,200
Merchandise inventory	150,000	160,000	(10,000)
Prepaid rent	3,000	2,000	1,000
Total current assets	$265,300	$248,000	$17,300
Current Liabilities			
Accounts payable	$ 87,000	$ 74,000	$13,000
Wages payable	1,800	2,300	(500)
Total current liabilities	$ 88,800	$ 76,300	$12,500
Working capital	$176,500	$171,700	$ 4,800

CASH FLOW FORMAT FOR STATEMENT OF CHANGES IN FINANCIAL POSITION

As mentioned earlier, *Opinion 19* specifies that the statement of changes in financial position may be presented in either a working capital or a cash flow format. The cash flow statement in Illustration 18.12 on the preceding page carries the title prescribed in the *Opinion* and also includes the detailed changes for working capital accounts. As presented, the statement would be supplemented with a separate schedule of cash from operations, like the one in Illustration 18.10.

GLOSSARY FOR SECTION 18.B

Accrual basis of accounting   A method of accounting by which an entity attempts to recognize revenues as soon as they have been earned and to match expenses with the revenues they helped to generate.

Cash basis of accounting   A method of accounting that recognizes revenues and expenses at the time that cash is received or paid out.

Cash cycle   The process by which cash is used in business operations to produce more cash.

Cash flow statement   A report that shows the sources and uses of cash for a period of time.

SELF-QUIZ ON OBJECTIVES FOR SECTION 18.B
Solutions to Self-Quiz begin on page B-56.

1. **OBJECTIVE 1.** Differentiate between accrual basis and cash basis accounting.

2. **OBJECTIVE 2.** Define the expression *cash flow statement*.

3. **OBJECTIVE 3.** List the steps in the preparation of a cash flow statement.

4. **OBJECTIVE 4.** Using the Trapid Corporation data provided in the self-quiz for the preceding section, prepare a cash flow statement for 19X4 accompanied by a separate schedule of cash from operations.

DISCUSSION QUESTIONS FOR SECTION 18.B

1. What kinds of questions can best be answered with the aid of a cash flow statement?

2. What is the major source of cash for most business concerns?

3. What is missing from the second sentence that follows?

    Cash inflow during a time period can be derived by adding the beginning Accounts Receivable balance to Sales for the period and subtracting the ending Accounts Receivable balance. An alternative approach is to reduce Sales by the _____ in Accounts Receivable or increase Sales by the _____ in Accounts Receivable.

4. Why is information about cash flow important to

   a. Managers?

   b. Creditors?

   c. Owners?

5. A manager was heard to say, "A cash flow statement is better than a statement showing working capital flows. A cash flow statement is in terms I can easily understand—movements of cash in and out of the business." Do you agree with the manager? Why?

EXERCISES FOR SECTION 18.B

18.B.1. Calculate the cash inflow from sales for 19X4 and 19X5, using the following information.

a.	Sales for 19X4	$248,000
	Accounts Receivable, 12/31/X3	67,000
	Accounts Receivable, 12/31/X4	42,000
b.	Sales for 19X5	$284,000
	Accounts Receivable, 12/31/X4	42,000
	Accounts Receivable, 12/31/X5	53,000

18.B.2. Calculate the cash inflow from sales for 19X4 and 19X5, using the information provided here.

a.	Sales for 19X4	$120,000
	Increase in Accounts Receivable during 19X4	31,000
b.	Sales for 19X5	$110,000
	Decrease in Accounts Receivable during 19X5	22,000

18.B.3. Calculate the cash paid out for merchandise using the following data.

Cost of Goods Sold	$780,000
Beginning Inventory	84,000
Ending Inventory	98,000
Beginning Accounts Payable	71,000
Ending Accounts Payable	59,000

18.B.4. Calculate the cash paid out for wages using the following data.

Wages Expense for 19X5	$390,000
Wages Payable, 12/31/X4	4,000
Wages Payable, 12/31/X5	6,000

18.B.5. Calculate the cash paid out for rent using the following data.

Rent Expense for 19X5	$96,000
Prepaid Rent, 12/31/X4	6,000
Prepaid Rent, 12/31/X5	8,000

18.B.6. Indicate for each of the following events whether there is an immediate cash inflow or outflow, or whether cash is unaffected at the time of the event.

    a. Taxes are paid.

    b. Merchandise is purchased on credit.

    c. Dividends are declared.

    d. Money is borrowed from a bank.

    e. Dividends are paid.

    f. Depreciation is recorded.

    g. A sale is made on credit.

    h. A utility bill is received.

    i. Accounts payable are paid.

PROBLEMS FOR SECTION 18.B
Alternate Problems for this section begin on page D-98.

18.B.7. Selected information for Bill's Tidy Service is provided here.

BILL'S TIDY SERVICE
Income Statement
For the Year Ended December 31, 19X5

Service revenue		$54,000
Expenses		
Salaries	$28,000	
Rent	3,600	
Insurance	1,200	
Total expenses		32,800
Net Income		$21,200

BILL'S TIDY SERVICE
Balance Sheet Information
As of December 31, 19X5 and 19X4

	19X5	19X4
ASSETS		
Accounts receivable	$4,100	$4,800
Prepaid insurance	400	600
LIABILITIES		
Salaries payable	$1,000	$2,000

Required

1) Calculate the cash inflow from revenue.

2) Calculate the cash outgo for expenses.

3) Calculate the net cash from operations.

18.B.8. Jane Junior, a college student, experienced the following events during September.

    a. Net wages for September after taxes and other deductions, $121.50.

    b. Purchased books at college bookstore on credit, $89.

    c. Received scholarship check, $1,000.

    d. Borrowed $2,500 from student loan fund.

    e. Paid tuition and room and board, $2,800.

    f. Paid annual insurance premium on motorcycle, $230.

    g. Purchased clothing on credit, $150.

    h. Paid charge account bill, $180.

    i. Lent money to a friend, $10.

    j. Miscellaneous cash expenditures for the month, $28.

Required

Prepare a personal cash flow statement for Jane for the month of September.

18.B.9. An income statement and comparative balance sheet for Columbia Corporation are shown here and on the next page.

COLUMBIA CORPORATION Income Statement For the Year Ended December 31, 19X5		
Sales		$2,120,000
Expenses		
Cost of goods sold	$1,180,000	
Wages	360,000	
Rent	164,000	
Insurance	48,000	
Interest	31,000	
Depreciation	42,000	
Other	175,000	
Total expenses		2,000,000
Net Income		$ 120,000

COLUMBIA CORPORATION
Comparative Balance Sheet
December 31, 19X5 and 19X4

	19X5	19X4
ASSETS		
Current		
Cash	$ 53,000	$ 125,000
Accounts receivable, net	212,000	180,000
Merchandise inventory	311,000	320,000
Unexpired insurance	32,000	18,000
Total current assets	$608,000	$ 643,000
Noncurrent		
Fixtures and equipment	$492,000	$ 460,000
Accumulated depreciation	(126,000)	(84,000)
Total noncurrent assets	$366,000	$ 376,000
Total Assets	$974,000	$1,019,000
LIABILITIES		
Current		
Accounts payable	$164,000	$ 152,000
Wages payable	15,000	12,000
Bank loan	100,000	220,000
Total current liabilities	$279,000	$ 384,000
Noncurrent		
Notes payable	180,000	210,000
Total Liabilities	$459,000	$ 594,000
SHAREHOLDERS' EQUITY		
Common stock	$120,000*	$ 100,000
Capital in excess of par	240,000*	200,000
Retained earnings	155,000*	125,000
Total Shareholders' Equity	$515,000	$ 425,000
Total Liabilities and Shareholders' Equity	$974,000	$1,019,000

*Issued $60,000 stock dividend and paid $30,000 cash dividend during 19X5.

Required

1) Prepare a schedule of cash from operations for 19X5.

2) Prepare a statement of changes in financial position on a cash basis for 19X5.

18.B.10. Statements for Tee Corporation are as follows.

```
TEE CORPORATION
Income Statement
For the Year Ended December 31, 19X5
```

Service revenue		$100,000
Expenses		
Salaries	$60,000	
Rent	17,000	
Gasoline	4,000	
Insurance	5,000	
Repairs	2,000	
Depreciation	4,500	92,500
Net Income		$ 7,500

```
TEE CORPORATION
Comparative Balance Sheet
December 31, 19X5 and 19X4
```

	19X5	19X4
ASSETS		
Cash	$ 8,000	$ 5,000
Accounts receivable	10,000	4,000
Equipment	40,000	40,000
Accumulated depreciation—equipment	(4,000)	(1,000)
Trucks	9,000	9,000
Accumulated depreciation—trucks	(2,000)	(500)
Total Assets	$61,000	$56,500
LIABILITIES		
Salaries payable	$ 5,000	$ 4,000
Rent payable	5,000	9,000
Notes payable to bank	30,000	27,500
Total Liabilities	$40,000	$40,500
SHAREHOLDERS' EQUITY		
Common stock	$15,000	$15,000
Retained earnings	6,000*	1,000
Total Shareholders' Equity	$21,000	$16,000
Total Liabilities and Shareholders' Equity	$61,000	$56,500

*A dividend of $2,500 was paid during 19X5.

Required

Prepare a statement of changes in financial position on a cash basis for the year ended December 31, 19X5.

SUMMARY OF CHAPTER 18

A statement of changes in financial position is most often prepared on a working capital basis. Working capital is the difference between current assets and current liabilities at a point in time. A comparative schedule of working capital shows changes in individual working capital accounts and the net change for the period. Changes in noncurrent account balances must be analyzed to ensure that all sources and uses of working capital are pinned down. The net change in working capital as shown on the statement of changes in financial position must agree with the net change calculated on the comparative schedule of working capital.

Because of the importance of cash, a statement showing inflows and outflows of cash during the accounting period is very helpful in managing and evaluating an entity. The preparation of a cash flow statement involves the conversion of accrual basis accounting data to a cash basis. Cash inflows and outflows for normal business operations are usually offset against each other, with net cash from operations shown as one source of cash. The final net change in cash as shown on a cash flow statement must agree with the actual amount by which the cash balance increased or decreased during the period.

PROBLEMS FOR CHAPTER 18
Alternate Problems for this chapter begin on page D-101.

18.1, An income statement and comparative balance sheet for Cuerpa Corporation are provided here.

CUERPA CORPORATION Income Statement For the Year Ended December 31, 19X5		
Sales		$800,000
Expenses		
Cost of goods sold	$500,000	
Salaries	120,000	
Rent	36,000	
Insurance	12,000	
Depreciation	20,000	
Other	46,000	
Total expenses		734,000
Net Income		$ 66,000

CUERPA CORPORATION
Comparative Balance Sheet
December 31, 19X5 and 19X4

	19X5	19X4
ASSETS		
Cash	$ 9,000	$ 5,000
Accounts receivable	12,000	6,000
Merchandise inventory	88,000	102,000
Furniture and equipment	220,000	180,000
Accumulated depreciation	(60,000)	(40,000)
Total Assets	$269,000	$253,000
LIABILITIES		
Accounts payable	$ 9,000	$ 11,000
Salaries payable	6,000	4,000
Notes payable (due in 19X8)	70,000	82,000
Total Liabilities	$ 85,000	$ 97,000
SHAREHOLDERS' EQUITY		
Common stock	$ 50,000	$ 40,000
Retained earnings	134,000*	116,000
Total Shareholders' Equity	$184,000	$156,000
Total Liabilities and Shareholders' Equity	$269,000	$253,000

*Cash dividends of $48,000 were paid during 19X5.

Required

1) Prepare a comparative schedule of working capital.

2) Prepare a statement of changes in financial position on a working capital basis for 19X5.

3) Prepare a cash flow statement for 19X5 accompanied by a separate schedule of cash from operations.

18.2. An income statement and comparative balance sheet for Harcor Corporation are shown here and on the next page.

HARCOR CORPORATION
Income Statement
For the Year Ended December 31, 19X5

Sales		$3,700,000
Cost of goods sold		2,590,000
Gross Profit		$1,110,000
Operating expenses		
Salaries	$920,000	
Rent	96,000	
Depreciation	73,000	
Other	47,000	
Total expenses		1,136,000
Net Loss		$ 26,000

	19X5	19X4
HARCOR CORPORATION Comparative Balance Sheets December 31, 19X5 and 19X4		
ASSETS		
Current		
Cash	$ 22,000	$ 12,000
Accounts receivable	61,000	72,000
Merchandise inventory	98,000	101,000
Prepaid rent	32,000	24,000
Total current assets	$213,000	$209,000
Noncurrent		
Furniture and fixtures	$460,000	$400,000
Accumulated depreciation	(141,000)	(68,000)
Total noncurrent assets	$319,000	$332,000
Total Assets	$532,000	$541,000
LIABILITIES		
Current		
Accounts payable	$ 90,000	$111,000
Salaries payable	31,000	24,000
Total current liabilities	$121,000	$135,000
Noncurrent		
Bank loan payable	65,000	50,000
Total Liabilities	$186,000	$185,000
SHAREHOLDERS' EQUITY		
Common stock	$200,000	$172,000
Retained earnings	146,000*	184,000
Total Shareholders' Equity	$346,000	$356,000
Total Liabilities and Shareholders' Equity	$532,000	$541,000

*Cash dividends of $12,000 were paid during 19X5.

Required

1) Prepare a schedule of cash from operations for 19X5.

2) Prepare a statement of changes in financial position on a cash basis for 19X5.

3) Prepare a comparative schedule of working capital.

4) Prepare a statement of changes in financial position on a working capital basis for 19X5.

18.3. An income statement, comparative balance sheet, and other data for the Grant Thompson Company are as follows.

GRANT THOMPSON COMPANY Income Statement For the Year Ended December 31, 19X5		
Service revenue		$2,348,000
Expenses		
Supplies	$927,000	
Wages	898,000	
Advertising	70,000	
Interest	25,000	
Depreciation	80,000	
Repairs	32,000	2,032,000
Net Operating Income		$ 316,000
Gain on sale of building		25,000
Net Income		$ 341,000

GRANT THOMPSON COMPANY Comparative Balance Sheet December 31, 19X5 and 19X4		
	19X5	**19X4**
ASSETS		
Current		
Cash	$ 3,000	$ 21,000
Accounts receivable	48,000	40,000
Supplies	94,000	98,000
Prepaid advertising	30,000	35,000
Total current assets	$175,000	$194,000
Noncurrent		
Buildings	$475,000	$250,000
Accumulated depreciation	(154,000)	(104,000)
Total noncurrent assets	$321,000	$146,000
Total Assets	$496,000	$340,000
LIABILITIES		
Current		
Accounts payable	$ 39,000	$ 41,000
Interest payable	10,000	15,000
Total current liabilities	$ 49,000	$ 56,000
Noncurrent		
Mortgage payable	120,000	160,000
Total Liabilities	$169,000	$216,000
OWNER'S EQUITY		
G. Thompson, capital	327,000	124,000
Total Liabilities and Owner's Equity	$496,000	$340,000

Other Data

1) During the year the company sold for $120,000 cash a building costing $125,000 and having a book value of $95,000.

2) Grant Thompson withdrew $138,000 for his personal use during 19X5.

Required

1) Prepare a schedule of cash from operations for 19X5.

2) Prepare a cash flow statement for 19X5.

3) Prepare a comparative schedule of working capital.

4) Prepare a statement of changes in financial position on a working capital basis for 19X5.

COMPREHENSION PROBLEMS FOR CHAPTER 18

18.4. Susan Smith started a trucking company under the name of S&S Trucking on December 31, 19X4. Although the income statement for 19X5 showed a profit of $80,000, the company's bank balance on December 31, 19X5, was only $6,000. Susan could not understand why the cash balance was so low, considering the amount of income earned during 19X5. Statements for S&S Trucking follow.

S&S TRUCKING Income Statement For the Year Ended December 31, 19X5		
Revenue		$320,000
Expenses		
Wages	$110,000	
Gasoline	40,000	
Insurance	20,000	
Repairs	10,000	
Depreciation	46,000	
Other	14,000	240,000
Net Income		$ 80,000

S&S TRUCKING Comparative Balance Sheet December 31, 19X5 and 19X4		
	19X5	**19X4**
ASSETS		
Cash	$ 6,000	$ 80,000
Accounts receivable	124,000	–0–
Unexpired insurance	10,000	–0–
Trucks	220,000	100,000
Accumulated depreciation	(46,000)	–0–
Total Assets	$314,000	$180,000
LIABILITIES		
Accounts payable	$ 30,000	$ –0–
Notes payable	60,000	–0–
Total Liabilities	$ 90,000	$ –0–
OWNER'S EQUITY		
S. Smith, capital	224,000	180,000
Total Liabilities and Owner's Equity	$314,000	$180,000

Required

1) Prepare a cash flow statement for S&S Trucking for 19X5.

2) Explain why Susan's cash balance has dwindled to $6,000.

18.5. The board of directors of Zicon Electronics Corporation has determined as a matter of policy that working capital should not fall below $10,000,000. At the beginning of the current fiscal year working capital stands at $10,500,000. Selected budget data for the current fiscal year are shown here.

a. Net income for the current fiscal year is projected to be $3,500,000.

b. Included among the current year's projections are depreciation, $200,000; patent amortization, $18,000; amortization of premium on bonds payable, $123,000.

c. Old equipment with a book value of $1,400,000 will be sold during the year. A prospective purchaser has agreed to pay $300,000 cash and sign a $750,000 note due one year after the date of the sale. The anticipated results of this event have been reflected in the projected net income for the year.

d. Zicon's managers plan to purchase new equipment during the year for $1,500,000 cash and a long-term note payable of $1,600,000. The first payment on the note will be due one year from the date of the purchase.

e. A short-term (current) note payable for $90,000 will be paid off during the year.

f. Long-term bonds payable will be retired during the year by paying cash in the amount of their carrying (book) value, which is $2,000,000.

Required

1) Use the information provided to project the level of working capital at the end of the current fiscal year.

2) Assuming that there is sufficient cash, can the board pay a $2,000,000 cash dividend at the end of the year without violating its own working capital policy? Explain.

CHAPTER **19**
Financial Statement Analysis

OBJECTIVES

In this chapter we deal with the analysis of financial data. At the conclusion of your study, you should be able to

1. Prepare horizontally analyzed statements, showing amounts and rates of change, using the following:
   a. Balance sheets for two points in time.
   b. Income statements for two accounting periods.

2. Vertically analyze the following:
   a. A balance sheet.
   b. An income statement.

3. Calculate turnover rates for the following:
   a. Receivables.
   b. Inventories.
   c. Assets.

4. Calculate rates of return on the following:
   a. Assets.
   b. Equity.
   c. Common equity.

5. State what is meant by the expression *trading on the equity*.

6. Calculate the following:
   a. Current ratio.
   b. Debt-equity ratio.
   c. Times interest earned.
   d. Price-earnings ratio.
   e. Dividend yield rate.

WHY ANALYZE?

Analysis involves comparisons. A bit of information standing alone is meaningless. One item can be judged only by comparison with one or more other items. Relative concepts such as merit, size, and temperature all involve comparisons. To judge anything as good, large, or hot requires some understanding of what lies between these points and their opposites: bad, small, and cold.

Accounting results, like other data, are judged by means of comparisons. To say that net income for a year is good implies comparison with prior years, other entities, or budgeted figures. A given amount of income may be good for a small company but poor for a larger one.

Analysis can help make financial data more useful to particular types of statement users. Creditors, for example, have interests that differ from those of owners. Long-term creditors may have different concerns from those of short-term creditors. And informational needs of institutional investors (banks, insurance companies, mutual funds, and so forth) are different from those of individual investors. Thus a purpose of financial statement analysis is to tailor information to the needs of its users.

THE DIFFERENT NEEDS OF DIFFERENT USERS

Creditors' Needs

The creditors of a company are primarily interested in the entity's ability to pay periodic interest and to repay loans on their due dates. Such payments are usually made with cash. Thus creditors really want to know whether the entity will have sufficient cash available to meet its debt obligations.

Accounting reports on past achievement and on business pictures at points in time. So far, accountants in the United States have been reluctant to vouch for projections into the future, although they do assist in preparing cash budgets and other pro forma reports. In this context, *pro forma simply means "projected" or "predicted."* Accountants have generally preferred to deal with facts (data) that are known to have occurred. There are indications, however, that accountants are coming under increasing pressure to supply pro forma statements, along with disclosures of the assumptions on which the projections are based.

Creditors have been compelled to use historical accounting data as a basis for judging a company's ability, and willingness, to meet future debt obligations. They have been most interested in the company's *liquid* position and in the rate at which the company has produced cash in the past. In other words, they have been primarily concerned with past liquidity as an indication of future debt-paying ability. *Liquidity* was defined in the previous chapter as nearness to cash. It refers to an entity's ability to turn assets into cash, and to the relative amount of cash and near-cash assets as compared to current debt obligations.

Owners' Needs

Shareholders, partners, and proprietors are usually most interested in the long-term *profitability* of their entities. Profitability is a relative concept—the relationship between an amount of net income (profit) for a period and some other measure. To gauge profitability, net income may be related to total revenues, invested assets, owners' equity, or combinations of these and other measures. And, once profitability rates are calculated, they are then usually compared with rates for other periods, other entities, budgeted figures, and/or industry averages.

Managers' Needs

The managers of an entity are concerned with gauging their own performance, as well as the performance of those who report to them. Presumably, they want to show that they have done a good job, but they are also interested in using accounting data to improve their future performance. For these purposes, managers may need data in more detail than is provided in the condensed accounting statements presented to owners and creditors.

Creditors, owners, and managers are often concerned about the same things, but for different reasons. An owner may be concerned about adequate liquidity so that dividends can be paid and expansion (growth) financed. Creditors like to deal with profitable entities because such entities are more likely to pay their debts. And managers must maintain a reasonable balance of liquidity and profitability to keep both creditors and owners satisfied.

BALANCE SHEET ANALYSIS

Horizontal Comparisons

Comparative statements present data side by side for two or more periods or points in time. In this way, statement users may easily *compare amounts on each line, an act referred to as horizontal analysis.* In horizontal analysis, the statement reader determines whether an item is larger or smaller than for a previous time. In fact, the reader usually wants to know *how much* change has occurred. For this reason, comparative statements are often prepared with a column that shows the amounts of increases and decreases that have occurred.

To get a better idea of *relative magnitudes* of change, rates of change may be shown in a separate column of a comparative statement. For determining amounts and rates of change between two times, the earlier time is usually taken as the *base* period. An amount of change is divided by the base period amount to obtain the rate of change.

The comparative balance sheet in Illustration 19.1 has been horizontally analyzed for the convenience of statement users. The $5,200 decrease in cash during 19X5 is divided by the $20,400 base amount to obtain the 25.5%

ILLUSTRATION 19.1

			Increase or (Decrease)	
	19X5	**19X4**	*Amount*	*Percent*
PERQUISITE CORPORATION Comparative Balance Sheet December 31, 19X5 and 19X4				
ASSETS				
Current				
Cash	$ 15,200	$ 20,400	$(5,200)	(25.5)%
Accounts receivable, net	100,000	80,000	20,000	25.0%
Merchandise inventory	120,000	130,000	(10,000)	(7.7)%
Prepaid rent	4,800	3,600	1,200	33.3%
Total current assets	$240,000	$234,000	$ 6,000	2.6%
Noncurrent				
Furniture and equipment, net	627,000	584,000	43,000	7.4%
Total Assets	$867,000	$818,000	$49,000	6.0%
LIABILITIES				
Current				
Accounts payable	$105,800	$ 86,600	$19,200	22.2%
Wages payable	1,200	1,400	(200)	(14.3)%
Total current liabilities	$107,000	$ 88,000	$19,000	21.6%
Noncurrent				
Bonds payable	300,000	300,000	–0–	–0–
Total Liabilities	$407,000	$388,000	$19,000	4.9%
SHAREHOLDERS' EQUITY				
Preferred stock, 8%, $100 par	$100,000	$100,000	$ –0–	–0–
Common stock, $10 par	200,000	200,000	–0–	–0–
Retained earnings	160,000	130,000	30,000	23.1%
Total Shareholders' Equity	$460,000	$430,000	$30,000	7.0%
Total Liabilities and Shareholders' Equity	$867,000	$818,000	$49,000	6.0%

NOTE: Cash dividends were paid during 19X5 in the amount of $59,000. There are no preferred dividend arrearages for 19X5 or prior years.

OBJECTIVE 1a. Prepare horizontally analyzed statements, showing amounts and rates of change, using balance sheets for two points in time.

rate of decrease. The other percentages shown were computed in a similar manner.

Note that percentages in horizontally analyzed statements do not sum vertically, as do the dollar amounts. That is because the base amount, which represents 100%, changes for each horizontal line. Each percentage rate is nothing more than the relationship between the amount of change and the figure for the earlier period. For example, the decrease in Cash during 19X5 is related to the base year figure as follows.

$$\frac{\text{Change}}{\text{Base}} = \frac{\$(5,200)}{\$20,400} = (25.5)\%$$

Thus we might say that Cash decreased by 25.5% during 19X5 or that the balance at the end of 19X5 is 25.5% less than at the end of 19X4.

Vertical Comparisons

For some purposes, *items in a statement can best be compared with other items in the same statement, an approach referred to as* **vertical analysis**. For instance, we might want to know what proportion of assets was in the form of cash, or how liabilities compared with assets.

The usual approach to vertical analysis is to relate all amounts in a statement to one base figure in that statement. When a balance sheet is vertically analyzed, total assets are usually taken as the base figure of 100%. The balance sheet in Illustration 19.2 on the next page has been vertically analyzed to assist the statement user.

As you can see, percentages in vertically analyzed statements total in the same manner as the dollar amounts. However, rounded approximations may need to be adjusted slightly before the percentages will sum vertically. The percentage column in Illustration 19.2 was achieved by dividing each balance sheet amount by the total assets and rounding the quotient to the nearest tenth of a percent. For instance, cash as a percentage of total assets was determined as follows.

$$\frac{\text{Account balance}}{\text{Total assets}} = \frac{\$15,200}{\$867,000} = 1.753172\%,$$
which rounds to 1.8%.

Common-Size Comparisons. A percentage expresses the proportionate relationship between two figures. By comparing one percentage with another, we can judge the relationship between two sets of amounts by looking at just two figures. Percentages calculated for one company may be compared to those for another company, or perhaps to average percentages for a whole industry. In a similar manner, a firm's percentages for one year may be compared to those calculated for one or more previous years.

Although entities differ from one another in size and many other respects, much can be learned by comparing one company with others. Investors, creditors, and managers like to measure a company's performance

ILLUSTRATION 19.2

**OBJECTIVE 2a. Vertically
analyze a balance sheet.**

PERQUISITE CORPORATION Balance Sheet December 31, 19X5		
ASSETS		
Current		
Cash	$ 15,200	1.8%
Accounts receivable, net	100,000	11.5
Merchandise inventory	120,000	13.8
Prepaid rent	4,800	0.6
Total current assets	$240,000	27.7%
Noncurrent		
Furniture and equipment, net	627,000	72.3
Total Assets	$867,000	100.0%
LIABILITIES		
Current		
Accounts payable	$105,800	12.2%
Wages payable	1,200	0.1
Total current liabilities	$107,000	12.3%
Noncurrent		
Bonds payable	300,000	34.6
Total Liabilities	$407,000	46.9%
SHAREHOLDERS' EQUITY		
Preferred stock, 8%, $100 par	$100,000	11.5%
Common stock, $10 par	200,000	23.1
Retained earnings	160,000	18.5
Total Shareholders' Equity	$460,000	53.1%
Total Liabilities and Shareholders' Equity	$867,000	100.0%

against the performance of other companies. The relative efficiency and position of different companies can be evaluated by comparing their vertically analyzed statements. The percentages, or ratios, can be compared, regardless of size differences. In fact, the dollar figures may be ignored when the statements of companies of unequal size are compared. For this reason, *reports that show two or more vertically analyzed columns may be referred to as common-size statements.* Common-size statements are often prepared for one company to show vertically analyzed figures for two or more accounting periods or points in time.

Dollar amounts are sometimes excluded from common-size statements, with only the percentages shown. The 19X5 percentages in the common-size balance sheet in Illustration 19.3 are the same as those shown in Illustration 19.2. The 19X4 percentages came from vertical analysis of the 19X4 balance sheet amounts presented in Illustration 19.1.

From Illustration 19.3, we can see that there were no drastic proportionate changes in the makeup of the balance sheet between 19X4 and 19X5. The Cash percentage declined slightly, and the proportionate increase in Accounts Receivable was largely offset by the decline in the Merchandise Inventory percentage. Similar observations may be made without having judgments clouded by absolute dollar amounts.

ILLUSTRATION 19.3

PERQUISITE CORPORATION Common-Size Comparative Balance Sheet December 31, 19X5 and 19X4		
	19X5	**19X4**
ASSETS		
Current		
Cash	1.8%	2.5%
Accounts receivable, net	11.5	9.8
Merchandise inventory	13.8	15.9
Prepaid rent	0.6	0.4
Total current assets	27.7%	28.6%
Noncurrent		
Furniture and equipment, net	72.3	71.4
Total Assets	100.0%	100.0%
LIABILITIES		
Current		
Accounts payable	12.2%	10.6%
Wages payable	0.1	0.1
Total current liabilities	12.3%	10.7%
Noncurrent		
Bonds payable	34.6	36.7
Total Liabilities	46.9%	47.4%
SHAREHOLDERS' EQUITY		
Preferred stock, 8%, $100 par	11.5%	12.2%
Common stock, $10 par	23.1	24.5
Retained earnings	18.5	15.9
Total Shareholders' Equity	53.1%	52.6%
Total Liabilities and Shareholders' Equity	100.0%	100.0%

Other Balance Sheet Analyses

Current Ratio.   In the previous chapter we were concerned with net current assets and working capital flows. A widely used measure called the *current ratio* indicates the relative size of total current assets as compared with total current liabilities at a point in time. The *current ratio is the number of dollars of current assets per dollar of current liabilities.* We can calculate the current ratio for Perquisite Corporation at December 31, 19X5, by using data provided in Illustration 19.2.

OBJECTIVE 6a.   Calculate the current ratio.

$$\text{Current ratio} = \frac{\text{Current assets}}{\text{Current liabilities}} :1 = \frac{\$240,000}{\$107,000} :1 = 2.24:1$$

A colon (:) is usually substituted for the word "to" when the ratio is written. The above ratio is read "2.24 to 1," and it means that on December 31, 19X5, Perquisite Corporation had $2.24 of current assets for each $1 of current liabilities.

Current ratios may be compared for different points in time. At December 31, 19X4, Perquisite Corporation had a current ratio of 2.66:1, which indicates that the current ratio declined by 42¢ per $1 of current liabilities during 19X5.

Current ratios may also be compared for different entities, to get some idea of their relative liquidity. However, keep in mind that liquidity needs vary with different types of entities. For example, banks and finance companies must remain very liquid, but attorneys and physicians can get by with little liquidity.

Actually, expected cash flow is usually a better indication of the *future* availability of cash than is a current ratio. As pointed out in Chapter 18, certain levels of current assets and current liabilities are needed on a more or less permanent basis for most concerns. A high current ratio does not necessarily mean that the concern has excess cash for paying dividends, or that it has current assets not needed in its day-to-day operations. Nor does a low current ratio prove that an entity will have any difficulty in meeting its financial obligations.

Acid-Test Ratio.   A more severe measure of liquidity can be calculated in the form of an acid-test ratio. *The **acid-test ratio**, sometimes referred to as the **quick ratio**, is the number of dollars of quick assets per dollar of current liabilities.* For this purpose, *quick assets are defined as cash plus marketable securities and current receivables.* At December 31, 19X5, Perquisite Corporation had an acid-test ratio of 1.08:1, calculated as follows.

$$\text{Acid-test ratio} = \frac{\text{Quick assets}}{\text{Current liabilities}} :1 = \frac{\$115,200}{\$107,000} = 1.08:1$$

Debt and Equity Ratios. Many people are interested in the relationships between liabilities, owners' equity, and assets. Recall the accounting equation.

Assets = Liabilities + Owners' equity

Since the three elements of the equation are interrelated, any ratio between two of the elements necessarily involves the third. For example, if liabilities are 60% of total assets, then owners' equity must necessarily be 40% of assets.

Debt and equity ratios are derived from vertical analysis of a balance sheet. In fact, the vertically analyzed balance sheets in Illustrations 19.2 and 19.3 show that total liabilities were 46.9% of total assets at December 31, 19X5, and that total owners' equity was 53.1% of total assets.

Liabilities may also be compared directly to owners' equity to get a debt-equity ratio. Depending on the needs of the users, any or all of the ratios in Illustration 19.4 may be determined. (Data from Illustration 19.2 are used in each case.)

The debt ratio is the proportion of the entity's assets financed by creditors, whereas the equity ratio is the proportion financed by the owners of the firm. The higher the debt ratio, the lower the equity ratio, since the sum of the two percentages is always 100%. Creditors usually prefer a high equity ratio to ensure an adequate reservoir of owners' equity for absorption of possible losses. Owners usually like a relatively high debt ratio so long as borrowed funds can be used to earn more than the related interest charges. The use of borrowed funds to increase rates of return to owners is discussed later.

Book Value per Share. You may recall from Chapter 14 that *book value* is the amount of equity shown in the accounts for a class of stock divided by the number of shares of stock outstanding. Book value per share is most often determined for common stock.

ILLUSTRATION 19.4

Debt ratio. Total liabilities as a percentage of total assets.

$$\frac{\text{Total liabilities}}{\text{Total assets}} = \frac{\$407,000}{\$867,000} = 46.9\%$$

Equity ratio. Total owners' equity as a percentage of total assets.

$$\frac{\text{Total owners' equity}}{\text{Total assets}} = \frac{\$460,000}{\$867,000} = 53.1\%$$

Debt-equity ratio. Total liabilities as a percentage of total owners' equity.

$$\frac{\text{Total liabilities}}{\text{Total owners' equity}} = \frac{\$407,000}{\$460,000} = 88.5\%$$

OBJECTIVE 6b. Calculate the debt-equity ratio.

To calculate book value per common share, we need to know the total number of outstanding shares and the equity of common shareholders. At December 31, 19X5, Perquisite Corporation had 20,000 shares of common stock outstanding, determined as follows.

$$\text{Shares outstanding} = \frac{\text{Common stock account balance}}{\text{Par value per share}}$$

$$= \frac{\$200,000}{\$10} = 20,000 \text{ shares outstanding}$$

The book value per common share for Perquisite Corporation at December 31, 19X5, is $18, calculated as follows.

$$\text{Book value per common share} = \frac{\text{Total equity} - \text{preferred equity}}{\text{Common shares outstanding}}$$

$$= \frac{\$460,000 - \$100,000}{20,000} = \$18 \text{ per share}$$

INCOME STATEMENT ANALYSIS

Horizontal Analysis

You saw earlier how balance sheets may be horizontally analyzed to show amounts and percentages of changes between two *points* in time. Horizontal analyses of income statements stress the amounts and rates of change between two *periods* of time, as shown in Illustration 19.5 on the next page. In each instance the change is divided by the base year (19X4) amount.

Vertical Analysis

For vertically analyzing income statements, the figure for net sales is usually taken as the base figure. The percentages in the Perquisite Corporation statement in Illustration 19.6 were calculated by dividing each amount in the income statement by the net sales figure.

The percentages may be viewed in terms of how net sales dollars are distributed. On the average, 63.2¢ of each dollar of net sales went toward the cost of inventory sold, leaving 36.8¢ to cover other expenses and net income. Operating expenses took 26.5¢, interest 1.3¢, and income taxes 3.4¢ of each dollar of net sales. Out of each dollar of net sales, 5.6¢ was left after all expenses were covered.

ILLUSTRATION 19.5

			Increase or (Decrease)	
	19X5	**19X4**	*Amount*	*Percent*
		PERQUISITE CORPORATION		
		Comparative Income Statement		
		For the Years Ended December 31, 19X5 and 19X4		
Net sales	$1,580,000	$1,520,000	$60,000	3.9%
Cost of goods sold	998,000	980,000	18,000	1.8%
Gross Profit on Sales	$ 582,000	$ 540,000	$42,000	7.8%
Operating expenses				
Selling	$ 313,000	$ 271,000	$42,000	15.5%
General and administrative	105,000	134,000	(29,000)	(21.6)%
Total operating expenses	$ 418,000	$ 405,000	$13,000	3.2%
Operating Income	$ 164,000	$ 135,000	$29,000	21.5%
Interest expense	21,000	22,000	(1,000)	(4.5)%
Income Before Income Taxes	$ 143,000	$ 113,000	$30,000	26.5%
Income taxes	54,000	41,000	13,000	31.7%
Net Income	$ 89,000	$ 72,000	$17,000	23.6%
Earnings per common share	$4.05*	$3.20	$0.85	26.6%

*Calculation of earnings per share is illustrated on page 816.

OBJECTIVE 1b. Prepare horizontally analyzed statements, showing amounts and rates of change, using income statements for two accounting periods.

Common-Size Income Statement.   The common-size income statement in Illustration 19.7 on the next page was prepared without dollar amounts so as to force the statement user to concentrate on ratios alone. The rates in the 19X5 column came from the income statement in Illustration 19.6; the 19X4 amounts came from a vertical analysis of the 19X4 column in Illustration 19.5.

ILLUSTRATION 19.6

	PERQUISITE CORPORATION	
	Income Statement	
	For the Year Ended December 31, 19X5	
Net sales	$1,580,000	100.0%
Cost of goods sold	998,000	63.2
Gross Profit on Sales	$ 582,000	36.8%
Operating expenses		
Selling	$ 313,000	19.8%
General and administrative	105,000	6.7
Total operating expenses	$ 418,000	26.5%
Operating Income	$ 164,000	10.3%
Interest expense	21,000	1.3
Income Before Income Taxes	$ 143,000	9.0%
Income taxes	54,000	3.4
Net Income	$ 89,000	5.6%

OBJECTIVE 2b. Vertically analyze an income statement.

ILLUSTRATION 19.7

PERQUISITE CORPORATION Common-Size Comparative Income Statement For the Years Ended December 31, 19X5 and 19X4		
	19X5	**19X4**
Net sales	100.0%	100.0%
Cost of goods sold	63.2	64.5
Gross Profit on Sales	36.8%	35.5%
Operating expenses		
Selling	19.8%	17.8%
General and administrative	6.7	8.8
Total operating expenses	26.5%	26.6%
Operating Income	10.3%	8.9%
Interest expense	1.3	1.5
Income Before Income Taxes	9.0%	7.4%
Income taxes	3.4	2.7
Net Income	5.6%	4.7%

From Illustration 19.7 we can see that the percentage cost of goods sold declined during 19X5, resulting in a higher rate of gross profit on sales. Also, the percentage increase for Selling Expenses was more than offset by the percentage decrease for General and Administrative Expenses. Other observations may be made without being influenced by the absolute dollar amounts for the two periods.

Times Interest Earned

Times interest earned is a measure of the number of times that interest expense for a period is divisible into income before interest and taxes. Perquisite Corporation earned 7.8 times its interest expense during 19X5, calculated as follows.

OBJECTIVE 6c. Calculate times interest earned.

$$\text{Times interest earned} = \frac{\text{Net income} + \text{Income taxes} + \text{Interest expense}}{\text{Interest expense}}$$
$$= \frac{\$89,000 + \$54,000 + \$21,000}{\$21,000} = \frac{\$164,000}{\$21,000}$$
$$= 7.8 \text{ times interest earned}$$

In this instance, the amount which is divided by interest is the operating income for 19X5. Operating income divided by interest expense will yield times interest earned provided that interest expense is the only nonoperating item on the income statement. The safest approach, however, is to add interest and income taxes to net income to get the numerator, as just illustrated.

Income taxes are added back because interest expense is deductible for tax purposes. A times interest earned of 7.8 means that future earning power could drop to about one-eighth of 19X5 earnings, and interest of $21,000 could still be paid. Thus it is a measure of the relative ability of the entity to pay the interest on its debt.

CROSS-STATEMENT ANALYSIS

Some measures require the use of data from both income statements and balance sheets. Various types of *turnover rates* and *rates of return* involve cross-statement analysis.

Turnover Rates

*A **turnover rate** expresses the number of times that a balance sheet quantity is divisible into an income statement measure of volume.* Turnover rates are used in judging the relative efficiency with which an entity's resources are employed.

Accounts Receivable Turnover. Receivables represent temporary delays in the receipt of cash. The higher the level of receivables, the fewer funds available for other purposes. In general, managers try to keep the level of receivables down by collecting them as quickly as possible.

Accounts receivable turnover is the number of times that the average amount of accounts receivable is divisible into net sales on account for a period. The higher the turnover rate, the faster the receivables are being collected.

When available, the amount of net sales on account for the period is used to calculate the turnover of receivables. Sales for cash involve no delays in cash collection, and consequently no collection periods. When the amount of sales on account is not known, we usually assume that all sales were made on account, since most business transactions in the world today are made on a credit basis.

Since the credit sales amount is for a period of time, it is best that we use as the divisor the *average* balance of Accounts Receivable during that period. If balances at shorter intervals are not readily available, the average is calculated by adding beginning and ending balances and dividing the result by 2. Using the data provided in Illustration 19.1 for the Perquisite Corporation, we get the following result.

$$
\begin{aligned}
\text{Average accounts receivable} &= \frac{\text{Beginning accounts receivable } + \text{ Ending accounts receivable}}{2} \\
&= \frac{\$80,000 + \$100,000}{2} \\
&= \$90,000
\end{aligned}
$$

Where even the beginning receivables balance is not available, we might assume that the ending balance is representative of the average balance.

Data for the following calculation of accounts receivable turnover during 19X5 came from Perquisite Corporation statements presented earlier. It is assumed that all of Perquisite's sales were on account. The result may than be compared with turnover rates for previous periods or other entities.

OBJECTIVE 3a. Calculate turnover rates for receivables.

$$\text{Accounts receivable turnover} = \frac{\text{Net sales on account}}{\text{Average accounts receivable}}$$

$$= \frac{\$1,580,000}{\$90,000} = 17.6 \text{ times during 19X5}$$

A variation of the turnover rate for receivables is the *average collection period,* *which is the average number of days that it took to collect an account receivable during the period.* Once the receivables turnover rate is known, the average collection period may be ascertained by dividing the number of days in the accounting period by the turnover rate. The average collection period for Perquisite Corporation for the year 19X5 is determined as follows.

$$\text{Average collection period} = \frac{\text{Days in accounting period}}{\text{Accounts receivable turnover rate}}$$

$$= \frac{365 \text{ days}}{17.6 \text{ times}} = 21 \text{ days}$$

Another variation of receivables turnover analysis is the determination of the *days sales in ending accounts receivable by dividing the ending Accounts Receivable balance by the average sales on account per day.* Either the actual number of business days or the number of calendar days during the accounting period may be used for determining the average sales, depending on the needs of the users and the data available. The following calculation for Perquisite Corporation uses the calendar days in a year.

$$\text{Average sales on account per day} = \frac{\text{Net sales on account}}{\text{Days in accounting period}}$$

$$= \frac{\$1,580,000}{365} = \$4,329$$

$$\text{Days' sales in ending accounts receivable} = \frac{\text{Ending accounts receivable}}{\text{Average sales on account per day}}$$

$$= \frac{\$100,000}{\$4,329} = 23 \text{ days}$$

The latter measure may be helpful in assessing the quality of the ending receivables. The more days' sales in ending receivables, the greater the likelihood that some of the receivables are rather old—and therefore less likely to be collected.[1] For example, we might be quite concerned if an entity's receivables represent 60 days of sales and we know that the entity sells on terms of 2/10, n/30. Since all accounts are supposed to be paid within 30 days, some of the accounts must be long overdue.

Inventory Turnover. *Inventory turnover is the number of times that the average inventory during a period is divisible into cost of goods sold for that period.* As with other turnover rates, we will use the best average balance we can calculate with the data available; often the average must be calculated with only the beginning and ending balances. The 19X5 inventory turnover rate for Perquisite Corporation is calculated as follows.

$$\text{Inventory turnover} = \frac{\text{Cost of goods sold}}{\text{Average inventory}}$$

$$= \frac{\$998,000}{\dfrac{\$130,000 + \$120,000}{2}}$$

$$= \frac{\$998,000}{\$125,000} = 8 \text{ times}$$

OBJECTIVE 3b. Calculate turnover rates for inventories.

We must be careful not to confuse the calculation of receivable turnover with that for inventory turnover. Accounts receivable are recorded at *selling* prices, as are sales. For inventory turnover, we divide the *cost* of goods sold by inventory, also recorded on a *cost* basis.

Days' sales in average inventory may be determined by dividing the days in the accounting period by the inventory turnover rate for the period. As with the average collection period of receivables, either the business days or the calendar days may be used, depending on the user's needs and the data available. Using calendar days, the days' sales in average inventory during 19X5 for Perquisite Corporation is determined as follows.

$$\text{Days' sales in average inventory} = \frac{\text{Days in accounting period}}{\text{Inventory turnover rate}}$$

$$= \frac{365 \text{ days}}{8 \text{ times}} = 46 \text{ days}$$

---

[1]For a discussion of the relationship between age of receivables and their estimated collectibility, see Section 6.B.

The foregoing calculation shows that on the average, the entity maintained an inventory balance equivalent to the cost of goods sold during 46 calendar days. This measure also says that, on the average, inventory items were held by the business for 46 calendar days before they were sold. *Remember, inventories are accounted for on a cost basis, so it is cost of goods sold, not sales, with which inventory balances must be compared.*

Managers of an entity normally attempt to maximize the inventory turnover rate and consequently minimize the days' sales in inventory. Naturally, there are other important considerations, such as the need to maintain an adequate selection and quantity of inventory items so that customers can be supplied with the goods they want.

Days in Operating Cycle. In Section 18.B we defined the *cash cycle* as the process by which cash is used in business operations to produce more cash. A closely related concept is that of the *operating cycle, which is the period of time between the purchase of goods and the realization of cash from their sales.* Since days' sales in average inventory is a measure of the average time it took to sell an inventory item, and since the average collection period is a measure of the average time it took to collect receivables, the sum of the two measures should approximate the length of the operating cycle.

For Perquisite Corporation, the average operating cycle during 19X5 was as follows.

$$\text{Days in operating cycle} = \text{Average collection period} + \text{Days' sales in avg. inv.}$$
$$= 21 + 46 = 67 \text{ days}$$

In other words, it took an average of 67 calendar days to turn a newly purchased item of merchandise into cash from its sale. The calculation is somewhat more involved for manufacturing concerns, since the time it takes to produce the goods must be included in the operating cycle. Still, the goal is the same: to keep the operating cycle as short as possible.

Asset Turnover. *An overall measure of the efficiency with which a firm's resources have been used is its asset turnover, calculated by dividing net sales for a period by the average assets during the period.* Perquisite Corporation had an asset turnover rate of 1.9 for 19X5, calculated as follows.

OBJECTIVE 3c. Calculate turnover rates for assets.

$$\text{Asset turnover} = \frac{\text{Net sales}}{\text{Average assets}} = \frac{\$1,580,000}{\dfrac{\$818,000 + \$867,000}{2}}$$

$$= \frac{\$1,580,000}{\$842,500} = 1.9 \text{ times}$$

The greater the asset turnover rate, the more sales are being made per dollar of assets employed. Perhaps some caution is in order concerning the use of asset turnover rates. Some types of concerns are expected to turn assets at a slower rate than others. For example, it would make no sense to compare asset turnover for a jewelry store with that of a produce market. A jewelry store sells high-priced (and high-profit) goods that do not spoil, while a produce market sells perishable goods at relatively low markups. Naturally, we would expect the produce market to have a higher turnover rate than the jewelry store.

Rates of Return

The ultimate measure of a business concern's success, at least insofar as accounting data are concerned, is the amount of net income produced with the resources that were employed. *A rate of return is calculated by dividing an amount of resources employed by an entity into the earnings that can be attributed to those sources.* A rate of return compares an amount of earnings with the size of the resource base employed to earn it.

Return on Assets. The *size* of a business is usually measured by the amount of its assets. A large company is expected to earn more net income than a small company. The relative productivity of a company's assets can be measured by computing a *return on assets, which is net income plus interest divided by the average assets used during the period.* Interest is added back to net income because it represents a return to the creditors who supplied a portion of the assets used.

Return on assets is a measure of the efficiency with which assets were used, regardless of whether they were financed with borrowed money or owners' funds. Perquisite Corporation earned 13.1% return on assets during 19X5, computed as follows.[2]

$$\text{Return on assets} = \frac{\text{Net income} + \text{Interest expense}}{\text{Average assets}} = \frac{\$89,000 + \$21,000}{\dfrac{\$818,000 + \$867,000}{2}}$$

$$= \frac{\$110,000}{\$842,500} = 13.1\%$$

OBJECTIVE 4a. Calculate rates of return on assets.

---

[2]The calculation may be refined for some purposes by adding back only the after-tax cost of the interest expense. If, for instance, the marginal income tax rate is 40%, the after-tax cost of interest is only 60% of the tax deductible interest accrued during the period. Under this approach, the rate of return on Perquisite's assets is determined as follows:

$$\text{Return on assets} = \frac{\$89,000 + 0.60(\$21,000)}{\$842,500} = 12.1\%$$

Some statement users are interested in the overall productivity of the firm's assets before any income taxes or returns to the suppliers of resources are considered. From this viewpoint, Perquisite's return on assets is calculated as follows:

$$\text{Return on assets} = \frac{\$89,000 + \$54,000 + \$21,000}{\$842,500} = 19.5\%$$

Perquisite produced a little better than 13¢ return for each dollar of average assets employed during 19X5. It is possible that the beginning and ending assets were not representative of the amount of assets used during the year. For example, inventories may be at a low point at year-end, as in a toy store immediately after Christmas. A more representative average would result from summing the total assets on hand at the end of each month and dividing by 12.

Return on Equity.   The owners of a business are interested in the return on assets as an indication of the effectiveness with which the company's assets have been used. They may be *more* concerned, however, about the **return on equity,** *which is the relationship between the net income and the average owners' equity.* The return on equity to Perquisite's stockholders is figured as follows.

OBJECTIVE 4b. Calculate rates of return on equity.

$$\text{Return on equity} = \frac{\text{Net income}}{\text{Average owners' equity}} = \frac{\$89,000}{\dfrac{\$430,000 + \$460,000}{2}}$$

$$= \frac{\$89,000}{\$445,000} = 20\%$$

Perquisite's return on equity for 19X5 indicates that 20¢ was earned for each dollar of stockholders' equity present during the year. The managers of this company were able to turn a 13.1% *return on assets* into a 20% *return on equity* by using borrowed funds, a practice known as *trading on the equity.*

OBJECTIVE 5. State what is meant by trading on the equity.

*Trading on the equity, sometimes called **financial leverage,** is the act of earning more on borrowed funds than they cost in interest.* Suppose, for example, that you could borrow money at 8% interest and lend it out for 10% interest. You would be able to keep the extra 2% for yourself. Of course, a lender may be reluctant to lend to you unless you have some assets of your own for security.

Creditors prefer to lend to companies that have an adequate equity base. Owners' equity is the *residual* claim of the owners, as depicted by the following arrangement of the basic accounting equation.

Assets − Liabilities = Owners' equity

Business losses are borne by the owners, so long as some owners' equity remains to absorb them. If accumulated business losses are so large that they exceed owners' equity, then assets will be insufficient to cover the liabilities, and the company is said to be *insolvent.* Although a legal definition is somewhat more involved, for our purposes it is enough to say that *insolvency is the state of owing more liabilities than one has in assets.*

Thus owners' equity acts as a *buffer* against losses for creditors. The more equity the owners have, the more likely it is that the creditors will be able to collect interest and repayments due them. When a business has an acceptable equity base, it can then borrow funds for use in business operations. In this way, the business trades on its equity base to achieve a higher return on equity for its owners.

We have seen how Perquisite's managers were able to parlay a 13.1% return on assets into a 20% return on equity. This resulted from employing low-interest bonds and interest-free current liabilities to help earn the 13.1% return on assets. We will see in the following paragraphs how the 8% preferred stock provided an additional trading on the equity benefit to common shareholders.

Return on Common Equity. Common shareholders' claims against a corporation represent the *residual* (last, final, underlying) equity of the entity. Where preferred stock is present, the preferred shareholders have a priority (superior) claim to the fixed returns that their shares are supposed to bear. Whatever is left of net income after covering preferred dividends belongs to the common shareholders. *Return on common equity is net income less preferred dividends divided by the average common equity for the period.*

The comparative balance sheet presented for Perquisite in Illustration 19.1 shows that there was $100,000 of 8% preferred stock outstanding throughout 19X5. Preferred dividends of $8,000 must have been paid for 19X5, since the note at the bottom of the statement says that there were no arrearages (unpaid amounts) at the end of 19X5.

The return on common equity for 19X5 is calculated as follows.

$$\text{Return on common equity} = \frac{\text{Net income} - \text{Preferred dividends}}{\text{Average common shareholders' equity}}$$

$$= \frac{\$89,000 - \$8,000}{\dfrac{\$330,000 + \$360,000}{2}} = \frac{\$81,000}{\$345,000} = 23.5\%$$

OBJECTIVE 4c. Calculate rates of return on common equity.

The return to common shareholders is even larger than the previously calculated return on equity, a result of additional trading on the equity benefits. A 13.1% *return on assets* was parlayed into a 20% *return on equity* and a 23.5% *return on common equity*. You can see that it pays to use the funds supplied by others, provided that a larger rate is earned on the funds than must be paid to those who supplied them.

Times Preferred Dividends Earned

Times preferred dividends earned is a measure of the number of times that preferred dividend requirements are divisible into net income. **Perquisite**

Corporation earned a net income for 19X5 that was 11.1 times the preferred dividends, determined as follows.

$$\text{Times preferred dividends earned} = \frac{\text{Net income}}{\text{Preferred dividends}}$$

$$= \frac{\$89,000}{\$8,000} = 11.1 \text{ times}$$

This measure helps to assess the relative likelihood that the corporation can continue to pay preferred dividends in the future. We can conclude that Perquisite's net income could decline by 90% and preferred dividends would still be covered by the remaining net income.

Earnings per Common Share

Earnings per common share are determined by dividing net income less preferred dividends by the average common shares outstanding during the period in which the income was earned. Present practice is to report earnings per common share on the face of annual income statements for corporations, usually at the bottom.[3] As pointed out in Chapter 15, earnings per share calculations may be complicated by the presence of common stock equivalents and other potential dilutions of common stock. If we assume that there are no outstanding stock rights, convertible securities, or other complicating items for Perquisite Corporation, the earnings per common share can be calculated for 19X5 as follows.

$$\text{Earnings per common share} = \frac{\text{Net income} - \text{Preferred dividends}}{\text{Average number of common shares}}$$

$$= \frac{\$89,000 - \$8,000}{20,000 \text{ shares}}$$

$$= \frac{\$81,000}{20,000 \text{ shares}} = \$4.05 \text{ per common share}$$

We know that there were 20,000 shares of common stock outstanding at the beginning and end of 19X5 because the Common Stock account shows a balance of $200,000 at each of those dates, and the balance sheet indicates that each common share has a $10 par value. Also, there is no evidence of any treasury shares, which would show up as a negative item in the shareholders' equity section of the balance sheet.

---

[3]*Opinions of the Accounting Principles Board No. 15*, "Earnings Per Share" (New York: American Institute of Certified Public Accountants, 1969), par. 12.

MARKET VALUE PER SHARE ANALYSES

The *market value* of a share of stock will usually be more or less than its *book value*. *Market value per share is the price for which a share of stock could currently be sold.* Market values of shares reflect investors' views of the current value of an entity as a going concern—and those views depend on the investors' expectations about the concern's future earning power.

Except under unusual circumstances, market values are not recorded into accounting systems until assets are sold.[4] Thus *book value per share* is based on the *cost* of reported assets less liabilities.

The market value of shares is important to investors. It determines how much must be paid to acquire new shares, and how much cash could be obtained from selling shares currently owned.

The previous day's prices of shares listed on major stock exchanges are printed in the financial sections of many newspapers. The current values of shares not traded on formal stock exchanges may be more difficult to pin down, but in many cases can be approximated in some way.

Price-Earnings Ratio

The price-earnings ratio for common shares represents the number of times that the current market value of a share is divisible by the reported earnings per share on the latest annual income statement. If Perquisite common stock sells for $26 per share on a day in 19X6, the price-earnings ratio is 6.4, determined as follows.

$$\text{Price-earnings ratio} = \frac{\text{Market value per share}}{\text{Earnings per share}} = \frac{\$26}{\$4.05} = 6.4$$

OBJECTIVE 6d. Calculate the price-earnings ratio.

It is probably worth noting that the reciprocal of the price-earnings ratio, the *earnings-price rate, is in effect the rate of return on a share's market value.* Thus, for the example we used, the earnings-price rate would be 0.156 or 15.6%, determined as follows.

$$\text{Earnings-price rate} = \frac{\text{Earnings per share}}{\text{Market value per share}} = \frac{\$4.05}{\$26} = 15.6\%$$

Price-earnings ratios are most familiar to investors, probably because they are frequently reported in the newspapers along with the current prices of stocks.

---

[4]One notable exception is the lower of cost or market concept. Accountants in some countries are moving toward value-based accounting systems, and in the United States, *FASB Statement No. 33* requires the largest of corporations to report certain supplemental data on a current cost basis (see Section 12.B).

Dividend Yield Rate

Another commonly reported measure is the *dividend yield rate for common shares, computed by dividing the dividends per common share for the previous year by the current market value per common share.* In 19X5 Perquisite paid $51,000 in cash dividends on 20,000 shares of common stock, which amounted to $2.55 per share. Therefore, Perquisite shares selling for $26 per share have a yield rate of 9.8%, determined as follows.

OBJECTIVE 6e. Calculate the dividend yield rate.

$$\text{Dividend yield rate} = \frac{\text{Common dividends per share}}{\text{Market value per common share}} = \frac{\$2.55}{\$26} = 9.8\%$$

TREND ANALYSIS

Most people who are interested in financial statement analysis are really interested in predicting what the future holds for the entity. An investor wants to know whether more securities should be purchased, or whether those held should be sold. A creditor must decide whether to extend more credit or to demand payment of what is already due. Union leaders must formulate wage demands, directors must decide whether corporate officers should be replaced—the list could go on and on.

One approach to predicting what might happen in the future is to study past trends. *Trend analysis is the study of the direction in which indicators have tended to move in the past, in an attempt to determine what is most likely to happen in the future.* Trend analysis assumes that past tendencies are likely to continue in the future. A concern whose sales have been steadily growing is more likely to be labeled a growth firm than is one whose sales have been decreasing. Trend analysis may concentrate on comparative dollar amounts, rates of change, or any other measure that can be compared over time and projected into the future.

PROJECTED DATA

As we have said, most users of financial data are ultimately concerned about what the future holds for the entitites being reported on. Managers of an entity spend a considerable amount of time trying to project future outcomes. Most concerns develop for their internal use formal predictions in the form of *budgets, which are financial plans for the future.* Techniques for arriving at reasonable budgets are discussed in later chapters.

Large, well-managed firms usually develop overall budgeting systems that go so far as to project *what financial statements are likely to show for future accounting periods, sometimes referred to as pro forma financial statements.* Some people believe that external users of accounting data should be provided with the projections developed internally by an entity's accountants and managers. However, accountants and managers have so far been reluctant to do this. They fear that such data may be used unwisely and that they will be criticized, and perhaps even sued for damages, should future results turn out to be substantially different from what was predicted. Also, the argument is advanced that competing companies might find ways to profit from knowledge about what an entity's managers are planning for the future.

Annual reports of corporations have sometimes provided limited remarks on future plans for the enterprise. The Securities and Exchange Commission seems to be requiring that increasing amounts of information about future plans be disclosed by corporations seeking approval to market new issues of securities. Accountants in a few countries have been moving more rapidly toward the inclusion of projected financial data in published annual reports than have accountants in the United States. It appears likely that as time passes, more and more projected data will be provided to users of financial statements.

SUMMARY OF CHAPTER 19

Financial data may be made more useful for particular users by means of analysis. There are many ways to analyze financial information, all involving comparisons of some kind. Some of the more commonly used comparative measures are summarized in the following outline.

Measure	Calculation
BALANCE SHEET MEASURES	
Current ratio	$\dfrac{\text{Current assets}}{\text{Current liabilities}}:1$
Acid-test ratio (Quick ratio)	$\dfrac{\text{Quick assets}}{\text{Current liabilities}}:1$
Debt ratio	$\dfrac{\text{Total liabilities}}{\text{Total assets}}$
Equity ratio	$\dfrac{\text{Total owners' equity}}{\text{Total assets}}$
Debt-equity ratio	$\dfrac{\text{Total liabilities}}{\text{Total owners' equity}}$
Book value per common share	$\dfrac{\text{Total equity} - \text{Preferred equity}}{\text{Common shares outstanding}}$
INCOME STATEMENT MEASURES	
Gross profit rate	$\dfrac{\text{Gross profit}}{\text{Net sales}}$
Net income rate	$\dfrac{\text{Net income}}{\text{Net sales}}$
Times interest earned	$\dfrac{\text{Net income} + \text{Income tax} + \text{Interest exp.}}{\text{Interest expense}}$
CROSS-STATEMENT MEASURES	
Accounts receivable turnover rate	$\dfrac{\text{Net sales on account}}{\text{Average accounts receivable}}$
Average collection period	$\dfrac{\text{Days in accounting period}}{\text{Accounts receivable turnover rate}}$
Day's sales in ending accounts receivable	$\dfrac{\text{Ending accounts receivable}}{\text{Average sales on account per day}}$
Inventory turnover rate	$\dfrac{\text{Cost of goods sold}}{\text{Average inventory}}$
Days' sales in average inventory	$\dfrac{\text{Days in accounting period}}{\text{Inventory turnover rate}}$
Days in operating cycle	Average collection period + Days sales in average inventory

Measure	Calculation
Asset turnover	$\dfrac{\text{Net sales}}{\text{Average assets}}$
Return on assets	$\dfrac{\text{Net income} + \text{Interest expense}}{\text{Average assets}}$
Return on equity	$\dfrac{\text{Net income}}{\text{Average owners' equity}}$
Return on common equity	$\dfrac{\text{Net income} - \text{Preferred dividends}}{\text{Average common shareholders' equity}}$
Times preferred dividends earned	$\dfrac{\text{Net income}}{\text{Preferred dividends}}$
Earnings per common share	$\dfrac{\text{Net income} - \text{Preferred dividends}}{\text{Average number of common shares}}$
MARKET VALUE PER SHARE MEASURES	
Price-earnings ratio	$\dfrac{\text{Market value per share}}{\text{Earnings per share}}$
Earnings-price rate	$\dfrac{\text{Earnings per share}}{\text{Market value per share}}$
Dividend yield rate	$\dfrac{\text{Common dividends per share}}{\text{Market value per common share}}$

GLOSSARY FOR CHAPTER 19

Accounts receivable turnover   A measure of the number of times that the average amount of accounts receivable is divisible into net sales on account for a period of time.

Acid-test ratio (quick ratio)   A measure of the number of dollars of quick assets per dollar of current liabilities.

Asset turnover   An overall measure of the efficiency with which a firm's resources have been used, computed by dividing net sales for a period by the average assets during the period.

Average collection period   The average number of days that it took to collect an account receivable during a period.

Budgets   Financial plans for the future.

Common-size statements   Reports that show two or more vertically analyzed columns.

Comparative statements   Statements that present data side by side for two or more periods or points in time.

Current ratio   A measure of the number of dollars of current assets per dollar of current liabilities.

Required

1) What was the amount and rate of change during fiscal year 19X5 in Belco's investment in noncurrent assets?

2) Has Belco's investment in noncurrent assets increased relative to total assets? Explain.

3) Has Belco's liquidity improved between 19X4 and 19X5? Explain.

4) Comment on the apparent quality of Belco's receivables. (All sales are made on credit with terms of 2/10, n/30.)

5) How long do you think it will take to convert the ending merchandise inventory to cash through the normal operating cycle?

6) Does Belco take effective advantage of trading on the equity? Explain.

PART VIII

MANUFACTURING OPERATIONS

ACCOUNTANTS IN THE WORKPLACE

NAME: Elmer D. Chinn

AFFILIATION: None

POSITION: Sole Proprietor

SPECIALIZATION: Personal Taxes, Estate Planning

Elmer Chinn is selective about the type of work he does. "I am not inclined to go out and seek new business for the sake of new business alone," says Chinn. He prefers to focus on those areas of accounting he enjoys: taxation and estate planning. In 15 years of private practice, Chinn has acquired a large number of clients, whom he describes as investors, not businesspeople. "I help them with their taxes and estates, often in conjunction with their lawyers and, occasionally, their stockbrokers."

Upon graduation from the University of Washington, Chinn began his career in the Los Angeles office of Price Waterhouse. After one year in auditing, five years in tax work, and two moves, he was asked to move again, this time out of the country. Chinn chose to resign.

"At first, I was interested in working in private industry," he recalls. Meanwhile he took on various accounting assignments—some from Price Waterhouse on a per diem basis, others through referrals. He found that he liked working for himself, more and more work came his way, and before long he was established in his own business.

Chinn tells potential employees that they may gain valuable experience at a larger firm, but that he prefers the independence of his own practice. His experience is a good example of how organizational decisions can affect a career. If he had not been asked to transfer out of the country, he might never have become a successful independent businessman.

NAME: Richard J. Kessler

AFFILIATION: Weyerhauser Corporation

POSITION: Regional Accounting Manager

SPECIALIZATION: Cost accounting

As a cost accounting manager, Richard J. Kessler sees to it that his region's books remain in good order. He also provides management with valuable data on manufacturing costs. "To properly do his job," says Kessler, "a cost accountant must know accounting principles thoroughly *and* manufacturing processes well. Only with this combined knowledge can he or she contribute fully to a company's success."

The key to successful cost accounting, in Kessler's opinion, is to devise systems that address the unique needs of the unit. He feels that accountants sometimes try to be too precise, thereby generating more work and expense for little, if any, benefit to management.

A graduate of the University of Puget Sound, Kessler began his career with Weyerhauser as an accountant trainee. Since then he has held a variety of jobs—"something that Weyerhauser encourages," he notes.

At present, Kessler oversees the finances for six separate profit centers. He and his staff prepare monthly financial statements for each center that must be "highly accurate and timely." They also furnish detailed analyses of costs and productivity to each unit manager.

Says Kessler: "Just looking at profits, you may get a mistaken view of productivity." It is important to provide data that allow managers to "see a difference when they make a procedural change"—to make sure that when profits rise, "operations have improved also."

CHAPTER 20
Manufacturing Accounting

OBJECTIVES

Chapter 20 deals with accounting for manufacturing concerns. At the conclusion of your study, you should be able to

1. Differentiate between manufacturing and merchandising operations.

2. Name and define the three types of inventories used in manufacturing operations.

3. Name the three elements of cost assigned to manufactured goods, and state what is included in each element.

4. Prepare the following items, given the necessary data for a manufacturing concern using a periodic inventory system:
   a. An end-of-period work sheet.
   b. A schedule of cost of goods completed.
   c. Entries to adjust inventory accounts and record cost of goods sold for the period.
   d. Closing entries.

THE NATURE OF MANUFACTURING

Manufacturing is the process of combining various resources to produce a good that did not previously exist. The word stems from two Latin words: *manu* meaning "by hand," and *factus* meaning "made." At one time, most manufactured goods were handmade by individuals or families within their homes.

During the Industrial Revolution, production processes shifted to factories, where workers went each day to specialize in certain production tasks. With the introduction of the corporate form of organization, numbers of investors were able to pool their wealth to build large, costly factories. Expensive machinery helped make labor much more productive. As a result, workers could be paid more, which in turn enabled them to buy the greater quantities of goods being produced.

In most societies today, people are dependent on one another for the goods and services they use. Few products are made in the home; most are manufactured in factories and purchased by people with the money they earn from their labors.

Manufacturing processes combine *factors of production* to create products that are sold to customers. The customers may be distributors, wholesalers, retailers, or consumers, depending on the circumstances. *A factor of production is a resource (ingredient, or element) that is used in a production process.* Various kinds of labor, materials, contracted services, building space, machinery, and other ingredients are combined as factors of production to manufacture the products that a manufacturing concern sells.

You may recall a discussion in Section 4.A about different types of *utility*. It was pointed out that manufacturing concerns concentrate primarily on the creation of *form* utility, although they are also involved in creating *time, place,* and other kinds of utilities.

The difference between the total value of goods produced during a period and the total cost of factors of production (resources) used up in producing the goods is a measure of the value of the utility that was created in the manufacturing process during that period. Illustration 20.1 depicts the manufacturing concept.

However, one must keep in mind that under the *cost concept,* manufactured goods on hand (Finished Goods) are accounted for on a cost basis. It is only upon the sale of goods that the *realization concept* permits the recognition of the value added through the creation of utility.

There are many different ways of accounting for manufacturing operations. This chapter will consider only those general aspects of manufacturing accounting that differ from those of accounting for merchandising concerns. Recall that merchandising concerns buy and resell goods without

ILLUSTRATION 20.1

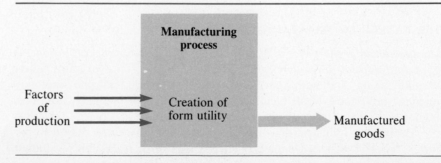

changing their form, whereas manufacturing concerns combine resources to produce goods that did not previously exist. (Chapter 21 will deal with the two types of cost accounting systems that are most often used in accounting for manufacturing operations on a perpetual basis.)

MANUFACTURING INVENTORIES

Most manufacturing concerns must store a certain amount of materials for future use in the production process. Also, at any point in time there may be goods at various stages of completion. Finally, certain quantities of finished goods may have to be stored until they are sold. The three types of manufacturing inventories are defined below.

TYPES OF MANUFACTURING INVENTORIES

Materials inventory. Materials on hand that have not yet been put into the production process.

Goods in process inventory. Incomplete products still in the production process.

Finished goods inventory. Completed goods awaiting sale.

Like other inventories on hand, manufacturing inventories are classified as current assets on a balance sheet.

PRODUCTION COST ELEMENTS

Costs associated with the manufacture of goods are sometimes referred to as product costs. The three main elements of product costs are discussed in the paragraphs that follow.

Direct Materials

Materials that have not already been processed by suppliers, or that have been processed only for general use, are sometimes referred to as raw materials. Iron ore is a raw material used in the production of pig iron; logs are used in the production of lumber; and so on. Sheet steel has been processed to a certain degree, but it is nevertheless considered a raw material for the production of automobiles and other products.

Materials that have been processed by suppliers for specific purposes are usually referred to as purchased parts. Headlights purchased from suppliers are purchased parts for the manufacture of automobiles, as are picture tubes for the manufacture of television sets. *Materials and parts that become embodied in finished products are called direct materials.*

Direct Labor

Services supplied by employees who work directly on goods being produced are referred to as direct labor. If you have ever been in a factory, you probably saw people applying direct labor to products as machine operators, packers, and so on. *The cost of both direct materials and direct labor are sometimes called direct costs or prime costs.*

Factory Overhead

Some factors of production are more difficult to identify with goods being produced than are direct materials and direct labor. *Costs that are not directly identifiable with goods being produced are sometimes referred to as indirect costs. The cost of indirect materials and indirect labor, and all other indirect manufacturing costs, are called factory overhead, manufacturing overhead, or factory burden.* Thus factory overhead includes all manufacturing costs other than direct materials and direct labor—in other words, all indirect manufacturing costs.

Indirect Materials. Some materials may be used indirectly in the operation of the factory, such as for maintenance and cleaning. Some accounting systems classify Supplies Inventory as a separate account, while others control all unused materials through one Materials Inventory account. Either way, *materials that are consumed in the factory without going directly into the goods being produced are referred to as indirect materials.* Costs of indirect materials are considered part of factory overhead.

As an expediency, the costs of incidental direct materials are sometimes classified as indirect. For instance, the cost of glue or staples used to seal cartons may be treated as overhead in order to simplify the accounting process.

Indirect Labor. *Services performed by factory employees who do not work directly on goods being produced are called indirect labor.* Indirect labor costs are viewed as part of factory overhead. Employees involved in factory maintenance, cleaning, supervision, timekeeping, plant protection, and similar factory activities contribute indirect labor.

ILLUSTRATION 20.2

OBJECTIVE 3. Name the elements of cost assigned to manufactured goods, and state what is included in each element.

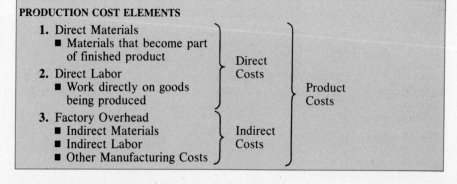

PRODUCTION COST ELEMENTS

1. Direct Materials
   - Materials that become part of finished product
2. Direct Labor
   - Work directly on goods being produced

} Direct Costs

3. Factory Overhead
   - Indirect Materials
   - Indirect Labor
   - Other Manufacturing Costs

} Indirect Costs

} Product Costs

Other Manufacturing Costs. Various other indirect costs incurred in the operation of a factory are regarded as part of factory overhead. Examples of these manufacturing costs are depreciation of machinery and factory buildings, insurance and property taxes on plant assets, and electricity used for lighting and air conditioning.

The various production cost elements may be summarized as shown in Illustration 20.2.

Illustration 20.3 provides an idea of how the various kinds of cost dollars are assumed to flow into the products being manufactured.

ILLUSTRATION 20.3

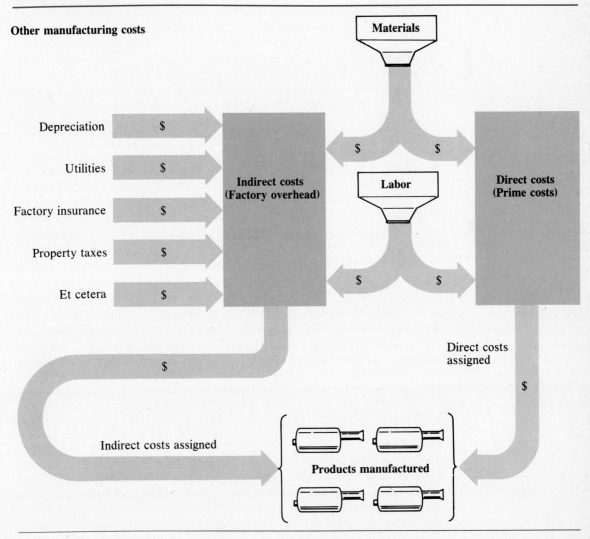

PERIODIC INVENTORY SYSTEM FOR PRODUCT COSTS

The manner in which manufacturing cost elements move through the accounts depends on whether inventory accounts are kept on a periodic or a perpetual basis. You may recall from Chapter 7 that under a periodic inventory system, inventory accounts are adjusted only at the end of each period. On the other hand, under a perpetual inventory system, inventory accounts show the flows of inventory quantities during the accounting period.

Product Cost Flows Through a Periodic System

In a periodic inventory system, product costs are accumulated throughout the period in temporary equity accounts. At the end of the accounting period, the temporary accounts are closed out and inventory accounts are corrected. The main difference between accounting for manufacturing and accounting for merchandising by means of a periodic inventory system is that end-of-period work is more complex with manufacturing systems.

A Manufacturing Summary account may be used for summarizing product costs and arriving at the cost of goods completed during the period. Illustration 20.4 shows one approach for moving product costs through the accounts within a periodic inventory system.

Under a periodic system, inventory accounts show beginning balances throughout an accounting period. Factory costs are accumulated in Materials Purchases, Factory Labor, and Other Manufacturing Costs accounts until the end of the period, at which time the balances in these accounts are transferred to the Manufacturing Summary account, as represented by the short dashed lines in Illustration 20.4. The beginning inventories of materials and goods in process are also transferred to the Manufacturing Summary account. The Manufacturing Summary account is then reduced by the ending inventories of materials and work in process (indicated by long dashed lines in the illustration), leaving as the Manufacturing Summary account balance at this point the cost of goods completed (finished) during the period. The cost of goods completed is then transferred to the Cost of Goods Sold account or perhaps, depending on the procedures used, to an Income Summary account. Under either approach, a further step is required in order to update the Finished Goods Inventory account to show the correct end-of-period balance.

Manufacturing Work Sheet

The main difference in the work sheets for manufacturing concerns, as compared with those for merchandising companies, is the use of an additional set of columns for summarizing the cost of goods completed during the period. The trial balance and adjustments columns have been omitted from the work sheet in Illustration 20.5 on page 846 in order to focus attention on

ILLUSTRATION 20.4

PRODUCT COST FLOWS
Periodic Inventory System

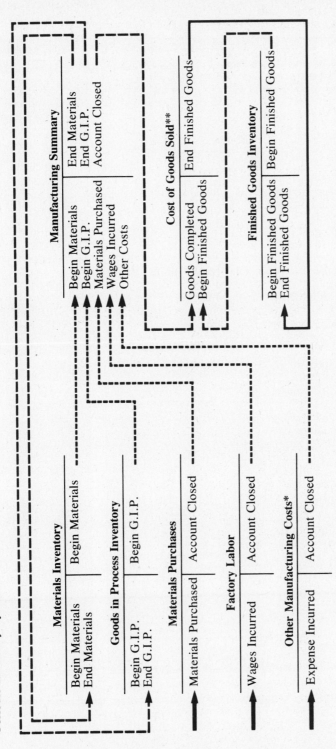

* These costs may be accumulated in any number of accounts, depending upon the circumstances and the informational needs.

** The Cost of Goods Sold account is closed to Retained Earnings along with the other temporary equity accounts.

845

ILLUSTRATION 20.5

OBJECTIVE 4a. Prepare
an end-of-period work
sheet for a manufacturing
concern using a periodic
inventory system.

PRODO MANUFACTURING CORP.
Work Sheet
For the Year Ended December 31, 19— —

Accounts	Adjusted Trial Balance	
	Debit	*Credit*
Cash	10,500	
Accounts Receivable	300,210	
Allowance for Doubtful Accounts		30,000
Beginning Inventories		
Materials	185,000	
Goods in Process	37,200	
Finished Goods	260,000	
Machinery and Equipment	433,000	
Accumulated Depreciation—Mach. and Equip.		120,000
Building	200,000	
Accumulated Depreciation—Building		60,000
Land	170,000	
Accounts Payable		251,640
Wages Payable		2,240
Income Taxes Payable		59,250
Mortgage Payable		200,000
Common Stock, $10 par		300,000
Retained Earnings		468,100
Sales		2,400,000
Materials Purchases	901,420	
Factory Labor	766,700	
Other Manufacturing Costs	382,910	
General and Administrative Expenses	73,680	
Selling Expenses	104,360	
Interest Expense	7,000	
Income Taxes	59,250	
	3,891,230	3,891,230
Ending Inventories		
Materials		
Goods in Process		
Finished Goods		
Cost of Goods Completed		
Net Income		

Manufacturing Summary		Income Statement		Balance Sheet	
Debit	*Credit*	*Debit*	*Credit*	*Debit*	*Credit*
				10,500	
				300,210	
					30,000
185,000					
37,200					
		260,000			
				433,000	
					120,000
				200,000	
					60,000
				170,000	
					251,640
					2,240
					59,250
					200,000
					300,000
					468,100
			2,400,000		
901,420					
766,700					
382,910					
		73,680			
		104,360			
		7,000			
		59,250			
	164,000			164,000	
	42,000			42,000	
			295,000	295,000	
2,273,230	206,000				
	2,067,230	2,067,230			
2,273,230	2,273,230	2,571,520	2,695,000	1,614,710	1,491,230
		123,480			123,480
		2,695,000	2,695,000	1,614,710	1,614,710

the manufacturing summary columns. Except for inventory adjustments, adjusting entries for manufacturing concerns are quite similar to those for other types of entities.

As pointed out before, there are a variety of acceptable procedures for doing bookkeeping and accounting. Prodo Manufacturing Corporation maintains control accounts for Other Manufacturing Costs, General and Administrative Expenses, and Selling Expenses in the general ledger, while maintaining more detailed classifications of these expense categories in separate subsidiary expense ledgers. For example, the manufacturing costs ledger contains separate subsidiary accounts for Property Tax, Expired Insurance, and Building Depreciation.

Do not let the way in which inventories are portrayed in the work sheet confuse you. The components of cost of goods completed are shown in the manufacturing summary columns, and the components of cost of goods sold appear in the income statement columns. The inventory accounts are adjusted with a separate set of entries, which are illustrated a little later in this chapter.

Schedule of Cost of Goods Completed

From the information contained in the Manufacturing Summary columns of the work sheet, we can prepare a *schedule of cost of goods completed. This schedule, sometimes called a* **manufacturing statement** *or* **statement of goods finished,** *supports the income statement in that it provides details about manufacturing costs that may be of interest to some statement users.*

The schedule shown in Illustration 20.6 contains information that came directly from the manufacturing summary columns of the work sheet.

ILLUSTRATION 20.6

OBJECTIVE 4b. Prepare a schedule of cost of goods completed.

PRODO MANUFACTURING CORPORATION
Schedule of Cost of Goods Completed
For the Year Ended December 31, 19--

Goods in process, Jan. 1		$ 37,200
Cost of materials used		
Materials inventory, Jan. 1	$ 185,000	
Materials purchases	901,420	
Cost of materials available	$1,086,420	
Materials inventory, Dec. 31	164,000	
Cost of materials used	$ 922,420	
Factory labor	766,700	
Other manufacturing costs	382,910	
Total cost added to process		2,072,030
Total cost in process		$2,109,230
Goods in process, Dec. 31		42,000
Cost of goods completed		$2,067,230

ILLUSTRATION 20.7

	MANUFACTURING ADJUSTMENTS		
Dec. 31	Manufacturing Summary	2,273,230	
	Materials Inventory		185,000
	Goods in Process		37,200
	Materials Purchases		901,420
	Factory Labor		766,700
	Other Manufacturing Costs		382,910
	To transfer to Manufacturing Summary the manufacturing accounts with debit balances.		
31	Materials Inventory	164,000	
	Goods in Process	42,000	
	Manufacturing Summary		206,000
	To remove ending materials and goods in process inventories from Manufacturing Summary.		
31	Cost of Goods Sold	2,067,230	
	Manufacturing Summary		2,067,230
	To transfer to Cost of Goods Sold the cost of goods completed during the year.		
31	Cost of Goods Sold	260,000	
	Finished Goods		260,000
	To transfer beginning finished goods to Cost of Goods Sold.		
31	Finished Goods	295,000	
	Cost of Goods Sold		295,000
	To set up ending finished goods inventory.		

OBJECTIVE 4c. Prepare entries to adjust inventory accounts and record cost of goods sold.

Adjustments for Cost of Goods Completed and Sold

Adjusting entries are needed to recognize the cost of goods completed and update the inventory accounts. Notice how the entries in Illustration 20.7 follow the cost-flow diagram shown earlier in Illustration 20.4.

The T-accounts in Illustration 20.8 on the next page show how the Manufacturing Summary account identifies the product costs for the period and how it ties in with Cost of Goods Sold.

Closing Entries

When inventories have been adjusted, and cost of goods sold determined, closing entries may be made for a manufacturing concern much the same as for other entities. Prodo's revenue and expense accounts may be closed to Retained Earnings by means of a single entry, as shown in Illustration 20.9 on the next page, or by any series of entries that arrive at the same end result. As in the case of service and merchandising concerns, some accountants prefer to use an Income Summary account in the closing process.

ILLUSTRATION 20.8

Manufacturing Summary			
Beg. Materials	185,000	End. Materials	164,000
Beg. Goods in Process	37,200	End. Goods in Process	42,000
Materials Purchases	901,420	Goods Completed	2,067,230
Factory Labor	766,700		
Manufacturing Expenses	382,910		
Cost of Goods Sold			
Goods Completed	2,067,230	End. Finished Goods	295,000
Beg. Finished Goods	260,000		

ILLUSTRATION 20.9

**OBJECTIVE 4d. Prepare
closing entries.**

	CLOSING ENTRY		
Dec. 31	Sales	2,400,000	
	Cost of Goods Sold		2,032,230
	General and Administrative Expenses		73,680
	Selling Expenses		104,360
	Interest Expense		7,000
	Income Taxes		59,250
	Retained Earnings		123,480
	To close revenue and expense accounts and reflect net income in Retained Earnings.		

FINANCIAL STATEMENTS FOR A MANUFACTURING CONCERN

Except for the schedule of cost of goods completed, financial statements for manufacturing concerns look much like those for merchandising entities. The main difference in the income statement is that cost of goods completed is substituted for merchandise purchases in the cost of goods sold calculation. If desired, a cost of goods sold schedule may be prepared separate from the income statement, with only the total cost of goods sold appearing in the income statement. And the schedule of cost of goods completed is sometimes combined with cost of goods sold as one integrated schedule supporting the income statement.

Unless they are condensed into one figure, three inventory categories will appear among the current assets on the balance sheet. As a rule, manufacturing companies show much larger investments in machinery, equipment, and buildings than do merchandising firms.

ILLUSTRATION 20.10

PRODO MANUFACTURING CORPORATION
Income Statement
For the Year Ended December 31, 19--

Sales		$2,400,000
Cost of goods sold		
Finished goods, Jan. 1	$ 260,000	
Cost of goods completed (see schedule)	2,067,230	
Goods available for sale	$2,327,230	
Finished goods, Dec. 31	295,000	2,032,230
Gross Profit		$ 367,770
Operating expenses		
General and administrative	$ 73,680	
Selling	104,360	178,040
Net Operating Income		$ 189,730
Interest expense		7,000
Net Income Before Income Taxes		$ 182,730
Income taxes		59,250
Net Income		$ 123,480
Earnings Per Share		$4.12

Illustrations 20.10 and 20.11 (next page) show how an income statement and balance sheet might appear for a relatively small and uncomplicated manufacturing entity. The retained earnings statement and statement of changes in financial position are not presented, since they are not prepared any differently for manufacturing concerns.

PRODUCT COST FLOWS THROUGH A PERPETUAL SYSTEM

In a perpetual inventory system, the inventory accounts reflect increases and decreases in inventory levels as they occur. Many manufacturing concerns use cost accounting systems that move costs through the inventory accounts as production activity takes place. There are many systems of accounting for production costs. Illustration 20.12 on page 853 is an oversimplified view of how product costs move through a perpetual system.

The approaches for accounting for products on a perpetual basis are explored in the following chapter. The presentation of financial statements is unaffected by the kind of cost system used.

ILLUSTRATION 20.11

PRODO MANUFACTURING CORPORATION
Balance Sheet
December 31, 19--

ASSETS

Current

Cash		$ 10,500
Accounts receivable	$300,210	
Less: Allowance for doubtful accounts	30,000	270,210

Inventories			
Materials	$164,000		
Goods in process	42,000		
Finished goods	295,000	501,000	
Total current assets			$ 781,710

Noncurrent

Machinery and equipment	$433,000		
Less: Accumulated depreciation	120,000	$313,000	
Building	$200,000		
Less: Accumulated depreciation	60,000	140,000	
Land		170,000	
Total noncurrent assets			623,000
Total Assets			$1,404,710

LIABILITIES

Current

Accounts payable	$251,640	
Wages payable	2,240	
Income taxes payable	59,250	
Total current liabilities		$313,130

Noncurrent

Mortgage payable		200,000
Total Liabilities		$ 513,130

SHAREHOLDERS' EQUITY

Common stock, $10 par	$300,000	
Retained earnings	591,580	
Total Shareholders' Equity		891,580
Total Liabilities and Shareholders' Equity		$1,404,710

ILLUSTRATION 20.12

PRODUCT COST FLOWS
Perpetual Inventory System

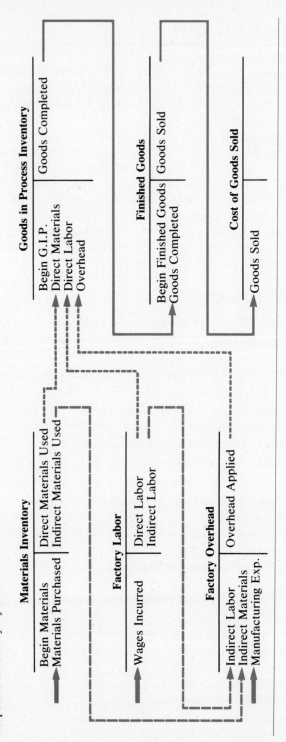

SUMMARY OF CHAPTER 20

Manufacturing concerns combine factors of production to create products that did not previously exist. Either a periodic or a perpetual system might be used for assigning product costs to inventory accounts. Manufacturing concerns normally have three inventory accounts: Materials, Goods in Process, and Finished Goods.

There are three elements of product costs: direct materials, direct labor, and factory overhead. Factory overhead consists of indirect materials, indirect labor, and all other indirect manufacturing expenses.

Manufacturing work sheets usually show the components of cost of goods completed in a separate set of manufacturing summary columns. A schedule of cost of goods completed is prepared to support the income statement for a manufacturing concern. When a periodic inventory system is used, the ending inventories may be updated by means of special manufacturing adjustments at the end of each period.

GLOSSARY FOR CHAPTER 20

Direct costs (prime costs)   The costs of both direct materials and direct labor.

Direct labor   Services supplied by employees who work directly on goods being produced.

Direct materials   Materials and parts that become embodied in finished products.

Factor of production   A resource that is used in a production process.

Factory overhead (manufacturing overhead, factory burden)   The costs of indirect materials and indirect labor, and all other indirect manufacturing costs.

Finished goods inventory   Completed goods awaiting sale.

Goods in process inventory   Incomplete products still in the production process.

Indirect costs   Costs that are not directly identifiable with goods being produced.

Indirect labor   Services performed by factory employees who do not work directly on goods being produced.

Indirect materials   Materials that are consumed in the factory without going directly into the goods being produced.

Manufacturing   The process of combining various resources to produce goods that did not previously exist.

Materials inventory   Materials on hand that have not yet been put into the production process.

Product costs   Costs associated with the manufacture of goods.

Purchased parts   Materials that have been processed by suppliers for specific purposes.

Raw materials   Materials that have not already been processed by suppliers, or that have been processed only for general use.

Schedule of cost of goods completed (manufacturing statement, statement of goods finished)   A schedule that supports the income statement in that it provides details about manufacturing costs.

SELF-QUIZ ON OBJECTIVES FOR CHAPTER 20
Solutions to Self-Quiz begin on page B-60.

1. **OBJECTIVE 1.** Differentiate between manufacturing and merchandising operations.

2. **OBJECTIVE 2.** Name and define the three types of inventories used in manufacturing operations.

3. **OBJECTIVE 3.** Name the three elements of cost assigned to manufactured goods, and state what is included in each element.

4. A trial balance and additional data are provided here and on the next page for Tempo Manufacturing Corporation. The account balances reflect all adjustments except the updating of inventory accounts and the recognition of cost of goods sold. Tempo uses a periodic inventory system for accounting for product costs.

	Debit	Credit
TEMPO MANUFACTURING CORPORATION		
Adjusted Trial Balance		
For the Year Ended December 31, 19 – –		
Cash	118,410	
Accounts Receivable	498,600	
Allowance for Doubtful Accounts		40,000
Beginning Inventories		
Materials	137,500	
Goods in Process	181,940	
Finished Goods	316,330	
Land	280,000	
Building	550,000	
Accumulated Depreciation—Building		150,000
Machinery and Equipment	424,000	
Accumulated Depreciation—Machinery and Equipment		180,000
Accounts Payable		385,200
Interest Payable		2,500
Income Taxes Payable		293,000
Bonds Payable		500,000
Common Stock, $5 par		200,000
Capital in Excess of Par		275,000
Retained Earnings		186,250
Sales		3,430,700
Materials Purchases	984,200	
Factory Labor	949,480	
Other Manufacturing Costs	478,140	
General and Administrative Expenses	182,300	
Selling Expenses	258,750	
Interest Expense	30,000	
Income Taxes	253,000	
	5,642,650	5,642,650

Ending Inventories	
Materials	$142,700
Goods in Process	159,230
Finished Goods	305,500

a. **OBJECTIVE 4a.** Prepare an end-of-period work sheet for Tempo Corporation, starting with the adjusted trial balance columns.

b. **OBJECTIVE 4b.** Prepare a schedule of cost of goods completed.

c. **OBJECTIVE 4c.** Make journal entries to adjust the inventory accounts and set up cost of goods sold for the year.

d. **OBJECTIVE 4d.** Make a closing entry (or entries) to close the temporary equity accounts that remain open after doing part (c).

DISCUSSION QUESTIONS FOR CHAPTER 20

1. Merchandising firms are concerned mainly with merchandise inventories. What are the three types of inventories used in manufacturing operations, and why does the nature of manufacturing make it desirable to separate the inventory types for accounting purposes?

2. Under what circumstances will the cost of goods completed equal the cost of goods sold?

3. How do the inventory accounts in a perpetual inventory system differ from the inventory accounts in a periodic inventory system?

4. What is the difference between direct costs and indirect costs?

5. What is the primary type of utility created by manufacturing firms?

6. Which of the following would most likely be included in factory overhead?
   a. Cost of machinery repairs
   b. Cost of sheet steel used by an automobile manufacturing company
   c. Fee charged by the CPA firm that audits the corporation's records
   d. Cost of factory insurance
   e. Cost of renting factory building
   f. Cost of advertising finished goods
   g. Depreciation on production equipment
   h. Wages paid to a machine operator
   i. Wages paid to factory managers
   j. Wages paid to plant security guards

7. Which inventory account would contain the cost of each of the asset items listed here?
   a. Soft drinks bottled and cased in a bottling plant
   b. Logs in the warehouse of a lumber mill

c. Tires awaiting sale in the warehouse of a rubber company

d. Cloth cut into pattern shape and size by workers for a clothing manufacturing firm

e. Partially completed TV sets in an electronics manufacturing firm

f. Sand stored in bins at a glass manufacturing plant

g. Flour bagged and on hand in a flour mill

h. Flour on hand in a commercial bakery

EXERCISES FOR CHAPTER 20

20.1. Use the following data to calculate the cost of materials used during the year.

Beginning Materials Inventory	$ 297,000
Ending Materials Inventory	184,000
Materials Purchases during the year	1,361,000
Beginning Goods in Process	78,000
Ending Goods in Process	89,000

20.2. Use the following data to calculate the cost of goods completed during the year.

Beginning Goods in Process	$ 58,000
Ending Goods in Process	89,000
Cost of Materials Used	942,000
Factory Labor	671,000
Other Manufacturing Costs	293,000
Beginning Finished Goods	345,000
Ending Finished Goods	310,000

20.3. Calculate the cost of goods sold for the year, using the data shown here.

Beginning Finished Goods	$ 169,000
Ending Finished Goods	186,000
Cost of Goods Completed	1,744,000
General and Administrative Expenses	88,000
Selling Expenses	142,000

20.4. Selected information from the adjusted trial balance at December 31 for Gordo Manufacturing Corporation is provided on the next page. Prepare a closing entry for the corporation at December 31.

	Debit	Credit
Materials Inventory	162,000	
Goods in Process	71,000	
Finished Goods	283,000	
Retained Earnings		10,400,000
Sales		4,870,000
Cost of Goods Sold	3,165,000	
General and Administrative Expense	384,000	
Selling Expense	651,000	
Interest Expense	22,000	
Income Taxes	128,000	

20.5. Use the following data to calculate the cost of goods completed during the year.

Increase in Materials Inventory during the year	$ 81,000
Increase in Goods in Process during the year	28,000
Materials Purchases	852,000
Factory Labor	184,000
Other Manufacturing Costs	68,000

20.6. Use the following data to calculate the cost of goods sold during the year.

Increase in Materials Inventory during the year	$ 114,000
Decrease in Goods in Process during the year	115,000
Decrease in Finished Goods during the year	90,000
Materials Purchases	1,000,000
Factory Labor	100,000
Other Manufacturing Costs	200,000

PROBLEMS FOR CHAPTER 20
Alternate Problems for this chapter begin on page D-109.

20.7. Selected data for Melva Company are as follows.

Materials Inventory, Jan. 1	$ 111,000
Materials Inventory, Dec. 31	208,000
Goods in Process, Jan. 1	97,000
Goods in Process, Dec. 31	83,000
Materials Purchases	2,088,000
Factory Labor	749,000
Other Manufacturing Costs	314,000

Required

1) Prepare a schedule of cost of goods completed.

2) Prepare adjusting entries to reflect cost of goods completed into Manufacturing Summary and to update the inventory accounts.

20.8. An adjusted trial balance and additional data are provided here for Quando Manufacturing Corporation. The account balances include all adjustments except the updating of inventory accounts and the recognition of cost of goods sold. Quando uses the periodic inventory system for accounting for product costs.

QUANDO MANUFACTURING CORPORATION Adjusted Trial Balance December 31, 19--	Debit	Credit
Cash	24,000	
Accounts Receivable	263,000	
Allowance for Doubtful Accounts		21,000
Beginning Inventories		
Materials	54,000	
Goods in Process	38,000	
Finished Goods	111,000	
Land	92,000	
Building	406,000	
Accumulated Depreciation—Building		84,000
Machinery and Equipment	364,000	
Accumulated Depreciation—Machinery and Equipment		122,000
Accounts Payable		212,000
Interest Payable		9,000
Income Taxes Payable		48,000
Bonds Payable		200,000
Common Stock, $10 par		250,000
Capital in Excess of Par		46,000
Retained Earnings		213,000
Sales		2,684,000
Materials Purchases	846,000	
Factory Labor	756,000	
Other Manufacturing Costs	433,000	
General and Administrative Expenses	96,000	
Selling Expenses	249,000	
Interest Expense	21,000	
Income Taxes	136,000	
	3,889,000	3,889,000

Ending Inventories	
Materials	$50,000
Goods in Process	49,000
Finished Goods	98,000

Required

1) Prepare a manufacturing work sheet similar to the one illustrated in the chapter.

2) Prepare a schedule of cost of goods completed.

3) Prepare an income statement.

4) Prepare a balance sheet.

20.9. An adjusted trial balance and additional data are provided here for Roritan Manufacturing, Inc. The account balances reflect all adjustments except the updating of inventory accounts and the recognition of cost of goods sold. Roritan uses a periodic inventory system.

RORITAN MANUFACTURING, INC. Adjusted Trial Balance December 31, 19--		
	Debit	**Credit**
Cash	31,000	
Accounts Receivable	88,000	
Beginning Inventories		
Materials	64,000	
Goods in Process	117,000	
Finished Goods	121,000	
Land	140,000	
Building	806,000	
Accumulated Depreciation—Building		202,000
Machinery and Equipment	480,000	
Accumulated Depreciation—Machinery and Equipment		198,000
Accounts Payable		104,000
Income Taxes Payable		61,000
Notes Payable (180 days)		280,000
Common Stock, no par		600,000
Retained Earnings		192,000
Sales		2,430,000
Materials Purchases	711,000	
Factory Labor	590,000	
Other Manufacturing Costs	298,000	
General and Administrative Expenses	169,000	
Selling Expenses	242,000	
Income Taxes	210,000	
	4,067,000	4,067,000

Ending Inventories	
Materials	$ 71,000
Goods in Process	122,000
Finished Goods	136,000

Required

1) Prepare an end-of-period work sheet for Roritan, Inc., starting with adjusted trial balance columns.

2) Prepare a schedule of cost of goods completed.

3) Make journal entries to adjust the inventory accounts and set up cost of goods sold for the year.

4) Make a closing entry (or entries) to close the temporary equity accounts that remain open after doing part (3).

5) Prepare an income statement.

6) Prepare a balance sheet.

20.10. Provided here are selected data for Jolly Corporation.

Materials Inventory, Jan. 1	$ 100,000
Materials Inventory, Dec. 31	198,000
Goods in Process, Jan. 1	54,000
Goods in Process, Dec. 31	54,000
Finished Goods, Jan. 1	368,000
Finished Goods, Dec. 31	270,000
Materials Purchases	1,863,000
Factory Labor	161,000
Other Manufacturing Costs	387,000

Required

Prepare a schedule of cost of goods sold that shows clearly (as part of the schedule) the components of cost of goods completed during the year.

20.11. An adjusted trial balance and additional data are provided on the next page for the Scarlet Corporation. The account balances have been adjusted except for updating the inventory accounts and recognizing cost of goods sold. The corporation accounts on a fiscal year ending June 30.

SCARLET CORPORATION Adjusted Trial Balance June 30, 19--		
	Debit	**Credit**
Cash	29,000	
Accounts Receivable	76,000	
Beginning Inventories		
Materials	18,000	
Goods in Process	34,000	
Finished Goods	40,000	
Land	108,000	
Depreciable Assets	636,000	
Accumulated Depreciation		222,000
Accounts Payable		58,000
Income Taxes Payable		–0–
Bonds Payable		250,000
Common Stock		300,000
Retained Earnings		70,000
Gain from Sale of Depreciable Assets		24,000
Sales		888,000
Materials Purchases	340,000	
Factory Labor	200,000	
Other Manufacturing Costs	92,000	
General and Administrative Expenses	84,000	
Selling Expenses	128,000	
Interest Expense	27,000	
Income Taxes	–0–	
	1,812,000	1,812,000

Ending Inventories	
Materials	$13,000
Goods in Process	26,000
Finished Goods	19,000

Required

1) Prepare a manufacturing work sheet similar to the one illustrated in the chapter.

2) Determine net *operating* income (or loss) for the year.

20.12. Ending inventory data and data from an adjusted trial balance for the Lion Company, Inc., are as follows.

Ending Inventories	
Materials	$12,000
Goods in Process	14,000
Finished Goods	24,000

Adjusted Trial Balance Data December 31, 19--	Debit	Credit
Beginning Inventories		
Materials	9,000	
Goods in Process	24,000	
Finished Goods	21,000	
Sales		550,000
Materials Purchases	90,000	
Factory Labor	190,000	
Other Manufacturing Costs	140,000	
General and Administrative Expenses	21,000	
Selling Expenses	59,000	
Interest Expense	8,000	
Income Taxes	13,000	

Required

1) Make journal entries to adjust inventory accounts and set up cost of goods sold for the year.

2) Make a closing entry (or entries) to close the temporary equity accounts that remain open after doing part (1).

3) Prepare a schedule of cost of goods completed and an income statement for the Lion Company, Inc.

COMPREHENSION PROBLEMS FOR CHAPTER 20

20.13. Shown here are manufacturing cost data, with some amounts missing, for Rutgers Manufacturing, Inc.

RUTGERS MANUFACTURING, INC.	Beginning	Ending
Materials Inventory	$48,000	$ a?
Goods in Process	67,000	51,000
Finished Goods	b?	14,000
For the Year Ended December 31		
Materials Purchases		$186,000
Cost of Materials Used		203,000
Factory Labor		c?
Other Manufacturing Costs		54,000
Cost Added to Process		d?
Cost of Goods Completed		353,000
Goods Available for Sale		360,000
Cost of Goods Sold		e?

Required

Determine the missing amounts (a) through (e), and prepare a schedule of cost of goods sold that presents clearly within the schedule the components of cost of goods completed.

20.14. Shown here are selected data, with some amounts missing, for Wooglin Corporation.

WOOGLIN CORPORATION		
	Beginning	**Ending**
Materials Inventory	$ a?	$ b?
Goods in Process	c?	221,000
Finished Goods	450,000	g?
For the Year Ended December 31		
Materials Purchases		$ 685,000
Cost of Materials Available		804,000
Cost of Materials Used		783,000
Factory Labor		354,000
Other Manufacturing Costs		d?
Total Cost Added to Process		1,206,000
Total Cost in Process during the year		e?
Cost of Goods Completed		1,183,000
Goods Available for Sale		f?
Cost of Goods Sold		1,411,000
Operating Expenses		314,000
Income Taxes		87,000
Sales		2,000,000
Number of common shares outstanding, 100,000		

Required

Determine the missing amounts (a) through (g), and prepare an income statement accompanied by a separate schedule of cost of goods completed.

Cost Accounting Systems

Perpetual cost systems attempt to identify costs with either customer orders (jobs) or production processes. Section A of Chapter 21 concentrates on job order cost systems, and Section B deals with process cost systems. Although the end objective of all product cost systems is to identify production costs with goods being produced, the methods may differ.

Section A first considers the purposes and limitations of cost systems and then introduces a simple job order cost system. The determination of a factory overhead rate and the disposition of underapplied or overapplied overhead are also covered in Section A.

Section B considers the nature of process cost systems and illustrates the flow of costs through a simple process system. An approach for calculating equivalent units of production is demonstrated. Equivalent unit data are then used in the transfer of costs as products move from department to department and eventually into finished goods inventory. Production reports for cost centers are also discussed and illustrated.

SECTION 21.A

Job Order Cost Systems

OBJECTIVES

This section concentrates on job order systems for accounting for manufacturing costs. At the conclusion of your study, you should be able to

1. State four general purposes of cost accounting systems.
2. State the circumstances under which a job order cost system is most likely to be used.
3. Calculate an overhead application rate, given total estimated costs of factory overhead and direct labor for a period.
4. Make journal entries to record the following, assuming use of a job order cost system:
   a. The cost of materials used for Goods in Process and Factory Overhead.
   b. The cost of factory labor charged to Goods in Process and Factory Overhead.
   c. The application of factory overhead to Goods in Process.
   d. The transfer of cost of completed jobs to Finished Goods.
   e. The sale of products, including recognition of Cost of Goods Sold.

PURPOSES OF COST SYSTEMS

Cost accounting involves the identification and control of costs and the processing and reporting of cost information. Although all types of costs are accounted for, the expression *cost accounting* usually refers to accounting for *product costs* in manufacturing concerns. In fact, accountants sometimes use the expressions *factory accounting* and *cost accounting* interchangeably.

A cost accounting system is usually just a part of the overall system of accounting for an entity. Although cost accounting systems serve many goals, their overall purposes may be stated as follows.

OBJECTIVE 1. State four general purposes of cost accounting systems.

> **PURPOSES OF COST SYSTEMS**
> Cost systems provide manufacturing cost data for
> 1. Preparing financial statements.
> 2. Controlling and minimizing current costs.
> 3. Evaluating past performance.
> 4. Planning for the future.

LIMITATIONS OF COST SYSTEMS

Many people attribute to product cost data more accuracy than the figures deserve. Cost accounting systems are merely systematic approaches for *approximating* product cost movements in a consistent manner. The more complex the production process, the more difficult it is to pin down cost allocations. Some students are shocked to learn that accountants cannot calculate with precision the cost of producing a new automobile, a gallon of gasoline, a cured ham, or any other product of a complicated manufacturing process.

There are a number of reasons why product costs usually cannot be precisely determined. The processing of accounting data is in itself a costly matter. Oftentimes, it is simply not practical to accurately identify particular cost elements with specific units of product. As pointed out in the previous chapter, costs are moved through a perpetual cost accounting system as production takes place during an accounting period. In order to provide timely data, costs are frequently estimated.

Owing to their indirect nature, factory overhead costs cannot be traced positively to product units. Instead they are *assumed* to flow in proportion to some direct measure such as direct labor or direct materials. Another problem area, somewhat akin to that of assigning overhead costs, is the allocation of joint costs.

Joint Costs

As pointed out in Chapter 20, direct costs of materials and labor can be associated with a product more easily than can indirect costs. However, where *joint products* are produced from a common raw material, we have no logical basis for allocating the materials cost between the different products. *Joint products result when two or more distinct goods are produced from a common raw material.* The production processes of refining petroleum, slaughtering animals, and sawing logs are just a few of the many instances where joint products result. Consider, for example, a barrel of crude oil, from which gasoline, fuel oil, motor oil, grease, wax, and a multitude of other products are refined.

*Joint costs, sometimes called **common costs**, are costs incurred in connection with the manufacture of two or more distinct products. **Joint materials costs** are the costs of materials from which two or more distinct goods are produced. **Joint processing costs** are the labor and overhead costs incurred in the production of joint products.* A barrel of petroleum may yield various grades of gasoline, kerosene, fuel oil, lubricating oil, benzene, petrochemicals, and other distinct products. Similarly, a number of meat products are derived from the slaughter of a pig, a number of lumber products from the sawing of logs, and so on.

Accountants are not able to determine exactly how much of either the joint materials costs or the joint processing costs are attributable to each joint product that results. For example, no one can say precisely how much of the cost of a pig, or the cost of slaughtering, is attributable to the pork chops.

As an expediency, an approach often used is to assign joint costs to products in proportion to their *relative market values*. If, for example, a bushel of corn costing $5 is milled to obtain cornmeal worth $4 and grits worth $6, the corn cost would be apportioned as follows.

RELATIVE MARKET VALUE FORMULA

$$\frac{\text{Value of one product}}{\text{Value of all products}} \times \text{Joint cost} = \text{Cost assigned to one product}$$

$$\frac{\$4}{\$4 + \$6} \times \$5 = \$2 \text{ corn cost assigned to meal}$$

$$\frac{\$6}{\$4 + \$6} \times \$5 = \$3 \text{ corn cost assigned to grits}$$

The relative market values approach simply assigns joint costs in proportion to a product's *ability to bear* the cost, as measured by its worth. This is not to say that joint costs logically flow in proportion to product values.

As you study cost systems, try to keep in mind that they are merely orderly and systematic methods for allocating manufacturing costs and for moving product costs through the accounts.

TYPES OF COST SYSTEMS

Manufacturing concerns, and the goods they produce, are many and varied. Every cost system should be tailored to meet an entity's particular needs. Basically, a cost system is a paper representation of production activity.

A complex production process can be viewed as consisting of *segments* of activity. Production processes may be broken down, or segmented, according to areas of management *responsibility*. A production department normally has a supervisor, or foreman, who is responsible for managing the activity of that department. Production activities may be segmented by departments, divisions, or other organizational subdivisions.

Costs are sacrifices of resources that are incurred in the operation of a business. Production costs are measures of the resources used up in the manufacturing process. A departmental supervisor is usually held responsible for the costs incurred by his or her department.

Those subdivisions of an entity that incur costs are called cost centers. *A **cost center** can be any identifiable activity area in which someone is held* *responsible for the costs incurred.* Cost accounting systems should provide information about an entity's cost centers.

JOBS AS COST CENTERS

Some manufacturing companies produce goods that have been specially ordered by buyers. In other words, products are created according to the specifications of contracts between the buyers and the producer. Each product (or group of products) is produced to the order of the purchaser. Since each order is unique, each job may be viewed as a cost center. *A job order cost system attempts to identify production costs with customer orders.* Aerospace companies, shipbuilders, manufacturers of special machines, and construction companies are all entities that use job order cost systems. Thus a job order cost system is most often used where products are made individually or in batches to the specifications of customers.

OBJECTIVE 2. State the circumstances under which a job order cost system is most likely to be used.

A job may be started and completed in one area of the plant or at one particular construction site. Direct materials are brought to the job site, and employees go to the site to perform their direct labor. Overhead may be assumed to flow to each job, as depicted by Illustration 21.1.

JOB COST SHEETS

Where a job order cost system is used, costs assigned to each job are usually accumulated on a job cost sheet. *A job cost sheet is a form for accumulating the direct materials, direct labor, and overhead costs assigned to a particular production job.* A job may consist of a single specialized product or a quantity of identical items produced especially for a customer. The job cost sheet in Illustration 21.2 on the next page is for a specially designed tank for storing chemicals.

Although job cost sheets may vary in format, they all provide some means of accumulating direct materials and direct labor as these costs are

ILLUSTRATION 21.1

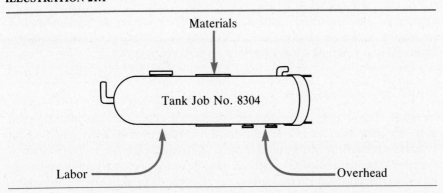

ILLUSTRATION 21.2

JOB COST SHEET

Job __8304__

Product __tank to order of Chem. Co.__　Quantity __1__

Started __January 11, 19--__　Completed __January 28, 19--__

Direct Materials			Direct Labor			
Date	Requisition	Amount		Date	Time Summary	Amount
19-- Jan. 11	1496	8,306 00		19-- Jan. 14	02	1,609 00
12	1504	824 00		21	03	396 00
18	1548	71 00		28	04	265 00
21	1575	92 00				2,270 00
		9,293 00				

Summary		
Direct Materials	9,293	00
Direct Labor	2,270	00
Overhead (_80_ % of Direct Labor)	1,816	00
Total Cost	13,379	00

---

applied to jobs. In many instances today, job costs are accumulated electronically, in which case the cost details for a job may be either displayed on a cathode ray tube or printed out as they are needed.

GOODS IN PROCESS

In a job cost system, the job cost sheets (or equivalent computer-stored data) for jobs in process are subsidiary records controlled by the Goods in Process account in the general ledger. Although changes in the Goods in Process account are usually aggregated and posted only at periodic intervals, it is nevertheless a *perpetual* inventory account. The frequency with which

ILLUSTRATION 21.3

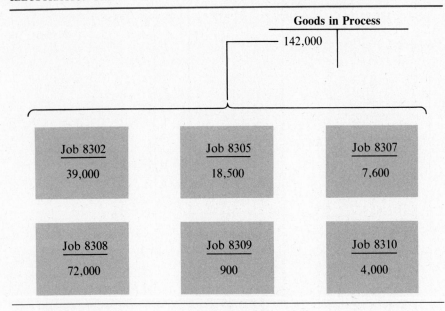

the account is updated varies according to the need for information and the preference of accountants.

As Illustration 21.3 implies, the total costs shown on the cost sheets for unfinished jobs should total to the balance of the Goods in Process account at any particular point in time.

RECORDING JOB COSTS

At the end of the previous chapter, a diagram was shown that depicted the flow of costs through a perpetual inventory system. That diagram is repeated in Illustration 21.4 on the next page so that you can refer to it as you study the movement of product costs through a simple job order cost system.

Materials

The materials inventory account, when maintained on a perpetual basis, must reflect purchases and uses of materials during an accounting period. You may recall from Chapter 7 how subsidiary inventory records are controlled by the inventory account in the general ledger when a perpetual system is used.

Factory materials are usually kept in a factory storeroom until they are issued for use. Factory workers must present a properly approved *materials*

ILLUSTRATION 21.4

PRODUCT COST FLOWS

Perpetual Inventory System

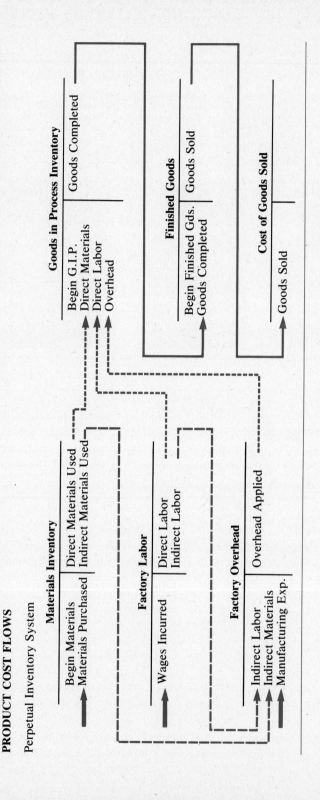

ILLUSTRATION 21.5

MATERIALS REQUISITION FORM

Date___1/11/--___   Materials Requisition No. 1496

___✓___Direct Materials   Job No.___8304___

_____Indirect Materials   Subsidiary Account No._____

Quantity	Material No.	Description	Unit Cost		Amount	
50	84	Sheet Steel, 8'x 4' x $\frac{3}{16}$"	166	12	8306	00

Approved	Issued	Received
C.J.L	M.K.M.	D.M.D

---

requisition form to the storeroom clerk as authorization to take materials from the storeroom. The materials requisition form should indicate the particular purpose for which the materials are to be used. The materials charged on January 11 to Job No. 8304, as shown on the job cost sheet in Illustration 21.2, were approved for issuance on the requisition form shown in Illustration 12.5.

Direct materials used are posted to job cost sheets either directly from materials requisition forms or from summaries of these forms. The requisition form also may be used as the basis for reducing the subsidiary inventory record for the quantities of materials withdrawn from the storeroom.

Materials issued for indirect use in the factory are so indicated on the materials requisition form. The Factory Overhead account in the general ledger may serve as a control account for an overhead cost subsidiary ledger, in which case the appropriate subsidiary account number will be noted on the materials requisition form. In the overhead subsidiary ledger, costs are summarized by categories—Maintenance, Machinery Depreciation, Electricity, Insurance, and so on.

At periodic intervals (daily, weekly, or monthly), the materials requisition forms are summarized for recording in the journal, as shown in Illustration 21.6 on the next page. Postings to an overhead subsidiary ledger may be made either from the materials requisition forms or from a summary of them.

ILLUSTRATION 21.6

OBJECTIVE 4a. Record the cost of materials used for Goods in Process and Factory Overhead.

JOB COST SHEET

Job ___8304___

Product _tank to order of Chem. Co._ Quantity __1__

Started _January 11, 19--_ Completed _January 28, 19--_

Direct Materials			Direct Labor		
Date	Requisition	Amount	Date	Time Summary	Amount
Jan. 11 19--	1496	8,306.00	Jan. 14 19--	02	1,609.00

MATERIALS REQUISITION FORM

Date ___1/11/--___   Materials Requisition No. 1496

✓ Direct Materials   Job No. ___8304___

___ Indirect materials   Subsidiary Account No. _____

Quantity	Material No.	Description	Unit Cost		Amount	
50	84	Steel Sheet 8' x 4' x 7/16"	166	12	8306	00

MATERIALS SUMMARY

Mat. Req. No.	Direct	Indirect
No. 1496	8,306	
No. 1497		972
Totals	335,000	30,850

MATERIALS LEDGER CARD		No. 84
Incr.	**Decr.**	**Bal.**
	8,306	XXX

General Journal

PAGE

Date	Account Names and Explanations	A/C #	Debit		Credit	
Jan. 31	Goods in Process		335,000	00		
	Factory Overhead		30,850	00		
	Materials Inventory				365,850	00
	To record materials used during					
	January.					

Labor

In a job order cost system, each job is charged with the cost of direct labor devoted to the job. Consequently, records must be maintained that allow direct labor to be identified with particular jobs. One approach is to have each employee fill out a time ticket upon completing a task. The time ticket identifies the job or overhead task worked on, the time involved, and the hourly rate of pay, as shown in Illustration 21.7.

ILLUSTRATION 21.7

```
┌─────────────────────────────────────────────────┐
│  Date ____1/11/--____      Time Ticket No. 7653   │
│                                                   │
│  Employee ___Sam Short___      __119__            │
│                  Name            No.              │
│                                                   │
│  Task ___Welding___                               │
│                                                   │
│  __✓__ Direct Labor      Job No. __8304__         │
│                                                   │
│  _____ Indirect Labor   Sub. Acct. No.____       │
│                                                   │
│  Started ___1:00___      Stopped ___4:00___       │
│                                                   │
│  Hours ___3:00___ Rate _$10.50_ Total _$31.50_    │
│                                                   │
│  Supervisor's Approval ___LD___                   │
└─────────────────────────────────────────────────┘
```

The time ticket may be summarized daily or weekly by job and overhead cost category. The time summary may then provide the information for postings to job cost sheets and overhead subsidiary accounts as well as the entry to record labor costs. Illustration 21.8 on the next page depicts the relationship between the time ticket and the other accounting records. The Factory Payroll account is debited as wages are paid in cash; a credit balance in Factory Payroll is a liability because it represents wages owed to employees.

Overhead

As pointed out in the previous chapter, factory overhead consists of indirect costs that are not easily traced to particular products. Nevertheless, it is an accepted accounting practice to assign to manufactured goods portions of the overhead costs incurred in the production process. The usual approach is to assign overhead costs to products in proportion to some identifiable base. The base most often used is direct labor dollars, but labor hours, machine hours, direct materials, and other bases are used when they are considered appropriate.

A predetermined *overhead rate* is calculated by relating the estimated total overhead for the period to the estimated base amount. For example, if total overhead cost for the year is expected to be $1,600,000, and if estimated direct labor cost for the same period is $2,000,000, a factory overhead rate of 80% may be determined as follows.

$$\frac{\text{Estimated total overhead}}{\text{Estimated total direct labor}} = \frac{\$1,600,000}{\$2,000,000} = 80\%$$

OBJECTIVE 3. Calculate an overhead application rate.

ILLUSTRATION 21.8

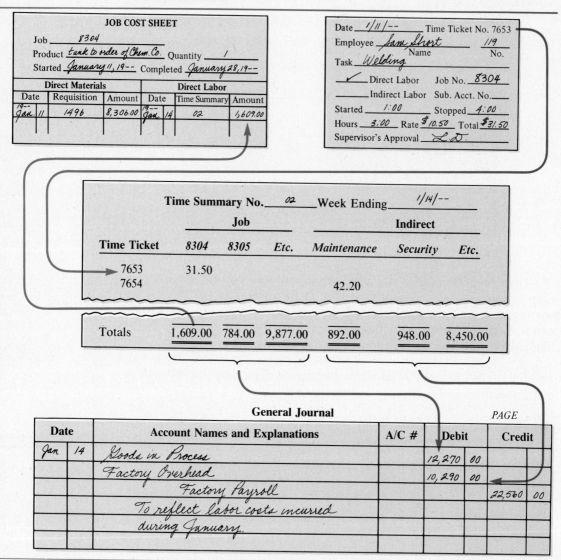

Thus *a factory overhead rate is the percentage of a determinable base amount that is used for purposes of assigning factory overhead costs to products.* For our example, 80¢ is assigned to a job for each dollar of direct labor identified with the job.

Overhead need not be applied to job cost sheets each time direct labor cost is posted. For the job cost sheet pictured earlier, the overhead was entered into the summary of total cost when the job was completed. Note that an 80% factory overhead rate was used for assigning overhead to the job.

At some point in time, an entry is made to reflect in the Goods in Process account the overhead costs applied to jobs. The following entry assumes that factory overhead is charged to Goods in Process on a monthly basis.

Jan. 31	Goods In Process	148,000	
	Factory Overhead		148,000
	Overhead applied to jobs at 80% of direct labor costs.		

OBJECTIVE 4c. Record the application of factory overhead to Goods in Process.

Underapplied and Overapplied Overhead. You can see from the Factory Overhead account in Illustration 21.9 that less overhead was applied for January than was incurred during the month. *A debit balance in an overhead account is referred to as* **underapplied overhead,** *since less overhead has been applied than was incurred for the period. A credit balance, on the other hand, is called* **overapplied overhead,** *because more overhead cost was applied than was incurred during the period.* Remember, an overhead application rate is based on estimations of both the overhead costs and the base for application, so it is not likely that overhead applications will exactly total to the actual overhead costs.

It is entirely possible that the underapplied overhead (debit balance) at the end of January will be canceled out by overapplications during other months of the year. Overhead costs may be high in some months and low in others owing to seasonal and other factors. For instance, electric bills are apt to be higher in very cold and very hot months because of heating and cooling requirements. Because of the tendency for overhead costs to vary,

ILLUSTRATION 21.9

	Factory Overhead			*ACCOUNT NO. 800*	
				Balance	
Date	**Item**	**Debit**	**Credit**	*Debit*	*Credit*
19--					
Jan. 7	Indirect Labor	8,460		8,460	
14	Indirect Labor	10,290		18,750	
21	Indirect Labor	9,720		28,470	
28	Indirect Labor	8,940		37,410	
31	Indirect Materials	30,850		68,260	
31	Other Mfg. Costs	84,600		152,860	
31	Applied to Goods in Process		148,000	4,860	

most accountants wait until the end of an accounting year to dispose of the Factory Overhead account balance.

When the year-end Factory Overhead balance (debit or credit) is small it is usually closed to Cost of Goods Sold; a large (significant) balance is usually apportioned between ending Goods in Process, Finished Goods, and Cost of Goods Sold for the year. The purpose of the apportionment is to adjust the applied overhead elements of each of the three accounts to the actual overhead for the year. Remember, overhead is applied during a year by means of an estimated overhead rate.

To illustrate the apportionment approach, let us assume that the entity has *underapplied overhead* of $400,000 at year-end, and that applied overhead components of ending Goods in Process, ending Finished Goods, and Cost of Goods Sold for the year are $100,000, $300,000, and $1,600,000, respectively. The apportionment process would increase the overhead in each account by 20%, as Illustration 21.10 shows.

The entry to dispose of the underapplied overhead would take the following form.

Dec. 31	Goods in Process	20,000	
	Finished Goods	60,000	
	Cost of Goods Sold	320,000	
	Factory Overhead		400,000
	To apportion underapplied factory overhead.		

Had there been an overapplied (credit) balance in the Factory Overhead account, the adjustment percentage would have been negative, and the adjustment amounts would have been credited to the Goods in Process, Finished Goods, and Cost of Goods Sold accounts.

ILLUSTRATION 21.10

APPORTIONMENT OF UNDERAPPLIED OVERHEAD

$$\frac{\text{Factory overhead balance}}{\text{Total overhead applied during the year}} = \text{Adjustment percentage}$$

$$\frac{\$400,000}{\$2,000,000} = 20\%$$

Account	Applied Overhead	×	Adjustment %	=	Dollar Adjustment
Goods in Process	$ 100,000	×	20%	=	$ 20,000
Finished Goods	300,000	×	20%	=	60,000
Cost of Goods Sold	1,600,000	×	20%	=	320,000
			Underapplied Overhead		$400,000

RECORDING COMPLETED JOBS

As jobs are completed, entries are made to transfer costs from Goods in Process to Finished Goods, as illustrated by the following entry.

Jan. 28	Finished Goods	13,379	
	Goods in Process		13,379
	Job 8304 completed and transferred to Finished Goods.		

OBJECTIVE 4d. Record the transfer of cost of completed jobs to Finished Goods.

RECORDING COST OF GOODS SOLD

As customers take legal title to the manufactured products, revenues are recognized and recorded. When a perpetual inventory system is used, Cost of Goods Sold is also recognized at the time that each sale is recorded. The following entry was made when the customer took possession of the tank manufactured as Job No. 8304.

Jan. 29	Accounts Receivable	18,000	
	Cost of Goods Sold	13,379	
	Sales		18,000
	Finished Goods		13,379
	Chem. Co. picked up Job No. 8304.		

OBJECTIVE 4e. Record the sale of products, including recognition of Cost of Goods Sold.

At this point you should review the cost-flow diagram shown earlier in Illustration 21.4. That diagram summarizes the flow of product costs through the general ledger control accounts. Under a perpetual inventory system, the Materials Inventory account is normally supported by subsidiary materials inventory records; Factory Overhead is supported by an overhead cost subsidiary ledger; Goods in Process by job cost sheets; and Finished Goods by finished goods inventory records.

GLOSSARY FOR SECTION 21.A

Cost accounting The identification and control of costs and the processing and reporting of cost information.

Cost center Any identifiable activity area in which someone is held responsible for the costs incurred.

Factory overhead rate The percentage of a determinable base amount that is used for purposes of assigning factory overhead costs to products.

Job cost sheet   A form for accumulating the direct materials, direct labor, and overhead costs assigned to a particular production job.

Job order cost system   A system that identifies production costs with customer orders.

Joint costs (common costs)   Costs that are incurred in connection with the manufacture of two or more distinct products.

Joint materials costs   Costs of materials from which two or more distinct goods are produced.

Joint processing costs   Labor and overhead costs incurred in the production of joint products.

Joint products   Two or more distinct goods produced from a common raw material.

Materials requisition form   A form that authorizes the taking of materials from a storeroom.

Overapplied overhead   A credit balance in an overhead account, indicating that more overhead cost has been applied than was incurred during the period.

Underapplied overhead   A debit balance in an overhead account, indicating that less overhead cost has been applied than was incurred for the period.

SELF-QUIZ ON OBJECTIVES FOR SECTION 21.A
Solutions to Self-Quiz begin on page B-64.

1. **OBJECTIVE 1.**   State four general purposes of cost accounting systems.

2. **OBJECTIVE 2.**   State the circumstances under which a job order cost system is most likely to be used.

3. **OBJECTIVE 3.**   Direct labor costs of Maxweld Manufacturing Company for a year are estimated to total $642,000, while factory overhead costs are estimated at $770,400. Calculate the overhead application rate, assuming that the basis for application is direct labor cost.

4. Maxweld Manufacturing Company shows the following data for materials used and labor incurred during March.

Total from Materials Summary	
Direct materials	$49,700
Indirect materials	13,900
Totals from Time Summary	
Direct labor	$52,800
Indirect labor	38,600

Make journal entries on March 31 to record the following:

a. **OBJECTIVE 4a.**   The cost of materials used in the Goods in Process and Factory Overhead accounts.

b. **OBJECTIVE 4b.** The cost of factory labor in the Goods in Process and Factory Overhead accounts.

c. **OBJECTIVE 4c.** The application of factory overhead to Goods in Process, using the overhead application rate you calculated for self-quiz item 3.

5. Maxweld Manufacturing Company shows that Job 314 was completed on March 14, with a total assigned cost of $62,000. Darby Company had ordered Job 314 on January 12, and had agreed to pay $84,000 30 days after receiving the goods. Darby took possession of (and title to) the products manufactured for the job on March 19. Make journal entries to record the following:

a. **OBJECTIVE 4d.** The completion of Job 314.

b. **OBJECTIVE 4e.** The acceptance of Job 314 goods by Darby Company.

DISCUSSION QUESTIONS FOR SECTION 21.A

1. Consider the following statement: "With care, accountants are able to precisely determine unit production costs, even where very complex production processes are used." Do you agree? Why?

2. What does the expression joint costs (common costs) mean, and what difficulties are caused by joint costs?

3. What is a cost center?

4. What purposes does a materials requisition form serve?

5. What is the difference between underapplied overhead and overapplied overhead?

6. How are ending balances in Factory Overhead handled?

7. The Gords Company ledger shows a credit balance of $6,800 in the Factory Overhead account at the close of the year. How was the credit balance brought about?

EXERCISES FOR SECTION 21.A

21.A.1. Direct labor costs for the year for Clarion Manufacturing, Inc., are expected to be $980,000, while factory overhead costs are expected to be $735,000. Calculate the overhead application rate, assuming that the basis for application is direct labor cost.

21.A.2. The Skidmore Corporation assigns factory overhead at 39% of direct materials cost. Calculate the overhead to be applied to job A163 when the job cost sheet shows total direct labor cost of $80,000 and total direct materials cost of $42,000.

21.A.3. Acre Company uses direct materials as the basis for applying overhead to jobs. It is estimated that factory overhead will total $1,860,000 for a year, while direct labor is estimated at $4,680,000 and direct materials at $3,220,000. Calculate the overhead rate.

Labor Used

Employees usually work in only one process cost center, and for the most part they specialize in just one or two tasks. Detailed time tickets are not needed under these circumstances, and employees can simply check themselves into and out of the factory by means of time clock cards. Labor costs can be summarized from the payroll records and recorded in the following manner.

OBJECTIVE 3b. Record the use of labor.

Mar. 31	Goods in Process, Casting	80,000	
	Goods in Process, Finishing	186,000	
	Factory Overhead	108,000	
	Factory Payroll		374,000
	Factory labor used in March.		

Overhead Applied

As with job order accounting, overhead may be applied on the basis of a predetermined rate. Keep in mind that overhead costs consist of more than just indirect materials and indirect labor. Skillet Corporation has established

ILLUSTRATION 21.12

				Balance	
Date	**Item**	**Debit**	**Credit**	**Debit**	**Credit**

Goods in Process, Casting

Date	Item	Debit	Credit	Debit	Credit
19--					
Mar. 1	Beginning Balance			5,000	
31	Direct Materials	220,000		225,000	
31	Direct Labor	80,000		305,000	
31	Factory Overhead	48,000		353,000	

Goods in Process, Finishing

Date	Item	Debit	Credit	Debit	Credit
19--					
Mar. 1	Beginning Balance			12,600	
31	Direct Materials	58,000		70,600	
31	Direct Labor	186,000		256,600	
31	Factory Overhead	93,000		349,600	

an overhead application rate of 60% of direct labor cost for casting and 50% of direct labor for finishing. The entry to apply overhead to Goods in Process at March 31 is as follows.

Mar. 31	Goods in Process, Casting	48,000	
	Goods in Process, Finishing	93,000	
	Factory Overhead		141,000
	Factory overhead applied at 60% of casting		
	direct labor and 50% of finishing direct labor.		

OBJECTIVE 3c. Record the application of factor overhead.

At this point the two Goods in Process accounts of Skillet Corporation appear as in Illustration 21.12. You can see from those accounts that so far there has been no transfer of costs from the casting department to the finishing department, nor has there been any recognition of the cost of the goods completed during the month.

UNIT AND TOTAL COSTS

Knowledge of costs per unit of product is helpful in determining the amounts to be transferred from one production process to the next. For purposes of determining unit and total product costs, it is generally easier to work with partially completed units in terms of their equivalence in completed units.

Equivalent Units

In many production processes, there are always some goods being worked on. For example, when employees leave the casting department of Skillet Corporation on the night of March 31, some freshly cast skillets may be left cooling in the molds. Since these skillets still must be removed from the molds, the casting department's work is only partially completed.

For the example just used, all the direct materials (units of iron) are put into process when the casting begins. Thus the goods in process are 100% complete insofar as casting materials are concerned. Let us assume that skillets cooling in the molds are 80% complete insofar as casting direct labor is concerned. Since overhead is applied in proportion to direct labor cost, the goods are also assumed to be 80% complete for purposes of assigning overhead costs.

To simplify matters, partially completed goods may be stated in terms of *equivalent units* of completed product. For example, the direct labor required to do 80% of the work on 500 units of product is equivalent to the direct labor required to fully complete 400 units of product. Thus *equivalent units are the number of completed units that could have been attained with the quantity of a resource (material, labor, or overhead) that went into a number of partially completed units.* Illustration 21.13 shows the equivalent units of production for the casting department during March.

ILLUSTRATION 21.13

		Materials		Labor and Overhead	
SKILLET CORPORATION Casting Department Equivalent Units Completed For the Month of March 19--					
	Actual Units	Stage of Completion	Equivalent Units for March	Stage of Completion	Equivalent Units for March
Goods in process, March 1	300	100%	–0–	80%	60
Started and completed	20,000	100%	20,000	100%	20,000
Goods in process, March 31	500	100%	500	80%	400
Completed in March	20,300*		20,500		20,460

*Actual units completed exclude the 500 units still in process at month-end.

The beginning units in process plus the units started and completed make up the total actual units completed during the month.

Note that during March no materials were added to the beginning goods in process because they were already 100% complete insofar as materials are concerned. However, since on March 1 beginning goods were only 80% complete for purposes of labor and overhead, the other 20% had to be added during March to finish the casting process. Thus the labor and overhead cost to be added in March is 20% of that required for 300 full units, or the cost of fully casting 60 equivalent whole units.

OBJECTIVE 2. Compute equivalent units of production for a period.

Owing to the nature of the finishing process, abrasives and oil are continually added during the process. Illustration 21.14 shows equivalent units

ILLUSTRATION 21.14

		Materials		Labor and Overhead	
SKILLET CORPORATION Finishing Department Equivalent Units Completed For the Month of March 19--					
	Actual Units	Stage of Completion	Equivalent Units for March	Stage of Completion	Equivalent Units for March
Goods in process, March 1	600	40%	360	20%	480
Started and completed	19,500	100%	19,500	100%	19,500
Goods in process, March 31	800	65%	520	30%	240
Completed in March	20,100		20,380		20,220

for the finishing department during March. The schedule disregards the work performed by the casting department before the units were received by the finishing department.

Production Reports

Production reports show how product costs are determined for a period of time. The report in Illustration 21.15 provides the information needed for transferring costs from casting to finishing. This report, as well as the other presentations that follow, assigns costs to ending units in process on a first-in, first-out (FIFO) basis. However, units are transferred to the next process, and to finished goods, on an average cost per unit basis.

The equivalent units in Illustration 21.15 came from Illustration 21.13. The cost per unit transferred ($17.0016) differs slightly from the total unit cost for March ($16.9878) because the unit cost of the beginning Goods in Process, brought over from the previous month, was somewhat higher than the unit cost for March.

Another way to calculate the cost of goods transferred to the finishing department is shown in Illustration 21.16 on the next page.

ILLUSTRATION 21.15

			Equivalent Units		Unit Cost
SKILLET CORPORATION					
Casting Department					
Production Report					
For the Month of March 19––					
Cost in process during March					
Goods in process, March 1	$ 5,000				
Direct materials added	220,000	÷	20,500	=	$10.7317
Direct labor added	80,000	÷	20,460	=	3.9101
Overhead applied	48,000	÷	20,460	=	2.3460
Total cost in process	$353,000				
Unit cost incurred in March					$16.9878
Cost assigned to 500 units in process					
Direct materials	$ 5,366	=	500	×	$10.7317
Direct labor	1,564	=	400	×	$ 3.9101
Factory overhead	938	=	400	×	$ 2.3460
Goods in process, March 31	$ 7,868				
Transferred to finishing department	$345,132	÷	20,300	=	$17.0016

ILLUSTRATION 21.16

COST OF UNITS TRANSFERRED TO FINISHING DEPARTMENT		
Goods in process, March 1, 300 units		$ 5,000
Cost to complete beginning goods in process		
Direct labor (60 equivalent units at $3.9101)	$235	
Factory overhead (60 equivalent units at $2.3460)	141	376
Cost of units started and completed		
20,000 units at $16.9878		339,756
Cost of 20,300 units transferred to finishing		
(average unit cost of $17.0016)		$345,132

The production report for the finishing department is shown in Illustration 21.17. Equivalent units came from Illustration 21.14. The cost per unit transferred ($33.6487) is slightly different from the unit cost for March ($33.6457) because of the effects of February costs in the beginning goods in process amount.

ILLUSTRATION 21.17

SKILLET CORPORATION Finishing Department Production Report For the Month of March 19--					
			Equivalent Units		Unit Cost
Cost in process during March					
Goods in process, March 1	$ 12,600				
Transferred from casting	345,132				$17.0016
Direct materials added	58,000	÷	20,380	=	2.8459
Direct labor added	186,000	÷	20,220	=	9.1988
Overhead applied	93,000	÷	20,220	=	4.5994
Total cost in process	$694,732				
Unit cost incurred in March					$33.6457
Cost assigned to 800 units in process					
Cost from casting department	$ 13,601	=	800	×	$17.0016
Direct materials	1,480	=	520	×	$ 2.8459
Direct labor	2,208	=	240	×	$ 9.1988
Factory overhead	1,104	=	240	×	$ 4.5994
Goods in process, March 31	$ 18,393				
Transferred to finished goods	$676,339	÷	20,100	=	$33.6487

ILLUSTRATION 21.18

COST OF UNITS TRANSFERRED TO FINISHED GOODS INVENTORY		
Goods in process, March 1, 600 units		$ 12,600
Cost to complete beginning goods in process		
Direct materials (360 equivalent units at $2.8459)	$1,025	
Direct labor (480 equivalent units at $9.1988)	4,415	
Factory overhead (480 equivalent units at $4.5994)	2,208	7,648
Cost of units started and completed		
19,500 at $33.6457		656,091
Cost of 20,100 units transferred to finished goods		
(average unit cost of $33.6487)		$676,339

Once again, the cost of goods transferred to Finished Goods inventory could be directly calculated as in Illustration 21.18.

Completed Goods

The cost of goods completed by the casting department is transferred to the finishing department by means of the following entry.

Mar. 31	Goods in Process, Finishing	345,132	
	Goods in Process, Casting		345,132
	Cost of goods completed by casting and		
	transferred to finishing.		

OBJECTIVE 3d. Record the transfer of cost from one production process to another.

Also, the following entry is needed to transfer the cost of goods completed by the finishing department to the Finished Goods inventory account.

Mar. 31	Finished Goods	676,339	
	Goods in Process, Finishing		676,339
	Cost of goods completed by finishing and		
	transferred to Finished Goods inventory.		

OBJECTIVE 3e. Record the transfer of cost of goods finished to the Finished Goods inventory account.

Cost of Goods Sold

Now suppose that Skillet Corporation had 5,000 finished skillets on hand on March 1 and 4,000 finished units on March 31. Furthermore, the beginning inventory units, completed in February, were carried in the records at a cost of $33.80 each. Assuming use of the first-in, first-out (FIFO) approach for finished goods, cost of goods sold for March may be calculated as shown at the top of page 895.

ILLUSTRATION 21.19

Goods in Process, Casting

Date	Item	Debit	Credit	Balance Debit	Balance Credit
19--					
Mar. 1	Beginning Balance			5,000	
31	Direct Materials	220,000		225,000	
31	Direct Labor	80,000		305,000	
31	Factory Overhead	48,000		353,000	
31	Transfer to Finishing		345,132	7,868	

Goods in Process, Finishing

Date	Item	Debit	Credit	Balance Debit	Balance Credit
19--					
Mar. 1	Beginning Balance			12,600	
31	Direct Materials	58,000		70,600	
31	Direct Labor	186,000		256,600	
31	Factory Overhead	93,000		349,600	
31	Transfer from Casting	345,132		694,732	
31	Transfer to Finished Goods		676,339	18,393	

Finished Goods Inventory

Date	Item	Debit	Credit	Balance Debit	Balance Credit
19--					
Mar. 1	Beginning Balance, 5,000 units at $33.80			169,000	
31	Completed, 20,100 at $33.6487	676,339		845,339	
31	Sold, 21,100 units		710,744	134,595	

Cost of Goods Sold

Date	Item	Debit	Credit	Balance Debit	Balance Credit
19--					
Mar. 31	Units sold in March	710,744		710,744	

	Units	Unit Cost	Total
Beginning finished goods	5,000	$33.8000	$169,000
Completed during March	20,100	$33.6487	676,339
Available for sale	25,100		$845,339
Ending finished goods	4,000	$33.6487	134,595
Goods sold	21,100		$710,744

The following entry recognizes Cost of Goods Sold for March on a first-in, first-out basis.

Mar. 31	Cost of Goods Sold
	    Finished Goods
	    5,000 skillets at $33.80 and 16,100 skillets at
	    $33.6487.
		710,744	710,744

After all the entries have been posted, the accounts will appear as in Illustration 21.19. The arrows indicate the flow of costs from one account to another.

GLOSSARY FOR SECTION 21.B

Equivalent units   The number of completed units that could have been attained with the quantity of a resource (material, labor, or overhead) that went into a number of partially completed units.

Process cost system   A set of procedures for accumulating product costs by processing operations or departments.

SELF-QUIZ ON OBJECTIVES FOR SECTION 21.B
Solutions to Self-Quiz begin on page B-65.

1. **OBJECTIVE 1.** State the circumstances under which a process cost system is most likely to be used.

2. **OBJECTIVE 2.** The mixing department of Tappe Corporation began the month of May with 12,000 units of product to which 80% of materials had been added and which were 60% complete insofar as labor and overhead were concerned. Of the 60,000 units that were *started* during May, 8,000 were still in process at month-end. Ending units were 40% complete for materials and 20% complete for labor and overhead. Determine the equivalent units of production in May for materials, labor, and overhead for the mixing department.

3. Selected data for May from the records of Tappe Corporation are provided here.

From materials use records	
Materials used directly in mixing department	$130,000
Materials used directly in canning department	46,000
Materials used indirectly	25,000
From factory payroll summary	
Direct labor in mixing department	$210,000
Direct labor in canning department	94,000
Indirect labor	173,000
Overhead application rate as percentage of direct labor cost	
Mixing department	120%
Canning department	82%
Completed by mixing department and transferred to canning department 560,000 units at a unit cost of $1.05 each	
Completed by canning department and transferred to finished goods 520,000 units at a unit cost of $1.50 each	

Prepare journal entries at May 31 to record the following:

a. **OBJECTIVE 3a.** The use of materials during May.

b. **OBJECTIVE 3b.** The distribution of factory labor costs for May.

c. **OBJECTIVE 3c.** The application of overhead to Goods in Process.

d. **OBJECTIVE 3d.** The transfer of goods from the mixing department to the canning department.

e. **OBJECTIVE 3e.** The transfer of completed goods from the canning department to Finished Goods inventory.

DISCUSSION QUESTIONS FOR SECTION 21.B

1. Why is it helpful to convert numbers of partially completed units in process to *equivalent* completed units?

2. Why are job order cost systems inadequate for accounting for standardized goods that are mass-produced for sale to anyone who will buy them?

3. How are cost centers in job order systems different from those in process systems?

4. Why might the equivalent units of materials in process be different from the equivalent units of labor in process for the same goods at a point in time?

5. Why are equivalent units of labor in process usually the same as the equivalent units of overhead in process for the same goods at a point in time?

6. Under what circumstances would the production costs of one department be included in the Goods in Process account of another department?

EXERCISES FOR SECTION 21.B

21.B.1. The Boro Corporation began June with 80,000 units in process that were 70% complete as to direct materials and 60% complete as to direct labor and overhead. Determine the equivalent units of production that it will take to complete the 80,000 units in June.

21.B.2. P.S. Manufacturing Company began operations during March. There were no units completed in March, but at March 31, 42,000 units were 90% complete as to direct materials and 80% complete as to direct labor and overhead. Calculate the company's equivalent production in March.

21.B.3. The assembly department of Mark Manufacturing began the month of September with 180 units of product to which 60% of direct materials had been added and which were 40% complete insofar as labor and overhead were concerned. Of the 250 units that were started during September, 40 were still in process at month-end. Ending units were 70% complete for materials and 40% complete for labor and overhead. Calculate the department's equivalent units of production in September.

21.B.4. Which of the following types of manufacturing companies would most likely use a job order system, and which would probably use a process system?

    a. Flour mill

    b. Machine tool manufacturer

    c. Brewery

    d. Textile mill

    e. Shipbuilder

    f. Cement plant

    g. Gasoline refinery

    h. Printing company

    i. Company making specialty electronics gear

    j. Paint manufacturer

21.B.5. Use the following data to calculate both the equivalent units of production for Process B during January and the actual number of units transferred from Process B to Process C.

January Production Data

Jan. 1   Beginning units on hand, 800; 25% completed. The units were finished by Process B and transferred to Process C during January.

    31   Units received from Process A, completed, and transferred to Process C during January, 6,000 units.

    31   Ending units on hand in Process B, 1,000; 40% completed.

21.B.6. Johnson Manufacturing Company uses three manufacturing processes: forming, grinding, and polishing. During August, 10,000 new units were started in the forming process. Beginning and ending goods in process were as follows.

| Process | August 1 | | August 31 | |
	Units	% Complete	Units	% Complete
Forming	800	75	900	33⅓
Grinding	500	40	600	50
Polishing	300	66⅔	500	60

Compute the equivalent units of production for each process.

PROBLEMS FOR SECTION 21.B
Alternate Problems for this section begin on page D-114.

21.B.7. Selected data for April from the records of the Herbie Manufacturing Company are provided here. Herbie employs a process cost system for accounting for manufacturing costs.

Materials
Used directly in assembly department	$210,000
Used directly in painting department	31,000
Used indirectly	46,000

Factory labor
Direct labor in assembly department	$340,000
Direct labor in painting department	44,000
Indirect labor	98,000

Overhead application rate as a percentage of direct labor cost
Assembly department	40%
Painting department	110%

Completed by assembly department and transferred to painting department
1,120 units at a cost of $480 each
Completed by painting department and transferred to finished goods
1,000 units at a cost of $555 each

Required
Prepare journal entries at April 30 to record the following:

1) The use of materials during April

2) The distribution of labor costs for April

3) The application of overhead to Goods in Process

4) The transfer of goods from the assembly department to the painting department

5) The transfer of completed goods from the painting department to Finished Goods inventory

21.B.8. A partially completed production report for the assembly department of the Max Mower Company is as follows.

			Equivalent Units		Unit Cost
MAX MOWER COMPANY Assembly Department Production Report For the Month of May 19———					
Cost in process during May					
Goods in process, May 1	$ 20,000				
Direct materials added	110,000	÷	3,120	=	$
Direct labor added	180,000	÷	3,090	=	
Overhead applied*		÷	3,090	=	
Total cost in process	$				
Unit cost incurred in May					$
Cost assigned to 400 units in process					
Direct materials	$	=	400	×	$
Direct labor		=	300	×	$
Factory overhead		=	300	×	$
Goods in process, May 31	$				
Transferred to painting department	$	÷	3,130	=	$

*Overhead is applied at 40% of direct labor.

Required

Complete the production report.

21.B.9. The Sloan Toy Company manufactures inexpensive plastic toys in a two-step process involving a molding department and a finishing department. Selected data are given here for the two departments for the month of April.

	Molding Department	Finishing Department
Goods in process, April 1	$ 2,000	$ 8,000
Direct labor to complete beginning goods in process	300	3,800
Factory overhead to complete beginning goods in process	136	1,596
Cost of units started and completed	27,400	41,500

Required

1) Calculate the cost of goods transferred to the finishing department during April.

2) Make an entry at April 30 to record the transfer of goods to the finishing department.

3) Calculate the cost of goods transferred to Finished Goods during April.

4) Make an entry at April 30 to record the transfer to Finished Goods.

21.B.10. Regency Garment Company uses two manufacturing processes, cutting and sewing. The Goods in Process accounts pictured do not include September transfers from cutting to sewing and from sewing to finished goods. The beginning inventory in each account was completed during September. Additional data about product units are provided here.

Goods in Process—Cutting			Goods in Process—Sewing	
9/1	1,800		9/1	3,020
9/30	6,000		9/30	1,100
9/30	2,000		9/30	5,500
9/30	2,000		9/30	2,200

	Cutting		Sewing	
	Units	*% Complete**	*Units*	*% Complete**
Beginning inventory	600	66⅔	400	50
Started and completed	1,700	100	1,800	100
Ending inventory	400	25	500	40

*Percentages shown are for materials, labor, and overhead usage.

Required

1) Compute equivalent units of production for each process.

2) Compute the unit cost added in each process during September.

3) Compute the total unit cost of production during September.

4) Compute the number of units transferred from cutting to sewing and from sewing to finished goods.

5) Compute the average unit cost of goods transferred from cutting to sewing and from sewing to finished goods.

SUMMARY OF CHAPTER 21

Cost accounting is done for all types of costs, but most people associate the expression with product costs. Cost accounting systems provide data for financial statements and aid in controlling and minimizing costs, evaluating performance, and planning. Contrary to what some people believe, cost systems are merely systematic approaches for approximating product cost movements in a consistent manner. Joint costs are particularly difficult to handle, since there are no logical bases for allocating them among the various products that are processed.

Cost systems should be tailored to meet an entity's particular needs. Job order cost systems treat customer orders as cost centers, whereas production processes are viewed as cost centers when process cost systems are used. Within job cost systems, job cost sheets constitute subsidiary records controlled by one Goods in Process account. Costs are viewed as flowing from one processing operation to another when process cost systems are used, and a separate Goods in Process account is employed for each processing center.

All cost systems attempt to identify the three product cost elements—direct materials, direct labor, and factory overhead—with goods being produced. Since factory overhead cannot be directly traced into the products, it is assigned at an overhead rate on some determinable base amount. The conversion of numbers of partially completed units in process to equivalent completed units is helpful in determining how much product cost to transfer along with the products as they move through the processing stages.

PROBLEMS FOR CHAPTER 21
Alternate Problems for this chapter begin on page D-116.

21.1. Selected data for September from the records of the Sojo Canning Corporation are shown here. Goods completed in the packing department go to Finished Goods inventory.

		Materials		Labor and Overhead	
	Actual Units	*Stage of Completion*	*Equivalent Units for Sept.*	*Stage of Completion*	*Equivalent Units for Sept.*
Goods in process, 9/1	4,800	98%		90%	
Started and completed	79,000	100%		100%	
Goods in process, 9/30	3,000	98%		80%	
Completed in September	83,800				

SOJO CANNING CORPORATION
Packing Department
Equivalent Units Completed
For the Month of September 19--

Overhead is applied at 54% of direct labor.

Cost in Process during September	
Goods in process, 9/1	$ 2,880
Direct materials added	7,000
Direct labor applied	18,000
Transferred from canning department (82,000 units)	42,000

Required

1) Calculate the equivalent units for September and finish the schedule provided in the problem.

2) Prepare a production report for the packing department for the month of September similar to the production reports illustrated in this chapter.

3) Make a journal entry at September 30 to record the transfer of the cost of goods completed to Finished Goods inventory.

21.2. The trial balance for the Dot Manufacturing Company at January 1 follows. The company uses a job order cost system with perpetual inventories. The transactions for March are presented in summarized form.

DOT MANUFACTURING COMPANY Trial Balance January 1, 19--		
	Debit	**Credit**
Cash	12,000	
Accounts Receivable	18,000	
Materials Inventory	10,000	
Goods in Process	15,000	
Finished Goods	20,000	
Factory Equipment	100,000	
Accumulated Depreciation		20,000
Accounts Payable		5,000
Factory Payroll		2,000
D. Kahl, Capital		148,000
	175,000	175,000

Summarized Transactions

a) Materials costing $21,000 were purchased on account.

b) Materials issued from the storeroom totaled $22,600; indirect materials, $2,600; and direct materials, $20,000.

c) Wages earned by factory employees were $34,000. Direct labor was $30,000 and indirect labor was $4,000.

d) Equipment depreciated by $1,000 during the month.

e) Other factory costs of $3,000 were credited to accounts payable.

f) $10,000 of factory overhead was applied to production.

g) Jobs costing $65,000 were completed.

h) Goods shipped to customers had a production cost of $65,000.

i) The goods shipped were billed to customers at $90,000.

j) Collections of accounts receivable were $88,000 for the month.

k) Wages paid to employees totaled $35,000.

l) $26,000 was paid on accounts payable.

m) $4,000 of selling expenses and $6,000 of administrative expenses were paid in cash.

Required

1) Journalize the summarized transactions.

2) Prepare a preclosing trial balance for January 31. (You may want to use T-accounts to compute ending balances.)

3) Close the Factory Overhead account. (Assume the entire balance is closed to Cost of Goods Sold.)

21.3. A trial balance for the Pickle Corporation follows. Summarized transaction and production data are provided for July. A case of pickles is one unit of production. A process cost system is used.

THE PICKLE CORPORATION Trial Balance June 30, 19--		
	Debit	**Credit**
Cash	12,000	
Accounts Receivable	20,000	
Materials Inventory	15,000	
Goods in Process—Pickling	6,000	
Goods in Process—Packing	3,000	
Finished Goods	8,000	
Prepaid Rent	7,000	
Unexpired Insurance	2,400	
Factory Equipment	150,000	
Accumulated Depreciation—Equipment		50,000
Accounts Payable		30,000
Factory Payroll		2,000
Notes Payable		15,000
Common Stock		100,000
Retained Earnings		21,100
Sales		200,000
Factory Overhead		300
Selling Expense	20,000	
Administrative Expense	15,000	
Cost of Goods Sold	160,000	
	418,400	418,400

Summarized Data

a) Materials purchased on account amounted to $20,000.

b) Factory costs to be recorded are as follows:

Expired rent	$1,000
Expired insurance	400
Depreciation	1,250
Miscellaneous credits to accounts payable	1,000

c) A summary of payroll records showed direct labor totals of $10,000 for pickling and $4,000 for packing. Indirect labor was $1,000.

d) The summary of materials requisitions showed direct materials of $23,100 used in pickling and $6,300 used in packing. Indirect materials costing $2,250 were issued.

e) Factory overhead is applied at 50% of direct labor cost.

f) The pickling department had 3,000 units in process two-thirds completed at the beginning of the month. Units started in process and completed were 9,700. Remaining in inventory were 4,000 units one-half completed. The cost added to each unit in the pickling department is $3. (Record the amount transferred from pickling to packing.)

g) The packing department transferred to finished stock 12,500 cases at an average cost of $4.

h) Customers bought 10,000 cases on account at a sale price of $5 per case. The cost of goods sold was $4 per case.

i) Additional common stock was issued for $50,000 cash.

j) Accounts receivable of $42,000 were collected.

k) Cash disbursements were as follows:

Factory Payroll	$16,000
Accounts Payable	46,000
Notes Payable	15,000
Selling Expense	4,000
Administrative Expense	4,000

Required

1) Journalize the summarized transactions for July.

2) Set up T-accounts and post the July entries.

3) Prepare a trial balance on July 31.

4) Prepare a balance sheet at July 31 and an income statement for the six months ended July 31, assuming that the revenue and expense data in the June 30 trial balance are for the first five months of the fiscal year starting February 1.

COMPREHENSION PROBLEM FOR CHAPTER 21

21.4. A condensed income statement and balance sheet for Farnsworth Specialty Corporation are presented here.

FARNSWORTH SPECIALTY CORPORATION
Income Statement
For the Year Ended December 31, 19X4

Sales	$1,800,000
Cost of goods sold	1,350,000
Gross Profit	$ 450,000
Operating expenses	290,000
Net Income before Taxes	$ 160,000
Income taxes	70,000
Net Income	$ 90,000
Earnings per share	$0.90

FARNSWORTH SPECIALTY CORPORATION
Balance Sheet
December 31, 19X4

ASSETS		LIABILITIES		
Cash	$ 10,000	Accounts payable	$120,000	
Receivables	85,000	Bank loans	500,000	
Inventories		Total Liabilities		$ 620,000
Materials	14,000			
Goods in process	189,000	SHAREHOLDERS' EQUITY		
Finished goods	–0–	Common stock	$ 50,000	
Plant and equipment (net)	860,000	Capital in excess of par	150,000	
		Retained earnings	338,000	
		Total Shareholders' Equity		538,000
		Total Liabilities and		
Total Assets	$1,158,000	Shareholders' Equity		$1,158,000

Farnsworth Specialty Corporation builds highly specialized equipment to the design specifications of its customers. A job order cost system is used to account for product costs. At the end of 19X4, there was only one job in process—a complex industrial robot to be used on a customer's assembly-line operation. The robot had been in process since August 10, 19X4. Of the total anticipated cost to build the robot, 90% of the materials, labor, and overhead had been applied by December 31. The job is expected to be completed by late January 19X5, at which time Farnsworth will receive the $300,000 sales price agreed upon.

During early January 19X5, Farnsworth's president, who is also the corporation's principal shareholder, complains to the concern's auditors that both the position and the performance of the corporation were better than the statements portray. He fears that the corporation's major creditor, a local bank, will be misled by the statements. The auditors have responded that the statements are fair because they are in accordance with generally accepted accounting principles.

Required

1) Do you agree with the president or the auditors? Explain.

2) Based on what you know about the corporation, what could you say to Farnsworth's bankers to help them evaluate the position and performance of Farnsworth?

PART IX

BUDGETS AND DECISION MAKING

ACCOUNTANTS IN THE WORKPLACE

NAME: Robert A. Lefkowitz

AFFILIATION: Coopers & Lybrand

POSITION: Tax Partner (Generalist)

SPECIALIZATION: Corporate Tax Planning

Why work for a Big Eight accounting firm? "We work with very high-level executives and have a large, diverse base of clients," explains Robert A. Lefkowitz, one of Coopers & Lybrand's 180 tax partners. Its 900 partners and staff distributed throughout the world provide C&L with "almost unlimited resources." Says Lefkowitz: "Our chief strength lies in the ability to draw on experts within the company to solve virtually any problem."

As a tax partner, Lefkowitz wears two hats. He serves as an "expert-on-call" for his audit colleagues, as they prepare year-end audits that are increasingly complicated by changing tax laws. As a tax consultant, he helps clients understand the tax consequences of an action *before* they take it. "I try to maintain a trusting relationship with my clients, so if a problem arises they feel free to pick up the phone and call me. Sometimes I'll be able to answer a question on the spot."

At other times, however, the case may require an indepth study. Then Lefkowitz, in conjunction with other C&L practitioners, will examine the situation thoroughly. For example, he cites the recent case of a manufacturing client about to acquire a furniture company. What and how complex were the many tax considerations?

First, Lefkowitz had to decide whether to recommend a taxable or nontaxable transaction. That meant choosing between buying the company with cash or with stock. Since issuing new stock would have diluted the manufacturing company's earnings per share, he recommended a cash purchase, or taxable transaction.

Second, he had to decide whether to advise his client to buy the company whole or to buy only specific assets. Since the whole company may have harbored hidden liabilities, he counseled buying specific assets.

Finally, how best could the $75 million purchase price be allocated over the assets purchased in order to maximize potential tax deductions relating to the purchase price? For help, Lefkowitz drew upon the expertise of other partners in C&L's Engineering and Valuation Department.

Lefkowitz also works with corporate executives on their personal tax problems. "Executives," he says, "are pleased if you can save their company $50,000. But they're no less pleased if you can save them $2,000 or $3,000 on their personal returns."

Lefkowitz is a graduate of the Wharton School and Georgetown Law School and holds a Master's degree in tax law from New York University. He chose accounting because it seemed to offer the best opportunity to work in the tax field. "Although technical knowledge remains the cornerstone of our business," he says, "our profession is also people oriented." For this reason, C&L prefers its employees to be "well rounded." Lefkowitz (himself an avid tennis and golf player) speaks regularly before accounting and business organizations on accounting and tax-related matters.

22
Budgetary Control

Planning is an important part of managing any entity, regardless of the entity's size, legal form, or goals. Accountants contribute to the planning process by quantifying projections and by arranging budgeted data in understandable schedules and reports. Section A of Chapter 22 explores the overall budgeting process, and Section B looks at the use of budgeted data for a period in evaluating performance for that period.

Section A differentiates managerial from financial accounting before discussing the purposes of budgeting. The way in which subbudgets make up a master budget is covered, and the process is illustrated by a simple example. Finally, the steps in preparing a master budget are summarized.

Section B commences with the purposes of responsibility accounting, goes on to define a responsibility center, and then discusses the circumstances under which costs may be controllable by managers. Performance reports showing the amounts by which actual costs for a period varied from budgeted costs for that period are illustrated.

SECTION 22.A

Budgeting

OBJECTIVES

This section deals with the preparation of the various subbudgets that make up a master budget for an entity. At the conclusion of your study, you should be able to

1. Differentiate between managerial accounting and financial accounting.
2. Prepare spread sheets for arriving at projected cash receipts from sales and projected cash payments for purchases.
3. Prepare a cash budget for one or more future time periods.
4. List in your own words the steps involved in making a master budget.

MANAGERIAL VERSUS FINANCIAL ACCOUNTING

Users of accounting reports range from owners and creditors to labor unions, government bureaus, consumer advocates, environmentalists—the list could go on and on. *The formal reports prepared primarily for people not directly involved in the management of a company are called **financial statements**. The process of gathering information for presentation in financial statements is called **financial accounting**.*

Accounting information is needed for the internal management of an entity, as well as for external reporting. *Accounting schedules and statements used internally by managers are called, not surprisingly, **management reports**. The process of gathering information for use in management reports is called **managerial accounting**.* Thus financial accounting is directed toward the provision of information for *external* users, whereas managerial accounting collects information for use by *internal* (management) users.

OBJECTIVE 1.
Differentiate between managerial and financial accounting.

This does not mean that entities maintain two distinctly different accounting systems for recording transactions and events. Usually, the financial accounting system is designed to provide the historical accounting information needed by managers. However, all kinds of data may be collected outside the main accounting system. For instance, a supervisor may record the length of an employee's lunch break on a desk calendar. The modern trend is toward integrated computer systems that maintain all kinds of data in interrelated data banks.

Managers need a great deal of information for coordinating an entity's activities, controlling its resources, and planning for its future. Managers must make decisions in the present that will affect future outcomes. Under current accounting practices, financial statements report only on events that have already occurred. But future projections, and present decisions, are necessarily based on data about the past. For example, decisions about which employees to promote, fire, or retain are usually based on records of past performance. And the goal of decisions of this kind is to improve *future* performance.

PURPOSES OF BUDGETING

All managers should devote some time to planning for the future. *Formal plans in quantitative terms are called budgets.* Budgets are based on predictions of future outcomes. *The process of predicting future outcomes and conditions is called forecasting.* Forecasting uses facts about the past and present to project future conditions. Business conditions, like the weather, become more difficult to predict as we look farther into the future. Still, even a long-range plan based on tenuous predictions is better than no plan at all.

Budgets aid managers not only in planning for the future but also in coordinating activities. For example, a projected increase in sales means that more goods must be available for sale, which in turn means that the level of production must be stepped up, and so on down the line. In other words, all kinds of activities will have to be coordinated to achieve the higher level of sales in the future.

Budgets also help control resources. When managers participate in the planning process, they are likely to feel responsible for meeting or bettering the budget. As an evaluation device, budgeted amounts may be compared with actual results when they are known, to determine how well managers have done toward attaining the budget goals. Some approaches for analyzing the differences (variances) between budgeted and actual results are discussed later in this chapter and in Chapter 24.

MASTER BUDGETS

An overall plan for a company is often referred to as a master budget. A master budget is made up of subbudgets for the various functional and responsibility areas of the entity. The subbudgets are interrelated and fit together to constitute the overall master budget for a company, as suggested by Illustration 22.1 on the next page.

Subbudgets

Many aspects of budgeting depend on the level of expected activity. The accounting measure of output activity (accomplishment) is revenue. The revenue for companies that sell goods is *sales.* Therefore, the logical starting point for budget preparation in merchandising and manufacturing enterprises is the estimation of sales.

Budget data should be obtained from the best possible sources. Managers who are responsible for sales should be in the best position to predict

ILLUSTRATION 22.1

MASTER BUDGET

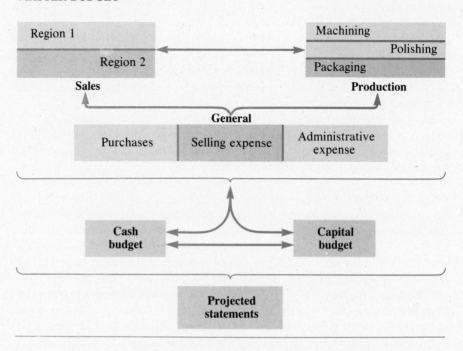

future sales. Salespeople may be asked to estimate how much they expect to sell in their territories. Regional sales managers then compile these predictions into estimates for their regions. The vice-president in charge of sales may be responsible for reviewing and combining regional estimates to arrive at total expected sales for the entity.

Production budgets, which should stem from sales expectations, suggest the need for purchasing raw materials, hiring employees, and obtaining other resources.

The expected sales and production levels, along with knowledge of the age and condition of plant and equipment, may suggest that new assets will be needed for replacement and expansion purposes. *The overall plan for acquisition of long-term assets is called the* **capital budget**. Here the term *capital* refers to long-term productive assets rather than to owners' equity.

Expected cash flows can be determined from information derived for the various other budgets. *The* **cash budget**, *showing the expected sources and uses of cash,* is usually prepared on a companywide basis. In effect, it is a variety of *projected cash flow statement,* though the form may vary from that used for reporting past cash flows. Cash budgets may show expected flows for short or long periods or for a combination of both.

A master budget is likely to contain a projected (pro forma) income statement for the budget period and a projected balance sheet for the end of the budget period. Also, the more detailed cash budget data may be combined to obtain a forecast statement of changes in financial position for the budget period.

Budgeting, like other aspects of accounting, should be designed to meet the needs of a particular entity. The number of subdivisions in the master budget should depend on the particular circumstances. The needs of the entity should also determine the time period (week, month, quarter, or year) for which it budgets.

Participation

Managers should be involved in budgeting for their own areas of responsibility; otherwise they may rebel at being held accountable for someone else's plan. When a budget is forced on a manager, it may be viewed as a straitjacket that interferes with job performance. Under these circumstances, managers attempt to outwit the persons in charge of the budget. They may attempt to distort reported data or to discredit the budget by showing that the projections are unrealistic.

Entities that involve their managers in the budgeting process generally derive more benefit from budgeting. A manager is more apt to think of his or her own budget as a helpful device for doing a better job. And if something goes wrong, a manager is somewhat more willing to accept responsibility for his or her own plan than for someone else's.

The overall formulation of a budget is generally guided and coordinated by a *budget committee,* made up of responsible members of the organization. The accountant's role in the budgeting process is to assist the managers by providing information about the past, by helping them quantify their plans, and by pulling together the various parts into formal budget schedules.

Techniques

Some people think of budgeting as a guessing game; others view it as clairvoyance—an uncanny ability to see into the future. Actually, budgeting is just the application of logic—common sense—to the task of forecasting what will probably happen.

In budgeting, we always start with yesterday's experience and today's conditions. This knowledge of the past and present is then amended by what is expected, or predicted, for the future. Your personal cash budget, though perhaps only a mental one, is probably derived in a similar manner. You know from experience how much cash you need for such things as food and clothing; you also know how much cash you now have; and you have some idea of how much cash you can expect to receive in the future, and when. From these facts and expectations you are able to formulate at least a vague program for your personal receipts and payments of cash in the near future.

Studying accounting data about the past makes relationships between events become apparent. For instance, sales necessarily imply the cost of goods sold. If managers know the kinds of goods likely to be sold, they can probably pin down the approximate cost of goods for a given amount of sales.

The technique of relating one thing to something else is used frequently in budgeting. *Establishing a dependent relationship between two or more happenings (variables) is called* **correlation**. The cost of goods sold correlates strongly with sales. Other costs may also correlate with sales, but the relationship may be weaker and less predictable. Other correlations can also be established for use in budgeting. For instance, interest expense varies with debt levels, wages relate to hours worked, automobile cost depends on miles driven—we could go on and on.

Budget Periods

Budgets may be prepared for time periods of any length, depending on the needs of the users. Budgets are usually prepared for accounting periods and parts of accounting periods. Quite frequently, they are prepared for each month of the upcoming accounting year, with the 12-month totals constituting the yearly budget.

Rolling budgets (evolving budgets) are continually maintained for some entities, in that a budget is added for another future month with the passing of each current month. In other words, the monthly budget for April 19X6 would be added to a 12-month rolling budget at the time that the budget for April 19X5 was dropped off. Each of the other 11 monthly budgets is also revised at the time that the budget for the twelfth month is added, so that the entire rolling budget reflects the latest information available.

SIMPLE BUDGETING ILLUSTRATION

Sales Budget

To keep matters simple, let us assume that Dumar Distributing Company handles only one type of good, which it sells to retailers for $50 per unit. Our focus is on the budgets for the first three months of 19X5.

Estimates of the number of units that are likely to be sold during each of the months have been compiled by the sales staff. These numbers of estimated units are then multiplied by the expected sales prices, as shown in Illustration 22.2.

Purchases Budget

Inventory practices vary, but let us assume that managers of Dumar attempt to maintain an inventory of approximately 5,000 units of stock on hand. At December 31, 19X4, there were 5,100 units on hand, purchased at a cost of $30 each. Suppliers' prices are expected to remain at $30 per unit during the first quarter of 19X5. For our simple example, the expected cost of purchases may be derived as in Illustration 22.3.

ILLUSTRATION 22.2

DUMAR DISTRIBUTING COMPANY Sales Budget For the First Quarter, 19X5			
	Estimated Sales		
Month	**Quantity**	**Price**	**Total Sales**
January	3,480	$50	$174,000
February	3,000	$50	150,000
March	4,320	$50	216,000
Total for quarter	10,800		$540,000

ILLUSTRATION 22.3

DUMAR DISTRIBUTING COMPANY Purchases Budget For the First Quarter, 19X5				
	January	**February**	**March**	**Quarter**
Projected units of sales	3,480	3,000	4,320	10,800
Desired ending inventory units	5,000	5,000	5,000	5,000
Total units needed	8,480	8,000	9,320	15,800
Less: Beginning inventory units	5,100	5,000	5,000	5,100
Purchases required in units	3,380	3,000	4,320	10,700
Cost per unit	× $30	× $30	× $30	× $30
Projected cost of purchases	$101,400	$90,000	$129,600	$321,000

Keep in mind that most merchandising concerns handle a number of kinds of goods, which considerably complicates the budgeting process. Further complicating the process for manufacturing concerns are the assortment of inventories (Materials, Goods in Process, and Finished Goods) and the manufacturing cost elements (direct materials, direct labor, and factory overhead) that must be projected.

Selling Expense Budget

Dumar expects variable selling expenses (such as sales commissions and travel) to run about 15% of sales revenue, and fixed selling expenses (such as sales manager's salary and depreciation) to amount to $10,000 per month. *A **variable cost** changes directly in relation to changes in activity levels, whereas **fixed cost** is not affected by the level of activity during an accounting or budget period.* These expressions are used throughout the remainder of this book.

ILLUSTRATION 22.4

DUMAR DISTRIBUTING COMPANY Selling Expense Budget For the First Quarter, 19X5				
	January	**February**	**March**	**Quarter**
Projected sales revenue	$174,000	$150,000	$216,000	$540,000
Variable expense percentage	× 15%	× 15%	× 15%	× 15%
Variable selling expense	$ 26,100	$ 22,500	$ 32,400	$ 81,000
Fixed selling expense	10,000	10,000	10,000	30,000
Projected selling expense	$ 36,100	$ 32,500	$ 42,400	$111,000

The selling expense budget in Illustration 22.4 reflects the conditions described in the previous paragraph.

Administrative Expense Budget

Administrative expenses, like selling expenses, may have both variable and fixed elements. However, we assume that Dumar's administrative expenses are all fixed, at least over the relatively short time span of a calendar quarter. The expected administrative expenses (made up of office salaries, supplies, depreciation, and so on) are projected in Illustration 22.5.

Capital Budget

Capital budgets are usually prepared for long periods ahead, because they are likely to involve very large investments of funds. Thus a capital budget may project outlays for long-term assets for five or more years. For our purposes, let us just say that the capital budget indicates that equipment will be purchased in February 19X5 with an estimated cash payment of $30,000.

Cash Budget

A cash budget is nothing more than a *projected* cash flow statement. It shows expected inflows and outflows of cash and the net change in cash

ILLUSTRATION 22.5

DUMAR DISTRIBUTING COMPANY Administrative Expense Budget For the First Quarter, 19X5	
Month	**Estimated Administrative Expenses**
January	$20,000
February	20,000
March	20,000
Total for quarter	$60,000

ILLUSTRATION 22.6

CASH BUDGETING PROCESS

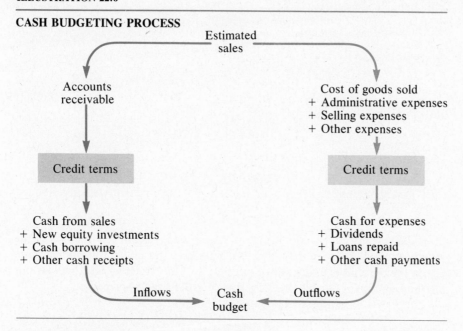

over a budget period. (Cash flow statements for *past* periods are discussed in Section 18.B.) As pointed out in Chapter 9, cash is a most desirable asset. Cash budgets are very helpful in controlling cash and in ensuring that future cash balances will be adequate, but not so large as to be wasteful.

A logical place to start a cash flow prediction is with the sales forecast. From Illustration 22.6 you can see how the cash budgeting process utilizes information derived from the other subbudgets of the master budget.

Projected Cash Inflows from Sales. The manner in which cash is expected to flow from Accounts Receivable depends upon credit terms and past experience. If, for example, all sales are made on account, and if customers normally pay in the month following a sale, then each month's sales represent expected cash collections in the following month—except, of course, for accounts that prove to be uncollectible.

Let us assume that Dumar Company sells only on terms of net 10 days, that sales occur at a uniform rate during each month, and that all accounts are collected. Under these circumstances, approximately two-thirds of each month's sales should be collected during the month of sale, with the remaining one-third collected in the following month. From the sales budget shown earlier, and assuming that sales during December 19X4 were $180,000, a spread sheet like the one in Illustration 22.7 on the next page can be prepared to approximate cash collections for the first quarter of 19X5.

Projected Cash Outflows for Purchases. Spread sheets similar to the one in Illustration 22.7 are also helpful for accumulating anticipated payments of

ILLUSTRATION 22.7

		Collections			
	Sales	January	February	March	Quarter

DUMAR DISTRIBUTING COMPANY
Projected Collections of Cash from Sales
For the First Quarter, 19X5

	Sales	January	February	March	Quarter
December	$180,000	$ 60,000			$ 60,000
January	174,000	116,000	$ 58,000		174,000
February	150,000		100,000	$ 50,000	150,000
March	216,000			144,000	144,000
Projected collections of receivables		$176,000	$158,000	$194,000	$528,000

cash. Dumar normally pays for about half of each month's purchases in the month of purchase, with the remainder being paid during the following month. Given the purchases budget developed earlier (Illustration 22.3), and assuming that purchases during December were $108,000, the projected payments for purchases would be as shown in Illustration 22.8.

Cash Flow Data.   As you have probably begun to suspect, cash budgeting for actual entities can become quite complicated. You will deal with some of the more involved budgeting techniques in advanced courses in accounting and finance. But for now, let us simply assume the following additional facts about Dumar Company:

1. Depreciation, a noncash expense, is included in selling expense projections at $6,000 per month and in administrative expense projections at $5,000 per month. The remaining selling and administrative expenses are expected to be paid in the months incurred.

ILLUSTRATION 22.8

DUMAR DISTRIBUTING COMPANY
Projected Payments of Cash for Purchases
For the First Quarter, 19X5

		Payments			
Purchases		January	February	March	Quarter
December	$108,000	$ 54,000			$ 54,000
January	101,400	50,700	$50,700		101,400
February	90,000		45,000	$ 45,000	90,000
March	129,600			64,800	64,800
Projected payments on account		$104,700	$95,700	$109,800	$310,200

2. Income taxes for 19X4 are due on March 15, 19X5, in the amount of $62,100.

3. Directors of Dumar expect to pay cash dividends of $10,000 during the month of March 19X5.

4. Managers of Dumar attempt to maintain a cash balance of about $20,000 in the firm's checking account. When the account balance drops below that amount by more than $1,000, sufficient marketable securities are sold to restore the balance to approximately $20,000. When marketable securities are not available, money is borrowed from the bank in even multiples of $1,000 to restore the balance to approximately the amount desired. When the account balance exceeds the desired balance by more than $1,000, the excess is applied to the payment of any outstanding bank loans, and any remaining excess amount is invested in government notes (marketable securities) in multiples of $1,000. In the interest of simplicity, interest on bank loans is ignored.

5. The balance sheet for Dumar at December 31, 19X4, appears in Illustration 22.9.

Cash Budget Format.   Cash budgets are prepared in a variety of formats. Some arrangements start with the beginning cash balance, add expected receipts, and then subtract projected payments to arrive at an estimated future balance. Other variations first subtract projected payments from estimated receipts to obtain the expected cash increase or decrease for the period, then combine that figure with the beginning balance to arrive at the

ILLUSTRATION 22.9

DUMAR DISTRIBUTING COMPANY Balance Sheet December 31, 19X4			
ASSETS		*LIABILITIES*	
Cash	$ 20,200	Accounts payable	$ 54,000
Inventory (5,100 units at $30)	153,000	Income taxes payable	62,100
Marketable securities	–0–	Bank loans payable	10,000
Accounts receivable	60,000	Total Liabilities	$126,100
Land	12,000		
Depreciable assets, at cost	187,000	*SHAREHOLDERS' EQUITY*	
Accumulated depreciation	(110,000)	Common stock	$ 50,000
		Retained earnings	146,100
		Total Shareholders' Equity	$196,100
		Total Liabilities and Shareholders' Equity	
Total Assets	$322,200		$322,200

ILLUSTRATION 22.10

	January	February	March	Quarter
DUMAR DISTRIBUTING COMPANY Cash Budget For the First Quarter, 19X5				
Projected cash receipts				
Collections of cash from sales[a]	$176,000	$158,000	$194,000	$528,000
Projected cash payments				
Payments of cash for purchases[b]	$104,700	$ 95,700	$109,800	$310,200
Selling expenses[c]	30,100	26,500	36,400	93,000
Administrative expenses[d]	15,000	15,000	15,000	45,000
Income taxes for 19X4			62,100	62,100
Purchase of equipment		30,000		30,000
Cash dividends			10,000	10,000
Total projected payments	$149,800	$167,200	$233,300	$550,300
Increase (Decrease) in Cash	$ 26,200	$ (9,200)	$(39,300)	$(22,300)
Beginning cash balance[e]	20,200	20,400	20,200	20,200
Total	$ 46,400	$ 11,200	$(19,100)	$ (2,100)
Increase (decrease) in bank loans[f]	(10,000)		32,000	22,000
(Increase) decrease in securities[g]	(16,000)	9,000	7,000	–0–
Projected ending cash balance	$ 20,400	$ 20,200	$ 19,900	$ 19,900

NOTES:

[a]From schedule of projected collections of cash from sales (Illustration 22.7).

[b]From schedule of projected payments of cash for purchases (Illustration 22.8).

[c]Projected selling expenses from selling expense budget (Illustration 22.4) less $6,000 depreciation per month.

[d]Projected administrative expenses from administrative expense budget (Illustration 22.5) less $5,000 depreciation per month.

[e]The beginning balance for January is the Cash balance on December 31, as shown in the balance sheet (Illustration 22.9).

[f]Additional borrowing from banks provides cash, whereas loan payments reduce cash.

[g]Cash is used to acquire additional securities, while sales of securities provide cash.

OBJECTIVE 3. Prepare a cash budget.

estimated ending cash balance. The cash budget in Illustration 22.10 uses the latter approach, but also shows at the bottom the anticipated changes in bank loans and marketable securities.

You can see how managers can anticipate the need for additional cash. And banks and other lending agencies look more favorably on concerns that plan sufficiently well to know in advance when borrowing may be required. A well-managed entity is a better lending risk than one whose managers do not know when borrowing will be necessary, or how much. Moreover, the budget alerts managers to the need for investing surplus cash. Idle cash is unproductive, bearing no return for the owners of an entity.

Projected Income Statement

The process of deriving the various subbudgets usually provides most of the information needed for preparing a projected (pro forma) income statement for the budget period. For example, the projected sales and expenses have

ILLUSTRATION 22.11

DUMAR DISTRIBUTING COMPANY Projected Income Statement For the Quarter Ended March 31, 19X5		
Sales[a]		$540,000
Cost of goods sold		
Beginning inventory (5,100 units at $30)[b]	$153,000	
Purchases (10,700 units at $30)[c]	321,000	
Available for sale	$474,000	
Ending inventory (5,000 units at $30)	150,000	324,000
Gross Profit		$216,000
Operating expenses		
Selling[d]	$111,000	
Administrative[e]	60,000	171,000
Net Income before Income Taxes		$ 45,000
Estimated income taxes[f]		14,000
Net Income after Income Taxes		$ 31,000

NOTES:

[a]From sales budget (Illustration 22.2).

[b]Same as ending inventory at December 31 (Illustration 22.9).

[c]From purchases budget (Illustration 22.3).

[d]From selling expense budget (Illustration 22.4).

[e]From administrative expense budget (Illustration 22.5).

[f]Based on the projected amount of net income before taxes.

already been determined for Dumar Company for the first quarter of 19X5, so that a projected income statement may be prepared, as shown in Illustration 22.11.

Projected Balance Sheet

You may have already noticed that the data needed for preparing a projected balance sheet is now readily available. Balances for Cash, Inventories, and Bank Loans Payable have been specifically pinned down. The other balance sheet items are not too difficult to derive, as Illustration 22.12 on the next page demonstrates.

STEPS IN BUDGET PREPARATION

The budgeting process involves a series of steps, some of which must occur in a particular order. For example, it would be foolish to try to predict the purchases for a period before the expected sales have been determined. In other instances, the sequence of steps may be varied somewhat without any harmful effects. For example, the projected income statement could be pre-

ILLUSTRATION 22.12

DUMAR DISTRIBUTING COMPANY			
Projected Balance Sheet			
March 31, 19X5			

ASSETS		*LIABILITIES*	
Cash	$ 19,900	Accounts payable	$ 64,800[d]
Inventory (5,000 at $30)	150,000	Income taxes payable	14,000[e]
Marketable securities	–0–	Bank loans payable	32,000[f]
Accounts receivable	72,000[a]	Total Liabilities	$110,800
Land	12,000		
Depreciable assets, at cost	217,000[b]	*SHAREHOLDERS' EQUITY*	
Accumulated depreciation	(143,000)[c]	Common stock	$ 50,000
		Retained earnings	167,100[g]
		Total Shareholders' Equity	$217,100
		Total Liabilities and	
Total Assets	$327,900	Shareholders' Equity	$327,900

NOTES

[a]Projected March sales	$216,000		[d]Projected March purchases	$129,600
Collections expected in March	144,000		Payments expected in March	64,800
Anticipated receivables	$ 72,000		Anticipated payables	$ 64,800
[b]Depreciable assets at 12/31/X4	$187,000		[e]From projected income statement	
Planned purchase in February	30,000		[f]From March column of cash budget	
Total	$217,000		[g]Retained earnings at 12/31/X4	$146,100
[c]Accumulated Depreciation at 12/31/X4	$110,000		Dividends in March	(10,000)
Selling depreciation (3 months at $6,000)	18,000		Projected net income	31,000
Administrative depreciation (3 months at $5,000)	15,000		Retained earnings, 3/31/X5	$167,100
Balance at 3/31/X5	$143,000			

ILLUSTRATION 22.13

MASTER BUDGETING PROCESS

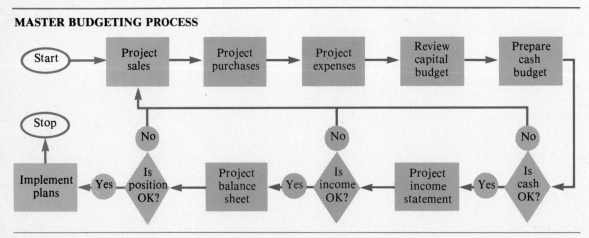

pared before the cash budget. The following list of steps shows one acceptable sequence in the preparation of a budget.

> **STEPS IN PREPARING A BUDGET**
>
> 1. Estimate quantities of sales for budget periods and multiply the projected sales units by expected selling prices to get total revenue projections.
> 2. Determine the numbers of units of goods that will be needed to meet the sales projections, taking into consideration the inventory quantities already on hand. For manufacturing concerns, the cost elements (direct materials, direct labor, and factory overhead) would then be determined for the needed production. For merchandising concerns, the projected costs of purchasing the needed units are somewhat easier to determine.
> 3. Determine the budgets for selling expenses and administrative expenses.
> 4. Review the capital budget to determine what outlays are planned during the master budget periods.
> 5. From the information derived for the subbudgets, prepare a cash budget for the budget period or periods.
> 6. From the projected revenues and expenses, prepare a projected (pro forma) income statement for the budget period.
> 7. Prepare a projected (pro forma) balance sheet for the end of the budget period.
> 8. Take any necessary steps to revise the subbudgets (plans) in order to achieve better results than are now predicted by the master budget.

OBJECTIVE 4. List the steps in making a master budget.

As suggested in step 8, budgets may be revised in an effort to achieve better results. As shown in Illustration 22.13, the critical factors are usually the adequacy of cash, net income, and financial position. When any or all of these elements are projected to be inadequate, the subbudgets are reviewed and reworked to come up with a plan that gives promise of achieving more favorable results.

GLOSSARY FOR SECTION 22.A

Budgets   Formal plans in quantitative terms.

Capital budget   The overall plan for acquisition of long-term assets.

Cash budget   A plan showing expected sources and uses of cash for a future period of time.

Correlation   The process of establishing a dependent relationship between two or more happenings (variables).

Financial accounting   The process of gathering information for presentation in financial statements prepared for external users.

Financial statements   Formal reports prepared primarily for people not directly involved in the management of a company.

Fixed cost   A cost that is not affected by the level of activity during an accounting or budget period.

Forecasting   The process of predicting future outcomes and conditions.

Management reports   Reports used internally by managers.

Managerial accounting   The process of gathering information for use in reports used mainly for internal decision making.

Master budget   An overall plan for a company.

Rolling budget (evolving budget)   A set of projections for which another future month's budget is added with the passing of each current month.

Variable cost   A cost that changes directly in relation to changes in activity levels.

SELF-QUIZ ON OBJECTIVES FOR SECTION 22.A
Solutions to Self-Quiz begin on page B-66.

1. **OBJECTIVE 1.** Differentiate between managerial accounting and financial accounting.

2. **OBJECTIVE 2.** Peggy's Cake Sales buys and resells various kinds of cakes. Sales are usually collected 50% in the month of sale, 40% in the month following sale, and 10% in the second month following sale. About 60% of purchases are paid for in the month of purchase, with the remainder being paid for in the following month. Prepare spread sheets for the *fourth quarter* of 19X5 to determine expected cash receipts from sales and cash payments for purchases based on the following projections. The spread sheets should show data by months and in totals for the quarter.

19X5	Projected Sales	Projected Purchases
August	$ 72,000	$48,000
September	66,000	40,000
October	84,000	50,000
November	78,000	46,000
December	122,000	74,000

3. **OBJECTIVE 3.** Use the spread sheets you made for self-quiz item (2), together with the following data, to prepare a cash budget for the fourth quarter 19X5 for Peggy's Cake Sales. Present figures by months and for the quarter in a format similar to the one illustrated in this Section.

Other Data

a) The cash balance at September 30, 19X5, is expected to be $5,000, the normal cash balance for Peggy's. When the balance falls below $5,000 by at least $1,000, marketable securities are liquidated, if available, in multiples of $1,000 to bring the balance to approximately $5,000. If securities are not available, funds are borrowed from the bank in multiples of $1,000 to achieve the desired balance. When the balance exceeds $5,000 by at least $1,000, the excess is applied in multiples of $1,000 against any bank loans outstanding. Excess funds still available after paying bank loans are used in $1,000 multiples to purchase marketable securities. No bank loans are expected to be owed at September 30, and no marketable securities are expected to be owned.

b) Selling and Administrative Expenses are estimated at $16,000 for October, $18,000 for November, and $20,000 for December 19X5. Selling and Administrative Expenses are generally paid in the month incurred, except for $5,000 of monthly depreciation that has been included in the figures.

c) Office furniture will be purchased in October 19X5 for $24,000 cash.

d) Peggy, the proprietor of the business, withdraws $2,000 of cash per month for personal living expenses.

4. **OBJECTIVE 4.** List in your own words the steps involved in making a master budget.

DISCUSSION QUESTIONS FOR SECTION 22.A

1. What are the purposes of having managers participate in the planning/budgeting process?

2. How do cash budgets aid managers?

3. What is meant by *correlation,* and how is it used in budgeting?

4. What is a *rolling budget,* and what advantages does a rolling budget have over a static budget?

5. Sales forecasts are often prepared by the salespeople. Do you think they are the proper people to provide such information? Would you have any reservations about sales forecasts prepared by salespeople? Explain.

6. James Marston operates a family-owned company. Business is very good, and the company has more cash than it needs for normal operations. When the company's new treasurer suggests that a cash budget be prepared, James argues that it would be a waste of time because the company has plenty of cash. Do you agree? Explain your answer.

7. What is a master budget?

8. What is a capital budget, and what does it have to do with a master budget?

9. What is the difference between a variable expense and a fixed expense?

EXERCISES FOR SECTION 22.A

22.A.1. Actual sales data for the Beta Corporation for the last quarter of 19X3 and a sales forecast for the first quarter of 19X4 are provided here. Assume that sales for each month are collected 60% in the month of sale, 30% in the month following sale, and 10% in the second month following sale. Prepare a spread sheet for the first quarter of 19X4 to derive the monthly expected cash receipts from sales.

Sales, 19X3		Sales Forecast, 19X4	
October	$ 80,000	January	$ 70,000
November	100,000	February	80,000
December	120,000	March	100,000

22.A.2. Actual purchases data for the Gamma Corporation for the last quarter of 19X1 and a purchases forecast for the first quarter of 19X2 are provided here. Assume that purchases during each month are paid 50% in the month of purchase, 30% in the month following purchase, and 20% in the second month following purchase. Prepare a spread sheet for the first quarter of 19X2 to derive the monthly expected cash payments for purchases.

Purchases, 19X1		Purchases Forecast, 19X2	
October	$100,000	January	$120,000
November	70,000	February	100,000
December	80,000	March	80,000

22.A.3. Data for Nulf, Inc., follow. Prepare a partial projected cash flow statement, showing net cash from operations for the month of March.

	February	March
Sales forecasts	$80,000	$120,000
Cost of Goods Sold forecasts	$48,000	$ 72,000
Administrative Expenses	$10,000	$ 10,000
Other Expenses as a % of Sales	10%	10%

Sales are collected 65% in the month of sale and 35% in the month after sale. Expenses, including cost of goods sold, are paid 90% in the month incurred and 10% in the next month.

22.A.4. Identify each of the following tasks as either financial accounting or managerial accounting.

    a. Preparation of an income statement

    b. Preparation of a projected balance sheet

c. Preparation of a performance report

d. Preparation of a capital budget

e. Preparation of a master budget

f. Journalizing a transaction

g. Preparation of a statement of changes in financial position

PROBLEMS FOR SECTION 22.A
Alternate Problems for this section begin on page D-119.

22.A.5. Poco Manufacturing Company collects 40% of sales in the month of sale, 40% in the month following sale, 15% in the second month following sale, and 4% in the third month following sale (1% of sales are uncollectible). About 70% of purchases are paid for in the month of purchase, with the remainder paid in the next month. Sales and purchases data follow.

	Sales	Purchases
ACTUAL		
April	$ 70,000	$40,000
May	80,000	50,000
June	80,000	70,000
PROJECTED		
July	90,000	90,000
August	130,000	60,000
September	90,000	50,000
October	90,000	40,000
November	60,000	30,000
December	50,000	30,000

Required

1) Prepare spread sheets for the last six months of the calendar year to determine expected cash receipts from sales and cash payments for purchases based on the foregoing actual and projected data. The spread sheets should show data by months and in total for the period.

2) If the company begins July with a cash balance of $1,000, in which months (if any) will there be a need to borrow cash? Consider your solution to part (1), but ignore other potential sources and uses of cash.

22.A.6. Actual credit sales for the last half of 19X4 and a sales forecast for the first half of 19X5 are shown on the next page for the Klingon Corporation. Assume that each month's credit sales are made evenly during the month and that, on the average, credit sales are collected 2½ months after they are made.

KLINGON CORPORATION			
Credit Sales, 19X4		*Credit Sales Forecast, 19X5*	
July	$ 60,000	January	$ 90,000
August	100,000	February	70,000
September	110,000	March	60,000
October	70,000	April	120,000
November	140,000	May	120,000
December	160,000	June	80,000

Required

Prepare a spread sheet for January through June 19X5 showing expected monthly and total cash inflows from credit sales.

22.A.7. Redram Supply Company buys large quantities of industrial supplies and resells them in smaller quantities to its customers. Sales are usually collected 60% in the month of sale, 30% in the month following sale, and 10% in the second month following sale. About 70% of purchases are paid for in the month of purchase, with the remainder being paid in the following month. Sales and purchases data are shown here, together with selected other data.

	Sales	**Purchases**
May	$ 80,000	$50,000
June	100,000	80,000

	Projected Sales	**Projected Purchases**
July	$ 60,000	$60,000
August	120,000	50,000
September	150,000	90,000

Other Data

1) Redram tries to maintain a cash balance of $6,000 and the balance at July 1 is exactly $6,000. When the balance falls to $4,000 or less, marketable securities are liquidated, if available, in multiples of $1,000 to bring the balance to approximately $6,000. If securities are not available, funds are borrowed against a line of credit at the bank in multiples of $1,000 to achieve the desired balance. When the balance exceeds $6,000 by at least $1,000, cash is applied in $1,000 increments against any outstanding bank loans to bring the balance down to approximately $6,000. Excess funds still available after paying bank loans are used in $1,000 multiples to purchase marketable securities. There is an outstanding bank loan of $2,000 at July 1.

2) Cash payments in addition to those made for purchases are expected to be as follows:

July	$21,000
August	54,000*
September	20,000

*Includes purchase of equipment

3) The owner of the business withdraws $3,000 of cash on the last day of each month for personal living expenses.

Required

1) Prepare quarterly spread sheets for July, August, and September to determine expected cash receipts from sales and cash payments for purchases. The spread sheets should show data by months and in total for the quarter.

2) Prepare a quarterly cash budget for July, August, and September. Present figures by months and for the quarter in a format similar to the one illustrated in this section.

SECTION 22.B

Responsibility Accounting

OBJECTIVES

This section deals with the reporting of information used in evaluating managers. At the end of your study, you should be able to

1. Define the following expressions:
   a. Responsibility accounting.
   b. Responsibility center.
   c. Controllable cost.
2. Prepare a performance report, given budgeted and actual cost data for a responsibility center.
3. State how responsibility accounting aids in the identification of trouble spots.

PURPOSES OF RESPONSIBILITY ACCOUNTING

As we have seen, managerial accounting deals with the collection and reporting of information for internal use by an entity's managers. The information helps managers make decisions and control the entity's resources. Budgets, for example, help managers make plans and coordinate activities.

OBJECTIVE 1a. Define responsibility accounting.

Another aspect of managerial accounting has to do with the evaluation of how well managers have performed in the past. Managers are accountable for the responsibilities assigned to them. *Responsibility accounting is the process of accumulating and reporting information for use in evaluating managers' performance. The device used for reporting on responsibility is called a performance report or responsibility report.* Lower-level managers report on their performance to higher-level managers, and higher-level managers use the performance reports in the evaluation of how well lower-level managers have performed.

Responsibilities generally follow from the authority that has been delegated from higher-level managers to those at lower levels. Let us assume, for example, that a corporation consists of two manufacturing plants, each with two production departments. The corporation president is delegated authority from the corporate directors, who represent the shareholders of the entity. Within the entity, the president delegates authority to the plant managers, and the plant managers in turn delegate authority to their department managers, as shown in Illustration 22.14.

If the corporation has a well-developed system of responsibility accounting, each lower-level manager will submit a performance report to the manager to whom he or she is responsible, and the manager in authority will use the report to evaluate the lower-level manager's performance. It

ILLUSTRATION 22.14

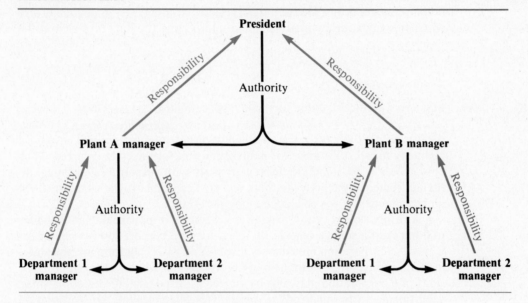

follows, then, that the principal purposes of responsibility accounting are to help managers report on their performance and to aid in performance evaluation. As suggested by Illustration 22.15, managers should also use performance reports in evaluating their own performance.

ILLUSTRATION 22.15

RESPONSIBILITY ACCOUNTING

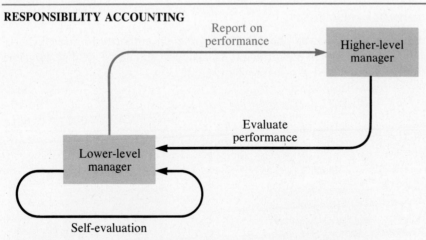

Purposes:
- To help managers report on their performance
- To aid in the evaluation of performance

We should keep in mind that responsibility reports are products of accounting systems designed and supervised by accountants. Accountants also assist in evaluation by analyzing and interpreting the data provided in the reports.

RESPONSIBILITY CENTERS

OBJECTIVE 1b. Define responsibility center.

Managers are accountable for their responsibilities. *A part of an entity for which a manager is responsible is called a responsibility center.* You may recall that a *cost center* was defined as an identifiable activity area in a company for which someone is held responsible for the costs incurred. Thus cost center is to some extent synonymous with responsibility center, although some people prefer to think of a cost center narrowly as the smallest identifiable center for cost accounting purposes.

A responsibility center may be any size, and it may include any number of other responsibility centers. In fact, an entire corporation is a center for which the corporation president is responsible. A corporation income statement is, in a sense, a responsibility report on the whole corporation. Divisions of a corporation may also be viewed as responsibility centers, as may departments within divisions. Consider, for example, the AB Corporation consisting primarily of two plants, each with two production departments. The responsibility centers for the AB Corporation might be identified as in Illustration 22.16.

An organization chart like the one in Illustration 22.17 shows the lines of authority downward and responsibility upward. And Illustration 22.18 shows the reporting on, and evaluation of, performance through just one line of responsibility/authority.

CONTROLLABLE COSTS

Managers should always be delegated sufficient authority to meet their responsibilities. Under this principle, a manager should be held responsible

ILLUSTRTION 22.16

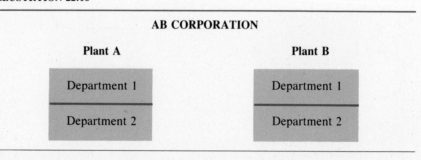

AB CORPORATION

Plant A	Plant B
Department 1	Department 1
Department 2	Department 2

ILLUSTRATION 22.17

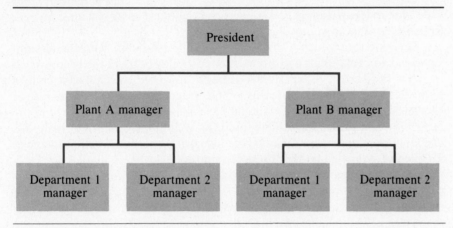

only for controllable costs. *A **controllable cost** is a cost that can be influenced by a manager at a specific responsibility level.*

OBJECTIVE 1c. Define controllable cost.

A performance report for a cost center should include only the costs controllable at that responsibility level, because those are the only costs for which the manager can reasonably answer. Remember, a performance report is by definition a device for reporting on responsibility. Costs that are not controllable by a particular manager can hardly be that manager's responsibility.

A responsibility report for Department 1 should show only the costs controlled by that department's manager. The manager of a production de-

ILLUSTRATION 22.18

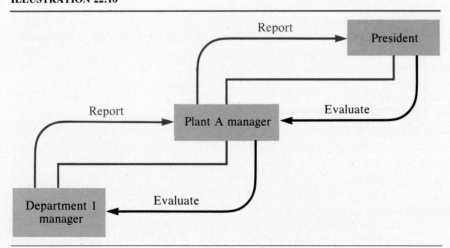

partment will usually have control over the direct materials and direct labor used in that department. Certain overhead (indirect) costs may also be controllable, at least to some degree, by a department head.

The extent to which a cost is controllable may vary with the circumstances. Direct materials and direct labor costs may be more easily controlled than overhead costs. A department manager, however, may not have control over the price paid for materials or the wage rate paid to departmental employees. Still, the manager should have some degree of control over the *quantities* of materials and labor used, as well as the *quality* of materials and labor. For example, it may be the manager's decision whether to assign a skilled or unskilled worker for a certain task.

Several managers at the same level may be able to influence a particular cost. Ideally, each manager is held responsible for that portion of a cost element that he or she controls. A purchasing manager should answer for the prices paid for materials; a production manager should answer for the quantities of materials used. Wage rates may be the responsibility of a personnel manager; and labor usage may be controlled by a department head.

PERFORMANCE REPORTS

Performance reports may be prepared in a variety of formats, including written explanations in paragraph form. In practice, however, performance reports usually present budgeted and actual figures for a period in comparative form. A third column may be used to show the *differences between budgeted and actual figures, referred to as* **variances.** *Favorable variances occur when actual results are better than the budget projections, whereas* **unfavorable variances** *result when actual results are worse than predicted.* The performance report in Illustration 22.19 is for Department 1 of AB Corporation's Plant A.

Keep in mind that the example in Illustration 22.19 has been simplified. It is likely that other manufacturing costs, and perhaps materials and labor as well, would be reported in greater detail than is shown here. Figures for factory utilities, insurance, property taxes, and other expenses are budgeted and later compared to actual amounts when they become available. Also, manufacturing concerns of any size are much more complex in organization than in our simple example.

The responsibility report for each plant incorporates the departmental reports and also shows costs (and revenues, if applicable) controlled directly at the plant level. Notice how the Plant A report in Illustration 22.20 presents only the total figures for each production department. (The Department 1 totals are the same as those shown at the bottom of that department's performance report.) In this way, the reports prepared for increasingly higher responsibility levels may be less cluttered and more understandable than they would be with all the detailed figures shown.

ILLUSTRATION 22.19

<table>
<tr><td colspan="4">**AB CORPORATION**
Department 1, Plant A
Performance Report
For the Month of January 19X4</td></tr>
<tr><td>Production: 10,000 Equivalent Units</td><td></td><td></td><td>**Variance:**
Favorable</td></tr>
<tr><td></td><td>**Budget**</td><td>**Actual**</td><td>**(Unfavorable)**</td></tr>
<tr><td>Direct materials</td><td>$ 80,000</td><td>$ 84,000</td><td>$(4,000)</td></tr>
<tr><td>Direct labor</td><td>64,000</td><td>62,000</td><td>2,000</td></tr>
<tr><td>Factory overhead</td><td></td><td></td><td></td></tr>
<tr><td>Indirect materials</td><td>11,000</td><td>12,000</td><td>(1,000)</td></tr>
<tr><td>Indirect labor</td><td>26,000</td><td>26,000</td><td>–0–</td></tr>
<tr><td>Other manufacturing costs</td><td>18,000</td><td>21,000</td><td>(3,000)</td></tr>
<tr><td>Total</td><td>$199,000</td><td>$205,000</td><td>$(6,000)</td></tr>
</table>

OBJECTIVE 2. Prepare a performance report.

By now you probably have a general idea of how lower-level data are incorporated and summarized as responsibility accumulates upward in an organization.

Management by Exception

The amount of time available to managers is limited and valuable. To manage effectively, managers must direct their energies toward areas that need the most attention, sometimes called trouble spots. *A system in which the at-*

ILLUSTRATION 22.20

<table>
<tr><td colspan="4">**AB CORPORATION**
Plant A
Performance Report
For Month of January, 19X4</td></tr>
<tr><td></td><td></td><td></td><td>**Variance:**
Favorable</td></tr>
<tr><td></td><td>**Budget**</td><td>**Actual**</td><td>**(Unfavorable)**</td></tr>
<tr><td>Department 1</td><td>$199,000</td><td>$205,000</td><td>$(6,000)</td></tr>
<tr><td>Department 2</td><td>240,000</td><td>238,000</td><td>2,000</td></tr>
<tr><td>Plant-level administration</td><td>85,000</td><td>86,000</td><td>(1,000)</td></tr>
<tr><td>Total</td><td>$524,000</td><td>$529,000</td><td>$(5,000)</td></tr>
</table>

OBJECTIVE 2. Prepare a performance report.

tention of managers is directed to unusual or unfavorable matters is sometimes referred to as **management by exception.**

The size and direction of variances shown in performance reports provide managers with one means of identifying trouble spots. Large variances, particularly those that are *unfavorable,* highlight exceptional circumstances that need to be investigated. A large variance can sometimes be explained as having resulted from matters beyond the control of the responsible manager. For instance, an unexpected increase in the market price of a raw material may force actual costs beyond the budgeted amount. But even here, alternatives may be available to managers. Perhaps a different kind of raw material might be substituted in the future. And if the price for which a finished product can be sold is inadequate to cover all costs, the product may have to be discontinued. If nothing else, budgets for future periods must reflect all known increases in resource costs.

Approaches for analyzing variances are explored further in Chapter 24.

GLOSSARY FOR SECTION 22.B

Controllable cost   A cost that can be influenced by a manager at a specific responsibility level.

Favorable variances   Differences by which actual results are better than budget projections.

Management by exception   A system in which the attention of managers is directed to unusual or unfavorable matters.

Organization chart   A chart showing the lines of authority and responsibility within an entity.

Performance report (responsibility report)   A device used for reporting on responsibility.

Responsibility accounting   The process of accumulating and reporting information for use in evaluating managers' performance.

Responsibility center   A part of an entity for which a manager is responsible.

Unfavorable variances   Differences by which actual results are worse than budget projections.

Variances   Differences between budgeted and actual figures.

SELF-QUIZ ON OBJECTIVES FOR SECTION 22.B
Solutions to Self-Quiz begin on page B-68.

1. **OBJECTIVE 1.** Define the following expressions:
   a. Responsibility accounting.
   b. Responsibility center.
   c. Controllable cost.

2. **OBJECTIVE 2.** The machining department of the Rockview Plant of Quizmo Corporation budgeted the following costs for October.

QUIZMO CORPORATION Machining Department—Rockview Plant Cost Budget For the Month of October 19– –	
Direct materials	$240,000
Direct labor	290,000
Factory overhead	
Indirect materials	76,000
Indirect labor	58,000
Other manufacturing costs	85,000
Total	$749,000

The machining department produced 50,400 equivalent units of product during October and incurred the following actual costs.

QUIZMO CORPORATION Machining Department—Rockview Plant Cost Report For the Month of October 19– –	
Direct materials	$225,000
Direct labor	302,000
Factory overhead	
Indirect materials	78,000
Indirect labor	53,000
Other manufacturing costs	86,000
Total	$744,000

Prepare a performance report for October for the machining department of Quizmo Corporation.

3. **OBJECTIVE 3.** State how responsibility accounting aids in the identification of trouble spots.

DISCUSSION QUESTIONS FOR SECTION 22.B

1. How do budgets aid managers in performance evaluation?

2. A basic principle of management is that a manager's responsibility and authority should be kept in balance. What is the justification for this principle?

3. Authority is delegated down through a business organization. Where does a corporation president's authority come from?

4. Responsibility rises upward through an organization. To whom is the board of directors of a corporation responsible?

5. What is meant by management by exception?

6. Why is it advisable to exclude noncontrollable costs from a manager's performance report?

7. What does an organization chart show?

EXERCISES FOR SECTION 22.B

22.B.1. Pick from the following items those most apt to be controllable by the manager of the grinding department in a large manufacturing plant.

a. Grinding department direct labor

b. Factory building depreciation

c. Fire insurance on the plant

d. Grinding department direct materials

e. Plant security costs

f. Grinding machine maintenance

g. Grinding machine depreciation

22.B.2. Indicate the portion of the chart opposite that represents the responsibility center for the manager of Plant 1. Also, indicate the responsibility center for the vice-president of production.

NORVAL CORPORATION
Organizational Chart

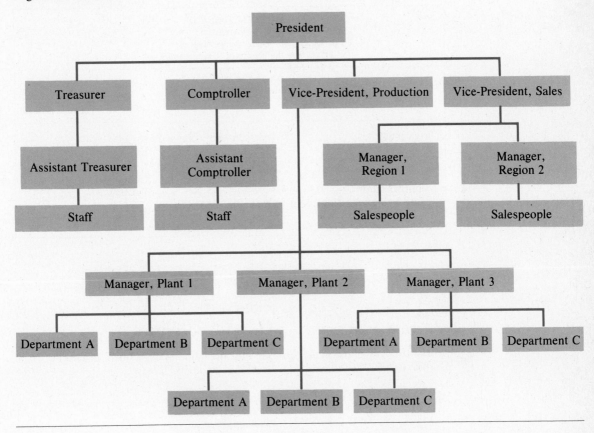

22.B.3. Determine the variance for each line in the following report, and indicate for each variance whether it is favorable or unfavorable.

I&O COMPANY **Department I** **Performance Report** **For the Month of September 19− −**			
	Budget	**Actual**	**Variance:** **Favorable** **(Unfavorable)**
Direct materials	$ 476,000	$ 482,000	
Direct labor	838,000	831,000	
Factory overhead			
Indirect materials	34,000	33,000	
Indirect labor	145,000	147,000	
Other manufacturing costs	72,000	75,000	
Total	$1,565,000	$1,568,000	

PROBLEMS FOR SECTION 22.B
Alternate Problems for this section begin on page D-122.

22.B.4. Budgeted and actual cost data for the painting department of DAG Corporation are as follows.

DAG CORPORATION **Painting Department** **For the Month of February 19− −**		
	Budget	**Actual**
Direct materials	$ 28,000	$ 33,000
Direct labor	86,000	92,000
Factory overhead		
Indirect materials	11,000	10,000
Indirect labor	18,000	18,000
Other manufacturing costs	31,000	33,000
Total	$174,000	$186,000

Required

1) Prepare a performance report for February for the painting department.

2) In your opinion, which variance shown in the performance report deserves the most serious attention from DAG's managers? Why?

22.B.5. The Aquapura Corporation manufactures pure fresh water from sea water. Budget and cost data are shown here for the electrolysis department.

AQUAPURA CORPORATION Electrolysis Department For the Month of August 19--		
Production: 4,980,000 Equivalent Units		
	Budget	**Actual**
Direct materials	$290,000	$311,000
Direct labor	180,000	168,000
Factory overhead		
Indirect materials	84,000	82,000
Indirect labor	23,000	24,000
Other manufacturing costs	41,000	48,000
Total	$618,000	$633,000

Required

1) Prepare a performance report for August for the electrolysis department of Aquapura Corporation.

2) Prepare a list of costs with unfavorable variances and their amounts. Indicate the percentage of variation from the budget for each of the costs listed.

22.B.6. Budgeted and actual data for the painting department of the Wellrock Corporation are shown here.

WELLROCK CORPORATION Painting Department For the Month of September 19--		
Production: 8,200 Equivalent Units		
	Budget	**Actual**
Direct materials	$ 8,000	$ 11,000
Direct labor	92,000	84,000
Factory overhead		
Indirect materials	3,000	4,000
Indirect labor	18,000	13,000
Other manufacturing costs	21,000	20,000
Total	$142,000	$132,000

Required

Prepare a performance report for September for the painting department.

Expenses incurred in the generation of revenue should be held to a minimum. A reduction in expense levels may actually be viewed as a type of accomplishment. Keep in mind that net income may be increased by either of the following accomplishments.

1. Increasing revenues by more than any accompanying increase in expenses
2. Decreasing expenses by more than any accompanying decrease in revenues

There is another reason for keeping asset costs as low as possible. Remember, one way to judge a company's performance is to relate its net income to the amount of assets employed in the company.

$$\frac{\text{Net income}}{\text{Average assets}} = \text{Rate of return on assets}$$

The smaller the amount of assets employed in earning a given amount of net income, the higher the rate of return. The overall goal of a business concern is to earn as much as possible (over the long run) with the assets employed—in other words, to operate the company efficiently. The more cost committed to assets, the higher the level of income needed to maintain a good rate of return.

Presumably, all segments of a competitive economy are better off when businesses operate efficiently. Consumers enjoy lower prices, shareholders earn higher returns, employees (including managers) receive higher wages, governments collect more taxes, and so on. The point is that costs should be carefully controlled, whether they are deferred as assets or matched in the current period as expenses.

TYPES OF COST

Costs may be categorized in a variety of ways. One way is to distinguish between unexpired and expired costs. Unexpired costs are assets; expired costs are expenses. Expired costs may be further categorized as follows.

Product Costs
Selling Expenses
Administrative Expenses
Other Expenses

The various product costs that go into cost of goods sold are discussed in Chapter 20. Product costs assigned to ending inventories do not expire until the inventory items are sold.

Selling Expenses and Administrative Expenses may be further broken down into object categories such as Salaries, Supplies Used, Depreciation, and so forth. Other Expenses are those that are difficult to classify and are likely to relate more generally to the whole entity than to any functional part of it. Interest Expense, the rental fee on borrowed funds, is a common example of Other Expenses.

COST RELATIONSHIPS

An income statement pictures the revenues for a period and the expenses that supposedly helped generate those revenues. The assumption, then, is that expenses (expired costs) can be related to (matched with) revenues.

Revenues result from the sale of goods or services during a period; the more goods sold or services rendered, the higher the level of revenues. In other words, the higher the level of sales *activity,* the greater the revenue.

Expenses for a period are the costs of achieving that period's activity level. Activity may be measured in units of sales (or services) as well as in dollars. If the number of units of sales for a future period can be predicted, this *activity level* can be used as a basis for predicting both the revenues (accomplishments) and expenses (sacrifices) for that period.

The dependence of one outcome (variable) on another can be illustrated graphically. Let us examine the simple cost relationships for the Miltap Company, which manufactures and sells miltaps as its only product.

Fixed Costs

*A **fixed cost** is one that is not affected by the level of activity during an accounting or budget period.* Building depreciation, administrative salaries, property taxes, and insurance are just a few examples of costs that do not tend to vary with activity levels.

OBJECTIVE 1.
Differentiate between fixed, step-fixed, variable, and mixed costs.

For illustration purposes, let us assume that the Miltap Company has the following costs each month.

FIXED COSTS PER MONTH	
Product	$ 60,000
Selling	10,000
Administrative	25,000
Other	5,000
Total	$100,000

The relationships between costs and activity levels may be pictured graphically. Illustration 23.1 on the next page depicts the fact that the total monthly fixed cost remains constant as the number of miltaps sold changes. The straight line representing total fixed cost can be stated in a simple equa-

ILLUSTRATION 23.1   **Total fixed cost per month**

OBJECTIVE 4. Select from a group of graphs the one that depicts behavior of a particular cost.

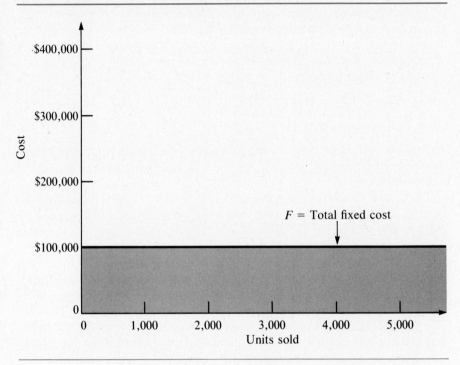

tion, where F represents fixed cost. Keep in mind that the total fixed cost line in the graph represents the sum of the individual cost lines for the various fixed costs.

> F = Total fixed cost per month

Costs that are fixed *in total* decline on a *per unit* basis as output activity increases. For example, a total fixed cost of $100,000 amounts to $100 per unit at 1,000 units of sales, falls to $50 per unit at 2,000 units of sales, and is further reduced to $20 per unit at 5,000 units of sales. Illustration 23.2 shows the fixed cost per unit for Miltap Company.

Step-Fixed Costs

As a practical matter, hardly any cost remains completely fixed as activity is continuously increased. Sooner or later, continued growth requires additional space and equipment, which results in increased rent, depreciation,

ILLUSTRATION 23.2   Fixed cost per unit

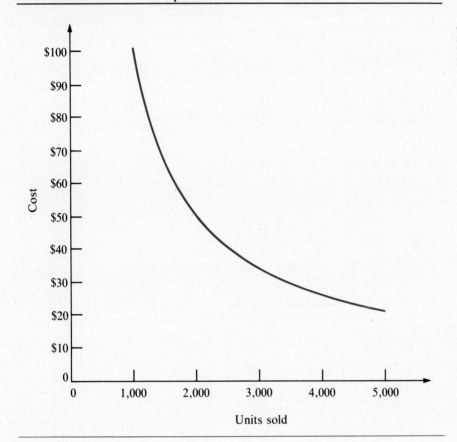

and other expenses. Similarly, at some point, more administrators will be needed, property taxes will increase, and so on. *A cost that remains constant except for one or more abrupt changes is referred to as a **step-fixed cost.***

Suppose, for example, that the total fixed cost must be increased to $150,000 per month for the company to attain sales of more than 5,000 miltaps each month. The jump in fixed cost is pictured in Illustration 23.3. On a *per unit* basis, the step in fixed cost will cause the unit cost to jump at 5,000 units, as shown in Illustration 23.4. Both illustrations are on the next page.

Of course, if an activity level beyond 5,000 units of sales per month is highly unlikely, we may just ignore what would happen at that point. Likewise, possible reductions of fixed costs at low activity levels may be ignored if it is not feasible to operate at such low levels. Thus if fixed costs are apt to remain constant over a relevant range of activity between 2,000 and 5,000

ILLUSTRATION 23.3   Step-fixed cost per month

OBJECTIVE 4.   Select from a group of graphs the one that depicts behavior of a particular cost.

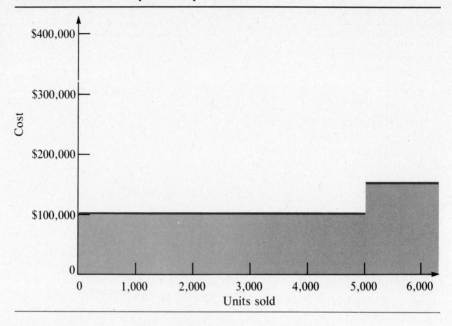

ILLUSTRATION 23.4   Step-fixed cost per unit

OBJECTIVE 4.   Select from a group of graphs the one that depicts behavior of a particular cost.

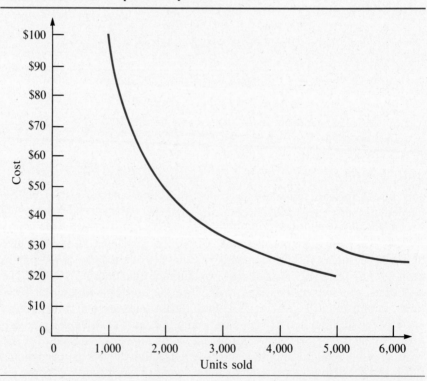

units of sales, then the fixed cost graph of Illustration 23.1 is adequate for planning purposes. *A **relevant range of activity** is the span between the low and high activity levels at which an entity might reasonably be expected to operate during a time period. In other words, it is the normal range of activity for a concern.* If, for example, the relevant range of activity for an entity were between 2,000 and 4,000 units, the step-fixed cost portrayed by the graph in Illustration 23.5 could be viewed as a fixed cost. No harm would be done by depicting the cost as one horizontal line, formed by the dashed extensions for activity levels below and above the relevant activity range.

Variable Costs

*A **variable cost** is one that changes directly in relation to changes in activity level.* Variable costs associated with products have been identified as direct materials, direct labor, and variable factory overhead. Certain nonproduct costs may also vary with changing activity levels. For example, commissions paid to salespeople vary with sales levels. Transportation, supplies, billing costs, and many other expenses may also vary (at least in part) as sales levels change.

OBJECTIVE 1.
Differentiate between fixed, step-fixed, variable, and mixed costs.

ILLUSTRATION 23.5   Step-fixed cost per month, viewed as fixed cost

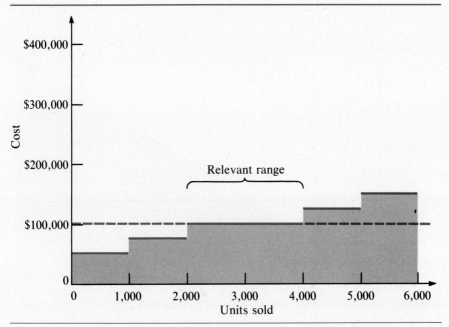

To keep matters simple, let us assume that variable costs may be identified with each miltap sold as follows.

VARIABLE COSTS PER UNIT	
Product	$30
Selling	20
Administrative	8
Other	2
Total per unit	$60

The total variable cost for the Miltap Company can be portrayed graphically, as in Illustration 23.6.

The variable cost for any given number of units of sales can be calculated by multiplying the variable cost per unit by the number of units. If v represents the variable cost per unit, and n represents the number of units, the equation for the line can be expressed as shown in the box at the top of the page opposite.

ILLUSTRATION 23.6   Total variable cost per month

OBJECTIVE 4. Select from a group of graphs the one that depicts behavior of a particular cost.

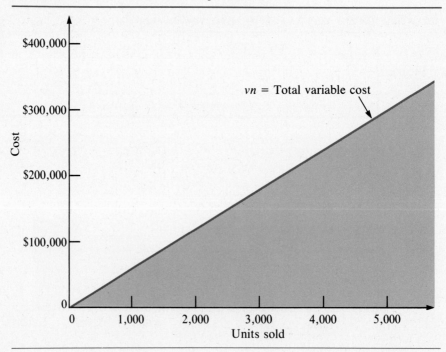

vn = Total variable cost

vn = Total variable cost

To find the total variable cost for 3,000 units of sales, we multiply $60 by 3,000 units:

vn = Total variable cost
$60(3,000) = $180,000

Variable cost viewed on a *per unit* basis becomes fixed. The graph in Illustration 23.7 shows that Miltap's variable cost remains at $60 per unit as volume increases.

ILLUSTRATION 23.7   Variable cost per unit

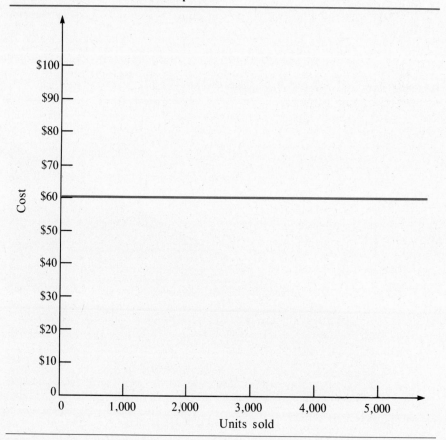

OBJECTIVE 4. Select from a group of graphs the one that depicts behavior of a particular cost.

The relationship between per unit and total cost behavior may be summarized as follows.

	Per Unit	Total
Variable cost	Constant	Changes
Fixed cost	Changes	Constant

Mixed Costs

OBJECTIVE 1.
Differentiate between fixed, step-fixed, variable, and mixed costs.

Costs that exhibit a combination of fixed and variable behavior are referred to as mixed costs. Consider, for example, the case where salespeople are paid base salaries plus a commission on what they sell. If base salaries total $10,000 per month, and if an additional sales commission of $5 is paid for each unit sold, total monthly compensation for salespeople would be pictured as in Illustration 23.8.

ILLUSTRATION 23.8   Mixed cost per month

OBJECTIVE 4. Select from a group of graphs the one that depicts behavior of a particular cost.

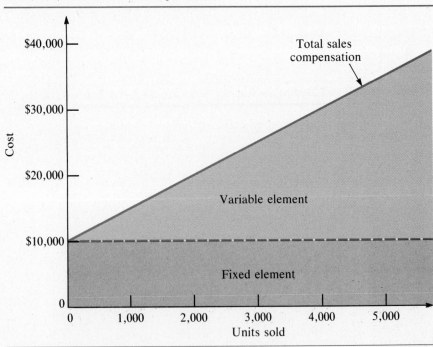

ILLUSTRATION 23.9   Combined total cost per month, viewed with fixed cost as a bottom layer

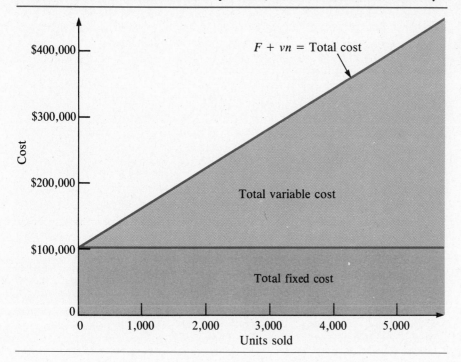

OBJECTIVE 3. Draw a graph that depicts combined total costs for an entity over a designated range of activity levels.

As a practical matter, mixed cost elements may be viewed separately. In the example just given, we can include the base salaries of salespeople along with other fixed costs and combine the sales commissions with other variable costs.

Combined Total Cost

Fixed and variable costs may be pictured together on the same graph, as in Illustration 23.9. An alternative arrangement shows fixed cost as a layer on top of variable cost, as in Illustration 23.10 on the next page.

The total cost formula that follows is stated both in general terms and for the Miltap Company in particular.

$$vn + F = \text{Total cost}$$
$$\$60n + \$100,000 = \text{Miltap total cost}$$

OBJECTIVE 2. Write a total cost formula for a one-product entity with linear cost relationships.

ILLUSTRATION 23.10   Combined total cost per month, viewed with fixed cost as a top layer

**OBJECTIVE 3. Draw a
graph that depicts
combined total costs for
an entity over a
designated range of
activity levels.**

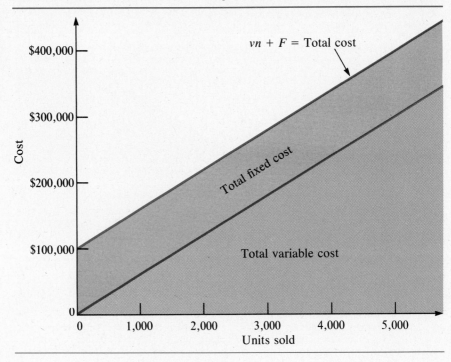

To calculate Miltap's total cost at 4,000 units of sales, we simply sub-stitute 4,000 for n.

$$\$60(4{,}000 \text{ units}) + \$100{,}000 = \$340{,}000 \text{ Total cost}$$

Should the fixed cost have a step in it within the relevant activity range, the total cost graph would appear as in Illustration 23.11.

Curvilinear Relationships

The relationships between costs and activity may take a variety of forms in actual practice. Sometimes the *rate* at which a cost changes varies as activity increases or decreases. Consider, for example, materials that cost less per unit as larger quantities are purchased because of quantity (volume) dis-counts. Transportation and handling costs may also decline on a *per unit* basis as larger quantities of materials are used. Variable costs that increase at a constantly *decreasing rate* will take the graphical form shown in Illus-

ILLUSTRATION 23.11 Combined total cost per month, when fixed cost is stepped

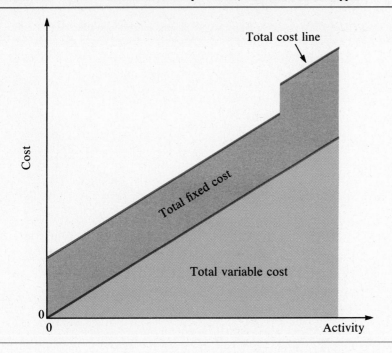

tration 23.12. Costs may also increase at an *increasing rate,* as pictured in Illustration 23.13 on the next page.

One example of an increasing cost rate is the cost of raw materials used by a cannery, materials that have to be hauled from increasing distances as

ILLUSTRATION 23.12 Total variable cost per month, with a decreasing rate

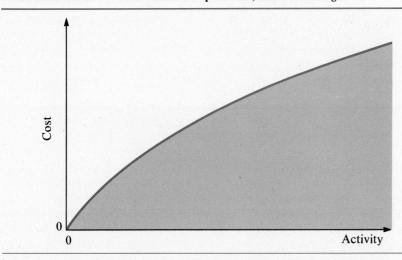

ILLUSTRATION 23.13   Total variable cost per month, with an increasing rate

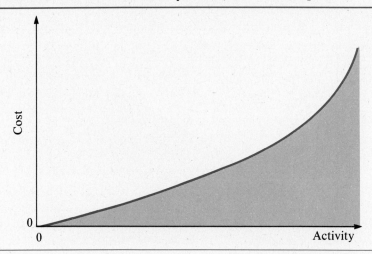

vegetable supplies in nearby areas are used up. Or costs may increase at a decreasing rate over a certain range of activity, after which they start increasing at an increasing rate as depicted in Illustration 23.14. For example, quantity discounts might be available on raw materials until local supplies are exhausted, after which additional materials become increasingly costly.

ILLUSTRATION 23.14   Total variable cost per month, with decreasing and increasing rates

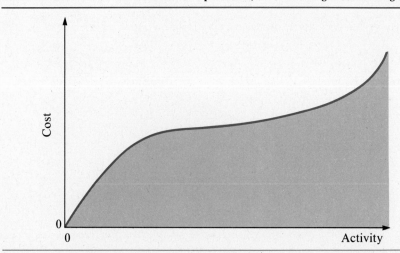

There is no limit to the number of possible relationships between costs and activity. You might try drawing lines of various shapes on a graph, and then see if you can think of cost relationships that would go with the lines you have drawn.

GLOSSARY FOR SECTION 23.A

Fixed cost   A cost that is not affected by the level of activity during an accounting or budget period.

Mixed cost   A cost that exhibits a combination of fixed and variable behavior.

Relevant range of activity   The span between the low and high activity levels at which an entity might reasonably be expected to operate during a time period. In other words, it is the normal range of activity for an entity.

Step-fixed cost   A cost that remains constant except for one or more abrupt changes.

Variable cost   A cost that changes directly in relation to changes in activity levels.

SELF-QUIZ ON OBJECTIVES FOR SECTION 23.A
Solutions to Self-Quiz begin on page B-68.

1. OBJECTIVE 1. In your own words, differentiate between fixed, step-fixed, variable, and mixed costs.

2. Experience shows that Elrod Company has fixed cost per month of $50,000, and that variable costs for its one product, L-rods, amount to $25 per unit.

   a. OBJECTIVE 2. Write a monthly total cost formula for Elrod Company, using the symbol n to represent units sold.

   b. OBJECTIVE 3. Draw a graph that pictures Elrod's combined total cost over activity levels from 0 to 5,000 units of sales.

3. OBJECTIVE 4. For each of the costs described here, indicate the number of the graph (see page 962) that probably pictures the behavior of the cost. A graph may represent more than one cost behavior or none of the behaviors described.

   a. Total fixed cost that jumps (steps) once at a given level of monthly activity

   b. Fixed cost per unit

   c. Variable cost per unit

   d. Total variable cost per month

   e. Monthly sales compensation that includes base salaries plus commissions for units sold

   f. Total monthly fixed cost that remains constant over the relevant range of activity

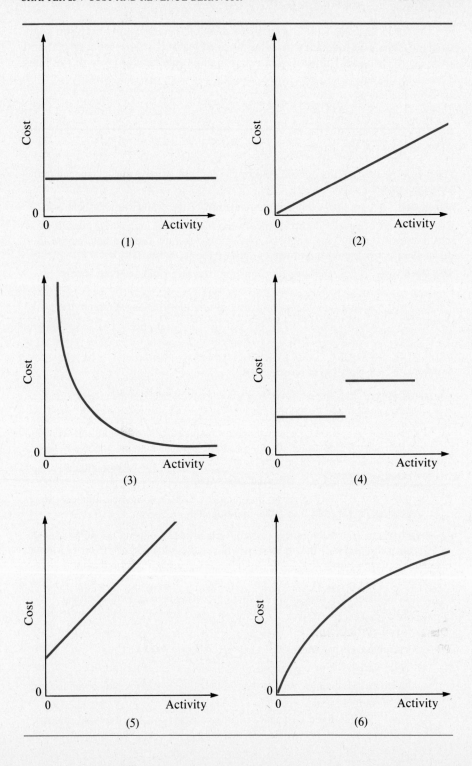

DISCUSSION QUESTIONS FOR SECTION 23.A

1. A fixed cost is one that remains constant as the level of activity changes. Some accountants argue that in the real world there is no such thing as a completely fixed cost. Does this argument have merit? Why?

2. What are the two basic accomplishments by which net income may be increased in the future?

3. On a *per unit* basis, fixed costs are variable and variable costs are fixed. Is this statement true or false? Why?

4. What is meant by the expression *relevant range,* and how does it relate to a step-fixed cost?

5. How and why does a graph of a mixed cost resemble an entity's total cost graph?

6. Under what circumstances might a cost increase at an increasing rate?

7. Under what circumstances might a cost increase at a decreasing rate?

8. Under what circumstances might a cost increase at a decreasing rate up to a point, after which it increases at an increasing rate?

EXERCISES FOR SECTION 23.A

23.A.1. Darth Corporation has a total fixed cost of $60,000 and a variable cost of 70¢ per unit. Calculate expected total cost at each of the following production levels:

  a. 100,000 units.

  b. 150,000 units.

  c. 0 units.

23.A.2. Calculate the *average* unit cost for each of the situations described in exercise 23.A.1(a) and (b). Why is the unit cost for (b) less than for (a)?

23.A.3. The Skoshi Corporation has total fixed costs per month of $90,000 and a variable cost for its one product of $2.50 per unit. Write a monthly total cost formula for Skoshi, using the symbol n to represent units produced.

23.A.4. Parr Manufacturing Company has total fixed costs of $80,000 for production of 0 through 100,000 units. For production between 100,001 and 200,000 units, fixed cost will increase by $30,000. Variable cost is $4 per unit. Draw a graph that portrays Parr's total cost from 0 through 200,000 units of production. Show fixed cost as a layer on top of the variable cost.

$$
\begin{array}{ll}
\text{Total revenue} - \text{Total cost} & = \text{Net income} \\
pn - (vn + F) & = \text{Net income} \\
pn - vn - F & = \text{Net income} \\
\$100n - \$60n - \$100{,}000 & = \text{Net income}
\end{array}
$$

The anticipated net income (or loss) at any level of sales may now be determined by substituting for n the number of units of sales. For example, sales of only 2,000 units would result in a net loss, as follows.

OBJECTIVE 3. Calculate net income or net loss.

$$
\begin{array}{lll}
\$100n - & \$60n & - \$100{,}000 = \text{Net income} \\
\$100(2{,}000) - & \$60(2{,}000) & - \$100{,}000 = \text{Net income} \\
\$200{,}000 - & \$120{,}000 & - \$100{,}000 = \$(20{,}000)^*
\end{array}
$$

*Parentheses denote loss

BREAK-EVEN POINT

*The **break-even point** for an entity is the particular volume of sales at which total revenue is equal to total cost.* The break-even point may be determined for the Miltap Company by designating a *zero* net income and solving for the value of n, as follows.

OBJECTIVE 2. Determine the break-even point in units.

$$
\begin{array}{ll}
pn - vn - F & = \text{Net income} \\
\$100n - \$60n - \$100{,}000 & = \$0 \\
\$40n & = \$100{,}000 \\
n & = 2{,}500 \text{ units sold}
\end{array}
$$

The Miltap Company should break even at 2,500 units of sales, where its total revenue would be equal to its total cost. In the graph in Illustration 23.16, the break-even point is the point at which the total revenue and total cost lines intersect.

Vertical distances between the total revenue and total cost lines represent *net incomes* above the break-even point and *net losses* below the break-even point.

CONTRIBUTION MARGIN

*The **contribution margin** is what is left over from revenue after allowing for variable costs.* Thus, the contribution margin *per unit* can be determined for the Miltap Company as follows.

OBJECTIVE 1. Determine the contribution margin per unit.

$$
\begin{array}{ll}
p - v & = \text{Contribution margin per unit} \\
\$100 - \$60 & = \$40 \text{ Contribution margin per unit}
\end{array}
$$

Now refer back to the break-even calculation and notice that the break-even point was determined by dividing the total fixed cost by the contribution margin per unit. In other words, the break-even point is the number of units that must be sold for the contribution margin per unit to accumulate to a sum sufficient to cover the total fixed cost for the period. For the Miltap Company, the break-even point is 2,500 units of sales, as illustrated here.

$$\frac{\text{Total fixed cost}}{\text{Contribution margin per unit}} = \text{Break-even point in sales units}$$

$$\frac{\$100,000}{\$40} = 2{,}500 \text{ units to break even}$$

OBJECTIVE 2. Determine the break-even point in units.

ILLUSTRATION 23.16   Break-even point

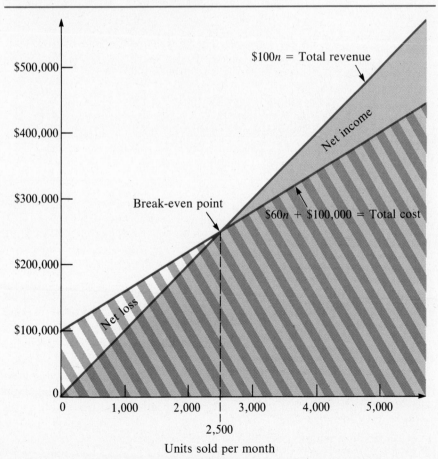

Units sold per month

ILLUSTRATION 23.17   Cost-volume-profit measures

OBJECTIVE 4.   Draw a graph depicting total variable cost, total cost, and total revenue.

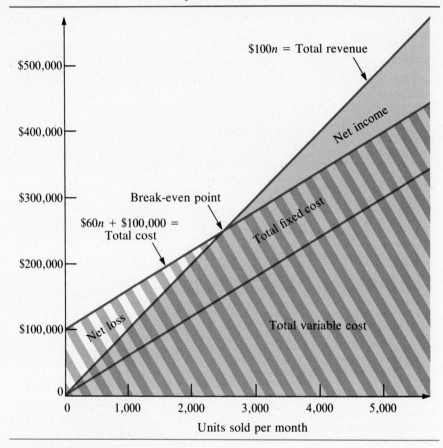

The *total* contribution margin at a given activity level can be measured on a graph as the distance between the total variable cost and the total revenue at that activity level. The blue revenue area above variable cost on the graph in Illustration 23.17 represents the measures of total contribution margin for the Miltap Company at various sales levels.

You can see that beyond the break-even point, the contribution margin per unit accumulates as net income. In other words, once the total fixed cost is covered, the contribution margin from additional units sold is all profit.

Contribution margin may also be stated as a percentage of revenue.

$$\frac{p - v}{p} = \text{Contribution margin percentage}$$

$$\frac{\$100 - \$60}{\$100} = \frac{\$40}{\$100} = 40\% \text{ contribution margin}$$

This means that the Miltap Company has 40¢ of each sales dollar left over after allowing for variable costs. The break-even point in sales revenue terms may be directly determined as follows.

$$\frac{\text{Total fixed cost}}{\text{Contribution margin percentage}} = \text{Break-even point in sales dollars}$$

$$\frac{\$100,000}{0.40} = \$250,000 \text{ break-even sales revenue}$$

OBJECTIVE 2. Determine the break-even point in dollars.

The more fixed cost a company has, the more sales needed to break even. On the other hand, a low variable cost rate means a high contribution margin. Highly mechanized manufacturing concerns, such as steelmaking, auto assembly, refining, and mining are usually saddled with heavy fixed costs. Consequently, they are apt to suffer huge losses when sales are low, and show enormous profits when sales are high.

MARGIN OF SAFETY

*The difference between the level of current sales and the break-even sales level is referred to as the **margin of safety**.* Margin of safety may be expressed in dollars, in units, or as a percentage. For example, when the Miltap Company achieves a sales level of $400,000 per month, it has a margin of safety of $150,000, or 1,500 units, in excess of break-even sales. Or the margin of safety may be stated in percentage terms as follows.

$$\frac{\text{Sales} - \text{Break-even sales}}{\text{Sales}} = \text{Margin of safety percentage}$$

$$\frac{\$400,000 - \$250,000}{\$400,000} = 37.5\%$$

EFFECTS OF CHANGES IN COST AND/OR REVENUE BEHAVIOR

The real world is anything but stable. Conditions are constantly changing, and planners attempt to incorporate predicted changes into planning processes. Even though we cannot predict what the future holds, we *can* speculate on the effects that various possible conditions may have on an entity.

Cost-volume-profit models may be manipulated to observe the effects of changing circumstances. For example, we can see from the graph in Illustration 23.18 how Miltap's break-even point would be increased if total fixed cost rose to $150,000 per month. The additional units of sales needed to cover the $50,000 increase in fixed cost can be determined as follows.

$$\frac{\text{Additional fixed cost}}{\text{Contribution margin per unit}} = \text{Additional units to break even}$$

$$\frac{\$50,000}{\$40} = 1,250 \text{ additional units}$$

ILLUSTRATION 23.18   Increase in total fixed cost

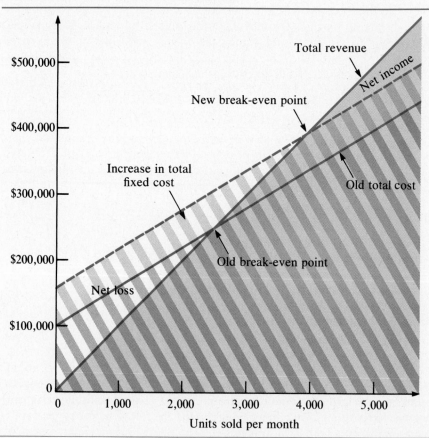

ILLUSTRATION 23.19   Increase in price per unit

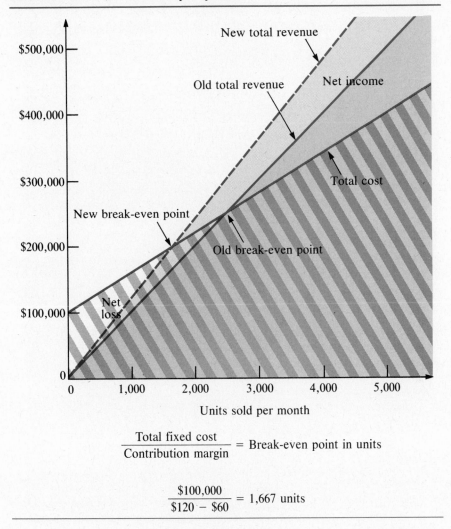

$$\frac{\text{Total fixed cost}}{\text{Contribution margin}} = \text{Break-even point in units}$$

$$\frac{\$100,000}{\$120 - \$60} = 1,667 \text{ units}$$

Thus the break-even point would increase from 2,500 units to 3,750 units per month as a result of the $50,000 increase in fixed cost.

Similarly, we can experiment with changes in unit prices and/or unit variable costs. The graph in Illustration 23.19 shows the effect of an increase in Miltap's unit selling price to $120. The graph in Illustration 23.20 on the next page shows the effect of an increase in unit variable cost to $70. In each case, all other factors are assumed to remain as they were originally. The break-even points for the changed conditions are also determined below the graphs by dividing the total fixed cost by the contribution margin per unit.

ILLUSTRATION 23.20   Increase in variable cost per unit

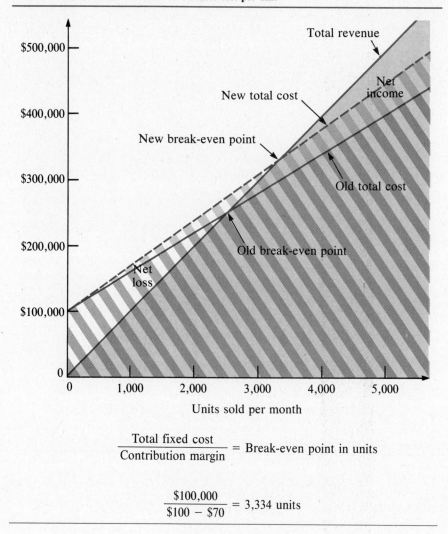

$$\frac{\text{Total fixed cost}}{\text{Contribution margin}} = \text{Break-even point in units}$$

$$\frac{\$100,000}{\$100 - \$70} = 3,334 \text{ units}$$

The results are rounded to whole numbers since it is assumed that only whole units are sold.

The complexities of working with curvilinear functions for revenues and costs are avoided at this level of your study. We are also ignoring the complications encountered with multiproduct companies. These factors make the planning process more difficult, but not impossible. The concepts of cost variability, contribution margin, and break-even point may become multi-dimensional, but they remain valid nevertheless.

GLOSSARY FOR SECTION 23.B

Break-even point　The particular volume of sales at which total revenue is equal to total cost.

Contribution margin　The amount that is left over from revenue after allowing for variable costs.

Margin of safety　The difference between the level of current sales and the break-even sales level.

SELF-QUIZ ON OBJECTIVES FOR SECTION 23.B
Solutions to Self-Quiz begin on page B-70.

Yutu Company produces and sells only yutus. Fixed costs total $40,000 per month, and variable costs run $6 per unit. Yutus are sold for a unit price of $8.

1. **OBJECTIVE 1.**　Determine the contribution margin per yutu sold.

2. **OBJECTIVE 2.**　Determine Yutu's monthly break-even point in both units and sales dollars.

3. **OBJECTIVE 3.**　Calculate Yutu's expected net income (or loss) at a sales volume of 30,000 units.

4. **OBJECTIVE 4.**　Draw a graph for Yutu that pictures its total variable cost, total cost, and total revenue for sales volumes from 0 to 50,000 units per month.

DISCUSSION QUESTIONS FOR SECTION 23.B

1. What is the general formula for deriving total revenue for a one-product company?

2. What is meant by a break-even point?

3. What is the term used to describe the amount that is left of revenue after allowing for variable costs?

4. What is the general break-even equation for a one-product company?

5. What are the simplifying assumptions that underlie a linear cost-volume-profit model?

6. What is meant by a margin of safety?

7. How is a margin of safety percentage determined?

8. What effect would a *decrease* in fixed cost per month have on a concern's break-even point? Explain.

9. What effect would a *decrease* in revenue per unit have on a concern's break-even point? Explain.

10. What effect would a *decrease* in variable cost per unit have on a concern's break-even point? Explain.

EXERCISES FOR SECTION 23.B

23.B.1. Mackey, Incorporated, sells only one product. By restricting sales to one product, the company is able to get quantity discounts on purchases and minimize its inventory carrying costs. Price and cost data are as follows:

Price	$ 400
Variable cost	$ 300
Monthly fixed cost	$6,000

 a. Calculate break-even sales in dollars.

 b. Assume that fixed costs increase by $500 a month. Calculate the *additional* sales *in dollars* required to break even.

23.B.2. The H&H Corporation manufactures pouches that sell for $3 each. The company has variable costs of $1.20 per unit and fixed costs per month of $8,000. During the month of June, the company expects to sell only 4,000 units.

 a. How much net income is expected for June?

 b. Would H&H be better off to close down for the month of June? Why?

23.B.3. Write a break-even equation and calculate the break-even point in units and dollars for the company whose costs and revenues are portrayed on the following graph.

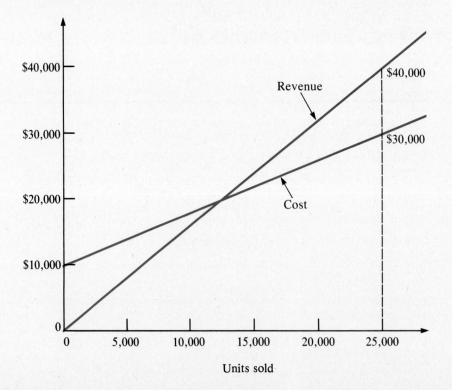

Units sold

23.B.4. The cost-volume-profit relationship for Adle Incorporated is portrayed by the following graph.

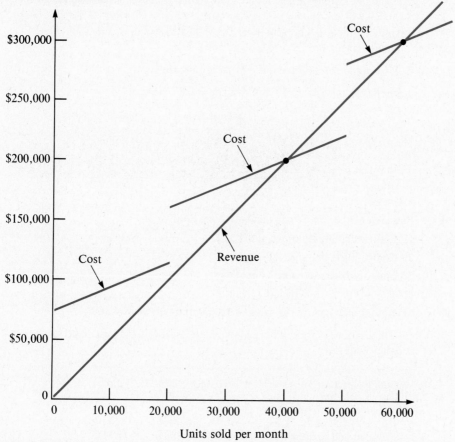

Units sold per month

a. What is the approximate break-even point in units as shown by the graph?

b. At approximately what level of activity is Adle's profit maximized?

23.B.5. Nifty Company had sales during the previous year of $800,000, total fixed cost of $264,000, and total variable cost of $448,000. Determine Nifty's margin of safety for the previous year and its margin of safety percentage. (*Hint:* First determine the contribution margin percentage.)

PROBLEMS FOR SECTION 23.B
Alternate Problems for this section begin on page D-127.

23.B.6. The Purple Paint Corporation produces and sells only purple paint. Fixed costs run about $90,000 per month, and variable costs run $7 per gallon. Purple sells its paint at a price of $9.50 per gallon.

Required

1) Calculate the contribution margin per gallon of paint sold.

2) Calculate Purple's break-even point in both gallons and sales dollars.

3) Calculate Purple's expected net income (or loss) at a sales volume of 30,000 gallons.

4) Draw a graph depicting Purple's total cost and total revenue for sales volumes from 0 to 50,000 gallons per month.

23.B.7. Price and cost data for three firms are provided:

	Unit Price	Unit Variable Cost	Monthly Fixed Cost
Firm 1	$4	$2.50	$15,000
Firm 2	$4	$2.50	$30,000
Firm 3	$4	$2.00	$30,000

Required

For each of the three firms, calculate the following:

1) Contribution margin per unit.

2) Contribution margin percentage.

3) Monthly break-even sales in units.

4) Monthly break-even sales in dollars.

5) Net income or loss for sales of 15,000 units during a month.

23.B.8. There are two break-even points for the Mauve Company. Cost and revenue data follow.

Selling price per unit	$10
Variable cost per unit	$7.50
Fixed cost per month	
Up to 10,000 units	$16,000
From 10,000 to 20,000 units	$32,000

Required

1) Calculate the units of sales required to break even at each of the two points, using the equation $pn = vn + F$.

2) Calculate the dollars of sales required to break even at each of the two points by dividing fixed cost by the contribution margin percentage.

3) Draw a graph portraying Mauve's break-even points.

23.B.9. The Leavy Manufacturing Company has a contribution margin of $5 for each unit of product sold. Fixed costs are $17,000 per month.

Required

1) Calculate the number of units of sales required to break even.

2) Plot the total contribution toward fixed cost and profit on a graph and plot total fixed cost on the same graph.

3) Where do the contribution line and the fixed cost line intersect? What is this point called?

SUMMARY OF CHAPTER 23

Costs may be viewed in terms of how they behave in relation to changes in activity levels. Fixed costs remain constant, while variable costs change along with activity levels. Cost relationships for single-product entities may be expressed as equations or pictured as graphs. A step-fixed cost may be viewed as a single horizontal line if the level of cost remains fixed over the relevant range of expected activity. A mixed cost can be viewed as consisting of fixed and variable elements.

A variable cost is fixed on a per unit basis, while fixed cost becomes ever smaller per unit as the activity level increases. Under some circumstances, variable cost relationships may be curvilinear, in that they increase at either decreasing or increasing rates as activity goes up.

Cost and revenue equations may be combined into a net income formula for a single-product entity. A break-even activity level can then be approximated by designating net income as zero. Cost and revenue equations may be pictured graphically so as to show the break-even point and the elements of net loss, net income, and contribution margin. The break-even point may be stated in either units or dollars of sales. Contribution margin can be stated in per unit, percentage of sales, or total terms. A margin of safety factor can be computed to show how far above the break-even point a firm is currently operating.

The effects of changes in revenues, variable costs, or fixed costs may be approximated by reflecting the changes in the cost-volume-profit model for a concern.

PROBLEMS FOR CHAPTER 23
Alternate Problems for this chapter begin on page D-129.

23.1. Four unrelated situations are described here.

  a. Arch Company has total monthly fixed costs of $40,000, sells its product units for $10 each, and breaks even at 8,000 units per month.

Required
Determine Arch's variable cost per unit.

  b. Bowen Company earned $20,000 net income last month from sales of 8,400 product units at a price of $7 per unit. Bowen has a variable cost of $4 per product unit.

Required
Calculate Bowen's fixed cost for the month.

  c. Callas Company has monthly fixed cost of $50,000 and variable cost of $1.20 per unit. Callas deals in one product that sells for $2 per unit. During the previous month, Callas incurred a net loss of $18,000.

Required

Determine the number of units that must have been sold by Callas during the previous month.

d. Dinah Company's monthly break-even point is 6,000 units of sales. Dinah has monthly fixed cost of $30,000 and sells its product for $9 per unit.

Required

Determine Dinah's variable cost per unit.

23.2. Lamont Gortz is an accounting student at East Stak University. He is planning to earn some money by selling sandwiches in the college residence halls. Lamont believes he can sell his sandwiches for $1 each. They will cost him 60¢ each to make, and he will have to pay a sales commission of 15¢ for each sandwich sold. A large microwave oven suitable for heating the sandwiches rents for $100 per month. Lamont will also have to rent storage and work space for $250 per month.

Required

1) Determine the number of sandwiches per month that Lamont must sell to break even.

2) How many sandwiches must be sold for Lamont to earn a net income of $300 per month?

3) Draw a graph for Lamont that pictures his total variable cost, total cost, and total revenue for sales volumes from 0 to 3,000 sandwiches per month.

COMPREHENSION PROBLEMS FOR CHAPTER 23

23.3. Mileau Company managers are considering a number of alternatives in an attempt to improve the company's performance. In the past, the concern has had a monthly fixed cost of $10,000 and a unit variable cost of $4, and it has sold its one product at $6 per unit. Monthly sales have averaged about 5,500 units, with little deviation over or under that sales level. The alternatives under consideration, and the expected consequences, are as follows.

a. Increase the sales price to $6.50 per unit, in which case it is likely that sales will fall to 4,000 units per month.

b. Reduce sales price to $5.60 per unit, in which case sales should rise to a level of 6,000 units per month.

c. Increase fixed cost by $5,000 per month, which will permit variable cost to be reduced to $3 per unit.

d. Substitute direct labor for some of the fixed cost, which will reduce fixed cost by $2,000 per month and increase unit variable cost by 30¢ per unit.

Alternatives (c) and (d) would have no effects on sales prices or sales levels. Either (a) or (b) may be selected, but not both. Likewise, only one choice could be made from (c) or (d). However, the sales price per unit could be changed simultaneously with a choice of either (c) or (d).

Required

Analyze the net income and break-even effects of the four alternatives, and make recommendations to Mileau's managers as to which alternatives they should implement.

23.4. Blip Company is capable of producing up to 50,000 blips per year in its plant. At January 1, 19X1, there were no beginning inventories on hand. During 19X1, orders were received from customers for 40,000 blips at a price of $18 per unit. Blip's cost structure is summarized here.

Variable costs on a per unit basis	
Direct materials	$2
Direct labor	3
Variable factory overhead	4
Variable selling cost (per unit sold)*	1
Fixed costs per year	
Fixed factory overhead	$180,000
Fixed administrative cost*	60,000

*All selling costs are variable and all administrative costs are fixed.

Blip's proprietor has suggested that the company produce goods for inventory with the idle plant capacity.

Required

1) Prepare an income statement for Blip, assuming that 40,000 units are produced and sold during 19X1.

2) Prepare an income statement for Blip, assuming that 50,000 units are produced during 19X1, with 10,000 units being carried over into 19X2 as finished goods inventory.

3) To what can the differences in net income be attributed?

4) Discuss the circumstances under which the production of the additional units of inventory would be desirable.

24

Flexible Budgets and Standard Costs

Budgeting is a chancy process. However, planning is essential to good management, no matter how uncertain the future. A knowledge of relationships between activity, revenues, and costs in the past can be used to estimate outcomes for a variety of circumstances that may arise. Flexible plans are generally superior to a single, fixed plan.

Chapter 24 contains two sections. Section A deals with the preparation and use of flexible budgets. A discussion of the nature and merits of flexible budgets is followed by an explanation of how to identify fixed and variable relationships by looking at historical data. Relationships, once identified, are used in predicting outcomes for various activity levels. Also, a flexible budget performance report is compared to a static budget report in order to illustrate the differences.

Section B concentrates on the use of standard costs and on the analysis of variances from standards. Standard costs are defined, their advantages are listed, and the components of a standard unit cost are identified. The remainder of the section primarily deals with techniques for analyzing materials, labor, and overhead variances. Approaches for disposing of variance account balances are briefly described.

SECTION 24.A

Flexible Budgets

OBJECTIVES

This section shows how cost-volume-profit concepts may be used to prepare flexible budgets. At the conclusion of your study, you should be able to

1. State three advantages of flexible budgets over static budgets.
2. Determine the apparent variable cost per unit of activity and the fixed cost per period, given cost data for an entity at two levels of activity.
3. Prepare a flexible budget performance report for a production department, given flexible budget data and actual costs for a period.

THE NATURE OF FLEXIBLE BUDGETS

In Chapter 22 you were introduced to budgets that were prepared for particular activity levels. *A budget prepared for just one activity level may be referred to as a **static budget**, a **fixed budget**, or a **rigid budget**.* Of course, it is unlikely that a predicted activity level will be achieved exactly. For this reason, many accountants and managers prefer *flexible budgets* over static budgets.

The best managers are those who can quickly adjust to changing conditions. Unexpected events, both good and bad, occur in the commercial world just as they do in our personal lives. Business managers must be ready to adjust their plans for changes in activity level (volume), as well as for other kinds of changes and catastrophes.

Managers' goals are somewhat like targets—they represent something to shoot for. One type of target, or goal, is the level of activity that is planned for a future period. The actual level of activity, however, may differ for a variety of reasons. Salespeople may sell less (or more) of the company's products than was anticipated; or there may be an unforeseen economic downswing (or upswing), or a change in consumer tastes, or the outbreak of war (or declaration of peace).

A decline (or increase) in sales affects the entire business entity. Purchases and production are necessarily tied to sales activity. The amount of cash to be realized from operations also depends on sales level, although cash flow may lag behind sales activity because of the effects of credit. The purchasing requirements, the need to employ a second shift, and the level of inventory needed are examples of items dictated by the level of sales activity.

A **flexible budget** *is a budget model for forecasting cost and revenue data for varying activity levels.* Flexible budgets are more useful than static budgets for planning purposes because they allow managers to speculate on the consequences of operating at activity levels other than the most likely, or the most desired, level. Managers may then be better able to coordinate and control operations when a predicted volume level is not attained or is surpassed.

Flexible budgets are also more useful than static budgets in identifying trouble spots that deserve special attention from managers. These problem areas may become apparent during the planning process, when outcomes at certain activity levels are considered unacceptable. On the other hand, the problem areas may be indicated at the end of the budget period by large variances between actual and predicted results.

Finally, flexible budgets are more useful than static budgets in evaluating performance, since actual results may be compared with budgeted amounts for the volume of actual activity. This is particularly important where the manager being evaluated has little or no control over the activity level. For example, a production manager has little to do with the quantity of goods that are sold—unless, of course, sales are lost because of production problems.

In summary, flexible budgets are superior to static budgets for at least three reasons.

OBJECTIVE 1. State three advantages of flexible budgets over static budgets.

1. Flexible budgets permit managers to speculate on the consequences of operating at activity levels other than the most likely (or most desired) level.
2. Flexible budgets are more useful in the identification of trouble spots.
3. Flexible budgets are more useful for evaluating performance.

VARIABLE VERSUS FIXED COSTS

The preparation of flexible budgets requires that costs be identified as either variable or fixed in relation to changes in activity levels. Some costs are relatively easy to categorize; building depreciation can safely be called fixed, while sales commissions are clearly variable. Other costs may not be so easily classified, although they may be forced into whatever category they seem to fit best.

Some approaches to differentiating fixed and variable elements of cost attempt to deduce the extent of variability from observable (or predicted) data. In doing this, we might work with data for a single cost, a group of costs, or total cost. To illustrate one such approach, let us assume that past monthly total costs of Flynn Company at various levels of activity were as indicated by the dots in the graph in Illustration 24.1. A ruled line may then be drawn through the clustering of points to represent an approximation of the relationship between total cost and activity levels.[1] The point at which

---

[1] A mathematical technique called the *method of least squares* may be used to derive a more precise line from the data available. Such refinements are left to more advanced courses in managerial and cost accounting.

ILLUSTRATION 24.1   Total monthly cost

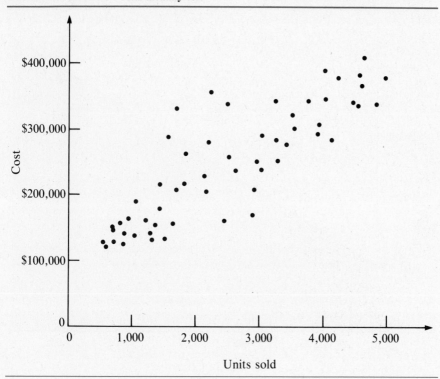

the total cost line intersects the vertical axis of the graph establishes the fixed cost element of total cost, as shown in Illustration 24.2 on the next page.

The variable cost per unit may be derived from the slope of the total cost line. Total cost increases from $100,000 to $400,000 as sales levels go from 0 to 5,000 units, so variable cost per unit may be determined as follows.

$$\frac{\text{Change in cost}}{\text{Change in activity}} = \text{Variable cost per unit}$$

$$\frac{\$300,000}{5,000 \text{ units}} = \$60 \text{ variable cost per unit}$$

Actually, variable and fixed cost elements are implied by total cost data for any two levels of activity. The process is shown in Illustration 24.3 on the next page for total cost data from two income statements of the Rowel Company, for which the numbers of units sold are as indicated.

ILLUSTRATION 24.2   Monthly cost

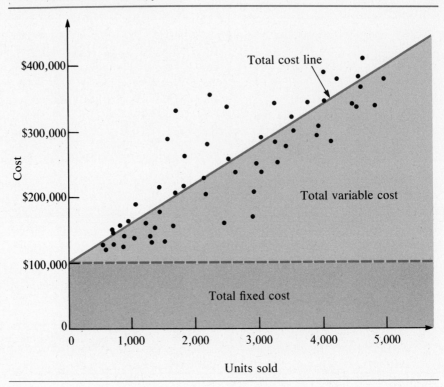

We must of course recognize that the relationship implied by the data in Illustration 24.3 might not represent normal results or expectations. In other words, the data we used might represent dots outside of a normal grouping that would appear on a graph like the one in Illustration 24.1.

ILLUSTRATION 24.3

OBJECTIVE 2. Determine the apparent variable cost per unit of activity and the fixed cost per period.

	19X3	19X2	Change
Sales in units	40,000	35,000	5,000
Total cost	$550,000	$500,000	$50,000
Less variable cost			
Units times $10 per unit*	400,000	350,000	
Fixed cost per year	$150,000	$150,000	

*Variable cost per unit: $\dfrac{\text{Change in cost}}{\text{Change in activity}} = \dfrac{\$50,000}{5,000 \text{ units}} = \$10$ variable cost per unit

PREPARING A FLEXIBLE BUDGET

Flexible budgets may be prepared for an entire entity as well as for any or all of its subdivisions. Projections into the future may be made at a variety of activity levels in order to foresee problems associated with particular budgets. The presentation in Illustration 24.4 shows both static and flexible budget data for a production department of AB Corporation.

The variable cost figures shown in the Flexible Budget columns are obtained by multiplying the unit costs by the production units chosen as a possible activity level. For example, the projected costs at 13,000 units are derived as follows.

Direct materials	$\$ 8 \times 13,000 = \$104,000$
Direct labor	$6 \times 13,000 = 78,000$
Variable overhead	$3 \times 13,000 = 39,000$
Total variable cost	$\$17 \times 13,000 = \$221,000$

Thus variable cost for Department 1 can be projected for any production level n by the following formula.

Direct material +	Direct labor +	Variable overhead =	Total variable cost
$\$8n$ +	$\$6n$ +	$\$3n$	= Total variable cost

ILLUSTRATION 24.4

AB CORPORATION
Department 1, Plant A
Production Budget
For the Month of April 19--

	Static (Expected) Budget	Flexible Budget			
		Variable per Unit	Fixed per Month	Possible Outcomes	
Units of production	12,000			13,000	14,000
Variable costs					
Direct materials	$ 96,000	$ 8		$104,000	$112,000
Direct labor	72,000	6		78,000	84,000
Variable overhead	36,000	3		39,000	42,000
Total variable	$204,000	$17		$221,000	$238,000
Fixed overhead	26,000		$26,000	26,000	26,000
Total cost	$230,000	$17	$26,000	$247,000	$264,000

ILLUSTRATION 24.5

	Unit Cost	Possible Units of Production			
		12,000	*13,000*	*14,000*	*15,000*

AB CORPORATION
Department 1, Plant A
Variable Overhead Budget
For the Month of April 19––

	Unit Cost	12,000	13,000	14,000	15,000
Machine maintenance	$0.80	$ 9,600	$10,400	$11,200	$12,000
Cleaning supplies	0.50	6,000	6,500	7,000	7,500
Timekeeping	0.30	3,600	3,900	4,200	4,500
Factory utilities	1.00	12,000	13,000	14,000	15,000
Other	0.40	4,800	5,200	5,600	6,000
Total variable overhead	$3.00	$36,000	$39,000	$42,000	$45,000

And, since fixed cost is assumed to remain constant, the monthly cost formula for Department 1 is as follows.

Variable cost   + Fixed cost = Total cost
$\$8n + \$6n + \$3n + \$26,000 = $ Total cost

Just as variable cost is broken down into direct materials, direct labor, and variable overhead elements, so can variable overhead be further divided into its components. The schedule in Illustration 24.5 shows how variable overhead might be portrayed on a flexible basis.

The individual costs that make up fixed overhead would also be projected, although they would be expected to be the same at all output levels.

FLEXIBLE BUDGET PERFORMANCE REPORTS

As previously pointed out, flexible budgets are more useful in evaluating performance because they permit actual results to be compared with what was expected to occur at the *same level of activity*. The presentations in Illustrations 24.6 and 24.7 show the difference between static and flexible budget performance reports when Department 1 produced at a level of 12,800 units during April.

Variances

Whereas the static budget performance report shows a total unfavorable variance of $11,984, a performance report based on a flexible budget shows a total *favorable* variance of $1,616. You can see how the production manager

ILLUSTRATION 24.6

	Static (Expected) Budget	Actual	Variance: Favorable (Unfavorable)
AB CORPORATION **Department 1, Plant A** **Static Budget Performance Report** **For the Month of April 19––**			
Units of production	12,000	12,800	
Variable costs			
Direct materials	$ 96,000	$ 99,996	$ (3,996)
Direct labor	72,000	78,988	(6,988)
Variable overhead	36,000	37,000	(1,000)
Total variable	$204,000	$215,984	$(11,984)
Fixed overhead	26,000	26,000	–0–
Total cost	$230,000	$241,984	$(11,984)

of Department 1 might be severely misjudged if only a static budget were prepared. The flexible budget report shows an unfavorable variance only for direct labor. Under the *management by exception* concept mentioned in Chapter 22, the attention of managers may be drawn to this unfavorable variance so that appropriate action can be taken to avoid a recurrence in the future.

ILLUSTRATION 24.7

	Flexible Budget	Actual	Variance: Favorable (Unfavorable)
AB CORPORATION **Department 1, Plant A** **Flexible Budget Performance Report** **For the Month of April 19––**			
Units of production	12,800	12,800	
Variable costs			
Direct materials	$102,400	$ 99,996	$2,404
Direct labor	76,800	78,988	(2,188)
Variable overhead	38,400	37,000	1,400
Total variable	$217,600	$215,984	$1,616
Fixed overhead	26,000	26,000	–0–
Total cost	$243,600	$241,984	$1,616

OBJECTIVE 3. Prepare a flexible budget performance report for a production department.

Although significant variances are less likely for fixed overhead costs, they are possible nevertheless. A substantial and unpredicted increase in property taxes, insurance premiums, or some other fixed cost category can bring about a sizable fixed cost variance.

Managers should also be interested in the reasons for large *favorable* variances. A favorable variance might have resulted from an erroneous initial estimate or from a change in circumstances during the period. For example, the cost of direct materials may have decreased because of an increased supply in the marketplace. If materials cost per unit is expected to be lower, the reduction should be reflected in budgets for future periods.

A favorable variance is not always cause for rejoicing. For example, the favorable direct materials variance on the flexible performance report may have resulted from the substitution of cheaper and inferior materials because high-quality materials were not available. If such an action resulted in lower product quality, product reputation could be damaged, lawsuits could result, or other dire consequences could occur in the future.

A look at the detailed variances attributable to cost subcategories may also be revealing. For example, the favorable $1,400 variance shown for variable overhead on the flexible budget report may have been the net result of the sizable offsetting individual variances indicated in Illustration 24.8.

A manager might be somewhat more curious about the $2,500 unfavorable variance for Factory Utilities than about a $1,400 favorable variance for total variable overhead. The next section deals with techniques for further analyzing variances and determining their underlying causes.

ILLUSTRATION 24.8

AB CORPORATION Department 1, Plant A Variable Overhead Performance Report For the Month of April 19--			
	Flexible Budget	Actual	Variance: Favorable (Unfavorable)
Units of production	12,800	12,800	
Machine maintenance	$10,240	$ 7,020	$3,220
Cleaning supplies	6,400	5,700	700
Timekeeping	3,840	3,900	(60)
Factory utilities	12,800	15,300	(2,500)
Other	5,120	5,080	40
Total variable overhead	$38,400	$37,000	$1,400

GLOSSARY FOR SECTION 24.A

Flexible budget   A budget model for forecasting cost and revenue data for varying activity levels.

Static budget (fixed budget, rigid budget)   A budget prepared for just one activity level.

SELF-QUIZ ON OBJECTIVES FOR SECTION 24.A
Solutions to Self-Quiz begin on page B-71.

1. **OBJECTIVE 1.** State three advantages of flexible budgets over static budgets.

2. **OBJECTIVE 2.** Determine the apparent variable cost per unit and fixed cost per month from the following data for Tickel Production Corporation.

	May	**June**
Sales in units	10,000	12,000
Total cost	$210,000	$238,000

3. **OBJECTIVE 3.** The following data are provided for the fishmeal production department of the Tet Foods Corporation. Prepare a flexible budget performance report for May.

Flexible Budget Information	
Variable production costs per bag of fishmeal	
Direct materials	$12
Direct labor	4
Variable overhead	6
Fixed overhead per month, $50,000	
Actual Production Costs for May 19X4	
Variable	
Direct materials	$506,000
Direct labor	163,800
Variable overhead	238,000
Fixed overhead	50,000
Fishmeal produced during May: 40,000 bags	

DISCUSSION QUESTIONS FOR SECTION 24.A

1. What is a *flexible budget,* and how does a flexible budget differ from a *static budget?*

2. Why are flexible budgets said to be better than static budgets for evaluating performance?

3. Why is sales activity usually the basis for flexible budgeting?

4. Why will variances shown in a flexible budget performance report generally be different from those shown in a static budget performance report?

5. Why is it necessary to differentiate variable and fixed costs for flexible budgeting purposes?

6. Why should budget variances be analyzed?

EXERCISES FOR SECTION 24.A

24.A.1. The stamping department of BG Manufacturing produced 48,000 units during 19X1 and 54,000 units during 19X2. Total cost was $359,000 in 19X1 and $395,000 in 19X2. Calculate the apparent variable cost per unit and the fixed cost per year.

24.A.2. Following are cost and revenue data for the Nelsby Corporation for August and September.

	August	**September**
Activity units	100,000	130,000
Total cost	$220,000	$265,000
Total revenue	$300,000	$390,000

a. Calculate variable cost per unit.

b. Calculate fixed cost per month.

c. Write a net income formula that can be used to project sales, variable cost, fixed cost, and net income for a one-month period.

24.A.3. Variable overhead costs per gallon for the juicing department of Alio Corporation have been estimated as follows:

Indirect labor	$0.60
Utilities	0.35
Supplies	0.23
Repair parts	0.10

Prepare a variable overhead budget for the month of May for possible production levels of 100,000, 125,000, and 150,000 units.

24.A.4. Virgo Corporation accountants have established from past experience that the splicing department has fixed overhead costs of approximately $80,000 per month, and that in the future variable costs per unit are expected to be as follows:

Direct materials	$20
Direct labor	30
Variable overhead	15

Set up a production budget showing possible outcomes for production levels of 20,000, 22,000, and 24,000 units per month.

PROBLEMS FOR SECTION 24.A
Alternate Problems for this section begin on page D-130.

24.A.5. The shaping department had overhead costs at two volume levels, which follow.

	Production Level	
Cost Category	*20,000 Units*	*30,000 Units*
Utilities	$ 10,000	$ 14,000
Depreciation	40,000	40,000
Timekeeping	8,000	8,000
Maintenance	22,000	30,000
Supervision	35,000	45,000
Supplies	7,000	10,000
Total overhead cost	$122,000	$147,000

Required

1) Prepare a schedule showing the variable cost per unit and fixed cost per month by individual cost category and for total overhead.

2) Speculate as to why some of the cost categories have both fixed and variable elements.

24.A.6. During the month of June the supervisor of Department 2 submitted the following budget for July to the vice-president for production.

JANCY CORPORATION **Department 2 Budget** **For the Month of July 19--**	
Expected production	60,000 Units
Variable costs	
Direct materials	$120,000
Direct labor	180,000
Variable overhead	75,000
Total variable costs	$375,000
Fixed overhead	210,000
Total cost	$585,000

During the month of July, 50,000 units were produced at a total production cost of $533,000. Of the total cost, $215,000 was considered fixed and the remainder variable. Materials usage records show that Department 2 used direct materials costing $95,000; payroll records show direct labor cost of $160,000 for Department 2 for July. Department 2 had no beginning or ending work in process for July.

Required

1) Prepare for Department 2 a static budget performance report for July.

2) Prepare for Department 2 a flexible budget performance report for July.

3) Explain as best you can the reasons for the differences in variances shown in the reports prepared for (1) and (2).

4) Give several possible reasons for the fixed overhead variance for July.

24.A.7. Michner Corporation produces a single product, which it attempts to sell for $80 per unit. During slow periods, selected customers are encouraged to purchase the product at reduced prices. Michner's costs are budgeted according to the following variable and fixed elements.

	Variable per Unit	**Fixed per Month**
Production costs	$20	$350,000
Selling costs	8	140,000
Administrative costs	–0–	130,000

All told, 45 percent of net income must be paid as federal, state, and local income taxes. During early October Michner's accountants prepared the following income statement for September.

MICHNER CORPORATION Income Statement For the Month of September 19––		
Sales (24,000 units)		$1,600,000
Cost of goods sold		880,000
Gross Profit		$ 720,000
Operating expenses		
Selling	$330,000	
Administrative	140,000	470,000
Net Income before Tax		$ 250,000
Income taxes		112,500
Net Income after Tax		$ 137,500

Required

1) Prepare a performance income statement for September which includes, in addition to the income statement columns, columns for flexible budget figures and variances of actual from budgeted amounts.

2) Write a formula for Michner's net income after tax based on the budget data given.

3) According to the budget data, at what sales level would Michner break even?

24.A.8. Molly Company accountants have estimated monthly fixed overhead of $90,000 for the firm's boring department. Direct materials for the boring department are expected to cost $1.20 per unit, direct labor is estimated at 80¢ per unit, and variable overhead is anticipated at 200% of direct labor cost. Production for the month of March is predicted at 60,000 units, although it is possible that the production level may fall as low as 58,000 units or run as high as 62,000 units for the month.

Required

1) Write a total cost formula for the boring department.

2) Prepare a flexible budget presentation showing predicted production costs for production levels of 58,000, 60,000, and 62,000 units of activity during the month of March.

SECTION 24.B

Standard Costs

OBJECTIVES

This section concentrates on standard costs and on the analysis of variances of actual costs from standard. At the conclusion of your study, you should be able to

1. Define the expression *standard cost*.
2. State three benefits of using standard costs.
3. Determine the following, given the necessary data:
   a. Materials rate variance.
   b. Materials quantity variance.
   c. Labor rate variance.
   d. Labor quantity variance.
   e. Overhead volume variance.
   f. Overhead budget variance.

WHAT ARE STANDARD COSTS?

In the cost systems illustrated in Chapter 21, we assumed that actual costs of direct materials and direct labor were charged to Goods in Process accounts. For simplicity, it was assumed that for process cost systems, cost flows were recorded in the ledger accounts only at the end of each month. However, if accounting records are to be maintained on a perpetual basis, they must be more frequently updated.

In many instances it is impractical, if not impossible, to pin down the actual unit costs of materials and labor on a timely basis. The solution is to apply production costs to Goods in Process on an estimated basis. After all, estimated costs are used for budgeting purposes, and it is to the budgeted (estimated) costs that actual costs are subsequently compared on performance reports. When estimated costs are applied to Goods in Process, the budgeted figures are taken into the accounting system, in much the same way as overhead was applied earlier at an estimated rate.

OBJECTIVE 1. Define standard cost.   *When estimated unit costs reflect what cost should be when resources are being effectively used, they are called* **standard costs**. Direct materials, direct labor, and factory overhead may all be charged to Goods in Process at standard rates, and product costs may be transferred on through the accounting system at standard cost per unit of product.

A distinction is sometimes made between *budgeted* costs and *standard* costs. Budgeted costs are simply estimated, whereas standard costs are determined by means of extensive research involving time and motion studies and other scientific approaches developed jointly by engineers, accountants, and managers. For our purposes, distinctions between budgeted, estimated, and standard costs are moot. However they are determined, costs applied at other than actual amounts may be, and should be, compared subsequently with actual results for analysis purposes.

ADVANTAGES OF STANDARD COSTS

One advantage of using standard cost rates has already been mentioned. Standard costs may be transferred through perpetual accounting systems before actual costs are known with certainty. In this way, cost accounting data may be accumulated on a more timely, and more useful, basis than would be possible otherwise.

Another benefit is that the standard costs serve as bases (standards) of comparison for evaluating actual costs. The analysis of variances of actual from standard costs is discussed later in this section.

Standard costs, once determined, are available for use in budgeting for the future. Standard costs may serve as goals because they represent what costs should be when resources are efficiently used.

Here, then, is a summary of the benefits to be derived from using standard costs.

1. Standard costs serve as reasonable unit cost measures for budgeting purposes.
2. Standard costs permit production costs to be transferred through the accounting system before actual costs are known with certainty.
3. Standard costs serve as bases (standards) of comparison for evaluating actual costs.

OBJECTIVE 2. State three benefits of using standard costs.

STANDARD COST RATES

Recall from the previous section the product costs that were used to project a flexible budget for Department 1, Plant A, of AB Corporation. Let us assume that the variable unit costs and the total fixed overhead cost per month have been carefully established as *standard* costs, and that they are used for charging costs to Goods in Process as production takes place.

In order to charge fixed overhead at a standard rate, some production level must be assumed. As pointed out in Chapter 23, fixed cost *per unit* declines as output increases. The following calculations show how the fixed overhead per month for Department 1 is spread thinner as production levels increase.

$$\frac{\text{Fixed overhead per month}}{\text{Units of production}} = \text{Fixed overhead per unit}$$

$$\frac{\$26,000}{12,000} = \$2.167$$

$$\frac{\$26,000}{13,000} = \$2.00$$

$$\frac{\$26,000}{14,000} = \$1.857$$

If standard monthly production is assumed to be 13,000 units, the fixed overhead rate would be $2 per unit produced. If 14,000 units were used as standard activity, then the rate would be $1.857.

In practice, both variable and fixed overhead are often related to direct labor cost or direct labor hours and assigned to Goods in Process on that basis. In other words, overhead is assigned to production in proportion to the direct labor used.

The variance analysis calculations in the remainder of this section compares actual outcomes with the following standards for Department 1.

STANDARD COST PER UNIT PRODUCED IN DEPARTMENT 1		
Direct materials, 4 pounds at $2 per pound		$ 8
Direct labor, 1 hour at $6 per hour		6
Factory overhead		5
Variable, $3 per direct labor hour	$3	
Fixed, $2 per direct labor hour	2	
Total standard cost per unit		$19

VARIANCE ANALYSIS

From the foregoing schedule, you can see that each standard cost component is made up of a standard quantity at a standard rate or price. For example, each product unit is expected to involve 4 pounds of material at a cost of $2 per pound, one hour of labor at $6 per hour, and a standard overhead cost of $5 for each hour of labor.

Either the actual quantities or the actual rates may vary from the standards for each of the cost components. *A **rate (price) variance** is the difference between the standard cost of the quantity used and the actual cost of that quantity. A **quantity (usage) variance** is the difference between the standard cost of the standard quantity and the standard cost of the actual quantity.*

Because overhead is indirect, and because a portion of overhead is fixed, overhead variances are analyzed somewhat differently from materials and labor variances. These differences are explained later.

Materials Variances

The difference between the standard quantity of materials at standard cost per pound and the actual cost of the materials used can be broken down into the rate (price) and quantity (usage) components.

Materials Rate Variance.   In a standard cost system, the materials rate (price) variance may be determined as materials are purchased and added to inventory. For instance, if 51,280 pounds of materials are purchased all at once during April at $1.95 per pound, the standard cost of the units purchased ($2 × 51,280) is charged to Materials Inventory and a variance account is credited for the cost saving of 5¢ per pound, as shown in the following entry.

Materials Inventory	102,560	
Accounts Payable		99,996
Materials Rate Variance		2,564

The amounts in the foregoing entry are calculated in the T-accounts shown in Illustration 24.9. The materials rate variance is simply the result of paying more or less than standard price for materials purchases.

MATERIALS RATE VARIANCE

(Standard rate − Actual rate) × Actual quantity purchased = Materials rate variance

($2 − $1.95)   ×   51,280 lb.   = $2,564 favorable

OBJECTIVE 3a. Determine materials rate variance.

We know that favorable variances occur when actual costs are less than those budgeted. In accounting, gains are registered as credits while expenses and losses are recorded as debits. The amount saved by paying 5¢ less per

ILLUSTRATION 24.9

Accounts Payable	
	Actual rate × Actual quantity purchased $1.95 per lb. × 51,280 lb. = $99,996

Materials Inventory	
Standard rate × Actual quantity purchased $2 per lb. × 51,280 lb. = $102,560	

Materials Rate Variance	
	(Standard rate − Actual rate) × Actual quantity ($2 − $1.95) × 51,280 lb. = $2,564 favorable

pound for materials purchased shows up on the credit side of the Materials Rate Variance account. This favorable rate variance may be the result of wise action by the purchasing department. On the other hand, it may simply reflect a temporary decline in market prices resulting from economic conditions. The person in charge of the purchasing department is usually responsible for explaining materials rate variances.

Materials Quantity Variance. Our example assumes that only one type of material is used (at least in Department 1) and that all materials go directly into process (none go into factory overhead as indirect materials). To further simplify matters, it is assumed that no goods are left in process (unfinished) at the end of a month.

Now let us suppose that 51,280 pounds of materials were used during April to produce 12,800 units of product. Standard materials usage at 4 pounds per product unit (12,800 units at 4 pounds each) would have been 51,200 pounds. The Goods in Process account is charged with the standard cost of standard quantity used ($2 × 51,200), as the following entry shows.

Goods in Process	102,400	
Materials Quantity Variance	160	
Materials Inventory		102,560

The T-accounts in Illustration 24.10 show just what goes into the ledger accounts. The unfavorable (debit) quantity variance resulted from the use of 80 pounds more than standard.

OBJECTIVE 3b. Determine materials quantity variance.

MATERIALS QUANTITY VARIANCE

(Standard quantity − Actual quantity used) × Standard rate = Materials quantity variance

| (51,200 | − | 51,280) | × | $2 | = $160 unfavorable |

ILLUSTRATION 24.10

Materials Inventory	
	Actual quantity used × Standard rate 51,280 × $2 = $102,560

Goods in Process	
Standard quantity × Standard rate 51,200 × $2 = $102,400	

Materials Quantity Variance	
(Standard quantity − Actual quantity) × Standard rate (51,200 − 51,280) × $2 = $160 unfavorable	

The manager of a production department is normally accountable for a materials quantity variance. Excess usage might be due to careless handling by workers, resulting in waste or spoilage. On the other hand, if excess usage results from the purchase of inferior materials, the purchasing department manager may be held accountable for the variance.

Labor Variances

A total labor variance consists of two elements: the rate variance stemming from variations of actual hourly costs from standard rates, and the quantity (efficiency) variance stemming from the difference between actual labor hours and standard hours.

To illustrate labor variances, we assume that 12,740 labor hours at $6.20 were used to produce the 12,800 product units during April. Since standard labor has been determined at one hour per unit at $6 per hour, the total labor variance can be figured as follows.

TOTAL LABOR VARIANCE	
Standard labor cost	
12,800 units of product × 1 hour × $6 =	$76,800
Actual labor cost	
12,740 hours at $6.20 =	78,988
Unfavorable labor variance	$ 2,188

Labor Rate Variance. The labor rate variance is the result of paying a different rate than standard for the actual hours used. For our example, the extra 20¢ per hour paid for 12,740 hours worked results in the following rate variance.

LABOR RATE VARIANCE
(Standard rate − Actual rate) × Actual hours = Labor rate variance
($6 − $6.20) × 12,740 = $2,548 unfavorable

OBJECTIVE 3c. Determine labor rate variance.

A labor rate variance may be due to an increase in wage rates, overtime work, or the assignment of highly paid workers to tasks normally done by lower-paid people. Responsibility for labor rate variances may be shared by personnel administrators and production managers, depending on who has control over decisions that result in variances.

Labor Quantity Variance. The labor quantity (efficiency) variance results from using more or less time than standard. The 12,740 actual hours used were fewer than the 12,800 standard hours (one hour per unit) for producing 12,800 units of product, resulting in the following favorable variance.

LABOR QUANTITY VARIANCE

(Standard hours − Actual hours) × Standard rate = Labor quantity variance
   (12,800   −   12,740)   × $6   = $360 favorable

A production supervisor is normally responsible for explaining the labor quantity variance. In this instance, production workers have performed efficiently, perhaps because they were so well paid (resulting in the unfavorable rate variance).

Summary of Labor Variances. The following entry and the T-accounts in Illustration 24.11 summarize the way in which labor variances may be determined in a standard cost system.

Goods in Process	76,800	
Labor Rate Variance	2,548	
Labor Quantity Variance		360
Wages Payable		78,988

One should keep in mind that cost systems in practice differ in many ways. Some standard cost systems, for example, do not identify materials and labor quantity variances until the point at which costs of completed goods are transferred from Goods in Process to Finished Goods accounts. Under these circumstances, materials and labor are charged to the Goods in Process account at the standard unit costs of actual units used.

ILLUSTRATION 24.11

Wages Payable	
	Actual hours × Actual rate 12,740 × $6.20 = $78,988
Goods in Process	
Standard hours × Standard rate 12,800 × $6 = $76,800	
Labor Rate Variance	
(Standard rate − Actual rate) × Actual hours ($6 − $6.20) × 12,740 = $2,548 unfavorable	
Labor Quantity Variance	
	(Standard hours − Actual hours) × Standard rate (12,800 − 12,740) × $6 = $360 favorable

Overhead Variances

Recall that variable and fixed overhead components are usually combined into one standard rate for application purposes. The two components, and the indirect nature of overhead, make the character of overhead variances considerably more complex than that of materials and labor variances.

The more labor applied to a process, the more the overhead application will be because direct labor hours serve as the basis for overhead application. Therefore, an unfavorable labor quantity (usage) variance means that extra overhead was also applied. If overhead is applied as a percentage of actual direct labor cost, both labor rate and labor quantity variances have overhead implications.

Overhead variances may be analyzed in a variety of ways. To minimize complications at this level of your study, the overhead variance is broken down into only two elements: the *volume variance* and the *budget variance*.

Overhead Volume Variance. *An overhead volume variance is the difference between applied fixed overhead and budgeted fixed overhead.* Because it results from operating at a level higher or lower than some predetermined capacity, the volume variance is sometimes referred to as the *capacity variance*.

Recall that the standard overhead rate for Department 1 is the combination of a $3 variable and $2 fixed cost rate per unit, and that the unit fixed cost resulted from spreading $26,000 of budgeted fixed cost over 13,000 hours of direct labor. Now, if overhead is applied on the basis of standard labor hours (one hour per product unit), fixed overhead would be *underapplied* during April, because there were only 12,800 standard labor hours for the month. The failure to attain the 13,000-hour production level by 200 hours means that $400 of budgeted fixed overhead was not applied to the process, as indicated here.

OVERHEAD VOLUME VARIANCE

(Scheduled volume   −   Budgeted volume) × Fixed overhead rate = Volume variance

(Standard labor hours − Budgeted labor hours) × Fixed overhead rate = Volume variance

    (12,800 hours   −   13,000 hours)   × $2   = $400 unfavorable

or

(Applied fixed overhead − Budgeted fixed overhead) = Volume variance

    (12,800 × $2)   − $26,000   = $400 unfavorable

An unfavorable volume variance may be cautiously viewed as a cost of unused production capacity. However, the validity of such a conclusion depends on how capacity has been defined and on the particular costs that have been identified as fixed. Some concerns use the practical maximum output level as capacity, while others use ideal capacity, normal production

OBJECTIVE 3e. Determine overhead volume variance.

ILLUSTRATION 24.12

Goods in Process	64,000	
Manufacturing Overhead		64,000
To apply overhead to process:		
12,800 hours at $5 per hour.		
Manufacturing Overhead	1,000	
Overhead Volume Variance	400	
Overhead Budget Variance		1,400
To close out the overapplied overhead		
balance and to identify overhead variances.		

level, or expected production level for determining their overhead application rates.

Overhead Budget Variance.   When we speak of *an overhead budget variance*, we refer to *the difference between the budgeted overhead for the production level achieved and the actual overhead incurred.* Because it is a measure of the success in holding down actual overhead costs, as compared with those predicted by means of a flexible budget, the budget variance is sometimes called the *spending variance* or the *controllable variance.*

    If actual overhead incurred during April were $63,000, the budget variance could be determined as follows.

OBJECTIVE 3f. Determine overhead budget variance.

> **OVERHEAD BUDGET VARIANCE**
>
> Flexible budget overhead − Actual overhead = Budget variance
>
> $\left(\begin{array}{c}\text{Standard} \\ \text{labor hours}\end{array} \times \begin{array}{c}\text{Variable} \\ \text{overhead rate}\end{array}\right) + \begin{array}{c}\text{Budgeted} \\ \text{fixed overhead}\end{array} - \begin{array}{c}\text{Actual} \\ \text{overhead}\end{array} = \text{Budget variance}$
>
> $(12,800 \quad \times \quad \$3) \quad + \quad \$26,000 \quad - \quad \$63,000 \quad = \quad \$1,400\ \text{favorable})$

Summary of Overhead Variances.   The entries in Illustration 24.12 and the T-accounts in Illustration 24.13 summarize the way that overhead variances are identified in a standard cost system.

ILLUSTRATION 24.13

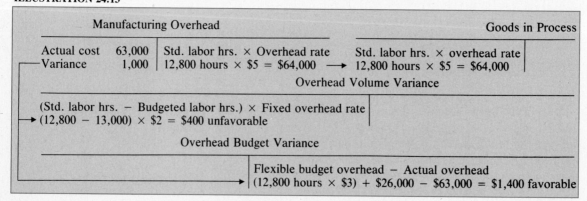

DISPOSING OF VARIANCE ACCOUNT BALANCES

Variance accounts in standard cost systems are normally allowed to accumulate until year-end, at which time they are closed out. Depending on circumstances, variances may be treated as losses or gains, allocated between Inventories and Cost of Goods Sold, or simply closed to Cost of Goods Sold. The most common approach is simply to close variances to Cost of Goods Sold for the year. Allocation between Inventories and Cost of Goods Sold roughly converts the costs from standard to actual.

Where standards are carefully determined and kept current during the year, there is some justification for viewing unfavorable variances as losses resulting from mismanagement, and favorable variances as gains resulting from good management. Of course, as pointed out previously, unfavorable variances may be due to circumstances beyond management's control (such as changes in economic conditions). Likewise, favorable variances are not always brought about by shrewd management decisions.

ANALYZING FLEXIBLE BUDGET VARIANCES

The techniques presented in this section for analyzing variances are not limited to standard cost systems. Where the needed data are available, they may be just as readily used for analyzing performance report variances. In fact, the data used in this section are consistent with the Department 1 performance report for April that was presented in the previous section on flexible budgets.

Suppose, for example, that the facts were as described in this section, except that the accounting system reflected actual rather than standard costs. (Even so, it is likely that factory overhead would be applied at an estimated rate.) Variances, other than possibly for overhead costs, would not then appear in the accounts. Nevertheless, the variances identified in a flexible budget performance report can still be analyzed (as shown in this section) to identify the rate and quantity variance components for materials and labor, as well as the volume and budget variance components for overhead.

GLOSSARY FOR SECTION 24.B

Overhead budget (spending, controllable) variance   The difference between the budgeted overhead for the production level achieved and the actual overhead incurred.

Overhead volume (capacity) variance   The difference between applied fixed overhead and budgeted fixed overhead.

Quantity (usage) variance   The difference between the standard cost of the standard quantity and the standard cost of the actual quantity.

Rate (price) variance   The difference between the standard cost of the quantity used and the actual cost of that quantity.

Standard costs   Carefully determined estimates of what costs should be when resources are effectively used.

SELF-QUIZ ON OBJECTIVES FOR SECTION 24.B
Solutions to Self-Quiz begin on page B-72.

1. **OBJECTIVE 1.** Define the expression *standard cost*.

2. **OBJECTIVE 2.** State three benefits to be derived from using standard costs.

3. **OBJECTIVE 3.** The following data are provided for the fishmeal production department of Tet Foods Corporation.

Standard Cost per Bag of Fishmeal		
Direct materials, 120 lb. at 10¢ per lb.		$12
Direct labor, ½ hour at $8 per hour		4
Factory overhead		
Variable, $12 per direct labor hour	$6	
Fixed, $2 per direct labor hour*	1	7
Total standard cost per bag		$23

*Fixed overhead rate = $50,000 total fixed per month ÷ 25,000 normal capacity labor hours.

Actual Production Costs for May	
Direct materials, 4,600,000 lb. at 11¢	$506,000
Direct labor, 21,000 hours at $7.80	163,800
Factory overhead	
Variable	238,000
Fixed	50,000
Fishmeal produced during May: 40,000 bags	

Determine the following for the month of May:

a. Materials rate variance.

b. Materials quantity variance.

c. Labor rate variance.

d. Labor quantity variance.

e. Overhead volume variance.

f. Overhead budget variance.

DISCUSSION QUESTIONS FOR SECTION 24.B

1. What is the difference between a rate variance and a quantity variance?

2. Who should be held responsible for a materials rate (price) variance?

3. Who should be held responsible for a materials quantity variance?

4. Under what circumstances will the labor quantity variance cause an unfavorable overhead budget variance?

5. Why is an overhead volume variance sometimes referred to as a *capacity variance?*

6. Why is an overhead budget variance sometimes referred to as a *controllable variance?*

7. Where variances are identified in separate accounts with standard cost systems, how are the variances treated (disposed of) at the end of an accounting period?

EXERCISES FOR SECTION 24.B

24.B.1. The flexible budget for a painting department shows an $18 standard materials cost based on use of two gallons of paint at $9 per gallon. During September, 8,420 gallons of paint were used, at an average cost of $9.40 per gallon, to complete 4,300 units of product. Compute the materials rate variance, the materials quantity variance, and the total materials variance for September for the painting department.

24.B.2. The machining department plans for the month of May called for production of 4,000 equivalent units using as direct materials 400 pounds of brass machine stock costing $12.50 per pound. Actual direct materials for May cost $5,720. Production for May consisted of 4,400 equivalent units for which 440 pounds of brass were used at a cost of $13 per pound. Determine rate and quantity components of the total materials variance.

24.B.3. Department B employs a standard cost system in which 3 hours of direct labor at $15 per hour is considered standard for processing one unit of product. During one week, in which 20,000 units of product were processed, 62,000 hours of labor were used at an average cost of $14.50 per hour. Prepare a journal entry which charges direct labor cost to Goods in Process, recognizes Wages Payable, and identifies labor rate and quantity variances for the week.

24.B.4. Cutting department assigns overhead to Goods in Process at a rate of $3 per standard direct labor hour. Of the $3 rate, $2 is considered variable and $1 fixed. The fixed overhead portion of the rate is based on 10,000 budgeted labor hours per month. During the month of May standard labor hours were 9,000, and actual overhead cost incurred was $31,000. Determine the overhead volume and budget variances for May.

PROBLEMS FOR SECTION 24.B
Alternate Problems for this section begin on page D-132.

24.B.5. Cintec Company has established the following standard costs for one of its production departments.

Direct materials, 10 grams at $5 per gram	$50
Direct labor, 3 hours at $15 per hour	45
Factory overhead	
Variable, $3 per direct labor hour	9
Fixed, $2 per direct labor hour	6

The fixed overhead rate was determined by dividing $40,000 of expected fixed overhead cost per month by 20,000 normal capacity direct labor hours.

During the month of July, the following costs were incurred in processing 6,000 units of product.

Direct materials, 59,000 grams at $5.10 per gram	$300,900
Direct labor, 18,500 hours at $14.80 per hour	273,800
Factory overhead	
Variable	58,000
Fixed	40,000

Required

Determine for the month of July the following variances.

1) Materials rate variance

2) Materials quantity variance

3) Labor rate variance

4) Labor quantity variance

5) Overhead volume variance

6) Overhead budget variance

24.B.6. Smithy Company produces one product and employs a standard cost system. Standard costs per product unit have been determined as follows.

Direct materials, 2 liters at $3 per liter		$ 6
Direct labor, 1 hour at $10 per hour		10
Factory overhead		
Variable, $2 per direct labor hour	$2	
Fixed, $5 per direct labor hour	5	7
Total standard cost per product unit		$23

The fixed overhead rate is based on $40,000 of expected fixed overhead per month spread over 8,000 budgeted direct labor hours (8,000 units of anticipated production at 1 hour of direct labor per unit). Smithy Company produces only for confirmed customer orders and carries little or no inventory on hand. There were no inventories on hand at the beginning of March, nor were there any at the end of March. The following events were experienced in producing and selling 7,600 units of product during March.

a. Purchased 15,500 liters of direct materials at $2.95 per liter. Terms were net 60 days.

b. The 15,500 liters of direct materials purchased during March were put into process.

c. Wages of $77,688 are owed for 7,800 hours of direct labor worked during March.

d. Actual manufacturing overhead costs for the month were $53,000.

Required

Prepare journal entries for March to:

1) Record the direct materials purchased and identify the materials rate variance.

2) Transfer the direct materials to Goods in Process and identify the materials quantity variance.

3) Record direct wages and identify labor rate and quantity variances.

4) Record actual manufacturing overhead costs. (*Note:* Credit the amount to an account titled Various Accounts.)

5) Charge overhead to Goods in Process.

6) Close the Manufacturing Overhead account and identify the overhead volume and budget variances. (*Note:* Assume the Overhead account is closed monthly.)

7) Transfer the Goods in Process balance to Finished Goods Inventory.

8) Transfer the Finished Goods Inventory to Cost of Goods Sold.

24.B.7. Normal capacity for Mileu Company is considered to be 10,000 units of product per month. Standard direct labor cost per product unit is $18, and manufacturing overhead is assigned to production at 150% of standard direct labor cost. The standard overhead rate is considered to be one-half variable and one-half fixed. During August, when 9,800 units were produced, actual overhead amounted to $265,000, of which $128,000 was variable and $137,000 was fixed.

Required

1) Prepare a journal entry to assign standard overhead to production for August.

2) Prepare the entry on August 31 to close the Manufacturing Overhead account and recognize overhead volume and budget variances for the month. (*Hint:* Total overhead variance less volume variance equals the budget variance.)

3) Interpret in words (what do they mean?) the overhead variances journalized in requirement (2). Was fixed overhead for the month more or less than one would have expected for the units produced? Explain.

SUMMARY OF CHAPTER 24

Whereas a static budget pictures expected results for only one activity level, flexible budgets may be used to forecast results for varying activity levels. Flexible budgets are more useful than static budgets for purposes of planning, identifying trouble spots, and evaluating performance. The extent of cost variability as activity levels change may be approximated by observing past data. Total cost for past periods may be plotted against activity levels, or the change in total cost between two output levels may be divided by the change in units of activity.

Actual costs may be compared with flexible budget amounts in performance reports. Variances of actual results from flexible budget expectations are more useful than variances from static budget figures.

Standard cost systems charge to production processes what costs should be when resources are being effectively employed. Variances of actual from standard costs are identified within the accounting system. Variances may be broken down in a variety of ways, but most standard cost systems identify rate and quantity variances for direct materials and direct labor. An overhead volume variance identifies the cost of unused production capacity, and an overhead budget volume indicates how much actual factory overhead varied from the overhead predicted by a flexible budget for the activity level actually achieved.

PROBLEMS FOR CHAPTER 24
Alternate Problems for this chapter begin on page D-134.

24.1. The following data are provided for the fertilizer division of Chemmo Chemicals, Incorporated.

Flexible Budget Information

Variable production cost per 100 lb. of fertilizer
Direct materials, 130 lb.* at 8¢ per lb.	$10.40
Direct labor, one-quarter hour at $4 per hour	1.00
Variable overhead, at $8 per direct labor hour	2.00

Fixed overhead per month, $80,000

---

*The ingredients are dried in the production process, resulting in a weight reduction.

Actual Production Costs for the month of January

Variable
Direct materials, 6,600,000 lb. at 7.5¢	$495,000
Direct labor, 13,750 hours at $4 per hour	55,000
Variable overhead	100,000
Fixed overhead	82,000

Fertilizer produced during January: 5,000,000 lb.

Required

1) Prepare a flexible budget performance report for January.

2) Determine the rate and quantity elements of the

    a) Direct materials variance.

    b) Direct labor variance.

24.2. The Mighty Mower Company assembles and sells one model of a home lawnmower. The accounting records disclose the following information for 19X5 and 19X4.

	19X5	**19X4**
Mowers produced and sold	1,600	1,100
Total cost	$154,000	$115,500
Sales	$280,000	$192,500

Required

1) Determine the apparent variable cost per unit and fixed cost per year.

2) Calculate the contribution margin per unit for 19X5.

3) Calculate the contribution margin percentage for 19X5.

4) Determine Mighty Mower's break-even point in both units and sales dollars for 19X5.

5) Calculate Mighty Mower's expected net income (or loss) at sales volumes of 300 mowers and 2,000 mowers.

24.3. A comparative income statement for the Nilte Corporation follows.

NILTE CORPORATION Income Statement For Years Ended December 31, 19X4 and 19X3		
	19X4	**19X3**
Sales	$15,000,000	$12,000,000
Cost		
Casting department	$ 6,000,000	$ 5,000,000
Grinding department	2,300,000	2,000,000
Selling and administrative	3,600,000	3,000,000
Total cost	$11,900,000	$10,000,000
Net Income	$ 3,100,000	$ 2,000,000

The selling price per product unit remained constant during 19X3 and 19X4 and is not expected to change during 19X5.

Required

1) Calculate variable cost per sales dollar and fixed cost per year for each department and for the selling and administrative function.

2) Write a net income formula that can be used to project variable cost per sales dollar, fixed cost per year for each department and the selling and administrative function, and total net income.

3) Prepare a projected income statement (flexible budget) for 19X5 similar to those shown for 19X3 and 19X4, assuming estimated sales of $21,000,000 for 19X5.

24.4. The gear box assembly department uses 24 specially hardened nuts and bolts for each gear box assembled. It takes one-half of a labor hour to assemble one gear box. The fixed costs for the department total $2,400 per month. One dozen nuts and bolts cost $3. Wages are $5 per hour. The department has no variable overhead (indirect) costs.

Required

1) Write a total cost formula that can be used to project direct materials, direct labor, fixed cost, and total cost for the gear box assembly department for a one-month period.

2) Project total cost at a production level of 5,000 gear boxes per month.

3) Write formulas for projecting (a) the number of nuts and bolts; and (b) the number of labor hours required for various levels of production.

4) What quantity of nuts and bolts, and of labor hours, should be budgeted for production of 6,400 gear boxes?

5) If the labor force puts in only 120 production hours a month per worker, how many workers must be hired to assemble 6,400 gear boxes per month?

COMPREHENSION PROBLEM FOR CHAPTER 24

24.5. Seetu Company has the capacity to manufacture 20,000 units of product per month. Standard direct materials usage is 2 pounds per product unit. During February, 40,000 pounds of direct materials were used to turn out 18,000 units of product. The production manager complains that the poor quality of direct materials used in February resulted in excess materials waste during the month. The purchasing agent states that she purchased materials from a new supplier at $5.60 per pound, whereas the standard cost of direct materials is $6 per pound.

Overhead is assigned to production at a standard overhead rate of $3.20 per pound of direct materials used. The variable overhead portion of the standard overhead rate is $2; the fixed portion is $1.20 (budgeted fixed overhead is $48,000 per month). Actual overhead cost for February was $132,000.

Required

1) Determine the materials rate and quantity variances for February.

2) Determine the overhead volume and budget variances for February.

3) State one or more possible reasons for assigning overhead on the basis of materials used.

4) Assuming that the entire materials quantity variance was due to inferior materials (as compared to the quality of materials purchased in previous months), evaluate the purchasing agent's decision to change suppliers. Consider in your analysis any identifiable relationships between materials variances and overhead variances.

CHAPTER **25**

Alternative Choice Decisions
(Capital Budgeting)

Intelligent decision making requires useful data. Many decisions are primarily based on accounting information. Decision makers, and those who advise them, must be able to select relevant data for use in comparing available choices.

Chapter 25 consists of two sections. Section A focuses on the identification and use of relevant data for decision making. The section first describes how to diagram available alternatives. The need for determining areas of difference between alternatives is discussed, and two tests of relevance are listed. The calculations of initial cash outlay, yearly net cash flows, and the net advantage for an alternative are illustrated. The section closes with a warning that some important considerations defy quantification.

Section B considers five different approaches for analyzing and comparing alternatives. A distinction is made between mutually exclusive and competing alternatives before the techniques, advantages, and disadvantages of the different approaches are discussed. Three cost-saving alternatives are used to illustrate the results obtained by using the various approaches. Finally, a table summarizes the resulting measures and rankings.

SECTION 25.A

Relevant Data

OBJECTIVES

In this section our concern is with the relevance of data for purposes of making alternative choices. At the conclusion of your study, you should be able to

1. State the two questions for testing whether information is relevant to a decision.
2. State what a sunk cost is, and explain why sunk costs are irrelevant for decision purposes.
3. Perform the following tasks, given information about two decision alternatives:
   a. Select the information that is relevant to the decision.
   b. Calculate the incremental after-tax net cash outlay.
   c. Calculate the net annual after-tax cash benefit on an incremental basis.
   d. Determine the net advantage (or disadvantage) on an incremental basis.

ALTERNATIVE CHOICES

Every management decision involves a choice between alternatives. The kinds of decisions vary with the area of management, the size of the entity, and other circumstances. Purchasing agents must decide what to buy and from whom; personnel managers must decide which job applicants to hire; other managers must decide whether to introduce new products, drop old ones, construct new plant facilities, borrow money—the list could go on and on.

ILLUSTRATION 25.1

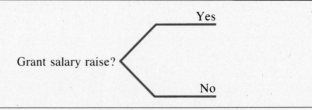

ILLUSTRATION 25.2

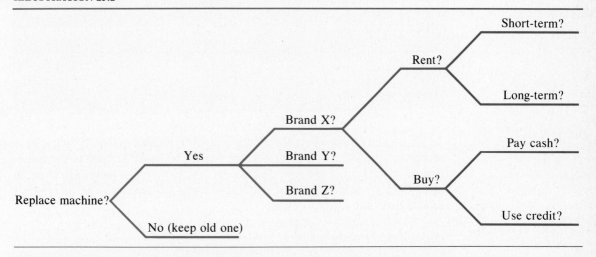

Sometimes a decision requires only a simple yes or no response. A manager may have to decide whether a specific employee will get a raise in salary. The decision may be diagramed as in Illustration 25.1. On other occasions, a decision may involve a multitude of alternatives. For example, deciding whether to replace a machine might require the kinds of considerations shown in Illustration 25.2.

A diagram like the one in Illustration 25.2, which shows alternatives available for a particular decision, is called a decision tree. Some decision trees become very involved. The diagram pictured here could be expanded to include different sources of credit. And, of course, the alternatives that branch out for brand X may also be applicable to brands Y and Z.

Some considerations are by their nature difficult to quantify. These hard-to-quantify variables are ignored until the end of the section, where they are discussed briefly.

INCREMENTAL ANALYSIS

Managers strive to achieve certain goals. Presumably, most of the goals of a *business* entity are consistent with profit maximization, at least in the long run. Therefore, managers should be concerned about the long-run effects of management decisions on the entity's profits. One approach is to estimate the company's total net income for one or more periods for each decision alternative being considered. The alternative that promises the greatest potential net income can then be selected as the superior one. For example, we might have the following situation for two alternatives under consideration.

DOOBLE STORES Projected for the Year 19X6		
	Alternative A	**Alternative B**
Total revenue	$900,000	$910,000
Total expense	800,000	795,000
Net income	$100,000	$115,000

It appears that alternative B is superior to alternative A because it promises a higher net income for the year. The extra $15,000 is the *incremental* advantage of B over A. Of course, the net income increment is made up of both a revenue difference and an expense difference. The increments can be determined as follows.

DOOBLE STORES Projected for the Year 19X6			
	Alternative A	**Alternative B**	**Difference**
Total revenue	$900,000	$910,000	$10,000
Total expense	800,000	795,000	(5,000)
Net income	$100,000	$115,000	$15,000

Thus we can say that B is superior to A for two reasons: revenue will be higher and expense will be lower.

It is not necessary to work with aggregate revenue and expense for the entire business, provided that *incremental* effects on revenue and expense can be determined. Assume, for example, that alternatives A and B represent two brands of power saws. Dooble Stores may choose to sell one brand or the other, but they will not be allowed to sell both. Assuming that other kinds of merchandise are also sold, the decision approach is to pin down the *differences* in revenue and expense for the two alternatives. Suppose that sales and cost of goods sold for saws are the only factors that will *differ* for the two alternatives, as shown here.

DOOBLE STORES Projected Sales and Costs of Saws for the Year 19X6			
	A	**B**	**Difference**
Expected saw sales	$40,000	$50,000	$10,000
Expected cost of saws sold	30,000	25,000	(5,000)
Effect on net income	$10,000	$25,000	$15,000

You can see from the simple example we have used that alternative B is superior to alternative A. The *relevant* data needed for this decision were the anticipated *future differences* in outcomes. These differences may be either incremental costs or incremental benefits between the alternatives under consideration. *An incremental (differential) cost is an additional sacrifice associated with a decision choice, whereas an incremental (differential) benefit is an additional advantage obtained from a decision choice.* In a sense, both the increase in revenue and the decrease in cost illustrated for Dooble Stores are incremental benefits to be derived from choice B.

Relevance Test

The word *relevant* is much used but seldom defined. It means appropriate, applicable, pertinent, or apropos. Thus *relevant data* are facts that are useful for, or pertinent to, the consideration of a particular problem. For our purposes, *relevant data are facts that are both significant and helpful to managers in making decisions that affect the future.*

OBJECTIVE 3a. Select information relevant to a decision.

The questions that follow may serve as a test for determining whether information is relevant to a decision. It is only when the answers to both questions are positive that the information is relevant.

INFORMATION RELEVANCE TEST

  1. Does the information pertain to *future* conditions?
  2. Is the information *different* for the alternatives being considered?

OBJECTIVE 1. State the two questions for testing whether information is relevant to a decision.

Relevant information may sometimes be in topsy-turvy form, at least when compared with historical reporting concepts. Accountants would never think of recording a cost that was *not* incurred by an entity. In decision making, however, a potential *cost saving* is relevant information, as is revenue that may have to be forgone. *A potential benefit that is forgone (lost) as a result of choosing an alternative is sometimes referred to as an opportunity cost.*

Consider the following information for alternatives X and Y.

	X	Y	Difference
Projected Revenues and Expenses			
Expected revenue	$68,000	$62,000	$(6,000)
Expected expense	54,000	41,000	(13,000)
Effect on net income	$14,000	$21,000	$ 7,000

If alternative Y is chosen, revenue will be reduced by the $6,000 of *opportunity cost*. On the other hand, alternative Y will permit a *cost saving* of $13,000. Since the cost saving exceeds the lost revenue, alternative Y appears to be the more attractive choice.

The remainder of this section concentrates on identifying the relevant effects of decisions on future cash flows.

Sunk Costs

Except for possible tax consequences, costs incurred in the past are not relevant to decisions about the future. *Past costs are often called sunk costs* because the expenditures cannot be reversed. The net book values of long-term assets are sunk costs and are therefore irrelevant data for purposes of decision making, as are depreciation expenses.

The current salvage values (market values) of assets *are* relevant data, however. In a sense, managers continuously reinvest the disposition value of assets by declining to sell them for what they would bring. Recall from our earlier discussion that a forgone benefit is an *opportunity cost*—and the net realizable value of any asset is the opportunity cost of continuing to hold that asset.

Tax Considerations

Taxes imposed by various tax laws are relevant considerations when decisions are being made. Income taxes have the effect of reducing the benefits from taxable revenues and reducing the real sacrifices of deductible expenses. Incremental benefits that are taxable result in a corresponding increase in taxable income and in a tax cost at the marginal rate of tax. For example, a taxable incremental benefit of $8,000 will be reduced to $4,800 when the marginal rate of tax is 40%, as illustrated here.

Incremental benefit	$8,000
Increase in tax (40% marginal tax rate)	3,200
Net after-tax benefit	$4,800

The after-tax benefit is 60% of the pretax amount when the marginal tax rate is 40%, as follows.

(1 − Marginal tax rate) × Pretax benefit = After-tax benefit
$$(1 - 0.40) \times \$8,000 = \$4,800$$

In a similar manner, the burden of an incremental cost that is tax-deductible is reduced by the tax savings. A $6,000 incremental cost that is deductible will save $2,400 in taxes at a 40% marginal tax rate.

Incremental cost	$6,000
Reduction in tax (40% marginal rate)	2,400
Net after-tax cost	$3,600

or

(1 − Marginal tax rate) × Pretax cost = After-tax cost
$$(1 - 0.40) \times \$6,000 = \$3,600$$

Certain current cost outlays, such as those for the purchase of long-term assets, are not deductible when they are incurred. The costs of some assets are apportioned (expired) over their useful lives as depreciation, depletion, or amortization. Whereas past *sunk costs* are irrelevant to decision making, the tax savings from deductible write-offs of past costs are quite relevant.

Consider, for example, write-offs of sunk costs as depreciation expenses. When depreciation is deductible for tax purposes, it acts as a *tax shield, offsetting some revenues that would otherwise be taxed.* Depreciation of $10,000 will shield $10,000 of revenues against income taxation. Thus dollars of deductible depreciation *save taxes* to the extent of the marginal tax rate multiplied by the annual depreciation amount. If, for example, the marginal tax rate is 40%, $10,000 of depreciation will save $4,000 that would otherwise have to be paid as income taxes.

The tax effects of book gains or losses from disposals of assets are also relevant. Taxable gains result in real tax costs, while tax-deductible losses save taxes.

Net Cash Outlay

The net cash required at the outset of an alternative is referred to as the net cash outlay, or net investment. If we are considering the outright purchase of a machine for cash, the net cash outlay is simply the cash price of the new machine. If, however, the decision involves the replacement of a currently owned machine with a different one, there are other relevant items to consider. Suppose, for example, that the facts listed in Illustration 25.3 apply to the decision at hand.

ILLUSTRATION 25.3

Cost of old machine	$ 80,000
Accumulated depreciation on old machine	$ 60,000
Current market (salvage) value of old machine	$ 30,000
Expected cash cost of new machine	$200,000
Marginal income tax rate	45%
Expected remaining life of either machine	10 years
Expected salvage value of either machine at end of 10 years	$ –0–

ILLUSTRATION 25.4

Cash cost of new machine			$200,000
Less: Cash cleared from sale of old machine			
Cash from sale		$30,000	
Less tax on gain			
Sale price	$30,000		
Book value	20,000		
Gain	$10,000		
Tax on gain ($10,000 × 45%)		4,500	
Cash cleared after tax			25,500
Net cash outlay for new machine			$174,500

The cash that could be cleared from the sale of the old machine might be applied toward the purchase price of the new one. The net cash outlay for the new machine would be determined as shown in Illustration 25.4.

Annual Net Cash Flows

Most decision alternatives affect outcomes in a number of future years. To properly evaluate alternatives, all incremental changes in cash flows should be considered. In this regard, the relevant data are the *future incremental* cash flows—the *differences* in cash flows that can be attributed to the decision at hand.

Let us assume that the expected future costs for machining 10,000 parts each year for ten years are as listed in Illustration 25.5 for each of the alternatives shown.

The relevant facts are those that represent *changes* in future cash flows. When the new machine is viewed as an alternative to keeping the old one, the direct materials cost may be ignored because it would remain the same. However, the new machine would make it possible to save $4 per unit in direct labor and $2 per unit in variable overhead, a *before-tax* saving of $6 per unit. Assuming that the marginal tax rate is expected to remain at 45%

ILLUSTRATION 25.5

	Old Machine	New Machine
Per unit costs		
Direct materials	$ 8	$8
Direct labor	$10	$6
Variable overhead	$ 5	$3
Depreciation per year		
$20,000 ÷ 10 years	$2,000	
$200,000 ÷ 10 years		$20,000

ILLUSTRATION 25.6

Incremental benefit before tax		
$6 per unit × 10,000 units		$60,000
Less income taxes each year		
Cost savings	$60,000	
Increase in depreciation expense	18,000	
Net taxable difference	$42,000	
Income taxes, $42,000 × 45%		18,900
Net annual benefit after taxes		$41,100

OBJECTIVE 3c. Calculate the net annual after-tax cash benefit on an incremental basis.

in the future, the annual net cash benefit can be determined as shown in Illustration 25.6.

A quick approach that arrives at the same result is as follows.

Incremental after-tax savings in cost:	
$60,000 × (1 − 0.45) =	$33,000
Plus taxes saved by depreciation shield:	
$18,000 × 0.45 =	8,100
Net annual benefit after taxes	$41,100

Net Advantage or Disadvantage

To get the net advantage or disadvantage of an alternative, we might compare the future net cash flows with the net cash outlay, as shown here.

Total net cash benefit − Net cash outlay = Net advantage
10 years × $41,100 − $174,500 = $236,500

OBJECTIVE 3d. Determine the net advantage (or disadvantage) on an incremental basis.

It would appear that the entity could expect to be better off by $236,500 over the ten-year period if the new machine were purchased. Had the result come out to be negative, it would represent a net disadvantage. A word of caution: the net advantage approach illustrated here is not altogether valid, for we have not yet considered the *present values* of future amounts of cash. That refinement of the incremental approach for evaluating alternatives comes in the next section.

HARD-TO-QUANTIFY CONSIDERATIONS

Because accountants are accustomed to working with quantified data they may overlook important elements that are difficult to quantify. Sometimes the overriding considerations in a decision stem from legal or moral obligations, or from the risks of loss should the predicted benefits not occur. The prejudices of managers, however irrational, often swing the decision choice to a particular alternative.

A teetotaling restaurant owner might refuse to serve alcoholic beverages, no matter how much incremental profit would result. Replacement of employees by automated machinery may be rejected because managers feel responsible for the welfare of company employees—or perhaps because of the anticipated effects of such an action on the morale of the remaining employees.

Managers are inclined to choose a secure alternative over a risky one that offers higher potential profits. And many companies maintain large idle cash balances or considerable investments in low-yield government securities as hedges against hard times. On the other hand, some managers plunge headfirst into new ventures about which they know little.

There is not much that accountants can do about subjective considerations, other than to help managers identify them on a conscious level.

GLOSSARY FOR SECTION 25.A

Decision tree   A diagram that shows alternatives available for a particular decision.

Incremental (differential) benefit   An additional advantage obtained from a decision choice.

Incremental (differential) cost   An additional sacrifice associated with a decision choice.

Net cash outlay (net investment)   The net cash required at the outset of an alternative.

Opportunity cost   A potential benefit that is forgone (lost) as a result of choosing an alternative.

Relevant data   Facts that are both significant and helpful to managers in making decisions that affect the future.

Sunk costs   Costs incurred in the past.

Tax shield   A deductible cost that acts as an offset against revenue that would otherwise be taxed.

SELF-QUIZ ON OBJECTIVES FOR SECTION 25.A
Solutions to Self-Quiz begin on page B-73.

1. **OBJECTIVE 1.** State the two questions for testing whether information is relevant to a decision.

2. **OBJECTIVE 2.** State what a sunk cost is, and state why sunk costs are irrelevant for decision purposes.

3. Managers of Zippy Dart Corporation are considering the replacement of an old dart-casting machine with a new one. About 100,000 darts per year are cast with the aid of a single casting machine. The following data are available.

	Old Machine	**Proposed New Machine**
Cost	$80,000	$100,000
Accumulated depreciation	$40,000	$ –0–
Current disposition value	$20,000	$100,000
Remaining life	5 years	5 years
Expected salvage value in 5 years	$–0–	$ –0–
Depreciation method	Straight line	Straight line
Marginal tax rate	46%	46%
Production costs		
Direct materials per dart	$0.20	$0.30
Direct labor per dart	$0.60	$0.40
Variable overhead per dart	$0.30	$0.20
Selling price per dart	$3	$3

a. **OBJECTIVE 3a.** Select the information that is relevant to deciding whether to replace the old machine with a new one.

b. **OBJECTIVE 3b.** Calculate the incremental after-tax net cash outlay required to purchase the new machine.

c. **OBJECTIVE 3c.** Calculate the net annual after-tax cash benefit on an incremental basis.

d. **OBJECTIVE 3d.** Determine the net advantage (or disadvantage) on an incremental basis.

DISCUSSION QUESTIONS FOR SECTION 25.A

1. What constitutes *relevant data* for decision making?

2. What is an *incremental cost?*

3. What is *opportunity cost?*

4. Depreciation expenses are usually considered irrelevant for decision purposes because they are write-offs of sunk costs. Why is depreciation relevant when it is deductible for tax purposes?

5. Fixed overhead, at least in the short run, is irrelevant to most decisions. Is this statement true or false? Why?

6. What effect does depreciation have on cash flows?

7. Consider an investment alternative that involves the replacement of an old piece of equipment by a newer model. The old equipment can only be disposed of at a loss; that is, for less than its book value. What is the effect of the loss on cash flows?

EXERCISES FOR SECTION 25.A

25.A.1. Identify the items in the following list that are relevant for decision making (ignore income tax effects):

   a. Cost of an existing asset.

   b. Cost of a replacement asset.

   c. Depreciation on a replacement asset.

   d. Depreciation on an existing asset.

   e. Cost of retraining employees to operate a replacement asset.

   f. Cost of lost production while installing a replacement asset.

   g. Incremental savings of operating costs.

   h. Loss resulting from disposal of existing asset.

25.A.2. The production manager for Bower Company is recommending that the manufacturing process be changed from a manual system to a highly automated system. The purchase of a sophisticated machine will allow both labor and materials cost savings. Costs related to the two processes follow.

	Old Process	New Process
Direct labor (total for 6 years)	$120,000	$51,000
Direct materials (total for 6 years)	$ 66,000	$60,000
Fixed overhead (total for 6 years)	$ 12,000	$12,000
Cost of machine	$ 30,000	$54,000
Present market value	$ –0–	$54,000
Useful life	6 years	6 years
Annual depreciation	$ 5,000	$ 9,000
Maintenance cost (total for 6 years)	$ 3,000	$ 6,000

Indicate the amounts relevant to the decision and determine the relevant incremental costs and benefits (ignore tax effects).

25.A.3. Suppose an asset is sold for $10,000 cash, which is $1,000 greater than the book value of the asset. Assuming a marginal tax rate of 40%, determine the effect of the gain on cash flows.

25.A.4. Assume that Jackson Corporation's marginal tax rate of 40% also applies to gains and losses on asset disposals. Calculate the after-tax effect on cash flows of each event in the following list.

   a. Interest expense, $5,000

   b. Labor cost savings, $12,000

   c. Payment for new machine, $40,000

   d. Increase in cost of goods sold, $10,000

   e. Disposal of an asset for its book value, $10,000

   f. Disposal of an asset for $8,000, which is $2,000 less than its book value

g. Disposal of an asset for $8,000, which is $2,000 more than its book value

h. An increase in depreciation of $6,000 per year

25.A.5. Basso, Incorporated, is considering the purchase of a new stamping machine that will produce additional revenue of $50,000 a year for three years. The new machine costs $60,000, has an estimated life of three years, and is expected to have no salvage value at the end of its life. There will be additional labor and materials costs of $10,000 per year for three years. The marginal tax rate is 40%. Calculate the annual net cash flows after taxes.

PROBLEMS FOR SECTION 25.A
Alternate Problems for this section begin on page D-135.

25.A.6. The DDQ Corporation is considering the replacement of an old pneumatic press with a new, more efficient model. The old press has a book value of $4,000 and will last four more years. It will not have any salvage value at the end of its life. The old press could be sold today for $4,000. The new press will also last four years and will have no salvage value. It will cost $10,400 and will reduce operating costs by $3,600 each year for four years. The marginal tax rate is 40%.

Required

1) Calculate the amount and timing of the cash flows resulting from the purchase of the new press.

2) Without regard to the time value of money, state whether the new press should be purchased. Why?

25.A.7. Jack Jarvis is a second-year accounting student. At the beginning of September he has an opportunity to move into a new apartment much closer to the college. Unfortunately, he has just paid two months' rent in advance for his present apartment. If he moves out, the rent paid in advance will not be refunded. He must take the new apartment immediately or not at all. Information relating to the two apartments follows.

	Old Apartment	New Apartment
Rent paid in advance	$220	$-0-
Monthly rent	110	90
Monthly utilities	16	16
Monthly carfare to college	8	-0-
Monthly TV cable rental	10	10
Remaining months in school year	9	9

Required

1) Prepare a schedule showing the rent payments required each month under the two alternatives, and calculate the differences.

2) Prepare a schedule showing other relevant information and the differences between the alternatives over the 9-month period.

3) Calculate the net savings (or loss) that would result from moving to the new apartment.

4) State which apartment Jack should choose and why.

25.A.8. Marlin Manufacturing Company, a partnership, makes its own components for assembly into marlins. One of the parts, a plastic brace, is available from an outside supplier at a cost of $1.80 each. Information concerning costs follows.

PLASTICS DEPARTMENT 19X3		
For 100,000 Braces	**Per Unit**	**Total**
Direct materials	$0.30	$ 30,000
Direct labor	0.70	70,000
Variable overhead	0.60	60,000
Fixed overhead	0.40	40,000
Manufacturing cost	$2.00	$200,000

Fixed overhead consists of allocations of general and administrative expenses and depreciation of the department's equipment. The book value of equipment is $200,000. Assume that for each of the next ten years the company will need the same number of braces as were produced in 19X3. The present equipment will last ten more years. The equipment has no market or salvage value. Assume the company has no alternative use for the space or equipment now used by the department to produce plastic braces. You may ignore tax considerations.

Required

1) Calculate the yearly manufacturing cost savings (or cost increases) Marlin can realize by purchasing plastic braces from the supplier.

2) State whether Marlin should make its own plastic braces or buy them from the supplier. Explain your answer.

3) List some qualitative factors that should be considered in make-or-buy situations like this one.

25.A.9. Arbo Corporation managers are thinking of replacing an old machine with a newer, more efficient model. The company expects to produce at a rate of 40,000 units per year for the next eight years. The corporation's marginal tax rate is 46%. Information about the two machines follows.

	Old Machine	New Machine
Cost	$40,000.00	$120,000.00
Book value	$ 8,000.00	$120,000.00
Market value	$ 6,000.00	$120,000.00
Useful life	8 years	8 years
Annual depreciation	$ 1,000.00	$ 15,000.00
Direct materials per unit	$ 1.80	$ 1.90
Direct labor per unit	$ 3.00	$ 2.30
Variable overhead per unit	$ 0.80	$ 0.75
Fixed overhead per unit	$ 1.00	$ 1.00
Employee retraining cost	$–0–	$ 1,300.00

Required

1) Calculate the net saving or the net cost for the new machine. Ignore the time value of money.

2) State whether the old machine should be replaced and why.

25.A.10. Westly Adams Company is considering the replacement of an old printing press with a more efficient up-to-date model. Data for the two machines follow.

	Old Press	New Press
Purchase cost	$10,000	$30,000
Book value	$ 1,000	$30,000
Current market value	$ 1,000	$30,000
Remaining life	10 years	10 years
Annual saving from new press		$ 5,000
Marginal tax rate	40%	40%
Depreciation method	Straight-line	Straight-line

Required

Calculate the net cash outlay and the net annual after-tax benefits that will result from the purchase of the new machine and the sale of the old one for its market value.

25.A.11. M&M Corporation is considering the replacement of a machine with a newer model that will cut costs. Information relative to the two machines follows.

	Old Machine	New Machine
Cost	$50,000	$110,000
Book value and market value	$25,000	$110,000
Remaining life	10 years	10 years
Annual depreciation	$ 2,500	$ 11,000
Annual operating cost	$83,000	$ 65,000
Employee retraining cost	$–0–	$ 5,000

Required

1) Prepare a schedule showing the information relevant to the decision and the incremental differences between the two alternatives over the 10-year life, assuming a marginal tax rate of 40%. Ignore the time value of money.

2) State whether you recommend replacement of the old machine and why.

SECTION 25.B

Ranking Alternatives

OBJECTIVES

In this section we consider different approaches to making investment choices from among available alternatives. At the conclusion of your study, you should be able to

1. Differentiate between mutually exclusive alternatives and competing alternatives.

2. State two limitations of the payback approach for evaluating investment alternatives, and state the circumstances under which the payback approach will nevertheless result in a reasonable ranking of alternatives.

3. Determine for two or more investment alternatives for which appropriate data are given:
   a. The payback periods.
   b. The net present values.
   c. The profitability indexes.
   d. The approximate rates of return.

4. Rank two or more investment alternatives according to relative profitability and defend the order of ranking.

MUTUALLY EXCLUSIVE VERSUS COMPETING ALTERNATIVES

Recall the *decision tree* shown in the previous section. The choices shown there are *mutually exclusive alternatives in that the choice of one automatically rejects the others.* Selection of brand X rules out brands Y and Z; purchase of the machine rules out renting it; and so on.

> **OBJECTIVE 1.**
> **Differentiate between mutually exclusive and competing alternatives.**

When any number of the available alternatives may be chosen, the choices are said to be *competing* for available funds. *Competing alternatives, then, are alternatives that do not conflict with one another; the choice of any one alternative does not exclude the choice of any other.* A proposal to expand the factory building, for example, is not in conflict with plans to replace old machinery; nor does it exclude the possibility of refurbishing the president's office, adding a product line, or making any number of other possible investments of the company's available funds.

Competing alternatives may be ranked according to their relative profitability in order to assist managers in making their choices. Alternatives can then be selected from the top down, until the available funds run out. Every alternative under consideration should, of course, offer some contribution to profits, since not much can be gained from investing in losing ventures. Thus only those projects that promise to contribute something toward future profits should be viewed as *competing* with one another.

The top-ranked alternative among a *mutually exclusive* group of choices is presumably the winner over the other available alternatives. A ranking of *competing* alternatives simply establishes the relative attractiveness of the choices that are competing for whatever resources are available. Here are some of the more popular approaches to ranking alternatives.

RETURN ON INVESTMENT APPROACH

There was a time when accountants and managers tried to evaluate incremental data with statement analysis techniques. Recall from Chapter 19 the *return on assets* measure, whereby net income plus interest is divided by the average assets employed during the period. Perhaps, so the thinking went, an *incremental* effect on net income could be divided by the average investment needed to earn that increment in order to obtain a measure of profitability for a particular choice. The *return on investment* calculation *divides an average increment to net income by the average investment in an alternative.*

$$\frac{\text{Average increment to net income}}{\text{Average investment in alternative}} = \text{Return on investment}$$

To illustrate approaches to ranking investments, consider three cost-saving decision alternatives for which the data in Illustration 25.7 are provided. The alternatives do not involve any dispositions of assets now held.

Return on investment rates for the three alternatives may be determined as shown in Illustration 25.8.

ILLUSTRATION 25.7

	R	S	T
Required cash investment in depreciable assets	$160,000	$90,000	$300,000
Expected life of project	10 years	10 years	10 years
Expected salvage value of assets	$-0-	$-0-	$-0-
Depreciation method used	Straight-line	Straight-line	Straight-line
Annual cash cost savings expected, excluding depreciation and before income taxes	$ 40,000	$25,000	$ 70,000
Marginal tax rate	40%	40%	40%

ILLUSTRATION 25.8

RETURN ON INVESTMENT APPROACH			
	R	S	T
Average Annual Increment to Net Income			
Annual cost savings	$40,000	$25,000	$70,000
Extra depreciation	16,000	9,000	30,000
Net savings before tax	$24,000	$16,000	$40,000
Tax at 40%	9,600	6,400	16,000
Increment to income after tax	$14,400	$ 9,600	$24,000
Average Investment			
$\dfrac{\text{Cost + Salvage}}{2}$	$80,000	$45,000	$150,000
Return on Investment			
$\dfrac{\text{Average increment to net income}}{\text{Average investment}}$	18.0%	21.3%	16.0%

Thus, using the return on investment approach, S would offer the highest return, followed by R, with T coming in last. If these were *mutually exclusive alternatives,* choices R and T would be rejected. If the alternatives were competing, available funds would be allocated first to S, then to R, and then to T if sufficient funds were available to finance all three—and provided no other competing alternatives offer greater returns.

Limitation of Return on Investment Approach

The main limitation of the return on investment approach is so serious that few modern managers or accountants support its use. This disabling limitation is that the approach fails to consider the *time value* of money. The faster money can be recovered from an alternative, the sooner it can be reinvested in another alternative. As pointed out in Appendix I of Chapter 16, the farther in the future an amount of money is, the less it is worth in present value terms.

PAYBACK APPROACH

One of the earliest attempts to recognize the time value of money, the *payback period approach*, is crude but still popular because of its simplicity. *The payback period for an investment is the number of years it will take to recover the initial cash paid out.* The faster cash is recovered, the shorter the payback period—and the better the investment is supposed to be.

ILLUSTRATION 25.9

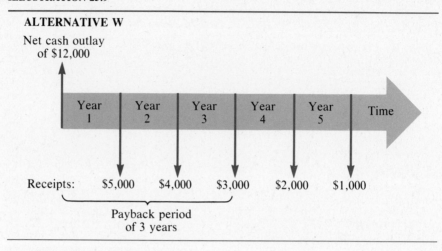

ALTERNATIVE W

When annual net cash flows are equal, the payback period can be determined by dividing the initial net cash outlay by the annual net after-tax cash flow, as illustrated here.

$$\frac{\text{Net cash outlay}}{\text{Annual net after-tax cash flow}} = \text{Payback period in years}$$

If net annual cash flows are unequal, the payback period must be determined by adding up the cash flows over time, starting with the first year. Illustration 25.9 shows an alternative paying back the initial cash outlay in three years.

The annual cash savings for the three alternatives introduced earlier are actually equivalent to cash inflows. That is, cash that does not have to be

ILLUSTRATION 25.10

OBJECTIVE 3a.
Determine payback
periods.

PAYBACK APPROACH			
	R	**S**	**T**
Net Cash Outlay	$160,000	$90,000	$300,000
Annual Net Cash Saving			
Cost saving after taxes			
(1 − 0.40) × Cost saving	$ 24,000	$15,000	$ 42,000
Tax saving from depreciation shield			
0.40 × Depreciation	6,400	3,600	12,000
Annual net after-tax cash saving	$ 30,400	$18,600	$ 54,000
Payback Period			
$\dfrac{\text{Net cash outlay}}{\text{Annual net after-tax cash saving}}$	5.263 yrs.	4.839 yrs.	5.556 yrs.

paid out is as good as extra cash coming in. Since the annual flows for these alternatives are expected to be level, the payback periods may be figured as in Illustration 25.10.

From these calculations, it would appear that S is the most attractive alternative, with R coming in second and T third.

Limitations of Payback Approach

Although the payback approach is easy to use, its limitations can be serious. The payback approach measures the *time* required to recover the initial cash outlay, but it does not consider *variations* in cash flow when annual receipts are not expected to be level. For example, alternatives G and H in Illustration 25.11 show equally good payback periods. But a close inspection shows that,

ILLUSTRATION 25.11

ALTERNATIVE G

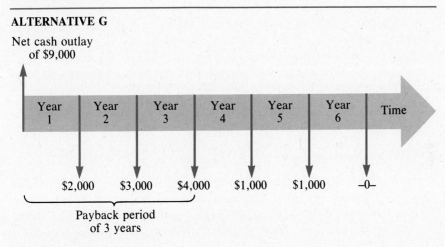

ALTERNATIVE H

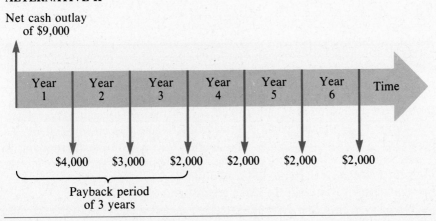

in year 1, alternative H promises to recover $2,000 more cash than G. This extra cash in the first year has more time value than the $2,000 of extra cash in year 3 under alternative G.

Another serious deficiency of the payback approach is that it does not consider either the amount or the timing of cash that is expected to be received *after* payback periods are over. Alternative H is expected to yield $2,000 in each of three years beyond the payback period, whereas alternative G offers only $1,000 in each of two additional years.

In summary, we must keep in mind the two rather serious handicaps of the payback approach.

OBJECTIVE 2. State two limitations of the payback approach, and state when this approach will nevertheless result in a reasonable ranking of alternatives.

> 1. The timing (variation) of cash flow during payback periods is not considered.
> 2. The timing and amount of cash flow beyond payback periods are not considered.

In spite of its limitations, the payback approach does rank alternatives reasonably well when all the alternatives have equal lives and when each alternative is expected to produce a level net annual cash flow in the future. The reasons for this conclusion become apparent when you study the rate of return approach later in the section.

PRESENT VALUE APPROACHES

Net Present Value Approach

Amounts of money at different points in time may be adjusted to equivalent values at one point in time. The most common practice is to adjust all amounts to *present values,* which simply means the equivalent values at the time the analysis is being done. In other words, a *present value is today's value of a future inflow or outflow of money.*

Net present value is the difference between the present value of cash inflows and the present value of cash outflows.

> Present value of inflows − Present value of outflows = Net present value

If the present value of inflows exceeds the present value of outflows, the net present value is positive. The *size* of the net present value of an alternative is a measure of its relative attractiveness as an investment. A negative net present value means an unattractive investment alternative.

A variation of the net present value formula offsets expected cash outflows of *future* years against inflows in those years, in which case the following equation will yield the same results as the preceding one.

Present value of annual net cash flows − Net cash outlay = Net present value

To determine present value, some *rate* must be used for discounting future amounts. The higher the rate used, the smaller the present value and vice versa. The problem is to select the rate that is most meaningful for a particular company.

Cost of Capital.   Any investment alternative should produce (or be worth) at least as much as the cost of the funds committed to it. *The cost of money used by a company, stated in annual percentage terms, is commonly referred to as the cost of capital.*

Some people contend that the cost of money used is the *incremental* cost of the funds to be committed to an alternative. In other words, if money can be borrowed at an annual interest rate of 8%, this is the cost of that particular batch of funds. Presumably, then, any return that can be generated in excess of the cost of the funds used leaves the company and its owners better off than they would otherwise be.

Others argue, however, that the incremental cost of funds depends on the existing relationship between debt and equity at any point in time. The amount of owners' equity represents a kind of buffer that is available for absorption of possible losses in future years. The more owners' equity there is, the greater the likelihood that lenders will get what is due them. The greater the amount of debt without any addition to owners' equity, the higher the rate of interest that must be paid. Thus the amount of current borrowing may affect the cost of future borrowing.

Something in the way of an *average* cost of the capital employed in the business is preferred by some over incremental cost. The problem here is to determine just what the cost of equity funds is. Is it the dividend (yield) rate, the rate of return on equity, or something in between? Equity holders surely expect something more from their investment than cash dividends. Earnings that are reinvested (retained) in the business offer a promise of future earnings growth and a corresponding increase in the value of owners' shares in a business. Perhaps the rate of return currently being earned on owners' equity is an approximate measure of what equity holders expect from their investment.

To obtain a reasonable average cost of capital, the cost of each segment of funds supplied must be *weighted* according to the amount of funds involved. In other words, if there is twice as much owners' equity than there is debt, the cost of equity should have twice as much effect on the cost of capital rate. Suppose, for example, that a corporation has been earning 12% on shareholders' equity and pays 6% after-tax interest on borrowed funds. If total shareholders' equity is now $200,000 and liabilities are $100,000, the average cost of capital can be figured as follows.

	Amount	Rate	Cost
Shareholders' equity	$200,000	12%	$24,000
Liabilities	100,000	6%	6,000
Total	$300,000		$30,000

$$\text{Average rate} = \frac{\$\ 30,000}{\$300,000} = 10\%$$

Thus this company had an average cost of capital of 10%.

Since interest is deductible for tax purposes, the after-tax cost of interest is less than the stated rate. For example, the after-tax cost of 10% interest is only 6% when the marginal tax rate is 40%, determined as follows.

$$(1 - 0.40) \times 0.10 = 0.06 = \text{After-tax cost}$$

You can see that the cost of capital concept is a tenuous one. From an overall point of view, the rate a company earns on new investments should be sufficient to at least maintain the entity's total current value, and preferably increase its value over time. Therefore, perhaps the current *rate of return on assets* should be the minimum earnings rate demanded for new alternatives.

Let us suppose that the *after-tax* cost of capital applicable to the alternatives R, S, and T presented earlier is 10%. The net present value of each alternative may then be determined as follows.

OBJECTIVE 3b.
Determine net present values.

NET PRESENT VALUE APPROACH			
	R	S	T
Annual net after-tax cash saving*	$ 30,400	$ 18,600	$ 54,000
Multiplied by annuity factor for 10 years, 10%†	× 6.145	× 6.145	× 6.145
Present value of cash saving	$186,808	$114,297	$331,830
Less: Net cash outlay	160,000	90,000	300,000
Net present value	$ 26,808	$ 24,297	$ 31,830

*As determined in Illustration 25.10.

†Refer to the present value factor tables that make up Appendix II of Chapter 16.

From a net present value standpoint, T seems to be the most attractive alternative, with R second and S last. However, this approach does not consider the size differences of the initial investments required to achieve the different net present values of the alternatives. The *relative* effectiveness of the investments may be measured by comparing the net present values with the net cash outlays required to obtain them.

Profitability Index. The effectiveness of an amount invested can be measured by relating it to the amount of net present value generated. This relationship can be shown by *dividing the net present value by the net cash outlay, which results in a **profitability index** for the alternatives.*

$$\frac{\text{Net present value}}{\text{Net cash outlay}} = \text{Profitability index}$$

The larger the profitability index, the more effective the alternative appears to be. Profitability indexes for the three alternatives introduced earlier are determined as follows.

OBJECTIVE 3c. Determine profitability indexes.

PROFITABILITY INDEX			
	R	S	T
$\dfrac{\text{Net present value}}{\text{Net cash outlay}}$ = profitability index	$\dfrac{\$26,808}{\$160,000} = 0.168$	$\dfrac{\$24,297}{\$90,000} = 0.270$	$\dfrac{\$31,830}{\$300,000} = 0.106$

As you can see, the profitability index is highest for S and lowest for T.

Rate of Return Approach

The need for arbitrarily choosing a cost of capital rate can be avoided by solving for the rate of return that an alternative promises. *The rate of return is the interest rate that will equate the present value of future net cash flows to the initial cash outlay.* In other words, we are looking for the rate that will satisfy the following equalities.

Present value of annual net after-tax cash flows = Net cash outlay

or

Present value of annual net after-tax cash flows − Net cash outlay = 0

We can approximate the rate of return promised by an alternative by solving for the present value annuity factor that equates the net cash outlay with the future cash flows. The factor, once determined, is compared with factors in a present value annuity table on the line for the number of periods involved. The factor closest to the one calculated identifies the approximate rate of return promised by the alternative.

Let us use the information for alternative R to illustrate the approach. The annual net after-tax cash flow multiplied by the annuity factor *f* must equal the net cash outlay.

$$\text{Annual net after-tax cash flow} \times f = \text{Net cash outlay}$$
$$\$30,400 \times f = \$160,000$$
$$f = \frac{\$160,000}{\$30,400}$$
$$f = 5.263$$

Thus when annual cash flows are level, the annuity factor is calculated in the same way as the payback period. By referring to the present value annuity table in Appendix II of Chapter 16, we see that on the 10-period line, 5.263 falls between the factors for 12% and 14%. The factor is so near to the one for 14% that we can say that alternative R promises a rate of return just under 14%.

OBJECTIVE 3d. Determine approximate rates of return.

The rates of return for each of the three alternatives are approximated as follows.

RATE OF RETURN APPROACH		
R	**S**	**T**
$\dfrac{\text{Net cash outlay}}{\text{Annual net cash flows}} = f$ $\dfrac{\$160,000}{\$30,400} = 5.263$	$\dfrac{\$90,000}{\$18,600} = 4.839$	$\dfrac{\$300,000}{\$54,000} = 5.556$
Approximate rate of return Just under 14%	Just under 16%	Just over 12%

Thus, as pointed out earlier, when the lives of alternatives are equal, and when net annual after-tax cash flows are expected to be level for each alternative, choices will be ranked in the same order by both the rate of return and payback approaches. This fact probably explains the continuing popularity of the simple payback approach for evaluating alternative choices.

COMPARISON OF RANKINGS

OBJECTIVE 4. Rank alternatives and defend the order of ranking.

The following presentation summarizes the rankings we obtained under the various approaches for evaluating the three alternatives.

Approach	Alternative R		Alternative S		Alternative T	
	Measure	*Rank*	*Measure*	*Rank*	*Measure*	*Rank*
Return on investment	18.0%	2	21.3%	1	16.0%	3
Payback period in years	5.263	2	4.839	1	5.556	3
Net present value	$26,808	2	$24,297	3	$31,830	1
Profitability index	.168	2	.270	1	.106	3
Approximate rate of return	14%	2	16%	1	12%	3

The net present value rankings are different from the others for alternatives S and T because the net present value approach does not consider the *relative effectiveness* of the net cash outlays. For example, whereas alternative T offers a net present value that is $5,022 greater than that offered by R, T requires $145,022 more net cash outlay than does R. As we have said, the profitability index measures the relative effectiveness of the amount invested in an alternative.

As *competing* alternatives, it would appear that S is most desirable, with R in second place and T placing last. However, if the alternatives are *mutually exclusive,* a manager may consider the higher net present value of T as important enough to rank it first, with R being ranked second. Much will depend on the amount of funds available for investment and on the possible alternative uses for the funds.

GLOSSARY FOR SECTION 25.B

Competing alternatives   Alternatives that do not conflict with each other; the choice of any one alternative does not exclude the choice of any other.

Cost of capital   The cost of funds used by a company, stated in annual percentage terms.

Mutually exclusive alternatives   Alternatives for which a choice of one automatically rejects the others.

Net present value   The difference between the present value of cash inflows and the present value of cash outflows.

Payback period   The number of years it will take to recover an amount of initial cash paid out.

Present value   Today's value of a future inflow or outflow of money.

Profitability index   The result obtained by dividing the net present value by the net cash outlay.

Rate of return   The interest rate that will equate the present value of future net cash flows to the initial cash outlay.

Return on investment   The result obtained by dividing an average increment to net income by the average investment in an alternative.

SELF-QUIZ ON OBJECTIVES FOR SECTION 25.B
Solutions to Self-Quiz begin on page B-74.

1. **OBJECTIVE 1.** Differentiate between mutually exclusive and competing alternatives.

2. **OBJECTIVE 2.** State two limitations of the payback approach for evaluating alternatives, and state the circumstances under which the payback approach will nevertheless result in a reasonable ranking of alternatives.

3. Information concerning two alternatives under consideration is provided here. No assets currently owned will need to be sold or retired.

	Alternative J	Alternative K
Annual cash proceeds before taxes	$ 70,000	$100,000
Cash cost of new depreciable asset	$300,000	$450,000
Expected life of new asset	15 years	15 years
Expected salvage value	$ –0–	$ –0–
Depreciation method used	Straight-line	Straight-line
Marginal tax rate	30%	30%
Approximate after-tax cost of capital	10%	10%

a. Determine the following for each alternative:

(1) OBJECTIVE 3a. Payback period.

(2) OBJECTIVE 3b. Net present value.

(3) OBJECTIVE 3c. Profitability index.

(4) OBJECTIVE 3d. Approximate rate of return.

b. OBJECTIVE 4. Choose the most attractive investment alternative, and defend your choice.

DISCUSSION QUESTIONS FOR SECTION 25.B

1. When considering mutually exclusive investment alternatives, why is it acceptable to choose only the best alternative, without having to rank the alternatives that are second best, third best, and so on? Explain.

2. What does the expression *cost of capital* mean?

3. What is an important shortcoming of the net present value approach for comparing investment alternatives?

4. Suppose you have $1,000 to invest and there are two alternatives available to you. Alternative A requires a $1,000 cash outlay now and will return $1,250 at the end of one year. Alternative B requires a $1,000 cash outlay now and will return $1,250 at the end of two years. Which alternative would you choose? Explain.

5. What does a payback period measure?

6. Why are shorter payback periods preferred to longer payback periods?

7. Suppose two competing investment alternatives each require a different initial outlay. What problem is encountered in using the net present value approach to compare the two alternatives? How can the problem be overcome?

8. Why does the rate of return approach often lead to a ranking of investment alternatives that differs from the net present value approach?

EXERCISES FOR SECTION 25.B

25.B.1. Use the present value tables in Appendix II of Chapter 16 to calculate the approximate amount to which $1,000 invested today at 10% per annum will accumulate over 40 years.

25.B.2. Calculate the payback period in years for an investment that requires a net cash outlay of $1,800,000 and has the potential to provide a net annual after-tax cash saving of $295,000.

25.B.3. Calculate the net present value for a net cash outlay of $1,800,000 that will produce an annual net after-tax cash saving of $295,000 for ten years, assuming a cost of capital of

   a. 10%.

   b. 12%.

25.B.4. Determine the approximate rate of return for the investment described in exercise 25.B.3.

25.B.5. A $1,000, 6% bond issued by the Frog Town Telephone Company is selling at a discount for $880. The bond matures in eight years. What is the approximate yield rate (rate of return) before taxes to someone who purchases the bond and holds it until maturity? (Assume that the interest is received at the end of each year.)

25.B.6. Rank the following investments according to payback period and rate of return.

Investment	Net Cash Outlay	Net Annual Cash Saving After Taxes	Years of Expected Life
A	$ 45,500	$12,000	5
B	101,700	18,000	10
C	58,000	11,000	10

PROBLEMS FOR SECTION 25.B
Alternate Problems for this section begin on page D-137.

25.B.7. Managers of Watz Corporation are thinking of replacing an old stamping press with a new, more efficient model. The old press has a book value of $40,000 and will last for four more years. It will not have any salvage value at the end of its life. The old press can be sold today for $40,000. The new press will last for four years and will have no salvage value. It will cost $104,000 and will reduce operating costs by $36,000 per year for four years. The marginal tax rate is 46%. Straight-line depreciation is used.

Required

  1) Assuming a 10% after-tax cost of capital, determine the net present value of investing in the new press.

2) Calculate the approximate rate of return offered by the new press.

3) Use the results in parts (1) and (2) to make a recommendation as to whether the new press should be purchased.

25.B.8. Information concerning three alternatives under consideration are provided here. No assets currently owned will need to be sold or retired.

	Alternative A	Alternative B	Alternative C
Initial cash outlay	$10,000	$20,000	$50,000
Annual net after-tax cash benefit	$2,100	$4,700	$9,800
Useful life in years	8	8	8

Assume that the after-tax cost of capital is 10%.

Required

1) Rank the alternatives by the following methods:

a) Net present value.

b) Profitability index.

c) Payback period.

d) Approximate rate of return.

2) Which ranking method(s) do you prefer? State the reasons for your choice.

25.B.9. Information concerning two alternatives under consideration are provided here.

	Alternative E	Alternative F
Annual net cash proceeds before tax	$100,000	$130,000
Cash cost of new asset	$400,000	$700,000
Expected life of new asset	10 years	10 years
Expected salvage value	$–0–	$–0–
Depreciation method	Straight-line	Straight-line
Marginal tax rate	40%	40%
After-tax cost of capital	12%	12%

If either E or F is selected, the company will dispose of assets with a book value of $40,000 for $10,000 cash. The present assets are being depreciated on a straight-line basis and have a remaining life of ten years with no expected salvage value. The marginal tax rate of 40% applies also to gains and losses on asset disposals.

Required

1) Determine the following for each alternative:

a) Payback period.

b) Net present value.

c) Approximate rate of return.

2) Choose the most attractive alternative and defend your choice.

25.B.10. The Giant Corporation purchased 100 electrostatic copy machines five years ago at a cost of $900,000. It was estimated at the time that the useful life of the machines would be fifteen years with no salvage value at the end of their life. The machines can be sold now for $400,000. New, more advanced, copy machines can be purchased today for $900,000. They will result in annual cost savings of $98,000 each year for the 10-year life of the new machines. At the end of ten years, the new machines can be sold for $100,000. The company's marginal tax rate is 40%. This rate also applies to gains and losses on asset disposals. Giant's after-tax cost of capital is 10%.

Required

1) Calculate on an incremental basis the net cash outlay and the annual net cash flows associated with the purchase of the new copy machines.

2) Calculate the net present value of the investment in the new copy machines and make a purchase recommendation.

25.B.11. After-tax cash flows for three investment alternatives are shown in the following diagrams.

ALTERNATIVE A

Net cash outlay: $8,000

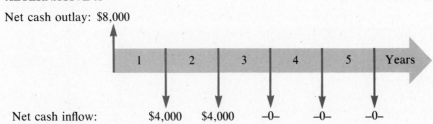

ALTERNATIVE B

Net cash outlay: $8,000

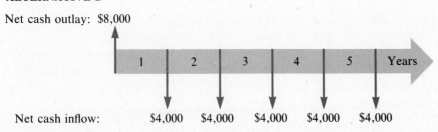

ALTERNATIVE C

Net cash outlay: $8,000

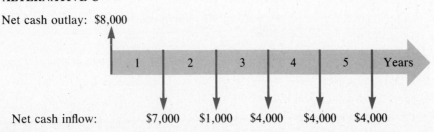

Required

1) Calculate the payback period for each of the investment alternatives.

2) How would you rank the alternatives, and why?

3) Comment on the limitations of the payback approach in evaluating these alternatives.

25.B.12. After-tax cash flows for three investment alternatives are shown in the following diagrams.

ALTERNATIVE J

Net cash outlay: $8,000

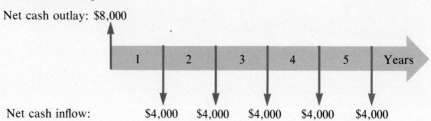

Net cash inflow: $4,000 $4,000 $4,000 $4,000 $4,000

ALTERNATIVE K

Net cash outlay: $8,000

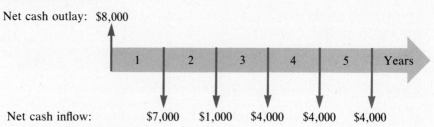

Net cash inflow: $7,000 $1,000 $4,000 $4,000 $4,000

ALTERNATIVE L

Net cash outlay: $60,000

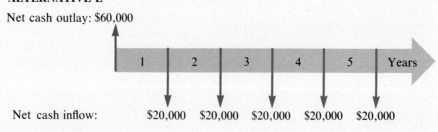

Net cash inflow: $20,000 $20,000 $20,000 $20,000 $20,000

Required

Assuming after-tax cost of capital of 8%, rank the alternatives according to their profitability index numbers.

SUMMARY OF CHAPTER 25

Alternative choices available to managers may be diagramed in the form of decision trees. Only incremental effects on future outcomes need be considered when decision choices are being analyzed. Sunk costs and other data that would otherwise be irrelevant become relevant to decision choices when they affect present and future payments for income taxes.

Various approaches are used for ranking alternative choices available to managers. The return on investment approach does not consider the time value of money and is therefore of little use for internal decision making. The payback approach is easy to apply and yields reasonable rankings for alternatives that have equal lives and produce level future cash flows. Profitability indexes may be calculated as a refinement of the net present value approach. The rate of return approach determines the approximate yield rates offered by various alternatives, without having to assume any cost of capital rate.

PROBLEMS FOR CHAPTER 25
Alternate Problems for this chapter begin on page D-138.

25.1. On September 1, 19X4, the Bitek Corporation purchased a new automatic programmable lathe at a cost of $75,000. The lathe has an expected useful life of five years and will have no salvage value at the end of its life. On September 2, 19X4, a saleswoman from another lathe manufacturer demonstrated that her company's new laser beam lathe could reduce Bitek's operating costs before depreciation by $25,000 per year as compared with the new lathe Bitek just purchased. The laser beam lathe costs $100,000, will last five years, and will have no salvage value at the end of its life. If the laser beam lathe is purchased, the present lathe could be sold for $35,000. Mr. Sooner, president of Bitek, says he cannot purchase the laser beam lathe because the sale of the present lathe would result in a $40,000 loss. By not purchasing the laser beam lathe, he says, the $40,000 loss would be avoided. The corporation's marginal tax rate is 40%. The 40% rate also applies to gains and losses on the disposal of assets. The company uses straight-line depreciation. Bitek's after-tax cost of capital is 12%.

Required

1) Prepare an incremental analysis of the relevant cash flows associated with the possible purchase of the laser beam lathe.

2) Calculate the net present value resulting from the purchase of the laser beam lathe and state whether the lathe should be purchased.

25.2. The bookkeeper for Turkey City Construction Company has prepared the following information on a proposed apartment building.

CASH ANALYSIS **Proposed Apartment Building**		
Construction and land cost		$1,400,000
Annual after-tax net cash inflow		$70,000
Useful life		40 years
Total cash inflow (40 × $70,000)	$2,800,000	
Less: Net cash outlay	1,400,000	
Net cash benefit	$1,400,000	

The company's after-tax cost of capital is 8%. Since the cash investment can be doubled over the life of the project, the bookkeeper has recommended investing in the project.

Required

1) Calculate the net present value of the project.

2) Calculate the approximate rate of return offered by the project.

3) Make a recommendation to the company regarding the project.

25.3. Beene Gurns, a local real estate developer, is considering the following investment alternatives:

Mini-Mall. Land for the mall may be purchased now for $200,000. Phase I construction costs of $400,000 will be due at the end of year 1. Phase II construction costs of $200,000 will be due at the end of year 2. Net cash proceeds after taxes for year 3 are estimated at $40,000, and for years 4 through 20 at $120,000 per year. The property would be sold at the end of 20 years for an amount that would leave $600,000 after taxes.

Fast-Food Franchise. The franchise requires an immediate cash payment of $120,000. An existing building can be leased for 20 years. Remodeling will require a cash payment of $50,000 at the end of year 1. After allowance for building lease and operating costs, the net annual after-tax cash proceeds will be $25,000 starting with the current year. Assume that cash flows occur at the end of each year. The franchise is expected to be worthless at the end of 20 years.

Required

1) Set up time diagrams, like those illustrated in this chapter, to show the cash flows for each alternative.

2) Evaluate the alternatives by means of the rate of return approach and make a recommendation to Mr. Gurns.

25.4. I&O Corporation has just purchased a new vacuum molding machine at a cost of $100,000 to produce plastic parts for automobile manufacturers. The machine has a useful life of five years. One week after the machine is put into use, a sales engineer from a company that produces vacuum molders calls on the company president to show him specifications on a new molder that costs $120,000 and has a useful life of five years with no salvage value expected at the end of its life. The new machine will reduce total manufacturing costs by $25,000 per year for five years. In addition, the machine will leave what used to be waste materials from the old machine in a form that can be sold for $5,000 of additional revenue each year. The plant comptroller argues that they are stuck with the machine just purchased, since its resale value is only $40,000. He would object to the $60,000 loss that would result from the disposal of the existing machine. I&O is taxed at a marginal rate of 46%, and its after-tax cost of capital rate is 14%.

Required

1) State whether the potential loss from disposal of the existing machine is a relevant consideration. Explain.

2) State whether the company should replace the machine it now has. Explain.

COMPREHENSION PROBLEMS FOR CHAPTER 25

25.5. Spring Corporation is considering either constructing or leasing additional floor space. The space required can be constructed for $100,000, and it can be used for a ten-year period with no salvage value expected. Spring would give the builder a down payment of $50,000 and would pay the remainder over ten years. A mortgage repayment schedule follows.

Year	Interest Payment	Principal Payment	Total Payment
1*	4,000	3,452	7,452
2	3,723	3,729	7,452
3	3,426	4,026	7,452
4	3,103	4,349	7,452
5	2,756	4,696	7,452
6	2,380	5,072	7,452
7	1,974	5,478	7,452
8	1,536	5,916	7,452
9	1,063	6,389	7,452
10	551	6,893	7,444

*The $50,000 down payment to the builder would be due now. The first payment on the mortgage is due on the first day of occupancy, one year from now.

The same amount of space can be acquired through a lease-purchase plan for $13,580 per year for ten years. The first payment would be due on the first day of occupancy, one year from now. After the tenth payment, the building would be turned over to Spring at no additional cost. Spring Corporation pays income taxes at a 40% marginal rate.

Required

1) Determine the amount and timing of the annual after-tax cash flows for both the construction alternative and the lease-purchase arrangement, and show the incremental difference between the alternatives.

2) State which alternative you would recommend, and why. For this requirement, be sure to consider the time value of money, using 12% as the after-tax cost of capital rate.

25.6. The Baluga Manufacturing Company has $800,000 of surplus cash to invest. The accounting department has prepared the following analysis of two available alternatives for the executive committee's consideration.

Alternative 1: Plant Expansion and New Product Development

Initial cash investment	$800,000
Useful life	10 years
Expected increase in annual net income after tax	$130,000
Average increase in assets	
($800,000 ÷ 2)	$400,000
Average return on investment	
($130,000 ÷ $400,000)	32.5%

Alternative 2: Renovation and Modernization of Plant and Equipment

Initial cash investment		$800,000
Useful life		10 years
Expected increase in net income after tax:		
Year 1	$ 350,000	
2	250,000	
3	100,000	
4	100,000	
5	50,000	
6	50,000	
7	50,000	
8	50,000	
9	50,000	
10	50,000	
Total	$1,100,000	
Average per year ($1,100,000 ÷ 10)		$110,000
Average increase in assets		
($800,000 ÷ 2)		$400,000
Average return on investment		
($110,000 ÷ $400,000)		27.5%

The accounting department notes that the company uses 12% as the minimum acceptable after-tax rate of return for the company. While both alternatives meet the minimum requirement, the accounting department recommends the plant expansion project because it offers the greater rate of return. Both alternatives require an immediate outlay of $800,000. The incremental net income figures can be converted to incremental cash inflows simply by adding back depreciation of $80,000 per year.

Required

Make your own recommendation to the committee, supported by your reasons and any additional analyses needed.

CHAPTER **26**

Income Tax
Considerations

OBJECTIVES

This chapter deals with some aspects of income taxation. At the conclusion of your study, you should be able to

1. Use the tax rate schedules provided in the chapter to determine the individual income tax for a given amount of taxable income.

2. Differentiate between tax deductions and tax credits.

3. Define the following tax expressions:
   a. Proportional tax.
   b. Progressive tax.
   c. Marginal tax rate.
   d. Adjusted gross income.
   e. Itemized deductions.
   f. Minimum tax.
   g. Tax credit.
   h. Investment tax credit.
   i. Capital gain.

4. Differentiate between tax avoidance, tax deferral, and tax evasion.

5. State the purpose of tax allocation accounting.

TAXES IN GENERAL

Federal, state, and local governments levy taxes of every conceivable description. *A tax is a charge imposed by a public authority upon a person or organization.* Most people and business entities are subject to some of the many forms of taxation on income, sales, transportation, amusements, gasoline, liquor, property, gambling—we could go on and on.

Each entity is burdened with the responsibility for complying with all the tax laws that apply to it. The more widespread a concern's operations, the greater its compliance burden. Company officials are presumed to be familiar with the tax requirements of the various townships, boroughs, school districts, and all other political subdivisions within whose boundaries the company operates. If a company operates internationally, its tax compliance problems are further compounded by the complexities of foreign tax laws.

As pointed out in Chapter 25, managers must consider the tax effects of their decisions. Managers should at least know enough about taxes to determine when they need advice from tax specialists. Large corporations employ their own tax specialists to give advice and counsel to corporate managers. Managers of small companies may seek advice from public accountants or attorneys who are knowledgeable about tax laws.

INCOME AS A TAX BASE

*An **income tax** is a tax based on income.* Income tax laws generally presume that the size of one's income is a measure of an *ability to pay* toward the costs of running a government entity. The higher one's level of income, the greater one's ability to pay tax.

Income subject to tax is called, naturally enough, *taxable income. Taxable income is defined in the statute by which the income tax was enacted, but we can state simply that it is the difference between taxable revenues and allowable deductions.*

OBJECTIVE 3a. Define proportional tax.

*When an income tax is levied at a constant rate on any amount of taxable income, it is said to be a **proportional tax.*** Each taxpayer then pays a fixed *proportion* of whatever taxable income he or she has. A state, for example, might levy a flat 5% tax on taxable income as defined in the state law. A taxpayer with a large taxable income will obviously pay more tax than one with a small taxable income, as shown here.

	Taxpayer A	Taxpayer B
Taxable income	$10,000	$100,000
Tax rate	× 0.05	× 0.05
Tax due	$ 500	$ 5,000

The *federal* income tax in the United States is based on the theory that one's ability to pay taxes increases *more* than proportionately as one has greater amounts of taxable income. The federal income tax is a *progressive tax in that the rates of tax increase with increasing amounts of taxable income.* The rate structure is occasionally changed by Congress. At the time of this writing, the *Internal Revenue Code* prescribes the tax rate schedules in Illustration 26.1 for the year 1984 and thereafter, subject to automatic adjustments of brackets for the effects of inflation. A single taxpayer with

OBJECTIVE 3b. Define progressive tax.

ILLUSTRATION 26.1

FEDERAL INCOME TAX RATE SCHEDULES			
Taxable Income			**Of the Amount Over**
Over	*But Not Over*	**Income Tax**	
Single Individuals			
$ –0–	$ 2,300	. . . 0%	$ –0–
$ 2,300	$ 3,400	$ –0– + 11%	$ 2,300
$ 3,400	$ 4,400	$ 121 + 12%	$ 3,400
$ 4,400	$ 6,500	$ 241 + 14%	$ 4,400
$ 6,500	$ 8,500	$ 535 + 15%	$ 6,500
$ 8,500	$ 10,800	$ 835 + 16%	$ 8,500
$ 10,800	$ 12,900	$ 1,203 + 18%	$ 10,800
$ 12,900	$ 15,000	$ 1,581 + 20%	$ 12,900
$ 15,000	$ 18,200	$ 2,001 + 23%	$ 15,000
$ 18,200	$ 23,500	$ 2,737 + 26%	$ 18,200
$ 23,500	$ 28,800	$ 4,115 + 30%	$ 23,500
$ 28,800	$ 34,100	$ 5,705 + 34%	$ 28,800
$ 34,100	$ 41,500	$ 7,507 + 38%	$ 34,100
$ 41,500	$ 55,300	$ 10,319 + 42%	$ 41,500
$ 55,300	$ 81,800	$ 16,115 + 48%	$ 55,300
$ 81,800	. . .	$ 28,835 + 50%	$ 81,800
Married Individuals Filing Joint Returns			
$ –0–	$ 3,400	. . . 0%	$ –0–
$ 3,400	$ 5,500	$ –0– + 11%	$ 3,400
$ 5,500	$ 7,600	$ 231 + 12%	$ 5,500
$ 7,600	$ 11,900	$ 483 + 14%	$ 7,600
$ 11,900	$ 16,000	$ 1,085 + 16%	$ 11,900
$ 16,000	$ 20,200	$ 1,741 + 18%	$ 16,000
$ 20,200	$ 24,600	$ 2,497 + 22%	$ 20,200
$ 24,600	$ 29,900	$ 3,465 + 25%	$ 24,600
$ 29,900	$ 35,200	$ 4,790 + 28%	$ 29,900
$ 35,200	$ 45,800	$ 6,274 + 33%	$ 35,200
$ 45,800	$ 60,000	$ 9,772 + 38%	$ 45,800
$ 60,000	$ 85,600	$ 15,168 + 42%	$ 60,000
$ 85,600	$109,400	$ 25,920 + 45%	$ 85,600
$109,400	$162,400	$ 36,630 + 49%	$109,400
$162,400	. . .	$ 62,600 + 50%	$162,400

NOTE: Rate schedules that apply to married individuals filing separate returns and to unmarried heads of households are not included here.

Taxable Income	Tax Rate
First $25,000	15%
Next $25,000	18%
Next $25,000	30%
Next $25,000	40%
Over $100,000	46%

As pointed out in Chapter 15, corporate income paid out as dividends is subject to double taxation in that the dividends are also taxed as personal income of the shareholders. The conditions under which the corporate form of business can serve as a tax advantage are outlined in Chapter 15.

INDIVIDUAL INCOME TAX

Essentially, the Internal Revenue Code provides that all revenues are subject to tax unless excluded specifically by the Code, and that no deductions are permitted unless allowed by the Code. Examples of receipts excluded from federal taxation are social security benefits (subject to limits), unemployment compensation (subject to limits), and interest on bonds issued by state and local governments. Revenues subject to federal income tax may be reduced by various deductions allowed by the Code. Some deductions are subtracted directly from gross income subject to tax, while other deductions must be subtracted in a later step from adjusted gross income. *Adjusted gross income is gross income less deductions permitted directly from gross income.*

OBJECTIVE 3d. Define adjusted gross income.

You may wonder why it makes any difference at what point deductions are made. Adjusted gross income must be accurately determined, because that amount influences other items—for instance, the amount of certain itemized deductions permitted—in the tax computation.

Deductions from Gross Income

Anyone engaged in a business, trade, or profession may deduct directly from gross income all the ordinary and necessary expenses of doing business. Persons receiving rents and royalties may deduct from gross income expenses related to the earnings of those items. Employees may deduct the unreimbursed cost of business travel and transportation directly from gross income. Also, deductions for capital losses and the exempt portion of long-term capital gains directly reduce gross income. Capital gains and losses are addressed later in this chapter. Taxpayers may also reduce gross income by alimony payments, qualified payments to retirement accounts, and a special deduction permitted working married couples who file joint returns. The special deduction is 10% of the earned income of the spouse with the smaller earnings for the year, not to exceed a maximum deduction of $3,000.

Deductions from Adjusted Gross Income

There are essentially two types of deductions from adjusted gross income: itemized (or alternate standard) deductions and personal exemptions.

Itemized (or Alternative Standard) Deductions.   Individual taxpayers are automatically allowed a flat standard deduction from adjusted gross income. The standard deduction allowance is built into the current tax rate schedule as a *zero bracket* amount. From the tax rate schedules in Illustration 26.1 you can see that single persons are automatically allowed a standard deduction of $2,300, while married persons filing joint returns are allowed $3,400. In other words, *a standard deduction (zero bracket amount) is an amount that a taxpayer may earn free of tax to take care of personal expenses that are deductible from adjusted gross income.*

Taxpayers may *elect* to itemize their deductions from adjusted gross income when they can substantiate more than the standard deduction amounts. Since standard deduction amounts are already built into the tax rate schedules, the total of itemized deductions must be reduced by the amount of the standard deduction allowed.

Itemized deductions are personal expenses allowed as deductions from adjusted gross income by the Code. We are not attempting to list everything that may be taken as an itemized deduction. Suffice it to say that medical costs, state and local taxes, interest payments, charitable contributions, casualty losses, and certain job-related expenses may be itemized. Only medical expenses in excess of 5% of adjusted gross income qualify as itemized deductions, and the amount of deductible charitable contributions is limited to a maximum percentage of adjusted gross income. You can begin to see why it is important to properly state adjusted gross income on tax returns.

OBJECTIVE 3e. Define itemized deductions.

Personal Exemptions.   *The Code allows each taxpayer to deduct from adjusted gross income a $1,000 personal exemption,* plus additional $1,000 personal exemptions for each qualifying dependent. An extra personal exemption is allowed if the taxpayer is over age 65 or blind. Like all other aspects of the Code, the amount allowed for each personal exemption is subject to change by Congress. The present law provides for automatic increases in the $1,000 exemption amount to compensate for inflation as it occurs.

Determining the Tax (or Refund) Due

Tax forms are designed to lead taxpayers through the various steps needed to arrive at the tax due the Internal Revenue Service or the refund due the taxpayer. It is not always clear from looking at the forms just where one

ILLUSTRATION 26.2

Gross Income Subject to Tax

Less: Deductions from gross income

Adjusted gross income

Less: Itemized deductions (or standard deduction)

Less: Personal exemptions

Taxable income

Tax rates

↓

Income tax

Less: Tax credit

Less: Prepaid tax

Tax due (or refund)

stage of the calculation stops and another begins. However, from the Code itself we can surmise that the determination of taxes due from or refundable to an individual taxpayer takes the steps shown in Illustration 26.2.

OBJECTIVE 3f. Define minimum tax.

Minimum Tax. *The Code provides for* **minimum tax** *on certain* **tax preference items,** *items that would otherwise escape taxation in the year they are deductible (or excluded) from taxable revenues.* Tax preference items, which are listed in the Code, include such things as accelerated depreciation on real property and leased assets. Corporations must pay a minimum rate of 15% on tax preference items in excess of $10,000 for the year.[1] The total tax paid by individuals must amount to a minimum of 20% on alternative minimum taxable income less an exemption of $30,000 for a single individual or $40,000 for a married couple filing jointly.[2] The main purpose of the minimum tax is to ensure that profitable corporations and prosperous individuals pay a respectable amount of taxes regardless of their ability to take

---

[1]Code Sec. 56.

[2]The concept of alternative minimum taxable income and other features of the minimum tax on individuals are covered in Code Sec. 55.

advantage of preferential provisions of the Code. The minimum tax, like most other matters covered in this chapter, involves rather complex provisions, limitations, and exceptions. Our purpose at this point is to make you aware of some of the important tax features one must consider when making decisions.

Tax Credits.   Various tax credits may be deducted from the income tax that is determined from taxable income. *Tax credits are direct offsets against income tax.* Credits may be allowed for foreign taxes paid, political contributions, investments in certain kinds of long-term productive assets, and other items specified in the Code at any one point in time. *The investment tax credit is a percentage of the cost of qualified productive assets purchased during the year.* The investment credit percentage is subject to change, depending on economic conditions, and is apt to be suspended during periods of economic prosperity.[3]

> **OBJECTIVE 3g.** Define tax credit.

> **OBJECTIVE 3h.** Define investment tax credit.

Some people confuse tax *deductions* with tax *credits*. Deductions reduce taxable income, whereas credits are offset directly against taxes due. Donations to various worthy causes are often solicited with the statement that "contributions can be taken off your income taxes." This statement is untrue, because contributions to worthy causes can be deducted only from taxable revenues—not from the tax itself.

> **OBJECTIVE 2.** Differentiate between tax deductions and tax credits.

Prepaid Tax.   Federal income taxes are withheld from the earnings of employees and remitted by employers to the federal government. Individuals are expected to voluntarily prepay tax on income not subject to withholding by filing *declarations of estimated tax* at specific times during the year. Failure to prepay at least 80% of taxes due may subject the taxpayer to interest charges on the unpaid amounts. As indicated by the schedule of steps pictured in Illustration 26.2, prepaid taxes are subtracted, along with tax credits, directly from the income tax.

TAXATION OF CAPITAL GAINS

*A **capital gain** is the difference between the cost of a capital asset and the proceeds obtained from its sale.* If the cost of a capital asset exceeds the proceeds of sale, a *capital loss* results. What is meant by a capital asset, as the item is used in tax laws, becomes quite involved. For our purposes, let us just say that *a **capital asset** is a property held as an investment.* For example, corporate stocks and bonds owned by individuals or other corporations are capital assets.

> **OBJECTIVE 3i.** Define capital gain.

Capital gains realized by individuals are subject to special tax treatment under the Internal Revenue code. Once again, the law is complex and difficult

---

[3]At this writing, the investment tax credit is 10%.

to explain in simple terms. For now, it is sufficient to say that 60% of the gains from the sale of capital assets owned longer than 12 months is not subject to the individual income tax. In other words, 60% of capital gains from the sale of long-term investments is tax free.[4]

Dividends paid to shareholders are taxed as ordinary income, whereas capital gains from the sale of corporate shares receive favorable tax treatment. Generally speaking, then, a corporation is encouraged to reinvest its earnings in ways that will cause the market value of its shares to rise over time. Shareholders may then be able to escape taxation on over half the gains that are realized upon the sale of shares they have owned.

TAX PLANNING

It is fairly safe to say that both individuals and corporations attempt to minimize the taxes they must pay. Federal, state, and local tax laws provide numerous opportunities for either avoiding taxation under certain circumstances or delaying payment.

Since most management decisions involve tax consequences, managers and accountants should learn as much as they can about the aspects of tax laws that relate to their particular areas of responsibility. At the very least, people should be sufficiently informed to know when they need advice from tax specialists.

Most aspects of planning involve tax consequences. Therefore, all planning should include the tax costs, or tax savings, associated with the planned outcomes.

The decision-making consequences of taxable incremental benefits and tax-deductible incremental costs are discussed in Chapter 25. Also discussed there are the benefits to be derived from *tax shields* provided by depreciation expense and book losses from asset dispositions that would otherwise be irrelevant to decision making.

Tax Avoidance

Federal income taxes may be avoided permanently by receiving income of a nontaxable nature, such as interest on municipal bonds or the excluded portion of capital gains. Also, revenue may be legally shielded from taxation by means of deductible expenses and losses, including certain personal expenditures for interest, contributions, local taxes, and so on. Finally, taxes may be avoided by legally offsetting them with investment credits, foreign tax credits, and other allowable tax credits. *Tax avoidance, then, is the act of legally bypassing tax obligations by taking advantage of provisions of (or loopholes in) the tax law.*

OBJECTIVE 4.
Differentiate between tax
avoidance, tax deferral,
and tax evasion.

---

[4]See Code Sec. 1201 and 1202 for treatment of capital gains and losses.

Tax Deferral

*Obligations to pay taxes on current revenues can sometimes be shifted to future periods, a process called **tax deferral**.* Taxes are most often deferred by deducting from current taxable revenues costs that would be more appropriately matched with revenues of future periods. For example, accelerated cost recovery methods might be employed for tax purposes when they cannot be justified under the *matching concept* of accounting. Of course, overstatements of current costs usually result in understatements of costs in future periods, since costs may be deducted only once. Similarly, taxable revenues deferred to future periods must be recognized, and taxed, in those subsequent periods.

*Discrepancies between the points in time when revenues or expenses are recognized for tax purposes and when they are recognized for financial reporting purposes are referred to as **timing differences**.* Taxpayers will normally delay the payment of taxes as long as the law permits, because of the time value of money. As pointed out in Appendix I of Chapter 16, the present value of future amounts of money is always less, because of the effects of discounting. It is for this reason that taxpayers should attempt to minimize the current payment of taxes, forestalling tax payments as long as they can.

OBJECTIVE 4.
Differentiate between tax avoidance, tax deferral, and tax evasion.

Tax Evasion

***Tax evasion** is the process of eluding taxes by illegal means.* Tax evasion occurs when taxpayers purposefully fail to report taxable revenues or when deductions or credits are intentionally overstated. Proved acts of tax cheating may result in severe penalties. Tax evasion should not be confused with tax avoidance or tax deferral. Taxpayers are expected to take advantage of all legal opportunities to minimize their current taxes. Tax evasion, on the other hand, is a criminal offense.

OBJECTIVE 4.
Differentiate between tax avoidance, tax deferral, and tax evasion.

TAX ALLOCATION

Timing differences between financial reporting and tax returns bring about a disparity between reported net income and the taxes due for the year. For example, let us consider a new machine purchased at the beginning of year 1 for $10,000, with an estimated five-year life and no anticipated salvage value. Let us assume that 3-year accelerated cost recovery system (ACRS) depreciation is used for tax purposes, while 5-year straight-line depreciation is used for financial reporting purposes.[5] The concern involved is taxed at

---

[5]As pointed out in Section 8.B, ACRS depreciation rates are selected from tables prescribed in the Code. Assets designated as "3-year property," which were bought during the years 1981 through 1984, are depreciated 25% in the year acquired, 38% the following year, and 37% the third year.

ILLUSTRATION 26.3

TAX EFFECTS OF TIMING DIFFERENCES						
	Year					
	1	*2*	*3*	*4*	*5*	**Total**
Depreciation						
Financial (straight-line)	$ 2,000	$ 2,000	$ 2,000	$2,000	$2,000	$10,000
Tax deduction (ACRS)	2,500	3,800	3,700	–0–	–0–	10,000
Taxable income over (under) net income	$ (500)	$(1,800)	$(1,700)	$2,000	$2,000	$ –0–
Tax overstatement (understatement) at 40% rate	$ (200)	$ (720)	$ (680)	$ 800	$ 800	$ –0–

a marginal rate of 40%. The schedule in Illustration 26.3 shows the tax effects of the timing differences.

From Illustration 26.3 it is apparent that the actual taxes due will be lower in the first three years, and higher in the last two years, than would have been the case had straight-line depreciation been used for tax purposes. Consequently, the actual taxes due will appear to be too low during the early years and too high during the later years, when compared with the net income reported on the income statements.

The solution is to *recognize the deferred tax obligation as a liability until such time as the taxes are paid, an approach referred to as* **tax allocation** *accounting.*[6] In addition to recognizing taxes actually payable for year 1, the concern would record a deferred tax liability for that year. Subsequently, the Deferred Tax Liability account would be drawn down during years when taxable income exceeds net income as a result of depreciation differences. Thus the purpose of tax allocation accounting is to minimize the disparity between reported net income and income tax due for the year. The entries in Illustration 26.4 show the means by which tax allocation accounting attempts to conform tax expense to the reported net income for the year.

OBJECTIVE 5. State the purpose of tax allocation accounting.

---

[6]Tax allocation accounting may also be employed when revenues are taxed in an earlier period than they are recognized for accounting purposes. In this case, the prepaid taxes are held in a Deferred Tax Charge account (a noncurrent asset) until the revenues are considered realized.

ILLUSTRATION 26.4

End of Year			
1	Income Tax Expense	XXX	
	Income Tax Payable		XXX
	Deferred Tax Liability		200
2	Income Tax Expense	XXX	
	Income Tax Payable		XXX
	Deferred Tax Liability		720
3	Income Tax Expense	XXX	
	Income Tax Payable		XXX
	Deferred Tax Liability		680
4	Income Tax Expense	XXX	
	Deferred Tax Liability	800	
	Income Tax Payable		XXX
5	Income Tax Expense	XXX	
	Deferred Tax Liability	800	
	Income Tax Payable		XXX

The following T-account shows how the obligation for deferred taxes is first built up and then subsequently drawn down.

Deferred Tax Liability			
		Year 1	200
		Year 2	720
		Year 3	680
Year 4	800		
Year 5	800		

SUMMARY OF CHAPTER 26

Individuals and entities are responsible for complying with all tax laws that apply to them. Managers, especially, must consider the various tax effects of the decisions they make, seeking advice from tax specialists when necessary.

Income taxes are imposed on individuals and corporations at progressive rates, in that marginal rates of tax increase as taxable income becomes larger. The federal income tax in the United States originated in 1913. The various revenue acts were first codified in 1939, then rewritten in 1954 into the Internal Revenue Code, which continues, although amended numerous times, to this date.

Tax deductions for individuals fall into two categories: those from gross income and those from adjusted gross income. Tax deductions should not be confused with tax credits, which are direct offsets against income tax.

Gains derived from the sale of capital assets held longer than 12 months are subject to special treatment in that 60% of the gains escapes taxation.

Legitimate steps to avoid or defer taxes should not be confused with tax evasion, which is illegal. Taxpayers usually prefer to delay the payment of taxes as long as possible because of the time value of money. A business entity may employ tax allocation accounting to minimize disparities between reported net income and the taxes for the year.

GLOSSARY FOR CHAPTER 26

Adjusted gross income Gross income less deductions permitted directly from gross income.

Capital asset A property held as an investment.

Capital gain The difference between the cost of a capital asset and the proceeds obtained from its sale.

Estate The properties, and the claims against them, of a deceased person, until such time as the properties are distributed to heirs and beneficiaries.

Income tax A tax based on income.

Internal Revenue Code The law that imposes the various federal taxes.

Investment tax credit A percentage of the cost of qualified productive assets purchased during the year.

Itemized deductions Personal expenses allowed as deductions from adjusted gross income by the Code.

Marginal tax rate   The rate at which a given amount of additional income is taxed.

Minimum tax   A tax on certain tax preference items.

Personal exemptions   Flat deductions from adjusted gross income allowed for each taxpayer and for qualifying dependents.

Progressive tax   An income tax that subjects increasing amounts of taxable income to increasing rates of tax.

Proportional tax   An income tax levied at a constant rate on any amount of taxable income.

Standard deduction (zero bracket amount)   An amount that a taxpayer may earn free of tax to take care of personal expenses that are deductible from adjusted gross income.

Tax   A charge imposed by a public authority upon a person or organization.

Taxable income   The difference between taxable revenues and allowable deductions.

Tax allocation accounting   The process of recognizing a deferred tax obligation as a liability until such time as the taxes are paid.

Tax avoidance   The act of legally bypassing tax obligations by taking advantage of provisions of (or loopholes in) the tax law.

Tax credits   Direct offsets against income tax.

Tax deferral   The process of shifting obligations to pay taxes to future periods.

Tax evasion   The process of eluding taxes by illegal means.

Tax preference items   Items that would otherwise escape taxation in the year they are deductible (or excluded) from taxable revenues.

Timing differences   Discrepancies between the points in time when revenues or expenses are recognized for tax purposes and when they are recognized for financial reporting purposes.

Trust   A fund of property that is being administered by a trustee, under a legal trust agreement, for the benefit of another.

SELF-QUIZ ON OBJECTIVES FOR CHAPTER 26
Solutions to Self-Quiz begin on page B-76.

1. **OBJECTIVE 1.** Paul and Sandra Pahr are filing a joint return on which they report their combined taxable income of $63,000. Determine their income tax for the year. (*Note:* Use the tax rate schedules provided in the chapter.)

2. **OBJECTIVE 2.** Differentiate tax deductions from tax credits.

3. **OBJECTIVE 3.** Define the following tax expressions:
   a. Proportional tax.
   b. Progressive tax.
   c. Marginal tax rate.
   d. Adjusted gross income.

    e. Itemized deductions.

    f. Minimum tax.

    g. Tax credit.

    h. Investment tax credit.

    i. Capital gain.

4. **OBJECTIVE 4.** Differentiate between tax avoidance, tax deferral, and tax evasion.

5. **OBJECTIVE 5.** State the purpose of tax allocation accounting.

DISCUSSION QUESTIONS FOR CHAPTER 26

1. What is the Internal Revenue Code?

2. What is the difference between an estate and a trust?

3. A proprietorship is viewed as a separate entity for accounting purposes. Is a proprietorship a separate taxable entity? If not, how does proprietorship income subject to taxation get reported to the Internal Revenue Service?

4. Is a partnership required to file an annual tax return?

5. Why must deductions from gross income be kept distinct from deductions from adjusted gross income?

6. Why is the standard deduction sometimes referred to as a zero bracket amount?

7. Which would you prefer, a $1,000 tax credit or a $1,000 tax deduction? Explain your answer.

8. Why is tax planning so important?

EXERCISES FOR CHAPTER 26

26.1. Refer to the tax rate schedules for individuals presented in this chapter to answer the following questions.

    a. What is the marginal tax rate for a single individual with a taxable income of $29,000?

    b. What is the marginal tax rate for married persons filing jointly with a taxable income of $29,000?

    c. What is the tax due for married individuals filing jointly with a taxable income of $50,000? What is the marginal rate? The average rate?

    d. If you are married and file jointly, and are already earning a taxable income of $50,000, what portion of every *additional* dollar of taxable income earned will you be able to keep (spend) after allowing for income tax?

26.2. John and Mary are considering marriage. Each expects to have a taxable income of $30,000 for the current year. Determine the total tax they would pay as single individuals, and compare that to the total tax they would pay as married individuals filing a joint return. Refer to the tax rate schedules in this chapter, and assume that total deductions will be the same under either approach except for a $3,000 special deduction for filing jointly as a working married couple.

26.3. Assuming a marginal tax rate of 40%, determine the after-tax effect on profits of each of the following events.

- **a.** An increase in taxable revenue of $50,000.
- **b.** An increase in deductible expenses of $50,000.
- **c.** An increase in tax credits of $50,000.

26.4. Refer to the individual tax rate schedules provided in this chapter to do the following.

- **a.** Compute the tax due for a single individual with a taxable income of $70,000.
- **b.** Compute the tax due for married individuals filing a joint return which shows a taxable income of $70,000.
- **c.** Determine the marginal and average tax rates for situations (a) and (b).

26.5. A piece of equipment was purchased in early January for $100,000. The equipment is expected to last for ten years and be of no value at the end of that period. Straight-line depreciation is being used for accounting purposes and double-declining-balance depreciation for tax purposes (the equipment does not qualify for ACRS depreciation). Assuming that the marginal tax rate is 46%, determine the amount and direction by which the Deferred Tax Liability account balance should change at the end of the first and second years of this equipment's life. Ignore any other tax allocation influences on the amount of deferred tax.

PROBLEMS FOR CHAPTER 26
Alternate Problems for this chapter begin on page D-140.

26.6. Refer to the tax rate schedule for single individuals.

Required

Calculate the amount of tax and determine the marginal tax rate and average tax rate for each of the following taxable incomes of single individuals.

1) $20,000

2) $40,000

3) $80,000

4) $160,000

26.7. Refer to the tax rate schedule for married individuals.

Required

Calculate the amount of tax and determine the marginal tax rate and average tax rate for each of the following taxable incomes of married couples filing joint returns.

1) $20,000

2) $40,000

3) $80,000

4) $160,000

26.8. Neely Corporation shows a before-tax net income of $90,000 for 19X1. The only difference between accounting for financial statements and tax reporting is that a machine purchased in early January 19X1 is being depreciated on a straight-line basis for financial reporting whereas the sum-of-years'-digits is used for tax purposes (assume that ACRS depreciation is not applicable here). The machine cost $108,000 and is expected to last eight years with no salvage value at the end of that time.

Required

1) Determine the annual machine depreciation for accounting purposes.

2) Determine the machine depreciation to be deducted on the 19X1 federal tax return.

3) Prepare the entry at December 31, 19X1, to recognize the Income Tax Expense for 19X1, the Income Tax Payable, and the Deferred Tax Liability under tax allocation procedures. (Refer to the corporate tax rates provided in the chapter.)

4) Assuming that Neely's before-tax net income for 19X2 is $120,000, make the entry at December 31, 19X2, to recognize the expense, payable, and deferred liability for federal income tax.

COMPREHENSION PROBLEMS FOR CHAPTER 26

26.9. Farley Nodler owns and manages a proprietorship which showed a net income of $120,000 for the past year, all subject to taxation on his personal tax return. Farley is unmarried and has personal exemptions and deductions for the year of $5,000, resulting in a taxable income of $115,000 (he had no income except from his business). Income from the business is expected to increase gradually as the concern expands in the future.

Farley has determined that a hired manager of a business such as his would earn an annual salary of $50,000. Consequently, he withdraws $50,000 each year and leaves the remaining profits in the business to finance expansion. Farley is considering incorporation of his business, with himself as the sole shareholder.

Required

Advise Farley on the advantages and disadvantages of incorporating his business. Include in your considerations a comparison of Farley's federal income tax for the past year with what might have been paid had the business been a corporation.

26.10. Marsha Miller owns a small corporation which employs her as its president. She earns a salary as president of $25,000 and receives $55,000 in dividends from the corporation each year. After appropriate deductions, Marsha's personal annual taxable income is $70,000. Marsha is unmarried. The corporation's annual income before tax is $120,000. The corporation does not qualify for Subchapter S treatment. Refer to the individual and corporate tax rate schedules provided in this chapter.

Required

1) Calculate the annual tax due on the corporation's earnings.

2) Calculate Marsha's annual personal income tax.

3) What steps might be taken to improve Marsha's tax situation?

APPENDIX A

International Dimensions of Accounting

WHAT IS INTERNATIONAL ACCOUNTING?

In spite of the recent recession, international business continues to be an important aspect of large U.S. companies. In some cases, the business involves primarily import/export operations, but in many others it also involves direct production and marketing investments in countries outside the United States. In addition to the many business problems encountered in operating in a variety of countries, there are a number of accounting problems as well.

Two major kinds of accounting problems confront firms that have investments abroad: (1) The books and records of the foreign branch or subsidiary may have to be kept in the language and accounting standards of the country where the investment is located; and (2) transactions recorded in a foreign currency have to be translated into U.S. dollars before they can be combined with results from U.S. operations and presented in domestic financial statements. Thus a study of international accounting involves an understanding of how accounting standards and practices vary worldwide and of some unique problems of dealing in foreign currencies.

DIFFERENCES IN ACCOUNTING STANDARDS AND PRACTICES

Accounting standards and practices vary worldwide for a variety of reasons, and they determine how economic events are recorded in a company's

This appendix was written by Lee H. Radebaugh, Associate Professor of Accounting, Graduate School of Management, Brigham Young University, Provo, Utah.

books and records. The problem that a multinational corporation faces is that these standards and practices may vary greatly from country to country, creating problems in evaluating performance and in reporting results to investors, creditors, and governments.

Reasons for Differences in Standards

Accounting standards are influenced by various interests, such as investors, creditors, government users (such as tax authorities) and regulators, environmental characteristics, international influences, and the accounting profession.

Investors and Creditors. As identified by the Financial Accounting Standards Board (FASB), investors and creditors are the major users of financial information outside the firm. In many countries, creditors are the most important users of corporate financial data. This is especially true in West Germany and Japan, where banks are institutional investors or provide very high leverage for expansion. In the United States, institutional investors actively influence the setting of standards because of the large blocks of stock they hold in major corporations. Noninstitutional investors in a broadly based capital market need quality information on which to base investment decisions. They are often represented by stockbrokers, who are able to prepare sophisticated analyses of financial data for them. It is clear that the investing public is a more active group in the United States than in most other countries, where governments and creditors tend to exert more influence.

Government Users. Governments are active in two major ways: use of information and regulation of activity. Primary users of information are tax authorities and planners. In France the tax authorities allow generous depreciation allowances, but these allowances must also be used for book purposes. This results in assets with unusually low values when compared to the actual useful life of the assets. In the United States, the difference between tax and book income is reflected in the deferred tax account, but countries that use tax laws as the basis for accounting do not allow this benefit. German accounting standards are reflected in law, which is tax-influenced. The legalistic approach is very different from that used in the United States where the FASB sets standards. Peru's accounting standards reflect the needs of government planners. The Peruvian government nationalized several industries and decided to take a stronger role in directing the economy during the early 1970s; it borrowed some concepts from the French uniform general accounting plan and developed its own uniform plan that all companies must use for tax purposes and for reporting to government planners. In the United States the Securities and Exchange Commission (SEC) is a good example of a government agency that influences accounting standards and practices through regulation rather than direct use.

Environmental Influences. In countries with high rates of inflation, as in many Latin American countries, procedures have been developed and used for many years to account for inflation. The Netherlands, a country with relatively low inflation historically, has had a highly refined approach to inflation accounting for several decades because of the heavy influence of economic thought in the education and training of accountants.

International Influences. Many international forces of an institutional rather than environmental nature have strongly influenced accounting principles worldwide. Prime examples were the colonial policies of England and France: Each of these countries carried their business and accounting philosophies to their colonies and instituted similar systems. The United States has also tended to do this as its economic influence has spread by means of foreign direct investment.

The Accounting Profession. In countries such as the United States, Canada, and the United Kingdom, the accounting profession can be an important influence in the development of accounting principles. The problem with accounting in many countries is that it is not recognized as a profession, making it difficult to attract top-flight people that can actively research and develop accounting standards.

Major Differences in Standards

Differences in accounting standards and practices do not imply superiority or inferiority of standards, but simply differences. Sometimes standards that seem perfectly reasonable in one economic and business environment are totally inappropriate in another environment. In a recent study of annual reports for companies from all over the world, it was determined that major differences exist in relation to consolidation practices and accounting for goodwill, deferred taxes, long-term leases, discretionary reserves, inflation, and foreign currency translation.[1] Without discussing each of the above, we can use consolidation practices to illustrate the variety that exists.

Consolidation practices include whether or not majority-owned subsidiaries are combined with parent company results and how less-than-majority-owned investments are recorded on the books of the parent. In some countries, such as Peru, consolidated financial statements are not permitted. In the United States, only consolidated statements are disclosed to shareholders. In most European countries parent company and consolidated financial statements are common. In the United States, firms are required to use the equity method for reporting the results of investees where the investor owns 20 percent or more of the voting stock, whereas the cost method is

---

[1] Choi, Frederick D. S. and Vinod B. Bavishi, "International Accounting Standards: Issues Needing Attention," *Journal of Accountancy* (March 1983), p. 65.

used for investments of less than 20 percent. In many countries, such as Japan, it is common to use the cost method for all investments. This affects not only the investment recorded on the balance sheet of the investor but also the amount and timing of income in the income statement.

Harmonization of Standards and Practices

The growth of international capital markets has probably had the greatest influence on the harmonization of standards worldwide, but only as related to international stock and bond issues rather than to the actual standards used by local firms in individual countries. International disclosures tend to follow more closely the practices of the United States and the United Kingdom.

International Accounting Standards Committee. The IASC is an organization composed of professional organizations from more than 50 countries. Its major objective is to set accounting standards that countries can put into practice. The standards often reflect a narrowing of alternative practices and improved disclosure rather than an attempt to identify one best way to account for something. Thus the standards result in harmonization rather than standardization. To date the IASC has set 21 standards covering a variety of topics. The U.S. representative to the IASC is the American Institute of Certified Public Accountants. Thus far there are no major differences between IASC standards and those issued by the FASB, so that adherence to U.S. generally accepted accounting principles reflects adherence to IASC standards as well.

United Nations. The UN has become involved in attempts to set accounting standards through the Commission on Transnational Corporations. The Commission's activities relate to accounting disclosure, primarily in nonfinancial areas such as the structure of the multinational corporation, the main activities of its affiliates, employment information, accounting policies, and transfer pricing policies. Although specific standards and guidelines have not yet been set by the Commission, its thoughts reflect many of the concerns of developing countries and could well become guidelines for legal requirements in those countries.

Organization for Economic Cooperation and Development. The OECD, an organization representing most of the industrial countries, has issued a code of conduct that has accounting ramifications. These guidelines are similar to those already used in practice in the United States, but future proposals in the area of employment disclosures and transfer pricing policies could depart from standards and practices in this country.

European Economic Community. One of the original goals of the ten-member EEC is the free flow of capital, which implies that accounting information should achieve some degree of comparability. The EEC periodically issues directives that must be incorporated into national law in each of the member countries. The Fourth Directive was issued in 1978 to provide the framework for a common standard of accounting disclosure. The directive is concerned with the format of the balance sheet and income statements (but not the statement of changes in financial position) and the valuation of accounts. Although these standards affect fewer countries than do the standards of the IASC or the UN, the enforcement mechanism is much more effective. All firms operating in EEC countries, including those owned by foreign investors, are required to adhere to the provisions passed into national law.[2]

FOREIGN CURRENCY TRANSLATION

Foreign Currency Transactions

Importers and exporters may find that they are entering into transactions denominated in a foreign currency and that they are carrying balances denominated in a foreign currency in their financial statements. Therefore these transactions need to be translated into dollars when they take place, and foreign currency receivables and payables need to be constantly updated to reflect any changes in exchange rates. The FASB standard that deals with these issues is *Statement No. 52,* "Foreign Currency Translation."

To illustrate, let's assume that on January 1, DataCorp purchases equipment from a British manufacturer for £500,000 with payment to be made on February 15. The exchange rate on January 1 was $1.55/£, on January 31 it was $1.53/£, and on February 15, it was $1.50/£. Following are the journal entries to record the acquisition of the machinery on January 1, the change in the dollar value of the liability on January 31, and the settlement of the liability on February 15.

Jan. 1	Machinery	775,000	
	Accounts Payable		775,000
Jan. 31	Accounts Payable	10,000	
	Foreign Exchange Gain		10,000
Feb. 15	Accounts payable	765,000	
	Foreign Exchange Gain		15,000
	Cash		750,000

---

[2]For a more complete discussion of the reasons for differences in accounting standards worldwide and their harmonization, see Jeffrey S. Arpan and Lee H. Radebaugh, *International Accounting and Multinational Enterprises* (New York: John Wiley & Sons, 1981), Chapters 2 and 3.

The machinery is carried on the books at the exchange rate in effect on the date of acquisition (the spot exchange rate), and the liability is also initially carried at that same exchange rate. However, at the end of the month when new financial statements are issued, the liability is revised to reflect the new spot exchange in effect. This restatement results in a foreign exchange gain, since the liability would require less dollars to liquidate than it would have when the transaction was originally recorded. At the date of settlement the importer must convert the liability into pounds sterling, and the exchange rate that is used is the spot rate on that date. Since the amount of cash expended is less than the book value of the liability, the transaction results in a gain.

Foreign Currency Financial Statements

The consolidated financial statements of U.S. companies with foreign operations contain information recorded originally in the currency of the country where the operations are located and then translated into dollars. This complex process of translation is controlled by *FASB Statement No. 52*. It identifies two ways in which financial statements can be translated and provides information to help firms choose between the methods. The guidance rules classify foreign operations into three categories and provide a translation method for each category.

The two translation methods are the *current rate* (known as the closing rate method in Europe) and the *temporal*. The current rate method is the simpler of the two because all assets and liabilities are translated into dollars at the spot rate in effect on the balance sheet date. In the stockholders' equity section of the balance sheet, capital stock is translated at the rate in effect when the capital stock was issued (the historical exchange rate), and retained earnings is the accumulation of earnings from prior years, combined with the translated income statement for the current year. The income statement is translated at the average exchange rate during the year. Since the balance sheet and income statement are translated at different exchange rates, it is possible that assets may not equal the total of liabilities and stockholders' equity after translation. The difference, called a translation adjustment, is a separate component of stockholders' equity under the current rate method.

The temporal method is more complex. Under that method, cash and most receivables and payables are translated at the current exchange rate, whereas nonmonetary assets that are carried at their historical costs are translated at the historical exchange rate (the rate in effect when the asset was acquired). Stockholders' equity is treated the same way as in the current rate method. In the income statement most revenues and expenses are translated at the average exchange rate. However, cost of sales and depreciation expense are translated at the rate in effect when the corresponding assets were acquired. Another major difference between the two methods is that the translation adjustment is included in the income statement as a translation gain or loss rather than taken directly to stockholders' equity.

Three categories of foreign operations are used for purposes of deciding whether to use the current rate method or the temporal method for translation purposes. To illustrate these categories, let's assume that a U.S. firm has subsidiaries in Japan, France, and Brazil. In the case of Japan let's assume that the functional currency is the Japanese yen, the currency in which the subsidiary primarily generates and expends cash. In this situation, the firm would use the current rate method to translate the financial statements recorded in yen into dollars before consolidation.

In the French case let's assume that the French subsidiary gets most of its components from the home office in the United States and provides most of its output for final assembly in the United States. Most of the cash movements would be in dollars and most of the decisions would be made in the United States rather than France. Thus the temporal method would be used rather than the current rate method. This reflects the attitude that the functional currency is really the dollar instead of the French franc.

In the Brazil situation the translation methodology depends on the inflation rate rather than on a definition of functional currency. The temporal method is always used when the cumulative rate of inflation in a country is approximately 100 percent or more for a three year period because high rates of inflation usually result in a rapidly depreciating currency, such as in Brazil. Using the current exchange rate to translate fixed assets from the local currency into U.S. dollars would result in distorted financial statements when the local currency is depreciating so much.

ACCOUNTING FOR INFLATION

Another major issue that has international ramifications is accounting for inflation. There are two interesting dimensions to this issue: (1) how inflation is accounted for in different countries; and (2) the unique problems faced by a multinational corporation in accounting for inflation. In the first situation, there are two major approaches to inflation accounting in countries other than the United States. The first is represented by practice in the United Kingdom, which decided to adopt current value accounting for its financial statements rather than general purchasing power adjustments (or a combination of the two as is the case in the United States). In the United Kingdom, firms are permitted to use current value accounting as supplementary financial statements or in place of historical cost statements as the primary financial statements. The Dutch also permit the use of current value information, and some Dutch firms use replacement values for nonmonetary assets rather than historical costs in the primary financial statements.

In many Latin American countries a different approach to accounting for inflation is used. An index, usually tied to consumer prices, is used to revalue fixed assets periodically. In Peru, for example, the government passes a decree (law) each year, which stipulates the percentage that must be used for the revaluation. That percentage is not necessarily tied to the cost of a specific asset, such as would be the case in replacement cost accounting, and may not even reflect consumer prices for that particular year. The objective is simply to revalue the assets so that depreciation charges can be brought more into line with other costs in the financial statements.

The other major inflation issue is how the multinational corporation has to deal with inflation in different countries in reporting to its shareholders and creditors. The supplementary inflation information contained in the annual report presents information for foreign countries as well as the United States. In general, current cost information is developed in the currency of the country where the foreign operation is located and then translated into U.S. dollars using the current rate translation method. For foreign operations where the functional currency is the dollar rather than the local currency, general purchasing power adjustments must also be made. This is accomplished by translating the local currency financial statements into dollars using the temporal method and then restating these financial statements for changes in the purchasing power of the dollar.

CONCLUSION

Obviously, there are other issues of international dimension that could be discussed, but those presented are some of the most important. Remember that accounting as practiced in different countries reflects differences in the business and economic environments of these countries. Also remember that multinational corporations face unique problems that most domestic firms don't, because of accounting standards and practices, currencies, and rates of inflation that vary from country to country.

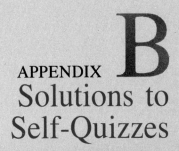

APPENDIX B
Solutions to
Self-Quizzes

SOLUTIONS TO SELF-QUIZ FOR SECTION 1.A

1. **a.** An income statement answers the question, how well did the organization do during the period covered?

    b. A balance sheet answers the question, where does the organization stand at a point in time?

    c. A statement of changes in financial position answers the questions, where did financial resources come from during the period and what were financial resources used for during the period?

2. Refer to the section glossary for definitions.

3. **a.** A bookkeeper performs clerical (routine, repetitive) tasks of accounting according to prescribed instructions. An accountant supervises bookkeepers; prepares, analyzes, and interprets financial reports; audits accounting records; and/or performs other complex accounting activities.

    b. Public accounting is performed by accountants who practice individually or in public accounting firms to provide services to others for a fee. Private accounting is performed by accountants who are salaried employees of the concerns they serve. Governmental accounting is performed by accountants who are salaried employees of government agencies.

    c. General accounting is the overall process of collecting, processing, and reporting financial data. Cost accounting concerns the identification and control of costs and the processing and reporting of cost information. Budgeting is the process of projecting future financial outcomes and subsequently comparing the projections to actual results. Auditing is the act of examining accounting records to determine whether they are accurate and reliable.

d. Financial accounting involves gathering and reporting financial information to users outside the organization, whereas managerial accounting is the process of providing useful information to managers of the organization being accounted for.

SOLUTIONS TO SELF-QUIZ FOR SECTION 1.B

1. Assets = Liabilities + Owner's Equity

   or

   Assets − Liabilities = Owner's Equity

   Note: The equation *Assets − Owner's Equity = Liabilities* is mathematically correct but conceptually misleading because owner's equity is the residual. Liability holders have a *legal* claim on assets; an owner has what is left after these claims are met.

2.

		Assets			=	Liabilities	+	Owner's Equity
	Cash	+	Office Supplies	+	Car	=	Note Payable	+	R. Flox, Capital
a)	+ 3,000							+	3,000
b)	− 20	+	20						
c)	− 500				+ 5,500		+ 5,000		
d)	− 400							−	400
e)	− 200						− 200		

3.

FLOX COMPANY
Balance Sheet
September 30, 19--

ASSETS		*LIABILITIES*	
Cash	$4,000	Note payable	$4,200
Office supplies	75		
Car	5,500		
		OWNER'S EQUITY	
		R. Flox, capital	5,375
	____	Total Liabilities and	
Total Assets	$9,575	Owner's Equity	$9,575

4.

	Assets		= **Liabilities** +		**Owner's Equity**

		Accounts			Accounts	
	Cash +	Receivable +	Gasoline =	Payable +	J. Ripe, Capital	
	1,000 +	500 +	280 =	330 +	1,450	
a) −	250				−	250 Rent expense
b)				+ 90	−	90 Utilities expense
c)			− 50		−	50 Gasoline expense
d) +	400				+	400 Service revenue
e)		+ 600			+	600 Service revenue

5.

ACORN TREE SERVICE Income Statement For the Month of January 19--		
Service revenue		$2,000
Expenses		
Wages	$500	
Depreciation	150	
Gasoline	200	
Rent	400	1,250
Net Income		$ 750

6. OBJECTIVE 4. Refer to section glossary for concept definitions.

SOLUTIONS TO SELF-QUIZ FOR SECTION 2.A

1. Refer to the section glossary for definitions.

2. A T-account is an abbreviated (shorthand) version of a ledger account that resembles the letter *T*. The left side is called the debit side.

3.

Cash				Truck			Note Payable	
a)	20,000	b)	5,000	b)	12,500		b)	7,500
c)	500	d)	2,000					

Wage Expense		Delivery Fees		I. M. Worthy, Capital	
d)	2,000	c)	500	a)	20,000

4. See the glossary for definitions of (and thus the differences between) a proprietorship, a partnership, and a corporation.

SOLUTIONS TO SELF-QUIZ FOR SECTION 2.B

1. **a.** Documenting
   b. Recording
   c. Summarizing
   d. Reporting

2. Refer to the section glossary for definitions. The documenting function is accomplished with source documents; recording is done in journals; data is summarized in ledgers; and reporting is accomplished through statements.

3. See the general journal entries on the page opposite.

4.

					Cash		ACCOUNT NO. 111

						Balance	
Date	Item	Ref.	Debit	Credit		*Debit*	*Credit*
19-- May 2		1	1,800			1,800	

					Pam Pence, Capital		ACCOUNT NO. 311

						Balance	
Date	Item	Ref.	Debit	Credit		*Debit*	*Credit*
19-- May 2		1		1,800			1,800

General Journal				PAGE 1
Date	**Account Names and Explanations**	**A/C #**	**Debit**	**Credit**

19--
May 2
	Cash
	  Pam Pence, Capital
	  Owner invested cash; Deposit No. 1.
		111
		311
			1,800	1,800

3	Sanding Machine
	  Cash
	  Note Payable
	  Purchased machine for cash and note; check No. 101.
			2,000	500
				1,500

4	Sanding Supplies on Hand
	  Accounts Payable
	  Purchased supplies from Gritty Co. on account.
			700	700

15	Cash
	  Sanding Revenue
	  Revenue received in cash; Deposit No. 2.
			900	900

15	Pam Pence, Withdrawals
	  Cash
	  Owner withdrew cash; Check No. 102.
			100	100

25	Rent Expense
	  Cash
	  Paid building rent for May; Check No. 103.
			300	300

25	Accounts Payable
	  Cash
	  Paid on account; Check No. 104.
			200	200

31	Wage Expense
	  Cash
	  Paid wage for May; Check No. 105.
			600	600

31	Accounts Receivable
	  Sanding Revenue
	  Billed customers for work performed in May.
			1,300	1,300

31	Depreciation Expense
	  Accumulated Depreciation—Sanding Machine
	  Depreciation for May.
			80	80

31	Sanding Supplies Expense
	  Sanding Supplies on Hand
	  Sanding supplies used during May.
			150	150

NOTES: Account titles used should be identical to those given in the chart of accounts.

Account numbers would not be written in the A/C # column until the entries are posted in the ledger.

SOLUTIONS TO SELF-QUIZ FOR SECTION 3.A

1. The purpose of accounting is to provide useful information. Information is most useful when it is accurate and up to date. Adjustment entries are necessary to record events that have not been noted (documented) and recorded in the usual way. In other words, adjusting entries update and correct information shown in the accounts.

2.

Date	Account Names and Explanations	A/C #	Debit	Credit
	ADJUSTING JOURNAL ENTRIES			
19--	*a)*			
Oct. 31	Accounts Receivable		850	
	Service Revenue			850
	To recognize unbilled revenue at October 31.			
	b)			
31	Interest Expense		40	
	Interest Payable			40
	Accrued interest on loan payable to the bank.			
	c)			
31	Service Revenue		500	
	Unearned Service Revenue			500
	To defer customer advances for services to be performed in November.			
	d)			
31	Prepaid Rent		800	
	Rent Expense			800
	To defer November and December rent paid in October.			
	e)			
31	Unearned Service Revenue		400	
	Service Revenue			400
	To recognize revenue earned during October.			
	f)			
31	Depreciation Expense—Automobile		150	
	Accum. Depr.—Automobile			150
	To recognize automobile depreciation for October.			

SOLUTIONS TO SELF-QUIZ FOR SECTION 3.B

1. See the work sheet at the top of pages B-8–B-9.

2.

DIBBS COMPANY Income Statement For the Month of April 19--		
Service revenue		$3,430
Expenses		
Wages	$1,750	
Supplies	320	
Depreciation	200	2,270
Net Income		$1,160

DIBBS COMPANY Statement of Owner's Capital For the Month of April 19--	
Capital balance, April 1	$15,850
Net income for April	1,160
Total	$17,010
Less: April withdrawals	850
Capital balance, April 30	$16,160

DIBBS COMPANY Balance Sheet April 30, 19--			
ASSETS			
Current			
Cash		$ 450	
Accounts receivable		750	
Supplies		120	
Total current assets			$ 1,320
Noncurrent			
Land		$ 5,000	
Building	$25,000		
Less: Accumulated depreciation	4,700	20,300	
Total noncurrent assets			25,300
Total Assets			$26,620
LIABILITIES			
Current			
Accounts payable	$ 110		
Wages payable	350		
Total current liabilities		$ 460	
Noncurrent			
Mortgage payable		10,000	
Total Liabilities			$10,460
OWNER'S EQUITY			
B. Dibbs, capital			16,160
Total Liabilities and Owner's Equity			$26,620

DIBBS COMPANY
Work Sheet
For the Month of April 19--

A/C #	Account	Unadjusted Trial Balance	
		Dr.	Cr.
111	Cash	450	
112	Accounts Receivable	520	
113	Supplies	190	
115	Land	5,000	
116	Building	25,000	
0116	Accumulated Depreciation—Building		4,500
211	Accounts Payable		110
212	Wages Payable		–0–
215	Mortgage Payable		10,000
311	B. Dibbs, Capital		15,850
312	B. Dibbs, Withdrawals	850	
411	Service Revenue		3,200
511	Wage Expense	1,400	
512	Supplies Expense	250	
513	Depreciation Expense	–0–	
	Net Income	33,660	33,660

3. An asset is usually classified as current if it can meet any of the following conditions within one year:

   a. If it can reasonably be expected to turn into cash

   b. If it can easily be converted to cash by the managers of the entity

   c. If it can take the place of cash (as with prepaid expenses)

   A liability is considered current if it can reasonably be expected to be paid within one year.

| Adjustments | | Adjusted Trial Balance | | Income Statement | | Balance Sheet | |
Dr.	Cr.	Dr.	Cr.	Dr.	Cr.	Dr.	Cr.
		450				450	
a) 230		750				750	
	c) 70	120				120	
		5,000				5,000	
		25,000				25,000	
	d) 200		4,700				4,700
			110				110
	b) 350		350				350
			10,000				10,000
			15,850				15,850
		850				850	
	a) 230		3,430		3,430		
b) 350		1,750		1,750			
c) 70		320		320			
d) 200		200		200			
850	850	34,440	34,440	2,270	3,430	32,170	31,010
				1,160			1,160
				3,430	3,430	32,170	32,170

Adjustment Explanations:
a) To recognize unbilled revenue at April 30.
b) Accrued wages at April 30.
c) Additional supplies used during April.
d) Building depreciation for April.

SOLUTIONS TO SELF-QUIZ FOR SECTION 3.C

1.

General Journal				PAGE 28
Date	**Account Names and Explanations**	**A/C #**	**Debit**	**Credit**
	CLOSING ENTRIES			
19-- Oct. 31	Service Revenue	41	1,100	
	Rent Expense	51		300
	Supplies Expense	52		150
	H. Van Allen, Capital	31		650
	To close revenue and expense accounts and reflect net income in the owner's capital account.			
31	H. Van Allen, Capital	31	600	
	H. Van Allen, Withdrawals	32		600
	To close withdrawals into capital account.			

H. Van Allen, Capital					ACCOUNT NO. 31	
					Balance	
Date	**Item**	**Ref.**	**Debit**	**Credit**	*Debit*	*Credit*
19-- Oct. 1	Balance	X				230
31	Closing (Net Income)	28		650		880
31	Closing (Withdrawals)	28	600			280

H. Van Allen, Withdrawals					ACCOUNT NO. 32	
					Balance	
Date	**Item**	**Ref.**	**Debit**	**Credit**	*Debit*	*Credit*
19-- Oct. 15		27	50		50	
31		27	550		600	
31	Closing	28		600	-0-	

Service Revenue				ACCOUNT NO. 41		
					Balance	
Date	Item	Ref.	Debit	Credit	Debit	Credit
19-- Oct. 10		27		500		500
25		27		390		890
31	Adjusting	27		210		1,100
31	Closing	28	1,100			–0–

Rent Expense				ACCOUNT NO. 51		
					Balance	
Date	Item	Ref.	Debit	Credit	Debit	Credit
19-- Oct. 15		27	300		300	
31	Closing	28		300	–0–	

Supplies Expense				ACCOUNT NO. 52		
					Balance	
Date	Item	Ref.	Debit	Credit	Debit	Credit
19-- Oct. 8		27	80		80	
17		27	70		150	
31	Closing	28		150	–0–	

SOLUTIONS TO SELF-QUIZ FOR SECTION 4.A

1. Refer to section glossary for definition.

2. Whereas retailing involves sales to consumers in relatively small quantities, wholesaling consists of selling goods in relatively large quantities to retailers or other merchants.

3. See the general journal entries on the following page.

Date	Account Names and Explanations	A/C #	Debit	Credit
19--				
Mar. 1	Purchases		8,000	
	Accounts Payable			8,000
	Purchased goods from Doby Supply Co.;			
	f.o.b. shipping point.			
2	Purchases		400	
	Cash			400
	Purchased goods with Check No. 5062.			
4	Transportation In (or Freight In)		60	
	Cash			60
	Paid freight charges on Mar. 1 purchase;			
	Check No. 5063.			
5	Cash		500	
	Sales			500
	Cash sales; Deposit No. 1055.			
7	Accounts Receivable		4,000	
	Sales			4,000
	Sold to Jay Mooney; f.o.b. destination.			
8	Transportation Out (or Freight Out)		40	
	Cash			40
	Paid freight charges on Mar. 7 sale;			
	Check No. 5064.			
9	Accounts Payable		8,000	
	Cash			8,000
	Paid for Mar. 1 purchase with Check No. 5065.			
14	Cash		4,000	
	Accounts Receivable			4,000
	Collected for Mar. 7 sale; Deposit No. 1056.			

4.

INLAND SALES COMPANY
Schedule of Cost of Goods Sold
For the Year Ended December 31, 19X5

Merchandise inventory at December 31, 19X4		$ 40,000
Purchases during 19X5	$500,000	
Transportation in	10,000	
Delivered cost of purchases		510,000
Cost of goods available for sale		$550,000
Merchandise inventory at December 31, 19X5		30,000
Cost of goods sold		$520,000

SOLUTIONS TO SELF-QUIZ FOR SECTION 4.B

1.

Date	Account Names and Explanations	A/C #	Debit	Credit
19--				
Apr. 4	Purchases		3,000	
	Accounts Payable			3,000
	Purchased goods from Duke Co. on terms of 2/10, n/30.			
6	Accounts Receivable		600	
	Sales			600
	Sold goods to Ray Co. on terms of 1/10, n/60.			
7	Accounts Payable		500	
	Purchases Returns and Allowances			500
	Allowance for goods missing from purchase of April 4 from Duke Co.			
9	Sales Returns and Allowances		100	
	Accounts Receivable			100
	Goods returned by Ray Co. from sale of April 6.			
13	Accounts Payable		2,500	
	Cash			2,450
	Purchases Discounts			50
	Paid balance due on April 4 purchase, after allowance of April 7.			
16	Cash		495	
	Sales Discounts		5	
	Accounts Receivable			500
	Received balance due on April 6 sale, after return of April 9.			

2.

ALLEY COMPANY
Schedule of Cost of Goods Sold
For the Year Ended December 31, 19--

Merchandise inventory at January 1			$ 30,000
Purchases		$400,000	
Less: Purchases discounts	$5,000		
Purchases returns and allowances	2,000	7,000	
Net purchases		$393,000	
Plus: Transportation in		10,000	
Delivered cost of purchases			403,000
Merchandise available for sale			$433,000
Merchandise inventory at December 31			45,000
Cost of goods sold			$388,000

3. a.

	Date	Account Names and Explanations	A/C #	Debit	Credit
(1)	19-- Mar. 5	Accounts Receivable		4,900	
		Sales			4,900
		Sold goods to Ace Co. for $5,000 on terms of 2/10, n/30.			
(2)	15	Cash		4,900	
		Accounts Receivable			4,900
		Collected for sale of March 5.			
(3)	30	Cash		5,000	
		Accounts Receivable			4,900
		Sales Discounts Forfeited			100
		Collected for sale of March 5.			

3. b.

	Date	Account Names and Explanations	A/C #	Debit	Credit
(1)	19-- Mar. 5	Purchases		4,900	
		Accounts Payable			4,900
		Goods purchased from Bee Co. for $5,000 on terms of 2/10, n/30.			
(2)	14	Accounts Payable		4,900	
		Cash			4,900
		Paid for purchase of March 5.			
(3)	29	Accounts Payable		4,900	
		Purchases Discounts Lost		100	
		Cash			5,000
		Paid for purchase of March 5.			

SOLUTIONS TO SELF-QUIZ FOR SECTION 4.C

1.

1) See the work sheet on pages B-16–B-17.

2)

DUXAL COMPANY
Income Statement
For the Year Ended September 30, 19X5

Sales		$215,000	
Less: Sales discounts	$2,000		
Sales returns and allowances	3,000	5,000	
Net Sales			$210,000
Cost of goods sold			
Merchandise inventory, 10/1/X4		$ 15,000	
Purchases	$130,000		
Less: Purchases discounts	$1,000		
Purchases returns and allowances	2,000	3,000	
Net purchases		$127,000	
Plus: Transportation in		5,000	
Delivered cost of net purchases		132,000	
Cost of goods available for sale		$147,000	
Merchandise inventory, 9/30/X5		7,000	
Cost of goods sold			140,000
Gross Profit			$ 70,000
Operating expenses			
Salaries		$35,000	
Advertising		3,000	
Utilities		4,000	
Depreciation		2,000	
Total operating expenses			44,000
Net Operating Income			$ 26,000
Other revenue			
Rent			5,000
Net Income			$ 31,000

DUXAL COMPANY
Work Sheet
For the Year Ended September 30, 19X5

A/C #	Account	Unadjusted Trial Balance Dr.	Unadjusted Trial Balance Cr.
	Cash	8,000	
	Accounts Receivable	25,000	
	Merchandise Inventory	15,000	
	Land	11,000	
	Building	60,000	
	Accumulated Depreciation—Building		22,000
	Accounts Payable		12,000
	Note Payable (Long-term)		20,000
	Francine Duxal, Capital		29,000
	Francine Duxal, Withdrawals	5,000	
	Sales		215,000
	Sales Discounts	2,000	
	Sales Returns and Allowances	3,000	
	Rent Revenue		5,000
	Purchases	130,000	
	Purchases Discounts		1,000
	Purchases Returns and Allowances		2,000
	Transportation In	5,000	
	Salaries Expense	35,000	
	Advertising Expense	3,000	
	Utilities Expense	4,000	
		306,000	306,000
	Depreciation Expense		
	Cost of Goods Sold		
	Net Income		

Adjustments		Adjusted Trial Balance		Income Statement		Balance Sheet	
Dr.	Cr.	Dr.	Cr.	Dr.	Cr.	Dr.	Cr.
		8,000				8,000	
		25,000				25,000	
g) 7,000	b) 15,000	7,000				7,000	
		11,000				11,000	
		60,000				60,000	
	a) 2,000		24,000				24,000
			12,000				12,000
			20,000				20,000
			29,000				29,000
		5,000				5,000	
			215,000		215,000		
		2,000		2,000			
		3,000		3,000			
			5,000		5,000		
	c) 130,000	–0–					
d) 1,000			–0–				
e) 2,000			–0–				
	f) 5,000	–0–					
		35,000		35,000			
		3,000		3,000			
		4,000		4,000			
a) 2,000		2,000		2,000			
b) 15,000	g) 7,000						
c) 130,000	d) 1,000	140,000		140,000			
f) 5,000	e) 2,000						
162,000	162,000	305,000	305,000	189,000	220,000	116,000	85,000
				31,000			31,000
				220,000	220,000	116,000	116,000

Adjustment Explanations:
a) Depreciation for the year.
b) Beginning inventory to Cost of Goods Sold.
c) Purchases to Cost of Goods Sold.
d) Purchases Discounts to Cost of Goods Sold.
e) Purchases Returns and Allowances to Cost of Goods Sold.
f) Transportation In to Cost of Goods Sold.
g) Set up ending inventory.

3)

	DUXAL COMPANY **Balance Sheet** **September 30, 19X5**		

ASSETS

Current

Cash		$ 8,000	
Accounts receivable		25,000	
Merchandise inventory		7,000	$40,000

Noncurrent

Land		$11,000	
Building	$60,000		
Less: Accumulated depreciation	24,000	36,000	47,000
Total Assets			$87,000

LIABILITIES

Current

Accounts payable		$12,000	

Noncurrent

Note payable		20,000	
Total Liabilities			$32,000

OWNER'S EQUITY

Francine Duxal, capital			55,000
Total Liabilities and Owner's Equity			$87,000

4) See the journal on the page opposite.

2. Refer to section glossary for definition.

4)

	General Journal			PAGE

Date	Account Names and Explanations	A/C #	Debit	Credit
	ADJUSTING ENTRIES			
19X5	*a)*			
Sept. 30	Depreciation Expense		2,000	
	Accumulated Depreciation—Building			2,000
	Building depreciation.			
	b)			
30	Cost of Goods Sold		15,000	
	Merchandise Inventory			15,000
	To transfer beginning inventory to			
	Cost of Goods Sold.			
	c)			
30	Cost of Goods Sold		130,000	
	Purchases			130,000
	To transfer purchases.			
	d)			
30	Purchases Discounts		1,000	
	Cost of Goods Sold			1,000
	To transfer purchases discounts.			
	e)			
30	Purchases Returns and Allowances		2,000	
	Cost of Goods Sold			2,000
	To transfer purchases returns and allowances.			
	f)			
30	Cost of Goods Sold		5,000	
	Transportation In			5,000
	To transfer transportation in.			
	g)			
30	Merchandise Inventory		7,000	
	Cost of Goods Sold			7,000
	To set up ending inventory.			
	CLOSING ENTRIES			
30	Sales		215,000	
	Rent Revenue		5,000	
	Sales Discounts			2,000
	Sales Returns and Allowances			3,000
	Salaries Expense			35,000
	Advertising Expense			3,000
	Utilities Expense			4,000
	Depreciation Expense			2,000
	Cost of Goods Sold			140,000
	Francine Duxal, Capital			31,000
	To close revenue and expense accounts			
	to owner's capital.			
30	Francine Duxal, Capital		5,000	
	Francine Duxal, Withdrawals			5,000
	To close withdrawals to owner's capital.			

SOLUTIONS TO SELF-QUIZ FOR SECTION 5.A

1. *Subsidiary ledgers* help keep the general ledger to a manageable size and help divide work and responsibility among employees so that transactions may be processed efficiently. *Special journals* help divide journalizing work into segments and improve efficiency by reducing journalizing effort, reducing posting effort, and permitting specialization.

2. See the special journals, general ledger accounts, and accounts receivable ledger accounts below and on the page opposite.

CASH RECEIPTS JOURNAL FOR THE MONTH OF September 19-- 　　　　PAGE CR25

Date	Accounts & Explanation	Ref.	General Debit	General Credit	Accounts Receivable Credit	Sales Credit	Sales Tax Payable Credit	Cash Debit
Sept. 30	Brought Forward		85.00	1,000.00	16,750.40	45,218.60	2,260.90	65,144.90
30	Archie Ball	✓			150.00			150.00
30	Cash sales					6,531.60	326.58	6,858.18
30			85.00	1,000.00	16,900.40	51,750.20	2,587.48	72,153.08
					(114)	(411)		

SALES JOURNAL FOR THE MONTH OF September 19-- 　　　　PAGE S16

Date	Customer	Invoice Number	Ref.	Accounts Receivable Debit	Sales Tax Payable Credit	Sales Credit
Sept. 30	Brought Forward			18,411.96	876.76	17,535.20
30	Alan Wahoo	1435	✓	210.00	10.00	200.00
30				18,621.96	886.76	17,735.20
				(114)		(411)

GENERAL LEDGER ACCOUNTS

Accounts Receivable 　　　*ACCOUNT NO. 114*

Date	Item	Ref.	Debit	Credit	Balance Debit	Balance Credit
19-- Sept. 1	Balance	X			8,460.75	
30		S16	18,621.96		27,082.71	
30		CR25		16,900.40	10,182.31	

					Balance	
		Sales				ACCOUNT NO. 411
Date	Item	Ref.	Debit	Credit	*Debit*	*Credit*
19——						
Sept. 30		S16		17,735.20		17,735.20
30		CR25		51,750.20		69,485.40

ACCOUNTS RECEIVABLE LEDGER ACCOUNTS

NAME   Archie Ball
ADDRESS   1436 Tee Street, Tarrytown, NY 10591

Date	Item	Ref.	Debit	Credit	Balance
19——					
Sept. 20		S15	150.00		150.00
30		CR25		150.00	–0–

NAME   Alan Wahoo
ADDRESS   3285 Bee Street, Tarrytown, NY 10591

Date	Item	Ref.	Debit	Credit	Balance
19——					
Sept. 1	Balance	X			240.00
10		CR24		240.00	–0–
30		S16	210.00		210.00

3.

> **NELLY COMPANY**
> **Schedule of Accounts Receivable**
> **September 30, 19——**
>
> | | |
> |---|---:|
> | Sheldon Artoo | $ 972.50 |
> | Ann Craft | 499.00 |
> | Farley Craig | 1,615.14 |
> | Jane Franz | 1,284.12 |
> | Ralph Hartle | 3,740.25 |
> | Mary Rooney | 1,530.50 |
> | Mark Stafford | 330.80 |
> | Alan Wahoo | 210.00 |
> | Total | $10,182.31 |

SOLUTIONS TO SELF-QUIZ FOR SECTION 5.B

1.

PURCHASES JOURNAL FOR THE MONTH OF <u>January 19--</u>   *PAGE P2*

Date	Creditor	P.O. No.	Invoice Date	Terms	Ref.	Amount
	Brought Forward					20,765
Jan. 30	Varco, Inc.	1361	1/28/--	n/30	√	620
31	Art Supply Company	1362	1/29/--	2/10, n/30	√	500
31	Purchases Dr., Accounts Payable Cr.					21,885
						(511)(211)

CASH PAYMENTS JOURNAL FOR THE MONTH OF <u>January 19--</u>   *PAGE CP2*

Date	Accounts and Explanation	Ck. No.	Ref.	General Debit	General Credit	Accounts Payable Debit	Purchases Discounts Credit	Cash Credit
	Brought Forward	2831		6,542	2,000	18,600	204	22,938
Jan. 31	Wage Expense	2832	612	2,400				2,400
31	Jazzy Corp.		√			600	12	588
31				8,942	2,000	19,200	216	25,926
						(211)		

GENERAL LEDGER ACCOUNTS

		Accounts Payable			ACCOUNT NO. 211	
					Balance	
Date	Item	Ref.	Debit	Credit	Debit	Credit
19--						
Jan. 1	Balance	X				10,400
31		P2		21,885		32,285
31		CP2	19,200			13,085

		Purchases			ACCOUNT NO. 511	
					Balance	
Date	Item	Ref.	Debit	Credit	Debit	Credit
19--						
Jan. 31		P2	21,885		21,885	

ACCOUNTS PAYABLE LEDGER ACCOUNTS

NAME Art Supply Company
ADDRESS 210 First Street, Clarion, PA 16214

Date	Item	Ref.	Debit	Credit	Balance
19-- Jan. 31		P2		500	500

NAME Jazzy Corporation
ADDRESS 2114 Fifth Ave., Knox, PA 16232

Date	Item	Ref.	Debit	Credit	Balance
19-- Jan. 23 31		P1 CP2	 600	600	600 –0–

2. **a.** Because of its liquidity, cash is a difficult asset to safeguard. When all cash payments are recorded in one book, it is somewhat easier to keep a close watch on where cash goes. Also, the responsibility for recording cash payments can be assigned to one individual.

   b. When the person who handles the cash does not have access to the books, that person will not be able to conceal a theft of cash for very long.

SOLUTIONS TO SELF-QUIZ FOR SECTION 6.A

1. **a.**

Date	Account Names and Explanations	A/C #	Debit	Credit
19X4 Dec. 1	Notes Receivable Accounts Receivable—Blake Co. Received 9%, 60-day note in settlement of overdue account.		4,000	 4,000
31	Interest Receivable Interest Revenue To accrue interest on Blake Co. note. (4,000 × 0.09 × 30/360)		30	 30
19X5 Jan. 30	Cash Notes Receivable Interest Receivable Interest Revenue Blake Co. note collected.		4,060	 4,000 30 30

b.

Date	Account Names and Explanations	A/C #	Debit	Credit
19X4 Dec. 1	Accounts Payable—Darling Co. Notes Payable Incurred 9%, 60-day note in settlement of an account payable.		4,000	4,000
31	Interest Expense Interest Payable To accrue interest on Darling Co. note.		30	30
19X5 Jan. 30	Notes Payable Interest Payable Interest Expense Cash Paid Darling Co. note.		4,000 30 30	4,060

2.

Date	Account Names and Explanations	A/C #	Debit	Credit
19-- June 10	Notes Receivable Accounts Receivable—Dundi Co. Received 12%, 90-day note in settlement of overdue account.		6,000.00	6,000.00

July 10	Cash
	    Notes Receivable
	    Interest Revenue
	Discounted Dundi Co. note at the bank.
			6,087.30	6000.00
				87.30

Sept. 8	Accounts Receivable Cash Dundi Co. note dishonored.		6,180.00	6,180.00

$$\text{Maturity value} = \$6,000 + (\$6,000 \times 0.12 \times 90/360) = \$6,180$$

$$\text{Discount} = \$6,180 \times 0.09 \times 60/360 = \$92.70$$

$$\text{Proceeds} = \$6,180 - \$92.70 = \$6,087.30$$

Note to student: If Notes Receivable—Discounted had been credited on July 10, a second entry would be necessary on September 8 to cancel out Notes Receivable—Discounted (with a debit) against Notes Receivable (credited).

3.   Refer to section glossary for definitions.

SOLUTIONS TO SELF-QUIZ FOR SECTION 6.B

1. a.

Date	Account Names and Explanations	A/C #	Debit	Credit
19-- July 5	Uncollectible Accounts Expense Accounts Receivable—J. Dobbs To write off an uncollectible account.		800	800

    b.

Date	Account Names and Explanations	A/C #	Debit	Credit
19-- Nov. 10	Accounts Receivable—J. Dobbs Uncollectible Accounts Expense To reinstate an account previously written off.		800	800
10	Cash Accounts Receivable—J. Dobbs To record the collection of an account.		800	800

2. a.

Date	Account Names and Explanations	A/C #	Debit	Credit
19-- Mar. 12	Allowance for Doubtful Accounts Accounts Receivable—R. Troup To write off uncollectible account.		700	700

    b.

Date	Account Names and Explanations	A/C #	Debit	Credit
19-- Sept. 14	Accounts Receivable—R. Troup Allowance for Doubtful Accounts To reinstate an account previously written off.		700	700
14	Cash Accounts Receivable—R. Troup To record the collection of an account.		700	700

3. **a.**

Date	Account Names and Explanations	A/C #	Debit	Credit
19-- Dec. 31	Uncollectible Accounts Expense Allowance for Doubtful Accounts To set up estimated uncollectibles at 1% of credit sales.		6,000	6,000

b.

Date	Account Names and Explanations	A/C #	Debit	Credit
19-- Dec. 31	Uncollectible Accounts Expense Allowance for Doubtful Accounts To increase the allowance balance to 5% of ending receivables. (5% × $90,000) − $200		4,300	4,300

4.

Date	Account Names and Explanations	A/C #	Debit	Credit
19-- Dec. 31	Uncollectible Accounts Expense Allowance for Doubtful Accounts To adjust the allowance account to the balance determined to be needed at year-end. ($624 + $1,055 + $1,000) + $600		3,279	3,279

5. Estimating uncollectibles by either the percentage of revenue method or the percentage of receivables balance method fails to consider the *quality* of receivables at the time the adjustment is being made. The longer a receivable remains unpaid, the more likely that it will have to be written off as uncollectible. The older an account is, the more likely that the customer will be unable or unwilling to pay it.

    A receivables aging schedule groups amounts due from customers according to the length of time the receivables have remained unpaid. This provides a much better basis for estimating uncollectibles than does the percentage of revenue method or the percentage of receivables balance method.

SOLUTIONS TO SELF-QUIZ FOR SECTION 7.A

1. It is usually desirable to make a cost-flow assumption for inventory costing purposes for two basic reasons: (a) to help prevent manipulation of accounting results and (b) to avoid the problems of identifying specific costs with particular units of inventory. (Where there are many kinds of items in inventory, it is impractical to identify actual costs with all the units of inventory on hand.)

2.   **a. FIFO**

Available for sale			$8,580
Cost of ending inventory			
Purchased on Aug. 11	120 units at $21	$2,520	
From purchase of June 20	10 units at 20	200	
Ending inventory	130 units		2,720
Cost of goods sold			$5,860

   b. LIFO

Available for sale			$8,580
Cost of ending inventory			
Inventory on Jan. 1	70 units at $18	$1,260	
From Mar. 6 purchase	60 units at 19	1,140	
Ending inventory	130		2,400
Cost of goods sold			$6,180

   c. WEIGHTED AVERAGE

Weighted average unit cost = $8,580 ÷ 440 units = $19.50

Available for sale	$8,580
Cost of ending inventory	
130 units at $19.50	2,535
Cost of goods sold	$6,045

3. The relative effects of using each of the three methods may be written in paragraph form, but should reflect the information presented in Illustration 7.3. Also, you might mention that the effects on income taxes due will follow from the effects on net income. FIFO will result in the highest taxes, LIFO the lowest, and weighted average will fall somewhere in between.

SOLUTIONS TO SELF-QUIZ FOR SECTION 7.B

1. Physical inventories on hand may differ from the accounting records for two basic reasons: (1) clerical mistakes are occasionally made during the recording and posting of merchandise purchased and sold, and (2) inventory units may disappear as a result of shoplifting, employee theft, or spoilage.

2. The principal reasons for using perpetual inventory systems are:

   a. To help discourage thefts of inventories.

   b. To help identify the types and numbers of inventory units available for sale.

   c. To help ensure that sufficient levels of inventories are maintained.

3. a.

FIFO Perpetual		
Cost of goods sold		
Sale of Jan. 10	3 at $500	$1,500
Sale of Jan. 20	⎰ 2 at 500	1,000
	2 at 520	1,040
	⎱ 1 at 540	540
Cost of goods sold		$4,080
Ending inventory		
From purchase of Jan. 15	3 at $540	$1,620

b.

LIFO Perpetual		
Cost of goods sold		
Sale of Jan. 10	⎰ 2 at $520	$1,040
	⎱ 1 at 500	500
Sale of Jan. 20	⎰ 4 at 540	2,160
	⎱ 1 at 500	500
Cost of goods sold		$4,200
Ending inventory		
From beginning inventory	3 at $500	$1,500

c.

Moving Average			Cost of Goods Sold
Beginning inventory	5 at $500.00	$2,500.00	
Purchased Jan. 5	2 at 520.00	1,040.00	
Available	7 at 505.71	$3,540.00*	
Sold Jan. 10	3 at 505.71	1,517.13	$1,517.13
Available	4 at 505.71	$2,022.87*	
Purchased Jan. 15	4 at 540.00	2,160.00	
Available	8 at 522.86	$4,182.87*	
Sold Jan. 20	5 at 522.86	2,614.30	2,614.30
Inventory, Jan. 31	3 at 522.86	$1,568.57*	
Cost of goods sold			$4,131.43

*Balances are residuals and are not exactly in agreement with units on hand times the rounded unit cost figures.

4. The LIFO method will usually show different results for the two systems because under the periodic system, a simplifying assumption is made that *all* purchases are made before any sales occur during the period. Under the perpetual system, a sale can be made (and recorded) only from stocks on hand at that date.

5. In the expression *lower of cost or market,* the word *market* refers to the market in which *purchases* are made. In this sense, market means *replacement cost.*

6.

Inventory Item	Quantity	Invoice Cost	Replacement Cost	Lower of Cost or Market
A	10	$ 50	$ 60	$ 500
B	30	10	8	240
C	5	80	85	400
D	22	32	30	660
E	4	100	100	400
F	15	16	20	240
Total Ending Inventory				$2,440

SOLUTIONS TO SELF-QUIZ FOR SECTION 7.C

1. Markup is the difference between the cost of an inventory item and its selling price. The total of all the markups on goods sold during a period is the gross profit for that period.

2. It may be desirable to estimate the amount of inventory (1) when interim statements are needed, (2) when auditors want to check the reasonableness of a physical inventory figure, and (3) when the approximate amount of an inventory loss must be established.

3. **a.**

Beginning inventory		$ 50,000
Purchases, Jan. 1 through Mar. 31		200,000
Available for sale		$250,000
Sales, Jan. 1 through Mar. 31	$300,000	
Less: Estimated gross profit (40% × $300,000)	120,000	
Estimated cost of goods sold		180,000
Estimated inventory at March 31		$ 70,000

b. $70,000 − $40,000 = $30,000 inventory loss

4. **a.**

	Cost		Retail		
Beginning inventory	$ 72,000		$100,000		
Purchases	558,000		800,000		
Goods available	$630,000	÷	$900,000	=	70%
Inventory at selling prices			$150,000	×	70% =
Inventory at approximate cost	$105,000	←			

b.

	Cost	Retail		
Goods available at retail		$900,000		
Sales		700,000		
Estimated inventory at retail		$200,000		
Actual inventory at retail		150,000		
Shortage at selling prices		$ 50,000	×	70% =
Shortage at estimated cost	$ 35,000			

SOLUTIONS TO SELF-QUIZ FOR SECTION 8.A

1.

Date		Account Names and Explanations	A/C #	Debit	Credit
19--					
Jan.	4	Machinery		20,140	
		Cash			20,140
		Purchased new shaving machine.			
	5	Machinery		300	
		Cash			300
		Freight charges on new shaving machine.			
	6	Machinery		700	
		Cash			700
		Cost of installing new shaving machine.			
	8	Cash		800	
		Accumulated Depreciation—Machinery		7,000	
		Loss on Sale of Machinery		200	
		Machinery			8,000
		Sold old grinding machine.			
	10	Automotive Equipment (new)		14,000	
		Accumulated Depreciation—Automotive Equipment		8,000	
		Automotive Equipment (old)			10,000
		Cash			12,000
		Traded in old truck for new one.			
	11	Building—Improvements (19--)		60,000	
		Cash			60,000
		Electronic smoke detector and burglar alarm installed in building.			
	15	Accumulated Depreciation—Machinery		4,000	
		Cash			4,000
		Old polishing machine was overhauled.			

NOTE: Losses, but not gains, are recognized when old depreciable assets are traded in on assets of like kind.

2. **a.** *Long-term assets* are expected to remain with an entity for more than one year. *Current assets* are expected to be used up or paid out within one year, or one operating cycle if longer than one year. In other words, long-term assets are noncurrent assets.

    b. *Tangible assets* are properties that have physical substance; *intangible assets* are property rights that have value but no physical substance.

    c. *Depreciation* is the process of converting portions of the cost of a long-term productive asset to expense as the asset is worn out in the process of generating revenue. *Depletion* is the allocation of natural resource cost to units that have been removed from land. *Amortization* is the allocation of the cost of an intangible asset to accounting periods.

SOLUTIONS TO SELF-QUIZ FOR SECTION 8.B

1. **a.**

Date	Account Names and Explanations	A/C #	Debit	Credit
19X4 Dec. 31	Depreciation Expense Accumulated Depreciation—Truck Depreciation for one-half year by straight-line time method. (½)($36,000 ÷ 8 yrs.)		2,250	2,250

b.

Date	Account Names and Explanations	A/C #	Debit	Credit
19X4 Dec. 31	Depreciation Expense Accumulated Depreciation—Truck Depreciation for one-half year by straight-line use method. (10,000)($36,000 ÷ 100,000)		3,600	3,600

c.

Date	Account Names and Explanations	A/C #	Debit	Credit
19X4 Dec. 31	Depreciation Expense Accumulated Depreciation—Truck Depr. for one-half year by double-declining-balance method. (½)(25% × $36,800)		4,600	4,600

d.

Date	Account Names and Explanations	A/C #	Debit	Credit
19X4 Dec. 31	Depreciation Expense Accumulated Depreciation—Truck Depr. for one-half year by sum-of-years'-digits method. (½)(8/36 × $36,000)		4,000	4,000

2.

Method	Size of Reported Net Income	Size of Reported Total Assets
Straight-line	1	1
Double-declining-balance	3	3
Sum-of-years'-digits	2	2

3.

Date	Account Names and Explanations	A/C #	Debit	Credit
19X4 Dec. 31	Ore Depletion Accumulated Depletion—Ore Deposits Cost of ore mined during the year. (15,000)($200,000 ÷ 100,000)		30,000	30,000

4.

Date	Account Names and Explanations	A/C #	Debit	Credit
19X4 Dec. 31	Copyright Amortization Expense Copyright Copyright amortization for the year. ($60,000 ÷ 5 yrs.)		12,000	12,000

SOLUTIONS TO SELF-QUIZ FOR SECTION 9.A

1. Accountants classify the following items as cash:

   a. Money in the form of coins and paper currency.

   b. Checking account balances.

   c. Checks and other items that banks will accept as deposits in checking accounts.

2. Control over cash is important because of its attractiveness to thieves owing to its portability and its acceptance as a medium of exchange, as well as to the difficulty of identification by its rightful owner. With cash, people can acquire most of the things they want. Some employees who work with an entity's cash may be tempted to pocket some of it—unless they are convinced that cash controls are likely to expose their acts.

3.

Date	Account Names and Explanations	A/C #	Debit	Credit
19-- Jan. 3	Petty Cash 　　Cash in Bank 　　Established a petty cash fund.		100	100
31	Postage Expense Office Expense Travel Expense 　　Cash in Bank 　　Reimbursed petty cash fund.		23 36 21	80

4. Here are the major types of control procedures discussed in the section:

   a. Separation of duties.

   b. Prompt documentation of cash receipts by means of cash registers, prenumbered receipt forms, and check listings.

   c. Daily intact deposits of cash.

   d. Payments by check.

   e. Use of a voucher system.

   f. Use of imprest funds.

   g. Bank reconciliations.

   h. Close attention to the business operation by an owner or manager of a small concern.

SOLUTIONS TO SELF-QUIZ FOR SECTION 9.B

1. The two overall reasons for differences between cash account and bank statement balances are time lags and errors.

2. Here are the four general steps for preparing a bank reconciliation:

   a. Compare deposits shown on the bank statement with deposits that have been recorded in the accounting records, noting any outstanding deposits or errors made in recording deposits.

   b. Arrange the canceled checks returned with the bank statement in numerical order, and compare them with the list of outstanding checks from the previous period and with checks recorded during the current period, noting any outstanding checks or errors made in recording checks.

   c. Identify any increases or decreases on the bank statement that have not already been recorded in the books.

   d. Reconcile both the bank statement balance and the Cash in Bank account balance to the correct disposable cash at the reconciliation date.

3. **1)**

	DUNKLE COMPANY			
	Bank Reconciliation			
	May 31, 19--			

BANK STATEMENT		*BOOKS*		
Statement balance	$3,785.40	Account balance		$1,523.13
Add: Deposits in transit	631.00	Plus: Error (Check No. 4126)		27.00
	$4,416.40			$1,550.13
Less: Outstanding checks	2,911.27	Less: Returned check	$32.00	
		Service charge	13.00	45.00
Disposable cash	$1,505.13	Disposable cash		$1,505.13

2)

Date	Account Names and Explanations	A/C #	Debit	Credit
19--				
May 31	Cash in Bank		27	
	Accounts Payable			27
	To adjust for error made in recording Check No. 4126.			
31	Accounts Receivable		32	
	Cash in Bank			32
	Customer's check returned for insufficient funds.			
31	Bank Service Charges		13	
	Cash in Bank			13
	Bank service charge for May.			

Or the adjustments may be combined into one entry, as follows.

Date	Account Names and Explanations	A/C #	Debit	Credit
19--				
May 31	Accounts Receivable		32	
	Bank Service Charges		13	
	Accounts Payable			27
	Cash in Bank			18
	To adjust cash per bank reconciliation of May 31.			

SOLUTIONS TO SELF-QUIZ FOR SECTION 10.A

1. Liabilities are generally paid with cash at some future time. Therefore, effective control over liabilities is essential to good cash control. Even valid (legal) liabilities must be carefully managed (controlled) to avoid over-committing a concern's ability to pay liabilities in the future.

2. The three major goals of a control system for liabilities are to ensure that (a) obligations to pay money are valid, (b) amounts are correctly stated, and (c) obligations are paid at the proper time.

3. **a.**

BUCKLEY COMPANY	**VOUCHER**	**No. X2-792**

Pay To *Tabby Supply Co.*   Voucher Date *July 2, 19--*
825 South Byers Street   Invoice Date *July 1, 19--*
Knox, PA   16232   Due Date *July 10, 19--*

Invoice No. *2175*   Gross Amount *$800.00*
P.O. No. *585*   Discount *16.00*
        Net *$784.00*

Verifications   Account Distribution

Quantities	*E.F.*	
Prices	*E.F.*	
Terms	*E.F.*	
Extensions and Footings	*B.A.*	
Account Distribution	*B.A.*	
Approved	*F. Malee*	

Account	Amount
Purchases	*$800.00*
Vouchers Payable (Cr.) $ *800.00*	

Paid: *7/10/--*   Check No. *1466*   Amount *$784.00*

b.

VOUCHER REGISTER				
Voucher No.	**Date**	**Payee**	**Paid**	
			Date	*Ck. No.*
X2–792	19-- July 2	Tabby Supply Company	19-- July 10	1466

c.

				CHECK REGISTER			PAGE 7
Check No.	Date	Payee	Voucher No.	Vouchers Payable Dr.	Purchases Discounts Cr.	Cash Cr.
1466	19-- July 10	Tabby Supply Company	X2–792	800	16	784

4. Here are the six basic steps for processing a voucher:
   a. Prepare a voucher.
   b. Record the voucher in the voucher register.
   c. File the unpaid voucher, with related forms, by due date.
   d. Pull the voucher packet and pay it on its due date.
   e. Record the check in the check register.
   f. File the voucher packet in an alphabetical file by the supplier's name.

							PAGE 8
Voucher Payable Cr.	Purchases Dr.	Freight In Dr.	Supplies Dr.	Salaries Dr.	Other Debits Account	Ref.	Amount
800	800						

SOLUTIONS TO SELF-QUIZ FOR SECTION 10.B

1. Three overall goals of payroll systems are as follows:

   a. To allow accruals of salaries and wages only for services actually rendered to the entity.

   b. To process data quickly enough to permit prompt payment of salaries and wages that are due.

   c. To comply with government regulations.

2. a.

Regular pay: 86 hours at $7	$602
Overtime premium: 6 hours at $3.50	21
Gross pay	$623

b.

Gross pay		$623.00
Deductions		
FICA: 7% × $623	$43.61	
Federal income tax	90.00	
State income tax	12.46	146.07
Net pay		$476.93

3. a.

Date	Account Names and Explanations	A/C #	Debit	Credit
Jan. 31	Wage Expense		12,640.00	
	FICA Taxes Payable			884.80
	Federal Income Taxes Payable			1,910.00
	State Income Taxes Payable			252.80
	Wages Payable			9,592.40
	To record wages for pay period ended Jan. 31.			

b.

Date	Account Names and Explanations	A/C #	Debit	Credit
Jan. 31	Payroll Tax Expense		1,327.20	
	FICA Taxes Payable			884.80
	State Unemployment Taxes Payable			341.28
	Federal Unemployment Taxes Payable			101.12
	Payroll tax expense for the pay period ended this date.			

SOLUTIONS TO SELF-QUIZ FOR CHAPTER 11

1. The four data processing functions are (a) collecting, (b) converting, (c) rearranging, and (d) communicating.

2. The three methods of processing data are (a) manual, (b) mechanical, and (c) electronic.

3. Advantages of EDP for internal control:

    a. Computers are faster, more accurate, and more consistent than people.

    b. Computers are never dishonest.

    c. Computers can help in reviewing, testing, and analyzing data. Various kinds of checks and balances may be incorporated right into computer programs.

    Disadvantages:

    a. Information may be in a format that is unfamiliar to people attempting to audit the records. Some information is inside the computer at certain points in time.

    b. The reduced number of employees needed in a computerized system makes it more difficult to divide duties among them so that they may check on one another. In other words, division of duties may become impractical.

    c. Computer breakdowns may result in serious problems.

4. The types of EDP input media include:

    a. Keyboard.

    b. Punched cards or tapes.

    c. Magnetic tapes or disks.

    d. Magnetic ink or optical characters.

    The types of EDP output media include:

    a. Type or print, including magnetic or optical characters.

    b. Cathode-ray tube display.

    c. Magnetic tapes or disks.

    d. Punched cards or tapes.

5. Refer to chapter glossary for definitions.

SOLUTIONS TO SELF-QUIZ FOR SECTION 12.A

1. The overall goal of accounting is to communicate the most useful information feasible with the means (resources) available.

2. a. *Entity concept:* Each organization for which we account is an independent entity, separate from its owners, managers, customers, creditors, and all other persons and entities with which it deals.

    b. *Monetary concept:* Transactions and events can be stated in terms of monetary units.

    c. *Cost concept:* Assets are recorded and maintained in the accounting records at their cost bases.

    d. *Time period concept:* The activities of an entity are capable of being identified with particular calendar accounting periods.

    e. *Realization concept:* Revenue arises at the point of sale of property, or upon the rendering of a service.

    f. *Matching concept:* Revenues should be matched with the expenses that were responsible for their generation.

    g. *Going concern concept:* The life of an entity is considered unlimited unless (or until) there is concrete evidence that it will end at some approximately determinable future time.

3. Refer to the section glossary for definitions.

4. An auditors' report is a statement of the scope of the work done by the auditors and an expression of the auditors' opinion about the fairness of the accounting statements.

SOLUTIONS TO SELF-QUIZ FOR SECTION 12.B

1. Stated simply, the price-level problem in accounting is that the quantification unit used in accounting (the monetary unit) is continually changing in value. Stated in somewhat more detail, the price-level problem in accounting is that communication is distorted, a conclusion based on the following statements.

Price-level Problem in Accounting

    a. Accounting data are communicated by means of statements and reports.

    b. Accounting data are reported (quantified) in terms of monetary units.

    c. Accounting statements and reports commonly include monetary units of different time periods.

    d. The value of monetary units is constantly changing over time.

    e. Accounting has traditionally ignored the changing value of monetary units over time.

    f. Unlike measuring units are combined in conventional accounting statements and reports.

    g. Therefore, accounting communication is distorted.

2. **a.** Assets: Understated.

    b. Net incomes: Overstated.

    c. Rates of return: Overstated.

    d. Sales growth trends: Overstated.

3. **a.** $(154/110) \times \$80,000 = \$112,000$ in 12/31/X9 dollars

   b.

	Nominal Dollars	
	12/31/X9	*12/31/X8*
Cash	$ 8,000	$ 6,000
Accounts receivable	60,000	40,000
Accounts payable	(50,000)	(60,000)
Net monetary assets	$ 18,000	$(14,000)

APPROXIMATION OF PURCHASING POWER GAIN		
	Nominal Dollars	Conversion Factor	Constant 12/31/X9 Dollars
Net monetary assets at 12/31/X8	$(14,000)	154/110	$(19,600)
Incr. in net monetary assets during year	32,000	154/132	37,333
			$17,733
Net monetary assets at 12/31/X9	$ 18,000	154/154	18,000
Purchasing power gain on net monetary items			$ 267

4. **a.** *Nominal dollar* reporting, sometimes referred to as *unit-of-money* or *mixed dollar* reporting, is the way in which conventional statements are shown in terms of actual numbers of monetary units recorded at the various times that transactions occurred, without any adjustments to make units equivalent.

   b. *Constant dollar, uniform dollar,* or *common dollar* reporting shows dollars that have been adjusted to a common point in time.

   c. *Current cost* reporting shows assets and expenses in terms of replacement costs.

5. The types of financial data that large corporations must disclose are:

   a. Income from continuing operations for the current fiscal year on both a constant dollar basis and a current cost basis

   b. The purchasing power gain or loss on net monetary items for the current fiscal year

   c. The current cost amounts of inventory and property, plant, and equipment at the end of the current fiscal year

   d. Increases or decreases for the current fiscal year in the current cost amounts of inventory and property, plant, and equipment, net of the effects of monetary inflation

   e. A five-year summary of selected financial data, adjusted for price-level changes, about revenues, income, assets, monetary gains and losses, dividends per common share, and market prices of common shares

SOLUTIONS TO SELF-QUIZ FOR CHAPTER 13

1. a,b.

Date	Account Names and Explanations	A/C #	Debit	Credit
19X4 Jan. 2	Cash		100,000	
	Traude, Capital			80,000
	Weil, Capital			20,000
	To record partners' investments.			
Dec. 31	Income Summary		24,000	
	Traude, Capital			9,000
	Weil, Capital			15,000
	To distribute net income.*			
31	Weil, Capital		10,800	
	Weil, Withdrawals			10,800
	To close Weil's withdrawals to the capital account.			

*	Traude	Weil	Total
Partner's salary	$ –0–	$10,800	$10,800
Partners' interest	6,400	1,600	8,000
Remaining income	2,600	2,600	5,200
Net income	$9,000	$15,000	$24,000

2. a. 1)

Date	Account Names and Explanations	A/C #	Debit	Credit
July 1	Reede, Capital		30,000	
	Farley, Capital		30,000	
	Lyon, Capital			60,000

	To record Lyon's purchase of a one-
	    third interest directly from Reede and
	    Farley.			

2)

Date	Account Names and Explanations	A/C #	Debit	Credit
July 1	Goodwill		30,000	
	Reede, Capital			15,000
	Farley, Capital			15,000
	To recognize goodwill as suggested by the amount Lyon is willing to pay for a one-third interest.			
1	Reede, Capital		35,000	
	Farley, Capital		35,000	
	Lyon, Capital			70,000
	To record Lyon's purchase of a one-third interest directly from Reede and Farley.			

b. 1)

Date	Account Names and Explanations	A/C #	Debit	Credit
July 1	Cash		96,000	
	Reede, Capital			2,000
	Farley, Capital			2,000
	Lyon, Capital			92,000
	To record Lyon's payment for a one-third interest in the partnership.			

2)

Date	Account Names and Explanations	A/C #	Debit	Credit
July 1	Goodwill		12,000	
	Reede, Capital			6,000
	Farley, Capital			6,000
	To recognize goodwill as suggested by the amount Lyon is willing to pay for a one-third interest.			
1	Cash		96,000	
	Lyon, Capital			96,000
	To record Lyon's admission to a one-third partnership interest.			

3. a.

LMN COMPANY Relative Ability of Partners to Absorb Losses At May 31, 19--				
	Total	**L**	**M**	**N**
Capital balances	$140,000	$60,000	$50,000	$30,000
Loss that would eliminate N's equity	− 90,000	− 30,000	− 30,000	− 30,000
Remainder	$ 50,000	$30,000	$20,000	$ −0−
Loss that would eliminate M's equity	− 40,000	− 20,000	− 20,000	
Remainder	$ 10,000	$10,000	$ −0−	

LMN COMPANY Cash Distribution Schedule From May 31, 19-- Forward				
Cash Available	**Liabilities**	**L**	**M**	**N**
First $160,000	All			
Next $10,000		All		
Next $40,000		½	½	
Remaining cash		⅓	⅓	⅓

b. 1)

LMN COMPANY Liquidation Schedule May 31, 19--						
				Equity		
	Cash	**Other Assets**	**Liabilities**	**L**	**M**	**N**
Balance before liquidation	$ 6,000	$294,000	$160,000	$60,000	$50,000	$30,000
Other assets sold	+ 249,000	− 294,000		− 15,000	− 15,000	− 15,000
	$255,000	$ −0−	$160,000	$45,000	$35,000	$15,000
Cash distributed	− 255,000		− 160,000	− 45,000	− 35,000	− 15,000
	$ −0−	$ −0−	$ −0−	$ −0−	$ −0−	$ −0−

2)

Date	Account Names and Explanations	A/C #	Debit	Credit
May 31	Cash		249,000	
	Loss on Sale of Assets		45,000	
	Other Assets			294,000
	Noncash assets sold.			
31	L, Capital		15,000	
	M, Capital		15,000	
	N, Capital		15,000	
	Loss on Sale of Assets			45,000
	Loss allocated to partners.			
31	Liabilities		160,000	
	Cash			160,000
	Liabilities paid.			
31	L, Capital		45,000	
	M, Capital		35,000	
	N, Capital		15,000	
	Cash			95,000
	Cash distributed to partners to close accounts.			

SOLUTIONS TO SELF-QUIZ FOR CHAPTER 14

1. Distinguishing features of corporations:
   a. Greater potential for accumulating equity capital
   b. Easy transferability of ownership
   c. Limited liability of owners for business debts
   d. Potential for unlimited life
   e. Tendency for separation of management from ownership
   f. Greater control by governments
   g. Obligation of the entity to pay income taxes

2.

SOLUTIONS TO SELF-QUIZ FOR SECTION 16.A

Da

19
Jai

1. A long-term liability is valued at the net present value of the resources required to satisfy the obligation.

2. Bonds will sell at a *discount* when the going market rate of interest exceeds the stated rate of interest. Bonds will sell at a *premium* when the market rate of interest is less than the stated rate.

Fe

3.

	Date	Account Names and Explanations	A/C #	Debit	Credit

a.	19X3
	Dec. 1
		Cash
		    Bonds Payable
		    Premium on Bonds Payable
		Bonds issued at 107.
				107,000	100,000
					7,000

b.	31	Bond Interest Expense Premium on Bonds Payable Bond Interest Payable To accrue interest on bonds for one month. ($\frac{1}{6}$)(4% × $107,000) = $713		713 37	750
c.	19X4 June 1	Bond Interest Expense Bond Interest Payable Premium on Bonds Payable Cash Semiannual bond interest payment. (4% × $107,000) − $713 = $3,567		3,567 750 183	4,500
d.	Dec. 1	Bond Interest Expense Premium on Bonds Payable Cash Semiannual bond interest payment. (4%)($107,000 − $37 − $183) = $4,271		4,271 229	4,500
e.	19Y3 Dec. 1	Bond Payable Cash Bonds retired at maturity.		100,000	100,000

Ju

A

4.

Date	Account Names and Explanations	A/C #	Debit	Credit
Aug. 1	Bonds Payable Premium on Bonds Payable Loss on Retirement of Bonds Cash Bonds called at 104.		1,000,000 15,000 25,000	1,040,000

SOLUTIONS TO SELF-QUIZ FOR SECTION 16.B

1. When both of the following conditions are met, investments in securities are classified as marketable.

   a. The securities are readily salable.

   b. The investing entity's managers view the securities as a ready source of cash.

   Securities that do not meet both of the foregoing tests are classified as long-term investments.

2.

Date	Account Names and Explanations	A/C #	Debit	Credit
19X4 Dec. 28	Bond Sinking Fund Cash Quarterly contribution to sinking fund.		30,000	30,000
31	Bond Sinking Fund Sinking Fund Revenue Sinking fund earnings as reported by trustee.		10,000	10,000
19X9 Jan. 10	Bonds Payable Cash Bond Sinking Fund Bonds retired and sinking fund closed out.		2,000,000 1,200	2,001,200

3.

Date	Account Names and Explanations	A/C #	Debit	Credit
Feb. 10	Investment in Merkle Stock Cash Purchased 4,000 shares of Merkle common at 8¼, plus broker's commission of $600.		33,600	33,600
Apr. 30	Investment in Doel Bonds Bond Interest Receivable Cash Purchased 20 Doel bonds at 100, plus accrued interest. (³⁄₆)(4% × $20,000) = $400		20,000 400	20,400
May 6	No entry required. However, the cost per share is now $33,600 ÷ 4,200 shares = $8.			

June 14	Cash
	    Investment in Merkle Stock
	    Gain on Sale of Securities
	Sold 1,000 shares of Merkle common at
	9½, less broker's commission of $150.
			9,350	8,000
				1,350

Aug. 1	Cash
	    Bond Interest Receivable
	    Bond Interest Revenue
	Received semiannual interest on Doel
	bonds.
			800	400
				400

Nov. 12	Dividends Receivable Dividend Revenue Dividend of 50¢ per share on 3,200 shares of Merkle common.		1,600	1,600
Dec. 10	Cash Dividends Receivable Received cash dividend on Merkle common.		1,600	1,600

4. Under the cost method of accounting for shares, cash dividends are recorded as revenues, and no recognition is given to income reported by the corporation that issued the shares. Under the equity method of accounting for investments in common shares, the investor recognizes a proportionate share of net income that is reported by the related company, and receipt of a cash dividend is recorded as a realization of part of the investment. The equity method is used only where the investing corporation owns enough of the voting stock of the related corporation to exercise significant influence on its operations.

SOLUTIONS TO SELF-QUIZ FOR SECTION 17.A

1.

HOME OFFICE JOURNAL				
Date	Account Names and Explanations	A/C #	Debit	Credit
Jan. 5	Eastside Branch Cash Cash transferred to new branch.		4,000	4,000
7	Eastside Branch Shipments to Eastside Branch Merchandise sent to branch.		12,000	12,000
20	Cash Eastside Branch Received cash from Eastside branch.		6,000	6,000

BRANCH JOURNAL				
Date	Account Names and Explanations	A/C #	Debit	Credit
Jan. 5	Cash Home Office Cash received from home office.		4,000	4,000
7	Shipments from Home Office Home Office Merchandise received from home office.		12,000	12,000
20	Home Office Cash Cash transferred to home office.		6,000	6,000

2. a.

PARKER COMPANY—HOME OFFICE Income Statement For the Year Ended December 31, 19--			
Sales			$600,000
Cost of goods sold			
Inventory, January 1		$ 80,000	
Purchases	$510,000		
Less: Shipments to branch	180,000	330,000	
Available for sale		$410,000	
Inventory, December 31		75,000	335,000
Gross Profit			$265,000
Operating expenses			
Rent		$ 60,000	
Wages		120,000	
Depreciation		5,000	
Utilities		11,000	
Miscellaneous		3,000	199,000
Net Income—Home Office			$ 66,000
Net Income—Eastside Branch			15,000
Total Net Income			$ 81,000

b.

	Home Office	Eastside Branch	Eliminations Debit	Eliminations Credit	Combined Income St.
PARKER COMPANY Work Sheet for Combining Income Statements For the Year Ended December 31, 19--					
Sales	600,000	270,000			870,000
Cost of goods sold					
Inventory, Jan. 1	80,000	–0–			80,000
Purchases	510,000				510,000
Shipments from home office		180,000		180,000	
Shipments to branch	(180,000)		180,000		
Inventory, Dec. 31	(75,000)	(15,000)			(90,000)
Cost of goods sold	335,000	165,000			500,000
Gross Profit	265,000	105,000			370,000
Operating expenses					
Rent	60,000	24,000			84,000
Wages	120,000	58,000			178,000
Depreciation	5,000				5,000
Utilities	11,000	7,000			18,000
Miscellaneous	3,000	1,000			4,000
Total operating expenses	199,000	90,000			289,000
Net Income	66,000	15,000	180,000	180,000	81,000

c.

EASTSIDE BRANCH JOURNAL

Date	Account Names and Explanations	A/C #	Debit	Credit
Dec. 31	Sales		270,000	
	Merchandise Inventory		15,000	
	Shipments from Home Office			180,000
	Rent Expense			24,000
	Wages Expense			58,000
	Utilities Expense			7,000
	Miscellaneous Expense			1,000
	Home Office			15,000
	To close temporary accounts, adjust inventory, and reflect net income into the home office account.			

ALTERNATIVE ENTRIES

Date	Account Names and Explanations	A/C #	Debit	Credit
Dec. 31	Merchandise Inventory		15,000	
	Cost of Goods Sold		165,000	
	Shipments from Home Office			180,000
	To set up ending inventory and cost of goods sold.			
31	Sales		270,000	
	Cost of Goods Sold			165,000
	Rent Expense			24,000
	Wages Expense			58,000
	Utilities Expense			7,000
	Miscellaneous Expense			1,000
	Home Office			15,000
	To close temporary accounts and reflect net income into the home office account.			

g.

$$\text{Debt-equity ratio} = \frac{\text{Total liabilities}}{\text{Total owners' equity}} = \frac{\$392,000}{\$429,400} = 91.3\%$$

h.

$$\text{Price-earnings ratio} = \frac{\text{Market value per share}}{\text{Earnings per share}} = \frac{\$75}{\$9.80} = 7.7$$

i.

$$\text{Dividend yield rate} = \frac{\text{Common dividends per share}}{\text{Market value per common share}} = \frac{\$9.63}{\$75} = 12.8\%$$

4. Trading on the equity is the act of earning more on borrowed funds than they cost in interest. Carriers, Inc., appears to be doing rather well trading on the equity, since a 15.9% return on assets was parlayed into a 42.9% return on common equity. The use of preferred stock equity was also beneficial to common shareholders, since the preferred dividend rate is only 9% of preferred stock par, or $9 per share per year.

Special note: The very high return of 42.9% on common equity suggests that Carriers's assets are stated at considerably less than the entity's market value. This is further suggested by the excess of market value per share over book value per share. Perhaps the firm has goodwill that is not included among the assets. The price-earnings ratio of 7.7 implies a rate of return on the market value of shares of 13%, which is a more reasonable investment return than the 42.9% calculated on the book value of shareholders' equity. Since assets are accounted for on a cost basis, the results referred to here are entirely possible, and perhaps to be expected.

SOLUTIONS TO SELF-QUIZ FOR CHAPTER 20

1. A manufacturing concern combines various resources to produce goods that did not previously exist. A merchandising firm, on the other hand, buys goods and resells them without changing their form.

2. **a.** *Materials inventory.* Materials on hand that have not yet been put into the production process.

   b. *Goods in process inventory.* Incomplete products still in the production process.

   c. *Finished goods inventory.* Completed goods awaiting sale.

3. **a.** *Direct materials.* Materials that become part of a finished product.

   b. *Direct labor.* Services supplied by employees who work directly on goods being produced.

   c. *Factory overhead.* Indirect manufacturing costs consisting of indirect materials, indirect labor, and all other indirect manufacturing expenses.

4. a. See the double-page work sheet on pages B-62 and B-63.

   b.

TEMPO MANUFACTURING CORPORATION Schedule of Cost of Goods Completed For the Year Ended December 31, 19--		
Goods in process, Jan. 1		$ 181,940
Cost of materials used		
Materials inventory, Jan. 1	$ 137,500	
Materials purchases	984,200	
Cost of materials available	$1,121,700	
Materials inventory, Dec. 31	142,700	
Cost of materials used	$ 979,000	
Factory labor	949,480	
Other manufacturing costs	478,140	
Total cost added to process		2,406,620
Total cost in process		$2,588,560
Goods in process, Dec. 31		159,230
Cost of goods completed		$2,429,330

   c.

Date	Account Names and Explanations	A/C #	Debit	Credit
	MANUFACTURING ADJUSTMENTS			
19-- Dec. 31	Manufacturing Summary		2,731,260	
	Materials Inventory			137,500
	Goods in Process			181,940
	Materials Purchases			984,200
	Factory Labor			949,480
	Other Manufacturing Costs			478,140
	To transfer to Manufacturing Summary the manufacturing accounts with debit balances.			
31	Materials Inventory		142,700	
	Goods in Process		159,230	
	Manufacturing Summary			301,930
	To remove ending materials and goods in process inventories from Manufacturing Summary.			
31	Cost of Goods Sold		2,429,330	
	Manufacturing Summary			2,429,330
	To transfer to Cost of Goods Sold the cost of goods completed during the year.			
31	Cost of Goods Sold		316,330	
	Finished Goods			316,330
	To transfer beginning finished goods to Cost of Goods Sold.			
31	Finished Goods		305,500	
	Cost of Goods Sold			305,500
	To set up ending finished goods inventory.			

NOTE: Other combinations of entries that accomplish the same results are acceptable.

a.

TEMPO MANUFACTURING CORP. Work Sheet For the Year Ended December 31, 19--		
	Adjusted Trial Balance	
Accounts	*Debit*	*Credit*
Cash	118,410	
Accounts Receivable	498,600	
Allowance for Doubtful Accounts		40,000
Beginning Inventories		
Materials	137,500	
Goods in Process	181,940	
Finished Goods	316,330	
Land	280,000	
Building	550,000	
Accumulated Depreciation—Building		150,000
Machinery and Equipment	424,000	
Accumulated Depreciation—Mach. and Equip.		180,000
Accounts Payable		385,200
Interest Payable		2,500
Income Taxes Payable		293,000
Bonds Payable		500,000
Common Stock, $5 par		200,000
Capital in Excess of Par		275,000
Retained Earnings		186,250
Sales		3,430,700
Materials Purchases	984,200	
Factory Labor	949,480	
Other Manufacturing Costs	478,140	
General and Administrative Expenses	182,300	
Selling Expenses	258,750	
Interest Expense	30,000	
Income Taxes	253,000	
	5,642,650	5,642,650
Ending Inventories		
Materials		
Goods in Process		
Finished Goods		
Cost of Goods Completed		
Net Income		

Manufacturing Summary		Income Statement		Balance Sheet	
Debit	*Credit*	*Debit*	*Credit*	*Debit*	*Credit*
				118,410	
				498,600	
					40,000
137,500					
181,940					
		316,330			
				280,000	
				550,000	
					150,000
				424,000	
					180,000
					385,200
					2,500
					293,000
					500,000
					200,000
					275,000
					186,250
			3,430,700		
984,200					
949,480					
478,140					
		182,300			
		258,750			
		30,000			
		253,000			
	142,700			142,700	
	159,230			159,230	
			305,500	305,500	
2,731,260	301,930				
	2,429,330	2,429,330			
2,731,260	2,731,260	3,469,710	3,736,200	2,478,440	2,211,950
		266,490			266,490
		3,736,200	3,736,200	2,478,440	2,478,440

d.

Date	Account Names and Explanations	A/C #	Debit	Credit
19-- Dec. 31	*CLOSING ENTRY* Sales		3,430,700	
	Cost of Goods Sold			2,440,160
	General and Administrative Expenses			182,300
	Selling Expenses			258,750
	Interest Expense			30,000
	Income Taxes			253,000
	Retained Earnings			266,490
	To close revenue and expense accounts and record net income in Retained Earnings.			

NOTE: Several closing entries and an Income Summary account could have been employed to accomplish the same overall result.

SOLUTIONS TO SELF-QUIZ FOR SECTION 21.A

1. The four general purposes of cost systems, as presented in this chapter, are to provide manufacturing cost data for

   a. Preparing financial statements.

   b. Controlling and minimizing current costs.

   c. Evaluating past performance.

   d. Planning for the future.

2. A job order cost system is most likely to be used where products are produced individually or in batches to the specifications of customers.

3. Overhead application rate $= \dfrac{\text{Estimated total overhead}}{\text{Estimated total direct labor}} = \dfrac{\$770,400}{\$642,000} = 120\%$

4.

Date	Account Names and Explanations	A/C #	Debit	Credit
Mar. 31	Goods in Process		49,700	
	Factory Overhead		13,900	
	Materials Inventory			63,600
	To record materials used during March.			
31	Goods in Process		52,800	
	Factory Overhead		38,600	
	Factory Payroll			91,400
	To record labor costs incurred during March.			
31	Goods in Process		63,360	
	Factory Overhead			63,360
	Overhead applied to jobs at 120% of direct labor costs.			

5.

Date	Account Names and Explanations	A/C #	Debit	Credit
Mar. 14	Finished Goods		62,000	
	Goods in Process			62,000
	Job 314 completed.			
19	Accounts Receivable		84,000	
	Cost of Goods Sold		62,000	
	Sales			84,000
	Finished Goods			62,000
	Job 314 accepted by Darby Company.			

SOLUTIONS TO SELF-QUIZ FOR SECTION 21.B

1. A process cost system is most likely to be used where standardized goods are produced on a more or less continuous basis.

2. One approach to determining equivalent units is by means of a schedule as follows.

TAPPE CORPORATION Mixing Department Equivalent Units Completed For the Month of May 19--					
		Materials		**Labor and Overhead**	
	Actual Units	*Stage of Completion*	*Equivalent Units for May*	*Stage of Completion*	*Equivalent Units for May*
Goods in process, May 1	12,000	80%	2,400	60%	4,800
Started and completed	52,000	100%	52,000	100%	52,000
Goods in process, May 31	8,000	40%	3,200	20%	1,600
Completed in May	64,000		57,600		58,400

3.

Date	Account Names and Explanations	A/C #	Debit	Credit
19--	*a)*			
May 31	Goods in Process, Mixing		130,000	
	Goods in Process, Canning		46,000	
	Factory Overhead		25,000	
	Materials Inventory			201,000
	Materials used in May.			
	b)			
31	Goods in Process, Mixing		210,000	
	Goods in Process, Canning		94,000	
	Factory Overhead		173,000	
	Factory Payroll			477,000
	Factory labor used in May.			
	c)			
31	Goods in Process, Mixing		252,000	
	Goods in Process, Canning		77,080	
	Factory Overhead			329,080
	Factory overhead applied at 120% of mixing direct labor and 82% of canning direct labor.			
	d)			
31	Goods in Process, Canning		588,000	
	Goods in Process, Mixing			588,000
	Cost of goods completed in mixing and transferred to canning.			
	e)			
31	Finished Goods		780,000	
	Goods in Process, Canning			780,000
	Cost of goods completed by canning and transferred to Finished Goods inventory.			

SOLUTIONS TO SELF-QUIZ FOR SECTION 22.A

1. The process of gathering information for presentation in financial statements prepared for external users is called financial accounting. The process of gathering information for use in preparing reports and other information mainly for internal decision making is called managerial accounting.

2.

PEGGY'S CAKE SALES
Projected Collections of Cash from Sales
For the Fourth Quarter, 19X5

Sales		Collections			
		October	November	December	Quarter
August	$ 72,000	$ 7,200			$ 7,200
September	66,000	26,400	$ 6,600		33 000
October	84,000	42,000	33,600	$ 8,400	84,000
November	78,000		39,000	31,200	70,200
December	122,000			61,000	61,000
Projected collections of cash		$75,600	$79,200	$100,600	$255,400

PEGGY'S CAKE SALES
Projected Payments of Cash for Purchases
For the Fourth Quarter, 19X5

Purchases		Payments			
		October	November	December	Quarter
September	$ 40,000	$16,000			$ 16,000
October	50,000	30,000	$20,000		50,000
November	46,000		27,600	$18,400	46,000
December	74,000			44,400	44,400
Projected payments		$46,000	$47,600	$62,800	$156,400

3.

PEGGY'S CAKE SALES
Cash Budget
For the Fourth Quarter, 19X5

	October	November	December	Quarter
Projected cash receipts				
Collections of cash from sales	$75,600	$79,200	$100,600	$255,400
Projected cash payments				
Payments of cash for purchases	$46,000	$47,600	$ 62,800	$156,400
Selling and administrative expenses	11,000	13,000	15,000	39,000
Purchase of furniture	24,000			24,000
Owner's withdrawals	2,000	2,000	2,000	6,000
Total projected payments	$83,000	$62,600	$ 79,800	$225,400
Increase (Decrease) in Cash	$(7,400)	$16,600	$ 20,800	$ 30,000
Beginning cash balance	5,000	4,600	5,200	5,000
Total	$(2,400)	$21,200	$ 26,000	$ 35,000
Increase (decrease) in bank loans	7,000	(7,000)	–0–	–0–
(Increase) decrease in securities	–0–	(9,000)	(21,000)	(30,000)
Projected ending cash balance	$ 4,600	$ 5,200	$ 5,000	$ 5,000

4. Your list may differ from the one that appears on page 925 in wording or in order of steps. However, the essential points should be included, and the order should follow a logical sequence.

SOLUTIONS TO SELF-QUIZ FOR SECTION 22.B

1. Refer to section glossary for definitions.

2.

QUIZMO CORPORATION Machining Department—Rockview Plant Performance Report For the Month of October 19--			
Production: 50,400 Equivalent Units	**Budget**	**Actual**	**Variance: Favorable (Unfavorable)**
Direct materials	$240,000	$225,000	$ 15,000
Direct labor	290,000	302,000	(12,000)
Factory overhead			
Indirect materials	76,000	78,000	(2,000)
Indirect labor	58,000	53,000	5,000
Other manufacturing costs	85,000	86,000	(1,000)
Total	$749,000	$744,000	$ 5,000

3. Responsibility accounting identifies differences (variances) between budgeted and actual costs. The size and direction of the variances helps to direct the attention of managers to exceptional situations that often uncover trouble spots in the organization. (This approach is sometimes referred to as *management by exception.*)

SOLUTIONS TO SELF-QUIZ FOR SECTION 23.A

1. A *fixed cost* remains constant as levels of activity change, whereas a *step-fixed cost* changes abruptly at one or more activity levels. A *variable cost* is one that changes directly in relation to activity levels. A *mixed cost* is simply a cost with both fixed and variable elements of behavior.

2. **a.** $25n + \$50,000 = $ Total cost

    b.

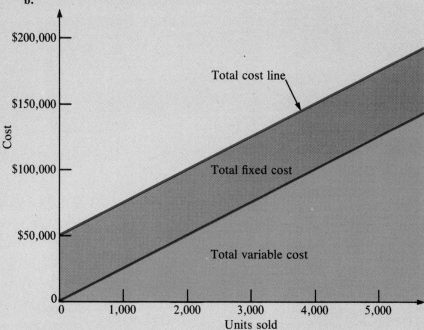

Or, as an alternative:

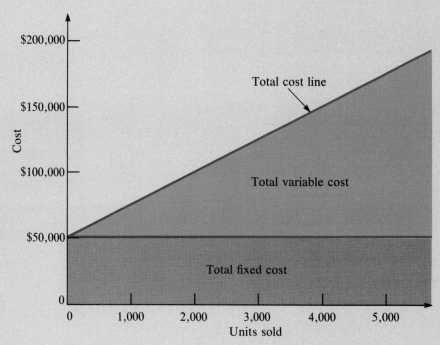

3. **a.** 4
   b. 3
   c. 1
   d. 2
   e. 5
   f. 1

SOLUTIONS TO SELF-QUIZ FOR SECTION 23.B

1. $p - v$ = Contribution margin per unit

   $\$8 - \$6 = \$2$

2. Break-even point in units:

   $pn - vn - \quad F \quad$ = Net income

   $\$8n - \$6n - \$40{,}000 = \$0$

   $\qquad\qquad \$2n \quad = \$40{,}000$

   $\qquad\qquad n \quad = 20{,}000$ units break-even sales

   or simply

   $$\frac{F}{p - v} = \frac{\$40{,}000}{\$2} = 20{,}000 \text{ units}$$

   Break-even point in sales dollars:

   $\$8 \times 20{,}000$ units $= \$160{,}000$ break-even sales

   or

   Let s = Sales in dollars

   $$\frac{\$6}{\$8} = 75\% \text{ variable cost as \% of price}$$

   $s - 0.75s - \$40{,}000 = \$0$

   $\qquad\qquad 0.25s = \$40{,}000$

   $\qquad\qquad s = \$160{,}000$ break-even sales

3. $\quad pn \quad - \quad vn \quad - \quad F \quad$ = Net income

   $\$8(30{,}000) - \$6(30{,}000) - \$40{,}000$ = Net income

   $\$240{,}000 \quad - \quad \$180{,}000 \quad - \$40{,}000$ = Net income

   $\qquad\qquad\qquad\qquad\qquad \$20{,}000$ = Net income

4.

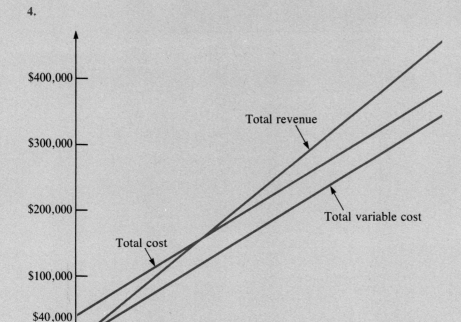

Units sold

SOLUTIONS TO SELF-QUIZ FOR SECTION 24.A

1. The three advantages of flexible budgets as stated in this section are:
   a. Flexible budgets permit managers to speculate on the consequences of operating at activity levels other than the most likely (or most desired) level.
   b. Flexible budgets are more useful in the identification of trouble spots.
   c. Flexible budgets are more useful for evaluating performance.

2. $\dfrac{\text{Change in cost}}{\text{Change in activity}}$ = Variable cost per unit

   $\dfrac{\$238,000 - \$210,000}{12,000 - 10,000} = \dfrac{\$28,000}{2,000} = \$14$ variable cost per unit

	May	June
Total cost	$210,000	$238,000
Less variable cost		
Units times $14	140,000	168,000
Fixed cost per month	$ 70,000	$ 70,000

3.

TET FOODS CORPORATION
Fishmeal Production Department
Flexible Budget Performance Report
For the Month of May 19--

	Flexible Budget	Actual	Variance Favorable (Unfavorable)
Units of production	40,000	40,000	
Variable costs			
Direct materials	$480,000	$506,000	$(26,000)
Direct labor	160,000	163,800	(3,800)
Variable overhead	240,000	238,000	2,000
Total variable	$880,000	$907,800	$(27,800)
Fixed overhead	50,000	50,000	–0–
Total cost	$930,000	$957,800	$(27,800)

SOLUTIONS TO SELF-QUIZ FOR SECTION 24.B

1. Standard costs are carefully determined estimates of what costs should be when resources are effectively used.

2. Benefits of Standard Costs:

   a. Standard costs serve as reasonable unit cost measures for budgeting purposes.

   b. Standard costs permit production costs to be transferred through the accounting system before actual costs are known with certainty.

   c. Standard costs serve as bases (standards) of comparison for evaluating actual costs.

3. a. **Actual pounds × (Standard price − Actual price) = Materials rate variance**
   4,600,000 × (10¢ − 11¢) = $46,000 unfavorable

   b. **(Standard pounds − Actual pounds) × Standard price = Materials quantity variance**
   (4,800,000 − 4,600,000) × 10¢ = $20,000 favorable
   120 pounds per bag × 40,000 bags produced

   c. **(Standard rate − Actual rate) × Actual hours = Labor rate variance**
   ($8 − $7.80) × 21,000 hours = $4,200 favorable

   d. **(Standard hours − Actual hours) × Standard rate = Labor quantity variance**

        (20,000   −   21,000)   × $8   = $8,000 unfavorable

       ½ hour per bag × 40,000 bags produced

   e.   **(Achieved volume   −   Budgeted volume) × Fixed overhead rate = Volume variance**

       (Standard labor hours − Budgeted labor hours) × Fixed overhead rate = Volume variance

          (20,000 hours   −   25,000 hours)   × $2   = $10,000 unfavorable

       ½ hour × 40,000 bags   Normal capacity

     or

      Applied fixed overhead − Budgeted fixed overhead = Volume variance

       (20,000 hours × $2) − $50,000   = $10,000 unfavorable

   f.   **Flexible budget overhead   − Actual overhead = Budget variance**

     (20,000 hours × $12) + $50,000 − $288,000   = $2,000 favorable

SOLUTIONS TO SELF-QUIZ FOR SECTION 25.A

1. Positive answers to the following questions indicate that information is relevant to a decision.

   a. Does the information pertain to future conditions?

   b. Is the information different for the alternatives under consideration?

2. A sunk cost is a cost incurred in the past. Sunk costs are irrelevant because they cannot be undone, regardless of which decision choices are made in the present or the future.

3. **a.** The relevant data are those that are boxed here, because they pertain to the future and are different for the alternatives. Also, the potential loss on the sale of the old machine, the difference in annual depreciation expense, and the marginal tax rates are relevant because of their effects on future tax payments.

	Old Machine	Proposed New Machine
Cost	$80,000	$100,000
Accumulated depreciation	$40,000	$ –0–
Current disposition value	$20,000	$100,000
Remaining life	5 years	5 years
Expected salvage value in 5 years	$ –0–	$ –0–
Depreciation method	Straight-line	Straight-line
Marginal tax rate	46%	46%
Production costs		
Direct materials per dart	$0.20	$0.30
Direct labor per dart	$0.60	$0.40
Variable overhead per dart	$0.30	$0.20
Selling price per dart	$3	$3

b.

Cash cost of new machine			$100,000
Less cash cleared from sale of old machine			
Cash from sale		$20,000	
Tax saved from loss on sale			
Sale price	$20,000		
Book value	40,000		
Loss	$20,000		
Tax saved by loss ($20,000 × 46%)		9,200	
Cash cleared after tax			29,200
Net cash outlay for the new machine			$ 70,800

c.

Incremental savings before tax			
20¢ per unit (100,000 units)			$20,000
Less income taxes each year			
Cost savings		$20,000	
Increase in depreciation expense			
New depreciation	$20,000		
Old depreciation	8,000	12,000	
Net taxable difference		$ 8,000	
Income taxes ($8,000 × 46%)			3,680
Net annual benefit after taxes			$16,320

d. 5 years × $16,320 − $70,800 = $10,800 net advantage

Caution: This solution does not take into consideration the time value of money.

SOLUTIONS TO SELF-QUIZ FOR SECTION 25.B

1. With mutually exclusive alternatives, the circumstances are such that the choice of one alternative automatically rules out the others being considered. Competing alternatives, however, are not in conflict with each other; they simply compete with each other for the funds that are available.

2. Two limitations of the payback approach are (a) that timings of cash flows during payback periods are not considered and (b) that timings and amounts of cash flows beyond payback periods are not considered. Nevertheless, when the lives of all alternatives are equal, and when net annual cash flows are expected to be level for each alternative, the payback approach will rank alternatives in the same order as will the rate of return approach.

3. a.

	J	K
Annual cash flows after tax		
Cash proceeds before tax	$70,000	$100,000
Times (1 − 0.30)	× 0.70	× 0.70
	$49,000	$ 70,000
Tax savings from depreciation shield		
0.30 × Depreciation	6,000	9,000
Annual cash flows after tax	$55,000	$ 79,000
(1)		
Payback period in years	$\dfrac{\$300,000}{\$55,000} = 5.455$	$\dfrac{\$450,000}{\$79,000} = 5.696$
(2)		
Net present value*	$118,330	$150,874
(3)		
Profitability index	$\dfrac{\$118,300}{\$300,000} = 0.394$	$\dfrac{\$150,874}{\$450,000} = 0.335$
(4)		
Rate of return†	Just over 16%	Just under 16%

*(Annual cash flows after taxes) (7.606) − Net cash outlay.

†The payback period figures are used as present value annuity factors, and the approximate rates of return are located by comparing the factors calculated with those on the 15-year line of the present value annuity table.

b. Alternative choice J appears to be more attractive than K. Alternative J comes out ahead under the *payback period, profitability index,* and *rate of return* approaches. However, if the alternatives are mutually exclusive, and if plenty of investment funds are available, alternative K might be chosen to obtain the extra $32,544 of net present value.

Note that the *additional* annual cash flow after taxes of $24,000 offered by K, when compared with the *additional* investment required of $150,000, implies a factor of 6.250. Thus the *incremental* investment in K will produce a return of just under 14%, which is well above the 10% cost of capital rate.

SOLUTIONS TO SELF-QUIZ FOR CHAPTER 26

1.

Tax on $60,000	$15,168
Plus: 42% of $3,000	1,260
Total tax for year	$16,428

2. Tax deductions are subtractions from taxable revenues to arrive at taxable income. Tax credits are direct offsets against income tax.

3. Refer to chapter glossary for definitions.

4. Tax avoidance is the act of legally bypassing tax obligations, whereas tax deferral is the process of delaying tax payments by legally shifting them to future periods. Tax evasion, on the other hand, is the act of eluding taxes by illegal means.

5. The purpose of tax allocation is to minimize the disparity between reported net income and tax due for the year.

Corporation Financial Statements
(General Motors Corporation)

CONSOLIDATED FINANCIAL STATEMENTS

General Motors Corporation
and Consolidated Subsidiaries

RESPONSIBILITIES FOR FINANCIAL STATEMENTS

The following financial statements of General Motors Corporation and consolidated subsidiaries were prepared by the management which is responsible for their integrity and objectivity. The statements have been prepared in conformity with generally accepted accounting principles and, as such, include amounts based on judgments of management. Financial information elsewhere in this Annual Report is consistent with that in the financial statements.

Management is further responsible for maintaining a system of internal accounting controls, designed to provide reasonable assurance that the books and records reflect the transactions of the companies and that its established policies and procedures are carefully followed. From a stockholder's point of view, perhaps the most important feature in the system of control is that it is continually reviewed for its effectiveness and is augmented by written policies and guidelines, the careful selection and training of qualified personnel, and a strong program of internal audit.

Deloitte Haskins & Sells, independent certified public accountants, are engaged to examine the financial statements of General Motors Corporation and its subsidiaries and issue reports thereon. Their examination is conducted in accordance with generally accepted auditing standards which comprehend a review of internal accounting controls and a test of transactions. The Accountants' Report appears on page 26.

The Board of Directors, through the Audit Committee (composed entirely of non-employe Directors), is responsible for assuring that management fulfills its responsibilities in the preparation of the financial statements. The Committee selects the independent public accountants annually in advance of the Annual Meeting of Stockholders and submits the selection for ratification at the Meeting. In addition, the Committee reviews the scope of the audits and the accounting principles being applied in financial reporting. The independent public accountants, representatives of management, and the internal auditors meet regularly (separately and jointly) with the Committee to review the activities of each and to ensure that each is properly discharging its responsibilities. To ensure complete independence, Deloitte Haskins & Sells have full and free access to meet with the Committee, without management representatives present, to discuss the results of their examination, the adequacy of internal accounting controls, and the quality of the financial reporting.

Chairman

Chief Financial Officer

SOURCE: General Motors Corporation, *1982 Annual Report*, Detroit, pp. 17–29.

—————————————————— ACCOUNTANTS' REPORT ——————————————————

**Deloitte
Haskins + Sells**
CERTIFIED PUBLIC ACCOUNTANTS

1114 Avenue of the Americas
New York, New York 10036

General Motors Corporation, its Directors and Stockholders: February 7, 1983

We have examined the Consolidated Balance Sheet of General Motors Corporation and consolidated subsidiaries as of December 31, 1982 and 1981 and the related Statements of Consolidated Income and Changes in Consolidated Financial Position for each of the three years in the period ended December 31, 1982. Our examinations were made in accordance with generally accepted auditing standards and, accordingly, included such tests of the accounting records and such other auditing procedures as we considered necessary in the circumstances.

In our opinion, these financial statements present fairly the financial position of the companies at December 31, 1982 and 1981 and the results of their operations and the changes in their financial position for each of the three years in the period ended December 31, 1982, in conformity with generally accepted accounting principles applied on a consistent basis.

Deloitte Haskins & Sells

STATEMENT OF CONSOLIDATED INCOME

For the Years Ended December 31, 1982, 1981 and 1980
(Dollars in Millions Except Per Share Amounts)

	1982	1981	1980
Net Sales (Note 2)	$60,025.6	$62,698.5	$57,728.5
Costs and Expenses			
Cost of sales and other operating charges, exclusive of items listed below	51,548.3	55,185.2	52,099.8
Selling, general and administrative expenses	2,964.9	2,715.0	2,636.7
Depreciation of real estate, plants and equipment	2,403.0	1,837.3	1,458.1
Amortization of special tools	2,147.5	2,568.9	2,719.6
Total Costs and Expenses	59,063.7	62,306.4	58,914.2
Operating Income (Loss)	961.9	392.1	(1,185.7)
Other income less income deductions—net (Note 4)	476.3	367.7	348.7
Interest expense (Note 1)	(1,415.4)	(897.9)	(531.9)
Income (Loss) before Income Taxes	22.8	(138.1)	(1,368.9)
United States, foreign and other income taxes (credit) (Note 6)	(252.2)	(123.1)	(385.3)
Income (Loss) after Income Taxes	275.0	(15.0)	(983.6)
Equity in earnings of nonconsolidated subsidiaries and associates (dividends received amounted to $412.7 in 1982, $189.7 in 1981 and $116.8 in 1980)	687.7	348.4	221.1
Net Income (Loss)	962.7	333.4	(762.5)
Dividends on preferred stocks	12.9	12.9	12.9
Earnings (Loss) on Common Stock	$ 949.8	$ 320.5	($ 775.4)
Average number of shares of common stock outstanding (in millions)	307.4	299.1	292.4
Earnings (Loss) Per Share of Common Stock (Note 7)	$3.09	$1.07	($2.65)

Reference should be made to notes on pages 20 through 26.

CONSOLIDATED BALANCE SHEET

December 31, 1982 and 1981
(Dollars in Millions Except Per Share Amounts)

ASSETS	1982	1981
Current Assets		
Cash	$ 279.6	$ 204.1
United States Government and other marketable securities and time deposits—at cost, which approximates market of $2,835.5 and $1,086.3	2,846.6	1,116.6
Total cash and marketable securities	3,126.2	1,320.7
Accounts and notes receivable (including GMAC and its subsidiaries—$312.0 and $636.2)—less allowances	2,864.5	3,643.3
Inventories (less allowances) (Note 1)	6,184.2	7,222.7
Prepaid expenses and deferred income taxes	1,868.2	1,527.1
Total Current Assets	14,043.1	13,713.8
Equity in Net Assets of Nonconsolidated Subsidiaries and Associates (principally GMAC and its subsidiaries—Note 8)	4,231.1	3,369.5
Other Investments and Miscellaneous Assets—at cost (less allowances)	1,550.0	1,783.5
Common Stock Held for the Incentive Program (Note 3)	35.2	71.5
Property		
Real estate, plants and equipment—at cost (Note 9)	37,687.2	34,811.5
Less accumulated depreciation (Note 9)	18,148.9	16,317.4
Net real estate, plants and equipment	19,538.3	18,494.1
Special tools—at cost (less amortization)	2,000.1	1,546.6
Total Property	21,538.4	20,040.7
Total Assets	$41,397.8	$38,979.0

LIABILITIES AND STOCKHOLDERS' EQUITY		
Current Liabilities		
Accounts payable (principally trade)	$ 3,600.7	$ 3,699.7
Loans payable (principally overseas) (Note 11)	1,182.5	1,727.8
Accrued liabilities (Note 10)	7,601.8	7,127.5
Total Current Liabilities	12,385.0	12,555.0
Long-Term Debt (Note 11)	4,452.0	3,801.1
Capitalized Leases	293.1	242.9
Other Liabilities (including GMAC and its subsidiaries—$876.0 and $424.0)	4,259.8	3,092.7
Deferred Credits (including investment tax credits—$1,158.7 and $1,111.1)	1,720.8	1,566.2
Stockholders' Equity (Notes 3 and 12)		
Preferred stocks ($5.00 series, $183.6; $3.75 series, $100.0)	283.6	283.6
Common stock (issued, 312,363,657 and 304,804,228 shares)	520.6	508.0
Capital surplus (principally additional paid-in capital)	1,930.4	1,589.5
Net income retained for use in the business	15,552.5	15,340.0
Total Stockholders' Equity	18,287.1	17,721.1
Total Liabilities and Stockholders' Equity	$41,397.8	$38,979.0

Reference should be made to notes on pages 20 through 26.
Certain amounts for 1981 have been reclassified to conform with 1982 classifications.

STATEMENT OF CHANGES
IN CONSOLIDATED FINANCIAL POSITION

For the Years Ended December 31, 1982, 1981 and 1980
(Dollars in Millions)

	1982	1981	1980
Source of Funds			
Net income (loss)	$ 962.7	$ 333.4	($ 762.5)
Depreciation of real estate, plants and equipment	2,403.0	1,837.3	1,458.1
Amortization of special tools	2,147.5	2,568.9	2,719.6
Deferred income taxes, undistributed earnings of nonconsolidated subsidiaries and associates, etc.—net	75.8	68.0	311.5
Total funds provided by current operations	5,589.0	4,807.6	3,726.7
Increase in long-term debt	2,497.4	2,172.7	1,305.1
Decrease (Increase) in other working capital items	1,306.2	(341.2)	4,267.7
Proceeds from sale of newly issued common stock	353.5	303.6	271.9
Other—net	1,459.2	1,703.3	95.2
Total	11,205.3	8,646.0	9,666.6
Use of Funds			
Dividends paid to stockholders (Note 12)	750.2	730.5	874.1
Expenditures for real estate, plants and equipment	3,611.1	6,563.3	5,160.5
Expenditures for special tools	2,601.0	3,178.1	2,600.0
Retirements of long-term debt	1,846.5	257.6	299.1
Investments in nonconsolidated subsidiaries and associates	591.0	311.0	4.1
Total	9,399.8	11,040.5	8,937.8
Increase (Decrease) in cash and marketable securities	1,805.5	(2,394.5)	728.8
Cash and marketable securities at beginning of the year	1,320.7	3,715.2	2,986.4
Cash and marketable securities at end of the year	$ 3,126.2	$ 1,320.7	$3,715.2
Decrease (Increase) in Other Working Capital Items by Element			
Accounts and notes receivable	$ 778.8	$ 125.1	$1,262.0
Inventories	1,038.5	72.3	844.1
Prepaid expenses and deferred income taxes	(341.1)	(820.6)	(243.1)
Accounts payable	(99.0)	(268.0)	586.4
Loans payable	(545.3)	51.3	752.4
Accrued liabilities	474.3	498.7	1,065.9
Decrease (Increase) in other working capital items	$ 1,306.2	($ 341.2)	$4,267.7

Reference should be made to notes on pages 20 through 26.
Certain amounts for 1981 and 1980 have been reclassified to conform with 1982 classifications and format.

NOTES TO FINANCIAL STATEMENTS

NOTE 1. Significant Accounting Policies

Principles of Consolidation

The consolidated financial statements include the accounts of the Corporation and all domestic and foreign subsidiaries which are more than 50% owned and engaged principally in manufacturing or wholesale marketing of General Motors products. General Motors' share of earnings or losses of nonconsolidated subsidiaries and of associates in which at least 20% of the voting securities is owned is generally included in consolidated income under the equity method of accounting.

Income Taxes

Investment tax credits are deferred and amortized over the lives of the related assets. The tax effects of timing differences between pretax accounting income and taxable income (principally related to depreciation, sales and product allowances, undistributed earnings of subsidiaries and associates, and benefit plans expense) are deferred. Provisions are made for estimated United States and foreign taxes, less available tax credits and deductions, which may be incurred on remittance of the Corporation's share of subsidiaries' undistributed earnings less those deemed to be permanently reinvested. Possible taxes beyond those provided would not be material.

Inventories

Inventories are stated generally at cost, which is not in excess of market. The cost of substantially all domestic inventories was determined by the last-in, first-out (LIFO) method. If the first-in, first-out (FIFO) method of inventory valuation had been used by the Corporation for U.S. inventories, it is estimated they would be $1,886.0 million higher at December 31, 1982, compared with $2,077.1 million higher at December 31, 1981. As a result of decreases in unit sales and actions taken to reduce inventories, certain LIFO inventory quantities carried at lower costs prevailing in prior years, as compared with the costs of current purchases, were liquidated in 1982, 1981 and 1980. These inventory adjustments favorably affected income (loss) before income taxes by approximately $305.0 million, $89.2 million and $259.2 million in the respective years. The cost of inventories outside the United States was determined generally by the FIFO or the average cost method.

Major Classes of Inventories

(Dollars in Millions)	1982	1981
Productive material, work in process and supplies	$3,774.4	$4,561.5
Finished product, service parts, etc.	2,409.8	2,661.2
Total	$6,184.2	$7,222.7

Depreciation and Amortization

Depreciation is provided on groups of property using, with minor exceptions, an accelerated method which accumulates depreciation of approximately two-thirds of the depreciable cost during the first half of the estimated lives of the property.

Expenditures for special tools are amortized, with the amortization applied directly to the asset account, over short periods of time because the utility value of the tools is radically affected by frequent changes in the design of the functional components and appearance of the product. Replacement of special tools for reasons other than changes in products is charged directly to cost of sales.

Pension Program

The Corporation and its subsidiaries have several pension plans covering substantially all of their employes, including certain employes in foreign countries. Benefits under the plans are generally related to an employe's length of service, wages and salaries, and, where applicable, contributions. The costs of these plans are determined on the basis of actuarial cost methods and include amortization of prior service cost over periods not in excess of 30 years from the later of October 1, 1979 or the date such costs are established. With the exception of certain overseas subsidiaries, pension costs accrued are funded within the limitations set by the Employee Retirement Income Security Act.

Product Related Expenses

Expenditures for advertising and sales promotion and for other product related expenses are charged to costs and expenses as incurred; provisions for estimated costs related to product warranty are made at the time the products are sold.

Expenditures for research and development are charged to expenses as incurred and amounted to $2,175.1 million in 1982, $2,249.6 million in 1981 and $2,224.5 million in 1980.

Foreign Exchange

Exchange and translation activity included in net income in 1982, 1981 and 1980 amounted to gains of $348.4 million, $226.2 million and $164.6 million, respectively. Statement of Financial Accounting Standards No. 8, Accounting for the Translation of Foreign Currency Transactions and Foreign Currency Financial Statements, was applied throughout the three-year period.

Interest Cost

Total interest cost incurred in 1982, 1981 and 1980 amounted to $1,544.6 million, $995.2 million and $567.1 million, respectively, of which $129.2 million, $97.3 million and $35.2 million related to certain real estate, plants and equipment acquired in those years was capitalized.

NOTE 2. Net Sales

(Dollars in Millions)	1982	1981	1980
Net sales includes sales to:			
Nonconsolidated subsidiaries and associates	$ 96.3	$ 130.4	$ 104.1
Dealerships operating under dealership assistance plans	$1,253.7	$1,688.9	$1,456.0

Unrealized intercompany profits on sales to nonconsolidated subsidiaries and to associates are deferred.

NOTES TO FINANCIAL STATEMENTS (continued)

NOTE 3. Incentive Program

The Incentive Program consists of the General Motors Bonus Plan, the General Motors Stock Option Plans and the General Motors Performance Achievement Plan. The By-Laws provide that the Plans in which directors or officers of the Corporation may participate shall be presented for action at a stockholders' meeting at least once in every five years. The Program was last approved by stockholders at the 1982 Annual Meeting which resulted in the adoption of a modified Bonus Plan, the new 1982 Stock Option Plan and the new Performance Achievement Plan.

The modified Bonus Plan includes a new formula, a reduction in the payout period for bonus instalments and provision for the payment of interest equivalents on undelivered cash awards. The 1982 Stock Option Plan includes incentive stock options as provided under the Economic Recovery Tax Act of 1981. The Performance Achievement Plan is based on the achievement of performance levels, established by the Bonus and Salary Committee, over periods of not less than two nor more than five years.

The Corporation maintains a reserve for purposes of the Bonus Plan. For any year, a maximum credit may be made to the reserve equal to the amount which the independent public accountants of the Corporation determine to be 8% of the net earnings which exceed $1 billion, but not in excess of the amount paid out as dividends on the common stock during the year. The Bonus and Salary Committee may, at its discretion, direct that for any year an amount less than the maximum amount available under the formula be credited. Further, the Committee may, but is not obligated to, award as bonus in any year the full amount available in the reserve for such awards. Bonus awards under the Bonus Plan and such other amounts arising out of the operation of the Bonus Plan as the Committee may determine are charged to the reserve.

As a result of low earnings in 1982 and 1981 and a net loss in 1980, no credits were made to the Reserve for the Bonus Plan. Accordingly, the Committee determined that there would be no bonus awards related to the years 1982, 1981 and 1980.

In addition, there was no accrual in 1982 for the Performance Achievement Plan.

Under the provisions of the Bonus Plan, as amended in 1982, participants receive their awards in instalments in as many as three years (five years in the case of awards prior to 1982). Performance Achievement Plan awards are to be paid as soon as is practicable following completion of the performance period. If participants in the Bonus and Stock Option Plans fail to meet conditions precedent to receiving undelivered instalments of bonus awards (and contingent credits related to the Stock Option Plan prior to 1977), the amount of any such instalments is credited to income. Upon the exercise of stock options, any related contingent credits are proportionately reduced and the amount of the reduction is credited to income.

Changes during 1980, 1981 and 1982 in the status of options granted under the Stock Option Plans are shown in the following table. The option prices are 100% of the average of the highest and lowest sales prices of General Motors common stock on the dates the options were granted as reported (1) on the New York Stock Exchange for options granted prior to 1976, and (2) on the Composite Tape of transactions on all major exchanges and nonexchange markets in the U.S. for options granted in 1976 and subsequent years. Incentive stock options expire ten years from date of grant. Nonqualified stock options granted prior to 1982 expire ten years from date of grant and nonqualified stock options granted in 1982 and thereafter expire ten years and two days from date of grant. Options are subject to earlier termination under certain conditions.

The Corporation intends to deliver newly issued stock upon the exercise of any of the options. The maximum number of shares for which additional options might be granted under the Plan was 1,582,170 at January 1, 1980, 1,230,055 at December 31, 1980 and 931,405 at December 31, 1981. Of the 7,500,000 shares authorized for grant under the 1982 Stock Option Plan, 740,420 shares were granted, 1,365 shares were terminated, and the maximum number of shares for which additional options might be granted was 6,760,945 at December 31, 1982.

	Years Granted	Option Prices	Shares Under Option
Outstanding at Jan. 1, 1980	1973-1979	$50.00-$73.38	1,307,024
Granted	1980	53.25	425,590
Terminated	1973-1980		(120,001)
Outstanding at Dec. 31, 1980			1,612,613
Granted	1981	50.00	464,255
Terminated	1973-1981		(269,195)
Outstanding at Dec. 31, 1981			1,807,673
Granted:	March 1982	38.25	897,150
	Oct. 1982	46.50	740,420
Exercised	1980-1981	53.25/50.00	(1,635)
Terminated	1973-1982		(191,469)
Outstanding at Dec. 31, 1982			3,252,139
Options outstanding at Dec. 31, 1982 consisted of:	1973	$73.38	43,956
	1974	50.00	76,718
	1976	65.19	51,960
	1977	66.57	179,510
	1978	63.75	216,075
	1979	59.50	262,770
	1980	53.25	370,230
	1981	50.00	428,310
	March 1982	38.25	883,555
	Oct. 1982	46.50	739,055
Total Shares Under Option			3,252,139

Common stock held for the Incentive Program is stated substantially at cost and used exclusively for payment of Program liabilities.

(Dollars in Millions)	1982 Shares	1982 Amount	1981 Shares	1981 Amount
Balance at Jan. 1	1,177,137	$71.5	2,037,978	$125.8
Acquired during the year	2,039	.1	2,833	.1
Sold to trustee of S-SPP	(2,723)	(.1)	(8,224)	(.5)
Delivered to participants	(584,246)	(36.3)	(855,450)	(53.9)
Balance at Dec. 31	592,207	$35.2	1,177,137	$ 71.5

NOTES TO FINANCIAL STATEMENTS (continued)

NOTE 4. Other Income Less Income Deductions

(Dollars in Millions)	1982	1981	1980
Other income:			
Interest	$483.6	$427.9	$392.1
Other	174.5*	123.6	81.7
Income deductions	(181.8)	(183.8)	(125.1)
Net	$476.3	$367.7	$348.7

*Includes $48.7 million gain from early retirement of long-term debt.

NOTE 5. Pension Program

Total pension expense of the Corporation and its consolidated subsidiaries amounted to $1,565.9 million in 1982, $1,493.8 million in 1981 and $1,922.1 million in 1980. For purposes of determining pension expense, the Corporation uses a variety of assumed rates of return on pension funds in accordance with local practice and regulations, which rates approximated 7% in 1982 and 1981 and 6% in 1980. The increase to 7% in the assumed rate of return used in determining retirement plan costs and other changes in actuarial assumptions made in 1981 reduced retirement plan costs for 1981 by $411.1 million and increased net income by $205.6 million ($0.69 per share). The following table compares accumulated plan benefits and plan net assets for the Corporation's defined benefit plans in the United States as of October 1 (the plans' anniversary date) of both 1982 and 1981:

(Dollars in Millions)	1982	1981
Actuarial present value of accumulated plan benefits:		
Vested	$16,347.8	$15,707.9
Nonvested	1,754.1	1,829.6
Total	$18,101.9	$17,537.5
Net assets available for benefits:		
Trustees	$11,381.7	$ 9,914.7
Insurance companies	3,051.1	2,956.7
Total	$14,432.8	$12,871.4

The assumed rates of return used in determining the actuarial present value of accumulated plan benefits (shown in the table above) were based upon those published by the Pension Benefit Guaranty Corporation, a public corporation established under the Employee Retirement Income Security Act (ERISA). Such rates averaged approximately 10¼% for 1982 and approximately 10% for 1981.

The Corporation's pension plans of subsidiaries outside the United States are not required to report to governmental agencies pursuant to ERISA and the actuarial value of accumulated benefits for these plans has not been determined in the manner calculated and shown above. The total of these plans' pension funds and balance sheet accruals, less pension prepayments and deferred charges, exceeded the actuarially computed value of vested benefits by approximately $242 million at December 31, 1982 and $226 million at December 31, 1981.

NOTE 6. United States, Foreign and Other Income Taxes (Credit)

(Dollars in Millions)	1982	1981	1980
Taxes estimated to be payable (refundable) currently:			
United States Federal	($168.6)	$442.9	($307.7)
Foreign	98.6	62.4	56.2
State and local	(8.1)	41.4	(36.9)
Total	(78.1)	546.7	(288.4)
Taxes deferred—net:			
United States Federal	(146.3)	(829.3)	(342.2)
Foreign	(35.0)	(57.9)	131.9
State and local	(40.4)	(89.6)	(39.0)
Total	(221.7)	(976.8)	(249.3)
Investment tax credits deferred—net:			
United States Federal	85.3	312.6	126.0
Foreign	(37.7)	(5.6)	26.4
Total	47.6	307.0	152.4
Total taxes (credit)	($252.2)	($123.1)	($385.3)

Investment tax credits entering into the determination of taxes estimated to be payable (refundable) currently amounted to $403.0 million in 1982, $592.1 million in 1981 and $350.9 million in 1980.

The deferred taxes (credit) for timing differences consisted principally of the following: 1982—($164.0) million for benefit plans expense, ($172.0) million for sales and product allowances and $275.0 million for depreciation; 1981—($546.3) million for benefit plans expense and ($267.2) million for sales and product allowances; and 1980—($232.1) million for sales and product allowances.

Income (loss) before income taxes included the following components:

(Dollars in Millions)	1982	1981	1980
Domestic income (loss)	$170.4	$288.7	($ 928.6)
Foreign income (loss)	(147.6)	(426.8)	440.3)
Total	$ 22.8	($138.1)	($1,368.9)

The consolidated income tax (credit) was different than the amount computed at the United States statutory income tax rate for the reasons set forth in the table below:

	1982	1981	1980
Expected tax (credit) at U.S. statutory income tax rate	$ 10.5	($ 63.5)	($629.7)
Investment tax credits amortized	(355.4)	(285.1)	(198.5)
Foreign tax rate differential	169.3	213.0	403.7
State and local income taxes	(26.2)	(26.0)	(41.0)
Other adjustments	(50.4)	38.5	80.2
Consolidated income tax (credit)	($252.2)	($123.1)	($385.3)

NOTE 7. Earnings (Loss) Per Share of Common Stock

Earnings (loss) per share of common stock are based on the average number of shares outstanding during each year. The effect on earnings (loss) per share resulting from the assumed exercise of outstanding options and delivery of bonus awards and contingent credits under the Incentive Program is not material.

NOTES TO FINANCIAL STATEMENTS (continued)

NOTE 8. General Motors Acceptance Corporation and Subsidiaries
Condensed Consolidated Balance Sheet (Dollars in Millions)

	1982	1981
Cash and investments in securities	$ 1,674.2	$ 1,709.9
Finance receivables—net (including GM and affiliates—$876.0 and $424.0)	41,771.1	39,692.5
Other assets	969.4	446.2
Total Assets	$44,414.7	$41,848.6
Short-term debt	$22,114.1	$23,256.1
Accounts payable and other liabilities (including GM and affiliates—$312.0 and $636.2)	2,689.0	2,507.5
Long-term debt	15,695.5	12,849.9
Stockholder's equity	3,916.1	3,235.1
Total Liabilities and Stockholder's Equity	$44,414.7	$41,848.6

Condensed Consolidated Statement of Income (Dollars in Millions)

	1982	1981	1980
Gross Revenue	$7,255.4	$6,153.9	$4,566.8
Interest and discount	4,482.1	4,174.7	2,889.6
Other expenses	2,085.3	1,614.0	1,446.2
Total Expenses	6,567.4	5,788.7	4,335.8
Net Income	$ 688.0	$ 365.2	$ 231.0

NOTE 9. Real Estate, Plants and Equipment and Accumulated Depreciation (Dollars in Millions)

	1982	1981
Real estate, plants and equipment (Note 11):		
Land	$ 361.8	$ 350.8
Land improvements	1,136.8	1,026.4
Leasehold improvements—less amortization	41.8	38.4
Buildings	7,921.3	7,159.6
Machinery and equipment	24,802.1	21,470.4
Furniture and office equipment	403.6	350.3
Capitalized leases	711.7	655.4
Construction in progress	2,308.1	3,760.2
Total	$37,687.2	$34,811.5
Accumulated depreciation:		
Land improvements	$ 576.5	$ 530.8
Buildings	3,650.6	3,409.4
Machinery and equipment	13,456.6	11,987.2
Furniture and office equipment	160.9	132.5
Capitalized leases	255.0	208.2
Extraordinary obsolescence	49.3	49.3
Total	$18,148.9	$16,317.4

NOTE 10. Accrued Liabilities
(Dollars in Millions)

	1982	1981
Taxes, other than income taxes	$ 885.1	$ 812.2
Payrolls	1,476.7	1,576.2
Employe benefits	1,111.4	263.8
Dealer and customer allowances, claims, discounts, etc.	2,990.8	2,685.4
Other	1,137.8	1,789.9
Total	$7,601.8	$7,127.5

NOTE 11. Long-Term Debt
(Dollars in Millions)

			1982	1981
GM:				
U.S. dollars:				
10% Notes		1984-86	$ 200.0	$ 200.0
8.05% Notes		1985	300.0	300.0
12.2% Notes		1986-88	200.0	200.0
8.03% Adjustable Rate Notes		1989	400.0	–
10% Notes		1991	237.5	200.0
8⅝% Debentures		2005	160.1	300.0
Other	6.5%	1984-2000	91.9	219.3
Other currencies	10.6%	1984-89	411.6	271.7
Consolidated subsidiaries:				
U.S. dollars	11.5%	1984-93	931.6	829.9
Spanish pesetas	14.0%	1984-90	680.0	188.3
Australian dollars	12.6%	1984-89	213.9	8.5
Brazilian cruzeiros	38.7%	1984-87	183.0	17.4
Austrian schillings	7.5%	1984-87	150.7	64.5
Venezuelan bolivars	14.7%	1984	127.9	60.0
Mexican pesos	20.1%	1984	65.1	4.8
French francs	13.9%	1984-86	49.9	25.9
German marks	7.6%	1984-96	38.9	248.3
Canadian dollars			–	687.9
Other currencies	Various	1984-2004	120.1	89.3
Total			4,562.2	3,915.8
Less unamortized discount (principally on 10% notes due 1991)			110.2	114.7
Total			$4,452.0	$3,801.1

At year-end 1982, the Corporation and its consolidated subsidiaries had unused short-term credit lines of approximately $2.4 billion and unused long-term credit agreements of approximately $2.7 billion. Long-term debt at December 31, 1982 and 1981 included approximately $2,032 million and $660 million, respectively, of short-term obligations which are intended to be renewed or refinanced under long-term credit agreements. Long-term debt (including current portion) bore interest at a weighted average rate of approximately 13.3% at December 31, 1982 and 12.7% at December 31, 1981.

(continued)

NOTES TO FINANCIAL STATEMENTS (continued)

NOTE 11. (concluded)

In 1981, the Corporation and a subsidiary arranged a private financing of $500 million in 10% notes due 1991, of which $400 million was outstanding at December 31, 1981 and $475 million at December 31, 1982. The difference between the 10% stated interest rate and the effective rates at dates of issuance (15.45%-1981; 12.07%-1982) reflects the discount which is being amortized over the lives of the notes. An option to acquire certain real estate in 1991 was also granted. The option holder may deliver the notes in payment for the real estate.

Under the sinking fund provisions of the trust indenture for the Corporation's 8⅝% Debentures due 2005, the Corporation is to make annual sinking fund payments of $11.8 million in each of the years 1998 through 2004.

Maturities of long-term debt in the years 1983 through 1987 are (in millions) $465.4 (included in loans payable at December 31, 1982), $1,068.7, $741.8, $615.9 and $313.7. Loans payable at December 31, 1981 included $186.4 million current portion of long-term debt.

NOTE 12. Stockholders' Equity (Dollars in Millions Except Per Share Amounts)	1982	1981	1980
Capital Stock:			
Preferred Stock, without par value, cumulative dividends (authorized, 6,000,000 shares), no change during the year:			
$5.00 series, stated value $100 per share, redeemable at Corporation option at $120 per share (issued, 1,875,366 shares; in treasury, 39,722 shares; outstanding, 1,835,644 shares)	$ 183.6	$ 183.6	$ 183.6
$3.75 series, stated value $100 per share, redeemable at Corporation option at $100 per share (issued and outstanding, 1,000,000 shares)	100.0	100.0	100.0
Common Stock, $1⅔ par value (authorized, 500,000,000 shares):			
Issued at beginning of the year (304,804,228 shares in 1982, 298,053,782 in 1981 and 292,472,499 in 1980)	508.0	496.7	487.4
Newly issued stock sold under provisions of the Stock Option Plans, Employe Stock Ownership Plans, Savings-Stock Purchase Programs and the Dividend Reinvestment Plan (6,459,429 shares in 1982, 6,750,446 in 1981 and 5,581,283 in 1980) and exchanged for long-term debt (1,100,000 shares in 1982)	12.6	11.3	9.3
Issued at end of the year (312,363,657 shares in 1982, 304,804,228 in 1981 and 298,053,782 in 1980)	520.6	508.0	496.7
Total capital stock at end of the year	804.2	791.6	780.3
Capital Surplus (principally additional paid-in capital):			
Balance at beginning of the year	1,589.5	1,297.2	1,034.6
Proceeds in excess of par value of newly issued common stock sold under provisions of the Stock Option Plans, Employe Stock Ownership Plans, Savings-Stock Purchase Programs and the Dividend Reinvestment Plan and, in 1982, exchanged for long-term debt	340.9	292.3	262.6
Balance at end of the year	1,930.4	1,589.5	1,297.2
Net Income Retained for Use in the Business:			
Balance at beginning of the year	15,340.0	15,737.1	17,373.7
Net income (loss)	962.7	333.4	(762.5)
Total	16,302.7	16,070.5	16,611.2
Cash dividends:			
Preferred stock, $5.00 series, $5.00 per share	9.2	9.2	9.2
Preferred stock, $3.75 series, $3.75 per share	3.7	3.7	3.7
Common stock, $2.40 per share in 1982 and 1981 and $2.95 in 1980	737.3	717.6	861.2
Total cash dividends	750.2	730.5	874.1
Balance at end of the year	15,552.5	15,340.0	15,737.1
Total Stockholders' Equity	$18,287.1	$17,721.1	$17,814.6

The preferred stock is subject to redemption at the option of the Board of Directors on any dividend date on not less than thirty days' notice at the redemption prices stated above plus accrued dividends.

The Certificate of Incorporation provides that no cash dividends may be paid on the common stock so long as current assets (excluding prepaid expenses) in excess of current liabilities of the Corporation are less than $75 per share of outstanding preferred stock. Such current assets (with inventories calculated on the FIFO basis) in excess of current liabilities were greater than $75 in respect of each share of outstanding preferred stock at December 31, 1982.

The equity of the Corporation and its consolidated subsidiaries in the accumulated net loss, since acquisition, of associates has been included in net income retained for use in the business.

NOTES TO FINANCIAL STATEMENTS (concluded)

NOTE 13. Segment Reporting

General Motors is a highly vertically-integrated business operating primarily in a single industry consisting of the manufacture, assembly and sale of automobiles, trucks and related parts and accessories classified as automotive products. Because of the high degree of integration, substantial interdivisional and intercompany transfers of materials and services are made. Consequently, any determination of income by area of operations or class of products is necessarily arbitrary because of the allocation and reallocation of costs, including Corporate costs, benefiting more than one division or product.

Substantially all of General Motors' products are marketed through retail dealers and through distributors and jobbers in the United States and Canada and through distributors and dealers overseas.

To assist in the merchandising of General Motors' products, GMAC and its subsidiaries offer financial services and certain types of automobile insurance to dealers and customers.

Net sales, net income (loss), total and net assets and average number of employes in the U.S. and in locations outside the U.S. for 1982, 1981 and 1980 are summarized below. Net income (loss) is after provisions for deferred income taxes applicable to that portion of the undistributed earnings deemed to be not permanently invested, less available tax credits and deductions, and appropriate consolidating adjustments for the geographic areas set forth below. Interarea sales are made at negotiated selling prices.

1982	United States	Canada	Europe	Latin America	All Other	Total[1]
Net Sales:			(Dollars in Millions)			
Outside	$45,650.1	$2,621.9	$7,150.5	$2,699.5	$1,903.6	$60,025.6
Interarea	4,673.8	5,350.7	234.3	310.2	192.9	–
Total net sales	$50,323.9	$7,972.6	$7,384.8	$3,009.7	$2,096.5	$60,025.6
Net Income (Loss)	$ 1,079.3	($ 33.5)	$ 6.2	($ 16.5)	($ 63.2)	$ 962.7
Total Assets	$29,227.4	$2,299.0	$5,952.3	$2,973.3	$1,063.5	$41,397.8
Net Assets	$15,756.0	$ 774.7	$ 803.3	$ 894.3	$ 170.7	$18,287.1
Average Number of Employes (in thousands)	441	34	114	38	30	657

1981						
Net Sales:						
Outside	$47,022.4	$4,099.2	$6,585.2	$2,730.0	$2,261.7	$62,698.5
Interarea	5,731.1	4,747.2	265.6	129.9	128.1	–
Total net sales	$52,753.5	$8,846.4	$6,850.8	$2,859.9	$2,389.8	$62,698.5
Net Income (Loss)	$ 763.3	($ 35.6)	($ 426.7)	($ 62.6)	$ 129.2	$ 333.4
Total Assets	$27,510.8	$2,772.8	$5,208.5	$2,642.8	$ 980.3	$38,979.0
Net Assets	$15,608.7	$ 832.6	$ 505.5	$ 640.7	$ 247.3	$17,721.1
Average Number of Employes (in thousands)	522	39	113	38	29	741

1980						
Net Sales:						
Outside	$41,637.4	$4,218.0	$7,437.6	$2,448.4	$1,987.1	$57,728.5
Interarea	5,287.1	3,876.7	317.5	72.3	64.3	–
Total net sales	$46,924.5	$8,094.7	$7,755.1	$2,520.7	$2,051.4	$57,728.5
Net Income (Loss)	($ 71.9)	($ 20.3)	($ 559.3)	$ 42.9	($ 150.8)	($ 762.5)
Total Assets	$25,494.2	$1,891.0	$4,319.3	$1,953.2	$1,029.9	$34,581.0
Net Assets	$15,753.6	$ 791.9	$ 670.6	$ 528.8	$ 152.0	$17,814.6
Average Number of Employes (in thousands)	517	37	125	37	30	746

[1]After elimination of interarea transactions.

NOTE 14. Contingent Liabilities

There are various claims and pending actions against the Corporation and its subsidiaries with respect to commercial matters, including warranties and product liability, governmental regulations including environmental and safety matters, civil rights, patent matters, taxes and other matters arising out of the conduct of the business. Certain of these actions purport to be class actions, seeking damages in very large amounts. The amounts of liability on these claims and actions at December 31, 1982 were not determinable but, in the opinion of the management, the ultimate liability resulting will not materially affect the consolidated financial position or results of operations of the Corporation and its consolidated subsidiaries.

SUPPLEMENTARY INFORMATION

Selected Quarterly Data (Dollars in Millions Except Per Share Amounts)

	1982 Quarters				1981 Quarters			
	1st	2nd	3rd	4th	1st	2nd	3rd	4th
Net sales	$14,721.4	$17,144.6	$14,282.6	$13,877.0	$15,723.9	$18,015.1	$13,410.2	$15,549.3
Operating income (loss)	(7.4)	863.3	(53.6)	159.6	267.4	1,029.2	(959.5)	55.0
Income (loss) before income taxes	(259.7)	665.4	(236.8)	(146.1)	261.5	892.4	(1,155.8)	136.2
United States, foreign and other income taxes (credit)	(256.8)	236.3	(151.5)	(80.2)	130.8	446.2	(585.0)	115.1
Income (loss) after income taxes	(2.9)	429.1	(85.3)	(65.9)	130.7	446.2	(570.8)	21.1
Equity in earnings of nonconsolidated subsidiaries and associates	131.2	130.9	214.7	210.9	59.6	68.4	102.6	117.8
Net income (loss)	128.3	560.0	129.4	145.0	190.3	514.6	(468.2)	96.7
Dividends on preferred stocks	3.2	3.3	3.2	3.2	3.2	3.3	3.2	3.2
Earnings (loss) on common stock	$ 125.1	$ 556.7	$ 126.2	$ 141.8	$ 187.1	$ 511.3	($ 471.4)	$ 93.5
Average number of shares of common stock outstanding (in millions)	304.7	306.8	307.6	310.5	297.2	298.2	299.2	301.6
Earnings (loss) per share of common stock*	$0.41	$1.82	$0.41	$0.45	$0.63	$1.72	($1.59)	$0.31
Dividends per share of common stock	$0.60	$0.60	$0.60	$0.60	$0.60	$0.60	$0.60	$0.60
Stock price range**								
High	$41.38	$47.13	$50.13	$64.50	$56.13	$58.00	$53.13	$46.50
Low	$34.00	$40.13	$39.63	$46.25	$43.88	$51.38	$42.63	$33.88

*Includes favorable (unfavorable) effects on EPS of: early retirement of long-term debt of $0.16 in the second quarter of 1982 (included in other income); foreign exchange/translation activity [1982: first quarter—$0.83, second quarter—$0.25, third quarter—($0.07), fourth quarter—$0.05; 1981: first quarter—$0.19, second quarter—$0.45, third quarter—$0.64, fourth quarter—($0.53)]; and reductions in accruals due to salaried policy modifications in the fourth quarter of 1981—$0.25.

**The principal market is the New York Stock Exchange and prices are based on the Composite Tape. Common stock is also listed on the Midwest, Pacific and Philadelphia stock exchanges. As of December 31, 1982, there were 1,035,162 holders of record of common stock.

The net credits for income taxes in the 1982 quarters reflect the relatively low level of earnings combined with the favorable impact of U.S. investment tax credits. The effective income tax rate (credit) in the fourth quarter of 1981 was higher than would be expected as a result of the combination of the high level of U.S. investment tax credits and the low level of earnings.

Selected Financial Data (Dollars in Millions Except Per Share Amounts)

	1982	1981	1980	1979	1978
Net sales	$60,025.6	$62,698.5	$57,728.5	$66,311.2	$63,221.1
Earnings (loss) on common stock	$ 949.8	$ 320.5	($ 775.4)	$ 2,879.8	$ 3,495.1
Dividends on common stock	737.3	717.6	861.2	1,520.3	1,712.6
Net income (loss) retained in the year	$ 212.5	($ 397.1)	($ 1,636.6)	$ 1,359.5	$ 1,782.5
Earnings (loss) on common stock—per share	$3.09	$1.07	($2.65)	$10.04	$12.24
Dividends on common stock—per share	2.40	2.40	2.95	5.30	6.00
Net income (loss) retained in the year—per share	$0.69	($1.33)	($5.60)	$ 4.74	$ 6.24
Average shares of common stock outstanding (in millions)	307.4	299.1	292.4	286.8	285.5
Dividends on capital stock as a percent of net income	77.9%	219.1%	N.A.	53.0%	49.2%
Expenditures for real estate, plants and equipment	$ 3,611.1	$ 6,563.3	$ 5,160.5	$ 3,351.3	$ 2,695.5
Expenditures for special tools	$ 2,601.0	$ 3,178.1	$ 2,600.0	$ 2,015.0	$ 1,826.7
Cash and marketable securities	$ 3,126.2	$ 1,320.7	$ 3,715.2	$ 2,986.4	$ 4,054.8
Working capital	$ 1,658.1	$ 1,158.8	$ 3,212.1	$ 6,751.0	$ 7,991.2
Total assets	$41,397.8	$38,979.0	$34,581.0	$32,215.8	$30,598.3
Long-term debt and capitalized leases	$ 4,745.1	$ 4,044.0	$ 2,058.3	$ 1,030.8	$ 1,124.5

EFFECTS OF INFLATION ON FINANCIAL DATA

Inflation remains the nemesis of the orderly conduct of business. Its adverse ramifications are dramatized when the effects of inflation are taken into account in the evaluation of comparative financial results.

The accompanying Schedules display the basic historical cost financial data adjusted for general inflation (constant dollar) and also for changes in specific prices (current cost) for use in such evaluation. The Schedules are intended to help readers of financial data assess results in the following specific areas:

    a. The erosion of general purchasing power,
    b. Enterprise performance,
    c. The erosion of operating capability, and
    d. Future cash flows.

In reviewing these Schedules, the following comments may be of assistance in understanding the reasons for the different "income" amounts and the uses of the data.

Financial statements—historical cost method

The objective of financial statements, and the primary purpose of accounting, is to furnish, to the fullest extent practicable, objective, quantifiable summaries of the results of financial transactions to those who need or wish to judge management's ability to manage. The data are prepared by management and audited by the independent public accountants.

The present accounting system in general use in the United States and the financial statements prepared by major companies from that system were never intended to be measures of relative economic value, but instead are basically a history of transactions which have occurred and by which current and potential investors and creditors can evaluate their expectations. There are many subjective, analytical, and economic factors which must be taken into consideration when evaluating a company. Those factors cannot be quantified objectively. Just as the financial statements cannot present in reasonable, objective, quantifiable form all of the data necessary to evaluate a business, they also should not be expected to furnish all the data needed to evaluate the effects of inflation on a company.

Data adjusted for general inflation—constant dollar method

Financial reporting is, of necessity, stated in dollars. It is generally recognized that the purchasing power of a dollar has deteriorated in recent years, and the costs of raw materials and other items as well as wage rates have increased and can be expected to increase further in the future. It is not as generally recognized, however, that profit dollars also are subject to the same degree of reduction in purchasing power. Far too much attention is given to the absolute level of profits rather than the relationship of profits to other factors in the business and to the general price level. For example, as shown in Schedule A, adjusting the annual amount of sales and net income (loss) to a constant 1967 dollar base, using the U.S. Bureau of Labor Statistics' Consumer Price Index for Urban Consumers (CPI-U), demonstrates that constant dollar profits have not changed in recent years in line with the changes in sales volume. This is reflected in the general decline in the net income (loss) as a percent of sales over that period as well as the decrease in the dividends paid in terms of constant dollars of purchasing power.

The constant dollar income statement contains only two basic adjustments. Most importantly, the provision for depreciation and amortization is recalculated. Historical dollar accounting understates the economic cost of property (including special tools) consumed in production because the depreciation and amortization charges are based on the original dollar cost of assets acquired over a

period of years. Constant dollar depreciation and amortization restates such expense based on asset values adjusted to reflect increases in the CPI-U subsequent to acquisition or construction of the related property. In addition to recalculating depreciation and amortization expense, cost of sales is adjusted to reflect changes in the CPI-U for the portion of inventories not stated on the last-in, first-out (LIFO) basis in the conventional financial statements. Other items of income and expense are not adjusted because they generally reflect transactions that took place in 1982 and, therefore, were recorded in average 1982 dollars.

Data adjusted for changes in specific prices—current cost method

Another manner in which to analyze the effects of inflation on financial data (and thus the business) is by adjusting the historical cost data to the current costs for the major balance sheet items which have been accumulated through the accounting system over a period of years and which thus reflect different prices for the same commodities and services.

The purpose of this type of restatement is to furnish estimates of the effects of price increases for replacement of inventories and property on the potential future net income of the business and thus assess the probability of future cash flows. Although these data may be useful for this purpose, they do not reflect specific plans for the replacement of property. A more meaningful estimate of the effects of such costs on future earnings is the estimated level of future capital expenditures which is set forth on page 16 in the Financial Review: Management's Discussion and Analysis.

Summary

In the accompanying Schedules, the effects of the application of the preceding methods on the last five years' and the current year's operations are summarized. Under both the constant dollar and the current cost methods, the net income of General Motors is lower (or the net loss is higher) than that determined under the historical cost method. This means that business, as well as individuals, is affected by inflation and that the purchasing power of business dollars also has declined. In addition, the costs of maintaining the productive capacity, as reflected in the current cost data (and estimate of future capital expenditures), have increased, and thus management must seek ways to cope with the effects of inflation through accounting methods such as the LIFO method of inventory valuation, which matches current costs with current revenues, and through accelerated methods of depreciation.

Another significant adjustment is the restatement of stockholders' equity—the investment base. The adjustment for general inflation puts all the expenditures for these items on a consistent purchasing power basis—the average 1967 dollar. This adjustment decreases the historical stockholders' equity, as represented by net assets in Schedule A, of about $18.3 billion at December 31, 1982 to a constant dollar basis of $10.1 billion. In other words, the $18.3 billion represented in the financial statements has only $10.1 billion of purchasing power expressed in 1967 dollars. The net assets adjusted for specific prices, as shown in Schedule A, amounted to $9.8 billion at December 31, 1982. This is $0.3 billion lower than that shown on a constant dollar basis due to the fact that the CPI-U index is not accelerating as rapidly as the indices of specific prices applicable to General Motors.

Finally, it must be emphasized that there is a continuing need for national monetary and fiscal policies designed to control inflation and to provide adequate capital for future business growth which, in turn, will mean increased productivity and employment.

SCHEDULE A

Comparison of Selected Data Adjusted for Effects of Changing Prices
(Dollars in Millions Except Per Share Amounts)
Historical cost data adjusted for general inflation (constant dollar) and changes in specific prices (current cost). (A)

	1982	1981	1980	1979	1978
Net Sales—as reported	$60,025.6	$62,698.5	$57,728.5	$66,311.2	$63,221.1
—in constant 1967 dollars	20,762.9	23,017.1	23,390.8	30,501.9	32,354.7
Net Income (Loss)—as reported	$ 962.7	$ 333.4	($ 762.5)	$ 2,892.7	$ 3,508.0
—in constant 1967 dollars	(38.9)(B)(	305.8) (	1,023.8) (	817.0	1,384.5
—in current cost 1967 dollars	71.7 (B)(	252.8) (	829.5)	829.5	
Earnings (Loss) per share of common stock					
—as reported	$3.09	$1.07	($2.65)	$10.04	$12.24
—in constant 1967 dollars	(0.14)(B)	(1.04)	(3.52)	2.83	4.83
—in current cost 1967 dollars	0.22 (B)	(0.86)	(2.86)	2.87	
Dividends per share of common stock—as reported	$2.40	$2.40	$2.95	$5.30	$6.00
—in constant 1967 dollars	0.83	0.88	1.20	2.44	3.07
Net income (loss) as a percent of sales					
—as reported	1.6%	0.5%	(1.3%)	4.4%	5.5%
—in constant 1967 dollars	(0.2)	(1.3)	(4.4)	2.7	4.3
—in current cost 1967 dollars	0.3	(1.1)	(3.5)	2.7	
Net income (loss) as a percent of stockholders' equity					
—as reported	5.3%	1.9%	(4.3%)	15.1%	20.0%
—in constant 1967 dollars	(0.4)	(3.0)	(9.4)	6.7	11.2
—in current cost 1967 dollars	0.7	(2.4)	(7.3)	6.4	
Net assets at year-end—as reported	$18,287.1	$17,721.1	$17,814.6	$19,179.3	$17,569.9
—in constant 1967 dollars	10,153.9	10,247.2	10,887.6	12,163.4	12,351.3
—in current cost 1967 dollars	9,818.3	10,450.9	11,377.2	12,982.7	
Unrealized gain from decline in purchasing power of dollars of net amounts owed	$ 130.5	$ 241.3	$ 182.3	$ 83.8	
Excess of increase in general price level over increase in specific prices of inventory and property	$ 861.2	$ 619.0	$ 689.2	$ 221.8	
Market price per common share at year-end					
—unadjusted	$62.38	$38.50	$45.00	$50.00	$53.75
—in constant 1967 dollars	21.58	14.13	18.23	23.00	27.51
Average Consumer Price Index	289.1	272.4	246.8	217.4	195.4

(A) Adjusted data have been determined by applying the Consumer Price Index —Urban to the data with 1967 (CPI-100) as the base year. Depreciation has been determined on a straight-line basis for this calculation.

(B) These amounts will differ from those shown for constant dollar and current cost in Schedule B because a different base year (1982) has been used in Schedule B in order to illustrate the effect of changing prices in an alternative form.

SCHEDULE B

Schedule of Income Adjusted for Changing Prices
For the Year Ended December 31, 1982
(Dollars in Millions Except Per Share Amounts)

	As Reported in the Financial Statements (Historical Cost)	Adjusted for General Inflation (1982 Constant Dollar)	Adjusted for Changes in Specific Prices (1982 Current Cost)
Net Sales	$60,025.6	$60,025.6	$60,025.6
Cost of sales	51,548.3	52,339.7	51,915.1
Depreciation and amortization expense	4,550.5	4,833.5	4,939.1
Other operating and nonoperating items—net	3,216.3	3,216.3	3,216.3
United States and other income taxes (credit)	(252.2)	(252.2)	(252.2)
Total costs and expenses	59,062.9	60,137.3	59,818.3
Net Income (Loss)	$ 962.7	($ 111.7)(A)	$ 207.3(A)
Earnings (Loss) per share of common stock	$3.09	($0.41)(A)	$0.63(A)
Unrealized gain from decline in purchasing power of dollars of net amounts owed		$ 377.4	$ 377.4
Excess of increase in general price level over increase in specific prices of inventory and property			$ 2,490.1(B)

(A) These amounts will differ from those shown for constant dollar and current cost in Schedule A because a different base year (1967) has been used in Schedule A in order to illustrate the effect of changing prices in an alternative form.

(B) At December 31, 1982, current cost of inventory was $8,070.2 million and current cost of property (including special tools), net of accumulated depre- ciation and amortization, was $29,750.1 million. The current cost of property owned and the related depreciation and amortization expense were cal- culated by applying (1) selected producer price indices to historical book values of machinery and equipment and (2) the Marshall Valuation Service index to buildings, and the use of assessed values for land.

APPENDIX **D**

Alternate Problems

ALTERNATE PROBLEMS FOR SECTION 1.B

Alternate 1.B.5. Donally Company shows the following selected data on June 30.

Accounts payable	$6,400
Equipment	7,000
Supplies	2,200
D. Donally, capital	?
Building	8,000
Land	2,000

Required

Prepare a balance sheet that includes the missing amount for owner's equity.

Servo Company's revenues and expenses for the accounting year ended September 30 are provided below

Service revenue	$110,000
Wage expense	68,000
Rent expense	3,600
Telephone and postage expense	1,700
Supplies expense	250
Insurance expense	2,800

Required

Prepare an income statement for the year.

D-1

ALTERNATE PROBLEMS FOR CHAPTER 1

Alternate 1.1. Paula Kimbal established her own advertising agency on May 1 of this year. She does not expect to be able to hire any employees for several months. During the first month of business, Kimbal Ad Agency experienced the following transactions.

Transactions

a) Paula deposited $15,000 of personal funds in a bank account in the firm's name.

b) Purchased office equipment for $8,640 on account. The equipment is expected to last for six years, after which it will be worthless.

c) Purchased advertising supplies for $690 cash.

d) Billed clients $1,200 for services rendered.

e) Paid $800 office rental charge for May.

f) Paid $5,000 on the account incurred for purchase of office equipment.

g) Billed clients $1,800 for services performed.

h) Collected $1,200 on accounts receivable.

i) Paula withdrew $1,300 of cash from the business for her own personal use.

j) Received a $210 electric bill for May. Payment of the bill is due on June 20.

k) Work was performed in May for which clients will be billed $660 during June. Paula could not find time during May to prepare and mail the bills.

l) A count of advertising supplies shows supplies costing $430 are still on hand at the end of May.

Required

1) Reflect the foregoing transactions, including any needed month-end adjustments, into an accounting equation like the following.

		Assets			=	**Liabilities**	+	**Owner's Equity**
		Accounts	Advertising	Office		Accounts		P. Kimbal,
Cash	+	Receivable	+ Supplies	+ Equipment	=	Payable	+	Capital

2) Total the account categories and make sure the equation is in balance.

3) Prepare an income statement for the month of May.

4) Prepare a balance sheet that shows the firm's position at month-end.

5) Which of the accounting concepts governed the way you chose to handle transaction (k)? Explain.

6) State why you did, or did not, include the owner's withdrawal—transaction (i)—in the income statement.

Alternate 1.2. Otto Randal, an instructor at Central College, decided to start a part-time accounting and tax practice. Otto Randal, CPA, was involved in the following transactions during January of this year, its first month of operations.

Transactions

a) Otto withdrew $6,000 from his personal savings account and deposited the amount in a business checking account for Otto Randal, CPA.

b) Otto wrote a check for $400 to pay January rental for office space.

c) Purchased a used desk-top printing calculator for $360 on account (for credit). The calculator is expected to last for three years, after which it will be worthless.

d) Wrote a $120 check for various office supplies.

e) Wrote a check for $3,840 for used office furniture. Otto plans to use the furniture for four years, after which he will junk it and purchase more suitable furniture.

f) Sent bills totaling $320 to clients for services rendered during January.

g) Wrote a check for $100 to apply against the obligation incurred for purchase of the calculator—transaction (c).

h) Otto wrote and cashed a $250 business check to obtain money for personal use.

i) Collected and deposited $120 of cash received on account from a client.

j) Received a $20 phone bill for the office telephone. The charges are for the month of January, but will not be paid until some time during February.

k) At month-end, Otto established that office supplies costing $80 are still on hand, the remainder having been used during January.

Required

1) Reflect the foregoing transactions, including any end-of-month adjustments that are necessary, into an accounting equation like the following. Then total the account categories to make sure the equation is in balance after all transactions are reflected.

Assets = **Liabilities + Owner's Equity**

	Accounts	Office			Accounts	Otto Randal,
Cash +	Receivable +	Supplies +	Calculator +	Furniture =	Payable +	Capital

2) Prepare an income statement for the month of January.

3) Prepare a balance sheet that shows the firm's position at month-end.

4) Which of the accounting concepts discussed in this chapter were involved in your month-end adjustments for office supplies and depreciation?

5) Comment on the implications of the net loss shown on the income statement for January. Do you think that such losses are unusual for new business concerns? Why?

ALTERNATE PROBLEMS FOR SECTION 2.A

Alternate 2.A.5. The following transactions were experienced by John's Laundry during July.

Transactions

a) John Bea invested $5,000 to start a commercial laundry business.

b) The business borrowed $4,000 from a bank by signing a note payable.

c) Equipment costing $10,000 was purchased for $3,000 cash and a note payable for the remainder.

d) Supplies costing $500 were purchased on account.

e) A $600 payment was made on notes payable.

f) Cash revenue of $2,100 was collected.

g) Revenue of $700 was earned but not yet collected.

h) Wages of $1,200 were paid in cash.

i) Rent expense of $700 was paid in cash.

j) Supplies worth $130 were still on hand at month-end.

k) Equipment depreciation of $200 was recognized.

l) John withdrew $1,000 from the business for personal use.

Required

1) Prepare T-accounts that reflect the July transactions.

2) Prepare an income statement for July.

3) Prepare a statement of owner's capital for July.

4) Prepare a balance sheet at month-end.

Alternate 2.A.6. The following transactions were experienced by the James Company.

Transactions

a) The owner, Harry James, invested $15,000 in the business.

b) The company borrowed $20,000 from the bank.

c) Machinery costing $10,000 was purchased for cash.

d) A payment of $2,000 was made on the bank loan.

e) Harry withdrew $700 from the business for his personal use.

f) Office supplies were purchased on credit for $50.

Required

1) Record each of the transactions in T-accounts by debiting and crediting the accounts affected.

2) The accounting equation $A = L + OE$ will exist if your work in requirement (1) was correctly done. Show that the sum of the asset T-account balances is equal to the sum of the liability and owner's equity T-account balances.

Alternate 2.A.7. The following T-accounts show the status of Green Company at April 30.

Cash		Accounts Payable		D. Green, Capital	
10,000	2,000		50		5,000
4,000	300				
	1,000				
	260				
	3,100				
	900				
	600				

Accounts Receivable		Note Payable		D. Green, Withdrawals	
4,000		300	5,000	800	

Office Supplies		Wage Expense		Service Revenue	
50	85	3,000			4,000
165					8,000

Equipment		Rent Expense	
5,000		1,400	

Accum. Depr. — Equip.		Supplies Expense	
	100	80	

Insurance Expense	
1,500	

Depreciation Expense	
100	

Required

1) Prepare an income statement for the month of April.

2) Prepare a balance sheet at April 30.

Alternate 2.A.8. Sue Smith established a dress shop during June. The following transactions took place during that month.

Transactions

a) Sue Smith invested $20,000 cash to start the business.

b) Purchased a piece of land for $15,000 and a building for $25,000 by paying $10,000 cash and assuming a $30,000 mortgage.

c) Equipment costing $2,500 was purchased on account.

d) Office supplies of $80 were purchased for cash.

e) Paid $1,200 on accounts payable.

f) Borrowed $8,000 cash from the bank by signing a note.

g) Acquired some adjacent land for $5,000 cash in order to expand parking facilities.

h) Paid $700 for office supplies.

i) Smith transferred equipment valued at $1,500 to the entity. This equipment had been used in another business owned by Smith.

Required

1) For each of the above transactions, indicate which accounts will be debited and which will be credited, and by how much.

2) Set up T-accounts and record the transactions.

3) Compute the balance in each T-account and prepare a list of account titles and balances.

4) Prepare a balance sheet for June 30.

ALTERNATE PROBLEMS FOR SECTION 2.B

Alternate 2.B.5. Alma Crual completed the requirements for a CPA certificate in June and decided to start her own accounting firm. The transactions for July for Alma Crual, CPA, are as follows:

Transactions

July 1	Alma deposited $3,000 in the new business's bank account (Deposit No. 1).
6	Purchased office furniture costing $2,000 on account.
10	Purchased office supplies costing $250 for cash (Check No. 101).
18	Purchased an electronic calculator for $850 cash (Check No. 102).
25	Alma invested another $1,000 cash in the business (Deposit No. 2).
28	Paid for furniture purchased on July 6, $2,000 (Check No. 103).
31	Purchased office supplies on account, $50.

Required

1) Make journal entries to record the July transactions. Use account titles that are brief and descriptive.

2) Set up ledger accounts and post the July journal entries to them.

3) Prepare a trial balance at July 31.

4) Prepare a balance sheet at July 31.

Alternate 2.B.6. Following are transactions for Ward Company for the month of April.

Transactions

Apr. 2   Collected $600 of accounts receivable that had been recorded in previous months (Deposit No. 410).

10   Collected $500 for services performed for customers in April (Deposit No. 411).

15   Paid April rent on building, $300 (Check No. 1032).

17   Paid balance due to College Service Station for gasoline purchased on credit during March, $250 (Check No. 1033).

20   Collected $675 for services performed for customers in April (Deposit No. 412).

26   Mary Ward withdrew $425 for personal use (Check No. 1034).

31   Paid employee wages for April, $950 (Check No. 1035).

31   Received bill for $230 from College Service Station for gasoline purchased on credit during April.

31   Billed customers $820 for services performed in April (cash to be collected in May).

31   Monthly depreciation on the company truck was $200.

Required

1) Journalize the foregoing transactions on journal page 20. Choose titles that are brief and descriptive.

2) From the transactions journalized, prepare an income statement for April (without posting the entries to ledger accounts).

Alternate 2.B.7. Following are June transactions and the chart of accounts for the Ford Company.

Transactions

June 4   Paid $500 on accounts payable (Check No. 701).

6   Owner withdrew $350 for personal use (Check No. 702).

7   Collected $320 of accounts receivable (Deposit No. 154).

9   Collected $625 cash for services rendered in June (Deposit No. 155).

10   Purchased equipment for $5,000, paying $500 down (Check No. 703) and signing a note for the remaining cost.

15   Paid June rent on building, $475 (Check No. 704).

30   Paid June wages of $1,500 (Check No. 705).

30   Received bill for utilities used in June, $100.

30   Billed customers $3,300 for services rendered in June (to be collected in July).

30   Equipment depreciation for June was $350.

FORD COMPANY
Chart of Accounts

100 Assets	*300 Owner's Equity*
111 Cash	311 T. Ford, Capital
112 Accounts Receivable	312 T. Ford, Withdrawals
121 Equipment	*400 Revenue*
0121 Accumulated Depreciation—	411 Service Revenue
Equipment	*500 Expenses*
	511 Rent Expense
200 Liabilities	512 Wage Expense
211 Accounts Payable	513 Utilities Expense
212 Note Payable	514 Depreciation Expense

Required

Journalize the transactions on journal page 3.

Alternate 2.B.8. A chart of accounts and a number of journal entries for the Scott Company follow. Georgia Scott started the business on March 1.

SCOTT COMPANY
Chart of Accounts

10 Assets	*30 Owner's Equity*
11 Cash	31 G. Scott, Capital
12 Accounts Receivable	32 G. Scott, Withdrawals
13 Supplies on Hand	*40 Revenue*
16 Equipment	41 Service Revenue
016 Accumulated Depreciation—	*50 Expenses*
Equipment	51 Rent Expense
20 Liabilities	52 Wage Expense
21 Accounts Payable	53 Supplies Expense
26 Notes Payable	54 Depreciation Expense

General Journal				PAGE 1
Date	**Account Names and Explanations**	**A/C #**	**Debit**	**Credit**
19-- Mar. 2	Cash 　　G. Scott, Capital 　　Owner invested cash; Deposit No. 10.		5,000	5,000
4	Equipment 　　Cash 　　Notes Payable 　　Purchased equipment for cash and note; Check No. 210.		4,000	500 3,500
5	Supplies on Hand 　　Accounts Payable 　　Purchased supplies on account from B&B.		500	500
10	Cash 　　Service Revenue 　　Cash revenue received; Deposit No. 11.		800	800
15	Rent Expense 　　Cash 　　Paid March rent; Check No. 211.		250	250
21	Cash 　　Service Revenue 　　Cash revenue received; Deposit No. 12.		750	750
26	G. Scott, Withdrawals 　　Cash 　　Owner withdrew cash for personal use; Check No. 212.		500	500
31	Wage Expense 　　Cash 　　Paid March wages; Check No. 213.		1,500	1,500
31	Accounts Receivable 　　Service Revenue 　　Billed customers for services performed in March.		930	930
31	Supplies Expense 　　Supplies on Hand 　　Supplies used in March.		175	175
31	Depreciation Expense 　　Accumulated Depreciation—Equipment 　　Depreciation for March.		200	200

Required

1) Set up ledger accounts and post the entries. Use account forms that provide for a running balance, and be sure to cross-reference the entries and postings.

2) Prepare a trial balance for Scott Company at March 31.

3) Prepare an income statement for March.

4) Prepare a statement of owner's capital for March.

5) Prepare a balance sheet at March 31.

ALTERNATE PROBLEMS FOR CHAPTER 2

Alternate 2.1. An opening trial balance at October 1 is shown for the Effo Company, a consulting firm. Following the trial balance is a list of transactions for October.

	EFFO COMPANY Trial Balance October 1, 19--		
A/C #	**Account**	**Debit**	**Credit**
111	Cash	1,800	
112	Accounts Receivable	1,600	
113	Office Supplies	150	
121	Office Equipment	900	
0121	Accumulated Depreciation—Office Equipment		30
211	Accounts Payable		420
212	Notes Payable		1,200
311	E. F. Flicker, Capital		2,800
312	E. F. Flicker, Withdrawals	–0–	
411	Consultant Fees		–0–
511	Rent Expense	–0–	
512	Secretarial Expense	–0–	
513	Supplies Expense	–0–	
514	Depreciation Expense	–0–	
		4,450	4,450

Transactions

Oct. 3   Received payment from client for September bill, $1,200 cash (Deposit No. 160).

8   Billed client for report completed today, $500.

10   Purchased supplies for $60 on account.

16   Made $50 payment on notes payable (Check No. 724).

28   Billed clients $4,200 for work completed in October.

30   Paid secretary wages, $425 (Check No. 725).

30   Owner withdrew $1,400 for personal use (Check No. 726).

30   Paid rent for October, $600 (Check No. 727).

30   Recognized depreciation on office equipment for October, $30.

30   Office supplies used from stockroom during October, $85.

Required

1) Journalize the October transactions.

2) Set up T-accounts with balances as shown on the October trial balance, and post the October journal entries to the T-accounts.

3) Prepare a trial balance at October 31.

4) Prepare an income statement for the month of October.

Alternate 2.2. The Ants Away Company's opening trial balance for January 1 is shown below, followed by a list of the January transactions.

	ANTS AWAY COMPANY **Trial Balance** **January 1, 19--**		
A/C #	**Account**	**Debit**	**Credit**
111	Cash	380	
112	Equipment	2,000	
0112	Accumulated Depreciation—Equipment		900
212	Note Payable		600
311	H. Stamps, Capital		880
411	Service Revenue		–0–
511	Chemicals Expense	–0–	
512	Truck Rental Expense	–0–	
513	Advertising Expense	–0–	
514	Depreciation Expense	–0–	
		2,380	2,380

Transactions

Jan. 8	Deposited $140 in fees collected from customers (Deposit No. 93).
10	Paid $150 charge for truck rental during January (Check No. 310).
10	Paid $30 for chemicals used on jobs performed (Check No. 311).
15	Deposited $180 in fees collected (Deposit No. 94).
15	Paid $50 for newspaper advertising (Check No. 312).
18	Paid $40 on note payable (Check No. 313).
25	Deposited $260 in fees collected (Deposit No. 95).
26	Paid $80 for chemicals used on jobs performed (Check No. 314).
31	Equipment depreciation for January, $60.

Required

1) Journalize the January transactions on general journal page 14.

2) Set up ledger accounts on forms that allow for a running balance, showing the opening balance at January 1 for the first five accounts. Post the journal entries to the ledger accounts, taking care to cross-reference the journal and ledger properly.

3) Prepare a trial balance at January 31.

4) Prepare an income statement and statement of owner's capital for January, as well as a balance sheet at January 31.

Alternate 2.3. Rubbish Collection Service was started on April 1. A chart of accounts and the April transactions for the new business are as follows.

RUBBISH COLLECTION SERVICE
Chart of Accounts

10 Assets

11 Cash
12 Accounts Receivable
13 Supplies
16 Truck
016 Accum. Depr.—Truck

20 Liabilities

21 Accounts Payable
22 Note Payable

30 Owner's Equity

31 C. Duncan, Capital
031 C. Duncan, Withdrawals

40 Revenue

41 Collection Fees

50 Expenses

51 Wage Expense
52 Supplies Expense
53 Gasoline Expense
54 Repairs Expense
55 Depreciation Expense

Transactions

Apr.	1	Carl Duncan invested $3,000 in the business (Deposit No. 10).
	2	A used truck for collecting rubbish was purchased for $6,000. A note was signed for $4,000, and the balance was paid with Check No. 101.
	4	Office and cleaning supplies were purchased for $60 cash (Check No. 102).
	6	Deposited $400 in collection fees (Deposit No. 11).
	6	Purchased gasoline on account for the truck, $15.
	15	Duncan withdrew $200 for personal use (Check No. 103).
	15	Paid employee wages of $250 (Check No. 104).
	17	Purchased gasoline on account for the truck, $20.
	18	Deposited $500 in collection fees (Deposit No. 12).
	20	Paid April payment on the truck note, $200 (Check No. 105).
	20	Paid $35 due for gasoline that was purchased earlier in the month (Check No. 106).
	22	Paid $50 to have the truck repaired (Check No. 107).
	22	Purchased gasoline on account for the truck, $25.
	25	Duncan withdrew $300 for personal use (Check No. 108).
	30	Billed customers for $600 in collection fees earned in April. Customers are expected to pay in May.
	30	Paid employee wages of $280 (Check No. 109).
	30	A check of supplies on hand shows that supplies costing $20 were used in April.
	30	Truck depreciation for April was $150.

Required

1) Journalize the April transactions, starting with page 1 of the general journal.

2) Set up ledger accounts on forms that allow for a running balance. Post entries to ledger accounts, taking care to cross-reference the entries and postings properly.

3) Prepare a trial balance at April 30.

4) Prepare an income statement and statement of owner's capital for April, and a balance sheet at April 30.

ALTERNATE PROBLEMS FOR SECTION 3.A

Alternate 3.A.6. Adjustments data are given below.

Adjustments Data

a) On April 1, the payment of $1,200 for one year of insurance coverage was recorded by debiting an asset, Prepaid Insurance, and crediting Cash. One month of the insurance coverage has expired.

b) The Office Supplies account shows a balance of $180. A check of supplies on hand shows unused supplies of only $85.

c) Service revenue from a job that was completed on April 30, for which a customer will be billed $1,500, has not yet been recorded.

d) Interest of $60 has accrued on a note payable, but has not yet been paid or recorded.

e) Depreciation on office furniture for April was $80.

Required

Prepare adjusting entries at April 30.

Alternate 3.A.7. The asset and liability account balances at April 30 for the King Company follow. Additional data needed for adjustments are also supplied.

KING COMPANY Selected Account Balances April 30, 19--		
	Debit	**Credit**
Cash	3,800	
Prepaid Rent	1,200	
Accounts Receivable	2,000	
Office Equipment	6,000	
Loan Payable		3,000
Unearned Service Revenue		1,000

Adjustments Data

a) Rent expense to be recognized for the month of April, $600.

b) Depreciation on office equipment for the month of April, $100.

c) Interest due April 30 on loan payable, $15.

d) Employee's salaries not paid as of April 30, $400.

e) On April 1, $1,000 was collected in advance from a client. The collection was recorded as a liability. Services valued at $500 were performed for the client in April.

Required

Make the necessary adjusting entries at April 30.

ALTERNATE PROBLEMS FOR SECTION 3.B

Alternate 3.B.3. A. Garvey, Surveyor, has the following trial balance and adjustments data at the end of his first year of practice.

A. GARVEY, SURVEYOR
Unadjusted Trial Balance
December 31, 19--

	Debit	Credit
Cash	4,230	
Accounts Receivable	13,750	
Equipment	50,000	
Supplies	520	
Accounts Payable		1,600
A. Garvey, Capital		7,000
Fees Earned		85,000
Salary Expense	16,000	
Utilities Expense	3,600	
Rent Expense	5,500	
	93,600	93,600

Adjustments Data

a) Office rent payable at the end of the year was $500.

b) Supplies inventory at December 31 was $350.

c) Depreciation expense on equipment was not recorded for the year. The equipment has a five-year life and is being depreciated on a straight-line basis.

Required

Prepare a ten-column work sheet.

Alternate 3.B.4. An unadjusted trial balance for Barn Company at October 31 is shown below. Also provided are adjustments data at October 31. The firm uses a monthly accounting period. No additional capital was contributed by the owner during October.

	BARN COMPANY Unadjusted Trial Balance October 31, 19--		
A/C #	**Account**	**Debit**	**Credit**
111	Cash	450	
112	Accounts Receivable	800	
113	Prepaid Insurance	300	
114	Truck	7,600	
0114	Accumulated Depreciation—Truck		1,800
211	Accounts Payable		390
212	Wages Payable		–0–
213	Interest Payable		–0–
214	Note Payable		2,000
311	E. Barn, Capital		5,900
312	E. Barn, Withdrawals	1,000	
411	Fees Earned		1,200
511	Rent Expense	500	
512	Gasoline Expense	40	
513	Wage Expense	600	
514	Interest Expense	–0–	
515	Depreciation Expense	–0–	
516	Insurance Expense	–0–	
		11,290	11,290

Adjustments Data

a) Accrued interest on note payable at October 31, $30.

b) Accrued wages payable to employees at October 31, $80.

c) Truck depreciation for October, $200.

d) Insurance expired during October, $100.

Required

1) Prepare a ten-column work sheet for Barn Company for the month of October.

2) Prepare an income statement and a statement of owner's capital for October, along with a classified balance sheet in report form at October 31.

3) Prepare adjusting journal entries at October 31.

ALTERNATE PROBLEMS FOR SECTION 3.C

Alternate 3.C.5. The adjusted trial balance for Fran's Hair Place is as follows.

FRAN'S HAIR PLACE Adjusted Trial Balance January 31, 19--		
	Debit	**Credit**
Cash	2,430	
Accounts Receivable	1,500	
Prepaid Rent	2,700	
Supplies on Hand	550	
Salon Equipment	12,000	
Accumulated Depreciation—Salon Equipment		3,600
Accounts Payable		1,200
Notes Payable		5,000
Interest Payable		300
Fran Nebo, Capital		8,000
Fran Nebo, Withdrawals	2,400	
Fees Earned		7,000
Salaries Expense	1,800	
Rent Expense	900	
Supplies Expense	120	
Depreciation Expense	400	
Interest Expense	300	
	25,100	25,100

Required

Prepare closing entries, assuming that

1) An Income Summary account is used.

2) An Income Summary account is not used.

Alternate 3.C.6. An adjusted trial balance for Garcia Company at October 31 follows.

GARCIA COMPANY Adjusted Trial Balance October 31, 19--			
A/C #	**Account**	**Debit**	**Credit**
111	Cash	1,900	
112	Accounts Receivable	3,180	
211	Accounts Payable		460
311	M. Garcia, Capital		3,200
312	M. Garcia, Withdrawals	1,600	
411	Fees Earned		9,000
511	Rent Expense	2,000	
512	Miscellaneous Expense	180	
513	Salary Expense	3,800	
		12,660	12,660

Required

1) Prepare closing entries.

2) Prepare a post-closing trial balance for the Garcia Company at October 31 assuming that the closing entries have been posted to ledger accounts.

ALTERNATE PROBLEMS FOR CHAPTER 3

Alternate 3.1. A chart of accounts and other data for Consultate Company are shown here.

CONSULTATE COMPANY
Chart of Accounts

Assets

111 Cash
112 Accounts Receivable
113 Prepaid Insurance
114 Supplies
115 Trucks
0115 Accumulated Depreciation—
       Trucks

Liabilities

211 Accounts Payable
212 Wages Payable
213 Interest Payable
214 Notes Payable (long-term)

Owner's Equity

311 J. Miles, Capital
312 J. Miles, Withdrawals

Revenue

411 Fees Earned

Expenses

511 Rent Expense
512 Insurance Expense
513 Wage Expense
514 Interest Expense
515 Gasoline Expense
516 Supplies Expense
517 Depreciation Expense

CONSULTATE COMPANY
Post-Closing Trial Balance
July 31, 19—

A/C #	Account	Debit	Credit
111	Cash	10,000	
112	Accounts Receivable	12,000	
113	Prepaid Insurance	3,300	
114	Supplies	700	
115	Trucks	18,000	
0115	Accumulated Depreciation—Trucks		1,800
211	Accounts Payable		9,410
214	Notes Payable (long-term)		7,000
311	J. Miles, Capital		25,790
		44,000	44,000

Transactions

Aug.   1   Received $3,000 cash for services rendered and billed in July (Deposit No. 2870).

      4   Purchased supplies costing $150 on account.

      8   Billed customers for August services, $8,000.

      9   Paid $4,000 on accounts payable (Check No. 5061).

    10   Purchased a truck for $6,000. Paid $1,000 cash (Check No. 5062) and signed a note for the balance.

    12   Paid employee wages, $5,000 (Check Nos. 5063–5073).

    20   Billed customers for services, $10,000.

    23   Collected $7,000 cash for services rendered and billed in July (Deposit No. 2871).

    26   Paid employee wages, $5,000 (Check Nos. 5074–5084).

    26   J. Miles withdrew $600 for personal use (Check No. 5085).

    30   Received bill for August rent, $4,000.

    30   Received bill for gasoline purchased and used during August, $840.

Adjustments Data

a) Insurance expired during August, $300.

b) Supplies used during August, $700.

c) Truck depreciation for August, $600.

d) Wages accrued but not paid at August 31, $500.

e) Accrued interest for August on notes payable, $120.

f) Fees earned but not billed for August, $450.

Required

1) Open new ledger accounts with August 1 balances.

2) Prepare general journal entries in good form on journal page 83 for the August transactions.

3) Post August journal entries to the ledger.

4) Prepare a ten-column work sheet for the month of August.

5) Prepare an income statement and a statement of owner's capital for August, and a classified balance sheet at August 31.

6) Prepare adjusting journal entries for August.

7) Prepare closing entries for August.

8) Post the adjusting and closing entries to the ledger and prepare the ledger accounts for the new period.

Alternate 3.2. A partially completed work sheet for Ace Flying Service is shown as follows.

ACE FLYING SERVICE
Work Sheet
for the Month of January 19—

A/C #	Account	Unadjusted Trial Balance		Adjustment		Adjusted Trial Balance	
		Dr.	Cr.	Dr.	Cr.	Dr.	Cr.
111	Cash	2,000				2,000	
112	Accounts Receivable	4,400		a) 800		5,200	
113	Supplies	500			b) 470	30	
116	Planes	250,000				250,000	
0116	Accumulated Depreciation—Planes		25,000		c) 1,500		26,500
211	Accounts Payable		5,000				5,000
212	Interest Payable		–0–		d) 950		950
213	Notes Payable (60 days)		6,000				6,000
214	Loans Payable (due in 5 years)		100,000				100,000
311	Fred Ace, Capital		118,100				118,100
312	Fred Ace, Withdrawals	4,000				4,000	
411	Charter Fees		15,450		a) 800		16,250
511	Salary Expense	6,000				6,000	
512	Gasoline Expense	1,650				1,650	
513	Rent Expense	1,000				1,000	
514	Interest Expense	–0–		d) 950		950	
515	Supplies Expense	–0–		b) 470		470	
516	Depreciation Expense	–0–		c) 1,500		1,500	
		269,550	269,550	3,720	3,720	272,800	272,800

Explanations:
a) Fees earned but not billed in January.
b) Supplies used in January.
c) Plane depreciation for January.
d) Interest accrued at January 31.

Required

1) Prepare a completed work sheet for Ace Flying Service.

2) Prepare an income statement and a statement of owner's capital for the month of January.

3) Prepare a classified balance sheet in report form at January 31.

4) Prepare adjusting and closing entries.

5) Prepare a post-closing trial balance.

Alternate 3.3. Ledger accounts at May 31 are given for Unicom Company, followed by adjustments information, on pages D-20–D-24.

	Cash				ACCOUNT NO. 111	
					Balance	
Date	**Item**	**Ref.**	**Debit**	**Credit**	**Debit**	**Credit**
19-- May 1	Balance	X			1,500	
2		20		1,300	200	
3		20	3,000		3,200	
15		20	4,000		7,200	
15		20		5,000	2,200	
16		20		400	1,800	
16		20		1,000	800	
19		20		100	700	
21		20	200		900	
30		20		300	600	

	Accounts Receivable				ACCOUNT NO. 112	
					Balance	
Date	**Item**	**Ref.**	**Debit**	**Credit**	**Debit**	**Credit**
19-- May 1	Balance	X			4,000	
3		20		3,000	1,000	
21		20		200	800	

	Supplies				ACCOUNT NO. 113	
					Balance	
Date	**Item**	**Ref.**	**Debit**	**Credit**	**Debit**	**Credit**
19-- May 1	Balance	X			400	
19		20	100		500	
21		20	800		1,300	

	Prepaid Insurance				ACCOUNT NO. 114	
					Balance	
Date	**Item**	**Ref.**	**Debit**	**Credit**	**Debit**	**Credit**
19-- May 1	Balance	X			400	

	Land				ACCOUNT NO. 116	
					Balance	
Date	**Item**	**Ref.**	**Debit**	**Credit**	**Debit**	**Credit**
19-- May 1	Balance	X			8,000	

	Building				ACCOUNT NO. 117	
					Balance	
Date	**Item**	**Ref.**	**Debit**	**Credit**	**Debit**	**Credit**
19-- May 1	Balance	X			52,000	

	Accumulated Depreciation—Building				ACCOUNT NO. 117	
					Balance	
Date	**Item**	**Ref.**	**Debit**	**Credit**	**Debit**	**Credit**
19-- May 1	Balance	X				1,450

	Accounts Payable				ACCOUNT NO. 211	
					Balance	
Date	**Item**	**Ref.**	**Debit**	**Credit**	**Debit**	**Credit**
19-- May 1	Balance	X				400
16		20	400			-0-
21		20		800		800
30		20	300			500

	Salaries Payable				ACCOUNT NO. 212	
					Balance	
Date	**Item**	**Ref.**	**Debit**	**Credit**	**Debit**	**Credit**
19-- May 1	Balance	X				300
30		20	300			-0-

Interest Payable   *ACCOUNT NO. 213*

Date	Item	Ref.	Debit	Credit	Balance Debit	Balance Credit

Mortgage Payable   *ACCOUNT NO. 218*

Date	Item	Ref.	Debit	Credit	Balance Debit	Balance Credit
19-- May 1	Balance	X				32,150

M. Barclay, Capital   *ACCOUNT NO. 311*

Date	Item	Ref.	Debit	Credit	Balance Debit	Balance Credit
19-- May 1	Balance	X				32,000

M. Barclay, Withdrawals   *ACCOUNT NO. 312*

Date	Item	Ref.	Debit	Credit	Balance Debit	Balance Credit
19-- May 15		20	5,000		5,000	

Fees Earned   *ACCOUNT NO. 411*

Date	Item	Ref.	Debit	Credit	Balance Debit	Balance Credit
19-- May 15		20		4,000		4,000

Salaries Expense   *ACCOUNT NO. 511*

Date	Item	Ref.	Debit	Credit	Balance Debit	Balance Credit
19-- May 2		20	1,000		1,000	
16		20	1,000		2,000	

Supplies Expense   *ACCOUNT NO. 512*

Date	Item	Ref.	Debit	Credit	Balance Debit	Balance Credit

Insurance Expense   *ACCOUNT NO. 513*

Date	Item	Ref.	Debit	Credit	Balance Debit	Balance Credit

Depreciation Expense   *ACCOUNT NO. 514*

Date	Item	Ref.	Debit	Credit	Balance Debit	Balance Credit

Interest Expense   *ACCOUNT NO. 515*

Date	Item	Ref.	Debit	Credit	Balance Debit	Balance Credit

Adjustments Data

a) Building depreciation for May, $120.

b) Accrued interest on mortgage payable at May 31, $250.

c) Supplies used during May, $700.

d) Accrued salaries at May 31, $1,100.

e) Insurance expired during May, $50.

Required

1) Prepare a ten-column work sheet for Unicom Company for May.

2) Prepare adjusting journal entries on journal page 21.

3) Prepare closing journal entries.

4) Post adjusting and closing entries to ledger accounts.

ALTERNATE PROBLEMS FOR SECTION 4.A

Alternate 4.A.6. The following transactions are for a merchandising firm that uses a periodic inventory system.

Transactions

Aug. 10   Purchased merchandise for $5,000 cash, f.o.b. destination (Check No. 6610).

12   Purchased merchandise on account at a cost of $14,000; f.o.b. shipping point.

13   Paid freight for merchandise purchased on August 12, $300 cash (Check No. 6611).

13   Sold merchandise for $500 cash (Deposit No. 190).

15   Sold merchandise on account for $8,000; goods shipped f.o.b. destination.

18   Paid freight bill of $150 for goods shipped August 15 (Check No. 6612).

Required

Journalize the transactions.

Alternate 4.A.7. The data below are for Norbert Sales Company.

Merchandise inventory, April 30	$ 85,000
Merchandise inventory, May 31	72,000
Purchases during May	610,000
Sales during May	980,000
Freight in during May	10,400
Freight out during May	4,800

Required

Prepare a schedule of cost of goods sold for Norbert Sales Company for the month of May.

Alternate 4.A.8. The Butterfield Store purchases merchandise for resale from Sanchez Dairy. Selected transactions for February are as follows.

Transactions

Feb. 5   Butterfield purchased merchandise on account from Sanchez Dairy at a cost of $2,500, f.o.b. destination. Freight charges of $100 were paid by Sanchez on this date.

15   Butterfield purchased merchandise on account from Sanchez Dairy at a cost of $800; f.o.b. shipping point.

18   Butterfield paid $40 freight charges on February 15 purchase.

Required

1) Journalize the transactions for Butterfield Store.

2) Journalize the appropriate transactions as they would appear in Sanchez's records.

ALTERNATE PROBLEMS FOR SECTION 4.B

Alternate 4.B.6. Purchases and sales transactions of the Bits and Pieces Antique Shop are listed below.

Transactions

Nov. 2   Sold merchandise on account, $6,000; terms 2/10, n/30.

4   Purchased merchandise on account, $5,000; terms 3/5, n/30.

7   Paid for November 4 purchase.

7   Customer returned damaged goods from November 2 sale, $400.

10   Received payment for goods sold November 2.

11   Purchased merchandise on account, $4,000; terms 1/10, n/30.

14   Returned damaged goods purchased November 11, $800.

18   Sold merchandise on account, $12,000; terms 2/10, n/30.

25   Paid for merchandise purchased November 11.

30   Received payment for goods sold November 18.

30   Sold merchandise for cash, $2,000.

Required

Make journal entries to record the transactions, assuming that

1) Purchases and sales are recorded at gross (before cash discounts).

2) Purchases and sales are recorded net of cash discounts.

Alternate 4.B.7. The following transactions were experienced by Chan Company, which records purchases and sales on a gross basis.

Transactions

Mar. 1   Sold merchandise for cash, $250.

3   Purchased merchandise on account for $5,000; terms 2/10, n/30.

6   Customer returned merchandise sold on March 1 for a cash refund.

12   Purchased merchandise on account for $6,000; terms 1/15, n/30.

15   Paid for merchandise purchased on March 3.

16   Returned part of the March 12 purchase to the vendor for credit. The returned merchandise had been invoiced at a gross cost of $1,000.

18   Sold merchandise on credit for $700; terms 3/10, n/30.

25   Paid for merchandise purchased on March 12, less returns and discounts.

26   Customer paid account for March 18 sale.

Required

Record the transactions in Chan's journal.

ALTERNATE PROBLEMS FOR SECTION 4.C

Alternate 4.C.4. A partially completed work sheet for Farkleberry Fabrics Store appears on the page opposite. The fabrics inventory at June 30 is $13,000.

Required

1) Prepare a completed work sheet for Farkleberry Fabrics.

2) Prepare an income statement for Farkleberry Fabrics Store for the month of June, and a balance sheet at June 30.

FARKLEBERRY FABRICS STORE
Work Sheet
For the Month Ended June 30, 19--

A/C #	Account	Unadjusted Trial Balance		Adjustments	
		Dr.	Cr.	Dr.	Cr.
11	Cash	2,000			
12	Accounts Receivable	12,000			
13	Fabrics Inventory, May 31	22,000			
16	Equipment	6,000			
016	Accumulated Depreciation—Equipment		2,000		a) 600
21	Accounts Payable		4,600		
25	Bank Loan Payable (due in 3 years)		8,000		
31	R. Nettles, Capital		20,280		
32	R. Nettles, Withdrawals	1,000			
41	Sales		15,000		
42	Sales Returns and Allowances	800			
43	Sales Discounts Forfeited		160		
51	Purchases	3,000			
52	Purchases Returns and Allowances		200		
53	Purchases Discounts Lost	50			
54	Freight In	100			
62	Salary Expense	2,000			
63	Advertising Expense	510			
64	Utilities Expense	180			
65	Rent Expense	600			
		50,240	50,240		
66	Depreciation Expense			a) 600	
67	Interest Expense			b) 40	
22	Interest Payable				b) 40
61	Cost of Goods Sold				

Adjustment Explanations:
a) Depreciation for June.
b) Accrued Interest Payable at June 30.

Alternate 4.C.5. An unadjusted trial balance for Chalski Company follows. Adjustments information for the fiscal year ended September 30 is also provided.

A/C #	Account	Debit	Credit
	CHALSKI COMPANY **Unadjusted Trial Balance** **September 30, 19X5**		
111	Cash	17,000	
112	Prepaid Insurance	2,500	
113	Accounts Receivable	258,000	
115	Merchandise Inventory, 9/30/X4	375,000	
116	Supplies	2,500	
118	Store Equipment	288,000	
0118	Accumulated Depreciation—Store Equipment		32,200
211	Accounts Payable		66,000
212	Notes Payable (due in 3 years)		44,000
311	S. Chalski, Capital		708,000
312	S. Chalski, Withdrawals	40,000	
411	Sales		970,000
412	Sales Returns and Allowances	12,000	
413	Sales Discounts	9,000	
420	Rental Income		5,000
512	Purchases	520,000	
513	Purchases Returns and Allowances		4,000
514	Purchases Discounts		7,800
515	Transportation In	2,000	
516	General Salaries Expense	60,000	
517	Advertising Expense	11,000	
518	Sales Salaries Expense	206,000	
519	Supplies Expense	–0–	
520	Depreciation Expense	–0–	
521	Rent Expense	34,000	
522	Insurance Expense	–0–	
511	Cost of Goods Sold	–0–	
		1,837,000	1,837,000

Adjustments Data

a) Insurance expired during fiscal year, $1,250.

b) Supplies on hand at September 30, $1,500.

c) Store equipment depreciation for fiscal year, $20,000.

d) Merchandise inventory at September 30, 19X5, $400,000.

Required

1) Prepare a ten-column work sheet for Chalski for the year ended September 30, 19X5.

2) Prepare a multiple-step income statement for the year.

3) Prepare a classified balance sheet at September 30.

4) Prepare adjusting and closing entries at September 30.

5) Prepare a condensed single-step income statement for the year supported by a separate schedule of cost of goods sold.

Alternate 4.C.6. Accountants use a variety of approaches for accomplishing end-of-period work. One work sheet approach carries all temporary accounts related to purchases directly into the income statement columns of the work sheet. The income statement columns also show the beginning Merchandise Inventory in the debit column and the ending Merchandise Inventory in the credit column.

Required

1) Use the unadjusted trial balance and adjustments data provided in problem Alt. 4.C.5 to prepare a work sheet for Chalski Company that follows the approach described above.

2) Prepare closing entries for Chalski Company that are consistent with the work sheet approach used for requirement 1. (*Hint:* The inventory account will be updated and accounts related to purchases closed, as part of the closing entries. One compound closing entry may be made for all items in the income statement columns.)

ALTERNATE PROBLEMS FOR CHAPTER 4

Alternate 4.1. Singh Supply sells merchandise at wholesale prices to retail stores. A post-closing trial balance at April 30, a list of transactions for May, and adjustments information are as follows.

SINGH SUPPLY
Post-Closing Trial Balance
April 30, 19--

A/C #	Account	Debit	Credit
111	Cash	30,000	
112	Accounts Receivable	65,000	
113	Merchandise Inventory	80,000	
116	Furnishings	148,000	
0116	Accumulated Depreciation—Furnishings		78,000
211	Accounts Payable		95,000
212	Wages Payable		–0–
213	Notes Payable (due in 2 years)		60,000
311	Kay Singh, Capital		90,000
312	Kay Singh, Withdrawals	–0–	
411	Sales		–0–
412	Sales Discounts	–0–	
413	Sales Returns and Allowances	–0–	
510	Cost of Goods Sold	–0–	
511	Purchases	–0–	
512	Purchases Discounts		–0–
513	Purchases Returns and Allowances		–0–
514	Transportation In	–0–	
611	Wage Expense	–0–	
612	Depreciation Expense	–0–	
613	Rent Expense	–0–	
		323,000	323,000

Transactions

May 2	Sold merchandise on account, $200,000; terms 2/10, n/30.
6	Customer returned goods sold on May 2, $4,000.
9	Received payment for May 2 sale.
10	Purchased merchandise on account, $60,000; terms 1/10, n/30.
15	Returned defective merchandise costing $1,000 from purchase of May 10.
20	Purchased merchandise on account, $90,000; terms 1/10, n/30.
20	Paid transportation charges on May 20 purchase, $400.
25	Sold merchandise on account, $50,000; terms 2/10, n/30.
26	Paid wages through May 25, $15,000.
27	Paid for May 20 purchase.
27	Paid for May 10 purchase.
29	Paid May rent, $4,000.
31	Received payments on accounts receivable, $25,000. These accounts were not subject to any discounts.
31	The proprietor, Kay Singh, withdrew $600 for personal use.

Adjustments Data

a) Wages accrued but not paid at May 31, $3,000.

b) Depreciation on furnishings for May, $2,000.

c) Merchandise inventory at May 31, $70,000.

Required

1) Make journal entries to record the May transactions; begin on journal page 84.

2) Open appropriate ledger accounts with beginning balances, and post the May transactions.

3) Prepare a work sheet for May.

4) Prepare a multiple-step income statement for May.

5) Prepare a classified balance sheet at May 31.

6) Prepare and post adjusting and closing entries at May 31.

Alternate 4.2. The following information is presented for Jancy Sales Company: post-closing trial balance at December 31, a list of transactions for January, and adjustments information at January 31.

	JANCY SALES COMPANY **Post-Closing Trial Balance** **December 31, 19– –**		
A/C #	**Account**	**Debit**	**Credit**
11	Cash	40,000	
12	Accounts Receivable	70,000	
13	Merchandise Inventory	50,000	
15	Furniture and Fixtures	84,000	
015	Accumulated Depreciation—Furniture and Fixtures		22,000
21	Accounts Payable		35,000
22	Salaries Payable		–0–
23	Interest Payable		600
24	Loan Payable (due in 3 years)		60,000
31	T. Jancy, Capital		126,400
32	T. Jancy, Withdrawals	–0–	
41	Sales		–0–
42	Sales Discounts	–0–	
43	Sales Returns and Allowances	–0–	
51	Cost of Goods Sold	–0–	
52	Purchases	–0–	
53	Purchases Discounts		–0–
54	Purchases Returns and Allowances		–0–
55	Freight In	–0–	
61	Salary Expense	–0–	
62	Rent Expense	–0–	
63	Depreciation Expense	–0–	
64	Interest Expense	–0–	
		244,000	244,000

Transactions

Jan.	4	Purchased merchandise on account, $15,000; terms 1/10, n/30.
	6	Returned damaged merchandise costing $2,000 from purchase of January 4.
	12	Paid for January 4 purchase.
	14	Sold merchandise on account, $30,000; terms 2/10, n/30.
	15	Customer returned goods sold on January 14, $600.
	17	Purchased merchandise on account, $28,000; terms 1/10, n/30.
	19	Paid freight charges on January 17 purchase, $500.
	20	Sold merchandise for cash, $20,000.
	22	Customer paid for merchandise sold January 14.
	23	Sold merchandise on account, $35,000; terms 2/10, n/30.
	27	Paid salaries through January 27, $14,000.
	29	Received payment for January 23 sale.
	30	Paid $19,000 on accounts payable. These accounts were not subject to any discounts.
	31	Paid January rent, $3,000.
	31	Paid for January 17 purchase.
	31	Cash withdrawn by owner, $1,000.

Adjustments Data

a) Additional interest accrued during January on loan payable, $600.

b) Depreciation for January, $700.

c) Salaries accrued but not paid at January 31, $3,500.

d) Merchandise inventory at January 31, $42,000.

Required

1) Make journal entries to record the January transactions; begin on journal page 129.

2) Open appropriate ledger accounts with beginning balances, and post the January transactions.

3) Prepare a work sheet for January.

4) Prepare a multiple-step income statement for January.

5) Prepare a classified balance sheet at January 31.

6) Prepare and post adjusting and closing entries at January 31.

ALTERNATE PROBLEMS FOR SECTION 5.A

Alternate 5.A.4. Makey Furniture Store commenced business on July 21. Following are transactions relating to sales and cash receipts during July.

Transactions

19--

July 21   Peg Makey deposited $60,000 in a checking account for her store.

24   Sold furniture on account to T. Riley for $800 plus 6% sales tax.

25   Sold furniture on account to A. Tolby for $1,200 plus 6% sales tax.

25   Sold furniture for $530 cash, of which $30 represents sales tax.

27   Sold furniture on account to F. Farley for $850 plus 6% sales tax.

28   Collected $300 from T. Riley to apply on his account.

28   Sold furniture on account to E. Pitts for $900 plus 6% sales tax.

29   Sold furniture on account to A. McCoy for $250 plus 6% sales tax.

30   Collected $901 on account from F. Farley.

30   Sold furniture on account to L. Gomez for $600 plus 6% sales tax.

31   Sold furniture for $1,325 cash, of which $75 represents sales tax.

Required

1) Record the July transactions in sales and cash receipts journals with column headings as indicated.

CASH RECEIPTS JOURNAL FOR THE MONTH OF_____   *PAGE____*

Date	Accounts and Explanation	Ref.	General Debit	General Credit	Accounts Receivable Credit	Sales Credit	Sales Tax Payable Credit	Cash Debit

SALES JOURNAL FOR THE MONTH OF_____   *PAGE____*

Date	Customer	Invoice Number	Ref.	Accounts Receivable Debit	Sales Tax Payable Credit	Sales Credit

2) Balance and rule the journals.

3) Set up subsidiary ledger accounts for customers, and post appropriate amounts from the journals to the accounts.

4) Set up general ledger accounts for Cash (111), Accounts Receivable (112), Sales Tax Payable (213), Peg Makey, Capital (311), and Sales (411). Make all necessary postings from the journals to the general ledger accounts.

5) Reconcile the customers' ledger to its control account by preparing a schedule of accounts receivable whose total equals the control account balance.

Alternate 5.A.5. Provided below are page CR18 of the cash receipts journal and page S5 of the sales journal for Nox Company. The beginning balances on March 1 for four general ledger accounts are as follows.

Account #	Account	Balance Debit	Balance Credit
111	Cash	3,600	
112	Accounts Receivable	2,800	
212	Sales Tax Payable		1,005
411	Sales		–0–

Required

1) Set up cash receipts and sales journals like those shown, and balance and rule the journals.

2) Set up four general ledger accounts to reflect the balances indicated, and post from the journals to the four accounts, taking care to properly cross-reference the postings.

CASH RECEIPTS JOURNAL FOR THE MONTH OF March 19--   PAGE CR18

Date	Accounts and Explanation	Ref.	General Debit	General Credit	Accounts Receivable Credit	Sales Credit	Sales Tax Payable Credit	Cash Debit
Mar. 31	Brought Forward		600	4,200	6,275	14,200	275	24,350
31	B. Roberts	√			750			750

SALES JOURNAL FOR THE MONTH OF March 19--   PAGE S5

Date	Customer	Invoice Number	Ref.	Accounts Receivable Debit	Sales Tax Payable Credit	Sales Credit
Mar. 28	Brought Forward			7,230	210	7,020
30	L. Bender	511	√	360	10	350
31	J. Gwin	512	√	541	15	526

Alternate 5.A.6. Provided below are the last three transactions for April, the April 1 balances for two general ledger accounts and two subsidiary accounts receivable accounts, page CR33 of the cash receipts journal, and page S18 of the sales journal.

Transactions

Apr. 30   Sold merchandise on account to Sara Roberts for $425 plus 5% sales tax (Invoice No. 604).

30   Received $360 on account from Phil Rose.

30   Cash sales for today were $2,400. Sales taxes of $120 were collected from customers in addition to the sales proceeds.

Selected Account Balances, April 1

Accounts Receivable (Account No. 112)	$3,700
Sales (Account No. 411)	–0–
Sara Roberts	215
Phil Rose	730

Required

1) Set up journal pages like those illustrated and record the three transactions.

2) Set up accounts receivable ledger accounts for Roberts and Rose and reflect any postings required by the transactions.

3) Total the journal columns, and balance and rule the journals.

4) Set up general ledger accounts for Accounts Receivable and Sales, and post from the journals to those accounts.

CASH RECEIPTS JOURNAL FOR THE MONTH OF April 19--   *PAGE CR33*

Date	Accounts and Explanation	Ref.	General Debit	General Credit	Accounts Receivable Credit	Sales Credit	Sales Tax Payable Credit	Cash Debit
Apr. 30	Brought Forward		400	2,800	6,200	4,925	246	13,771

SALES JOURNAL FOR THE MONTH OF April 19--   *PAGE S18*

Date	Customer	Invoice Number	Ref.	Accounts Receivable Debit	Sales Tax Payable Credit	Sales Credit
Apr. 29	Brought Forward			7,536	471	7,065

ALTERNATE PROBLEMS FOR SECTION 5.B

Alternate 5.B.4. Marco Toy Company commenced business on March 16. Following are transactions relating to purchases and cash payments during March.

Transactions

Mar. 17	Purchased toys from Nifty Company for $1,200 on account; terms 1/10, n/30.
17	Purchased toys from Rider Company for $700 on account; terms 3/10, n/30.
18	Purchased toys from Imex, Inc., for $2,000 on account; terms n/60.
19	Purchased toys from Zemo Company for $350 cash (Check No. 1001).
23	Paid Nifty Company account incurred on March 17 (Check No. 1002).
25	Paid Rider Company account incurred on March 17 (Check No. 1003).
28	Paid employee wages of $820 (Check No. 1004).
29	Purchased toys from Nifty Company for $2,400; terms 1/10, n/30.
30	T. Marco, the owner, withdrew $600 cash from the business for his personal use (Check No. 1005).
30	Purchased toys from Milo Company for $1,500; terms 2/10, n/30.
31	Paid building rent for March, $1,200 (Check No. 1006).
31	Purchased toys from Rider Company for $3,100; terms 3/10, n/30.

Required

1) Record the March transactions in purchases and cash payments journals with column headings indicated here.

PURCHASES JOURNAL FOR THE MONTH OF _____				PAGE __
Date	Creditor	Terms	Ref.	Amount

CASH PAYMENTS JOURNAL FOR THE MONTH OF _____   PAGE __

Date	Accounts and Explanation	Ck. No.	Ref.	General Debit	General Credit	Accounts Payable Debit	Purchases Discounts Credit	Cash Credit

2) Balance and rule the journals.

3) Set up subsidiary ledger accounts for creditors, and post appropriate amounts from the journals to the accounts.

4) Set up general ledger accounts for Cash (111), Accounts Payable (201), T. Marco, Withdrawals (302), Purchases (501), Purchases Discounts (502), Wages (604), and Building Rent (608). (*Note:* Assume that the owner invested $80,000 in the business, and include that amount in the Cash account on March 16 with a reference to the cash receipts journal page CR1.) Make all necessary postings.

5) Reconcile the creditor ledger to its control account by preparing a schedule of accounts payable whose total equals the control account balance.

Alternate 5.B.5. Provided below and on the following page are the last three transactions for the month of July, page 28 of the purchases journal, and page 23 of the cash payments journal. Two general ledger accounts and two accounts from the subsidiary accounts payable ledger are also provided.

Transactions

July 31 Paid Polce Company invoice dated July 12 (Check No. 2468). The invoice amount is $760, and credit terms are 2/10, n/30.

31 Paid JDK Corporation invoice dated July 18 (Check No. 2469). The invoice amount is $850 and credit terms are 2/10, n/30.

31 Received merchandise from the Polce Company at a cost of $490 (Purchase Order No. PO743). Invoice dated July 30; terms 2/10, n/30.

PURCHASES JOURNAL FOR THE MONTH OF July 19--   *PAGE P28*

Date	Creditor	P.O. No.	Invoice Date	Terms	Ref.	Amount
July 30	Brought Forward Polce Company	PO 742	7/20	2/10, n/30		31,750 490

CASH PAYMENTS JOURNAL FOR THE MONTH OF July 19--   *PAGE CP23*

Date	Accounts and Explanation	Ck. No.	Ref.	General Debit	General Credit	Freight In Debit	Accounts Payable Debit	Purchases Discounts Credit	Cash Credit
July 19	Brought Forward Office Supplies	2467	115	8,750 95	2,950	520	42,000	780	47,540 95

GENERAL LEDGER ACCOUNTS

| | | | | | Balance | |
	Accounts Payable			ACCOUNT NO. 211		
Date	Item	Ref.	Debit	Credit	Debit	Credit
19-- July 1	Balance	X				15,800

| | | | | | Balance | |
	Purchases			ACCOUNT NO. 511		
Date	Item	Ref.	Debit	Credit	Debit	Credit

ACCOUNTS PAYABLE LEDGER ACCOUNTS

NAME   JDK Corporation
ADDRESS   205 Park Ave., Watertown, NY

Date	Item	Ref.	Debit	Credit	Balance
19-- July 18		P27		850	850

NAME   Polce Company
ADDRESS   342 Forest Rd., Brookside, NY

Date	Item	Ref.	Debit	Credit	Balance
19-- July 12		P26		760	760

Required

1) Set up journals like those shown, and record the three transactions.

2) Total the journal columns, and balance and rule the cash payments and purchases journals.

3) Post from the journals to ledger accounts like those shown, taking care to reference the postings properly.

Alternate 5.B.6. The last page of a cash payments journal for October is as follows.

				General		Freight In	Accounts Payable	Purchases Discounts	Cash
Date	Accounts and Explanation	Ck. No.	Ref.	Debit	Credit	Debit	Debit	Credit	Credit
	Brought Forward			25,000	7,350	95	13,200	80	30,865
Oct. 20	Williams, Inc.	0147					720	14	720
25	Equipment	0148		2,500					
28	Sample Company	0149					1,570		1,570

CASH PAYMENTS JOURNAL FOR THE MONTH OF <u>October 19--</u>   *PAGE CP30*

Required

1) Set up a journal like the one shown, and balance and rule the journal. If the journal is not in balance, locate and correct the error(s) by lining through incorrect amounts and writing in the correct amounts. Check stubs show that Check No. 0147 was written for $720; No. 0148 for $2,500; and No. 0149 for $1,750.

2) Set up ledger accounts with balances as indicated, and post from the journal to the accounts.

	GENERAL LEDGER ACCOUNTS	
A/C #	Account	Balance Oct. 1
111	Cash	$39,000
116	Equipment	50,000
211	Accounts Payable	32,000
513	Purchases Discounts	–0–
514	Freight In	–0–

ACCOUNTS PAYABLE LEDGER ACCOUNTS			
Date	Ref.	Credit	Balance
Williams, Inc.			
Oct. 12	P8	$1,850	$1,850
16	P8	940	2,790
Sample Company			
Oct. 3	P8	$1,750	$1,750

ALTERNATE PROBLEMS FOR CHAPTER 5

Alternate 5.1. Provided below and on the page opposite are a company's last six transactions for the month of February, page 20 of the purchases journal, page 19 of the sales journal, page 13 of the cash payments journal, and page 21 of the cash receipts journal. Beginning balances for four general ledger accounts and the February 25 balances for four subsidiary accounts are also provided.

Transactions

Feb. 26   Sold merchandise on account to D. Ferred for $800 plus 7% sales tax (Invoice No. 4627).

26   Received $400 on account from B. T. Park.

27   Paid Enco Corporation invoice dated February 20 (Check No. 4151). The invoice amount is $1,500 and credit terms are 1/10, n/60.

28   Received merchandise from Skoshi Company at a cost of $2,200 (Purchase Order No. PO41). Invoice dated February 24; terms 2/10, n/30.

28   Paid Skoshi Company invoice dated February 1 (Check No. 4152). The invoice amount is $2,000, and credit terms are 2/10, n/30.

28   Cash sales for today were $3,000. Sales taxes of $210 were collected from customers and placed in the cash register along with the proceeds from the cash sales.

PURCHASES JOURNAL FOR THE MONTH OF February 19--   *PAGE P20*

Date	Creditor	P.O. No.	Invoice Date	Terms	Ref.	Amount
Feb. 22	Brought Forward Gluck Corporation	PO46	2/20	2/10, n/30	√	19,800 400

SALES JOURNAL FOR THE MONTH OF February 19--   *PAGE S19*

Date	Customer	Invoice Number	Ref.	Accounts Receivable *Debit*	Sales Tax Payable *Credit*	Sales *Credit*
Feb. 20	Brought Forward M. Parde	4626	√	64,850 963	3,850 63	61,000 900

CASH PAYMENTS JOURNAL FOR THE MONTH OF February 19--   PAGE CP13

Date	Accounts and Explanation	Ck. No.	Ref.	General Debit	General Credit	Freight In Debit	Accounts Payable Debit	Purchases Discounts Credit	Cash Credit
	Brought Forward			750	3,200	650	27,400	480	25,120

CASH RECEIPTS JOURNAL FOR THE MONTH OF February 19--   PAGE CR21

Date	Accounts and Explanation	Ref.	General Debit	General Credit	Accounts Receivable Credit	Sales Credit	Sales Tax Payable Credit	Cash Debit
	Brought Forward		6,100	7,000	8,700	21,400	1,260	32,260

GENERAL LEDGER ACCOUNTS

Account #	Title	Feb. 1 Balance Debit	Feb. 1 Balance Credit
111	Cash	19,500	
112	Accounts Receivable	11,800	
211	Accounts Payable		19,800
411	Sales		100,000

SUBSIDIARY LEDGER ACCOUNTS

Name	Feb. 25 Balance Debit	Feb. 25 Balance Credit
Receivables		
D. Ferred	1,000	
B. T. Park	400	
Payables		
Enco Corporation		1,500
Skoshi Company		3,000

Required

1) Set up journal pages with brought forward and entry amounts like those illustrated, and record the six transactions.

2) Total the journal columns; balance and rule the journals.

3) Set up the four general ledger accounts and four subsidiary accounts, and post to them from the journals.

Alternate 5.2. Case Company has a monthly accounting cycle. Following are the last six transactions for April and adjustments information for April. In addition, the four special journals, post-closing trial balance at March 31, list of receivable and payable balances at April 26 and general ledger accounts provided in problem 5.2 are to be used for this problem.

Transactions

Apr. 27   Paid Alex Company invoice dated April 20 (Check No. 412). The invoice amount is $1,500, and credit terms are 1/10, n/30.

28   Sold merchandise on account to B. Quano for $600 plus 6% sales tax (Invoice No. 2186).

29   Received merchandise from Ace Wholesale at a cost of $4,500 (Purchase Order No. PO71). Invoice dated April 26; terms 2/20, n/30.

30   Paid wages for the period April 16 through April 30, $4,700 (Check No. 413).

30   Cash sales for today were $2,200. Sales taxes of $132 were collected from customers and placed in the cash register along with the proceeds from cash sales.

30   Received $500 on account from B. Quano.

Adjustments Data

a) Depreciation expense (equipment) for April, $150.

b) Interest expense accrued but not paid during April, $60.

c) Merchandise inventory at April 30, $36,900.

Required

1) Set up journal pages for four special journals like those shown in problem 5.2, and record the six transactions just listed.

2) Total the journal columns, and balance and rule the journals.

3) Set up general ledger accounts for the accounts included on the post-closing trial balance of March 31 given in problem 5.2. Include appropriate balances as shown on the trial balance and the additional postings shown in the ledger accounts illustrated in problem 5.2.

4) Set up an accounts receivable ledger account for B. Quano and accounts payable ledger accounts for Ace Wholesale and Alex Company. Reflect purchases of $1,500 and $500 on April 20, both referenced as P19 in the Alex Company account.

5) Post from the journals to the general and subsidiary ledger accounts.

6) Prepare a work sheet for the month of April.

7) Prepare schedules of the subsidiary receivable and payable account balances at April 30, and reconcile to the general ledger control accounts.

8) Prepare an income statement for April.

9) Prepare a balance sheet at April 30.

10) Prepare adjusting and closing entries for April on general journal page 8.

11) Post adjusting and closing entries to the ledger accounts.

Alternate 5.3. Selected general and subsidiary ledger accounts for Scott Company are listed here with their balances at September 1. Also provided is a list of September transactions that involve cash receipts and cash payments.

GENERAL LEDGER ACCOUNTS			
A/C #	Title	Debit	Credit
111	Cash	$ 5,400	
112	Accounts Receivable	15,250	
212	Notes Payable		$8,000

ACCOUNTS RECEIVABLE LEDGER ACCOUNTS		
A/C #	Account Name	Amount
AR4	T. T. Fulton	$ 800
AR12	J. Howard	1,200

Transactions

19−−

Sept. 2   Purchased equipment for cash, $1,600 (Check No. 1201).

6   Received $300 on account from T. T. Fulton.

8   Borrowed $15,000 from the bank by signing a note payable due 90 days from today with interest at 12%.

10   Paid salary to P. Rhodes, $1,400 (Check No. 1202).

12   Paid Kennedy for merchandise purchased on account on September 4 (Check No. 1203). Invoice cost, $1,700; terms 2/10, n/30.

15   Cash sales for today were $700. Sales taxes of $28 were collected from customers in addition to the sales proceeds.

18   Paid freight charges to JSV Trucking on merchandise delivered today, $124 (Check No. 1204).

20   Purchased merchandise for cash, $340 (Check No. 1205).

22   Received $600 on account from J. Howard.

23   Cash sales for today were $920. Sales taxes of $36 were collected from customers in addition to the sales proceeds.

24   Paid Johnson Suppliers for merchandise purchased on September 6 (Check No. 1206). Invoice cost, $1,550; terms 1/10, n/30.

Required

1) Set up a cash payments journal (page 12) and a cash receipts journal (page 10), and record the transactions given for September. (*Note:* Review the transactions to determine the special columns you want to include in the journals.)

2) Balance and rule the journals.

3) Set up the three general ledger accounts and two customer accounts to reflect the September 1 balances provided, and post to the accounts from the journals.

ALTERNATE PROBLEMS FOR SECTION 6.A

Alternate 6.A.7. On September 1 Rogers Company accepted a 120-day, 9% note (dated September 1) for $20,000 from JSV Company in settlement of an overdue account receivable. On October 1 Rogers discounted the note at the bank at a 12% per annum discount rate. The note was paid by JSV on its due date, and Rogers received notice from the bank of the payment.

Required

1) Make general journal entries to reflect the foregoing events for

   a) Rogers Company.

   b) JSV Company.

2) Assume instead that the interest rate had been 10% and the discount rate 9%. Make the necessary entries for

   a) Rogers Company.

   b) JSV Company.

Alternate 6.A.8. Stewart Company experienced the following events during the year.

a. Insurance premiums of $9,500 for the twelve-month period of October 1, last year, through September 30, this year, were paid on March 20, this year. Equivalent insurance premiums apply to the following twelve-month period.

b. On September 1 a $5,000, 12%, 180-day note was received from James Corporation. The note was dated September 1.

c. Borrowed $10,000 from the bank on November 1 by signing a 12% per annum note due in 120 days.

Required

Make any adjusting journal entries needed on Stewart's books at December 31. Stewart accounts on a calendar-year basis and records adjusting entries only at year-end.

Alternate 6.A.9. On October 1, 19X4, Smarto Company accepted an $8,000, 180-day, 9% note (dated October 1, 19X4) from B&J Stores in settlement of an overdue account receivable.

Required

1) Make general journal entries for Smarto to record the note, the accrual of interest at December 31, 19X4, and the collection of the note on its due date.

2) Make the general journal entries for B&J Stores to record issuance of the note, the accrual of interest at December 31, and payment at the note's due date.

ALTERNATE PROBLEMS FOR SECTION 6.B

Alternate 6.B.6. Bruce Company uses an aging schedule to estimate uncollectibles. The results of an aging schedule at December 31 are as follows.

	0–30 Days	31–90 Days	Over 90 Days
Accounts Receivable	$72,000	$24,000	$9,000
Estimated Loss Rate	1%	5%	15%

Required

1) Assume that Allowance for Doubtful Accounts shows a credit balance of $425 at December 31. Make the entry to adjust the allowance account.

2) Assume that Allowance for Doubtful Accounts shows a debit balance of $425. Make the entry to adjust the allowance account.

Alternate 6.B.7. Weaver Company offers its credit customers terms of 3/10, n/30. At December 31 Accounts Receivable includes $25,000 of customer accounts still subject to the 3% discount. In the past, 90% of the customers have taken advantage of sales discounts.

Required

1) Make an adjusting entry at December 31 to allow for the ending receivables that will probably not be collected because of sales discounts.

2) Assume that a $2,500 receivable included in the December 31 balance is collected on January 5, net of the 3% discount. Make the required journal entry.

Alternate 6.B.8. On December 31, 19X4, Whitfield Company estimated that during 19X5 customers will return (or request allowance for) about $800 worth of goods sold in 19X4.

Required

1) Make an adjusting entry at December 31, 19X4, to record this estimate.

2) Assume that a customer returns merchandise and receives a cash refund of $90 on January 25, 19X5. The sale had been made on December 29, 19X4. Make the required journal entry.

ALTERNATE PROBLEMS FOR CHAPTER 6

Alternate 6.1. Following are selected events experienced by Arcane Company.

19X3

Dec. 31   Arcane estimates uncollectibles at 2% of sales. Sales for 19X3 were $900,000. Allowance for Doubtful Accounts showed a debit balance of $800 before the year-end adjustment.

19X4

Jan. 3   A 60-day, 9% note (dated January 3) for $5,000 was accepted from Barko Company in settlement of an overdue account receivable.

6   A $1,000 account receivable from UYA, Inc., was judged uncollectible.

13   The Barko Company note was discounted at the bank at a 6% per annum discount rate.

Feb. 14   UYA paid the $1,000 balance due that was written off on January 6.

Mar. 5   Arcane was notified by the bank that Barko Company defaulted on its note due March 4. Arcane paid the bank the maturity amount.

Apr. 3   Barko paid the maturity amount of the note defaulted on March 5 plus interest at 9% per annum calculated from the due date of the note.

Nov. 25   A 90-day, 8% note (dated November 25) for $12,000 was accepted from Nolo Company in settlement of an overdue account receivable.

Dec. 17   Various customer accounts totaling $16,500 were written off as uncollectible.

Dec. 31   Adjusting entries were made for uncollectible accounts expense and to accrue interest on the Nolo Company note. Sales for 19X4 were $920,000.

19X5

Feb. 23   Cash was received in settlement of the Nolo Company note plus interest.

Required

Record in Arcane's general journal all entries required by the foregoing events.

Alternate 6.2. Adjustments data for R. H. Mays Company are as follows.

Adjustments Data

a) On April 1, 19X4, a three-year insurance premium of $1,800 was paid.

b) Depreciation on furniture and equipment is $2,000 per year.

c) The bank loan was signed November 1, 19X4. It requires interest at 10% per annum to be paid quarterly and falls due on November 1, 19X6.

d) Experience indicates that 4% of ending Accounts Receivable turn out to be uncollectible.

e) The note receivable is dated October 2, 19X4, and bears 12% interest payable when the note matures on January 30, 19X5.

f) The merchandise inventory at December 31, 19X4, is $18,000.

Required

1) Use the partial work sheet provided in problem 6.2 and the adjustments data just provided to complete a ten-column work sheet for R. H. Mays Company.

2) Prepare an income statement for 19X4.

3) Prepare a balance sheet at December 31, 19X4.

Alternate 6.3. Following are a list of accounts receivable for Archboy Company at December 31 and a summary of loss experience.

Accounts Receivable		
Transaction Date	**Name**	**Amount Due**
Nov. 20	J. Able	$ 6,000
Oct. 15	M. Baker	5,000
Dec. 1	D. Chaps	2,000
Jan. 30	V. Dalby	1,500
Aug. 27	T. Early	2,950
Dec. 16	W. Falk	4,100
Dec. 2	R. Jones	3,300
Dec. 28	P. Kole	4,000
Dec. 12	B. Lamb	13,000
Dec. 30	E. Mohl	8,100
Oct. 15	C. Nold	2,200
Dec. 10	F. Ochs	6,000

Loss Experience	
Account Age	% Uncollectible
1–30 days	1/2
31–60 days	2
61–120 days	4
Over 120 days	30

Required

1) Prepare a receivables aging schedule at December 31. Group the accounts as follows: 1–30 days, 31–60 days, 61–120 days, and over 120 days.

2) Assume that Allowance for Doubtful Accounts shows a credit balance of $600. Make the adjusting entry for estimated uncollectibles at December 31.

3) What proportion of the adjusted Allowance for Doubtful Accounts applies to accounts that are 1–30 days old? 31–60 days old? 61–120 days old? Over 120 days?

4) At which account age group should the most collection effort be directed? Why?

ALTERNATE PROBLEMS FOR SECTION 7.A

Alternate 7.A.4. Inventory and purchasing data for one kind of inventory held by Hilo Company are shown here. Hilo employs a periodic inventory system.

Jan. 1	Beginning inventory	500 units at $50	$25,000
Feb. 28	Purchased	1,000 units at 52	52,000
May 16	Purchased	200 units at 52	10,400
Oct. 20	Purchased	150 units at 60	9,000
Dec. 1	Purchased	300 units at 65	19,500
Dec. 31	Ending inventory	350 units	

Required

Determine the cost of ending inventory and cost of goods sold, using

1) The LIFO method.

2) The FIFO method.

3) The weighted average method.

Alternate 7.A.5. Inventory and purchasing data for one type of inventory sold by Siegel Company are as shown. A periodic inventory system is used.

Jan. 1	Beginning inventory	10,000 units at 10¢
Feb. 15	Purchased	9,000 units at 12¢
July 30	Purchased	7,500 units at 15¢
Sept. 30	Purchased	6,000 units at 16¢
Dec. 31	Ending inventory	5,000 units

Required

1) Determine the cost of ending inventory and cost of goods sold using

   a) The FIFO method.

   b) The LIFO method.

   c) The weighted average method.

2) Assume that Siegel's purchases on February 15, July 30, and September 30 were all at units costing 10¢. Determine the cost of ending inventory and the cost of goods sold using

   a) The FIFO method.

   b) The LIFO method.

   c) The weighted average method.

Alternate 7.A.6. The following data relate to R&V Grain Supply. A periodic inventory system is used.

Nov. 1	Beginning inventory of corn	10,000 bushels at $2.50	$ 25,000
6	Purchased	15,000 bushels at 2.75	41,250
15	Purchased	20,000 bushels at 3.00	60,000
20	Purchased	25,000 bushels at ?	?
30	Ending inventory	5,000 bushels at ?	?
Cost of goods sold			$201,250

Required

Assuming use of the LIFO method:

1) Determine the cost of the ending inventory.

2) Determine the unit cost and total cost of the November 20 purchase.

ALTERNATE PROBLEMS FOR SECTION 7.B

Alternate 7.B.4. The Caloric Coal Company's inventory records are shown here for the month of April.

Apr.	1	Beginning inventory	100 tons at $18	$ 1,800
	4	Purchased	400 tons at 22	8,800
	8	Sold	200 tons at 40	8,000
	10	Sold	100 tons at 40	4,000
	15	Purchased	500 tons at 23	11,500
	17	Sold	600 tons at 40	24,000
	20	Purchased	300 tons at 25	7,500
	26	Sold	200 tons at 40	8,000

Required

1) Determine the cost of ending inventory, the cost of goods sold, and the gross profit for April using the periodic inventory system and

   a) The LIFO method.

   b) The FIFO method.

   c) The weighted average method.

2) Determine the cost of ending inventory, the cost of goods sold, and the gross profit for April using the perpetual inventory system and

   a) The LIFO method.

   b) The FIFO method.

   c) The moving average method.

Alternate 7.B.5. Inventory data for a merchandise item stocked by Chung Company are as follows.

AC45–21 ELBOWS			
		Units	**Unit Cost**
Sept.	1	Beginning inventory	160	$1.50
	4	Purchased	210	1.80
	20	Sold	150	
	24	Purchased	200	2.00
	30	Sold	250	

Required

1) Compute the cost of goods sold during September and the ending inventory at September 30, using the perpetual inventory system and the FIFO method.

2) Compute the cost of goods sold during September and the ending inventory at September 30, using the perpetual inventory system and the LIFO method.

3) Compute the cost of goods sold during September and the ending inventory at September 30, using the perpetual inventory system and the moving average method.

Alternate 7.B.6. Kifer Company uses a perpetual inventory system and the LIFO method. Inventory data for Part X–9 are shown here.

PART X–9			
		Units	**Unit Cost**
May 1	Beginning inventory	100	$50
7	Purchased	80	52
10	Sold	50	
15	Sold	90	
25	Purchased	70	55
30	Sold	80	

Required

Record the beginning inventory, purchases, cost of goods sold, and inventory balance on a subsidiary inventory record card.

ALTERNATE PROBLEMS FOR SECTION 7.C

Alternate 7.C.5. On June 15, Forest Sporting Goods was robbed of a large part of its inventory of sporting equipment. Selected data are as shown here.

	Cost	**Retail**
Beginning inventory, January 1	$ 72,000	$120,000
Purchases through June 14	336,000	560,000
Sales through June 14		480,000
Inventory remaining after robbery		20,000

Required

Estimate the cost of the stolen inventory.

Alternate 7.C.6. The following data are available from the records of the Mary Ann Dress Shop.

Inventory at Jan. 1	
At selling prices	$ 80,000
At cost	60,000
Purchases, Jan. 1 through Dec. 31	
At selling prices	$750,000
At cost	562,500

The December 31 inventory at selling prices was $125,000.

Required

Reduce the December 31 inventory to approximate cost, using the retail inventory method.

Alternate 7.C.7. Slocum Company inventory at December 31, 19X4, taken on a retail basis, is $540,000. Other data relative to the company follow.

	Cost	Retail
Sales for 19X4		$7,050,000
Purchases during 19X4	$4,455,000	6,750,000
Inventory at December 31, 19X3	594,000	900,000

Required

1) Reduce the retail inventory at December 31, 19X4, to cost, using retail inventory procedure.

2) The owner of the company suspects that shoplifting has been widespread during the year. Estimate the cost of the inventory that was stolen or that otherwise disappeared during 19X4.

ALTERNATE PROBLEMS FOR CHAPTER 7

Alternate 7.1. The Growrite Farm Supply custom-mixes fertilizer for its customers. Growrite uses a periodic inventory system. During the quarter ended March 31, one of the chemicals used in the basic mix has fallen sharply in price. Inventory and sales data for the chemical follow.

			Tons	Cost/Ton	Selling Price/Ton
Jan.	1	Beginning inventory	500	$24	
	3	Purchases	300	23	
	15	Sales	200		$32
	30	Sales	200		32
Feb.	4	Purchases	1,000	21	
	20	Sales	600		31
Mar.	1	Purchases	2,000	19	
	8	Sales	800		31
	15	Purchases	1,000	18	
	27	Sales	1,200		30

Required

1) Identify the inventory method that will result in the most reported net income for the quarter.

2) Identify the inventory method that will show the least net income.

3) How much more (or less) gross profit will result from using the first-in, first-out method than from using the last-in, first-out method?

4) The use of FIFO will result in the same inventory figure under either a periodic or a perpetual system, whereas LIFO inventory will differ with the two systems. Explain why these differences will occur.

Alternate 7.2. The Lee Company sells only one product. Inventories are costed on a first-in, first-out basis, using a periodic inventory system. An unadjusted trial balance and adjustments information follow.

	THE LEE COMPANY Unadjusted Trial Balance December 31, 19X4		
A/C #	Account	Debit	Credit
111	Cash	15,000	
112	Prepaid Insurance	–0–	
113	Prepaid Advertising	–0–	
115	Accounts Receivable	72,000	
0115	Allowance for Doubtful Accounts	340	
116	Merchandise Inventory	98,000	
118	Equipment	60,000	
0118	Accumulated Depreciation—Equipment		12,000
211	Accounts Payable		12,500
212	Bank Loan Payable		20,000
213	Interest Payable		–0–
311	S. Lee, Capital		51,340
312	S. Lee, Withdrawals	4,500	
411	Sales		650,000
412	Sales Returns and Allowances	6,000	
511	Purchases	390,000	
512	Purchases Discounts		2,200
513	Purchases Returns and Allowances		600
514	Freight In	2,800	
610	Cost of Goods Sold	–0–	
611	Salary Expense	70,000	
612	Rent Expense	12,000	
613	Insurance Expense	8,400	
614	Advertising Expense	5,800	
615	Utilities Expense	3,800	
616	Depreciation Expense	–0–	
617	Interest Expense	–0–	
618	Uncollectible Accounts Expense	–0–	
		748,640	748,640

Adjustments Data

a) Equipment depreciation for the year, $6,000.

b) A one-year fire insurance premium was paid on July 1, 19X4. Insurance Expense was debited for the entire amount, $1,400.

c) On October 1 the company paid $4,000 in advance for ads that were to appear in four monthly issues of a magazine, starting with November 19X4. The entire amount was debited to Advertising Expense.

d) The bank loan payable was incurred on September 2, 19X4, when a note bearing interest at 9% per annum was signed. Interest is to be paid on February 28, 19X5, the due date of the note.

e) It is expected that 1% of Accounts Receivable will prove to be uncollectible.

f) Inventory Activity

Jan. 1	Beginning inventory	980 units @ $100
Jan. 12	Purchased	1,269 units @ 100
Feb. 10	Purchased	800 units @ 102
Mar. 15	Sold	1,500 units
May 10	Purchased	1,100 units @ 105
July 20	Sold	580 units
Sept. 29	Sold	1,669 units
Nov. 26	Purchased	600 units @ 110
Dec. 24	Sold	700 units

Required

Prepare a ten-column work sheet for the year 19X4.

Alternate 7.3. Baker Company has provided the following information to the accounting firm that does its annual audit.

Inventory, January 1, 19X4	$ 200,000
Purchases during 19X4	2,500,000
Inventory, December 31, 19X4	582,000
Sales during 19X4	3,265,000
Average gross profit rate during previous four years	35%

Required

1) Describe an approach for testing the reasonableness of the ending inventory figure.

2) Use the approach you just described to test the ending inventory figure, and indicate whether you would consider the inventory within reason.

Alternate 7.4. Reported data for M. J. Stores are as follows.

	Cost	Retail
Beginning inventory	$ 53,760	$ 84,000
Purchases	1,006,620	1,560,000
Sales		1,359,000
Ending inventory	103,525	
Historic gross profit rate	35%	

Required

Test the reasonableness of the reported cost of ending inventory by two estimating methods, and indicate whether you consider the reported figure to be reasonable.

ALTERNATE PROBLEMS FOR SECTION 8.A

Alternate 8.A.5. On July 1 the WST Company purchased a drill press, serial number BA–2076, for $19,000. The drill press was installed in Building C. Costs of machines are charged to a general ledger control account titled Machinery and Equipment. Freight on the machine was $500, which was paid July 5. The estimated useful life of the machine is 10 years, after which it is expected to have a salvage value of $1,000.

Required

Set up a subsidiary plant ledger record card similar to the one in the section, showing the preceding information on the card. Include half a year's straight-line depreciation recorded on December 31.

Alternate 8.A.6. Selected events for July are as follows.

July 10 Traded an old car for a new car that had a list price of $10,000. The car dealer allowed $3,000 for the old car, and the remaining cost, $7,000, was paid in cash. The old car had cost $6,000 and had accumulated depreciation of $4,000 at the time it was traded.

17 Sold an old press for $3,000 cash. The machine had originally cost $15,000 and had accumulated depreciation to date of $9,600. Factory machinery and equipment are controlled by a general ledger account titled Machinery.

28 An old grinding machine that had originally cost $20,000 and had accumulated depreciation of $18,000 and a remaining life of 2 years was overhauled at a cash cost of $3,250. As a result of the overhaul, the machine is expected to last for 3 additional years (a total of 5 years of life remaining).

30 A new lighting system was installed in a 10-year-old building that has a remaining life of 25 years. The new lighting system cost $125,000, which was paid in cash.

Required

Make journal entries to record the preceding events.

Alternate 8.A.7. On June 10, 19X4, the Bender Company purchased a custom-made piece of equipment at a cost of $120,000. Terms of the sale were 5/30, n/60. Freight charges of $3,600 and installation costs of $2,400 were paid on June 10, 19X4. The machine was paid for on June 25, 19X4. It is the company's policy to use straight-line depreciation and to record depreciation on long-lived assets as if they were acquired on the first day of the month of purchase. The equipment is expected to have a useful life of 10 years and a salvage value of $12,000. On

January 2, 19X8, the company paid $13,300 cash for a major overhaul of the equipment. As a result of the overhaul, the machine has an expected useful life of 8 years from the date of the overhaul, with an expected salvage value of $10,000.

Required

Make journal entries to record the transactions just described, including depreciation for the years ended December 31, 19X4 through 19X8.

ALTERNATE PROBLEMS FOR SECTION 8.B

Alternate 8.B.8. Sutton Adjusters purchased four delivery vans on November 1, 19X4, at a total cost of $49,000. The vans have an expected life of 4 years and an estimated total salvage value of $1,000.

Required

Make the adjusting journal entry at December 31, 19X4, assuming use of

1) The straight-line time method.

2) The straight-line use method (the vans are expected to be useful for a total of 320,000 miles; they were driven 21,000 miles through December 31).

3) The double-declining-balance method.

4) The sum-of-years'-digits method.

Alternate 8.B.9. The TGY Company purchased a steamroller on January 2, 19X3, at a cost of $392,000. Freight charges of $8,000 for delivery of the steamroller were also paid on January 2. The estimated useful life is 5 years, after which the expected salvage value is $40,000.

Required

Prepare a chart like the one that follows, showing the depreciation that would be recorded at the end of each year and the total for each method.

Date	Depreciation			
	Straight-Line	*Sum-of-Years'-Digits*	*Double-Declining-Balance*	*150% Declining-Balance*
12/31/X3				
12/31/X4				
12/31/X5				
12/31/X6				
12/31/X7				
Total				

Alternate 8.B.10. On July 1, 19X4, Bold Company purchased 800 acres of land for a cash cost of $2,560,000. Core-drilling samples indicated that the land contained approximately 3,000,000 tons of ore reserves. It is estimated that after all the ore is removed, the land will have a residual value of $160,000. During 19X4, 450,000 tons of ore were removed. During 19X5, 500,000 tons were removed. On May 15, 19X6, the land was sold for $2,500,000 cash. From January 1, 19X6, through May 15, 19X6, 300,000 tons of ore were removed.

Required

Make journal entries to record

1) The purchase of the land.

2) Depletion for 19X4, 19X5, and 19X6.

3) The sale of the land.

ALTERNATE PROBLEMS FOR CHAPTER 8

Alternate 8.1. Barton Company purchased a stamping machine on July 1, 19X4, at a cash cost of $36,000. On the same date, installation charges of $1,400 were paid. The machine has an expected useful life of 8 years and an estimated salvage value of $2,000. The company rounds depreciation calculations to the nearest whole dollar.

Required

1) Make journal entries to record the acquisition of the machine.

2) Make adjusting journal entries to record depreciation at December 31, 19X4, and December 31, 19X5, assuming use of

 a) The straight-line time method.

 b) The double-declining-balance method.

 c) The sum-of-years'-digits method.

Alternate 8.2. On January 3, 19X4, GB III Company traded in an obsolete computer for a modern computer that had a list price of $430,000. The computer vendor allowed $50,000 for the old computer, and the remaining cost of $380,000 was paid in cash. The old computer had cost $180,000 and had accumulated depreciation of $140,000. GB III Company uses the double-declining-balance method of depreciation. The new computer is expected to last 10 years and have a salvage value of $40,000.

Required

1) Make the journal entry at January 3, 19X4, to record the acquisition of the new computer.

2) Make the adjusting entry at December 31, 19X4, to record the year's depreciation on the new computer.

3) Make the adjusting entry to record depreciation on the computer for 19X5.

4) On January 2, 19X6, the computer was sold for $250,000 cash. Record the sale of the computer.

5) Make the entry on January 2, 19X6, to record the sale of the computer for $250,000, assuming that straight-line time depreciation had been used (instead of the double-declining-balance method).

Alternate 8.3. An unadjusted trial balance for the Nodrah Company is as shown here, followed by adjustments information.

NODRAH COMPANY **Unadjusted Trial Balance** **December 31, 19X4**		
	Debit	**Credit**
Cash	21,000	
Accounts Receivable	40,000	
Land	25,000	
Machinery	22,600	
Accumulated Depreciation—Machinery		6,000
Automotive Equipment	30,000	
Accumulated Depreciation—Automotive Equipment		15,600
Building	140,000	
Accumulated Depreciation—Building		20,213
Accounts Payable		20,000
Notes Payable (due 6/30/X5)		12,000
Mortgage Payable		82,000
M. Nodrah, Capital		66,787
Fees		280,000
Salary Expense	180,000	
Utilities Expense	7,000	
Supplies Expense	12,000	
Interest Expense	6,200	
Gasoline Expense	7,800	
Other Expense	11,000	
	502,600	502,600

Adjustments Data

1) All machinery was purchased during January, 19X3. Estimated life is 6 years, with a salvage value of $1,600. The sum-of-years'-digits depreciation method is used.

2) All automotive equipment was purchased during January, 19X1. Estimated life is 5 years, with a salvage value of $4,000. The straight-line time depreciation method is used.

3) The building was occupied during January, 19X2. Estimated life is 20 years, with an estimated scrap value of $18,000. The depreciation method used is 150% declining-balance (150% of the straight-line rate).
(*Suggestion:* For convenience, calculate depreciation to the nearest whole dollar.)

Required

1) Prepare a ten-column work sheet.

2) Prepare an income statement for the year ended December 31, 19X4.

3) Prepare a balance sheet at December 31, 19X4.

Alternate 8.4. On January 3, 19X4, the Jacqueline Company purchased a stamping machine, serial number SM–461, for $85,000. A cash payment of $40,000 was made, and a note was signed for the balance. The stamping machine was installed in the Frogtown Plant on January 4, 19X4. An installation fee of $2,100 was paid in cash on that date. The cost of the machine is to be charged to a general ledger control account titled Machinery. The estimated useful life of the stamping machine is 16 years, after which it is expected to have a salvage value of $2,750. The company follows the practice of rounding all depreciation calculations to the nearest whole dollar.

Required

1) Make general journal entries to record the events just described.

2) Fill in information for the stamping machine on a subsidiary plant ledger record card like the one illustrated in the chapter.

3) Make an adjusting journal entry at December 31, 19X4, to record depreciation on the stamping machine. The company uses the double-declining-balance depreciation method.

4) Indicate the first year's depreciation on the subsidiary record card.

ALTERNATE PROBLEMS FOR SECTION 9.A

Alternate 9.A.7. Events relating to petty cash for Philber Company are shown here.

July 2   Established a $100 petty cash fund.

6   Reimbursed employee for entertainment expense related to the business, $35.

10   Paid delivery charge (freight in), $12.

15   Reimbursed an employee for travel expenses, $24.

18   Replenished petty cash fund for expenditures through this date.

25   Increased petty cash fund to $150.

Required

1) Assume that the July 6 expenditure was to reimburse M. Tight, and that payment was approved by his supervisor, Jane Biggs. Prepare a petty cash voucher similar to the one illustrated in the section.

2) Make general journal entries to record the aforementioned events.

Alternate 9.A.8. The following events relating to petty cash are provided for the B&J Company.

July 2   Established a $150 petty cash fund.

10   Paid for cleaning supplies, $22.

16   Paid freight in, $68.

24   Paid delivery cost, $9.

28   The fund was replenished. When vouchers were summarized, it was discovered that the fund was short $2.

Required

Make appropriate journal entries to record the foregoing events.

Alternate 9.A.9. Events relating to petty cash for Bower Company follow.

Mar. 3   Established a $75 petty cash fund.

8   Purchased office supplies, $12.

10   Paid delivery charges (freight in) to TDY Freight Company, $8.

16   Purchased postage stamps, $24.

18   Paid delivery charges (freight in), $12.

22   Received a collect telegram, $5.

30   Replenished petty cash fund for expenditures made through this date.

30   Increased petty cash fund to $125 balance.

Required

1) Prepare a petty cash voucher for the March 10 expenditure. Use fictitious names and initials where necessary.

2) Make the journal entries needed to record the aforementioned events.

ALTERNATE PROBLEMS FOR SECTION 9.B

Alternate 9.B.6. The following information is provided for the Sockorelli Company.

a. The bank statement balance at October 31 was $9,423.54.

b. The cash in bank account balance at October 31 was $11,811.11.

c. Check Nos. 2411, 2415, and 2416 totaling $2,100.43 were outstanding.

d. Deposits in transit at October 31 totaled $4,600.

e. A payment on account of $1,192 was recorded in the cash payments journal as $1,129.

f. The bank returned a paid check drawn by the Soccer Company for $812 with the other paid checks.

g. A credit memo for $1,000 was listed on the statement for a note collected by the bank on the company's behalf.

h. The bank statement included a service charge of $13 that was not recorded by the company.

Required

1) Prepare a two-part bank reconciliation at October 31 for the Sockorelli Company.

2) Make an entry (or entries) to adjust the Cash in Bank account balance at October 31.

Alternate 9.B.7. Information is shown here for the Barbarino and Alexander Company.

a. Bank statement balance at August 31, $5,751.60.

b. Cash in Bank account balance at August 31, $994.60.

c. Outstanding deposits at August 31, $950.

d. Outstanding checks at August 31, $2,655.

e. A customer's check for $75 marked "insufficient funds" was included with the bank statement.

f. A bank service charge of $8 appeared on the bank statement but was not recorded by the company.

g. Check No. 1311 for $461 in payment on Accounts Payable was recorded as $416.

h. The bank collected a customer's note receivable for $3,000, and interest of $180, and credited the proceeds directly to the company's account on October 31.

Required

1) Prepare a two-part bank reconciliation at August 31.

2) Make an entry (or entries) to adjust the Cash in Bank account to the correct balance at August 31.

Alternate 9.B.8. The Macy Company received a bank statement showing a balance of $5,530 at December 31. The company's Cash in Bank account indicated a balance of $7,031 on the same day. The following information has been gathered.

a. Outstanding deposits at December 31, $625.

b. Outstanding checks at December 31, $1,090.

c. The bank erroneously deducted from Macy's account a $160 check written by the James Company.

d. A deposit of $2,000 was erroneously recorded by the bank as $200.

e. There was an unrecorded bank service charge of $6.

Required

1) Prepare a two-part bank reconciliation at December 31.

2) Make an entry (or entries) to adjust the Cash in Bank account to the correct balance at December 31.

3) State what action Macy Company should take as a result of the errors made by the bank.

ALTERNATE PROBLEMS FOR CHAPTER 9

Alternate 9.1. John Attle opened his first checking account when he went away to college. He was very surprised early during the semester when the college bookstore called him to say that a $24 check he had written had been returned to the bookstore marked NSF for nonsufficient funds. John pieced together the following information from his sketchy records, his memory, and the September 30 bank statement that he had thrown in his desk drawer without reading.

    a. His checkbook record showed a balance of $60.16 on September 30.

    b. The September 30 bank statement showed a balance of $21.06.

    c. John had never recorded Check No. 28 in the amount of $18.60.

    d. John had made an error in subtracting a check from the checkbook balance, which resulted in overstating the balance by $10.

    e. There was a $5 check-printing charge that John had not recorded.

    f. There was a deposit in transit of $25.

    g. There were outstanding checks in the amounts of $24 and $45.50.

    h. John had recorded a $50 deposit twice in his checkbook.

Required

Find John's correct amount of disposable cash by preparing a two-part bank reconciliation at September 30.

Alternate 9.2. Selected information follows for the JG Company.

    a. Bank statement balance at October 31, $9,430.

    b. Cash in Bank account balance at October 31, $12,854.

    c. Check No. 1325 for $46 had been cashed by the bank and was returned with the statement. JG Company had issued a stop-payment order to the bank four days before the check was cashed.

    d. Check No. 1336 for $150 was written on October 31 to replenish the petty cash fund. It was not included with the canceled checks.

    e. A bank service charge of $9 appeared on the bank statement.

    f. Cash receipts for October 31 of $3,519 were not deposited in the bank until November 3.

Required

    1) Prepare a two-part bank reconciliation at October 31.

    2) Make an entry (or entries) to adjust the Cash in Bank account at October 31.

    3) State what should be done about check No. 1325.

    4) Give a possible explanation for the fact that check No. 1336 did not clear, even though it was written to Petty Cash and did not have to be mailed anywhere.

Alternate 9.3. Selected information is as follows for the Stacy Company.

    a. Bank statement balance at July 31, $34,124.

    b. Cash in Bank account balance at July 31, $29,258.

c. The bank statement included a late payment charge of $135 that was erroneously deducted by the bank from Stacy's account.

d. The deposit for July 24 of $5,375 was erroneously recorded in Stacy's books as $3,575.

e. There were a number of outstanding checks totaling $2,090.

f. A customer's check for $495 was returned with the notation "insufficient funds."

g. Deposits in transit at July 31 totaled $894.

h. A credit amount for $2,500 was listed on the statement for a note collected by the bank on the company's behalf.

Required

1) Prepare a two-part bank reconciliation at July 31.

2) The bookkeeper who prepared the reconciliation complained about the large number of outstanding checks for small amounts. Many of these checks were written for delivery charges, miscellaneous purchases of supplies, and postage. Suggest ways that the company might improve its cash control and reduce the number of checks written for small amounts each month.

ALTERNATE PROBLEMS FOR SECTION 10.A

Alternate 10.A.4. A list of invoices received by D&M Company is shown here. D&M Company uses a voucher system. Quantities, prices, and terms shown on a voucher are verified by B. Looper. Extensions and footings and account distributions are verified by Q. Arkle. Vouchers are approved for payment by R. Gifford.

Invoice					Account		
Date	*No.*	**P.O. No.**	**Payable To**	**Amount**	*Name*	*No.*	**Terms**
19--							
Mar. 2	2131	616–P	Zeno Petroleum	$ 980	Gas Exp.	54	1/10, n/30
3	M–64	611–P	Bobbie Jeans, Inc.	620	Purchases	51	n/30
7			Learned Hand, Esq.	1,500	Legal Exp.	55	n/30
8	A218	619–P	B&G Suppliers	108	Supplies	14	2/10, n/30
11	1516	608–P	Moldo Products	2,700	Purchases	51	n/30
13	486	609–P	Major Equipment	1,600	Equipment	18	2/10, n/30
20	2121	618–P	B-Imports	2,100	Purchases	51	2/10, n/30
21	1211		Electric Edison Co.	518	Util. Exp.	56	n/30
26	616	610–P	Redram, Inc.	2,200	Purchases	51	n/30

Required

1) Prepare Voucher No. 4141, dated March 4, for the first invoice just listed.

2) Record the invoices in a voucher register starting with Voucher No. 4141. Assume that in each case vouchers were prepared two days after the invoice date.

3) Balance and rule the register, and note appropriate account reference numbers as they would appear after postings to ledger accounts have been completed. (Vouchers Payable is Account No. 21.)

Alternate 10.A.5. Three situations for the Hauhart Company are described here.

Oct. 4   Received an invoice, dated October 1, from Baker Manufacturing for a stamping machine (Equipment account). The amount of the invoice was $12,300 for the machine and $400 for installation, terms 2/10, n/30. The invoice was paid on October 13 with Check No. 2808.

     8   Check No. 2802 for $260 was made payable to Petty Cash to replenish petty cash and to increase the amount of the fund by $100. Expenditures from petty cash consisted of $130 for travel expense, $10 for postage expense, and $20 for freight in.

   12   Merchandise was received on a C.O.D. shipment. Check No. 2807 was drawn to Fast Freight Company for $2,118. The merchandise cost $2,081 and the freight charge, including the C.O.D. charge, was $37.

Required

1) Prepare a voucher form to reflect the information provided for each situation. (Number vouchers serially starting with No. 101.)

2) Record the three vouchers in a voucher register.

3) Record payments of the vouchers in a check register, and note the payments properly in the voucher register.

Alternate 10.A.6. State's Department Store received the following invoice from Top Wholesale. Susan Bean verified the invoice on the date received, November 14. D. D. Stover approved the voucher. The merchandise was ordered on Purchase Order No. X4–232.

INVOICE			NO. 500015
	TOP WHOLESALE 145 Stoneage Road New York, NY		
Sold to:			*November 13, 19--*
State' Department Store *New York, NY*			

Quantity	Item	Unit Price	Amount
540	*Dresses*	*28.00*	*15,120.00*
Terms: *2/10, n/30*			

Required

Prepare Voucher No. 7852, dated November 15, for the invoice shown.

ALTERNATE PROBLEMS FOR SECTION 10.B

Alternate 10.B.7. The Harol Company incurred wage expenses of $20,800 for the pay period ended February 28. FICA taxes were withheld from all earnings at a 7% rate. Additionally, $3,150 was withheld for federal income taxes, and $675 was withheld for a credit union savings plan.

Required

1) Make a general journal entry to record the payroll, assuming actual payment of wages is made at another time.

2) Make a general journal entry to record the employer's payroll tax expense for the pay period. Assume a state unemployment tax rate of 2.7% and a federal unemployment tax rate of 0.8% on the total amount of wages.

3) Prepare a single general journal entry to take the place of the two preceding entries.

Alternate 10.B.8. A payroll register for Axelrod Associates is as follows. Axelrod pays its employees biweekly, five days after the payroll period ends.

PAYROLL REGISTER					FOR BIWEEKLY PERIOD ENDED _JUNE 30, 19--_	
			Deductions			
Name	Gross Pay	Fed. Inc. Tax	FICA Tax	Union Dues	Total	Net Pay
T. Aimes	1,600.00	209.00	112.00	15.00	336.00	1,264.00
K. Okonkwo	960.00	82.40	67.20	15.00	164.60	795.40
S. Petruski	960.00	93.60	67.20	15.00	175.80	784.20
R. Stiner	1,500.00	180.00	105.00	15.00	300.00	1,200.00
W. Wertz	2,400.00	511.00	168.00	–0–	679.00	1,721.00
Total	7,420.00	1,076.00	519.40	60.00	1,655.40	5,764.60

Required

1) Make an entry in general journal form to record the payroll on June 30.
2) Record the employer's FICA tax expense for the June 30 payroll.
3) Make an entry on July 5 to record the transfer of cash to a payroll bank account for payment to employees.
4) Assume that the taxes related to the June 30 payroll are deposited with a bank on July 10. Make the appropriate journal entry.

Alternate 10.B.9. Jim Bruce works for Strong Mobile Homes as a carpenter for $12 an hour. He receives an overtime premium of one-half his regular rate for hours worked in excess of 40 each week. For the biweekly pay period ended June 15 he worked 43 hours and 46 hours, respectively. He is married and claims four exemption allowances. Mr. Bruce's wages are subject to deductions for FICA tax at 7%, federal income tax, and union dues of $12 each biweekly period.

Required

Using the foregoing data and the federal withholding tax table provided in Illustration 10.10, fill in the first line of an employee's individual earnings record for Mr. Bruce.

ALTERNATE PROBLEMS FOR CHAPTER 10

Alternate 10.1. Selected transactions for the Zorton Company are listed below.

Transactions

Nov. 3   Paid freight charges to the Queens Freight Company driver for delivery of merchandise, $31 (Check No. 1193).

4	Purchased merchandise on account from the Williams Company; terms 2/10, n/30, $4,100.
9	Received invoice from the General Oil Company for October's Gasoline Expense, $790.
12	Paid for merchandise purchased November 4 from the Williams Company (Check No. 1194).
13	Purchased supplies for cash from B&G Suppliers, $86 (Check No. 1195).
30	Wrote a check for $4,600 payable to Payroll Bank Account for November salaries (Check No. 1196).
30	Replenished petty cash fund, $88 (Check No. 1197). Expenditures from petty cash were $28 (Freight In), $40 (Travel Expense), and $20 (Postage Expense).

Required

Record the transactions in a voucher register and a check register. Start with Voucher No. 7611 and remember to make appropriate notations of payments in the voucher register.

Alternate 10.2. Shown below and on the following page are the last few transactions for the month of July, a voucher register, and a check register for the Kropcheck Company.

Transactions

July 27	Paid freight charges to the Speedy Delivery Company for merchandise delivery, $86 (Check No. 2132).
29	Paid for merchandise purchased July 21 from the Proper Company, Voucher No. 3131, invoice, $5,800, terms 2/10, n/30 (Check No. 2133).
29	Received invoice from the Marciano Fuel Company for heating oil used from June 15 through July 15 (Heating Expense), $780.
31	Wrote check No. 2134 to the payroll account for salaries for July, $8,756.

Required

1) Record the events in a voucher register and a check register. (Start with Voucher No. 3469.)
2) Set up ledger accounts for the following:
   a) Vouchers Payable—Account No. 212, July 1 balance, $10,000.
   b) Purchases—Account No. 511, July 1 balance, $40,000.
   c) Heating Expense—Account No. 618, July 1 balance, $5,000.
3) Balance and rule the registers, and post appropriate amounts to the ledger accounts set up in part (2).

VOUCHER REGISTER				
			Paid	
Voucher No.	**Date**	**Payee**	*Date*	*Ck. No.*
	19-- July 26	Brought Forward		

CHECK REGISTER						*PAGE 38*
				Vouchers Payable	**Purchases Discounts**	**Cash**
Check No.	**Date**	**Payee**	**Voucher No.**	*Dr.*	*Cr.*	*Cr.*
	19-- July 27	Brought Forward		12,560.48	92.61	12,467.87

Alternate 10.3. The Dinko Company employs six people. The cumulative earnings through July 30 and the earnings for the biweekly pay period ended August 13 follow.

Employee	Cumulative Earnings Through July 30	Earnings 7/31–8/13	Exemption Allowances Claimed
J. Bently	$26,100	$1,756	7
J. Farkle	3,180	1,060	1
M. Jones	28,500	2,900	4
F. Plotts	17,400	1,040	5
H. Vicker	5,060	980	0
S. Xavier	8,370	1,080	2
Total	$88,610	$8,816	

FICA taxes are 7% on the first $30,000 earned; state unemployment taxes are 2.7% on the first $7,000 earned; federal unemployment taxes are 0.8% on the first $7,000. Employees contribute 5% of their gross pay to a retirement plan, and the employer matches their contributions. Both the employees' and the employer's retirement contributions are paid to an insurance company quarterly. All the employees are married.

					Other Debits		
Vouchers Payable	Purchases	Freight In	Supplies	Salaries			PAGE 49
Cr.	Dr.	Dr.	Dr.	Dr.	Account	Ref.	Amount
18,176.49	7,849.56	1,192.70	361.21	7,651.02			1,122.00

Required

1) Calculate the total deductions for payroll taxes and retirement contributions for the period ended August 13. (*Note:* Refer to the tax withholding table in Illustration 10.10.)

2) Calculate the amount of the payroll taxes levied on the employer and the amount of the employer's contribution to the retirement plan for the period ended August 13.

3) Make general journal entries to record the payroll, the employer's payroll tax expense, and the employer's retirement contributions expense for the pay period.

Alternate 10.4. The Frogtown Storm Window Company is subject to the Fair Labor Standards Act, the Federal Insurance Contributions Act (assume 7% on the first $30,000 of earnings), and federal and state unemployment taxes at 0.8% federal and 2.7% state on the first $7,000 of earnings. The company employs five people as follows.

Name	Title	Pay Class
B. Carter	Laborer	$6.00 per hour
C. Doctor	Laborer	$5.00 per hour
H. Frank	Laborer	$6.00 per hour
Q. Porks	Manager	Salary
G. Redram	Salesperson	$6.50 per hour

The company pays on the Monday following the end of the pay period and transfers the amount of the net payroll to a special payroll bank account on each payday. The manager, Q. Porks, earns a biweekly gross salary of $1,000. The February payroll periods and pay dates were as follows.

For the Biweekly Period Ended	Pay Date
February 13	February 15
February 27	March 1

Transactions for Acorn and a partial list of accounts are as follows.

Transactions

Nov. 9   Purchased merchandise for cash, $1,880.75.

     11   Sold merchandise on account to Jack Alexander (Subsidiary Account No. 112), $195.60.

     20   Purchased equipment paying $400 cash and promising to pay the balance of $600 to the Kingsville Equipment Company (Subsidiary Account No. 214) in 30 days.

     24   Collected $248 on account from Roger Morely (Subsidiary Account No. 126).

PARTIAL LIST OF ACCOUNTS	
111	Cash
112	Accounts Receivable
121	Equipment
211	Accounts Payable
411	Sales
511	Purchases

Required

Start with transaction No. 1101, and code the transactions in a twenty-three-digit format like the one illustrated in this problem. Write zeros in any of the 23 spaces not otherwise used.

ALTERNATE PROBLEMS FOR SECTION 12.A

Alternate 12.A.5. Jim Gwen operates a bowling alley. He lives in a soundproof apartment behind the bowling alley, which represents approximately one-third of the building space. Jim's bookkeeper has prepared the following income statement for 19X4.

GWEN BOWLING ALLEY
Income Statement
For the Year Ended December 31, 19X4

Revenues		
Service revenue	$96,000	
Sales	34,000	$130,000
Expenses		
Cost of goods sold	$22,100	
Salaries	18,000	
Depreciation	28,000	
Utilities	3,200	
Maintenance	4,200	
Gasoline	2,700	78,200
Net Income		$ 51,800

A balance sheet prepared for December 31, 19X4, showed total business assets of $500,000, and owner's equity of $320,000.

An audit of the accounting records turned up the following facts.

a. The entire bowling alley building is included as a business asset at a net book value on December 31 of $240,000. Building depreciation for the entire building in the amount of $24,000 was included in depreciation expense for 19X4. About one-fourth of the $3,200 for utilities was applicable to the residence portion of the building.

b. A pickup truck was included among business assets at a net book value at December 31 of $12,000. Truck depreciation in the amount of $4,000 was charged to depreciation expense during 19X4. The pickup, which had Gwen Bowling Alley printed on the sides, was used for business and personal use. The owner agreed that about 50% of the pickup use was personal. The total gasoline bill of $2,700 was included as a business expense.

c. About one-sixth of the maintenance expense was attributable to the personal part of the building.

Required

1) State the accounting concept that has been most violated in accounting for the bowling alley, and defend your answer.

2) Under three columns like those that follow, show the effects of correcting for each situation just described, and determine the corrected net income, total assets, and owner's equity figures.

| | 19X4 Net Income | December 31, 19X4 | |
		Assets	Owner's Equity
As Reported	$51,800	$500,000	$320,000

Alternate 12.A.6. Jay Company insured the life of one of its key employees for $500,000. The cash surrender value of the insurance policy is carried in an account titled *Cash Surrender Value of Life Insurance*. On April 15, 19X4, the insured employee died. On that date, the cash surrender value of the policy was carried at $240,000.

Required

1) Suggest reasons why a company may wish to insure the life of a key employee.

2) Prepare an entry on April 15 to record the death of the employee. Assume that the receivable will be collected from the insurance company at a later date. Devise descriptive titles for the accounts affected by the entry.

3) State whether you think the entry you made conveys the real economic consequences of the employee's death, and give reasons why you answered as you did.

ALTERNATE PROBLEMS FOR SECTION 12.B

Alternate 12.B.7. Selected balance sheet data for Jason Company are as follows.

	12/31/X2	12/31/X1
Cash	$108,000	$108,000
Inventory	200,000	200,000
Land	190,000	190,000
Mortgage payable (credit balance)	(30,000)	(30,000)

Price index numbers were as follows.

12/31/X1	160
12/31/X2	176
Average for 19X2	168

Required

1) Assuming that the land was purchased on December 31, 19X1, calculate its cost stated in dollars of December 31, 19X2.

2) Assuming the Cash, Inventory, and Mortgage Payable balances remained constant throughout 19X2, calculate the purchasing power gain or loss on monetary items that occurred during 19X2.

Alternate 12.B.8. Tara Company purchased land on January 1, 19X4, for $100,000. Tara also had $22,000 cash in a special bank checking account throughout 19X4, and owed $60,000 to a noteholder during the entire year. Assume that the price index was 200 at January 1, 19X4, 176 at December 31, 19X4, and that the average index during 19X4 was 188.

Required

1) Determine the land cost in equivalent end-of-year dollars.

2) Determine the purchasing power gain or loss that resulted from holding the cash during the year.

3) Determine the purchasing power gain or loss that resulted from owing the money during the year.

Alternate 12.B.9. Janice's Dress Shop maintains inventory on a last-in, first-out (LIFO) basis. Cost of goods sold was reported on the current income statement as follows.

Beginning inventory	$ 59,000
Purchases	148,000
Goods available	$207,000
Less: Ending inventory	73,000
Cost of goods sold	$134,000

The beginning inventory was purchased when the price index was 125. Purchases were made evenly over the year. The price index at December 31 was 150. The average index for the year was 142.

Required

Prepare the cost of goods sold section of the income statement in end-of-year equivalent dollars.

ALTERNATE PROBLEMS FOR CHAPTER 12

Alternate 12.1. Redram Company started business on December 31, 19X4. A comparative balance sheet for Redram shows data at 12/31/X4 and 12/31/X5.

REDRAM COMPANY Comparative Balance Sheet		
	12/31/X5	**12/31/X4**
ASSETS		
Cash	$ 42,000	$ 42,000
Accounts receivable	160,000	–0–
Inventory (LIFO basis)	30,000	30,000
Building and equipment (net)	182,000	190,000
Land	30,000	30,000
Total Assets	$444,000	$292,000
LIABILITIES		
Accounts payable	$ 15,000	$ –0–
Note payable	40,000	40,000
Total Liabilities	$ 55,000	$ 40,000
OWNER'S EQUITY		
T. Redram, capital	$389,000	$252,000
Total Liabilities and Owner's Equity	$444,000	$292,000

Price index numbers were as follows.

December 31, 19X4	180
Average for 19X5	198
December 31, 19X5	207

Assume that current receivables and payables grew evenly over the year, and other assets and liabilities remained constant throughout the year except that the net book value of Buildings and Equipment declined evenly as depreciation accrued.

Required

1) Calculate the purchasing power gain or loss on monetary items that occurred during 19X5.

2) Restate (prepare) the comparative balance sheet for Redram in 12/31/X5 equivalent dollars.

3) In regard to the restated balance sheet, identify any departures from conventional accounting concepts, and state whether you think the departures are justified.

Alternate 12.2. An income statement for Redram Company for the year 19X5 follows. Refer when necessary to the comparative balance sheet presented in the previous problem.

REDRAM COMPANY
Income Statement
For the Year Ended December 31, 19X5

Sales		$600,000
Cost of goods sold		325,000
Gross Profit		$275,000
Operating expenses		
Depreciation	$ 8,000	
Other	150,000	158,000
Net Income		$117,000

Price index numbers were as follows.

December 31, 19X4	180
Average for 19X5	198
December 31, 19X5	207

Assume that sales and expenses were evenly spread over the year, and that the Building and Equipment for which depreciation is shown were acquired at December 31, 19X4.

Required

1) Convert the income statement to equivalent December 31, 19X5 dollars. Include in the income statement the effect of the purchasing power gain or loss from holding monetary items.

2) In regard to the restated income statement, identify any departures from conventional accounting concepts, and state whether you think the departures are justified.

Alternate 12.3. A balance sheet for Carland Company and other data are as follows.

CARLAND COMPANY
Balance Sheet
December 31, 19X8

ASSETS		
Cash		$ 40,000
Accounts receivable		63,000
Inventory (LIFO)		150,000
Building and furniture (net)		650,000
Land		180,000
Total Assets		$1,083,000
LIABILITIES		
Accounts payable	$110,000	
Mortgage payable	550,000	
Total Liabilities		$ 660,000
OWNER'S EQUITY		
J. Carland, capital		423,000
Total Liabilities and Owner's Equity		$1,083,000

Other data:

a. The same average balances have been maintained in the Cash and Accounts Receivable accounts since the company was started in early 19X1.

b. Inventory is maintained on a LIFO basis, and has been held at the same level since the corporation began.

c. Land, building, and furniture were all purchased on 1/2/X1.

d. The company has maintained the same average balances in the Accounts Payable and the Mortgage Payable accounts since operations began.

e. Price index data are assumed as follows.

Index at 1/2/X1	95
Average index for 19X8	168
Index at 12/31/X7	163
Index at 12/31/X8	171

Required

1) Use the information provided to prepare a balance sheet in 12/31/X8 equivalent dollars.

2) How would your solution have been different if inventory had been maintained on a FIFO basis? Your answer may be in nonspecific terms.

3) Explain how the statement you presented can be in constant dollars when monetary account balances were not converted.

ALTERNATE PROBLEMS FOR CHAPTER 13

Alternate 13.6. Ward and Shaw are equal partners with capital balances of $60,000 each at September 1.

Required

Record Sail's purchase of a one-third interest in the Ward-Shaw Company on September 1, assuming the following:

1) Sail pays cash of $36,000 directly to each of the old partners, and

   a) The amount of the payment is ignored by the accountant.

   b) Goodwill is recognized at the time Sail is admitted.

2) Sail pays cash of $30,000 directly to each of the old partners and the amount of the payment is ignored.

Alternate 13.7. Gray, Knight, and Green are partners with capital balances of $70,000 each on May 1.

Required

Record Black's purchase of a one-fourth interest in the GKG Company on May 1 assuming the following:

1) Black pays cash of $50,000 into the partnership, and

   a) An appropriate bonus is credited to the new partner.

   b) Goodwill of $20,000 is brought to the firm in the form of the new partner's business contacts and previous experience.

   c) The price paid by the new partner reflects the fact that one of the firm's assets, Land, is overstated by $60,000.

2) Black pays cash of $72,000 into the partnership, and

   a) The bonus approach is used in making the entry.

   b) Goodwill is recognized at the time that Black is admitted.

Alternate 13.8. The partners who own the Gongia Company have agreed to liquidate the partnership. A condensed balance sheet at August 31 is shown here. The partners share profits and losses equally, and all partners are personally wealthy.

GONGIA COMPANY			
Condensed Balance Sheet			
August 31, 19--			
Cash	$ 20,000	Liabilities	$160,000
Other assets	380,000	A, capital	120,000
		B, capital	80,000
		C, capital	40,000
Total	$400,000	Total	$400,000

Required

1) Assuming that noncash assets are sold for $302,000 cash on August 31,

   a) Prepare a partnership liquidation schedule.

   b) Prepare formal entries to record the liquidation of the partnership, assuming that all cash is distributed on August 31.

2) Assuming that noncash assets are sold for $125,000 cash on August 31,

   a) Prepare a partnership liquidation schedule.

   b) Prepare formal entries to record the liquidation of the partnership, assuming that all cash is distributed on August 31.

ALTERNATE PROBLEMS FOR CHAPTER 14

Alternate 14.9. Selected events pertaining to Flip Corporation are described here.

Jan. 15   Incorporators of Flip Corporation paid $80,000 in legal and other organization costs.

15   The charter obtained for Flip Corporation authorized the issuance of 1,000,000 shares of $10 par common stock and 200,000 shares of $100 par, 8% cumulative preferred stock. Incorporators had previously obtained subscriptions for 50,000 shares of common stock at $30 per share.

30   Collected $500,000 of the subscriptions receivable.

Feb. 15   Issued 20,000 shares of preferred stock for $100 cash per share.

20   Collected remaining subscriptions receivable and issued common stock.

July 15   Reacquired as treasury stock 1,000 shares of common stock at $32 per share.

Aug. 13   Reissued at $34 per share the treasury stock acquired on May 15.

18   Paid amount due incorporators for organization costs.

Required

Prepare general journal entries for Flip Corporation to record the foregoing events.

Alternate 14.10. An adjusted trial balance for RJM, Incorporated, is shown here.

<table>
<tr><td colspan="3" align="center">**RJM INCORPORATED**
Adjusted Trial Balance
December 31, 19——</td></tr>
<tr><td></td><td align="center">**Debits**</td><td align="center">**Credits**</td></tr>
<tr><td>Cash</td><td>150,000</td><td></td></tr>
<tr><td>Marketable securities</td><td>510,000</td><td></td></tr>
<tr><td>Subscriptions receivable—Common</td><td>40,000</td><td></td></tr>
<tr><td>Accounts receivable</td><td>410,000</td><td></td></tr>
<tr><td>Buildings and equipment</td><td>1,500,000</td><td></td></tr>
<tr><td>Accumulated depreciation—Buildings and equipment</td><td></td><td>456,000</td></tr>
<tr><td>Accounts payable</td><td></td><td>210,000</td></tr>
<tr><td>Notes payable</td><td></td><td>460,000</td></tr>
<tr><td>Preferred stock</td><td></td><td>500,000</td></tr>
<tr><td>Common stock</td><td></td><td>600,000</td></tr>
<tr><td>Common stock subscribed</td><td></td><td>50,000</td></tr>
<tr><td>Capital in excess of par</td><td></td><td>140,000</td></tr>
<tr><td>Capital from reissue of treasury stock</td><td></td><td>36,000</td></tr>
<tr><td>Treasury stock</td><td>198,000</td><td></td></tr>
<tr><td>Retained earnings</td><td></td><td>231,000</td></tr>
<tr><td>Sales</td><td></td><td>980,000</td></tr>
<tr><td>Salaries expense</td><td>340,000</td><td></td></tr>
<tr><td>Rent expense</td><td>96,000</td><td></td></tr>
<tr><td>Other expenses</td><td>419,000</td><td></td></tr>
<tr><td></td><td>3,663,000</td><td>3,663,000</td></tr>
</table>

Required

Prepare a balance sheet at December 31.

Alternate 14.11. The shareholders' equity section of a balance sheet for Malaby Corporation is as shown here.

<table>
<tr><td colspan="3" align="center">**SHAREHOLDERS' EQUITY**</td></tr>
<tr><td>Preferred stock, $100 par, 9%, 20,000 shares
  authorized, 20,000 shares issued</td><td>$2,000,000</td><td></td></tr>
<tr><td>Common stock, $10 par, 100,000 shares authorized,
  30,000 shares issued</td><td>300,000</td><td></td></tr>
<tr><td>Capital in excess of par</td><td>1,955,000</td><td></td></tr>
<tr><td>Capital from reissue of treasury stock</td><td>10,000</td><td></td></tr>
<tr><td>Retained earnings (the cost of treasury stock,
  $58,000, unavailable for dividends)</td><td>480,000</td><td></td></tr>
<tr><td></td><td>$4,745,000</td><td></td></tr>
<tr><td>Less: Treasury stock at cost, 1,000 shares</td><td>58,000</td><td></td></tr>
<tr><td>Total Shareholders' Equity</td><td></td><td>4,687,000</td></tr>
</table>

Required

1) Calculate the book value per common share.

2) Calculate the new book value per common share after an additional 10,000 shares of common stock are issued at $100 per share.

Alternate 14.12. At May 31, the records of the Jenkins Corporation provided the following information.

$100 par value common shares issued	200,000
Common shares subscribed	28,000
Treasury stock shares	8,000
Preferred shares issued	20,000
Total shareholders' equity	$42,690,000
Preferred shareholders' equity	$2,000,000
Market value per common share	$360

Required

1) Calculate the book value per common share at May 31.

2) Assume that the common stock is split 2 for 1 on June 1. Calculate the par value, book value, and probable market value per share immediately after the stock split.

3) Can you think of any practical reason for splitting the stock?

ALTERNATE PROBLEMS FOR CHAPTER 15

Alternate 15.7. Following are selected events for Zebo, Inc.

Events

June 1 Directors of Zebo, Inc. declared common dividends of $1.10 per share to be paid in cash on August 15 to stockholders of record on June 30. There are 2,000,000 shares of common stock outstanding.

15 Directors earmarked $500,000 of Retained Earnings for possible loss from a breach of contract lawsuit.

30 Date of record for cash dividend.

Aug. 15 Common dividends paid in cash.

Oct. 1 Directors declared a 3% stock dividend to be issued on November 15 to stockholders of record on October 19. There are 2,000,000 shares outstanding, market value $40 per share, par value $10 per share.

19 Date of record for stock dividend.

| Nov. | 15 | Stock dividend shares issued to common shareholders. |
| | 20 | The lawsuit prompting the directors' action on June 15 was settled out of court with a cash payment by Zebo of $360,000 to the plaintiff. |

Required

Make all journal entries needed to reflect the foregoing events.

Alternate 15.8. Shanon Corporation had net income after taxes for 19X5 of $21,000,000. Preferred dividends of $360,000 were paid during 19X4. There were 1,800,000 shares of common stock outstanding at January 1, 19X5, and 80,000 shares of common stock were issued on July 1, 19X5.

Required

1) Calculate earnings per share for 19X5.

2) State where earnings per share figures are normally shown in the accounting statements.

Alternate 15.9. Selected data follow for the Winston Corporation.

SELECTED DATA For the Fiscal Year Ended December 31, 19X4.	
Sales	$212,000,000
Cost of goods sold	137,000,000
Selling, administrative, and general expenses	15,000,000
Interest expense	20,000,000
Federal income taxes	15,000,000
Cash dividends paid on common stock	8,000,000
Cash dividends paid on preferred stock	2,000,000
Retained earnings at January 1, 19X4	110,400,000
Retained earnings at December 31, 19X4	125,400,000
Average number of common shares outstanding: 2,300,000	

Required

Prepare a combined statement of income and retained earnings for Winston for the year ended December 31, 19X4. Be sure to include earnings per share in your statement.

Alternate 15.10. The balance in the Retained Earnings account of the Carcase Corporation at January 1, 19X5, is $10,440,328. Selected transactions are as follows.

Transactions

19X5

| Jan. | 5 | Common dividends of $903,400 declared October 15, 19X4, are paid. |

Mar.	15	Directors declared a 5% stock dividend to be distributed on May 10 to stockholders of record on April 15. There are 2,000,000 shares of $10 par value stock outstanding, market value $20 per share.
Apr.	15	Date of record for stock dividend.
May	10	Stock dividend shares issued to common stockholders.
	13	Acquired 205,000 shares of treasury stock at a cost of $19.50 per share.
June	15	Directors declared common dividends of 52¢ per share to be paid in cash on September 1 to stockholders of record on July 30. There are 2,100,000 shares of issued stock, including 205,000 shares of treasury stock.
July	30	Date of record for cash dividend.
Sept.	1	Cash dividend paid.

Required

1) Make journal entries needed to reflect the foregoing events.

2) Open a Retained Earnings ledger account at January 1, 19X5, and post entries made in part (1). Disregard cross-referencing numbers.

ALTERNATE PROBLEMS FOR SECTION 16.A

Alternate 16.A.6. On October 31, 19X2, the Gordo Corporation issued bonds with a face value of $10,000,000. The bonds pay $500,000 in interest on April 30 and October 31 of each year of their 15-year life (10% per annum).

Required

1) Assume that the bonds were issued at 108⅛, a price that yields about 9% per annum effective interest rate. Using the effective interest method, make journal entries to

a) Record the bond issuance of October 31, 19X2

b) Recognize the accrued interest on the bonds at December 31, 19X2, the end of the accounting year

c) Record payment of bond interest on April 30, 19X3

d) Record payment of bond interest on October 31, 19X3

e) Record the retirement of the bonds on October 31, 19Y7, assuming that the entry to record the final interest payment has already been made

2) Make the required entries, assuming that the bonds were issued at 92¾, a price that yields about 11% per annum effective interest rate.

Alternate 16.A.7. The following 10-year bonds were issued by various companies on the dates shown.

Bond Issue	Issue Date	Face Amount	Issue Price	Annual Interest Paid	Effective Interest
a	9/1/X4	$1,000,000	87½	6%	8%
b	10/1/X4	$1,000,000	93¼	7%	8%
c	11/1/X4	$1,000,000	107	10%	9%
d	12/1/X4	$1,000,000	92⅜	9%	10%
e	12/1/X4	$1,000,000	100	8%	8%

Each bond pays interest semiannually.

Required

Using the effective interest method, make journal entries to record accrued interest expense for each bond at December 31, 19X4.

ALTERNATE PROBLEMS FOR SECTION 16.B

Alternate 16.B.5. Following are selected transactions for the Case Corporation.

Transactions

Jan. 20   Purchased 6,000 shares of Jenks common stock at 44¼ plus broker's commission of $2,600. These shares represent about 4% of total Jenks shares outstanding.

Feb. 10   Received 60 shares of Jenks common as a 1% stock dividend on the shares acquired January 20.

     28   Purchased 50 bonds of Fay Corporation at 100 plus five months' accrued interest plus broker's commission of $500. The bonds have a face amount of $1,000 each, bear 10% per annum interest, and pay interest semiannually on March 31 and September 30.

Mar. 31   Received semiannual interest on Fay Corporation bonds.

May 13   Sold 2,000 shares of Jenks common at 48 less brokerage commission of $900.

Sept. 30   Received semiannual interest on Fay Corporation bonds.

Oct. 30   Jenks Corporation declared a $1 per share common dividend to be paid on December 5 to shareholders of record on November 20.

Dec. 5   Received cash dividend on Jenks stock that had been declared on October 30.

Required

Record the foregoing transactions in the journal of Case Corporation.

Alternate 16.B.6. Selected transactions of Arno Corporation are shown here.

Transactions

19X3

Sept. 1 Purchased as a long-term investment 10 $1,000, 12% bonds of TKO Corporation at 123, a price that yields 8% per annum effective interest. The bonds pay interest semiannually on March 1 and September 1.

1 Purchased as a long-term investment 10 $1,000, 8% bonds of West Corporation at 77, a price that yields 12% per annum effective interest. The bonds pay interest semiannually on March 1 and September 1.

Dec. 31 Adjusted for accrued interest on TKO and West bonds.

19X4

Mar. 1 Received interest check from TKO Corporation.

1 Received interest check from West Corporation.

Sept. 1 Received interest check from TKO Corporation.

1 Received interest check from West Corporation.

Required

Make general journal entries to reflect the foregoing events on the investor's books, using the effective interest method for recognizing interest earned. Round all computations to the nearest cent.

ALTERNATE PROBLEMS FOR CHAPTER 16

Alternate 16.1. The following selected events were experienced by Dawson Corporation.

Events

19X4

Aug. 10 Issued 50,000 shares of $5 par common stock at $14 per share.

Oct. 1 Issued 10-year bonds with a face value of $600,000 at 93½, a price to yield effective interest of 9% per annum, compounded semiannually. The bonds provide for paying 8% per annum interest on April 1 and October 1.

15 Purchased 1,500 shares of Que Corporation $10 par common stock for $16 per share. All the remaining 60,000 shares of Que stock are closely owned within one family.

Nov. 1 Purchased 50 $1,000 bonds of Driden Corporation at 105. The bonds provide for 10% per annum interest payable on May 1 and November 1 of each year. The bonds will be held for several years and bear effective interest at 9% per annum.

19X5

Jan. 26   Received a check for $1,200 in payment of dividends of 80¢ per share on Que Corporation common stock.

Feb. 8   Cash dividends of 40¢ per share on 50,000 shares were declared and paid by Dawson Corporation.

Apr. 1   Paid semiannual interest on bonds.

May   1   Received check for semiannual interest on Driden bonds purchased November 1, 19X4.

Required

1) Prepare for Dawson Corporation, in general journal form, entries for the events listed, including any needed adjusting entries at December 31, 19X4, the end of Dawson's accounting Year.

2) Explain why you did (or did not) accrue dividends on December 31, 19X4.

Alternate 16.2. The Barnes Corporation issued $1,000,000 face amount bonds on September 1, 19X4, at 94¼, a price that yields about 12% per annum effective interest rate. The bonds pay $55,000 of interest on March 1 and September 1 of each year of their 10-year life (11% per annum).

Required

1) Use the effective interest method to complete the following table for the first three years of bond life.

Six-Month Period	Interest Payment	Effective Interest	Discount Amortization	Discount Balance	Gross Bond Liability
At issue				$57,500	$942,500
1	$55,000				
2					
3					
4					
5					
6					

2) Make journal entries to record the bond issue; accrued interest at December 31, 19X4; interest payments on March 1, 19X5, and September 1, 19X5; and accrued interest at December 31, 19X5.

3) On their issue date, TTA Corporation acquired as a long-term investment one-tenth of the Barnes bonds. Make general journal entries on TTA books to record the acquisition of the bonds; accrued interest on December 31, 19X4; receipt of interest on March 1, 19X5, and September 1, 19X5; and accrued interest at December 31, 19X5. TTA employs the effective interest method for amortizing discounts on long-term investments.

ALTERNATE PROBLEMS FOR SECTION 17.A

Alternate 17.A.7. The following events pertain to Onebo Company and its branch operation.

Events

Nov. 4   The Onebo Company established Branch A by transferring $40,000 cash to a bank account in the branch name.

   8   Merchandise costing $24,000 transferred from the home office to Branch A.

   16   Excess merchandise costing $4,000 returned by Branch A to the home office.

   29   Branch A transferred $8,000 cash to the home office.

Required

Prepare journal entries for both home office and branch books to reflect the foregoing events.

Alternate 17.A.8. A trial balance for the Brisbee branch of Boom Industries follows.

BOOM INDUSTRIES—BRISBEE BRANCH Trial Balance December 31, 19--		
	Debit	**Credit**
Cash	8,000	
Accounts Receivable	60,000	
Merchandise Inventory, January 1*	192,000	
Accounts Payable		99,000
Home Office		83,000
Sales		780,000
Purchases	80,000	
Shipments from Home Office	530,000	
Wage Expense	60,000	
Rent Expense	24,000	
Other Expense	8,000	
	962,000	962,000

*Merchandise Inventory, December 31, $87,000.

Required

1) Prepare an income statement for the branch for the year ended December 31.

2) Prepare a balance sheet for the branch at December 31.

3) Make the journal entry on the home office books to recognize branch income (or loss) for the year.

Alternate 17.A.9. Trial balance figures at December 31 are provided here for the Zobo Company home office and Erdo Branch. The company accounts on a calendar-year basis. Adjustments have been made for everything except inventories and cost of goods sold. Ending inventory figures are provided.

	ZOBO COMPANY Trial Balance December 31, 19--			
	Home Office		**Erdo Branch**	
	Debit	*Credit*	*Debit*	*Credit*
Cash	21,000		12,000	
Accounts Receivable	52,000		27,000	
Merchandise Inventory, January 1	55,000		-0-	
Erdo Branch	32,000			
Furniture and Fixtures	90,000			
Accumulated Depreciation		20,000		
Accounts Payable		46,000		17,000
Notes Payable		18,000		
Home Office				32,000
Common Stock		80,000		
Retained Earnings		60,000		
Sales		900,000		266,000
Purchases	500,000		90,000	
Shipments to Erdo Branch		53,000		
Shipments from Home Office			53,000	
Rent Expense	198,000		40,000	
Wage Expense	200,000		80,000	
Depreciation Expense	4,000			
Utilities Expense	18,000		10,000	
Miscellaneous Expense	7,000		3,000	
	1,177,000	1,177,000	315,000	315,000

Inventory, December 31	
Home Office	$50,000
Erdo Branch	$20,000

Required

1) Prepare a work sheet for combining home office and branch income statements.

2) Prepare an income statement for the home office.

3) Prepare a closing entry (or entries) at December 31 for the Erdo Branch books. If the inventory adjustment is not included as part of the closing entry, make a separate adjusting entry to set up ending inventory.

4) Prepare a work sheet for combining home office and branch balance sheets.

ALTERNATE PROBLEMS FOR SECTION 17.B

Alternate 17.B.6. A balance sheet for the Band Corporation is shown here.

BAND CORPORATION Balance Sheet March 31, 19--		
ASSETS		
Cash		$ 41,000
Accounts receivable		170,000
Furniture and fixtures	$690,000	
Less: Accumulated depreciation	180,000	510,000
Total Assets		$721,000
LIABILITIES		
Accounts Payable	$160,000	
Notes payable	130,000	
Total Liabilities		$290,000
SHAREHOLDERS' EQUITY		
Common stock	$300,000	
Retained earnings	131,000	
Total Shareholders' Equity		431,000
Total Liabilities and Shareholders' Equity		$721,000

On April 1 Band Corporation formed a wholly owned subsidiary by transferring $40,000 cash to a bank account in the name of the Carlo Corporation, for which Band received 8,000 shares of $5 par Carlo stock. There were no other transactions on April 1.

Required

1) Make journal entries for Band and Carlo Corporations to record the April 1 event.

2) Prepare a work sheet for consolidating balance sheets for the two corporations at April 1.

3) Prepare a consolidated balance sheet at April 1.

Alternate 17.B.7. BTP Corporation owns 90% of the outstanding shares of IFF Corporation. All the goods sold by IFF were purchased during the year from BTP, and all of IFF's Accounts Payable are owed to BTP. IFF's Notes Payable are owed to banks. Partial consolidating work sheets are shown here.

BTP AND IFF CORPORATIONS
Work Sheet for Consolidating Balance Sheets
December 31, 19--

	BTP Corp.	IFF Corp.	Eliminations Debit	Eliminations Credit	Consol. Bal. Sheet
Cash	30,000	11,000			
Accounts receivable	180,000	30,000			
Investment in IFF Corp.	94,500				
Other assets	389,500	110,000			
Total Assets	694,000	151,000			
Accounts payable	140,000	32,000			
Notes payable	80,000	14,000			
Common stock—BTP	200,000				
Retained earnings—BTP	274,000				
Common stock—IFF		70,000			
Retained earnings—IFF		35,000			
Minority interest					
Total Liabilities and Shareholders' Equity	694,000	151,000			

BTP AND IFF CORPORATIONS
Work Sheet for Consolidating Income Statements
For Year Ended December 31, 19--

	BTP Corp.	IFF Corp.	Eliminations Debit	Eliminations Credit	Consol. Inc. St.
Sales	800,000	260,000			
Cost of goods sold	650,000	110,000			
Gross Profit	150,000	150,000			
Operating expenses	180,000	50,000			
Net Income	(30,000)	100,000			

Required

Set up and complete work sheets like those shown.

Alternate 17.B.8. JK Corporation is a wholly owned subsidiary of TTV Corporation. TTV purchases merchandise from various producers and sells wholesale to JK for sale in retail stores. All TTV's sales are made to JK. Income statements for the two corporations are shown here.

TTV CORPORATION Income Statement For the Year Ended December 31, 19--	
Sales	$575,000
Cost of goods sold	402,500
Gross Profit	$172,500
Operating expenses	138,500
Net Income	$ 34,000

JK CORPORATION Income Statement For the Year Ended December 31, 19--	
Sales	$865,000
Cost of goods sold	575,000
Gross Profit	$290,000
Operating expenses	202,000
Net Income	$ 88,000

Required

1) Prepare a work sheet for consolidating income statements.

2) Prepare a consolidated income statement for TTV and JK Corporations.

ALTERNATE PROBLEMS FOR CHAPTER 17

Alternate 17.1. Summarized transactions for the first month's operations of the Eastern Branch of Dallo, Inc., are as follows.

Transactions

Sept. 1 Received $50,000 from home office.

4 Received merchandise costing $238,000 from home office.

8 Sales on account, $109,000.

10 Purchased merchandise on account, $57,500.

17 Cash sales, $10,000; sales on account, $38,000.

24 Sales on account, $144,000.

25 Collected $54,000 on account.

30 Paid rent for September, $2,800.

30 Paid salaries for September, $37,500.

30 Paid $26,000 on accounts payable.

30 Transferred $10,000 cash to home office.

Merchandise inventory at September 30 was $22,500.

Required

1) Record the transactions in the branch general journal.

2) Prepare an income statement for the branch.

3) Prepare a closing entry (or entries) at September 30 for the branch. If you do not set up ending inventory as part of the closing entry, prepare a separate adjusting entry to do so.

4) Make an entry on the home office books to recognize branch net income (or net loss).

Alternate 17.2. Ace Corporation owns 80% of the common stock of King Corporation. King operates a branch store for which separate accounting records are maintained. Trial balances at year-end for Ace, King, and King's branch store are presented here. King's Purchases balance represents merchandise purchased from Ace, whereas the Purchases account for King Branch represents goods purchased from unrelated suppliers. King's Accounts Payable are all due to Ace, while the Accounts Payable of King Branch are due to unrelated firms. Ignore any problems associated with possible intercompany markups in inventories.

Trial Balances
June 30, 19X5

	Ace		King		King Branch	
	Debit	*Credit*	*Debit*	*Credit*	*Debit*	*Credit*
Cash	30,000		15,000		12,000	
Accounts Receivable	150,000		75,000		60,000	
Merchandise Inventory, July 1, 19X4	260,000		88,000		74,000	
Investment in King Corporation	332,000					
King Branch			105,000			
Other Assets	518,000		262,000		33,000	
Accounts Payable		146,000		50,000		34,000
King Home Office						105,000
Common Stock		500,000		200,000		
Retained Earnings		614,000		215,000		
Sales		800,000		490,000		360,000
Purchases	420,000		330,000		90,000	
Shipments to King Branch				110,000		
Shipments from King Home Office					110,000	
Rent Expense	130,000		40,000		15,000	
Wage Expense	140,000		100,000		70,000	
Other Expense	80,000		50,000		35,000	
	2,060,000	2,060,000	1,065,000	1,065,000	499,000	499,000
Inventory, June 30, 19X5	270,000		95,000		69,000	

Required

1) Prepare a work sheet for combining the income statements of King and its branch store.

2) Prepare one or more entries for King Branch to update the Merchandise Inventory balance and close the branch's temporary equity accounts at June 30.

3) Prepare entries for King to recognize the branch net income for the year, update King's Merchandise Inventory balance, and close King's temporary equity accounts at June 30.

4) Prepare a work sheet for combining the balance sheets of King and its branch store. Keep in mind that the balances of some permanent accounts have been changed by the entries made for requirements (2) and (3).

5) Prepare a work sheet for consolidating the income statement of Ace with the combined income statement of King that resulted from requirement (1).

6) Prepare entries for Ace to recognize its share of King's net income, update Ace's Merchandise Inventory balance, and close Ace's temporary equity accounts at June 30.

7) Prepare a work sheet for consolidating the balance sheet of Ace with the combined balance sheet of King that resulted from requirement (4). Keep in mind that the balances of some of Ace's permanent accounts have been changed by the entries made for requirement (6).

8) Assume for purposes of this requirement that King's beginning and ending inventories (but not its branch inventories) were all purchased from Ace and that Ace consistently realizes a gross profit rate of 25% on sales. What further changes would need to be made in the consolidated statements you have prepared? Why?

Alternate 17.3. Walker Corporation has for some years operated a branch in another city. The post-closing trial balances at the end of the fiscal year are shown here for the corporation and on the next page for its Jogger Branch. There are no intracompany receivables or payables at March 31.

WALKER CORPORATION Trial Balance March 31, 19X5		
Cash	40,000	
Accounts Receivable	600,000	
Merchandise Inventory	700,000	
Jogger Branch	380,000	
Other Assets	500,000	
Accounts Payable		900,000
Common Stock		500,000
Capital in Excess of Par		220,000
Retained Earnings		600,000
	2,220,000	2,220,000

WALKER CORPORATION—JOGGER BRANCH Trial Balance March 31, 19X5		
Cash	18,000	
Accounts Receivable	110,000	
Merchandise Inventory	200,000	
Other Assets	152,000	
Accounts Payable		100,000
Home Office		380,000
	480,000	480,000

On April 1, 19X5, before conducting any business for the new year, the branch operation was incorporated as Jogger Corporation. The branch assets and liabilities were taken over by the new corporation at their book values, and 30,000 shares of $10 par common stock in Jogger Corporation were issued to Walker Corporation.

Required

1) Prepare a work sheet for combining the Walker Corporation and Jogger Branch balance sheets at March 31, 19X5.

2) Make general journal entries to record the effects of terminating Jogger Branch and creating Jogger Corporation:

   a) In Walker Corporation's journal.

   b) In Jogger Branch's journal.

   c) In Jogger Corporation's journal.

3) Prepare a work sheet for consolidating the balance sheets of Walker Corporation and Jogger Corporation immediately after Jogger's formation on April 1.

4) In what ways are the work sheets prepared for requirements (1) and (3) different? Explain why both procedures reach the same results.

ALTERNATE PROBLEMS FOR SECTION 18.A

Alternate 18.A.6. An income statement and comparative balance sheet for Banks, Incorporated, are as follows.

BANKS, INC.
Income Statement
For the Year Ended June 30, 19X5

Sales		$3,600,000
Cost of goods sold		2,000,000
Gross Profit		$1,600,000
Operating expenses		
Wages	$1,200,000	
Rent	98,000	
Depreciation	46,000	
Miscellaneous	54,000	
Total expenses		1,398,000
Net Income		$ 202,000

BANKS, INC.
Comparative Balance Sheet
June 30, 19X5 and 19X4

	19X5	19X4
ASSETS		
Current		
Cash	$ 32,000	$ 40,000
Accounts receivable	180,000	135,000
Merchandise inventory	310,000	340,000
Prepaid rent	10,000	4,000
Total current assets	$532,000	$519,000
Noncurrent		
Furniture and equipment	$526,000	$390,000
Accumulated depreciation	(147,000)	(101,000)
Total noncurrent assets	$379,000	$289,000
Total Assets	$911,000	$808,000
LIABILITIES		
Current		
Accounts payable	$230,000	$245,000
Wages payable	36,000	40,000
Total current liabilities	$266,000	$285,000
Noncurrent		
Notes payable	250,000	181,000
Total Liabilities	$516,000	$466,000
SHAREHOLDERS' EQUITY		
Common stock	$120,000	$100,000
Capital in excess of par	51,000	40,000
Retained earnings	224,000*	202,000
Total Shareholders' Equity	$395,000	$342,000
Total Liabilities and Shareholders' Equity	$911,000	$808,000

*Cash dividends of $180,000 were paid during 19X5.

Required

1) Prepare a comparative schedule of working capital.
2) Prepare a statement of changes in financial position on a working capital basis for fiscal year ending June 30, 19X5.

Alternate 18.A.7. Statements for L&K Beauty Shops, Inc., are provided here.

L&K BEAUTY SHOPS, INC. Income Statement For the Year Ended December 31, 19X5		
Revenue		$1,515,000
Expenses		
Salaries and wages	$976,000	
Depreciation	140,000	
Rent	190,000	
Advertising	54,000	1,360,000
Net Income		$ 155,000

L&K BEAUTY SHOPS, INC. Comparative Balance Sheet December 31, 19X5 and 19X4	19X5	19X4	Increase (Decrease)
ASSETS			
Cash	$ 94,000	$ 86,000	$ 8,000
Accounts receivable	105,000	130,000	(25,000)
Building	600,000	300,000	300,000
Accumulated depreciation	(200,000)	(60,000)	(140,000)
Total Assets	$599,000	$456,000	$143,000
LIABILITIES			
Accounts payable	$ 87,000	$ 95,000	$ (8,000)
Salaries payable	53,000	47,000	6,000
Long-term notes payable	250,000	150,000	100,000
Total Liabilities	$390,000	$292,000	$ 98,000
SHAREHOLDERS' EQUITY			
Common stock	$125,000	$125,000	$ -0-
Retained earnings	84,000*	39,000	45,000
Total Shareholders' Equity	$209,000	$164,000	$ 45,000
Total Liabilities and Shareholders' Equity	$599,000	$456,000	$143,000

*Dividends paid during 19X5, $110,000.

Required

Use the foregoing data to prepare a statement of changes in financial position on a working capital basis for the year ended December 31, 19X5.

Alternate 18.A.8. An income statement and comparative balance sheet for BAC Corporation are provided here.

BAC CORPORATION Income Statement For the Year Ended December 31, 19X5		
Service revenue		$109,300
Expenses		
Salaries	$70,000	
Rent	12,000	
Advertising	6,500	
Insurance	3,000	
Supplies	2,800	
Depreciation	6,000	100,300
Net Income		$ 9,000

BAC CORPORATION Comparative Balance Sheet December 31, 19X5 and 19X4		
	19X5	**19X4**
ASSETS		
Cash	$15,000	$ 4,000
Accounts receivable	23,000	24,000
Equipment	60,000	60,000
Accumulated depreciation—equipment	(12,000)	(6,000)
Total Assets	$86,000	$82,000
LIABILITIES		
Salaries payable	$ 7,000	$ 6,000
Rent payable	6,000	4,000
Notes payable (noncurrent)	45,000	50,000
Total Liabilities	$58,000	$60,000
SHAREHOLDERS' EQUITY		
Common stock	$12,000	$12,000
Retained earnings	16,000*	10,000
Total Shareholders' Equity	$28,000	$22,000
Total Liabilities and Shareholders' Equity	$86,000	$82,000

*Dividends of $3,000 paid during 19X5.

Required

1) Calculate the change in working capital during 19X5.

2) Calculate working capital provided by 19X5 operations.

3) Prepare a statement of changes in financial position for 19X5 on a working capital basis.

ALTERNATE PROBLEMS FOR SECTION 18.B

Alternate 18.B.7. Selected information for R&N Travel Agency is provided here.

R&N TRAVEL AGENCY Income Statement For the Year Ended December 31, 19X5		
Service revenue		$69,000
Expenses		
Salaries	$34,000	
Rent	5,600	
Advertising	1,500	
Total expenses		41,100
Net Income		$27,900

R&N TRAVEL AGENCY Balance Sheet Information As of December 31, 19X5 and 19X4		
	19X5	**19X4**
ASSETS		
Accounts receivable	$2,750	$2,350
Prepaid advertising	500	250
LIABILITIES		
Salaries payable	$3,400	$1,700

Required

1) Calculate the cash inflow from revenue.

2) Calculate the cash outgo for expenses.

3) Calculate the net cash from operations.

Alternate 18.B.8. Brad Green, a professional football player, experienced the following events during January.

    a. Net wages for January after taxes and other deductions, $8,750.28.

    b. Paid cash for sports car from local car dealer, $25,000.

    c. Purchased gasoline at local gas station on credit, $35.

    d. Received super bowl bonus check, $50,000.

    e. Won state lottery, $1,000.

    f. Paid mortgage on property, $6,600.

    g. Paid annual insurance premium on property, $5,400.

    h. Purchased furniture on credit, $890.

    i. Paid cleaning and laundry bill, $23.

    j. Paid utility bills for January, $425.

Required

Prepare a personal cash flow statement for Brad for the month of January.

Alternate 18.B.9. An income statement and comparative balance sheet for Raritan Corporation are shown here and on the next page.

RARITAN CORPORATION Income Statement For the Year Ended December 31, 19X5		
Sales		$5,000,000
Expenses		
Cost of goods sold	$4,180,000	
Wages	400,000	
Rent	164,000	
Insurance	48,000	
Interest	40,000	
Depreciation	46,000	
Other	200,000	
Total expenses		5,078,000
Net Loss		$ 78,000

RARITAN CORPORATION
Comparative Balance Sheet
December 31, 19X5 and 19X4

	19X5	19X4
ASSETS		
Current		
Cash	$ 42,000	$ 125,000
Accounts receivable, net	310,000	180,000
Merchandise inventory	300,000	320,000
Unexpired insurance	30,000	18,000
Total current assets	$ 682,000	$ 643,000
Noncurrent		
Fixtures and equipment	$ 490,000	$ 460,000
Accumulated depreciation	(130,000)	(84,000)
Total noncurrent assets	$ 360,000	$ 376,000
Total Assets	$1,042,000	$1,019,000
LIABILITIES		
Current		
Accounts payable	$ 195,000	$ 152,000
Wages payable	18,000	12,000
Bank loan	120,000	220,000
Total current liabilities	$ 333,000	$ 384,000
Noncurrent		
Notes payable	180,000	28,000
Total Liabilities	$ 513,000	$ 412,000
SHAREHOLDERS' EQUITY		
Common stock	$ 120,000*	$ 90,000
Capital in excess of par	240,000*	180,000
Retained earnings	169,000*	337,000
Total Shareholders' Equity	$ 529,000	$ 607,000
Total Liabilities and Shareholders' Equity	$1,042,000	$1,019,000

*Issued $90,000 stock dividend.

Required

1) Prepare a schedule of cash from operations for 19X5.

2) Prepare a statement of changes in financial position on a cash basis for 19X5.

ALTERNATE PROBLEMS FOR CHAPTER 18

Alternate 18.1. An income statement and comparative balance sheet for Clarion Corporation are provided here.

CLARION CORPORATION
Income Statement
For the Year Ended December 31, 19X5

Sales		$700,000
Expenses		
Cost of goods sold	$450,000	
Salaries	98,000	
Rent	32,000	
Insurance	12,000	
Depreciation	20,000	
Other	42,000	
Total expenses		654,000
Net Income		$ 46,000

CLARION CORPORATION
Comparative Balance Sheet
December 31, 19X5 and 19X4

	19X5	19X4
ASSETS		
Cash	$ 6,000	$ 8,000
Accounts receivable	14,000	5,000
Merchandise inventory	99,000	94,000
Furniture and equipment	220,000	180,000
Accumulated depreciation	(60,000)	(40,000)
Total Assets	$279,000	$247,000
LIABILITIES		
Accounts payable	$ 15,000	$ 12,000
Salaries payable	8,000	5,000
Notes payable (due in 19X8)	72,000	82,000
Total Liabilities	$ 95,000	$ 99,000
SHAREHOLDERS' EQUITY		
Common stock	$ 65,000	$ 40,000
Retained earnings	119,000*	108,000
Total Shareholders' Equity	$184,000	$148,000
Total Liabilities and Shareholders' Equity	$279,000	$247,000

*Cash dividends of $35,000 were paid during 19X5.

WILLIAM RUTGERS COMPANY
Income Statement
For the Year Ended December 31, 19X5

Sales		$5,600,000
Expenses		
Cost of goods sold	$3,400,000	
Wages	1,500,000	
Rent	300,000	
Insurance	56,000	
Depreciation	60,000	
Miscellaneous	42,000	5,358,000
Net Operating Income		$ 242,000
Gain on sale of equipment		20,000
Net Income		$ 262,000

WILLIAM RUTGERS COMPANY
Comparative Balance Sheet
December 31, 19X5 and 19X4

	19X5	19X4
ASSETS		
Current		
Cash	$ 15,000	$ 15,000
Accounts receivable	92,000	98,000
Merchandise inventory	160,000	141,000
Unexpired insurance	16,000	12,000
Total current assets	$283,000	$266,000
Noncurrent		
Furniture and equipment	$380,000	$320,000
Accumulated depreciation	(98,000)	(62,000)
Total noncurrent assets	$282,000	$258,000
Total Assets	$565,000	$524,000
LIABILITIES		
Current		
Accounts payable	$121,000	$116,000
Rent payable	18,000	6,000
Total current liabilities	$139,000	$122,000
Noncurrent		
Notes payable	54,000	114,000
Total Liabilities	$193,000	$236,000
OWNER'S EQUITY		
W. Rutgers, capital	372,000	288,000
Total Liabilities and Owner's Equity	$565,000	$524,000

Other Data

1) During the year the company sold, for $76,000 cash, equipment costing $80,000 and having a book value of $56,000.

2) William Rutgers withdrew $178,000 for his personal use during 19X5.

Required

1) Prepare a schedule of cash from operations for 19X5.

2) Prepare a cash flow statement for 19X5.

3) Prepare a comparative schedule of working capital.

4) Prepare a statement of changes in financial position on a working capital basis for 19X5.

ALTERNATE PROBLEMS FOR CHAPTER 19

Alternate 19.11. A comparative balance sheet for the Trig Corporation follows.

	19X5	19X4
TRIG CORPORATION **Comparative Balance Sheet** **December 31, 19X5 and 19X4**		
ASSETS		
Current		
Cash	$ 13,800	$ 12,400
Accounts receivable	97,800	68,000
Merchandise inventory	170,000	160,000
Prepaid rent	3,000	2,500
Total current assets	$284,600	$242,900
Noncurrent		
Equipment	$480,000	$352,000
Accumulated depreciation	(186,000)	(132,000)
Total noncurrent assets	$294,000	$220,000
Total Assets	$578,600	$462,900
LIABILITIES		
Current		
Accounts payable	$ 87,000	$ 73,500
Wages payable	12,000	2,300
Total current liabilities	$ 99,000	$ 75,800
Noncurrent		
Notes payable	140,000	110,000
Total Liabilities	$239,000	$185,800
SHAREHOLDERS' EQUITY		
Common stock	$ 55,000	$ 51,000
Capital in excess of par	75,000	31,000
Retained earnings	209,600	195,100
Total Shareholders' Equity	$339,600	$277,100
Total Liabilities and Shareholders' Equity	$578,600	$462,900

Required

1) Horizontally analyze the balance sheet by showing amounts and rates of change.

2) Vertically analyze the 19X5 balance sheet column shown for the Trig Corporation.

3) Explain why percentages on vertically analyzed statements may be summed, while those on horizontally analyzed statements cannot.

Alternate 19.12. An income statement for the Trig Corporation for the year ended December 31, 19X5, is shown here.

TRIG CORPORATION Income Statement For the Year Ended December 31, 19X5	
Net sales	$1,000,000
Cost of goods sold	530,000
Gross Profit on Sales	$ 470,000
Operating expenses	
Selling	$ 255,200
General and administrative	91,000
Total operating expenses	$ 346,200
Operating Income	$ 123,800
Interest expense	11,200
Income Before Income Taxes	$ 112,600
Income taxes	52,000
Net Income	$ 60,600

Required

1) Vertically analyze the income statement.

2) Interpret the percentages in terms of what they represent as cents out of each dollar of net sales.

Alternate 19.13. A comparative income statement for the Lave Corporation is as follows.

LAVE CORPORATION Comparative Income Statement For the Years Ended December 31, 19X5 and 19X4		
	19X5	**19X4**
Net sales	$850,000	$940,000
Cost of goods sold	510,000	570,000
Gross Profit	$340,000	$370,000
Operating expenses		
Salaries	$130,000	$125,000
Rent	30,000	36,000
Insurance	10,000	12,000
Depreciation	20,000	28,000
Other	8,000	9,000
Total operating expenses	$198,000	$210,000
Operating Income	$142,000	$160,000
Interest expense	28,000	28,000
Income Before Income Taxes	$114,000	$132,000
Income taxes	44,000	53,000
Net Income	$ 70,000	$ 79,000

Required

1) Horizontally analyze the income statement by showing the amounts and rates of change.

2) Give reasons why net income decreased proportionately more than gross profit did.

Alternate 19.14. A comparative balance sheet and an income statement are shown here for Xeno Corporation.

	19X5	19X4
XENO CORPORATION **Comparative Balance Sheet** **December 31, 19X5 and 19X4**		
ASSETS		
Current		
Cash	$ 53,000	$ 75,000
Accounts receivable, net	218,000	180,000
Merchandise inventory	300,000	340,000
Unexpired insurance	32,000	28,000
Total current assets	$603,000	$623,000
Noncurrent		
Fixtures and equipment	$452,000	$460,000
Accumulated depreciation	(116,000)	(84,000)
Total noncurrent assets	$336,000	$376,000
Total Assets	$939,000	$999,000
LIABILITIES		
Current		
Accounts payable	$164,000	$172,000
Wages payable	10,000	12,000
Bank loan	100,000	200,000
Total current liabilities	$274,000	$384,000
Noncurrent		
Notes payable	183,000	210,000
Total Liabilities	$457,000	$594,000
SHAREHOLDERS' EQUITY		
Preferred stock, 9%, $100 par	$100,000	$100,000
Common stock, $10 par	110,000*	100,000
Capital in excess of par, common	130,000*	100,000
Retained earnings	142,000*	105,000
Total Shareholders' Equity	$482,000	$405,000
Total Liabilities and Shareholders' Equity	$939,000	$999,000

*Issued $40,000 stock dividends and paid $63,000 cash dividends (including preferred) during 19X5. There are no preferred dividend arrearages for 19X5 or prior years. At December 31, 19X5, common shares were selling for $79.75; at December 31, 19X4, common shares were selling for $76.

XENO CORPORATION Comparative Income Statement For the Years Ended December 31, 19X5 and 19X4		
	19X5	19X4
Net sales	$2,120,000	$2,980,000
Cost of goods sold	1,200,000	2,000,000
Gross Profit	$ 920,000	$ 980,000
Operating expenses		
Selling	$ 550,000	$ 560,000
General and administrative	110,000	120,000
Total operating expenses	$ 660,000	$ 680,000
Operating Income	$ 260,000	$ 300,000
Interest expense	30,000	40,000
Income Before Income Taxes	$ 230,000	$ 260,000
Income taxes	90,000	100,000
Net Income	$ 140,000	$ 160,000

Required

Calculate the following for 19X5 or, where appropriate, at December 31, 19X5:

1) Accounts receivable turnover rate (all sales were made on account)

2) Inventory turnover rate

3) Asset turnover

4) Return on assets

5) Return on equity

6) Return on common equity

7) Current ratio

8) Debt-equity ratio

9) Times interest earned

10) Price-earnings ratio

11) Dividend yield rate

ALTERNATE PROBLEMS FOR CHAPTER 20

Alternate 20.7. Selected data for Shelly Company are as follows.

Materials Inventory, Jan. 1	$ 349,000
Materials Inventory, Dec. 31	97,000
Goods in Process, Jan. 1	65,000
Goods in Process, Dec. 31	48,000
Materials Purchases	1,465,000
Factory Labor	823,000
Other Manufacturing Costs	276,000

Required

1) Prepare a schedule of cost of goods completed.

2) Prepare adjusting entries to reflect cost of goods completed into Manufacturing Summary and to update the inventory accounts.

Alternate 20.8. An adjusted trial balance and additional data are provided here for Acorn Manufacturing Corporation. The account balances reflect all adjustments except the updating of inventory accounts and the recognition of cost of goods sold. Acorn uses the periodic inventory system for accounting for product costs.

ACORN MANUFACTURING CORPORATION Adjusted Trial Balance December 31, 19--		
	Debit	**Credit**
Cash	30,000	
Accounts Receivable	305,000	
Allowance for Doubtful Accounts		32,000
Beginning Inventories		
Materials	42,000	
Goods in Process	49,000	
Finished Goods	100,000	
Land	80,000	
Building	418,000	
Accumulated Depreciation—Building		79,000
Machinery and Equipment	350,000	
Accumulated Depreciation—Machinery and Equipment		120,000
Accounts Payable		200,000
Interest Payable		9,000
Income Taxes Payable		45,000
Bonds Payable		190,000
Common Stock, $10 par		250,000
Capital in Excess of Par		45,000
Retained Earnings		230,000
Sales		2,675,000
Materials Purchases	850,000	
Factory Labor	730,000	
Other Manufacturing Costs	333,000	
General and Administrative Expenses	196,000	
Selling Expenses	238,000	
Interest Expense	24,000	
Income Taxes	130,000	
	3,875,000	3,875,000

Ending Inventories	
Materials	$40,000
Goods in Process	30,000
Finished Goods	89,000

Required

1) Prepare a manufacturing work sheet similar to the one illustrated in the chapter.

2) Prepare a schedule of cost of goods completed.

3) Prepare an income statement.

4) Prepare a balance sheet.

Alternate 20.9. An adjusted trial balance and additional data are provided here for Wako Manufacturing, Inc. The account balances reflect all adjustments except the updating of inventory accounts and the recognition of cost of goods sold. Wako uses a periodic inventory system.

WAKO MANUFACTURING, INC. Adjusted Trial Balance December 31, 19 – –		
	Debit	Credit
Cash	131,000	
Accounts Receivable	188,000	
Beginning Inventories		
Materials	164,000	
Goods in Process	217,000	
Finished Goods	221,000	
Land	240,000	
Building	906,000	
Accumulated Depreciation—Building		402,000
Machinery and Equipment	680,000	
Accumulated Depreciation—Machinery and Equipment		398,000
Accounts Payable		204,000
Income Taxes Payable		161,000
Notes Payable (180 days)		480,000
Common Stock, no par		700,000
Retained Earnings		122,000
Sales		3,000,000
Materials Purchases	811,000	
Factory Labor	690,000	
Other Manufacturing Costs	398,000	
General and Administrative Expenses	269,000	
Selling Expenses	342,000	
Income Taxes	210,000	
	5,467,000	5,467,000

Ending Inventories	
Materials	$171,000
Goods in Process	222,000
Finished Goods	110,000

Required

1) Prepare an end-of-period work sheet for Wako, starting with adjusted trial balance columns.

2) Prepare a schedule of cost of goods completed.

3) Make journal entries to adjust the inventory accounts and set up cost of goods sold for the year.

4) Make a closing entry (or entries) to close the temporary equity accounts that remain open after doing part (3).

5) Prepare an income statement.

6) Prepare a balance sheet.

ALTERNATE PROBLEMS FOR SECTION 21.A

Alternate 21.A.7. Crenshaw Manufacturing Corporation incurred labor cost and used materials during November, as shown here.

Materials used	
Direct materials	$111,100
Indirect materials	32,000
Labor cost incurred	
Direct labor	$ 70,000
Indirect labor	52,200

Required

Make journal entries on November 30 to record the following:

1) The cost of materials used, in the Goods in Process and Factory Overhead accounts.

2) The cost of factory labor, in the Goods in Process and Factory Overhead accounts.

3) The application of factory overhead to Goods in Process, using a 70% overhead application rate based on direct labor cost.

Alternate 21.A.8. Harcorp Manufacturing completed Job 7468, a custom spot-welding machine, on April 15. Job cost sheets show that the total cost assigned to Job 7468 was $30,300. Job 7468 was ordered by SHM Company on April 1, and that firm agreed to pay $51,800 30 days after receiving the equipment. On May 1, SHM took title to the welder manufactured by Harcorp.

Required

1) Make journal entries on Harcorp's books to record the following:

   a) The completion of Job 7468.

    b) The acceptance of Job 7468 by the SHM Company.

    c) The collection of SHM's account on May 31.

  2) Make journal entries on SHM's books to record the following:

    a) The acceptance of Job 7468.

    b) The payment on May 31 for Job 7468.

Alternate 21.A.9. A partial list of events for the Tara Manufacturing Company follows.

Events

a) Materials costing $4,500 were purchased on credit.

b) Received $2,400 utility bill for heat and power used in factory.

c) Totals in the summary of materials requisitions showed indirect materials used of $5,700 and direct materials used of $36,400.

d) Depreciation on factory equipment was $9,400.

e) The labor distribution summary showed total direct labor of $60,000 and total indirect labor of $5,800.

f) Factory overhead is applied at 80% of direct labor cost.

g) A summary of completed job cost sheets showed total cost applied of $145,800.

h) Jobs shipped from the finished goods storeroom had a total cost of $138,000.

Required

Journalize the summarized transactions, assuming use of a job order cost system and perpetual inventories.

ALTERNATE PROBLEMS FOR SECTION 21.B

Alternate 21.B.7. Selected data for October from the records of the BG Manufacturing Company are provided here. BG employs a process cost system for accounting for manufacturing costs.

Materials	
Used directly in welding department	$108,000
Used directly in grinding department	85,000
Used indirectly	52,000
Factory labor	
Direct labor in welding department	$210,000
Direct labor in grinding department	180,000
Indirect labor	60,000
Overhead application rate as a percentage of direct labor cost	
Welding department	30%
Grinding department	50%
Completed by welding department and transferred to grinding department	
2,200 units at a cost of $130 each	
Completed by grinding department and transferred to finished goods	
1,900 units at a cost of $260 each	

Required

Prepare journal entries at October 31 to record the following:

1) The use of materials during October

2) The distribution of labor costs for October

3) The application of overhead to Goods in Process

4) The transfer of goods from the welding department to the grinding department

5) The transfer of completed goods from the grinding department to Finished Goods inventory

Alternate 21.B.8. A partially completed production report for the assembly department of the Moss Camera Company is shown on the page opposite.

MOSS CAMERA COMPANY
Assembly Department
Production Report
For the Month of January, 19--

			Equivalent Units		Unit Cost
Cost in process during January					
Goods in process, January 1	$ 48,000				
Direct materials added	220,000	÷	2,400	=	$
Direct labor added	300,000	÷	2,200	=	
Overhead applied*		÷	2,200	=	
Total cost in process	$				
Unit cost incurred in January					$
Cost assigned to 320 units in process					
Direct materials	$	=	320	×	$
Direct labor		=	290	×	$
Factory overhead		=	290	×	$
Goods in process, January 31	$				
Transferred to finishing department	$	÷	2,150	=	$

*Overhead is applied at 60% of direct labor.

Required

Complete the production report.

Alternate 21.B.9. The Reed Liquid Cleanser Company receives liquid cleanser in bulk form and bottles it for sale to stores. Selected data are given here for Reed's two departments for the month of October.

	Bottling Department	Packing Department
Goods in process, October 1	$ 3,400	$ 9,700
Direct labor to complete beginning goods in process	875	1,750
Factory overhead to complete beginning goods in process	294	560
Cost of units started and completed	30,230	52,780

Required

1) Calculate the cost of goods transferred to the packing department during October.

2) Make an entry at October 31 to record the transfer of goods to the packing department.

3) Calculate the cost of goods transferred to finished goods during October.

4) Make an entry at October 31 to record the transfer to finished goods.

ALTERNATE PROBLEMS FOR CHAPTER 21

Alternate 21.1. Selected data for August from the records of the TDM Corporation are shown here. Goods completed in the washing department go to Finished Goods inventory.

		Materials		Labor and Overhead	
	Actual Units	Stage of Completion	Equivalent Units for Aug.	Stage of Completion	Equivalent Units for Aug.
TDM CORPORATION Washing Department Equivalent Units Completed For the Month of August 19--					
Goods in process, 8/1	3,000	97%		92%	
Started and completed	88,000	100%		100%	
Goods in process, 8/31	4,200	96%		85%	
Completed in August	91,000				

Overhead is applied at 42% of direct labor.

Cost in Process during August	
Goods in process, 8/1	$ 14,000
Direct materials added	92,000
Direct labor applied	214,000
Transferred from grinding department (92,200 units)	86,000

Required

1) Calculate the equivalent units for August and finish the schedule provided in the problem.

2) Prepare a production report for the washing department for the month of August similar to the production report illustrated in this chapter.

3) Make a journal entry at August 31 to record the transfer of the cost of goods completed to Finished Goods inventory.

Alternate 21.2. The trial balance for the KS Manufacturing Company at November 1 follows. The company uses a job order cost system with perpetual inventories. The transactions for November are presented in summarized form.

KS MANUFACTURING COMPANY Trial Balance November 1, 19--		
	Debit	Credit
Cash	24,000	
Accounts Receivable	32,000	
Materials Inventory	15,000	
Goods in Process	12,000	
Finished Goods	17,000	
Factory Equipment	175,000	
Accumulated Depreciation		37,000
Accounts Payable		25,000
Factory Payroll		5,000
K. Stewart, Capital		208,000
	275,000	275,000

Summarized Transactions

a) Materials costing $42,000 were paid for with cash.

b) Materials issued from the storeroom totaled $34,200; indirect materials, $4,200; and direct materials, $30,000.

c) Wages earned by factory employees were $56,000. Direct labor was $50,000 and indirect labor was $6,000.

d) Equipment depreciated by $2,500 during the month.

e) Other factory costs of $4,500 were credited to accounts payable.

f) $18,000 of factory overhead was applied to production.

g) Jobs costing $80,000 were completed.

h) Goods shipped to customers had a production cost of $60,000.

i) The goods shipped were billed to customers at $98,000.

j) Collections of accounts receivable were $89,000 for the month.

k) Wages paid to employees totaled $28,000.

l) $25,000 was paid on accounts payable.

m) $5,500 of selling expense and $7,200 of administrative expense were paid in cash.

Required

1) Journalize the summarized transactions.

2) Prepare a preclosing trial balance for November 30. (You may want to use T-accounts to compute ending balances.)

3) Close the Factory Overhead account. (Assume the entire balance is closed to Cost of Goods Sold.)

Alternate 21.3. A trial balance for the Scott Corporation follows. Summarized transaction and production data are provided for June. The company consists of two departments: spinning and weaving. A process cost system is used.

THE SCOTT CORPORATION Trial Balance May 31, 19--		
	Debit	**Credit**
Cash	14,400	
Accounts Receivable	24,000	
Materials Inventory	18,000	
Goods in Process—Spinning	3,500	
Goods in Process—Weaving	3,600	
Finished Goods	9,600	
Prepaid Rent	8,400	
Prepaid Advertising	2,880	
Factory Equipment	180,000	
Accumulated Depreciation—Equipment		60,000
Accounts Payable		33,800
Factory Payroll		2,500
Mortgage Payable		40,000
Common Stock		120,000
Retained Earnings		23,720
Sales		240,000
Factory Overhead		360
Selling Expense	35,000	
Administrative Expense	29,000	
Cost of Goods Sold	192,000	
	520,380	520,380

Summarized Data

a) Materials purchased on account amounted to $24,000.

b) Factory costs to be recorded are as follows:

Expired rent	$1,200
Expired advertising	480
Depreciation	3,500
Miscellaneous credits to accounts payable	1,200

c) A summary of payroll records showed direct labor totals of $12,000 for spinning and $4,800 for weaving. Indirect labor was $1,200.

d) The summary of materials requisitions showed direct materials of $27,720 used in spinning and $7,560 used in weaving. Indirect materials costing $2,700 were issued.

e) Factory overhead is applied at 60% of direct labor cost.

f) The spinning department had 4,000 units in process one-fourth completed at the beginning of the month. Units started in process and completed were 8,000. Remaining in inventory were 2,000 units three-fourths completed. The cost added to each unit in the spinning department is $3.50. (Record the amount transferred from spinning to weaving.)

g) The weaving department transferred to finished stock 11,000 units at an average cost of $5.

h) Customers bought 12,000 units on account at a sale price of $7.50 per unit. The cost of goods sold was $5 per unit.

i) Additional common stock was issued for $80,000 cash.

j) Accounts receivable of $50,400 were collected.

k) Cash disbursements were as follows:

Factory Payroll	$19,200
Accounts Payable	50,200
Mortgage Payable	20,000
Selling Expense	4,800
Administrative Expense	5,200

Required

1) Journalize the summarized transactions for June.

2) Set up T-accounts and post the June entries.

3) Prepare a trial balance on June 30.

4) Prepare a balance sheet at June 30 and an income statement for the six months ended June 30, assuming that the revenue and expense data in the May 31 trial balance are for the first five months of the fiscal year starting January 1.

ALTERNATE PROBLEMS FOR SECTION 22.A

Alternate 22.A.5. Minx Manufacturing Company collects 30% of sales in the month of sale, 50% in the month following sale, 15% in the second month following sale, and 4% in the third month following sale (1% of sales are uncollectible). About 80% of purchases are paid for in the month of purchase, with the remainder paid in the next month. Sales and purchases data follow.

	Sales	Purchases
ACTUAL		
October	$ 60,000	$40,000
November	80,000	50,000
December	80,000	70,000
PROJECTED		
January	80,000	90,000
February	80,000	90,000
March	90,000	50,000
April	150,000	40,000
May	60,000	30,000
June	50,000	30,000

Required

1) Prepare spread sheets for the first six months of the calendar year to determine expected cash receipts from sales and cash payments for purchases based on the actual and projected data just provided. The spread sheets should show data by months and in total for the period.

2) If the company begins January with a cash balance of $10,000, in which months (if any) will there be a need to borrow cash? Consider your solution to part (1), but ignore other potential sources and uses of cash.

Alternate 22.A.6. Actual credit sales for the first half of 19X8 and a sales forecast for the second half of 19X8 are shown here for the CSC Corporation. Assume that each month's credit sales are made evenly during the month and that, on the average, credit sales are collected 2½ months after they are made.

CSC CORPORATION			
Credit Sales, 19X8		*Credit Sales Forecast, 19X9*	
January	$120,000	July	$120,000
February	80,000	August	80,000
March	80,000	September	70,000
April	90,000	October	90,000
May	100,000	November	100,000
June	150,000	December	140,000

Required

Prepare a spread sheet for July through December 19X8 showing expected monthly and total cash inflows from credit sales.

Alternate 22.A.7. Tam Wholesale Company buys large quantities of goods and resells them in smaller quantities to its customers. Sales are usually collected 50% in the month of sale, 40% in the month following sale, and 10% in the second month following sale. About 70% of purchases are paid for in the month of purchase, with the remainder being paid in the next month. Sales and purchases information and selected other data are shown here.

	Sales	Purchases
February	$150,000	$90,000
March	90,000	60,000

	Projected Sales	Projected Purchases
April	$ 90,000	$90,000
May	100,000	80,000
June	120,000	50,000

Other Data

1) Tam tries to maintain a cash balance of $5,000. The balance at April 1 is $5,000. When the balance falls to $4,000 or less, marketable securities are liquidated, if available, in multiples of $1,000 to bring the balance to approximately $5,000. If securities are not available, funds are borrowed against a line of credit at the bank in multiples of $1,000 to achieve the desired balance. When the balance exceeds $5,000 by at least $1,000, cash is applied in $1,000 increments against any outstanding bank loans to bring the balance down to approximately $5,000. Excess funds still available after paying bank loans are used in $1,000 multiples to purchase marketable securities. There are $6,000 in marketable securities owned at April 1.

2) Cash payments in addition to those made for purchases are expected to be as follows:

April	$15,000
May	60,000*
June	10,000

*Includes purchase of machinery

3) The owner of the business withdraws $2,000 of cash on the last day of each month for personal living expenses.

Required

1) Prepare quarterly spread sheets for April, May, and June to determine expected cash receipts from sales and cash payments for purchases. The spread sheets should show data by months and in total for the quarter.

2) Prepare a quarterly cash budget for April, May, and June. Present figures by months and for the quarter in a format similar to the one illustrated in this section.

ALTERNATE PROBLEMS FOR SECTION 22.B

Alternate 22.B.4. Budgeted and actual cost data for the galvanizing department of Zinco Corporation are shown here.

ZINCO CORPORATION Galvanizing Department For the Month of March 19--		
	Budget	**Actual**
Direct materials	$ 30,000	$ 33,000
Direct labor	88,000	92,000
Factory overhead		
Indirect materials	10,000	10,000
Indirect labor	19,000	18,000
Other manufacturing costs	28,000	33,000
Total	$175,000	$186,000

Required

1) Prepare a performance report for March for the galvanizing department.

2) In your opinion, which variance shown in the performance report deserves the most serious attention from Zinco's managers? Why?

Alternate 22.B.5. The Markwade Corporation manufactures ski boots. Budget and cost data are shown here for the finishing department.

MARKWADE CORPORATION Finishing Department For the Month of June 19--		
Production: 148,000 Equivalent Units	**Budget**	**Actual**
Direct materials	$348,000	$373,000
Direct labor	216,000	202,000
Factory overhead		
Indirect materials	100,000	98,000
Indirect labor	27,000	28,000
Other manufacturing costs	49,000	57,000
Total	$740,000	$758,000

Required

1) Prepare a performance report for June for the finishing department of Markwade Corporation.

2) Prepare a list of costs with unfavorable variances and their amounts. Indicate the percentage of variation from the budget for each of the costs listed.

Alternate 22.B.6. Budgeted and actual data for the molding department of the Bethwick Corporation follow.

BETHWICK CORPORATION Molding Department For the Month of November 19--		
Production: 7,800 Equivalent Units	**Budget**	**Actual**
Direct materials	$ 12,000	$ 11,000
Direct labor	88,000	90,000
Factory overhead		
Indirect materials	5,000	3,000
Indirect labor	15,000	19,000
Other manufacturing costs	34,000	36,000
Total	$154,000	$159,000

Required

Prepare a performance report for November for the molding department.

ALTERNATE PROBLEMS FOR CHAPTER 22

Alternate 22.1. Shown here are a balance sheet and selected other data for TTV Corporation.

TTV CORPORATION Balance Sheet April 30, 19--		
ASSETS		
Cash		$ 30,000
Accounts receivable		42,000
Inventory		12,000
Land		83,000
Building	$198,000	
Less: Accumulated depreciation	72,000	126,000
Equipment	$ 72,000	
Less: Accumulated depreciation	24,000	48,000
Total Assets		$341,000
LIABILITIES		
Accounts payable		$ 60,000
SHAREHOLDERS' EQUITY		
Common stock	$120,000	
Retained earnings	161,000	
Total Shareholders' Equity		281,000
Total Liabilities and Shareholders' Equity		$341,000

Other Data

a) Accounts receivable are collected during the month following sale.

b) Accounts payable are paid in the month following purchase.

c) Expected cash sales during May are $28,000, and expected credit sales are $70,000.

d) Building depreciation is $1,200 per month, and equipment depreciation is $1,800 per month.

e) All expenses other than depreciation and wages are incurred on account. Total expenses for May are projected to be $79,400.

f) Equipment costing $6,000 will be purchased in May by signing a note payable.

g) Wages totaling $14,400 will be paid in May.

h) Net income for May is expected to be $18,600.

i) Dividends declared and paid in May will be $24,000.

j) All other figures and interrelationships, except cash, will remain unchanged.

Required

Prepare a projected (pro forma) balance sheet at May 31.

Alternate 22.2. J. S. Steele is concerned about his ability to finance his next quarter at college. He has prepared the following projection of personal cash flows for the coming quarter.

	March	April	May
J. S. STEELE			
Projected Cash Flow			
March–May 19– –			
Cash balance, March 1	$1,500		
Work study income	150	$150	$150
Track scholarship	1,000		
Payment for books	125		
Deposit on lab equipment	50		
Refund on lab equipment			40
Payments on car	75	75	75
Room and board	300	300	300
Clothes	200	40	40
Tuition and fees	950		
Entertainment	25	25	25
Ski trip to Vermont	300		
Spring break vacation in Florida		500	
Graduation expenses			100

Required

1) Prepare a personal cash budget for J. S. for the months of March, April, and May.

2) Suggest possible actions that J. S. might take to cover any cash shortages indicated by the budget.

Alternate 22.3. On December 31, 19X4, Stewart Corporation had on hand 20,000 units of inventory which had cost $6 per unit. Stewart's managers intend to reduce the inventory level to 12,000 units during 19X5. The $6 unit cost of purchases is expected to remain stable in the future.

The sales staff of Stewart anticipate that 180,000 units will be sold during 19X5 at the present sales price of $10 per unit. As in the past, selling expenses are expected to average about 12% of sales, and administrative expenses tend to run about $15,000 per month. No other expenses are anticipated except for federal, state, and local income taxes, which amount to a combined rate of 46% of net income before tax.

Required

1) Prepare in condensed form a projected income statement for Stewart for 19X5. Support the statement with a separate schedule of cost of goods sold.

2) In 19X5 Stewart sold 170,000 units at $10 per unit, but purchase costs were incurred at the rate of $6.50 per unit. At year-end, Stewart had on hand 13,000 units of inventory at a cost of $6.50 per unit. Selling expenses for 19X5 amounted to $204,000, and administrative expenses totaled $180,000 for the year.

a) Prepare in comparative form a four-column statement that shows both the projected and the actual income statement figures along with variances stated both in dollars and in percentages.

b) Would you consider the statement you prepared for (a) to be a responsibility report? Why? Which manager or official is responsible for the overall performance of a corporation?

c) Comment on the relative significance of the variances shown.

ALTERNATE PROBLEMS FOR SECTION 23.A

Alternate 23.A.6. The Zinfandel Company has fixed costs of $100,000 per month. Variable costs for its one product amount to $200 per unit.

Required

1) Write a monthly total cost formula for Zinfandel Company, using the symbol n to represent units sold.

2) Draw a graph that represents Zinfandel's total cost over activity levels from 0 to 3,000 units of sales.

3) What is total cost at 2,500 units?

Alternate 23.A.7. A number of cost graphs are pictured here.

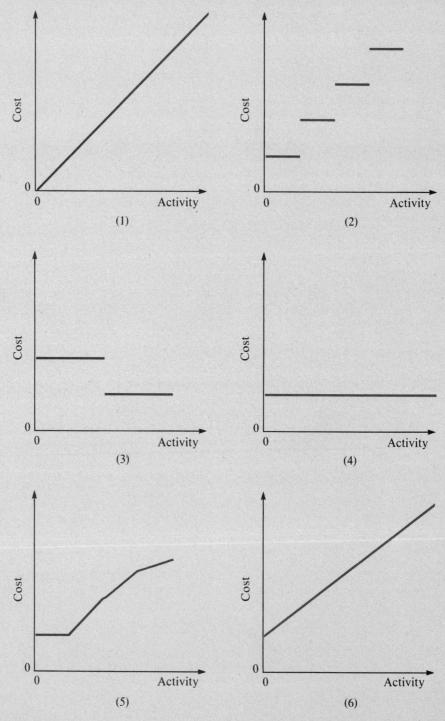

Required

Select the graph from among those shown that probably portrays each cost in the following list.

1) Total rent of $3,000 a month

2) A mobile home saleswoman is paid a salary of $400 per month plus $400 for each mobile home she sells

3) Total salaries of cable TV installers, where an installer is needed for each 300 installations per month

4) Total rent on a building provided by the City Redevelopment Authority, whereby rent is reduced in amount when a certain number of people are employed for the entire month

5) Water charges amounting to a fixed charge for the first 5,000 gallons used, 5¢ per gallon for the next 5,000 gallons, 4¢ per gallon for the next 5,000 gallons and 3¢ per gallon for usage over 15,000 gallons

6) Total materials cost when materials for each unit cost 50¢

Alternate 23.A.8. Banner Company's total cost was observed to be $200,000 during a month when 5,000 units of product were sold and $290,000 during a month when 8,000 units were sold. No unusual circumstances occurred during either month. Assume that relationships between costs and sales are linear. Banner sells product units at $50 each.

Required

1) Construct a graph that shows total variable cost and total cost for sales from 0 to 10,000 units per month.

2) Write a total cost formula for Banner that includes the variable cost per unit and Banner's fixed cost per month.

3) What would you expect total cost to be during a month in which 6,200 units were sold?

4) Calculate net income (or net loss) for Banner for a monthly sales level of

   a) 7,200 units.

   b) 5,000 units.

5) At what unit sales level would the total sales be expected to equal total cost?

ALTERNATE PROBLEMS FOR SECTION 23.B

Alternate 23.B.6. The Petite Corporation produces and sells only one product. Fixed costs run about $100,000 per month, and variable costs run $6 per unit. Petite sells its product at a price of $9 per unit.

Required

1) Calculate the contribution margin per unit sold.

2) Calculate Petite's break-even point in both units and sales dollars.

3) Calculate Petite's expected net income (or loss) at a sales volume of 40,000 units.

4) Draw a graph depicting Petite's total cost and total revenue for sales volume from 0 to 50,000 units per month.

Alternate 23.B.7. Price and cost data for three firms are provided:

	Unit Price	Unit Variable Cost	Monthly Fixed Cost
Firm 1	$6	$3.75	$22,500
Firm 2	$6	$3.75	$33,750
Firm 3	$6	$4.50	$33,750

Required

For each of the three firms, calculate the following:

1) Contribution margin per unit.

2) Contribution margin percentage.

3) Monthly break-even sales in units.

4) Monthly break-even sales in dollars.

5) Net income or loss for sales of 15,000 units during a month.

Alternate 23.B.8. There are two break-even points for the Sands Company. Cost and revenue data follow.

Selling price per unit	$20
Variable cost per unit	$14
Fixed cost per month	
Up to 5,000 units	$24,000
From 5,000 to 10,000 units	$48,000

Required

1) Calculate the units of sales required to break even at each of the two points, using the equation $pn = vn + F$.

2) Calculate the dollars of sales required to break even at each of the two points by dividing fixed cost by the contribution margin percentage.

3) Draw a graph portraying Sands's break-even points.

ALTERNATE PROBLEMS FOR CHAPTER 23

Alternate 23.1. Four unrelated situations are described here.

   a. Seth Company has total monthly fixed costs of $50,000, sells its product units for $15 each, and breaks even at 10,000 units per month.

Required

Determine Seth's variable cost per unit.

   b. Maxon Company earned $26,000 net income last month from sales of 7,500 product units at a price of $5 per unit. Maxon has a variable cost of $2.50 per product unit.

Required

Calculate Maxon's fixed cost for the month.

   c. Doran Company has monthly fixed cost of $75,000 and variable cost of $1.80 per unit. Doran deals in one product that sells for $2.70 per unit. During the previous month, Doran earned a net income of $15,000.

Required

Determine the number of product units that must have been sold during the previous month.

   d. J&N Company's monthly break-even point is 800 units of sales. The company has monthly fixed cost of $40,000 and sells its product for $150 per unit.

Required

Determine the variable cost per unit.

Alternate 23.2. Mary Scott is planning to earn extra money for college by setting up a cross-country ski rental shop in a nearby forest. The complete ski package will cost her $3.50 per unit each day to rent. This ski package will then be rented out for public use at $8 per day. Mary will have to rent a building at a cost of $200 per month and pay utilities of $100 each month. A college friend has agreed to help Mary if he can earn 50¢ for each ski package that is rented. Assume that ski packages will be rented by Mary only after they have been reserved by customers.

Required

   1) Determine the number of ski packages per month that must be rented to break even.

   2) How many ski packages must be rented for Mary to earn a net income of $500?

   3) Draw a graph for Mary that pictures her total variable cost, total cost, and total revenue for sales volumes from 0 to 300 ski packages per month.

ALTERNATE PROBLEMS FOR SECTION 24.A

Alternate 24.A.5. The forming department had overhead costs at two volume levels as follows.

Cost Category	Production Level	
	40,000 Units	*60,000 Units*
Utilities	$ 20,000	$ 26,000
Depreciation	80,000	80,000
Timekeeping	10,000	10,000
Maintenance	16,000	20,000
Supervision	60,000	70,000
Supplies	8,000	9,000
Total overhead cost	$194,000	$215,000

Required

1) Prepare a schedule showing the variable cost per unit and fixed cost per month by individual cost category and for total overhead.

2) Speculate as to why some of the cost categories have both fixed and variable elements.

Alternate 24.A.6. During the month of October the following budget was prepared for Department X.

CONNOR CORPORATION Department X Budget For the Month of November 19--	
Expected production	80,000 Units
Variable costs	
Direct materials	$240,000
Direct labor	320,000
Variable overhead	96,000
Total variable	$656,000
Fixed overhead	204,000
Total cost	$860,000

During the month of November, 80,500 units were produced at a total production cost of $868,000. Of the total cost, $204,000 was considered fixed and the remainder variable. Materials usage records show that Department X used direct materials costing $242,000; payroll records show direct labor cost of $324,000 for Department X for November. Department X had no beginning or ending work in process for November.

Required

1) Prepare for Department X a static budget performance report for November.

2) Prepare for Department X a flexible budget performance report for November.

3) Explain as best you can the reasons for the differences in variances shown in the reports prepared for (1) and (2).

Alternate 24.A.7. Tooler Corporation produces a single product, which it attempts to sell for $120 per unit. During slow periods, selected customers are encouraged to purchase the product at reduced prices. Tooler's costs are budgeted according to the following variable and fixed elements.

	Variable per Unit	Fixed per Month
Production costs	$30	$520,000
Selling costs	10	100,000
Administrative costs	–0–	275,000

Fifty-two percent of net income must be paid as federal, state, and local income taxes. During August the following income statement for July was prepared.

TOOLER CORPORATION
Income Statement
For the Month of July 19––

Sales (15,000 units)		$1,800,000
Cost of goods sold		990,000
Gross Profit		$ 810,000
Operating expenses		
Selling	$255,000	
Administrative	273,000	528,000
Net Income before Tax		$ 282,000
Income taxes		146,640
Net Income after Tax		$ 135,360

Required

1) Prepare a performance income statement for July which includes, in addition to the income statement columns, columns for flexible budget figures and variances of actual from budgeted amounts.

2) Write a formula for Tooler's net income after tax based on the budget data given.

3) According to the budget data, at what sales level would Tooler break even?

ALTERNATE PROBLEMS FOR SECTION 24.B

Alternate 24.B.5. Hahn Company has established the following standard costs for one of its production departments.

Direct materials, 20 pounds at $7 per pound	$140
Direct labor, 5 hours at $12 per hour	60
Factory overhead	
Variable, $4 per direct labor hour	20
Fixed, $3 per direct labor hour	15

The fixed overhead rate was determined by dividing $75,000 of expected fixed overhead cost per month by 25,000 normal capacity direct labor hours.

During the month of March, the following costs were incurred in processing 4,000 units of product.

Direct materials, 82,000 lb. at $6.90 per lb.	$565,800
Direct labor, 19,500 hours at $12.40 per hour	241,800
Factory overhead	
Variable	83,000
Fixed	76,000

Required

Determine for the month of March the following variances.

1) Materials rate variance

2) Materials quantity variance

3) Labor rate variance

4) Labor quantity variance

5) Overhead volume variance

6) Overhead budget variance

Alternate 24.B.6. Grant Company produces one product and employs a standard cost system. Standard costs per product unit have been determined as follows.

Direct materials, 3 gallons at $5 per gallon		$15
Direct labor, 2 hours at $8 per hour		16
Factory overhead		
Variable, $3 per direct labor hour	$ 6	
Fixed, $6 per direct labor hour	12	18
Total standard cost per product unit		$49

The fixed overhead rate is based on $34,800 of expected fixed overhead per month spread over 5,800 budgeted direct labor hours (2,900 units of anticipated production at 2 hours of direct labor per unit). Grant Company produces only for firm customer orders and carries little or no inventory on hand. There were no inventories on hand at the beginning of May, nor were there any at the end of May. The following events were experienced in producing and selling 2,850 units of product during May.

a. Purchased 8,400 gallons of direct materials at $5.05 per gallon. Terms were net 60 days.

b. The 8,400 gallons of direct materials purchased during May were put into process.

c. Wages of $46,110 are owed for 5,800 hours of direct labor worked during May.

d. Actual manufacturing overhead costs for the month were $51,000.

Required

Prepare journal entries for May to:

1) Record the direct materials purchased and identify the materials rate variance.

2) Transfer the direct materials to Goods in Process and identify the materials quantity variance.

3) Record direct wages and identify labor rate and quantity variances.

4) Record actual manufacturing overhead costs. (*Note:* Credit the amount to an account titled Various Accounts.)

5) Charge overhead to Goods in Process.

6) Close the Manufacturing Overhead account and identify the overhead volume and budget variances. (*Note:* Assume the Overhead account is closed monthly.)

7) Transfer the Goods in Process balance to Finished Goods Inventory.

8) Transfer the Finished Goods Inventory to Cost of Goods Sold.

Alternate 24.B.7. Normal capacity for Stover Company is considered to be 20,000 units of product per month. Standard direct labor cost per product unit is $15, and manufacturing overhead is assigned to production at 140% of standard direct labor cost. The standard overhead rate is considered to be one-half variable and one-half fixed. During April, when 19,600 units were produced, actual overhead amounted to $430,000, of which $205,000 was variable and $225,000 was fixed.

Required

1) Prepare a journal entry to assign standard overhead to production for April.

2) Prepare the entry on April 30 to close the Manufacturing Overhead account and recognize overhead volume and budget variances for the month.

3) Interpret in words (what do they mean?) the overhead variances journalized in requirement (2). Was fixed overhead for the month more or less than one would have expected for the units produced? Explain.

ALTERNATE PROBLEMS FOR CHAPTER 24

Alternate 24.1. The following data are provided for the Darion Plant of Triped, Incorporated.

Flexible Budget Information	
Variable production cost per unit	
Direct materials, 50 lb. at $3 per lb.	$150.00
Direct labor, 5 hours at $5 per hour	25.00
Variable overhead, at $7.50 per direct labor hour	37.50
Fixed overhead per month, $120,000	
Actual Production Costs for the Month of October	
Variable	
Direct materials, 51,500 lb. at $3.10	$159,650
Direct labor, 5,000 hours at $5 per hour	25,000
Variable overhead	37,000
Fixed overhead	118,000
Produced during October: 1,010 units	

Required

1) Prepare a flexible budget performance report for October.

2) Determine the rate and quantity elements of the

   a) Direct materials variance

   b) Direct labor variance

Alternate 24.2. The Grinch Company assembles and sells one model of a grinch. The accounting records disclose the following information for 19X2 and 19X1.

	19X2	**19X1**
Grinches produced and sold	18,000	11,000
Total cost	$558,000	$411,000
Sales	$792,000	$484,000

Required

1) Determine the apparent variable cost per unit and fixed cost per year.

2) Calculate the contribution margin per unit for 19X2.

3) Calculate the contribution margin percentage for 19X2.

4) Determine Grinch's break-even point in both units and sales dollars for 19X2.

5) Calculate Grinch's expected net income (or loss) at sales volumes of 7,000 grinches and 9,000 grinches.

Alternate 24.3. A comparative income statement for the Dexter Corporation follows.

DEXTER CORPORATION Income Statement For Years Ended December 31, 19X6 and 19X5		
	19X6	**19X5**
Sales	$175,000	$150,000
Cost		
Grinding department	$ 68,000	$ 60,000
Sanding department	34,000	30,000
Selling and administrative	45,000	40,000
Total cost	$147,000	$130,000
Net Income	$ 28,000	$ 20,000

The selling price per unit remained constant during 19X5 and 19X6 and is not expected to change during 19X7.

Required

1) Calculate variable cost per sales dollar and fixed cost per year for each department and for the selling and administrative function.

2) Write a net income formula that can be used to project variable cost per sales dollar, fixed cost per year for each department and the selling and administrative function, and total net income.

3) Prepare a projected income statement (flexible budget) for 19X7 similar to those for 19X5 and 19X6, assuming estimated sales of $200,000 for 19X7.

ALTERNATE PROBLEMS FOR SECTION 25.A

Alternate 25.A.6. The Doville Press purchased a typesetting machine five years ago at a cost of $15,000. It was estimated that the machine's total useful life would be 15 years and that it would have no salvage value at the end of its life. The machine can be sold now for $10,500. A new automatic typesetter will cost $30,000. As a special offer, the new machine can be purchased for $20,000 down, with the $10,000 balance to be paid at the end of one year. This will permit a saving on labor of $3,000 a year for its 10-year life. It is estimated that the machine's salvage value at the end of 10 years will be $2,000. The company's marginal tax rate is 46%. This rate also applies to gains and losses on asset disposals.

Required

1) Calculate the amount and timing of the incremental after-tax cash flows.

2) Without regard to the time value of money, state whether you recommend purchase of the automatic typesetter. Explain your answer.

Alternate 25.A.7. Sandra Mavis is a junior accountant in a large city. At the beginning of January she has an opportunity to rent a different apartment much closer to her office. Unfortunately, Sandra will have to forfeit a $1,000 rental deposit on the old apartment if she moves; otherwise she must fulfill her agreement to rent the apartment for another year. She must take the new apartment immediately or not at all. Information relating to the two apartments follows.

	Old Apartment	New Apartment
Rental deposit	$1,000	$-0-
Monthly rent	500	400
Monthly utilities	60	60
Monthly train fare	80	-0-
Monthly TV cable rental	10	10
Months obligated	12	12

Required

1) Prepare a schedule showing the rent payments required each month under the two alternatives, and calculate the differences.

2) Prepare a schedule showing other relevant information and the differences between the alternatives over the 12-month period.

3) Calculate the net saving (or loss) that would result from moving to the new apartment.

4) State which apartment Sandra should rent and why.

Alternate 25.A.8. Wayne Manufacturing Company, a family corporation, makes its own components for assembly into clocks. Internal clockworks are available from a foreign supplier at a cost of $3 per unit. Information concerning costs follows.

CLOCKWORKS DEPARTMENT 19X8		
For 200,000 Sets	**Per Unit**	**Total**
Direct materials	$0.70	$140,000
Direct labor	1.20	240,000
Variable overhead	0.60	120,000
Fixed overhead	0.90	180,000
Manufacturing cost	$3.40	$680,000

Fixed overhead consists of allocations of general administrative expense and depreciation of the department's equipment. The book value of equipment is $300,000. Assume that for each of the next 10 years the company will need the same number of clockworks as were produced in 19X8. The present equipment will last 10 more years. The equipment has no market or salvage value. Assume the company has no alternative use for the space or equipment now used by the department to produce clockworks. You may ignore tax considerations.

Required

1) Calculate the yearly manufacturing cost savings (or cost increases) Wayne can realize by purchasing clockworks from the foreign supplier.

2) State whether Wayne should make its own clockworks or buy them from the supplier. Explain your answer.

3) List some qualitative factors that should be considered in make-or-buy situations like this one.

ALTERNATE PROBLEMS FOR SECTION 25.B

Alternate 25.B.7. The president of Ringo Company is thinking of replacing an old drilling machine with a new, more efficient model. The old machine has a book value of $35,000 and will last for five more years. It will not have any salvage value at the end of its life. The old machine can be sold today for $35,000. The new machine will last for five years and will have no salvage value. It will cost $80,000 and will reduce operating costs by $30,000 per year for five years. The marginal tax rate is 46%. Straight-line depreciation is used.

Required

1) Assuming a 12% after-tax cost of capital, determine the net present value of investing in the new machine.

2) Calculate the approximate rate of return offered by the new machine.

3) Use the results in parts (1) and (2) to make a recommendation as to whether the new machine should be purchased.

Alternate 25.B.8. Information concerning three alternatives under consideration are provided here. No assets now owned will need to be sold or retired.

	Alternative X	Alternative Y	Alternative Z
Initial cash outlay	$8,000	$50,000	$22,000
Annual net after-tax cash benefit	$2,000	$9,000	$4,500
Useful life in years	8	8	8

Assume that the after-tax cost of capital is 10%.

Required

1) Rank the alternatives by the following methods:

   a) Net present value.

   b) Profitability index.

    c) Payback period.

    d) Approximate rate of return.

2) Which ranking method(s) do you prefer? State the reasons for your choice.

Alternate 25.B.9. Information concerning two alternatives under consideration is as follows. No assets now owned will need to be sold or retired.

	Alternative A	Alternative B
Annual net cash proceeds before tax	$200,000	$300,000
Cash cost of new asset	$800,000	$1,100,000
Expected life of new asset	12 years	14 years
Expected salvage value	$-0-	$100,000
Depreciation method	Straight-line	Straight-line
Marginal tax rate	40%	40%
After-tax cost of capital	10%	10%

Required

1) Determine the following for each alternative:

    a) Payback period.

    b) Net present value.

    c) Approximate rate of return.

2) Choose the most attractive alternative and defend your choice.

ALTERNATE PROBLEMS FOR CHAPTER 25

Alternate 25.1. On April 15, 19X4, the Aardvark Company purchased a new vacuum molder at a cost of $100,000. The molder has an expected useful life of eight years and will have no salvage value at the end of its life. On April 16, 19X4, a salesman from another manufacturer demonstrated that his company's new computer-controlled vacuum molder could reduce Aardvark's operating costs before depreciation by $30,000 per year as compared with the new molder Aardvark just purchased. The computerized molder costs $124,000, will last eight years, and will have no salvage value at the end of its life. If the computerized molder is purchased, the present molder could be sold for $40,000. Ms. Aarron, president of Aardvark, says she cannot purchase the new molder because the sale of the present molder would result in a $60,000 loss. By not purchasing the computerized molder, she says, the company would avert the $60,000 loss. The corporation's marginal tax rate is 46%. The 46% rate also applies to gains and losses on the disposal of assets. The company uses straight-line depreciation. Aardvark's after-tax cost of capital is 10%.

Required

1) Prepare an incremental analysis of the relevant cash flows associated with the possible purchase of the computer-controlled molder.

2) Calculate the net present value resulting from the purchase of the computerized molder and state whether the molder should be purchased.

Alternate 25.2. A manager of Nimble Development Company has prepared the following information on a proposed building that would be leased to commercial tenants.

CASH ANALYSIS		
Proposed Commercial Building		
Construction and land cost		$2,000,000
Annual after-tax net cash inflow		$200,000
Useful life		30 years
Total cash inflow (30 × $200,000)	$6,000,000	
Less: Net cash outlay	2,000,000	
Net cash benefit	$4,000,000	

The company's after-tax cost of capital is 10%. Since the cash investment can be tripled over the life of the project, the manager has recommended investing in the project.

Required

1) Calculate the net present value of the project.

2) Calculate the approximate rate of return offered by the project.

3) Make a recommendation to the company regarding the project.

Alternate 25.3. Karen Mort is considering the following investment alternatives:

Skating Rink. Land for the rink may be purchased now for $300,000. Phase I construction costs of $800,000 will be due at the end of year 1. Phase II construction costs of $300,000 will be due at the end of year 2. Net cash proceeds after taxes for year 3 are estimated at $90,000, and for years 4 through 15 at $200,000 per year. Assume that annual cash flows occur at the end of each year. The property would be sold at the end of 15 years for an amount that would leave $500,000 after taxes.

Tax Return Franchise. The franchise requires an immediate cash payment of $200,000. An existing building can be leased for 15 years. Remodeling will require a cash payment of $80,000 at the end of year 1. Net annual after-tax cash proceeds will be $40,000 starting with the current year. Assume that annual cash flows occur at the end of each year. The franchise is expected to be worthless at the end of 15 years.

Required

1) Set up time diagrams, like those illustrated in this chapter, to show the cash flows for each alternative.

2) Evaluate the alternatives by means of the rate of return approach and make a recommendation to Ms. Mort.

ALTERNATE PROBLEMS FOR CHAPTER 26

Alternate 26.6. Refer to the tax rate schedule for single individuals (page 1053).

Required

Calculate the amount of tax and determine the marginal tax rate and average tax rate for each of the following taxable incomes of single individuals.

1) $15,000

2) $30,000

3) $60,000

4) $120,000

Alternate 26.7. Refer to the tax rate schedule for married individuals (page 1053).

Required

Calculate the amount of tax and determine the marginal tax rate and average tax rate for each of the following taxable incomes of married couples filing joint returns.

1) $15,000

2) $30,000

3) $60,000

4) $120,000

Alternate 26.8. Early Corporation shows a before-tax net income of $115,000 for 19X5. The only difference between accounting for financial statements and tax reporting is that a machine purchased in early January 19X5 is being depreciated on a straight-line basis for financial reporting while sum-of-years'-digits is used for tax purposes (assume that ACRS depreciation is not applicable here). The machine cost $126,000 and is expected to last six years with no salvage value at the end of that time.

Required

1) Determine the annual machine depreciation for accounting purposes.

2) Determine the machine depreciation to be deducted on the 19X5 federal tax return.

3) Prepare the entry at December 31, 19X5, to recognize the Income Tax Expense for 19X5, the Income Tax Payable, and the Deferred Tax Liability under tax allocation procedures. (Refer to the corporate tax rates provided in the chapter.)

4) Assuming that Early's before-tax net income for 19X6 is $95,000, make the entry at December 31, 19X6, to recognize the expense, payable, and deferred liability for federal income tax.

Index